THE ODYSSEY READER

IDEAS AND STYLE

THE ODYSSEY READER

ODYSSEY PRESS NEW YORK

IDEAS AND STYLE

Newman P. Birk & Genevieve B. Birk

TUFTS UNIVERSITY

ACKNOWLEDGMENTS

The authors are grateful to the following writers, publishers, and literary agents for permission to use the materials listed below.

AAUP Bulletin: "Scholarly Style, or the Lack Thereof" by Sheridan Baker in the *AAUP Bulletin,* Autumn 1956, pages 464–470.

George Allen and Unwin, Ltd.: passage from *The Interpretation of Dreams* by Sigmund Freud, translated and edited by James Strachey.

Walter Allen, "And Now the Mid-Atlantic Man" in *The New York Times Book Review,* December 27, 1964. © 1964 by The New York Times Company. Reprinted by permission.

Appleton-Century-Crofts, Inc.: "The Intrinsic Value of Art" from *The Principles of Aesthetics,* Second Edition, by DeWitt H. Parker. Copyright 1920, 1946 by F. S. Crofts & Co., Inc. Reprinted by permission of Appleton-Century-Crofts. Passage from *Science and Christian Tradition* by Thomas Henry Huxley.

Edward Arnold, Ltd.: passage from *The Human Situation* by W. Macneile Dixon.

The Atlantic Monthly: "A Reasonable Life in a Mad World" by Irwin Edman, "Grammar for Today" by Bergen Evans. Copyright © March 1949/March 1960 by The Atlantic Monthly Company, Boston, Mass. 02116. Reprinted with permission.

Sheridan Baker: "Scholarly Style, or the Lack Thereof" in the *AAUP Bulletin,* Autumn 1956, pages 464–470.

Basic Books, Inc.: passage from *The Interpretation of Dreams* by Sigmund Freud, translated and edited by James Strachey, Basic Books, Inc., Publishers, New York, 1955.

Beacon Press: "Notes of a Native Son" from *Notes of a Native Son* by James Baldwin, reprinted by permission of the Beacon Press, copyright © 1955 by James Baldwin.

Brandt & Brandt: "The Principles of Newspeak" from *Nineteen Eighty-four* by George Orwell.

The Clarendon Press: passage from *The Manual of Epictetus* (translated by P. E. Matheson); selections from *A Dictionary of Modern English Usage,* Second Edition, by H. W. Fowler, both by permission of the Clarendon Press, Oxford.

Sir Kenneth Clark: "The Blot and the Diagram."

Norman Cousins: "The Computer and the Poet" in *Saturday Review,* July 23, 1966.

Doubleday and Company, Inc.: passage from *Zen Buddhism: Selected Writings of D. T. Suzuki,* copyright © 1956 by William Barrett; selections from *The Theatre of the Absurd,* copyright © 1961 by Martin Esslin, both reprinted by permission of Doubleday & Company, Inc.

The Economist: "Not Just America," from *The Economist,* August 21, 1965.

Les Éditions Nagel: passage from *L'Existentialisme Est un Humanisme* by Jean-Paul Sartre (trans. Philip Mairet).

Estate of Irwin Edman: "A Reasonable Life in a Mad World" by Irwin Edman in *The Atlantic Monthly,* March, 1949, copyright © 1960 by The Atlantic Monthly Company, Boston, Mass. 02116. Reprinted with permission.

Bergen Evans: "Grammar for Today" in *The Atlantic Monthly,* March, 1960. Copyright © March 1960 by The Atlantic Monthly Company, Boston, Mass. 02116. Reprinted with permission.

Farrar, Straus & Giroux, Inc.: "My Negro Problem—and Ours" from *Doings and Undoings* by Norman Podhoretz. Copyright © 1963 by Norman Podhoretz. Reprinted with permission of Farrar, Straus & Giroux, Inc. "Settling the Colonel's Hash," reprinted with permission of Farrar, Straus & Giroux, Inc. from *On the Contrary* by Mary McCarthy. Copyright © 1961 by Mary McCarthy. "My Mother and the Animals," reprinted with permission of Farrar, Straus & Giroux from *My Mother's House* by Colette. Copyright 1953 by Farrar, Straus & Young.

John Fischer: "Substitutes for Violence." Copyright © 1965 by Harper's Magazine, Inc. Reprinted from the January, 1966, issue of Harper's Magazine by permission of the author.

J. Glenn Gray: "Salvation on the Campus." Copyright © 1965 by Harper's Magazine, Inc. Reprinted from the May, 1965, issue of Harper's Magazine by permission of the author.

Harcourt, Brace & World, Inc.: "I Get a Colt to Break In" from *The Autobiography of Lincoln Steffens,* copyright, 1931, by Harcourt, Brace & World, Inc.; renewed, 1959, by Peter Steffens. Reprinted by permission of the publishers. "Lincoln Speaks at Gettysburg" condensed from *Abraham Lincoln: The War Years* by Carl Sandburg, copyright, 1939, by Harcourt, Brace & World, Inc.; renewed, 1967, by Carl Sandburg. Reprinted by permission of the publishers. "Why I Write" from *Such, Such Were the Joys* by George Orwell, copyright, 1945, 1952, 1953, by Sonia Brownell Orwell. Reprinted by permission of Harcourt, Brace & World, Inc. "The Genesis of a Mood" from *The Modern Temper* by Joseph Wood Krutch, copyright, 1929, by Harcourt, Brace & World, Inc.; renewed, 1957, by Joseph Wood Krutch. Reprinted by permission of the publishers. Passage from *A Walker in the City,* copyright, 1951, by Alfred Kazin. Reprinted by permission of Harcourt, Brace & World, Inc.

Harper & Row, Publishers, Inc.: Introduction by Aldous Huxley to the *Bhagavad-Gita* translated by Swami Prabhavananda and Christopher Isherwood. Copyright 1944, 1951 by the Vedanta Society of Southern California. "Calculating Machine" from *The Second Tree from the Corner* by E. B. White. Copyright 1951 by E. B. White. "Walden" from *One Man's Meat* by E. B. White. Copyright 1939 by E. B. White. "The Ideal of Individual Fulfillment" from *Excellence: Can We Be Equal and Excellent Too?* by John W. Gardner. Copyright © by John W. Gardner. Passages from *Kennedy* by Theodore C. Sorensen. Copyright © 1965 by Theodore C. Sorensen. Chapter 9 of *The Autobiography of Mark Twain* edited by Charles Neider. Copyright © 1959 by The Mark Twain Company. Copyright © 1959 by Charles Neider. All reprinted by permission of Harper & Row, Publishers.

Harper's Magazine: "Substitutes for Violence" by John Fischer. Copyright © 1965, by Harper's Magazine, Inc. Reprinted from the January, 1966, issue of Harper's

Magazine by permission of the author. "Salvation on the Campus" by J. Glenn Gray. Copyright © 1965 by Harper's Magazine, Inc. Reprinted from the May, 1965, issue of Harper's Magazine by permission of the author.

Harvard Today: "The Problem of People" by Roger Revelle in *Harvard Today,* Autumn 1965.

Harvard University Press: "The Idea of a Multiversity." Reprinted by permission of the publishers from Clark Kerr, *The Uses of the University.*

A. M. Heath & Company, Limited: "The Principles of Newspeak" from *Nineteen Eighty-four* by George Orwell. Reprinted by permission of Miss Sonia Brownell; Martin Secker & Warburg, Limited; A. M. Heath & Company, Limited.

Holt, Rinehart and Winston, Inc.: excerpts from *The Sane Society* by Erich Fromm. Copyright © 1955 by Erich Fromm. Reprinted by permission of Holt, Rinehart and Winston, Inc.

Houghton Mifflin Company: "The Crisis of American Masculinity" from *The Politics of Hope* by Arthur M. Schlesinger, Jr.; the passage "Prologue: January 1961" from *A Thousand Days: John F. Kennedy in the White House* by Arthur M. Schlesinger, Jr.

Leon H. Keyserling: "Something for Everybody" in *The New York Times Book Review,* February 27, 1966. © by The New York Times Company. Reprinted by permission.

Alfred A. Knopf, Inc.: "Father Opens My Mail" from *Life With Father,* by Clarence Day. Copyright 1934 by Clarence Day and renewed 1962 by Katharine B. Day. Reprinted by permission of Alfred A. Knopf, Inc. Selections from Chapter 5 from *The Spirit of Tragedy,* by Herbert J. Muller. Copyright 1956 by Herbert J. Muller. Reprinted by permission of Alfred A. Knopf, Inc. Excerpts from *The Myth of Sisyphus,* by Albert Camus. Copyright 1955 by Alfred A. Knopf, Inc. Reprinted by permission.

Joseph Wood Krutch: "Some Unsentimental Confessions of a Nature Writer" in *The New York Herald Tribune Book Review,* June 15, 1952, and "Life, Liberty, and the Pursuit of Welfare," 1961.

John Lear: "Men, Moonships, and Morality" in *Saturday Review,* January 7, 1967.

Longmans, Green & Company, Inc.: passage from *The Will to Believe* by William James.

F. L. Lucas: "On the Fascination of Style." Reprinted by special permission of the author and Holiday, copyright 1960, by The Curtis Publishing Co.

John Lukacs: "It's Halfway to 1984" in *The New York Times Magazine,* January 2, 1966. © 1966 by The New York Times Company. Reprinted by permission.

The Macmillan Company: passage from "Universities and Their Function" from *The Aims of Education* by Alfred North Whitehead. Copyright 1929 by The Macmillan Company; renewed 1957 by Evelyn Whitehead. Reprinted with the permission of The Macmillan Company. Passage from *The Problem of Pain* by C. S. Lewis, first published in the United States in 1943 by The Macmillan Company.

McGraw-Hill Book Company: "What If We Succeed?" from *We Are Not Alone* by Walter Sullivan. Copyright © 1964, 1966 by Walter Sullivan. Used by permission.

Julian Messner: "The Creative Mind," reprinted by permission of Julian Messner, Division of Simon and Schuster, Inc., from *Science and Human Values* by J. Bronowski. Copyright © 1956, by J. Bronowski.

Emmanuel G. Mesthene: "Learning to Live with Science" in *Saturday Review*, July 17, 1965.

Methuen and Company, Ltd.: passage from *Existentialism and Humanism* by Jean-Paul Sartre, translated by Philip Mairet.

The Michigan Quarterly Review: "Two Heresies" by Geoffrey Crowther in *The Michigan Alumnus Quarterly Review*, LXVI (Summer 1960), 266–271. Reprinted by permission of the University of Michigan and *The Michigan Quarterly Review*, successor to *The Michigan Alumnus Quarterly Review*.

Elting E. Morison: "It's Two-Thirds of a Century—We've Made It, So Far" in *The New York Times Magazine*, April 24, 1966. © 1966 by The New York Times Company. Reprinted by permission.

Lewis Mumford: "The American Way of Death." Reprinted from *The New York Review of Books*, copyright © 1966, Lewis Mumford.

The New York Times Book Review: "And Now the Mid-Atlantic Man" by Walter Allen, December 27, 1964; "Something for Everybody" by Leon H. Keyserling, February 27, 1966. © 1964/1966 by The New York Times Company. Reprinted by permission.

The New York Times Magazine: "It's Halfway to 1984" by John Lukacs in the *Times Magazine*, January 2, 1966; "It's Two-Thirds of a Century—We've Made It, So Far" by Elting E. Morison, April 24, 1966. © 1966 by The New York Times Company.

The New York University Press: "The Case for Determinism" by Brand Blanshard, from *Determinism and Freedom in the Age of Modern Science*.

W. W. Norton and Company, Inc.: passage from "Science and Poetry" by I. A. Richards. Copyright 1926 and copyright 1951 by W. W. Norton and Company, Inc. Reprinted by permission of W. W. Norton and Company, Inc.

The Odyssey Press, Inc.: selections from *The Way of Philosophy* (Rev. Ed.) by Philip Wheelwright.

Mario Pei: "The Dictionary as a Battlefront" by Mario Pei in *Saturday Review* Education Supplement, July 21, 1962.

A. D. Peters and Co.: Selection from *Man Stands Alone* by Julian Huxley. Reprinted by permission of A. D. Peters and Co.

Philosophical Library, Inc.: "Science and Religion" from *Out of My Later Years* by Albert Einstein; "Does Human Nature Change?" by John Dewey, first published in *The Rotarian* and later in *Problems of Men*. Reprinted by permission.

Princeton University Press: "The Anti-Hero" from *Radical Innocence: Studies in the Contemporary American Novel* by Ihab Hassan. Reprinted by permission of Princeton University Press. © 1961.

Random House, Inc.: William Faulkner's Nobel Prize Address; Adlai E. Stevenson's Speech of Acceptance at the Democratic National Convention, 1952.

Henry Regnery Company: "Ultimate Terms in Contemporary Rhetoric" from *The Ethics of Rhetoric* by Richard M. Weaver.

St. Martin's Press, Inc.: passage from *The Human Situation* by W. Macneile Dixon.

Saturday Review, Inc.: "The Dictionary as a Battlefront" by Mario Pei in the Education Supplement of *Saturday Review*, July 21, 1962; "Learning to Live with Science" by Emmanuel G. Mesthene, July 17, 1965; "Confessions of a Scientist-Humanist" by Warren Weaver, May 28, 1966; "The Computer and the Poet" by

Norman Cousins, July 23, 1966; "Men, Moonships, and Morality" by John Lear, January 7, 1967.

Charles Scribner's Sons: "The Lantern-Bearers" by Robert Louis Stevenson.

Martin Secker & Warburg, Ltd.: passage from *My Mother's House* by Colette. Reprinted by permission of Martin Secker & Warburg, Limited. Passage from *Nineteen Eighty-four* by George Orwell, reprinted by permission of Miss Sonia Brownell and Secker & Warburg.

Simon and Schuster, Inc.: "The Monster" from *Of Men and Music* by Deems Taylor, copyright 1937 by Deems Taylor. Reprinted by permission of Simon and Schuster, Inc. "Prospects in the Arts and Sciences" from *The Open Mind* by J. Robert Oppenheimer, copyright © 1955 by J. Robert Oppenheimer. Reprinted by permission of Simon and Schuster, Inc.

Estate of James Thurber: "Which" from *Ladies' and Gentlemen's Guide to Modern English Usage.* Copr. © 1931, 1959 James Thurber. From *The Owl In the Attic,* published by Harper & Row. Originally printed in *The New Yorker.*

The Viking Press, Inc.: "The Jew and the Christian" from *Viking Portable World Bible* edited by Robert O. Ballou. Copyright 1939, 1944, 1967 by Robert O. Ballou. Reprinted by permission of The Viking Press, Inc. All Rights Reserved. "Former Teachers" from *Philosopher's Holiday* by Irwin Edman. Copyright 1938 by Irwin Edman, © 1966 by Mrs. Lester Markel. Reprinted by permission of The Viking Press, Inc.

Warren Weaver: "Confessions of a Scientist-Humanist" in *Saturday Review,* May 28, 1966.

Nils Y. Wessell: "The Opportunity for Change," Matriculation Speech, 1965, Tufts University.

World Journal Tribune: "Some Unsentimental Confessions of a Nature Writer" by Joseph Wood Krutch in the *Herald Tribune Book Review,* June 15, 1952. Reprinted by permission of the World Journal Tribune and the author.

Yale University Press: "The Ideal Democracy" from *Modern Democracy* by Carl L. Becker. Copyright © 1941 by Yale University Press.

PREFACE

In selecting and editing material for *The Odyssey Reader: Ideas and Style,* we were guided by several assumptions. The first assumption is that when students come to college their minds are as vital as they ever will be; that freshmen and sophomores can think and want to think; that they are ready for, and deserve to have, stirring intellectual experiences; and that their young, live minds are receptive to the thought and the wisdom of good and great minds, past and present. The purpose in choosing many of these readings has been to provide a real intellectual experience for the student and an enlarged understanding both of his intellectual heritage and of the contemporary world.

A closely related assumption is that a major aim of liberal education should be not only to stir the questioning mind but also to offer a choice of answers. In the readings in this book there is conflict, sometimes clear contradiction, as well as harmony, among the writers' views. The diversity both in range of material and in points of view will, it is hoped, stimulate the student to examine his own beliefs and attitudes and help him to choose meaningful values on which to build a personal philosophy.

Finally, as the subtitle *Ideas and Style* suggests, another assumption is that studying, analyzing, and judging the rhetorical principles and the techniques in good prose will improve students' writing. Students become more aware of rhetorical choices open to them when they write, and they become newly aware, as they read, of the importance of the way ideas are phrased and developed. The text repeatedly stresses the oneness of content and form, mind and manner, ideas and style.

Different teachers will, of course, use this book differently. Students should probably read carefully the "Introduction to Rhetorical Analysis," which discusses more fully some of the ideas sketched in this preface but is intended particularly to give students tools for analysis and suggestions about reading. Since, however, this book is long, instructors are likely to select from the readings, and they may well not wish to follow the plan shown in the "Contents."

"Part One, Ways of Ordering Ideas and Experience" is designed to emphasize organization and to supply clear examples of some ways of ordering material. Comments and questions following each reading give special emphasis to organization and to techniques of coherence and development within the larger pattern; but they deal too (as do comments and questions throughout the book) with the writer's ideas and with other aspects of his style and tone. The essays in Part One need not be read in the sequence in which they appear; the general arrangement, however, is from material most easily read to material more complex in content and organization. Readings in "Part Two, Ideas and Values," the longest and probably the most significant part of the book, are grouped by theme; numbers after each sub-section refer to other readings relevant to the theme or to the authors represented in the unit. "Part Three, Autobiography and Personal Essays" illustrates and comments on techniques that may be especially helpful to the student if he does this kind of writing from personal experience.

The table of contents of *The Odyssey Reader* will reveal, too, another principle operative in the choice of readings: interested in range and diversity, we have also thought it useful to include, in a number of instances, more than one sample of an author's writing. Several selections from Plato, for example, give students some acquaintance with the Socratic-Platonic philosophy and provide background for the references to Plato and to Greek thought that occur in other readings. For rather different reasons, Irwin Edman, Joseph Wood Krutch, George Orwell, Arthur M. Schlesinger, Jr., and E. B. White are among the skillful modern writers represented by more than one selection. Comparison and contrast of the ideas, style, and persona in two or more samples of an author's writing may be fruitful subjects for discussion or writing.

As indicated earlier, comments and questions follow each reading in the book. Although some teachers may find this sort of critical-analytical apparatus an encumbrance, we have found that most students profit from it: Well-planned questions will often lead students to notice what, without guidance, they might have missed, and so may make them more perceptive and judicious readers and eventually more conscious and effective writers. Such analytical apparatus may also free the teacher to go his own way in class, assuming that his students have worked and thought through the questions and that he need not cover the same ground. Teachers who prefer not to use the Comment and Questions can, of course, ignore them, even tell their students to ignore them. The students, no doubt, will be happy to comply.

I am grateful to colleagues and students at Tufts University and to many other friends who have commented on these readings and have suggested possible new readings. For help in preparing the manuscript and for criticism of the final drafts, I am indebted to Patricia Martin-Jenkins Hartwell and especially to Beatrice Blane Silber.

Before his death my husband, Newman Peter Birk, had done much of the planning, the selecting of material, and the writing in the following pages. It is only proper that his name be on the title page of the *Reader* that he did not see completed but that has, in fact, been our joint project.

GENEVIEVE B. BIRK

CONTENTS

PART TWO | Ideas and Values

PART THREE | Autobiography and Personal Essays

THE
ODYSSEY READER

IDEAS AND
STYLE

AN INTRODUCTION
TO RHETORICAL ANALYSIS

How does a composition come into being? How, as Robert Frost once said of a poem, does it assume direction and end in a clarification? Writers work, of course, in different ways; but, given an idea, a body of information, a set of values, or an experience which a writer wants to communicate, he is likely to be faced, simultaneously, with a number of questions: What general order or arrangement is best suited to my material? How can I make this order clear? How can I develop meaningfully the parts of the material? Answers to such questions usually depend on another question: What kind of audience am I writing for? Consideration of audience leads to still further questions: What shall be my attitude toward my audience and my material? What "voice," or what image of myself, do I wish to project? And, finally—in the actual process of writing—what kind of language and what rhetorical devices will best fit my total purpose in this communication? Shaping a composition involves making choices.

Some of these choices may be inevitable or automatic. For example, if the writer merely wants to give a clear account of a process, then a step-by-step chronological order may seem inevitable; if he knows that he is addressing an audience of nonspecialists, he knows, too, that he must avoid or must explain technical language; and his attitude toward his material may be purely objective. More often, though, the writer's choices are not predetermined by material or situation; he makes them consciously and thoughtfully, guided by his conception of the impact he wants his writing to have on the reader. As a writer or as a perceptive reader, one needs to be aware of possible choices—of organization, of tone, and of modes of expression—which we shall discuss in the following pages.

I. WAYS OF ORDERING IDEAS AND EXPERIENCE

Perhaps we should begin this section by elaborating a statement made earlier. Writers work in different ways; it is therefore difficult, if not impossible, to give an exact account of their procedure in organizing their material. Except in very short and simple pieces, the writer is likely to go through a period of somewhat random thinking, and then of rough planning in which he tentatively fixes on the main divisions of his subject, on a possible sequence of main ideas, on sub-units within the major divisions, and on methods of ordering and developing those smaller units. The process may be in some ways analogous to the arranging of materials in a chest of drawers—deciding what should go into which drawer and how the contents of each are best arranged for order and convenience. Working by trial and error and impelled by sudden new ideas, the writer may make choices and changes that extend from total reorganization to, in the last stages, choices of particular words and even of punctuation marks. By means of a process in itself perhaps disorderly, the successful writer arrives at an orderly presentation; a coherent pattern emerges finally from his struggle with his material.

The classification and description of such final patterns is to some degree artificial because the patterns are often used in combination in a complex piece of writing (or even in a single paragraph) and because the ways of ordering material overlap: a definition may also be an analysis; narration may be a primary method of showing a cause–effect relationship. What might be called the general or dominant order of ideas frequently splinters into other orders, as when a broad thesis supported by reasons is developed in detail by paragraphs of contrast and comparison. The listing below (and in Part I of the readings) is therefore meant to call the reader's attention to some ways of ordering ideas and to aid him in recognizing and evaluating the pattern or patterns chosen by the authors he reads. What the reader requires is that there be some kind of order, by means of which the writer ends in a clarification.

Thesis and Examples.   The writer may state his thesis or generalization early and support it by short or long examples. Or he may start with examples from which he arrives at a thesis or conclusion. Or he may begin and end with general statements, both supported by the examples he supplies. The reader's response to a piece of writing using this organization will depend largely on the intrinsic interest of the examples and their aptness in supporting the thesis.

Thesis and Reasons.   Using this order, the writer often states early his belief, judgment, or recommendation (thesis), and then gives reasons for believing as he does. Part of his reasoning may consist of anticipating and countering possible objections to the position he is taking.

Generalization and Qualification.   This pattern is akin to Thesis and

Reasons. It occurs when the writer wishes to state a thesis which, taken literally, sounds like a sweeping generalization. He may qualify (that is, modify, limit, or restrict) by defining terms and by negation or exclusion —showing what he does *not* mean by, or what he excludes from, his original generalization. Having qualified and clarified, he usually restates his generalization at the end.

Narration. The most common order in nonfictional narration is chronological arrangement, or the setting down of events in the time-order in which they occur. When events occur simultaneously, in different places, narration may also involve space-order. And, in complex narration, the writer may have reasons (which should be made clear to the reader) for moving about in time and space—for starting his narrative in the middle, for example, or at the end, of a sequence of events.

Analysis. Analysis is the method of dividing a complex subject into its main parts, examining each of the parts, and showing their relationship to each other and to the whole. In a formal analysis, the main parts may in turn be divided, each subdivision may be further divided, and so on down to the last possible unit. When a writer says, "Four problems face the Security Council," or "There are many reasons for unrest on the campus," he is introducing an analysis of a subject too complex to be treated as a whole. The section you are now reading is an analysis of "ways of ordering ideas and experience."

Contrast and Comparison. The writer using this pattern sets side by side two or more people, things, or situations, and considers the differences, or similarities, or differences and similarities between them. One might, for example, compare the passive resistance of Gandhi with that of Martin Luther King, or compare and contrast the relationship of the individual and society in two or more modern novels. If the subjects being compared are complex, the writer may break them by analysis into their main parts and contrast or compare them part by part. He may discuss the topics, or the parts of them, in combination, or he may present one topic first and then compare the other with it.

Cause and Effect. In this pattern of organization a writer discusses the cause of an event or a situation and then the effect—for example, the cause of the growth of large universities and the effect of that growth. Within the general cause–effect order, the writer often uses analysis; that is, he divides "cause" into three or four main causes, and "effect" into three or four main effects. He may also reverse the order, starting with the effects of a development or event, and then discussing its causes.

Question-to-Answer or **Problem-to-Solution.** The writer using this order may need to clarify the question or problem by means of facts, examples, quotations, definition, or analysis. His proposed answer or solution is usually arrived at and supported by examples, reasons, statistics, and other kinds of amplifying detail.

Definition. Extended definition (of a term, an idea, or a mood, for example) attempts, like brief definition, to put the subject into a genus or class and to differentiate it from other members of that class. It also clarifies the subject in one or more of these ways: (1) by giving examples; (2) by comparing the subject with something familiar to the reader; (3) by comparing and contrasting it with related subjects; (4) by tracing its history or development; (5) by negating or excluding—showing what it does not mean or does not include in this context; (6) by restating the essentials of the definition; (7) by analyzing—breaking the subject into its components and examining each part.

As we have suggested earlier, the patterns of organization described above (and we have not exhausted the list of possible patterns, but have merely named the most common ones) are used in developing paragraphs as well as longer pieces of writing; a cause–effect organization may therefore contain paragraphs or even larger units of definition, analysis, contrast and comparison, etc. We might note in passing that many of these ways of ordering material are also used in single sentences. For example, "I believe that objective examinations should be abolished because they often test knowledge of unimportant details and because they do not stimulate thought" is a sentence of thesis and reasons; "Mankind must put an end to war or war will put an end to mankind" is a sentence of contrast or antithesis. Antithetical structures like the last one are also, of course, aspects of a writer's style.

One further point about the ordering of ideas and experience: We have thus far been dealing with logical order. Another consideration for the writer may be psychological order. A writer may be primarily concerned with informing, persuading, convincing, communicating an attitude or experience, or moving to action. In the light of his intention, what arrangement of points, examples, or reasons will be most interesting, pleasing, moving, or convincing? What strategy will be most effective in achieving his aims? We shall return later to this matter of psychological order.

II. CLARITY AND COHERENCE

When the writer has decided on the logical order best suited to his material, he uses four major devices for making that order (and the material) clear to his readers.

1. He may use his title or his opening paragraphs, or both, to signal his organization to the reader. A title like "The Problem of People," for example, suggests definition and analysis of the problem and possibly a proposed solution.

2. The writer uses paragraphs to mark the units of his discourse, to

indicate to the reader that one phase of his discussion has ended and another is beginning. He may use section numbers, headings, or transitional paragraphs to mark off the main divisions of his thought. Often, though certainly not always, the writer begins his paragraphs with topic sentences; when he does, these first sentences provide an outline of the piece of writing. The skillful writer generally develops his paragraphs fully, by using one or more of the ways of ordering ideas discussed in the preceding pages; each paragraph is an organized block in the whole structure of the composition.

3. The writer uses transitional devices to link his paragraphs and to carry the reader smoothly from one unit of the composition into the next. A good writer is like a man who knows just where he is going, attended by a friend who is in a dark and unfamiliar area. In this analogy, transitions are ways of saying "turn right" or "turn left" or "now we go straight ahead for a while," and the reader is like a blind man whose mental steps the writer is directing. One of the marks of the skillful writer is the deft and unobtrusive use of transitions. Common transitional devices are: (a) concluding a paragraph with a sentence which introduces the next phase of the discussion; (b) using in the first sentence of a new paragraph a connective like *therefore, in addition, on the contrary;* (c) beginning a paragraph with a sentence that refers clearly, perhaps by pronoun references or the repetition of key words, or synonyms, to material in the preceding paragraph. The passage below consists of the last two sentences of a paragraph and the opening sentence of the following paragraph. The transitional devices are italicized.

So regarded, the term democracy refers primarily to a form of government, and it has always meant government by the many as opposed to government by the one—government by the people as opposed to government by a tyrant, a dictator, or an absolute monarch. This is the most *general meaning* of the *word* as men have commonly understood *it.*

In *this antithesis* there are, *however,* certain implications, always tacitly understood, which give a *more precise meaning* to *the term.*—CARL L. BECKER, *Modern Democracy*

4. The writer may use brief summaries or restatement to emphasize his central idea, to conclude a major division of his discussion, or to establish the relationship between parts of the material.

Being alert to any such signals which the writer provides will help the reader to follow the development of the composition.

III. AUDIENCE, ASSUMPTIONS, TONE, PERSONA

Sometimes unconsciously, but more often consciously, the writer makes certain assumptions about his audience. His readers are, for example, knowledgeable about his subject or they are uninformed; they consider his subject important or they need to be persuaded that it is important to them; they are likely to be receptive to his ideas or they are likely to be hostile; they will respond to subtleties of wit and irony or they will be confused by such subtleties. Effective communication depends, as Cardinal Newman pointed out, on initial agreements, "tacit understandings," between reader and writer. In so far as he can, the able writer needs to determine what attitudes or shared beliefs or interests he can safely count on and use as a starting point for further discussion. If he anticipates opposition to his ideas, he may try to establish initial agreements of another kind—for example, common interests in other areas, or the agreement that unorthodox ideas deserve a hearing; he may use interest-arousing devices, such as an opening anecdote or a startling initial statement or question to capture the reader's attention and persuade him to read on. When a communication is to be spoken (as some of the readings in this book were), the writer may make further assumptions in the light of the occasion: his audience will expect a formal address, or they will expect an informal discussion; the occasion calls for the establishing of an easy, personal relationship with the audience, or it does not. All such assumptions will help to shape what we have earlier called the psychological order or the strategy of the composition, and they will profoundly influence the writer's style and his tone.

Tone may be defined as the manner of verbal expression that a speaker or writer adopts. It is the expression of his attitudes toward his audience, himself, and his material. For example, his attitude toward his audience may be friendly or reserved; his attitude toward himself may be over-confident or modest; his attitude toward his material may be enthusiastic or indignant, emotional or objective. In expressing his attitude toward his subject a writer consciously or unconsciously slants his material by the way he selects facts, words, and emphasis to produce a favorable or unfavorable response. Slanting, whether blatant and deliberate or subtle and perhaps even unintentional, can be examined by studying the author's bias in selecting or omitting facts, his preference for favorably or unfavorably charged words (a politician may be called a "patriot" or a "demagogue"), and his use of proportion and position in developing his ideas to achieve the desired emphasis.

Related to tone is the *persona*—the "voice," the role, the personality, which, consciously or unconsciously, the writer adopts in a particular communication. The writer, of course, may be, and often is, simply himself, honestly expressing his views. "Self," however, is many-sided; we all have various selves, some consciously, some unconsciously, revealed; we have the capacity for looking at a subject in different ways, with different selves. President Kennedy, for example, parodied his own famous Inaugural Address—"ask not what . . . ask . . . "—at a Democratic fund-raising dinner. His serious address revealed his serious, idealistic side, and his fund-raising speech revealed his sense of humor. Thus a writer, without dishonesty or hypocrisy, may write dispassionately on something about which he has strong feelings: his analytic self dominates his emotional self for the purposes of his communication. An angry man may adopt the role of a reasonable man; he may deliberately understate in order to avoid the appearance of overstating. A writer sometimes assumes a personality wholly unlike his own, seeming to approve when he actually disapproves; in this case he trusts his readers to see through the assumed persona, to perceive and appreciate his irony, and so to share his real attitudes. Persona is the writer's presence in a piece of writing, his revelation of himself, of which the perceptive reader is aware.

IV. STYLE

Style is compounded of many elements, including the writer's personality, his way of thinking, his conscious or unconscious slanting, his tone, his choice of words, his arrangement of words, the length and rhythm of his sentences. We shall suggest here some of the characteristics which the good reader notices as he analyzes a writer's style in relation to the writer's ideas.[1] Many of these aspects of style are interdependent and overlapping; and some may be conspicuously present, subtly present, or even conspicuously absent in a particular piece of writing.

The general formality or informality of the style and its appropriateness to the writer's material. Vocabulary, sentence structure, and length of sentences are important elements in this quality of style. So are the writer's tone and sometimes, specifically, his use of contractions and his use of pronouns (*I, you, we, one*), which are part of the persona. The following passage about a boy and his colt is an example of informal style:

Yes, conceit. I was full of it, and the colt was quite as bad. One day my chum Hjalmar came into town on his Black Bess, blanketed. She had had a great fistula cut out of her shoulder and had to be kept warm. I expected to see her weak and dull, but no, the good old mare was champing and dancing, like my colt.

"What is it makes her so?" I asked, and Hjalmar said he didn't know, but he thought she was proud of the blanket. A great idea. I had a gaudy horse blanket. I put it on the colt, and I could hardly hold her. We rode down the main street together, both horses, and both boys, so full of vanity that everybody stopped to smile. We thought they admired, and maybe they did. But some boys on the street gave us another angle. They, too, stopped and looked, and as we passed, one of them said, "Think you're hell, don't you?"

Spoilsport!

---

[1] Any unfamiliar terms used in this discussion are defined in the Glossary, pages 895–899.

We did, as a matter of fact; we thought we were hell.—*The Autobiography of Lincoln Steffens*

The following paragraph, on a very different subject, illustrates a much more formal style. The author uses longer sentences, a more formal vocabulary, and, particularly, more complex sentence structures, including sustained parallelism and appositive structures.

In the long history of man on earth there comes a time when he remembers something of what has been, anticipates something that will be, knows the country he has traversed, wonders what lies beyond—the moment when he becomes aware of himself as a lonely, differentiated item in the world. Sooner or later there emerges for him the most devastating of all facts, namely, that in an indifferent universe which alone endures, he alone aspires, endeavors to attain, and attains only to be defeated in the end. From that moment his immediate experience ceases to be adequate, and he endeavors to project himself beyond it by creating ideal worlds of semblance, Utopias of other time or place in which all has been, may be, or will be well.—CARL L. BECKER, *Modern Democracy*

Sentence length and variety in length. In the first of the passages quoted above, the sentences are either very short or are of medium length; in the second, the sentences are consistently long. The able writer usually varies his sentence length, not necessarily in a single passage, but in the whole composition, and often for purposes of emphasis. A short sentence among long ones, for example, is given emphasis by contrast. In the following passage, a complex sentence of more than seventy words is followed by a simple six-word sentence.

Were nature constant in her intentions we might hope to understand them, but how at odds with herself this Lady Bountiful, mother of all living, when she counsels one species of her own creation, providing an armoury the most ingenious, claws and fangs and suckers, instruments of death, that one tribe of her offspring might the better murder the members of another, a device, to our poor uninstructed vision, neither lovely nor divine. Nature is no believer in disarmament.—W. MACNEILE DIXON, *The Human Situation*

Sentence structure and variety in structure. Variety in structure as well as in length is illustrated in the preceding passage. Skillful writers avoid monotony; they vary their structures by intermingling loose and periodic sentences; by using parallel and balanced constructions as a change from simpler constructions; by use and arrangement of subordinate clauses, modifiers, and appositive structures; by occasional departures from the normal subject–verb–object order of English sentences. Conspicuous use of any of these rhetorical techniques can be a distinguishing mark of a writer's style.

The first of the following sentences about the Emperor Marcus Aurelius, an example of formal nineteenth-century prose, is an elaborate periodic sentence; the second is a simple loose sentence with a short introductory modifier:

Inasmuch then as the theology of Christianity did not appear to him true or of divine origin; inasmuch as this strange history of a crucified God was not credible to him, and a system which purported to rest entirely upon a foundation to him so wholly unbelievable, could not be foreseen by him to be that renovating agency which, after all abatements, it has in fact proved to be; the gentlest and most amiable of philosophers and rulers, under a solemn sense of duty, authorized the persecution of Christianity. To my mind this is one of the most tragical facts in all history.—JOHN STUART MILL, *On Liberty*

In the following passage, an example of less formal modern style, the first and third sentences begin with subject–verb; the second, longer sentence has three parallel phrases and begins with a subordinate clause:

I am not able, and I do not want, completely to abandon the world view that I acquired in childhood. So long as I remain alive and well I shall continue to feel strongly about prose style, to love the surface of the earth, and to take a pleasure in solid objects and scraps of useless information. It is no use trying to suppress that side of myself.—GEORGE ORWELL, "Why I Write"

The following sentence, part of Winston Churchill's report on the evacuation of Dunkirk in World War II, further illustrates parallel phrasing and also a high degree of subordination and modification:

I have, myself, full confidence that if all do their duty, if nothing is neglected, and if the best arrangements are made, as they are being made, we shall prove ourselves once again able to defend our Island home, to ride out the storm of war, and to outlive the menace of tyranny, if necessary for years, if necessary alone.

Triple parallel constructions, called triads, which are more characteristic of formal than of informal style, are noticeable in the preceding sentence in the three *if* clauses (*if all . . . , if nothing . . . , if the best arrangements . . . .*) and in the three infinitive phrases (*to defend . . . , to ride . . . , to outlive . . . .*).

In the passage below, the first three sentences are similarly constructed, on a pattern of contrast or antithesis. The last two sentences illustrate inversion, or departure from conventional sentence order: three objects (*almanac, solstice, equinox*) precede the subject and verb. The whole passage builds effectively to a climax with the three clauses in the last sentence and the figure of speech at the end.

The civilized man has built a coach, but has lost the use of his feet. He is supported on crutches, but lacks so much support of muscle. He has a fine Geneva watch, but he fails of the skill to tell the hour by the sun. A Greenwich nautical almanac he has, and so being sure of the information when he wants it, the man in the street does not know a star in the sky. The solstice he does not observe, the equinox he knows as little; and the whole bright calendar of the year is without a dial in his mind.—RALPH WALDO EMERSON, "Self-Reliance"

The first of the three sentences below begins, not with the subject, but with an adverb and part of the verb, and ends with parallel phrases. The second is an example of balance and antithesis. In the third, the main verb and the object twice precede the subject. Words taken out of their normal order and placed at the beginning or the end of a sentence are given emphasis by their unconventional position. Try rearranging the sentence elements in this passage, beginning each sentence or clause with its subject and verb, to see what emphasis is gained by the inverted order.

Never have the nations of the world had so much to lose or so much to gain. Together we shall save our planet or together we shall perish in its flames. Save it we can, and save it we must, and then shall we earn the eternal thanks of mankind and, as peacemakers, the eternal blessing of God.—JOHN F. KENNEDY, Address to the United Nations, September 25, 1961.

It is possible, of course, to overuse some of the rhetorical devices we have been illustrating. An appropriate simplicity can also be a characteristic of good style.

Repetition. Needless and wordy repetition of words or ideas is the mark of the incompetent rather than the competent writer. Skillful repetition, however, can impress key words and phrases on the reader's mind, bind together the parts of a paragraph or composition, and create emotional effects. Skillful repetition of words is illustrated in the passage above from President Kennedy's address to the United Nations: *so much . . . so much, Together . . . together, Save it . . . save it, eternal . . . eternal.* Parallel structures and effectively repeated sentence patterns are also techniques of repetition for emphasis and rhythm.

In the passage below, the author doubly emphasizes his main idea of simplicity by the repetition of words in very short sentences. (This passage is a good example, too, of variety in sentence length and sentence structure.)

Our life is frittered away by detail. An honest man has hardly need to count more than his ten fingers, or in extreme cases he may add his ten toes, and lump the rest. Simplicity, simplicity, simplicity! I say, let your affairs be as two or three, and not a hundred or a thousand; instead of a million count half a dozen, and keep your accounts on your thumb-nail. In the midst of this chopping sea of civilized life, such are the clouds and storms and quicksands and thousand-and-one items to be allowed for, that a man has to live, if he would not founder and go to the bottom and not make his port at all, by dead reckoning, and he must be a great calculator indeed who succeeds. Simplify, simplify.

Instead of three meals a day, if it be necessary eat but one; instead of a hundred dishes, five; and reduce other things in proportion.—HENRY DAVID THOREAU, *Walden*

Repetition of words and structures is used for a different effect in the following paragraph; the sentence rhythms imitate the "tick-tock deliberation" of the clock:

In many a country cottage over the land, a tall old clock in a quiet corner told time in a tick-tock deliberation. Whether the orchard branches hung with pink-spray blossoms or icicles of sleet, whether the outside news was seedtime or harvest, rain or drought, births or deaths, the swing of the pendulum was right and left and right and left in a tick-tock deliberation.—CARL SANDBURG, *Abraham Lincoln: The War Years*

The prose writer, like the poet, may also use repeated patterns of sound, such as alliteration, for special effects; a brief example is the repetition of *l* sounds in this excerpt from President Kennedy's Inaugural Address: "*l*et us go forth to *l*ead the *l*and we *l*ove."

Abstract and concrete language. Abstract words generally name qualities (*intelligence, honor*), concepts (*evolution, scientific method*), and conditions (*poverty, insanity*). Concrete words generally refer to things that exist in the physical world and can be perceived by the senses: *chair, apple, light bulb, rose bush.* Abstract words are necessary in language for expressing general ideas and arriving at judgments and conclusions; frequently, however, they do not have the same meaning for different people, and highly abstract language may leave the reader with only a vague impression of what the writer had in mind. Concrete words and details give supporting facts, statistics, reasons, and examples; they answer such questions as: What kind? What color? How large? How far? How many? Why? In what way? What is an illustration? The good writer therefore communicates his meaning by judicious choice and combination of abstract and concrete language. The good reader judges the effectiveness of the details by which abstractions are supported, clarified, illustrated, or defined.

Figurative language is often used to make a general and abstract idea clear and vivid by associating it with something concrete and familiar. The most common figures of speech are simile—a nonliteral comparison usually introduced by *like* or *as*: "Still we live meanly, *like ants*"; metaphor—an implied nonliteral comparison: "Time is *but the stream I go a-fishing in*"; and analogy—a sustained comparison of two dissimilar ideas or situations. Adlai E. Stevenson, on hearing of the death of Eleanor Roosevelt, said:

She would rather light candles than curse the darkness, and her glow has warmed the world.

The figurative statement, with its extension of the meaning of *light* in *glow* and *warmed*, evokes images and feeling; it concentrates meaning. Compare a literal and colorless statement like "She was not content to complain about things as they are and do nothing about them; she worked successfully in small ways to benefit the world." Figurative language is a marked trait of some styles and not of others; but it is more common in good prose, and a greater contributor to good prose, than many people realize.

Diction. This large term may cover much of what we have been discussing in the preceding pages. We shall use it here to refer to the writer's choice of words: the exactness of his words in denotation and connotation; the economy of his expression—economy not in the sense of brevity but in the sense of his choice of words that work, that warrant the space they take in the sentence; his fresh combinations of words; his use of factual or of emotionally charged language and its appropriateness to content; his choice of words for purposes of wit, humor, or irony.

Diction must be judged, of course, in the context of the whole composition and of the author's intention and tone; but even in brief passages the reader may have an immediate sense of the rightness of the author's words. We have quoted earlier a passage from Carl L. Becker, part of which is "the moment when he [man] becomes aware of himself as a lonely, differentiated item in the world." *Lonely* and *differentiated* do not have the same meaning: *lonely* suggests man's emotion, his unhappiness in his isolation, *differentiated* his sense of difference from other species; together the words carry complex meaning; and *item*, in addition to continuing the idea of separateness in *differentiated*, further connotes insignificance and depersonalization. When Winston Churchill said, ". . . we shall prove ourselves once again able to defend our Island home," *prove ourselves* (rather than "find ourselves") suggested meeting a test and establishing a truth; *once again* was a reminder that the British people had met tests before; and *Island home* had a deeper emotional meaning than "country" or "land," and also suggested, perhaps, the presence of the sea as a protective barrier. In the sentences below, spoken at a memorial service for Winston Churchill, one of the eloquent speakers of the twentieth century paid tribute to another. One feels that the words, the combinations of words, and the image at the end all are exactly right.

We shall hear no longer the remembered eloquence and wit, the old courage and defiance, the robust serenity of indomitable faith. Our world is thus poorer, our political dialogue is diminished, and the sources of public inspiration run more thinly for all of us. There is a lonesome place against the sky.—ADLAI E. STEVENSON, January 28, 1965

Emphasis. We have mentioned earlier several techniques of emphasis: the use of slanting and charged language; the use of the emphatic short sentence among longer ones; the emphasis given a word when it is moved from its normal position to the beginning or end of a sentence; and controlled repetition of structures, words, or ideas.

In general, beginnings and endings are important. A classic piece of advice to inexperienced writers is: "Strike out your first paragraph, strike out your last paragraph, and strike out your favorite sentence." *Favorite sentence* refers to the falsely eloquent or pretentious sentence of which the writer may be unjustly proud; and the advice about paragraphs usually means that the conclusion is a weak summary of the content of a short paper and that the opening paragraph is a dull and wasted leading up to the subject. Experienced writers use their beginning paragraphs for one or more of these purposes: to launch vigorously and directly into the subject, to arouse interest, to establish an appropriate tone or writer–audience relationship. Although some of the readings in this book are excerpts from longer works, many of them are complete essays and addresses; when they are, the author's beginning, and his probable reasons for using the emphatic opening position as he does, are worth particular consideration.

The end-position is usually even more emphatic than the beginning. The strongest sentences build to a climax; the writer uses the ending, followed by the period-pause, for a word, a phrase, or an idea which he wishes to emphasize. Good paragraphs, too, are likely to end strongly; and chapters and whole compositions end with the idea—sometimes a restatement of the main theme—which the writer wants to impress on the reader's mind. Part of analytical reading is noting the writer's ending, considering his emphasis, and thinking about how logically his conclusion is derived from the preceding material or for what psychological reasons he gave major emphasis to his concluding statements.

Within sections of the composition, too, one may observe a climactic order. If the author is giving a series of arguments or examples, why has he arranged them as he has? Is his arrangement dictated by logic, or is it the most emphatic psychological order?

Emphasis is also achieved by proportion—by the amount of space, the length of development, given to parts of the material. The writer generally gives something like equal development to ideas or aspects of the subject which seem to him of equal significance and the fullest development to his most significant ideas. The attentive reader is aware of proportion; at times he may ask himself why the writer has chosen to give emphasis by development to certain parts of the material and whether his reasons are primarily logical or psychological.

In the analysis of narrative writing (some of the personal and autobiographical essays in the last sections of this book, for example), the term *pace* is commonly used to refer to the proportions of summary and presentation. Summary is general statement which gives the net result of action; presentation is the dramatic development of scenes, in which characters, in a setting, speak and act. The skillful writer of narrative usually quickens his pace by summarizing, and so de-emphasizing, unimportant events; he slows his pace to present and give emphasis to significant actions and experiences. In a somewhat different sense, one may speak of the pace or movement of a piece of expository writing. When, for example, the writer develops an illustration at length or supplies numerous instances or concrete details to support a generalization, he may do so in order to be clear, interesting, or convincing; but he is also emphasizing the point to which he is giving this full development.

V. READING FOR IDEAS AND STYLE

Some of the most able students who come to college have read widely but superficially. They have not had the experience of reading in depth; and, called upon to do close analytical reading of complex material, they may have one or more of these difficulties: missing main ideas or confusing minor points with major points; failing to see the connections between points and being unclear about the broad development of the theme or idea; not understanding, or misunderstanding, the author's vocabulary and so missing the meaning of sections of the material. Although no simple remedy can be prescribed for these weaknesses, many students improve their reading when they adopt a systematic method of reading for study. One practical method consists of two stages. The first is reading the material through to see the whole development, without stopping to puzzle long over difficult passages, to look up words, to underline, or to take notes. (Students sometimes block themselves in reading—and also lose the thread of thought—by delaying over a passage that will be clarified by the later context; and they are not in a good position to underline or to take notes until they know what ideas are most significant.) This first reading should be as rapid as is consistent with the student's general comprehension of the material, and the reading should be continuous, to give a sense of the sequence and relationship of ideas. The second step is careful re-reading, in which the student examines the development of the main ideas, studies the texture of thought, is attentive to the author's language and tone, and works out the meaning of difficult passages. He may need to consult his dictionary in order to understand the author's words or allusions; more often he needs to study the context and the author's explanation of troublesome terms. If the reader is using his own book, he may be wise in this stage of reading to underline important ideas or to develop a system of marginal notation or numbering which shows the relationship between ideas. Part of this attentive re-reading should be active thought about the material presented.

Another common difficulty in reading comes from twisting the writer's words, distorting the meaning because it is alien or uncongenial to the reader. Not able to believe that anyone could hold such views, the reader reads what he wants to read instead of what is written. Reading Plato's *Symposium* without understanding the Greek attitude toward homosexual love, or reading an essay based on the assumption that "God is dead," or reading a discussion of the unreality of the phenomenal world, students have at times been led by their disbelief or disapproval into reading something the author has not intended and has not said. This difficulty stems, basically, less from habits of reading than from attitudes, habits of mind.

What are the attitudes, the obligations, and the pleasures or satisfactions of the good reader?

His first attitude should be curiosity, openness to new points of view, and willingness to suspend judgment until he has understood and thought about the writer's ideas. His first obligation, therefore, is to be fair to the writer and to make a real effort to understand exactly what is said. In trying to understand, he will be aided by a method of study like the one suggested early in this section. He may also find it helpful to outline complex pieces of writing and to form the habit of summarizing in his own words the writer's central ideas and the sequence of ideas. Sometimes a piece of writing (usually argument or persuasion) can be very briefly summarized in the form of a syllogism or a series of syllogisms. A syllogism is a three-part statement consisting of two premises and a conclusion drawn from the premises. For example:

> Men cut off from the past lose a sense of personal identity. (Major premise)
> Modern man is cut off from the past. (Minor premise)
> Therefore, modern man has lost a sense of personal identity. (Conclusion)

Phrasing such syllogisms, when it is possible to do so, may clarify the author's argument and also enable the reader to think about how, and how convincingly, the writer has established his premises and how valid his conclusion is.

Full understanding of a piece of writing may depend, however, on more than an ability to summarize the factual content, important though that is. Understanding may depend, for example, on awareness of the context of circumstances—the time, the occasion, the type of audience for whom the communication was written.[2] Such knowledge may help to explain the author's assumptions, the kind of language and illustration he chooses, and his tone. The reader also, in so far as he can, needs to determine the author's intention. On the surface, the author may be analyzing or giving information; but he may at the same time want his readers to respond in

---

[2] In the headnotes to the readings we have supplied some of this information.

certain ways, and he uses words to evoke feelings and attitudes as well as to inform. "Serious" writing is not always consistently serious in tone; the writer may use humor, irony, overstatement, or understatement as devices of persuasion. The reader misreads when he misunderstands the full intention and takes with deadly literalness what is meant to be facetious, ironical, or deliberately extravagant.

If, after his best efforts to understand a piece of writing, the reader still finds himself perplexed by parts of it, he may well consider another attitude and obligation of the good reader. The poet Coleridge phrased this "golden rule": "Until you understand a writer's ignorance, presume yourself ignorant of his understanding." Coleridge, reading one of Plato's Dialogues, found unintelligible passages in it and thought of dismissing the meaningless portions as Platonic jargon. But then he recalled his delight with the wisdom in Plato's other writing; he remembered passages in Plato, now thoroughly comprehensible, which had once seemed equally unintelligible; and he considered the reverence accorded Plato by the numerous great men who had studied his works. Unable to resolve the inconsistency of Plato's genius and a use of meaningless words, Coleridge wrote, "Therefore, utterly baffled in all my attempts to understand the ignorance of Plato, *I conclude myself ignorant of his understanding*."[3] In marked contrast is the pronouncement of a college freshman: "Plato is dull."

The good reader, then, is receptive and willing to credit the writer with having something to say that is worth understanding; but he is also critical in his reading. He judges the fundamental clarity (as distinct from the immediate transparency), the interest, and the logic of the writer's presentation. He knows that good logicians do not make sweeping statements without needed qualifications; do not base generalizations on too few examples; do not rest their cases on unsupported assumptions that an audience is unlikely to accept; do not use words in special senses without defining them; do not distort meaning by taking statements out of their context; do not use analogies (excellent devices for clarifying or persuading) as substitutes for solid argument or proof. The critical reader considers the appropriateness and effectiveness of language, examples, tone, and emphasis, in the light of what he knows of the circumstances and the author's intention. Finally, having understood as fully as possible and thought about the material, the reader makes a personal evaluation—of the appeal, the interest, the worth, or the truth of this communication for him.

We have not spoken directly of the pleasures or satisfactions of good reading, though some of them have been implied: the satisfaction of understanding; the satisfaction of encountering ideas which may give

---

[3] *Biographia Literaria*, Chapter XII.

form to the unexpressed thoughts of the reader or which may challenge him, disturb him, but open new vistas of thought; the satisfaction of arriving at sound judgments, of weighing conflicting values and making choices of one's own—for awareness of alternatives increases freedom of choice; the pleasure in language used well. Above all, perhaps, the good reader has the pleasure, even excitement, of seeing a mind at work— a clever, or good, or great mind, thinking; ordering ideas; qualifying, supporting, amplifying; selecting the words, the sentence patterns, the tone, and the emphasis to communicate his meaning to another mind. The reader may be chiefly impressed by a writer's thought, or chiefly impressed by his personality or his craft or art. The very best prose reflects the whole man—reason, imagination, character, and feeling; in it the good reader discovers a harmonious fusion of mind and manner, ideas and style.

PART ONE

Ways of Ordering Ideas

and Experience

THESIS AND EXAMPLES

[1] *James Thurber*: Which

JAMES THURBER (1894–1961) was an American essayist, well known, particularly to readers of *The New Yorker*, for his witty and satiric prose pieces and drawings. His books include *My Life and Hard Times, The Middle-Aged Man on the Flying Trapeze, Let Your Mind Alone, Fables for Our Time, My World—and Welcome to It, Thurber Country*, and *Alarms and Diversions*. "Which" is a section of "Ladies' and Gentlemen's Guide to Modern English Usage," published in 1929 in *The New Yorker*. The reference to Fowler in the opening sentences is to H. W. Fowler, whose *Dictionary of Modern English Usage* Thurber is quoting.

[1] The relative pronoun "which" can cause more trouble than any other word, if recklessly used. Foolhardy persons sometimes get lost in which-clauses and are never heard of again. My distinguished contemporary, Fowler, cites several tragic cases, of which the following is one: "It was rumoured that Beaconsfield intended opening the Conference with a speech in French, his pronunciation of which language leaving everything to be desired . . ." That's as much as Mr. Fowler quotes because, at his age, he was afraid to go any farther. The young man who originally got into that sentence was never found. His fate, however, was not as terrible as that of another adventurer who became involved in a remarkable which-mire. Fowler has followed his devious course as far as he safely could on foot: "Surely what applies to games should also apply to racing, the leaders of which being the very people from whom an example might well be looked for . . ." Not even Henry James could have successfully emerged from a sentence with "which," "whom," and "being"

in it. The safest way to avoid such things is to follow in the path of the American author, Ernest Hemingway. In his youth he was trapped in a which-clause one time and barely escaped with his mind. He was going along on solid ground until he got into this: "It was the one thing of which, being very much afraid—for whom has not been warned to fear such things—he . . ." Being a young and powerfully built man, Hemingway was able to fight his way back to where he had started, and begin again. This time he skirted the treacherous morass in this way: "He was afraid of one thing. This was the one thing. He had been warned to fear such things. Everybody has been warned to fear such things." Today Hemingway is alive and well, and many happy writers are following along the trail he blazed.

[2] What most people don't realize is that one "which" leads to another. Trying to cross a paragraph by leaping from "which" to "which" is like Eliza crossing the ice. The danger is in missing a "which" and falling in. A case in point is this: "He went up to a pew which was in the gallery, which brought him under a colored window which he loved and always quieted his spirit." The writer, worn out, missed the last "which"—the one that should come just before "always" in that sentence. But supposing he had got it in! We would have: "He went up to a pew which was in the gallery, which brought him under a colored window which he loved and which always quieted his spirit." Your inveterate whicher in this way gives the effect of tweeting like a bird or walking with a crutch, and is not welcome in the best company.

[3] It is well to remember that one "which" leads to two and that two "whiches" multiply like rabbits. You should never start out with the idea that you can get by with one "which." Suddenly they are all around you. Take a sentence like this: "It imposes a problem which we either solve, or perish." On a hot night, or after a hard day's work, a man often lets himself get by with a monstrosity like that, but suppose he dictates that sentence bright and early in the morning. It comes to him typed out by his stenographer and he instantly senses that something is the matter with it. He tries to reconstruct the sentence, still clinging to the "which," and gets something like this: "It imposes a problem which we either solve, or which, failing to solve, we must perish on account of." He goes to the water cooler, gets a drink, sharpens his pencil, and grimly tries again. "It imposes a problem which we either solve or which we don't solve and . . ." He begins once more: "It imposes a problem which we either solve, or which we do not solve, and from which . . ." The more times he does it the more "whiches" he gets. The way out is simple: "We must either solve this problem, or perish." Never monkey with "which." Nothing except getting tangled up in a typewriter ribbon is worse.

--◄{ COMMENT AND QUESTIONS }►--

1.   The author states his general thesis in his opening sentence and restates it in his final sentences. What particular kinds of trouble with *which* do his further statements and his examples emphasize or clarify?

2.   What assumptions is Thurber making about the readers of this essay?

3.   Examine the diction in paragraph 1. What is the effect of the expressions *recklessly, foolhardy, tragic cases, His fate . . . was not as terrible, barely escaped with his mind?* "Foolhardy persons sometimes get lost in which-clauses" introduces a sustained figure of speech. What is the implied comparison, and what expressions carry it through the paragraph?

4.   Is the comparison at the beginning of paragraph 2 related to the sustained figure in paragraph 1? Explain.

5.   How might the illustrative sentence in paragraph 2 (*He went up to a pew . . . .*) be improved?

6.   Examine the last sentence of paragraph 2. What are the connotations of *inveterate whicher?* What are the suggestions of *tweeting like a bird* and *walking with a crutch?* Does the sentence end strongly?

7.   *Multiply like rabbits* in the first sentence of paragraph 3 is ordinarily a cliché. What keeps it from seeming trite in this context?

8.   In paragraph 3 Thurber shifts to direct address to the reader (*You should never*) and to imperative mood (*Take a sentence . . . . Never monkey with "which"*). In the sentence beginning *On a hot night,* however, he shifts to third person. Why do you think he makes these shifts?

9.   What is the effect of the final sentence of the essay?

10.   Revise the following which-mire:
This article, which comes from *Ladies' and Gentlemen's Guide to Modern English Usage,* which was published in 1929, was written by James Thurber, who was a contributor to *The New Yorker* in which magazine appeared many of his stories and drawings which depict human beings who are caught in a society which is frustrating.

THESIS AND REASONS

[2]   *Geoffrey Crowther*: Two Heresies

SIR GEOFFREY CROWTHER (1907–   ) is an English economist and journalist, former editor of *The Economist,* and Chairman of the Central Advisory Council for Education (in England) from 1956 to 1960. In June, 1960, he received an honorary LL.D. degree from the University of Michigan and delivered, on that occasion, the following commencement address.

[¹] Mr. President, Regents of the University, members of the faculty, fellow graduates, ladies and gentlemen: I have been coming to Ann Arbor, on and off, for more than thirty years. I have made many friendships here. I have played some part in sending you a steady stream of graduate students from my own country. I have watched with affection and amazement the gigantic growth of this great institution. Of all the state universities of America, this is the one where I feel most at home.

[²] Yet never in my wildest moments did I dream that I should be admitted to the dignity of becoming an honorary graduate of The University of Michigan, and I am still overwhelmed by it. It is impossible to stand here, in this great stadium, before such a gathering, surrounded as we are by the spreading buildings of a great campus, without feelings of deep emotion, of humility, but also of pride, to know that one is to be a member of your body. I know that in this I can speak for all my fellow honorary graduates. In the words of the Prayer Book, for being made partakers in all this, we give you most humble and hearty thanks.

[³] On me you have conferred the supreme privilege of being permitted to address you. I would not for the world miss the honor. But it carries a very heavy burden with it. For what can be said in a commencement address that has not been said a thousand times before? Shall I extol the glories of the tradition of learning that leads from the monks' cells of the Middle Ages to the great universities of today? Those glories would gain nothing from anything I could say. Shall I sound the alarm for academic freedom? It seems to me to be in less danger today than at many other times. Should I perhaps address myself exclusively to the graduating class? Should I preach the ancient moral virtues to you? It would be an impertinence. Should I remind you of your duty to the community that has done so much for you? It would be an insult. Should I take the oldest and most shopworn theme of all, and remind you that this is a commencement, a beginning, not an ending? You wouldn't listen to me if I did. Should I try to give you the only thing that the old can give to the young—that is, the fruits of experience? But the chief thing you learn from experience is that no one will learn from other people's experience. No, members of the class of 1960, I can do nothing for you. The campuses of the country have been ringing all week long with high moral sentiments, and I haven't the heart to try to add to them.

[4] I must presume, Mr. President, that you had some deliberate purpose in choosing for your speaker this afternoon a foreigner—and one, moreover, who has been engaged for some years past in an intensive study of the educational system of his own country. I read in that a hint that you wanted to hear something of what an American university looks like from the outside to one who has been put by chance in the position to make some comparison between American universities and those of other countries. If that is your wish, I shall try to comply.

[5] But even then my dilemma is not quite resolved. Should I speak only of what I admire in the American university? That, indeed, would be easy. The words would come quickly to my mouth, because I spend so much of my time when I am at home in England pressing on our own universities some of your practices. I admire so much your generosity—not only your generosity of money, but your generosity of spirit, your deep sense of service to the community, the way you convince the individual—be he freshman or doctor—that you exist to serve him, not he to serve the institution. I admire the way you are forever breaking down the barriers between you and the rest of the community—not hiding behind hedges of aloofness and superiority, as too many of the academic institutions in my own country do. I admire the eagerness with which the pursuit of knowledge is carried on here. In Europe one is sometimes made to feel that the pursuit is over, that knowledge has been caught and tamed and made to live comfortably ever after. I admire the structure of graduate schools superimposed on a liberal arts college—a structure that, in my opinion, we should do well to adopt in England.

[⁶] There is so much to admire. But it would be a poor compliment to you to assume that all you wanted to hear was praise. The purpose of an address, after all, is communication from one mind to another, and if I am to succeed in setting you thinking, I must give you something to think about. So as I pondered what I would say to you this afternoon, I slowly screwed up my courage to the conviction that I can best return the compliment you pay me by telling of some of the things in the American university to which, in my opinion, you should be giving your serious critical attention. Having so often landed into trouble at home for singing the praises of the American university too loud, I had better run the risk of getting into trouble here for the opposite reason. So I determined to pick out this afternoon a couple of points on which I find myself beset with doubts. I am the more emboldened to do this because they are points which, so far as I can observe, do not seem to disturb you. That is why I gave myself the title of "Two Heresies" because I am going to challenge what is usually taken for granted.

[⁷] Let me state my two heresies quite bluntly so that you will see what I am getting at, and then I will try to defend them one after the other. My first heresy is to think that there are too many college students. And my second heresy is to think that they work too hard.

[⁸] When I say that there are too many college students, I don't mean here, at Michigan. There are, indeed, a goodly number here, but I would not presume to say that there are too many. There is a great deal to be said for the small college. And there is a great deal also to be said for the big college—though it is less often said. From what I know of Michigan, I would not say that it is too big—not yet. In any case, that is not my argument. I am not arguing about big colleges and small colleges. I am asking whether, in the United States, as a whole, there are not too many college students altogether—whether the proportion of the population that goes to college is not too large.

[⁹] Now I know that it has always been one of the fundamental doctrines of the American people that there must be no special privileges, no select class, that every boy and girl has a right to go to college if he or she can make the grade and can find, borrow, or earn enough money to stay alive for four years. I am not challenging that great American principle. Heretic though I may be, I am not trying to preach any old-world doctrine of a privileged aristocracy. No, I am trying, now that I am to be admitted to your society, to be a good American democrat (with a small "d"). Certainly, the right exists. But then it always has existed. What is new within the past decade or so—what is new and different and doubtful —is the doctrine that almost every American boy or girl should be encouraged and assisted to claim his right. There is also a right to travel freely on the highway. But even in Michigan you can't all do it at once. Indeed, if you try to claim this right all at once the only result is that nobody gets any benefit from it. It is possible to believe passionately in the existence of a right, and yet to hope that not everyone will claim it.

[10] Where is the process of universal education to stop? Is everyone to go to school until he is twenty-five or thirty—or thirty-five? I have had no opportunity to go back to the statistics, but my impression is that college going, as a percentage of the age group, is now in this country just about where high-school going was two generations ago. Now you know what has happened to the high school. I believe the nation-wide figure is that 85 per cent of the eighteen-year-olds are in high school. The same thing is now visibly happening to college going. If you include the junior colleges, it won't be long before the proportion reaches the halfway mark, and there is no reason to suppose that it will stop there.

[11] In my observation most Americans seem to take it for granted that this is a good thing. Perhaps it is—but not self-evidently so. There must, after all, be a limit somewhere. There must be some age at which universal education—the keeping of everyone in school—should stop. Is it not conceivable that the limit has been reached?

[12] Why do I say this? Chiefly because of the effect this movement towards universal college education is having on the colleges themselves. I will single out two of its effects. The first is that it must be lowering the average intellectual standard of the colleges of the country as a whole. That follows almost mathematically. If the process goes on until every boy and girl is in college, then the average standard of intelligence in the colleges in the country as a whole will be an I.Q. of exactly 100, which is a great deal lower than it has been hitherto. I am no mathematician, and it is a matter of constant surprise to me to discover that as many as half of all the people in the country are below average in intelligence. I am completely assured, however, that it is so. And what is more, that even with all the resources of modern science, there is nothing that can be done about it.

[13] It cannot help the colleges if more and more of their students come to them not because of any genuine desire to continue their education in any real sense of the word, but because it is socially the thing to do. If this is the general picture, then colleges, like this one, which want to maintain and even improve their standards, are forced into being more and more selective. Every good college in the country is besieged by applicants and at its wit's end to know how to choose among them. I do not think that it is good for the front-rank colleges if everyone who gets in has the feeling that he has succeeded in going through the eye of the needle to get there. And I do not think it is good for the country. Thus this great democratic principle of everyone having a college education is in fact creating a new privileged class—those who manage to get a good college education.

[14] The second consequence is this—that if nearly everybody goes to college, then increasingly all those who aspire to enter the professions or the higher ranks of business and administration—in a word all those who want to follow one of the careers for which college used to be the preparation—all these are now forced to go to a graduate school as well. Now, as I said before, I have nothing but admiration for the graduate schools. But they were never intended to serve 15 or 20 per cent of the age group. Moreover, what will happen to them when more and more of their students are there, not because they have any real interest in more study, not even because what they learn will really be useful to them, but simply because they are under some compulsion to appear better educated—which is taken to mean longer educated—than the mass, simply because they can't get the sort of job they want without a second set of letters after their names?

[15] More and more careers, for this reason, and among the highest careers, cannot begin until the age of twenty-four—or even twenty-six or twenty-seven if there is selective service to be done. Now think what this means. I suppose one can say that active life—that is, the life of the conscious mind—begins at or about the age of six or seven when one learns to read. At the other end, retirement from gainful occupation is more and more being pushed down towards sixty. In other words, in the normal life, there are not much more than fifty years or so between infancy and retirement. Is it really good sense that for the intellectual leaders of the country—the most intelligent quarter of the whole—as many as twenty out of those fifty-plus years should be spent in learning and only a bit more than thirty in doing? Is that really a rational employment of the scarcest of all scarce resources—human talent? Isn't there something to be said for the view that there should be less preparation for life and more living? Is America right to keep its young longer and longer on the leash, and to rely for the productive work of the nation more and more on the middle-aged? Only a very rich country could do it at all. But is it a wise application of your riches? When it comes to fighting, the job has to be done by the young. Is war the only activity in which the qualities of youth are needed? Must we in everything else be studied, overtrained, and elderly?

[16] Let me quickly turn, before the brickbats begin to fly, to my second heresy. In saying that the student of today has to work too hard, I can, I think, reasonably anticipate the sympathy of at least part of my audience. But perhaps I don't mean quite what they think I mean.

[17] I was speaking just a moment ago of the pressure that the good colleges are under to defend their standards. It is their duty to do so. If it is a privilege to be admitted to one of these institutions of the first rank, then no student should be allowed to remain there who does not continue

to measure up to the highest standards. I am not criticizing this concern for standards. Indeed, I am supporting it.

[18] But how, by what means, have the standards been enforced and maintained? From what I see and hear, I suspect that far too many colleges are doing it by what is the easy way for them—by demanding an ever higher total of hours put in—of hours, what is more, that have to be devoted to doing what the professor says must be done. Assignments become heavier and are more rigorously enforced. I have no doubt at all that the student of today who wants to secure a good average has to work for much longer hours than he did thirty years ago, when I first knew the American colleges. I don't mean that the student of the last generation led an easy life. His mind was active for as many hours a day as now: But I do think that he didn't have his nose held so close to the grindstone of requirements. He was freer to roam and follow his fancy. Now, it seems to me, he goes very much more in harness. Indeed, I have heard the head of a famous institution—not in Michigan—openly boast that they weed out the weaklings in the first year, not by any considerations of intellectual capacity or promise, but by deliberately setting an almost impossibly heavy schedule of assigned study in order to see who can take it.

[19] Now this all seems to me to be a mistake. Let us indeed have high standards, the highest possible. But high standards of what? Of diligence? Or of intelligence? The two are by no means the same thing. Indeed, they can be, and I suspect often are, at variance with each other, since the high intelligence, the really original mind, is likely to be the first to revolt against a drudgery which, in his case at least, is pointless and unnecessary.

[20] Let us get back to the fundamentals. What does a university exist for? What is the purpose of education? Is it to absorb a defined quantity of instruction? Or to learn how to think? Is it to accumulate knowledge? Or to acquire understanding? No doubt you know the old comparison between the two different ways of regarding the student's mind. You can think of it either as a pitcher that has to be filled up with factual knowledge or as a fire that has to be set alight. Put it in that way, and the right choice, I think, immediately becomes clear. The proper question for educators to be asking themselves every day is not "Am I cramming my students with the proper facts?" but "Am I succeeding in setting their minds ablaze?" And we all know that what is needed for a good roaring blaze is plenty of fresh air.

[21] Please don't misunderstand me. I am not asking for soft options. I don't want the students to live lives of leisure. I want them to be under the heaviest pressure. I want them to lead the most vigorous and rigorous lives. I want them to have to meet the severest tests. But let them be tests of intellect, of understanding, of expression, of imagination, of judgment, of purpose—and not just of the ability to stay awake.

[²²] I have one special reason for this plea. We hear a great deal now-adays of the danger of overspecialization, of the confining of the world of learning within narrow compartments which are unable, or unwilling, to say anything to each other. This is a real danger. There has been much discussion in my own country of the emergence of two cultures, the scientific and the humanitarian, which are increasingly separate from, and even hostile to, each other. I think this is an understatement of the danger. It is not two cultures with which we are threatened, but twenty-two. There is nothing in the world of learning more urgent than to find means of breaking down this separatism and moving back, so far as we can, to the time when educated men could travel in each other's territories without passports or interpreters. This is the authentic university tradition. It is indeed what the word means. Let us never forget that this great institution is a university. It ought not to be allowed to become a diversity.

[²³] Now I am simple enough to believe that the way to get a meeting of minds is to let them meet. You cannot solve the problem by prescribing courses, chemistry for the historian, or aesthetics for the engineer. You can prescribe the course all right but you can't prescribe the interest in the subject which alone makes it worthwhile. The only way you can get a real cross-fertilization between the different disciplines is to give a generous allowance of time for people of varying interests to explore each other's minds. I would plead that everyone in a university, from the freshman to the president, should make himself much less busy. He will find as a result—of this I am sure—that his mind is much more active.

[²⁴] I hope that I shall be forgiven for asking you to think about my two heresies. Of course, I have exaggerated them. I have been trying to use that powerful stimulus to thought, indignation. But why, after all, should I try to make you cross? There is, I repeat, so very much more to admire than to criticize. It is precisely because so much depends on the American universities that one wants to see them perfect. It is on you, more than on anyone else, that the hopes of liberal civilization in the world rest. You will remember that during the war the United States was often described as the arsenal of freedom—and how rightly. But the moral is in the long run so much more important than the material, and what will in the end determine the shape of the world in which our grandchildren live is not how many rockets or space ships or tanks America can build but the ideas to which Americans attach their faith. You attract to yourselves in your universities, and nowhere more than here in Michigan, so much of the best in the outside world and you give it back with such generosity. It is here that the links are forged that bind the free world together.

[²⁵] So you must not think of me, I hope, as a critic, or even as a candid friend, but simply as the newest of your graduates, full of ambition for the growth in grace and power of his Alma Mater. My prayer for this great university is the prayer that A. C. Benson uttered for his native country:

> Land of Hope and Glory, Mother of the Free!
> How can we extol thee, who are born of thee?
> Wider yet and wider may thy bounds be set,
> God, who made thee mighty, make thee mightier yet.

COMMENT AND QUESTIONS

1. Any commencement address is governed, in part, by certain established conventions: the speaker, in his introductory remarks, is expected to pay tribute to the college or university, to express gratitude for the honorary degree he is receiving, and to comment on the honor of being chosen to give the commencement address. Crowther observes all of these conventions, certainly, but he goes beyond them—both in the depth and extent of his expression of appreciation and in the extent of his introductory remarks: six paragraphs, approximately a fourth of the speech, precede the actual statement of his thesis. These paragraphs are in part logical preparation for the two heresies, but they also establish a psychological relationship with his audience. This is particularly important because the speaker, an Englishman, an outsider, proposes to criticize some theories and practices in American education. What kind of speaker–audience relationship is established in the first two paragraphs?

2. What is the purpose of paragraph 3—the enumeration of subjects that Crowther might discuss but will not?

3. Paragraphs 4 and 5 make an approach to the speaker's topic and also make a significant contribution to tone. What are the purposes in these paragraphs of the various references to the English system of education? Four sentences in paragraph 5 begin with "I admire." What keeps the sentences in this paragraph from being monotonous?

4. In paragraph 6, what attitudes toward his audience does the speaker express and imply? What attitudes toward himself? What persona has been revealed by the end of the first six paragraphs?

5. What possible misunderstandings of his first heresy is Crowther careful to remove? Comment on the effectiveness of his analogy of the right to go to college and the right to travel.

6. What are Crowther's reasons for thinking that the time may have come for the process of universal college education to stop? Much of this section of the speech has a cause–effect development. What are the effects of universal education as Crowther sees them? Why does he use repeated question-patterns at the end of paragraph 15 instead of making his points in declarative sentences?

7. Are Crowther's reasons for believing that there are too many college students convincing to you? The trend toward universal college education has, of course, increased in the years since this address was given. Would it be desirable to stop or to reverse the trend? Would it be practically possible to do so?

8. With his second heresy, as with his first, the speaker takes pains to correct possible misinterpretations. What kinds of high standards does he think the colleges have been inclined to adopt and enforce? What different high standards would he establish? What are his reasons for urging less busyness? What desirable effects would it produce? Do you find anything especially deft in the last two sentences of paragraph 22?

9. What is the purpose of education, according to Crowther, and what is "the authentic university tradition"? Do you think that decreased assigned work would indeed have the results he foresees?

10. Crowther's style is interesting and good in many ways. Examine paragraphs 19 and 21 to see one of his techniques of repeating and yet varying his sentence length and structure.

11. The last two paragraphs turn from criticism and return to the tone of the opening section of the address. What additional tribute does Crowther pay to American universities in paragraph 24? The closing prayer of A. C. Benson (an English writer, 1862–1925) was probably selected for its tone and the relationship of *Mother* and *Alma Mater*. What part of the prayer is also directly relevant to the central ideas of the address?

12. As you think about the whole speech, do you see any logical or psychological reasons for the order in which Crowther presents his two heresies?

GENERALIZATION
AND QUALIFICATION

℘

[3]   *Nils Y. Wessell*: The Opportunity for Change

NILS Y. WESSELL (1914–   ), whose doctoral degree is in psychology,
was president of Tufts University from 1953 to 1966, and is now head of the
Institute for Educational Development. "The Opportunity for Change" was
a matriculation address, given in September, 1965, to the entering members
of the Tufts classes of 1969.

[1] If we were to assemble here this evening all of the joys and worries,
all of the concerns and enthusiasms, and all of the hopes and doubts that
have marked the months and years between your individual decisions to
apply to Tufts and your arrival on this campus this week, they would fill
this room and the cage beyond to overflowing. Add to these what your
teachers and parents and other members of your family have experienced
and all of the buildings of this University would not provide capacity
enough. There is excitement in your finally being here, for all of us, your
teachers and counselors who are the faculty and adminstration of Tufts,
as well as for you. The reason is simple. Great hope and great promise
combine as you begin an adventure which you have in your own power to
make the most meaningful of your lives.

[2] I grant that some limits will be set on your accomplishments by
factors not now possible of substantial modification, but I would urge you
tonight and in the next year or two ahead of you that you seek to uncover

those ways in which your growth has not been predestined by what has gone before. This does not mean that I have cast off a bias of the last twenty-five years of my life which gives the nod to nature over nurture, to biology over psychology, to heredity over environment in the development of human traits and in the setting of goals and standards of achievement. What I am attempting to say is that even with whatever predestination you bring with you, biological or otherwise, there are opportunities for growth and maturation and achievement which, if anything, go beyond your present expectations.

[3] One form of predestination never did provide for me a compelling case. This is the Freudian notion that the experiences, traumatic and otherwise, of the first three or four years of life determine adult personality in a substantial and almost irrevocable way—at least irrevocable without psychoanalysis. I do not mean to denigrate early childhood experiences. In fact, there is much we need yet to learn about their role. What I do say is that such influences during infancy do not make impossible at age eighteen significant changes for the better and the development of personal qualities during the college years of a mature and healthy sort. In short, do not assume that it is too late to make fundamental changes in the level of your intellectual achievement or in your personal traits or in your sense of values or in your commitment to ideals. Granted that the change may be negative as well as positive. In the academic community, however, to quote the popular song of a generation ago, we "accentuate the positive."

[4] It is quite possible for you who are shy to develop social poise and confidence; for you who are a bit too arrogant to learn that a measure of humility is both more effective and more attractive; for you who are self-centered to learn the nobler pursuits stemming from a sense of social concern; for you who consider yourself fated to save the world to learn you must save yourself first; for you who would conform completely to the social and personal code of your contemporaries to know the rewards of some individuality; for you who bristle at the slightest imposition of authority to discover that freedom is really the opportunity for self discipline; and for you who have but parroted back what your teachers have taught you to experience the joy and the excitement of personal discovery and invention.

[5] These are but a few illustrations of the potential for change which is within you and it is during the next two years that much of the change can be accomplished. You do not come to college fully formed. Neither computers nor human intuition can define exactly and predict completely your personal and intellectual qualities and the limits of their development.

[6] Your heredity, your early childhood, your home life over the last

eighteen years, and the role of your teachers in influencing you are of course still important. To make sure I am not misunderstood let me turn the coin over for a minute and examine the other side.

[⁷] The role of heredity in determining many of your traits and characteristics and capacities is real even though not fully understood. Molecular biology and biochemistry however are on the threshold of startling breakthroughs in our understanding of genetic mechanisms. Clearly some of you are blessed with greater potential than others, whether that potential involves quantitative reasoning or verbal facility or physical size and attractiveness or speed of foot. You would be wise to seek the most objective appraisal you can get of what your abilities in any or all of these areas are, provided you do not then set for yourself ceilings of achievement that are arbitrary and fixed or premature.

[⁸] If you are presently five feet, two inches tall or weigh one hundred twenty pounds or take twenty-two seconds to run the one hundred yard dash, it is most unlikely that you will ever become a professional basketball or football player. If you scored eight hundred on the verbal part of the scholastic aptitude test all three times you took it, and between 350 and 400 on the quantitative part on the same three occasions, and if the scores are reflected also in your grades over the last several years, then engineering or physics might well not be the best choice of a major field you can make. It is not true that anyone can do anything he wants to provided he is sufficiently motivated. If you do not agree with me, I suggest you try flying to the moon without benefit of rocket or capsule.

[⁹] Of course, all these illustrations are exaggerated by design. They are cited to make sure that you do not interpret my remarks to mean that there are no bounds to what you can achieve intellectually or personally. Trusting that this simple but important point has been made, I turn to my main thesis which is to persuade and to remind you that there is much indeed you can accomplish and that the next two years are critical in determining what your levels of aspiration will be.

[¹⁰] As many college teachers will testify, the change that takes place in students from freshman to senior year seems to defy generalization and analysis. Individual differences in students seem to cover so wide a range that anything meaningful and valid and inclusive is difficult to state. But I am willing to try, for I believe that the most important thing I can provide assurance about as you begin your college career is that change— important change—is very much within your power to achieve.

[¹¹] There is evidence that people differ widely in the age at which they reach their ceilings of mental ability. Substantial gains can be made in certain intellectual characteristics, such as reasoning, even after the age of thirty. There is also evidence that the more intelligent persons of a particular age are not only increasing in measured ability at a faster rate than less intelligent persons of the same age, but also have farther to go in reaching their maximum ability. Your developing your ability to the full is, of course, your first goal and ours to assist you in attaining.

[¹²] Just as there is evidence that intellectual development does not reach a ceiling by age fifteen or sixteen, so is there evidence to contradict the notion that personality development reaches its fixed characteristics by a similar age. Your personalities are not fully formed by the time you enter college.

[¹³] The college environment is one which is highly favorable to change. Learning is change and learning is our chief concern. Entering college students face a high degree of independence in comparison with their prior school and home experiences. College students have yet to take on the commitments and the encumbrances typical of young people immediately after the age of twenty-two.

[¹⁴] Your attitudes as college students toward change are also somewhat contradictory in that your confidence frequently does not match your aspiration. You look upon college as being a circumstance which by some magic process will bring about the realization of many of your dreams. Somehow college will do this to you and for you. Actually, any of your dreams that are realized will be realized because of your own efforts and not because of some mysterious process which exerts its influence through your mere passive attendance at college.

[¹⁵] Your coming to a fuller realization of the potential for change that is within you and subject to your own efforts, your intimate familiarity with change, and your grasp of the factors which make for change grow in importance almost daily, for the world in general is evolving at an accelerated pace. A few decades ago the curve of knowledge could be described as a gently rising plateau. This is no longer so. The line seems to be approaching the vertical. The individual who has not learned to live with change and to effect change in himself will be obsolete the day he receives his diploma. If college graduates are not so educated and prepared, who else in society will be? The unpredictability of the physical world is clearly being matched by the unpredictability of the political and social world.

[¹⁶] There are two cautions and a hope I would express as you face the opportunity for change and the prospect of change which will mark your college years. The first is that you avoid being premature in the new commitments you make with respect to intellectual or moral or personal standards. New concepts with respect to such standards should be studied and weighed and discussed and evaluated and even some of them in time made deeply and unequivocally your own. However, I do suggest that you postpone for a while at least the complete identification and the complete espousal of a cause or standard or way of life until you have satisfied yourself that you have brought all the objectivity you can muster to the issues involved and have examined fairly and carefully more than one point of view. Commitment should come and will come in time, and will before the end of four undergraduate years on many issues in many cases; but do not cast the die too early in your college career.

[17] My second caution is that you do not permit rebellion to be the chief architect of your way of life and of your standards of behavior. Of course it is natural that you should consider yourself more responsible and more prepared to exercise freedom than your parents believe you to be, but beware of the easy trap into which you can fall of determining all of your attitudes on the basis of rebellion to constituted authority or the older generation. May I remind you that you will all too soon be the older generation yourselves and that the generation now called older by you was not too long ago aged eighteen to twenty-two. But more than this, your standards and your ideas and your aspirations should be positive and not reactionary, should be built out of your own experience as contributing, maturing individuals. Living a life only of protest makes no more personal sense than taking in each other's laundry makes economic sense. Protest, yes, injustice and indignity. But you will find only futility in protesting the fact that there are people older than you.

[18] And finally may I express a hope, a hope that in this university and in American society generally there will develop a sense of community out of which will come a realization to the full of the true dignity of the individual and of the common goals and aspirations of all persons of good will, whether they be eighteen or twenty-two or thirty-five or sixty-four and whether they be called students or faculty or administration or the younger generation or the Establishment or what-have-you. That sense of community will enable us to realize to the maximum the potential in all of us, will make of the intellectual experience that is college something both exciting and satisfying, and will result in our personal relations being characterized by mutual respect, confidence and warmth.

[19] By many roads you have traveled to this campus. In a real sense you are all equals in the opportunities now before you and in the potential you possess to capitalize upon these opportunities. It is truly an adventure that awaits you, to prepare yourself for change by changing yourself.

---## COMMENT AND QUESTIONS ##---

1. How would you describe the tone of the opening paragraph? What relationship with his audience is the speaker establishing?
2. In each of the first three paragraphs, Wessell states and restates parts of

his central thesis: "... you begin an adventure which you have in your own power to make the most meaningful of your lives" (paragraph 1); "... there are opportunities for growth and maturation and achievement which, if anything, go beyond your present expectations" (paragraph 2); "... do not assume that it is too late to make fundamental changes in the level of your intellectual achievement or in your personal traits or in your sense of values or in your commitment to ideals" (paragraph 3). In the second and third paragraphs, how does he qualify these generalizations?

3. Paragraph 4 is a paragraph of examples of possible changes. Notice that the paragraph is a single sentence, with sustained parallel phrasing. Is there a logical or a psychological order, or both, in the arrangement of the examples?

4. Paragraph 5 restates the central idea: "You do not come to college fully formed," and paragraph 6 introduces further qualifications. What are the qualifications, and how are they developed in paragraphs 7 and 8?

5. What is the function of paragraph 9?

6. Paragraph 10 ends with another assurance that important change is possible. Do you find any qualifications in this paragraph?

7. Paragraph 13 states that the college environment is highly favorable to change. In what sense is paragraph 14 a qualification of 13?

8. What does paragraph 15 contribute to the development of the main idea of the speech?

9. What are Wessell's two cautions, and how are they related to the central theme of change? Are there qualifications here too (paragraphs 16 and 17)?

10. Do you think that paragraph 18 was included chiefly for content or for tone? Explain.

11. Examine the final paragraph of the composition. How is "By many roads" related to the earlier content? The author has granted that the students he is addressing are not equal in heredity, background, and potential. In what sense is the second sentence of the last paragraph true? In what ways is the last sentence an effective ending?

NARRATION

[4]   *Robert O. Ballou*: The Jew and the Christian

ROBERT O. BALLOU (1892–1962) was an American writer and publisher, and editor of *The Bible of the World* and a condensation, *The Portable World Bible*. The aim of *The Portable World Bible,* from which this selection is taken, is to present compactly the central ideas of the world's eight great religions—Hinduism, Buddhism, Zoroastrianism, Judeo-Christianity, Mohammedanism, Confucianism, and Taoism. "The Jew and the Christian" is Ballou's introduction to selections from the Old and New Testaments.

[¹] Out of the land of Egypt, out of a swamp of bulrushes, out of the loins of a slave woman 1200 years before the birth of Christ, came the child who was to become the supreme lawmaker of all time. The religion of Judaism, for which he laid the foundation, and that of Christianity, which was its child, are to-day the strong bases of Western religious culture.

[²] There is no story of the miraculous conception or birth of Moses such as those which record the origins of Jesus, of Gautama Buddha, and of Zarathushtra. There were no voices of angels singing to herald the coming of the great Hebrew leader, no moving star or other phenomena of nature to lead shepherds and wise men to the bed of the child, no bending down of trees over the mother, as in the story of the birth of the Buddha, no luminosity about the place of *accouchement,* such as that which we are told shone about Zarathushtra's birthplace three days before his birth. There were no prophets either at his birth or during his

39

childhood to proclaim his divinity. Nor did Moses ever claim for himself any divine qualities which set him apart from other mortals.

[³] The greatest of all the leaders of the Jews was a child of his people, hidden at birth in the bulrushes on the bank of an Egyptian river by his mother in order that he might escape the edict of Pharaoh that every child of the Hebrews should be killed. And though we are told that he later saw God, talked with him, and received directly from the omnipotent hand the stone tablets containing the Ten Commandments, he remained a man of his people to the day of his death and beyond.

[⁴] From time immemorial the Jews had prophesied the coming of a Messiah. Christians believe that the prophecy was fulfilled in the birth of Jesus. The orthodox Jews' dissension from this belief does not arise from protestation that Moses was this long-heralded Messiah. They still await a divine leader in human form, and are content to regard one of the world's most dramatic stories—that of the life of Moses—as the narrative of a natural phenomenon and Moses as a thoroughly human being. They are satisfied to say, in the words of Deuteronomy, "There arose not a prophet since in Israel like unto Moses, whom the Lord knew face to face."

[⁵] Yet if a religion which is swayed by so many cross currents and has so many leaders in it as has Judaism may be said to have a personal founder, surely that man is Moses. With Aaron as his lieutenant, he led the Children of Israel out of their bondage in Egypt and during forty years of wandering held them together, strengthened them in their heart-breaking discouragements, instructed them, laid down laws for them which he enforced with an iron hand, and gave them the Ten Commandments in the form recognized to-day by both Jew and Christian. By pleading, demonstration, threats, denunciations, and even ruthless slaughter of the recalcitrant, he induced them to worship only Jehovah, thus paving the way for the monotheism which is the basis of Western theology.

[⁶] To understand the complex pattern of the Jewish religion, it is necessary to look back to times long prior to the birth of Moses, to a time probably before the Iranian branch of Indo-Europeans migrated to Persia.

[⁷] The Jews were then a group of Semitic tribes wandering on the Arabian desert and slowly drifting towards Palestine, constantly seeking better pastures for their herds of sheep and goats.

[⁸] There is evidence that even at this early date they recognized a code of laws enunciated in ten sentences which they called "the Ten Commands." Some of these are identical in meaning with edicts of the Ten Commandments. Some are not. But they are undoubtedly the parent of the later code. (See *The Bible of the World*, p. 1368.) The stories of the origins of the earth and of man may already have been established much as we have them today in Genesis. The story of Adam and Eve in its essentials may, or may not, have had some relation to a basic legend believed by that other great race of religious men, the Indo-Europeans, who told the story of Mashya and Mashyoi in Persia and that of Yama and Pami in India. The story of the flood and the ark which Noah built appears in its essential details in the earlier Babylonian *Epic of Gilgamish*. (See *The Bible of the World*, pp. 1366, 1367.) Some of the laws later enunciated in the Old Testament (notably those of exact retaliation) are from the Code of Hammurabai, a Babylonian king who ruled about 2250 B.C. who is probably identical with the King Amraphel of Genesis 14, 1. According to the Babylonian story this code, inscribed on tablets, was given to Hammurabai by the sun god himself, an almost exact parallel to the story of Jehovah giving Moses the Ten Commandments.

[⁹] Obviously, then, Judaism owes much to earlier religions. But it has contributed to the present much more than it has borrowed from the past.

[¹⁰] That contribution began even before the birth of Moses when, about 2000 B.C., the Jews wandered from "Ur of the Chaldees" westward to found a nation. Because in their migration they crossed the Euphrates River, they were called "Hebrews" from a word which means "to cross over." Genesis tells us that they were led by the patriarch Abraham.

[¹¹] Some scholars now question the existence of the individual man Abraham, believing rather that this was the designation of a tribe, but the name stands in Jewish belief for one of the greatest of all the early patriarchs, the first of the strong Jewish leaders whose names have been preserved, the "father of the faithful," and the "friend of God."

[¹²] At the time of Abraham his people believed in many gods. These gods had been given names after first having been worshipped merely as natural phenomena or objects. The Hebrews accorded their worship to individual deities as their fancies—or their beliefs in relative godly strengths—dictated. But the God of Abraham was *Yaweh,* Yaweh the strong, Yaweh whose power, so Abraham said, was far greater than the combined strength of all the other gods. Abraham and Yaweh had made a compact whereby the great god had agreed to accept the Hebrews as his chosen people, to take a special interest in them, and to further their well-being so long as they acknowledged him alone as their god, gave no homage to other gods, and did his will.

[¹³] Now the doing of his will was a complex matter. Sacrifices, burnt offerings heaped upon an altar, prayers and incantations—these he wanted, but they were not in themselves enough. The will of Yaweh was that the people of Abraham should, in their daily lives, follow a course of conduct which had in view the well-being and happiness of their fellow tribesmen. Thus an ethical pattern was woven into the religion along with its rites and ceremonies. It did not yet include the concept of world brotherhood. Ethical conduct towards members of the tribe of

Abraham was one thing—that to others, another. But even here was the beginning of an ethical code which later was to dominate the Western World.

[14] Abraham's compact with Yaweh did not constitute the monotheism, the belief that there is one God only, which Judaism and its child Christianity accept to-day, but was rather "henotheism," the worship of one god, while recognizing others. Until long after the death of Moses the existence of other gods was believed in by the Jews. The first commandment did not say "Thou shalt believe that there are no other gods but me," but rather "Thou shalt have no other gods before me." This tacit recognition of the existence of other gods was reinforced by such admonitions as "Revile not the gods." When God appeared to Moses in the burning bush he did not say, "I am the only God," nor did he apparently feel that the simple words "I am God" were enough to make him known. He identified himself among the gods by saying "I am the God of thy father, the God of Abraham, the God of Isaac, and the God of Jacob." Even years later, when Moses' leadership had ended with his death and Joshua, having led his people through a long lifetime, was about to die, he urged them to "put away the strange gods which are among you, and incline your hearts unto the Lord God of Israel."

[15] Directly descended from Abraham, through his son Isaac, was Jacob, twin brother of Esau. Jacob, whose name later became Israel, was the father of twelve sons who became heads of the twelve tribes of Israel. Esau meanwhile headed another tribe near Canaan who became known as the Edomites.

[16] The story of the twelve sons of Jacob—how one of them, Joseph, was sold by his brothers and carried into Egypt, how Joseph rose to leadership under the powerful Pharaoh, of how he brought his people to live there in a land of plenty, how he and his master died, and how another Pharaoh enslaved the Hebrews—is told in the later part of Genesis and the first part of Exodus.

[17] Then arose the mighty figure of Moses, the son of a Hebrew slave named Levi, who was adopted by the daughter of Pharaoh when she found him hidden in the bulrushes. As a son of the royal household he might have cast his lot in with the Egyptian overlords. But the Pharaoh's daughter had engaged Moses' own mother (who had thrust herself forward through subterfuge) to nurse him, and from her he must have been well schooled in the manner of his birth and the history of his people. When as a young man he saw the burdens laid upon the Hebrews, he was overcome with sadness. This rapidly grew into anger and drove Moses to kill an Egyptian who was beating a Jew. Escaping from the wrath of the Pharaoh, he went into the land of Midian where he married and had the first of several encounters with Yaweh who, speaking from the midst of a burning bush, said that his name was "I Am" (just as, in

the later Hinduist *Upanishads*, Yama tells Nachiketas that God can be named only by the words "He Is"). Reaffirming the ancient covenant with Abraham, Yaweh said that he had come to strengthen his people. With Moses acting as his spokesman and executive, he would lead them out of their captivity.

[18] How Moses courageously faced the Pharaoh, demanding and finally accomplishing the release of the Hebrews (with the help of "I Am" and the plagues he sent upon the Egyptians), how he led them across the Red Sea and to the very edge of the Promised Land with the fire by night and the cloud by day which Yaweh sent to guide them, is told in the magnificent story of Exodus. This story is of primary importance in the belief of devout Jews to this day, for they have not forgotten Yaweh's ancient covenant with Abraham, and God's help in their deliverance from Egypt is one of the basic evidences that he fulfilled his part of that compact.

[19] After the death of Moses the Hebrew people passed through centuries of vicissitudes as a nation. These are important from a religious point of view only in so far as the changing circumstances influenced their religious, and therefore, their ethical concepts—those two forces which, as early as Abraham, were becoming so strongly enmeshed with tribal feeling that the three were to become one. Their attitude towards God, their attitude towards themselves as a united and exclusive people, and their standards of ethical conduct merged in the one mighty phenomenon of Judaism.

[20] For nearly a century in the time of the kings they enjoyed prosperity and peace. Then, during the reign of Rehoboam, when the nation was in the throes of political dissension and revolt against high taxation, once more the people were divided. Now the two groups became a northern and a southern kingdom, "Israel" and "Judah." In both kingdoms prosperity brought luxury and with it a falling away from the ancient worship of Yaweh. Many adopted the licentious practices of the Canaanitish religion and worshipped the Canaanitish gods. Their covenant with Yaweh forgotten, an increase in the commercial spirit brought with it exploitation, extortion, the selling of the poor into slavery for debts, immorality, and wars.

[21] Rising to the need of the times came a succession of great leaders. They have been called prophets, but perhaps it would be more accurate to call them sociologists and religious truth-tellers. For their teachings were based upon a deep understanding of the human heart and mind, a keen knowledge of the ills and needs of their people, and an exalted vision of righteous justice.

[22] One can only speculate on how much or how little they were influenced by other similar religious phenomena which were occurring throughout the world. This great age of religious awakening took place a little more than half a millennium before the birth of Christ and gave

the *Upanishads* with their conception of the supreme Brahma, Gautama Buddha, and Mahavira to India, Confucius and Lao Tze to China, and the great monotheistic and work-revering Zarathushtra to Persia. In Greece men sought elevation of the human soul through beauty in one of the world's greatest periods of art. Rome was spreading its civilization through conquest and leaving its mark indelibly upon world society through the Roman genius in law making.

[23] In Israel these seers and moral leaders saw the threatened disintegration of national unity and morality, and reminded their people over and over of their covenant with Yaweh and their debt to him for their deliverance from slavery. They warned them that greed, dishonesty, cruelty, intolerance, lasciviousness, materialism, and sloth were the instruments of national suicide. Perhaps they were strongly influenced by contemporary Zoroastrianism, for whereas Jehovah had previously been represented as the source of all things, both good and evil, he was now credited only with good while Satan (parallel of the Zoroastrian Angra Mainyu) was thought to create evil. Other evidences point to possible extensive borrowing of concepts from the fertile and vital religion of the great Persian.

[24] But regardless of how much Judaism may have taken from Zoroastrianism or other religions, its own utterances at this time were vastly more important. It was combining, with such force, conviction, and practicality as had never before been achieved, a theology and a social code. It was building an ethical religion in which man was to achieve salvation through co-operation with the one God, omnipotent Lord of the universe and loving, merciful father of us all, in whose godhead we could participate through righteousness and love in the service of our fellow-men.

[25] Considering the later prophets and the earlier leaders as one group, no other religious history has within it such an assembly of giants—Abraham and Moses, Elijah (who is reported to have raised a man from the dead and miraculously filled a widow's pitcher with milk centuries before Christ was said to have performed similar miracles), Elisha, Amos, Hosea, Joel, Micah, the dour and sorrowful Jeremiah (first to suggest that others besides Jews might share in the blessings of Jehovah-worship), Nahum, Habbakuk, Zephaniah, Ezekiel, Job of the many trials and great faith, Isaiah to whose loving Father-God all men were equal regardless of race, colour, or time or place of their births, and the deep-throated Daniel, saved by faith from the jaws of lions, who could dream and sing while he told of the holiness of Jehovah, and the glory which slept in the souls of men, waiting only for a reign of human righteousness to awaken it and vivify the human world.

[26] But no nation has ever realized the visions of greatness seen by its spiritual leaders. Century by century the moral and religious practices of

no part of the intention or effort of any one of these to overthrow the religion of his fathers and set up a new religion in its place. Many of Christ's most forceful admonitions, including his great commandments— "The Lord thy God is one God. Thou shalt love the Lord thy God with all thy heart, and thy neighbour as thyself"—were direct quotations from the Old Testament. The Golden Rule he quoted (with a slight change to make it positive instead of negative) from Hillel. He announced his purpose (Luke 4:18–19) in the words of an Old Testament prophet: "The Lord anointed me to preach good tidings to the poor. He hath sent me to proclaim release to the captives and recovering of sight to the blind, to set at liberty them that are bruised, to proclaim the acceptable year of the Lord." (Isaiah 61:1–2.) He said that he had come not to destroy, but to fulfil, the Jewish laws. He at all times observed the Jewish religious ceremonies rigorously. Even his cry of despair on the cross, "My God, my God, why hast thou forsaken me?" evidenced his preoccupation with Hebrew religious texts, for it is a direct quotation from an Old Testament Psalm.

[31] Racially and religiously Christ was born, lived, and died a loyal Jew. He sought merely to strengthen observance of the Jewish law and widen his people's understanding of the merciful, loving, Father-God whose Lordship was attested by the Jewish spiritual leaders who preceded him. He wanted to impress upon his people the doctrine that devotion to God was meaningless unless it was expressed first of all in devotion to one's fellowmen.

[32] The life of Jesus is shrouded in mystery and mysticism. As in the earlier stories of Gautama Buddha and Zarathushtra, the scriptural story tells of the miraculous conception of Jesus, of homage paid to him at birth by wise men (probably Zoroastrian priests) who recognized his divinity, of his temptation by Satan (as Buddha was tempted by Mara and Zarathushtra assaulted by a personification of evil), of many miracles which he performed during his ministry, and, as a last proof of his divinity, of his resurrection after death.

[33] Jesus' reception during his life was a stormy one. The multitudes, drawn by his tremendous personal magnetism and his never failing understanding and kindness, flocked to him, proclaimed his goodness and greatness, and many of them acknowledged him as the Son of God and the long-awaited Messiah. But powerful forces in the Jewish congregation, jealous of his popularity, incensed by his denunciation of some of them, and bitterly critical of his disregard for formalism, his willingness to violate some of the minor laws of the Jews, and his heretical claim that he was the Son of God, repudiated him, conspired to kill him, saw him crucified, and, after his death, persecuted his followers.

[34] It is probably to that persecution that we owe the spread of Judeo-Christianity to the West and its influence upon modern life, for reaction

the Jews declined until, like coins which become so worn that their original values cannot be deciphered, they had little in common with the teachings of the great prophets. It was time for a new vision and a new leader.

[27] Twelve hundred years after the death of Moses, about the time when Krishna in the *Bhagavad Gita* was calling India to righteous living and devotion to God, when Buddhism was flooding eastward into China and Japan, and Zoroastrianism was falling away from the greatness which its founder had brought to it, there was born in Bethlehem of Judea a Jew who was to descend upon the Hebrew congregation like a storm from heaven. Crying for repentance and rededication to God, he offered salvation in holy loving kindness to all who would follow him.

[28] Jesus of Nazareth was well versed in the religion of his fathers and dedicated, as were those great religious leaders whose concepts he carried on, to worship of "the God of Abraham, the God of Isaac, and the God of Jacob," Jehovah, who was now seen as the one God, omnipotent ruler of the universe and loving father of mankind. As he grew to manhood Jesus saw a Hebrew nation whose religious life consisted largely in external observances, in rituals and sacrifices, in petty dietary laws and other domestic rules, rather than in that spiritual co-operation with God through humility, social righteousness, and faith of which the later prophets spoke. He saw a priestly class who hypocritically held themselves above others— as the priests of Hinduism did at the time of Gautama's birth—and a people who believed that they were the chosen of God and thus the superiors of all other peoples. Intolerance, bigotry, hypocrisy, and materialism were like acid poisons eating away the soul of Israel.

[29] There were other great Jewish leaders who saw these things, others who were carrying on and advancing the religious thought of the prophets. One of the most notable of these, the incomparable Rabbi Hillel, was still living when Jesus was born. He preached the Golden Rule of Reciprocity (which Confucius had taught in China and Gautama Buddha in India more than half a millennium before) and other principles of humility, worship of the one God, and universal brotherhood, which became such essential parts of Christ's doctrine. But the Hebrew nation as a whole heeded these exhortations as little as they had those of Isaiah— as little as the Christian nations of the twentieth century heed the doctrines of Jesus Christ.

[30] The mission which Jesus set for himself was essentially no different from that to which Isaiah, Amos, Jeremiah, Ezekiel, Hillel, and the other great Jewish leaders had devoted their lives. Each of these and Jesus tried to bring understanding and a reawakened consciousness of the need of righteousness to his people, just as Confucius and Lao Tze in China, Gautama Buddha in India, and Zarathushtra in Persia had done. It was

from it produced the ministry of Paul. In the beginning those who followed the doctrines of Jesus, the Jew from Nazareth, were thought of merely as the representatives of a new Jewish sect, just as the first Buddhists were merely representatives of a new sect in Hinduism. There was nothing startling or revolutionary in the appearance of one more sect. Judaism had survived many divisions and the infusions of many interpretations. But the doctrine of Jesus, after his death, was singularly unsuccessful among the Jews. It was only when the convert, Paul, turned from the persecuting Jews and began his almost fanatic proselytizing among the Gentiles that the doctrine spread into Greece and Rome and thence to the rest of the Western World.

[35] During Paul's ministry, in the first century after the death of Jesus, the followers of Christ's doctrine (or more properly the followers of Christ's doctrine as interpreted by Paul and his colleagues) definitely left the Jewish congregation, called themselves Christians, and established the Christian Church at Antioch. Thus occurred the greatest and most tragic schism in the religious history of the Western World, and one which Christ himself never intended and never foresaw.

[36] None of the story of Jesus in any form which is now extant was recorded during his lifetime. The earliest writings of the New Testament are in the Acts of the Apostles and the Pauline Epistles, written A.D. 50–65. The four Gospels, which tell the story of Christ's life, were written A.D. 65–150. The three called "the Synoptics" because they "see together" or present substantially the same point of view (Matthew, Mark, and Luke) were written first. The last, the Gospel of John, was written much later and presents a somewhat different theological concept which has much that relates it to the religions of India and China. "In the beginning was the Word," John writes, "and the Word was with God, and the Word was God." Thus he was presenting a concept which was very like that of the Tao in Taoism and the Brahman of the *Upanishads*. Indeed, Chinese translations of the Gospel of John begin, "In the beginning was the *Tao*, and the *Tao* was with God, and the *Tao* was God," repeating the concept of one of the verses of the *Tao-Te King*, basic scripture of Taoism.

[37] There are logical questions to be asked, pertinent to contemporary social problems, in view of the history of New Testament writing. Would the Gospels, and thus the story of the life of Christ, ever have been written at all and preserved for us had it not been for the passionate ministry of Paul and his colleagues? How much of the point of view in the Gospels, the Acts of the Apostles, and the Epistles, how much of the point of view of the Christian Church to-day, and how much of the separation between Jew and Gentile to-day, rise directly from Paul's point of view rather than from the doctrines of Christ himself? These questions have been asked many times and no attempt to answer them will be made here. They are

raised simply because they are healthy questions for the mind of any one approaching the subject of Christ's place in the religious history of the Western World or the subject of a world emerging from the most destructive war in history and hoping for a society based upon the brotherhood of man. They are raised because they emphasize once more the indisputable fact that Jesus (regardless of the question of his special divinity, which Christians assert and Jews deny) was one in a long line of great Jewish spiritual leaders who together gave the world the religious and ethical foundations of Western civilization which are threatened to-day by a vast complex of international antagonisms.

[38] The Christian cannot, if he wishes to understand his own beliefs, separate Christ from his predecessors, nor can the Jew, if he wishes to understand the full flowering of the religious thought of his Old Testament prophets, ignore its logical development in the doctrine of Jesus Christ. That there should ever have been any separation between the doctrines of Israel and those of Christianity is a sad commentary on the Jew's lack of understanding of Isaiah, Ezekiel, Hillel, and his other great leaders, and the Christian's lack of understanding of the Jew whom he calls Saviour.

[39] The sacred books of the Jew and the Christian are contained in what the Western World calls the Holy Bible, of which the Old Testament only is acknowledged by the orthodox Jew, while the Christian Church has added to it the New Testament containing the Gospels, the Pauline writings, and certain other books. During the early years of the Christian Church there was a movement by the Christians to abolish the Old Testament entirely and to accept only the New as the Christian Bible. Fortunately it failed, else Christianity would have been robbed of far the greater part of its scriptures, including the scriptural bases on which Christ built his doctrine.

[40] The Old Testament of Judaism contains 24 books arranged in three groups known as the Law (the first five books, called the *Torah* by Jews and the *Pentateuch* by Christians), the Prophets, and the Writings. These books are still read in the original (Hebrew, with the exception of about half the book of Daniel, parts of Ezra, and one verse of Jeremiah, which are in Aramaic) in all orthodox Jewish synagogues. In the Christian Bible they have been rearranged into 39 books. The New Testament consists of 27 books which were originally written in Greek during the first century of the Christian era.

[41] There are also other books, which are considered apocryphal by many. But those of the Old Testament Apocrypha are still included in the Bibles of the Greek and Roman Catholic Churches, which also take some of their traditions from the New Testament Apocrypha, though they do not include the books of this group in their Bible.

⚜ COMMENT AND QUESTIONS ⚜

1. In narrating the history of Judaism and Christianity, Ballou follows a generally chronological order and shows the relationship of events or developments by time-connectives like *even at this early date, Then arose the mighty figure of Moses, After the death of Moses,* etc. However, he sometimes departs from chronological order, and he sometimes expands his focus on Judeo-Christianity into a world view, using space–time connectives to relate the development of Judaism and Christianity to other religious and philosophical movements. Ballou's first departure from chronological order occurs in the first six paragraphs of the essay. What are his purposes in starting with Moses and then, in paragraph 6, moving back to an earlier time? Why does the last sentence in paragraph 5 make a strong ending, not only for the paragraph, but also for the introductory section about Moses?

2. Ballou is not content with setting down facts, but is concerned with making his account vivid and dramatic. Examine the sentences in the first two paragraphs. How do they lend a quality of interest and drama to the material?

3. Paragraphs 6 and 7, each consisting of a single sentence, make a transition to an earlier period, and might have been written as one paragraph. In fact, paragraphs 6, 7, and 8 could have been written as a single paragraph dealing with the situation and the beliefs (or possible beliefs) of the ancient Jews. Can you justify or explain Ballou's paragraphing?

4. What is the function of paragraph 9, and why do you think Ballou made a separate paragraph of its two sentences instead of attaching them to the preceding or the following paragraph?

5. What is the importance of the content of paragraphs 12 and 13 in the history of Judaism?

6. Paragraph 14 (in which Ballou again departs from strict chronology) states and supports a thesis. What is the thesis and how is it supported?

7. In paragraph 19, what are the three forces which "merged in the one mighty phenomenon of Judaism"? How has this merging of forces been prepared for earlier in the essay? Where is it later re-emphasized?

8. Paragraph 22 is one example of Ballou's world view. What appear to be the purposes of such brief surveys of world developments? Do they contribute effectively to the central narrative, or are they a distraction for the reader?

9. According to Ballou (paragraphs 28–31), what was the mission Jesus set for himself, and what did it have in common with the mission of other Jewish leaders?

10. The account of Jesus' life (paragraphs 28–33) does not follow a chronological pattern. Examine Ballou's arrangement of material in this section of the essay and try to determine the reasons for the arrangement.

11. How does Ballou support the statement (paragraph 31) that "racially and religiously Christ was born, lived, and died a loyal Jew"?

12. What, according to Ballou (paragraphs 34–37), was the importance of Paul in the history of Judeo-Christianity?

13. What lack of understanding by Christians and by Jews does Ballou see in the split between Christianity and Judaism?

14. Does Ballou's essay build to a climax at the end, or does it seem to end anticlimactically? Does the context of the essay (see the headnote) help to explain the last three paragraphs?

15. Consider the statements and implications in this essay about the debt of Judaism to other religions, the debt of Christianity to Judaism, and the recurrence of similar traditions and ideas in the world's various religions. Does a knowledge of such debts, dependencies, and interrelationships seem to you to detract from the validity of a particular religious faith, or does it seem to you to enrich it? Explain your attitude.

ANALYSIS

[5] *George Orwell*: Why I Write

GEORGE ORWELL (1903–1950), whose real name was Eric Blair, was
an English author and critic, probably best known for his novel *Nineteen
Eighty-Four*. The following essay, from *Such, Such Were the Joys*, was
written in 1947, the year before Orwell wrote *Nineteen Eighty-Four*.

[¹] From a very early age, perhaps the age of five or six, I knew that
when I grew up I should be a writer. Between the ages of about seventeen and twenty-four I tried to abandon this idea, but I did so with the
consciousness that I was outraging my true nature and that sooner or later
I should have to settle down and write books.

[²] I was the middle child of three, but there was a gap of five years on
either side, and I barely saw my father before I was eight. For this and
other reasons I was somewhat lonely, and I soon developed disagreeable
mannerisms which made me unpopular throughout my schooldays. I had
the lonely child's habit of making up stories and holding conversations
with imaginary persons, and I think from the very start my literary ambitions were mixed up with the feeling of being isolated and undervalued.
I knew that I had a facility with words and a power of facing unpleasant
facts, and I felt that this created a sort of private world in which I could
get my own back for my failure in everyday life. Nevertheless the volume
of serious—*i.e.* seriously intended—writing which I produced all through
my childhood and boyhood would not amount to half a dozen pages. I
wrote my first poem at the age of four or five, my mother taking it down
to dictation. I cannot remember anything about it except that it was about

a tiger and the tiger had "chair-like teeth"—a good enough phrase, but I fancy the poem was a plagiarism of Blake's "Tiger, Tiger." At eleven, when the war of 1914–18 broke out, I wrote a patriotic poem which was printed in the local newspaper, as was another, two years later, on the death of Kitchener. From time to time, when I was a bit older, I wrote bad and usually unfinished "nature poems" in the Georgian style. I also, about twice, attempted a short story which was a ghastly failure. That was the total of the would-be serious work that I actually set down on paper during all those years.

[³] However, throughout this time I did in a sense engage in literary activities. To begin with there was the made-to-order stuff which I produced quickly, easily and without much pleasure to myself. Apart from school work, I wrote *vers d'occasion*, semi-comic poems which I could turn out at what now seems to me astonishing speed—at fourteen I wrote a whole rhyming play, in imitation of Aristophanes, in about a week—and helped to edit school magazines, both printed and in manuscript. These magazines were the most pitiful burlesque stuff that you could imagine, and I took far less trouble with them than I now would with the cheapest journalism. But side by side with all this, for fifteen years or more, I was carrying out a literary exercise of a quite different kind: this was the making up of a continuous "story" about myself, a sort of diary existing only in the mind. I believe this is a common habit of children and adolescents. As a very small child I used to imagine that I was, say, Robin Hood, and picture myself as the hero of thrilling adventures, but quite soon my "story" ceased to be narcissistic in a crude way and became more and more a mere description of what I was doing and the things I saw. For minutes at a time this kind of thing would be running through my head: "He pushed the door open and entered the room. A yellow beam of sunlight, filtering through the muslin curtains, slanted on to the table, where a matchbox, half open, lay beside the inkpot. With his right hand in his pocket he moved across to the window. Down in the street a tortoise-shell cat was chasing a dead leaf," etc., etc. This habit continued till I was about twenty-five, right through my non-literary years. Although I had to search, and did search, for the right words, I seemed to be making this descriptive effort almost against my will, under a kind of compulsion from outside. The "story" must, I suppose, have reflected the styles of the various writers I admired at different ages, but so far as I remember it always had the same meticulous descriptive quality.

[⁴] When I was about sixteen I suddenly discovered the joy of mere words, *i.e.* the sounds and associations of words. The lines from *Paradise Lost*—

> So hee with difficulty and labour hard
> Moved on: with difficulty and labour hee,

which do not now seem to me so very wonderful, sent shivers down my backbone; and the spelling "hee" for "he" was an added pleasure. As for the need to describe things, I knew all about it already. So it is clear what kind of books I wanted to write, in so far as I could be said to want to write books at that time. I wanted to write enormous natural- istic novels with unhappy endings, full of detailed descriptions and arrest- ing similes, and also full of purple passages in which words were used partly for the sake of their sound. And in fact my first completed novel, *Burmese Days*, which I wrote when I was thirty but projected much earlier, is rather that kind of book.

[5] I give all this background information because I do not think one can assess a writer's motives without knowing something of his early development. His subject matter will be determined by the age he lives in—at least this is true in tumultuous, revolutionary ages like our own— but before he ever begins to write he will have acquired an emotional attitude from which he will never completely escape. It is his job, no doubt, to discipline his temperament and avoid getting stuck at some immature stage, or in some perverse mood: but if he escapes from his early influences altogether, he will have killed his impulse to write. Put- ting aside the need to earn a living, I think there are four great motives for writing, at any rate for writing prose. They exist in different degrees in every writer, and in any one writer the proportions will vary from time to time, according to the atmosphere in which he is living. They are:

[6] (1) Sheer egoism. Desire to seem clever, to be talked about, to be remembered after death, to get your own back on grownups who snubbed you in childhood, etc., etc. It is humbug to pretend that this is not a motive, and a strong one. Writers share this characteristic with scientists, artists, politicians, lawyers, soldiers, successful businessmen—in short, with the whole top crust of humanity. The great mass of human beings are not acutely selfish. After the age of about thirty they abandon indi- vidual ambition—in many cases, indeed, they almost abandon the sense of being individuals at all—and live chiefly for others, or are simply smothered under drudgery. But there is also the minority of gifted, wilful people who are determined to live their own lives to the end, and writers belong in this class. Serious writers, I should say, are on the whole more vain and self-centred than journalists, though less interested in money.

[7] (2) Esthetic enthusiasm. Perception of beauty in the external world, or, on the other hand, in words and their right arrangement. Pleasure in the impact of one sound on another, in the firmness of good prose or the rhythm of a good story. Desire to share an experience which one feels is valuable and ought not to be missed. The esthetic motive is very feeble in a lot of writers, but even a pamphleteer or a writer of text- books will have pet words and phrases which appeal to him for non- utilitarian reasons; or he may feel strongly about typography, width of

margins, etc. Above the level of a railway guide, no book is quite free from esthetic considerations.

[8] (3) Historical impulse. Desire to see things as they are, to find out true facts and store them up for the use of posterity.

[9] (4) Political purpose—using the word "political" in the widest possible sense. Desire to push the world in a certain direction, to alter other people's idea of the kind of society that they should strive after. Once again, no book is genuinely free from political bias. The opinion that art should have nothing to do with politics is itself a political attitude.

[10] It can be seen how these various impulses must war against one another, and how they must fluctuate from person to person and from time to time. By nature—taking your "nature" to be the state you have attained when you are first adult—I am a person in whom the first three motives would outweigh the fourth. In a peaceful age I might have written ornate or merely descriptive books, and might have remained almost unaware of my political loyalties. As it is I have been forced into becoming a sort of pamphleteer. First I spent five years in an unsuitable profession (the Indian Imperial Police, in Burma), and then I underwent poverty and the sense of failure. This increased my natural hatred of authority and made me for the first time fully aware of the existence of the working classes, and the job in Burma had given me some understanding of the nature of imperialism: but these experiences were not enough to give me an accurate political orientation. Then came Hitler, the Spanish civil war, etc. By the end of 1935 I had still failed to reach a firm decision. I remember a little poem that I wrote at that date, expressing my dilemma:

> A happy vicar I might have been
> Two hundred years ago,
> To preach upon eternal doom
> And watch my walnuts grow;
>
> But born, alas, in an evil time,
> I missed that pleasant haven,
> For the hair has grown on my upper lip
> And the clergy are all clean-shaven.
>
> And later still the times were good,
> We were so easy to please,
> We rocked our troubled thoughts to sleep
> On the bosoms of the trees.
>
> All ignorant we dared to own
> The joys we now dissemble;
> The greenfinch on the apple bough
> Could make my enemies tremble.

But girls' bellies and apricots,
Roach in a shaded stream,
Horses, ducks in flight at dawn,
All these are a dream.

It is forbidden to dream again;
We maim our joys or hide them;
Horses are made of chromium steel
And little fat men shall ride them.

I am the worm who never turned,
The eunuch without a harem;
Between the priest and the commissar
I walk like Eugene Aram;[1]

And the commissar is telling my fortune
While the radio plays,
But the priest has promised an Austin Seven,
For Duggie always pays.[2]

I dreamed I dwelt in marble halls,
And woke to find it true;
I wasn't born for an age like this;
Was Smith? Was Jones? Were you?

The Spanish war and other events in 1936–7 turned the scale and thereafter I knew where I stood. Every line of serious work that I have written
since 1936 has been written directly or indirectly, *against* totalitarianism
and *for* democratic socialism, as I understand it. It seems to me nonsense,
in a period like our own, to think that one can avoid writing of such
subjects. Everyone writes of them in one guise or another. It is simply a
question of which side one takes and what approach one follows. And
the more one is conscious of one's political bias, the more chance one has
of acting politically without sacrificing one's esthetic and intellectual
integrity.

[11] What I have most wanted to do throughout the past ten years is to
make political writing into an art. My starting point is always a feeling
of partisanship, a sense of injustice. When I sit down to write a book, I
do not say to myself, "I am going to produce a work of art." I write it
because there is some lie that I want to expose, some fact to which I want
to draw attention, and my initial concern is to get a hearing. But I could
not do the work of writing a book, or even a long magazine article, if it
were not also an esthetic experience. Anyone who cares to examine my
work will see that even when it is downright propaganda it contains

[1] Eugene Aram (1704–1757) was an English schoolmaster and a murderer.
[2] A common British saying, used ironically; "Duggie" is an expression equivalent
to our "bookie."

much that a full-time politician would consider irrelevant. I am not able, and I do not want, completely to abandon the world-view that I acquired in childhood. So long as I remain alive and well I shall continue to feel strongly about prose style, to love the surface of the earth, and to take a pleasure in solid objects and scraps of useless information. It is no use trying to suppress that side of myself. The job is to reconcile my ingrained likes and dislikes with the essentially public, nonindividual activities that this age forces on all of us.

[12] It is not easy. It raises problems of construction and of language, and it raises in a new way the problem of truthfulness. Let me give just one example of the cruder kind of difficulty that arises. My book about the Spanish civil war, *Homage to Catalonia,* is, of course, a frankly political book, but in the main it is written with a certain detachment and regard for form. I did try very hard in it to tell the whole truth without violating my literary instincts. But among other things it contains a long chapter, full of newspaper quotations and the like, defending the Trotskyists who were accused of plotting with Franco. Clearly such a chapter, which after a year or two would lose its interest for any ordinary reader, must ruin the book. A critic whom I respect read me a lecture about it. "Why did you put in all that stuff?" he said. "You've turned what might have been a good book into journalism." What he said was true, but I could not have done otherwise. I happened to know, what very few people in England had been allowed to know, that innocent men were being falsely accused. If I had not been angry about that I should never have written the book.

[13] In one form or another this problem comes up again. The problem of language is subtler and would take too long to discuss. I will only say that of late years I have tried to write less picturesquely and more exactly. In any case I find that by the time you have perfected any style of writing, you have always outgrown it. *Animal Farm* was the first book in which I tried, with full consciousness of what I was doing, to fuse political purpose and artistic purpose into one whole. I have not written a novel for seven years, but I hope to write another fairly soon. It is bound to be a failure, every book is a failure, but I do know with some clarity what kind of book I want to write.

[14] Looking back through the last page or two, I see that I have made it appear as though my motives in writing were wholly public-spirited. I don't want to leave that as the final impression. All writers are vain, selfish and lazy, and at the very bottom of their motives there lies a mystery. Writing a book is a horrible, exhausting struggle, like a long bout of some painful illness. One would never undertake such a thing if one were not driven on by some demon whom one can neither resist nor understand. For all one knows that demon is simply the same instinct that makes a baby squall for attention. And yet it is also true that one can write

nothing readable unless one constantly struggles to efface one's own personality. Good prose is like a window pane. I cannot say with certainty which of my motives are the strongest, but I know which of them deserve to be followed. And looking back through my work, I see that it is invariably where I lacked a *political* purpose that I wrote lifeless books and was betrayed into purple passages, sentences without meaning, decorative adjectives and humbug generally.

COMMENT AND QUESTIONS

1. This essay has three major divisions: (a) background information—an account of Orwell's "nonliterary years" (paragraphs 1–4); (b) an analysis of the four great motives for writing (paragraphs 5–9); (c) an analysis of the author's primarily political motive in writing (paragraphs 10–14). Material in the first of these divisions is roughly, but not wholly, chronological in arrangement. What departures from chronological order do you find in paragraphs 1–4? What are the principal transitional devices by which Orwell links the experiences and activities of his early years? Examine with particular care the sentences in paragraph 3 to see how the author links ideas within a paragraph.

2. The first four paragraphs of the essay might be called an analysis within a larger analysis. In paragraphs 2–4, what particular experiences, attitudes, and habits contribute to what Orwell later calls the world-view acquired in childhood? How do these experiences determine the kind of book (paragraph 4) which, at the age of about twenty-five, he wanted to write?

3. What are Orwell's attitudes toward himself and toward his early literary activities (paragraphs 1–4)? How are the attitudes expressed?

4. At the end of his example, in paragraph 3, of the descriptive story he told himself (and again in paragraph 6), the author uses *etc., etc.*—a practice frequently discouraged by teachers of composition because the expression may be a substitute for thoughtful or accurate detail. Can you justify Orwell's *etc., etc.*? What tone, or attitude toward his audience and material, does it communicate?

5. Paragraph 5 serves the double purpose of explaining why the author has given the background information and of introducing the four motives for writing. How are the background and the motives related? What examples of qualification do you find in paragraph 5?

6. In the analysis of motives (paragraphs 6–9), how do you account for the fact that the first two motives—sheer egoism and esthetic enthusiasm—are given considerably more development than the last two?

7. Notice the sentence structure in paragraphs 6–9. What is the effect of the incomplete sentences following each of the headings? In paragraph 6, Orwell's sentences are notably varied in structure and in length. What is

the effect of this variety? What words or combinations of words seem particularly well selected?

8. The beginning of paragraph 10 restates in different terms what Orwell has said near the end of paragraph 5 about the fluctuations of the four impulses or motives. How is his statement that "by nature" he was one "in whom the first three motives would outweigh the fourth" supported by what we already know of his early experience?

9. Paragraphs 10–14 might be regarded as different levels of analysis: paragraphs 10 and 11 analyze Orwell's political purpose (the last of the four central motives), first by giving the causes or reasons for its development, and second by explaining his desire to make political writing into an art; paragraphs 12 and 13 are an analysis of the problems involved in making political writing an art; and paragraph 14 is a final appraisal of his motives and his writing. What were the reasons (paragraph 10) for his decision to write politically? In what ways does the poem included in paragraph 10 help the reader to understand the difficulty of his choice? (The first line of the last stanza is a near-quotation of a line from Balfe's opera *The Bohemian Girl.* In the song, the marble halls are part of lost wealth and social position. What do the marble halls appear to mean in Orwell's poem?) How does the last sentence of paragraph 10 make an emphatic ending and at the same time lead into the next paragraph?

10. What aspects of the world-view acquired in childhood are referred to in paragraph 11?

11. At the beginning of paragraph 12, Orwell says that combining political and artistic purposes raises problems of construction, language, and truthfulness. Which problems are chiefly emphasized in the example in paragraph 12? In the material in paragraph 13?

12. What is the tone of paragraph 13?

13. What seems to be the purpose of the last paragraph of the essay? What is the meaning of the sentence "Good prose is like a window pane," and how is it related to the baby squalling for attention? In the next-to-last sentence of the paragraph, Orwell says that although he cannot be sure which of his motives are strongest, he knows which deserve to be followed. The *which* in the last part of the sentence is plural; in the context of the whole essay, what does *which* refer to? The last sentence of the paragraph emphasizes, rightly of course, the importance of the political purpose. In the last clause of that last sentence, why is *betrayed* a well-chosen word? How are the four parallel phrases ending the sentence and the essay related to earlier content?

14. What is your impression of the persona, the total personality, revealed in this essay?

CONTRAST
AND COMPARISON

[6] *John Lukacs*: It's Halfway to 1984

J O H N L U K A C S is an essayist, teacher, and historian, author of *A History of the Cold War* and *Decline and Rise of Europe*. The following essay was published in *The New York Times Magazine*, January 2, 1966.

[1] We are now halfway to 1984. George Orwell, the author of "1984," finished his book in 1948. That was 18 years ago, and it is not more than another 18 years before that ominous date rolls around.

[2] It is *ominous*, in every sense of that antique adjective. There is reason to believe that 18 years from now thousands of people will experience a feeling of uneasiness, perhaps a light little shudder of trepidation, as they first encounter that new year's numerals in print. In the English-speaking world, at least, "1984" has become a household term, suggesting some kind of inhuman totalitarian nightmare. And since millions who have not read the book now recognize the term, it is reasonable to assume that both the theme and the title of the book have corresponded to an emerging consciousness among many people in the otherwise progressive-minded English-speaking democracies, to the effect that things are *not* getting better all the time—no, not at all.

[3] The plot of "1984" is well-known but it may be useful to sum it up briefly. By 1984 most of the world has been divided by three super-states—Oceania, Eurasia and Eastasia. They are perpetually at war with one other, but no one of them is completely able to subdue the others.

This state of war enables the rulers of these states (the ruler of Oceania being Big Brother) to keep their peoples both ignorant and submissive. This is achieved by totalitarian and technical methods, by the absoluteness of one-party rule and by a kind of censorship that controls not only the behavior but even the thinking process of individuals. The hero of "1984," Winston Smith, born in 1945 (both the date and the first name are significant), is a simple party member and a functionary of the Ministry of Truth in London, which is the chief city of Airstrip One, for that is what Britain became after she had been absorbed by the United States to form Oceania. (Continental Europe, having been absorbed by the Soviet Union, had become Eurasia.)

[4] Winston is a weak and forlorn intellectual who, however, is sickened not only by the dreary living conditions in 1984 but by the prevalence of official lying and the almost complete absence of personal privacy. One day he stumbles into a love affair, which in itself is a dangerous thing since the party punishes illicit relationships severely. Winston experiences happiness and a sense of personal fulfillment, especially as Julia shares his hatred of the existing system.

[5] There is a high official in the Ministry of Truth, O'Brien, whom Winston instinctively trusts. He and Julia confide in O'Brien. They are deceived. All along, O'Brien has set a trap for them: they are arrested in their secret little room. They are tortured. Winston, despite his strong residue of convictions, not only confesses to everything imaginable, but in the end, faced by an especially horrible torture, he even betrays Julia. He is finally released; he is a completely broken man; he has even come to believe in the almightiness and goodness of Big Brother.

[6] But it is not this plot, it is rather Orwell's description of everyday life in 1984 that is the principal matter of the novel and, one may suppose, the principal matter of interest to its readers. Life in 1984 is a mixture of horror and dreariness. What is horrible is not so much war as the shriveling of personal freedoms and privacy with the planners of the superstate controlling vast portions of once-independent lives. What is dreary is that within these totalitarian conditions the living standards of masses of people in what were once civilized and prosperous countries are reduced: Food and drink are little better than standardized slop; mass entertainments are primitive and vulgar; personal property has virtually disappeared.

[7] One of the profound differences between "1984" and Aldous Huxley's "Brave New World" (published in 1932, the latter still had many of the marks of the light-headed twenties; its philosophy compared with that of "1984" is a rather irresponsible *jeu d'esprit*) lies in Orwell's view of the past rather than of the future. Looking back from 1984, conditions in the early, capitalistic portion of the 20th century seem romantic and almost idyllic to Winston Smith, so much so that on a solemn occasion he

offers a toast "to the past." Unemployment, revolutions, Fascism and, to some extent, even Nazism and Communism are lesser evils than what is going on in Oceania in 1984, since by that time the rulers of the state have perfected brainwashing and thought-control to the point that the memories of entire generations, and hence their opinions about the past, have been eliminated.

[8] This, of course, does not happen overnight: It is a brutal but gradual development. In "1984," Orwell set the decisive turning point in the middle sixties, "the period of the great purges in which the original leaders of the Revolution were wiped out once and for all. By 1970 none of them was left, except Big Brother himself."

[9] Let us keep in mind that "1984" is the work of a novelist and not of a prophet; Orwell ought not be criticized simply because some of his visions have not been borne out. On the other hand, Orwell was concerned in the late forties with certain tendencies of evil portent; and "1984" was a publishing success because around 1950, for great numbers of people, the picture of a society such as he described was not merely fantastic but to some extent plausible.

[10] It is still plausible today, but not quite in the way in which Orwell envisaged the future 18 years ago. Halfway to 1984 we can say, fortunately, that most of Orwell's visions have proved wrong. It is true that the United States, the Soviet Union and China correspond to some extent to the superpowers Oceania, Eurasia and Eastasia. But the United States has not annexed Britain, the Soviet Union has fallen far short of conquering all of Europe, and even China does not extend much beyond her traditional boundaries.

[11] What is more important, the superpowers are not at war with one another. It is true that during the so-called cold war between the United States and the Soviet Union many of the practices of traditional and civilized diplomacy were abandoned; but the cold war has given place to something like a cold peace between these two superpowers. Even the dreadful and ominous war in Asia is marked by the reluctance of the United States and China directly to attack each other.

[12] Orwell proved correct in saying that "war . . . is no longer the desperate, annihilating struggle that it was in the early decades of the 20th century. It is a warfare of limited aims between combatants who are unable to destroy one another. . . ." Yet Orwell was interested principally not in international but in internal developments. For example, in "1984" the peoples of Oceania are isolated; travel is forbidden except for a small minority of the élite; and the press is controlled to the extent that no meaningful information from the outside world is available to the public.

[13] But now, halfway to 1984, the opposite has been happening. It is not warfare but torrents of automobiles and mass tourism that threaten

to destroy entire landscapes and cityscapes; great amounts of information are available to us about an undigestible variety of matters; and at times it seems that the cultural traditions of great Western nations are endangered less by the persistence of isolationism than by a phony internationalism drummed up by a kind of pervasive publicity that drowns out the once truer music of the arts.

[14] Also, in the world of "1984" most people are ill-fed, badly clothed, run-down. But this, too, has not happened. Now, halfway to 1984, almost everywhere in the world, living standards have risen, and the danger is not, as Orwell envisaged it, that entire generations of once-prosperous countries will no longer know such things as wine, oranges, lemons and chocolate; it is, rather, that our traditional tastes and table habits may be washed away by a flood of frozen and synthetic foods of every possible kind, available to us every hour of the day.

[15] The reasons why Orwell's visions of 1984 have been wrong seem to be bound up with the time and the circumstances of the book's conception. About the circumstances Orwell himself was supposed to have said that "1984" "wouldn't have been so gloomy if I had not been so ill." He wrote most of the book in self-imposed isolation on a rain-shrouded Scottish island, finishing it in an English country hospital in late 1948. Shortly thereafter, he was moved to a hospital in London, where in January, 1950, he died. As for the time of writing, in the late nineteen-forties Orwell's imagination succumbed, at least in part, to the temptation of conceiving the future as an increasingly acute continuation of what seems to be going on at the present. (In one of his earlier essays, Orwell had criticized the American writer James Burnham for this very fault.) Around 1949, when most intellectuals had come around to recognizing that Stalin's tyranny was hardly better than Hitler's, many of them concluded that it is in the nature of totalitarianism to become more and more tyrannical as time goes on. Indeed, some of them established their reputations by the ponderous books they produced on this theme. (Hannah Arendt's "The Origins of Totalitarianism" is an example.) Yet only a few years later, events in Eastern Europe and in Russia showed that history is unpredictable and that the projections of intellectuals are often oversimplified. But this Orwell did not live to see.

[16] He foresaw the horrible features of 1984 as the consequences of totalitarianism, of political tyranny, of the despotism of a dictator. But halfway to 1984 we can see, for example, that the era of totalitarian dictatorship is sliding away, into the past. Even the Soviet Union seems to be moving in the direction of what one may call "post-totalitarian"; all over Eastern Europe (though not yet in Asia) we can perceive regimes that, though dictatorial, are no longer totalitarian. The danger for us is, rather, the obverse: the possibility of totalitarian democracy.

[17] Totalitarian democracy? The words seem paradoxical; our eyes and ears are unaccustomed to the sight and the sound of them in combination. Yet I believe that we ought to accustom our imaginations to the possibility of a democratic society in which universal popular suffrage exists while freedom of speech, press and assembly are hardly more than theoretical possibilities for the individual, whose life and ideas, whose rights to privacy, to family autonomy and to durable possessions are regimented by government and rigidly molded by mass production and by mass communications.

[18] Let me, at this point, fall back on a personal illustration. For a long time the term "1984" evoked, to me, the image of a police state of the Eastern European type. But when I think of 1984 now, the image that swims into my mind is that of a gigantic shopping center and industrial complex—something like the one which has been erected a few miles from where I live in eastern Pennsylvania.

[19] The undulating rural landscape around Valley Forge, with its bright dots of houses and its crossroads, has been transformed. There is now the eerie vastness of the General Electric Space Center whose square edifices spread across hundreds of acres. Beyond it stand other flat windowless blocks of buildings—the King of Prussia shopping center, around the trembling edges of which bulldozers roar from morning to night, boring their brutal tracks into the clayey soil which they must churn to mud before it can be covered by concrete. The predominant material is concrete, horizontal and vertical concrete. Twice a day, thousands of people pour into and out of this compound, in a tremendous metallic flow. But no one lives there. At night and on Sundays, these hundreds of acres resemble a deserted airport, with a few autombiles clustering here and there, or slowly cruising on one of the airstrips, occasionally peered at by uniformed guards. Why fly to the moon? Stand on a cold January night in the middle of a parking lot in a large shopping center in the American North. It is a man-made moonscape. This is how the moon will look after our Herculean efforts, after we reach it, colonize it, pour concrete over it.

[20] This is how 1984 looks to me, in the middle sixties, but I know and feel that this view is neither solitary nor unusual. There are millions of Americans who, passing a similar space-age complex of buildings, will say "1984," covering up their resignation with a thin coat of defensive humor. What strikes us is not just the ugliness of the buildings but something else, something that is not so much the reaction of middle-aged earthmen against brave new worlds as it is the expression of a feeling which is, alas, close to the Orwellian nightmare vision: a sense of impersonality together with a sense of powerlessness.

[21] The impersonality is there, in the hugeness of the Organization and in the anonymous myriads of the interchangeable human beings who

make up most of their personnel. The powerlessness is the feeling which I share with so many of my neighbors—that we cannot stop what in America is called the March of Progress, the cement trucks coming toward us any day from across the hill; the knowledge that our voices, our votes, our appeals, our petitions amount to near-nothing at a time when people have become accustomed to accepting the decisions of planners, experts and faraway powerful agencies. It is a sickening inward feeling that the essence of self-government is becoming more and more meaningless at the very time when the outward and legal forms of democracy are still kept up.

[22] Let us not fool ourselves: Now, halfway to 1984, with all of the recent advances of civil rights, with all of the recent juridical extensions of constitutional freedoms, we *are* facing the erosion of privacy, of property and—yes—even of liberty. This has nothing to do with the Communist Conspiracy or with Ambitious Government Bureaucrats—that is where our New Conservatives go wrong. It has nothing to do with Creeping Socialism. It has very much to do with Booming Technology. The dangers which our modern societies in the West, and particularly the United States, face now, halfway to 1984, are often new kinds of dangers, growing out of newly developing conditions. What ought to concern us is the rootlessness of a modern, technological, impersonal society, with interchangeable people, on all levels of education.

[23] We ought to dwell less on the possibility of unemployment arising out of automation, in a society which, after all, feels obligated to produce full employment; rather, we ought to consider the growing purposelessness of occupations in a society where by now more people are employed in administration that in production. And in such a society we ought to prattle less about the need for more "creative leisure" when the problem is that work becomes less and less creative. We ought to worry not about the insufficient availability of products but about the increasing impermanence of possessions. We ought to think deeply not so much about the growth of the public sectors of the public economy at the expense of private enterprise (which, at any rate, is no longer very "private"), but rather, about the cancerous growth of the public sectors of our existence at the expense of the private autonomy of our personal lives.

[24] We ought to concern ourselves less with the depreciation of money and more with the depreciation of language; with the breakdown of interior, even more than with the state of exterior, communications—or, in other words, with the increasing practices of Orwell's Doubletalk and Doublethink, and with their growing promotion not so much by political tyrannies as by all kinds of techniques, in the name of Progress.

[25] I cannot—and, perhaps, I need not—explain or illustrate these concerns in greater detail. They are, in any event, 1966 concerns about the future, not 1948 ones. Still, while many of the phantoms that haunted

Orwell's readers 18 years ago have not materialized, the public currency
of the term 1984 has lost none of its poignancy. The tone of our literature,
indeed of our entire cultural atmosphere, is far more pessimistic than it
was 18 years ago. "Alienation" and "hopelessness" are no longer Central
European words; they are very American. This broad, and often near-
nihilistic, cultural apathy and despair is relatively new on the American
(and also on the British) scene. Its existence suggests that, despite the
errors of Orwell's visions, the nightmare quality of "1984" continues to
obsess our imagination, and not merely as the sickly titillation of a horror
story. It haunts millions who fear that life may become an Orwellian
nightmare even without the political tyranny that Orwell had predicted.

[26] "It is by his political writings," Bertrand Russell once wrote, "that
Orwell will be remembered." If this is so—and at this moment, halfway
to 1984, it still seems so—he will be remembered for the wrong reasons,
and one can only hope that the slow corrective tides of public opinion in
the long run will redress the balance.

[27] Orwell was not so much concerned with the degeneration of justice as with the degeneration of truth. For Orwell, both in the beginning
and in the end was The Word. This is true of "1984," too, which had three
levels. On the top level there is the "plot," the love affair of Winston and
Julia, which is really flat and inconsequential. On the second level there
is the political vision which, as we have seen, sometimes holds up, sometimes not. It is the third level, of what is happening to words and to print,
to speech and to truth in 1984, which agitated Orwell the most. Indeed,
this spare and economical writer chose to end the novel "1984" by adding
an appendix on "The Principles of Newspeak." Orwell was frightened less
by the prospects of censorship than by the potential falsification of history,
and by the mechanization of speech.

[28] The first of these protracted practices would mean that the only
possible basis for a comparison with conditions other than the present
would disappear; the second, that the degeneration of traditional language would lead to a new kind of mechanical talk and print which would
destroy the meaning of private communications between persons. This
prospect haunted Orwell throughout the last 12 years of his life. Some of
his best essays dealt with this theme of falsifications of truth—even more
than totalitarianism, this was his main concern. As long as people can
talk to one another meaningfully, as long as they have private beliefs, as
long as people retain some of the qualities of Winston Smith's mother
(she had not been an "unusual woman, still less an intelligent one; and
yet she had possessed a kind of nobility, a kind of purity, simply because
the standards she obeyed were private ones. Her feelings were her own,
and could not be altered from the outside . . ."), tyranny was vulnerable;
it could not become total.

[29] Orwell was wrong in believing that the development of science

was incompatible with totalitarianism (by 1984, "science, in the old sense, has almost ceased to exist. In Newspeak there is no word for science"). As we have seen, he foresaw a decay of technology ("the fields are cultivated by horse-ploughs while books are written by machinery"). This is not what has happened; now, halfway to 1984, the fields are cultivated by bulldozers while books are written by machine-men. But Orwell was right in drawing attention to Double-think, "the power of holding two contradictory beliefs in one's mind simultaneously, and accepting both of them," and to the desperate prospects of Doubletalk, of the degeneration of standards of language through varieties of supermodern jargon, practiced by political pitchmen as well as by professional intellectuals. There is reason to believe that, were he alive today, Orwell would have modified his views on the nature of the totalitarian menace; and that, at the same time, he would be appalled by many of the present standards and practices in mass communications, literature and publishing, even in the West, and perhaps especially in the United States.

[30] In short, the 1984 that we ought to fear is now, in 1966, different from the 1948 version. Politically speaking, Tocqueville saw further in the eighteen-thirties than Orwell in the nineteen-forties. The despotism which democratic nations had to fear, Tocqueville wrote, would be different from tyranny: "It would be more extensive and more mild; it would degrade men without tormenting them. . . . The same principle of equality which facilitates despotism tempers its rigor." In an eloquent passage Tocqueville described some of the features of such a society: Above the milling crowds "stands an immense and tutelary power, which takes upon itself alone to secure their gratifications and to watch over their fate. That power is absolute, minute, regular, provident and mild. . . ." But when such a government, no matter how provident and mild, becomes omnipotent, "what remains but to spare [people] all the care of thinking and all the trouble of living?"

[31] Orwell's writing is as timely as Tocqueville's not when he is concerned with forms of polity but when he is concerned with evil communication. In this regard the motives of this English Socialist were not at all different from the noble exhortation with which Tocqueville closed one of his chapters in "Democracy in America": "Let us, then, look forward to the future with that salutary fear which makes men keep watch and ward for freedom, not with that faint and idle terror which depresses and enervates the heart." Present and future readers of "1984" may well keep this distinction in mind.

--·⊰{ COMMENT AND QUESTIONS }⊱·--

1. The first two paragraphs of the essay elaborate the title and discuss the meaning that the term *1984* has for millions of people in the English-speaking world. The date 1984 is *ominous*, the author says, "in every sense of that antique adjective." What are the senses of *ominous*?

2. At the end of paragraph 2, Lukacs states an assumption: the theme and title of Orwell's book have corresponded to an emerging consciousness that things are *not* getting better all the time. Does this assumption follow logically from the preceding material? Explain.

3. Paragraphs 3–5 summarize the plot of *Nineteen Eighty-Four*. Is the summary useful even though, as Lukacs says, the plot is well known? What is the significance (paragraph 4) of the birth-date and the first name of Winston Smith? In paragraph 5, the author uses a number of short sentences and short independent clauses—a departure from the style of the two preceding paragraphs of summary. What is the purpose of these simpler structures?

4. The opening sentence of paragraph 6 makes a transition from the plot to the quality of everyday life in 1984, which is developed in paragraphs 6–8. What distinction is made between the horror and the dreariness of life in 1984? What purpose is served by the brief contrast, in paragraph 7, of Aldous Huxley's and Orwell's views? In what way does paragraph 8 conclude direct discussion of Orwell's novel and mark a return to the central idea of Lukacs' essay?

5. Paragraph 9 introduces the idea that some of Orwell's visions of the future have not been borne out and so prepares for the analysis (paragraphs 10–16) of the world of 1966, halfway to 1984, in comparison to the world Orwell envisaged. This section of the essay is predominantly a series of contrasts, carefully qualified, between what Orwell foresaw and what has happened. In what specific ways have Orwell's visions proved wrong? What explanations does the author give for Orwell's failure as a prophet?

6. In this section of contrast (paragraphs 10–16), what suggestions do you find that developments opposite to those foreseen by Orwell are not in themselves desirable?

7. The end of paragraph 16 introduces the possibility of totalitarian democracy, which is described in paragraph 17. What does this totalitarian democracy have in common with the society of *Nineteen Eighty-four*?

8. In the illustration (paragraphs 18–19) of the author's image of 1984, what words and details best convey his attitudes toward this image of the future world? What devices of emphasis does Lukacs use?

9. Paragraph 20 states directly what has been stated indirectly before: that the Orwellian nightmare vision is already to some extent a reality. Paragraphs 17–25, in fact, deal with both similarities and differences between 1966 and *Nineteen Eighty-Four*. What characteristics of the Orwellian

nightmare are developed in paragraphs 20 and 21? Do the details Lukacs gives adequately support his generalizations?

10. Paragraph 22, developed by restatement and by cause–effect, introduces a series of new problems that should concern us now, halfway to 1984. What are these concerns (paragraphs 22–24)? At the beginning of paragraph 25, the author says that he cannot and perhaps need not explain or illustrate the concerns in greater detail. Would more illustration and detail have helped to clarify his ideas? Can you supply examples of each of these matters of concern?

11. Although the problems facing us in the nineteen-sixties are in many ways unlike the problems of *Nineteen Eighty-Four,* what relationship does the author see between the concept of 1984 and pessimism and "alienation" today? To what extent is the last sentence of paragraph 25 a summary of the content of the essay thus far?

12. Paragraph 26 makes a transition to the last main section of the essay— a discussion of Orwell's primary concern with the degeneration of language and the falsification of truth. If you have read Orwell's essay "Why I Write" (page 51), consider this question: Lukacs says that if Orwell is remembered for his political writing, he will be remembered for the wrong reasons. Does Lukacs mean by "political writing" exactly what Orwell himself meant?

13. Point out examples of contrast and comparison in the last section of the essay (paragraphs 27–31).

14. What are the purposes of the quotations from Tocqueville (paragraphs 30 and 31)? What, precisely, is the "distinction" referred to in the last sentence of the essay? Why is it emphasized by its position at the end of the essay?

CAUSE AND EFFECT

❦

[7] *Erich Fromm*: Alienation: Quantification, Abstractification

ERICH FROMM (1900–), a German-born, naturalized-American psychoanalyst, has taught and lectured at a number of American colleges. His books include *Escape from Freedom, Man for Himself, Psychoanalysis and Religion, The Sane Society, The Art of Loving, May Man Prevail,* and *The Heart of Man.* The following selection is part of Chapter Five of *The Sane Society.* "The alienated person," Fromm says, "is out of touch with himself as he is out of touch with any other person. He, like the others, is experienced as things are experienced; with the senses and with common sense, but at the same time without being related to oneself and to the world outside productively."

[1] We must introduce the discussion of alienation by speaking of one of the fundamental economic features of Capitalism, the process of *quantification* and *abstractification*.

[2] The medieval artisan produced goods for a relatively small and known group of customers. His prices were determined by the need to make a profit which permitted him to live in a style traditionally commensurate with his social status. He knew from experience the costs of production, and even if he employed a few journeymen and apprentices, no elaborate system of bookkeeping or balance sheets was required for the operation of his business. The same held true for the production of the peasant, which required even less quantifying abstract methods. In

69

contrast, the modern business enterprise rests upon its balance sheet. It cannot rest upon such concrete and direct observation as the artisan used to figure out his profits. Raw material, machinery, labor costs, as well as the product can be expressed in the same money value, and thus made comparable and fit to appear in the balance equation. All economic occurrences have to be strictly quantifiable, and only the balance sheets, the exact comparison of economic processes quantified in figures, tell the manager whether and to what degree he is engaged in a profitable, that is to say, a meaningful business activity.

[3] This transformation of the concrete into the abstract has developed far beyond the balance sheet and the quantification of the economic occurrences in the sphere of production. The modern businessman not only deals with millions of dollars, but also with millions of customers, thousands of stockholders, and thousands of workers and employees; all these people become so many pieces in a gigantic machine which must be controlled, whose effects must be calculated; each man eventually can be expressed as an abstract entity, as a figure, and on this basis economic occurrences are calculated, trends are predicted, decisions are made.

[4] Today, when only about 20 per cent of our working population is self-employed, the rest work for somebody else, and a man's life is dependent on someone who pays him a wage or a salary. But we should say "something," instead of "someone," because a worker is hired and fired by an institution, the managers of which are impersonal parts of the enterprise, rather than people in personal contact with the men they employ. Let us not forget another fact: in precapitalistic society, exchange was to a large extent one of goods and services; today, all work is rewarded with money, the abstract expression of work—that is to say, we receive different quantities of the same for different qualities; and we give money for what we receive—again exchanging only different quantities for different qualities. Practically nobody, with the exception of the farm population, could live for even a few days without receiving and spending money, which stands for the abstract quality of concrete work.

[5] Another aspect of capitalist production which results in increasing abstractification is the increasing division of labor. Division of labor as a whole exists in most known economic systems, and, even in most primitive communities, in the form of division of labor between the sexes. What is characteristic of capitalistic production is the degree to which this division has developed. While in the medieval economy there was a division of labor let us say between agricultural production and the work of the artisan, there was little such division within each sphere of production itself. The carpenter making a chair or table made the whole chair or the whole table, and even if some preparatory work was done by his apprentices, he was in control of the production, overseeing it in its entirety. In the modern industrial enterprise, the worker is not in touch

with the whole product at any point. He is engaged in the performance of one specialized function, and while he might shift in the course of time from one function to another, he is still not related to the concrete product *as a whole*. He develops a specialized function, and the tendency is such, that the function of the modern industrial worker can be defined as working in a machinelike fashion in activities for which machine work has not yet been devised or which would be costlier than human work. The only person who is in touch with the whole product is the manager, but to him the product is an abstraction, whose essence is exchange value, while the worker, for whom it is concrete, never works on it as a whole.

[⁶] Undoubtedly without quantification and abstractification modern mass production would be unthinkable. But in a society in which economic activities have become the main preoccupation of man, this process of quantification and abstractification has transcended the realm of economic production, and spread to the attitude of man to things, to people, and to himself.

[⁷] In order to understand the abstractification process in modern man, we must first consider the ambiguous function of abstraction in general. It is obvious that abstractions in themselves are not a modern phenomenon. In fact, an increasing ability to form abstractions is characteristic of the cultural development of the human race. If I speak of "a table," I am using an abstraction; I am referring, not to a specific table in its full concreteness, but to the genus "table" which comprises all possible concrete tables. If I speak of "a man" I am not speaking of this or that person, in his concreteness and uniqueness, but of the genus "man," which comprises all individual persons. In other words, I make an abstraction. The development of philosophical or scientific thought is based on an increasing ability for such abstractification, and to give it up would mean to fall back into the primitive way of thinking.

[⁸] However, there are *two* ways of relating oneself to an object: one can relate oneself to it in its full concreteness; then the object appears with all its specific qualities, and there is no other object which is identical with it. And one can relate oneself to the object in an abstract way, that is, emphasizing only those qualities which it has in common with all other objects of the same genus, and thus accentuating some and ignoring other qualities. The full and productive relatedness to an object comprises this polarity of perceiving it in its uniqueness, and at the same time in its generality; in its concreteness, and at the same time in its abstractness.

[⁹] In contemporary Western culture this polarity has given way to an almost exclusive reference to the abstract qualities of things and people, and to a neglect of relating oneself to their concreteness and uniqueness. Instead of forming abstract concepts where it is necessary and useful, everything, including ourselves, is being abstractified; the concrete reality of people and things to which we can relate with the reality of our own person, is replaced by abstractions, by ghosts that embody different qualities.

[10] It is quite customary to talk about a "three-million-dollar bridge," a "twenty-cent cigar," a "five-dollar watch," and this not only from the standpoint of the manufacturer or the consumer in the process of buying it, but as the essential point in the description. When one speaks of the "three-million-dollar bridge," one is not primarily concerned with its usefulness or beauty, that is, with its concrete qualities, but one speaks of it as of a commodity, the main quality of which is its exchange value, expressed in a quantity, that of money. This does not mean, of course, that one is not concerned also with the usefulness or beauty of the bridge, but it does mean that its concrete (use) value is *secondary* to its abstract (exchange) value in the way the object is experienced. The famous line by Gertrude Stein "a rose is a rose is a rose," is a protest against this abstract form of experience; for most people a rose is just *not* a rose, but a flower in a certain price range, to be bought on certain social occasions; even the most beautiful flower, provided it is a wild one, costing nothing, is not experienced in its beauty, compared to that of the rose, because it has no exchange value.

[11] In other words, things are experienced as commodities, as embodiments of exchange value, not only while we are buying or selling, but in our attitude toward them when the economic transaction is finished. A thing, even after it has been bought, never quite loses its quality as a commodity in this sense, it is expendable, always retaining its exchange-value quality. A good illustration of this attitude is to be found in a report of the Executive Secretary of an important scientific organization as to how he spent a day in his office. The organization had just bought and moved into a building of their own. The Executive Secretary reports that during one of the first days after they had moved into the building, he got a call from a real estate agent, saying that some people were interested in buying the building and wanted to look at it. Although he knew that it was most unlikely that the organization would want to sell the building a few days after they had moved in, he could not resist the temptation to know whether the value of the building had risen since they had bought it, and spent one or two valuable hours in showing the real estate agent around. He writes: "very interested in fact we can get an offer for more than we have put in building. Nice coincidence that offer comes while treasurer is in the office. All agree it will be good for Board's morale to learn that the building will sell for a good deal more than it cost. Let's see what happens." In spite of all the pride and pleasure in the new building, it had still retained its quality as a commodity, as something expendable, and to which no full sense of possession or use is attached. The same attitude is obvious in the relationship of people to the cars they

buy; the car never becomes fully a thing to which one is attached, but retains its quality as a commodity to be exchanged in a successful bargain; thus, cars are sold after a year or two, long before their use value is exhausted or even considerably diminished.

[12] This abstractification takes place even with regard to phenomena which are not commodities sold on the market, like a flood disaster; the newspapers will headline a flood, speaking of a "million-dollar catastrophe," emphasizing the abstract quantitative element rather than the concrete aspects of human suffering.

[13] But the abstractifying and quantifying attitude goes far beyond the realm of things. People are also experienced as the embodiment of a quantitative exchange value. To speak of a man as being "worth one million dollars," is to speak of him not any more as a concrete human person, but as an abstraction, whose essence can be expressed in a figure. It is an expression of the same attitude when a newspaper headlines an obituary with the words "Shoe Manufacturer Dies." Actually a *man* has died, a man with certain human qualities, with hopes and frustrations, with a wife and children. It is true that he manufactured shoes, or rather, that he owned and managed a factory in which workers served machines manufacturing shoes; but if it is said that a "Shoe Manufacturer Dies," the richness and concreteness of a human life is expressed in the abstract formula of economic function.

[14] The same abstractifying approach can be seen in expressions like "Mr. Ford produced so many automobiles," or this or that general "conquered a fortress"; or if a man has a house built for himself, he says, "I built a house." Concretely speaking, Mr. Ford did not manufacture the automobiles; he directed automobile production which was executed by thousands of workers. The general never conquered the fortress; he was sitting in his headquarters, issuing orders, and his soldiers did the conquering. The man did not build a house; he paid the money to an architect who made the plans and to workers who did the building. All this is not said to minimize the significance of the managing and directing operations, but in order to indicate that in this way of experiencing things, sight of what goes on concretely is lost, and an abstract view is taken in which one function, that of making plans, giving orders, or financing an activity, is identified with the whole concrete process of production, or of fighting, or of building, as the case may be.

[15] The same process of abstractification takes place in all other spheres. The New York *Times* recently printed a news item under the heading: "B.Sc. + Ph.D. = $40,000." The information under this somewhat baffling heading was that statistical data showed that a student of engineering who had acquired his Doctor's degree will earn, in a lifetime, $40,000 more than a man who has only the degree of Bachelor of

Sciences. As far as this is a fact it is an interesting socioeconomic datum, worth while reporting. It is mentioned here because the way of expressing the fact as an equation between a scientific degree and a certain amount of dollars is indicative of the abstractifying and quantifying thinking in which knowledge is experienced as the embodiment of a certain exchange value on the personality market. It is to the same point when a political report in a news magazine states that the Eisenhower administration feels it has so much "capital of confidence" that it can risk some unpopular measures, because it can "afford" to lose some of that confidence capital. Here again, a human quality like confidence is expressed in its abstract form, as if it were a money investment to be dealt with in terms of a market speculation. How drastically commercial categories have entered even religious thinking is shown in the following passage by Bishop Sheen, in an article on the birth of Christ. "Our reason tells us," so writes the author, "that if anyone of the claimants (for the role of God's son) came from God, the least that God could do to support His Representative's claim would be to preannounce His coming. Automobile manufacturers tell us when to expect a new model."[1] Or, even more drastically, Billy Graham, the evangelist, says: "I am selling the greatest product in the world; why shouldn't it be promoted as well as soap?"[2]

[16] The process of abstractification, however, has still deeper roots and manifestations than the ones described so far, roots which go back to the very beginning of the modern era; to the *dissolution* of any *concrete frame of reference* in the process of life.

[17] In a primitive society, the "world" is identical with the tribe. The tribe is in the center of the Universe, as it were; everything outside is shadowy and has no independent existence. In the medieval world, the Universe was much wider; it comprised this globe, the sky and the stars above it; but it was seen with the earth as the center and man as the purpose of Creation. Everything had its fixed place, just as everybody had his fixed position in feudal society. With the fifteenth and sixteenth centuries, new vistas opened up. The earth lost its central place, and became one of the satellites of the sun; new continents were found, new sea lanes discovered; the static social system was more and more loosened up; everything and everybody was moving. Yet, until the end of the nineteenth century, nature and society had not lost their concreteness and definiteness. Man's natural and social world was still manageable, still had definite contours. But with the progress in scientific thought, technical discoveries and the dissolution of all traditional bonds, this definiteness and concreteness is in the process of being lost. Whether we think of our new cosmological picture, or of theoretical physics, or of atonal music, or abstract

[1] From *Collier's* magazine, 1953. (Fromm)
[2] *Time* Magazine, October 25, 1954. (Fromm)

as we progress we tend to abstractify + quantify

art—the concreteness and definiteness of our frame of reference is disappearing. We are not any more in the center of the Universe, we are not any more the purpose of Creation, we are not any more the masters of a manageable and recognizable world—we are a speck of dust, we are a nothing, somewhere in space—without any kind of concrete relatedness to anything. We speak of millions of people being killed, of one third or more of our population being wiped out if a third World War should occur; we speak of billions of dollars piling up as a national debt, of thousands of light years as interplanetary distances, of interspace travel, of artificial satellites. Tens of thousands work in one enterprise, hundreds of thousands live in hundreds of cities.

[18] The dimensions with which we deal are figures and abstractions; they are far beyond the boundaries which would permit of any kind of concrete experience. There is no frame of reference left which is manageable, observable, which is adapted to *human dimensions*. While our eyes and ears receive impressions only in humanly manageable proportions, our concept of the world has lost just that quality; it does not any longer correspond to our human dimensions.

[19] This is especially significant in connection with the development of modern means of destruction. In modern war, one individual can cause the destruction of hundreds of thousands of men, women and children. He could do so by pushing a button; he may not feel the emotional impact of what he is doing, since he does not know the people whom he kills; it is almost as if his act of pushing the button and their death had no real connection. The same man would probably be incapable of even slapping, not to speak of killing, a helpless person. In the latter case, the concrete situation arouses in him a conscience reaction common to all normal men; in the former, there is no such reaction, because the act and his object are alienated from the doer, his act is not *his* any more, but has, so to speak, a life and a responsibility of its own.

[20] Science, business, politics, have lost all foundations and proportions which make sense humanly. We live in figures and abstractions; since nothing is concrete, nothing is real. Everything is possible, factually and morally. Science fiction is not different from science fact, nightmares and dreams from the events of next year. Man has been thrown out from any definite place whence he can overlook and manage his life and the life of society. He is driven faster and faster by the forces which originally were created by him. In this wild whirl he thinks, figures, busy with abstractions, more and more remote from concrete life.

automation brings impersonality

--◀{ C O M M E N T   A N D   Q U E S T I O N S }▶--

1. One way of analyzing this selection is to examine its different levels of cause–effect relationships. In the large pattern, the "process of quantification and abstractification" is a cause of the alienation of man in modern Western society. This process of quantification and abstractification, in turn, has several causes: (a) the characteristics of capitalist mass production; (b) the related habit of applying the values of economic production to things which are not actually commodities; (c) the deeper cause of a changing concept of the world in which a concrete human frame of reference is lost. The effect of all this is that modern man lives in a "wild whirl . . . busy with abstractions, more and more remote from concrete life."

    Fromm's opening paragraph indicates that he is using the terms *quantification* and *abstractification* to refer to a single phenomenon: ". . . *one* of the fundamental economic features . . . *the process* of quantification and abstractification." What is the difference in meaning of the two words? Why does Fromm use both of the rather cumbersome terms instead of only one?

2. Paragraph 2 is developed by contrast. What are the significant differences between medieval production and modern business enterprise?

3. In paragraphs 3 and 4, how has the transformation of the concrete into the abstract developed beyond the balance sheet? What words and phrases does Fromm use to emphasize the loss of concrete and personal experience in economic relations?

4. In what specific ways does increasing division of labor (paragraph 5) result in greater abstractification, and, eventually, in alienation?

5. Paragraph 6 is transitional. What connection does it establish between mass production and a changed attitude toward things and people?

6. In the discussion of abstractness and concreteness (paragraphs 7–9), what, according to Fromm, is the value of abstraction? What is the best, or most productive, way of relating oneself to an object? What kind of relating is characteristic of contemporary Western culture? What is the reason for the emphasis, at the end of paragraph 9, on the difference between quantity and quality?

7. What central idea is developed by means of the examples in paragraphs 10–12?

8. In what way does paragraph 12 lead into paragraph 13?

9. Paragraphs 13–15 are developed largely by examples. What slightly different points are made by the examples in each of the three paragraphs?

10. Paragraph 16 introduces a deeper cause of the process of abstractification, which is developed in paragraphs 17–19. What method or methods of development are used in paragraph 17? What does Fromm mean by saying that we have "no frame of reference . . . adapted to *human dimensions*"?

What idea is further developed by the discussion of modern war in paragraph 19?

11. This selection is part of a chapter "Man in Capitalistic Society," an analysis of the socio-economic conditions which create the social character of modern Western man and which are responsible for disturbances in his mental health. Are the statements made in paragraph 20 (the conclusion of one section of the chapter) adequately supported by the preceding material in this selection, or do some of them depend for meaning on a larger context?

12. Look back at the paragraph beginnings in "Alienation: Quantification and Abstractification." How does Fromm use his paragraph beginnings to establish transitions and to keep his organization clear?

QUESTION-TO-ANSWER OR PROBLEM-TO-SOLUTION

॰

[8]   *Arthur M. Schlesinger, Jr.*: The Crisis
of American Masculinity

ARTHUR M. SCHLESINGER, JR. (1917–   ) has been a professor
of history at Harvard and a special assistant to President Kennedy; he is now
Albert Schweitzer Professor of the Humanities, City University of New York.
Among his books are *The Age of Jackson,* winner of the 1945 Pulitzer Prize
for history; *The Vital Center;* three volumes of *The Age of Roosevelt* (*The
Crisis of the Old Order, 1919–1933, The Coming of the New Deal, The
Politics of Upheaval*); and *A Thousand Days: John F. Kennedy in the White
House,* which received the 1965 Pulitzer Prize for biography and the National
Book Award in history and biography. The following essay, first published
in *Esquire* in November, 1958, was later reprinted in *The Politics of Hope,*
a collection of Schlesinger's essays on American politics and culture.

[1] What has happened to the American male? For a long time, he
seemed utterly confident in his manhood, sure of his masculine role in
society, easy and definite in his sense of sexual identity. The frontiersmen
of James Fenimore Cooper, for example, never had any concern about
masculinity; they were men, and it did not occur to them to think twice
about it. Even well into the twentieth century, the heroes of Dreiser, of
Fitzgerald, of Hemingway remain men. But one begins to detect a new
theme emerging in some of these authors, especially in Hemingway: the

78

theme of the male hero increasingly preoccupied with proving his virility to himself. And by mid-century, the male role had plainly lost its rugged clarity of outline. Today men are more and more conscious of maleness not as a fact but as a problem. The ways by which American men affirm their masculinity are uncertain and obscure. There are multiplying signs, indeed, that something has gone badly wrong with the American male's conception of himself.

[2] On the most superficial level, the roles of male and female are increasingly merged in the American household. The American man is found as never before as a substitute for wife and mother—changing diapers, washing dishes, cooking meals and performing a whole series of what once were considered female duties. The American woman meanwhile takes over more and more of the big decisions, controlling them indirectly when she cannot do so directly. Outside the home, one sees a similar blurring of function. While men design dresses and brew up cosmetics, women become doctors, lawyers, bank cashiers and executives. "Women now fill many 'masculine' roles," writes the psychologist, Dr. Bruno Bettelheim, "and expect their husbands to assume many of the tasks once reserved for their own sex." They seem an expanding, aggressive force, seizing new domains like a conquering army, while men, more and more on the defensive, are hardly able to hold their own and gratefully accept assignments from their new rulers. A recent book bears the stark and melancholy title *The Decline of the American Male*.

[3] Some of this evidence, it should be quickly said, has been pushed too far. The willingness of a man to help his wife around the house may as well be evidence of confidence in masculinity as the opposite; such a man obviously does not have to cling to masculine symbols in order to keep demonstrating his maleness to himself. But there is more impressive evidence than the helpful husband that this is an age of sexual ambiguity. It appears no accident, for example, that the changing of sex—the Christine Jorgensen phenomenon—so fascinates our newspaper editors and readers; or that homosexuality, that incarnation of sexual ambiguity, should be enjoying a cultural boom new in our history. Such developments surely express a deeper tension about the problem of sexual identity.

[4] Consider the theatre, that faithful mirror of a society's preoccupations. There have been, of course, popular overt inquiries into sexual ambiguities, like *Compulsion* or *Tea and Sympathy*. But in a sense these plays prove the case too easily. Let us take rather two uncommonly successful plays by the most discussed young playwrights of the United States and Great Britain—Tennessee Williams's *Cat On A Hot Tin Roof* and John Osborne's *Look Back in Anger*. Both deal with the young male in a singular state of confusion and desperation. In *Cat On A Hot Tin Roof*, Brick Pollitt, the professional football player, refuses to sleep with

his wife because of guilty memories of his relations with a dead team mate. In *Look Back in Anger*, Jimmy Porter, the embittered young intellectual who can sustain a relationship with his wife only by pretending they are furry animals together, explodes with hatred of women and finds his moments of happiness rough-housing around the stage with a male pal.

[5] Brick Pollitt and Jimmy Porter are all too characteristic modern heroes. They are, in a sense, castrated; one is stymied by fear of homosexuality, the other is an unconscious homosexual. Neither is capable of dealing with the woman in his life: Brick surrenders to a strong woman, Jimmy destroys a weak one. Both reject the normal female desire for full and reciprocal love as an unconscionable demand and an intolerable burden. Now not many American males have been reduced to quite the Pollitt-Porter condition. Still the intentness with which audiences have watched these plays suggests that exposed nerves are being plucked— that the Pollitt-Porter dilemma expresses in vivid and heightened form something that many spectators themselves feel or fear.

[6] Or consider the movies. In some ways, the most brilliant and influential American film since the war is *High Noon*. That remarkable movie, which invested the Western with the classic economy of myth, can be viewed in several ways: as an existentialist drama, for example, or as a parable of McCarthyism. It can also be viewed as a mordant comment on the effort of the American woman to emasculate the American man. The sheriff plainly did not suffer from Brick Pollitt's disease. But a large part of the story dealt with the attempt of his girl to persuade him not to use force—to deny him the use of his pistol. The pistol is an obvious masculine symbol, and, in the end, it was the girl herself, in the modern American manner, who used the pistol and killed a villain. (In this connection, one can pause and note why the Gary Coopers, Cary Grants, Clark Gables and Spencer Tracys continue to play romantic leads opposite girls young enough to be their daughters; it is obviously because so few of the younger male stars can project a convincing sense of masculinity.)

[7] Psychoanalysis backs up the theatre and the movies in emphasizing the obsession of the American male with his manhood. "Every psychoanalyst knows," writes one of them, "how many emotional difficulties are due to those fears and insecurities of neurotic men who are unconsciously doubting their masculinity." "In our civilization," Dr. Theodor Reik says, "men are afraid that they will not be men enough." Reik adds significantly: "And women are afraid that they might be considered only women." Why is it that women worry, not over whether they can fill the feminine role, but whether filling that role is enough, while men worry whether they can fill the masculine roll at all? How to account for this rising tide of male anxiety? What has unmanned the American man?

[8] There is currently a fashionable answer to this question. Male anxiety, many observers have declared, is simply the result of female ag-

gression: what has unmanned the American man is the American woman. The present male confusion and desperation, it is contended, are the inevitable consequence of the threatened feminization of American society. The victory of women is the culmination of a long process of masculine retreat, beginning when Puritanism made men feel guilty about sex and the frontier gave women the added value of scarcity. Fleeing from the reality of femininity, the American man, while denying the American woman juridical equality, transformed her into an ideal of remote and transcendent purity with overriding authority over the family, the home, the school and culture. This habit of obeisance left the male psychologically disarmed and vulnerable when the goddess stepped off the pedestal and demanded in addition equal economic, political and legal rights. In the last part of the nineteenth century, women won their battle for equality. They gained the right of entry into one occupation after another previously reserved for males. Today they hold the key positions of personal power in our society and use this power relentlessly to consolidate their mastery. As mothers, they undermine masculinity through the use of love as a technique of reward and punishment. As teachers, they prepare male children for their role of submission in an increasingly feminine world. As wives, they complete the work of subjugation. Their strategy of conquest is deliberately to emasculate men—to turn them into Brick Pollitts and Jimmy Porters.

[9] Or so a standard indictment runs; and no doubt there is something in it. American women have unquestionably gained through the years a place in our society which American men have not been psychologically prepared to accept. Whether because of Puritanism or the frontier, there has been something immature in the traditional American male attitude toward women—a sense of alarm at times amounting to panic. Almost none of the classic American novels, for example, presents the theme of mature and passionate love. Our nineteenth-century novelists saw women either as unassailable virgins or abandoned temptresses—never simply as women. One looks in vain through *Moby Dick* and *The Adventures of Huckleberry Finn*, through Cooper and Poe and Whitman, for an adult portrayal of relations between men and women. "Where," Leslie Fiedler has asked, "is the American *Madame Bovary, Anna Karenina, Wuthering Heights,* or *Vanity Fair*?"

[10] Yet the implication of the argument that the American man has been unmanned by the emancipation of the American woman is that the American man was incapable of growing up. For the nineteenth-century sense of masculinity was based on the psychological idealization and the legal subjection of women; masculinity so spuriously derived could never—and should never—have endured. The male had to learn to live at some point with the free and equal female. Current attempts to blame "the decline of the American male" on the aggressiveness of the

American female amount to a confession that, under conditions of free competition, the female was bound to win. Simple observation refutes this supposition. In a world of equal rights, some women rise; so too do some men; and no pat generalization is possible about the sexual future of society. Women have gained power in certain ways; in others, they have made little progress. It is safe to predict, for example, that we will have a Roman Catholic, perhaps even a Jew, for President before we have a woman. Those amiable prophets of an impending American matriarchy (all men, by the way) are too pessimistic.

[11] Something more fundamental is involved in the unmanning of American men than simply the onward rush of American women. Why is the American man so unsure today about his masculine identity? The basic answer to this is surely because he is so unsure about his identity in general. Nothing is harder in the whole human condition than to achieve a full sense of identity—than to know who you are, where you are going, and what you mean to live and die for. From the most primitive myths to the most contemporary novels—from Oedipus making the horrified discovery that he had married his mother, to Leopold Bloom and Stephen Dedalus searching their souls in Joyce's Dublin and the haunted characters of Kafka trying to make desperate sense out of an incomprehensible universe—the search for identity has been the most compelling human problem. That search has always been ridden with trouble and terror. And it can be plausibly argued that the conditions of modern life make the quest for identity more difficult than it has ever been before.

[12] The pre-democratic world was characteristically a world of status in which people were provided with ready-made identities. But modern western society—free, equalitarian, democratic—has swept away all the old niches in which people for so many centuries found safe refuge. Only a few people at any time in human history have enjoyed the challenge of "making" themselves; most have fled from the unendurable burden of freedom into the womblike security of the group. The new age of social mobility may be fine for those strong enough to discover and develop their own roles. But for the timid and the frightened, who constitute the majority in any age, the great vacant spaces of equalitarian society can become a nightmare filled with nameless horrors. Thus mass democracy, in the very act of offering the individual new freedom and opportunity, offers new moral authority to the group and thereby sets off a new assault on individual identity. Over a century ago Alexis de Tocqueville, the perceptive Frenchman who ruminated on the contradictions of equality as he toured the United States in the Eighteen Thirties, pointed to the "tyranny of the majority" as a central problem of democracy. John Stuart Mill, lamenting the decline of individualism in Great Britain, wrote: "That so few now dare to be eccentric marks the chief danger of the time." How much greater that danger seems a century later!

[13] For our own time has aggravated the assault on identity by adding economic and technological pressures to the political and social pressures of the nineteenth century. Modern science has brought about the growing centralization of the economy. We work and think and live and even dream in larger and larger units. William H. Whyte, Jr., has described the rise of "the organization man," working by day in immense business concerns, sleeping by night in immense suburban developments, deriving his fantasy life from mass-produced entertainments, spending his existence, not as an individual, but as a member of a group and coming in the end to feel guilty and lost when he deviates from his fellows. Adjustment rather than achievement becomes the social ideal. Men no longer fulfill an inner sense of what they *must be;* indeed, with the cult of the group, that inner sense itself begins to evaporate. Identity consists, not of self-realization, but of smooth absorption into the group. Nor is this just a matter of passive acquiescence. The group is aggressive, imperialistic, even vengeful, forever developing new weapons with which to overwhelm and crush the recalcitrant individual. Not content with disciplining the conscious mind, the group today is even experimenting with means of violating the subconscious. The subliminal invasion represents the climax of the assault on individual identity.

[14] It may seem a long way from the loss of the sense of self to the question of masculinity. But if people do not know *who* they are, it is hardly surprising that they are no longer sure what sex they are. Nigel Dennis's exuberant novel, *Cards of Identity,* consists of a series of brilliant variations on the quest for identity in contemporary life. It reaches one of its climaxes in the tale of a person who was brought up by enlightened parents to believe that there was no such thing as pure male or female— everyone had elements of both—and who accepted this proposition so rigorously that he (she) could not decide what his (her) own sex was. "In what identity do you intend to face the future?" someone asks. "It seems that nowadays," comes the plaintive reply, "one must choose between being a woman who behaves like a man, and a man who behaves like a woman. In short, I must choose to be one in order to behave like the other." If most of us have not yet quite reached that condition of sexual chaos, yet the loss of a sense of identity is obviously a fundamental step in the decay of masculinity. And the gratification with which some American males contemplate their own decline should not obscure the fact that women, for all their recent legal and economic triumphs, are suffering from a loss of identity too. It is not accidental that the authors of one recent book described modern woman as the "lost sex."

[15] If this is true, then the key to the recovery of masculinity does not lie in any wistful hope of humiliating the aggressive female and restoring the old masculine supremacy. Masculine supremacy, like white supremacy, was the neurosis of an immature society. It is good for men as well

as for women that women have been set free. In any case, the process is
irreversible; that particular genie can never be put back into the bottle.
The key to the recovery of masculinity lies rather in the problem of
identity. When a person begins to find out *who* he is, he is likely to find
out rather soon what sex he is.

[¹⁶] For men to become men again, in short, their first task is to recover
a sense of individual spontaneity. And to do this a man must visualize
himself as an individual apart from the group, whatever it is, which
defines his values and commands his loyalty. There is no reason to suppose
that the group is always wrong: to oppose the group automatically is
nearly as conformist as to surrender to it automatically. But there is every
necessity to recognize that the group is one thing and the individual—
oneself—is another. One of the most sinister of present-day doctrines is
that of *togetherness.* The recovery of identity means, first of all, a new
belief in apartness. It means a determination to resist the overpowering
conspiracy of blandness, which seeks to conceal all tension and conflict in
American life under a blanket of locker-room affability. And the rebirth
of spontaneity depends, at bottom, on changes of attitude *within* people—
changes which can perhaps be described, without undue solemnity, as
moral changes. These changes will no doubt come about in as many ways
as there are individuals involved. But there are some general suggestions
that can be made about the techniques of liberation. I should like to
mention three such techniques: satire, art, and politics.

[¹⁷] Satire means essentially the belief that nothing is sacred—that
there is no person or institution or idea which cannot but benefit from
the exposure of comedy. Our nation in the past has reveled in satire; it is,
after all, the nation of Abraham Lincoln, of Mark Twain, of Finley Peter
Dunne, of H. L. Mencken, of Ring Lardner. Indeed, the whole spirit of
democracy is that of satire; as Montaigne succinctly summed up the
democratic faith: "Sit he on never so high a throne, a man still sits on his
own bottom." Yet today American society can only be described as a
pompous society, at least in its official manifestations. Early in 1958 Mort
Sahl, the night-club comedian, made headlines in New York because he
dared make a joke about J. Edgar Hoover! It was not an especially good
joke, but the fact that he made it at all was an encouraging sign. One
begins to feel that the American people can only stand so much reverence
—that in the end our native skepticism will break through, sweep aside
the stuffed shirts and the stuffed heads and insist that platitudes are plati-
tudinous and the great are made, among other things, to be laughed at.
Irony is good for our rulers; and it is even better for ourselves because it
is a means of dissolving the pomposity of society and giving the individual
a chance to emerge.

[¹⁸] If irony is one source of spontaneity, art is another. Very little can
so refresh our vision and develop our vision and develop our values as

the liberating experience of art. The mass media have cast a spell on us: the popular addiction to prefabricated emotional clichés threatens to erode our capacity for fresh and direct aesthetic experience. Individual identity vanishes in the welter of machine-made reactions. But thoughtful exposure to music, to painting, to poetry, to the beauties of nature, can do much to restore the inwardness, and thereby the identity, of man. There is thus great hope in the immense cultural underground of our age—the paper-bound books, the long-playing records, the drama societies, the art festivals, the new interest in painting and sculpture. All this represents a disdain for existing values and goals, a reaching out for something more exacting and more personal, an intensified questing for identity.

[19] And politics in a true sense can be a means of liberation—not the banal politics of rhetoric and self-congratulation, which aims at burying all real issues under a mass of piety and platitude; but the politics of responsibility, which tries to define the real issues and present them to the people for decision. Our national politics have become boring in recent years because our leaders have offered neither candid and clear-cut formulations of the problems nor the facts necessary for intelligent choice. A virile political life will be definite and hardhitting, respecting debate and dissent, seeking clarity and decision.

[20] As the American male develops himself by developing his comic sense, his aesthetic sense and his moral and political sense, the lineaments of personality will at last begin to emerge. The achievement of identity, the conquest of a sense of self—these will do infinitely more to restore American masculinity than all the hormones in the test tubes of our scientists. "Whoso would be a *man*," said Emerson, "must be a nonconformist"; and, if it is the present writer who adds the italics, nonetheless one feels that no injustice is done to Emerson's intention. How can masculinity, femininity, or anything else survive in a homogenized society, which seeks steadily and benignly to eradicate all differences between the individuals who compose it? If we want to have *men* again in our theatres and our films and our novels—not to speak of in our classrooms, our business offices and our homes—we must first have a society which encourages each of its members to have a distinct identity.

--⊰ COMMENT AND QUESTIONS ⊱--

1. Schlesinger's essay has four main parts: the first section (paragraphs 1–7), which begins and ends with similar questions, develops a problem; the second section (paragraphs 8–10) supplies one current answer to the ques-

tions, an answer which the author considers inadequate; the third section (paragraphs 11–15) explores a deeper cause of the problem; and the last section (paragraphs 16–20) suggests a solution. Within this framework of problem-to-solution, Schlesinger uses contrast and comparison as well as cause–effect development.

Examine paragraph 1 of the essay. What makes it an effective beginning? How is the paragraph developed? How are the sentences within the paragraph linked? Why is *rugged* ("*rugged* clarity of outline," sentence 4) a better word than, for example, "unmistakable"? What are the two functions of the last sentence of paragraph 1?

2. Paragraphs 2–7 support the author's thesis that the American male is uncertain of his masculinity. What kinds of evidence does Schlesinger give? What examples of qualification do you find in this section (see especially paragraphs 3, 5, and 6)?

3. What contrasts and comparisons are used to develop paragraph 5?

4. What is the currently fashionable answer to the question of what has unmanned the American man? What are Schlesinger's reasons (paragraphs 9–10) for finding this answer not wholly satisfactory?

5. Paragraph 9 explicitly introduces the idea of some deficiency in American men themselves. In paragraphs 9 and 10, what direct and indirect references do you find to the idea of immaturity in the American man's attitude toward women?

6. Examine the organization and the transitions in the first two divisions of the essay (paragraphs 1–10) by re-reading, and perhaps underlining, the following sentences: the first and last sentences of paragraph 1; the first and fourth sentences of paragraph 2; the first and third sentences of paragraph 3; the first sentences of paragraphs 4, 5, and 6; the first and last sentences of paragraph 7; the first two sentences of paragraph 8; the first two sentences of paragraph 9; and the first sentence of paragraph 10. What are Schlesinger's principal devices for keeping the sequence of ideas and the relationship of ideas clear?

7. Paragraph 11 states a new thesis (a "basic answer" to the problem of American masculinity), supported in paragraphs 12 and 13. What is the thesis? What contrasts are used in paragraph 12? How is paragraph 12 linked to paragraph 13? How is paragraph 13 developed?

8. What is the function of paragraph 14? Do the concluding sentences, about women, violate the unity of the paragraph and of the essay on masculinity?

9. What is the reference of *this* ("If *this* is true") at the beginning of paragraph 15? Paragraph 15 is largely summary and restatement. What ideas and themes discussed earlier are drawn together in this paragraph?

10. Paragraph 16 introduces a solution to the problem of lost identity and, at the end, introduces three techniques for recovery of self. Comment on Schlesinger's diction in this paragraph; specifically, what are the connotations and contributions to tone of *spontaneity, sinister* (applied to "togetherness"), *overpowering conspiracy of blandness, blanket of locker-room affability, liberation*? What instances of qualification do you find in the paragraph?

11. In paragraphs 17–19, exactly what does Schlesinger mean by satire, art,

and politics? How may each of these help to restore identity? Are they related to the idea of maturity (or immaturity) discussed earlier in the essay? In recommending satire, art, and politics, is the author addressing the average American man, or a particular kind of American man? Would you add other "techniques of liberation" to the three he suggests?

12. Examine the sentences in paragraphs 18 and 19. What distinctive traits of style do you notice? In paragraph 18, why does Schlesinger use the term "immense cultural *underground*" in reference to paperback books, records, etc.? In the last sentence of paragraph 19, what words are particularly well chosen to fit the context of the whole essay?

13. What are the functions of the first two sentences of paragraph 20? In the next-to-last sentence of paragraph 20, why does the author mention femininity as well as masculinity? What are the connotations of *homogenized society*? What is the effect of the compounded adverbs *steadily and benignly*?

14. The structure of the concluding sentence gives major emphasis to having men in theatres, films, and novels, and less emphasis to having men in classrooms, offices, and homes. Does this emphasis follow logically from the content of the essay?

DEFINITION

ℰ

[9]   *Carl L. Becker*: The Ideal Democracy

CARL L. BECKER (1873–1945) was a distinguished American historian
who taught at Pennsylvania State College, Dartmouth, the Universities of
Kansas and Minnesota, and after 1917 at Cornell. Among his books are *The
Heavenly City of the Eighteenth Century Philosophers, Every Man His Own
Historian, New Liberties for Old, How New Will the Better World Be?* and
Modern Democracy, from which this selection is taken. "The Ideal Democracy"
was originally delivered as a lecture at the University of Virginia in 1940.
References to then-current world affairs date the essay in minor ways, but
it remains contemporary as an illuminating definition and discussion of the
historical development of democracy.

[1] Democracy, like liberty or science or progress, is a word with which
we are all so familiar that we rarely take the trouble to ask what we mean
by it. It is a term, as the devotees of semantics say, which has no "referent"
—there is no precise or palpable thing or object which we all think of
when the word is pronounced. On the contrary, it is a word which connotes different things to different people, a kind of conceptual Gladstone
bag which, with a little manipulation, can be made to accommodate
almost any collection of social facts we may wish to carry about in it. In it
we can as easily pack a dictatorship as any other form of government. We
have only to stretch the concept to include any form of government
supported by a majority of the people, for whatever reasons and by
whatever means of expressing assent, and before we know it the empire
of Napoleon, the Soviet regime of Stalin, and the Fascist systems of

Mussolini and Hitler are all safely in the bag. But if this is what we mean by democracy, then virtually all forms of government are democratic, since virtually all governments, except in times of revolution, rest upon the explicit or implicit consent of the people. In order to discuss democracy intelligently it will be necessary, therefore, to define it, to attach to the word a sufficiently precise meaning to avoid the confusion which is not infrequently the chief result of such discussions.

[2] All human institutions, we are told, have their ideal forms laid away in heaven, and we do not need to be told that the actual institutions conform but indifferently to these ideal counterparts. It would be possible then to define democracy either in terms of the ideal or in terms of the real form—to define it as government of the people, by the people, for the people; or to define it as government of the people, by the politicians, for whatever pressure groups can get their interests taken care of. But as a historian, I am naturally disposed to be satisfied with the meaning which, in the history of politics, men have commonly attributed to the word—a meaning, needless to say, which derives partly from the experience and partly from the aspirations of mankind. So regarded, the term democracy refers primarily to a form of government, and it has always meant government by the many as opposed to government by the one—government by the people as opposed to government by a tyrant, a dictator, or an absolute monarch. This is the most general meaning of the word as men have commonly understood it.

[3] In this antithesis there are, however, certain implications, always tacitly understood, which give a more precise meaning to the term. Peisistratus, for example, was supported by a majority of the people, but his government was never regarded as a democracy for all that. Caesar's power derived from a popular mandate, conveyed through established republican forms, but that did not make his government any less a dictatorship. Napoleon called his government a democratic empire, but no one, least of all Napoleon himself, doubted that he had destroyed the last vestiges of the democratic republic. Since the Greeks first used the term, the essential test of democratic government has always been this: the source of political authority must be and remain in the people and not in the ruler. A democratic government has always meant one in which the citizens, or a sufficient number of them to represent more or less effectively the common will, freely act from time to time, and according to established forms, to appoint or recall the magistrates and to enact or revoke the laws by which the community is governed. This I take to be the meaning which history has impressed upon the term democracy as a form of government. It is, therefore, the meaning which I attach to it in these lectures.

[4] The most obvious political fact of our time is that democracy as thus defined has suffered an astounding decline in prestige. Fifty years

ago it was not impossible to regard democratic government, and the liberties that went with it, as a permanent conquest of the human spirit. In 1886 Andrew Carnegie published a book entitled *Triumphant Democracy*. Written without fear and without research, the book was not an achievement of the highest intellectual distinction perhaps; but the title at least expressed well enough the prevailing conviction—the conviction that democracy had fought the good fight, had won the decisive battles, and would inevitably, through its inherent merits, presently banish from the world the most flagrant political and social evils which from time immemorial had afflicted mankind. This conviction could no doubt be most easily entertained in the United States, where even the tradition of other forms of government was too remote and alien to color our native optimism. But even in Europe the downright skeptics, such as Lecky, were thought to be perverse, and so hardheaded a historian as J. B. Bury could proclaim with confidence that the long struggle for freedom of thought had finally been won.

[5] I do not need to tell you that within a brief twenty years the prevailing optimism of that time has been quite dispelled. One European country after another has, willingly enough it seems, abandoned whatever democratic institutions it formerly enjoyed for some form of dictatorship. The spokesmen of Fascism and Communism announce with confidence that democracy, a sentimental aberration which the world has outgrown, is done for; and even the friends of democracy support it with declining conviction. They tell us that democracy, so far from being triumphant, is "at the crossroads" or "in retreat," and that its future is by no means assured. What are we to think of this sudden reversal in fortune and prestige? How explain it? What to do about it?

– II –

[6] One of the presuppositions of modern thought is that institutions, in order to be understood, must be seen in relation to the conditions of time and place in which they appear. It is a little difficult for us to look at democracy in this way. We are so immersed in its present fortunes that we commonly see it only as a "close-up," filling the screen to the exclusion of other things to which it is in fact related. In order to form an objective judgment of its nature and significance, we must therefore first of all get it in proper perspective. Let us then, in imagination, remove from the immediate present scene to some cool high place where we can survey at a glance five or six thousand years of history, and note the part which democracy has played in human civilization. The view, if we have been accustomed to take democratic institutions for granted, is a bit bleak and disheartening. For we see at once that in all this long time, over the habitable globe, the great majority of the human race has neither known nor apparently much cared for our favorite institutions.

[⁷] Civilization was already old when democracy made its first notable appearance among the small city states of ancient Greece, where it flourished brilliantly for a brief century or two and then disappeared. At about the same time something that might be called democracy appeared in Rome and other Italian cities, but even in Rome it did not survive the conquest of the world by the Roman Republic, except as a form of local administration in the cities of the empire. In the twelfth and thirteenth centuries certain favorably placed medieval cities enjoyed a measure of self-government, but in most instances it was soon replaced by the dictatorship of military conquerors, the oligarchic control of a few families, or the encroaching power of autocratic kings. The oldest democracy of modern times is the Swiss Confederation, the next oldest is the Dutch Republic. Parliamentary government in England does not antedate the late seventeenth century, the great American experiment is scarcely older. Not until the nineteenth century did democratic government make its way in any considerable part of the world—in the great states of continental Europe, in South America, in Canada and Australia, in South Africa and Japan.

[⁸] From this brief survey it is obvious that, taking the experience of mankind as a test, democracy has as yet had but a limited and temporary success. There must be a reason for this significant fact. The reason is that democratic government is a species of social luxury, at best a delicate and precarious adventure which depends for success upon the validity of certain assumptions about the capacities and virtues of men, and upon the presence of certain material and intellectual conditions favorable to the exercise of these capacities and virtues. Let us take the material conditions first.

[⁹] It is a striking fact that until recently democracy never flourished except in very small states—for the most part in cities. It is true that in both the Persian and the Roman empires a measure of self-government was accorded to local communities, but only in respect to purely local affairs; in no large state as a whole was democratic government found to be practicable. One essential reason is that until recently the means of communication were too slow and uncertain to create the necessary solidarity of interest and similarity of information over large areas. The principle of representation was well enough known to the Greeks, but in practice it proved impracticable except in limited areas and for special occasions. As late as the eighteenth century it was still the common opinion that the republican form of government, although the best ideally, was unsuited to large countries, even to a country no larger than France. This was the view of Montesquieu, and even of Rousseau. The view persisted into the nineteenth century, and English conservatives, who were opposed to the extension of the suffrage in England, consoled themselves with the notion that the American Civil War would confirm it—would demonstrate that government by and for the people would perish, if not from off the earth at least from large countries. If their hopes were confounded the reason is that the means of communication, figuratively speaking, were making large countries small. It is not altogether fanciful to suppose that, but for the railroad and the telegraph, the United States would today be divided into many small republics maneuvering for advantage and employing war and diplomacy for maintaining an unstable balance of power.

[10] If one of the conditions essential to the success of democratic government is mobility, ease of communication, another is a certain measure of economic security. Democracy does not flourish in communities on the verge of destitution. In ancient and medieval times democratic government appeared for the most part in cities, the centers of prosperity. Farmers in the early Roman Republic and in the Swiss Cantons were not wealthy to be sure, but equality of possessions and of opportunity gave them a certain economic security. In medieval cities political privilege was confined to the prosperous merchants and craftsmen, and in Athens and the later Roman Republic democratic government was found to be workable only on condition that the poor citizens were subsidized by the government or paid for attending the assemblies and the law courts.

[11] In modern times democratic institutions have, generally speaking, been most successful in new countries, such as the United States, Canada, and Australia, where the conditions of life have been easy for the people; and in European countries more or less in proportion to their industrial prosperity. In European countries, indeed, there has been a close correlation between the development of the industrial revolution and the emergence of democratic institutions. Holland and England, the first countries to experience the industrial revolution, were the first also (apart from Switzerland, where certain peculiar conditions obtained) to adopt democratic institutions; and as the industrial revolution spread to France, Belgium, Germany, and Italy, these countries in turn adopted at least a measure of democratic government. Democracy is in some sense an economic luxury, and it may be said that in modern times it has been a function of the development of new and potentially rich countries, or of the industrial revolution which suddenly dowered Europe with unaccustomed wealth. Now that prosperity is disappearing round every next corner, democracy works less well than it did.

[12] So much for the material conditions essential for the success of democratic government. Supposing these conditions to exist, democratic government implies in addition the presence of certain capacities and virtues in its citizens. These capacities and virtues are bound up with the assumptions on which democracy rests, and are available only in so far as the assumptions are valid. The primary assumption of democratic

government is that its citizens are capable of managing their own affairs. But life in any community involves a conflict of individual and class interests, and a corresponding divergence of opinion as to the measures to be adopted for the common good. The divergent opinions must be somehow reconciled, the conflict of interests somehow compromised. It must then be an assumption of democratic government that its citizens are rational creatures, sufficiently so at least to understand the interests in conflict; and it must be an assumption that they are men of good will, sufficiently so toward each other at least to make those concessions of individual and class interest required for effecting workable compromises. The citizens of a democracy should be, as Pericles said the citizens of Athens were, if not all originators at least all sound judges of good policy.

[13] These are what may be called the minimum assumptions and the necessary conditions of democratic government anywhere and at any time. They may be noted to best advantage, not in any state, but in small groups within the state—in clubs and similar private associations of congenial and like-minded people united for a specific purpose. In such associations the membership is limited and select. The members are, or may easily become, all acquainted with each other. Everyone knows, or may easily find out, what is being done and who is doing it. There will of course be differences of opinion, and there may be disintegrating squabbles and intrigues. But on the whole, ends and means being specific and well understood, the problems of government are few and superficial; there is plenty of time for discussion; and since intelligence and good will can generally be taken for granted there is the disposition to make reasonable concessions and compromises. The analogy must be taken for what it is worth. States may not be the mystical blind Molochs of German philosophy, but any state is far more complex and intangible than a private association, and there is little resemblance between such associations and the democracies of modern times. Other things equal, the resemblance is closest in very small states, and it is in connection with the small city states of ancient Greece that the resemblance can best be noted.

[14] The Greek states were limited in size, not as is often thought solely or even chiefly by the physiography of the country, but by some instinctive feeling of the Greek mind that a state is necessarily a natural association of people bound together by ties of kinship and a common tradition of rights and obligations. There must then, as Aristotle said, be a limit:

For if the citizens of a state are to judge and distribute offices according to merit, they must know each other's characters; where they do not possess this knowledge, both the elections to offices and the decisions in the law courts will go wrong. Where the population is very large they are manifestly settled by haphazard, which clearly ought not to be. Besides, in over-populous states foreigners and metics will readily acquire citizenship, for who will find them out?

It obviously did not occur to Aristotle that metics and foreigners should be free to acquire citizenship. It did not occur to him, or to any Greek of his time, or to the merchants of the self-governing medieval city, that a state should be composed of all the people inhabiting a given territory. A state was rather an incorporated body of people within, but distinct from, the population of the community.

[15] Ancient and medieval democracies had thus something of the character of a private association. They were, so to speak, purely pragmatic phenomena, arising under very special conditions, and regarded as the most convenient way of managing the affairs of people bound together by community of interest and for the achievement of specific ends. There is no suggestion in Aristotle that democracy (polity) is intrinsically a superior form of government, no suggestion that it derives from a special ideology of its own. If it rests upon any superiority other than convenience, it is the superiority which it shares with any Greek state, that is to say, the superiority of Greek over barbarian civilization. In Aristotle's philosophy it is indeed difficult to find any clear-cut distinction between the democratic form of government and the state itself; the state, if it be worthy of the name, is always, whatever the form of government, "the government of freemen and equals," and in any state it is always necessary that "the freemen who compose the bulk of the people should have absolute power in some things." In Aristotle's philosophy the distinction between good and bad in politics is not between good and bad types of government, but between the good and the bad form of each type. Any type of government—monarchy, aristocracy, polity—is good provided the rulers aim at the good of all rather than at the good of the class to which they belong. From Aristotle's point of view neither democracy nor dictatorship is good or bad in itself, but only in the measure that it achieves, or fails to achieve, the aim of every good state, which is that "the inhabitants of it should be happy." It did not occur to Aristotle that democracy (polity), being in some special sense in harmony with the nature of man, was everywhere applicable, and therefore destined by fate or the gods to carry throughout the world a superior form of civilization.

[16] It is in this respect chiefly that modern democracy differs from earlier forms. It rests upon something more than the minimum assumptions. It is reinforced by a full-blown ideology which, by endowing the individual with natural and imprescriptible rights, sets the democratic form of government off from all others as the one which alone can achieve the good life. What then are the essential tenets of the modern democratic faith?

– III –

[17] The liberal democratic faith, as expressed in the works of eighteenth- and early nineteenth-century writers, is one of the formulations

of the modern doctrine of progress. It will be well, therefore, to note briefly the historical antecedents of that doctrine.

[18] In the long history of man on earth there comes a time when he remembers something of what has been, anticipates something that will be, knows the country he has traversed, wonders what lies beyond—the moment when he becomes aware of himself as a lonely, differentiated item in the world. Sooner or later there emerges for him the most devastating of all facts, namely, that in an indifferent universe which alone endures, he alone aspires, endeavors to attain, and attains only to be defeated in the end. From that moment his immediate experience ceases to be adequate, and he endeavors to project himself beyond it by creating ideal worlds of semblance, Utopias of other time or place in which all has been, may be, or will be well.

[19] In ancient times Utopia was most easily projected into the unknown past, pushed back to the beginning of things—to the time of P'an Ku and the celestial emperors, to the Garden of Eden, or the reign of King Chronos when men lived like gods free from toil and grief. From this happy state of first created things there had obviously been a decline and fall, occasioned by disobedience and human frailty, and decreed as punishment by fate or the angry gods. The mind of man was therefore afflicted with pessimism, a sense of guilt for having betrayed the divine purpose, a feeling of inadequacy for bringing the world back to its original state of innocence and purity. To men who felt insecure in a changing world, and helpless in a world always changing for the worse, the future had little to offer. It could be regarded for the most part only with resignation, mitigated by individual penance or well-doing, or the hope of some miraculous intervention by the gods, or the return of the god-like kings, to set things right again, yet with little hope that from this setting right there would not be another falling away.

[20] This pervasive pessimism was gradually dispelled in the Western world, partly by the Christian religion, chiefly by the secular intellectual revolution occurring roughly between the fifteenth and the eighteenth centuries. The Christian religion gave assurance that the lost golden age of the past would be restored for the virtuous in the future, and by proclaiming the supreme worth of the individual in the eyes of God enabled men to look forward with hope to the good life after death in the Heavenly City. Meantime, the secular intellectual revolution, centering in the matter-of-fact study of history and science, gradually emancipated the minds of men from resignation to fate and the angry gods. Accumulated knowledge of history, filling in time past with a continuous succession of credible events, banished all lost golden ages to the realm of myth, and enabled men to live without distress in a changing world since it could be regarded as not necessarily changing for the worse. At the same time, a more competent observation and measurement of the action of material

things disclosed an outer world of nature, indifferent to man indeed, yet behaving, not as the unpredictable sport of the gods, but in ways understandable to human reason and therefore ultimately subject to man's control.

[21] Thus the conditions were fulfilled which made it possible for men to conceive of Utopia, neither as a lost golden age of the past nor as a Heavenly City after death prepared by the gods for the virtuous, but as a future state on earth of man's own devising. In a world of nature that could be regarded as amenable to man's control, and in a world of changing social relations that need not be regarded as an inevitable decline and fall from original perfection, it was possible to formulate the modern doctrine of progress: the idea that, by deliberate intention and rational direction, men can set the terms and indefinitely improve the conditions of their mundane existence.

[22] The eighteenth century was the moment in history when men first fully realized the engaging implications of this resplendent idea, the moment when, not yet having been brought to the harsh appraisal of experience, it could be accepted with unclouded optimism. Never had the universe seemed less mysterious, more open and visible, more eager to yield its secrets to common-sense questions. Never had the nature of man seemed less perverse, or the mind of man more pliable to the pressure of rational persuasion. The essential reason for this confident optimism is that the marvels of scientific discovery disclosed to the men of that time a God who still functioned but was no longer angry. God the Father could be conceived as a beneficient First Cause who, having performed his essential task of creation, had withdrawn from the affairs of men, leaving them competently prepared and fully instructed for the task of achieving their own salvation. In one tremendous sentence Rousseau expressed the eighteenth-century world view of the universe and man's place in it. "Is it simple," he exclaimed, "is it natural that God should have gone in search of Moses in order to speak to Jean Jacques Rousseau?"

[23] God had indeed spoken to Rousseau, he had spoken to all men, but his revelation was contained, not in Holy Writ interpreted by Holy Church, but in the great Book of Nature which was open for all men to read. To this open book of nature men would go when they wanted to know what God had said to them. Here they would find recorded the laws of nature and of nature's God, disclosing a universe constructed according to a rational plan; and that men might read these laws aright they had been endowed with reason, a bit of the universal intelligence placed within the individual to make manifest to him the universal reason implicit in things and events. "Natural law," as Volney so clearly and confidently put it, "is the regular and constant order of facts by which God rules the universe; the order which his wisdom presents to the sense and reason

of men, to serve them as an equal and common rule of conduct, and to guide them, without distinction of race or sect, toward perfection and happiness." Thus God had devised a planned economy, and had endowed men with the capacity for managing it: to bring his ideas, his conduct, and his institutions into harmony with the universal laws of nature was man's simple allotted task.

[24] At all times political theory must accommodate itself in some fashion to the prevailing world view, and liberal-democratic political theory was no exception to this rule. From time immemorial authority and obedience had been the cardinal concepts both of the prevailing world view and of political and social theory. From time immemorial men had been regarded as subject to overruling authority—the authority of the gods, and the authority of kings who were themselves gods, or descended from gods, or endowed with divine authority to rule in place of gods; and from time immemorial obedience to such divine authority was thought to be the primary obligation of men. Even the Greeks, who were so little afraid of their gods that they could hob-nob with them in the most friendly and engaging way, regarded mortals as subject to them; and when they lost faith in the gods they deified the state as the highest good and subordinated the individual to it. But the eighteenth-century world view, making man the measure of all things, mitigated if it did not destroy this sharp contrast between authority and obedience. God still reigned but he did not govern. He had, so to speak, granted his subjects a constitution and authorized them to interpret it as they would in the supreme court of reason. Men were still subject to an overruling authority, but the subjection could be regarded as voluntary because self-imposed, and self-imposed because obedience was exacted by nothing more oppressive than their own rational intelligence.

[25] Liberal-democratic political theory readily accommodated itself to this change in the world view. The voice of the people was now identified with the voice of God, and all authority was derived from it. The individual instead of the state or the prince was now deified and endowed with imprescriptible rights; and since ignorance or neglect of the rights of man was the chief cause of social evils, the first task of political science was to define these rights, the second to devise a form of government suited to guarantee them. The imprescriptible rights of man were easily defined, since they were self-evident: "All men are created equal, [and] are endowed by their Creator with certain inalienable rights, among which are life, liberty, and the pursuit of happiness." From this it followed that all just governments would remove those artificial restraints which impaired these rights, thereby liberating those natural impulses with which God had endowed the individual as a guide to thought and conduct. In the intellectual realm, freedom of thought and the competi-

tion of diverse opinion would disclose the truth, which all men, being rational creatures, would progressively recognize and willingly follow. In the economic realm, freedom of enterprise would disclose the natural aptitudes of each individual, and the ensuing competition of interests would stimulate effort, and thereby result in the maximum of material advantage for all. Liberty of the individual from social constraint thus turned out to be not only an inherent natural right but also a preordained natural mechanism for bringing about the material and moral progress of mankind. Men had only to follow reason and self-interest: something not themselves, God and Nature, would do whatever else was necessary for righteousness.

[26] Thus modern liberal-democracy is associated with an ideology which rests upon something more than the minimum assumptions essential to any democratic government. It rests upon a philosophy of universally valid ends and means. Its fundamental assumption is the worth and dignity and creative capacity of the individual, so that the chief aim of government is the maximum of individual self-direction, the chief means to that end the minimum of compulsion by the state. Ideally considered, means and ends are conjoined in the concept of freedom: freedom of thought, so that the truth may prevail; freedom of occupation, so that careers may be open to talent; freedom of self-government, so that no one may be compelled against his will.

[27] In the possibility of realizing this ideal the prophets and protagonists of democracy exhibited an unquestioned faith. If their faith seems to us somewhat naïve, the reason is that they placed a far greater reliance upon the immediate influence of good will and rational discussion in shaping the conduct of men than it is possible for us to do. This difference can be conveniently noted in a passage from the *Autobiography* of John Stuart Mill, in which he describes his father's extraordinary faith in two things—representative government and complete freedom of discussion:

So complete was my father's reliance on the influence of reason over the minds of mankind, whenever it was allowed to reach them, that he felt as if all would be gained if the whole population were taught to read, if all sorts of opinions were allowed to be addressed to them by word and writing, and if by means of the suffrage they could nominate a legislature to give effect to the opinions they adopted. He thought that when the legislature no longer represented a class interest, it would aim at the general interest, honestly and with adequate wisdom; since the people would be sufficiently under the guidance of educated intelligence to make in general good choice of persons to represent them, and having done so to leave to those whom they had chosen a liberal discretion. Accordingly, artistocratic rule, the government of the few in any of its shapes, being in his eyes the only thing that stood between mankind and the administration of its affairs by the best wisdom to be found amongst them, was the object of his sternest disapprobation, and a democratic suffrage the principal article of his political creed.

[28] The beliefs of James Mill were shared by the little group of Philosophical Radicals who gathered about him. They were, indeed, the beliefs of all those who in the great crusading days placed their hopes in democratic government as a panacea for injustice and oppression. The actual working of democratic government, as these devoted enthusiasts foresaw it, the motives that would inspire men and the objects they would pursue in that ideal democracy which so many honest men have cherished and fought for, have never been better described than by James Bryce in his *Modern Democracies*. In this ideal democracy, says Bryce,

the average citizen will give close and constant attention to public affairs, recognizing that this is his interest as well as his duty. He will try to comprehend the main issues of policy, bringing them an independent and impartial mind, which thinks first not of its own but of the general interest. If, owing to inevitable differences of opinion as to what are the measures needed for the general welfare, parties become inevitable, he will join one, and attend its meetings, but will repress the impulses of party spirit. Never failing to come to the polls, he will vote for his party candidate only if satisfied by his capacity and honesty. He will be ready to . . . be put forward as a candidate for the legislature (if satisfied of his own competence), because public service is recognized as a duty. With such citizens as electors, the legislature will be composed of upright and capable men, single-minded in their wish to serve the nation. Bribery in constituencies, corruption among public servants, will have disappeared. Leaders may not always be single-minded, nor assemblies always wise, nor administrators efficient, but all will be at any rate honest and zealous, so that an atmosphere of confidence and goodwill will prevail. Most of the causes that make for strife will be absent, for there will be no privileges, no advantages to excite jealousy. Office will be sought only because it gives opportunity for useful public service. Power will be shared by all, and a career open to all alike. Even if the law does not—perhaps it cannot—prevent the accumulation of fortunes, these will be few and not inordinate, for public vigilance will close the illegitimate paths to wealth. All but the most depraved persons will obey and support the law, feeling it to be their own. There will be no excuse for violence, because the constitution will provide a remedy for every grievance. Equality will produce a sense of human solidarity, will refine manners, and increase brotherly kindness.

[29] Such is the ideal form of modern democracy laid away in heaven. I do not need to tell you that its earthly counterpart resembles it but slightly.

---**⊰ C O M M E N T   A N D   Q U E S T I O N S ⊱**---

1. One of the best ways to study the very skillful organization of this essay is to examine the first and last sentences of each paragraph, noticing how they state or emphasize topic ideas, and how they establish transitions between paragraphs and sections. What phase of the subject is treated in each of the three major divisions of the essay, and how are the three divisions related?

2. What methods of definition are used in paragraphs 1–3?

3. Paragraph 4 (developed by contrast and example) states a thesis which is further developed and supported in paragraph 5. What is the thesis? Is it still supportable today, almost thirty years after Becker wrote "The Ideal Democracy"?

4. What is Becker's attitude toward Andrew Carnegie's book (paragraph 4)? What expressions particularly reveal the attitude? How would you describe Becker's tone in this passage?

5. Which of the three questions at the end of section I is most directly answered in section II?

6. The last sentence of paragraph 6 and the first sentence of paragraph 8 state, in different words, a generalization about democracy. How is the generalization supported in paragraph 7?

7. Paragraph 8 introduces reasons for the limited success of democracy in human history. Upon what material conditions does democracy depend (paragraphs 9–11)? What minimum assumptions does democracy make about the capacities and virtues of its citizens (paragraph 12)? Some Americans at the present time find it difficult to understand why people of other countries—the developing nations, for example—have not been and are not enthusiastic about democratic government. In what ways might Becker's discussion of the history of democracy throw light on the fact that the institutions which seem obviously valuable to us are not equally attractive to all people?

8. What are the purposes in the essay of paragraphs 13–16?

9. Paragraphs 18–21 are developed by time-order and by cause and effect. What were the historical causes of (a) man's creation of ideal worlds or Utopias; (b) the pessimism, in ancient times, about the future; (c) the gradual dispelling of this pessimism; (d) the formulation of the modern doctrine of progress?

10. This essay, like all of Carl Becker's writing, is notable for its lucid and polished style. Study the writing in paragraphs 18–21, noticing the rhythm and flow of the sentences and the way the sentences are structured to end strongly. What particular qualities of style seem to you especially effective?

11. Examine the diction in paragraph 22. What words and expressions convey a sense of the magnificence of the eighteenth-century world view? At the same time, how does Becker indicate his own reservations about that optimistic view?

12. What contrasts are established in paragraph 24, and how are the contrasts emphasized? Explain how the world view of the eighteenth century affected political theory and produced the modern democratic ideology (paragraphs 24–26).

13. One way of supporting a thesis or generalization is the use of apt quotation. Comment on Becker's use of quotation in this essay and on the purposes served by the quoted material.

14. Becker ends with an assumption: "I do not need to tell you . . . ." In your opinion, in what marked ways does the "earthly counterpart" of democracy differ from the ideal form?

15. Since "The Ideal Democracy" is the first of three lectures on democracy, it is somewhat inconclusive: the author does not answer all the questions he raises at the end of the first section, and he may leave in doubt his own opinion of democracy as a form of government. That opinion is stated in the following passage from another of Becker's books, *New Liberties for Old:*

> To have faith in the dignity and worth of the individual man as an end in himself, to believe that it is better to be governed by persuasion than by coercion, to believe that fraternal good will is more worthy than a selfish and contentious spirit, to believe that in the long run all values are inseparable from the love of truth and the disinterested search for it, to believe that knowledge and the power it confers should be used to promote the welfare and happiness of all men rather than to serve the interests of those individuals and classes whom fortune and intelligence endow with temporary advantage—these are the values which are affirmed by the traditional democratic ideology. . . . The case for democracy is that it accepts the rational and humane values as ends, and proposes as the means of realizing them the minimum of coercion and the maximum of voluntary assent. We may well abandon the cosmological temple in which the democratic ideology originally enshrined these values without renouncing the faith it was designed to celebrate. The essence of that faith is belief in the capacity of man, as a rational and humane creature, to achieve the good life by rational and humane means. The chief virtue of democracy, and the sole reason for cherishing it, is that with all its faults it still provides the most favorable conditions for achieving that end by those means.

What is meant, in the third-from-the-last sentence in the quotation above, by "*the cosmological temple* in which the democratic ideology originally enshrined these values"? What difference do you see between the view of democracy which Becker expresses in the last two sentences of the quotation above and the view of the writers quoted in the last section of "The Ideal Democracy"?

PART TWO

Ideas and Values

EDUCATION AND THE
INQUIRING MIND

℘

[10]   *Plato*: Apology

IN 399 B.C., SOCRATES, Greek philosopher and teacher, was accused
of impiety and of corrupting the youth of Athens with false doctrines, and
was tried and condemned to death by a court of 501 Athenian citizens.
According to Athenian law, the accused acted as his own attorney and spoke
to the court in his own behalf. If he was judged guilty of the charges, and if
no punishment for the offense was established by Athenian law, his accusers
proposed a penalty, and the defendant might propose an alternate penalty;
the court then chose between them. The *Apology*, or *Defense* (the Greek
word did not imply expression of regret, as our word *apology* may), is
Socrates' speech to the court, reported by his pupil Plato. It gives us a
picture of a human being, an almost legendary thinker, who has helped
to shape Western thought, and whose voice still says over the centuries that
wisdom and virtue come only from thought and inquiry, and that the
unexamined life is not worth living.

[¹] How you, O Athenians, have been affected by my accusers, I cannot
tell; but I know that they almost made me forget who I was—so persua-
sively did they speak; and yet they have hardly uttered a word of truth.
But of the many falsehoods told by them, there was one which quite
amazed me;—I mean when they said that you should be upon your guard
and not allow yourselves to be deceived by the force of my eloquence.
To say this, when they were certain to be detected as soon as I opened

This selection was translated by Benjamin Jowett.

my lips and proved myself to be anything but a great speaker, did indeed appear to me most shameless—unless by the force of eloquence they mean the force of truth; for if such is their meaning, I admit that I am eloquent. But in how different a way from theirs! Well, as I was saying, they have scarcely spoken the truth at all; but from me you shall hear the whole truth; not, however, delivered after their manner in a set oration duly ornamented with words and phrases. No, by heaven! but I shall use the words and argument which occur to me at the moment; for I am confident in the justice of my cause: at my time of life I ought not to be appearing before you, O men of Athens, in the character of a juvenile orator—let no one expect it of me. And I must beg of you to grant me a favour:—if I defend myself in my accustomed manner, and you hear me using the words which I have been in the habit of using in the agora, at the tables of the money-changers, or anywhere else, I would ask you not to be surprised, and not to interrupt me on this account. For I am more than seventy years of age, and appearing now for the first time in a court of law, I am quite a stranger to the language of the place; and therefore I would have you regard me as if I were really a stranger, whom you would excuse if he spoke in his native tongue, and after the fashion of his country:—Am I making an unfair request of you? Never mind the manner, which may or may not be good; but think only of the truth of my words, and give heed to that: let the speaker speak truly and the judge decide justly.

[2] And first, I have to reply to the older charges and to my first accusers, and then I will go on to the later ones. For of old I have had many accusers, who have accused me falsely to you during many years; and I am more afraid of them than of Anytus and his associates, who are dangerous, too, in their own way. But far more dangerous are the others, who began when you were children, and took possession of your minds with their falsehoods, telling of one Socrates, a wise man, who speculated about the heaven above, and searched into the earth beneath, and made the worse appear the better cause. The disseminators of this tale are the accusers whom I dread; for their hearers are apt to fancy that such enquirers do not believe in the existence of the gods. And they are many, and their charges against me are of ancient date, and they were made by them in the days when you were more impressible than you are now—in childhood, or it may have been in youth—and the cause when heard went by default, for there was none to answer. And hardest of all, I do not know and cannot tell the names of my accusers; unless in the chance case of a comic poet. All who from envy and malice have persuaded you—some of them having first convinced themselves—all this class of men are most difficult to deal with; for I cannot have them up here, and cross-examine them, and therefore I must simply fight with shadows in my own defence,

and argue when there is no one who answers. I will ask you then to assume with me, as I was saying, that my opponents are of two kinds; one recent, the other ancient: and I hope that you will see the propriety of my answering the latter first, for these accusations you heard long before the others, and much oftener.

[3] Well, then, I must make my defence, and endeavour to clear away in a short time, a slander which has lasted a long time. May I succeed, if to succeed be for my good and yours, or likely to avail me in my cause! The task is not an easy one; I quite understand the nature of it. And so leaving the event with God, in obedience to the law I will now make my defence.

[4] I will begin at the beginning, and ask what is the accusation which has given rise to the slander of me, and in fact has encouraged Meletus to prefer this charge against me. Well, what do the slanderers say? They shall be my prosecutors, and I will sum up their words in an affidavit: "Socrates is an evildoer, and a curious person, who searches into things under the earth and in heaven, and he makes the worse appear the better cause; and he teaches the aforesaid doctrines to others." Such is the nature of the accusation: it is just what you have yourselves seen in the comedy of Aristophanes, who has introduced a man whom he calls Socrates, going about and saying that he walks in air, and talking a deal of nonsense concerning matters of which I do not pretend to know either much or little— not that I mean to speak disparagingly of any one who is a student of natural philosophy. I should be very sorry if Meletus could bring so grave a charge against me. But the simple truth is, O Athenians, that I have nothing to do with physical speculations. Very many of those here present are witnesses to the truth of this, and to them I appeal. Speak then, you who have heard me, and tell your neighbours whether any of you have ever known me hold forth in few words or in many upon such matters. . . . You hear their answer. And from what they say of this part of the charge you will be able to judge of the truth of the rest.

[5] As little foundation is there for the report that I am a teacher and take money; this accusation has no more truth in it than the other. Although, if a man were really able to instruct mankind, to receive money for giving instruction would, in my opinion, be an honour to him. There is Gorgias of Leontium, and Prodicus of Ceos, and Hippias of Elis, who go the round of the cities, and are able to persuade the young men to leave their own citizens by whom they might be taught for nothing, and come to them whom they not only pay, but are thankful if they may be allowed to pay them. There is at this time a Parian philosopher residing in Athens, of whom I have heard; and I came to hear of him in this way:— I came across a man who has spent a world of money on the Sophists, Callias, the son of Hipponicus, and knowing that he had sons, I asked

him: "Callias," I said, "if your two sons were foals or calves, there would be no difficulty in finding some one to put over them; we should hire a trainer of horses, or a farmer, probably, who would improve and perfect them in their own proper virtue and excellence; but as they are human beings, whom are you thinking of placing over them? Is there any one who understands human and political virtue? You must have thought about the matter, for you have sons; is there any one?" "There is," he said. "Who is he?" said I; "and of what country? and what does he charge?" "Evenus the Parian," he replied; "he is the man, and his charge is five minae." Happy is Evenus, I said to myself, if he really has this wisdom, and teaches at such a moderate charge. Had I the same, I should have been very proud and conceited; but the truth is that I have no knowledge of the kind.

[⁶] I dare say, Athenians, that some one among you will reply, "Yes, Socrates, but what is the origin of these accusations which are brought against you; there must have been something strange which you have been doing? All these rumours and this talk about you would never have arisen if you had been like other men: tell us, then, what is the cause of them, for we should be sorry to judge hastily of you." Now, I regard this as a fair challenge, and I will endeavor to explain to you the reason why I am called wise and have such an evil fame. Please to attend then. And although some of you may think that I am joking, I declare that I will tell you the entire truth. Men of Athens, this reputation of mine has come of a certain sort of wisdom which I possess. If you ask me what kind of wisdom, I reply, wisdom such as may perhaps be attained by man, for to that extent I am inclined to believe that I am wise; whereas the persons of whom I was speaking have a superhuman wisdom, which I may fail to describe, because I have it not myself; and he who says that I have, speaks falsely, and is taking away my character. And here, O men of Athens, I must beg you not to interrupt me, even if I seem to say something extravagant. For the word which I will speak is not mine. I will refer you to a witness who is worthy of credit; that witness shall be the God of Delphi—he will tell you about my wisdom, if I have any, and of what sort it is. You must have known Chaerephon; he was early a friend of mine, and also a friend of yours, for he shared in the recent exile of the people, and returned with you. Well, Chaerephon, as you know, was very impetuous in all his doings, and he went to Delphi and boldly asked the oracle to tell him whether—as I was saying, I must beg you not to interrupt—he asked the oracle to tell him whether any one was wiser than I was, and the Pythian prophetess answered, that there was no man wiser. Chaerephon is dead himself; but his brother, who is in court, will confirm the truth of what I am saying.

[⁷] Why do I mention this? Because I am going to explain to you why I have such an evil name. When I heard the answer, I said to myself,

What can the God mean? and what is the interpretation of his riddle? for I know that I have no wisdom, small or great. What then can he mean when he says that I am the wisest of men? And yet he is a god, and cannot lie; that would be against his nature. After long consideration, I thought of a method of trying the question. I reflected that if I could only find a man wiser than myself, then I might go to the god with a refutation in my hand. I should say to him, "Here is a man who is wiser than I am; but you said that I was the wisest." Accordingly I went to one who had the reputation of wisdom, and observed him—his name I need not mention; he was a politician whom I selected for examination—and the result was as follows: When I began to talk with him, I could not help thinking that he was not really wise, although he was thought wise by many, and still wiser by himself; and thereupon I tried to explain to him that he thought himself wise, but was not really wise; and the consequence was that he hated me, and his enmity was shared by several who were present and heard me. So I left him, saying to myself, as I went away: Well, although I do not suppose that either of us knows anything really beautiful and good, I am better off than he is—for he knows nothing, and thinks that he knows; I neither know nor think that I know. In this latter particular, then, I seem to have slightly the advantage of him. Then I went to another who had still higher pretensions to wisdom, and my conclusion was exactly the same. Whereupon I made another enemy of him, and of many others besides him.

[8] Then I went to one man after another, being not unconscious of the enmity which I provoked, and I lamented and feared this: but necessity was laid upon me,—the word of God, I thought, ought to be considered first. And I said to myself, Go I must to all who appear to know, and find out the meaning of the oracle. And I swear to you, Athenians, by the dog I swear!—for I must tell you the truth—the result of my mission was just this: I found that the men most in repute were all but the most foolish; and that others less esteemed were really wiser and better. I will tell you the tale of my wanderings and of the "Herculean" labours, as I may call them, which I endured only to find at last the oracle irrefutable. After the politicians, I went to the poets; tragic, dithyrambic, and all sorts. And there, I said to myself, you will be instantly detected; now you will find out that you are more ignorant than they are. Accordingly I took them some of the most elaborate passages in their own writings, and asked what was the meaning of them—thinking that they would teach me something. Will you believe me? I am almost ashamed to confess the truth, but I must say that there is hardly a person present who would not have talked better about their poetry than they did themselves. Then I knew that not by wisdom do poets write poetry, but by a sort of genius and inspiration; they are like diviners or soothsayers who also say many fine things, but do not understand the meaning of them. The poets ap-

peared to me to be much in the same case; and I further observed that upon the strength of their poetry they believed themselves to be the wisest of men in other things in which they were not wise. So I departed, conceiving myself to be superior to them for the same reason that I was superior to the politicians.

[⁹] At last I went to the artisans. I was conscious that I knew nothing at all, as I may say, and I was sure that they knew many fine things; and here I was not mistaken, for they did know many things of which I was ignorant, and in this they certainly were wiser than I was. But I observed that even the good artisans fell into the same error as the poets;—because they were good workmen they thought that they also knew all sorts of high matters, and this defect in them overshadowed their wisdom; and therefore I asked myself on behalf of the oracle, whether I would like to be as I was, neither having their knowledge nor their ignorance, or like them in both; and I made answer to myself and to the oracle that I was better off as I was.

[¹⁰] This inquisition has led to my having many enemies of the worst and most dangerous kind, and has given occasion also to many calumnies. And I am called wise, for my hearers always imagine that I myself possess the wisdom which I find wanting in others; but the truth is, O men of Athens, that God only is wise; and by his answer he intends to show that the wisdom of men is worth little or nothing; he is not speaking of Socrates, he is only using my name by way of illustration, as if he said, He, O men, is the wisest, who, like Socrates, knows that his wisdom is in truth worth nothing. And so I go about the world obedient to the god, and search and make enquiry into the wisdom of any one, whether citizen or stranger, who appears to be wise; and if he is not wise, then in vindication of the oracle I show him that he is not wise; and my occupation quite absorbs me, and I have no time to give either to any public matter of interest or to any concern of my own, but I am in utter poverty by reason of my devotion to the god.

[¹¹] There is another thing:—young men of the richer classes, who have not much to do, come about me of their own accord; they like to hear the pretenders examined, and they often imitate me, and proceed to examine others; there are plenty of persons, as they quickly discover, who think that they know something, but really know little or nothing; and then those who are examined by them instead of being angry with themselves are angry with me: This confounded Socrates, they say; this villainous misleader of youth!—and then if somebody asks them, Why, what evil does he practise or teach? they do not know, and cannot tell; but in order that they may not appear to be at a loss, they repeat the ready-made charges which are used against all philosophers about teaching things up in the clouds and under the earth, and having no gods, and making the worst appear the better cause; for they do not like to confess that their pretence of knowledge has been detected—which is the truth; and as they are numerous and ambitious and energetic, and are drawn up in battle array and have persuasive tongues, they have filled your ears with their loud and inveterate calumnies. And this is the reason why my three accusers, Meletus and Anytus and Lycon, have set upon me; Meletus, who has a quarrel with me on behalf of the poets; Anytus, on behalf of the craftsmen and politicians; Lycon, on behalf of the rhetoricians: and, as I said at the beginning, I cannot expect to get rid of such a mass of calumny all in a moment. And this, O men of Athens, is the truth and the whole truth; I have concealed nothing, I have dissembled nothing. And yet, I know that my plainness of speech makes them hate me, and what is their hatred but a proof that I am speaking the truth? Hence has arisen the prejudice against me; and this is the reason of it, as you will find out either in this or in any future enquiry.

[12] I have said enough in my defence against the first class of my accusers; I turn to the second class. They are headed by Meletus, that good man and true lover of his country, as he calls himself. Against these, too, I must try to make a defence:—Let their affidavit be read: it contains something of this kind: It says that Socrates is a doer of evil, who corrupts the youth; and who does not believe in the gods of the State, but has other new divinities of his own. Such is the charge; and now let us examine the particular counts. He says that I am a doer of evil, and corrupt the youth; but I say, O men of Athens, that Meletus is a doer of evil, in that he pretends to be in earnest when he is only in jest, and is so eager to bring men to trial from a pretended zeal and interest about matters in which he really never had the smallest interest. And the truth of this I will endeavour to prove to you.

[13] Come hither, Meletus, and let me ask a question of you. You think a great deal about the improvement of youth?

Yes, I do.

Tell the judges, then, who is their improver; for you must know, as you have taken the pains to discover their corrupter, and are citing and accusing me before them. Speak, then, and tell the judges who their improver is.—Observe, Meletus, that you are silent, and have nothing to say. But is not this rather disgraceful, and a very considerable proof of what I was saying, that you have no interest in the matter? Speak up, friend, and tell us who their improver is.

The laws.

But that, my good sir, is not my meaning. I want to know who the person is, who, in the first place, knows the laws.

The judges, Socrates, who are present in court.

What, do you mean to say, Meletus, that they are able to instruct and improve youth?

Certainly they are.

What, all of them, or some only and not others?

All of them.

By the goddess Here, that is good news! There are plenty of improvers, then. And what do you say of the audience,—do they improve them?

Yes, they do.

And the senators?

Yes, the senators improve them.

But perhaps the members of the assembly corrupt them?—or do they improve them?

They improve them.

Then every Athenian improves and elevates them; all with the exception of myself; and I alone am their corrupter? Is that what you affirm?

That is what I stoutly affirm.

I am very unfortunate if you are right. But suppose I ask you a question: How about horses? Does one man do them harm and all the world good? Is not the exact opposite the truth? One man is able to do them good, or at least not many;—the trainer of horses, that is to say, does them good, and others who have to do with them rather injure them? Is not that true, Meletus, of horses, or of any other animal? Most assuredly it is; whether you and Anytus say yes or no. Happy indeed would be the condition of youth if they had one corrupter only, and all the rest of the world were their improvers. But you, Meletus, have sufficiently shown that you never had a thought about the young: your carelessness is seen in your not caring about the very things which you bring against me.

And now, Meletus, I will ask you another question—by Zeus I will: Which is better, to live among bad citizens, or among good ones? Answer, friend, I say; the question is one which may be easily answered. Do not the good do their neighbours good, and the bad do them evil?

Certainly.

And is there any one who would rather be injured than benefited by those who live with him? Answer, my good friend, the law requires you to answer—does any one like to be injured?

Certainly not.

And when you accuse me of corrupting and deteriorating the youth, do you allege that I corrupt them intentionally or unintentionally?

Intentionally, I say.

But you have just admitted that the good do their neighbours good, and the evil do them evil. Now, is that a truth which your superior wisdom has recognized thus early in life, and am I, at my age, in such darkness and ignorance as not to know that if a man with whom I have to live is corrupted by me, I am very likely to be harmed by him; and yet I corrupt him, and intentionally, too—so you say, although neither I nor any other human being is ever likely to be convinced by you. But either I do not corrupt them, or I corrupt them unintentionally; and on either view of the case you lie. If my offence is unintentional, the law has no cognizance of unintentional offences: you ought to have taken me privately, and warned and admonished me; for if I had been better advised, I should have left off doing what I only did unintentionally—no doubt I should; but you would have nothing to say to me and refused to teach me. And now you bring me up in this court, which is a place not of instruction, but of punishment.

It will be very clear to you, Athenians, as I was saying, that Meletus has no care at all, great or small, about the matter. But still I should like to know, Meletus, in what I am affirmed to corrupt the young. I suppose you mean, as I infer from your indictment, that I teach them not to acknowledge the gods which the State acknowledges, but some other new divinities or spiritual agencies in their stead. These are the lessons by which I corrupt the youth, as you say.

Yes, that I say emphatically.

Then, by the gods, Meletus, of whom we are speaking, tell me and the court, in somewhat plainer terms, what you mean! For I do not as yet understand whether you affirm that I teach other men to acknowledge some gods, and therefore that I do believe in gods, and am not an entire atheist—this you do not lay to my charge,—but only you say that they are not the same gods which the city recognizes—the charge is that they are different gods. Or, do you mean that I am an atheist simply, and a teacher of atheism?

I mean the latter—that you are a complete atheist.

What an extraordinary statement! Why do you think so, Meletus? Do you mean that I do not believe in the godhead of the sun or moon, like other men?

I assure you judges, that he does not: for he says that the sun is stone, and the moon earth.

Friend Meletus, you think that you are accusing Anaxagoras: and you have but a bad opinion of the judges, if you fancy them illiterate to such a degree as not to know that these doctrines are found in the books of Anaxagoras the Clazomenian, which are full of them. And so, forsooth, the youth are said to be taught them by Socrates, when there are not infrequently exhibitions of them at the theatre (price of admission one drachma at the most); and they might pay their money, and laugh at Socrates if he pretends to father these extraordinary views. And so, Meletus, you really think that I do not believe in any god?

I swear by Zeus that you believe absolutely in none at all.

Nobody will believe you, Meletus, and I am pretty sure that you do not believe yourself. I cannot help thinking, men of Athens, that Meletus is reckless and impudent, and that he has written this indictment in a spirit of mere wantonness and youthful bravado. Has he not compounded a riddle, thinking to try me? He said to himself:—I shall see whether the wise Socrates will discover my facetious contradiction, or whether I shall be able to deceive him and the rest of them. For he certainly does appear to me to contradict himself in the indictment as much as if he said that Socrates is guilty of not believing in the gods, and yet of believing in them—but this is not like a person who is in earnest.

I should like you, O men of Athens, to join me in examining what I conceive to be his inconsistency; and do you, Meletus, answer. And I must remind the audience of my request that they would not make a disturbance if I speak in my accustomed manner:

Did ever man, Meletus, believe in the existence of human things, and not of human beings? . . . I wish, men of Athens, that he would answer, and not be always trying to get up an interruption. Did ever any man believe in horsemanship, and not in horses? or in flute-playing, and not in flute-players? No, my friend; I will answer to you and to the court, as you refuse to answer for yourself. There is no man who ever did. But now please to answer the next question: Can a man believe in spiritual and divine agencies, and not in spirits or demigods?

He cannot.

How lucky I am to have extracted that answer, by the assistance of the court! But then you swear in the indictment that I teach and believe in divine or spiritual agencies (new or old, no matter for that); at any rate, I believe in spiritual agencies,—so you say and swear in the affidavit; and yet if I believe in divine beings, how can I help believing in spirits or demigods;—must I not? To be sure I must; and therefore I may assume that your silence gives consent. Now what are spirits or demigods? are they not either gods or the sons of gods?

Certainly they are.

But this is what I call the facetious riddle invented by you: the demigods or spirits are gods, and you say first that I do not believe in gods, and then again that I do believe in gods; that is, if I believe in demigods. For if the demigods are the illegitimate sons of gods, whether by the nymphs or by any other mothers, of whom they are said to be the sons— what human being will ever believe that there are no gods if they are the sons of Gods? You might as well affirm the existence of mules, and deny that of horses and asses. Such nonsense, Meletus, could only have been intended by you to make trial of me. You have put this into the indictment because you had nothing real of which to accuse me. But no one who has a particle of understanding will ever be convinced by you that the same men can believe in divine and superhuman things, and yet not believe that there are gods and demigods and heroes.

[14] I have said enough in answer to the charge of Meletus: any elaborate defence is unnecessary; but I know only too well how many are the enmities which I have incurred, and this is what will be my destruction if I am destroyed;—not Meletus, nor yet Anytus, but the envy and detrac-

tion of the world, which has been the death of many good men, and will probably be the death of many more; there is no danger of my being the last of them.

[15] Some one will say: And are you not ashamed, Socrates, of a course of life which is likely to bring you to an untimely end? To him I may fairly answer: There you are mistaken: a man who is good for anything ought not to calculate the chance of living or dying; he ought only to consider whether in doing anything he is doing right or wrong—acting the part of a good man or of a bad. Whereas, upon your view, the heroes who fell at Troy were not good for much, and the son of Thetis above all, who altogether despised danger in comparison with disgrace; and when he was so eager to slay Hector, his goddess mother said to him, that if he avenged his companion Patroclus, and slew Hector, he would die himself—"Fate," she said, in these or the like words, "waits for you next after Hector"; he, receiving this warning, utterly despised danger and death, and instead of fearing them, feared rather to live in dishonour, and not to avenge his friend. "Let me die forthwith," he replied, "and be avenged of my enemy, rather than abide here by the beaked ships, a laughingstock and a burden of the earth." Had Achilles any thought of death and danger? For wherever a man's place is, whether the place which he has chosen or that in which he has been placed by a commander, there he ought to remain in the hour of danger; he should not think of death or of anything but of disgrace. And this, O men of Athens, is a true saying.

[16] Strange, indeed, would be my conduct, O men of Athens, if I, who, when I was ordered by the generals whom you chose to command me at Potidaea and Amphipolis and Delium, remained where they placed me, like any other man, facing death—if now, when, as I conceive and imagine, God orders me to fulfill the philosopher's mission of searching into myself and other men, I were to desert my post through fear of death, or any other fear; that would indeed be strange, and I might justly be arraigned in court for denying the existence of the gods, if I disobeyed the oracle because I was afraid of death, fancying that I was wise when I was not wise. For the fear of death is indeed the pretence of wisdom, and not real wisdom, being a pretence of knowing the unknown; and no one knows whether death, which men in their fear apprehend to be the greatest evil, may not be the greatest good. Is not this ignorance of a disgraceful sort, the ignorance which is the conceit that a man knows what he does not know? And in this respect only I believe myself to differ from men in general, and may perhaps claim to be wiser than they are:—that whereas I know but little of the world below, I do not suppose that I know: but I do know that injustice and disobedience to a better, whether God or man, is evil and dishonourable, and I will never fear or avoid a possible good rather than a certain evil. And therefore if you let me go now, and are not convinced by Anytus, who said that since I had been

prosecuted I must be put to death; (or if not that I ought never to have been prosecuted at all); and that if I escape now, your sons will all be utterly ruined by listening to my words—if you say to me, Socrates, this time we will not mind Anytus, and you shall be let off, but upon one condition, that you are not to enquire and speculate in this way any more, and that if you are caught doing so again you shall die;—if this was the condition on which you let me go, I should reply: Men of Athens, I honour and love you; but I shall obey God rather than you, and while I have life and strength I shall never cease from the practice and teaching of philosophy, exhorting any one whom I meet and saying to him after my manner: You, my friend,—a citizen of the great and mighty and wise city of Athens,—are you not ashamed of heaping up the greatest amount of money and honour and reputation, and caring so little about wisdom and truth and the greatest improvement of the soul, which you never regard or heed at all? And if the person with whom I am arguing, says: Yes, but I do care; then I do not leave him or let him go at once; but I proceed to interrogate and examine and cross-examine him, and if I think that he has no virtue in him, but only says that he has, I reproach him with undervaluing the greater, and overvaluing the less. And I shall repeat the same words to every one whom I meet, young and old, citizen and alien, but especially to the citizens, inasmuch as they are my brethren. For know that this is the command of God; and I believe that no greater good has ever happened in the State than my service to the God. For I do nothing but go about persuading you all, old and young alike, not to take thought for your persons or your properties, but first and chiefly to care about the greatest improvement of the soul. I tell you that virtue is not given by money, but that from virtue comes money and every other good of man, public as well as private. This is my teaching, and if this is the doctrine which corrupts the youth, I am a mischievous person. But if any one says that this is not my teaching, he is speaking an untruth. Wherefore, O men of Athens, I say to you, do as Anytus bids or not as Anytus bids, and either acquit me or not; but whichever you do, understand that I shall never alter my ways, not even if I have to die many times.

[17] Men of Athens, do not interrupt, but hear me; there was an understanding between us that you should hear me to the end: I have something more to say, at which you may be inclined to cry out; but I believe that to hear me will be good for you, and therefore I beg that you will not cry out. I would have you know, that if you kill such an one as I am, you will injure yourselves more than you will injure me. Nothing will injure me, not Meletus nor yet Anytus—they cannot, for a bad man is not permitted to injure a better than himself. I do not deny that Anytus may, perhaps, kill him, or drive him into exile, or deprive him of civil

rights; and he may imagine, and others may imagine, that he is inflicting a great injury upon him: but there I do not agree. For the evil of doing as he is doing—the evil of unjustly taking away the life of another—is greater far.

[¹⁸] And now, Athenians, I am not going to argue for my own sake, as you may think, but for yours, that you may not sin against the God by condemning me, who am his gift to you. For if you kill me you will not easily find a successor to me, who, if I may use such a ludicrous figure of speech, am a sort of gadfly, given to the State by God; and the State is a great and noble steed who is tardy in his motions owing to his very size, and requires to be stirred into life. I am that gadfly which God has attached to the State, and all day long and in all places am always fastening upon you, arousing and persuading and reproaching you. You will not easily find another like me, and therefore I would advise you to spare me. I dare say that you may feel out of temper (like a person who is suddenly awakened from sleep), and you think that you might easily strike me dead as Anytus advises, and then you would sleep on for the remainder of your lives, unless God in his care of you sent you another gadfly. When I say that I am given to you by God, the proof of my mission is this:—if I had been like other men, I should not have neglected all my own concerns or patiently seen the neglect of them during all these years, and have been doing yours, coming to you individually like a father or elder brother, exhorting you to regard virtue; such conduct, I say, would be unlike human nature. If I had gained anything, or if my exhortations had been paid, there would have been some sense in my doing so; but now, as you will perceive, not even the impudence of my accusers dares to say that I have ever exacted or sought pay of any one; of that they have no witness. And I have a sufficient witness to the truth of what I say—my poverty.

[¹⁹] Some one may wonder why I go about in private giving advice and busy myself with the concerns of others, but do not venture to come forward in public and advise the State. I will tell you why. You have heard me speak at sundry times and in divers places of an oracle or sign which comes to me, and is the divinity which Meletus ridicules in the indictment. This sign, which is a kind of voice, first began to come to me when I was a child; it always forbids but never commands me to do anything which I am going to do. This is what deters me from being a politician. And rightly, as I think. For I am certain, O men of Athens, that if I had engaged in politics, I should have perished long ago, and done no good either to you or to myself. And do not be offended at my telling you the truth: for the truth is, that no man who goes to war with you or any other multitude, honestly striving against the many lawless and unrighteous deeds which are done in a state, will save his life; he who will fight for the right, if he would live even for a brief space, must have a private station and not a public one.

[20] I can give you convincing evidence of what I say, not words only, but what you value far more—actions. Let me relate to you a passage of my own life which will prove to you that I should never have yielded to injustice from any fear of death and that "as I should have refused to yield" I must have died at once. I will tell you a tale of the courts, not very interesting perhaps, but nevertheless true. The only office of State which I ever held, O men of Athens, was that of senator: the tribe Antiochis, which is my tribe, had the presidency at the trial of the generals who had not taken up the bodies of the slain after the battle of Arginusae; and you proposed to try them in a body, contrary to law, as you all thought afterwards; but at the time I was the only one of the Prytanes who was opposed to the illegality, and I gave my vote against you; and when the orators threatened to impeach and arrest me, and you called and shouted, I made up my mind that I would run the risk, having law and justice with me, rather than take part in your injustice because I feared imprisonment and death. This happened in the days of the democracy. But when the oligarchy of the Thirty was in power, they sent for me and four others into the rotunda, and bade us bring Leon the Salaminian from Salamis, as they wanted to put him to death. This was a specimen of the sort of commands which they were always giving with the view of implicating as many as possible in their crimes; and then I showed, not in word only but in deed, that, if I may be allowed to use such an expression, I cared not a straw for death, and that my great and only care was lest I should do an unrighteous or unholy thing. For the strong arm of that oppressive power did not frighten me into doing wrong; and when we came out of the rotunda the other four went to Salamis and fetched Leon, but I went quietly home. For which I might have lost my life, had not the power of the Thirty shortly afterwards come to an end. And many will witness to my words.

[21] Now, do you really imagine that I could have survived all these years, if I had led a public life, supposing that like a good man I had always maintained the right and had made justice, as I ought, the first thing? No, indeed, men of Athens, neither I nor any other man. But I have been always the same in all my actions, public as well as private, and never have I yielded any base compliance to those who are slanderously termed my disciples, or to any other. Not that I have any regular disciples. But if any one likes to come and hear me while I am pursuing my mission, whether he be young or old, he is not excluded. Nor do I converse only with those who pay; but any one, whether he be rich or poor, may ask and answer me and listen to my words; and whether he turns out to be a bad man or a good one, neither result can be justly imputed to me; for

I never taught or professed to teach him anything. And if any one says that he has ever learned or heard anything from me in private which all the world has not heard, let me tell you that he is lying.

[22] But I shall be asked, Why do people delight in continually conversing with you? I have told you already, Athenians, the whole truth about this matter: they like to hear the cross-examination of the pretenders to wisdom; there is amusement in it. Now, this duty of cross-examining other men has been imposed upon me by God; and has been signified to me by oracles, visions, and in every way in which the will of divine power was ever intimated to any one. This is true, O Athenians; or, if not true, would be soon refuted. If I am or have been corrupting the youth, those of them who are now grown up and have become sensible that I gave them bad advice in the days of their youth should come forward as accusers, and take their revenge; or if they do not like to come themselves, some of their relatives, fathers, brothers, or other kinsmen, should say what evil their families have suffered at my hands. Now is their time. Many of them I see in the court. There is Crito, who is of the same age and of the same deme with myself, and there is Critobulus his son, whom I also see. Then again there is Lysanias of Sphettus, who is the father of Aeschines—he is present; and also there is Antiphon of Cephisus, who is the father of Epigenes; and there are the brothers of several who have associated with me. There is Nicostratus the son of Theosdotides, and the brother of Theodotus (now Theodotus himself is dead, and therefore he, at any rate, will not seek to stop him); and there is Paralus the son of Demodocus, who had a brother Theages; and Adeimantus the son of Ariston, whose brother Plato is present; and Aeantodorus, who is the brother of Apollodorus, whom I also see. I might mention a great many others, some of whom Meletus should have produced as witnesses in the course of his speech; and let him still produce them, if he has forgotten— I will make way for him. And let him say, if he has any testimony of the sort which he can produce. Nay, Athenians, the very opposite is the truth. For all these are ready to witness on behalf of the corrupter, of the injurer of their kindred, as Meletus and Anytus call me; not the corrupted youth only—there might have been a motive for that—but their uncorrupted elder relatives. Why should they too support me with their testimony? Why, indeed, except for the sake of truth and justice, and because they know that I am speaking the truth, and that Meletus is a liar.

[23] Well, Athenians, this and the like of this is all the defence which I have to offer. Yet a word more. Perhaps there may be some one who is offended at me, when he calls to mind how he himself on a similar, or even a less serious occasion, prayed and entreated the judges with many tears, and how he produced his children in court, which was a moving spectacle, together with a host of relations and friends; whereas I, who am

probably in danger of my life, will do none of these things. The contrast may occur to his mind, and he may be set against me, and vote in anger because he is displeased at me on this account. Now, if there be such a person among you,—mind, I do not say that there is,—to him I may fairly reply: My friend, I am a man, and like other men, a creature of flesh and blood, and not "of wood or stone," as Homer says; and I have a family, yes, and sons, O Athenians, three in number, one almost a man, and two others who are still young; and yet I will not bring any of them hither in order to petition you for an acquittal. And why not? Not from any self-assertion or want of respect for you. Whether I am or am not afraid of death is another question, of which I will not now speak. But, having regard to public opinion, I feel that such conduct would be discreditable to myself, and to you, and to the whole State. One who has reached my years, and who has a name for wisdom, ought not to demean himself. Whether this opinion of me be deserved or not, at any rate the world has decided that Socrates is in some way superior to other men. And if those among you who are said to be superior in wisdom and courage, and any other virtue, demean themselves in this way, how shameful is their conduct! I have seen men of reputation, when they have been condemned, behaving in the strangest manner; they seem to fancy that they were going to suffer something dreadful if they died, and that they could be immortal if you only allowed them to live; and I think that such are a dishonour to the State, and that any stranger coming in would have said of them that the most eminent men of Athens, to whom the Athenians themselves give honour and command, are no better than women. And I say that these things ought not to be done by those of us who have a reputation; and if they are done, you ought not to permit them; you ought rather to show that you are far more disposed to condemn the man who gets up a doleful scene and makes the city ridiculous, than him who holds his peace.

[24] But, setting aside the question of public opinion, there seems to be something wrong in asking a favour of a judge, and thus procuring an acquittal, instead of informing and convincing him. For his duty is, not to make a present of justice, but to give judgment; and he has sworn that he will judge according to the laws, and not according to his own good pleasure; and we ought not to encourage you, nor should you allow yourselves to be encouraged, in this habit of perjury—there can be no piety in that. Do not then require me to do what I consider dishonourable and impious and wrong, especially now, when I am being tried for impiety on the indictment of Meletus. For if, O men of Athens, by force of persuasion and entreaty I could overpower your oaths, then I should be teaching you to believe that there are no gods, and in defending should simply convict myself of the charge of not believing in them. But that it is not so—far otherwise. For I do believe that there are gods, and in a sense higher

than that in which any of my accusers believe in them. And to you and to God I commit my cause, to be determined by you as is best for you and me.

[The vote is taken and Socrates is convicted.]

[25] There are many reasons why I am not grieved, O men of Athens, at the vote of condemnation. I expected it, and am only surprised that the votes are so nearly equal; for I had thought that the majority against me would have been far larger; but now, had thirty votes gone over to the other side, I should have been acquitted. And I may say, I think, that I have escaped Meletus. I may say more; for without the assistance of Anytus and Lycon, any one may see that he would not have had a fifth part of the votes, as the law requires, in which case he would have incurred a fine of a thousand drachmae.

[26] And so he proposes death as the penalty. And what shall I propose on my part, O men of Athens? Clearly that which is my due. And what is my due? What returns shall be made to the man who has never had the wit to be idle during his whole life; but has been careless of what the many care for—wealth, and family interests, and military offices, and speaking in the assembly, and magistracies, and plots, and parties. Reflecting that I was really too honest a man to be a politician and live, I did not go where I could do no good to you or to myself; but where I could do the greatest good privately to every one of you, thither I went, and sought to persuade every man among you that he must look to himself, and seek virtue and wisdom before he looks to his private interests, and look to the State before he looks to the interests of the State; and that this should be the order which he observes in all his actions. What shall be done to such an one? Doubtless some good thing, O men of Athens, if he has his reward; and the good should be of a kind suitable to him. What would be a reward suitable to a poor man who is your benefactor, and who desires leisure that he may instruct you? There can be no reward so fitting as maintenance in the Prytaneum, O men of Athens, a reward which he deserves far more than the citizen who has won the prize at Olympia in the horse or chariot race, whether the chariots were drawn by two horses or by many. For I am in want, and he has enough; and he only gives you the appearance of happiness, and I give you the reality. And if I am to estimate the penalty fairly, I should say that maintenance in the Prytaneum is the just return.

[27] Perhaps you think that I am braving you in what I am saying now, as in what I said before about the tears and prayers. But this is not so. I speak rather because I am convinced that I never intentionally wronged any one, although I cannot convince you—the time has been too short; if there were a law at Athens, as there is in other cities, that a capital cause should not be decided in one day, then I believe that I should have con-

vinced you. But I cannot in a moment refute great slanders; and, as I am convinced that I never wronged another, I will assuredly not wrong myself. I will not say of myself that I deserve any evil, or propose any penalty. Why should I? Because I am afraid of the penalty of death which Meletus proposes? When I do not know whether death is a good or an evil, why should I propose a penalty which would certainly be an evil? Shall I say imprisonment? And why should I live in prison, and be the slave of the magistrate of the year—of the Eleven? Or shall the penalty be a fine, imprisonment until the fine is paid? There is the same objection. I should have to lie in prison, for money I have none, and cannot pay. And if I say exile (and this may possibly be the penalty which you will affix), I must indeed be blinded by the love of life, if I am so irrational as to expect that when you, who are my own citizens, cannot endure my discourses and words, and have found them so grievous and odious that you will have no more of them, others are likely to endure me. No, indeed, men of Athens, that is not very likely. And what a life should I lead, at my age, wandering from city to city, ever changing my place of exile, and always being driven out! For I am quite sure that wherever I go, there, as here, the young men will flock to me; and if I drive them away, their elders will drive me out at their request; and if I let them come, their fathers and friends will drive me out for their sakes.

[28] Some one will say: Yes, Socrates, but cannot you hold your tongue, and then you may go into a foreign city, and no one will interfere with you? Now, I have great difficulty in making you understand my answer to this. For if I tell you that to do as you say would be a disobedience to the God, and therefore that I cannot hold my tongue, you will not believe that I am serious; and if I say again that daily to discourse about virtue, and of those other things about which you hear me examining myself and others is the greatest good of man, and that the unexamined life is not worth living, you are still less likely to believe me. Yet I say what is true, although a thing of which it is hard for me to persuade you. Also, I have never been accustomed to think that I deserve to suffer any harm. Had I money I might have estimated the offence at what I was able to pay, and not have been much the worse. But I have none, and therefore I must ask you to proportion the fine to my means. Well, perhaps I could afford a mina, and therefore I propose that penalty: Plato, Crito, Critobulus, and Apollodorus, my friends here, bid me say thirty minae, and they will be the sureties. Let thirty minae be the penalty; for which sum they will be ample security to you.

[*Socrates is condemned to death.*]

[29] Not much time will be gained, O Athenians, in return for the evil name which you will get from the detractors of the city, who will say that you killed Socrates, a wise man; for they will call me wise, even though I

am not wise, when they want to reproach you. If you had waited a little while, your desire would have been fulfilled in the course of nature. For I am far advanced in years, as you may perceive, and not far from death. I am speaking now not to all of you, but only to those who have condemned me to death. And I have another thing to say to them: You think that I was convicted because I had no words of the sort which would have procured my acquittal—I mean, if I had thought fit to leave nothing undone or unsaid. Not so; the deficiency which led to my conviction was not of words—certainly not. But I had not the boldness or impudence or inclination to address you as you would have liked me to do, weeping and wailing and lamenting, and saying and doing many things which you have been accustomed to hear from others, and which, as I maintain, are unworthy of me. I thought at the time that I ought not to do anything common or mean when in danger: nor do I now repent of the style of my defence; I would rather die having spoken after my manner, than speak in your manner and live. For neither in war nor yet at law ought I or any man to use every way of escaping death. Often in battle there can be no doubt that if a man will throw away his arms, and fall on his knees before his pursuers, he may escape death; and in other dangers there are other ways of escaping death; if a man is willing to say and do anything. The difficulty, my friends, is not to avoid death, but to avoid unrighteousness; for that runs faster than death. I am old and move slowly, and the slower runner has overtaken me, and my accusers are keen and quick, and the faster runner, who is unrighteousness, has overtaken them. And now I depart hence condemned by you to suffer the penalty of death,—they too go their ways condemned by the truth to suffer the penalty of villainy and wrong; and I must abide by my award— let them abide by theirs. I suppose that these things may be regarded as fated,—and I think that they are well.

[30] And now, O men who have condemned me, I would fain prophesy to you; for I am about to die, and in the hour of death men are gifted with prophetic power. And I prophesy to you who are my murderers, that immediately after my departure punishment far heavier than you have inflicted on me will surely await you. Me you have killed because you wanted to escape the accuser, and not to give an account of your lives. But that will not be as you suppose: far otherwise. For I say that there will be more accusers of you than there are now; accusers whom hitherto I have restrained: and as they are younger they will be more inconsiderate with you, and you will be more offended at them. If you think that by killing men you can prevent some one from censuring your evil lives, you are mistaken; that is not a way of escape which is either possible or honourable; the easiest and the noblest way is not to be disabling others, but to be improving yourselves. This is the prophecy which I utter before my departure to the judges who have condemned me.

[³¹] Friends, who would have acquitted me, I would like also to talk with you about the thing which has come to pass, while the magistrates are busy, and before I go to the place at which I must die. Stay then a little, for we may as well talk with one another while there is time. You are my friends, and I should like to show you the meaning of this event which has happened to me. O my judges—for you I may truly call judges —I should like to tell you of a wonderful circumstance. Hitherto the divine faculty of which the internal oracle is the source has constantly been in the habit of opposing me even about trifles, if I was going to make a slip or error in any matter; and now as you see there has come upon me that which may be thought, and is generally believed to be, the last and worst evil. But the oracle made no sign of opposition, either when I was leaving my house in the morning, or when I was on my way to the court, or while I was speaking, at anything which I was going to say; and yet I have often been stopped in the middle of a speech, but now in nothing I either said or did touching the matter in hand has the oracle opposed me. What do I take to be the explanation of this silence? I will tell you. It is an intimation that what has happened to me is a good, and that those of us who think that death is an evil are in error. For the customary sign would surely have opposed me had I been going to evil and not to good.

[³²] Let us reflect in another way, and we shall see that there is great reason to hope that death is a good; for one of two things—either death is a state of nothingness and utter unconsciousness, or, as men say, there is a change and migration of the soul from this world to another. Now, if you suppose that there is no consciousness, but a sleep like the sleep of him who is undisturbed even by dreams, death will be an unspeakable gain. For if a person were to select the night in which his sleep was undisturbed even by dreams, and were to compare with this the other days and nights of his life, and then were to tell us how many days and nights he had passed in the course of his life better and more pleasantly than this one, I think that any man, I will not say a private man, but even the great king will not find many such days or nights, when compared with the others. Now, if death be of such a nature, I say that to die is gain; for eternity is then only a single night. But if death is the journey to another place, and there, as men say, all the dead abide, what good, O my friends and judges, can be greater than this? If, indeed, when the pilgrim arrives in the world below, he is delivered from the professors of justice in this world, and finds the true judges who are said to give judgment there, Minos and Rhadamanthus and Aeacus and Triptolemus, and other sons of God who were righteous in their own life, that pilgrimage will be worth making. What would not a man give if he might converse with Orpheus and Musaeus and Hesiod and Homer? Nay, if this be true, let me die again and again. I myself, too, shall have a wonderful interest in there meeting and conversing with Palamedes, and Ajax the son of Telamon, and any other ancient hero who has suffered death through an unjust judgment; and there will be no small pleasure, as I think, in comparing my own sufferings with theirs. Above all, I shall then be able to continue my search into true and false knowledge; as in this world, so also in the next; and I shall find out who is wise, and who pretends to be wise, and is not. What would not a man give, O judges, to be able to examine the leader of the great Trojan expedition; or Odysseus or Sisyphus, or numberless others, men and women too! What infinite delight would there be in conversing with them and asking them questions! In another world they do not put a man to death for asking questions; assuredly not. For besides being happier than we are, they will be immortal, if what is said is true.

[33] Wherefore, O judges, be of good cheer about death, and know of a certainty, that no evil can happen to a good man, either in life or after death. He and his are not neglected by the gods; nor has my own approaching end happened by mere chance. But I see clearly that the time had arrived when it was better for me to die and be released from trouble; wherefore the oracle gave no sign. For which reason, also, I am not angry with my condemners, or with my accusers; they have done me no harm, although they did not mean to do me any good; and for this I may gently blame them.

[34] Still, I have a favour to ask of them. When my sons are grown up, I would ask you, O my friends, to punish them; and I would have you trouble them, as I have troubled you, if they seem to care about riches, or anything, more than about virtue; or if they pretend to be something when they are really nothing,—then reprove them, as I have reproved you, for not caring about that for which they ought to care, and thinking that they are something when they are really nothing. And if you do this, both I and my sons will have received justice at your hands.

[35] The hour of departure has arrived, and we go our ways—I to die, and you to live. Which is better God only knows.

⊸⊷{ COMMENT AND QUESTIONS }⊶⊷⊸

1. The opening paragraph of the *Apology* is an interesting study in speaker–audience relationship. What is Socrates' attitude toward his audience? What persuasive facts does he give about himself, and what impressions does he give of himself and of his accusers?

2. Socrates believes that more dangerous to him than the immediate accusations of Meletus, Anytus, and Lycon is the body of rumor and misapprehension about him which has grown over a period of time. What false ideas about himself does he attempt to correct in the opening section of his defense?

3. Exactly what did the oracle say about Socrates? What, according to Socrates, did the oracle mean? What is the special character of Socrates' wisdom?

4. In paragraph 12 Socrates states the charges brought against him by Meletus and the second class of his accusers. He replies to these charges by countercharges against Meletus which describe the latter as "a doer of evil, in that he pretends to be earnest when he is only in jest, and is so eager to bring men to trial from a pretended zeal and interest about matters in which he really never had the smallest interest." In your judgment (see paragraph 13 and the many short paragraphs following) how successful is Socrates in supporting the charges he makes against Meletus? Does Socrates use any questionable reasoning in exposing his accuser? If so, where?

5. Socrates asks Meletus who is the improver of the youth. What answer would you give to this question about the youth of the present day?

6. Read again paragraphs 14–35. What are the three or four most important topics Socrates is discussing? What are his main ideas about each topic?

7. Socrates sometimes makes skillful use of comparisons or figures of speech— for example, the youth–horses analogy in his questioning of Meletus, the comparison of the good man's duty to a man's duty in war (paragraph 15), the gadfly analogy (paragraph 18), the figure of unrighteousness as a fast runner, faster than death (paragraph 29), and the comparison of death and sleep (paragraph 32). Which of these figures and comparisons seem to you most apt and memorable? Why?

8. One way to analyze the persona or character of Socrates as it appears in the *Apology* is to examine a list of traits and then to consider which ones Socrates notably possesses or does not possess. What judgment do you arrive at about each of the following, and how can you support your opinion?

courage	piety	spite or malice
tact	intractableness	reasonableness
humility	self-respect	didacticism
self-righteousness	humor	fanaticism
false modesty	hatred	open-mindedness in search
self-centeredness	respect for law	of truth
vanity	intolerance	pride
		integrity

9. John Stuart Mill, in "On the Liberty of Thought and Discussion" (page 134), speaks of the conviction of Socrates as one of "those dreadful mistakes which excite the astonishment and horror of posterity." If you had been a member of the jury hearing Socrates' speeches, how do you think you would have voted, and why?

10. Socrates lived some four hundred years before Jesus. In what ways are his ideas and values similar to and different from Christian ideas and values? (Perhaps see the "Sermon on the Mount," page 217.)

[11]   *Plato*: The Myth of the Cave

THE FOLLOWING selection from Book VII of *The Republic* by the Greek philosopher Plato (427–347 B.C.) is close to the center of Platonic thought. It touches on Plato's doctrine of Ideas or Forms—the theory that beyond the forms of the physical world there exist ideal Forms or Verities, of which the things of the visible world are only imperfect manifestations. And it discusses the education of Plato's philosopher-kings, the wise men and lovers of wisdom to whom the government of Plato's ideal Republic will be entrusted. Like all myths, "The Myth of the Cave" has a number of closely related applications: describing the education of the philosopher-kings, it also describes the ascent of the soul from the prison-house of the senses to the intellectual world of pure Being; and it may be read as a description of any process of education or enlightenment whereby one moves, at first with pain and confusion, from a world of familiar shadows into a brighter world of new concepts and realities.

[¹] And now, I said, let me show in a figure how far our nature is enlightened or unenlightened:—Behold! human beings living in an underground den, which has a mouth open towards the light and reaching all along the den; here they have been from their childhood, and have their legs and necks chained so that they can not move, and can only see before them, being prevented by the chains from turning round their heads. Above and behind them a fire is blazing at a distance, and between the fire and the prisoners there is a raised way; and you will see, if you look, a low wall built along the way, like the screen which marionette players have in front of them, over which they show the puppets.

I see.

And do you see, I said, men passing along the wall carrying all sorts of vessels, and statues and figures of animals made of wood and stone and various materials, which appear over the wall? Some of them are talking, others silent.

This selection was translated by Benjamin Jowett. (We have arbitrarily inserted paragraph numbers here and there to facilitate reference to particular passages.)

You have shown me a strange image, and they are strange prisoners.

[2] Like ourselves, I replied; and they see only their own shadows, or the shadows of one another, which the fire throws on the opposite wall of the cave?

True, he said; how could they see anything but the shadows if they were never allowed to move their heads?

And of the objects which are being carried in like manner they would only see the shadows?

Yes, he said.

And if they were able to converse with one another, would they not suppose that they were naming what was actually before them?

Very true.

And suppose further that the prison had an echo which came from the other side, would they not be sure to fancy when one of the passers-by spoke that the voice which they heard came from the passing shadow?

No question, he replied.

To them, I said, the truth would be literally nothing but the shadows of the images.

That is certain.

[3] And now look again, and see what will naturally follow if the prisoners are released and disabused of their error. At first, when any of them is liberated and compelled suddenly to stand up and turn his neck round and walk and look towards the light, he will suffer sharp pains; the glare will distress him, and he will be unable to see the realities of which in his former state he had seen the shadows; and then conceive some one saying to him, that what he saw before was an illusion, but that now, when he is approaching nearer to being and his eye is turned towards more real existence, he has a clearer vision,—what will be his reply? And you may further imagine that his instructor is pointing to the objects as they pass and requiring him to name them,—will he not be perplexed? Will he not fancy that the shadows which he formerly saw are truer than the objects which are now shown to him?

Far truer.

[4] And if he is compelled to look straight at the light, will he not have a pain in his eyes which will make him turn away to take refuge in the objects of vision which he can see, and which he will conceive to be in reality clearer than the things which are now being shown to him?

True, he said.

[5] And suppose once more, that he is reluctantly dragged up a steep and rugged ascent, and held fast until he is forced into the presence of the sun himself, is he not likely to be pained and irritated? When he approaches the light his eyes will be dazzled, and he will not be able to see anything at all of what are now called realities.

Not all in a moment, he said.

[6] He will require to grow accustomed to the sight of the upper world. And first he will see the shadows best, next the reflections of men and other objects in the water, and then the objects themselves; then he will gaze upon the light of the moon and the stars and the spangled heaven; and he will see the sky and the stars by night better than the sun or the light of the sun by day?

Certainly.

[7] Last of all he will be able to see the sun, and not mere reflections of him in the water, but he will see him in his own proper place, and not in another; and he will contemplate him as he is.

Certainly.

[8] He will then proceed to argue that this is he who gives the season and the years, and is the guardian of all that is in the visible world, and in a certain way the cause of all things which he and his fellows have been accustomed to behold.

Clearly, he said, he would first see the sun and then reason about him.

[9] And when he remembered his old habitation, and the wisdom of the den and his fellow-prisoners, do you not suppose that he would felicitate himself on the change, and pity them?

Certainly, he would.

And if they were in the habit of conferring honors among themselves on those who were quickest to observe the passing shadows and to remark which of them went before, and which followed after, and which were together; and who were therefore best able to draw conclusions as to the future, do you think that he would care for such honors and glories, or envy the possessors of them? Would he not say with Homer,

"Better to be the poor servant of a poor master,"

and to endure anything, rather than think as they do and live after their manner?

Yes, he said, I think that he would rather suffer anything than entertain these false notions and live in this miserable manner.

Imagine once more, I said, such an one coming suddenly out of the sun to be replaced in his old situation; would he not be certain to have his eyes full of darkness?

To be sure, he said.

And if there were a contest, and he had to compete in measuring the shadows with the prisoners who had never moved out of the den, while his sight was still weak, and before his eyes had become steady (and the time which would be needed to acquire this new habit of sight might be very considerable), would he not be ridiculous? Men would say of him that up he went and down he came without his eyes; and that it was better not even to think of ascending; and if any one tried to loose another and lead him up to the light, let them only catch the offender, and they would put him to death.

No question, he said.

[10] This entire allegory, I said, you may now append, dear Glaucon, to the previous argument; the prisonhouse is the world of sight, the light of the fire is the sun, and you will not misapprehend me if you interpret the journey upwards to be the ascent of the soul into the intellectual world according to my poor belief, which, at your desire, I have expressed—whether rightly or wrongly God knows. But, whether true or false, my opinion is that in the world of knowledge the idea of good appears last of all, and is seen only with an effort; and, when seen, is also inferred to be the universal author of all things beautiful and right, parent of light and of the lord of light in this visible world, and the immediate source of reason and truth in the intellectual; and that this is the power upon which he who would act rationally either in public or private life must have his eye fixed.

I agree, he said, as far as I am able to understand you.

[11] Moreover, I said, you must not wonder that those who attain to this beatific vision are unwilling to descend to human affairs; for their souls are ever hastening into the upper world where they desire to dwell; which desire of theirs is very natural, if our allegory may be trusted.

Yes, very natural.

And is there anything surprising in one who passes from divine contemplations to the evil state of man, misbehaving himself in a ridiculous manner; if, while his eyes are blinking and before he has become accustomed to the surrounding darkness, he is compelled to fight in courts of law, or in other places, about the images or the shadows of images of justice, and is endeavoring to meet the conceptions of those who have never yet seen absolute justice?

Anything but surprising, he replied.

[12] Any one who has common sense will remember that the bewilderments of the eyes are of two kinds, and arise from two causes, either from coming out of the light or from going into the light, which is true of the mind's eye, quite as much as of the bodily eye; and he who remembers this when he sees any one whose vision is perplexed and weak, will not be too ready to laugh; he will first ask whether that soul of man has come out of the brighter life, and is unable to see because unaccustomed to the dark, or having turned from darkness to the day is dazzled by excess of light. And he will count the one happy in his condition and state of being, and he will pity the other; or, if he have a mind to laugh at the soul which comes from below into the light, there will be more reason in this than in the laugh which greets him who returns from above out of the light into the den.

That, he said, is a very just distinction.

But then, if I am right, certain professors of education must be wrong when they say that they can put a knowledge into the soul which was not there before, like sight into blind eyes.

They undoubtedly say this, he replied.

[13] Whereas, our argument shows that the power and capacity of learning exists in the soul already; and that just as the eye was unable to turn from darkness to light without the whole body, so too the instrument of knowledge can only by the movement of the whole soul be turned from the world of becoming into that of being, and learn by degrees to endure the sight of being, and of the brightest and best of being, or in other words, of the good.

Very true.

And must there not be some art which will effect conversion in the easiest and quickest manner; not implanting the faculty of sight, for that exists already, but has been turned in the wrong direction, and is looking away from the truth?

Yes, he said, such an art may be presumed.

[14] And whereas the other so-called virtues of the soul seem to be akin to bodily qualities, for even when they are not originally innate they can be implanted later by habit and exercise, the virtue of wisdom more than anything else contains a divine element which always remains, and by this conversion is rendered useful and profitable; or, on the other hand, hurtful and useless. Did you never observe the narrow intelligence flashing from the keen eye of a clever rogue—how eager he is, how clearly his paltry soul sees the way to his end; he is the reverse of blind, but his keen eye-sight is forced into the service of evil, and he is mischievous in proportion to his cleverness?

Very true, he said.

[15] But what if there had been a circumcision of such natures in the days of their youth; and they had been severed from those sensual pleasures, such as eating and drinking, which, like leaden weights, were attached to them at their birth, and which drag them down and turn the vision of their souls upon the things that are below—if, I say, they had been released from these impediments and turned in the opposite direction, the very same faculty in them would have seen the truth as keenly as they see what their eyes are turned to now.

Very likely.

[16] Yes, I said; and there is another thing which is likely, or rather a necessary inference from what has preceded, that neither the uneducated and uninformed of the truth, nor yet those who never make an end of their education, will be able ministers of State; not the former, because they have no single aim of duty which is the rule of all their actions, private as well as public; nor the latter, because they will not act at all

except upon compulsion, fancying that they are already dwelling apart in
the islands of the blest.

Very true, he replied.

[17] Then, I said, the business of us who are the founders of the State
will be to compel the best minds to attain that knowledge which we have
already shown to be the greatest of all—they must continue to ascend
until they arrive at the good; but when they have ascended and seen
enough we must not allow them to do as they do now.

What do you mean?

[18] I mean that they remain in the upper world: but this must not be
allowed; they must be made to descend again among the prisoners in the
den, and partake of their labors and honors, whether they are worth
having or not.

But is not this unjust? he said; ought we to give them a worse life, when
they might have a better?

[19] You have again forgotten, my friend, I said, the intention of the
legislator, who did not aim at making any one class in the State happy
above the rest; the happiness was to be in the whole State, and he held
the citizens together by persuasion and necessity, making them benefactors of the State, and therefore benefactors of one another; to this end he
created them, not to please themselves, but to be his instruments in binding up the State.

True, he said, I had forgotten.

[20] Observe, Glaucon, that there will be no injustice in compelling our
philosophers to have a care and providence of others; we shall explain to
them that in other States, men of their class are not obliged to share in the
toils of politics: and this is reasonable, for they grow up at their own
sweet will, and the government would rather not have them. Being self-
taught, they can not be expected to show any gratitude for a culture
which they have never received. But we have brought you into the world
to be rulers of the hive, kings of yourselves and of the other citizens, and
have educated you far better and more perfectly than they have been
educated, and you are better able to share in the double duty. Wherefore
each of you, when his turn comes, must go down to the general underground abode, and get the habit of seeing in the dark. When you have
acquired the habit, you will see ten thousand times better than the inhabitants of the den, and you will know what the several images are, and
what they represent, because you have seen the beautiful and just and
good in their truth. And thus our State, which is also yours, will be a
reality, and not a dream only, and will be administered in a spirit unlike
that of other States, in which men fight with one another about shadows
only and are distracted in the struggle for power, which in their eyes is a
great good. Whereas the truth is that the State in which the rulers are

most reluctant to govern is always the best and most quietly governed, and the State in which they are most eager, the worst.

Quite true, he replied.

--◄ C O M M E N T   A N D   Q U E S T I O N S ►--

1. In this dialogue, Socrates, the principal speaker, leads Glaucon, by a series of planned steps and questions, to arrive at certain foreseen conclusions. This progressive question–answer mode of teaching and discussion, used by Socrates in his informal teaching and by Plato in his Dialogues, is called "the Socratic method." How is it like or different from the methods of teaching to which you are accustomed? What are its advantages and disadvantages?

2. Socrates says that he is attempting to "show in a figure how far our nature is enlightened or unenlightened." He makes his meaning clear by elaborating and interweaving two basic figures, the figures of light and the figures of ascent and descent. Listed on the left below are items from "The Myth of the Cave" which have symbolic meaning. Listed on the right, not in order, are meanings which the items represent. Think through the myth, and try to pair the symbols in the left-hand column with the ideas in the right-hand column. Does it seem to you that any of the symbolic meanings are unclear, or are inaccurately stated? Explain.

the prisoners	philosophers
the shadows of images seen by the prisoners	the process of education
	illusions, false notions
the firelight	unenlightened people
the steep ascent	the reality of the physical world
the upper world	the intellectual world of reality
the sun	the good, author of all things
freed prisoners who have become adjusted to the upper world	beautiful and right

3. What is the experience of the prisoner when he is first turned around and then dragged up out of the den?

4. What is the reaction of the cave-dwellers to the freed prisoner when he first returns to the cave?

5. According to Socrates, what kind of wisdom or knowledge is possessed by each of the following: (a) the chained prisoners in the cave; (b) the "clever rogue" described in paragraphs 14 and 15; (c) the philosopher who returns to serve the State (paragraph 20)?

6. For what two reasons may one's vision be perplexed and weak?

7. Why must the enlightened ones, in Plato's ideal State, descend to the den once more? What can they accomplish there?

8. Can you apply the allegory of the cave to any intellectual or spiritual experience of your own?

9. If you have read Nils Y. Wessell's "The Opportunity for Change," page 33, what agreements and disagreements about the nature of education do you find between Plato and Wessell?

10. If you have read John Dewey's "Does Human Nature Change?" page 348, do you think that Dewey and Plato are in agreement on the changeability of human nature? Do the two educators, separated in time by more than two thousand years, agree on the nature of the educative process? Explain.

[12]   *John Stuart Mill*: On the Liberty of Thought and Discussion

THE FOLLOWING selection is a sustained logical argument in favor of freedom of thought and opinion. Although most students will need to spend at least three hours on the essay in order to follow the close reasoning and understand the clear but very complex structure of the argument, the time will be well spent. John Stuart Mill (1806–1873) was an English writer, economist, and logician who has been called "the saint of rationalism." "On the Liberty of Thought and Discussion" is Chapter Two of his famous essay *On Liberty*, published in 1859.

[1] The time, it is to be hoped, is gone by, when any defence would be necessary of the "liberty of the press" as one of the securities against corrupt or tyrannical government. No argument, we may suppose, can now be needed, against permitting a legislature or an executive, not identified in interest with the people, to prescribe opinions to them, and determine what doctrines or what arguments they shall be allowed to hear. This aspect of the question, besides, has been so often and so triumphantly enforced by preceding writers, that it needs not be specially insisted on in this place. Though the law of England, on the subject of the press, is as servile to this day as it was in the time of the Tudors, there is little danger of its being actually put in force against political discussion, except during some temporary panic, when fear of insurrection drives ministers and judges from their propriety; and, speaking generally, it is not, in constitutional countries, to be apprehended that the government, whether completely responsible to the people or not, will often attempt to control the expression of opinion, except when in doing

so it makes itself the organ of the general intolerance of the public. Let us suppose, therefore, that the government is entirely at one with the people, and never thinks of exerting any power of coercion unless in agreement with what it conceives to be their voice. But I deny the right of the people to exercise such coercion, either by themselves or by their government. The power itself is illegitimate. The best government has no more title to it than the worst. It is as noxious, or more noxious, when exerted in accordance with public opinion, than when in opposition to it. If all mankind minus one were of one opinion, and only one person were of the contrary opinion, mankind would be no more justified in silencing that one person, than he, if he had the power, would be justified in silencing mankind. Were an opinion a personal possession of no value except to the owner; if to be obstructed in the enjoyment of it were simply a private injury, it would make some difference whether the injury was inflicted only on a few persons or on many. But the peculiar evil of silencing the expression of an opinion is, that it is robbing the human race; posterity as well as the existing generation; those who dissent from the opinion, still more than those who hold it. If the opinion is right, they are deprived of the opportunity of exchanging error for truth: if wrong, they lose, what is almost as great a benefit, the clearer perception and livelier impression of truth, produced by its collision with error.

[2] It is necessary to consider separately these two hypotheses, each of which has a distinct branch of the argument corresponding to it. We can never be sure that the opinion we are endeavouring to stifle is a false opinion; and if we were sure, stifling it would be an evil still.

[3] First: the opinion which it is attempted to suppress by authority may possibly be true. Those who desire to suppress it, of course deny its truth; but they are not infallible. They have no authority to decide the question for all mankind, and exclude every other person from the means of judging. To refuse a hearing to an opinion, because they are sure that it is false, is to assume that *their* certainty is the same thing as *absolute* certainty. All silencing of discussion is an assumption of infallibility. Its condemnation may be allowed to rest on this common argument, not the worse for being common.

[4] Unfortunately for the good sense of mankind, the fact of their fallibility is far from carrying the weight in their practical judgment which is always allowed to it in theory; for while every one well knows himself to be fallible, few think it necessary to take any precautions against their own fallibility, or admit the supposition that any opinion, of which they feel very certain, may be one of the examples of the error to which they acknowledge themselves to be liable. Absolute princes, or others who are accustomed to unlimited deference, usually feel this complete confidence in their own opinions on nearly all subjects. People more happily situated,

who sometimes hear their opinions disputed, and are not wholly unused to be set right when they are wrong, place the same unbounded reliance only on such of their opinions as are shared by all who surround them, or to whom they habitually defer; for in proportion to a man's want of confidence in his own solitary judgment, does he usually repose, with implicit trust, on the infallibility of "the world" in general. And the world, to each individual, means the part of it with which he comes in contact; his party, his sect, his church, his class of society; the man may be called, by comparison, almost liberal and large-minded to whom it means anything so comprehensive as his own country or his own age. Nor is his faith in this collective authority at all shaken by his being aware that other ages, countries, sects, churches, classes, and parties have thought, and even now think, the exact reverse. He devolves upon his own world the responsibility of being in the right against the dissentient worlds of other people; and it never troubles him that mere accident has decided which of these numerous worlds is the object of his reliance, and that the same causes which make him a Churchman in London, would have made him a Buddhist or a Confucian in Pekin. Yet it is as evident in itself, as any amount of argument can make it, that ages are no more infallible than individuals; every age having held many opinions which subsequent ages have deemed not only false but absurd; and it is as certain that many opinions now general will be rejected by future ages, as it is that many, once general, are rejected by the present.

[5] The objection likely to be made to this argument would probably take some such form as the following. There is no greater assumption of infallibility in forbidding the propagation of error, than in any other thing which is done by public authority on its own judgment and responsibility. Judgment is given to men that they may use it. Because it may be used erroneously, are men to be told that they ought not to use it all? To prohibit what they think pernicious, is not claiming exemption from error, but fulfilling the duty incumbent on them, although fallible, of acting on their conscientious conviction. If we were never to act on our opinions, because those opinions may be wrong, we should leave all our interests uncared for, and all our duties unperformed. An objection which applies to all conduct can be no valid objection to any conduct in particular. It is the duty of governments, and of individuals, to form the truest opinions they can; to form them carefully, and never impose them upon others unless they are quite sure of being right. But when they are sure (such reasoners may say), it is not conscientiousness but cowardice to shrink from acting on their opinions, and allow doctrines which they honestly think dangerous to the welfare of mankind, either in this life or in another, to be scattered abroad without restraint, because other people, in less enlightened times, have persecuted opinions now believed to be true. Let us take care, it may be said, not to make the same mistake: but govern-

ments and nations have made mistakes in other things, which are not denied to be fit subjects for the exercise of authority: they have laid on bad taxes, made unjust wars. Ought we therefore to lay on no taxes, and, under whatever provocation, make no wars? Men, and governments, must act to the best of their ability. There is no such thing as absolute certainty, but there is assurance sufficient for the purposes of human life. We may, and must, assume our opinion to be true for the guidance of our own conduct: and it is assuming no more when we forbid bad men to pervert society by the propagation of opinions which we regard as false and pernicious.

[6] I answer, that it is assuming very much more. There is the greatest difference between presuming an opinion to be true, because, with every opportunity for contesting it, it has not been refuted, and assuming its truth for the purpose of not permitting its refutation. Complete liberty of contradicting and disproving our opinion is the very condition which justifies us in assuming its truth for purposes of action; and on no other terms can a being with human faculties have any rational assurance of being right.

[7] When we consider either the history of opinion, or the ordinary conduct of human life, to what is it to be ascribed that the one and the other are no worse than they are? Not certainly to the inherent force of the human understanding; for, on any matter not self-evident, there are ninety-nine persons totally incapable of judging of it for one who is capable; and the capacity of the hundredth person is only comparative; for the majority of the eminent men of every past generation held many opinions now known to be erroneous, and did or approved numerous things which no one will now justify. Why is it, then, that there is on the whole a preponderance among mankind of rational opinions and rational conduct? If there really is this preponderance—which there must be unless human affairs are, and have always been, in an almost desperate state—it is owing to a quality of the human mind, the source of everything respectable in man either as an intellectual or as a moral being, namely, that his errors are corrigible. He is capable of rectifying his mistakes, by discussion and experience. Not by experience alone. There must be discussion, to show how experience is to be interpreted. Wrong opinions and practices gradually yield to fact and argument; but facts and arguments, to produce any effect on the mind, must be brought before it. Very few facts are able to tell their own story, without comments to bring out their meaning. The whole strength and value, then, of human judgment, depending on the one property, that it can be set right when it is wrong, reliance can be placed on it only when the means of setting it right are kept constantly at hand. In the case of any person whose judgment is really deserving of confidence, how has it become so? Because he has kept his mind open to criticism of his opinions and conduct. Because it has been his practice to

listen to all that could be said against him; to profit by as much of it as was just, and expound to himself, and upon occasion to others, the fallacy of what was fallacious. Because he has felt, that the only way in which a human being can make some approach to knowing the whole of a subject, is by hearing what can be said about it by persons of every variety of opinion, and studying all modes in which it can be looked at by every character of mind. No wise man ever acquired his wisdom in any mode but this; nor is it in the nature of human intellect to become wise in any other manner. The steady habit of correcting and completing his own opinion by collating it with those of others, so far from causing doubt and hesitation in carrying it into practice, is the only stable foundation for a just reliance on it: for, being cognizant of all that can, at least obviously, be said against him, and having taken up his position against all gain-sayers—knowing that he has sought for objections and difficulties, instead of avoiding them, and has shut out no light which can be thrown upon the subject from any quarter—he has a right to think his judgment better than that of any person, or any multitude, who have not gone through a similar process.

[8] It is not too much to require that what the wisest of mankind, those who are best entitled to trust their own judgment, find necessary to warrant their relying on it, should be submitted to by that miscellaneous collection of a few wise and many foolish individuals, called the public. The most intolerant of churches, the Roman Catholic Church, even at the canonisation of a saint, admits, and listens patiently to, a "devil's advo-cate." The holiest of men, it appears, cannot be admitted to posthumous honours, until all that the devil could say against him is known and weighed. If even the Newtonian philosophy were not permitted to be questioned, mankind could not feel as complete assurance of its truth as they now do. The beliefs which we have most warrant for have no safe-guard to rest on, but a standing invitation to the whole world to prove them unfounded. If the challenge is not accepted, or is accepted and the attempt fails, we are far enough from certainty still; but we have done the best that the existing state of human reason admits of; we have neg-lected nothing that could give the truth a chance of reaching us: if the lists are kept open, we may hope that if there be a better truth, it will be found when the human mind is capable of receiving it; and in the meantime we may rely on having attained such approach to truth as is possible in our own day. This is the amount of certainty attainable by a fallible being, and this the sole way of attaining it.

[9] Strange it is, that men should admit the validity of the arguments for free discussion, but object to their being "pushed to an extreme"; not seeing that unless the reasons are good for an extreme case, they are not good for any case. Strange that they should imagine that they are not assuming infallibility, when they acknowledge that there should be free

discussion on all subjects which can possibly be *doubtful,* but think that some particular principle or doctrine should be forbidden to be questioned because it is so *certain,* that is, because *they are certain* that it is certain. To call any proposition certain, while there is any one who would deny its certainty if permitted, but who is not permitted, is to assume that we ourselves, and those who agree with us, are the judges of certainty, and judges without hearing the other side.

[10] In the present age—which has been described as "destitute of faith, but terrified at scepticism"—in which people feel sure, not so much that their opinions are true, as that they should not know what to do without them—the claims of an opinion to be protected from public attack are rested not so much on its truth, as on its importance to society. There are, it is alleged, certain beliefs so useful, not to say indispensable, to well-being that it is as much the duty of governments to uphold those beliefs, as to protect any other of the interests of society. In a case of such necessity, and so directly in the line of their duty, something less than infallibility may, it is maintained, warrant, and even bind, governments to act on their own opinion, confirmed by the general opinion of mankind. It is also often argued, and still oftener thought, that none but bad men would desire to weaken these salutary beliefs; and there can be nothing wrong, it is thought, in restraining bad men, and prohibiting what only such men would wish to practise. This mode of thinking makes the justification of restraints on discussion not a question of the truth of doctrines, but of their usefulness; and flatters itself by that means to escape the responsibility of claiming to be an infallible judge of opinions. But those who thus satisfy themselves, do not perceive that the assumption of infallibility is merely shifted from one point to another. The usefulness of an opinion is itself a matter of opinion: as disputable, as open to discussion, and requiring discussion as much as the opinion itself. There is the same need of an infallible judge of opinions to decide an opinion to be noxious, as to decide it to be false, unless the opinion condemned has full opportunity of defending itself. And it will not do to say that the heretic may be allowed to maintain the utility or harmlessness of his opinion, though forbidden to maintain its truth. The truth of an opinion is part of its utility. If we would know whether or not it is desirable that a proposition should be believed, is it possible to exclude the consideration of whether or not it is true? In the opinion, not of bad men, but of the best men, no belief which is contrary to truth can be really useful: and can you prevent such men from urging that plea, when they are charged with culpability for denying some doctrine which they are told is useful, but which they believe to be false? Those who are on the side of received opinions never fail to take all possible advantage of this plea; you do not find *them* handling the question of utility as if it could be completely abstracted from that of truth: on the contrary, it is, above all, because their doctrine

is "the truth," that the knowledge or the belief of it is held to be so indispensable. There can be no fair discussion of the question of usefulness when an argument so vital may be employed on one side, but not on the other. And in point of fact, when law or public feeling do not permit the truth of an opinion to be disputed, they are just as little tolerant of a denial of its usefulness. The utmost they allow is an extenuation of its absolute necessity, or of the positive guilt of rejecting it.

[11] In order more fully to illustrate the mischief of denying a hearing to opinions because we, in our own judgment, have condemned them, it will be desirable to fix down the discussion to a concrete case; and I choose, by preference, the cases which are least favourable to me—in which the argument against freedom of opinion, both on the score of truth and on that of utility, is considered the strongest. Let the opinions impugned be the belief in a God and in a future state, or any of the commonly received doctrines of morality. To fight the battle on such ground gives a great advantage to an unfair antagonist; since he will be sure to say (and many who have no desire to be unfair will say it internally), Are these the doctrines which you do not deem sufficiently certain to be taken under the protection of law? Is the belief in a God one of the opinions to feel sure of which you hold to be assuming infallibility? But I must be permitted to observe, that it is not the feeling sure of a doctrine (be it what it may) which I call an assumption of infallibility. It is the undertaking to decide that question *for others,* without allowing them to hear what can be said on the contrary side. And I denounce and reprobate this pretension not the less, if put forth on the side of my most solemn convictions. However positive any one's persuasion may be, not only of the falsity but of the pernicious consequences—not only of the pernicious consequences, but (to adopt expressions which I altogether condemn) the immorality and impiety of an opinion; yet if, in pursuance of that private judgment, though backed by the public judgment of his country or his contemporaries, he prevents the opinion from being heard in its defence, he assumes infallibility. And so far from the assumption being less objectionable or less dangerous because the opinion is called immoral or impious, this is the case of all others in which it is most fatal. These are exactly the occasions on which the men of one generation commit those dreadful mistakes which excite the astonishment and horror of posterity. It is among such that we find the instances memorable in history, when the arm of the law has been employed to root out the best men and the noblest doctrines; with deplorable success as to the men, though some of the doctrines have survived to be (as if in mockery) invoked in defence of similar conduct towards those who dissent from *them,* or from their received interpretation.

[12] Mankind can hardly be too often reminded, that there was once a man named Socrates, between whom and the legal authorities and pub-

lic opinion of his time there took place a memorable collision. Born in an age and country abounding in individual greatness, this man has been handed down to us by those who best knew both him and the age, as the most virtuous man in it; while *we* know him as the head and prototype of all subsequent teachers of virtue, the source equally of the lofty inspiration of Plato and the judicious utilitarianism of Aristotle, "*i maëstri di color che sanno,*" the two headsprings of ethical as of all other philosophy. This acknowledged master of all the eminent thinkers who have since lived—whose fame, still growing after more than two thousand years, all but outweighs the whole remainder of the names which make his native city illustrious—was put to death by his countrymen, after a judicial conviction, for impiety and immorality. Impiety, in denying the gods recognised by the State; indeed his accuser asserted (see the "Apologia") that he believed in no gods at all. Immorality, in being, by his doctrines and instructions, a "corrupter of youth." Of these charges the tribunal, there is every ground for believing, honestly found him guilty, and condemned the man who probably of all then born had deserved best of mankind, to be put to death as a criminal.

[13] To pass from this to the only other instance of judicial iniquity, the mention of which, after the condemnation of Socrates, would not be an anti-climax: the event which took place on Calvary rather more than eighteen hundred years ago. The man who left on the memory of those who witnessed his life and conversation such an impression of his moral grandeur that eighteen subsequent centuries have done homage to him as the Almighty in person, was ignominiously put to death, as what? As a blasphemer. Men did not merely mistake their benefactor; they mistook him for the exact contrary of what he was, and treated him as that prodigy of impiety which they themselves are now held to be for their treatment of him. The feelings with which mankind now regard these lamentable transactions, especially the latter of the two, render them extremely unjust in their judgment of the unhappy actors. These were, to all appearance, not bad men—not worse than men commonly are, but rather the contrary; men who possessed in a full, or somewhat more than a full measure, the religious, moral, and patriotic feelings of their time and people: the very kind of men who, in all times, our own included, have every chance of passing through life blameless and respected. The highpriest who rent his garments when the words were pronounced, which, according to all the ideas of his country, constituted the blackest guilt, was in all probability quite as sincere in his horror and indignation as the generality of respectable and pious men now are in the religious and moral sentiments they profess; and most of those who now shudder at his conduct, if they had lived in his time, and been born Jews, would have acted precisely as he did. Orthodox Christians who are tempted to think that those who stoned to death the first martyrs must have been worse

men than they themselves are, ought to remember that one of those persecutors was Saint Paul.

[14] Let us add one more example, the most striking of all, if the impressiveness of an error is measured by the wisdom and virtue of him who falls into it. If ever any one, possessed of power, had grounds for thinking himself the best and most enlightened among his contemporaries, it was the Emperor Marcus Aurelius.[1] Absolute monarch of the whole civilized world, he preserved through life not only the most unblemished justice, but what was less to be expected from his Stoical breeding, the tenderest heart. The few failings which are attributed to him, were all on the side of indulgence: while his writings, the highest ethical product of the ancient mind, differ scarcely perceptibly, if they differ at all, from the most characteristic teachings of Christ. This man, a better Christian in all but the dogmatic sense of the word, than almost any of the ostensibly Christian sovereigns who have since reigned, persecuted Christianity. Placed at the summit of all the previous attainments of humanity, with an open, unfettered intellect, and a character which led him of himself to embody in his moral writings the Christian ideal, he yet failed to see that Christianity was to be a good and not an evil to the world, with his duties to which he was so deeply penetrated. Existing society he knew to be in a deplorable state. But such as it was, he saw, or thought he saw, that it was held together, and prevented from being worse, by belief and reverence of the received divinities. As a ruler of mankind, he deemed it his duty not to suffer society to fall in pieces; and saw not how, if its existing ties were removed, any others could be formed which could again knit it together. The new religion openly aimed at dissolving these ties: unless, therefore, it was his duty to adopt that religion, it seemed to be his duty to put it down. Inasmuch then as the theology of Christianity did not appear to him true or of divine origin; inasmuch as this strange history of a crucified God was not credible to him, and a system which purported to rest entirely upon a foundation to him so wholly unbelievable, could not be foreseen by him to be that renovating agency which, after all abatements, it has in fact proved to be; the gentlest and most amiable of philosophers and rulers, under a solemn sense of duty, authorized the persecution of Christianity. To my mind this is one of the most tragical facts in all history. It is a bitter thought, how different a thing the Christianity of the world might have been, if the Christian faith had been adopted as the religion of the empire under the auspices of Marcus Aurelius instead of those of Constantine. But it would be equally unjust to him and false to truth, to deny, that no one plea which can be urged for punishing anti-Christian teaching, was wanting to Marcus Aurelius for punishing, as he did, the propagation of Christianity. No Christian more

---

[1] See the selection from the *Meditations* of Marcus Aurelius, page 207.

firmly believes that Atheism is false, and tends to the dissolution of society, than Marcus Aurelius believed the same things of Christianity; he who, of all men then living, might have been thought the most capable of appreciating it. Unless any one who approves of punishment for the promulgation of opinions, flatters himself that he is a wiser and better man than Marcus Aurelius—more deeply versed in the wisdom of his time, more elevated in his intellect above it—more earnest in his search for truth, or more singleminded in his devotion to it when found; let him abstain from that assumption of the joint infallibility of himself and the multitude, which the great Antoninus made with so unfortunate a result. . . .[2]

[15] But, indeed, the dictum that truth always triumphs over persecution is one of those pleasant falsehoods which men repeat after one another till they pass into commonplaces, but which all experience refutes. History teems with instances of truth put down by persecution. If not suppressed for ever, it may be thrown back for centuries. To speak only of religious opinions: the Reformation broke out at least twenty times before Luther, and was put down. Arnold of Brescia was put down. Fra Dolcino was put down. Savonarola was put down. The Albigeois were put down. The Vaudois were put down. The Lollards were put down. The Hussites were put down. Even after the era of Luther, whatever persecution was persisted in, it was successful. In Spain, Italy, Flanders, the Austrian empire, Protestantism was rooted out; and, most likely, would have been so in England, had Queen Mary lived, or Queen Elizabeth died. Persecution has always succeeded, save where the heretics were too strong a party to be effectually persecuted. No reasonable person can doubt that Christianity might have been extirpated in the Roman Empire. It spread, and became predominant, because the persecutions were only occasional, lasting but a short time, and separated by long intervals of almost undisturbed propagandism. It is a piece of idle sentimentality that truth, merely as truth, has any inherent power denied to error of prevailing against the dungeon and the stake. Men are not more zealous for truth than they often are for error, and a sufficient application of legal or even of social penalties will generally succeed in stopping the propagation of either. The real advantage which truth has consists in this, that when an opinion is true, it may be extinguished once, twice, or many times, but in the course of ages there will generally be found persons to rediscover it, until some one of its reappearances falls on a time when from favourable circumstances it escapes persecution until it has made such head as to withstand all subsequent attempts to suppress it. . . .

[2] We have made occasional cuts in Mill's chapter. In the passage omitted here, Mill discusses the objection that "persecution is an ordeal through which truth ought to pass, and always passes successfully." Paragraph 15 is Mill's answer to this objection.

[¹⁶] Let us now pass to the second division of the argument, and dismissing the supposition that any of the received opinions may be false, let us assume them to be true, and examine into the worth of the manner in which they are likely to be held, when their truth is not freely and openly canvassed. However unwillingly a person who has a strong opinion may admit the possibility that his opinion may be false, he ought to be moved by the consideration that, however true it may be, if it is not fully, frequently, and fearlessly discussed, it will be held as a dead dogma, not a living truth.

[¹⁷] There is a class of persons (happily not quite so numerous as formerly) who think it enough if a person assents undoubtingly to what they think true, though he has no knowledge whatever of the grounds of the opinion, and could not make a tenable defence of it against the most superficial objections. Such persons, if they can once get their creed taught from authority, naturally think that no good, and some harm, comes of its being allowed to be questioned. Where their influence prevails, they make it nearly impossible for the received opinion to be rejected wisely and considerately, though it may still be rejected rashly and ignorantly; for to shut out discussion entirely is seldom possible, and when it once gets in, beliefs not grounded on conviction are apt to give way before the slightest semblance of an argument. Waiving, however, this possibility—assuming that the true opinion abides in the mind, but abides as a prejudice, a belief independent of, and proof against, argument—this is not the way in which truth ought to be held by a rational being. This is not knowing the truth. Truth, thus held, is but one superstition the more, accidentally clinging to the words which enunciate a truth.

[¹⁸] If the intellect and judgment of mankind ought to be cultivated, a thing which Protestants at least do not deny, on what can these faculties be more appropriately exercised by any one, than on the things which concern him so much that it is considered necessary for him to hold opinions on them? If the cultivation of the understanding consists in one thing more than in another, it is surely in learning the grounds of one's own opinions. Whatever people believe, on subjects on which it is of the first importance to believe rightly, they ought to be able to defend against at least the common objections. But, some one may say, "Let them be *taught* the grounds of their opinions. It does not follow that opinions must be merely parroted because they are never heard controverted. Persons who learn geometry do not simply commit the theorems to memory, but understand and learn likewise the demonstrations; and it would be absurd to say that they remain ignorant of the grounds of geometrical truths, because they never hear any one deny, and attempt to disprove them." Undoubtedly: and such teaching suffices on a subject like mathematics, where there is nothing at all to be said on the wrong side of the question. The peculiarity of the evidence of mathematical truths is that all the argument is on one side. There are no objections, and no answers to objections. But on every subject on which difference of opinion is possible, the truth depends on a balance to be struck between two sets of conflicting reasons. Even in natural philosophy, there is always some other explanation possible of the same facts; some geocentric theory instead of heliocentric, some phlogiston instead of oxygen; and it has to be shown why that other theory cannot be the true one: and until this is shown, and until we know how it is shown, we do not understand the grounds of our opinion. But when we turn to subjects infinitely more complicated, to morals, religion, politics, social relations, and the business of life, three-fourths of the arguments for every disputed opinion consist in dispelling the appearance which favour some opinion different from it. The greatest orator, save one, of antiquity, has left it on record that he always studied his adversary's case with as great, if not still greater, intensity than even his own. What Cicero practised as the means of forensic success requires to be imitated by all who study any subject in order to arrive at the truth. He who knows only his own side of the case, knows little of that. His reasons may be good, and no one may have been able to refute them. But if he is equally unable to refute the reasons on the opposite side; if he does not so much as know what they are, he has no ground for preferring either opinion. The rational position for him would be suspension of judgment, and unless he contents himself with that, he is either led by authority, or adopts, like the generality of the world, the side to which he feels most inclination. Nor is it enough that he should hear the arguments of adversaries from his own teachers, presented as they state them, and accompanied by what they offer as refutations. That is not the way to do justice to the arguments, or bring them into real contact with his own mind. He must be able to hear them from persons who actually believe them; who defend them in earnest, and do their very utmost for them. He must know them in their most plausible and persuasive form; he must feel the whole force of the difficulty which the true view of the subject has to encounter and dispose of; else he will never really possess himself of the portion of truth which meets and removes that difficulty. Ninety-nine in a hundred of what are called educated men are in this condition; even of those who can argue fluently for their opinions. Their conclusion may be true, but it might be false for anything they know: they have never thrown themselves into the mental position of those who think differently from them, and considered what such persons may have to say; and consequently they do not, in any proper sense of the word, know the doctrine which they themselves profess. They do not know those parts of it which explain and justify the remainder; the considerations which show that a fact which seemingly conflicts with another is reconcilable with it, or that, of two apparently strong reasons, one and not the other ought to be preferred. All that part of the truth which turns the scale, and decides the judgment of a completely informed mind, they are strangers to; nor is it ever really known, but to those who have attended equally and impartially to both sides, and endeavoured to see the reasons of both in the strongest light. So essential is this discipline to a real understanding of moral and human subjects, that if opponents of all important truths do not exist, it is indispensable to imagine them, and supply them with the strongest arguments which the most skilful devil's advocate can conjure up.

[19] To abate the force of these considerations, an enemy of free discussion may be supposed to say, that there is no necessity for mankind in general to know and understand all that can be said against or for their opinions by philosophers and theologians. That it is not needful for common men to be able to expose all the misstatements or fallacies of an ingenious opponent. That it is enough if there is always somebody capable of answering them, so that nothing likely to mislead uninstructed persons remains unrefuted. That simple minds, having been taught the obvious grounds of the truths inculcated on them, may trust to authority for the rest, and being aware that they have neither knowledge nor talent to resolve every difficulty which can be raised, may repose in the assurance that all those which have been raised have been or can be answered, by those who are specially trained to the task.

[20] Conceding to this view of the subject the utmost that can be claimed for it by those most easily satisfied with the amount of understanding of truth which ought to accompany the belief of it; even so, the argument for free discussion is no way weakened. For even this doctrine acknowledges that mankind ought to have a rational assurance that all objections have been satisfactorily answered; and how are they to be answered if that which requires to be answered is not spoken? or how can the answer be known to be satisfactory, if the objectors have no opportunity of showing that it is unsatisfactory? If not the public, at least the philosophers and theologians who are to resolve the difficulties, must make themselves familiar with those difficulties in their most puzzling form; and this cannot be accomplished unless they are freely stated, and placed in the most advantageous light which they admit of. The Catholic Church has its own way of dealing with this embarrassing problem. It makes a broad separation between those who can be permitted to receive its doctrines on conviction, and those who must accept them on trust. Neither, indeed, are allowed any choice as to what they will accept; but the clergy, such at least as can be fully confided in, may admissibly and meritoriously make themselves acquainted with the arguments of opponents, in order to answer them, and may, therefore, read heretical books; the laity, not unless by special permission, hard to be obtained. This discipline recognises a knowledge of the enemy's case as beneficial to the

teachers, but finds means, consistent with this, of denying it to the rest of the world: thus giving to the *élite* more mental culture, though not more mental freedom, than it allows to the mass. By this device it succeeds in obtaining the kind of mental superiority which its purposes require; for though culture without freedom never made a large and liberal mind, it can make a clever *nisi prius* advocate of a cause. But in countries professing Protestantism, this resource is denied; since Protestants hold, at least in theory, that the responsibility for the choice of a religion must be borne by each for himself, and cannot be thrown off upon teachers. Besides, in the present state of the world, it is pratically impossible that writings which are read by the instructed can be kept from the uninstructed. If the teachers of mankind are to be cognizant of all that they ought to know, everything must be free to be written and published without restraint.

[21] If, however, the mischievous operation of the absence of free discussion, when the received opinions are true, were confined to leaving men ignorant of the grounds of those opinions, it might be thought that this, if an intellectual, is no moral evil, and does not affect the worth of the opinions, regarded in their influence on the character. The fact, however, is, that not only the grounds of the opinion are forgotten in the absence of discussion, but too often the meaning of the opinion itself. The words which convey it cease to suggest ideas, or suggest only a small portion of those they were originally employed to communicate. Instead of a vivid conception and a living belief, there remain only a few phrases retained by rote; or, if any part, the shell and husk only of the meaning is retained, the finer essence being lost. The great chapter in human history which this fact occupies and fills, cannot be too earnestly studied and meditated on.

[22] It is illustrated in the experience of almost all ethical doctrines and religious creeds. They are all full of meaning and vitality to those who originate them, and to the direct disciples of the originators. Their meaning continues to be felt in undiminished strength, and is perhaps brought out into even fuller consciousness, so long as the struggle lasts to give the doctrine or creed an ascendancy over other creeds. At last it either prevails, and becomes the general opinion, or its progress stops; it keeps possession of the ground it has gained, but ceases to spread further. When either of these results has become apparent, controversy on the subject flags, and gradually dies away. The doctrine has taken its place, if not as a received opinion, as one of the admitted sects or divisions of opinion: those who hold it have generally inherited, not adopted it; and conversion from one of these doctrines to another, being now an exceptional fact, occupies little place in the thoughts of their professors. Instead of being, as at first, constantly on the alert either to defend themselves against the world, or to bring the world over to them, they have subsided into

acquiescence, and neither listen, when they can help it, to arguments against their creed, nor trouble dissentients (if there be such) with arguments in its favour. From this time may usually be dated the decline in the living power of the doctrine. We often hear the teachers of all creeds lamenting the difficulty of keeping up in the minds of believers a lively apprehension of the truth which they nominally recognise, so that it may penetrate the feelings, and acquire a real mastery over the conduct. No such difficulty is complained of while the creed is still fighting for its existence: even the weaker combatants then know and feel what they are fighting for, and the difference between it and other doctrines; and in that period of every creed's existence, not a few persons may be found, who have realised its fundamental principles in all the forms of thought, have weighed and considered them in all their important bearings, and have experienced the full effect on the character which belief in that creed ought to produce in a mind thoroughly imbued with it. But when it has come to be an hereditary creed, and to be received passively, not actively —when the mind is no longer compelled, in the same degree as at first, to exercise its vital powers on the questions which its belief presents to it, there is a progressive tendency to forget all of the belief except the formularies, or to give it a dull and torpid assent, as if accepting it on trust dispensed with the necessity of realising it in consciousness, or testing it by personal experience, until it almost ceases to connect itself at all with the inner life of the human being. Then are seen the cases, so frequent in this age of the world as almost to form the majority, in which the creed remains as it were outside the mind, incrusting and petrifying it against all other influences addressed to the higher parts of our nature; manifesting its power by not suffering any fresh and living conviction to get in, but itself doing nothing for the mind or heart except standing sentinel over them to keep them vacant.

[23] To what an extent doctrines intrinsically fitted to make the deepest impression upon the mind may remain in it as dead beliefs, without being ever realized in the imagination, the feelings, or the understanding, is exemplified by the manner in which the majority of believers hold the doctrines of Christianity. By Christianity I here mean what is accounted such by all churches and sects—the maxims and precepts contained in the New Testament. These are considered sacred, and accepted as laws, by all professing Christians. Yet it is scarcely too much to say that no one Christian in a thousand guides or tests his individual conduct by reference to those laws. The standard to which he does refer it, is the custom of his nation, his class, or his religious profession. He has thus, on the one hand, a collection of ethical maxims, which he believes to have been vouchsafed to him by infallible wisdom as rules for his government; and on the other, a set of everyday judgments and practices, which go a certain length with some of those maxims, not so great a length with others,

stand in direct opposition to some, and are, on the whole, a compromise between the Christian creed and the interests and suggestions of worldly life. To the first of these standards he gives his homage; to the other his real allegiance. All Christians believe that the blessed are the poor and humble, and those who are ill-used by the world; that it is easier for a camel to pass through the eye of a needle than for a rich man to enter the kingdom of heaven; that they should judge not, lest they be judged; that they should swear not at all; that they should love their neighbor as themselves; that if one take their cloak, they should give him their coat also; that they should take no thought for the morrow; that if they would be perfect, they should sell all that they have and give it to the poor. They are not insincere when they say that they believe these things. They do believe them, as people believe what they have always heard lauded and never discussed. But in the sense of that living belief which regulates conduct, they believe these doctrines just up to the point to which it is usual to act upon them. The doctrines in their integrity are serviceable to pelt adversaries with; and it is understood that they are to be put forward (when possible) as the reasons for whatever people do that they think laudable. But any one who reminded them that the maxims require an infinity of things which they never even think of doing, would gain nothing but to be classed among those very unpopular characters who affect to be better than other people. The doctrines have no hold on ordinary believers—are not a power in their minds. They have an habitual respect for the sound of them, but no feeling which spreads from the words to the things signified, and forces the mind to take *them* in, and make them conform to the formula. Whenever conduct is concerned, they look round for Mr. A and B to direct them how far to go in obeying Christ. . . .

[24] It still remains to speak of one of the principal causes which make diversity of opinion advantageous, and will continue to do so until mankind shall have entered a stage of intellectual advancement which at present seems at an incalculable distance. We have hitherto considered only two possibilities: that the received opinion may be false, and some other opinion, consequently, true; or that, the received opinion being true, a conflict with the opposite error is essential to a clear apprehension and deep feeling of its truth. But there is a commoner case than either of these; when the conflicting doctrines, instead of being one true and the other false, share the truth between them; and the nonconforming opinion is needed to supply the remainder of the truth, of which the received doctrine embodies only a part. Popular opinions, on subjects not palpable to sense, are often true, but seldom or never the whole truth. They are a part of the truth; sometimes a greater, sometimes a smaller part, but exaggerated, distorted, and disjointed from the truths by which they ought to be accompanied and limited. Heretical opinions, on the other hand, are

generally some of these suppressed and neglected truths, bursting the bonds which kept them down, and either seeking reconciliation with the truth contained in the common opinion, or fronting it as enemies, and setting themselves up, with similar exclusiveness, as the whole truth. The latter case is hitherto the most frequent, as, in the human mind, one-sidedness has always been the rule, and many-sidedness the exception. Hence, even in revolutions of opinion, one part of the truth usually sets while another rises. Even progress, which ought to superadd, for the most part only substitutes, one partial and incomplete truth for another; improvement consisting chiefly in this, that the new fragment of truth is more wanted, more adapted to the needs of the time, than that which it displaces. Such being the partial character of prevailing opinions, even when resting on a true foundation, every opinion which embodies some-what of the portion of truth which the common opinion omits, ought to be considered precious, with whatever amount of error and confusion that truth may be blended. No sober judge of human affairs will feel bound to be indignant because those who force on our notice truths which we should otherwise have overlooked, overlook some of those which we see. Rather, he will think that so long as popular truth is one-sided, it is more desirable than otherwise that unpopular truth should have one-sided assertors too; such being usually the most energetic, and the most likely to compel reluctant attention to the fragment of wisdom which they pro-claim as if it were the whole.

[25] Thus, in the eighteenth century, when nearly all the instructed, and all those of the uninstructed who were led by them, were lost in admiration of what is called civilisation, and of the marvels of modern science, literature, and philosophy, and while greatly overrating the amount of unlikeness between the men of modern and those of ancient times, indulged the belief that the whole of the difference was in their own favour; with what a salutary shock did the paradoxes of Rousseau explode like bombshells in the midst, dislocating the compact mass of one-sided opinion, and forcing its elements to recombine in a better form and with additional ingredients. Not that the current opinions were on the whole farther from the truth than Rousseau's were; on the contrary, they were nearer to it; they contained more of positive truth, and very much less of error. Nevertheless there lay in Rousseau's doctrine, and has floated down the stream of opinion along with it, a considerable amount of exactly those truths which the popular opinion wanted; and these are the deposit which was left behind when the flood subsided. The superior worth of simplicity of life, the enervating and demoralising effect of the trammels and hypocrisies of artificial society, are ideas which have never been entirely absent from cultivated minds since Rousseau wrote; and they will in time produce their due effect, though at present needing to

be asserted as much as ever, and to be asserted by deeds, for words, on this subject, have nearly exhausted their power.

[26] In politics, again, it is almost a commonplace, that a party of order or stability, and a party of progress or reform, are both necessary elements of a healthy state of political life; until the one or the other shall have so enlarged its mental grasp as to be a party equally of order and of progress, knowing and distinguishing what is fit to be preserved from what ought to be swept away. Each of these modes of thinking derives its utility from the deficiencies of the other; but it is in a great measure the opposition of the other that keeps each within the limits of reason and sanity. Unless opinions favourable to democracy and to aristocracy, to property and to equality, to co-operation and to competition, to luxury and to abstinence, to sociality and individuality, to liberty and discipline, and all the other standing antagonisms of practical life, are expressed with equal freedom, and enforced and defended with equal talent and energy, there is no chance of both elements obtaining their due; one scale is sure to go up, and the other down. Truth, in the great practical concerns of life, is so much a question of the reconciling and combining of opposites, that very few have minds sufficiently capacious and impartial to make the adjust-ment with an approach to correctness, and it has to be made by the rough process of a struggle between combatants fighting under hostile banners. On any of the great open questions just enumerated, if either of the two opinions has a better claim than the other, not merely to be tolerated, but to be encouraged and countenanced, it is the one which happens at the particular time and place to be in a minority. That is the opinion which, for the time being, represents the neglected interests, the side of human well-being which is in danger of obtaining less than its share. I am aware that there is not, in this country, any intolerance of differences of opinion on most of these topics. They are adduced to show, by admitted and multiplied examples, the universality of the fact, that only through diversity of opinion is there, in the existing state of human intellect, a chance of fair play to all sides of the truth. When there are persons to be found who form an exception to the apparent unanimity of the world on any subject, even if the world is in the right, it is always probable that dissentients have something worth hearing to say for themselves, and that truth would lose something by their silence.

[27] It may be objected, "But *some* received principles, especially on the highest and most vital subjects, are more than half-truths. The Chris-tian morality, for instance, is the whole truth on that subject, and if any one teaches a morality which varies from it, he is wholly in error." As this is of all cases the most important in practice, none can be fitter to test the general maxim. But before pronouncing what Christian morality is or is not, it would be desirable to decide what is meant by Christian moral-

ity. If it means the morality of the New Testament, I wonder that any one who derives his knowledge of this from the book itself, can suppose that it was announced, or intended, as a complete doctrine of morals. The Gospel always refers to a pre-existing morality, and confines its precepts to the particulars in which that morality was to be corrected, or superseded by a wider and higher; expressing itself, moreover, in terms most general, often impossible to be interpreted literally, and possessing rather the impressiveness of poetry or eloquence than the precision of legislation. To extract from it a body of ethical doctrine, has never been possible without eking it out from the Old Testament, that is, from a system elaborate indeed, but in many respects barbarous, and intended only for a barbarous people. St. Paul, a declared enemy to this Judaical mode of interpreting the doctrine and filling up the scheme of his Master, equally assumes a pre-existing morality, namely that of the Greeks and Romans; and his advice to Christians is in a great measure a system of accommodation to that; even to the extent of giving an apparent sanction to slavery. What is called Christian, but should rather be termed theological, morality, was not the work of Christ or the Apostles, but is of much later origin, having been gradually built up by the Catholic Church of the first five centuries, and though not implicitly adopted by moderns and Protestants, has been much less modified by them than might have been expected. For the most part, indeed, they have contented themselves with cutting off the additions which had been made to it in the Middle Ages, each sect supplying the place by fresh additions, adapted to its own character and tendencies. That mankind owe a great debt to this morality, and to its early teachers, I should be the last person to deny; but I do not scruple to say of it that it is, in many important points, incomplete and one-sided, and that unless ideas and feelings, not sanctioned by it, had contributed to the formation of European life and character, human affairs would have been in a worse condition than they now are. Christian morality (so called) has all the characters of a reaction; it is, in great part, a protest against Paganism. Its ideal is negative rather than positive; passive rather than active; Innocence rather than Nobleness; Abstinence from Evil, rather than energetic Pursuit of Good; in its precepts (as has been well said) "thou shalt not" predominates unduly over "thou shalt." In its horror of sensuality, it made an idol of asceticism, which has been gradually compromised away into one of legality. It holds out the hope of heaven and the threat of hell, as the appointed and appropriate motives to a virtuous life: in this falling far below the best of the ancients, and doing what lies in it to give to human morality an essentially selfish character, by disconnecting each man's feelings of duty from the interests of his fellow-creatures, except so far as a self-interested inducement is offered to him for consulting them. It is essentially a doctrine of passive obedience; it inculcates submission to all authorities found established; who indeed are not to be actively obeyed when they command what religion forbids, but who are not to be resisted, far less rebelled against, for any amount of wrong to ourselves. And while, in the morality of the best Pagan nations, duty to the State holds even a disproportionate place, infringing on the just liberty of the individual; in purely Christian ethics, that grand department of duty is scarcely noticed or acknowledged. It is in the Koran, not the New Testament, that we read the maxim—"A ruler who appoints any man to an office, when there is in his dominions another man better qualified for it, sins against God and against the State." What little recognition the idea of obligation to the public obtains in modern morality is derived from Greek and Roman sources, not from Christian; as, even in the morality of private life, whatever exists of magnanimity, highmindedness, personal dignity, even the sense of honour, is derived from the purely human, not the religious part of our education, and never could have grown out of a standard of ethics in which the only worth, professedly recognised, is that of obedience.

[28] I am as far as any one from pretending that these defects are necessarily inherent in the Christian ethics in every manner in which it can be conceived, or that the many requisites of a complete moral doctrine which it does not contain do not admit of being reconciled with it. Far less would I insinuate this of the doctrines and precepts of Christ himself. I believe that the sayings of Christ are all that I can see any evidence of their having been intended to be; that they are irreconcilable with nothing which a comprehensive morality requires; that everything which is excellent in ethics may be brought within them, with no greater violence to their language than has been done to it by all who have attempted to deduce from them any practical system of conduct whatever. But it is quite consistent with this to believe that they contain, and were meant to contain, only a part of the truth; that many essential elements of the highest morality are among the things which are not provided for, nor intended to be provided for, in the recorded deliverances of the Founder of Christianity, and which have been entirely thrown aside in the system of ethics erected on the basis of those deliverances by the Christian Church. And this being so, I think it a great error to persist in attempting to find in the Christian doctrine that complete rule for our guidance which its author intended it to sanction and enfcrce, but only partially to provide. I believe, too, that this narrow theory is becoming a grave practical evil, detracting greatly from the moral training and instruction which so many well-meaning persons are now at length exerting themselves to promote. I much fear that by attempting to form the mind and feelings on an exclusively religious type, and discarding those secular standards (as for want of a better name they may be called) which

heretofore coexisted with and supplemented the Christian ethics, receiving some of its spirit, and infusing into it some of theirs, there will result, and is even now resulting, a low, abject, servile type of character, which, submit itself as it may to what it deems the Supreme Will, is incapable of rising to or sympathising in the conception of Supreme Goodness. I believe that other ethics than any which can be evolved from exclusively Christian sources, must exist side by side with Christian ethics to produce the moral regeneration of mankind; and that the Christian system is no exception to the rule, that in an imperfect state of the human mind the interests of truth require a diversity of opinions. It is not necessary that in ceasing to ignore the moral truths not contained in Christianity men should ignore any of those which it does contain. Such prejudice, or oversight, when it occurs, is altogether an evil; but it is one from which we cannot hope to be always exempt, and must be regarded as the price paid for an inestimable good. The exclusive pretension made by a part of the truth to be the whole, must and ought to be protested against; and if a reactionary impulse should make the protestors unjust in their turn, this one-sidedness, like the other, may be lamented, but must be tolerated. If Christians would teach infidels to be just to Christianity, they should themselves be just to infidelity. It can do truth no service to blink the fact, known to all who have the most ordinary acquaintance with literary history, that a large portion of the noblest and most valuable moral teaching has been the work, not only of men who did not know, but of men who knew and rejected, the Christian faith.

[29] I do not pretend that the most unlimited use of the freedom of enunciating all possible opinions would put an end to the evils of religious or philosophical sectarianism. Every truth which men of narrow capacity are in earnest about, is sure to be asserted, inculcated, and in many ways even acted on, as if no other truth existed in the world, or at all events none that could limit or qualify the first. I acknowledge that the tendency of all opinions to become sectarian is not cured by the freest discussion, but is often heightened and exacerbated thereby; the truth which ought to have been, but was not, seen, being rejected all the more violently because proclaimed by persons regarded as opponents. But it is not on the impassioned partisan, it is on the calmer and more disinterested bystander, that this collision of opinions works its salutary effect. Not the violent conflict between parts of the truth, but the quiet suppression of half of it, is the formidable evil; there is always hope when people are forced to listen to both sides; it is when they attend only to one that errors harden into prejudices, and truth itself ceases to have the effect of truth, by being exaggerated into falsehood. And since there are few mental attributes more rare than that judicial faculty which can sit in intelligent judgment between two sides of a question, of which only one is represented by an advocate before it, truth has no chance but in proportion as

every side of it, every opinion which embodies any fraction of the truth, not only finds advocates, but is so advocated as to be listened to.

[30] We have now recognised the necessity to the mental well-being of mankind (on which all their other well-being depends) of freedom of opinion, and freedom of the expression of opinion, on four distinct grounds; which we will now briefly recapitulate.

[31] First, if any opinion is compelled to silence, that opinion may, for aught we can certainly know, be true. To deny this is to assume our own infallibility.

[32] Secondly, though the silenced opinion be an error, it may, and very commonly does, contain a portion of truth; and since the general or prevailing opinion on any subject is rarely or never the whole truth, it is only by the collision of adverse opinions that the remainder of the truth has any chance of being supplied.

[33] Thirdly, even if the received opinion be not only true, but the whole truth; unless it is suffered to be, and actually is, vigorously and earnestly contested, it will, by most of those who receive it, be held in the manner of a prejudice, with little comprehension or feeling of its rational grounds. And not only this, but, fourthly, the meaning of the doctrine itself will be in danger of being lost, or enfeebled, and deprived of its vital effect on the character and conduct: the dogma becoming a mere formal profession, inefficacious for good, but cumbering the ground, and preventing the growth of any real and heartfelt conviction, from reason or personal experience. . . .

---❀{ COMMENT AND QUESTIONS }❀---

1. In the first paragraph, which should be read very carefully, Mill limits the subject, states his point of view, and introduces the first two major sections of the essay. Then he proceeds to support his opinion by presenting arguments in favor of it and by anticipating and refuting objections which might be raised. In the last paragraphs of this selection he summarizes his case. What assumptions is Mill making about his audience? How do his assumptions influence his tone and his choice of material?

2. The following rough outline was written by an able student. Not intended to be a model outline, it illustrates the kind of notes an intelligent reader may take as an aid to understanding the development and main ideas of a complex piece of writing. Such notes are of value, too, when one wishes to review material previously read. The outline is printed here to illustrate one type of note-taking, and to give a general view of the content of the

essay. As you read it, recall the detailed development of each point, and read again parts of the essay that you remember only vaguely.

Evil of silencing opinion is that it robs the human race. If opinion is right, people are deprived of opportunity of exchanging error for truth. If opinion is wrong, they lose the clearer perception of truth produced by collision with error.

I. Opinion to be suppressed may be true.
    A. People who want to suppress it say it is false, but people and ages are not infallible.
    B. Man is capable of rectifying his mistakes only through experience and discussion.
        1. Beliefs can be relied on only when there has been a standing invitation to prove them wrong.
        2. Even RC church has devil's advocate.
        3. The lists must be kept open, to give a chance of receiving a better truth.
    C. Poor argument that "useful" beliefs should be protected.
        1. Usefulness of an opinion is itself a matter of opinion.
        2. Truth of an opinion is part of its utility.
    D. Illustrations of mischief of denying a hearing to opinions because we condemn them. When the opinion is called impious or immoral, men of one generation most often make dreadful mistakes which horrify posterity.
        1. Socrates—impiety and immorality.
        2. Jesus—blasphemy.
        3. Christianity itself—dissolution of society.
    E. Idea that truth triumphs over persecution is false. It can be put down. Truth has only this advantage—in the course of ages it will generally be rediscovered in more favorable circumstances.

II. Opinion to be suppressed may not be true; but consider how beliefs are held if discussion on them is not allowed.
    A. If not fearlessly discussed, a belief becomes a dead dogma.
    B. Blind belief, proof against argument, is prejudice, superstition; this is not the way truth should be held by a rational being.
    C. He who knows only his side of the case knows little of that. One really knows a doctrine by knowing the arguments against it.
    D. Not knowing grounds of opinion is a moral evil as well as an intellectual one: in the absence of discussion, not only the grounds of the belief but the meaning of it is forgotten. New creeds have meaning in the lives and characters of members; later, when hereditary and passively accepted, the belief is outside the mind, encrusting it against other perhaps more vital influences. Doctrines of Christianity used as an example here.

III. Conflicting doctrines often share the truth between them.
    A. We should consider precious, dissenting doctrines which contain some portion of the truth.

B. Since popular truth is one-sided, unpopular truth should have one-sided assertors too.

C. Rousseau in 18th century emphasized a neglected side of truth.

D. Minority opinion needs to be heard; it represents neglected interests.

E. Argument that Christian morality is not the whole truth of morality.
 1. What is it?
  a. New Testament refers to pre-existent morality of Old Testament, in many respects barbarous.
  b. St. Paul assumes pre-existing morality of Greece and Rome (slavery).
  c. Morality actually built up by Catholic Church in first five centuries.
 2. Christian morality is negative, passive, obedient, selfish—not social.
 3. Sayings of Christ contain and were meant to contain only part of truth.
 4. Ethics derived from other sources must exist with Christian ethics for moral regeneration of mankind.

F. There is always hope when people are forced to listen to both sides; when they hear only one, error hardens into prejudice and truth is exaggerated into falsehood.

IV. Conclusion.
 A. Opinion compelled to silence may be true. To deny this is to assume infallibility.
 B. Though silenced opinion be error, it may contain a portion of the truth.
 C. Even if popular opinion is true, without discussion it will be held as prejudice, with no comprehension of rational grounds.
 D. The meaning of the uncontested doctrine will be lost or enfeebled, deprived of any vital effect on character or conduct.

3. In the last sentence of paragraph 4, Mill speaks of opinions once generally accepted and now thought false. What examples of such opinions can you give from your knowledge of history, science, and the like?

4. How is Mill's discussion of the canonization of a saint (paragraph 8) relevant to his argument?

5. In paragraph 10 and elsewhere, what does Mill mean by "received opinions"? What are examples of received opinions in our own society?

6. What distinction does Mill make between feeling sure of a doctrine and assuming infallibility? What is his attitude toward each?

7. What fact is Mill attempting to establish in his discussion of Socrates (paragraph 12) and of Jesus (paragraph 13)? Has Mill chosen effective examples to prove his point? Explain. Comment on the last sentence in paragraph 13.

8. What further or different point is he making in his discussion of Marcus

Aurelius (paragraph 14)? Has he shown skill in choosing an example? Can you reduce the last sentence of the paragraph to a syllogism?

9. In paragraph 15, how does Mill support his idea that truth does not always triumph over persecution? How does he explain the survival of persecuted truth?

10. In paragraphs 21–23, Mill discusses the "decline in the living power of the [uncontested] doctrine." Just what does he mean? How does he support his thesis? Is his supporting material convincing to you?

11. In paragraph 25, Mill speaks favorably of Rousseau. Why? And how is Rousseau related to Mill's main argument?

12. Summarize the views of Christian morality expressed in paragraphs 27–28. See the "Sermon on the Mount," page 217. Do you find evidence that Mill has been unfair in his comments? Explain.

13. What is the major premise for Mill's whole argument? (See Mill's summary, paragraphs 30–33.)

14. In one or two sentences, phrase your own very brief summary of Mill's essay.

15. To what extent do you agree with Mill's argument in favor of complete freedom of thought and expression? If you disagree with, or have reservations about, any parts of Mill's position, exactly where do you disagree, and how would you justify your position?

[13] *John Henry Newman*: Enlargement of Mind

STUDENTS COME to college, we say, to get an education. But what should the nature of this education be? To this question, from the time of Plato to the present, there have been many answers. In *The Idea of a University*, originally a series of lectures given in 1852, John Henry Newman (1801–1890) analyzed the scope and nature of university education; Walter Pater called his work "the perfect handling of a theory." The following excerpt from Newman's sixth lecture, "Knowledge Viewed in Relation to Learning," defines what he considers the essence, the *sine qua non*, of a liberal education.

Churchman, theologian, educator, leader of the Oxford Movement in the Anglican Church and later cardinal in the Roman Catholic Church, Newman was one of the intellectual leaders in the nineteenth century and was perhaps the greatest prose stylist in a period of great writers of prose. The good reader will attend not only to what Newman has to say but to his manner of saying it.

TOPIC

[1] I suppose the *primâ-facie* view which the public at large would take of a University, considering it as a place of Education, is nothing more or less than a place for acquiring a great deal of knowledge on a great many subjects. Memory is one of the first developed of mental faculties; a boy's business when he goes to school is to learn, that is, to store up things in his memory. For some years his intellect is little more than an instrument for taking in facts, or a receptacle for storing them; he welcomes them as fast as they come to him; he lives on what is without; he has his eyes ever about him; he has a lively susceptibility of impressions; he imbibes information of every kind; and little does he make his own in a true sense of the word, living rather upon his neighbors all around him. He has opinions, religious, political, and literary, and, for a boy, is very positive in them and sure about them; but he gets them from his schoolfellows, or his masters, or his parents, as the case may be. Such as he is in his other relations, such also is he in his school exercises; his mind is observant, sharp, ready, retentive; he is almost passive in the acquisition of knowledge. I say this in no disparagement of the idea of a clever boy. Geography, chronology, history, language, natural history, he heaps up the matter of these studies as treasures for a future day. It is the seven years of plenty with him; he gathers in by handfuls, like the Egyptians, without counting; and though, as time goes on, there is exercise for his argumentative powers in the Elements of Mathematics, and for his taste in the Poets and Orators, still, while at school, or at least, till quite the last years of his time, he acquires, and little more; and when he is leaving for the University, he is mainly the creature of foreign influences and circumstances, and made up of accidents, homogeneous or not, as the case may be. Moreover, the moral habits, which are a boy's praise, encourage and assist this result; that is, diligence, assiduity, regularity, despatch, persevering application; for these are the direct conditions of acquisition, and naturally lead to it. Acquirements, again, are emphatically producible, and at a moment; they are a something to show, both for master and scholar; an audience, even though ignorant themselves of the subjects of an examination, can comprehend when questions are answered and when they are not. Here again is a reason why mental culture is in the minds of men identified with the acquisition of knowledge.

[2] The same notion possesses the public mind, when it passes on from the thought of a school to that of a University: and with the best of reasons so far as this, that there is no true culture without acquirements, and that philosophy presupposes knowledge. It requires a great deal of reading, or a wide range of information, to warrant us in putting forth our opinions on any serious subject; and without such learning the most original mind may be able indeed to dazzle, to amuse, to refute, to per-

plex, but not to come to any useful result or any trustworthy conclusion. There are indeed persons who profess a different view of the matter, and even act upon it. Every now and then you will find a person of vigorous or fertile mind, who relies upon his own resources, despises all former authors, and gives the world, with the utmost fearlessness, his views upon religion, or history, or any other popular subject. And his works may sell for a while; he may get a name in his day; but this will be all. His readers are sure to find in the long run that his doctrines are mere theories, and not the expression of facts, that they are chaff instead of bread, and then his popularity drops as suddenly as it rose.

[³] Knowledge then is the indispensable condition of expansion of mind, and the instrument of attaining to it; this cannot be denied; it is ever to be insisted on; I begin with it as a first principle; however, the very truth of it carries men too far, and confirms to them the notion that it is the whole of the matter. A narrow mind is thought to be that which contains little knowledge; and an enlarged mind, that which holds a great deal; and what seems to put the matter beyond dispute is, the fact of the great number of studies which are pursued in a University, by its very profession. Lectures are given on every kind of subject; examinations are held; prizes awarded. There are moral, metaphysical, physical Professors; Professors of languages, of history, of mathematics, of experimental science. Lists of questions are published, wonderful for their range and depth, variety and difficulty; treatises are written, which carry upon their very face the evidence of extensive reading or multifarious information; what then is wanting for mental culture to a person of large reading and scientific attainments? what is grasp of mind but acquirement? where shall philosophical repose be found, but in the consciousness and enjoyment of large intellectual possessions?

[⁴] And yet this notion is, I conceive, a mistake, and my present business is to show that it is one, and that the end of a Liberal Education is not mere knowledge, or knowledge considered in its *matter;* and I shall best attain my object, by actually setting down some cases, which will be generally granted to be instances of the process of enlightenment or enlargement of mind, and others which are not, and thus, by the comparison, you will be able to judge for yourselves, Gentlemen, whether Knowledge, that is, acquirement, is after all the real principle of the enlargement, or whether that principle is not rather something beyond it.

[⁵] For instance, let a person, whose experience has hitherto been confined to the more calm and unpretending scenery of these islands, . . . go for the first time into parts where physical nature puts on her wilder and more awful forms, whether at home or abroad, as into mountainous districts; or let one, who has ever lived in a quiet village, go for the first time to a great metropolis,—then I suppose he will have a sensation which perhaps he never had before. He has a feeling not in addition or increase of former feelings, but of something different in its nature. He will perhaps be borne forward, and find for a time that he has lost his bearings. He has made a certain progress, and he has a consciousness of mental enlargement; he does not stand where he did, he has a new centre, and a range of thoughts to which he was before a stranger.

[6] Again, the view of the heavens which the telescope opens upon us, if allowed to fill and possess the mind, may almost whirl it round and make it dizzy. It brings in a flood of ideas, and is rightly called an intellectual enlargement, whatever is meant by the term.

[7] And so again, the sight of beasts of prey and other foreign animals, their strangeness, the originality (if I may use the term) of their forms and gestures and habits and their variety and independence of each other, throw us out of ourselves into another creation, and as if under another Creator, if I may so express the temptation which may come on the mind. We seem to have new faculties, or a new exercise for our faculties, by this addition to our knowledge; like a prisoner, who, having been accustomed to wear manacles or fetters, suddenly finds his arms and legs free.

[8] Hence Physical Science generally, in all its departments, as bringing before us the exuberant riches and resources, yet the orderly course of the Universe, elevates and excites the student, and at first, I may say, almost takes away his breath, while in time it exercises a tranquilizing influence upon him. *Science can enlarge the mind*

[9] Again, the study of history is said to enlarge and enlighten the mind, and why? because, as I conceive, it gives it a power of judging of passing events, and of all events, and a conscious superiority over them, which before it did not possess.

[10] And in like manner, what is called seeing the world, entering into active life, going into society, travelling, gaining acquaintance with the various classes of the community, coming into contact with the principles and modes of thought of various parties, interests, and races, their views, aims, habits and manners, their religious creeds and forms of worship,—gaining experience how various yet how alike men are, how low-minded, how bad, how opposed, yet how confident in their opinions; all this exerts a perceptible influence upon the mind, which it is impossible to mistake, be it good or be it bad, and is popularly called its enlargement. *Switches point of view — Transition paragraph*

[11] And then again, the first time the mind comes across the arguments and speculations of unbelievers, and feels what a novel light they cast upon what he has hitherto accounted sacred; and still more, if it gives into them and embraces them, and throws off as so much prejudice what it has hitherto held, and, as if waking from a dream, begins to realize to its imagination that there is now no such thing as law and the transgression of law, that sin is a phantom, and punishment a bugbear, that it is free to sin, free to enjoy the world and the flesh; and still further, when it does enjoy them, and reflects that it may think and hold just *Against religion*

Power of judging past events

what it will, that "the world is all before it where to choose," and what
system to build up as its own private persuasion; when this torrent of
wilful thoughts rushes over and inundates it, who will deny that the fruit
of the tree of knowledge, or what the mind takes for knowledge, has
made it one of the gods, with a sense of expansion and elevation,—an
intoxication in reality, still, so far as the subjective state of the mind
goes, an illumination? Hence the fanaticism of individuals or nations,
who suddenly cast off their Maker. Their eyes are opened; and, like the
judgment-stricken king in the Tragedy, they see two suns, and a magic
universe, out of which they look back upon their former state of faith and
innocence with a sort of contempt and indignation, as if they were then
but fools, and the dupes of imposture.

[12] On the other hand, Religion has its own enlargement, and an enlargement, not of tumult, but of peace. It is often remarked of uneducated
persons, who have hitherto thought little of the unseen world, that, on
their turning to God, looking into themselves, regulating their hearts,
reforming their conduct, and meditating on death and judgment, heaven
and hell, they seem to become, in point of intellect, different beings from
what they were. Before, they took things as they came, and thought no
more of one thing than another. But now every event has a meaning; they
have their own estimate of whatever happens to them; they are mindful
of times and seasons, and compare the present with the past; and the
world, no longer dull, monotonous, unprofitable, and hopeless, is a
various and complicated drama, with parts and an object, and an awful
moral.

[13] Now from these instances, to which many more might be added,
it is plain, first, that the communication of knowledge certainly is either
a condition or the means of that sense of enlargement or enlightenment,
of which at this day we hear so much in certain quarters: this cannot be
denied; but next, it is equally plain, that such communication is not the
whole of the process. The enlargement consists, not merely in the passive
reception into the mind of a number of ideas hitherto unknown to it, but
in the mind's energetic and simultaneous action upon and towards and
among those new ideas, which are rushing in upon it. It is the action of
a formative power, reducing to order and meaning the matter of our
acquirements; it is a making the objects of our knowledge subjectively
our own, or, to use a familiar word, it is a digestion of what we receive,
into the substance of our previous state of thought; and without this no
enlargement is said to follow. There is no enlargement, unless there be
a comparison of ideas one with another, as they come before the mind,
and a systematizing of them. We feel our minds to be growing and expanding *then*, when we not only learn, but refer what we learn to what
we know already. It is not the mere addition to our knowledge that is
the illumination; but the locomotion, the movement onwards, of that

mental centre, to which both what we know, and what we are learning, the accumulating mass of our acquirements, gravitates. And therefore a truly great intellect, and recognized to be such by the common opinion of mankind, such as the intellect of Aristotle, or of St. Thomas, or of Newton, or of Goethe, . . . is one which takes a connected view of old and new, past and present, far and near, and which has an insight into the influence of all these one on another; without which there is no whole, and no centre. It possesses the knowledge, not only of things, but also of their mutual and true relations; knowledge, not merely considered as acquirement but as philosophy.

[14] Accordingly, when this analytical, distributive, harmonizing process is away, the mind experiences no enlargement, and is not reckoned as enlightened or comprehensive, whatever it may add to its knowledge. For instance, a great memory, as I have already said, does not make a philosopher, any more than a dictionary can be called a grammar. There are men who embrace in their minds a vast multitude of ideas, but with little sensibility about their real relations towards each other. These may be antiquarians, annalists, naturalists; they may be learned in the law; they may be versed in statistics; they are most useful in their own place; I should shrink from speaking disrespectfully of them; still, there is nothing in such attainments to guarantee the absence of narrowness of mind. If they are nothing more than well-read men, or men of information, they have not what specially deserves the name of culture of mind, or fulfills the type of Liberal Education.

[15] In like manner, we sometimes fall in with persons who have seen much of the world, and of the men who, in their day, have played a conspicuous part in it, but who generalize nothing, and have no observation, in the true sense of the word. They abound in information, in detail, curious and entertaining, about men and things; and, having lived under the influence of no very clear or settled principles, religious or political, they speak of every one and every thing, only as so many phenomena, which are complete in themselves, and lead to nothing, not discussing them, or teaching any truth, or instructing the hearer, but simply talking. No one would say that these persons, well informed as they are, had attained to any great culture of intellect or to philosophy.

[16] The case is the same still more strikingly where the persons in question are beyond dispute men of inferior powers and deficient education. Perhaps they have been much in foreign countries, and they receive, in a passive, otiose, unfruitful way, the various facts which are forced upon them there. Seafaring men, for example, range from one end of the earth to the other; but the multiplicity of external objects, which they have encountered, forms no symmetrical and consistent picture upon their imagination; they see the tapestry of human life, as it were on the wrong side, and it tells no story. They sleep, and they rise up, and they find

themselves, now in Europe, now in Asia; they see visions of great cities and wild regions; they are in the marts of commerce, or amid the islands of the South; they gaze on Pompey's Pillar, or on the Andes; and nothing which meets them carries them forward or backward, to any idea beyond itself. Nothing has a drift or relation; nothing has a history or a promise. Every thing stands by itself, and comes and goes in its turn, like the shifting scenes of a show, which leave the spectator where he was. Perhaps you are near such a man on a particular occasion, and expect him to be shocked or perplexed at something which occurs; but one thing is much the same to him as another, or, if he is perplexed, it is not knowing what to say, whether it is right to admire, or to ridicule, or to disapprove, while conscious that some expression of opinion is expected from him; or in fact he has no standard of judgment at all, and no landmarks to guide him to a conclusion. Such is mere acquisition, and, I repeat, no one would dream of calling it philosophy.

[17] Instances, such as these, confirm, by the contrast, the conclusion I have already drawn from those which preceded them. That only is true enlargement of mind which is the power of viewing many things at once as one whole, of referring them severally to their true place in the universal system, of understanding their respective values, and determining their mutual dependence. Thus is that form of Universal Knowledge, of which I have on a former occasion spoken, set up in the individual intellect, and constitutes its perfection. Possessed of this real illumination, the mind never views any part of the extended subject-matter of Knowledge without recollecting that it is but a part, or without the associations which spring from this recollection. It makes every thing in some sort lead to every thing else; it would communicate the image of the whole to every separate portion, till that whole becomes in imagination like a spirit, every where pervading and penetrating its component parts, and giving them one definite meaning. Just as our bodily organs, when mentioned, recall their function in the body, as the word "creation" suggests the Creator, and "subjects" a sovereign, so, in the mind of the Philosopher, as we are abstractedly conceiving of him, the elements of the physical and moral world, sciences, arts, pursuits, ranks, offices, events, opinions, individualities, are all viewed as one, with correlative functions, and as gradually by successive combinations converging, one and all, to the true centre.

[18] To have even a portion of this illuminative reason and true philosophy is the highest state to which nature can aspire, in the way of intellect; it puts the mind above the influences of chance and necessity, above anxiety, suspense, unsettlement, and superstition, which is the lot of the many. Men whose minds are possessed with some one object, take exaggerated views of its importance, are feverish in the pursuit of it, make it the measure of things which are utterly foreign to it, and are

startled and despond if it happens to fail them. They are ever in alarm
or in transport. Those on the other hand who have no object or principle
whatever to hold by, lose their way, every step they take. They are thrown
out, and do not know what to think or say, at every fresh juncture; they
have no view of persons, or occurrences, or facts, which come suddenly
upon them, and they hang upon the opinion of others, for want of internal
resources. But the intellect which has been disciplined to the perfection
of its powers, which knows, and thinks while it knows, which has learned
to leaven the dense mass of facts and events with the elastic force of
reason, such an intellect cannot be partial, cannot be exclusive, cannot be
impetuous, cannot be at a loss, cannot but be patient, collected, and
majestically calm, because it discerns the end in every beginning, the
origin in every end, the law in every interruption, the limit in each delay;
because it ever knows where it stands, and how its path lies from one
point to another. It is the τετράγωνος of the Peripatetic,[1] and has the "nil
admirari"[2] of the Stoic,—   *You must know both sides*

> Felix qui potuit rerum cognoscere causas,
> Atque metus omnes, et inexorabile fatum
> Subjecit pedibus, strepitumque Acherontis avari.[3]

There are men who, when in difficulties, originate at the moment vast
ideas or dazzling projects; who, under the influence of excitement, are
able to cast a light, almost as if from inspiration, on a subject or course
of action which comes before them; who have a sudden presence of mind
equal to any emergency, rising with the occasion, and an undaunted magnanimous bearing, and an energy and keenness which is but made intense
by opposition. This is genius, this is heroism; it is the exhibition of a
natural gift, which no culture can teach, at which no Institution can
aim; here, on the contrary, we are concerned, not with mere nature, but
with training and teaching. That perfection of the Intellect, which is
the result of Education, and its *beau ideal*, to be imparted to individuals
in their respective measures, is the clear, calm accurate vision and comprehension of all things, as far as the finite mind can embrace them, each
in its place, and with its own characteristics upon it. It is almost prophetic
from its knowledge of history; it is almost heart-searching from its knowledge of human nature; it has almost supernatural charity from its freedom
from littleness and prejudice; it has almost the repose of faith, because
nothing can startle it; it has almost the beauty and harmony of heavenly
contemplation, so intimate is it with the eternal order of things and the
music of the spheres.

[1] An allusion to Aristotle's *Ethics*—the good and *foursquare* man.
[2] To be amazed at nothing.
[3] Happy the man who can understand the causes of things, and thus spurn all fear
and inexorable fate and the roar of greedy Acheron.

--◄[**COMMENT AND QUESTIONS**]►--

1. In this selection Newman's essential purpose is to define an abstract concept—what he calls mental enlargement, mental illumination, or philosophical knowledge—and to persuade the reader that the achieving of such mental enlargement is the true end of education. In the "Introduction to Rhetorical Analysis" we have said that extended definitions, like brief definitions, put the subject into a genus or class, and differentiate it from other members of its class with which it might be confused. Extended definitions also clarify the subject in one or more of these ways: (a) by giving examples; (b) by comparing the subject with something familiar to the reader; (c) by comparing and contrasting it with related subjects; (d) by tracing its history or development; (e) by negating or excluding—showing what it does not mean or does not include as the author is using it; (f) by restating in different words the essentials of the definition; (g) by analyzing—breaking the subject into its components, and examining each part.

    Which of these methods of definition has Newman used? Where, in your judgment, has he used one or more of the methods most effectively?

2. Do you agree that enlargement of mind should be the chief end of education? What other aims or ends might be considered equally important?

3. To see Newman's skill in organizing his thought, read the first sentences only in paragraphs 1, 2, 3, 13, 14, 17, 18. Note that these sentences provide the framework upon which the development rests and also supply a kind of sentence outline and summary of the essay.

4. Now look at the development more closely by examining paragraphs 5 through 12. What makes these paragraph a unit? How has the author secured transitions from one paragraph to another? Newman is famous for his ability to see various sides of a question—an ability illustrated in paragraphs 11 and 12. Considering his strong religious beliefs, do you see a reason why paragraph 12 follows rather than precedes paragraph 11? Is paragraph 12 more effective because it is preceded by paragraph 11? Explain your answer.

5. Follow in detail the development of the thought in paragraphs 13 through 17. What is the unifying idea? What purpose is served by each paragraph?

6. In the last paragraph (18) Newman makes certain claims for the kind of education he has been describing and also admits that there are some powers which are beyond the reach of such an education. Just what claims does he make? Do the admissions add to or detract from his whole argument in favor of liberal education?

7. Some aspects of Newman's style which are particularly worthy of notice are his use of sustained parallelism to make his long sentences perfectly clear, his use of balance and antithesis and climactic arrangement, the varied pace and rhythm of his sentences, the subtle use of alliteration, the

choice of figures of speech (the tapestry figure in paragraph 16, for example). Can you find examples of these stylistic traits in this selection?

8. Plato in "The Myth of the Cave" is also writing about education. If you have read this selection, what major points of agreement and disagreement do you find between Newman and Plato?

[14] *Alfred North Whitehead*: Universities and Their Function

ALFRED NORTH WHITEHEAD (1861–1947) was a distinguished philosopher, mathematician, and educator. Widely respected both as a scholar and as a teacher, he was for many years a professor of philosophy at Harvard. His books include *Principia Mathematica* (written with Bertrand Russell), *Science and the Modern World, Adventures of Ideas, Process and Reality,* and *The Aims of Education* (1929) from which this essay is taken.

[1] The expansion of universities is one marked feature of the social life in the present age. All countries have shared in this movement, but more especially America, which thereby occupies a position of honor. It is, however, possible to be overwhelmed even by the gifts of good fortune; and this growth of universities, in number of institutions, in size, and in internal complexity of organization, discloses some danger of destroying the very sources of their usefulness, in the absence of a widespread understanding of the primary functions which universities should perform in the service of a nation. These remarks, as to the necessity for reconsideration of the function of universities, apply to all the more developed countries. They are only more especially applicable to America, because this country has taken the lead in a development which, under wise guidance, may prove to be one of the most fortunate forward steps which civilization has yet taken.

[2] This article will only deal with the most general principles, though the special problems of the various departments in any university are, of course, innumerable. But generalities require illustration, and for this purpose I choose the business school of a university. This choice is dictated by the fact that business schools represent one of the newer developments of university activity. They are also more particularly relevant

to the dominant social activities of modern nations, and for that reason are good examples of the way in which the national life should be affected by the activities of its universities. Also at Harvard, where I have the honor to hold office, the new foundation of a business school on a scale amounting to magnificence has just reached its completion.

[3] There is a certain novelty in the provision of such a school of training, on this scale of magnitude, in one of the few leading universities of the world. It marks the culmination of a movement which for many years past has introduced analogous departments throughout American universities. This is a new fact in the university world; and it alone would justify some general reflections upon the purpose of a university education, and upon the proved importance of that purpose for the welfare of the social organism.

[4] The novelty of business schools must not be exaggerated. At no time have universities been restricted to pure abstract learning. The University of Salerno in Italy, the earliest of European universities, was devoted to medicine. In England, at Cambridge, in the year 1316, a college was founded for the special purpose of providing "clerks for the King's service." Universities have trained clergy, medical men, lawyers, engineers. Business is now a highly intellectualized vocation, so it well fits into the series. There is, however, this novelty: the curriculum suitable for a business school, and the various modes of activity of such a school, are still in the experimental stage. Hence the peculiar importance of recurrence to general principles in connection with the molding of these schools. It would, however, be an act of presumption on my part if I were to enter upon any consideration of details, or even upon types of policy affecting the balance of the whole training. Upon such questions I have no special knowledge, and therefore have no word of advice.

– ii –

[5] The universities are schools of education, and schools of research. But the primary reason for their existence is not to be found either in the mere knowledge conveyed to the students or in the mere opportunities for research afforded to the members of the faculty.

[6] Both these functions could be performed at a cheaper rate, apart from these very expensive institutions. Books are cheap, and the system of apprenticeship is well understood. So far as the mere imparting of information is concerned, no university has had any justification for existence since the popularization of printing in the fifteenth century. Yet the chief impetus to the foundation of universities came after that date, and in more recent times has even increased.

[7] The justification for a university is that it preserves the connection between knowledge and the zest of life, by uniting the young and the old in the imaginative consideration of learning. The university imparts in-

formation, but it imparts it imaginatively. At least, this is the function which it should perform for society. A university which fails in this respect has no reason for existence. This atmosphere of excitement, arising from imaginative consideration, transforms knowledge. A fact is no longer a bare fact: it is invested with all its possibilities. It is no longer a burden on the memory: it is energizing as the poet of our dreams, and as the architect of our purposes.

[8] Imagination is not to be divorced from the facts: it is a way of illuminating the facts. It works by eliciting the general principles which apply to the facts, as they exist, and then by an intellectual survey of alternative possibilities which are consistent with those principles. It enables men to construct an intellectual vision of a new world, and it preserves the zest of life by the suggestion of satisfying purposes.

[9] Youth is imaginative, and if the imagination be strengthened by discipline this energy of imagination can in great measure be preserved through life. The tragedy of the world is that those who are imaginative have but slight experience, and those who are experienced have feeble imaginations. Fools act on imagination without knowledge; pedants act on knowledge without imagination. The task of a university is to weld together imagination and experience.

[10] The initial discipline of imagination in its period of youthful vigor requires that there be no responsibility for immediate action. The habit of unbiased thought, whereby the ideal variety of exemplifications is discerned in its derivation from general principles, cannot be acquired when there is the daily task of preserving a concrete organization. You must be free to think rightly and wrongly, and free to appreciate the variousness of the universe undisturbed by its perils.

[11] These reflections upon the general functions of a university can be at once translated in terms of the particular functions of a business school. We need not flinch from the assertion that the main function of such a school is to produce men with a greater zest for business. It is a libel upon human nature to conceive that zest for life is the product of pedestrian purposes directed toward the narrow routine of material comforts. Mankind by its pioneering instinct, and in a hundred other ways, proclaims falsehood of that lie.

[12] In the modern complex social organism, the adventure of life cannot be disjoined from intellectual adventure. Amid simpler circumstances, the pioneer can follow the urge of his instinct, directed toward the scene of his vision from the mountain top. But in the complex organizations of modern business the intellectual adventure of analysis, and of imaginative reconstruction, must precede any successful reorganization. In a simpler world, business relations were simpler, being based on the immediate contact of man with man and on immediate confrontation with all relevant material circumstances. Today business organization requires

an imaginative grasp of the psychologies of populations engaged in differing modes of occupation; of populations scattered through cities, through mountains, through plains; of populations on the ocean, and of populations in mines, and of populations in forests. It requires an imaginative grasp of conditions in the tropics, and of conditions in temperate zones. It requires an imaginative grasp of the interlocking interests of great organizations, and of the reactions of the whole complex to any change in one of its elements. It requires an imaginative understanding of laws of political economy, not merely in the abstract, but also with the power to construe them in terms of the particular circumstances of a concrete business. It requires some knowledge of the habits of government, and of the variations of those habits under diverse conditions. It requires an imaginative vision of the binding forces of any human organization, a sympathetic vision of the limits of human nature and of the conditions which evoke loyalty of service. It requires some knowledge of the laws of health, and of the laws of fatigue, and of the conditions for sustained reliability. It requires an imaginative understanding of the social effects of the conditions of factories. It requires a sufficient conception of the rôle of applied science in modern society. It requires that discipline of character which can say "yes" and "no" to other men, not by reason of blind obstinacy, but with firmness derived from a conscious evaluation of relevant alternatives.

[13] The universities have trained the intellectual pioneers of our civilization—the priests, the lawyers, the statesmen, the doctors, the men of science, and the men of letters. They have been the home of those ideals which lead men to confront the confusion of their present times. The Pilgrim Fathers left England to found a state of society according to the ideals of their religious faith; and one of their earlier acts was the foundation of Harvard University in Cambridge, named after that ancient mother of ideals in England, to which so many of them owed their training. The conduct of business now requires intellectual imagination of the same type as that which in former times has mainly passed into those other occupations; and the universities are the organizations which have supplied this type of mentality for the service of the progress of the European races.

[14] In early medieval history the origin of universities was obscure and almost unnoticed. They were a gradual and natural growth. But their existence is the reason for the sustained, rapid progressiveness of European life in so many fields of activity. By their agency the adventure of action met the adventure of thought. It would not have been possible antecedently to have divined that such organizations would have been successful. Even now, amid the imperfections of all things human, it is sometimes difficult to understand how they succeed in their work. Of

course there is much failure in the work of universities. But, if we take a broad view of history, their success has been remarkable and almost uniform. The cultural histories of Italy, of France, of Germany, of Holland, of Scotland, of England, of the United States, bear witness to the influence of universities. By "cultural history" I am not chiefly thinking of the lives of scholars; I mean the energizing of the lives of those men who gave to France, to Germany, and to other countries that impress of types of human achievement which, by their addition to the zest of life, form the foundation of our patriotism. We love to be members of society which can do those things.

[15] There is one great difficulty which hampers all the higher types of human endeavor. In modern times this difficulty has even increased in its possibilities for evil. In any large organization the younger men, who are novices, must be set to jobs which consist in carrying out fixed duties in obedience to orders. No president of a large corporation meets his youngest employee at his office door with the offer of the most responsible job which the work of that corporation includes. The young men are set to work at a fixed routine, and only occasionally even see the president as he passes in and out of the building. Such work is a great discipline. It imparts knowledge, and it produces reliability of character; also it is the only work for which the young men, in that novice stage, are fit, and it is the work for which they are hired. There can be no criticism of the custom, but there may be an unfortunate effect—prolonged routine work dulls the imagination.

[16] The result is that qualities essential at a later stage of a career are apt to be stamped out in an earlier stage. This is only an instance of the more general fact, that necessary technical excellence can only be acquired by a training which is apt to damage those energies of mind which should direct the technical skill. This is the key fact in education, and the reason for most of its difficulties.

[17] The way in which a university should function in the preparation for an intellectual career, such as modern business or one of the older professions, is by promoting the imaginative consideration of the various general principles underlying that career. Its students thus pass into their period of technical apprenticeship with their imaginations already practiced in connecting details with general principles. The routine then receives its meaning, and also illuminates the principles which give it that meaning. Hence, instead of a drudgery issuing in a blind rule of thumb, the properly trained man has some hope of obtaining an imagination disciplined by detailed facts and by necessary habits.

[18] Thus the proper function of a university is the imaginative acquisition of knowledge. Apart from this importance of the imagination, there is no reason why business men, and other professional men, should not

pick up their facts bit by bit as they want them for particular occasions. A university is imaginative or it is nothing—at least nothing useful.

- III -

[19] Imagination is a contagious disease. It cannot be measured by the yard, or weighed by the pound, and then delivered to the students by members of the faculty. It can only be communicated by a faculty whose members themselves wear their learning with imagination. In saying this, I am only repeating one of the oldest of observations. More than two thousand years ago the ancients symbolized learning by a torch passing from hand to hand down the generations. That lighted torch is the imagination of which I speak. The whole art in the organization of a university is the provision of a faculty whose learning is lighted up with imagination. This is the problem of problems in university education; and unless we are careful the recent vast extension of universities in number of students and in variety of activities—of which we are so justly proud— will fail in producing its proper results, by the mishandling of this problem.

[20] The combination of imagination and learning normally requires some leisure, freedom from restraint, freedom from harassing worry, some variety of experiences, and the stimulation of other minds diverse in opinion and diverse in equipment. Also there is required the excitement of curiosity, and the self-confidence derived from pride in the achievements of the surrounding society in procuring the advance of knowledge. Imagination cannot be acquired once and for all, and then kept indefinitely in an ice box to be produced periodically in stated quantities. The learned and imaginative life is a way of living, and is not an article of commerce.

[21] It is in respect to the provision and utilization of these conditions for an efficient faculty that the two functions of education and research meet together in a university. Do you want your teachers to be imaginative? Then encourage them to research. Do you want your researchers to be imaginative? Then bring them into intellectual sympathy with the young at the most eager, imaginative period of life, when intellects are just entering upon their mature discipline. Make your researchers explain themselves to active minds, plastic and with the world before them; make your young students crown their period of intellectual acquisition by some contact with minds gifted with experience of intellectual adventure. Education is discipline for the adventure of life; research is intellectual adventure; and the universities should be homes of adventure shared in common by young and old. For successful education there must always be a certain freshness in the knowledge dealt with. It must either be new in itself or it must be invested with some novelty of application to the new world of new times. Knowledge does not keep any better than fish.

You may be dealing with knowledge of the old species, with some old truth; but somehow or other it must come to the students, as it were, just drawn out of the sea and with the freshness of its immediate importance.

[22] It is the function of the scholar to evoke into life wisdom and beauty which, apart from his magic, would remain lost in the past. A progressive society depends upon its inclusion of three groups—scholars, discoverers, inventors. Its progress also depends upon the fact that its educated masses are composed of members each with a tinge of scholarship, a tinge of discovery, and a tinge of invention. I am here using the term "discovery" to mean the progress of knowledge in respect to truths of some high generality, and the term "invention" to mean the progress of knowledge in respect to the application of general truths in particular ways subservient to present needs. It is evident that these three groups merge into each other, and also that men engaged in practical affairs are properly to be called inventors so far as they contribute to the progress of society. But any one individual has his own limitation of function, and his own peculiar needs. What is important for a nation is that there shall be a very close relation between all types of its progressive elements, so that the study may influence the market place, and the market place the study. Universities are the chief agencies for this fusion of progressive activities into an effective instrument of progress. Of course they are not the only agencies, but it is a fact that today the progressive nations are those in which universities flourish.

[23] It must not be supposed that the output of a university in the form of original ideas is solely to be measured by printed papers and books labeled with the names of their authors. Mankind is as individual in its mode of output as in the substance of its thoughts. For some of the most fertile minds composition in writing, or in a form reducible to writing, seems to be an impossibility. In every faculty you will find that some of the more brilliant teachers are not among those who publish. Their originality requires for its expression direct intercourse with their pupils in the form of lectures, or of personal discussion. Such men exercise an immense influence; and yet, after the generation of their pupils has passed away, they sleep among the innumerable unthanked benefactors of humanity. Fortunately, one of them is immortal—Socrates.

[24] Thus it would be the greatest mistake to estimate the value of each member of a faculty by the printed work signed with his name. There is at the present day some tendency to fall into this error; and an emphatic protest is necessary against an attitude on the part of authorities which is damaging to efficiency and unjust to unselfish zeal.

[25] But, when all such allowances have been made, one good test for the general efficiency of a faculty is that as a whole it shall be producing in published form its quota of contributions of thought. Such a quota is to be estimated in weight of thought, and not in number of words.

[26] This survey shows that the management of a university faculty has no analogy to that of a business organization. The public opinion of the faculty, and a common zeal for the purposes of the university, form the only effective safeguards for the high level of university work. The faculty should be a band of scholars, stimulating each other, and freely determining their various activities. You can secure certain formal requirements, that lectures are given at stated times and that instructors and students are in attendance. But the heart of the matter lies beyond all regulation.

[27] The question of justice to the teachers has very little to do with the case. It is perfectly just to hire a man to perform any legal services under any legal conditions as to times and salary. No one need accept the post unless he so desires.

[28] The sole question is, What sort of conditions will produce the type of faculty which will run a successful university? The danger is that it is quite easy to produce a faculty entirely unfit—a faculty of very efficient pedants and dullards. The general public will only detect the difference after the university has stunted the promise of youth for scores of years.

[29] The modern university system in the great democratic countries will only be successful if the ultimate authorities exercise singular restraint, so as to remember that universities cannot be dealt with according to the rules and policies which apply to the familiar business corporations. Business schools are no exception to this law of university life. There is really nothing to add to what the presidents of many American universities have recently said in public on this topic. But whether the effective portion of the general public, in America or other countries, will follow their advice appears to be doubtful. The whole point of a university, on its educational side, is to bring the young under the intellectual influence of a band of imaginative scholars. There can be no escape from proper attention to the conditions which—as experience has shown—will produce such a band.

--⊰ C O M M E N T   A N D   Q U E S T I O N S ⊱--

1. What are the major purposes of the first section of Whitehead's essay?
2. The opening sentence of paragraph 7 is a key sentence containing a key word which Whitehead will use again and again. What is the key word? What other key words and phrases does the author use? In the last sentence of paragraph 7, Whitehead says that an atmosphere of excitement transforms knowledge so that facts are "energizing as the poet of our dreams, and as the architect of our purposes." How could the sense of the

quotation be restated? Can you illustrate Whitehead's meaning from your own experience or general knowledge?

3. Paragraphs 7, 8, and 9 might have been written as one paragraph on the importance of imagination. What might have been Whitehead's reasons for writing them as three paragraphs?

4. Examine the style of paragraphs 9 and 12. What notable qualities do you find in the writing?

5. Examine the figurative language in paragraphs 19–21. Which figures seem to you particularly effective?

6. What seems to be Whitehead's attitude toward what is popularly called "publish or perish"—the policy of requiring publication by members of college and university faculties?

7. According to Whitehead, of what service are teachers to students? Of what service are students to teachers?

8. Does Whitehead place chief emphasis on the role of the university in promoting the progress of society, or does he place it on the effect the university has on the students it educates? Explain.

9. In the first paragraph of the essay, the author has referred to possible danger in the expansion of universities. By the end of the essay, what dangers or problems has he discussed? Has he suggested ways of avoiding the dangers or solving the problems?

10. Read again the endings of sections II and III. What makes them effective endings?

11. If you have read Crowther's "Two Heresies," Wessell's "The Opportunity for Change," and Newman's "Enlargement of Mind," what points of agreement and disagreement do you see between their views of education and those of Whitehead?

[15] *Clark Kerr*: The Idea of a Multiversity

CLARK KERR (1911–   ), an economist and author of a number of books on industrial relations, was president of the University of California from 1958 to 1967 and is now head of the Carnegie Study of Higher Education. The following selection consists of two sections of the opening chapter of *The Uses of the University*, published in 1963.

[1] The university started as a single community—a community of masters and students. It may even be said to have had a soul in the sense of a central animating principle. Today the large American university is, rather, a whole series of communities and activities held together by

a common name, a common governing board, and related purposes. This great transformation is regretted by some, accepted by many, gloried in, as yet, by few. But it should be understood by all.

[²] The university of today can perhaps be understood, in part, by comparing it with what it once was—with the academic cloister of Cardinal Newman, with the research organism of Abraham Flexner.[1] Those are the ideal types from which it has derived, ideal types which still constitute the illusions of some of its inhabitants. The modern American university, however, is not Oxford nor is it Berlin; it is a new type of institution in the world. As a new type of institution, it is not really private and it is not really public; it is neither entirely of the world nor entirely apart from it. It is unique.

[³] "The Idea of a University" was, perhaps, never so well expressed as by Cardinal Newman when engaged in founding the University of Dublin a little over a century ago. His views reflected the Oxford of his day whence he had come. A university, wrote Cardinal Newman, is "the high protecting power of all knowledge and science, of fact and principle, of inquiry and discovery, of experiment and speculation; it maps out the territory of the intellect, and sees that . . . there is neither encroachment nor surrender on any sides." He favored "liberal knowledge," and said that "useful knowledge" was a "deal of trash."

[⁴] Newman was particularly fighting the ghost of Bacon who some 250 years before had condemned "a kind of adoration of the mind . . . by means whereof men have withdrawn themselves too much from the contemplation of nature, and the observations of experience, and have tumbled up and down in their own reason and conceits." Bacon believed that knowledge should be for the benefit and use of men, that it should "not be as a courtesan, for pleasure and vanity only, or as a bond-woman, to acquire and gain to her master's use; but as a spouse, for generation, fruit and comfort."

[⁵] To this Newman replied that "Knowledge is capable of being its own end. Such is the constitution of the human mind, that any kind of knowledge, if it really be such, is its own reward." And in a sharp jab at Bacon he said: "The Philosophy of Utility, you will say, Gentlemen, has at least done its work; and I grant it—it aimed low, but it has fulfilled its aim." Newman felt that other institutions should carry on research, for "If its object were scientific and philosophical discovery, I do not see why a University should have any students"—an observation sardonically echoed by today's students who often think their professors are not interested in them at all but only in research. A University training, said Newman, "aims at raising the intellectual tone of society, at cultivating the public mind, at purifying the national taste,

[1] An American educator, director of the Institute for Advanced Study at Princeton in 1930.

at supplying true principles to popular enthusiasm and fixed aims to popular aspirations, at giving enlargement and sobriety to the ideas of the age, at facilitating the exercise of political powers, and refining the intercourse of private life." It prepares a man "to fill any post with credit, and to master any subject with facility."

[6] This beautiful world was being shattered forever even as it was being so beautifully portrayed. By 1852, when Newman wrote, the German universities were becoming the new model. The democratic and industrial and scientific revolutions were all well underway in the western world. The gentleman "at home in any society" was soon to be at home in none. Science was beginning to take the place of moral philosophy, research the place of teaching.

[7] "The Idea of a Modern University," to use Flexner's phrase, was already being born. "A University," said Flexner in 1930, "is not outside, but inside the general social fabric of a given era. . . . It is not something apart, something historic, something that yields as little as possible to forces and influences that are more or less new. It is on the contrary . . . an expression of the age, as well as an influence operating upon both present and future."

[8] It was clear by 1930 that "Universities have changed profoundly— and commonly in the direction of the social evolution of which they are part." This evolution had brought departments into universities, and still new departments; institutes and ever more institutes; created vast research libraries; turned the philosopher on his log into a researcher in his laboratory or the library stacks; taken medicine out of the hands of the profession and put it into the hands of the scientists; and much more. Instead of the individual student, there were the needs of society; instead of Newman's eternal "truths in the natural order," there was discovery of the new; instead of the generalist, there was the specialist. The university became, in the words of Flexner, "an institution consciously devoted to the pursuit of knowledge, the solution of problems, the critical appreciation of achievement and the training of men at a really high level." No longer could a single individual "master any subject"—Newman's universal liberal man was gone forever.

[9] But as Flexner was writing of the "Modern University," it, in turn, was ceasing to exist. The Berlin of Humboldt[2] was being violated just as Berlin had violated the soul of Oxford. The universities were becoming too many things. Flexner himself complained that they were "secondary schools, vocational schools, teacher-training schools, research centers, 'uplift' agencies, businesses—these and other things simultaneously." They engaged in "incredible absurdities," "a host of inconsequential things." They "needlessly cheapened, vulgarized and mechanized

2 Wilhelm von Humboldt (1767–1835) was a German philologist and statesman who was instrumental in founding the University of Berlin in 1810.

themselves." Worst of all, they became "'service stations' for the general public."

[10] Even Harvard. "It is clear," calculated Flexner, "that of Harvard's total expenditures not more than one-eighth is devoted to the *central* university disciplines at the level at which a university ought to be conducted." He wondered: "Who has forced Harvard into this false path? No one. It does as it pleases; and this sort of thing pleases." It obviously did not please Flexner. He wanted Harvard to disown the Graduate School of Business and let it become, if it had to survive at all, the "Boston School of Business." He would also have banished all Schools of Journalism and Home Economics, football, correspondence courses, and much else.

[11] It was not only Harvard and other American universities, but also London. Flexner asked "in what sense the University of London is a university at all." It was only "a federation."

[12] By 1930, American universities had moved a long way from Flexner's "Modern University" where "The heart of a university is a graduate school of arts and sciences, the solidly professional schools (mainly, in America, medicine and law) and certain research institutes." They were becoming less and less like a "genuine university," by which Flexner meant "an organism, characterized by highness and definiteness of aim, unity of spirit and purpose." The "Modern University" was as nearly dead in 1930 when Flexner wrote about it, as the old Oxford was in 1852 when Newman idealized it. History moves faster than the observer's pen. Neither the ancient classics and theology nor the German philosophers and scientists could set the tone for the really modern university—the multiversity.

[13] "The Idea of a Multiversity" has no bard to sing its praises; no prophet to proclaim its vision; no guardian to protect its sanctity. It has its critics, its detractors, its transgressors. It also has its barkers selling its wares to all who will listen—and many do. But it also has its reality rooted in the logic of history. It is an imperative rather than a reasoned choice among elegant alternatives.

[14] President Nathan Pusey wrote in his latest annual report to the members of the Harvard Board of Overseers that the average date of graduation of the present Board members was 1924; and much has happened to Harvard since 1924. Half of the buildings are new. The faculty has grown five-fold, the budget nearly fifteen-fold. "One can find almost anywhere one looks similar examples of the effect wrought in the curriculum and in the nature of the contemporary university by widening international awareness, advancing knowledge, and increasingly sophisticated methods of research. . . . Asia and Africa, radio telescopes, masers and lasers and devices for interplanetary exploration unimagined in 1924 —these and other developments have effected such enormous changes in

the intellectual orientation and aspiration of the contemporary university as to have made the university we knew as students now seem a strangely underdeveloped, indeed a very simple and an almost unconcerned kind of institution. And the pace of change continues."

[15] Not only at Harvard. The University of California last year had operating expenditures from all sources of nearly half a billion dollars, with almost another 100 million for construction; a total employment of over 40,000 people, more than IBM and in a far greater variety of endeavors; operations in over a hundred locations, counting campuses, experiment stations, agricultural and urban extension centers, and projects abroad involving more than fifty countries; nearly 10,000 courses in its catalogues; some form of contact with nearly every industry, nearly every level of government, nearly every person in its region. Vast amounts of expensive equipment were serviced and maintained. Over 4,000 babies were born in its hospitals. It is the world's largest purveyor of white mice. It will soon have the world's largest primate colony. It will soon also have 100,000 students—30,000 of them at the graduate level; yet much less than one third of its expenditures are directly related to teaching. It already has nearly 200,000 students in extension courses—including one out of every three lawyers and one out of every six doctors in the state. And Harvard and California are illustrative of many more.

[16] Newman's "Ideal of a University" still has its devotees—chiefly the humanists and the generalists and the undergraduates. Flexner's "Idea of a Modern University" still has its supporters—chiefly the scientists and the specialists and the graduate students. "The Idea of a Multiversity" has its practitioners—chiefly the administrators, who now number many of the faculty among them, and the leadership groups in society at large. The controversies are still around in the faculty clubs and the student coffee houses; and the models of Oxford and Berlin and modern Harvard all animate segments of what was once a "community of masters and students" with a single vision of its nature and purpose. These several competing visions of true purpose, each relating to a different layer of history, a different web of forces, cause much of the malaise in the university communities of today. The university is so many things to so many different people that it must, of necessity, be partially at war with itself.

[17] How did the multiversity happen? No man created it; in fact, no man visualized it. It has been a long time coming about and it has a long way to go. What is its history? How is it governed? What is life like within it? What is its justification? Does it have a future?

LIFE IN THE MULTIVERSITY

[18] The "Idea of a University" was a village with its priests. The "Idea of a Modern University" was a town—a one-industry town—with

its intellectual oligarchy. "The Idea of a Multiversity" is a city of infinite variety. Some get lost in the city; some rise to the top within it; most fashion their lives within one of its many subcultures. There is less sense of community than in the village but also less sense of confinement. There is less sense of purpose than within the town but there are more ways to excel. There are also more refuges of anonymity—both for the creative person and the drifter. As against the village and the town, the "city" is more like the totality of civilization as it has evolved and more an integral part of it; and movement to and from the surrounding society has been greatly accelerated. As in a city, there are many separate endeavors under a single rule of law.

[19] The students in the "city" are older, more likely to be married, more vocationally oriented, more drawn from all classes and races than the students in the village; and they find themselves in a most intensely competitive atmosphere. They identify less with the total community and more with its subgroups. Burton R. Clark and Martin Trow have a particularly interesting typology of these subcultures: the "collegiate" of the fraternities and sororities and the athletes and activities majors; the "academic" of the serious students; the "vocational" of the students seeking training for specific jobs; and the "nonconformist" of the political activists, the aggressive intellectuals, and the bohemians. These subcultures are not mutually exclusive, and some of the fascinating pageantry of the multiversity is found in their interaction one on another.

[20] The multiversity is a confusing place for the student. He has problems of establishing his identity and sense of security within it. But it offers him a vast range of choices, enough literally to stagger the mind. In this range of choices he encounters the opportunities and the dilemmas of freedom. The casualty rate is high. The walking wounded are many. *Lernfreiheit*—the freedom of the student to pick and choose, to stay or to move on—is triumphant.

[21] Life has changed also for the faculty member. The multiversity is in the mainstream of events. To the teacher and the researcher have been added the consultant and the administrator. Teaching is less central than it once was for most faculty members; research has become more important. This has given rise to what has been called the "non-teacher" —"the higher a man's standing, the less he has to do with students"— and to a threefold class structure of what used to be "the faculty": those who only do research, those who only teach (and they are largely in an auxiliary role), and those who still do some of both. In one university I know, the proportions at the Ph.D. level or its equivalent are roughly one researcher to two teachers to four who do both.

[22] Consulting work and other sources of additional income have given rise to what is called the "affluent professor," a category that does include some but by no means all of the faculty. Additionally, many

faculty members, with their research assistants and teaching assistants, their departments and institutes, have become administrators. A professor's life has become, it is said, "a rat race of business and activity, managing contracts and projects, guiding teams and assistants, bossing crews of technicians, making numerous trips, sitting on committees for government agencies, and engaging in other distractions necessary to keep the whole frenetic business from collapse."

[23] The intellectual world has been fractionalized as interests have become much more diverse; and there are fewer common topics of conversation at the faculty clubs. Faculty government has become more cumbersome, more the avocation of active minorities; and there are real questions whether it can work effectively on a large scale, whether it can agree on more than preservation of the status quo. Faculty members are less members of the particular university and more colleagues within their national academic discipline groups.

[24] But there are many compensations. "The American professoriate" is no longer, as Flexner once called it, "a proletariat." Salaries and status have risen considerably. The faculty member is more a fully participating member of society, rather than a creature on the periphery; some are at the very center of national and world events. Research opportunities have been enormously increased. The faculty member within the big mechanism and with all his opportunities has a new sense of independence from the domination of the administration or his colleagues; much administration has been effectively decentralized to the level of the individual professor. In particular, he has a choice of roles and mixtures of roles to suit his taste as never before. He need not leave the Groves for the Acropolis unless he wishes; but he can, if he wishes. He may even become, as some have, essentially a professional man with his home office and basic retainer on the campus of the multiversity but with his clients scattered from coast to coast. He can also even remain the professor of old, as many do. There are several patterns of life from which to choose. So the professor too has greater freedom. *Lehrfreiheit,* in the old German sense of the freedom of the professor to do as he pleases, also is triumphant.

[25] What is the justification of the modern American multiversity? History is one answer. Consistency with the surrounding society is another. Beyond that, it has few peers in the preservation and dissemination and examination of the eternal truths; no living peers in the search for new knowledge; and no peers in all history among institutions of higher learning in serving so many of the segments of an advancing civilization. Inconsistent internally as an institution, it is consistently productive. Torn by change, it has the stability of freedom. Though it has not a single soul to call its own, its members pay their devotions to truth.

[26] The multiversity in America is perhaps best seen at work, adapting

and growing, as it responded to the massive impact of federal programs beginning with World War II. A vast transformation has taken place without a revolution, for a time almost without notice being taken. The multiversity has demonstrated how adaptive it can be to new opportunities for creativity; how responsive to money; how eagerly it can play a new and useful role; how fast it can change while pretending that nothing has happened at all; how fast it can neglect some of its ancient virtues. . . .

⸺⸮ COMMENT AND QUESTIONS ⸏⸺

1. Look again at the opening paragraph of the selection (also the opening paragraph of Kerr's book). What words and phrases in the first two sentences are echoed later in the selection? How are the choice and arrangement of words in the last two sentences effective?
2. What purposes are served by Kerr's historical approach, beginning in paragraph 2, to the university of today? What appear to be his attitudes toward the works of Newman and Flexner?
3. Examine paragraph 13. What is its function? What characteristics of style and tone do you notice?
4. What is the purpose, in paragraphs 14–15, of the detailed cataloguing of developments and activities at Harvard and, particularly, at the University of California?
5. What techniques of style and of paragraph development are noteworthy in paragraph 18?
6. Does life for the student in the multiversity, as Kerr describes it in paragraphs 19–20, seem attractive to you? Explain.
7. In the discussion of life for the faculty member in the multiversity (paragraphs 21–24) are there any implications that the student's educational experience is adversely affected? Support your answer with references to what Kerr says.
8. Paragraph 25 is well written. By what means does the author make it a good paragraph?
9. Kerr is notably fair in presenting the advantages and disadvantages of the multiversity. What is your response to the multiversity as he describes it?
10. If you have read Whitehead's "Universities and Their Function," do you think that Whitehead and Kerr could agree in any ways about the function of universities?

[16] *John W. Gardner*: Excellence: The Ideal of Individual Fulfillment

JOHN W. GARDNER (1912–   ) has been a college teacher, president of the Carnegie Corporation and of the Carnegie Foundation for the Advancement of Teaching, and Secretary of the Department of Health, Education and Welfare; in 1964 he received the Presidential Medal of Freedom. The following selection is Chapter XIII of a book published in 1961, *Excellence: Can We Be Equal and Excellent Too?*

THE PERSON ONE COULD BE

[1] Some years ago I had a memorable conversation with the ten-year-old son of one of my fellow professors. I was walking to class and he was headed for his violin lesson. We fell into conversation, and he complained that he couldn't play any real pieces on the violin yet—only those tiresome exercises. I suggested that this would be remedied as he improved, which led him to respond with melancholy: "But I don't want to improve. I expect I may even get worse."

[2] The idea of excellence is attractive to most people and inspiring to some. But taken alone it is a fairly abstract notion. It is not the universally powerful moving force that one might wish. We must therefore ask ourselves what are the moving and meaningful ideas that will inspire and sustain people as they strive for excellence.

[3] In our own society one does not need to search far for an idea of great vitality and power which can and should serve the cause of excellence. It is our well-established ideal of individual fulfillment. This ideal is implicit in our convictions concerning the worth of the individual. It undergirds our belief in equality of opportunity. It is expressed in our conviction that every individual should be enabled to achieve the best that is in him.

[4] The chief instrument we have devised to further the ideal of individual fulfillment is the educational system. But in our understandable preoccupation with perfecting that instrument, we have tended to forget the broader objectives it was designed to serve. Most Americans honor education; few understand its larger purposes. Our thinking about the aims of education has too often been shallow, constricted and lacking in reach or perspective. Our educational purposes must be seen in the

broader framework of our convictions concerning the worth of the individual and the importance of individual fulfillment.

[5] Education in the formal sense is only a part of the society's larger task of abetting the individual's intellectual, emotional and moral growth. *What we must reach for is a conception of perpetual self-discovery, perpetual reshaping to realize one's best self, to be the person one could be.*

[6] This is a conception which far exceeds formal education in scope. It includes not only the intellect but the emotions, character and personality. It involves not only the surface, but deeper layers of thought and action. It involves adaptability, creativeness and vitality.

[7] And it involves moral and spiritual growth. We say that we wish the individual to fulfill his potentialities, but obviously we do not wish to develop great criminals or great rascals. Learning for learning's sake isn't enough. Thieves learn cunning, and slaves learn submissiveness. We may learn things that constrict our vision and warp our judgment. We wish to foster fulfillment within the framework of rational and moral strivings which have characterized man at his best. In a world of huge organizations and vast social forces that dwarf and threaten the individual, we must range ourselves whenever possible on the side of individuality; but we cannot applaud an irresponsible, amoral or wholly self-gratifying individuality.

[8] America's greatness has been the greatness of a free people who shared certain moral commitments. Freedom without moral commitment is aimless and promptly self-destructive. It is an ironic fact that as individuals in our society have moved toward conformity in their outward behavior, they have moved away from any sense of deeply-shared purposes. We must restore *both* a vigorous sense of individuality *and* a sense of shared purposes. Either without the other leads to consequences abhorrent to us.

[9] To win our deepest respect the individual must both find himself and lose himself. This is not so contradictory as it sounds. We respect the man who places himself at the service of values which transcend his own individuality—the values of his profession, his people, his heritage, and above all the religious and moral values which nourished the ideal of individual fulfillment in the first place. But this "gift of himself" only wins our admiration if the giver has achieved a mature individuality and if the act of giving does not involve an irreparable crippling of that individuality. We cannot admire faceless, mindless servants of The State or The Cause or The Organization who were never mature individuals and who have sacrificed all individuality to the Corporate Good.

WASTE ON A MASSIVE SCALE

[10] In our society today, large numbers of young people never fulfill their potentialities. Their environment may not be such as to stimulate

such fulfillment, or it may actually be such as to stunt growth. The family trapped in poverty and ignorance can rarely provide the stimulus so necessary to individual growth. The neighborhood in which delinquency and social disintegration are universal conditions cannot create an atmosphere in which educational values hold a commanding place. In such surroundings, the process by which talents are blighted begins long before kindergarten, and survives long afterward.

[11] The fact that large numbers of American boys and girls fail to attain their full development must weigh heavily on our national conscience. And it is not simply a loss to the individual. At a time when the nation must make the most of its human resources, it is unthinkable that we should resign ourselves to this waste of potentialities. Recent events have taught us with sledge hammer effectiveness the lesson we should have learned from our own tradition—that our strength, creativity and further growth as a society depend upon our capacity to develop the talents and potentialities of our people.

[12] Any adequate attack on this problem will reach far beyond formal educational institutions. It will involve not only the school but the home, the church, the playground and all other institutions which shape the individual. The child welfare society, the adoption service, the foundlings' home, the hospital and clinic—all play their part. And so do slum clearance projects and social welfare programs that seek to create the kind of family and neighborhood environment which fosters normal growth.

[13] But it is not only in childhood that we face obstacles to individual fulfillment. Problems of another sort emerge at a later stage in the life span.

[14] Commencement speakers are fond of saying that education is a lifelong process. And yet that is something that no young person with a grain of sense needs to be told. Why do the speakers go on saying it? It isn't that they love sentiments that are well worn with reverent handling (though they do). It isn't that they underestimate their audience. The truth is that they know something their young listeners do not know— something that can never be fully communicated. No matter how firm an intellectual grasp the young person may have on the idea that education is a lifelong process, he can never know it with the poignancy, with the deeply etched clarity, with the overtones of satisfaction and regret that an older person knows it. The young person has not yet made enough mistakes that cannot be repaired. He has not yet passed enough forks in the road that cannot be retraced.

[15] The commencement speaker may give in to the temptation to make it sound as though the learning experiences of the older generation were all deliberate and a triumph of character—character that the younger generation somehow lacks. We can forgive him that. It is not easy to tell young people how unpurposefully we learn, how life tosses us head over

heels into our most vivid learning experiences, how intensely we resist many of the increments in our own growth.

[16] But we cannot forgive him as readily if he leaves out another part of the story. And that part of the story is that the process of learning through life is by no means continuous and by no means universal. If it were, age and wisdom would be perfectly correlated, and there would be no such thing as an old fool—a proposition sharply at odds with common experience. The sad truth is that for many of us the learning process comes to an end very early indeed. And others learn the wrong things.

[17] The differences among people in their capacity for continued growth are so widely recognized that we need not dwell on them. They must not be confused with differences in the degree of success—as the world measures success—which individuals achieve. Many whom the world counts as unsuccessful have continued learning and growing throughout their lives; and some of our most prominent people stopped learning literally decades ago.

[18] We still have a very imperfect understanding of why some people continue to learn and grow while others do not. Sometimes one can point to adverse circumstances as the cause of a leveling off of individual growth. But we cannot identify the conditions which have hindered or fostered development.

[19] Of course, people are never quite as buffeted by circumstance as they appear to be. The man who experiences great personal growth as a result of some accidental circumstance may have been ready to grow in any case. Pasteur said that chance favors the prepared mind. The man defeated by circumstance might have triumphed had he been made of other stuff. We all know individuals whose growth and learning can only be explained in terms of an inner drive, a curiosity, a seeking and exploring element in their personalities. Captain Cook said, "I . . . had ambition not only to go farther than any man had ever been before, but as far as it was possible for a man to go." Just as Cook's restless seeking led him over the face of the earth, so other men embark on Odysseys of the mind and spirit.

[20] It is a concern both for the individual and for the nation that moves the commencement speaker. Perhaps many men will always fall into ruts. Perhaps many will always let their talents go to waste. But the waste now exists on such a massive scale that sensible people cannot believe that it is all inevitable.

[21] Unfortunately, the conception of individual fulfillment and lifelong learning which animates the commencement speaker finds no adequate reflection in our social institutions. For too long we have paid pious lip service to the idea and trifled with it in practice. Like those who confine their religion to Sunday and forget it the rest of the week, we have segregated the idea of individual fulfillment into one compartment of our

national life, and neglect it elsewhere. We have set "education" off in a separate category from the main business of life. It is something that happens in schools and colleges. It happens to young people between the ages of six and twenty-one. It is not something—we seem to believe— that need concern the rest of us in our own lives.

[22] This way of thinking is long overdue for a drastic change. If we believe what we profess concerning the worth of the individual, then the idea of individual fulfillment within a framework of moral purpose must become our deepest concern, our national preoccupation, our passion, our obsession. We must think of education as relevant for everyone every-where—at all ages and in all conditions of life.

[23] Aside from our formal educational system there is little evidence of any such preoccupation. Some religious groups are doing excellent work. Our libraries and museums are a legitimate source of pride. Adult education programs have become increasingly effective. Certain of our organizations concerned with social welfare and with mental health play profoundly important roles.

[24] But what about moving pictures, radio and television, with their great possibilities for contributing to the growth of the individual? It would be fair to say that these possibilities have not dominated the imagi-nation of the men who control these media. On the contrary, these media have all too often permitted the triumph of cupidity over every educa-tional value. And what about newspapers and magazines, with their obvious potentialities for furthering the intellectual and moral growth of the individual? At best, a small fraction of the publishers accepts such a responsibility. Book publishers are less vulnerable to criticism, but they are not without fault.

[25] Serious pursuit of the goal of individual fulfillment will carry us even farther afield. Unions, lodges, professional organizations and social clubs can all contribute importantly to individual growth and learning if they are so inclined. Only sporadically have they been so inclined. There are innumerable opportunities open to the employer who is willing to acknowledge his responsibility for furthering the individual development of men and women in his employ. Some forward-looking companies have made a highly significant beginning in accepting that responsibility.

[26] What we are suggesting is that every institution in our society should contribute to the fulfillment of the individual. Every institution must, of course, have its own purposes and preoccupations, but over and above everything else that it does, it should be prepared to answer this question posed by society: "What is the institution doing to foster the development of the individuals within it?"

[27] Now what does all of this mean? It means that we should very greatly enlarge our ways of thinking about education. We should be painting a vastly greater mural on a vastly more spacious wall. What we

are trying to do is nothing less than to build a greater and more creative civilization. We propose that the American people accept as a universal task the fostering of individual development within a framework of rational and moral values. We propose that they accept as an all-encompassing goal the furtherance of individual growth and learning at every age, in every significant situation, in every conceivable way. By doing so we shall keep faith with our ideal of individual fulfillment and at the same time insure our continued strength and creativity as a society.

[28] If we accept this concern for individual fulfillment as an authentic national preoccupation, the schools and colleges will then be the heart of a national endeavor. They will be committed to the furthering of a national objective and not—as they now often find themselves—swimming upstream against the interests of a public that thinks everything else more urgent. The schools and colleges will be greatly strengthened if their task is undergirded by such a powerful public conception of the goal to be sought.

[29] And both schools and colleges will be faced with a challenge beyond anything they have yet experienced. We have said that much will depend upon the individual's attitude toward learning and toward his own growth. This defines the task of the schools and colleges. Above all they must equip the individual for a never-ending process of learning; they must gird his mind and spirit for the constant reshaping and re-examination of himself. They cannot content themselves with the time-honored process of stuffing students like sausages or even the possibly more acceptable process of training them like seals. It is the sacred obligation of the schools and colleges to instill in their students the attitudes toward growth and learning and creativity which will in turn shape the society. With other institutions at work on other parts of this task, the schools and colleges must of course give particular attention to the intellectual aspects of growth. This is uniquely their responsibility.

[30] If we accept without reservation these implications of our traditional belief in individual fulfillment, we shall have enshrined a highly significant purpose at the heart of our national life—a purpose that will lift all American education to a new level of meaning. We shall have accepted a commitment which promises pervasive consequences for our way of thinking about the purpose of democratic institutions. And we shall have embraced a philosophy which gives a rich personal meaning to the pursuit of excellence.

⊶⊷ COMMENT AND QUESTIONS ⊷⊶

1. What is the relationship of the ideas in the three opening paragraphs of this selection? Could the sequence of material in the three paragraphs be changed?

2. The author says in paragraph 4: "Our thinking about the aims of education has too often been shallow, constricted and lacking in reach or perspective." What are the different shades of meaning in the three descriptive terms? Where and in what ways does Gardner expand and clarify this sentence?

3. In what ways do paragraphs 7–9 qualify a central thesis about the importance of individual fulfillment?

4. What two major wastes of potentialities does Gardner discuss in the second section of his chapter? To which does he give greater emphasis by development? Can you see a reason for this emphasis?

5. What appear to be the author's attitudes toward the commencement speakers (paragraph 14 and the paragraphs following)?

6. What is the purpose of the distinction made in paragraph 17 between growth and success? Can you think of examples to support the statement in the last sentence of that paragraph?

7. Summarize as clearly as you can Gardner's criticism of our social institutions. Does the criticism seem to you justified? Gardner's book was published in 1961. Do you know of changes in the direction he is recommending that have occurred since then?

8. Paragraph 27 is perhaps the most complete statement of the central ideas of the selection. What techniques of style and of emphasis do you find in the paragraph?

9. What will be the new position and the clearly defined responsibility of the schools and colleges in the more excellent society Gardner hopes for? To what extent do you think that the schools and colleges are now occupying that position and assuming that responsibility? Explain.

10. If you have read the selections about education preceding this one, what similarities and what differences in ideas or emphasis do you find between Gardner and other writers concerned with education?

THE
QUEST FOR VALUES:
SOME TIMELESS
PHILOSOPHIES

ᛆ

[17] *Plato*: from the Symposium

THE FOLLOWING excerpt from the *Symposium* (or Banquet) presents
Plato's idea of love. Although the term "Platonic love" as it is generally used
carries little of Plato's meaning, it is derived from his concept of love as a
bridge between the material and the spiritual, by which one moves from the
love of earthly objects to the love of absolute beauty. The situation that Plato
establishes in the dialogue is this: Socrates and his friends, assembled for a
banquet, decide to devote the evening to conversation and to speeches in honor
of Love. When it is Socrates' turn to speak, he tells the company that he
learned of love from a wise woman, Diotima of Mantineia, and that he will
repeat what she said to him. In the dialogue that follows, Diotima asks
the questions, and Socrates answers. (For further notes on Plato, see pages
105 and 127.)

[1] "For there is nothing which men love but the good. Is there anything?" "Certainly, I should say, that there is nothing." "Then," she said,
"the simple truth is, that men love the good." "Yes," I said. "To which must

This selection was translated by Benjamin Jowett.

be added that they love the possession of the good?" "Yes, that must be added." "And not only the possession, but the everlasting possession of the good?" "That must be added too." "Then love," she said, "may be described generally as the love of the everlasting possession of the good?" "That is most true."

[²] "Then if this be the nature of love, can you tell me further," she said, "what is the manner of the pursuit? What are they doing who show all this eagerness and heat which is called love? and what is the object which they have in view? Answer me." "Nay, Diotima," I replied, "if I had known, I should not have wondered at your wisdom, neither should I have come to learn from you about this very matter." "Well," she said, "I will teach you:—The object which they have in view is birth in beauty, whether of body or soul." "I do not understand you," I said; "the oracle requires an explanation." "I will make my meaning clearer," she replied. "I mean to say, that all men are bringing to the birth in their bodies and in their souls. There is a certain age at which human nature is desirous of procreation—procreation which must be in beauty and not in deformity; and this procreation is the union of man and woman, and is a divine thing; for conception and generation are an immortal principle in the mortal creature, and in the inharmonious they can never be. But the deformed is always inharmonious with the divine, and the beautiful harmonious. Beauty, then, is the destiny or goddess of parturition who presides at birth, and therefore, when approaching beauty, the conceiving power is propitious, and diffusive, and benign, and begets and bears fruit: at the sight of ugliness she frowns and contracts and has a sense of pain, and turns away, and shrivels up, and not without a pang refrains from conception. And this is the reason why, when the hour of conception arrives, and the teeming nature is full, there is such a flutter and ecstasy about beauty whose approach is the alleviation of the pain of travail. For love, Socrates, is not, as you imagine, the love of the beautiful only." "What then?" "The love of generation and of birth in beauty." "Yes," I said. "Yes, indeed," she replied. "But why of generation?" "Because to the mortal creature, generation is a sort of eternity and immortality," she replied; "and if, as has been already admitted, love is of the everlasting possession of the good, all men will necessarily desire immortality together with good: Wherefore love is of immortality."

[³] All this she taught me at various times when she spoke of love. And I remember her once saying to me, "What is the cause, Socrates, of love, and the attendant desire? See you not how all animals, birds, as well as beasts, in their desire of procreation, are in agony when they take the infection of love, which begins with the desire of union; whereto is added the care of offspring, on whose behalf the weakest are ready to battle against the strongest even to the uttermost, and to die for them, and will let themselves be tormented with hunger or suffer anything in order to maintain their young? Man may be supposed to act thus from reason; but why should animals have these passionate feelings? Can you tell me why?" Again I replied that I did not know. She said to me: "And do you expect ever to become a master in the art of love, if you do not know this?" "But I have told you already, Diotima, that my ignorance is the reason why I come to you; for I am conscious that I want a teacher; tell me then the cause of this and of the other mysteries of love." "Marvel not," she said, "if you believe that love is of the immortal, as we have several times acknowledged; for here again, and on the same principle too, the mortal nature is seeking as far as is possible to be everlasting and immortal: and this is only to be attained by generation, because generation always leaves behind a new existence in the place of the old. Nay, even in the life of the same individual there is succession and not absolute unity: a man is called the same, and yet in the short interval which elapses between youth and age, and in which every animal is said to have life and identity, he is undergoing a perpetual process of loss and reparation—hair, flesh, bones, blood, and the whole body are always changing. Which is true not only of the body, but also of the soul, whose habits, tempers, opinions, desires, pleasures, pains, fears, never remain the same in any one of us, but are always coming and going; and equally true of knowledge, and what is still more surprising to us mortals, not only do the sciences in general spring up and decay, so that in respect of them we are never the same; but each of them individually experiences a like change. For what is implied in the word 'recollection,' but the departure of knowledge, which is ever being forgotten, and is renewed and preserved by recollection, and appears to be the same although in reality now, according to that law of succession by which all mortal things are preserved, not absolutely the same, but by substitution, the old worn-out mortality leaving another new and similar existence behind—unlike the divine, which is always the same and not another? And in this way, Socrates, the mortal body, or mortal anything, partakes of immortality; but the immortal in another way. Marvel not then at the love which all men have of their offspring; for that universal love and interest is for the sake of immortality."

[4] I was astonished at her words, and said: "Is this really true, O thou wise Diotima?" And she answered with all the authority of an accomplished Sophist: "Of that, Socrates, you may be assured;—think only of the ambition of men, and you will wonder at the senselessness of their ways, unless you consider how they are stirred by the love of an immortality of fame. They are ready to run all risks greater far than they would have run for their children, and to spend money and undergo any sort of toil, and even to die, for the sake of leaving behind them a name which shall be eternal. Do you imagine that Alcestis would have died to save Admetus, or Achilles to avenge Patroclus, or your own Codrus in order to preserve the kingdom for his sons, if they had not imagined

that the memory of their virtues, which still survive among us, would be immortal? Nay," she said, "I am persuaded that all men do all things, and the better they are the more they do them, in hope of the glorious fame of immortal virtue; for they desire the immortal.

[5] "Those who are pregnant in the body only, betake themselves to women and beget children—this is the character of their love; their off-spring, as they hope, will preserve their memory and give them the blessedness and immortality which they desire in the future. But souls which are pregnant—for there certainly are men who are more creative in their souls than in their bodies—conceive that which is proper for the soul to conceive or contain. And what are these conceptions?—wisdom and virtue in general. And such creators are poets and all artists who are deserving of the name inventor. But the greatest and fairest sort of wis-dom by far is that which is concerned with the ordering of states and families, and which is called temperance and justice. And he who in youth has the seed of these implanted in him and is himself inspired, when he comes to maturity desires to beget and generate. He wanders about seek-ing beauty that he may beget offspring—for in deformity he will beget nothing—and naturally embraces the beautiful rather than the deformed body; above all, when he finds a fair and noble and well-nurtured soul, he embraces the two in one person, and to such an one he is full of speech about virtue and the nature and pursuits of a good man; and he tries to educate him; and at the touch of the beautiful which is ever present to his memory, even when absent, he brings forth that which he had conceived long before, and in company with him tends that which he brings forth; and they are married by a far nearer tie and have a closer friendship than those who beget mortal children, for the childen who are their common offspring are fairer and more immortal. Who, when he thinks of Homer and Hesiod and other great poets, would not rather have their children than ordinary human ones? Who would not emulate them in the creation of children such as theirs, which have preserved their memory and given them everlasting glory? Or who would not have such children as Lycurgus left behind him to be the saviours, not only of Lacedaemon, but of Hellas, as one may say? There is Solon, too, who is the revered father of Athenian laws; and many others there are in many other places, both among Hellenes and barbarians, who have given to the world many noble works, and have been the parents of virtue of every kind; and many temples have been raised in their honour for the sake of children such as theirs; which were never raised in honour of any one, for the sake of his mortal children.

[6] "These are the lesser mysteries of love, into which even you, Soc-rates, may enter; to the greater and more hidden ones which are the crown of these, and to which, if you pursue them in a right spirit, they will lead, I know not whether you will be able to attain. But I will do

my utmost to inform you, and do you follow if you can. For he who would proceed aright in this matter should begin in youth to visit beautiful forms; and first, if he be guided by his instructor aright, to love one such form only—out of that he should create fair thoughts; and soon he will of himself perceive that the 'beauty of one form is akin to the beauty of another; and then if beauty of form in general is his pursuit, how foolish would he be not to recognize that the beauty in every form is one and the same! And when he perceives this he will abate his violent love of the one, which he will despise and deem a small thing, and will become a lover of all beautiful forms; in the next stage he will consider that the beauty of the mind is more honourable than the beauty of the outward form. So that if a virtuous soul have but a little comeliness, he will be content to love and tend him, and will search out and bring to the birth thoughts which may improve the young, until he is compelled to contemplate and see the beauty of institutions and laws, and to understand that the beauty of them all is of one family, and that personal beauty is a trifle; and after laws and institutions he will go on to the sciences, that he may see their beauty, being not like a servant in love with the beauty of one youth or man or institution, himself a slave mean and narrow-minded, but drawing towards and contemplating the vast sea of beauty, he will create many fair and noble thoughts and notions in boundless love of wisdom; until on that shore he grows and waxes strong, and at last the vision is revealed to him of a single science, which is the science of beauty everywhere. To this I will proceed; please to give me your very best attention:

[7] "He who has been instructed thus far in the things of love, and who has learned to see the beautiful in due order and succession, when he comes towards the end will suddenly perceive a nature of wondrous beauty (and this, Socrates, is the final cause of all our former toils)— a nature which in the first place is everlasting, not growing and decaying, or waxing and waning; secondly, not fair in one point of view and foul in another, or at one time or in one relation or at one place fair, at another time or in another relation or at another place foul, as if fair to some and foul to others, or in the likeness of a face or hands or any other part of the bodily frame, or in any form of speech or knowledge, or existing in any other being, as, for example, in an animal, or in heaven, or in earth, or in any other place, but beauty absolute, separate, simple, and everlasting, which without diminution and without increase, or any change, is imparted to the ever-growing and perishing beauties of all other things. He who from these ascending under the influence of true love, begins to perceive that beauty, is not far from the end. And the true order of going, or being led by another, to the things of love, is to begin from the beauties of earth and mount upwards for the sake of that other beauty, using these as steps only, and from one going on to two, and from two

to all fair forms, and from fair forms to fair practices, and from fair practices to fair notions, until from fair notions he arrives at the notion of absolute beauty, and at last knows what the essence of beauty is. This, my dear Socrates," said the stranger of Mantineia, "is that life above all others which man should live, in the contemplation of beauty absolute; a beauty which if you once beheld, you would see not to be after the measure of gold, and garments, and fair boys and youths, whose presence now entrances you; and you and many an one would be content to live seeing them only and conversing with them without meat or drink, if that were possible—you only want to look at them and to be with them. But what if man had eyes to see the true beauty—the divine beauty, I mean, pure and clear and unalloyed, not clogged with the pollutions of mortality and all the colours and vanities of human life—thither looking, and holding converse with the true beauty simple and divine? Remember how in that communion only, beholding beauty with the eye of the mind, he will be enabled to bring forth, not images of beauty, but realities (for he has hold not of an image but of a reality), and bringing forth and nourishing true virtue to become the friend of God and be immortal, if mortal man may. Would that be an ignoble life?"

COMMENT AND QUESTIONS

In the pages of the *Symposium* preceding the excerpt printed here, Diotima has told Socrates that love is a spirit who mediates between gods and men, that love is the offspring of Poverty and Plenty, and that love is love of the beautiful and good. In the selection printed here, the wise woman further explains that since love is of the everlasting possession of the beautiful and good, it is necessarily of the love of immortality, or of generation and birth in beauty, which to mortal creatures is a sort of eternity and immortality. The creative body inspired by love will produce children who provide one kind of immortality; the creative soul inspired by love will produce works of art and works of wisdom and virtue, fairer and more immortal than mortal children. All these things, Diotima says, are the lesser mysteries of love. The greater mystery and the highest experience of love is the experience of moving upward from the love of material objects to the love of spiritual things and finally to a perception of perfect Beauty and Good.

Below are four translations of the short passage in which Diotima summarizes the ascent, step by step, to the highest vision of love. Reading it in somewhat different language may help to clarify this key idea:

1. And the true order of going, or being led by another to the things of love is to begin from the beauties of earth and mount upwards for the sake

of that other beauty, using these as steps only, and from one going on to two, and from two to all fair forms, and from fair forms to fair practices, and from fair practices to fair notions, until from fair notions he arrives at the notion of absolute beauty, and at last knows what the essence of beauty is.

2. For such as discipline themselves upon this system, or are conducted by another begin to ascend through these transitory objects which are beautiful, towards that which is beauty itself, proceeding as on steps from the love of one form to that of two, and from that of two, to that of all forms which are beautiful; and from beautiful forms to beautiful habits and institutions, and from institutions to beautiful doctrines; until, from the meditation of many doctrines, they arrive at that which is nothing else than the doctrine of the supreme beauty itself, in the knowledge and contemplation of which at length they repose.

3. For let me tell you, the right way to approach the things of love, or to be led there by another, is this: beginning from these beautiful things, to mount for that beauty's sake ever upwards, as by a flight of steps, from one to two, and from two to all beautiful bodies, and from beautiful bodies to beautiful pursuits and practices, and from practices to beautiful learnings, so that from learnings he may come at last to that perfect learning which is the learning solely of that beauty itself, and may know at last that which is the perfection of beauty.

4. Those who learn the order of love, or are led by another, beginning with beautiful objects will move upward to beauty itself, proceeding as by steps from one fair form to all fair forms, from all fair forms to all fair actions, from all fair actions to all fair ideas, and thence, from the contemplation of fair ideas, to the knowledge of the very essence of beauty.

1. When Plato's idea is clear to you, give concrete examples of the steps or stages in this progression of love.
2. A less important part of Diotima's teaching is her comment on change. Examine the passage beginning in the middle of paragraph 3 with "Nay, even in the life of the same individual there is succession . . . ," and consider whether or not you agree with the statements made.
3. What particular parts of Diotima's discourse on "the lesser mysteries of love" (paragraphs 1–5) do you find interesting? Do you disagree with anything she says? Explain.
4. The words *sciences* and *science* used in this translation do not have the meaning we commonly assign to them. Examine the use of the words in the passage referred to in question 2 and in the next-to-last sentence of paragraph 6, and try to determine their meaning from context.
5. A. E. Taylor, an authority on Plato, says that the *Symposium* describes "the travel of the soul from temporality to eternity." What does this statement mean? Does it seem accurate to you? Explain your answer.
6. If you have read Plato's "Myth of the Cave," what parallels and what differences do you see between the ascent from the cave to the upper world and the ascent to a knowledge of perfect beauty?

[18] *Epicurus*: Letter to a Friend

EPICURUS (340?–270 B.C.) was a Greek philosopher who founded the Epicurean school. The following letter expresses and explains the central idea of his philosophy, that happiness or pleasure is the greatest good of life—an idea simplified and corrupted by followers who called themselves Epicureans.

[¹] We must consider that of desires some are natural, others empty; that of the natural some are necessary, others not; and that of the necessary some are necessary for happiness, others for bodily comfort, and others for life itself. A right understanding of these facts enables us to direct all choice and avoidance toward securing the health of the body and tranquility of the soul; this being the final aim of a blessed life. For the aim of all actions is to avoid pain and fear; and when this is once secured for us the tempest of the soul is entirely quelled, since the living animal no longer needs to wander as though in search of something he lacks, hunting for that by which he can fulfill some need of soul or body. We feel a need of pleasure only when we grieve over its absence; when we stop grieving we are in need of pleasure no longer. Pleasure, then, is the beginning and end of the blessed life.¹ For we recognize it as a good which is both primary and kindred to us. From pleasure we begin every act of choice and avoidance; and to pleasure we return again, using the feeling as the standard by which to judge every good.

[²] Now since pleasure is the good that is primary and most natural to us, for that very reason we do not seize all pleasures indiscriminately; on the contrary we often pass over many pleasures, when greater discomfort accrues to us as a result of them. Similarly we not infrequently judge pains better than pleasures, when the long endurance of a pain yields us a greater pleasure in the end. Thus every pleasure because of its natural kinship to us is good, yet not every pleasure is to be chosen; just as every pain also is an evil, yet that does not mean that all pains are necessarily to be shunned. It is by a scale of comparison and by the consideration of advantages and disadvantages that we must form our

From Epicurus' Letter to Menoecius, preserved in Diogenes Laertius, *Lives of the Philosophers*, Bk. X. Translated by Philip Wheelwright in *The Way of Philosophy* (Odyssey Press), pp. 423–25.

¹ I.e., since it is a product of that health of body and tranquility of soul mentioned above.

judgment on these matters. On particular occasions we may have reason to treat the good as bad, and the bad as good.

[3] Independence of circumstances we regard as a great good: not because we wish to dispense altogether with external advantages, but in order that, if our possessions are few, we may be content with what we have, sincerely believing that those enjoy luxury most who depend on it least, and that natural wants are easily satisfied if we are willing to forego superfluities. Plain fare yields as much pleasure as a luxurious table, provided the pain of real want is removed; bread and water can give exquisite delight to hungry and thirsty lips. To form the habit of a simple and modest diet, therefore, is the way to health: it enables us to perform the needful employments of life without shrinking, it puts us in better condition to enjoy luxuries when they are offered, and it renders us fearless of fortune.

[4] Accordingly, when we argue that pleasure is the end and aim of life, we do not mean the pleasure of prodigals and sensualists, as some of our ignorant or prejudiced critics persist in mistaking us. We mean the pleasure of being free from pain of body and anxiety of mind. It is not a continual round of drunken debauches and lecherous delights, nor the enjoyment of fish and other delicacies of a wealthy table, which produce a pleasant life; but sober reasoning, searching out the motives of choice and avoidance, and escaping the bondage of opinion, to which the greatest disturbances of spirit are due.

[5] The first step and the greatest good is prudence—a more precious thing than philosophy even, for all the other virtues are sprung from it. By prudence we learn that we can live pleasurably only if we live prudently, honorably, and justly, while contrariwise to live prudently, honorably, and justly guarantees a life that is pleasurable as well. The virtues are by nature bound up with a pleasant life, and a pleasant life is inseparable from them in turn.

[6] Is there any better and wiser man than he who holds reverent beliefs about the gods, is altogether free from the fear of death, and has serenely contemplated the basic tendencies of natural law? Such a man understands that the limit of good things is easy to attain, and that evils are slight either in duration or in intensity. He laughs at Destiny, which so many accept as all-powerful. Some things, he observes, occur of necessity, others by chance, and still others through our own agency. Necessity is irresponsible, chance is inconstant, but our own actions are free, and it is to them that praise and blame are properly attached. It would be better even to believe the myths about the gods than to submit to the Destiny which the natural philosophers teach. For the old superstitions at least offer some faint hope of placating the gods by worship, but the Necessity of the scientific philosophers is absolutely unyielding. As to

chance, the wise man does not deify it as most men do; for if it were divine it would not be without order. Nor will he accept the view that it is a universal cause even though of a wavering kind; for he believes that what chance bestows is not the good and evil that determine a man's blessedness in life, but the starting-points from which each person can arrive at great good or great evil. He esteems the misfortune of the wise above the prosperity of a fool; holding it better that well chosen courses of action should fail than that ill chosen ones should succeed by mere chance.

[7] Meditate on these and like precepts day and night, both privately and with some companion who is of kindred disposition. Thereby shall you never suffer disturbance, waking or asleep, but shall live like a god among men. For a man who lives constantly among immortal blessings is surely more than mortal.

⊰ COMMENT AND QUESTIONS ⊱

1. Read each sentence in paragraph 1 thoughtfully. What are examples of the different kinds of desires mentioned in the opening sentence? Do you agree that "the final aim of a blessed life" is "securing the health of the body and the tranquility of the soul"? Are you satisfied with the statement that "the aim of all actions is to avoid pain and fear," or do you believe there are other and more valid aims? If so, what are they? If you have read the "Sermon on the Mount," what different aim or aims are implicit in it?

2. Under what circumstances, according to Epicurus, should we choose to endure pain or deny ourselves pleasure? Can you illustrate from your own experience?

3. What is the meaning of "Independence of circumstances" at the beginning of paragraph 3?

4. What particular virtues does Epicurus think necessary for a pleasant life?

5. The *New World Dictionary* defines *epicure* as follows: "1. a person who enjoys and has a discriminating taste for foods and liquors. 2. a person who is especially fond of luxury and sensuous pleasures." It defines the adjective *Epicurean:* "1. of Epicurus or his philosophy. 2. fond of luxury and sensuous pleasure, especially that of eating and drinking. 3. suited to or characteristic of an epicure." Compare these definitions with Epicurus' own statement of his beliefs.

6. Part of Epicurus' teaching was designed to relieve human beings of two common anxieties: fear of the gods and fear of death. The gods, Epicurus believed, did not interfere in human lives; being gods, they were above the

affairs of men; nor was there an inflexible Destiny controlling men, predetermining their lives and fortunes. As to the fear of death, Epicurus argued that death is simply nonexistence; it is the ceasing of sensation, not to be feared because while we live death is not with us, and when death comes we have no sensations with which to experience it. With these ideas in mind, summarize in your own words the main ideas of paragraph 6.

7. It has been said that Epicureanism is a purely personal, and not a social, philosophy. On the basis of this selection do you agree or disagree with that judgment?

8. If you have read the *Apology*, compare and contrast the ideas of Epicurus and of Socrates. Do you think that Epicurus would have approved of the speech and actions of Socrates?

[19] The Stoic View

Epictetus: The Quiet Mind

Marcus Aurelius: from the Meditations

S T O I C I S M , founded late in the fourth century B.C. by the Greek philosopher Zeno, later became a patchwork of various beliefs. The teaching of Epictetus, however, represented a return to an earlier creed, and Marcus Aurelius read and was profoundly influenced by the *Discourses* of Epictetus. In general, the Stoic philosophy holds that the universe is a vast machine, directed by divine intelligence and ultimately good; all men, part of the great system of nature, are brothers. The wise man keeps his will "in harmony with nature"; he accepts things as they are and regards pleasure, pain, and all external circumstances as matters of indifference; he believes that virtue and perfection of soul are the greatest good of man and that the virtuous man, freed of all passion and desire, is also the happy man.

Epictetus was a Greek philosopher who lived as a slave in Rome in the first century A.D. and later taught in Rome and Epirus. Like Socrates, he left no writing, but his teaching was recorded by his pupil Flavius Arrianus. *The Manual* (or *Enchiridion*), from which the selection we have called "The Quiet Mind" is taken, sets down a brief, sometimes overlapping statement of the main doctrines of Epictetus' philosophy.

The first selection is from *The Manual* of Epictetus, translated by P. E. Matheson. Reprinted with permission of Clarendon Press. The selection from Marcus Aurelius's *Meditations* was translated by George Long.

Marcus Aurelius (121–180) was a Roman Emperor whom John Stuart
Mill called "the gentlest and most amiable of philosophers and rulers."[1]
The *Meditations* consists of twelve books of short passages which Marcus
Aurelius addressed to himself for the purpose of guiding his own conduct.
(The original title was *Marcus Aurelius to Himself*.) We have selected
from the whole work a number of representative passages.

Epictetus: The Quiet Mind

Of all existing things some are in our power, and others are not in our
power. In our power are thought, impulse, will to get and will to avoid,
and, in a word, everything which is our own doing. Things not in our
power include the body, property, reputation, office, and, in a word,
everything which is not our own doing. Things in our power are by nature
free, unhindered, untrammelled; things not in our power are weak,
servile, subject to hindrance, dependent on others. Remember then that
if you imagine that what is naturally slavish is free and what is naturally
another's is your own, you will be hampered, you will mourn, you will
be put to confusion, you will blame gods and men; but if you think that
only your own belongs to you, and that what is another's is indeed another's, no one will ever put compulsion or hindrance on you, you will
blame none, you will accuse none, you will do nothing against your will,
no one will harm you, you will have no enemy, for no harm can touch you.

1. Aiming then at these high matters, you must remember that to
attain them requires more than ordinary effort; you will have to give up
some things entirely, and put off others for the moment. And if you
would have these also—office and wealth—it may be that you will fail
to get them, just because your desire is set on the former, and you will
certainly fail to attain those things which alone bring freedom and
happiness.

Make it your study then to confront every harsh impression with the
words, "You are but an impression, and not at all what you seem to be."
Then test it by those rules that you possess; and first by this—the chief
test of all—"Is it concerned with what is in our power or with what is
not in our power?" And if it is concerned with what is not in our power,
be ready with the answer that it is nothing to you.

2. Remember that the will-to-get promises attainment of what you
will, and the will-to-avoid promises escape from what you avoid; and he
who fails to get what he wills is unfortunate, and he who does not escape
what he wills to avoid is miserable. If then you try to avoid only what is
unnatural in the region within your control, you will escape from all that

---

[1] For Mill's discussion of Marcus Aurelius see pages 142–43.

you avoid; but if you try to avoid disease or death or poverty you will be miserable.

Therefore let your will-to-avoid have no concern with what is not in man's power; direct it only to things in man's power that are contrary to nature. But for the moment you must utterly remove the will-to-get; for if you will to get something not in man's power you are bound to be unfortunate; while none of the things in man's power that you could honourably will to get is yet within your reach. Impulse to act and not to act, these are your concern; yet exercise them gently and without strain, and provisionally.

3. When anything, from the meanest thing upwards, is attractive or serviceable or an object of affection, remember always to say to yourself, "What is its nature?" If you are fond of a jug, say you are fond of a jug; then you will not be disturbed if it be broken. If you kiss your child or your wife, say to yourself that you are kissing a human being, for then if death strikes it you will not be disturbed.

4. When you are about to take something in hand, remind yourself what manner of thing it is. If you are going to bathe put before your mind what happens in the bath—water pouring over some, others being jostled, some reviling, others stealing; and you will set to work more securely if you say to yourself at once: "I want to bathe, and I want to keep my will in harmony with nature," and so in each thing you do; for in this way, if anything turns up to hinder you in your bathing, you will be ready to say, "I did not want only to bathe, but to keep my will in harmony with nature, and I shall not so keep it, if I lose my temper at what happens."

5. What disturbs men's minds is not events but their judgments on events. For instance, death is nothing dreadful, or else Socrates would have thought it so. No, the only dreadful thing about it is men's judgment that it is dreadful. And so when we are hindered, or disturbed, or distressed, let us never lay the blame on others, but on ourselves, that is, on our own judgments. To accuse others for one's own misfortunes is a sign of want of education; to accuse oneself shows that one's education has begun; to accuse neither oneself nor others shows that one's education is complete.

6. Be not elated at an excellence which is not your own. If the horse in his pride were to say, "I am handsome," we could bear with it. But when you say with pride, "I have a handsome horse," know that the good horse is the ground of your pride. You ask then what you can call your own. The answer is—the way you deal with your impressions. Therefore when you deal with your impressions in accord with nature, then you may be proud indeed, for your pride will be in a good which is your own.

7. When you are on a voyage, and your ship is at anchorage, and you disembark to get fresh water, you may pick up a small shellfish or a truffle

by the way, but you must keep your attention fixed on the ship, and keep looking towards it constantly, to see if the Helmsman calls you; and if he does, you have to leave everything, or be bundled on board with your legs tied like a sheep. So it is in life. If you have a dear wife or child given you, they are like the shellfish or the truffle, they are very well in their way. Only, if the Helmsman call, run back to your ship, leave all else, and do not look behind you. And if you are old, never go far from the ship, so that when you are called you may not fail to appear.

8. Ask not that events should happen as you will, but let your will be that events should happen as they do, and you shall have peace.

9. Sickness is a hindrance to the body, but not to the will, unless the will consent. Lameness is a hindrance to the leg, but not to the will. Say this to yourself at each event that happens, for you shall find that though it hinders something else, it will not hinder you.

10. When anything happens to you, always remember to turn to yourself and ask what faculty you have to deal with it. If you see a beautiful boy or a beautiful woman, you will find continence the faculty to exercise there; if trouble is laid on you, you will find endurance; if ribaldry, you will find patience. And if you train yourself in this habit your impressions will not carry you away.

11. Never say of anything, "I lost it," but say, "I gave it back." Has your child died? It was given back. Has your wife died? She was given back. Has your estate been taken from you? Was not this also given back? But you say, "He who took it from me is wicked." What does it matter to you through whom the Giver asked it back? As long as He gives it you, take care of it, but not as your own; treat it as passers-by treat an inn.

12. If you wish to make progress, abandon reasonings of this sort: "If I neglect my affairs I shall have nothing to live on"; "If I do not punish my son, he will be wicked." For it is better to die of hunger, so that you be free from pain and free from fear, than to live in plenty and be troubled in mind. It is better for your son to be wicked than for you to be miserable. Wherefore begin with little things. Is your drop of oil spilt? Is your sup of wine stolen? Say to yourself, "This is the price paid for freedom from passion, this is the price of a quiet mind." Nothing can be had without a price. When you call your slave-boy, reflect that he may not be able to hear you, and if he hears you, he may not be able to do anything you want. But he is not so well off that it rests with him to give you peace of mind.

13. If you wish to make progress, you must be content in external matters to seem a fool and a simpleton; do not wish men to think you know anything, and if any should think you to be somebody, distrust yourself. For know that it is not easy to keep your will in accord with nature and at the same time keep outward things; if you attend to one you must needs neglect the other.

14. It is silly to want your children and your wife and your friends to live for ever, for that means that you want what is not in your control to be in your control, and what is not your own to be yours. In the same way if you want your servant to make no mistakes, you are a fool, for you want vice not to be vice but something different. But if you want not to be disappointed in your will to get, you can attain to that.

Exercise yourself then in what lies in your power. Each man's master is the man who has authority over what he wishes or does not wish, to secure the one or to take away the other. Let him then who wishes to be free not wish for anything or avoid anything that depends on others; or else he is bound to be a slave.

15. Remember that you must behave in life as you would at a banquet. A dish is handed round and comes to you; put out your hand and take it politely. It passes you; do not stop it. It has not reached you; do not be impatient to get it, but wait till your turn comes. Bear yourself thus towards children, wife, office, wealth, and one day you will be worthy to banquet with the gods. But if when they are set before you, you do not take them but despise them, then you shall not only share the gods' banquet, but shall share their rule. For by so doing Diogenes and Heraclitus and men like them were called divine and deserved the name.

16. When you see a man shedding tears in sorrow for a child abroad or dead, or for loss of property, beware that you are not carried away by the impression that it is outward ills that make him miserable. Keep this thought by you: "What distresses him is not the event, for that does not distress another, but his judgment on the event." Therefore do not hesitate to sympathize with him so far as words go, and if it so chance, even to groan with him; but take heed that you do not also groan in your inner being.

17. Remember that you are an actor in a play, and the Playwright chooses the manner of it: if he wants it short, it is short; if long, it is long. If he wants you to act a poor man you must act the part with all your powers; and so if your part be a cripple or a magistrate or a plain man. For your business is to act the character that is given you and act it well; the choice of the cast is Another's.

18. When a raven croaks with evil omen, let not the impression carry you away, but straightway distinguish in your own mind and say, "These portents mean nothing to me; but only to my bit of a body or my bit of property or name, or my children or my wife. But for me all omens are favourable if I will, for, whatever the issue may be, it is in my power to get benefit therefrom."

19. You can be invincible, if you never enter on a contest where victory is not in your power. Beware then that when you see a man raised to honour or great power or high repute you do not let your impression carry you away. For if the reality of good lies in what is in our power,

there is no room for envy or jealousy. And you will not wish to be praetor, or prefect or consul, but to be free; and there is but one way to freedom—to despise what is not in our power.

20. Remember that foul words or blows in themselves are no outrage, but your judgment that they are so. So when any one makes you angry, know that it is your own thought that has angered you. Wherefore make it your first endeavour not to let your impressions carry you away. For if once you gain time and delay, you will find it easier to control yourself.

21. Keep before your eyes from day to day death and exile and all things that seem terrible, but death most of all, and then you will never set your thoughts on what is low and will never desire anything beyond measure.

22. If you set your desire on philosophy you must at once prepare to meet with ridicule and the jeers of many who will say, "Here he is again, turned philosopher. Where has he got these proud looks?" Nay, put on no proud looks, but hold fast to what seems best to you, in confidence that God has set you at this post. And remember that if you abide where you are, those who first laugh at you will one day admire you, and that if you give way to them, you will get doubly laughed at.

23. If it ever happen to you to be diverted to things outside, so that you desire to please another, know that you have lost your life's plan. Be content then always to be a philosopher; if you wish to be regarded as one too, show yourself that you are one and you will be able to achieve it.

24. Let not reflections such as these afflict you: "I shall live without honour, and never be of any account"; for if lack of honour is an evil, no one but yourself can involve you in evil any more than in shame. Is it your business to get office or to be invited to an entertainment?

Certainly not.

Where then is the dishonour you talk of? How can you be "of no account anywhere," when you ought to count for something in those matters only which are in your power, where you may achieve the highest worth?

"But my friends," you say, "will lack assistance."

What do you mean by "lack assistance"? They will not have cash from you and you will not make them Roman citizens. Who told you that to do these things is in our power, and not dependent upon others? Who can give to another what is not his to give?

"Get them then," says he, "that we may have them."

If I can get them and keep my self-respect, honour, magnanimity, show the way and I will get them. But if you call on me to lose the good things that are mine, in order that you may win things that are not good, look how unfair and thoughtless you are. And which do you really prefer? Money, or a faithful, modest friend? Therefore help me rather to keep these qualities, and do not expect from me actions which will make me lose them.

"But my country," says he, "will lack assistance, so far as lies in me."

Once more I ask, What assistance do you mean? It will not owe colonnades or baths to you. What of that? It does not owe shoes to the blacksmith or arms to the shoemaker; it is sufficient if each man fulfils his own function. Would you do it no good if you secured to it another faithful and modest citizen?

"Yes."

Well, then, you would not be useless to it.

"What place then shall I have in the city?"

Whatever place you can hold while you keep your character for honour and self-respect. But if you are going to lose these qualities in trying to benefit your city, what benefit, I ask, would you have done her when you attain to the perfection of being lost to shame and honour?

25. Has some one had precedence of you at an entertainment or a levée or been called in before you to give advice? If these things are good you ought to be glad that he got them; if they are evil, do not be angry that you did not get them yourself. Remember that if you want to get what is not in your power, you cannot earn the same reward as others unless you act as they do. How is it possible for one who does not haunt the great man's door to have equal shares with one who does, or one who does not go in his train equality with one who does; or one who does not praise him with one who does? You will be unjust then and insatiable if you wish to get these privileges for nothing, without paying their price. What is the price of a lettuce? An obol perhaps. If then a man pays his obol and gets his lettuces, and you do not pay and do not get them, do not think you are defrauded. For as he has the lettuces so you have the obol you did not give. The same principle holds good too in conduct. You were not invited to some one's entertainment? Because you did not give the host the price for which he sells his dinner. He sells it for compliments, he sells it for attentions. Pay him the price then, if it is to your profit. But if you wish to get the one and yet not give up the other, nothing can satisfy you in your folly.

What! you say, you have nothing instead of the dinner?

Nay, you have this, you have not praised the man you did not want to praise, you have not had to bear with the insults of his doorstep.

26. It is in our power to discover the will of Nature from those matters on which we have no difference of opinion. For instance, when another man's slave has broken the wine-cup we are very ready to say at once, "Such things must happen." Know then that when your own cup is broken, you ought to behave in the same way as when your neighbour's was broken. Apply the same principle to higher matters. Is another's child or wife dead? Not one of us but would say, "Such is the lot of man"; but when one's own dies, straightway one cries, "Alas! miserable am I."

But we ought to remember what our feelings are when we hear it of another.

27. As a mark[2] is not set up for men to miss it, so there is nothing intrinsically evil in the world.

Marcus Aurelius: Meditations

1. Begin the morning by saying to thyself, I shall meet with the busy-body, the ungrateful, arrogant, deceitful, envious, unsocial. All these things happen to them by reason of their ignorance of what is good and evil. But I who have seen the nature of the good that it is beautiful, and of the bad that it is ugly, and the nature of him who does wrong, that it is akin to me, not only of the same blood or seed, but that it participates in the same intelligence and the same portion of the divinity, I can neither be injured by any of them, for no one can fix on me what is ugly, nor can I be angry with my kinsman, nor hate him. For we are made for co-operation, like feet, like hands, like eyelids, like the rows of the upper and lower teeth. To act against one another then is contrary to nature; and it is acting against one another to be vexed and to turn away.

2. Every moment think steadily as a Roman and a man to do what thou hast in hand with perfect and simple dignity, and feeling of affection, and freedom, and justice; and to give thyself relief from all other thoughts. And thou wilt give thyself relief, if thou doest every act of thy life as if it were the last, laying aside all carelessness and passionate aversion from the commands of reason, and all hypocrisy, and self-love, and discontent with the portion which has been given to thee. Thou seest how few the things are, the which if a man lays hold of, he is able to live a life which flows in quiet, and is like the existence of the gods; for the gods on their part will require nothing more from him who observes these things.

3. Of human life the time is a point, and the substance is in a flux, and the perception dull, and the composition of the whole body subject to putrefaction, and the soul a whirl, and fortune hard to divine, and fame a thing devoid of judgement. And, to say all in a word, everything which belongs to the body is a stream, and what belongs to the soul is a dream and vapour, and life is a warfare and a stranger's sojourn, and after-fame is oblivion. What then is that which is able to conduct a man? One thing and only one, philosophy. But this consists in keeping the daemon[3] within

[2] That is, happiness, the result of virtue, is the mark set up for men to aim at.
[3] The inner spirit or spark of divinity in man.

a man free from violence and unharmed, superior to pains and pleasures, doing nothing without a purpose, nor yet falsely and with hypocrisy, not feeling the need of another man's doing or not doing anything; and besides, accepting all that happens, and all that is allotted, as coming from thence, wherever it is, from whence he himself came; and finally, waiting for death with a cheerful mind, as being nothing else than a dissolution of the elements of which every living being is compounded. But if there is no harm to the elements themselves in each continually changing into another, why should a man have any apprehension about the change and dissolution of all the elements? For it is according to nature, and nothing is evil which is according to nature.

4. We ought to observe also that even the things which follow after the things which are produced according to nature contain something pleasing and attractive. For instance, when bread is baked some parts are split at the surface, and these parts which thus open, and have a certain fashion contrary to the purpose of the baker's art, are beautiful in a manner, and in a peculiar way excite a desire for eating. And again, figs, when they are quite ripe, gape open; and in the ripe olives the very circumstance of their being near to rottenness adds a peculiar beauty to the fruit. And the ears of corn bending down, and the lion's eyebrows, and the foam which flows from the mouth of wild boars, and many other things—though they are far from being beautiful, if a man should examine them severally—still, because they are consequent upon the things which are formed by nature, help to adorn them, and they please the mind; so that if a man should have a feeling and deeper insight with respect to the things which are produced in the universe, there is hardly one of those which follow by way of consequence which will not seem to him to be in a manner disposed so as to give pleasure. And so he will see even the real gaping jaws of wild beasts with no less pleasure than those which painters and sculptors show by imitation; and in an old woman and an old man he will be able to see a certain maturity and comeliness; and the attractive loveliness of young persons he will be able to look on with chaste eyes; and many such things will present themselves, not pleasing to every man, but to him only who has become truly familiar with nature and her works.

5. Be like the promontory against which the waves continually break, but it stands firm and tames the fury of the water around it.

Unhappy am I, because this has happened to me.—Not so, but happy am I, though this has happened to me, because I continue free from pain, neither crushed by the present nor fearing the future. For such a thing as this might have happened to every man; but every man would not have continued free from pain on such an occasion. Why then is that rather a misfortune than this a good fortune? And dost thou in all cases call that a man's misfortune, which is not a deviation from man's nature? And does a thing seem to thee to be a deviation from man's nature, when it is not contrary to the will of man's nature? Well, thou knowest the will of nature. Will then this which has happened prevent thee from being just, magnanimous, temperate, prudent, secure against inconsiderate opinions and falsehood; will it prevent thee from having modesty, freedom, and everything else, by the presence of which man's nature obtains all that is its own? Remember too on every occasion which leads thee to vexation to apply this principle: not that this is a misfortune, but that to bear it nobly is good fortune.

6. One man, when he has done a service to another, is ready to set it down to his account as a favour conferred. Another is not ready to do this, but still in his own mind he thinks of the man as his debtor, and he knows what he has done. A third in a manner does not even know what he has done, but he is like a vine which has produced grapes, and seeks for nothing more after it has once produced its proper fruit. As a horse when he has run, a dog when he has tracked the game, a bee when it has made the honey, so a man, when he has done a good act, does not call out for others to come and see, but he goes on to another act, as a vine goes on to produce again the grapes in season.—Must a man then be one of these, who in a manner act thus without observing it?—Yes.

7. In the gymnastic exercises suppose that a man has torn thee with his nails, and by dashing against thy head has inflicted a wound. Well, we neither show any signs of vexation, nor are we offended, nor do we suspect him afterwards as a treacherous fellow; and yet we are on our guard against him, not however as an enemy, nor yet with suspicion, but we quietly get out of his way. Something like this let thy behaviour be in all the other parts of life; let us overlook many things in those who are like antagonists in the gymnasium. For it is in our power, as I said, to get out of the way, and to have no suspicion nor hatred.

8. When thou wishest to delight thyself, think of the virtues of those who live with thee; for instance, the activity of one, and the modesty of another, and the liberality of a third, and some other good quality of a fourth. For nothing delights so much as the examples of the virtues, when they are exhibited in the morals of those who live with us and present themselves in abundance, as far as is possible. Wherefore we must keep them before us.

9. To the jaundiced, honey tastes bitter, and to those bitten by mad dogs water causes fear; and to little children the ball is a fine thing. Why then am I angry? Dost thou think that a false opinion has less power than the bile in the jaundiced or the poison in him who is bitten by a mad dog?

10. No man will hinder thee from living according to the reason of thy own nature: nothing will happen to thee contrary to the reason of the universal nature.

11. This is the chief thing: Be not perturbed, for all things are accord-

ing to the nature of the universal; and in a little time thou wilt be nobody and nowhere, like Hadrian and Augustus. In the next place, having fixed thy eyes steadily on thy business, look at it, and at the same time remembering that it is thy duty to be a good man, and what man's nature demands, do that without turning aside; and speak as it seems to thee most just, only let it be with a good disposition and with modesty and without hypocrisy.

12. Pain is either an evil to the body—then let the body say what it thinks of it—or to the soul; but it is in the power of the soul to maintain its own serenity and tranquillity, and not to think that pain is an evil. For every judgement and movement and desire and aversion is within, and no evil ascends so high.

13. Wipe out thy imaginations by often saying to thyself: now it is in my power to let no badness be in this soul, nor desire nor any perturbation at all; but looking at all things I see what is their nature, and I use each according to its value.—Remember this power which thou hast from nature.

14. If thou art pained by an external thing, it is not this thing that disturbs thee, but thy own judgement about it. And it is in thy power to wipe out this judgement now. But if anything in thy own disposition gives thee pain, who hinders thee from correcting thy opinion? And even if thou art pained because thou art not doing some particular thing which seems to thee to be right, why dost thou not rather act than complain?— But some insuperable obstacle is in the way?—Do not be grieved then, for the cause of its not being done depends not on thee.

15. A cucumber is bitter.—Throw it away.—There are briars in the road.—Turn aside from them.—This is enough. Do not add, And why were such things made in the world? For thou wilt be ridiculed by a man who is acquainted with nature, as thou wouldst be ridiculed by a carpenter and shoemaker if thou didst find fault because thou seest in their workshop shavings and cuttings from the things which they make. And yet they have places into which they can throw these shavings and cuttings; and the universal nature has no external space; but the wondrous part of her art is that though she has circumscribed herself, everything within her which appears to decay and to grow old and to be useless she changes into herself, and again makes other new things from these very same, so that she requires neither substance from without nor wants a place into which she may cast that which decays. She is content then with her own space, and her own matter and her own art.

16. Do not despise death, but be well content with it, since this too is one of those things which nature wills. For such as it is to be young and to grow old, and to increase and to reach maturity, and to have teeth and beard and grey hairs, and to beget, and to be pregnant and to bring forth, and all the other natural operations which the seasons of thy life bring,

such also is dissolution. This, then, is consistent with the character of a reflecting man, to be neither careless nor impatient nor contemptuous with respect to death, but to wait for it as one of the operations of nature. As thou now waitest for the time when the child shall come out of thy wife's womb, so be ready for the time when thy soul shall fall out of this envelope. But if thou requirest also a vulgar kind of comfort which shall reach thy heart, thou wilt be made best reconciled to death by observing the objects from which thou art going to be removed, and the morals of those with whom thy soul will no longer be mingled. For it is no way right to be offended with men, but it is thy duty to care for them and to bear with them gently; and yet to remember that thy departure will be not from men who have the same principles as thyself. For this is the only thing, if there be any, which could draw us the contrary way and attach us to life, to be permitted to live with those who have the same principles as ourselves. But now thou seest how great is the trouble arising from the discordance of those who live together, so that thou mayest say, Come quick, O death, lest perchance I, too, should forget myself.

17. Either the gods have no power or they have power. If, then, they have no power, why dost thou pray to them? But if they have power, why dost thou not pray for them to give thee the faculty of not fearing any of the things which thou fearest, or of not desiring any of the things which thou desirest, or not being pained at anything, rather than pray that any of these things should not happen or happen? for certainly if they can co-operate with men, they can co-operate for these purposes. But perhaps thou wilt say, the gods have placed them in thy power. Well, then, is it not better to use what is in thy power like a free man than to desire in a slavish and abject way what is not in thy power? And who has told thee that the gods do not aid us even in the things which are in our power? Begin, then, to pray for such things, and thou wilt see. One man prays thus: How shall I be able to lie with that woman? Do thou pray thus: How shall I not desire to lie with her? Another prays thus: How shall I be released from this? Another prays: How shall I not desire to be released? Another thus: How shall I not lose my little son? Thou thus: How shall I not be afraid to lose him? In fine, turn thy prayers this way, and see what comes.

18. When thou art offended with any man's shameless conduct, immediately ask thyself, Is it possible, then, that shameless men should not be in the world? It is not possible. Do not, then, require what is impossible. For this man also is one of those shameless men who must of necessity be in the world. Let the same considerations be present to thy mind in the case of the knave, and the faithless man, and of every man who does wrong in any way. For at the same time that thou dost remind thyself that it is impossible that such kind of men should not exist, thou wilt become more kindly disposed towards every one individually. It is useful to per-

ceive this, too, immediately when the occasion arises, what virtue nature has given to man to oppose to every wrongful act. For she has given to man, as an antidote against the stupid man, mildness, and against another kind of man some other power. And in all cases it is possible for thee to correct by teaching the man who is gone astray; for every man who errs misses his object and is gone astray. Besides wherein hast thou been injured? For thou wilt find that no one among those against whom thou art irritated has done anything by which thy mind could be made worse; but that which is evil to thee and harmful has its foundation only in the mind. And what harm is done or what is there strange, if the man who has not been instructed does the acts of an uninstructed man? Consider whether thou shouldst not rather blame thyself, because thou didst not expect such a man to err in such a way. For thou hadst means given thee by thy reason to suppose that it was likely that he would commit this error, and yet thou hast forgotten and art amazed that he has erred. But most of all when thou blamest a man as faithless or ungrateful, turn to thyself. For the fault is manifestly thy own, whether thou didst trust that a man who had such a disposition would keep his promise, or when conferring thy kindness thou didst not confer it absolutely, nor yet in such way as to have received from thy very act all the profit. For what more dost thou want when thou hast done a man a service? Art thou not content that thou hast done something conformable to thy nature, and dost thou seek to be paid for it? Just as if the eye demand a recompense for seeing, or the feet for walking. For as these members are formed for a particular purpose, and by working according to their several constitutions obtain what is their own; so also as man is formed by nature to acts of benevolence, when he has done anything benevolent or in any other way conducive to the common interest, he has acted conformably to his constitution, and he gets what is his own.

19. Wilt thou, then, my soul, never be good and simple and one and naked, more manifest than the body which surrounds thee? Wilt thou never enjoy an affectionate and contented disposition? Wilt thou never be full and without a want of any kind, longing for nothing more, nor desiring anything, either animate or inanimate, for the enjoyment of pleasures? Nor yet desiring time wherein thou shalt have longer enjoyment, or place, or pleasant climate, or society of men with whom thou mayest live in harmony? But wilt thou be satisfied with thy present condition, and pleased with all that is about thee, and wilt thou convince thyself that thou hast everything and that it comes from the gods, that everything is well for thee, and will be well whatever shall please them, and whatever they shall give for the conservation of the perfect living being, the good and just and beautiful, which generates and holds together all things, and contains and embraces all things which are dissolved for the production of other like things? Wilt thou never be such that thou shalt so dwell

in community with gods and men as neither to find fault with them at all, nor to be condemned by them?

20. Whether the universe is a concourse of atoms, or nature is a system, let this first be established, that I am a part of the whole which is governed by nature; next, I am in a manner intimately related to the parts which are of the same kind with myself. For remembering this, inasmuch as I am a part, I shall be discontented with none of the things which are assigned to me out of the whole; for nothing is injurious to the part, if it is for the advantage of the whole. For the whole contains nothing which is not for its advantage; and all natures indeed have this common principle, but the nature of the universe has this principle besides, that it cannot be compelled even by any external cause to generate anything harmful to itself. By remembering, then, that I am a part of such a whole, I shall be content with everything that happens. And inasmuch as I am in a manner intimately related to the parts which are of the same kind with myself, I shall do nothing unsocial, but I shall rather direct myself to the things which are of the same kind with myself, and I shall turn all my efforts to the common interest, and divert them from the contrary. Now, if these things are done so, life must flow on happily, just as thou mayest observe that the life of a citizen is happy, who continues a course of action which is advantageous to his fellow-citizens, and is content with whatever the state may assign to him.

21. When thou hast assumed these names, good, modest, true, rational, a man of equanimity, and magnanimous, take care that thou dost not change these names; and if thou shouldst lose them, quickly return to them. And remember that the term Rational was intended to signify a discriminating attention to every several thing and freedom from negligence; and that Equanimity is the voluntary acceptance of the things which are assigned to thee by the common nature; and that Magnanimity is the elevation of the intelligent part above the pleasurable or painful sensations of the flesh, and above that poor thing called fame, and death, and all such things. If, then, thou maintainest thyself in the possession of these names, without desiring to be called by these names by others, thou wilt be another person and wilt enter on another life. For to continue to be such as thou hast hitherto been, and to be torn in pieces and defiled in such a life, is the character of a very stupid man and one overfond of his life, and like those half-devoured fighters with wild beasts, who though covered with wounds and gore, still intreat to be kept to the following day, though they will be exposed in the same state to the same claws and bites. Therefore fix thyself in the possession of these few names: and if thou art able to abide in them, abide as if thou wast removed to certain islands of the Happy. But if thou shalt perceive that thou fallest out of them and dost not maintain thy hold, go courageously into some nook where thou shalt maintain them, or even depart at once from life, not in

passion, but with simplicity and freedom and modesty; after doing this one laudable thing at least in thy life, to have gone out of it thus. In order, however, to the remembrance of these names, it will greatly help thee, if thou rememberest the gods, and that they wish not to be flattered, but wish all reasonable beings to be made like themselves; and if thou rememberest that what does the work of a fig-tree is a fig-tree, and what does the work of a dog is a dog, and that what does the work of a bee is a bee, and that what does the work of a man is a man.

22. Short is the little time which remains to thee of life. Live as on a mountain. For it makes no difference whether a man lives there or here, if he lives everywhere in the world as in a state (political community). Let men see, let them know a real man who lives according to nature. If they cannot endure him, let them kill him. For that is better than to live thus as men do.

23. What is that which as to this material (our life) can be done or said in the way most conformable to reason. For whatever this may be, it is in thy power to do it or to say it, and do not make excuses that thou art hindered. Thou wilt not cease to lament till thy mind is in such a condition that, what luxury is to those who enjoy pleasure, such shall be to thee, in the matter which is subjected and presented to thee, the doing of the things which are conformable to man's constitution; for a man ought to consider as an enjoyment everything which it is in his power to do according to his own nature. And it is in his power everywhere.

24. The healthy eye ought to see all visible things and not to say, I wish for green things; for this is the condition of a diseased eye. And the healthy hearing and smelling ought to be ready to perceive all that can be heard and smelled. And the healthy stomach ought to be with respect to all food just as the mill with respect to all things which it is formed to grind. And accordingly the healthy understanding ought to be prepared for everything which happens; but that which says, Let my dear children live, and let all men praise whatever I may do, is an eye which seeks for green things, or teeth which seek for soft things.

25. As those who try to stand in thy way when thou art proceeding according to right reason, will not be able to turn thee aside from thy proper action, so neither let them drive thee from thy benevolent feelings towards them, but be on thy guard equally in both matters, not only in the matter of steady judgement and action, but also in the matter of gentleness towards those who try to hinder or otherwise trouble thee. For this also is a weakness, to be vexed at them, as well as to be diverted from thy course of action and to give way through fear; for both are equally deserters from their post, the man who does it through fear, and the man who is alienated from him who is by nature a kinsman and a friend.

26. The things are three of which thou art composed, a little body,

a little breath (life), intelligence. Of these the first two are thine, so far as it is thy duty to take care of them; but the third alone is properly thine. Therefore if thou shalt separate from thyself, that is, from thy understanding, whatever others do or say, and whatever thou hast done or said thyself, and whatever future things trouble thee because they may happen, and whatever in the body which envelops thee or in the breath (life), which is by nature associated with the body, is attached to thee independent of thy will, and whatever the external circumfluent vortex whirls round, so that the intellectual power exempt from the things of fate can live pure and free by itself, doing what is just and accepting what happens and saying the truth: if thou wilt separate, I say, from this ruling faculty the things which are attached to it by the impressions of sense, and the things of time to come and of time that is past, and wilt make thyself like Empedocles' sphere,

All round, and in its joyous rest reposing;

and if thou shalt strive to live what is really thy life, that is, the present—then thou wilt be able to pass that portion of life which remains for thee up to the time of thy death, free from perturbations, nobly, and obedient to thy own daemon (to the god that is within thee).

27. When thou art troubled about anything, thou hast forgotten this, that all things happen according to the universal nature; and forgotten this, that a man's wrongful act is nothing to thee; and further thou hast forgotten this, that everything which happens, always happened so and will happen so, and now happens so everywhere; forgotten this too, how close is the kinship between a man and the whole human race, for it is a community, not of a little blood or seed, but of intelligence. And thou hast forgotten this too, that every man's intelligence is a god, and is an efflux of the deity; and forgotten this, that nothing is a man's own, but that his child and his body and his very soul came from the deity; forgotten this, that everything is opinion; and lastly thou hast forgotten that every man lives the present time only, and loses only this.

28. Man, thou hast been a citizen in this great state (the world): what difference does it make to thee whether for five years (or three)? For that which is conformable to the laws is just for all. Where is the hardship then, if no tyrant nor yet an unjust judge sends thee away from the state, but nature who brought thee into it? The same as if a praetor who has employed an actor dismisses him from the stage.—'But I have not finished the five acts, but only three of them.'—Thou sayest well, but in life the three acts are the whole drama; for what shall be a complete drama is determined by him who was once the cause of its composition, and now of its dissolution: but thou art the cause of neither. Depart then satisfied, for he also who releases thee is satisfied.

--◦◦{ C O M M E N T   A N D   Q U E S T I O N S }◦◦--

1. Because both of the preceding selections are a series of separate teachings, maxims, or reflections, they have no planned organization, and the numbered sections frequently repeat and overlap. In reviewing each selection, consider what the main ideas of each author are. How could the main ideas of Epictetus be expressed in a related, organized way? How could the main ideas of Marcus Aurelius similarly be expressed? On what matters are the two Stoics most completely in agreement? On what do their ideas and their emphasis appear to differ?

2. What does Epictetus mean in the first sentence of section 1 by "these high matters"?

3. What is the meaning of the word *impression* as Epictetus uses it in the second paragraph of section 1? What is the meaning of the sentence (section 5), "What disturbs men's minds is not events but their judgments on events"? Are the two ideas, about impressions and about judgments on events similar, or are they the same? Explain.

4. According to Epictetus, with what, in general, is the wise man not concerned? What are some of the particular things and events by which he is not disturbed? What methods does he use to keep himself undisturbed?

5. How does the closing statement of "The Quiet Mind," that there is nothing intrinsically evil in the world, follow logically from the preceding material?

6. It has been said that the coldness and austerity of Stoicism make it a philosophy few men can live by; that it makes almost impossible demands on human nature. What examples or statements in these two selections would seem to you to support that view? On the other hand, do you find in the Stoic philosophy any basic wisdom which might be useful to all men? In considering the last question, think about experiences which have caused you perturbation or unhappiness. Possible examples might be: (a) You have failed to receive an important, expected telephone call or letter. (b) You have fallen behind in your studies; the pressure of work has been enormous, and the situation has seemed hopeless. (c) You have been caught in a rush-hour traffic jam. (d) You have received a low grade on a paper or an examination. (e) You have heard of spiteful gossip directed at you. (f) You have wanted to study, but the dormitory has been noisy. (g) The person you have been in love with has married someone else. How would the Stoic react to these or similar situations?

7. Matthew Arnold called Marcus Aurelius "perhaps the most beautiful figure in history" and said that while the sentences of Epictetus fortify the character, the sentences of Marcus Aurelius touch the soul with the "gentleness and sweetness" of his morality. If you agree with this judgment, what particular examples can you give of the gentleness and sweetness in Marcus Aurelius?

8. The attitudes of Marcus Aurelius toward humanity or human beings in general are complex. What attitudes does he express?

9. Both Epictetus and Marcus Aurelius make skillful use of concrete words and examples and of figurative language. What details and figures of speech in the two selections are most memorable to you?

[20] *Jesus*: Sermon on the Mount

A HEADNOTE which attempted to state the importance and meaning of the Sermon on the Mount would be presumptuous and unnecessary. We shall merely say that it is the fullest single statement in the Bible of the basic doctrines of Jesus. According to the *New Standard Bible Dictionary*, the Sermon on the Mount is "at any rate in large measure, a compilation of the sayings of Jesus . . . gradually collected and massed in the present elaborate composition," and it constitutes "a general summary of what Matthew understands to have been Jesus' teachings about the disciple's relationship to duty and to God." The translation presented here is that of the King James version; students who prefer to read another version can find this passage in Matthew, chapters 5, 6, and 7.

CHAPTER 5

And seeing the multitudes, he went up into a mountain: and when he was set, his disciples came unto him:

2 And he opened his mouth, and taught them, saying,

3 Blessed *are* the poor in spirit: for theirs is the kingdom of heaven.

4 Blessed *are* they that mourn: for they shall be comforted.

5 Blessed *are* the meek: for they shall inherit the earth.

6 Blessed *are* they which do hunger and thirst after righteousness: for they shall be filled.

7 Blessed *are* the merciful: for they shall obtain mercy.

8 Blessed *are* the pure in heart: for they shall see God.

9 Blessed *are* the peacemakers: for they shall be called the children of God.

10 Blessed *are* they which are persecuted for righteousness' sake: for theirs is the kingdom of heaven.

11 Blessed are ye, when *men* shall revile you, and persecute *you,* and shall say all manner of evil against you falsely, for my sake.

12 Rejoice, and be exceeding glad: for great *is* your reward in heaven: for so persecuted they the prophets which were before you.

13 Ye are the salt of the earth: but if the salt have lost his savour, wherewith shall it be salted? it is thenceforth good for nothing, but to be cast out, and to be trodden under foot of men.

14 Ye are the light of the world. A city that is set on an hill cannot be hid.

15 Neither do men light a candle, and put it under a bushel, but on a candlestick; and it giveth light unto all that are in the house.

16 Let your light so shine before men, that they may see your good works, and glorify your Father which is in heaven.

17 Think not that I am come to destroy the law, or the prophets: I am not come to destroy, but to fulfil.

18 For verily I say unto you, Till heaven and earth pass, one jot or one tittle shall in no wise pass from the law, till all be fulfilled.

19 Whosoever therefore shall break one of these least commandments, and shall teach men so, he shall be called the least in the kingdom of heaven: but whosoever shall do and teach *them,* the same shall be called great in the kingdom of heaven.

20 For I say unto you, That except your righteousness shall exceed *the righteousness* of the scribes and Pharisees, ye shall in no case enter into the kingdom of heaven.

21 Ye have heard that it was said by them of old time, Thou shalt not kill; and whosoever shall kill shall be in danger of the judgment:

22 But I say unto you, That whosoever is angry with his brother without a cause shall be in danger of the judgment: and whosoever shall say to his brother, Raca, shall be in danger of the council: but whosoever shall say, Thou fool, shall be in danger of hell fire.

23 Therefore if thou bring thy gift to the altar, and there rememberest that thy brother hath ought against thee;

24 Leave there thy gift before the altar, and go thy way; first be reconciled to thy brother, and then come and offer thy gift.

25 Agree with thine adversary quickly, whiles thou art in the way with him; lest at any time the adversary deliver thee to the judge, and the judge deliver thee to the officer, and thou be cast into prison.

26 Verily I say unto thee, Thou shalt by no means come out thence, till thou hast paid the uttermost farthing.

27 Ye have heard that it was said by them of old time, Thou shalt not commit adultery:

28 But I say unto you, That whosoever looketh on a woman to lust after her hath committed adultery with her already in his heart.

29 And if thy right eye offend thee, pluck it out, and cast *it* from thee: for it is profitable for thee that one of thy members should perish, and not *that* thy whole body should be cast into hell.

30 And if thy right hand offend thee, cut it off, and cast *it* from thee: for it is profitable for thee that one of thy members should perish, and not *that* thy whole body should be cast into hell.

31 It hath been said, Whosoever shall put away his wife, let him give her a writing of divorcement:

32 But I say unto you, That whosoever shall put away his wife, saving for the cause of fornication, causeth her to commit adultery: and whosoever shall marry her that is divorced committeth adultery.

33 Again, ye have heard that it hath been said by them of old time, Thou shalt not forswear thyself, but shalt perform unto the Lord thine oaths:

34 But I say unto you, Swear not at all; neither by heaven; for it is God's throne:

35 Nor by the earth; for it is his footstool: neither by Jerusalem; for it is the city of the great King.

36 Neither shalt thou swear by thy head, because thou canst not make one hair white or black.

37 But let your communication be, Yea, yea; Nay, nay: for whatsoever is more than these cometh of evil.

38 Ye have heard that it hath been said, An eye for an eye, and a tooth for a tooth:

39 But I say unto you, That ye resist not evil: but whosoever shall smite thee on thy right cheek, turn to him the other also.

40 And if any man will sue thee at the law, and take away thy coat, let him have *thy* cloke also.

41 And whosoever shall compel thee to go a mile, go with him twain.

42 Give to him that asketh thee, and from him that would borrow of thee turn not thou away.

43 Ye have heard that it hath been said, Thou shalt love thy neighbour, and hate thine enemy.

44 But I say unto you, Love your enemies, bless them that curse you, do good to them that hate you, and pray for them which despitefully use you, and persecute you;

45 That ye may be the children of your Farther which is in heaven: for he maketh his sun to rise on the evil and on the good, and sendeth rain on the just and on the unjust.

46 For if ye love them which love you, what reward have ye? do not even the publicans the same?

47 And if ye salute your brethren only, what do ye more *than others?* do not even the publicans so?

48 Be ye therefore perfect, even as your Father which is in heaven is perfect.

CHAPTER 6

Take heed that ye do not your alms before men, to be seen of them: otherwise ye have no reward of your Father which is in heaven.

2 Therefore when thou doest *thine* alms, do not sound a trumpet before thee, as the hypocrites do in the synagogues and in the streets, that they may have glory of men. Verily I say unto you, They have their reward.

3 But when thou doest alms, let not thy left hand know what thy right hand doeth:

4 That thine alms may be in secret: and thy Father which seeth in secret himself shall reward thee openly.

5 And when thou prayest, thou shalt not be as the hypocrites *are:* for they love to pray standing in the synagogues and in the corners of the streets, that they may be seen of men. Verily I say unto you, They have their reward.

6 But thou, when thou prayest, enter into thy closet, and when thou hast shut thy door, pray to thy Father which is in secret; and thy Father which seeth in secret shall reward thee openly.

7 But when ye pray, use not vain repetitions, as the heathen *do:* for they think that they shall be heard for their much speaking.

8 Be not ye therefore like unto them: for your Father knoweth what things ye have need of, before ye ask him.

9 After this manner therefore pray ye: Our Father which art in heaven, Hallowed be thy name.

10 Thy kingdom come. Thy will be done in earth, as *it is* in heaven.

11 Give us this day our daily bread.

12 And forgive us our debts, as we forgive our debtors.

13 And lead us not into temptation, but deliver us from evil: For thine is the kingdom, and the power, and the glory, for ever. Amen.

14 For if ye forgive men their trespasses, your heavenly Father will also forgive you:

15 But if ye forgive not men their trespasses, neither will your Father forgive your trespasses.

16 Moreover when ye fast, be not, as the hypocrites, of a sad countenance: for they disfigure their faces, that they may appear unto men to fast. Verily I say unto you, They have their reward.

17 But thou, when thou fastest, anoint thine head, and wash thy face;

18 That thou appear not unto men to fast, but unto thy Father which is in secret: and thy Father, which seeth in secret, shall reward thee openly.

19 Lay not up for yourselves treasures upon earth, where moth and rust doth corrupt, and where thieves break through and steal:

20 But lay up for yourselves treasures in heaven, where neither moth nor rust doth corrupt, and where thieves do not break through nor steal:

21 For where your treasure is, there will your heart be also.

22 The light of the body is the eye: if therefore thine eye be single, thy whole body shall be full of light.

23 But if thine eye be evil, thy whole body shall be full of darkness. If therefore the light that is in thee be darkness, how great *is* that darkness!

24 No man can serve two masters: for either he will hate the one, and love the other; or else he will hold to the one, and despise the other. Ye cannot serve God and mammon.

25 Therefore I say unto you, Take no thought for your life, what ye shall eat, or what ye shall drink; nor yet for your body, what ye shall put on. Is not the life more than meat, and the body than raiment?

26 Behold the fowls of the air: for they sow not, neither do they reap, nor gather into barns; yet your heavenly Father feedeth them. Are ye not much better than they?

27 Which of you by taking thought can add one cubit unto his stature?

28 And why take ye thought for raiment? Consider the lilies of the field, how they grow; they toil not, neither do they spin:

29 And yet I say unto you, That even Solomon in all his glory was not arrayed like one of these.

30 Wherefore, if God so clothe the grass of the field, which to day is, and to morrow is cast into the oven, *shall he* not much more *clothe* you, O ye of little faith?

31 Therefore take no thought, saying, What shall we eat? or, What shall we drink? or, Wherewithal shall we be clothed?

32 (For after all these things do the Gentiles seek:) for your heavenly Father knoweth that ye have need of all these things.

33 But seek ye first the kingdom of God, and his righteousness; and all these things shall be added unto you.

34 Take therefore no thought for the morrow: for the morrow shall take thought for the things of itself. Sufficient unto the day *is* the evil thereof.

CHAPTER 7

Judge not, that ye be not judged.

2 For with what judgment ye judge, ye shall be judged: and with what measure ye mete, it shall be measured to you again.

3 And why beholdest thou the mote that is in thy brother's eye, but considerest not the beam that is in thine own eye?

4 Or how wilt thou say to thy brother, Let me pull out the mote out of thine eye; and, behold, a beam *is* in thine own eye?

5 Thou hypocrite, first cast out the beam out of thine own eye; and then shalt thou see clearly to cast out the mote out of thy brother's eye.

6 Give not that which is holy unto the dogs, neither cast ye your pearls

before swine, lest they trample them under their feet, and turn again and rend you.

7 Ask, and it shall be given you; seek, and ye shall find; knock, and it shall be opened unto you:

8 For every one that asketh receiveth; and he that seeketh findeth; and to him that knocketh it shall be opened.

9 Or what man is there of you, whom if his son ask bread, will he give him a stone?

10 Or if he ask a fish, will he give him a serpent?

11 If ye then, being evil, know how to give good gifts unto your children, how much more shall your Father which is in heaven give good things to them that ask him?

12 Therefore all things whatsoever ye would that men should do to you, do ye even so to them: for this is the law and the prophets.

13 Enter ye in at the strait gate: for wide *is* the gate, and broad *is* the way, that leadeth to destruction, and many there be which go in thereat:

14 Because strait *is* the gate, and narrow *is* the way, which leadeth unto life, and few there be that find it.

15 Beware of false prophets, which come to you in sheep's clothing, but inwardly they are ravening wolves.

16 Ye shall know them by their fruits. Do men gather grapes of thorns, or figs of thistles?

17 Even so every good tree bringeth forth good fruit; but a corrupt tree bringeth forth evil fruit.

18 A good tree cannot bring forth evil fruit, neither *can* a corrupt tree bring forth good fruit.

19 Every tree that bringeth not forth good fruit is hewn down, and cast into the fire.

20 Wherefore by their fruits ye shall know them.

21 Not every one that saith unto me, Lord, Lord, shall enter into the kingdom of heaven; but he that doeth the will of my Father which is in heaven.

22 Many will say to me in that day, Lord, Lord, have we not prophesied in thy name? and in thy name have cast out devils? and in thy name done many wonderful works?

23 And then will I profess unto them, I never knew you: depart from me, ye that work iniquity.

24 Therefore whosoever heareth these sayings of mine, and doeth them, I will liken him unto a wise man, which built his house upon a rock:

25 And the rain descended, and the floods came, and the winds blew, and beat upon that house; and it fell not: for it was founded upon a rock.

26 And every one that heareth these sayings of mine, and doeth them not, shall be likened unto a foolish man, which built his house upon the sand:

27 And the rain descended, and the floods came, and the winds blew, and beat upon that house; and it fell: and great was the fall of it.

28 And it came to pass, when Jesus had ended these sayings, the people were astonished at his doctrine:

29 For he taught them as *one* having authority, and not as the scribes.

COMMENT AND QUESTIONS

Richard G. Moulton, editor of *The Modern Reader's Bible,* states that the Sermon on the Mount, like many sections in the Bible, has a sevenfold structure and "follows a literary form prominent in the Hebrew philosophy we call wisdom literature." Each of these sections consists, he says, of a maxim supported by comment. Students who wish to follow this pattern may find the following outline useful.

Section 1. Matt. 5:3–12; the maxim is 3.
Section 2. Matt. 5:13; the maxim is "Ye are the salt of the earth."
Section 3. Matt. 5:14–16; the maxim is "Ye are the light of the world."
Section 4. Matt. 5:17–48; the maxim is 17.
Section 5. Matt. 6:1–18; the maxim is 1.
Section 6. Matt. 6:19–34; the maxim is 19–20.
Section 7. Matt. 7:1–29 (i.e., the whole of 7); the maxim is 1. Mr. Moulton points out that this seventh section is miscellaneous (another characteristic feature of wisdom literature) and that the number of sayings in it is seven.

1. It has been said that the expression "poor in spirit" (5:3) is a general expression clarified by the statements that follow it. Just what do you take the expression to mean?

2. In 5:13–15 Jesus is using figures of speech to clarify an idea. Explain the figures of speech and their meaning. Whom is Jesus addressing with the pronoun *ye* in these lines?

3. In 5:17 (and again in 7:12) Jesus refers to "the law" and "the prophets." What specific laws and prophets do you think may be referred to? If you have read "The Jew and the Christian," page 39, what statements made by Ballou are supported by this passage?

4. In 6:22–23 Jesus is again using figurative language. What is the literal meaning?

5. In 6:24 it is stated, "Ye cannot serve God and mammon." What is the relationship between this statement and 6:19–21? How does your dictionary define *mammon*? How would you define what is meant by *mammon* in terms of modern life?

6. John Stuart Mill in "On the Liberty of Thought and Discussion," pages 151–54, comments at some length on Christian morality. Do you think that what Mill says there is true of the Sermon on the Mount? Explain.

7. In your opinion, which of the precepts of Jesus are most difficult to follow in modern living? If you were to follow these precepts strictly, what changes would you have to make in your present way of life?
8. If you have read the *Apology*, what similarities and what differences do you find in the teaching of Socrates and of Jesus?
9. If you have read the selections from Epicurus, Epictetus, and Marcus Aurelius, you are familiar with the basic concepts of three views of life—the Epicurean, the Stoic, and the Christian. Which of these three philosophies do you think it would be most difficult to live by? Which would be most deeply rewarding?

[21]   *Aldous Huxley*: The Bhagavad-Gita and the Perennial Philosophy

THE BHAGAVAD-GITA, or Song of God, is the epic and gospel of the Hindu faith. The following essay, written by Aldous Huxley as an introduction to a translation of the *Bhagavad-Gita* by Swami Prabhavananda and Christopher Isherwood,[1] is largely a discussion of the elements which the author believes all the great religions of the world have in common. Aldous Huxley (1894–1963) was an English novelist and essayist, grandson of Thomas Huxley and brother of Julian Huxley; among his works are *Antic Hay, Point Counter Point, Brave New World, The Perennial Philosophy, Brave New World Revisited,* and *Literature and Science.*

[1] More than twenty-five centuries have passed since that which has been called the Perennial Philosophy was first committed to writing; and in the course of those centuries it has found expression, now partial, now complete, now in this form, now in that, again and again. In Vedanta and Hebrew prophecy, in the Tao Teh King and the Platonic dialogues, in the Gospel according to St John and Mahayana theology, in Plotinus and the Areopagite, among the Persian Sufis and the Christian mystics of the Middle Ages and the Renaissance—the Perennial Philosophy has spoken almost all the languages of Asia and Europe and has made use of the terminology and traditions of every one of the higher religions. But under all this confusion of tongues and myths, of local histories and particularist doctrines, there remains a Highest Common Factor, which is the Peren-

[1] This translation of the *Bhagavad-Gita* is available in an inexpensive Mentor Edition.

nial Philosophy in what may be called its chemically pure state. This final purity can never, of course, be expressed by any verbal statement of the philosophy, however undogmatic that statement may be, however deliberately syncretistic. The very fact that it is set down at a certain time by a certain writer, using this or that language, automatically imposes a certain sociological and personal bias on the doctrines so formulated. It is only in the act of contemplation, when words and even personality are transcended, that the pure state of the Perennial Philosophy can actually be known. The records left by those who have known it in this way make it abundantly clear that all of them, whether Hindu, Buddhist, Hebrew, Taoist, Christian or Mohammedan, were attempting to describe the same essentially indescribable Fact.

[2] The original scriptures of most religions are poetical and unsystematic. Theology, which generally takes the form of a reasoned commentary on the parables and aphorisms of the scriptures, tends to make its appearance at a later stage of religious history. The Bhagavad-Gita occupies an intermediate position between scripture and theology; for it combines the poetical qualities of the first with the clear cut methodicalness of the second. The book may be described, writes Ananda K. Coomaraswamy in his admirable *Hinduism and Buddhism,* "as a compendium of the whole Vedic doctrine to be found in the earlier Vedas, Brahmanas and Upanishads, and being therefore the basis of all the later developments, it can be regarded as the focus of all Indian religion." But this "focus of Indian religion" is also one of the clearest and most comprehensive summaries of the Perennial Philosophy ever to have been made. Hence its enduring value, not only for Indians, but for all mankind.

[3] At the core of the Perennial Philosophy we find four fundamental doctrines.

[4] First: the phenomenal world of matter and of individualized consciousness—the world of things and animals and men and even gods— is the manifestation of a Divine Ground within which all partial realities have their being, and apart from which they would be nonexistent.

[5] Second: human beings are capable not merely of knowing *about* the Divine Ground by inference; they can also realize its existence by a direct intuition, superior to discursive reasoning. This immediate knowledge unites the knower with that which is known.

[6] Third: man possesses a double nature, a phenomenal ego and an eternal Self, which is the inner man, the spirit, the spark of divinity within the soul. It is possible for a man, if he so desires, to identify himself with the spirit and therefore with the Divine Ground, which is of the same or like nature with the spirit.

[7] Fourth: man's life on earth has only one end and purpose: to identify himself with his eternal Self and so to come to unitive knowledge of the Divine Ground.

[⁸] In Hinduism the first of these four doctrines is stated in the most categorical terms. The Divine Ground is Brahman, whose creative, sustaining and transforming aspects are manifested in the Hindu trinity. A hierarchy of manifestations connects inanimate matter with man, gods, High Gods and the undifferentiated Godhead beyond.

[⁹] In Mahayana Buddhism the Divine Ground is called Mind or the Pure Light of the Void, the place of the High Gods is taken by the Dhyani-Buddhas.

[¹⁰] Similar conceptions are perfectly compatible with Christianity and have in fact been entertained, explicitly or implicitly, by many Catholic and Protestant mystics, when formulating a philosophy to fit facts observed by super-rational intuition. Thus, for Eckhart and Ruysbroeck, there is an Abyss of Godhead underlying the Trinity, just as Brahman underlies Brahma, Vishnu and Shiva. Suso has even left a diagrammatic picture of the relations subsisting between Godhead, triune God and creatures. In this very curious and interesting drawing, a chain of manifestation connects the mysterious symbol of the Divine Ground with the three Persons of the Trinity, and the Trinity in turn is connected in a descending scale with angels and human beings. These last, as the drawing vividly shows, may make one of two choices. They can either lead the life of the outer man, the life of separative selfhood; in which case they are lost (for, in the words of the Theologia Germanica, "nothing burns in hell but the self"). Or else they can identify themselves with the inner man, in which case it becomes possible for them, as Suso shows, to ascend again, through unitive knowledge, to the Trinity and even, beyond the Trinity, to the ultimate Unity of the Divine Ground.

[¹¹] Within the Mohammedan tradition such a rationalization of the immediate mystical experience would have been dangerously unorthodox. Nevertheless, one has the impression, while reading certain Sufi texts, that their authors did in fact conceive of *al haqq*, the Real, as being the Divine Ground or Unity of Allah, underlying the active and personal aspects of the Godhead.

[¹²] The second doctrine of the Perennial Philosophy—that it is possible to know the Divine Ground by a direct intuition higher than discursive reasoning—is to be found in all the great religions of the world. A philosopher who is content merely to know about the ultimate Reality—theoretically and by hearsay—is compared by Buddha to a herdsman of other men's cows. Mohammed uses an even homelier barnyard metaphor. For him the philosopher who has not realized his metaphysics is just an ass bearing a load of books. Christian, Hindu and Taoist teachers wrote no less emphatically about the absurd pretensions of mere learning and analytical reasoning. In the words of the Anglican Prayer Book, our eternal life, now and hereafter, "stands in the knowledge of God"; and this knowledge is not discursive but "of the heart," a super-rational intuition, direct, synthetic and timeless.

[13] The third doctrine of the Perennial Philosophy, that which affirms the double nature of man, is fundamental in all the higher religions. The unitive knowledge of the Divine Ground has, as its necessary condition, self-abnegation and charity. Only by means of self-abnegation and charity can we clear away the evil, folly and ignorance which constitute the thing we call our personality and prevent us from becoming aware of the spark of divinity illuminating the inner man. But the spark within is akin to the Divine Ground. By identifying ourselves with the first we can come to unitive knowledge of the second. These empirical facts of the spiritual life have been variously rationalized in terms of the theologies of the various religions. The Hindus categorically affirm that thou art That—that the indwelling Atman is the same as Brahman. For orthodox Christianity there is not an identity between the spark and God. Union of the human spirit with God takes place—union so complete the word "deification" is applied to it; but it is not the union of identical substances. According to Christian theology, the saint is "deified," not because Atman *is* Brahman, but because God has assimilated the purified human spirit into the divine substance by an act of grace. Islamic theology seems to make a similar distinction. The Sufi, Mansur, was executed for giving to the words "union" and "deification" the literal meaning which they bear in the Hindu tradition. For our present purposes, however, the significant fact is that these words are actually used by Christians and Mohammedans to describe the empirical facts of metaphysical realization by means of direct, super-rational intuition.

[14] In regard to man's final end, all the higher religions are in complete agreement. The purpose of human life is the discovery of Truth, the unitive knowledge of the Godhead. The degree to which this unitive knowledge is achieved here on earth determines the degree to which it will be enjoyed in the posthumous state. Contemplation of truth is the end, action the means. In India, in China, in ancient Greece, in Christian Europe, this was regarded as the most obvious and axiomatic piece of orthodoxy. The invention of the steam engine produced a revolution, not merely in industrial techniques, but also and much more significantly in philosophy. Because machines could be made progressively more and more efficient, western man came to believe that men and societies would automatically register a corresponding moral and spiritual improvement. Attention and allegiance came to be paid, not to Eternity, but to the Utopian future. External circumstances came to be regarded as more important than states of mind about external circumstances, and the end of human life was held to be action, with contemplation as a means to that end. These false and, historically, aberrant and heretical doctrines are now

systematically taught in our schools and repeated, day in, day out, by those anonymous writers of advertising copy who, more than any other teachers, provide European and American adults with their current philosophy of life. And so effective has been the propaganda that even professing Christians accept the heresy unquestioningly and are quite unconscious of its complete incompatibility with their own or anybody else's religion.

[15] These four doctrines constitute the Perennial Philosophy in its minimal and basic form. A man who can practise what the Indians call Jnana yoga (the metaphysical discipline of discrimination between the Real and the apparent) asks for nothing more. This simple working hypothesis is enough for his purposes. But such discrimination is exceedingly difficult and can hardly be practised, at any rate in the preliminary stages of the spiritual life, except by persons endowed with a particular kind of mental constitution. That is why most statements of the Perennial Philosophy have included another doctrine, affirming the existence of one or more human Incarnations of the Divine Ground, by whose mediation and grace the worshipper is helped to achieve his goal—that unitive knowledge of the Godhead, which is man's eternal life and beatitude. The Bhagavad-Gita is one such statement. Here, Krishna is an Incarnation of the Divine Ground in human form. Similarly, in Christian and Buddhist theology, Jesus and Gotama are Incarnations of divinity. But whereas in Hinduism and Buddhism more than one Incarnation of the Godhead is possible (and is regarded as having in fact taken place), for Christians there has been and can be only one.

[16] An Incarnation of the Godhead and, to a lesser degree, any theocentric saint, sage or prophet is a human being who knows Who he is and can therefore effectively remind other human beings of what they have allowed themselves to forget: namely, that if they choose to become what potentially they already are, they too can be eternally united with the Divine Ground.

[17] Worship of the Incarnation and contemplation of his attributes are for most men and women the best preparation for unitive knowledge of the Godhead. But whether the actual knowledge itself can be achieved by this means is another question. Many Catholic mystics have affirmed that, at a certain stage of that contemplative prayer in which, according to the most authoritative theologians, the life of Christian perfection ultimately consists, it is necessary to put aside all thoughts of the Incarnation as distracting from the higher knowledge of that which has been incarnated. From this fact have arisen misunderstandings in plenty and a number of intellectual difficulties. Here, for example, is what Abbot John Chapman writes in one of his admirable Spiritual Letters: "The problem of *reconciling* (not merely uniting) mysticism with Christianity is more

difficult. The Abbot (Abbot Marmion) says that St John of the Cross is like a sponge full of Christianity. You can squeeze it all out, and the full mystical theory remains. Consequently, for fifteen years or so, I hated St John of the Cross and called him a Buddhist. I loved St Teresa, and read her over and over again. She is first a Christian, only secondarily a mystic. Then I found that I had wasted fifteen years, so far as prayer was concerned." And yet, he concludes, in spite of its "Buddhistic" character, the practice of mysticism (or, to put it in other terms, the realization of the Perennial Philosophy) makes good Christians. He might have added that it also makes good Hindus, good Buddhists, good Taoists, good Moslems and good Jews.

[18] The solution to Abbot Chapman's problem must be sought in the domain, not of philosophy, but of psychology. Human beings are not born identical. There are many different temperaments and constitutions; and within each psycho-physical class one can find people at very different stages of spiritual development. Forms of worship and spiritual discipline which may be valuable for one individual may be useless or even positively harmful for another belonging to a different class and standing, within that class, at a lower or higher level of development. All this is clearly set forth in the Gita, where the psychological facts are linked up with general cosmology by means of the postulate of the *gunas*.[2] Krishna, who is here the mouthpiece of Hinduism in all its manifestations, finds it perfectly natural that different men should have different methods and even apparently different objects of worship. All roads lead to Rome—provided, of course, that it is Rome and not some other city which the traveller really wishes to reach. A similar attitude of charitable inclusiveness, somewhat surprising in a Moslem, is beautifully expressed in the parable of Moses and the Shepherd, told by Jalaluddin Rumi in the second book of the Masnavi. And within the more exclusive Christian tradition these problems of temperament and degree of development have been searchingly discussed in their relation to the way of Mary and the way of Martha in general, and in particular to the vocation and private devotion of individuals.

[19] We now have to consider the ethical corollaries of the Perennial Philosophy. "Truth," says St Thomas Aquinas, "is the last end for the entire universe, and the contemplation of truth is the chief occupation of wisdom." The moral virtues, he says in another place, belong to contemplation, not indeed essentially, but as a necessary predisposition. Virtue, in other words, is not the end, but the indispensable means to the knowledge of divine reality. Shankara, the greatest of the Indian commentators on

---

[2] In Hinduism the basis of all mind and matter, called *Prakriti*, is composed of three forces or *gunas*.

the Gita, holds the same doctrine. Right action is the way to knowledge; for it purifies the mind, and it is only to a mind purified from egotism that the intuition of the Divine Ground can come.

[20] Self-abnegation, according to the Gita, can be achieved by the practice of two all-inclusive virtues—love and non-attachment. The latter is the same thing as that "holy indifference," on which St François de Sales is never tired of insisting. "He who refers every action to God," writes Camus, summarizing his master's teaching, "and has no aims save His Glory, will find rest everywhere, even amidst the most violent commotions." So long as we practise this holy indifference to the fruits of action, "no lawful occupation will separate us from God; on the contrary, it can be made a means of closer union." Here the word "lawful" supplies a necessary qualification to a teaching which, without it, is incomplete and even potentially dangerous. Some actions are intrinsically evil or inexpedient; and no good intentions, no conscious offering of them to God, no renunciation of the fruits can alter their essential character. Holy indifference requires to be taught in conjunction not merely with a set of commandments prohibiting crimes, but also with a clear conception of what in Buddha's Eightfold Path is called "right livelihood." Thus, for the Buddhist, right livelihood was incompatible with the making of deadly weapons and of intoxicants; for the mediæval Christian, with the taking of interest and with various monopolistic practices which have since come to be regarded as legitimate good business. John Woolman, the American Quaker, provides a most enlightening example of the way in which a man may live in the world, while practising perfect non-attachment and remaining acutely sensitive to the claims of right livelihood. Thus, while it would have been profitable and perfectly lawful for him to sell West Indian sugar and rum to the customers who came to his shop, Woolman refrained from doing so, because these things were the products of slave labour. Similarly, when he was in England, it would have been both lawful and convenient for him to travel by stage coach. Nevertheless, he preferred to make his journeys on foot. Why? Because the comforts of rapid travel could only be bought at the expense of great cruelty to the horses and the most atrocious working conditions for the post-boys. In Woolman's eyes, such a system of transportation was intrinsically undesirable, and no amount of personal non-attachment could make it anything but undesirable. So he shouldered his knapsack and walked.

[21] In the preceding pages I have tried to show that the Perennial Philosophy and its ethical corollaries constitute a Highest Common Factor, present in all the major religions of the world. To affirm this truth has never been more imperatively necessary than at the present time. There will never be enduring peace unless and until human beings come to accept a philosophy of life more adequate to the cosmic and psychological facts than the insane idolatries of nationalism and the advertising

man's apocalyptic faith in Progress towards a mechanized New Jerusalem. All the elements of this philosophy are present, as we have seen, in the traditional religions. But in existing circumstances there is not the slightest chance that any of the traditional religions will obtain universal acceptance. Europeans and Americans will see no reason for being converted to Hinduism, say, or Buddhism. And the people of Asia can hardly be expected to renounce their own traditions for the Christianity professed, often sincerely, by the imperialists who, for four hundred years and more, have been systematically attacking, exploiting and oppressing, and are now trying to finish off the work of destruction by "educating" them. But happily there is the Highest Common Factor of all religions, the Perennial Philosophy which has always and everywhere been the metaphysical system of the prophets, saints and sages. It is perfectly possible for people to remain good Christians, Hindus, Buddhists or Moslems and yet to be united in full agreement on the basic doctrines of the Perennial Philosophy.

[22] The Bhagavad-Gita is perhaps the most systematic scriptural statement of the Perennial Philosophy. To a world at war, a world that, because it lacks the intellectual and spiritual prerequisites to peace, can only hope to patch up some kind of precarious armed truce, it stands pointing, clearly and unmistakably, to the only road of escape from the self-imposed necessity of self-destruction.

COMMENT AND QUESTIONS

1. What are the purposes of the opening paragraph of Huxley's essay?
2. This essay is very well organized. What pattern or patterns of organization does Huxley use? What are his principal devices for keeping his organization clear?
3. Compare the four fundamental doctrines of the Perennial Philosophy (paragraphs 4–14) with the doctrines of the church in which you were brought up, or with those of any church whose doctrines are familiar to you.
4. In paragraph 14 Huxley speaks of "false and, historically, aberrant and heretical doctrines." Exactly what does he mean? Do you agree with his judgment of these doctrines? Explain.
5. What, according to Huxley, are the ethical corollaries of the Perennial Philosophy?
6. In Huxley's view, what is the value of the Bhagavad-Gita, and what is the importance of the Perennial Philosophy? Do you agree with his reasoning in the last two paragraphs of the essay?

7. State what you think Huxley's intentions were in writing this introduction to the *Bhagavad-Gita*. Is he simply informing, or is he also evaluating and persuading? Justify your answer.
8. How many of the writers on religion or ethics whom you have read (for example, Plato, Epicurus, Epictetus, Marcus Aurelius, Emerson, James, Einstein, Newman in "Doubt and Faith," Sartre) do you think would agree wholly or in part with the doctrines and ethical corollaries of the Perennial Philosophy? Explain.

[22]   *William Barrett*: Zen for the West

WILLIAM BARRETT (1913–   ), editor of *The Partisan Review* from 1946 to 1953, is a professor of philosophy at New York University and author of *What Is Existentialism?* and *Irrational Man*. The following selection is part of his introduction to *Zen Buddhism: Selected Writings of D. T. Suzuki*.

– I –

[¹] What we call the Western tradition is formed by two major influences, Hebraic and Greek, and both these influences are profoundly dualistic in spirit. That is, they divide reality into two parts and set one part off against the other. The Hebrew makes his division on religious and moral grounds: God absolutely transcends the world, is absolutely separate from it; hence there follow the dualisms of God and creature, the Law and the erring members, spirit and flesh. The Greek, on the other hand, divides reality along intellectual lines. Plato, who virtually founded Western philosophy single-handed—Whitehead has remarked that 2500 years of Western philosophy is but a series of footnotes to Plato—absolutely cleaves reality into the world of the intellect and the world of the senses. The great achievement of the Greeks was to define the ideal of rationality for man; but in doing so, Plato and Aristotle not only made reason the highest and most valued function, they also went so far as to make it the very center of our personal identity. The Orientals never succumbed to this latter error; favoring intuition over reason, they grasped intuitively a center of the personality which held in unity the warring opposites of reason and unreason, intellect and senses, morality and nature. So far as we are Westerners, we inherit these dualisms, they are part of us: an irrationally nagging conscience from the Hebrews, an excessively dividing rational mind from the Greeks. Yet the experience

of modern culture, in the most diverse fields, makes them less and less
acceptable.

[²] Medieval Christianity still lives in the rational world of the Greeks.
The universe of St. Thomas Aquinas is the same bandbox universe of
Aristotle, a tight tiny tidy rational whole, where all is in apple-pie order,
and everything occupies its logical and meaningful place in the absolute
hierarchy of Being. When we turn from such humanized universes to
Indian thought, we are at first staggered by the vision of vast spaces,
endless aeons of time, universe upon universe, against which man
looks very small and meaningless; then we realize these are the spaces and
times of modern astronomy, and the Indian idea is therefore closer to us.
The distinguished Protestant theologian Paul Tillich has described the
essential experience of modern man as an encounter with "meaninglessness": lost in the vastness of the universe, man begins to think that his own
existence and that of the universe are "meaningless." The God of Theism,
says Tillich echoing Nietzsche, is dead, and Western man must find a
God beyond the God of Theism: the God offered us by rational theology
is no longer acceptable. From the point of view of the medieval Catholic
(and many still survive) the very premises of Buddhist thinking would
look "meaningless"; they are also more difficult and grim, but they look
much closer to what we moderns may have to swallow.

[³] In science itself, modern developments have combined to make
our inherited rationalism more shaky. Physics and mathematics, the two
most advanced of Western sciences, have in our time become paradoxical: that is, arrived at the state where they breed paradoxes for reason
itself. One hundred fifty years ago the philosopher Kant attempted to
show that there were ineluctable limits to reason, but the Western
mind, positivistic to the core, could be expected to take such a conclusion
seriously only when it showed up in science itself. Well, science in this
century has at last caught up with Kant: almost simultaneously Heisenberg in physics, and Godel in mathematics, have shown ineluctable limits
to human reason. Heisenberg's Principle of Indeterminacy shows essential limits to our ability to know and predict physical states of affairs,
and opens up to us the glimpse of a nature irrational and chaotic at bottom. Godel's results would seem to have even more far-reaching consequences when one reflects that in the Western tradition, from the Py-
thagoreans and Plato onward, mathematics has inspired the most absolute
claims of rationalism. Now it turns out that even in his most precise
science—in the province where his reason had seemed omnipotent—man
cannot escape his essential finitude: every system of mathematics that
he constructs is doomed to incompleteness. Mathematics is like a ship
in mid-ocean that has sprung leaks (paradoxes) which have been temporarily plugged, but our reason can never guarantee that the ship will
not spring other leaks. That this human insecurity should manifest it-

self in what had hitherto been the very citadel of reason, mathematics, marks a new turn in Western thinking. The next step would be to recognize the essentially paradoxical nature of reason itself.

[4] This step has been taken by some modern philosophers. The most original and influential philosopher now alive on the European continent is the German Existentialist Martin Heidegger. A German friend of Heidegger told me that one day when he visited Heidegger he found him reading one of Suzuki's books; "If I understand this man correctly," Heidegger remarked, "this is what I have been trying to say in all my writings." This remark may be the slightly exaggerated enthusiasm of a man under the impact of a book in which he recognizes some of his own thoughts; certainly Heidegger's philosophy in its tone and temper and sources is Western to its core, and there is much in him that is not in Zen, but also very much more in Zen that is not in Heidegger; and yet the points of correspondence between the two, despite their disparate sources, are startling enough. For what, after all, is Heidegger's final message but that Western philosophy is a great error, the result of the dichotomizing intellect that has cut man off from unity with Being itself and from his own Being. This error begins (in Plato) with locating truth in the intellect; the world of nature thereby becomes a realm of objects set over against the mind, eventually objects to be manipulated by scientific and practical calculation. Twenty-five hundred years of Western metaphysics move from Plato's intellectualism to Nietzsche's Will to Power, and concurrently man does become in fact the technological master of the whole planet; but the conquest of nature merely estranges him from Being itself and from his own Being and delivers him over to an ever ascending, ever more frantic will to power. "Divide and conquer" might thus be said to be the motto which Western man has adopted toward Being itself; but this of course is the counsel of power not of wisdom. Heidegger repeatedly tells us that this tradition of the West has come to the end of its cycle; and as he says this, one can only gather that he himself has already stepped beyond that tradition. Into the tradition of the Orient? I should say at least that he has come pretty close to Zen.

[5] If these happenings in science and philosophy indicate changed ways of thinking in the West, our modern art would seem to indicate very new ways of feeling. Whatever may be said on the thorny subject of modern art, the one fact that is clear is that to the artistic conservative it represents a scandal and a break with the tradition. Our modern art presents a surface so irrational, bizarre, and shocking that it must be considered a break with the older more rational canons of Western art. That Western painters and sculptors in this century have gone outside their tradition to nourish themselves with the art of the rest of the world— Oriental, African, Melanesian—signifies that what we knew as *the* tradition is no longer able to nourish its most creative members; its confining

mould has broken, under pressures from within. Our painting has detached itself from three-dimensional space, the arena of Western man's power and mobility; detached itself from the object, the supreme fixation of Western man's extroversion; and it has become subjective, contrary to the whole tenor of our Western life. Is all this merely malaise and revolt, or prophecy of a different spirit to come? In the past, new styles in painting have often been thus prophetic. In the art of literature, of course, the writer can be vocal about the new and revolutionary thing, and we find a novelist like D. H. Lawrence preaching against the bloodless rationalism of his culture. Lawrence urged the necessity of something he called "mindlessness," of becoming "mindless," if the meddlesome and self-conscious intellect were not in the end to cut off Western man irreparably from nature and even the possibility of real sexual union. Oddly enough, this "mindlessness" of Lawrence is a groping intuition after the doctrine of "no-mind" which Zen Buddhism had elaborated a thousand years before. Unlike Lawrence, however, the Zen masters developed this doctrine without falling into primitivism and the worship of the blood. In Lawrence's behalf it must be remembered that his culture gave him no help at all on these matters, and he had to grope in the dark pretty much on his own. And to change to one final literary example that involves no preaching or thesis whatsoever: the most considerable work of prose in English in this century is probably James Joyce's *Ulysses*, and this is so profoundly Oriental a book that the psychologist C. G. Jung recommended it as a long-needed bible for the white-skinned peoples. Joyce shattered the aesthetic of the Georgians that would divide reality into a compartment of the Beautiful forever separate from the opposite compartments of the Ugly or Sordid. *Ulysses*, like the Oriental mind, succeeds in holding the opposites together: light and dark, beautiful and ugly, sublime and banal. The spiritual premise of this work is an acceptance of life that no dualism—whether puritanical or aesthetic—could ever possibly embrace.

[6] Admittedly, all these happenings I have cited—from science, philosophy, art—make up a very selective list; this list could be expanded greatly; nevertheless even as it stands, these instances make up a body of "coincidence" so formidable that they must make us pause. When events run parallel this way, when they occur so densely together in time and in such diverse fields, they can no longer be considered as mere meaningless "coincidence" but as very meaningful symptoms; in this case symptoms that the West in its own depths begins to experience new things, begins in fact to experience its own opposite. In this new climate a concern with something like Zen Buddhism can no longer be taxed as idle exoticism, for it has to do with the practical daily bread of the spirit.

[7] The really somber paradox about all these changes is that they have happened in the deep and high parts of our culture, while in the areas

in between everything goes on as usual. Despite the discoveries of its artists, philosophers, theoretical scientists, the West, in its public and external life at any rate, is just as Western as ever, if not more so. Gadgets and traffic accumulate, the American way of life (or else the Russian) spreads all over the globe, the techniques for externalizing life become year by year more slick and clever. All of which may only show what a creature of contradictions Western man has become. And now that at last his technology has put in his hands the hydrogen bomb, this fragmented creature has the power to blow himself and his planet to bits. Plain common sense would seem to advise that he turn to look inward a little.

– II –

[8] None of the above considerations has to do with Zen itself. Or rather—to put it abruptly as Zen likes to do—Zen has nothing at all to do with them. They deal with the complicated abstractions of the intellect— philosophy, culture, science, and the rest—and what Zen seeks above all is the concrete and the simple that lie beyond the snarled tangles of intellectualization. Zen *is* the concrete itself. Zen eschews abstractions, or uses them only to get beyond them. Even when Zen declares against abstractions, it has to put the matter concretely: thus when the great Master Tokusan has his enlightenment, he does not merely say in pallid fashion that concepts are not enough; no, he burns all his philosophic texts, declaring, "All our understanding of the abstractions of philosophy is like a single hair in the vastness of space." Let the Western reader fasten upon this image and he will find it harder to miss the point. Or when another Master remarks on the difficulty of solving one of the Zen questions— which is equivalent to answering the riddle of existence itself—he does not merely say that it is difficult or so very very difficult that it is well-nigh impossible, but this: "It is like a mosquito trying to bite into an iron bull." The image lives because the image suggests the meaning beyond conceptualization.

[9] Now it is just this concreteness of expression, this extraordinary profusion of images and examples, that can make Zen most helpful to the Westerner, who in fact derives from a more highly abstract culture. But it would be a mistake for the Western reader to imagine that these are merely so many literary devices or adornments adopted by the Zen masters. On the contrary, the language of Zen is of the essence, the manner of expression is one with the matter. Zen expresses itself concretely because Zen is above all interested in facts not theories, in realities and not those pallid counters for reality which we know as concepts. "Fact" may suggest to the Western mind something merely quantitative or statistical—therefore also a lifeless and abstract thing. Zen wants, rather, the facts as living and concrete. In this sense, Zen might be described as Radical Intuitionism—if the Westerner wishes a handle by which to lay

hold of it. This does not mean that it is merely a philosophy of intuition like Bergson's, though it agrees with Bergson that the conceptualizing intellect does not reach reality; rather, it is radical intuition in the act itself. Radical Intuitionism means that Zen holds that thinking and sensing live, move, and have their being within the vital medium of intuition. We see with the two eyes only insofar as we are also seeing (though we may not know it) with the third eye—the eye of intuition. Hence, any sensory facts will do for Zen provided they serve to awaken the third eye, and we encounter in the Zen writings the most extraordinary incidents of illumination in connection with the most humble objects. In the end all language is pointing: we use language to point beyond language, beyond concepts to the concrete. The monk asks the Master, "How may I enter in the Way?," and the Master, pointing to the mountain spring, responds, "Do you hear the sound of that torrent? There you may enter." Another time Master and monk are walking upon the mountain, and the Master asks, "Do you smell the mountain laurel?" "Yes." "There, I have held nothing back from you."

[10] In its emphasis upon the living fact over the mere idea, Zen is true to the essential teaching of Buddha. Buddha cared very little for the philosophers; there were said to be already some 63 schools in existence in his time, and he had occasion to observe from their wrangling how imprisoned in the labyrinths of the intellect the human spirit can become. Thus Zen itself is not a philosophy (the Western reader must be warned here), though there lie behind it some of the great philosophies of Mahayana Buddhism. Though Buddha began by opposing the philosophers, nevertheless in the course of its history Buddhism evolved one of the greatest and most profound philosophies ever created. Is this a contradiction of the original spirit of the founder? No; for Buddhist philosophy is activated by an altogether different purpose from that of Western philosophy: Buddhism takes up philosophy only as a device to save the philosopher from his conceptual prison; its philosophy is, as it were, a non-philosophy, a philosophy to undo philosophy. A comparison of the mind of Buddha and Plato—probably the greatest intellects of East and West— may make us understand how sharply East and West diverge on this crucial point. For Plato philosophy is a discipline that leads us from the lower to the higher world, from the world of the senses to the world of ideas, to leave us abiding in this latter world as much as is humanly possible; for the Buddhist, philosophy should lead us beyond the intellect back into the one real world that was always there in its undivided wholeness. Zen presupposes this view of philosophy, but goes beyond the mere restatement of it to make actual use of it in its practical and concrete Chinese fashion.

[11] This passion for the living fact accounts for that quality in the Zen masters which must seem most amazing to the Westerner: their supreme

matter-of-factness. "What is the Tao (the way, the truth)?" asks the disciple. "Your everyday mind," replies the Master; and he goes on to amplify: "When I am hungry, I eat; when tired, I sleep." The disciple is puzzled, and asks whether this is not what everybody else does too. No, the Master replies; most people are never wholly in what they are doing; when eating, they may be absent-mindedly preoccupied with a thousand different fantasies; when sleeping, they are not sleeping. The supreme mark of the thoroughly integrated man is to be without a divided mind. This matter-of-fact spirit of Zen is expressed in another paradoxical statement: "Before you have studied Zen, mountains are mountains and rivers are rivers; while you are studying it, mountains are no longer mountains and rivers no longer rivers; but once you have had Enlightenment, mountains are once again mountains and rivers are rivers." The stories of their arduous struggles for Enlightenment teach us that this matter-of-fact spirit of the Zen masters is not a thing easily come by: they are indeed awesome figures who have crossed the mountains and rivers, floods and fires of the spirit in order to come back sole and whole to the most banal things of daily life. The nearest thing to this, so far as I know, that the West has produced is Kierkegaard's wonderful comparison of the Knight of Resignation and the Knight of Faith: the former all fidgets and romanticism, aspiring after the infinite but never at home with the finite, while the Knight of Faith sits so solidly in his existence that from without he looks as prosaic and matter-of-fact as a tax-collector. But this ideal of being in direct and unmediated relation to ordinary reality was something that poor Kierkegaard, who waged a feverish lifelong struggle against the mediating and devouring power of his intelligence, could only aspire after but never realize.

[¹²] In this striving for an unmediated relation to reality, as well as in its doctrine of an enlightenment (satori) that goes beyond reason, Zen would seem to be a form of Mysticism. But Zen is not mysticism as the West understands mysticism. The mystic, as defined by William James in *Varieties of Religious Experience* (James did not know about Zen), is one who pierces the veil of the natural or sensuous world in order to experience direct union with the higher reality. This formula holds for most of the great Western mystics from Plotinus onward, but it would not hold of Zen, which would reject this kind of mysticism as dualistic through and through, since it divides reality into lower and higher worlds. For Zen, higher and lower are one world; and in the records of Zen enlightenment which Suzuki sets before us there does not seem to occur anywhere the blurring of consciousness, the trancelike or semi-hallucinated state, which you will find among Western mystics. Even where it seems to move closest to mysticism, Zen remains supremely matter-of-fact. Nor is Zen to be confused with anything like pantheism, even though the Zen writings abound in statements that the Buddha-nature is to be found everywhere, in the dried up dirt-scraper, the cypress tree in the courtyard, etc. etc. Pantheism involves a division between the God who penetrates nature and nature itself as the phenomenal garment of God. But this too is a dualism that Zen leaves behind.

[13] Neither a philosophy, then, in the Western sense, nor a mysticism, not Pantheism and not Theism, Zen might seem to the reader at this point so much a matter of subtlety and nuance as to be devoid of all practical value. On the contrary; for the greatest contemporary tribute to the practicality of Zen comes not from philosophers or artists, but from two prominent *practicing* psychiatrists, C. G. Jung and Karen Horney, who became passionately interested in Zen for its therapeutic possibilities. Jung has written about Zen, and before her death Karen Horney visited Japan to observe the life of a Zen monastery at first hand. What attracted Jung to Zen was its remarkable pursuit of psychological wholeness. Horney saw something similar, but in terms of her own psychology: namely, the search for self-realization without either the false image of an idealized self ("We are saved such as we are," says the Zen master), or without the resigned and dependent clinging to external props like family, social group, or church (after his enlightenment the disciple slaps the Master Obaku's face, remarking "There is not, after all, very much in the Buddhism of Obaku," and the master is pleased, for the disciple shows he can now stand on his own two feet). Certainly the Zen masters, as we read of them in Suzuki's pages, give us the powerful impression of fully individuated individuals, carved out of one whole and solid block. What is most incredible to the Westerner is that this demand for the individuation of the disciple should be made by a *religion!* Western religions have always been willing to settle for less, very much less, from the believer—his filial obedience or docility, let him be a miserable psychological fragment otherwise. The reason is that Western religion has always placed the weight of emphasis upon the religious object outside the individual— God beyond the world, the Mosaic Law, the Church, the divine personality of Jesus. One can hardly imagine a Western religion producing a saying like the Zen Master's to his monks, "When you utter the name of Buddha, wash your mouth out." Zen is individualistic, and so iconoclastic and antinomian in its individualism that it will seem irreverent to many Westerners; but this is only because Zen wishes to strip the individual naked in order to return him to himself: in the end he cannot lean even upon the image of Buddha. Here precisely is the aspect of Zen Buddhism which is the greatest challenge to Western religions, and which needs to be studied most by us Westerners; for the march of our own history, as the great world of medieval religious images recedes ever further from our grasp and an increasingly secularized society engulfs us, has stripped Western man naked and left no rocklike security anywhere to lean upon. Here there looms before the frightened eyes of the Westerner what Bud-

dhism calls the Great Emptiness; but if he does not run away in fear, this great void may bloom with all manner of miracles, and heaven and earth, in consort once again, engender effortlessly all their ancient marvels.

[14] As to what Zen is, I leave the reader to discover in Suzuki's own pages that follow; what I have provided have been but a few negative warnings, signposts not to stray off the road, which come out of my own earlier failures of understanding. But there is one final misgiving I imagine taking shape in the reader's mind, because it has been taking shape in mine as I write, which needs to be faced before we are done; and it is this: Must not Buddhism forever remain an alien form to the Westerner? something he cannot appropriate and make his own? Are not the conditions that make ourselves and our lives what they are such that something like Zen could never be lived here? The question cannot be shirked; Zen itself would insist upon it, since Zen holds that it is not the abstract or bookish truth but the lived truth that counts. Indeed, the question looms so intensely before my mind that it seems almost to take on the imaginary body of some Zen master shaking his stick, threatening thirty blows and crying, "Speak quick, quick!" Well then, quickly: I would agree with Suzuki when he holds that Zen is the living fact in all religions East or West; or, a little more modestly, that Zen touches what is the living fact in all religions. For the readers of this book the question will hardly arise of becoming a Buddhist, but that does not lessen the importance of Zen to them: for however small the fragment of Zen that makes live contact with the Westerner, its influence is bound to work through, and he will never be quite the same again. In the beautiful words of the Master Hoyen: *When water is scooped up in the hands, the moon is reflected in them; when flowers are handled, the scent soaks into the robe.*

◄ COMMENT AND QUESTIONS ►

1. The author's vocabulary may cause some difficulty in understanding this selection. Use your dictionary to determine the meaning of any of the following words which are not clear to you in context: *dualistic* (paragraph 1); *Theism* (paragraph 2); *ineluctable, positivistic, finitude* (paragraph 3); *dichotomizing* (paragraph 4); *extroversion, primitivism* (paragraph 5); *externalizing* (paragraph 7); *eschews, conceptualization* (paragraph 8); *unmediated* (paragraph 11); *pantheism* (paragraph 12); *individuated, iconoclastic, antinomian* (paragraph 13).

2. What methods of paragraph development are used in paragraph 1? In this paragraph what particular expressions reveal Barrett's attitudes toward the dualisms of the Western tradition?

3. In paragraphs 2–7, how has the author made his organization clear?

4. Barrett says in paragraph 6 that the changes he has described cannot be regarded as mere coincidence but that they are meaningful symptoms. Does the material in paragraphs 3–5 seem to you to justify this conclusion? Explain.

5. In the first sentence of paragraph 7, what is meant by *the deep and high parts of our culture*? Why does Barrett call the paradox *somber*?

6. By the end of section I, in what ways has the author indicated, directly and indirectly, that Zen has something to say to the West?

7. In section II, what major characteristics of Zen emerge from Barrett's discussion? Which of the examples and comparisons in this section are most helpful to you in clarifying the nature of Zen?

8. Examine the writing in the last two sentences of paragraph 13. What traits of style do you observe?

9. Does Barrett answer the questions he raises in paragraph 14? Explain.

10. In the second section of his introduction, what further points does the author make about the importance of Zen for the West?

11. If you have read Aldous Huxley's essay on the Perennial Philosophy, do you think that the four fundamental doctrines of that philosophy are present in Zen?

THE
QUEST FOR VALUES:
SOME LATER VIEWS

ℰ

[23] *Ralph Waldo Emerson*: Self-Reliance

THE FOLLOWING essay is an assertion of the importance of the individual and a plea for independent, nonconformist thought and action. Many students will find its statements extreme, its advice almost impossible to put into practice in complex present-day society. The good reader, however, will bear in mind the historical context of the essay (the United States in 1840), and also, realizing that the colorful, dramatic overstatement is a technique of emphasis, will look through the sometimes-extravagant expression to the solid core of what the author has to say to any generation. Ralph Waldo Emerson (1803–1882) was an American essayist and poet, and a leader in the Transcendentalist movement of the nineteenth century. "Self-Reliance" was published in *Essays* in 1841.

[1] I read the other day some verses written by an eminent painter which were original and not conventional. The soul always hears an admonition in such lines, let the subject be what it may. The sentiment they instil is of more value than any thought they may contain. To believe your own thought, to believe that what is true for you in your private heart is true for all men,—that is genius. Speak your latent conviction, and it shall be the universal sense; for the inmost in due time becomes the outmost,—and our first thought is rendered back to us by the trumpets

of the Last Judgment. Familiar as the voice of the mind is to each, the highest merit we ascribe to Moses, Plato, and Milton is, that they set at naught books and traditions, and spoke not what men, but what *they* thought. A man should learn to detect and watch that gleam of light which flashes across his mind from within, more than the lustre of the firmament of bards and sages. Yet he dismisses without notice his thought, because it is his. In every work of genius we recognize our own rejected thoughts: they come back to us with a certain alienated majesty. Great works of art have no more affecting lesson for us than this. They teach us to abide by our spontaneous impression with good-humored inflexibility then most when the whole cry of voices is on the other side. Else tomorrow a stranger will say with masterly good sense precisely what we have thought and felt all the time, and we shall be forced to take with shame our own opinion from another.

[2] There is a time in every man's education when he arrives at the conviction that envy is ignorance; that imitation is suicide; that he must take himself for better, for worse, as his portion; that though the wide universe is full of good, no kernel of nourishing corn can come to him but through his toil bestowed on that plot of ground which is given to him to till. The power which resides in him is new in nature, and none but he knows what that is which he can do, nor does he know until he has tried. Not for nothing one face, one character, one fact, makes much impression on him, and another none. This sculpture in the memory is not without pre-established harmony. The eye was placed where one ray should fall, that it might testify of that particular ray. We but half express ourselves, and are ashamed of that divine idea which each of us represents. It may be safely trusted as proportionate and of good issues, so it be faithfully imparted, but God will not have his work made manifest by cowards. A man is relieved and gay when he has put his heart into his work and done his best; but what he has said or done otherwise, shall give him no peace. It is a deliverance which does not deliver. In the attempt his genius deserts him; no muse befriends; no invention, no hope.

[3] Trust thyself: every heart vibrates to that iron string. Accept the place the divine providence has found for you, the society of your contemporaries, the connection of events. Great men have always done so, and confided themselves childlike to the genius of their age, betraying their perception that the absolutely trustworthy was seated at their heart, working through their hands, predominating in all their being. And we are now men, and must accept in the highest mind the same transcendent destiny; and not minors and invalids in a protected corner, not cowards fleeing before a revolution, but guides, redeemers, and benefactors, obeying the Almighty effort, and advancing on Chaos and the Dark.

[4] What pretty oracles nature yields us on this text, in the face and behavior of children, babes, and even brutes! That divided and rebel

mind, that distrust of a sentiment because our arithmetic has computed the strength and means opposed to our purpose, these have not. Their mind being whole, their eye is as yet unconquered, and when we look in their faces, we are disconcerted. Infancy conforms to nobody: all conform to it, so that one babe commonly makes four or five out of the adults who prattle and play to it. So God has armed youth and puberty and manhood no less with its own piquancy and charm, and made it enviable and gracious and its claims not to be put by, if it will stand by itself. Do not think the youth has no force, because he cannot speak to you and me. Hark! in the next room his voice is sufficiently clear and emphatic. It seems he knows how to speak to his contemporaries. Bashful or bold, then, he will know how to make us seniors very unnecessary.

[5] The nonchalance of boys who are sure of a dinner, and would disdain as much as a lord to do or say aught to conciliate one, is the healthy attitude of human nature. A boy is in the parlor what the pit is in the playhouse; independent, irresponsible, looking out from his corner on such people and facts as pass by, he tries and sentences them on their merits, in the swift, summary way of boys, as good, bad, interesting, silly, eloquent, troublesome. He cumbers himself never about consequences, about interests; he gives an independent, genuine verdict. You must court him: he does not court you. But the man is, as it were, clapped into jail by his consciousness. As soon as he has once acted or spoken with *éclat*, he is a committed person, watched by the sympathy or the hatred of hundreds, whose affections must now enter into his account. There is no Lethe for this. Ah, that he could pass again into his neutrality! Who can thus avoid all pledges, and having observed, observe again from the same unaffected, unbiassed, unbribable, unaffrighted innocence, must always be formidable. He would utter opinions on all passing affairs, which being seen to be not private, but necessary, would sink like darts into the ear of men, and put them in fear.

[6] These are the voices which we hear in solitude, but they grow faint and inaudible as we enter into the world. Society everywhere is in conspiracy against the manhood of every one of its members. Society is a joint-stock company, in which the members agree, for the better securing of his bread to each shareholder, to surrender the liberty and culture of the eater. The virtue in most request is conformity. Self-reliance is its aversion. It loves not realities and creators, but names and customs.

[7] Whoso would be a man must be a non-conformist. He who would gather immortal palms must not be hindered by the name of goodness, but must explore if it be goodness. Nothing is at last sacred but the integrity of your own mind. Absolve you to yourself, and you shall have the suffrage of the world. I remember an answer which when quite young I was prompted to make to a valued adviser, who was wont to importune

me with the dear old doctrines of the church. On my saying, "What have I to do with the sacredness of traditions, if I live wholly from within?" my friend suggested: "But these impulses may be from below, not from above." I replied: "They do not seem to me to be such; but if I am the Devil's child, I will live then from the Devil." No law can be sacred to me but that of my nature. Good and bad are but names very readily transferable to that or this; the only right is what is after my constitution, the only wrong what is against it. A man is to carry himself in the presence of all opposition, as if everything were titular and ephemeral but him. I am ashamed to think how easily we capitulate to badges and names, to large societies and dead institutions. Every decent and well-spoken individual affects and sways me more than is right. I ought to go upright and vital, and speak the rude truth in all ways. If malice and vanity wear the coat of philanthropy, shall that pass? If an angry bigot assumes this bountiful cause of Abolition, and comes to me with his last news from Barbadoes, why should I not say to him: "Go love thy infant; love thy wood-chopper: be good-natured and modest: have that grace; and never varnish your hard, uncharitable ambition with this incredible tenderness for black folk a thousand miles off. Thy love afar is spite at home." Rough and graceless would be such greeting, but truth is handsomer than the affectation of love. Your goodness must have some edge to it,—else it is none. The doctrine of hatred must be preached as the counteraction of the doctrine of love when that pules and whines. I shun father and mother and wife and brother, when my genius calls me. I would write on the lintels of the door-post, *Whim*. I hope it is somewhat better than whim at last, but we cannot spend the day in explanation. Expect me not to show cause why I seek or why I exclude company. Then, again, do not tell me, as a good man did to-day, of my obligation to put all poor men in good situations. Are they *my* poor? I tell thee, thou foolish philanthropist, that I grudge the dollar, the dime, the cent, I give to such men as do not belong to me and to whom I do not belong. There is a class of persons to whom by all spiritual affinity I am bought and sold; for them I will go to prison, if need be; but your miscellaneous popular charities; the education at college of fools; the building of meeting-houses to the vain end to which many now stand; alms to sots; and the thousand-fold Relief Societies;—though I confess with shame I sometimes succumb and give the dollar, it is a wicked dollar which by and by I shall have the manhood to withhold. . . .

[8] What I must do is all that concerns me, not what the people think. This rule, equally arduous in actual and in intellectual life, may serve for the whole distinction between greatness and meanness. It is the harder, because you will always find those who think they know what is your duty better than you know it. It is easy in the world to live after the world's

opinion; it is easy in solitude to live after our own; but the great man is he who in the midst of the crowd keeps with perfect sweetness the independence of solitude.

[9] The objection to conforming to usages that have become dead to you is, that it scatters your force. It loses your time and blurs the impression of your character. If you maintain a dead church, contribute to a dead Bible society, vote with a great party either for the government or against it, spread your table like base housekeepers,—under all these screens I have difficulty to detect the precise man you are. And, of course, so much force is withdrawn from your proper life. But do your work, and I shall know you. Do your work, and you shall reinforce yourself. A man must consider what a blind-man's-buff is this game of conformity. If I know your sect, I anticipate your argument. I hear a preacher announce for his text and topic the expediency of one of the institutions of his church. Do I not know beforehand that not possibly can he say a new and spontaneous word? Do I not know that, with all this ostentation of examining the grounds of the institution, he will do no such thing? Do I not know that he is pledged to himself not to look but at one side,—the permitted side, not as a man, but as a parish minister? He is a retained attorney, and these airs of the bench are the emptiest affectation. Well, most men have bound their eyes with one or another handkerchief, and attached themselves to some one of these communities of opinion. This conformity makes them not false in a few particulars, authors of a few lies, but false in all particulars. Their every truth is not quite true. Their two is not the real two, their four is not the real four; so that every word they say chagrins us, and we know not where to begin to set them right. Meantime nature is not slow to equip us in the prison-uniform of the party to which we adhere. We come to wear one cut of face and figure, and acquire by degrees the gentlest asinine expression. There is a mortifying experience in particular, which does not fail to wreak itself also in the general history; I mean "the foolish face of praise," the forced smile which we put on in company where we do not feel at ease in answer to conversation which does not interest us. The muscles, not spontaneously moved, but moved by a low usurping wilfulness, grow tight about the outline of the face with the most disagreeable sensation.

[10] For non-conformity the world whips you with its displeasure. And therefore a man must know how to estimate a sour face. The by-standers look askance on him in the public street or in the friend's parlor. If this aversion had its origin in contempt and resistance like his own, he might well go home with a sad countenance; but the sour faces of the multitude, like their sweet faces, have no deep cause, but are put on and off as the wind blows and a newspaper directs. Yet is the discontent of the multitude more formidable than that of the senate and the college. It is easy enough for a firm man who knows the world to brook the rage of the

cultivated classes. Their rage is decorous and prudent, for they are timid as being very vulnerable themselves. But when to their feminine rage the indignation of the people is added, when the ignorant and the poor are aroused, when the unintelligent brute force that lies at the bottom of society is made to growl and mow, it needs the habit of magnanimity and religion to treat it godlike as a trifle of no concernment.

[11] The other terror that scares us from self-trust is our consistency; a reverence for our past act or word, because the eyes of others have no other data for computing our orbit than our past acts, and we are loath to disappoint them.

[12] But why should you keep your head over your shoulder? Why drag about this corpse of your memory, lest you contradict somewhat you have stated in this or that public place? Suppose you should contradict yourself; what then? It seems to be a rule of wisdom never to rely on your memory alone, scarcely even in acts of pure memory, but to bring the past for judgment into the thousand-eyed present, and live ever in a new day. In your metaphysics you have denied personality to the Deity: yet when the devout motions of the soul come, yield to them heart and life, though they should clothe God with shape and color. Leave your theory, as Joseph his coat in the hand of the harlot, and flee.

[13] A foolish consistency is the hobgoblin of little minds, adored by little statesmen and philosophers and divines. With consistency a great soul has simply nothing to do. He may as well concern himself with his shadow on the wall. Speak what you think now in hard words and to-morrow speak what to-morrow thinks in hard words again, though it contradict everything you said to-day.—"Ah, so you shall be sure to be misunderstood?"—Is it so bad, then, to be misunderstood? Pythagoras was misunderstood, and Socrates, and Jesus, and Luther, and Copernicus, and Galileo, and Newton, and every pure and wise spirit that ever took flesh. To be great is to be misunderstood.

[14] I suppose no man can violate his nature. All the sallies of his will are rounded in by the law of his being, as the inequalities of Andes and Himmaleh are insignificant in the curve of the sphere. Nor does it matter how you gauge and try him. A character is like an acrostic or Alexandrian stanza;—read it forward, backward, or across, it still spells the same thing. In this pleasing, contrite wood-life which God allows me, let me record day by day my honest thought without prospect or retrospect, and, I cannot doubt, it will be found symmetrical, though I mean it not and see it not. My book should smell of pines and resound with the hum of insects. The swallow over my window should interweave that thread or straw he carries in his bill into my web also. We pass for what we are. Character teaches above our wills. Men imagine that they communicate their virtue or vice only by overt actions, and do not see that virtue or vice emit a breath every moment.

[¹⁵] There will be an agreement in whatever variety of actions, so they be each honest and natural in their hour. For of one will, the actions will be harmonious, however unlike they seem. These varieties are lost sight of at a little distance, at a little height of thought. One tendency unites them all. The voyage of the best ship is a zigzag line of a hundred tacks. See the line from a sufficient distance, and it straightens itself to the average tendency. Your genuine action will explain itself, and will explain your other genuine actions. Your conformity explains nothing. Act singly, and what you have already done singly will justify you now. . . .

[¹⁶] I hope in these days we have heard the last of conformity and consistency. Let the words be gazetted and ridiculous henceforward. Instead of the gong for dinner, let us hear a whistle from the Spartan fife. Let us never bow and apologize more. A great man is coming to eat at my house. I do not wish to please him; I wish that he should wish to please me. I will stand here for humanity, and though I would make it kind, I would make it true. Let us affront and reprimand the smooth mediocrity and squalid contentment of the times, and hurl in the face of custom, and trade, and office, the fact which is the upshot of all history, that there is a great responsible Thinker and Actor working wherever a man works; that a true man belongs to no other time or place, but is the centre of things. Where he is, there is nature. He measures you, and all men, and all events. Ordinarily, everybody in society reminds us of somewhat else, or of some other person. Character, reality, reminds you of nothing else; it takes place of the whole creation. The man must be so much, that he must make all circumstances indifferent. Every true man is a cause, a country, and an age; requires infinite spaces and numbers and time fully to accomplish his design;—and posterity seems to follow his steps as a train of clients. A man Cæsar is born, and for ages after we have a Roman Empire. Christ is born, and millions of minds so grow and cleave to his genius, that he is confounded with virtue and the possible of man. An institution is the lengthened shadow of one man; as Monachism, of the Hermit Antony; the Reformation, of Luther; Quakerism, of Fox; Methodism, of Wesley; Abolition, of Clarkson. Scipio, Milton called "the height of Rome"; and all history resolves itself very easily into the biography of a few stout and earnest persons.

[¹⁷] Let a man then know his worth, and keep things under his feet. Let him not peep or steal, or skulk up and down with the air of a charity-boy, a bastard, or an interloper, in the world which exists for him. But the man in the street, finding no worth in himself which corresponds to the force which built a tower or sculptured a marble god, feels poor when he looks on these. To him a palace, a statue, or a costly book have an alien and forbidding air, much like a gay equipage, and seem to say like that, "Who are you sir?" Yet they all are his suitors for his notice, petitioners to his faculties that they will come out and take possession. The picture waits for my verdict: it is not to command me, but I am to settle its claims to praise. That popular fable of the sot who was picked up dead drunk in the street, carried to the duke's house, washed and dressed and laid in the duke's bed, and, on his waking, treated with all obsequious ceremony like the duke, and assured that he had been insane, owes its popularity to the fact, that it symbolizes so well the state of man, who is in the world a sort of sot, but now and then wakes up, exercises his reason and finds himself a true prince.

[18] Our reading is mendicant and sycophantic. In history, our imagination plays us false. Kingdom and lordship, power and estate, are a gaudier vocabulary than private John and Edward in a small house and common day's work; but the things of life are the same to both; the sum total of both are the same. Why all this deference to Alfred, and Scanderbeg, and Gustavus? Suppose they were virtuous; did they wear out virtue? As great a stake depends on your private act to-day, as followed their public and renowned steps. When private men shall act with original views, the lustre will be transferred from the actions of kings to those of gentlemen. . . .

[19] The magnetism which all original action exerts is explained when we inquire the reason of self-trust. Who is the Trustee? What is the aboriginal Self, on which a universal reliance may be grounded? What is the nature and power of that science-baffling star, without parallax, without calculable elements, which shoots a ray of beauty even into trivial and impure actions, if the least mark of independence appear? The inquiry leads us to that source, at once the essence of genius, of virtue, and of life, which we call Spontaneity or Instinct. We denote this primary wisdom as Intuition, whilst all later teachings are tuitions. In that deep force, the last fact behind which analysis cannot go, all things find their common origin. For, the sense of being which in calm hours rises, we know not how, in the soul, is not diverse from things, from space, from light, from time, from man, but one with them, and proceeds obviously from the same source whence their life and being also proceed. We first share the life by which things exist, and afterwards see them as appearances in nature, and forget that we have shared their cause. Here is the fountain of action and of thought. Here are the lungs of that inspiration which giveth man wisdom, and which cannot be denied without impiety and atheism. We lie in the lap of immense intelligence, which makes us receivers of its truth and organs of its activity. When we discern justice, when we discern truth, we do nothing of ourselves, but allow a passage to its beams. If we ask whence this comes, if we seek to pry into the soul that causes, all philosophy is at fault. Its presence or its absence is all we can affirm. Every man discriminates between the voluntary acts of his mind, and his involuntary perceptions, and knows that to his involuntary perceptions a perfect faith is due. He may err in the expression of them, but he knows

that these things are so, like day and night, not to be disputed. My wilful actions and acquisitions are but roving;—the idlest revery, the faintest native emotion, command my curiosity and respect. Thoughtless people contradict as readily the statements of perceptions as of opinions, or rather much more readily; for, they do not distinguish between perception and notion. They fancy that I choose to see this or that thing. But perception is not whimsical, it is fatal. If I see a trait, my children will see it after me, and in course of time, all mankind,—although it may chance that no one has seen it before me. For my perception of it is as much a fact as the sun.

[20] The relations of the soul to the divine spirit are so pure, that it is profane to seek to interpose helps. It must be that when God speaketh he should communicate, not one thing, but all things; should fill the world with his voice; should scatter forth light, nature, time, souls, from the centre of the present thought; and new date and new create the whole. Whenever a mind is simple, and receives a divine wisdom, old things pass away,—means, teachers, texts, temples, fall; it lives now, and absorbs past and future into the present hour. All things are made sacred by relation to it,—one as much as another. All things are dissolved to their centre by their cause, and, in the universal miracle, petty and particular miracles disappear. If, therefore, a man claims to know and speak of God, and carries you backward to the phraseology of some old mouldered nation in another country, in another world, believe him not. Is the acorn better than the oak which is its fulness and completion? Is the parent better than the child into whom he has cast his ripened being? Whence, then, this worship of the past? The centuries are conspirators against the sanity and authority of the soul. Time and space are but physiological colors which the eye makes, but the soul is light; where it is, is day; where it was, is night; and history is an impertinence and an injury, if it be anything more than a cheerful apologue or parable of my being and becoming.

[21] Man is timid and apologetic; he is no longer upright; he dares not say, "I think," "I am," but quotes some saint or sage. He is ashamed before the blade of grass or the blowing rose. These roses under my window make no reference to former roses or to better ones; they are for what they are; they exist with God to-day. There is no time to them. There is simply the rose; it is perfect in every moment of its existence. Before a leaf-bud has burst, its whole life acts; in the full-blown flower there is no more; in the leafless root there is no less. Its nature is satisfied, and it satisfies nature, in all moments alike. But man postpones or remembers; he does not live in the present, but with reverted eye laments the past, or, heedless of the riches that surround him, stands on tiptoe to foresee the future. He cannot be happy and strong until he too lives with nature in the present, above time.

[22] This should be plain enough. Yet see what strong intellects dare not

yet hear God himself, unless he speak the phraseology of I know not what David, or Jeremiah, or Paul. We shall not always set so great a price on a few texts, on a few lives. We are like children who repeat by rote the sentences of grandames and tutors, and, as they grow older, of the men of talents and character they chance to see,—painfully recollecting the exact words they spoke; afterwards, when they come into the point of view which those had who uttered these sayings, they understand them, and are willing to let the words go; for, at any time, they can use words as good when occasion comes. If we live truly, we shall see truly. It is as easy for the strong man to be strong, as it is for the weak to be weak. When we have new perception, we shall gladly disburden the memory of its hoarded treasures as old rubbish. When a man lives with God, his voice shall be as sweet as the murmur of the brook and the rustle of the corn.

[23] And now at last the highest truth on this subject remains unsaid: probably cannot be said; for all that we say is the far-off remembering of the intuition. That thought, by what I can now nearest approach to say it, is this. When good is near you, when you have life in yourself, it is not by any known or accustomed way; you shall not discern the footprints of any other; you shall not see the face of man; you shall not hear any name; the way, the thought, the good, shall be wholly strange and new. It shall exclude example and experience. You take the way from man, not to man. All persons that ever existed are its forgotten ministers. Fear and hope are alike beneath it. There is somewhat low even in hope. In the hour of vision, there is nothing that can be called gratitude, nor properly joy. The soul raised over passion beholds identity and eternal causation, perceives the self-existence of Truth and Right, and calms itself with knowing that all things go well. Vast spaces of nature, the Atlantic Ocean, the South Sea,—long intervals of time, years, centuries,—are of no account. This which I think and feel underlay every former state of life and circumstances, as it does underlie my present, and what is called life, and what is called death.

[24] Life only avails, not the having lived. Power ceases in the instant of repose; it resides in the moment of transition from a past to a new state, in the shooting of the gulf, in the darting to an aim. This one fact the world hates, that the soul *becomes;* for that forever degrades the past, turns all riches to poverty, all reputation to a shame, confounds the saint with the rogue, shoves Jesus and Judas equally aside. Why, then, do we prate of self-reliance? Inasmuch as the soul is present, there will be power not confident but agent. To talk of reliance is a poor external way of speaking. Speak rather of that which relies, because it works and is. Who has more obedience than I masters me, though he should not raise his finger. Round him I must revolve by the gravitation of spirits. We fancy it rhetoric, when we speak of eminent virtue. We do not yet see that virtue is Height, and that a man or a company of men, plastic and per-

meable to principles, by the law of nature must overpower and ride all cities, nations, kings, rich men, poets, who are not.

[25] This is the ultimate fact which we so quickly reach on this, as on every topic, the resolution of all into the ever-blessed ONE. Self-existence is the attribute of the Supreme Cause, and it constitutes the measure of good by the degree in which it enters into all lower forms. All things real are so by so much virtue as they contain. Commerce, husbandry, hunting, whaling, war, eloquence, personal weight, are somewhat, and engage my respect as examples of its presence and impure action. I see the same law working in nature for conservation and growth. Power is in nature the essential measure of right. Nature suffers nothing to remain in her kingdoms which cannot help itself. The genesis and maturation of a planet, its poise and orbit, the bended tree recovering itself from the strong wind, the vital resources of every animal and vegetable, are demonstrations of the self-sufficing, and, therefore, self-relying soul.

[26] Thus all concentrates; let us not rove; let us sit at home with the cause. Let us stun and astonish the intruding rabble of men and books and institutions, by a simple declaration of the divine fact. Bid the invaders take the shoes from off their feet, for God is here within. Let our simplicity judge them, and our docility to our own law demonstrate the poverty of nature and fortune beside our native riches. . . .

[27] The populace think that your rejection of popular standards is a rejection of all standard, and mere antinomianism; and the bold sensualist will use the name of philosophy to gild his crimes. But the law of consciousness abides. There are two confessionals, in one or the other of which we must be shriven. You may fulfil your round of duties by clearing yourself in the *direct*, or in the *reflex* way. Consider whether you have satisfied your relations to father, mother, cousin, neighbor, town, cat, and dog; whether any of these can upbraid you. But I may also neglect this reflex standard, and absolve me to myself. I have my own stern claims and perfect circle. It denies the name of duty to many offices that are called duties. But if I can discharge its debts, it enables me to dispense with the popular code. If any one imagines that this law is lax, let him keep its commandment one day.

[28] And truly it demands something godlike in him who has cast off the common motives of humanity, and has ventured to trust himself for a taskmaster. High be his heart, faithful his will, clear his sight, that he may in good earnest be doctrine, society, law, to himself, that a simple purpose may be to him as strong as iron necessity is to others!

[29] If any man consider the present aspects of what is called by distinction *society*, he will see the need of these ethics. The sinew and heart of man seem to be drawn out, and we are become timorous, desponding whimperers. We are afraid of truth, afraid of fortune, afraid of death, and afraid of each other. Our age yields no great and perfect persons. We

want men and women who shall renovate life and our social state, but we see that most natures are insolvent, cannot satisfy their own wants, have an ambition out of all proportion to their practical force, and do lean and beg day and night continually. Our housekeeping is mendicant, our arts, our occupations, our marriages, our religion, we have not chosen, but society has chosen for us. We are parlor soldiers. We shun the rugged battle of fate, where strength is born.

[30] If our young men miscarry in their first enterprises, they lose all heart. If the young merchant fails, men say he is *ruined*. If the finest genius studies at one of our colleges, and is not installed in an office within one year afterwards in the cities or suburbs of Boston or New York, it seems to his friends and to himself that he is right in being disheartened, and in complaining the rest of his life. A sturdy lad from New Hampshire or Vermont, who in turn tries all the professions, who *teams it, farms it, peddles*, keeps a school, preaches, edits a newspaper, goes to Congress, buys a township, and so forth, in successive years, and always, like a cat, falls on his feet, is worth a hundred of these city dolls. He walks abreast with his days, and feels no shame in not "studying a profession," for he does not postpone his life, but lives already. He has not one chance, but a hundred chances. Let a Stoic open the resources of man, and tell men they are not leaning willows, but can and must detach themselves; that with the exercise of self-trust, new powers shall appear; that a man is the word made flesh, born to shed healing to the nations, that he should be ashamed of our compassion, and that the moment he acts from himself, tossing the laws, the books, idolatries, and customs out of the window, we pity him no more, but thank and revere him,—and that teacher shall restore the life of man to splendor, and make his name dear to all history.

[31] It is easy to see that a greater self-reliance must work a revolution in all the offices and relations of men; in their religion; in their education; in their pursuits; their modes of living; their associations; in their property; in their speculative views.

1. In what prayers do men allow themselves! That which they call a holy office is not so much as brave and manly. Prayer looks abroad and asks for some foreign addition to come through some foreign virtue, and loses itself in endless mazes of natural and supernatural, and mediatorial and miraculous. Prayer that craves a particular commodity,—anything less than all good,—is vicious. Prayer is the contemplation of the facts of life from the highest point of view. It is the soliloquy of a beholding and jubilant soul. It is the spirit of God pronouncing his works good. But prayer as a means to effect a private end is meanness and theft. It supposes dualism and not unity in nature and consciousness. As soon as the man is at one with God, he will not beg. He will then see prayer in all action. The prayer of the farmer kneeling in his field to weed it, the prayer of the rower kneeling with the stroke of his oar, are true prayers

heard throughout nature, though for cheap ends. Caratach, in Fletcher's *Bonduca,* when admonished to inquire the mind of the god Audate, replies,—

> His hidden meaning lies in our endeavors;
> Our valors are our best gods.

[32] Another sort of false prayers are our regrets. Discontent is the want of self-reliance: it is infirmity of will. Regret calamities, if you can thereby help the sufferer: if not, attend your own work, and already the evil begins to be repaired. Our sympathy is just as base. We come to them who weep foolishly, and sit down and cry for company, instead of imparting to them truth and health in rough electric shocks, putting them once more in communciation with their own reason. The secret of fortune is joy in our hands. Welcome evermore to gods and men is the self-helping man. For him all doors are flung wide: him all tongues greet, all honors crown, all eyes follow with desire. Our love goes out to him and embraces him, because he did not need it. We solicitously and apologeti-cally caress and celebrate him, because he held on his way and scorned our disapprobation. The gods love him because men hated him. "To the persevering mortal," said Zoroaster, "the blessed Immortals are swift."

[33] As men's prayers are a disease of the will, so are their creeds a disease of the intellect. They say with those foolish Israelites, "Let not God speak to us lest we die. Speak thou, speak any man with us, and we will obey." Everywhere I am hindered of meeting God in my brother, because he has shut his own temple doors, and recites fables merely of his brother's or his brother's brother's God. Every new mind is a new classification. If it prove a mind of uncommon activity and power, a Locke, a Lavoisier, a Hutton, a Bentham, a Fourier, it imposes its classi-fication on other men, and lo! a new system. In proportion to the depth of the thought, and so to the number of the objects it touches and brings within reach of the pupil, is his complacency. But chiefly is this apparent in creeds and churches, which are also classifications of some powerful mind acting on the elemental thought of duty, and man's relation to the Highest. Such is Calvinism, Quakerism, Swedenborgism. The pupil takes the same delight in subordinating everything to the new terminology, as a girl who has just learned botany in seeing a new earth and new seasons thereby. It will happen for a time, that the pupil will find his intellectual power has grown by the study of his master's mind. But in all unbalanced minds, the classification is idolized, passes for the end, and not for a speedily exhaustible means, so that the walls of the system blend to their eye in the remote horizon with the walls of the universe; the luminaries of heaven seem to them hung on the arch their master built. They cannot imagine how you aliens have any right to see,—how you can see; "it must be somehow that you stole the light from us." They do

not yet perceive, that light, unsystematic, indomitable, will break into any cabin, even into theirs. Let them chirp awhile and call it their own. If they are honest and do well, presently their neat new pinfold will be too strait and low, will crack, will lean, will rot and vanish, and the immortal light, all young and joyful, million-orbed, million-colored, will beam over the universe as on the first morning.

2. It is for want of self-reliance that the superstition of Travelling, whose idols are Italy, England, Egypt, retains its fascination for all educated Americans. They who made England, Italy, or Greece venerable in the imagination did so by sticking fast where they were, like an axis of the earth. In manly hours, we feel that duty is our place. The soul is no traveller; the wise man stays at home, and when his necessities, his duties, on any occasion, call him from his house, or into foreign lands, he is at home still, and shall make men sensible, by the expression of his countenance, that he goes the missionary of wisdom and virtue, and visits cities and men like a sovereign, and not like an interloper or a valet.

[34] I have no churlish objection to the circumnavigation of the globe, for the purposes of art, of study, and benevolence, so that the man is first domesticated or does not go abroad with the hope of finding somewhat greater than he knows. He who travels to be amused, or to get somewhat which he does not carry, travels away from himself, and grows old even in youth among old things. In Thebes, in Palmyra, his will and mind have become old and dilapidated as they. He carries ruins to ruins.

[35] Travelling is a fool's paradise. Our first journeys discover to us the indifference of places. At home I dream that at Naples, at Rome, I can be intoxicated with beauty, and lose my sadness. I pack my trunk, embrace my friends, embark on the sea, and at last wake up in Naples, and there beside me is the stern fact, the sad self, unrelenting, identical, that I fled from. I seek the Vatican, and the palaces. I affect to be intoxicated with sights and suggestions, but I am not intoxicated. My giant goes with me wherever I go.

3. But the rage of travelling is a symptom of a deeper unsoundness affecting the whole intellectual action. The intellect is vagabond, and our system of education fosters restlessness. Our minds travel when our bodies are forced to stay at home. We imitate; and what is imitation but the travelling of the mind? Our houses are built with foreign taste; our shelves are garnished with foreign ornaments; our opinions, our tastes, our faculties, lean, and follow the Past and the Distant. The soul created the arts wherever they have flourished. It was in his own mind that the artist sought his model. It was an application of his own thought to the thing to be done and the conditions to be observed. And why need we copy the Doric or the Gothic model? Beauty, convenience, grandeur of thought, and quaint expression are as near to us as to any, and if the American artist will study with hope and love the precise thing to be done by him,

considering the climate, the soil, the length of the day, the wants of the people, the habit and form of the government, he will create a house in which all these will find themselves fitted, and taste and sentiment will be satisfied also.

[36] Insist on yourself; never imitate. Your own gift you can present every moment with the cumulative force of a whole life's cultivation; but of the adopted talent of another, you have only an extemporaneous, half possession. That which each can do best, none but his Maker can teach him. No man yet knows what it is, nor can, till that person has exhibited it. Where is the master who could have taught Shakespeare? Where is the master who could have instructed Franklin, or Washington, or Bacon, or Newton? Every great man is a unique. The Scipionism of Scipio is precisely that part he could not borrow. Shakespeare will never be made by the study of Shakespeare. Do that which is assigned you, and you cannot hope too much or dare too much. There is at this moment for you an utterance brave and grand as that of the colossal chisel of Phidias, or trowel of the Egyptians, or the pen of Moses, or Dante, but different from all these. Not possibly will the soul all rich, all eloquent, with thousand-cloven tongue, deign to repeat itself; but if you can hear what these patriarchs say, surely you can reply to them in the same pitch of voice; for the ear and the tongue are two organs of one nature. Abide in the simple and noble regions of thy life, obey thy heart, and thou shalt reproduce the Foreworld again.

4. As our Religion, our Education, our Art look abroad, so does our spirit of society. All men plume themselves on the improvement of society, and no man improves. . . .

[37] The civilized man has built a coach, but has lost the use of his feet. He is supported on crutches, but lacks so much support of muscle. He has a fine Geneva watch, but he fails of the skill to tell the hour by the sun. A Greenwich nautical almanac he has, and so being sure of the information when he wants it, the man in the street does not know a star in the sky. The solstice he does not observe, the equinox he knows as little; and the whole bright calendar of the year is without a dial in his mind. His note-books impair his memory; his libraries overload his wit; the insurance office increases the number of accidents; and it may be a question whether machinery does not encumber; whether we have not lost by refinement some energy, by a Christianity intrenched in establishments and forms, some vigor of wild virtue. For every Stoic was a Stoic; but in Christendom where is the Christian? . . .

[38] The reliance on Property, including the reliance on governments which protect it, is the want of self-reliance. Men have looked away from themselves and at things so long, that they have come to esteem the religious, learned, and civil institutions as guards of property, and they deprecate assaults on these, because they feel them to be assaults on

property. They measure their esteem of each other by what each has, and
not by what each is. But a cultivated man becomes ashamed of his property, out of new respect for his nature. Especially he hates what he has,
if he see that it is accidental,—came to him by inheritance, or gift, or
crime; then he feels that it is not having; it does not belong to him, has
no root in him, and merely lies there, because no revolution or no robber
takes it away. But that which a man is, does always by necessity acquire,
and what the man acquires is living property, which does not wait the
beck of rulers, or mobs, or revolutions, or fire, or storm, or bankruptcies,
but perpetually renews itself wherever the man breathes. . . .

[39] Nothing can bring you peace but yourself. Nothing can bring you
peace but the triumph of principles.

---◄ COMMENT AND QUESTIONS ►---

In thinking about this essay, it may be helpful to know something of the philosophical and literary movement called Transcendentalism, for which Emerson
was an important spokesman. Not a systematic philosophy, Transcendentalism
was compounded of many elements, including Platonism, Hebraism and Christianity, and ideas from Eastern philosophies and religions. Its tenets and expression differed with different writers, but Transcendentalists held in common two
closely related beliefs: that knowledge transcends the senses ("We denote this
primary wisdom as Intuition," Emerson says), and that an embracing divinity
dwells in all things—in everything in nature and in the individual souls of men.
Man could feel the indwelling God in the laws and beauty of nature, and he
could fulfill his part in the divine unity by listening to and acting on the prompt-
ings of his individual soul which was one with the world-soul. Optimism, self-
trust, and reliance on intuition rather than on outside authority and tradition
were therefore natural corollaries of the Transcendentalist philosophy. To it
Emerson added his own boundless faith in the worth and potentiality of each
individual, and in the individual genius of this country.

1. Emerson says: "There is a time in every man's education when he arrives
   at the conviction that envy is ignorance; that imitation is suicide; that he
   must take himself for better, for worse, as his portion. . . ." Is Emerson
   advocating complacency, acceptance of ourselves as we are, without striving for improvement? Explain.
2. According to Emerson, what two terrors frighten us from self-trust? Where
   in the essay do you find the clearest statements of the essential reason for
   self-reliance?
3. Emerson frequently acted with the independence and indifference to
   public opinion advocated in "Self-Reliance." At the same time, he was
   personally kind, gentle, courteous, sociable, generous and helpful to others.

Examine paragraph 7. Does it sound harsh and unconcerned for the welfare of others? Does it reveal the generous and social side of Emerson? How would you summarize the meaning of the paragraph?

4. "Self-Reliance," like much of Emerson's writing, is loosely organized; we have cut the essay without injury to the continuity of ideas, and it would be possible in a number of places to rearrange the paragraphs without loss. Emerson's power lies not in the organization and structure of the whole essay, but in separate paragraphs, and chiefly in pithy, picturesque, hard-hitting individual sentences. Vivid concrete language, often figurative, accounts for much of the quality of his style. Analyze the writing in paragraphs 12–13, 21, and 34–35, particularly for concrete language and techniques of emphasis. Point out other passages in the essay in which the phrasing is memorable.

5. Explain the statement in paragraph 24: "To talk of reliance is a poor external way of speaking. Speak rather of that which relies, because it works and is."

6. At the beginning of paragraph 31 Emerson says that a greater self-reliance must work a revolution in all the offices and relations of men. What particular changes does he consider desirable? Do you agree that the changes would be desirable?

7. We have heard a great deal in recent years about conformity and nonconformity in modern society. What kinds of nonconformity do you think that Emerson would approve? What kinds would he probably not approve?

8. A college student, after reading this essay, remarked that Emerson was recommending an easy, self-indulgent sort of life—just following your impulses and doing as you please. Emerson did not so regard the principles of self-reliance; he speaks of the "stern duties" imposed by being true to one's own nature, and says, "If any one imagines that this law is lax, let him keep its commandments one day." What would you do—precisely how would you act—if you followed the commandments of self-reliance for a day? Would it be easy?

9. Think about the following quotations from "Self-Reliance." Which ones seem to you wholly true or sound? Which ones partially true? With which ones can you not agree?

In every work of genius we recognize our own rejected thoughts.

We but half express ourselves, and are ashamed of the divine idea which each of us represents.

Society everywhere is in conspiracy against the manhood of every one of its members.

Whoso would be a man must be a non-conformist.

What I must do is all that concerns me, not what the people think.

A foolish consistency is the hobgoblin of little minds, adored by little statesmen and philosophers and divines.

As men's prayers are a disease of the will, so are their creeds a disease of the intellect.

Travelling is a fool's paradise.

Insist on yourself; never imitate.

10. It has sometimes been said that Emerson, with his faith in the individual, ignored the realities of human nature: there are people who, following their natural bent or the law of their own nature, would not fulfill a divine idea but would be injurious to themselves and to others. What is your reaction to this criticism of Emerson's philosophy?

11. If you have read the *Apology,* compare the ideas of Socrates and of Emerson. How do they agree and disagree in their attitudes toward conventional opinion, the principles by which men should be guided, and the source of wisdom?

[24] *Henry David Thoreau*: from Walden

HENRY DAVID THOREAU (1817–1862) was a friend of Emerson, influenced by Emerson's doctrine of self-reliance and by the Transcendentalist attitude toward nature.[1] Believing that "the mass of men lead lives of quiet desperation," that they are slaves to their property, and are distracted by superfluities and complexities and petty details from the real business of living, Thoreau went to live for two years (1845–1847) in the woods by Walden Pond, near Concord, Massachusetts. Here he hoped "so to love wisdom as to live according to its dictates, a life of simplicity, independence, magnanimity, and trust . . . to solve some of the problems of life, not only theoretically, but practically." The following selection from the book *Walden* gives some of Thoreau's philosophy and some of the experience of his sojourn in the woods.

[1] I was seated by the shore of a small pond, about a mile and a half south of the village of Concord and somewhat higher than it, in the midst of an extensive wood between that town and Lincoln, and about two miles south of that our only field known to fame, Concord Battle Ground; but I was so low in the woods that the opposite shore, half a mile off, like the rest, covered with wood, was my most distant horizon. For the first week, whenever I looked out on the pond it impressed me like a tarn high up on the side of a mountain, its bottom far above the surface of other lakes, and, as the sun arose, I saw it throwing off its nightly clothing of

[1] See Emerson's "Self-Reliance," page 242, and the comment on Transcendentalism, page 257.

mist, and here and there, by degrees, its soft ripples or its smooth reflecting surface was revealed, while the mists, like ghosts, were stealthily withdrawing in every direction into the woods, as at the breaking up of some nocturnal conventicle. The very dew seemed to hang upon the trees later into the day than usual, as on the sides of mountains.

[2] This small lake was of most value as a neighbor in the intervals of a gentle rain-storm in August, when, both air and water being perfectly still, but the sky overcast, midafternoon had all the serenity of evening, and the wood thrush sang around, and was heard from shore to shore. A lake like this is never smoother than at such a time; and the clear portion of the air above it being shallow and darkened by clouds, the water, full of light and reflections, becomes a lower heaven itself so much the more important. From a hilltop nearby, where the wood had been recently cut off, there was a pleasing vista southward across the pond, through a wide indentation in the hills which form the shore there, where their opposite sides sloping toward each other suggested a stream flowing out in that direction through a wooded valley, but stream there was none. That way I looked between and over the near green hills to some distant and higher ones in the horizon, tinged with blue. Indeed, by standing on tiptoe I could catch a glimpse of some of the peaks of the still bluer and more distant mountain ranges in the northwest, those true-blue coins from heaven's own mint, and also of some portion of the village. But in other directions, even from this point, I could not see over or beyond the woods which surrounded me. It is well to have some water in your neighborhood, to give buoyancy to and float the earth. One value even of the smallest well is, that when you look into it you see that earth is not continent but insular. This is as important as that it keeps butter cool. When I looked across the pond from this peak toward the Sudbury meadows, which in time of flood I distinguished elevated perhaps by a mirage in their seething valley, like a coin in a basin, all the earth beyond the pond appeared like a thin crust insulated and floated even by this small sheet of intervening water, and I was reminded that this on which I dwelt was but *dry land*.

[3] Though the view from my door was still more contracted, I did not feel crowded or confined in the least. There was pasture enough for my imagination. The low shrub oak plateau to which the opposite shore arose stretched away toward the prairies of the West and the steppes of Tartary, affording ample room for all the roving families of men. "There are none happy in the world but beings who enjoy freely a vast horizon,"—said Damodara, when his herds required new and larger pastures.

[4] Both place and time were changed, and I dwelt nearer to those parts of the universe and to those eras in history which had most attracted me. Where I lived was as far off as many a region viewed nightly by

astronomers. We are wont to imagine rare and delectable places in some remote and more celestial corner of the system, behind the constellation of Cassiopeia's Chair, far from noise and disturbance. I discovered that my house actually had its site in such a withdrawn, but forever new and unprofaned, part of the universe. If it were worth the while to settle in those parts near to the Pleiades or the Hyades, to Aldebaran or Altair, then I was really there, or at an equal remoteness from the life which I had left behind, dwindled and twinkling with as fine a ray to my nearest neighbor, and to be seen only in moonless nights by him. Such was that part of creation where I had squatted;—

> There was a shepherd that did live,
>   And held his thoughts as high
> As were the mounts whereon his flocks
>   Did hourly feed him by.

What should we think of the shepherd's life if his flocks always wandered to higher pastures than his thoughts?

[5] Every morning was a cheerful invitation to make my life of equal simplicity, and I may say innocence, with Nature herself. I have been as sincere a worshipper of Aurora as the Greeks. I got up early and bathed in the pond; that was a religious exercise, and one of the best things which I did. They say that characters were engraven on the bathing tub of King Tching-thang to this effect: "Renew thyself completely each day; do it again, and again, and forever again." I can understand that. Morning brings back the heroic ages. I was as much affected by the faint hum of a mosquito making its invisible and unimaginable tour through my apartment at earliest dawn, when I was sitting with door and windows open, as I could be by any trumpet that ever sang of fame. It was Homer's requiem; itself an Iliad and Odyssey in the air, singing its own wrath and wanderings. There was something cosmical about it; a standing advertisement, till forbidden, of the everlasting vigor and fertility of the world. The morning, which is the most memorable season of the day, is the awakening hour. Then there is least somnolence in us; and for an hour, at least, some part of us awakes which slumbers all the rest of the day and night. Little is to be expected of that day, if it can be called a day, to which we are not awakened by our Genius, but by the mechanical nudgings of some servitor, are not awakened by our own newly acquired force and aspirations from within, accompanied by the undulations of celestial music, instead of factory bells, and a fragrance filling the air— to a higher life than we fell asleep from; and thus the darkness bear its fruit, and prove itself to be good, no less than the light. That man who does not believe that each day contains an earlier, more sacred, and auroral hour than he has yet profaned, has despaired of life, and is pursuing a descending and darkening way. After a partial cessation of

his sensuous life, the soul of man, or its organs rather, are reinvigorated each day, and his Genius tries again what noble life it can make. All memorable events, I should say, transpire in morning time and in a morning atmosphere. The Vedas say, "All intelligences awake with the morning." Poetry and art, and the fairest and most memorable of the actions of men, date from such an hour. All poets and heroes, like Memnon, are the children of Aurora, and emit their music at sunrise. To him whose elastic and vigorous thought keeps pace with the sun, the day is a perpetual morning. It matters not what the clocks say or the attitudes and labors of men. Morning is when I am awake and there is a dawn in me. Moral reform is the effort to throw off sleep. Why is it that men give so poor an account of their day if they have not been slumbering? They are not such poor calculators. If they had not been overcome with drowsiness, they would have performed something. The millions are awake enough for physical labor; but only one in a million is awake enough for effective intellectual exertion, only one in a hundred millions to a poetic or divine life. To be awake is to be alive. I have never yet met a man who was quite awake. How could I have looked him in the face?

[6] We must learn to reawaken and keep ourselves awake, not by mechanical aids, but by an infinite expectation of the dawn, which does not forsake us in our soundest sleep. I know of no more encouraging fact than the unquestionable ability of man to elevate his life by a conscious endeavor. It is something to be able to paint a particular picture, or to carve a statue, and so to make a few objects beautiful; but it is far more glorious to carve and paint the very atmosphere and medium through which we look, which morally we can do. To affect the quality of the day, that is the highest of arts. Every man is tasked to make his life, even in its details, worthy of the contemplation of his most elevated and critical hour. If we refused, or rather used up, such paltry information as we get, the oracles would distinctly inform us how this might be done.

[7] I went to the woods because I wished to live deliberately, to front only the essential facts of life, and see if I could not learn what it had to teach, and not, when I came to die, discover that I had not lived. I did not wish to live what was not life, living is so dear; nor did I wish to practise resignation, unless it was quite necessary. I wanted to live deep and suck out all the marrow of life, to live so sturdily and Spartan-like as to put to rout all that was not life, to cut a broad swath and shave close, to drive life into a corner, and reduce it to its lowest terms, and, if it proved to be mean, why then to get the whole and genuine meanness of it, and publish its meanness to the world; or if it were sublime, to know it by experience, and be able to give a true account of it in my next excursion. For most men, it appears to me, are in a strange uncertainty about it, whether it is of the devil or of God, and have *somewhat hastily*

concluded that it is the chief end of man here to "glorify God and enjoy him forever."

[8] Still we live meanly, like ants; though the fable tells us that we were long ago changed into men; like pygmies we fight with cranes; it is error upon error, and clout upon clout, and our best virtue has for its occasion a superfluous and evitable wretchedness. Our life is frittered away by detail. An honest man has hardly need to count more than his ten fingers, or in extreme cases he may add his ten toes, and lump the rest. Simplicity, simplicity, simplicity! I say, let your affairs be as two or three, and not a hundred or a thousand; instead of a million count half a dozen, and keep your accounts on your thumb-nail. In the midst of this chopping sea of civilized life, such are the clouds and storms and quicksands and thousand-and-one items to be allowed for, that a man has to live, if he would not founder and go to the bottom and not make his port at all, by dead reckoning, and he must be a great calculator indeed who succeeds. Simplify, simplify. Instead of three meals a day, if it be necessary eat but one; instead of a hundred dishes, five; and reduce other things in proportion. Our life is like a German Confederacy, made up of petty states, with its boundary forever fluctuating, so that even a German cannot tell you how it is bounded at any moment. The nation itself, with all its so-called internal improvements, which, by the way, are all external and superficial, is just such an unwieldy and overgrown establishment, cluttered with furniture and tripped up by its own traps, ruined by luxury and heedless expense, by want of calculation and a worthy aim, as the million households in the land; and the only cure for it, as for them, is in a rigid economy, a stern and more than Spartan simplicity of life and elevation of purpose. It lives too fast. Men think that it is essential that the *Nation* have commerce, and export ice, and talk through a telegraph, and ride thirty miles an hour, without a doubt, whether *they* do or not; but whether we should live like baboons or like men, is a little uncertain. If we do not get out sleepers, and forge rails, and devote days and nights to the work, but go to tinkering upon our *lives* to improve *them*, who will build railroads? And if railroads are not built, how shall we get to Heaven in season? But if we stay at home and mind our business, who will want railroads? We do not ride on the railroad; it rides upon us. Did you ever think what those sleepers are that underlie the railroad? Each one is a man, an Irishman, or a Yankee man. The rails are laid on them, and they are covered with sand, and the cars run smoothly over them. They are sound sleepers, I assure you. And every few years a new lot is laid down and run over; so that, if some have the pleasure of riding on a rail, others have the misfortune to be ridden upon. And when they run over a man that is walking in his sleep, a supernumerary sleeper in the wrong position, and wake him up, they suddenly stop the cars, and make a hue and cry about it, as if this were an excep-

tion. I am glad to know that it takes a gang of men for every five miles to keep the sleepers down and level in their beds as it is, for this is a sign that they may sometime get up again.

[⁹] Why should we live with such hurry and waste of life? We are determined to be starved before we are hungry. Men say that a stitch in time saves nine, and so they take a thousand stitches to-day to save nine tomorrow. As for *work*, we haven't any of any consequence. We have the Saint Vitus' dance, and cannot possibly keep our heads still. If I should only give a few pulls at the parish bell-rope, as for a fire, that is, without setting the bell, there is hardly a man on his farm in the outskirts of Concord, notwithstanding that press of engagements which was his excuse so many times this morning, nor a boy, nor a woman, I might almost say, but would forsake all and follow that sound, not mainly to save property from the flames, but, if we will confess the truth, much more to see it burn, since burn it must, and we, be it known, did not set it on fire,—or to see it put out, and have a hand in it, if that is done as handsomely; yes, even if it were the parish church itself. Hardly a man takes a half-hour's nap after dinner, but when he wakes he holds up his head and asks, "What's the news?" as if the rest of mankind had stood his sentinels. Some give directions to be waked every half-hour, doubtless for no other purpose; and then, to pay for it, they tell what they have dreamed. After a night's sleep the news is as indispensable as the breakfast. "Pray tell me anything new that has happened to a man anywhere on this globe,"—and he reads it over his coffee and rolls, that a man has had his eyes gouged out this morning on the Wachito River; never dreaming the while that he lives in the dark unfathomed mammoth cave of this world, and has but the rudiment of an eye himself.

[¹⁰] For my part, I could easily do without the post-office. I think that there are very few important communications made through it. To speak critically, I never received more than one or two letters in my life—I wrote this some years ago—that were worth the postage. The penny-post is, commonly, an institution through which you seriously offer a man that penny for his thoughts which is so often safely offered in jest. And I am sure that I never read any memorable news in a newspaper. If we read of one man robbed, or murdered, or killed by accident, or one house burned, or one vessel wrecked, or one steamboat blown up, or one cow run over on the Western Railroad, or one mad dog killed, or one lot of grasshoppers in the winter,—we never need read of another. One is enough. If you are acquainted with the principle, what do you care for a myriad instances and applications? To a philosopher all *news*, as it is called, is gossip, and they who edit and read it are old women over their tea. Yet not a few are greedy after this gossip. There was such a rush, as I hear, the other day at one of the offices to learn the foreign news by the last arrival, that several large squares of plate glass belonging to the establishment were broken by the pressure,—news which I seriously think a ready wit might write a twelve-month, or twelve years, beforehand with sufficient accuracy. As for Spain, for instance, if you know how to throw in Don Carlos and the Infanta, and Don Pedro and Seville and Granada, from time to time in the right proportions,—they may have changed the names a little since I saw the papers,—and serve up a bullfight when other entertainments fail, it will be true to the letter, and give us as good an idea of the exact state or ruin of things in Spain as the most succinct and lucid reports under this head in the newspapers: and as for England, almost the last significant scrap of news from that quarter was the revolution of 1649; and if you have learned the history of her crops for an average year, you never need attend to that thing again, unless your speculations are of a merely pecuniary character. If one may judge who rarely looks into the newspapers, nothing new does ever happen in foreign parts, a French revolution not excepted.

[11] What news! how much more important to know what that is which was never old! "Kieou-he-yu (great dignitary of the state of Wei) sent a man to Khoung-tseu to know his news. Khoung-tseu caused the messenger to be seated near him, and questioned him in these terms: What is your master doing? The messenger answered with respect: My master desires to diminish the number of his faults, but he cannot come to the end of them. The messenger being gone, the philosopher remarked: What a worthy messenger! What a worthy messenger!" The preacher, instead of vexing the ears of drowsy farmers on their day of rest at the end of the week,—for Sunday is the fit conclusion of an ill-spent week, and not the fresh and brave beginning of a new one,—with this one other draggletail of a sermon, should shout with thundering voice, "Pause! Avast! Why so seeming fast, but deadly slow?"

[12] Shams and delusions are esteemed for soundest truths, while reality is fabulous. If men would steadily observe realities only, and not allow themselves to be deluded, life, to compare it with such things as we know, would be like a fairy tale and the Arabian Nights' Entertainments. If we respected only what is inevitable and has a right to be, music and poetry would resound along the streets. When we are unhurried and wise, we perceive that only great and worthy things have any permanent and absolute existence, that petty fears and petty pleasures are but the shadow of the reality. This is always exhilarating and sublime. By closing the eyes and slumbering, and consenting to be deceived by shows, men establish and confirm their daily life of routine and habit everywhere, which still is built on purely illusory foundations. Children, who play life, discern its true law and relations more clearly than men, who fail to live it worthily, but who think that they are wiser by experience, that is, by failure. I have read in a Hindoo book, that "there was a king's son, who, being expelled in infancy from his native city, was brought up by a forester,

and, growing up to maturity in that state, imagined himself to belong to the barbarous race with which he lived. One of his father's ministers having discovered him, revealed to him what he was, and the misconception of his character was removed, and he knew himself to be a prince. So soul," continues the Hindoo philosopher, "from the circumstances in which it is placed, mistakes its own character, until the truth is revealed to it by some holy teacher, and then it knows itself to be *Brahme*." I perceive that we inhabitants of New England live this mean life that we do because our vision does not penetrate the surface of things. We think that that *is* which *appears* to be. If a man should walk through this town and see only the reality, where, think you, would the "Mill-dam" go to? If he should give us an account of the realities he beheld there, we should not recognize the place in his description. Look at a meeting-house, or a court-house, or a jail, or a shop, or a dwelling-house, and say what that thing really is before a true gaze, and they would all go to pieces in your account of them. Men esteem truth remote, in the outskirts of the system, behind the farthest star, before Adam and after the last man. In eternity there is indeed something true and sublime. But all these times and places and occasions are now and here. God himself culminates in the present moment, and will never be more divine in the lapse of all the ages. And we are enabled to apprehend at all what is sublime and noble only by the perpetual instilling and drenching of the reality that surrounds us. The universe constantly and obediently answers to our conceptions; whether we travel fast or slow, the track is laid for us. Let us spend our lives in conceiving then. The poet or the artist never yet had so fair and noble a design but some of his posterity at least could accomplish it.

[13] Let us spend one day as deliberately as Nature, and not be thrown off the track by every nutshell and mosquito's wing that falls on the rails. Let us rise early and fast, or break fast, gently and without perturbation; let company come and let company go, let the bells ring and the children cry,—determined to make a day of it. Why should we knock under and go with the stream? Let us not be upset and overwhelmed in that terrible rapid and whirlpool called a dinner, situated in the meridian shallows. Weather this danger and you are safe, for the rest of the way is down hill. With unrelaxed nerves, with morning vigor, sail by it, looking another way, tied to the mast like Ulysses. If the engine whistles, let it whistle till it is hoarse for its pains. If the bell rings, why should we run? We will consider what kind of music they are like. Let us settle ourselves, and work and wedge our feet downward through the mud and slush of opinion, and prejudice, and tradition, and delusion, and appearance, that alluvion which covers the globe, through Paris and London, through New York and Boston and Concord, through Church and State, through poetry and philosophy and religion, till we come to a hard bottom

and rocks in place, which we can call *reality*, and say, This is, and no mistake; and then begin, having a *point d'appui*, below freshet and frost and fire, a place where you might found a wall or a state, or set a lamp-post safely or perhaps a gauge, not a Nilometer, but a Realometer, that future ages might know how deep a freshet of shams and appearances had gathered from time to time. If you stand right fronting and face to face to a fact, you will see the sun glimmer on both its surfaces, as if it were a cimeter, and feel its sweet edge dividing you through the heart and marrow, and so you will happily conclude your mortal career. Be it life or death, we crave only reality. If we are really dying, let us hear the rattle in our throats and feel cold in the extremities; if we are alive, let us go about our business.

[14] Time is but the stream I go a-fishing in. I drink at it; but while I drink I see the sandy bottom and detect how shallow it is. Its thin current slides away, but eternity remains. I would drink deeper; fish in the sky, whose bottom is pebbly with stars. I cannot count one. I know not the first letter of the alphabet. I have always been regretting that I was not as wise as the day I was born. The intellect is a cleaver; it discerns and rifts its way into the secret of things. I do not wish to be any more busy with my hands than is necessary. My head is hands and feet. I feel all my best faculties concentrated in it. My instinct tells me that my head is an organ for burrowing, as some creatures use their snout and fore paws, and with it I would mine and burrow my way through these hills. I think that the richest vein is somewhere hereabouts; so by the divining-rod and thin rising vapors I judge; and here I will begin to mine.

--- COMMENT AND QUESTIONS ---

1. The first four paragraphs of this selection are mainly descriptive. What reflective and philosophical elements do they also contain?

2. Paragraph 5, beginning with Thoreau's mornings at Walden Pond, builds into a larger idea. What is the figurative meaning of *morning* by the end of the paragraph? What is the meaning of the last two sentences of the paragraph?

3. In paragraph 6 Thoreau says: "It is something to be able to paint a particular picture, or to carve a statue, and so to make a few objects beautiful; but it is far more glorious to carve and paint the very atmosphere and medium through which we look, which morally we can do. To affect the quality of the day, that is the highest of arts." Do you agree with this statement? Would one who devoted himself to this "highest of arts" live solely for himself, and not for others?

4. What traits of style do you notice in paragraph 7? Thoreau says that he "wished to live deliberately, to front only the essential facts of life." What does he appear to mean by the essential facts of life? What things does he regard as superficial or nonessential? What things, in his opinion, are actually detrimental to a good life?

5. Early in *Walden,* Thoreau, who infrequently left the town in which he was born, says, "I have travelled a good deal in Concord." In what ways does he also travel a good deal at Walden Pond? In what ways does he settle and "live deep"? Do the two terms, *travel* and *live deep,* have the same or a similar meaning?

6. What are *sleepers* in paragraph 8? Comment on Thoreau's language in his discussion of the sleepers and of the railroads in general.

7. In his discussion of news (paragraphs 9–11) Thoreau is taking pleasure in overstatement. Which of his details do you find entertaining? Do you find any solid points in what he has to say? Explain.

8. Explain what is meant, in paragraph 12, by *shams and delusions* and by *reality.* How has Thoreau's use of the terms been prepared for by earlier context? How are the terms clarified in this paragraph?

9. Paragraphs 13 and 14 are particularly rich in figurative language. In the shifting figures of speech, is there a continuity or a central theme? What does Thoreau mean by saying, in paragraph 14, "I cannot count one. I know not the first letter of the alphabet"? What echoes do you find in these two paragraphs of ideas discussed in the preceding paragraphs of the selection?

[25] *Thomas Henry Huxley*: Agnosticism and Christianity

THOMAS HENRY HUXLEY (1825–1895) was a distinguished English biologist and teacher, known particularly for his defense of Darwin's theory of evolution, and for his lectures and writings explaining science to general audiences. The following selection is part of the essay "Agnosticism and Christianity," first printed in 1889.

[1] The present discussion has arisen out of the use, which has become general in the last few years, of the terms "Agnostic" and "Agnosticism."

From *Science and Christian Tradition* by Thomas Henry Huxley. Published by Appleton-Century-Crofts, Inc.

[2] The people who call themselves "Agnostics" have been charged with doing so because they have not the courage to declare themselves "Infidels." It has been insinuated that they have adopted a new name in order to escape the unpleasantness which attaches to their proper denomination. To this wholly erroneous imputation, I have replied by showing that the term "Agnostic" did, as a matter of fact, arise in a manner which negatives it; and my statement has not been, and cannot be refuted. Moreover, speaking for myself, and without impugning the right of any other person to use the term in another sense, I further say that Agnosticism is not properly described as a "negative" creed, nor indeed as a creed of any kind, except in so far as it expresses absolute faith in the validity of a principle which is as much ethical as intellectual. This principle may be stated in various ways, but they all amount to this: that it is wrong for a man to say that he is certain of the objective truth of any proposition unless he can produce evidence which logically justifies that certainty. This is what Agnosticism asserts; and, in my opinion, it is all that is essential to Agnosticism. That which Agnostics deny and repudiate, as immoral, is the contrary doctrine, that there are propositions which men ought to believe, without logically satisfactory evidence; and that reprobation ought to attach to the profession of disbelief in such inadequately supported propositions. The justification of the Agnostic principle lies in the success which follows upon its application, whether in the field of natural, or in that of civil, history; and in the fact that, so far as these topics are concerned, no sane man thinks of denying its validity.

[3] Still speaking for myself, I add, that though Agnosticism is not, and cannot be, a creed, except in so far as its general principle is concerned; yet that the application of that principle results in the denial of, or the suspension of judgment concerning, a number of propositions respecting which our contemporary ecclesiastical "gnostics" profess entire certainty. And, in so far as these ecclesiastical persons can be justified in their old-established custom (which many nowadays think more honoured in the breach than the observance) of using opprobrious names to those who differ from them, I fully admit their right to call me and those who think with me "Infidels"; all I have ventured to urge is that they must not expect us to speak of ourselves by that title.

[4] The extent of the region of the uncertain, the number of the problems the investigation of which ends in a verdict of not proven, will vary according to the knowledge and the intellectual habits of the individual Agnostic. I do not very much care to speak of anything as "unknowable." What I am sure about is that there are many topics about which I know nothing; and which, so far as I can see, are out of reach of my faculties. But whether these things are knowable by any one else is exactly one of

those matters which is beyond my knowledge, though I may have a tolerably strong opinion as to the probabilities of the case. Relatively to myself, I am quite sure that the region of uncertainty—the nebulous country in which words play the part of realities—is far more extensive than I could wish. Materialism and Idealism; Theism and Atheism; the doctrine of the soul and its mortality or immortality—appear in the history of philosophy like the shades of Scandinavian heroes, eternally slaying one another and eternally coming to life again in a metaphysical "Nifelheim."[1] It is getting on for twenty-five centuries, at least, since mankind began seriously to give their minds to these topics. Generation after generation, philosophy has been doomed to roll the stone uphill; and, just as all the world swore it was at the top, down it has rolled to the bottom again. All this is written in innumerable books; and he who will toil through them will discover that the stone is just where it was when the work began. Hume saw this; Kant saw it; since their time, more and more eyes have been cleaned of the films which prevented them from seeing it; until now the weight and number of those who refuse to be the prey of verbal mystifications has begun to tell in practical life.

[5] It was inevitable that a conflict should arise between Agnosticism and Theology; or rather, I ought to say, between Agnosticism and Ecclesiasticism. For Theology, the science, is one thing; and Ecclesiasticism, the championship of a foregone conclusion as to the truth of a particular form of Theology, is another. With scientific Theology, Agnosticism has no quarrel. On the contrary, the Agnostic, knowing too well the influence of prejudice and idiosyncrasy, even on those who desire most earnestly to be impartial, can wish for nothing more urgently than that the scientific theologian should not only be at perfect liberty to thresh out the matter in his own fashion; but that he should, if he can, find flaws in the Agnostic position; and, even if demonstration is not to be had, that he should put, in their full force, the grounds of the conclusions he thinks probable. The scientific theologian admits the agnostic principle, however widely his results may differ from those reached by the majority of Agnostics.

[6] But, as between Agnosticism and Ecclesiasticism, or, as our neighbours across the Channel call it, Clericalism, there can be neither peace nor truce. The Cleric asserts that it is morally wrong not to believe certain propositions, whatever the results of a strict scientific investigation of the evidence of these propositions. He tells us that "religious error is, in itself, of an immoral nature." He declares that he has prejudged certain conclusions, and looks upon those who show cause for arrest of judgment as emissaries of Satan. It necessarily follows that, for him, the attainment of faith, not the ascertainment of truth, is the highest aim of mental life.

[1] Mist home.

And, on careful analysis of the nature of this faith, it will too often be found to be, not the mystic process of unity with the Divine, understood by the religious enthusiast; but that which the candid simplicity of a Sunday scholar once defined it to be. "Faith," said this unconscious plagiarist of Tertullian, "is the power of saying you believe things which are incredible."

[7] Now I, and many other Agnostics, believe that faith, in this sense, is an abomination; and though we do not indulge in the luxury of self-righteousness so far as to call those who are not of our way of thinking hard names, we do feel that the disagreement between ourselves and those who hold this doctrine is even more moral than intellectual. It is desirable there should be an end of any mistakes on this topic. If our clerical opponents were clearly aware of the real state of the case, there would be an end of the curious delusion, which often appears between the lines of their writings, that those whom they are so fond of calling "Infidels" are people who not only ought to be, but in their hearts are, ashamed of themselves. It would be discourteous to do more than hint the antipodal opposition of this pleasant dream of theirs to facts.

[8] The clerics and their lay allies commonly tell us, that if we refuse to admit that there is good ground for expressing definite convictions about certain topics, the bonds of human society will dissolve and mankind lapse into savagery. There are several answers to this assertion. One is that the bonds of human society were formed without the aid of their theology; and, in the opinion of not a few competent judges, have been weakened rather than strengthened by a good deal of it. Greek science, Greek art, the ethics of old Israel, the social organisation of old Rome, contrived to come into being, without the help of any one who believed in a single distinctive article of the simplest of the Christian creeds. The science, the art, the jurisprudence, the chief political and social theories, of the modern world have grown out of those of Greece and Rome—not by favour of, but in the teeth of, the fundamental teachings of early Christianity, to which science, art, and any serious occupation with the things of this world, were alike despicable.

[9] Again, all that is best in the ethics of the modern world, in so far as it has not grown out of Greek thought, or Barbarian manhood, is the direct development of the ethics of old Israel. There is no code of legislation, ancient or modern, at once so just and so merciful, so tender to the weak and poor, as the Jewish law; and, if the Gospels are to be trusted, Jesus of Nazareth himself declared that he taught nothing but that which lay implicitly, or explicitly, in the religious and ethical system of his people.

And the scribe said unto him, Of a truth, Teacher, thou hast well said that he is one; and there is none other but he and to love him with all the heart, and with all the understanding, and with all the strength, and to love his neighbour as himself, is much more than all the whole burnt offerings and sacrifices. (Mark xii:32, 33.)

[10] Here is the briefest of summaries of the teaching of the prophets of Israel of the eighth century; does the Teacher, whose doctrine is thus set forth in his presence, repudiate the exposition? Nay; we are told, on the contrary, that Jesus saw that he "answered discreetly," and replied, "Thou are not far from the kingdom of God."

[11] So that I think that even if the creeds, from the so-called "Apostles'" to the so-called "Athanasian," were swept into oblivion; and even if the human race should arrive at the conclusion that, whether a bishop washes a cup or leaves it unwashed, is not a matter of the least consequence, it will get on very well. The causes which have led to the development of morality in mankind, which have guided or impelled us all the way from the savage to the civilized state, will not cease to operate because a number of ecclesiastical hypotheses turn out to be baseless. And, even if the absurd notion that morality is more the child of speculation than of practical necessity and inherited instinct, had any foundation; if all the world is going to thieve, murder, and otherwise misconduct itself as soon as it discovers that certain portions of ancient history are mythical; what is the relevance of such arguments to any one who holds by the Agnostic principle?

[12] Surely, the attempt to cast out Beelzebub by the aid of Beelzebub is a hopeful procedure as compared to that of preserving morality by the aid of immorality. For I suppose it is admitted that an Agnostic may be perfectly sincere, may be competent, and may have studied the question at issue with as much care as his clerical opponents. But, if the Agnostic really believes what he says, the "dreadful consequence" argufier (consistently, I admit, with his own principles) virtually asks him to abstain from telling the truth, or to say what he believes to be untrue, because of the supposed injurious consequences to morality. "Beloved brethren, that we may be spotlessly moral, before all things let us lie," is the sum total of many an exhortation addressed to the "Infidel." Now, as I have already pointed out, we cannot oblige our exhorters. We leave the practical application of the convenient doctrines of "Reserve"[2] and "Non-natural interpretation" to those who invented them.

[13] I trust that I have now made amends for any ambiguity, or want of fulness, in my previous exposition of that which I hold to be the essence of the Agnostic doctrine. Henceforward, I might hope to hear no more of the assertion that we are necessarily Materialists, Idealists, Atheists, Theists, or any other ists, if experience had led me to think that the proved falsity of a statement was any guarantee against its repetition.

[2] Withholding of perplexities from the lay mind.

And those who appreciate the nature of our position will see, at once, that when Ecclesiasticism declares that we ought to believe this, that, and the other, and are very wicked if we don't, it is impossible for us to give any answer but this: We have not the slightest objection to believe anything you like, if you will give us good grounds for belief; but, if you cannot, we must respectfully refuse, even if that refusal should wreck morality and insure our own damnation several times over. We are quite content to leave that to the decision of the future. The course of the past has impressed us with the firm conviction that no good ever comes of falsehood, and we feel warranted in refusing even to experiment in that direction.

--⊷ COMMENT AND QUESTIONS ⊶--

1. The agnostic principle, Huxley says, is "that it is wrong for a man to say that he is certain of the objective truth of any proposition unless he can produce evidence which logically justifies that certainty." What is the importance of the word *objective* in this statement of the agnostic position? How does agnosticism differ from atheism? From infidelism?
2. Can you supply examples to support Huxley's statement, at the end of paragraph 2, that outside the area of religion no sane man thinks of denying the validity of the agnostic principle?
3. What are examples of the "propositions" and "topics" about which opponents of agnosticism express certainty, and about which Huxley feels that he knows nothing?
4. What are the implications in Huxley's statement in paragraph 4: "I do not very much care to speak of anything as 'unknowable' "?
5. What distinction does Huxley make between theology and ecclesiasticism? Why does agnosticism have no quarrel with the former? Why must it be at war with the latter?
6. What are Huxley's answers to the assertion that mankind would lapse into savagery if certain ecclesiastical propositions were abandoned? On the basis of your reading, to what extent do you agree with his answers?
7. Explain the last sentence of paragraph 11: "And, even if the absurd notion that morality is more the child of speculation than of practical necessity and inherited instinct, had any foundation . . . what is the relevance of such arguments to any one who holds by the Agnostic principle?"
8. In what sense, according to Huxley, is the agnostic position a moral and ethical one? Do you agree with his claims? Explain.
9. How would you describe the tone of this selection and the persona revealed? Can you see reasons for Huxley's tone?

[26] *William James*: Religious Faith

WILLIAM JAMES (1842–1910) was an American psychologist, philosopher, and distinguished teacher at Harvard. "Religious Faith" is an excerpt from *The Will to Believe*, a collection of essays and lectures published in 1897.

[1] And now, in turning to what religion may have to say to the question,[1] I come to what is the soul of my discourse. Religion has meant many things in human history; but when from now onward I use the word I mean to use it in the supernaturalist sense, as declaring that the so-called order of nature, which constitutes this world's experience, is only one portion of the total universe, and that there stretches beyond this visible world an unseen world of which we now know nothing positive, but in its relation to which the true significance of our present mundane life consists. A man's religious faith (whatever more special items of doctrine it may involve) means for me essentially his faith in the existence of an unseen order of some kind in which the riddles of the natural order may be found explained. In the more developed religions the natural world has always been regarded as the mere scaffolding or vestibule of a truer, more eternal world, and affirmed to be a sphere of education, trial, or redemption. In these religions, one must in some fashion die to the natural life before one can enter into life eternal. The notion that this physical world of wind and water, where the sun rises and the moon sets, is absolutely and ultimately the divinely aimed-at and established thing, is one which we find only in very early religions, such as that of the most primitive Jews. It is this natural religion (primitive still, in spite of the fact that poets and men of science whose goodwill exceeds their perspicacity keep publishing it in new editions tuned to our contemporary ears) that, as I said a while ago, has suffered definitive bankruptcy in the opinion of a circle of persons, among whom I must count myself, and who are growing more numerous every day. For such persons the physical order of nature, taken simply as science knows it, cannot be held to reveal any one harmonious spiritual intent. It is mere *weather*, as Chauncey Wright called it, doing and undoing without end.

[2] Now, I wish to make you feel, if I can in the short remainder of this

---

[1] The question of the meaning of life.

hour, that we have a right to believe the physical order to be only a partial order; that we have a right to supplement it by an unseen spiritual order which we assume on trust, if only thereby life may seem to us better worth living again. But as such a trust will seem to some of you sadly mystical and execrably unscientific, I must first say a word or two to weaken the veto which you may consider that science opposes to our act.

[3] There is included in human nature an ingrained naturalism and materialism of mind which can only admit facts that are actually tangible. Of this sort of mind the entity called "science" is the idol. Fondness for the word "scientist" is one of the notes by which you may know its votaries; and its short way of killing any opinion that it disbelieves in is to call it "unscientific." It must be granted that there is no slight excuse for this. Science has made such glorious leaps in the last three hundred years, and extended our knowledge of nature so enormously both in general and in detail; men of science, moreover, have as a class displayed such admirable virtues,—that it is no wonder if the worshippers of science lose their head. In this very University, accordingly, I have heard more than one teacher say that all the fundamental conceptions of truth have already been found by science, and that the future has only the details of the picture to fill in. But the slightest reflection on the real conditions will suffice to show how barbaric such notions are. They show such a lack of scientific imagination, that it is hard to see how one who is actively advancing any part of science can make a mistake so crude. Think how many absolutely new scientific conceptions have arisen in our own generation, how many new problems have been formulated that were never thought of before, and then cast an eye upon the brevity of science's career. It began with Galileo, not three hundred years ago. Four thinkers since Galileo, each informing his successor of what discoveries his own lifetime had seen achieved, might have passed the torch of science into our hands as we sit here in this room. Indeed, for the matter of that, an audience much smaller than the present one, an audience of some five or six score people, if each person in it could speak for his own generation, would carry us away to the black unknown of the human species, to days without a document or monument to tell their tale. Is it credible that such a mushroom knowledge, such a growth overnight as this, *can* represent more than the minutest glimpse of what the universe will really prove to be when adequately understood? No! our science is a drop, our ignorance a sea. Whatever else be certain, this at least is certain,—that the world of our present natural knowledge *is* enveloped in a larger world of *some* sort of whose residual properties we at present can frame no positive idea.

[4] Agnostic positivism, of course, admits this principle theoretically in the most cordial terms, but insists that we must not turn it to any practical

use. We have no right, this doctrine tells us, to dream dreams, or suppose anything about the unseen part of the universe, merely because to do so may be for what we are pleased to call our highest interests. We must always wait for sensible evidence for our beliefs; and where such evidence is inaccessible we must frame no hypotheses whatever. Of course this is a safe enough position *in abstracto.* If a thinker had no stake in the unknown, no vital needs, to live or languish according to what the unseen world contained, a philosophic neutrality and refusal to believe either one way or the other would be his wisest cue. But, unfortunately, neutrality is not only inwardly difficult, it is also outwardly unrealizable, where our relations to an alternative are practical and vital. This is because, as the psychologists tell us, belief and doubt are living attitudes, and involve conduct on our part. Our only way, for example, of doubting or refusing to believe, that a certain thing *is,* is continuing to act as if it were *not.* If, for instance, I refuse to believe that the room is getting cold, I leave the windows open and light no fire just as if it still were warm. If I doubt that you are worthy of my confidence, I keep you uninformed of all my secrets just as if you were *un*worthy of the same. If I doubt the need of insuring my house, I leave it uninsured as much as if I believed there were no need. And so if I must not believe that the world is divine, I can only express that refusal by declining ever to act distinctively as if it were so, which can only mean acting on certain critical occasions as if it were *not* so, or in an irreligious way. There are, you see, inevitable occasions in life when inaction is a kind of action, and must count as action, and when not to be for is to be practically against; and in all such cases strict and consistent neutrality is an unattainable thing.

[⁵] And, after all, is not this duty of neutrality, where only our inner interests would lead us to believe, the most ridiculous of commands? Is is not sheer dogmatic folly to say that our inner interests can have no real connection with the forces that the hidden world may contain? In other cases divinations based on inner interests have proved prophetic enough. Take science itself! Without an imperious inner demand on our part for ideal logical and mathematical harmonies, we should never have attained to proving that such harmonies lie hidden between all the chinks and interstices of the crude natural world. Hardly a law has been established in science, hardly a fact ascertained, which was not first sought after, often with sweat and blood, to gratify an inner need. Whence such needs come from we do not know: we find them in us, and biological psychology so far only classes them with Darwin's "accidental variations." But the inner need of believing that this world of nature is a sign of something more spiritual and eternal than itself is just as strong and authoritative in those who feel it, as the inner need of uniform laws of causation ever can be in a professionally scientific head. The toil of many generations has proved the latter need prophetic. Why *may* not the former one be prophetic, too? And if needs of ours outrun the visible universe, why *may* not that be a sign that an invisible universe is there? What, in short, has authority to debar us from trusting our religious demands? Science as such assuredly has no authority, for she can only say what is, not what is not; and the agnostic "thou shalt not believe without coercive sensible evidence" is simply an expression (free to any one to make) of private personal appetite for evidence of a certain peculiar kind.

[6] Now, when I speak of trusting our religious demands, just what do I mean by "trusting"? Is the word to carry with it license to define in detail an invisible world, and to anathematize and excommunicate those whose trust is different? Certainly not! Our faculties of belief were not primarily given us to make orthodoxies and heresies withal; they were given us to live by. And to trust our religious demands means first of all to live in the light of them, and to act as if the invisible world which they suggest were real. It is a fact of human nature, that men can live and die by the help of a sort of faith that goes without a single dogma of definition. The bare assurance that this natural order is not ultimate but a mere sign or vision, the eternal staging of a many-storied universe, in which spiritual forces have the last word and are eternal,—this bare assurance is to such men enough to make life seem worth living in spite of every contrary presumption suggested by its circumstances on the natural plane. Destroy this inner assurance, however, vague as it is, and all the light and radiance of existence is extinguished for these persons at a stroke. Often enough the wild-eyed look at life—the suicidal mood—will then set in.

[7] And now the application comes directly home to you and me. Probably to almost everyone of us here the most adverse life would seem well worth living, if we only could be *certain* that our bravery and patience with it were terminating and eventuating and bearing fruit somewhere in an unseen spiritual world. By granting we are not certain, does it then follow that a bare trust in such a world is a fool's paradise and lubberland, or rather that it is a living attitude in which we are free to indulge? Well, we are free to trust at our own risks anything that is not impossible, and that can bring analogies to bear in its behalf. That the world of physics is probably not absolute, all the converging multitude of arguments that make in favor of idealism tend to prove; and that our whole physical life may lie soaking in a spiritual atmosphere, a dimension of being that we at present have no organ for apprehending, is vividly suggested to us by the analogy of our domestic animals. Our dogs, for example, are in our human life but not of it. They witness hourly the outward body of events whose inner meaning cannot, by any possible operation, be revealed to their intelligence,—events in which they themselves often play the cardinal part. My terrier bites a teasing boy, and the father demands damages. The dog may be present at every step of the negotiations, and see the

money paid, without an inkling of what it all means, without a suspicion that it has anything to do with *him;* and he never *can* know in his natural dog's life. Or take another case which used greatly to impress me in my medical-student days. Consider a poor dog whom they are vivisecting in a laboratory. He lies strapped on a board and shrieking at his executioners, and to his own dark consciousness is literally in a sort of hell. He cannot see a single redeeming ray in the whole business; and yet all these diabolical-seeming events are often controlled by human intentions with which, if his poor benighted mind could only be made to catch a glimpse of them, all that is heroic in him would religiously acquiesce. Healing truth, relief to future sufferings of beast and man, are to be bought by them. It may be genuinely a process of redemption. Lying on his back on the board there he may be performing a function incalculably higher than any that prosperous canine life admits of; and yet, of the whole performance, this function is the one portion that must remain absolutely beyond his ken.

[8] Now turn from this to the life of man. In the dog's life we see the world invisible to him because we live in both worlds. In human life, although we only see our world, and his within it, yet encompassing both these worlds a still wider world may be there, as unseen by us as our world is by him; and to believe in that world *may* be the most essential function that our lives in this world have to perform. But "*may* be! *may* be!" one now hears the positivist contemptuously exclaim; "what use can a scientific life have for maybes?" Well, I reply, the "scientific" life itself has much to do with maybes, and human life at large has everything to do with them. So far as man stands for anything, and is productive or originative at all, his entire vital function may be said to have to deal with maybes. Not a victory is gained, not a deed of faithfulness or courage is done, except upon a maybe; not a service, not a sally of generosity, not a scientific exploration or experiment or text-book, that may not be a mistake. It is only by risking our persons from one hour to another that we live at all. And often enough our faith beforehand in an uncertified result *is the only thing that makes the result come true.* Suppose, for instance, that you are climbing a mountain, and have worked yourself into a position from which the only escape is by a terrible leap. Have faith that you can successfully make it, and your feet are nerved to its accomplishment. But mistrust yourself, and think of all the sweet things you have heard the scientists say of *maybes,* and you will hesitate so long that, at last, all unstrung and trembling, and launching yourself in a moment of despair, you roll in the abyss. In such a case (and it belongs to an enormous class), the part of wisdom as well as of courage is to *believe what is in the line of your needs,* for only by such belief is the need fulfilled. Refuse to believe, and you shall indeed be right, for you shall irretrievably perish. But believe, and again you shall be right, for you

shall save yourself. You make one or the other of two possible universes true by your trust or mistrust,—both universes having been only *maybes,* in this particular, before you contributed your act.

[⁹] Now, it appears to me that the question whether life is worth living is subject to conditions logically much like these. It does, indeed, depend on you *the liver.* If you surrender to the nightmare view and crown the evil edifice by your own suicide, you have indeed made a picture totally black. Pessimism, completed by your act, is true beyond a doubt, so far as your world goes. Your mistrust of life has removed whatever worth your own enduring existence might have given to it; and now, throughout the whole sphere of possible influence of that existence, the mistrust has proved itself to have had divining power. But suppose, on the other hand, that instead of giving way to the nightmare view, you cling to it that this world is not the *ultimatum.* Suppose you find yourself a very wellspring, as Wordsworth says, of—

> Zeal and the virtue to exist by faith
> As soldiers live by courage; as, by strength
> Of heart, the sailor fights with roaring seas.

Suppose, however thickly evils crowd upon you, that your unconquerable subjectivity proves to be their match, and that you find a more wonderful joy than any passive pleasure can bring in trusting ever in the larger whole. Have you not now made life worth living on these terms? What sort of a thing would life really be, with your qualities ready for a tussle with it, if it only brought fair weather and gave these higher faculties of yours no scope? Please remember that optimism and pessimism are definitions of the world, and that our own reactions on the world, small as they are in bulk, are integral parts of the whole thing, and necessarily help to determine the definition. They may even be the decisive elements in determining the definition. A large mass can have its unstable equilibrium overturned by the addition of a feather's weight; a long phrase may have its sense reversed by the addition of the three letters *n-o-t.* This life *is* worth living, we can say, *since it is what we make it, from the moral point of view;* and we are determined to make it from that point of view, so far as we have anything to do with it, a success.

[¹⁰] Now, in this description of faiths that verify themselves I have assumed that our faith in an invisible order is what inspires those efforts and that patience which make this visible order good for moral men. Our faith in the seen world's goodness (goodness now meaning fitness for successful moral and religious life) has verified itself by leaning on our faith in the unseen world. But will our faith in the unseen world similarly verify itself? Who knows?

[¹¹] Once more it is a case of *maybe;* and once more *maybes* are the essence of the situation. I confess that I do not see why the very existence of an invisible world may not in part depend on the personal response which any one of us may make to the religious appeal. God himself, in short, may draw vital strength and increase of very being from our fidelity. For my own part, I do not know what the sweat and blood and tragedy of this life mean, if they mean anything short of this. If this life be not a real fight, in which something is eternally gained for the universe by success, it is no better than a game of private theatricals from which one may withdraw at will. But it *feels* like a real fight,—as if there were something really wild in the universe which we, with all our idealities and faithfulnesses, are needed to redeem; and first of all to redeem our own hearts from atheisms and fears. For such a half-wild, half-saved universe our nature is adapted. The deepest thing in our nature is this *Binnenleben* (as a German doctor lately has called it), this dumb region of the heart in which we dwell alone with our willingnesses and unwillingnesses, our faiths and fears. As through the cracks and crannies of caverns those waters exude from the earth's bosom which then form the fountain-heads of springs, so in these crepuscular depths of personality the sources of all our outer deeds and decisions take their rise. Here is our deepest organ of communication with the nature of things; and compared with all these concrete movements of our soul all abstract statements and scientific arguments—the veto, for example, which the strict positivist pronounces upon our faith—sound to us like mere chatterings of the teeth. For here possibilities, not finished facts, are the realities with which we have acutely to deal; and to quote my friend William Salter, of the Philadelphia Ethical Society, "as the essence of courage is to stake one's life on a possibility, so the essence of faith is to believe that the possibility exists."

[12] These, then, are my last words to you: Be *not* afraid of life. Believe that life *is* worth living, and your belief will help create the fact. The "scientific proof" that you are right may not be clear before the day of judgment (or some stage of being which that expression may serve to symbolize) is reached. But the faithful fighters of this hour, or the beings that then and there will represent them, may turn to the faint-hearted, who here decline to go on, with words like those with which Henry IV greeted the tardy Crillon after a great victory had been gained: "Hang yourself, brave Crillon! we fought at Arques, and you were not there."

⊶⊰ COMMENT AND QUESTIONS ⊱⊷

1. A pragmatic philosophy—the position that the worth of an idea depends on its practical effects—underlies this selection. Summarize in a sentence James' pragmatic argument for faith in an unseen order.

2. James anticipates objections to his thesis that we have a right to assume on trust an unseen spiritual order. By what means does he attempt to counter the objections?

3. How does James qualify *trusting* in his statement about trusting our religious demands?

4. If you have read Thomas Huxley's "Agnosticism and Christianity," you will see that Huxley and James disagree in some ways about religious faith; indeed, paragraph 4 of James' essay is a direct argument against the agnostic position defended by Huxley. What are James' arguments against (a) agnostic neutrality; (b) reliance on scientific evidence alone? Is there an area of agreement between James and Huxley in their attitudes toward religious orthodoxy? Do they agree on any other matters about science and religion?

5. William James is very skillful in the use of persuasive example and analogy. What point is he making by means of each of the following: the man who does not believe the room is getting cold; the dog in the laboratory; the mountain climber faced with a jump over an abyss?

6. Study the sentence structures and rhythms in paragraph 8, and try to determine by what techniques James achieves a vivid, forceful style.

7. How effectively, in your opinion, does James support his idea that life is worth living? What conditions are necessary for a successful life as he defines it?

8. Examine paragraph 11. What concept of God and of the relationship of God and human beings does James appear to hold?

9. In what ways is paragraph 12 an effective ending for James' lecture?

[27] *Albert Einstein*: Science and Religion

ALBERT EINSTEIN (1879–1955), German-born, naturalized-American theoretical physicist, is well known for his theory of relativity and his later generalized theory of gravitation. The following selection, first printed in 1941, has been reprinted as Part II of a longer essay "Science and Religion" in *Out of My Later Years*, a collection of Einstein's essays and addresses published in 1950.

[1] It would not be difficult to come to an agreement as to what we understand by science. Science is the century-old endeavor to bring together by means of systematic thought the perceptible phenomena of this world into as thoroughgoing an association as possible. To put it boldly,

it is the attempt at the posterior reconstruction of existence by the process of conceptualization. But when asking myself what religion is, I cannot think of the answer so easily. And even after finding an answer which may satisfy me at this particular moment, I still remain convinced that I can never under any circumstances bring together, even to a slight extent, all those who have given this question serious consideration.

[2] At first, then, instead of asking what religion is, I should prefer to ask what characterizes the aspirations of a person who gives me the impression of being religious: a person who is religiously enlightened appears to me to be one who has, to the best of his ability, liberated himself from the fetters of his selfish desires and is preoccupied with thoughts, feelings, and aspirations to which he clings because of their super-personal value. It seems to me that what is important is the force of this super-personal content and the depth of the conviction concerning its over-powering meaningfulness, regardless of whether any attempt is made to unite this content with a Divine Being, for otherwise it would not be possible to count Buddha and Spinoza as religious personalities. Accordingly, a religious person is devout in the sense that he has no doubt of the significance and loftiness of those super-personal objects and goals which neither require nor are capable of rational foundation. They exist with the same necessity and matter-of-factness as he himself. In this sense religion is the age-old endeavor of mankind to become clearly and completely conscious of these values and goals and constantly to strengthen and extend their effects. If one conceives of religion and science according to these definitions then a conflict between them appears impossible. For science can only ascertain what *is*, but not what should be, and outside of its domain value judgments of all kinds remain necessary. Religion, on the other hand, deals only with evaluations of human thought and action; it cannot justifiably speak of facts and relationships between facts. According to this interpretation, the well-known conflicts between religion and science in the past must all be ascribed to a misapprehension of the situation which has been described.

[3] For example, a conflict arises when a religious community insists on the absolute truthfulness of all statements recorded in the Bible. This means an intervention on the part of religion into the sphere of science; this is where the struggle of the Church against the doctrines of Galileo and Darwin belongs. On the other hand, representatives of science have often made an attempt to arrive at fundamental judgments with respect to values and ends on the basis of scientific method, and in this way have set themselves in opposition to religion. These conflicts have all sprung from fatal errors.

[4] Now, even though the realms of religion and science in themselves are clearly marked off from each other, nevertheless there exist between the two, strong reciprocal relationships and dependencies. Though reli-

gion may be that which determines the goal, it has, nevertheless, learned from science, in the broadest sense, what means will contribute to the attainment of the goals it has set up. But science can only be created by those who are thoroughly imbued with the aspiration towards truth and understanding. This source of feeling, however, springs from the sphere of religion. To this there also belongs the faith in the possibility that the regulations valid for the world of existence are rational, that is comprehensible to reason. I cannot conceive of a genuine scientist without that profound faith. The situation may be expressed by an image: science without religion is lame, religion without science is blind.

[5] Though I have asserted above, that in truth a legitimate conflict between religion and science cannot exist, I must nevertheless qualify this assertion once again on an essential point, with reference to the actual content of historical religions. This qualification has to do with the concept of God. During the youthful period of mankind's spiritual evolution, human fantasy created gods in man's own image, who, by the operations of their will were supposed to determine, or at any rate to influence, the phenomenal world. Man sought to alter the disposition of these gods in his own favor by means of magic and prayer. The idea of God in the religions taught at present is a sublimation of that old conception of the gods. Its anthropomorphic character is shown, for instance, by the fact that men appeal to the Divine Being in prayers and plead for the fulfilment of their wishes.

[6] Nobody, certainly, will deny that the idea of the existence of an omnipotent, just and omnibeneficent personal God is able to accord man solace, help, and guidance; also, by virtue of its simplicity the concept is accessible to the most undeveloped mind. But, on the other hand, there are decisive weaknesses attached to this idea in itself, which have been painfully felt since the beginning of history. That is, if this Being is omnipotent, then every occurrence, including every human action, every human thought, and every human feeling and aspiration is also His work; how is it possible to think of holding men responsible for their deeds and thoughts before such an Almighty Being? In giving out punishment and rewards He would to a certain extent be passing judgment on himself. How can this be combined with the goodness and righteousness ascribed to Him?

[7] The main source of the present-day conflicts between the spheres of religion and of science lies in this concept of a personal God. It is the aim of science to establish general rules which determine the reciprocal connection of objects and events in time and space. For these rules, or laws of nature, absolutely general validity is required—not proven. It is mainly a program, and faith in the possibility of its accomplishment in principle is only founded on partial success. But hardly anyone could be found who would deny these partial successes and ascribe them to

human self-deception. The fact that on the basis of such laws we are able to predict the temporal behavior of phenomena in certain domains with great precision and certainty, is deeply embedded in the consciousness of the modern man, even though he may have grasped very little of the contents of those laws. He need only consider that planetary courses within the solar system may be calculated in advance with great exactitude on the basis of a limited number of simple laws. In a similar way, though not with the same precision, it is possible to calculate in advance the mode of operation of an electric motor, a transmission system, or of a wireless apparatus, even when dealing with a novel development.

[8] To be sure, when the number of factors coming into play in a phenomenological complex is too large, scientific method in most cases fails us. One need only think of the weather, in which case prediction even for a few days ahead is impossible. Nevertheless no one doubts that we are confronted with a causal connection whose causal components are in the main known to us. Occurrences in this domain are beyond the reach of exact prediction because of the variety of factors in operation, not because of any lack of order in nature.

[9] We have penetrated far less deeply into the regularities obtaining within the realm of living things, but deeply enough nevertheless to sense at least the rule of fixed necessity. One need only think of the systematic order in heredity, and in the effect of poisons, as for instance alcohol on the behavior of organic beings. What is still lacking here is a grasp of connections of profound generality, but not a knowledge of order in itself.

[10] The more a man is imbued with the ordered regularity of all events, the firmer becomes his conviction that there is no room left by the side of this ordered regularity for causes of a different nature. For him neither the rule of human nor the rule of Divine Will exists as an independent cause of natural events. To be sure, the doctrine of a personal God interfering with natural events could never be *refuted*, in the real sense, by science, for this doctrine can always take refuge in those domains in which scientific knowledge has not yet been able to set foot.

[11] But I am persuaded that such behavior on the part of the representatives of religion would not only be unworthy but also fatal. For a doctrine which is able to maintain itself not in clear light but only in the dark, will of necessity lose its effect on mankind, with incalculable harm to human progress. In their struggle for the ethical good, teachers of religion must have the stature to give up the doctrine of a personal God, that is, give up that source of fear and hope which in the past placed such vast power in the hands of priests. In their labors they will have to avail themselves of those forces which are capable of cultivating the Good, the True, and the Beautiful in humanity itself. This is, to be sure, a more difficult but an incomparably more worthy task. After religious teachers accomplish the refining process indicated, they will surely rec-

ognize with joy that true religion has been ennobled and made more profound by scientific knowledge.

[12] If it is one of the goals of religion to liberate mankind as far as possible from the bondage of egocentric cravings, desires, and fears, scientific reasoning can aid religion in yet another sense. Although it is true that it is the goal of science to discover rules which permit the association and foretelling of facts, this is not its only aim. It also seeks to reduce the connections discovered to the smallest possible number of mutually independent conceptual elements. It is in this striving after the rational unification of the manifold that it encounters its greatest successes, even though it is precisely this attempt which causes it to run the greatest risk of falling a prey to illusions. But whoever has undergone the intense experience of successful advances made in this domain, is moved by profound reverence for the rationality made manifest in existence. By way of the understanding he achieves a far-reaching emancipation from the shackles of personal hopes and desires, and thereby attains that humble attitude of mind towards the grandeur of reason incarnate in existence, which, in its profoundest depths, is inaccessible to man. This attitude, however, appears to me to be religious, in the highest sense of the word. And so it seems to me that science not only purifies the religious impulse of the dross of its anthropomorphism, but also contributes to a religious spiritualization of our understanding of life.

[13] The further the spiritual evolution of mankind advances, the more certain it seems to me that the path to genuine religiosity does not lie through the fear of life, and the fear of death, and blind faith, but through striving after rational knowledge. In this sense I believe that the priest must become a teacher if he wishes to do justice to his lofty educational mission.

--✌{ COMMENT AND QUESTIONS }✌--

1. A religiously enlightened person, Einstein says, is one preoccupied with superpersonal goals and values. What examples can you supply of such superpersonal goals and values?
2. To what extent do you agree or disagree with Einstein's definitions of "a religious person" and "religion"?
3. In paragraph 3 Einstein gives some examples of past conflicts between science and religion—conflicts caused by the intervention of one into the sphere of the other. What further examples can you give of such intervention and conflict?

4. Examine the image at the end of paragraph 4. Would there be a loss if the terms were reversed so that the statement read: science without religion is blind, religion without science is lame?

5. Explain clearly what Einstein means by an anthropomorphic personal God and why he believes that this concept of God is incompatible with scientific knowledge.

6. State as clearly as you can what you think Einstein's intentions were in writing this essay.

7. We have said earlier that the ability to grasp the essentials of a piece of writing and to summarize it in precise, packed language is very useful to a college student. Read carefully the two summaries of Einstein's essay printed below; each was written on a quiz in class, in fifteen minutes, by an able student.

[1] Science is the attempt to associate and explain the phenomena of the world; religion is harder to define. The religiously enlightened man is concerned with and convinced of the importance of super-personal thoughts and goals which neither have nor need a rational basis. The understanding of these thoughts and the achievement of these goals is, then, the purpose of religion.

Viewed thus, science, which deals with what *is,* and religion, which deals with what *should be,* cannot conflict except through the overstepping of their limits. This occurs when religion tries to assume full truth for the Bible and conflicts with, for instance, Darwin, or when science attempts value judgments.

Although religion and science are strictly divided, they are interdependent. Religion needs science to point the way to the achievement of its goals; science needs the desire for truth and the faith in future success that religion gives.

In spite of theoretical absence of conflict, the actual content of present religions presents a great conflict in the doctrine of a personal God, which developed from the ancient conception of one or many almighty beings controlling the world. This idea gives comfort and aid and is easily conceived, but it is logically weak. How can God control the thoughts and actions of all beings, yet hold them responsible for these very thoughts and actions? He is judging Himself.

As science has pursued the determining of natural laws (rules interrelating objects and events in time and space), it has failed only through number and variety of factors, not through lack of order in nature. This increasingly manifest logic rules out control of the world by any other factor, human or Divine. Religious teachers must courageously abandon the powerful doctrine of a personal God, utilizing instead the forces for good extant within humanity itself.

Since the purpose of science is also to reduce natural laws to a few basic concepts, it helps religion in another way, for such achievement brings profound respect for the logic of existence and a resulting uplift to the super-personal thoughts and ideals which are the goal of religion.

Science, then, not only purifies religion by disproving the false concept of a personal God, but also contributes to religious spiritualization in the understanding of the phenomenal world. The road to true religion lies not through blind faith, but through science, the search for rational knowledge.

[2]   Science deals with what is—the facts of the physical world and their relationship. Religion is concerned with what should be—superpersonal ideals and values. Defined this way, science and religion should not conflict, but should be mutually helpful—religion providing the goals, and science the way of attaining the religious values. They conflict only when one wrongly intrudes into the other's proper realm. At present such conflict occurs when religious groups insist on the idea of a personal anthropomorphic God who intervenes and changes natural law in answer to prayer. Scientific knowledge reveals a great ordered regularity in the universe which allows no room for such independent causes or interference. Religious leaders should therefore give up the idea of the personal God and should work, with the aid of science, to teach reverence for the great rationality manifest in existence, and to cultivate the True, Good and Beautiful in humanity itself.

Both of these summaries are good. Which seems to you better, and why; or do you think that they have different virtues and weaknesses?

8. It is also useful to a student to be able to phrase very briefly the central ideas of a piece of writing. Write a concentrated statement of no more than a sentence or two which does this for Einstein's essay.

9. If you have read the selections preceding this one, compare and contrast the attitudes toward science and religion of Thomas Huxley, James, and Einstein.

[28]   *John Henry Newman*: Doubt and Faith

THE FOLLOWING selection is an excerpt from Part VII of *Apologia Pro Vita Sua* (1864), an autobiography in which the author, a leader in the Anglican Church and later cardinal in the Roman Catholic Church, traces and defends his spiritual and religious development. In Part III of the *Apologia* Newman, writing of his early years, has said that he distrusted the reality of material phenomena and rested "in the thought of two and two only supreme and luminously self-evident beings, myself and my Creator." For a further note on Newman see page 158.

[¹] Starting then with the being of a God (which, as I have said, is as certain to me as the certainty of my own existence, though when I try to put the grounds of that certainty into logical shape I find a difficulty in doing so in mood and figure to my satisfaction), I look out of myself into the world of men, and there I see a sight which fills me with unspeakable distress. The world seems simply to give the lie to that great truth, of which my whole being is so full; and the effect upon me is, in consequence, as a matter of necessity, as confusing as if it denied that I am in existence myself. If I looked into a mirror, and did not see my face, I should have the sort of feeling which actually comes upon me, when I look into this living busy world, and see no reflection of its Creator. This is, to me, one of the great difficulties of this absolute primary truth, to which I referred just now. Were it not for this voice, speaking so clearly in my conscience and my heart, I should be an atheist, or a pantheist, or a polytheist when I looked into the world. I am speaking for myself only; and I am far from denying the real force of the arguments in proof of a God, drawn from the general facts of human society, but these do not warm me or enlighten me; they do not take away the winter of my desolation, or make the buds unfold and the leaves grow within me, and my moral being rejoice. The sight of the world is nothing else than the prophet's scroll, full of "lamentations, and mourning, and woe."

[²] To consider the world in its length and breadth, its various history, the many races of man, their starts, their fortunes, their mutual alienation, their conflicts; and then their ways, habits, governments, forms of worship; their enterprises, their aimless courses, their random achievements and acquirements, the impotent conclusion of long-standing facts, the tokens so faint and broken, of a superintending design, the blind evolution of what turn out to be great powers or truth, the progress of things, as if from unreasoning elements, not towards final causes, the greatness and littleness of man, his far-reaching aims, his short duration, the curtain hung over his futurity, the disappointments of life, the defeat of good, the success of evil, physical pain, mental anguish, the prevalence and intensity of sin, the pervading idolatries, the corruptions, the dreary hopeless irreligion, that condition of the whole race, so fearfully yet exactly described in the Apostle's words, "having no hope and without God in the world"— all this is a vision to dizzy and appall; and inflicts upon the mind the sense of a profound mystery which is absolutely beyond human solution.

[³] What shall be said to this heart-piercing, reason-bewildering fact? I can only answer that either there is no Creator, or this living society of men is in a true sense discarded from His presence. Did I see a boy of good make and mind, with the tokens on him of a refined nature, cast upon the world without provision, unable to say whence he came, his birthplace or his family connections, I should conclude that there was some mystery connected with his history, and that he was one, of whom, from one cause or other, his parents were ashamed. Thus only should I be able to account for the contrast between the promise and condition of his being. And so I argue about the world—*if* there be a God, *since* there is a God, the human race is implicated in some terrible aboriginal calamity. It is out of joint with the purposes of its Creator. This is a fact, a fact as true as the fact of its existence; and thus the doctrine of what is theologically called original sin becomes to me almost as certain as that the world exists, and as the existence of God.

[4] And now, supposing it were the blessed and loving will of the Creator to interfere in this anarchical condition of things, what are we to suppose would be the methods which might be necessarily or naturally involved in His object of mercy? Since the world is in so abnormal a state, surely it would be no surprise to me if the interposition were of necessity equally extraordinary—or what is called miraculous. But that subject does not directly come into the scope of my present remarks. Miracles as evidence involve an argument; and of course I am thinking of some means which does not immediately run into argument. I am rather asking what must be the face-to-face antagonist, by which to withstand and baffle the fierce energy of passion and the all-corroding, all-dissolving skepticism of the intellect in religious inquiries? I have no intention at all to deny that truth is the real object of our reason, and that, if it does not attain to truth, either the premise or the process is in fault; but I am not speaking of right reason, but of reason as it acts in fact and concretely in fallen man. I know that even the unaided reason, when correctly exercised, leads to a belief in God, in the immortality of the soul, and in a future retribution; but I am considering it actually and historically; and in this point of view, I do not think I am wrong in saying that its tendency is towards a simple unbelief in matters of religion. No truth, however sacred, can stand against it, in the long run; and hence it is that in the pagan world, when our Lord came, the last traces of the religious knowledge of former times were all but disappearing from those portions of the world in which the intellect had been active and had had a career.

[5] And in these latter days, in like manner, outside the Catholic Church things are tending, with far greater rapidity than in that old time from the circumstance of the age, to atheism in one shape or another. What a scene, what a prospect, does the whole of Europe present at this day! and not only Europe, but every government and every civilization through the world, which is under the influence of the European mind! . . .

[6] Supposing then it to be the Will of the Creator to interfere in human affairs, and to make provisions for retaining in the world a knowledge of Himself, so definite and distinct as to be proof against the energy of human skepticism, in such a case—I am far from saying that there was

no other way—but there is nothing to surprise the mind, if He should think fit to introduce a power into the world, invested with the prerogative of infallibility in religious matters. Such a provision would be a direct, immediate, active, and prompt means of withstanding the difficulty; it would be an instrument suited to the need; and, when I find that this is the very claim of the Catholic Church, not only do I feel no difficulty in admitting the idea, but there is a fitness in it, which recommends it to my mind. And thus I am brought to speak of the Church's infallibility, as a provision, adapted by the mercy of the Creator, to preserve religion in the world, and to restrain that freedom of thought, which of course in itself is one of the greatest of our natural gifts, and to rescue it from its own suicidal excesses. And let it be observed that, neither here nor in what follows, shall I have occasion to speak directly of the revealed body of truths, but only as they bear upon the defense of natural religion. I say that a power, possessed of infallibility in religious teaching, is happily adapted to be a working instrument, in the course of human affairs, for smiting hard and throwing back the immense energy of the aggressive intellect—and in saying this, as in the other things that I have to say, it must still be recollected that I am all along bearing in mind my main purpose, which is a defense of myself.

---⚜{ COMMENT AND QUESTIONS }⚜---

1. Newman starts with an "absolute primary truth." What is the source of his certainty about the existence of God? In the two opening paragraphs of the selection, what other certainties does he express?
2. Examine the figurative language near the end of paragraph 1. In what ways is it effective?
3. Paragraph 2 is a long periodic sentence. Does there seem to you to be a logical or a psychological order in Newman's arrangement of details in the sentence, or is the arrangement purely random and impressionistic?
4. What is the purpose in paragraph 3 of the example of the "boy of good make and mind"? Comment on the appropriateness and effectiveness of the example as Newman uses it.
5. What is the meaning of the statement in paragraph 4, "Miracles as evidence involve an argument"?
6. State in your own words the conclusions or inferences that Newman draws from his premises about the existence of God and the condition of the world. Does he present his conclusions dogmatically? If not, how does he avoid the appearance of dogmatism?

7. In the next-to-last sentence of paragraph 6, what does Newman seem to mean by "natural religion"?
8. What are Newman's attitudes in this selection toward human reason and intellect? What words seem to you particularly well chosen to express those attitudes and to make needed qualifications and distinctions?

[29] C. S. Lewis: The Problem of Pain

c. s. lewis (1898–1963) was an English scholar, critic, theologian, and novelist. Among his works are *A Preface to Paradise Lost, The Screwtape Letters, The Pilgrim's Regress,* and *Miracles.* The following selection is the opening chapter of *The Problem of Pain,* published in 1940. Footnotes are the author's.

> *I wonder at the hardihood with which such persons undertake to talk about God. In a treatise addressed to infidels they begin with a chapter proving the existence of God from the works of Nature . . . this only gives their readers grounds for thinking that the proofs of our religion are very weak. . . . It is a remarkable fact that no canonical writer has ever used Nature to prove God.*
> pascal, Pensées, IV, 242, 243.

[1] Not many years ago when I was an atheist, if anyone had asked me, "Why do you not believe in God?" my reply would have run something like this: "Look at the universe we live in. By far the greatest part of it consists of empty space, completely dark and unimaginably cold. The bodies which move in this space are so few and so small in comparison with the space itself that even if every one of them were known to be crowded as full as it could hold with perfectly happy creatures, it would still be difficult to believe that life and happiness were more than a by-product to the power that made the universe. As it is, however, the scientists think it likely that very few of the suns of space—perhaps none of them except our own—have any planets; and in our own system it is improbable that any planet except the Earth sustains life. And Earth herself existed without life for millions of years and may exist for millions more when life has left her. And what is it like while it lasts? It is so arranged that all the forms of it can live only by preying upon one an-

other. In the lower forms this process entails only death, but in the higher there appears a new quality called consciousness which enables it to be attended with pain. The creatures cause pain by being born, and live by inflicting pain, and in pain they mostly die. In the most complex of all the creatures, Man, yet another quality appears, which we call reason, whereby he is enabled to foresee his own pain which henceforth is proceeded with acute mental suffering, and to foresee his own death while keenly desiring permanence. It also enables men by a hundred ingenious contrivances to inflict a great deal more pain than they otherwise could have done on one another and on the irrational creatures. This power they have exploited to the full. Their history is largely a record of crime, war, disease, and terror, with just sufficient happiness interposed to give them, while it lasts, an agonised apprehension of losing it, and, when it is lost, the poignant misery of remembering. Every now and then they improve their condition a little and what we call a civilisation appears. But all civilisations pass away and, even while they remain, inflict peculiar sufferings of their own probably sufficient to outweigh what alleviations they may have brought to the normal pains of man. That our own civilisation has done so, no one will dispute; that it will pass away like all its predecessors is surely probable. Even if it should not, what then? The race is doomed. Every race that comes into being in any part of the universe is doomed; for the universe, they tell us, is running down, and will sometime be a uniform infinity of homogeneous matter at a low temperature. All stories will come to nothing: all life will turn out in the end to have been a transitory and senseless contortion upon the idiotic face of infinite matter. If you ask me to believe that this is the work of a benevolent and omnipotent spirit, I reply that all the evidence points in the opposite direction. Either there is no spirit behind the universe, or else a spirit indifferent to good and evil, or else an evil spirit."

[²] There was one question which I never dreamed of raising. I never noticed that the very strength and facility of the pessimists' case at once poses us a problem. If the universe is so bad, or even half so bad, how on earth did human beings ever come to attribute it to the activity of a wise and good Creator? Men are fools, perhaps; but hardly so foolish as that. The direct inference from black to white, from evil flower to virtuous root, from senseless work to a workman infinitely wise, staggers belief. The spectacle of the universe as revealed by experience can never have been the ground of religion: it must always have been something in spite of which religion, acquired from a different source, was held.

[³] It would be an error to reply that our ancestors were ignorant and therefore entertained pleasing illusions about nature which the progress of science has since dispelled. For centuries, during which all men believed, the nightmare size and emptiness of the universe was already known. You will read in some books that the men of the Middle Ages thought the Earth flat and the stars near, but that is a lie. Ptolemy had told them that the Earth was a mathematical point without size in relation to the distance of the fixed stars—a distance which one mediæval popular text estimates as a hundred and seventeen million miles. And in times yet earlier, even from the beginnings, men must have got the same sense of hostile immensity from a more obvious source. To prehistoric man the neighbouring forest must have been infinite enough, and the utterly alien and infest which we have to fetch from the thought of cosmic rays and cooling suns, came snuffing and howling nightly to his very doors. Certainly at all periods the pain and waste of human life was equally obvious. Our own religion begins among the Jews, a people squeezed between great warlike empires, continually defeated and led captive, familiar as Poland or Armenia with the tragic story of the conquered. It is mere nonsense to put pain among the discoveries of science. Lay down this book and reflect for five minutes on the fact that all the great religions were first preached, and long practised, in a world without chloroform.

[4] At all times, then, an inference from the course of events in this world to the goodness and wisdom of the Creator would have been equally preposterous; and it was never made.[1] Religion has a different origin. In what follows it must be understood that I am not *primarily* arguing the truth of Christianity but describing its origin—a task, in my view, necessary if we are to put the problem of pain in its right setting.

[5] In all developed religion we find three strands or elements, and in Christianity one more. The first of these is what Professor Otto calls the experience of the *Numinous*. Those who have not met this term may be introduced to it by the following device. Suppose you were told there was a tiger in the next room: you would know that you were in danger and would probably feel fear. But if you were told "There is a ghost in the next room," and believed it, you would feel, indeed, what is often called fear, but of a different kind. It would not be based on the knowledge of danger, for no one is primarily afraid of what a ghost may do to him, but of the mere fact that it is a ghost. It is "uncanny" rather than dangerous, and the special kind of fear it excites may be called Dread. With the Uncanny one has reached the fringes of the Numinous. Now suppose that you were told simply "There is a mighty spirit in the room," and believed it. Your feelings would then be even less like the mere fear of danger: but the disturbance would be profound. You would feel wonder and a certain shrinking—a sense of inadequacy to cope with such a visitant and of prostration before it—an emotion which might be expressed in Shakespeare's words "Under it my genius is rebuked." This feeling may be described as awe, and the object which excites it as the *Numinous*.

---

[1] *I.e.*, never made at the beginnings of a religion. *After* belief in God has been accepted, "theodicies" explaining, or explaining away, the miseries of life, will naturally appear often enough.

[⁶] Now nothing is more certain than that man, from a very early period, began to believe that the universe was haunted by spirits. Professor Otto perhaps assumes too easily that from the very first such spirits were regarded with numinous awe. This is impossible to prove for the very good reason that utterances expressing awe of the Numinous and utterances expressing mere fear of danger may use identical language—as we can still say that we are "afraid" of a ghost or "afraid" of a rise in prices. It is therefore theoretically possible that there was a time when men regarded these spirits simply as dangerous and felt towards them just as they felt towards tigers. What is certain is that now, at any rate, the numinous experience exists and that if we start from ourselves we can trace it a long way back.

[⁷] A modern example may be found (if we are not too proud to seek it there) in *The Wind in the Willows* where Rat and Mole approach Pan on the island.

[⁸] " 'Rat,' he found breath to whisper, shaking, 'Are you afraid?' 'Afraid?' murmured the Rat, his eyes shining with unutterable love. 'Afraid? of Him? O, never, never. And yet—and yet—O Mole, I am afraid.' "

[⁹] Going back about a century we find copious examples in Wordsworth—perhaps the finest being that passage in the first book of the *Prelude* where he describes his experience while rowing on the lake in the stolen boat. Going back further we get a very pure and strong example in Malory,[2] when Galahad "began to tremble right hard when the deadly (= mortal) flesh began to behold the spiritual things." At the beginning of our era it finds expression in the Apocalypse where the writer fell at the feet of the risen Christ "as one dead." In Pagan literature we find Ovid's picture of the dark grove on the Aventine of which you would say at a glance *numen inest*[3]—the place is haunted, or there is a Presence here; and Virgil gives us the palace of Latinus "awful (*horrendum*) with woods and sanctity (*religione*) of elder days."[4] A Greek fragment attributed, but improbably, to Æschylus, tells us of earth, sea, and mountain shaking beneath the "dread eye of their Master."[5] And far further back Ezekiel tells us of the "rings" in his Theophany that "they were so high that they were dreadful"[6]: and Jacob, rising from sleep, says "How dreadful is this place!"[7]

[¹⁰] We do not know how far back in human history this feeling goes. The earliest men almost certainly believed in things which would excite

---

[2] XVII, xxii.
[3] *Fasti*, III, 296.
[4] *Aen.* VII, 172.
[5] Fragm, 464. Sidgwick's edition.
[6] Ezek. i, 18.
[7] Gen. xxviii, 17.

the feeling in us if *we* believed in them, and it seems therefore probable that numinous awe is as old as humanity itself. But our main concern is not with its dates. The important thing is that somehow or other it has come into existence, and is widespread, and does not disappear from the mind with the growth of knowledge and civilisation.

[11] Now this awe is not the result of an inference from the visible universe. There is no possibililty of arguing from mere danger to the uncanny, still less to the fully Numinous. You may say that it seems to you very natural that early man, being surrounded by real dangers, and therefore frightened, should invent the uncanny and the Numinous. In a sense it is, but let us understand what we mean. You feel it to be natural because, sharing human nature with your remote ancestors, you can imagine yourself reacting to perilous solitudes in the same way; and this reaction is indeed "natural" in the sense of being in accord with human nature. But it is not in the least "natural" in the sense that the idea of the uncanny or the Numinous is already contained in the idea of the dangerous, or that any perception of danger or any dislike of the wounds and death which it may entail could give the slightest conception of ghostly dread or numinous awe to an intelligence which did not already understand them. When man passes from physical fear to dread and awe, he makes a sheer jump, and apprehends something which could never be *given*, as danger is, by the physical facts and logical deductions from them. Most attempts to explain the Numinous presuppose the thing to be explained—as when anthropologists derive it from fear of the dead, without explaining why dead men (assuredly the least dangerous kind of men) should have attracted this peculiar feeling. Against all such attempts we must insist that dread and awe are in a different dimension from fear. They are in the nature of an interpretation man gives to the universe, or an impression he gets from it; and just as no enumeration of the physical qualities of a beautiful object could ever include its beauty, or give the faintest hint of what we mean by beauty to a creature without aesthetic experience, so no factual description of any human environment could include the uncanny and the Numinous or even hint at them. There seem, in fact, to be only two views we can hold about awe. Either it is a mere twist in the human mind, corresponding to nothing objective and serving no biological function, yet showing no tendency to disappear from that mind at its fullest development in poet, philosopher, or saint: or else it is a direct experience of the really supernatural, to which the name Revelation might properly be given.

[12] The Numinous is not the same as the morally good, and a man overwhelmed with awe is likely, if left to himself, to think the numinous object "beyond good and evil." This brings us to the second strand or element in religion. All the human beings that history has heard of acknowledge some kind of morality; that is, they feel towards certain

proposed actions the experiences expressed by the words "I ought" or "I ought not." These experiences resemble awe in one respect, namely that they cannot be logically deduced from the environment and physical experiences of the man who undergoes them. You can shuffle "I want" and "I am forced" and "I shall be well advised" and "I dare not" as long as you please without getting out of them the slightest hint of "ought" and "ought not." And, once again, attempts to resolve the moral experience into something else always presuppose the very thing they are trying to explain—as when a famous psychoanalyst deduces it from prehistoric parricide. If the parricide produced a sense of guilt, that was because men felt that they ought not to have committed it: if they did not so feel, it could produce no sense of guilt. Morality, like numinous awe, is a jump; in it, man goes beyond anything that can be "given" in the facts of experience. And it has one characteristic too remarkable to be ignored. The moralities accepted among men may differ—though not, at bottom, so widely as is often claimed—but they all agree in prescribing a behaviour which their adherents fail to practise. All men alike stand condemned, not by alien codes of ethics, but by their own, and all men therefore are conscious of guilt. The second element in religion is the consciousness not merely of a moral law, but of a moral law at once approved and disobeyed. This consciousness is neither a logical, nor an illogical, inference from the facts of experience; if we did not bring it to our experience we could not find it there. It is either inexplicable illusion, or else revelation.

[13] The moral experience and the numinous experience are so far from being the same that they may exist for quite long periods without establishing a mutual contact. In many forms of Paganism the worship of the gods and the ethical discussions of the philosophers have very little to do with each other. The third stage in religious development arises when men identify them—when the Numinous Power of which they feel awe is made the guardian of the morality to which they feel obligation. Once again, this may seem to you very "natural." What can be more natural than for a savage haunted at once by awe and by guilt to think that the power which awes him is also the authority which condemns his guilt? And it is, indeed, natural to humanity. But it is not in the least obvious. The actual behaviour of that universe which the Numinous haunts bears no resemblance to the behaviour which morality demands of us. The one seems wasteful, ruthless, and unjust; the other enjoins upon us the opposite qualities. Nor can the identification of the two be explained as a wish fulfilment, for it fulfils no one's wishes. We desire nothing less than to see that Law whose naked authority is already unsupportable armed with the incalculable claims of the Numinous. Of all the jumps that humanity takes in its religious history this is certainly the most surprising. It is not unnatural that many sections of the human race refused it; non-

moral religion, and non-religious morality, existed and still exist. Perhaps only a single people, as a people, took the new step with perfect decision —I mean the Jews: but great individuals in all times and places have taken it also, and only those who take it are safe from the obscenities and barbarities of unmoralised worship or the cold, sad self-righteousness of sheer moralism. Judged by its fruits, this step is a step towards increased health. And though logic does not compel us to take it, it is very hard to resist—even on Paganism and Pantheism morality is always breaking in, and even Stoicism finds itself willy-nilly bowing the knee to God. Once more, it may be madness—a madness congenital to man and oddly fortunate in its results—or it may be revelation. And if revelation, then it is most really and truly in Abraham that all peoples shall be blessed, for it was the Jews who fully and unambiguously identified the awful Presence haunting black mountain-tops and thunderclouds with "the *righteous* Lord" who "loveth righteousness."[8]

[14] The fourth strand or element is a historical event. There was a man born among these Jews who claimed to be, or to be the son of, or to be "one with," the Something which is at once the awful haunter of nature and the giver of the moral law. The claim is so shocking—a paradox, and even a horror, which we may easily be lulled into taking too lightly—that only two views of this man are possible. Either he was a raving lunatic of an unusually abominable type, or else He was, and is, precisely what He said. There is no middle way. If the records make the first hypothesis unacceptable, you must submit to the second. And if you do that, all else that is claimed by Christians becomes credible—that this Man, having been killed, was yet alive, and that His death, in some manner incomprehensible to human thought, has effected a real change in our relations to the "awful" and "righteous" Lord, and a change in our favour.

[15] To ask whether the universe as we see it looks more like the work of a wise and good Creator or the work of chance, indifference, or malevolence, is to omit from the outset all the relevant factors in the religious problem. Christianity is not the conclusion of a philosophical debate on the origins of the universe: it is a catastrophic historical event following on the long spiritual preparation of humanity which I have described. It is not a system into which we have to fit the awkward fact of pain: it is itself one of the awkward facts which have to be fitted into any system we make. In a sense, it creates, rather than solves, the problem of pain, for pain would be no problem unless, side by side with our daily experience of this painful world, we had received what we think a good assurance that ultimate reality is righteous and loving.

[16] Why this assurance seems to me good, I have more or less indicated. It does not amount to logical compulsion. At every stage of religious development man may rebel, if not without violence to his

[8] Ps. xi, 8.

own nature, yet without absurdity. He can close his spiritual eyes against the Numinous, if he is prepared to part company with half the great poets and prophets of his race, with his own childhood, with the richness and depth of uninhibited experience. He can regard the moral law as an illusion, and so cut himself off from the common ground of humanity. He can refuse to identify the Numinous with the righteous, and remain a barbarian, worshipping sexuality, or the dead, or the life-force, or the future. But the cost is heavy. And when we come to the last step of all, the historical Incarnation, the assurance is strongest of all. The story is strangely like many myths which have haunted religion from the first, and yet it is not like them. It is not transparent to the reason: we could not have invented it ourselves. It has not the suspicious *a priori* lucidity of Pantheism or of Newtonian physics. It has the seemingly arbitrary and idiosyncratic character which modern science is slowly teaching us to put up with in this wilful universe, where energy is made up in little parcels of a quantity no one could predict, where speed is not unlimited, where irreversible entropy gives time a real direction and the cosmos, no longer static or cyclic, moves like a drama from a real beginning to a real end. If any message from the core of reality ever were to reach us, we should expect to find in it just that unexpectedness, that wilful, dramatic anfractuosity which we find in the Christian faith. It has the master touch—the rough, male taste of reality, not made by us, or, indeed, for us, but hitting us in the face.

[17] If, on such grounds, or on better ones, we follow the course on which humanity has been led, and become Christians, we then have the "problem" of pain.

⋙ COMMENT AND QUESTIONS ⋘

1. What purposes are served by the long introductory paragraph presenting the atheist's views?
2. How would you describe the author's tone in paragraphs 3 and 4?
3. By what methods does Lewis define the Numinous in paragraph 5? In the following paragraphs how does he support his thesis that the numinous experience exists and is something not inferred from the visible world? Do you find any qualification of this particular thesis?
4. What do the numinous experience and the moral experience have in common? How do they differ?
5. What is meant by the statement in paragraph 13: "We desire nothing less than to see that Law whose naked authority is already unsupportable armed with the incalculable claims of the Numinous"?

6. Look again at Lewis' discussion (paragraphs 4–13) of the three strands or elements present in developed religions. Do you find his reasoning questionable at any point? Do his conclusions follow logically from his material? Explain.

7. In paragraph 14 the author uses some highly charged language. Do his charged words seem to you accurate? Are they effective? Do you agree that "there is no middle way" between the two hypotheses about Jesus?

8. What does Lewis mean, in paragraph 15, by calling Christianity "a *catastrophic* historical event"?

9. In paragraph 16 Lewis concedes that at every stage of religious development a man may, without absurdity, rebel. By what techniques does he make such rebellion seem undesirable?

10. The author uses the words *idiosyncratic* and *anfractuosity*, words which may have unfavorable connotations, in his discussion of the Christian faith (paragraph 16). What do the words mean? In this context, what favorable connotations do they have?

11. Comment on the author's reasoning in the last two paragraphs of the selection. Does he seem to you to make any unwarranted assumptions or inferences? Explain.

12. C. S. Lewis is an interesting writer. What qualities of style seem to you particularly good or noticeable in this selection?

[30] *Jean-Paul Sartre*: Existentialism

THE FOLLOWING discussion of existentialism, originally a lecture, is taken from *Existentialism and Humanism,* published in 1948. Jean-Paul Sartre (1905–   ), French novelist, short story writer, playwright, and philosopher, is a leading spokesman for the philosophy which he is explaining and defending in this selection. Assuming a universe without purpose, in which the individual alone determines what he will be, Sartre considers existentialism a philosophy not of pessimism and passivity, but of optimism and action. Among Sartre's other works are *Being and Nothingness, The Flies, No Exit, Nausea,* and *The Words.*

[1] What, then, is this that we call existentialism? Most of those who are making use of this word would be highly confused if required to explain its meaning. For since it has become fashionable, people cheerfully declare that this musician or that painter is "existentialist." A

This selection was translated by Philip Mairet.

columnist in *Clartés* signs himself "The Existentialist," and, indeed, the word is now so loosely applied to so many things that it no longer means anything at all. It would appear that, for the lack of any novel doctrine such as that of surrealism, all those who are eager to join in the latest scandal or movement now seize upon this philosophy in which, however, they can find nothing to their purpose. For in truth this is of all teachings the least scandalous and the most austere: it is intended strictly for technicians and philosophers. All the same, it can easily be defined.

[2] The question is only complicated because there are two kinds of existentialists. There are, on the one hand, the Christians, amongst whom I shall name Jaspers and Gabriel Marcel, both professed Catholics; and on the other the existential atheists, amongst whom we must place Heidegger as well as the French existentialists and myself. What they have in common is simply the fact that they believe that *existence* comes before *essence*—or, if you will, that we must begin from the subjective. What exactly do we mean by that?

[3] If one considers an article of manufacture—as, for example, a book or a paper-knife—one sees that it has been made by an artisan who had a conception of it; and he has paid attention, equally, to the conception of a paper-knife and to the pre-existent technique of production which is a part of that conception and is, at bottom, a formula. Thus the paper-knife is at the same time an article producible in a certain manner and one which, on the other hand, serves a definite purpose, for one cannot suppose that a man would produce a paper-knife without knowing what it was for. Let us say, then, of the paper-knife that its essence—that is to say the sum of the formulae and the qualities which made its production and its definition possible—precedes its existence. The presence of such-and-such a paper-knife or book is thus determined before my eyes. Here, then, we are viewing the world from a technical standpoint, and we can say that production precedes existence.

[4] When we think of God as the creator, we are thinking of him, most of the time, as a supernal artisan. Whatever doctrine we may be considering, whether it be a doctrine like that of Descartes, or of Leibnitz himself, we always imply that the will follows, more or less, from the understanding or at least accompanies it, so that when God creates he knows precisely what he is creating. Thus, the conception of man in the mind of God is comparable to that of the paper-knife in the mind of the artisan: God makes man according to a procedure and a conception, exactly as the artisan manufactures a paper-knife, following a definition and a formula. Thus each individual man is the realization of a certain conception which dwells in the divine understanding. In the philosophic atheism of the eighteenth century, the notion of God is suppressed, but not, for all that, the idea that essence is prior to existence; something of that idea we still find everywhere, in Diderot, in Voltaire and even in

Kant. Man possesses a human nature; that "human nature," which is the conception of human being, is found in every man; which means that each man is a particular example of a universal conception, the conception of Man. In Kant, this universality goes so far that the wild man of the woods, man in the state of nature and the bourgeois are all contained in the same definition and have the same fundamental qualities. Here again, the essence of man precedes that historic existence which we confront in experience.

[5] Atheistic existentialism, of which I am a representative, declares with greater consistency that if God does not exist there is at least one being whose existence comes before its essence, a being which exists before it can be defined by any conception of it. That being is man or, as Heidegger has it, the human reality. What do we mean by saying that existence precedes essence? We mean that man first of all exists, encounters himself, surges up in the world—and defines himself afterwards. If man as the existentialist sees him as not definable, it is because to begin with he is nothing. He will not be anything until later, and then he will be what he makes of himself. Thus, there is no human nature, because there is no God to have a conception of it. Man simply is. Not that he is simply what he conceives himself to be, but he is what he wills, and as he conceives himself after already existing—as he wills to be after that leap towards existence. Man is nothing else but that which he makes of himself. That is the first principle of existentialism. And this is what people call its "subjectivity," using the word as a reproach against us. But what do we mean to say by this, but that man is of a greater dignity than a stone or a table? For we mean to say that man primarily exists— that man is, before all else, something which propels itself towards a future and is aware that it is doing so. Man is, indeed, a project which possesses a subjective life, instead of being a kind of moss, or a fungus or a cauliflower. Before that projection of the self nothing exists; not even in the heaven of intelligence: man will only attain existence when he is what he purposes to be. Not, however, what he may wish to be. For what we usually understand by wishing or willing is a conscious decision taken— much more often than not—after we have made ourselves what we are. I may wish to join a party, to write a book or to marry—but in such a case what is usually called my will is probably a manifestation of a prior and more spontaneous decision. If, however, it is true that existence is prior to essence, man is responsible for what he is. Thus, the first effect of existentialism is that it puts every man in possession of himself as he is, and places the entire responsibility for his existence squarely upon his own shoulders. And, when we say that man is responsible for himself, we do not mean that he is responsible only for his own individuality, but that he is responsible for all men. The word "subjectivism" is to be understood in two senses, and our adversaries play upon only one of them.

Subjectivism means, on the one hand, the freedom of the individual subject and, on the other, that man cannot pass beyond human subjectivity. It is the latter which is the deeper meaning of existentialism. When we say that man chooses himself, we do mean that every one of us must choose himself; but by that we also mean that in choosing for himself he chooses for all men. For in effect, of all the actions a man may take in order to create himself as he wills to be, there is not one which is not creative, at the same time, of an image of man such as he believes he ought to be. To choose between this or that is at the same time to affirm the value of that which is chosen; for we are unable ever to choose the worse. What we choose is always the better; and nothing can be better for us unless it is better for all. If, moreover, existence precedes essence and we will to exist at the same time as we fashion our image, that image is valid for all and for the entire epoch in which we find ourselves. Our responsibility is thus much greater than we had supposed, for it concerns mankind as a whole. If I am a worker, for instance, I may choose to join a Christian rather than a Communist trade union. And if, by that membership, I choose to signify that resignation is, after all, the attitude that best becomes a man, that man's kingdom is not upon this earth, I do not commit myself alone to that view. Resignation is my will for everyone, and my action is, in consequence, a commitment on behalf of all mankind. Or if, to take a more personal case, I decide to marry and to have children, even though this decision proceeds simply from my situation, from my passion or my desire, I am thereby committing not only myself, but humanity as a whole, to the practice of monogamy. I am thus responsible for myself and for all men, and I am creating a certain image of man as I would have him to be. In fashioning myself I fashion man.

[6] This may enable us to understand what is meant by such terms—perhaps a little grandiloquent—as anguish, abandonment and despair. As you will soon see, it is very simple. First, what do we mean by anguish? The existentialist frankly states that man is in anguish. His meaning is as follows—When a man commits himself to anything, fully realizing that he is not only choosing what he will be, but is thereby at the same time a legislator deciding for the whole of mankind—in such a moment a man cannot escape from the sense of complete and profound responsibility. There are many, indeed, who show no such anxiety. But we affirm that they are merely disguising their anguish or are in flight from it. Certainly, many people think that in what they are doing they commit no one but themselves to anything: and if you ask them, "What would happen if everyone did so?" they shrug their shoulders and reply, "Everyone does not do so." But in truth, one ought always to ask oneself what would happen if everyone did as one is doing; nor can one escape from that disturbing thought except by a kind of self-deception. The man

who lies in self-excuse, by saying "Everyone will not do it" must be ill at ease in his conscience, for the act of lying implies the universal value which it denies. By its very disguise his anguish reveals itself. This is the anguish that Kierkegaard called "the anguish of Abraham." You know the story: An angel commanded Abraham to sacrifice his son: and obedience was obligatory, if it really was an angel who had appeared and said, "Thou, Abraham, shalt sacrifice thy son." But anyone in such a case would wonder, first, whether it was indeed an angel and secondly, whether I am really Abraham. Where are the proofs? A certain mad woman who suffered from hallucinations said that people were telephoning to her, and giving her orders. The doctor asked, "But who is it that speaks to you?" She replied: "He says it is God." And what, indeed, could prove to her that it was God? If an angel appears to me, what is the proof that it is an angel; or, if I hear voices, who can prove that they proceed from heaven and not from hell, or from my own subconsciousness or some pathological condition? Who can prove that they are really addressed to me?

[7] Who, then, can prove that I am the proper person to impose, by my own choice, my conception of man upon mankind? I shall never find any proof whatever; there will be no sign to convince me of it. If a voice speaks to me, it is still I myself who must decide whether the voice is or is not that of an angel. If I regard a certain course of action as good, it is only I who choose to say that it is good and not bad. There is nothing to show that I am Abraham: nevertheless I also am obliged at every instant to peform actions which are examples. Everything happens to every man as though the whole human race had its eyes fixed upon what he is doing and regulated its conduct accordingly. So every man ought to say, "Am I really a man who has the right to act in such a manner that humanity regulates itself by what I do?" If a man does not say that, he is dissembling his anguish. Clearly, the anguish with which we are concerned here is not one that could lead to quietism or inaction. It is anguish pure and simple, of the kind well known to all those who have borne responsibilities. When, for instance, a military leader takes upon himself the responsibility for an attack and sends a number of men to their death, he chooses to do it and at bottom he alone chooses. No doubt he acts under a higher command, but its orders, which are more general, require interpretation by him and upon that interpretation depends the life of ten, fourteen or twenty men. In making the decision, he cannot but feel a certain anguish. All leaders know that anguish. It does not prevent their acting, on the contrary it is the very condition of their action, for the action presupposes that there is a plurality of possibilities, and in choosing one of these, they realize that it has value only because it is chosen. Now it is anguish of that kind which existentialism describes, and moreover, as we shall see, makes

explicit through direct responsibility towards other men who are concerned. Far from being a screen which could separate us from action, it is a condition of action itself.

[8] And when we speak of "abandonment"—a favorite word of Heidegger—we only mean to say that God does not exist, and that it is necessary to draw the consequences of his absence right to the end. The existentialist is strongly opposed to a certain type of secular moralism which seeks to suppress God at the least possible expense. Towards 1880, when the French professors endeavored to formulate a secular morality, they said something like this:—God is a useless and costly hypothesis, so we will do without it. However, if we are to have morality, a society and a law-abiding world, it is essential that certain values should be taken seriously; they must have an *à priori* existence ascribed to them. It must be considered obligatory *à priori* to be honest, not to lie, not to beat one's wife, to bring up children and so forth; so we are going to do a little work on this subject, which will enable us to show that these values exist all the same, inscribed in an intelligible heaven although, of course, there is no God. In other words—and this is, I believe, the purport of all that we in France call radicalism—nothing will be changed if God does not exist; we shall rediscover the same norms of honesty, progress and humanity, and we shall have disposed of God as an out-of-date hypothesis which will die away quietly of itself. The existentialist, on the contrary, finds it extremely embarrassing that God does not exist, for there disappears with Him all possibility of finding values in an intelligible heaven. There can no longer be any good *à priori*, since there is no infinite and perfect consciousness to think it. It is nowhere written that "the good" exists, that one must be honest or must not lie, since we are now upon the plane where there are only men. Dostoevsky once wrote "If God did not exist, everything would be permitted"; and that, for existentialism, is the starting point. Everything is indeed permitted if God does not exist, and man is in consequence forlorn, for he cannot find anything to depend upon either within or outside himself. He discovers forthwith, that he is without excuse. For if indeed existence precedes essence, one will never be able to explain one's action by reference to a given and specific human nature; in other words, there is no determinism—man is free, man *is* freedom. Nor, on the other hand, if God does not exist, are we provided with any values or commands that could legitimize our behavior. Thus we have neither behind us, nor before us in a luminous realm of values, any means of justification or excuse. We are left alone, without excuse. That is what I mean when I say that man is condemned to be free. Condemned, because he did not create himself, yet is nevertheless at liberty, and from the moment that he is thrown into this world he is responsible for everything he does. The existentialist does not believe in the power of passion. He will never regard a grand passion as a destructive torrent upon which

a man is swept into certain actions as by fate, and which, therefore, is an excuse for them. He thinks that man is responsible for his passion. Neither will an existentialist think that a man can find help through some sign being vouchsafed upon earth for his orientation: for he thinks that the man himself interprets the sign as he chooses. He thinks that every man, without any support or help whatever, is condemned at every instant to invent man. As Ponge has written in a very fine article, "Man is the future of man." That is exactly true. Only, if one took this to mean that the future is laid up in Heaven, that God knows what it is, it would be false, for then it would no longer even be a future. If, however, it means that, whatever man may now appear to be, there is a future to be fashioned, a virgin future that awaits him—then it is a true saying. But in the present one is forsaken.

[⁹] As an example by which you may the better understand this state of abandonment, I will refer to the case of a pupil of mine, who sought me out in the following circumstances. His father was quarrelling with his mother and was also inclined to be a "collaborator";[1] his elder brother had been killed in the German offensive of 1940 and this young man, with a sentiment somewhat primitive but generous, burned to avenge him. His mother was living alone with him, deeply afflicted by the semi-treason of his father and by the death of her eldest son, and her one consolation was in this young man. But he, at this moment, had the choice between going to England to join the Free French Forces or of staying near his mother and helping her to live. He fully realized that this woman lived only for him and that his disappearance—or perhaps his death—would plunge her into despair. He also realized that, concretely and in fact, every action he performed on his mother's behalf would be sure of effect in the sense of aiding her to live, whereas anything he did in order to go and fight would be an ambiguous action which might vanish like water into sand and serve no purpose. For instance, to set out for England he would have to wait indefinitely in a Spanish camp on the way through Spain; or, on arriving in England or in Algiers he might be put into an office to fill up forms. Consequently, he found himself confronted by two very different modes of action; the one concrete, immediate, but directed towards only one individual; and the other an action addressed to an end infinitely greater, a national collectivity, but for that very reason ambiguous—and it might be frustrated on the way. At the same time, he was hesitating between two kinds of morality; on the one side the morality of sympathy, of personal devotion and, on the other side, a morality of wider scope but of more debatable validity. He had to choose between those two. What could help him to choose? Could the Christian doctrine? No. Christian doctrine says: Act with charity, love your neighbour, deny

---

[1] A Frenchman who cooperated with the Germans in World War II.

yourself for others, choose the way which is hardest, and so forth. But which is the harder road? To whom does one owe the more brotherly love, the patriot or the mother? Which is the more useful aim, the general one of fighting in and for the whole community, or the precise aim of helping one particular person to live? Who can give an answer to that *à priori*? No one. Nor is it given in any ethical scripture. The Kantian ethic says, Never regard another as a means, but always as an end. Very well; if I remain with my mother, I shall be regarding her as the end and not as a means: but by the same token I am in danger of treating as means those who are fighting on my behalf; and the converse is also true, that if I go to the aid of the combatants I shall be treating them as the end at the risk of treating my mother as a means.

[10] If values are uncertain, if they are still too abstract to determine the particular, concrete case under consideration, nothing remains but to trust in our instincts. That is what this young man tried to do; and when I saw him he said, "In the end, it is feeling that counts; the direction in which it is really pushing me is the one I ought to choose. If I feel that I love my mother enough to sacrifice everything else for her—my will to be avenged, all my longings for action and adventure—then I stay with her. If, on the contrary, I feel that my love for her is not enough, I go." But how does one estimate the strength of a feeling? The value of his feeling for his mother was determined precisely by the fact that he was standing by her. I may say that I love a certain friend enough to sacrifice such or such a sum of money for him, but I cannot prove that unless I have done it. I may say, "I love my mother enough to remain with her," if actually I have remained with her. I can only estimate the strength of this affection if I have performed an action by which it is defined and ratified. But if I then appeal to this affection to justify my action, I find myself drawn into a vicious circle.

[11] Moreover, as Gide has very well said, a sentiment which is play-acting and one which is vital are two things that are hardly distinguishable one from another. To decide that I love my mother by staying beside her, and to play a comedy the upshot of which is that I do so—these are nearly the same thing. In other words, feeling is formed by the deeds that one does; therefore I cannot consult it as a guide to action. And that is to say that I can neither seek within myself for an authentic impulse to action, nor can I expect, from some ethic, formulae that will enable me to act. You may say that the youth did, at least, go to a professor to ask for advice. But if you seek counsel—from a priest, for example—you have selected that priest; and at bottom you already knew, more or less, what he would advise. In other words, to choose an adviser is nevertheless to commit oneself by that choice. If you are a Christian, you will say, Consult a priest; but there are collaborationists, priests who are resisters and priests who wait for the tide to turn: which will you choose? Had

this young man chosen a priest of the resistance, or one of the collaboration, he would have decided beforehand the kind of advice he was to receive. Similarly, in coming to me, he knew what advice I should give him, and I had but one reply to make. You are free, therefore choose—that is to say, invent. No rule of general morality can show you what you ought to do: no signs are vouchsafed in this world. The Catholics will reply, "Oh, but they are!" Very well; still, it is I myself, in every case, who have to interpret the signs. While I was imprisoned,[2] I made the acquaintance of a somewhat remarkable man, a Jesuit, who had become a member of that order in the following manner. In his life he had suffered a succession of rather servere setbacks. His father had died when he was a child, leaving him in poverty, and he had been awarded a free scholarship in a religious institution, where he had been made continually to feel that he was accepted for charity's sake, and, in consequence, he had been denied several of those distinctions and honors which gratify children. Later, about the age of eighteen, he came to grief in a sentimental affair; and finally, at twenty-two—this was a trifle in itself, but it was the last drop that overflowed his cup—he failed in his military examination. This young man, then, could regard himself as a total failure: it was a sign —but a sign of what? He might have taken refuge in bitterness or despair. But he took it—very cleverly for him—as a sign that he was not intended for secular successes, and that only the attainments of religion, those of sanctity and of faith, were accessible to him. He interpreted his record as a message from God, and became a member of the Order. Who can doubt but that this decision as to the meaning of the sign was his, and his alone? One could have drawn quite different conclusions from such a series of reverses—as, for example, that he had better become a carpenter or a revolutionary. For the decipherment of the sign, however, he bears the entire responsibility. That is what "abandonment" implies, that we ourselves decide our being. And with this abandonment goes anguish.

[12] As for "despair," the meaning of this expression is extremely simple. It merely means that we limit ourselves to a reliance upon that which is within our wills, or within the sum of the probabilities which render our action feasible. Whenever one wills anything, there are always these elements of probability. If I am counting upon a visit from a friend, who may be coming by train or by tram, I presuppose that the train will arrive at the appointed time, or that the tram will not be derailed. I remain in the realm of possibilities; but one does not rely upon any possibilities beyond those that are strictly concerned in one's action. Beyond the point at which the possibilities under consideration cease to affect my action, I ought to disinterest myself. For there is no God and no prevenient design, which can adapt the world and all its possibilities to my will. When

[2] As a German prisoner of war in World War II.

Descartes said, "Conquer yourself rather than the world," what he meant was, at bottom, the same—that we should act without hope.

[13] Marxists, to whom I have said this, have answered: "Your action is limited, obviously, by your death; but you can rely upon the help of others. That is, you can count both upon what the others are doing to help you elsewhere, as in China and in Russia, and upon what they will do later, after your death, to take up your action and carry it forward to its final accomplishment which will be the revolution. Moreover you must rely upon this; not to do so is immoral." To this I rejoin, first, that I shall always count upon my comrades-in-arms in the struggle, in so far as they are committed, as I am, to a definite, common cause; and in the unity of a party or a group which I can more or less control—that is, in which I am enrolled as a militant and whose movements at every moment are known to me. In that respect, to rely upon the unity and the will of the party is exactly like my reckoning that the train will run to time or that the tram will not be derailed. But I cannot count upon men whom I do not know, I cannot base my confidence upon human goodness or upon man's interest in the good of society, seeing that man is free and that there is no human nature which I can take as foundational. I do not know where the Russian revolution will lead. I can admire it and take it as an example in so far as it is evident, today, that the proletariat plays a part in Russia which it has attained in no other nation. But I cannot affirm that this will necessarily lead to the triumph of the proletariat: I must confine myself to what I can see. Nor can I be sure that comrades-in-arms will take up my work after my death and carry it to the maximum perfection, seeing that those men are free agents and will freely decide, tomorrow, what man is then to be. Tomorrow, after my death, some men may decide to establish Fascism, and the others may be so cowardly or so slack as to let them do so. If so, Fascism will then be the truth of man, and so much the worse for us. In reality, things will be such as men have decided they shall be. Does that mean that I should abandon myself to quietism? No. First I ought to commit myself and then act my commitment, according to the time-honored formula that "one need not hope in order to undertake one's work." Nor does this mean that I should not belong to a party, but only that I should be without illusion and that I should do what I can. For instance, if I ask myself "Will the social ideal as such, ever become a reality?" I cannot tell, I only know that whatever may be in my power to make it so, I shall do; beyond that, I can count upon nothing.

[14] Quietism is the attitude of people who say, "let others do what I cannot do." The doctrine I am presenting before you is precisely the opposite of this, since it declares that there is no reality except in action. It goes further, indeed, and adds, "Man is nothing else but what he purposes, he exists only in so far as he realizes himself, he is therefore nothing else but the sum of his actions, nothing else but what his life is."

Hence we can well understand why some people are horrified by our teaching. For many have but one resource to sustain them in their misery, and that is to think, "Circumstances have been against me, I was worthy to be something much better than I have been. I admit I have never had a great love or a great friendship; but that is because I never met a man or a woman who were worthy of it; if I have not written any very good books, it is because I had not the leisure to do so; or, if I have had no children to whom I could devote myself it is because I did not find the man I could have lived with. So there remains within me a wide range of abilities, inclinations and potentialities, unused but perfectly viable, which endow me with a worthiness that could never be inferred from the mere history of my actions." But in reality and for the existentialist, there is no love apart from the deeds of love; no potentiality of love other than that which is manifested in loving; there is no genius other than that which is expressed in works of art. The genius of Proust is the totality of the works of Proust; the genius of Racine is the series of his tragedies, outside of which there is nothing. Why should we attribute to Racine the capacity to write yet another tragedy when that is precisely what he did not write? In life, a man commits himself, draws his own portrait and there is nothing but that portrait. No doubt this thought may seem comfortless to one who has not made a success of his life. On the other hand, it puts everyone in a position to understand that reality alone is reliable; that dreams, expectations and hopes serve to define a man only as deceptive dreams, abortive hopes, expectations unfulfilled; that is to say, they define him negatively, not positively. Nevertheless, when one says, "You are nothing else but what you live," it does not imply that an artist is to be judged solely by his works of art, for a thousand other things contribute no less to his definition as a man. What we mean to say is that a man is no other than a series of undertakings, that he is the sum, the organization, the set of relations that constitute these undertakings.

COMMENT AND QUESTIONS

1. Explain clearly the following existentialist beliefs: (a) that existence precedes essence; (b) that man makes himself; (c) that man is responsible for all men.
2. In paragraph 2 and particularly in paragraph 5, Sartre equates the idea that "existence precedes essence" with the idea of "subjectivity." What does the term *subjectivity* mean in this context?
3. Sartre says in paragraph 5, "To choose between this or that is at the same time to affirm the value of that which is chosen; for we are unable ever

to choose the worse." Do you agree or disagree with the logic of this statement? Explain.

4. When Sartre says (at the end of paragraph 5), "In fashioning myself I fashion man" and later (in paragraph 7), "I also am obliged at every instant to perform actions which are examples," is he assuming that there is one truth or one good way of life for all men, or is his meaning different? Explain.

5. What is the relevance of the example of the mad woman, at the end of paragraph 6, to the point Sartre is making?

6. How do *anguish, abandonment,* and *despair,* as Sartre uses the words, differ in meaning? Could one term be used to convey all three meanings? Explain.

7. What does Sartre mean by saying that man is condemned to be free?

8. Explain the statement that "there is no reality except in action."

9. In what sense is existentialism an optimistic philosophy? In what sense does it dignify man?

10. If you have read the selections from Epictetus and Marcus Aurelius (page 200), do you find points of agreement between the Stoic philosophers and Sartre?

11. If you have read the selections from Plato printed in this book, what contrasts do you see between the Socratic or Platonic view and the existentialist view of man? Are there any parallels or similarities between the two philosophies?

[31]   *Albert Camus*: from The Myth of Sisyphus

THE FOLLOWING selection is part of a long philosophical essay, first published in France in 1942, in which the author explores the concept of the Absurd—the encounter of the mind that desires rationality with an irrational universe—and the problem of suicide as a solution to the Absurd. Albert Camus (1913–1960) was a distinguished Algerian French writer, winner of the Nobel Prize for Literature in 1957. His major works include *The Stranger, The Plague, The Fall, Exile and the Kingdom, The Rebel,* and *Resistance, Rebellion, and Death.*

[1] Of whom and of what indeed can I say: "I know that!" This heart within me I can feel, and I judge that it exists. This world I can touch, and I likewise judge that it exists. There ends all my knowledge, and the rest is construction. For if I try to seize this self of which I feel sure, if I try to define and to summarize it, it is nothing but water slipping

through my fingers. I can sketch one by one all the aspects it is able to assume, all those likewise that have been attributed to it, this upbringing, this origin, this ardor or these silences, this nobility or this vileness. But aspects cannot be added up. This very heart which is mine will forever remain indefinable to me. Between the certainty I have of my existence and the content I try to give to that assurance, the gap will never be filled. Forever I shall be a stranger to myself. In psychology as in logic, there are truths but no truth. Socrates' "Know thyself" has as much value as the "Be virtuous" of our confessionals. They reveal a nostalgia at the same time as an ignorance. They are sterile exercises on great subjects. They are legitimate only in precisely so far as they are approximate.

[2] And here are trees and I know their gnarled surface, water and I feel its taste. These scents of grass and stars at night, certain evenings when the heart relaxes—how shall I negate this world whose power and strength I feel? Yet all the knowledge on earth will give me nothing to assure me that this world is mine. You describe it to me and you teach me to classify it. You enumerate its laws and in my thirst for knowledge I admit that they are true. You take apart its mechanism and my hope increases. At the final stage you teach me that this wondrous and multi-colored universe can be reduced to the atom and that the atom itself can be reduced to the electron. All this is good and I wait for you to continue. But you tell me of an invisible planetary system in which electrons gravitate around a nucleus. You explain this world to me with an image. I realize then that you have been reduced to poetry: I shall never know. Have I the time to become indignant? You have already changed theories. So that science that was to teach me everything ends up in a hypothesis, that lucidity founders in metaphor, that uncertainty is resolved in a work of art. What need had I of so many efforts? The soft lines of these hills and the hand of evening on this troubled heart teach me much more. I have returned to my beginning. I realize that if through science I can seize phenomena and enumerate them, I cannot, for all that, apprehend the world. Were I to trace its entire relief with my finger, I should not know any more. And you give me the choice between a description that is sure but that teaches me nothing and hypotheses that claim to teach me but that are not sure. A stranger to myself and to the world, armed solely with a thought that negates itself as soon as it asserts, what is this condition in which I can have peace only by refusing to know and to live, in which the appetite for conquest bumps into walls that defy its assaults? To will is to stir up paradoxes. Everything is ordered in such a way as to bring into being that poisoned peace produced by thoughtlessness, lack of heart, or fatal renunciations.

[3] Hence the intelligence, too, tells me in its way that this world is absurd. Its contrary, blind reason, may well claim that all is clear; I was waiting for proof and longing for it to be right. But despite so many

pretentious centuries and over the heads of so many eloquent and persuasive men, I know that it is false. On this plane, at least, there is no happiness if I cannot know. That universal reason, practical or ethical, that determinism, those categories that explain everything are enough to make a decent man laugh. They have nothing to do with the mind. They negate its profound truth, which is to be enchained. In this unintelligible and limited universe, man's fate henceforth assumes its meaning. A horde of irrationals has sprung up and surrounds him until his ultimate end. In his recovered and now studied lucidity, the feeling of the absurd becomes clear and definite. I said that the world is absurd, but I was too hasty. This world in itself is not reasonable, that is all that can be said. But what is absurd is the confrontation of this irrational and the wild longing for clarity whose call echoes in the human heart. The absurd depends as much on man as on the world. For the moment it is all that links them together. It binds them one to the other as only hatred can weld two creatures together. This is all I can discern clearly in this measureless universe where my adventure takes place. Let us pause here. If I hold to be true that absurdity that determines my relationship with life, if I become thoroughly imbued with that sentiment that seizes me in face of the world's scenes, with that lucidity imposed on me by the pursuit of a science, I must sacrifice everything to these certainties and I must see them squarely to be able to maintain them. Above all, I must adapt my behavior to them and pursue them in all their consequences. I am speaking here of decency. But I want to know beforehand if thought can live in those deserts. . . .

[4] Now the main thing is done, I hold certain facts from which I cannot separate. What I know, what is certain, what I cannot deny, what I cannot reject—this is what counts. I can negate everything of that part of me that lives on vague nostalgias, except this desire for unity, this longing to solve, this need for clarity and cohesion. I can refute everything in this world surrounding me that offends or enraptures me, except this chaos, this sovereign chance and this divine equivalence which springs from anarchy. I don't know whether this world has a meaning that transcends it. But I know that I do not know that meaning and that it is impossible for me just now to know it. What can a meaning outside my condition mean to me? I can understand only in human terms. What I touch, what resists me—that is what I understand. And these two certainties—my appetite for the absolute and for unity and the impossibility of reducing this world to a rational and reasonable principle—I also know that I cannot reconcile them. What other truth can I admit without lying, without bringing in a hope I lack and which means nothing within the limits of my condition?

[⁵] If I were a tree among trees, a cat among animals, this life would have a meaning, or rather this problem would not arise, for I should belong to this world. I should *be* this world to which I am now opposed by my whole consciousness and my whole insistence upon familiarity. This ridiculous reason is what sets me in opposition to all creation. I cannot cross it out with a stroke of the pen. What I believe to be true I must therefore preserve. What seems to me so obvious, even against me, I must support. And what constitutes the basis of that conflict, of that break between the world and my mind, but the awareness of it? If therefore I want to preserve it, I can through a constant awareness, ever revived, ever alert. This is what, for the moment, I must remember. At this moment the absurd, so obvious and yet so hard to win, returns to a man's life and finds its home there. At this moment, too, the mind can leave the arid, dried-up path of lucid effort. That path now emerges in daily life. It encounters the world of the anonymous impersonal pronoun "one," but henceforth man enters in with his revolt and his lucidity. He has forgotten how to hope. This hell of the present is his Kingdom at last. All problems recover their sharp edge. Abstract evidence retreats before the poetry of forms and colors. Spiritual conflicts become embodied and return to the abject and magnificent shelter of man's heart. None of them is settled. But all are transfigured. Is one going to die, escape by the leap, rebuild a mansion of ideas and forms to one's own scale? Is one, on the contrary, going to take up the heart-rending and marvelous wager of the absurd? Let's make a final effort in this regard and draw all our conclusions. The body, affection, creation, action, human nobility will then resume their places in this mad world. At last man will again find there the wine of the absurd and the bread of indifference on which he feeds his greatness.

[⁶] Let us insist again on the method: it is a matter of persisting. At a certain point on his path the absurd man is tempted. History is not lacking in either religions or prophets, even without gods. He is asked to leap. All he can reply is that he doesn't fully understand, that it is not obvious. Indeed, he does not want to do anything but what he fully understands. He is assured that this is the sin of pride, but he does not understand the notion of sin; that perhaps hell is in store, but he has not enough imagination to visualize that strange future; that he is losing immortal life, but that seems to him an idle consideration. An attempt is made to get him to admit his guilt. He feels innocent. To tell the truth, that is all he feels— his irreparable innocence. This is what allows him everything. Hence what he demands of himself is to live *solely* with what he knows, to accommodate himself to what is, and to bring in nothing that is not certain. He is told that nothing is. But this at least is a certainty. And it is with this that he is concerned: he wants to find out if it is possible to live *without appeal.*

[⁷] Now I can broach the notion of suicide. It has already been felt what solution might be given. At this point the problem is reversed. It was previously a question of finding out whether or not life had to have a meaning to be lived. It now becomes clear, on the contrary, that it will be lived all the better if it has no meaning. Living an experience, a particular fate, is accepting it fully. Now, no one will live this fate, knowing it to be absurd, unless he does everything to keep before him that absurd brought to light by consciousness. Negating one of the terms of the opposition on which he lives amounts to escaping it. To abolish conscious revolt is to elude the problem. The theme of permanent revolution is thus carried into individual experience. Living is keeping the absurd alive. Keeping it alive is, above all, contemplating it. Unlike Eurydice, the absurd dies only when we turn away from it. One of the only coherent philosophical positions is thus revolt. It is a constant confrontation between man and his own obscurity. It is an insistence upon an impossible transparency. It challenges the world anew every second. Just as danger provided man the unique opportunity of seizing awareness, so metaphysical revolt extends awareness to the whole of experience. It is that constant presence of man in his own eyes. It is not aspiration, for it is devoid of hope. That revolt is the certainty of a crushing fate, without the resignation that ought to accompany it.

[⁸] This is where it is seen to what a degree absurd experience is remote from suicide. It may be thought that suicide follows revolt—but wrongly. For it does not represent the logical outcome of revolt. It is just the contrary by the consent it presupposes. Suicide, like the leap, is acceptance at its extreme. Everything is over and man returns to his essential history. His future, his unique and dreadful future—he sees and rushes toward it. In its way, suicide settles the absurd. It engulfs the absurd in the same death. But I know that in order to keep alive, the absurd cannot be settled. It escapes suicide to the extent that it is simultaneously awareness and rejection of death. It is, at the extreme limit of the condemned man's last thought, that shoelace that despite everything he sees a few yards away, on the very brink of his dizzying fall. The contrary of suicide, in fact, is the man condemned to death.

[⁹] That revolt gives life its value. Spread out over the whole length of a life, it restores its majesty to that life. To a man devoid of blinders, there is no finer sight than that of the intelligence at grips with a reality that transcends it. The sight of human pride is unequaled. No disparagement is of any use. That discipline that the mind imposes on itself, that will conjured up out of nothing, that face-to-face struggle have something exceptional about them. To impoverish that reality whose inhumanity constitutes man's majesty is tantamount to impoverishing him himself. I understand then why the doctrines that explain everything to me also debilitate me at the same time. They relieve me of the weight of my own life, and yet I must carry it alone. At this juncture, I cannot conceive that a skeptical metaphysics can be joined to an ethics of renunciation.

[10] Consciousness and revolt, these rejections are the contrary of renunciation. Everything that is indomitable and passionate in a human heart quickens them, on the contrary, with its own life. It is essential to die unreconciled and not of one's own free will. Suicide is a repudiation. The absurd man can only drain everything to the bitter end, and deplete himself. The absurd is his extreme tension, which he maintains constantly by solitary effort, for he knows that in that consciousness and in that day-to-day revolt he gives proof of his only truth, which is defiance. This is a first consequence.

[11] If I remain in that prearranged position which consists in drawing all the conclusions (and nothing else) involved in a newly discovered notion, I am faced with a second paradox. In order to remain faithful to that method, I have nothing to do with the problem of metaphysical liberty. Knowing whether or not man is free doesn't interest me. I can experience only my own freedom. As to it, I can have no general notions, but merely a few clear insights. The problem of "freedom as such" has no meaning. For it is linked in quite a different way with the problem of God. Knowing whether or not man is free involves knowing whether he can have a master. The absurdity peculiar to this problem comes from the fact that the very notion that makes the problem of freedom possible also takes away all its meaning. For in the presence of God there is less a problem of freedom than a problem of evil. You know the alternative: either we are not free and God the all-powerful is responsible for evil. Or we are free and responsible but God is not all-powerful. All the scholastic subtleties have neither added anything to nor subtracted anything from the acuteness of this paradox.

[12] This is why I cannot get lost in the glorification or the mere definition of a notion which eludes me and loses its meaning as soon as it goes beyond the frame of reference of my individual experience. I cannot understand what kind of freedom would be given me by a higher being. I have lost the sense of hierarchy. The only conception of freedom I can have is that of the prisoner or the individual in the midst of the State. The only one I know is freedom of thought and action. Now if the absurd cancels all my chances of eternal freedom, it restores and magnifies, on the other hand, my freedom of action. That privation of hope and future means an increase in man's availability.

[13] Before encountering the absurd, the everyday man lives with aims, a concern for the future or for justification (with regard to whom or what is not the question). He weighs his chances, he counts on "someday," his retirement or the labor of his sons. He still thinks that something in his life can be directed. In truth, he acts as if he were free, even if all the facts

make a point of contradicting that liberty. But after the absurd, everything is upset. That idea that "I am," my way of acting as if everything has a meaning (even if, on occasion, I said that nothing has)—all that is given the lie in vertiginous fashion by the absurdity of a possible death. Thinking of the future, establishing aims for oneself, having preferences—all this presupposes a belief in freedom, even if one occasionally ascertains that one doesn't feel it. But at that moment I am well aware that that higher liberty, that freedom *to be,* which alone can serve as basis for a truth, does not exist. Death is there as the only reality. After death the chips are down. I am not even free, either, to perpetuate myself, but a slave, and, above all, a slave without hope of an eternal revolution, without recourse to contempt. And who without revolution and without contempt can remain a slave? What freedom can exist in the fullest sense without assurance of eternity?

[14] But at the same time the absurd man realizes that hitherto he was bound to that postulate of freedom on the illusion of which he was living. In a certain sense, that hampered him. To the extent to which he imagined a purpose to his life, he adapted himself to the demands of a purpose to be achieved and became the slave of his liberty. Thus I could not act otherwise than as the father (or the engineer or the leader of a nation, or the post-office sub-clerk) that I am preparing to be. I think I can choose to be that rather than something else. I think so unconsciously, to be sure. But at the same time I strengthen my postulate with the beliefs of those around me, with the presumptions of my human environment (others are so sure of being free, and that cheerful mood is so contagious!). However far one may remain from any presumption, moral or social, one is partly influenced by them and even, for the best among them (there are good and bad presumptions), one adapts one's life to them. Thus the absurd man realizes that he was not really free. To speak clearly, to the extent to which I hope, to which I worry about a truth that might be individual to me, about a way of being or creating, to the extent to which I arrange my life and prove thereby that I accept its having a meaning, I create for myself barriers between which I confine my life. I do like so many bureaucrats of the mind and heart who only fill me with disgust and whose only vice, I now see clearly, is to take man's freedom seriously.

[15] The absurd enlightens me on this point: there is no future. Henceforth this is the reason for my inner freedom. I shall use two comparisons here. Mystics, to begin with, find freedom in giving themselves. By losing themselves in their god, by accepting his rules, they become secretly free. In spontaneously accepted slavery they recover a deeper independence. But what does that freedom mean? It may be said, above all, that they *feel* free with regard to themselves, and not so much free as liberated.

Likewise, completely turned toward death (taken here as the most obvious absurdity), the absurd man feels released from everything outside that passionate attention crystallizing in him. He enjoys a freedom with regard to common rules. It can be seen at this point that the initial themes of existential philosophy keep their entire value. The return to consciousness, the escape from everyday sleep represent the first steps of absurd freedom. But it is existential *preaching* that is alluded to, and with it that spiritual leap which basically escapes consciousness. In the same way (this is my second comparison) the slaves of antiquity did not belong to themselves. But they knew that freedom which consists in not feeling responsible. Death, too, has patrician hands which, while crushing, also liberate.

[16] Losing oneself in that bottomless certainty, feeling henceforth sufficiently remote from one's own life to increase it and take a broad view of it—this involves the principle of a liberation. Such new independence has a definite time limit, like any freedom of action. It does not write a check on eternity. But it takes the place of the illusions of *freedom*, which all stopped with death. The divine availability of the condemned man before whom the prison doors open in a certain early dawn, that unbelievable disinterestedness with regard to everything except for the pure flame of life—it is clear that death and the absurd are here the principles of the only reasonable freedom: that which a human heart can experience and live. This is a second consequence. The absurd man thus catches sight of a burning and frigid, transparent and limited universe in which nothing is possible but everything is given, and beyond which all is collapse and nothingness. He can then decide to accept such a universe and draw from it his strength, his refusal to hope, and the unyielding evidence of a life without consolation.

[17] But what does life mean in such a universe? Nothing else for the moment but indifference to the future and a desire to use up everything that is given. Belief in the meaning of life always implies a scale of values, a choice, our preferences. Belief in the absurd, according to our definitions, teaches the contrary. But this is worth examining.

[18] Knowing whether or not one can live *without appeal* is all that interests me. I do not want to get out of my depth. This aspect of life being given me, can I adapt myself to it? Now, faced with this particular concern, belief in the absurd is tantamount to substituting the quantity of experiences for the quality. If I convince myself that this life has no other aspect than that of the absurd, if I feel that its whole equilibrium depends on that perpetual opposition between my conscious revolt and the darkness in which it struggles, if I admit that my freedom has no meaning except in relation to its limited fate, then I must say that what

counts is not the best living but the most living. It is not up to me to wonder if this is vulgar or revolting, elegant or deplorable. Once and for all, value judgments are discarded here in favor of factual judgments. I have merely to draw the conclusions from what I can see and to risk nothing that is hypothetical. Supposing that living in this way were not honorable, then true propriety would command me to be dishonorable. . . .

[19] By what is an odd inconsistency in such an alert race, the Greeks claimed that those who died young were beloved of the gods. And that is true only if you are willing to believe that entering the ridiculous world of the gods is forever losing the purest of joys, which is feeling, and feeling on this earth. The present and the succession of presents before a constantly conscious soul is the ideal of the absurd man. But the word "ideal" rings false in this connection. It is not even his vocation, but merely the third consequence of his reasoning. Having started from an anguished awareness of the inhuman, the meditation on the absurd returns at the end of its itinerary to the very heart of the passionate flames of human revolt.

[20] Thus I draw from the absurd three consequences, which are my revolt, my freedom, and my passion. By the mere activity of consciousness I transform into a rule of life what was an invitation to death—and I refuse suicide. I know, to be sure, the dull resonance that vibrates throughout these days. Yet I have but a word to say: that it is necessary. When Nietzsche writes: "It clearly seems that the chief thing in heaven and on earth is to *obey* at length and in a single direction: in the long run there results something for which it is worth the trouble of living on this earth as, for example, virtue, art, music, the dance, reason, the mind— something that transfigures, something delicate, mad, or divine," he elucidates the rule of a really distinguished code of ethics. But he also points the way of the absurd man. Obeying the flame is both the easiest and the hardest thing to do. However, it is good for man to judge himself occasionally. He is alone in being able to do so.

[21] "Prayer," says Alain, "is when night descends over thought." "But the mind must meet the night," reply the mystics and the existentials. Yes, indeed, but not that night that is born under closed eyelids and through the mere will of man—dark, impenetrable night that the mind calls up in order to plunge into it. If it must encounter a night, let it be rather that of despair, which remains lucid—polar night, vigil of the mind, whence will arise perhaps that white and virginal brightness which outlines every object in the light of the intelligence. At that degree, equivalence encounters passionate understanding. Then it is no longer even a question of judging the existential leap. It resumes its place amid the age-old fresco of human attitudes. For the spectator, if he is conscious, that leap is still absurd. In so far as it thinks it solves the paradox, it

reinstates it intact. On this score, it is stirring. On this score, everything resumes its place and the absurd world is reborn in all its splendor and diversity.

[22] But it is bad to stop, hard to be satisfied with a single way of seeing, to go without contradiction, perhaps the most subtle of all spiritual forces. The preceding merely defines a way of thinking. But the point is to live.

--◦◄ C O M M E N T   A N D   Q U E S T I O N S ►◦--

1. In the first two paragraphs, what similarities are there between Camus' inability to know himself and his inability to know the world?

2. Paragraph 3 is a central statement about the Absurd. In sentence 2 of that paragraph, what is the meaning of *blind reason,* the contrary of intelligence? The Absurd binds man and the world, Camus says, "as only hatred can bind two creatures together." Why is *hatred* a better word than *love*? What is the meaning of *decency* in the next-to-last sentence?

3. We have omitted material between the paragraphs numbered 3 and 4. Paragraph 4 is in part a restatement of the absurd situation described in paragraph 3. What differences in tone do you notice in the two paragraphs?

4. Do Camus' reasons (paragraph 5) for wishing to preserve the Absurd through constant awareness of it seem convincing to you? Explain.

5. In an earlier section of *The Myth of Sisyphus* Camus has discussed existential philosophies which begin with a sense of the Absurd but make a logical "leap" to a position which denies or suppresses the Absurd. There are, Camus says, many ways of leaping or escaping. In paragraphs 5 and 6 what way or ways of leaping does he seem to refer to? What is the relationship of the leap and the life "without appeal"?

6. Explain what Camus means by revolt and by the statement that revolt gives life its value.

7. Do you agree with Camus' reasoning (paragraph 8) that suicide is not the logical outcome of revolt? Explain.

8. Summarize what seem to you Camus' most important ideas about the Absurd man's freedom.

9. In the discussion of Absurd freedom, Camus does not explicitly relate this freedom to the rejection of suicide. What relationship do you see between the two ideas?

10. By what reasoning does Camus arrive at the idea that the most living rather than the best living is what counts?

11. Camus ends the long essay from which we have taken this selection with a discussion of the legend of Sisyphus, condemned by the gods to the endless torment of rolling a rock to a mountain top from which it would

roll back down again. Each time Sisyphus leaves the heights, Camus says, he has an hour of consciousness; but he is superior to his fate, stronger than his rock, and one must imagine that Sisyphus is happy. What is the relevance of this myth and Camus' interpretation of it to the selection that you have read?

12. Some critics call Camus an existentialist writer; others do not. If you have read the selection by Sartre, to what degree do you find the existentialist philosophy, as Sartre explains it, present in this selection by Camus?

[32] *J. Glenn Gray*: Salvation on the Campus:
Why Existentialism Is Capturing the Students

J . GLENN GRAY , chairman of the philosophy department at Colorado College, is an authority on German Existentialism and author of *The Warriors: Reflections on Men In Battle*. The following article was published in *Harper's Magazine* in May, 1965.

[¹] "Our Tom looked like a bum when he came home for Christmas. His clothes were filthy, he was wearing a mandarin beard, and his hair hadn't been cut since September. Last fall we gave him permission to live alone off-campus and cook for himself. Now he has trench mouth, a bad case of athlete's foot, and some kind of mysterious virus."

[²] Our neighbor was both exasperated and amused as she thus described her son, a senior at a famous Ivy League college. He is a superior student who had hitherto seemed anything but a beatnik. For years his parents have let him steer his own course and supported him financially at some sacrifice. What, then, is he rebelling against? Is this merely a ludicrous episode in his development or a sign of a severe disorder? His mother doesn't know.

[³] Many other enlightened parents are equally perplexed by the bizarre actions of their college sons and daughters. Nor can professors and university administrators shed much light on the moods and motivations of students in the 'sixties. They have been baffled by the rioting at Berkeley last fall and other less publicized incidents elsewhere.

[⁴] For today's student is a very different creature from his predecessors. In my own college days in the 'thirties, if I had come home at

Christmas in Tom's condition, my parents would probably have had me committed to a different sort of institution. What lies behind the change?

[5] For one thing, today's student is more affluent than we were, more comfortably housed, and better equipped with the materials of scholarship. But his college life is also more impersonal and competitive, less humane. It is harder for him to know his professors, the administration, or even his all too numerous fellow students. Learning is increasingly packaged and is sometimes referred to, shamelessly, as the "knowledge business." Knowledge itself expands at a rate that makes him feel like an impostor if he seeks to be broadly educated, and walls him off from others if he specializes. His professors are less attached to the institution where they teach and more to their disciplines. And they have less time to give him or the college. In this situation, the traditional college spirit— of either the rah-rah variety or the community of learners—may seem to the students as outmoded as the raccoon coat and the hip flask.

[6] If he has reached the age of reflection, today's student is seeking above all to differentiate himself from the crowd. Thirty years ago it was distinctive merely to be a college man. Now he must struggle to be more than a grade-point average, an anonymous statistic with a college and home address. Often he expresses this yearning for uniqueness in ways that parents, administrators, professors, and other outsiders consider illegitimate. Well publicized are the bearded, sloppily dressed students, defiant of even minimal administrative regulations, studious enough, but incontinent in their demands for alcoholic and sexual freedoms, fiercely insistent on leading their own lives.

[7] Typical of this state of mind is a student's letter in a recent issue of our college newspaper. "The trouble is that they [administration and faculty] take it all as seriously as the rest of the piety we get about law and morality and the intellectual purpose of our existence. The most ironic thing on this campus is that they believe in their own hypocrisy. . . . One of the reasons that administration and much of the faculty alike draw grotesque pictures of students is that they probably have never talked with one, not that they'd listen if they did. For years the same situations occur, the same opinions are given, the same pleas are voiced, and the same nothing happens."

[8] The desire for self-definition often goes hand in hand with an inner need—more or less conscious—for a compelling authority to make freedom meaningful. In the 'thirties, economic pressures for existence and our opposition to the fascist menace rescued us from this dilemma. In the 'forties there was the war and, afterward, the threat of the Bomb to distract attention from inner conflicts. For some students in the 'sixties the civil-rights struggle has become a Cause—a clear-cut issue on which to act and to argue. But as yet this movement has not reached anything

like the numbers nor hit with anything like the impact that we experienced with fascism, communism, the war, and the Bomb.

[⁹] Lacking an embracing cause and a fervent ideology, the student's search for a durable purpose is likely to become aggressive, extremist, at times despairing. It can easily turn into preoccupation with subjective feelings and plain egotism. As André Gide has put it, "Each human being who has only himself for aim suffers from a horrible void." Paradoxical as it sounds, the real problem of our college youth is to discover some authority, both private and public, that will make possible authentic individuality.

THEIR FAVORITE REBEL

[¹⁰] I have learned something about this search over the past fifteen years as one of the professors conducting a senior seminar called Freedom and Authority. Before generalizing, perhaps I should say a word about Colorado College, where I teach philosophy. It is a fairly typical small, private liberal-arts institution, founded in 1874 by New England Congregationalists before Colorado was a state. It has long since cut loose from church ties, drifting—like Grinnell, Carleton, Pomona, and others—into secularism. Our students are drawn from many states; after Colorado, California and Illinois contribute the most.

[¹¹] We are not as selective as the Ivy League colleges nor as equalitarian as the state institutions. Since—like those of most private colleges—our costs are high, our students come largely from upper-middle-class families. (Some are shockingly rich. A few years back when we banned automobiles for freshmen, a Texas girl wired our admissions committee, requesting in good faith that she be permitted to bring her private airplane.)

[¹²] I was originally lured out here by a dean who painted an enticing picture of Back Bay Boston accents mixed with Western ranch drawls. But the percentage of students from ranches, farms, and the working class has steadily declined, and drawls are now rare. In sum, our students and their families are, economically and socially, very much like you who are reading this magazine. They represent an important—if not typical—sample of American college students.

[¹³] Our Freedom and Authority seminar is a very freewheeling, wide-ranging course. Though we constantly change the readings, a few books have remained by nearly unanimous consent from the beginning. The first of these is Plato's account of the trial, imprisonment, and death of Socrates in the *Apology*, *Crito*, and end of *Phaedo*. These short dialogues, conveniently grouped in one paperback, are probably exerting a profounder influence on the campus today than such best-sellers as Golding, Salinger, and Baldwin, which bloom and fade in campus popularity.

[14] Why does Socrates appeal to contemporary students? They respond to his fearless assertion of his right to determine his own conduct despite powerful opposition from the majority of his fellow citizens. The conflict between individual freedom and sociopolitical authority which he dramatizes expresses their own central dilemma. These students have outgrown the discipline of parents. In college, various authorities—the college administration, campus mores, and student cliques—vie for their allegiance. They are also uneasily conscious of the different standards of the professional and business worlds they are about to enter. The sensitive student, confused by these uncertain values, is thrilled when Socrates, the original rebel who became the "father" of philosophy, tells his fellow Athenians that he loves and cherishes them, but chooses to obey only his own vision of the right and good. Socrates' example can still engender a revolutionary fervor in youthful hearts. It was hardly an accident that the campus rebellions at Berkeley and earlier at the University of Colorado were led by philosophy majors.*

[15] Less acceptable to my students than Socrates' idea of freedom is his concept of authority, which leads him to refuse a proffered escape from prison after he has been sentenced to death. He likens the laws of Athens to parents, who must always be obeyed even if they chastise their children unjustly. At this point, my students begin to protest, and their identification with Socrates is broken. As one of them put it last fall, "I can't imagine anything less comparable to my parents than the U.S. government."

[16] There are exceptions. One girl, for example, last November reconciled the seeming contradictions in Socrates' philosophy in this fashion: "In the *Apology* individual determination of conduct challenges and defeats all other values, including Athenian law. However, the reverse is not what happens in the *Crito*. Here, Athenian law is weighted *with* his personal laws of conduct *against* a solitary value, his life. His natural desire to flee for his life, not his individualism, is challenged here. . . . As part of his personal conduct code, Socrates could not destroy Athenian law simply because it was being used to destroy a lesser value, his life on earth. 'To injure in turn when ill-treated' was against his moral structure also, so that his personal conduct code forced him to abide by Athenian law. Of the three values considered in the *Apology* and the *Crito*, Socrates held individual determination of conduct most important, Athenian law second, and his own life least important."

[17] All of us blessed her, a rank beginner in philosophy, for the kind of insight that an unburdened mind often brings to a complex issue. In

---

* Similarly, the unprecedented student demonstration at Yale in March was a protest against the administration's failure to give tenure to an admired philosophy teacher.

the ensuing discussion, her classmates were intellectually persuaded that Socrates' freedom was sustained by his lifelong membership in the community of Athens. But how could his example be helpful today? Since patriotism is hardly an operable emotion among contemporary students, Socratic freedom, though intellectually appealing, does not in the end provide a satisfying answer. After all, Socrates was an old man with secure roots in a small community, a situation quite opposite to that of young people in our huge, fast-changing, incredibly complex society.

"JUST LIKE MY OLD MAN"

[18] As a contrast to Socrates, we study *The Death of Ivan Ilych,* Tolstoi's powerful short story in which a modern man must face an agonizing death with no resources save the polite conventions of an artificial society. Slowly dying, daily more isolated and desperate, Ivan asks:

"Then what does it mean? Why? It can't be that life is so senseless and horrible. But if it really has been so horrible and senseless, why must I die and die in agony? There is something wrong!

"Maybe I did not live as I ought to have done," it suddenly occurred to him. "But how could that be, when I did everything properly," he replied, and immediately dismissed from his mind this, the sole solution of all the riddles of life and death, as something quite impossible.

But he cannot dismiss these fears for long.

He lay on his back and began to pass his life in review in quite a new way. In the morning when he saw first his footman, then his wife, then his daughter, and then the doctor, their every word and movement confirmed to him the awful truth that had been revealed to him during the night. In them he saw himself—all that for which he had lived—and saw clearly that it was not real at all, but a terrible and huge deception which had hidden both life and death. This consciousness intensified his suffering tenfold.

[19] In the end, Tolstoi rescues Ivan from utter meaninglessness and absurdity via his own (Tolstoi's) passionate faith in primitive Christianity. But this does little to alleviate the atmosphere of controlled terror and doom.

[20] The story has a stunning impact on our students. If they find Socrates wholly admirable but a size larger than life, Ivan is all too human, the anonymous Everyman of our day, painfully contemporary. I have overheard more than one of my students breathe, "My God, he is just like my old man!" They do not identify with him for he is too much like adults they know and dislike—a portrait of what modern life may force them eventually to become. Though they hardly aspire to be heroes like Socrates, they desperately want to escape being victims like Ivan.

THE SIN OF PHONINESS

[21] Ivan's "inauthentic" life has become a rich source for the Existentialists in their indictment of modern society. On the campus Existentialism—which is both a mood and a metaphysics—is compounded of anxiety about being lost in the crowd and the lack of closeness or intimacy with fellow students. Sometimes the despairing response to these feelings is sexual promiscuity; more often it is expressed in eccentric dress and flamboyant behavior. Such climates of opinion are contagious and often attract spurious reactions. These can be downright funny, as in the reported case of the student who used to telephone his girl friend and say, "Honey, I'm in the abyss again. How about going out for a beer?"

[22] But in fact the underlying mood is quite different from the perennial depressions of late adolescence. These students are anxiously concerned with the problem of being themselves. Authenticity is the element of Existentialism that strikes the deepest note for them. The highest virtue is honesty with themselves and others while phoniness in whatever form is the greatest vice. "The thing that's wrong with this class," a senior burst out recently, "is that none of us is spontaneous. We're all trying to be so clever and to impress each other. I think we are simply afraid to be ourselves. I'm sick of my own pretending."

[23] To be a genuine or authentic person is not primarily a moral matter, in the sense that older Americans think of morality. For Existentialists authenticity means freely choosing what is one's own in behavior, attitude, and mode of living, however singular these may appear to others. The kind of society we are building—or that is being built around us—is, for them, a major obstacle to the attainment of authentic individuality.

TRIGGERS OF SELF-DISCOVERY

[24] The difficult art of becoming oneself can hardly be more than begun by the age of twenty-two or twenty-three. Hence the important question is: How long does the search continue? Graduates of our Freedom and Authority seminar often write to their old professors and many of them return to campus annually, from as far away as Pennsylvania and California. We hold an informal seminar with them at Homecoming, usually based on a book which we have assigned in advance.

[25] Surprises about the future development of one's students are the rule for a college professor. But I am still disconcerted when the students I counted on fail me and the least promising prove to be "late bloomers."

[26] In the last category is a pretty Connecticut girl who seemed quite unremarkable when she left my seminar section a couple of years ago and proceeded to a government job in Washington. Soon afterward an FBI agent came to my office for a routine loyalty check and I gave him the

expected replies. But meanwhile someone denounced her as an associate of Communists at college, and she was subjected to a thorough investigation. She secured help from the American Civil Liberties Union, an organization she had first heard of in our course. The investigation ended harmlessly at a hearing where one government agent testified that she was "an innocuous person."

[27] When she returned to campus last spring for a visit this characterization was much on her mind. "That agent was right," she told me. "Up till now I have been just that, an innocuous person, but I intend to be innocuous no longer." She asked me to support her application for law school, which she entered last fall. She had decided to become a defender of civil liberties in a private capacity, not to practice law. This winter she wrote me long letters displaying an unsuspected spirit and passion and marking her as a person who has attained security of mind. She has already resolved not to take the loyalty oath required of members of the bar in the state where she is studying, to make a court case of the matter. She has also become a militant pacifist. It was apparently the description of her as "innocuous" that triggered all these responses—all dormant in her college days.

[28] The death of President Kennedy had a similar transforming effect on another unlikely student whose undistinguished college career included a troubled progress through my Freedom and Authority course. He married and went to work for a national soap company where he was rising rapidly. But the Kennedy assassination disrupted his world. Soon afterward he wrote to me asking for "a philosopher's point of view." "I felt a strong sense of identity with him," he wrote, expressing a feeling widespread at that time. "Perhaps this is because he was young, or because we shared similar political views (weak and irresolute as mine are) or because he was an 'intellectual' President, or because . . . I felt guilt because of his murder, and I feel dead because of his death."

[29] He had tried, he said, to cope with the disaster, to reason it through, but in vain. "I usually end up saying 'God damn,' with an incredulous shake of the head. Surely there must be more grief written in people's hearts than what is written on their faces. Aside from a few hours at the funeral, all seems to be normal with the people I see and know. But for me this one act has made all other acts irrelevant and trivial; it has displaced time with paranoia, good with evil, relative simplicity with incomprehensibility, an ideal with dirt."

[30] He could no longer remain in the business world. Despite his wife and children, he decided to return to graduate school to prepare himself for work in international education. He is now immersed in the study of foreign languages and Existentialism. Wearing a heavy beard, he has lost all resemblance to the young executive of a year ago. For the first time in his life, he told me recently, he is truly "engaged" in discovering the

meaning of existence through commitment to thought and action rather than middle-class drift.

[31] These two cases are, of course, exceptions. Relatively few of our young alumni have made much progress toward attaining a distinctive individuality after leaving college. The demands of business and professional life on the men, of home-making and child-rearing on the women, tend either to halt the search or even to induce surrender to reigning values. It would seem that the very prosperity which permits college students to spend time pondering important issues of existence acts as a sedative in their early adulthood. Affluence, not religion, might be called the opiate of the 'sixties. The immediate requirements of making a living and getting ahead in the status race seem to dull the passions and despair which obsessed many of them in college. There is, of course, nothing surprising in this. Many of us escape the need to give meaning to our existence through the age-old expedient of producing the next generation and letting them struggle with the problem.

THE APPEAL OF NOTHINGNESS

[32] The Existentialist preoccupation with the Absurd, Nothingness, *Angst*, etc.—at least as metaphysical concepts—did not until recently have much of a grip on the English-speaking countries. When I first began teaching the leading Existentialists about 1950, interest in a Kierkegaard, Heidegger, or Sartre was likely to be a matter of either curiosity or fashion. Their very names were strange and most Americans had difficulty pronouncing the word Existentialism. In those years my colleagues frequently asked me to give a coffee-break explanation of the movement.

[33] Now discussions are far more earnest and passionate. I conduct a Wednesday evening seminar on Existentialism at my home. Frequently I have to push the students out after several hours, if I am to simmer down and get any sleep that night. Often they continue heated arguments elsewhere till the small hours. In colleges all over America, courses dealing with Existentialists are currently very popular, to the disgust of the disciples of Language Analysis—an Oxford import—who once felt confident of dominating academic philosophy. The rapid availability of translations from German and French Existentialist writings and sales of large editions attest to the surprising new demand.

[34] What accounts for it? Undeniably, there is a large element of the modish, for Americans have always been susceptible to philosophic imports from the Continent and England. (In philosophy, it has been said, we are still largely a colony of Europe.) I must also admit, rather shamefacedly, that even philosophy is not immune to the attraction of "the hottest thing in town." After the war it was Oxford Analysis, now it is Existentialism.

[35] There is, however, much more to the matter. Existentialists draw their insights and inspiration from literature rather than science. They are concerned with the individual and with personal experience in an age that threatens to overwhelm individuality. This is why they attract so many American playwrights and novelists who have begun the process of Americanizing the European mood. Because the specific possibilities and frustrations of our everyday life are sharply different from those in France or Germany we were slow to accept the Existentialist mood and metaphysics. Now that our writers have succeeded in "translating" them into our American idiom, we are feeling their delayed impact.

[36] The students I know best seem to have an intuitive grasp of what Heidegger and Sartre mean when they write of man's exposure to Nothingness. In a few extreme cases Nothingness means a profound feeling of disengagement with American culture, if not Western civilization itself. Other students who say in the privacy of my office, "I am at the end of my rope," are feeling only a temporary despair, perhaps little more than the romantic storm and stress of late adolescence. Sometimes I respond with a gentle joshing, and refuse to take them too seriously. With others I am far from sure.

[37] The latter group includes students who often do superb work in my classes but who are quite as likely to be on academic probation as on the Dean's list. (One of them recently spent three semesters in the near-failing and three in the excellent category.)

[38] These are brilliant, alienated young people. Generally, they do not care for Karl Jaspers, the Existentialist who identifies himself most closely with conventional philosophy. They respond to the philosophers radically at odds with the whole tradition of modern culture. They want Kierkegaard's either-or—the leap of faith or gross sensuality; Sartre's good faith or self-deception; Heidegger's nearness to Being or nihilism.

[39] The ablest student I ever taught at Colorado College was of this kind. He wrote better commentaries on these philosophers than are found in the published literature. His poems, which I alone was allowed to see, were also first-rate. But it was a trial to keep him in college from one semester to another. Again and again he would disappear into the mountains, by himself for days. My wife and I constantly feared his suicide. When he finally graduated I easily secured fellowships for him to three graduate schools. He turned down all of them and proceeded to wander over the country, supporting himself at odd jobs. In his college years I was, in effect, struggling with him for his very soul; it is now sadly clear that I lost.

TURNING INWARD

[40] In an earlier day, before the disillusionment with communism, some such students found release in action, in attachment to a utopian

authority which gave them a feeling of belonging. For others, the crude menace of Hitler served to unite them with Western values. Today a few find a sense of belonging in Southern racism. Others in the civil-rights movement or in the Peace Corps with its opportunities for genuine service.

[41] What these students need above all is action, not further study, yet how can I counsel them to give up their studies before the degree? To serve with any significance in our specialized society they will need more formal schooling than they have or want before they have "found" themselves. The plight of dropouts on the lower academic rungs is well known. Equally poignant is the problem of those at the top—often even in graduate school—who do not know where they are headed nor whether they should stay in college at all.

[42] Ironically, our technological society appears to widen the spheres of freedom while making it even harder to escape from the toils of "the system" as students call it. Students today travel far more than we did in the 'thirties and 'forties; learn and see more and participate in a much larger range of activities. At an early stage the choice of many different careers is open to them. But once they have chosen anything specific, whether it be a "major" or marriage, they are soon past the point of no return.

[43] In this situation Existentialism appeals. Its deepest conviction is that through his choices each individual makes himself. Its emphasis is not only on the absurd character of social reality, in some cases, of the world as a whole, but also on Possibility. In an inner sense everyone determines his own course. He can choose to lead an authentic existence or choose to be lost in the crowd. If the overwhelming majority opt for the latter condition, this does not prevent the exceptional person from standing alone as an authentic "single one." To a man, Existentialists are against group activities. They never tire of reminding us that "existence" literally means to "stand out from."

[44] "I have decided that I am simply different from all the others," a brilliant youth told me the other day, explaining how even his close friends saw no point whatever to his poetry. "I must think and write for myself from now on." Both resolution and pathos were in his voice.

WHAT, IF NOT ABSURD?

[45] I doubt that Existentialist philosophy can ultimately satisfy the search for authority. So far, few of these thinkers have provided guidelines for social or political action, though all of them stress the necessity for individual commitment. However, for students who are not yet able or ready to act, Existentialism offers a great deal. At the least it presents an escape from the morass of conformity, *la dolce vita,* boredom, and the meaningless competitiveness in which they see so many of their elders caught.

[46] Furthermore, those who go behind Sartre to the Danish and German originators of this movement discover a choice between an absurd or tragic view of human destiny. The absurd view is that existence is finally meaningless and futile, a defiant if admirable gesture in a void. The tragic conviction acknowledges the fragile and exposed character of individuality but discovers meaning and purpose in the individual's struggle to locate himself in nature and society. Though his personal life is of short duration, and subject to chance and misfortune while it lasts, his actions are of great importance in the moral sum of things. Tragedy links us to what has been in the history of our species and binds us in faith to the future. It teaches that there are things worth living and dying for, ideas, ancestors, and descendants.

[47] On the other hand, the metaphysical idea that "life is a tale told by an idiot, full of sound and fury, signifying nothing" can do none of these things. The conviction of absurdity cuts all ties to history and nature and with them the nerve of meaningful action. Which version of Existentialism will be accepted by students in the rest of the 'sixties?

[48] The answer will be important. It has been a favorite taunt of European critics that in America there are no tragedies, only mistakes. The quality of current experience is rapidly dissipating any remaining truth in this ancient charge. Yet young people inevitably find it hard to learn the price in pain and suffering necessary to pay for the tragic vision. Falling into a persuasion of absurdity and meaninglessness is, on the surface at least, much easier. The polar choices again are between the life of Socrates and that of Ivan Ilych.

[49] That the tragic and absurd should be competing for students' minds in the 'sixties is not surprising, when one remembers that many of their parents were fighting World War II while they were infants and that they have grown up in a world changing at an incredible pace. Indeed, were young people not constitutionally adaptable and preoccupied with the immediate present, they would be in a much worse plight than they are. The wonder is that so many are sane and resilient.

RIFT BETWEEN GENERATIONS

[50] Nevertheless, there has hardly been a time, in my experience, when students needed more attention and patient listening to by experienced professors than today. The pity is that so many of us retreat into research, government contracts, and sabbatical travel, leaving counsel and instruction to junior colleagues and graduate assistants. In so doing we deepen the rift between the generations and at the same time increase the sense of impersonality, discontinuity, and absence of community that makes college life less satisfactory in this decade than it used to be. What is needed are fewer books and articles by college professors and

more cooperative search by teacher and taught for an authority upon which to base freedom and individuality.

[51] After surviving so many turbulent decades of this century, some of us may feel a certain confidence that the present will prove no harder than the past has been. But we should remind ourselves that peace and affluence have their own perils as surely as do wars and depressions. Though our students increasingly come to us better prepared in the traditions of Western civilization, how many of them care more deeply about these traditions than did students in the bad old days? My pessimistic sense of catastrophe has lessened somewhat since 1960, but I find that deep uneasiness about the course of American higher education has grown. Nowadays nearly everyone looks to education for salvation as once we looked to religion or to a political ideology. But before we succeed in building the great society, we shall need to resolve the doubt and bafflement about its validity and worth in the minds of those now in college who should serve as leaders. Many of the harassed young men and women I teach, at any rate, have not yet decided what sense, if any, their existence has.

COMMENT AND QUESTIONS

1. Within his larger pattern of thesis and reasons Gray uses several methods of development, including the question-to-answer pattern of the opening section. Summarize his answers to the question (in paragraph 4) of what lies behind the change in college students. What were his probable reasons for arranging the answers in their present order? Do the answers seem to you valid for you and your contemporaries? Explain.
2. What is the purpose of the comment on Colorado College in paragraphs 10–12?
3. What points is the author making in discussing the students' responses to Socrates and to Ivan Ilych?
4. Gray says in paragraph 22 that for the students he knows "the highest virtue is honesty with themselves and others while phoniness in whatever form is the greatest vice." Is this statement true of the students you know? How would you define and illustrate *honesty* and *phoniness*?
5. According to Gray, what is the essential appeal of existentialism for students? What can it offer them?
6. If you have read the preceding selections from Sartre and from Camus (who is often called an existentialist writer), do you find that you share some or all of the attitudes of Gray's students toward existentialism? What is most meaningful to you in the existentialist view?

7. The author has called his essay "Salvation on the Campus." Does the content of the essay in any sense qualify this title? Explain.

8. Does Gray's entire picture of college life and of the situation of college students seem to you optimistic or pessimistic, encouraging or discouraging? Does it seem accurate? Explain.

9. How would you describe the persona revealed in Gray's essay?

HUMAN NATURE
AND THE HUMAN
SITUATION

卐

[33] *Philip Wheelwright*: What Is a Self?

THE FOLLOWING selection, an examination of various views and theories of *self*, is a chapter of a philosophy text, *The Way of Philosophy*, published in 1960. Philip Wheelwright (1901–   ) has taught philosophy at a number of American colleges and universities and before his retirement was a professor of philosophy at the University of California at Riverside. Among his other books are *A Critical Introduction to Ethics*, *The Burning Fountain*, *Heraclitus*, and *The Presocratics*. (Footnotes, with the exception of 9 and 10, are Wheelwright's.)

[1] Everyone tends to speak and think of himself quite naturally in the first person singular. "I think . . . ," "I want . . . ," "I feel . . ." are familiar everyday expressions. Such ways of speaking express a personal standpoint; they are reminders that subjectivity is an ineradicable component of all human intercourse and all human intelligibility. Even the most objective inquiries into truth have some implicit reference to the collective standpoint of the individual *I*'s who grasp the question and appraise the evidence in that way rather than some other. Especially in questions that have an existential rather than a technical character there is an underlying assumption of personal identity and valuation, an assumption of *I*-hood.

[²] So central is the *I* in all experience and all inquiry that Descartes, in a celebrated passage, has taken the self-awareness of *I*-hood to be the necessary starting-point of all philosophical reflection:

I will suppose that all the things which I see are false; I will persuade myself that none of the things which my fallible memory presents to me as having happened ever really existed; that my senses tell me nothing about a world beyond myself; that body, figure, extension, movement, and place are but fictions of my mind. What, then, can be esteemed as true? Nothing?

But I myself—am I not something? Even if I am deceived in thinking that I have senses and a body, am I so dependent on body and senses that I cannot exist without them? But I have said I will persuade myself that nothing in the world has the existence that I attribute to it; hence that my body with its sense organs is but a figment of my imagination—much as if I were to dream that I had some entirely different kind of body. If I am persuaded that all these things have no real existence, may I not further persuade myself that I, too, do not exist? No, that is impossible. I most surely exist so long as I am persuading myself of something. Grant that I may be deceived about as much else as you will, there is one thing about which I cannot possibly be deceived, and that is that at the moment of being deceived I must exist. The proposition, "I am," "I exist," is necessarily true each time that I mentally conceive it.[1]

[³] Up to a point Descartes stands upon irrefutable ground. There is a sense in which I most certainly do exist at the moment when I am questioning my existence. But the logic of the situation does not carry me any farther than that one abstract admission. Descartes proceeds in his later Meditations to "deduce," as he thinks, certain further characteristics of the self whose existence has been demonstrated by this logical *tour de force*. But his alleged deductions have by no means the same self-evident character as his original theorem. *That* I am is entirely certain at the moment when I reflect upon it; *what* I am is a question of labyrinthine complexity, which, when answered on introspection, allows of any amount of error, doubt, and self-deception. Is there any valid sense in which we can answer the *What?* The question, "What am I?" involves such questions as these: In what sense am I the same person that I was as a child? What, if anything, am "I" during a deep and dreamless sleep? And what, if anything, remains of me after death? Not "What is my body" but "What am I who know and to some extent manage my body?" In short, what does it mean to be a *self?*

THE SOUL-SUBSTANCE DOCTRINE

[⁴] To such questions the average man would doubtless exclaim, "Oh, you're asking about my *soul!*" And according to the current of opinions in which he happened to be moving he would express either conviction

---

[1] Paraphrased from the second of Descartes' *Meditations*.

or disbelief in this supposed entity. But what does the word "soul" mean? Sometimes it is spoken lightly, to connote no more than the generally acceptable word "self"—as when we say, "A bit of hardship is good for the soul," or as when we read that some character in a novel felt joy or grief or shame "in the very depths of his soul." Historically, however, the word has connoted much more than that, and the fuller meaning has always been a part of the orthodox tradition in Christian teaching. Christian thinkers have traditionally regarded the soul as a substance—not, of course, as a material substance having its existence in space, but as a permanent something which underlies and supports the various psychic phenomena which belong to it.

[5] The most celebrated pre-Christian expression of this view is found in Plato's Dialogue, *Phaedo*. Socrates, who is in prison and enjoying the company of certain friends for the last time before he must drink the hemlock, discusses the possibility of continuing to live after the body's death—i.e., whether the soul, or self, can survive the body. The discussion naturally involves the questions of the nature of the soul or self, and its relation to the body during what we call life. Socrates deals with the last question first, drawing from Simmias the following admission:

SOCRATES. When does the soul attain to truth? For we have agreed, have we not, that when she seeks to investigate anything in collaboration with the body she is deceived?

SIMMIAS. True.

SOCRATES. Then if she is to attain truth at all, it must become known to her by thought?

SIMMIAS. Yes.

SOCRATES. And can she not think best when none of the senses, whether of sound or sight or pleasure or pain, is distracting her? That is to say, when she draws herself away from the body and frees herself so far as she can from all contact with it, striving to be wholly alone with herself in order to seek what is really true?

SIMMIAS. Certainly.

Later in the discussion, with Cebes now as interlocutor, Socrates proceeds to a consideration of the soul's real nature:

SOCRATES. Should we not ask ourselves what kind of thing it is that is subject to dispersion, and hence in danger of being destroyed? And should we not then proceed to inquire whether the soul is that kind of thing? And should not our hopes and fears for our own souls be governed by our answer?

CEBES. That is true.

SOCRATES. Now it is compound things that are naturally capable of being broken up; for having been put together they can be taken apart. But merely what is uncompounded must be the one kind of thing that is indissoluble, if anything is?

CEBES. Yes, I should think so.

The uncompound, then, is that which we need not fear will be destroyed. But Socrates' second question is still to be answered: Is the soul composite or simple? Socrates begins by distinguishing sharply between the ever changing things and occurrences of the visible world, which are perceived through the ever changing sense-channels of the body, and the changeless "forms" of things, the enduring standards by which they can be compared and appraised, such as equality and beauty, which must be known by a part of ourselves that is equally unchanging, and this is the soul.

SOCRATES. Now then, Cebes: does it not follow from all we have been saying, that the soul is of the nature of the divine—in that it is immortal, and has the power of thought, and is indissoluble and unchangeable? And that the body is of the nature of the human—being mortal, and without the power of thought; and multiform, and so dissoluble and changeable? Can there be any reasonable denial of this, my dear Cebes?

CEBES. None whatever.

SOCRATES. Then if that is true, shall we not say that while the body is liable to rapid dissolution, the soul is wholly or at least very nearly indissoluble?

CEBES. Yes, indeed.[2]

ASSOCIATIONISM

[6] The argument that man's soul must be immortal because it is not composite and therefore not liable to change or dissolution, was revived by various theological writers in the seventeenth and eighteenth centuries, notably by Bishop Butler in his widely read *Analogy of Religion*. The dubious logic of the argument stirred David Hume, a generation later, to a diametrically opposite avowal:

For my part, when I enter most intimately into what I call *myself*, I always stumble on some particular perception or other, of heat or cold, light or shade, love or hatred, pain or pleasure. I never can catch *myself* at any time without a perception, never can observe anything but the perception. When my perceptions are removed for any time, as by sound sleep, so long am I insensible of *myself*, and may truly be said not to exist. And were all my perceptions removed by death, and could I neither think nor feel nor see nor love nor hate after the dissolution of my body, I should be entirely annihilated, nor do I conceive what is farther requisite to make me a perfect non-entity.

Hume concludes, therefore, that a self is "nothing but a bundle or collection of different perceptions, which succeed each other with an inconceivable rapidity, and are in a perpetual flux and movement." And sparing no pains to avoid being misunderstood, he adds this carefully qualified simile:

[2] The three passages are from Plato's *Phaedo*, 65, 78–80.

The mind is a kind of theatre, where several perceptions successively make their appearance; pass, re-pass, glide away, and mingle in an infinite variety of postures and situations. There is properly no *simplicity* in it at one time, nor *identity* in different—whatever natural propension we may have to imagine that simplicity and identity. The comparison of the theatre must not mislead us. They are the successive perceptions only, that constitute the mind; nor have we the most distant notion of the place where these scenes are represented, or of the materials of which it is composed.[3]

[7] Thus an associationistic theory, such as Hume's, regards the mind, and indeed the entire self, as nothing more than a lot of sensations, ideas and feelings, which follow or accompany one another according to the laws of mental association. Indeed, the very words "mind" and "self" are taken to be no more than convenient labels for the activity of such associations. To be sure, associationism does have a certain value in that it calls attention to the qualitative diversity and unceasing change of mental phenomena. The "stream of consciousness" technique employed by some modern novelists gives concrete embodiments to the associationist standpoint. Nevertheless, diversity and change are not the entire story; nor is man merely a looker-on at his own mental array. Associationism tends to ignore the humanistic view that a person is somehow more than the sum of his parts, and that within modest limits he is an initiator and director.

BEHAVIORISM

[8] If associationism involves a denial of the unity and directive power of mind, behaviorism goes still farther by denying the reality of mind altogether. The behavioristic theory arose out of experiments in animal psychology. The types of experiment to which animals such as white rats can be subjected do not assume any consciousness in them; what is to be observed is simply the relation between given stimuli, such as the smell of cheese in a maze, and the animal's behavior. The more extreme behaviorists, such as John B. Watson, undertook to deal with human behavior in basically the same way. In *Psychology from the Standpoint of a Behaviorist* (1919), the book that may be regarded as the first forthright statement of the behavioristic position, Watson declares that in his exposition "the reader will find no discussion of consciousness and no reference will be made to such terms as sensation, perception, attention, will, image and the like." He rejects such concepts and the problems arising from them on two grounds: that he finds them superfluous in carrying out the type of investigation that interests him, and that it is impossible to use them with the same rigorous objectivity as strictly behavioristic correlations. Consequently, as another American psycholo-

[3] David Hume, *A Treatise of Human Nature*, Part IV, Sec. 6.

gist has remarked in describing early American behaviorism, "The experimenter treated and recorded his own observations of the subject, but he denied himself the use of the subject's observations."[4]

[9] In Russia after the Revolution the development of animal psychology and consequently of behavioristic method became chiefly associated with the experiments of Pavlov on dogs. A bell would be rung and while the dog was in an attitude of attention to it a piece of meat would be offered. The dog would seize and eat the meat, its saliva flowing. After several repetitions of the same procedure it was observed that the sound of the bell alone would be enough to produce the salivation. The dog's subsequent salivation to the sound of a bell was described as a conditioned reflex.[5]

[10] The more extreme American behaviorists attempted a systematic reduction of all human expressions, mental as well as physical, to such definite types of physical behavior as neurological, muscular, and glandular activities, culminating in Watson's declaration that "Thought is nothing but a vibration of the larynx." A more temperate behaviorist K. L. Lashley, however, in the late 'twenties performed laboratory experiments which showed that when a subject "thinks about" the same thing on two separate occasions—as evidenced, say, by the word he writes on paper— the pattern of neurological vibrations on his larynx is often utterly different. The Lashley experiments thus gave some evidential support to the view that vibrations of the larynx are not sufficient to account for the unities and diversities of thought. The extreme irregularity of connections between stimulus and response in a human organism was explained by later behaviorists by what Tolman has called "intervening variables"—an assumption going beyond any actual evidence, but making it possible to hold on to the view that "organisms, their behavior and the environmental and organic conditions which induce the latter, are all that there are to be studied."[6]

[11] In general, behavioristic method works on its subjects entirely from the outside. Consequently it tends to encourage a manipulative rather than a sympathetic or coöperative attitude toward one's fellow-beings. The method is designed to discover what makes people tick and consequently—as Watson frankly admits—to control them:

Give me a dozen healthy infants, well-formed, and my own specified world to bring them up in and I'll guarantee to take any one at random and train him to become any type of specialist I might select—doctor, lawyer, artist,

---

[4] Knight Dunlap, *Old and New Viewpoints in Psychology* (1925), p. 56.

[5] Ivan Pavlov, *Conditioned Reflexes* (Oxford University Press, 1927); *Conditioned Reflexes and Psychiatry* (International Publishers, 1941).

[6] Edward C. Tolman, *Purposive Behavior in Animals and Men* (1932), p. 417.

merchant-chief and, yes, even beggar-man and thief, regardless of his talents, penchants, tendencies, abilities, vocations, and race of his ancestors.[7]

Whether Watson or any other behaviorist can make good so sweeping a boast is open to question. But in any case the boasting reveals the intent that lies behind the method. Behaviorism treats human beings as things to be manipulated—complex things no doubt, but still *things* rather than self-governing persons. There is a deep moral and metaphysical issue here —the problem of the right relation between self and self. . . .

[12] In the present context we need only observe the limited conception of selfhood which behaviorism implies. Its method *excludes from consideration* any part of what I think of as "myself" other than what can be detected in the form of bodily movements. Hence, as its basic concepts are geared to its method, behaviorism dismisses my conscious states as "unreal," or at any rate inconsequential. My toothache, to the behaviorist, is nothing more than its publicly observable manifestations— the vibrating dental nerves, the clenched fists, the laryngeal disturbances as the so-called "cries of pain" are suppressed, etc. And thus he artificially limits his conception of selfhood to those aspects of it which his method is capable of handling.

THEORY OF THE SUBCONSCIOUS

[13] The psychoanalytic interpretation of the self seeks objectivity in another way. It is less doctrinaire than behaviorism: it does not deny so immediately obvious a fact as consciousness, or conscious phenomena; and indeed Franz Alexander has declared that "the first assumption made by every psychoanalyst is that minds can study minds."[8] However, the theory holds that consciousness, while actual, is incomplete; it likens the mind to a deep well, the ripples on whose surface are caused by unseen currents in the dark depths. The ripples, properly interpreted, give clues to the hidden movements below the surface; many a slip of the tongue, many a sudden "irrational" impulse, testifies to more powerful causes at work than those found in any conscious awareness and intent. Freud even goes so far, in *The Psychopathology of Everyday Life*, as to declare that the woman who loses her wedding ring "really" wishes she were not married, and that the physician who forgets the name of his rival "really" wishes the name were blotted out of existence. The conscious mind shies away from admitting such unpleasant explanations of its quirks, and consoles itself with "rationalizations"—that is, with

[7] John B. Watson, *Behaviorism* (Norton, rev. ed., 1930), p. 82.

[8] Franz Alexander, M.D., *The Basic Principles of Psychoanalysis* (1954), p. 33. As a corollary of the above statement Dr. Alexander adds that the behaviorist, because he observes only the outward manifestations of the inner life, "does not deserve, strictly speaking, to be called a psychologist."

rationally plausible explanations that seem to justify the dubious action or omission but that have no basis in determinable fact.

[¹⁴] Since introspection is no trustworthy guide as to the character and motives of the unconscious part of the psyche, Freud successively tried out three other methods of investigation. His earliest experiments, influenced by the success of the French neurologist Charcot in treating hysteria patients, were with hypnosis. Often under hypnosis a patient's memory can be tapped and the origin of the symptoms discovered. But Freud encountered two difficulties: many neurotic patients could not be hypnotized, and hypnosis did not in all cases effect a cure. He next came under the influence of the Viennese physician Josef Breuer, and tried out the possibilities of "free association"—i.e., of encouraging the patient to talk out his emotional difficulties, thereby tapping his unconscious memory through mental associations made when he is fully relaxed. It is a slower method, but Freud found that it was effective for more patients and generally led to a more thorough catharsis. Thirdly, he employed dream analysis, on the hypothesis that a dream is a symbolic expression of the dreamer's libido, or unconscious desire.[9] Thus Freud draws heavily upon the data of abnormal psychology—on the hypothesis that individuals who are normal, those who are psychoneurotic (i.e., emotionally unbalanced), and those who are psychotic (i.e., the insane) are not sharply different in kind but simply exhibit different degrees of tendencies that all of them share.

Freudian analysis of the self

[¹⁵] In the later development of his theory Freud comes to conceive of the self, whether normal or abnormal, as consisting of three interacting psychic forces. The *ego* is the conscious intelligence, the discriminating part of the self. Freud postulates that the ego is entirely selfish, always calculating for its own supposed benefit; that it acts with forethought and seeks to satify its individual wants by taking account of and consciously manipulating or coming to terms with the social and physical environment. The *id* is the blind unconscious driving power of the self. In his earlier writings Freud tended to identify it with the sex instinct. In his more mature thought he conceives of it as formed of two opposing drives —*eros* and *arachne,* the love and death instincts. These move us without foresight of consequences; they strive peremptorily for satisfaction except so far as they are controlled by one of the other main elements. Freud interprets the newborn babe as being almost entirely *id;* the ego develops from it in the process of meeting social realilty. The *superego* (earlier called the "censor") provides the sense of *ought.* It is the seat of the "ego

---

[9] See the selection from Freud, "Dreams of the Death of Persons of Whom the Dreamer Is Fond," page 616. (Editors' note)

ideal," and is the great socializing force. It corresponds roughly to what we ordinarily call conscience; with the proviso that, in Freud's theory, it is entirely developed out of the child's early conflicts, both his fears and his admirations, toward the environing world.

[16] Somewhat analogously to the ancient Greek physicians who conceived of health as a right proportion of elements in an organic body, so Freud conceives of it as a harmonious state of balance and non-conflict among the ego, the id, the superego, and external reality. He describes such harmony by a phrase adapted from Fechner, "the principle of stability." Such desired balance, however, is continually being upset or threatened, and much human behavior is an expression of the resulting conflicts. The aim of psychoanalysis is to employ associational techniques to bring unconscious conflicts into the open and so to destroy their power, thus delivering the individual from psychic illness and establishing his psychic health.

Beyond Freud

[17] Despite Freud's fame, neither his concepts nor his presuppositions should be taken as the last word. He has made valuable contributions to psychotherapy. But the conceptual scheme from which he works is open to critical disagreement. One avenue of disagreement is opened up by comparing the Freudian triad with the Platonic. In Plato's simile of the charioteer and his two horses[10] it is evident that the sluggish horse corresponds roughly to the Freudian id. But elsewhere the correspondence is inexact and obscure. The charioteer is like the ego in being fully conscious, and the spirited horse is like the superego in providing the aspirational force in action directed toward ideal goals. But in Plato's view it is not the spirited horse that discerns the goals, it is the charioteer, which is to say the conscious mind. For the charioteer as Plato conceives him is the rightful master who utilizes the nobler horse's spiritual energy but reserves to himself the right and the responsibility of saying how that energy should be directed.

[18] Again, Freud's identification of the id with the Love and Death instincts and his sexual or quasi-sexual interpretation of these has been regarded by many psychologists as too narrow and doctrinaire. Particularly Freud's one-time disciple Alfred Adler came early to the conclusion that there is something more fundamental than sexuality at the root of human neuroses. The primary source of conflict, he maintained, is a feeling of inferiority. The most powerful human urge is the will to power, the will to dominate, and to be recognized. This instinct takes many forms, but

[10] A later discussion of Plato's simile, in paragraph 27, will clarify the discussion here. (Editors' note)

each individual must either make himself superior in some way or, if frustrated in that, build up fantasies of superiority. The first and healthier way is illustrated by Demosthenes who overcame his stuttering by learning to speak with pebbles in his mouth and eventually developed into the greatest orator in Greece, or by a boy poor at sports who learns to draw satisfaction from success in his studies or in debating or in social popularity. The other way, the way of fantasy, is memorably represented in James Thurber's short story, *The Secret Life of Walter Mitty,* where an intimidated husband meets every fresh assault of a nagging wife by an elaborate daydream of self-gratification. Thus Adler regards the self-assertive impulse and not the sex impulse as the dominant force in the human psyche. It is the source of all great achievement on the one hand, but when it is frustrated either by circumstance or by the individual's own hypersensitiveness it becomes the main cause of maladjustment and misconduct.

[19] Finally, one may challenge Freud's interpretation of the superego —the conscience—as merely the product of frustrations arising out of conflicts between the id and the external world. The Freudian case is put with considerable strength by the British psychologist J. C. Flügel, who analyzes the superego as partly (1) an "introjection" into the subconscious mind of the precepts and attitudes of one's fellowmen; partly (2) a development out of childhood aggressive impulses against one's parents, which later turn against one's self and become masochistic; and partly (3) a compensation for the defects of one's actual self by building up an ego-ideal which one would like to attain. The third component in Flügel's analysis is characteristically Adlerian. It becomes evident that Freud, Adler, and Flügel are alike in taking for granted that the superego must be exhaustively explainable in terms of calculable elements in the individual's organism and environment. That this limiting hypothesis can be challenged is shown by William James' contrary hypothesis that the superego (although he does not employ that word) may sometimes be a channel whereby "the conscious person is continuous with a wider reality through which saving experiences come."

[20] All in all, the theory of the subconscious should be taken for what it is—a theory which combines empirical evidences with considerable speculative extensions of thought. The extensions are justified by the same postulate of ontological continuity that justifies us in assuming that a pencil lies in a desk drawer during the entire time-interval between being put in and being taken out. . . . The theory of the subconscious provides a way of giving an intelligible context to the discontinuities and apparent absurdities that can be observed in conscious mental phenomena. That is its general justification: in particular human instances it is justified insofar as it succeeds in resolving the more unmanageable psychic conflicts and producing an increase in psychic harmony and joy.

TWO MARKS OF SELFHOOD

[21] The truth about selfhood needs to be stated in a way that neither inflates nor dwarfs the reality in question. The soul-substance doctrine says too much: not only does it allege an absolute unity and permanence that goes far beyond any possibility of verification in experience; it also is hard to reconcile with certain data of abnormal psychology, such as split personality, schizophrenia, and the like. Associationism and behaviorism, on the other hand, leave out too much that is essential. The one stresses exclusively the flow and succession of psychic events through time; while the other confines its attention to outward manifestations, ignoring the inward life and awareness that make such manifestations humanly significant. Neither of these theories does justice to the integral character and integrating activity of the self; and neither of them offers a ground for applying appropriate value-categories. Depth psychology, with its postulation of the subconscious, goes considerably beyond them in the richness of its field of exploration; but how adequately it develops and interprets its potentialities depends on the assumptions and methods that are particularly employed.

[22] Certain guiding ideas about selfhood, then, are needed in order to judge whether a given theory is adequate or not; and since direct acquaintance with selfhood is in the possession of everyone, the truth of such ideas has to be tested in the last resort by honest self-inquiry. Selfhood is distinguished by at least two main characteristics—intentiveness and self-integration. Certain other characteristics, to be discussed in subsequent chapters, may be regarded as of no less human importance; but these two are *logically prior*, in that a self would lose its character of selfhood if either of them were lacking.

Intentiveness

[23] The essence of an act of consciousness lies in its intentive relationship. . . . Every psychic phenomenon essentially involves something as object, although not every one in the same way. In imagination something is imagined, in judgment something is recognized or rejected, in love something is loved.[11]

[24] Selfhood is potentially conscious. Although one's actual consciousness may be intermittent, yet if it were to vanish utterly and permanently, there would be no self any longer existing. Now one firm fact about consciousness is that it always involves an object. The phrase "to be conscious" is always incomplete; it needs to be supplemented by a preposition. We are not simply conscious, we are conscious *of*. Mind exists only

---

[11] Franz Brentano (1838–1917), *Die Psychologie vom empirischen Standpunkt*. The Scholastic doctrine of *intentio* had stressed this characteristic of consciousness; more recently the idea has been developed by Edmund Husserl and others. Brentano's word *Intentionalität*, often translated "intentionality," is here translated "intentiveness."

in the act of grasping or trying to grasp, and in any case of reaching out for, something beyond itself. Thus it may be argued that the existence of a mental act involves and in a sense indicates the existence of something more than the mental act itself; but this general theorem does not give any clue as to what that something specifically is.

Self-integration

[25] The soul-substance theory goes too far, paying too high an intellectual price, in its effort to do justice to the integral character of the self. What is needed is the concept of a kind of unity that is not static but dynamic, not absolute but concretely pertinent to the purposes and life-context of the individual, yet effectively real.

[26] As a matter of fact, Plato, in other Dialogues than the *Phaedo* which was previously quoted, makes suggestions that appear to stem from such a concept. In the *Symposium* he describes the soul as a lover, always somehow incomplete and seeking completion and fulfillment by joining with the object that it loves. The object of love may be one of several kinds, which Plato summarizes under three heads—physical, social (interpersonal), and intellectual. What they have in common is that, to the soul that aspires to know them, each of them is *kalos*—the principal Greek word connoting intrinsic value; it may be translated "fine," "splendid," "beautiful." The simile of the lover suggests the further consideration that the aspiring soul desires not only to possess the beautiful and so far as possible to become one with it, but also to "create in the beautiful." As the physical lover consummates his love by creating flesh-and-blood offspring, the lover of beautiful forms is inspired by them to create a new spiritual vision and make it somehow effective in the integration of his own person and of the world around him.

[27] What is it in one's own person that needs to be integrated? In both the *Phaedrus* and the *Republic* Plato analyzes the soul into three "parts," or functional aspects: it has carnal desires (*epithymia*), spiritual energies (*thymos*), and mental illumination (*noêsis*). A man is pulled both by appetites (to eat and drink, to gratify the sex urge, to indulge in idle forms of amusement) and by aspirations (the zest of action and accomplishment). In a celebrated simile Plato likens these two kinds of motivation to a pair of horses drawing a chariot, the one both sluggish and lascivious, the other so spirited that he can hardly be restrained. But fortunately the chariot (the soul) has a driver (the conscious mind) who manages the inferior horse by alternately spurring it on and sharply checking it when its evil desires threaten to pull the chariot off the road; while he treats the nobler horse as an ally, guiding rather than commanding him.

[28] Whereas Plato's philosophy contains an unresolved tension be-

tween two concepts of the soul, the substantial and the functional, his pupil and independent follower Aristotle stresses the functional aspect exclusively. Aristotle defines soul as the primary *entelecheia* of a natural body possessing organs, and as the "determining principle" of a living body.[12] Since the Greek word *telos* means an end or aim, the word *entelecheia* connotes that the end toward which the bodily movements are directed is essentially an end given by the nature of the organism itself. Soul, in short, is the basic faculty of organization of an organic body. In man it may become rational—i.e., a conscious intention of self-direction; whereas in lower animals it is more or less blindly instinctive. But in no case is it something separate or separable from the body. Although superior to the body during life, it vanishes into nothingness when the body dies.

Health of the soul

[29] What is the "end given by the nature of the organism itself"? The natural end of any organism is *health* in the broadest sense of the word. Health involves maximal fullness of life, the most harmonious fulfillment of such life processes as a given species of organism is capable of. Health consists—not only to Aristotle but to virtually all the Greeks—in right proportion and due measure. The importance of right proportion and right blending for the health of the body is stressed by the Greek medical writers, particularly by those belonging to the school of the great Hippocrates:

The human constitution contains the salty and the bitter, the sweet and the acid, the astringent and the insipid, and many other elements possessing properties that vary both in number and in strength. These, when mixed and compounded with one another, are not noticed and do not injure their possessor; but when one of them is separated off and stands alone, then it becomes both noticeable and injurious.[13]

[30] Socrates extended the idea of health from the body to the soul, the Greek word for which is *psyche*. Thus when Crito solicits him to break the law by letting his friends bribe the jailor and escaping from prison where he is under sentence of death, Socrates replies:

SOCRATES. If by following the advice of those who do not understand such matters we cripple that part of us which is improved by health and injured by disease, would life thus crippled be worth living? The reference here is to the body, is it not?
CRITO. Yes.

[12] Aristotle, *De Anima*, II. i, iv.
[13] From the Hippocratic treatise, *On Ancient Medicine*, Chap. 14.

SOCRATES. Would life be worth living with the body in a crippled and bad condition?

CRITO. Of course not.

SOCRATES. Similarly, will life be worth living if we cripple that part of us which is improved by justice and injured by injustice? Do we regard the part of ourselves that has to do with justice and injustice as less important than the body?

CRITO. By no means.

SOCRATES. But even more worthwhile?

CRITO. Yes, far more.[14]

In Socrates, Plato, and Aristotle alike, notwithstanding metaphysical differences, the practical emphasis is on the soul's health; and they agree, too, that health consists in a harmonization and rightly proportioned blending of the soul's several faculties under the guidance of reason.

Transition to other problems

[31] In describing the natural action of the self as intentive and self-integrative there is no implication as to how continuously, how well, or how explicitly the processes go on in an individual instance. Nor is it implied that the double characterization is sufficient. Perhaps there are certain further characteristics too, that are essential, not accidental, to the life of the self. Some philosophers have maintained that the self cannot exist or be conceived apart from its interrelations with other selves—that is, apart from what Hocking has called "intersubjectivity," Buber "the I-thou relationship," and Calogero "dialogue."[15] Admittedly the self cannot be described fully if its natural responsiveness to other selves is ignored. . . . Enough has been said to indicate the basic paradox —that it is the essence of selfhood to transcend its own bare existence. It does so in at least two ways—by cognitively intending an object and by vitally intending its own significant continuance. These are both recognizable facts to anyone who reflects on how he consciously operates, but they are a queer kind of fact to anyone who habitually takes his ontological models from the space-time objects of the physical world. On the basis of their recognition a number of other philosophical questions have to be erected.

[14] Plato, *Crito*, 47E–48A.

[15] William Ernest Hocking, *Human Nature and its Remaking* (1923) and *The Meaning of God in Human Experience* (1912); Martin Buber, *I and Thou* (1937) and *Between Man and Man* (1947); Guido Calogero, *Logo e dialogo* (Milan, 1950).

--•{ COMMENT AND QUESTIONS }•--

1. This selection has a general question-to-answer pattern, and it might also be called an analysis of various concepts of *self*. What other methods of development does the author use?

2. In the preface to the text from which "What Is a Self?" is taken, Wheelwright discusses two extremes to be avoided by the writer of a book in philosophy: the extreme of entirely suppressing his own point of view and the extreme of putting it forward too insistently. In seeking a middle path between the two extremes, the author has presented and illustrated the theories of self and has also included his judgments of them. What are his criticisms of or reservations about the soul-substance doctrine, associationism, behaviorism, and the theory of the subconscious?

3. What are your own reactions to the four theories of self as you understand them from Wheelwright's discussion and from other reading you have done?

4. For a full understanding of "What Is a Self?" you will need to understand a number of words and phrases, some used in special senses. Look up in your dictionary any of the following italicized words which are not clear to you in context, and try to paraphase the sentences in which they occur; numbers refer to the paragraph in which the expression is first used: *existential* (1), *metaphysical* (11), *doctrinaire* (13), *catharsis* (14), *postulates* (15), *empirical* (20), *ontological* (20), *intentiveness* (22), the *substantial* and the *functional* (28), by *cognitively intending* an object and by *vitally intending* its own significant continuance (31).

5. State as concisely as you can what you think Wheelwright's concept of self is.

6. The author discusses self-integration and health of the soul under separate headings. Why? Is not integration an essential part of health of the soul?

7. What is the meaning of the statement near the end of paragraph 31 that facts about how the self operates "are a queer kind of fact to anyone who habitually takes his ontological models from the space-time objects of the physical world"?

8. A number of writers in this section (and elsewhere in the book) are concerned about the human self, spirit, or soul. For example, Joseph Wood Krutch says, in "The Genesis of a Mood," that modern man "is feeling about love, for example, much as the troubadour felt, but he thinks about it in a very different way. Try as he may, the two halves of his soul can hardly be made to coalesce. . . ." What does Krutch appear to mean by *soul*? What problems of self discussed by Wheelwright is Krutch concerned with?

9. Terms in common use in recent years, such as *alienation, loss of self, quest for identity*, reflect an anxiety about or a search for self. What do these terms mean to you? To what parts of Wheelwright's discussion would you relate them?

[34]   *John Dewey*: Does Human Nature Change?

JOHN DEWEY (1859–1952) was an American philosopher and educator,[1] a follower of William James, and the founder of the progressive-school movement. "Does Human Nature Change?" is a selection from *Problems of Men*, published in 1946.

[1] I have come to the conclusion that those who give different answers to the question I have asked in the title of this article are talking about different things. This statement in itself, however, is too easy a way out of the problem to be satisfactory. For there is a real problem, and so far as the question is a practical one instead of an academic one, I think the proper answer is that human nature *does* change.

[2] By the practical side of the question, I mean the question whether or not important, almost fundamental, changes in the ways of human belief and action have taken place and are capable of still taking place. But to put this question in its proper perspective, we have first to recognize the sense in which human nature does not change. I do not think it can be shown that the innate needs of men have changed since man became man or that there is any evidence that they will change as long as man is on the earth.

[3] By "needs" I mean the inherent demands that men make because of their constitution. Needs for food and drink and for moving about, for example, are so much a part of our being that we cannot imagine any condition under which they would cease to be. There are other things not so directly physical that seem to me equally engrained in human nature. I would mention as examples the need for some kind of companionship; the need for exhibiting energy, for bringing one's powers to bear upon surrounding conditions; the need for both coöperation with and emulation of one's fellows for mutual aid and combat alike; the need for some sort of aesthetic expression and satisfaction; the need to lead and to follow, etc.

[4] Whether my particular examples are well chosen or not does not matter so much as does recognition of the fact that there are some tendencies so integral a part of human nature that the latter would not be human nature if they changed. These tendencies used to be called instincts. Psychologists are now more chary of using that word than they

[1] See the portrayal of Dewey in Irwin Edman's essay "Former Teachers," p. 863.

used to be. But the word by which the tendencies are called does not matter much in comparison to the fact that human nature has its own constitution.

[5] Where we are likely to go wrong, after the fact is recognized that there is something unchangeable in the structure of human nature, is the inference we draw from it. We suppose that the manifestation of these needs is also unalterable. We suppose that the manifestations we have got used to are as natural and as unalterable as are the needs from which they spring.

[6] The need for food is so imperative that we call the persons insane who persistently refuse to take nourishment. But what kinds of food are wanted and used are a matter of acquired habit influenced by both physical environment and social custom. To civilized people today, eating human flesh is an entirely unnatural thing. Yet there have been peoples to whom it seemed natural because it was socially authorized and even highly esteemed. There are well-accredited stories of persons needing support from others who have refused palatable and nourishing foods because they were not accustomed to them; the alien foods were so "unnatural" they preferred to starve rather than eat them.

[7] Aristotle spoke for an entire social order as well as for himself when he said that slavery existed by nature. He would have regarded efforts to abolish slavery from society as an idle and utopian effort to change human nature where it was unchangeable. For according to him it was not simply the desire to be a master that was engrained in human nature. There were persons who were born with such an inherently slavish nature that it did violence to human nature to set them free.

[8] The assertion that human nature cannot be changed is heard when social changes are urged as reforms and improvements of existing conditions. It is always heard when the proposed changes in institutions or conditions stand in sharp opposition to what exists. If the conservative were wiser, he would rest his objections in most cases, not upon the unchangeability of human nature, but upon the inertia of custom; upon the resistance that acquired habits offer to change after they are once acquired. It is hard to teach an old dog new tricks and it is harder yet to teach society to adopt customs which are contrary to those which have long prevailed. Conservatism of this type would be intelligent, and it would compel those wanting change not only to moderate their pace, but also to ask how the changes they desire could be introduced with a minimum of shock and dislocation.

[9] Nevertheless, there are few social changes that can be opposed on the ground that they are contrary to human nature itself. A proposal to have a society get along without food and drink is one of the few that are of this kind. Proposals to form communities in which there is no cohabitation have been made and the communities have endured for a

time. But they are so nearly contrary to human nature that they have not endured long. These cases are almost the only ones in which social change can be opposed simply on the ground that human nature cannot be changed.

[10] Take the institution of war, one of the oldest, most socially reputable of all human institutions. Efforts for stable peace are often opposed on the ground that man is by nature a fighting animal and that this phase of his nature is unalterable. The failure of peace movements in the past can be cited in support of this view. In fact, however, war is as much a social pattern as is the domestic slavery which the ancients thought to be an immutable fact.

[11] I have already said that, in my opinion, combativeness is a constituent part of human nature. But I have also said that the manifestations of these native elements are subject to change because they are affected by custom and tradition. War does not exist because man has combative instincts, but because social conditions and forces have led, almost forced, these "instincts" into this channel.

[12] There are a large number of other channels in which the need for combat has been satisfied, and there are other channels not yet discovered or explored into which it could be led with equal satisfaction. There is war against disease, against poverty, against insecurity, against injustice, in which multitudes of persons have found full opportunity for the exercise of their combative tendencies.

[13] The time may be far off when men will cease to fulfill their need for combat by destroying each other and when they will manifest it in common and combined efforts against the forces that are enemies of all men equally. But the difficulties in the way are found in the persistence of certain acquired social customs and not in the unchangeability of the demand for combat.

[14] Pugnacity and fear are native elements of human nature. But so are pity and sympathy. We send nurses and physicians to the battlefield and provide hospital facilities as "naturally" as we charge bayonets and discharge machine guns. In early times there was a close connection between pugnacity and fighting, for the latter was done largely with the fists. Pugnacity plays a small part in generating wars today. Citizens of one country do not hate those of another nation by instinct. When they attack or are attacked, they do not use their fists in close combat, but throw shells from a great distance at persons whom they have never seen. In modern wars, anger and hatred come after the war has started; they are effects of war, not the cause of it.

[15] It is a tough job sustaining a modern war; all the emotional reactions have to be excited. Propaganda and atrocity stories are enlisted. Aside from such extreme measures there has to be definite organization, as we saw in the two World Wars, to keep up the morale of even non-

combatants. And morale is largely a matter of keeping emotions at a certain pitch; and unfortunately fear, hatred, suspicion, are among the emotions most easily aroused.

[16] I shall not attempt to dogmatize about the causes of modern wars. But I do not think that anyone will deny that they are social rather than psychological, though psychological appeal is highly important in working up a people to the point where they want to fight and in keeping them at it. I do not think, moreover, that anyone will deny that economic conditions are powerful among the social causes of war. The main point, however, is that whatever the sociological causes, they are affairs of tradition, custom, and institutional organization, and these factors belong among the changeable manifestations of human nature, not among the unchangeable elements.

[17] I have used the case of war as a typical instance of what is changeable and what is unchangeable in human nature, in their relation to schemes of social change. I have selected the case because it is an extremely difficult one in which to effect durable changes, not because it is an easy one. The point is that the obstacles in the way are put there by social forces which do change from time to time, not by fixed elements of human nature. This fact is also illustrated in the failures of pacifists to achieve their ends by appeal simply to sympathy and pity. For while, as I have said, the kindly emotions are also a fixed constituent of human nature, the channel they take is dependent upon social conditions.

[18] There is always a great outburst of these kindly emotions in time of war. Fellow feeling and the desire to help those in need are intense during war, as they are at every period of great disaster that comes home to observation or imagination. But they are canalized in their expression; they are confined to those upon our side. They occur simultaneously with manifestation of rage and fear against the other side, if not always in the same person, at least in the community generally. Hence the ultimate failure of pacifist appeals to the kindly elements of native human nature when they are separated from intelligent consideration of the social and economic forces at work.

[19] William James made a great contribution in the title of one of his essays, *The Moral Equivalent of War*. The very title conveys the point I am making. Certain basic needs and emotions are permanent. But they are capable of finding expression in ways that are radically different from the ways in which they now currently operate.

[20] An even more burning issue emerges when any fundamental change in economic institutions and relations is proposed. Proposals for such sweeping change are among the commonplaces of our time. On the other hand, the proposals are met by the statement that the changes are impossible because they involve an impossible change in human nature. To this statement, advocates of the desired changes are only too likely to

reply that the present system or some phase of it is contrary to human nature. The argument *pro* and *con* then gets put on the wrong ground.

[21] As a matter of fact, economic institutions and relations are among the manifestations of human nature that are most susceptible of change. History is living evidence of the scope of these changes. Aristotle, for example, held that paying interest is unnatural, and the Middle Ages reëchoed the doctrine. All interest was usury, and it was only after economic conditions had so changed that payment of interest was a customary and in that sense a "natural" thing, that usury got its present meaning.

[22] There have been times and places in which land was held in common and in which private ownership of land would have been regarded as the most monstrous of unnatural things. There have been other times and places when all wealth was possessed by an overlord and his subjects held wealth, if any, subject to his pleasure. The entire system of credit so fundamental in contemporary financial and industrial life is a modern invention. The invention of the joint-stock company with limited liability of individuals has brought about a great change from earlier facts and conceptions of property. I think the need of owning something is one of the native elements of human nature. But it takes either ignorance or a very lively fancy to suppose that the system of ownership that exists in the United States in 1946, with all its complex relations and its interweaving with legal and political supports, is a necessary and unchangeable product of an inherent tendency to appropriate and possess.

[23] Law is one of the most conservative of human institutions; yet through the cumulative effect of legislation and judicial decisions it changes, sometimes at a slow rate, sometimes rapidly. The changes in human relations that are brought about by changes in industrial and legal institutions then react to modify the ways in which human nature manifests itself, and this brings about still further changes in institutions, and so on indefinitely.

[24] It is for these reasons that I say that those who hold that proposals for social change, even of rather a profound character, are impossible and utopian because of the fixity of human nature confuse the resistance to change that comes from acquired habits with that which comes from original human nature. The savage, living in a primitive society, comes nearer to being a purely "natural" human being than does civilized man. Civilization itself is the product of altered human nature. But even the savage is bound by a mass of tribal customs and transmitted beliefs that modify his original nature, and it is these acquired habits that make it so difficult to transform him into a civilized human being.

[25] The revolutionary radical, on the other hand, overlooks the force of engrained habits. He is right, in my opinion, about the indefinite plasticity of human nature. But he is wrong in thinking that patterns of desire, belief, and purpose do not have a force comparable to the inertia,

the resistance to movement, possessed by these same objects when they are at rest. Habit, not original human nature, keeps things moving most of the time, about as they have moved in the past.

[26] If human nature is unchangeable, then there is no such thing as education and all our efforts to educate are doomed to failure. For the very meaning of education is modification of native human nature in formation of those new ways of thinking, of feeling, of desiring, and of believing that are foreign to raw human nature. If the latter were unalterable, we might have training but not education. For training, as distinct from education, means simply the acquisition of certain skills. Native gifts can be trained to a point of higher efficiency without that development of new attitudes and dispositions which is the goal of education. But the result is mechanical. It is like supposing that while a musician may acquire by practice greater technical ability, he cannot rise from one plane of musical appreciation and creation to another.

[27] The theory that human nature is unchangeable is thus the most depressing and pessimistic of all possible doctrines. If it were carried out logically, it would mean a doctrine of predestination from birth that would outdo the most rigid of theological doctrines. For according to it, persons are what they are at birth and nothing can be done about it, beyond the kind of training that an acrobat might give to the muscular system with which he is originally endowed. If a person is born with criminal tendencies, a criminal he will become and remain. If a person is born with an excessive amount of greed, he will become a person living by predatory activities at the expense of others; and so on. I do not doubt at all the existence of differences in natural endowment. But what I am questioning is the notion that they doom individuals to a fixed channel of expression. It is difficult indeed to make a silk purse out of a sow's ear. But the particular form which, say, a natural musical endowment will take depends upon the social influences to which one is subjected. Beethoven in a savage tribe would doubtless have been outstanding as a musician, but he would not have been the Beethoven who composed symphonies.

[28] The existence of almost every conceivable kind of social institution at some time and place in the history of the world is evidence of the plasticity of human nature. This fact does not prove that all these different social systems are of equal value, materially, morally, and culturally. The slightest observation shows that such is not the case. But the fact in proving the changeability of human nature indicates the attitude that should be taken toward proposals for social changes. The question is primarily whether they, in special cases, are desirable or not. And the way to answer that question is to try to discover what their consequences would be if they were adopted. Then if the conclusion is that they are desirable, the further question is how they can be accomplished with a minimum of waste, destruction, and needless dislocation.

[29] In finding the answer to this question, we have to take into account the force of existing traditions and customs; of the patterns of action and belief that already exist. We have to find out what forces already at work can be reinforced so that they move toward the desired change and how the conditions that oppose change can be gradually weakened. Such questions as these can be considered on the basis of fact and reason.

[30] The assertion that a proposed change is impossible because of the fixed constitution of human nature diverts attention from the question of whether or not a change is desirable and from the other question of how it shall be brought about. It throws the question into the arena of blind emotion and brute force. In the end, it encourages those who think that great changes can be produced offhand and by the use of sheer violence.

[31] When our sciences of human nature and human relations are anything like as developed as are our sciences of physical nature, their chief concern will be with the problem of how human nature is most effectively modified. The question will not be whether it is capable of change, but of how it is to be changed under given conditions. This problem is ultimately that of education in its widest sense. Consequently, whatever represses and distorts the processes of education that might bring about a change in human dispositions with the minimum of waste puts a premium upon the forces that bring society to a state of deadlock, and thereby encourages the use of violence as a means of social change.

COMMENT AND QUESTIONS

1. Dewey qualifies his thesis that human nature does change by means of an analysis of "human nature." What aspects of human nature does he consider unchangeable? What aspects are alterable? What examples does he give of each?
2. How does Dewey support his idea that profound changes in social and economic institutions and relations are not contrary to human nature? What accounts for the fact that such changes are difficult to bring about?
3. Can you think of current proposals for social or economic change that have been resisted on the ground that they are contrary to human nature? What attitude would Dewey recommend that one take toward these proposals?
4. According to the philosophy of pragmatism, to which Dewey subscribed, the worth or validity of an action or an idea is to be judged by the practical results it produces. What evidence can you see in this essay of Dewey's pragmatism?

5. What relationships does Dewey, who devoted much of his life to education, see between education and the changeability of human nature?
6. If you have read Newman's "Enlargement of Mind," compare his ideas and Dewey's on the meaning of education.
7. We have mentioned Dewey's initial qualification of his central thesis. His essay contains many examples of lesser qualifications and of care in avoiding sweeping generalizations. Notice, for example, in paragraph 28, "*almost* every conceivable kind," "*This fact does not prove,*" "The question is *primarily* whether they, *in special cases.*" Point out other examples in the essay of this kind of careful qualification.
8. Understanding a writer's ideas often depends on understanding key words and phrases—terms which he uses to make distinctions or to define, and which he may repeat for purposes of emphasis or unity. Explain clearly how and why Dewey uses each of the following terms: *needs, manifestations, inertia of custom, acquired habits, combativeness, war, social patterns, channel, plasticity of human nature, education, training, waste and dislocation, use of violence.*

[35] *Erich Fromm*: The Human Situation

THE FOLLOWING description of the human situation is the first section of Chapter Three of *The Sane Society*, published in 1955. For a note on Erich Fromm, see page 69.

[¹] Man, in respect to his body and his physiological functions, belongs to the animal kingdom. The functioning of the animal is determined by instincts, by specific action patterns which are in turn determined by inherited neurological structures. The higher an animal is in the scale of development, the more flexibility of action pattern and the less completeness of structural adjustment do we find at birth. In the higher primates we even find considerable intelligence; that is, use of thought for the accomplishment of desired goals, thus enabling the animal to go far beyond the instinctively prescribed action pattern. But great as the development within the animal kingdom is, certain basic elements of existence remain the same.

[²] The animal "is lived" through biological laws of nature; it is part of nature and never transcends it. It has no conscience of a moral nature, and no awareness of itself and of its existence; it has no reason, if by reason we mean the ability to penetrate the surface grasped by the senses and to understand the essence behind that surface; therefore the animal has no concept of the truth, even though it may have an idea of what is useful.

[3] Animal existence is one of harmony between the animal and nature; not, of course, in the sense that the natural conditions do not often threaten the animal and force it to a bitter fight for survival, but in the sense that the animal is equipped by nature to cope with the very conditions it is to meet, just as the seed of a plant is equipped by nature to make use of the conditions of soil, climate, etcetera, to which it has become adapted in the evolutionary process.

[4] At a certain point of animal evolution, there occurred a unique break, comparable to the first emergence of matter, to the first emergence of life, and to the first emergence of animal existence. This new event happens when in the evolutionary process, action ceases to be essentially determined by instinct; when the adaptation of nature loses its coercive character; when action is no longer fixed by hereditarily given mechanisms. When the animal transcends nature, when it transcends the purely passive role of the creature, when it becomes, biologically speaking, the most helpless animal, *man is born.* At this point, the animal has emancipated itself from nature by erect posture, the brain has grown far beyond what it was in the highest animal. This birth of man may have lasted for hundreds of thousands of years, but what matters is that a new species arose, transcending nature, that *life became aware of itself.*

[5] Self-awareness, reason and imagination disrupt the "harmony" which characterizes animal existence. Their emergence has made man into an anomaly, into the freak of the universe. He is part of nature, subject to her physical laws and unable to change them, yet he transcends the rest of nature. He is set apart while being a part; he is homeless, yet chained to the home he shares with all creatures. Cast into this world at an accidental place and time, he is forced out of it, again accidentally. Being aware of himself, he realizes his powerlessness and the limitations of his existence. He visualizes his own end: death. Never is he free from the dichotomy of his existence: he cannot rid himself of his mind, even if he should want to; he cannot rid himself of his body as long as he is alive—and his body makes him want to be alive.

[6] Reason, man's blessing, is also his curse; it forces him to cope everlastingly with the task of solving an insoluble dichotomy. Human existence is different in this respect from that of all other organisms; it is in a state of constant and unavoidable disequilibrium. Man's life cannot "be lived" by repeating the pattern of his species; *he* must live. Man is the only animal that can be *bored,* that can feel evicted from paradise. Man is the only animal who finds his own existence a problem which he has to solve and from which he cannot escape. He cannot go back to the

prehuman state of harmony with nature; he must proceed to develop his reason until he becomes the master of nature, and of himself.

[7] But man's birth ontogenetically as well as phylogenetically is essentially a *negative* event. He lacks the instinctive adaptation to nature, he lacks physical strength, he is the most helpless of all animals at birth, and in need of protection for a much longer period of time than any of them. While he has lost the unity with nature, he has not been given the means to lead a new existence outside of nature. His reason is most rudimentary, he has no knowledge of nature's processes, nor tools to replace the lost instincts; he lives divided into small groups, with no knowledge of himself or of others; indeed, the biblical Paradise myth expresses the situation with perfect clarity. Man, who lives in the Garden of Eden, in complete harmony with nature but without awareness of himself, begins his history by the first act of freedom, disobedience to a command. Concomitantly, he becomes aware of himself, of his separateness, of his helplessness; he is expelled from Paradise, and two angels with fiery swords prevent his return.

[8] Man's evolution is based on the fact that he has lost his original home, nature—and that he can never return to it, can never become an animal again. There is only one way he can take: to emerge fully from his natural home, to find a new home—one which he creates, by making the world a human one and by becoming truly human himself.

[9] When man is born, the human race as well as the individual, he is thrown out of a situation which was definite, as definite as the instincts, into a situation which is indefinite, uncertain and open. There is certainty only about the past, and about the future as far as it is death—which actually is return to the past, the inorganic state of matter.

[10] The problem of man's existence, then, is unique in the whole of nature; he has fallen out of nature, as it were, and is still in it; he is partly divine, partly animal; partly infinite, partly finite. *The necessity to find ever-new solutions for the contradictions in his existence, to find ever-higher forms of unity with nature, his fellow men and himself, is the source of all psychic forces which motivate man, of all his passions, affects and anxieties.*

[11] The animal is content if its physiological needs—its hunger, its thirst and its sexual needs—are satisfied. Inasmuch as man is *also* animal, these needs are likewise imperative and must be satisfied. *But inasmuch as man is human, the satisfaction of these instinctual needs is not sufficient to make him happy; they are not even sufficient to make him sane. The archimedic point of the specifically human dynamism lies in this uniqueness of the human situation; the understanding of man's psyche must be based on the analysis of man's needs stemming from the conditions of his existence.*

[12] The problem, then, which the human race as well as each indi-

vidual has to solve is that of being born. Physical birth, if we think of the individual, is by no means as decisive and singular an act as it appears to be. It is, indeed, an important change from intrauterine into extrauterine life; but in many respects the infant after birth is not different from the infant before birth; it cannot perceive things outside, cannot feed itself; it is completely dependent on the mother, and would perish without her help. Actually, the process of birth continues. The child begins to recognize outside objects, to react affectively, to grasp things and to coordinate his movements, to walk. But birth continues. The child learns to speak, it learns to know the use and function of things, it learns to relate itself to others, to avoid punishment and gain praise and liking. Slowly, the growing person learns to love, to develop reason, to look at the world objectively. He begins to develop his powers; to acquire a sense of identity, to overcome the seduction of his senses for the sake of an integrated life. Birth then, in the conventional meaning of the word, is only the beginning of birth in the broader sense. The whole life of the individual is nothing but the process of giving birth to himself; indeed, we should be fully born, when we die—although it is the tragic fate of most individuals to die before they are born.

[13] From all we know about the evolution of the human race, the birth of man is to be understood in the same sense as the birth of the individual. When man had transcended a certain threshold of minimum instinctive adaptation, he ceased to be an animal; but he was as helpless and unequipped for human existence as the individual infant is at birth. The birth of man began with the first members of the species homo sapiens, and human history is nothing but the whole process of this birth. It has taken man hundreds of thousands of years to take the first steps into human life; he went through a narcissistic phase of magic omnipotent orientation, through totemism, nature worship, until he arrived at the beginnings of the formation of conscience, objectivity, brotherly love. In the last four thousand years of his history, he has developed visions of the fully born and fully awakened man, visions expressed in not too different ways by the great teachers of man in Egypt, China, India, Palestine, Greece and Mexico.

[14] The fact that man's birth is primarily a negative act, that of being thrown out of the original oneness with nature, that he cannot return to where he came from, implies that the process of birth is by no means an easy one. Each step into his new human existence is frightening. It always means to give up a secure state, which was relatively known, for one which is new, which one has not yet mastered. Undoubtedly, if the infant could think at the moment of the severance of the umbilical cord, he would experience the fear of dying. A loving fate protects us from this first panic. But at any new step, at any new stage of our birth, we are afraid again. We are never free from two conflicting tendencies: one to

emerge from the womb, from the animal form of existence into a more human existence, from bondage to freedom; another, to return to the womb, to nature, to certainty and security. In the history of the individual, and of the race, the progressive tendency has proven to be stronger, yet the phenomena of mental illness and the regression of the human race to positions apparently relinquished generations ago, show the intense struggle which accompanies each new act of birth.[1]

COMMENT AND QUESTIONS

1. In the first three paragraphs, Fromm says that the functioning of animals is determined by instinctively prescribed action patterns; that the animal has no reason and no concept of the truth; and that animal existence is one of harmony between the animal and nature. How is each of these statements qualified?

2. Fromm's vocabulary may produce some difficulty in reading this selection. Paraphrase and explain each of the following statements: (a) "The animal 'is lived' through biological laws of nature" (paragraph 2); (b) The "emergence [of self-awareness, reason and imagination] has made man into an anomaly . . . . never is he free from the dichotomy of his existence" (paragraph 5); (c) "Human existence . . . is in a state of constant and unavoidable disequilibrium" (paragraph 6); (d) "But man's birth ontogenetically as well as phylogenetically is essentially a *negative* event" (paragraph 7).

3. Explain the paradox at the end of paragraph 12: "it is the tragic fate of most individuals to die before they are born."

4. In the whole selection, what contrasts does Fromm make between animals and men?

5. What parallels are drawn between the experience of the individual and the evolution of the human race?

6. Summarize in one or two sentences the cause–effect development of this selection.

7. What solution to the problem of human existence does Fromm appear to suggest?

8. If you have read Fromm's "Alienation: Quantification, Abstractification," page 69, what relationship do you see between "The Human Situation" and that later section of the same book?

---

[1] It is in this polarity that I see the true kernel in Freud's hypothesis of the existence of a life and death instinct; the difference to Freud's theory is, that the forward-going and the retrogressive impulse have not the same biologically determined strength, but that normally, the forward-going life instinct is stronger and increases in relative strength the more it grows. (Fromm)

9. If you have read John Dewey's essay "Does Human Nature Change?" do you think that Dewey and Fromm agree about the changeability of human nature?

[36] *W. Macneile Dixon*: Human Nature and the Human Situation

THE FOLLOWING analysis is part of Chapter IV of a book called *The Human Situation,* which was originally delivered as the Gifford Lectures in the University of Glasgow, 1935–37. This book, available in an inexpensive edition, is one that we should like to recommend to all thoughtful college students. W. Macneile Dixon (1886–1946) was Professor of English Language and Literature in the University of Glasgow, and is the author of a number of books including *Tragedy, The Englishman,* and *An Apology for the Arts.*

[1] The first and fundamental wonder is existence itself. That I should be alive, conscious, a person, a part of the whole, that I should have emerged out of nothingness, that the Void should have given birth not merely to things, but to me. Among the many millions who throughout the centuries have crossed the stage of time, probably not more than a handful have looked about them with astonishment, or found their own presence within the visible scene in any way surprising. Our immediate impressions and requirements, the daily doings, comings and goings of others like ourselves absorb in the years of infancy all our attention. Life steals imperceptibly upon us, without any sudden shock or sense of strangeness. How quietly we accommodate ourselves to the situation! In our early years, when all is fresh and new, we take the miracle for granted, and find abundant occupation and endless variety of interest. We are busy looking about us, and grow accustomed to living, and nothing appears startling to which we are accustomed. Thus it is that in the existence of the world or ourselves there appears for most of us no cause for amazement. So far from asking with Coleridge the unanswerable question, "Why should there be anything at all, any world at all?" we accept life without wonder and without curiosity. One might almost imagine that we were here on well-known ground, and but revisiting a country with which we had a previous acquaintance. Yet let the mind once awake—and distress of mind is the great awakener of mind—and

this emergence from the womb of the immeasurable universe rises to its full significance, to tower above all other thoughts, the wonder of wonders, beyond digestion into speech. To find oneself a member of a particular family and society, among innumerable other families and societies, engaged in a round of activities, to feel, think, love, hate, to eat, drink, sleep, to be involved in all these multitudinous affairs, not knowing in the least why this state of things should be ours, how we came into possession of this peculiar nature, acquired these needs, powers and passions, how or why we were launched upon this most extraordinary adventure—once give way to thoughts like these, and you are a prisoner for life, the prisoner of philosophy. But you will remain one of a negligible minority. And if it be a delusion to suppose that many human beings have been concerned with such musings, it is equally a delusion to suppose they have been spiritually minded, anxious about the state of their souls, eager for communion with God. All but the slenderest of minorities have been immersed in a struggle for existence, for material satisfactions, have sought the pleasures of the senses, or followed after power or wealth. Most have died, whatever their pursuits, in the full vigour of their sensuality, and all in the full tide of their ignorance. If there has been one God, universally acknowledged, universally worshipped, in all ages and countries, it is money.

What is here?
'Gold? yellow, precious, glittering gold?'

The inhabitants of Norwich in 1650 petitioned Parliament to grant them the land and other materials "of that vast and altogether useless cathedral of Norwich" towards the building of a workhouse and repairing piers.

[2] However it came about, here we find ourselves, and in many and most delicately balanced ways, adjusted to the business in hand. Had the adjustment been perfect, had the whole worked without friction, as the earth moves through the heavens without a disturbing ripple, our lives like those of the plants, without desire or pain, possibly a dim sense of happiness, a gentle, unruffled dream might have been ours. Nature appears to have begun, if she ever did begin, her great undertaking with insensate things, and it mattered not at all what she did with them. Whirling suns, seas, mountains, even plants, trees, flowers of all varieties might have come into and passed out of existence without disturbance of the great calm of eternity. But with the entrance upon the scene of that disturbing visitor, the soul, that singular entity which suffers and enjoys, with the coming of beings capable of sharp pains and acute desires, there arose a formidable situation. These entities sought satisfaction for their wishes and avoidance of suffering. They became struggling creatures, in possession of life, but not the life they desired. Every man goes

about arm in arm with disappointment. They discovered a harsh limit to their power over things. They found an enemy in the field, an evil thing, figured in all religions as the Adversary, the Opponent, the ἀντίθεόν, Ahriman in the Persian system, Lucifer or Satan in the Christian.

[3] How unfortunate, some theologians tell us, that man gave way to mental curiosity, and so forfeited his happy lot in the Garden of Eden, rising to a level of intelligence above the lowlier, unaspiring animals, content with pasture, with satisfactions of food and sex. They fared better, and ours, but for the great aboriginal catastrophe, would have been a like existence, without expectations or searchings of heart, without souls embittered by fruitless desires. The knowledge of good and evil was the fatal departure from the original design—Nature's error, or, as in the Christian view, the fault of man himself. The pursuit of wisdom brought misery, and to intelligence was attached a penalty.

[4] There is a saying that nature does nothing in vain. Yet if she created automatic machines, and some thinkers like the behaviourists insist we are no more, why did she proceed to the blunder, for assuredly a blunder it was, of conferring upon them an unnecessary sensitivity to pain and pleasure? Without sensitivity machines work very well. How much better had she been content with insensate things. But we are not stones or trees, and in making sensitive beings nature went clean out of her way. Consciousness is an unpardonable blot upon her scheme, and for this philosophy an inexplicable enigma. So it is that, in the midst of nature, man appears not as her child, but as a changeling. Exiled from his native home of innocence, elevated to kingly rank in the creation, the bond between mother and son was snapped. She reared a disappointed and rebellious child, a critic of his parent, judging her morals detestable, counselling, as did Huxley, resistance to her rule and defiance of her authority. Cosmic nature, he declares, is "no school of virtue," but the headquarters of its enemy.

[5] That the world is not to their mind has never ceased to surprise, if not to exasperate the philosophers. Its pattern displeases them, and they would remould it nearer to their hearts' desire. Some religions think it past mending, but the passion for reforming the world and one's neighbours has afflicted all the schools of thought, nor has it yet been abandoned. Yet the patterns they would substitute have never been divulged. The most dissatisfied are chary of offering alternative and superior worlds, nor does it appear that they know of any with which our own unfavourably compares. By some natural talent they perceive its deficiencies, but the plan of operations is kept a secret. Alfonso the Wise of Spain, indeed, remarked that "he could have suggested improvements in the universe had the Creator consulted him." Unfortunately at that moment a terrible thunderstorm burst over the Alcazar, and there is no record of his proposals, if he had any.

[6] The world has been called *theatrum Dei,* God's theatre. And if we were merely players on the stage, repeating words put into our mouths, performing actions assigned to us, and like them really unconcerned, appearing to suffer and yet not suffering, the situation were beyond rebuke. It is unhappily quite otherwise. Feeling entered the world and let loose a torrent of ills—the sick heart, the ailing body, the distressed mind.

> All thoughts that rive the heart are here, and all are vain,
> Horror, and scorn, and hate, and fear, and indignation.

[7] It is a curious speculation, yet not irrelevant to our enquiry, how human lots are cast, so strangely varied they are. You are born and no reasons given, a man or a woman, an Arab or an Andaman islander, an African pygmy or an Egyptian Pharaoh, a Chinese coolie or an English gentleman, a St. Thomas or an Ivan the Terrible. You are ushered into the world in the Stone Age, the fifth or fifteenth century, a vegetarian or a cannibal, of base or noble stock, the child of half-witted parents or of Viking breed, an imbecile or a fanatic. You inherit, according to the accident of your birth, a family blood-feud, a belief in Voodoo and a string of fantastic fetishes, or a Christian creed of love and charity. You are a warrior or a serf as Heaven decrees, are exposed as an infant born in ancient Sparta, die in middle life bitten by a poisonous snake in India, or live a respectable German merchant to a ripe old age. One of a million million possible lots is yours. Is it accidental, an act of God, or, as some have conjectured, a selection made by yourself in a previous state? How profound a mystery lies behind these so manifestly unequal conditions of human existence! And what justice is it, if one man languishes most of his life on a bed of sickness, and another enjoys health and happiness or sits upon an imperial throne? Nature strews these inequalities of place, time, heredity, circumstances with a monstrous partiality. On what principles you are allotted good looks, a musical ear, a sunny temper, an affectionate disposition, a talent for figures, or denied these qualities does not appear. We are, the maxim runs, as God made us, and there the matter perforce must end.

[8] Nor is it only our nature and disposition that we inherit, but the habits and traditions of some community, a Pagan, a Buddhistic or a Mohammedan creed, the *mos majorum,* the custom of our ancestors; and, with few exceptions, by these our lives are governed. These bodies of ours, as it would seem at haphazard distributed, are not negligible, or to be treated with cavalier indifference. From their tiresome demands and complaints there is no escape. They do very much as they please with us, often lame our best intentions and enforce our most sensual. To keep them in repair is a constant anxiety. What a despot is the stomach, whose caprices make us moody or cheerful, bland or irritable. Listen to the enormous laughter of Rabelais while he recounts the indignities to which

the body subjects the mind, making indecency an intimate part of our lives. He mocks at nature, which delights in shaming us. Our pride revolts, we are nauseated by ourselves, as was Swift, or nervously and shamefacedly avert our eyes from the dishonours we must endure.

[9] If nature gave us logic, she appears to be singularly lacking in what she bestows. For she herself drives no straight furrow, and exhibits an inconsistency which in a man would be accounted madness. Her habit is to turn upon herself, wound and afflict herself, undoing with her left hand what she has done with her right. What more inharmonious than that she should send hailstones to the destruction of her own blossoms and fruits, tempests upon the crops she has herself ripened to the harvest? The meteorite that, in 1908, fell in Siberia, about 100 tons in weight, destroyed the forest in which it fell for a radius of about forty miles. The lightning splits the tree, and sets the forest aflame. The sand of the desert or the encroaching sea turns fertile fields into barren wastes, and reduces whole populations to distress or starvation. It is her own features which nature thus rends and mangles. Wild beasts destroy 3000 persons every year in India, and 20,000 die of snake-bite. There are 700 million sufferers from malaria in the world. Forty per cent of the children born in Central China perish from cold or famine before they are a year old.

[10] When people talk of nature, what do they mean? Is it the immensity, the sublimity, the grandeur, or the indifference, the inhumanity she exhibits, of which they are thinking? We know her wonders and splendours, we know also her disorders, her cataclysms, her tempests. Nature is everything we admire and fear, everything we love, and everything we hate. She is "the sum of all phenomena." A perfectly ordered world, exact as a geometrical pattern, is the world desired by the logical mind. But how different the reality. Before its irrationalities reason trembles. The eruption of Krakatoa, in 1783, destroyed 40,000 human beings; the Quito, in 1797, also 40,000; the Lisbon earthquake, in 1755, twice that number. Is human life a bubble? Within the present century, in 1908, and again, in 1920, similar disturbances in Sicily and China eliminated half a million lives in sixty seconds. The eruption of Mount Pelé, in less than a quarter of an hour, laid the capital of Martinique in ruins, with the loss of 30,000 lives. During the Yangtse floods in 1931 over a million perished by drowning. Etna wakes and Messina perishes. Islands are submerged with their human freights, like ships at sea. In 1929 Ninaforu, in the Pacific, simply disappeared with all its inhabitants into the ocean depths. Would these things be "if the King of the universe were our friend"? The larks are not always in the sky on an April morning.

[11] Professor Bosanquet thought it exceedingly improbable that an earthquake would destroy London. His reason for thinking so was not a geological one. It would be, he believed, contrary to "the world-wisdom."

Such a preference by nature for London over Tokio or California is indeed very flattering to us as a nation, and very comforting. But what are we to think of a philosopher who says such things? You say nothing: you close his book.

[12] Nature does not seem to know her own mind, or else she speaks an equivocal language. Are her powers, perhaps, limited, and hers an imperium divided among satraps, or governors, not wholly in subordination to her central authority? For if not, why should there be a discord between her animate and inanimate provinces? The human mind looks for unity, yet everywhere in nature's realm contending powers are in conflict. You have the physical world indifferent to living things, unconcerned whether they exist or do not exist. In its turn, upon the insecure foundation of the body, the living organism, rises the mind, incapable, it would seem, of any independent existence. So that thought, love, hope, the soul and its affections, the whole intellectual structure of human life, are perilously poised in a trembling insecurity upon the material elements, themselves in continual flux.

[13] Were nature constant in her intentions we might hope to understand them, but how at odds with herself this Lady Bountiful, mother of all living, when she counsels one species of her own creation, providing an armoury the most ingenious, claws and fangs and suckers, instruments of death, that one tribe of her offspring might the better murder the members of another, a device, to our poor uninstructed vision, neither lovely nor divine. Nature is no believer in disarmament. The bird preys upon the insect and the worm, the glow-worm feeds upon the snail, the ichneumon lays its eggs upon the caterpillar, which, when the grubs emerge, will serve as their food. There are animals which seem an incarnation of malice, like that dweller in darkness, the blood-sucking vampire bat. How difficult to think of Christ as the son of the God of nature! Nature encourages internecine strife. Nor has she any favourites among her creatures, unless it be the insect tribe. There are not less than ten million varieties of them in existence. "In India alone the loss of crops, of timber, and of animal products by insect damage is estimated at over 150 million pounds annually, and the death roll due to insect-borne diseases at over a million and a half lives."[1]

[14] Life is one throughout the universe, yet its parts are in conflict. Nature has her racks and thumbscrews. You cannot instruct her in any of the torturer's or executioner's arts. There is no kindness in the sea, no benevolence in the forest. If you complain that men are a cruel breed, you need not enquire whence they derived the propensity. It is inherited, and from the mother's side.

[15] Perhaps these things should not be mentioned. Truth is a thorny

[1] *The World of Nature*, by H. C. Knapp-Fisher, p. 295.

rose. Sentimental writers do not dwell upon this theme. These star-gazers do not remind us of the *bellum omnium contra omnes*.[2] How tiresome are the one-eyed philosophies. There will be brave men born after us who will not attempt to build up their spiritual lives on a diet of lies. All forms of life, all organisms in which it is manifested, are engaged in an unceasing struggle to maintain themselves against the disintegrating forces of nature. All are in conflict with each other for the means of life, clan against clan, individual against individual. Each exists at the expense of others, and keeps its foothold only by success over the rest. Here is a telegram from South Australia, dated Nov. 6, 1934. "It is estimated that the farmers in Adelaide will lose at least three-quarters of their crops through the depredations of grass-hoppers, which are advancing in uncontrollable swarms on a front of 250 miles." How deep it goes, this warfare, you may conjecture if you remind yourself that the very trees of the forest are battling with each other for the light of the sun, and that the plants have their defensive armour, the rose and thistle their thorns, the nettle its sting. Make your heart iron within you, when you remember that to live you must kill, either plants or animals. "To live, my Lucilius, is to make war." Hunger for food, hunger for life, of which war is merely the continuation, are the presiding issues.

[16] It is no doubt necessary to think in terms of right and wrong, yet how much more convincing would be our moralists if they began at the beginning, if they could bring themselves to think first in terms of life and death. Who is ignorant that good and evil go everywhere hand in hand, in the closest, indeed inseparable, partnership? The misfortunes of one community make the fortunes of another. If England secures the world markets, they are lost to Germany. If oil becomes the necessary and universal fuel, the oil-producing districts flourish at the expense of those which have none. Among the competitors for a post, or the hand of a lady, one only can prove successful, and not invariably the most deserving. The magistrate and police depend for their livelihood on the swindler and the burglar, the physician upon the sick and disabled. Scarcity of food brings destitution to the poor and high prices to the farmer, and the higher a nation's standard of intellect and skill the worse for the incapable and unintelligent.

[17] We are not sure of what best nourishes, or what damages, the delicate machinery of nerve and brain. We guess at the causes of our physical lassitude. Poisons circulate in our blood from origins unknown. We are surrounded by unseen foes. Nor are our souls less vulnerable than our bodies. Affections spring up in us only to be thwarted or forbidden, or we discover too late that they have been foolishly misplaced and are betrayed. Our very sympathies lead us astray. We are imposed upon by

---

[2] war of all against all.

falsehoods and depressed by misunderstandings. The whole region of the emotions is subject to doubts, misgivings, confusion, and those who have shallow natures, feeling little, appear to be best suited for life. Instinct and desire point one way and mature reflection another. Duties conflict not merely with our wishes, but with opposing duties, so that we are in doubt where our loyalty is first due, which cause we should espouse, to which of the arguing voices we should give ear. And, do what we will, to live at all without inflicting injuries upon others is well-nigh, if not altogether impossible. "A terrible thing is life," says Socrates in the *Gorgias*. He thought it a disease, and left with his friend, Crito, a commission to sacrifice a cock as a thank-offering for his deliverance.

[18] Yet within this "odious scene of violence and cruelty," as Mill, rising to a moral superiority over the universe, called it, there runs a counter current. So that in nature's speech there is an equivocation, an irony, an irony clearly discerned, with that unclouded vision of theirs, by the Greeks, and even by the simpler peoples of the earth. A recent traveller reports the philosophy of an African tribe: "They said that although God is good, and wishes good for everybody, unfortunately he has a half-witted brother, who is always interfering with what he does. This half-witted brother keeps on obtruding himself, and does not give God a chance." How kindly a view of Satan! And what is irony? It is a double-speaking, it is language which, since it is open to two interpretations, hides the speaker's meaning, in which a sense is wrapped other than the obvious sense, language which says one thing and yet means another. There is the irony, too, of circumstances, promising what they do not perform, or it may be performing what they do not promise, or by the event baffling confident expectation. For this ironical language nature has a fondness. Observe that this nature which wars upon herself is the nature which constructs the exquisite fabric of the living organism, and with a physician's arts ministers to the diseases she inflicts, produces in the body anti-toxins to defeat the toxins, administers anaesthetics, and exercises a *vis medicatrix*[3] all her own. How difficult to recognise in the ferocities we see around us the subtle power which made the brain, which elaborated with consummate exactness the mechanism of the heart and lungs, all the devices by which the body maintains its existence! That nature should create a world full of difficulties and dangers, and thereupon proceed to place within it fabrics of an infinite delicacy and complexity to meet these very dangers and difficulties is a contradiction that baffles the understanding. With a cunning past all human thought she solves the problems she has, as it were, absent-mindedly set herself. The flood and the earthquake have no consideration for the plant or animal, yet nature which sends the flood and earthquake has provided, with foresight or in a dream, for the

[3] healing power.

living things they destroy. She both smiles and frowns upon her own creation, and is at once friendly and unfriendly. Like a scarlet thread it runs through her dominion, this inconsistency. Side by side with the undeniable and admirable adjustment between things organic and inorganic, you have the hostility, the discordance. What wonder that men, bewildered by this inexplicable procedure, have supposed her governments distributed among a hierarchy of squabbling deities, persecuting or protecting this or that race of men—Zeus the Greeks, Jehovah the Jews? What wonder they supposed even the trees to be the better of protecting deities, the olive Athena, the vine Dionysus? Ah, nature! subtle beyond all human subtlety, enigmatic, profound, life-giver and life-destroyer, nourishing mother and assassin, inspirer of all that is best and most beautiful, of all that is most hideous and forbidding!

[19] That the world is a unity the philosophers and men of science reiterate with a wearisome persistence. That it is united, they have the sense not to proclaim. How the world became disunited they have not told us. Yet in this procession of time and tears it is not so much the rivers of blood which flow through history, it is the broken hearts that appal us. What elicits human horror and indignation is not so much the suffering that the strong may with courage endure as the suffering at random inflicted upon the weak and innocent and defenceless. I read not long since of a child, who trustingly looked up the chimney to see the coming of Santa Claus. Her clothing took fire, and she was burnt to death. A painful world we might school ourselves to combat, were it only rational, but the conjunction of pain and senselessness is hard to bear. Nor would the heroic race of men, "toil-worn since being began," shrink from grief and wounds were it only assigned a noble task. But nature prescribes no tasks. She calls for no volunteers for a great essay. For the asking she might have millions. She points willing climbers to no Everest. The discovery of the goal—by far the most difficult task—she leaves to us. We are mountaineers by nature, but born blind, and must find for ourselves the Himalayan peak, if there be any peak, we are built to ascend, or else while away the time till the great axe falls, and the futilities are done with. Go where you will through nature, you find no directions for travellers. You choose your path, uncounselled and at your own peril, and the unlikely track may prove to be the best. To be clear-sighted is often to be short-sighted, as when the molluscs and crustaceans, protecting themselves with heavy defensive armour, entered with all their care and caution a blind alley, while naked, unaccommodated man, selecting the more dangerous path, advanced to the headship of living creatures.

[20] Life is a unique experience. There is nothing with which to compare it, no measure of its value in terms of some other thing, and money will not purchase it. Yet with this pearl of price we know not what to do. Schopenhauer loves to dwell, in illustration of his pessimistic thesis, upon

the boredom of life, and cites card-playing, a kill-time device, as "quite peculiarly an indication of the miserable side of humanity." That mortals should desire immortality, and yet find difficulty in passing an afternoon —if you have a fancy for paradoxes, here is a pretty one. We contemplate eternity without horror, and find an hour of our own society intolerable. "How dreary it is to be alive, gentlemen!" And how poverty-stricken is the human soul, which, even when armed with supernatural powers, can find no occupation for itself. Marlowe's Faustus, with Mephistopheles to gratify his every wish, can make nothing of his transcendent opportunity.

[21] Tacitus draws a terrible picture of the *taedium vitae*[4] which in imperial times descended upon the Roman aristocracy:

> In his cool hall, with haggard eyes,
> The Roman noble lay:
> He drove abroad, in furious guise,
> Along the Appian Way.
>
> He made a feast, drank fierce and fast,
> And crown'd his head with flowers—
> No easier nor no quicker pass'd
> The impracticable hours.

Or if, by good fortune, we inherit a nature abundant in resource, which finds every moment full of charm, and think the world a divine playground; another shadow darkens the windows of the soul. As the child, enchanted with the fairy spectacle upon the stage, the joyous bustle and the glittering lights, whispered to its mother—"Mother, this is not going to end soon, is it?" we are startled to discover that

> in the very temple of delight
> Veil'd melancholy has her sovran shrine.

To foresee the end of happiness poisons the springs of happiness. It will end, and soon. We are permitted an hour at the pageant and the curtain falls.

[22] It may be that, although appearances are against her, nature meant well by us, that her powers were limited. She has done what she could, giving us a "second best," since the best was beyond her. It lay within her strength to confer life, but not to preserve it. Yet one cannot refrain from asking, was it necessary that man's superiority should prove his bane, that his aspirations should end in the grave? To create immortal longings in the ephemeral being of an hour, to implant in him passions never to be gratified, for knowledge never to be attained, for understanding never to be fulfilled, to give him imagination, a fatal dowry, poverty of his possessions with the abundance of his cravings—

---

[4] weariness of life.

was this necessary? It appears either a refinement of malicious irony, or a promise of fulfilment, but which? The gods are silent

> Or is it that some Force, too wise, too strong,
> Even for yourselves to conjure or beguile,
> Sweeps earth, and heaven, and men, and gods along,
> Like the broad volume of the insurgent Nile?
> And the great powers we serve, themselves may be
> Slaves of a tyrannous necessity? . . .
>
> Oh, wherefore cheat our youth, if thus it be,
> Of one short joy, one lust, one pleasant dream?
> Stringing vain words of powers we cannot see,
> Blind divinations of a will supreme;
> Lost labour! when the circumambient gloom
> But hides, if Gods, Gods careless of our doom?

[23] There is, among her inconsistencies, another persuasive artifice of nature, for which, by any mechanical philosophy it is difficult, indeed, to account—the artifice by which she induced men to interest in a future they could not hope to see. She persuades them to self-sacrifice, to loss of life for their offspring, for their race, their country, to martyrdom for their faiths, for shadowy, intangible notions, less substantial than gossamer. By what arrangement of cranks, wheels and levers did she cozen this creature of a day to look beyond his own instant profit, his obvious gain? Why should hope have a place, heroism a place, renunciation a place in this automaton? Is cajolery among her talents? Manifestly the Spartans at Thermopylae were flattered to their ruin by a ridiculous pride of race.

[24] View life as a whole, exert all your powers of fancy, take all history into your account, the embarrassing contradiction remains. On all sides it raises its sphinx-like, ironical countenance. Another and final illustration will suffice. At the heart of existence there lies an undeniable sweetness, which no philosophy has fathomed, and no railing accusation against life can dislodge. The complaints against it are legion. In all ages and societies goes up the bitter cry, "Vanity of vanities, all is vanity." "All that exists," wrote Leopardi, "is evil, that anything exists is an evil; everything exists only to achieve evil; existence itself is an evil, and destined to evil. There is no other good than nonexistence."

[25] So much for life: not a pennyworth of value anywhere. Yet the doctrines and religions, and they are numerous, which condemn existence, offer no adequate explanation of the clinging attraction for a state they censure and profess to despise. From this so undesirable a possession their adherents are, for the most part, curiously unwilling to part. "What sort of a pessimist is this," asks Nietzsche, "who plays the flute?" The pessimists are not alone in vilifying life. They have the support of Christian preachers. "The whole world," says Donne, "is but a universal churchyard,

but our common grave." Christianity has little good to say of life, yet how reluctant the best Christians are to become angels. Like the worldlings they, too, are intoxicated with the pleasures of sense. They marry and are given in marriage. They succumb at times to song and laughter. Cheerfulness keeps lurking in odd corners of the horrid gloom. There is some magic at work here. Is it possible that something may be said for this vale of sorrows? Though not to be compared with the ineffable bliss we demand, yet as an alternative to nothing a case for existence can be stated. In fairness to nature you must enter this natural sweetness in the ledger of your account with her. The ecstasy of lovers, the joy in activity, the glow, the radiance, the sunlight, the perfume—omit these, and it is a caricature you have drawn, not the landscape. There is a music in the air.

> Riding adown the country lanes;
>   The larks sang high—
> O heart, for all thy griefs and pains
>   Thou shalt be loath to die.

[26] Many philosophers have been defeatists. Diogenes and Zeno, Epictetus and Marcus Aurelius, Schopenhauer and Spinoza. Ἀπάθεια, ἀταραξ, ία, *nil admirari*, indifference, impassivity, passionlessness, they are all one. Stoicism, Epicureanism, Taoism, how many creeds and doctrines are in their essence, withdrawals from life? For them it is not an adventure but a weary pilgrimage. They take no pleasure in it. Sick of time, they take refuge in eternity. And we seem forced to the strange conclusion that Paganism suits world conditions better. Perhaps it should, indeed, be expected. For why should the haters of life be more at home in it than its lovers? The creed of the Northmen, for example, left room for activity and prowess, for skill and enterprise, for courage and adventure. They had a liking for the risks and dangers of existence, which gave a zest to living, and for a worthy antagonist, who put them on their mettle. *Calculated pauses*

[27] Life is like the sea, never at rest, untamed, moody, capricious, perilous. Many a man who knows the sea has sworn, and sworn again, that once on land he would never more embark upon so inclement, so treacherous, so hateful an element. And few who have so sworn have not heard with aching hearts her call, and longed for her bitter and incomparable society. Like life she lays a spell upon them, a spell not resident in her smiles, though smile she can, nor in her calm, though, like life, she, too, has her seasons of calm, her sheltered lagoons and quiet havens. Men are said to love flattery. The sea never flatters. They are said to love ease. She offers toil. Like life, she deals in every form of danger, and many modes of death—famine, thirst, fire, cold, shipwreck. Like life she strips men of their pretensions and vanities, exposes the weakness of the weak and the folly of the fool. Wherein then lies the fascination, against

which the soft Lydian airs cannot with men that are men prevail? It flings a challenge and human nature rises to a challenge. Men are by nature striving creatures, heroically stubborn, as is the mind itself.

> Still nursing the unconquerable hope,
> Still clutching the inviolable shade.

They love best what they do for themselves, for what they themselves make they have a great affection; what is given them out of charity they value less. The world seems somehow so made as to suit best the adventurous and courageous, the men who, like Nelson, wear all their stars, like Napoleon's marshals their most splendid uniforms, not that they may be less but more conspicuous and incur greater dangers than their fellows. Leonidas at Thermopylae, resolved to stand and die for his country's cause, wished to save two lads by sending them home with a message to Sparta. He was met by the answer, "We are not here to carry messages, but to fight." However it comes about, such men are more inspiring figures than the defeatists.

[28] Matthew Arnold quotes with admiration Pope's rendering of the passage in Homer in which Sarpedon urges his friend Glaucus into the fight, the passage which in the original Lord Granville quoted on his deathbed.

> Could all our care elude the gloomy grave
> Which claims no less the fearful than the brave,
> For lust of fame I should not vainly dare
> In fighting fields, nor urge thy soul to war;
> But since, alas! ignoble age must come,
> Disease, and death's inexorable doom;
> The life which others pay, let us bestow,
> And give to fame what we to nature owe.

Cogito, ergo sum, said Descartes. "I think, therefore I am." He desired a platform, or rather an undeniable proposition as the foundation of his philosophic thought. His successors have not found it either undeniable or sufficient. They have rejected, too, such alternatives as "I act, therefore I am." "I desire, therefore I am." Let me suggest still another. No philosophers, or men of science, have so far had the hardihood, as far as I know, to deny us our pains. They relieve us of all else. They have taken from us our personality, our freedom, our souls, our very selves. They have, however, left us our sorrows. Let us take, then, as our foundation the proposition "I suffer, therefore I am." And let us add to it the converse and equally true statement, "I am, therefore I suffer." The privilege, if it be a privilege, of existence is ours and we have paid the price required. We have discharged our debts. We have not had something for nothing. We have free minds, and can look around us with a smile. Nothing can any longer intimidate us.

⊶❧ COMMENT AND QUESTIONS ❧⊷

1. The human situation, as Dixon sees it, is full of irony, paradox, contradiction. What irony or irrationality does he find in each of the following: (a) the fact that man has imagination, and is sensitive to pleasure and pain; (b) the existence of natural phenomena such as floods, earthquakes, and volcanic eruptions; (c) the relationship of the mind and the body; (d) the relationship between species of living things; (e) the fact that nature cures and heals; (f) the human desire for immortality; (g) human self-sacrifice for race or country or a faith; (h) the sweetness of life?

2. The passages below express attitudes toward nature that were very common in the nineteenth century.

> The indescribable innocence and beneficence of Nature,—of sun and wind and rain, of summer and winter,—such health, such cheer, they afford forever! and such sympathy have they ever with our race, that all Nature would be affected and the sun's brightness fade, and the winds would sigh humanely, and the clouds rain tears, and the woods shed their leaves and put on mourning in midsummer, if any man should ever for a just cause grieve.—HENRY DAVID THOREAU, *Walden*

> And I have felt
> A presence that disturbs me with the joy
> Of elevated thoughts; a sense sublime
> Of something far more deeply interfused,
> Whose dwelling is the light of setting suns,
> And the round ocean and the living air,
> And the blue sky, and in the mind of man:
> A motion and a spirit, that impels
> All thinking things, all objects of all thought,
> And rolls through all things. Therefore am I still
> A lover of the meadows and the woods,
> And mountains; and of all that we behold
> From this green earth; of all the mighty world
> Of eye, and ear,—both what they half create,
> And what perceive; well pleased to recognise
> In nature and the language of the sense
> The anchor of my purest thoughts, the nurse,
> The guide, the guardian of my heart, and soul
> Of all my moral being.—WILLIAM WORDSWORTH,
> "Lines Composed a Few Miles Above Tintern Abbey"

Compare Dixon's view of nature with the views held by Thoreau and Wordsworth. Which view are you inclined to hold? Which seems to you more nearly true?

3. "Every man goes about arm in arm with disappointment," the author says. Do you agree or disagree with this statement? Do you think that intelligent men are likely to feel more or less disappointment than unintelligent men; or do you think intelligence has no relevance to disappointment?

4. In paragraph 22, Dixon restates an idea he has touched on earlier: "It may be that, although appearances are against her, nature meant well by us, that her powers were limited." A more conventional idea is that nature (or God) is all-powerful. Does one of these ideas seem to you more satisfying than the other? If so, why?

5. Do you think the author is implying that life is purposeless? Do you think he is implying that it is not worth living? Explain.

6. Given the human situation presented in the essay, what attitudes toward life does the author think an intelligent human being should hold? How should he live?

7. If you have read Fromm's "The Human Situation," the selection preceding this one, you will have noticed that Dixon and Fromm touch on many of the same points about the human condition; the authors agree, for example, that men are struggling creatures exiled from their home of innocence, that penalties are attached to intelligence and consciousness, that men have a sense of powerlessness and an awareness of death. The tone of the two selections, the attitude toward the material, is very different. How would you describe Dixon's tone?

8. Dixon is an interesting stylist. Choose several passages from this selection that seem to you particularly good and analyze them carefully. Notice the sentence structure and variety in length and structure; the use of apt quotations, allusions, and examples; the use of figurative language; the touches of humor and irony; and the diction.

[37] *Joseph Wood Krutch*: The Genesis of a Mood

JOSEPH WOOD KRUTCH (1893–   ) has been a professor of dramatic literature at Columbia University and drama critic for *The Nation;* in recent years he has lived in Arizona and has devoted himself exclusively to writing. Among his many books are *The American Drama Since 1918, Henry David Thoreau, The Twelve Seasons, The Desert Year, The Measure of Man,* and *Human Nature and the Human Condition.* The following selection is Chapter One of Krutch's most famous book, *The Modern Temper,* published in 1929. In a preface to a 1956 edition of *The Modern Temper,* Krutch explained that some of his views had changed but that the description he gave of the origin of the modern temper "and the consequences likely to follow from it seem to me as valid as they ever were. It is only my own attitude toward it which is different. What I described and shared in I still describe but no longer accept. Hence the situation which *The Modern Temper* presents as hopeless does not now seem to me entirely so. But by the diagnosis I will still stand." Students will find Krutch's later attitudes expressed in *The Measure of Man* (1954), in *Human Nature and the Human Condition* (1959), and also in the two essays which follow this selection.

[1] It is one of Freud's quaint conceits that the child in its mother's womb is the happiest of living creatures. Into his consciousness no conflict has yet entered, for he knows no limitations to his desires and the universe is exactly as he wishes it to be. All his needs are satisfied before even he becomes aware of them, and if his awareness is dim that is but the natural result of a complete harmony between the self and the environment, since, as Spencer pointed out in a remote age, to be omniscient and omnipotent would be to be without any consciousness whatsoever. The discomfort of being born is the first warning which he receives that any event can be thrust upon him; it is the first limitation of his omnipotence which he perceives, and he is cast upon the shores of the world wailing his protest against the indignity to which he has been subjected. Years pass before he learns to control the expression of enraged surprise which arises within him at every unpleasant fact with which he is confronted, and his parents conspire so to protect him that he will learn only by very slow stages how far is the world from his heart's desire.

[2] The cradle is made to imitate as closely as may be the conditions, both physical and spiritual, of the womb. Of its occupant no effort is demanded, and every precaution is taken to anticipate each need before it can arise. If, as the result of any unforeseen circumstance, any unsatisfied desire is born, he need only raise his voice in protest to cause the entire world in so far as he knows it—his nurse or his parents—to rush to his aid. The whole of his physical universe is obedient to his will and he is justified by his experience in believing that his mere volition controls his destiny. Only as he grows older does he become aware that there are wills other than his own or that there are physical circumstances rebellious to any human will. And only after the passage of many years does he become aware of the full extent of his predicament in the midst of a world which is in very few respects what he would wish it to be.

[3] As a child he is treated as a child, and such treatment implies much more than the physical coddling of which Freud speaks. Not only do those who surround him co-operate more completely than they ever will again to satisfy his wishes in material things, but they encourage him to live in a spiritual world far more satisfactory than their own. He is carefully protected from any knowledge of the cruelties and complexities of life; he is led to suppose that the moral order is simple and clear, that virtue

triumphs, and that the world is, as the desires of whole generations of mankind have led them to try to pretend that it is, arranged according to a pattern which would seem reasonable and satisfactory to human sensibilities.] He is prevented from realizing how inextricably what men call good and evil are intertwined, how careless is Nature of those values called mercy and justice and righteousness which men have come, in her despite, to value; and he is, besides, encouraged to believe in a vast mythology peopled with figments which range all the way from the Saints to Santa Claus and which represent projections of human wishes which the adult has come to recognize as no more than projections but which he is willing that the child, for the sake of his own happiness, should believe real. Aware how different is the world which experience reveals from the world which the spirit desires, the mature, as though afraid that reality could not be endured unless the mind had been gradually inured to it, allow the child to become aware of it only by slow stages, and little by little he learns, not only the limitations of his will, but the moral discord of the world. Thus it is, in a very important sense, true that the infant does come trailing clouds of glory from that heaven which his imagination creates, and that as his experience accumulates he sees it fade away into the light of common day.

[4] Now races as well as individuals have their infancy, their adolescence, and their maturity. Experience accumulates not only from year to year but from generation to generation, and in the life of each person it plays a little larger part than it did in the life of his father. As civilization grows older it too has more and more facts thrust upon its consciousness and is compelled to abandon one after another, quite as the child does, certain illusions which have been dear to it. Like the child, it has instinctively assumed that what it would like to be true is true, and it never gives up any such belief until experience in some form compels it to do so. Being, for example, extremely important to itself, it assumes that it is extremely important to the universe also. The earth is the center of all existing things, man is the child and the protégé of those gods who transcend and who will ultimately enable him to transcend all the evils which he has been compelled to recognize. The world and all that it contains were designed for him, and even those things which seem noxious have their usefulness only temporarily hid. Since he knows but little he is free to imagine, and imagination is always the creature of desire.

– II –

[5] The world which any consciousness inhabits is a world made up in part of experience and in part of fancy. No experience, and hence no knowledge, is complete, but the gaps which lie between the solid fragments are filled in with shadows. Connections, explanations, and reasons are supplied by the imagination, and thus the world gets its patterned

completeness from material which is spun out of the desires. But as time goes on and experience accumulates there remains less and less scope for the fancy. The universe becomes more and more what experience has revealed, less and less what imagination has created, and hence, since it was not designed to suit man's needs, less and less what he would have it be. With increasing knowledge his power to manipulate his physical environment increases, but in gaining the knowledge which enables him to do so he surrenders insensibly the power which in his ignorance he had to mold the universe. The forces of nature obey him, but in learning to master them he has in another sense allowed them to master him. He has exchanged the universe which his desires created, the universe made for man, for the universe of nature of which he is only a part. Like the child growing into manhood, he passes from a world which is fitted to him into a world for which he must fit himself.

[6] If, then, the world of poetry, mythology, and religion represents the world as a man would like to have it, while science represents the world as he gradually comes to discover it, we need only compare the two to realize how irreconcilable they appear. For the cozy bowl of the sky arched in a protecting curve above him he must exchange the cold immensities of space and, for the spiritual order which he has designed, the chaos of nature. God he had loved *because* God was anthropomorphic, because He was made in man's own image, with purposes and desires which were human and hence understandable. But Nature's purpose, if purpose she can be said to have, is no purpose of his and is not understandable in his terms. Her desire merely to live and to propagate in innumerable forms, her ruthless indifference to his values, and the blindness of her irresistible will strike terror to his soul, and he comes in the fullness of his experience to realize that the ends which he proposes to himself—happiness and order and reason—are ends which he must achieve, if he achieve them at all, in her despite. Formerly he had believed in even his darkest moments that the universe was rational if he could only grasp its rationality, but gradually he comes to suspect that rationality is an attribute of himself alone and that there is no reason to suppose that his own life has any more meaning than the life of the humblest insect that crawls from one annihilation to another. Nature, in her blind thirst for life, has filled every possible cranny of the rotting earth with some sort of fantastic creature, and among them man is but one—perhaps the most miserable of all, because he is the only one in whom the instinct of life falters long enough to enable it to ask the question "Why?" As long as life is regarded as having been created, creating may be held to imply a purpose, but merely to have come into being is, in all likelihood, merely to go out of it also.

[7] Fortunately, perhaps, man, like the individual child, was spared in his cradle the knowledge which he could not bear. Illusions have been

lost one by one. God, instead of disappearing in an instant, has retreated step by step and surrendered gradually his control of the universe. Once he decreed the fall of every sparrow and counted the hairs upon every head; a little later he became merely the original source of the laws of nature, and even today there are thousands who, unable to bear the thought of losing him completely, still fancy that they can distinguish the uncertain outlines of a misty figure. But the rôle which he plays grows less and less, and man is left more and more alone in a universe to which he is completely alien. His world was once, like the child's world, three-quarters myth and poetry. His teleological concepts molded it into a form which he could appreciate and he gave to it moral laws which would make it meaningful, but step by step the outlines of nature have thrust themselves upon him, and for the dream which he made is substituted a reality devoid of any pattern which he can understand.

[8] In the course of this process innumerable readjustments have been made, and always with the effort to disturb as little as possible the myth which is so much more full of human values than the fact which comes in some measure to replace it. Thus, for example, the Copernican theory of astronomy, removing the earth from the center of the universe and assigning it a very insignificant place among an infinitude of whirling motes, was not merely resisted as a fact but was, when finally accepted, accepted as far as possible without its implications. Even if taken entirely by itself and without the whole system of facts of which it is a part, it renders extremely improbable the assumption, fundamental in most human thought, that the universe has man as its center and is hence understandable in his terms, but this implication was disregarded just as, a little later, the implications of the theory of evolution were similarly disregarded. It is not likely that if man had been aware from the very beginning that his world was a mere detail in the universe, and himself merely one of the innumerable species of living things, he would ever have come to think of himself, as he even now tends to do, as a being whose desires must be somehow satisfiable and whose reason must be matched by some similar reason in nature. But the myth, having been once established, persists long after the assumptions upon which it was made have been destroyed, because, being born of desire, it is far more satisfactory than any fact.

[9] Unfortunately, perhaps, experience does not grow at a constant, but at an accelerated, rate. The Greeks who sought knowledge, not through the study of nature but through the examination of their own minds, developed a philosophy which was really analogous to myth, because the laws which determined its growth were dictated by human desires and they discovered few facts capable of disturbing the pattern which they devised. The Middle Ages retreated still further into themselves, but with the Renaissance man began to surrender himself to nature, and the sci-

ences, each nourishing the other, began their iconoclastic march. Three centuries lay between the promulgation of the Copernican theory and the publication of the *Origin of Species,* but in sixty-odd years which have elapsed since that latter event the blows have fallen with a rapidity which left no interval for recovery. The structures which are variously known as mythology, religion, and philosophy, and which are alike in that each has as its function the interpretation of experience in terms which have human values, have collapsed under the force of successive attacks and shown themselves utterly incapable of assimilating the new stores of experience which have been dumped upon the world. With increasing completeness science maps out the pattern of nature, but the latter has no relation to the pattern of human needs and feelings.

[10] Consider, for example, the plight of ethics. Historical criticism having destroyed what used to be called by people of learning and intelligence "Christian Evidences," and biology having shown how unlikely it is that man is the recipient of any transcendental knowledge, there remains no foundation in authority for ideas of right and wrong; and if, on the other hand, we turn to the traditions of the human race anthropology is ready to prove that no consistent human tradition has ever existed. Custom has furnished the only basis which ethics have ever had, and there is no conceivable human action which custom has not at one time justified and at another condemned. Standards are imaginary things, and yet it is extremely doubtful if man can live well, either spiritually or physically, without the belief that they are somehow real. Without them society lapses into anarchy and the individual becomes aware of an intolerable disharmony between himself and the universe. Instinctively and emotionally he is an ethical animal. No known race is so low in the scale of civilization that it has not attributed a moral order to the world, because no known race is so little human as not to suppose a moral order so innately desirable as to have an inevitable existence. It is man's most fundamental myth, and life seems meaningless to him without it. Yet, as that systematized and cumulative experience which is called science displaces one after another the myths which have been generated by need, it grows more and more likely that he must remain an ethical animal in a universe which contains no ethical element.

– III –

[11] Mystical philosophers have sometimes said that they "accepted the universe." They have, that is to say, formed of it some conception which answered the emotional needs of their spirit and which brought them a sense of being in harmony with its aims and processes. They have been aware of no needs which Nature did not seem to supply and of no ideals which she too did not seem to recognize. They have felt themselves one with her because they have had the strength of imagination to make

her over in their own image, and it is doubtful if any man can live at peace who does not thus feel himself at home. But as the world assumes the shape which science gives it, it becomes more and more difficult to find such emotional correspondences. Whole realms of human feeling, like the realm of ethics, find no place for themselves in the pattern of nature and generate needs for which no satisfaction is supplied. What man knows is everywhere at war with what he wants.

[12] In the course of a few centuries his knowledge, and hence the universe of which he finds himself an inhabitant, has been completely revolutionized, but his instincts and his emotions have remained, relatively at least, unchanged. He is still, as he always was, adjusted to the orderly, purposeful, humanized world which all peoples unburdened by experience have figured to themselves, but that world no longer exists. He has the same sense of dignity to which the myth of his descent from the gods was designed to minister, and the same innate purposefulness which led him to attribute a purpose to nature, but he can no longer think in terms appropriate to either. The world which his reason and his investigation reveal is a world which his emotions cannot comprehend.

[13] Casually he accepts the spiritual iconoclasm of science, and in the detachment of everyday life he learns to play with the cynical wisdom of biology and psychology, which explain away the awe of emotional experience just as earlier science explained away the awe of conventional piety. Yet, under the stress of emotional crises, knowledge is quite incapable of controlling his emotions or of justifying them to himself. In love, he calls upon the illusions of man's grandeur and dignity to help him accept his emotions, and faced with tragedy he calls upon illusion to dignify his suffering; but lyric flight is checked by the rationality which he has cultivated, and in the world of metabolism and hormones, repressions and complexes, he finds no answer for his needs. He is feeling about love, for example, much as the troubadour felt, but he thinks about it in a very different way. Try as he may, the two halves of his soul can hardly be made to coalesce, and he cannot either feel as his intelligence tells him that he should feel or think as his emotions would have him think, and thus he is reduced to mocking his torn and divided soul. In the grip of passion he cannot, as some romanticist might have done, accept it with a religious trust in the mystery of love, nor yet can he regard it as a psychiatrist, himself quite free from emotion, might suggest—merely as an interesting specimen of psychical botany. Man *qua* thinker may delight in the intricacies of psychology, but man *qua* lover has not learned to feel in its terms; so that, though complexes and ductless glands may serve to explain the feelings of another, one's own still demand all those symbols of the ineffable in which one has long ceased to believe.

[14] Time was when the scientist, the poet, and the philosopher walked hand in hand. In the universe which the one perceived the other found

himself comfortably at home. But the world of modern science is one in which the intellect alone can rejoice. The mind leaps, and leaps perhaps with a sort of elation, through the immensities of space, but the spirit, frightened and cold, longs to have once more above its head the inverted bowl beyond which may lie whatever paradise its desires may create. The lover who surrendered himself to the Implacable Aphrodite or who fancied his foot upon the lowest rung of the Platonic ladder of love might retain his self-respect, but one can neither resist nor yield gracefully to a carefully catalogued psychosis. A happy life is a sort of poem, with a poem's elevation and dignity, but emotions cannot be dignified unless they are first respected. They must seem to correspond with, to be justified by, something in the structure of the universe itself; but though it was the function of religion and philosophy to hypostatize some such correspondence, to project a humanity upon nature, or at least to conceive of a humane force above and beyond her, science finds no justification for such a process and is content instead to show how illusions were born.

[15] The most ardent love of truth, the most resolute determination to follow nature no matter to what black abyss she may lead, need not blind one to the fact that many of the lost illusions had, to speak the language of science, a survival value. Either individuals or societies whose life is imbued with a cheerful certitude, whose aims are clear, and whose sense of the essential rightness of life is strong, live and struggle with an energy unknown to the skeptical and the pessimistic. Whatever the limitations of their intellects as instruments of criticism, they possess the physical and emotional vigor which is, unlike critical intelligence, analogous to the processes of nature. They found empires and conquer wildernesses, and they pour the excess of their energy into works of art which the intelligence of more sophisticated peoples continues to admire even though it has lost the faith in life which is requisite for the building of a Chartres or the carving of a Venus de Milo. The one was not erected to a law of nature or the other designed to celebrate the libido, for each presupposed a sense of human dignity which science nowhere supports.

[16] Thus man seems caught in a dilemma which his intellect has devised. Any deliberately managed return to a state of relative ignorance, however desirable it might be argued to be, is obviously out of the question. We cannot, as the naïve proponents of the various religions, new and old, seem to assume, believe one thing and forget another merely because we happen to be convinced that it would be desirable to do so; and it is worth observing that the new psychology, with its penetrating analysis of the influence of desire upon belief, has so adequately warned the reason of the tricks which the will can play upon it that it has greatly decreased the possibility of beneficent delusion and serves to hold the mind in a steady contemplation of that from which it would fain escape. Weak and uninstructed intelligences take refuge in the monotonous repe-

tition of once living creeds, or are even reduced to the desperate expedient of going to sleep amid the formulae of the flabby pseudo-religions in which the modern world is so prolific. But neither of these classes affords any aid to the robust but serious mind which is searching for some terms upon which it may live.

[17] And if we are, as by this time we should be, free from any teleological delusion, if we no longer make the unwarranted assumption that every human problem is somehow of necessity solvable, we must confess it may be that for the sort of being whom we have described no survival is possible in any form like that which his soul has now taken. He is a fantastic thing that has developed sensibilities and established values beyond the nature which gave him birth. He is of all living creatures the one to whom the earth is the least satisfactory. He has arrived at a point where he can no longer delude himself as to the extent of his predicament, and should he either become modified or disappear the earth would continue to spin and the grass to grow as it has always done. Of the thousands of living species the vast majority would be as unaware of his passing as they are unaware now of his presence, and he would go as a shadow goes. His arts, his religions, and his civilizations—these are fair and wonderful things, but they are fair and wonderful to him alone. With the extinction of his poetry would come also the extinction of the only sensibility for which it has any meaning, and there would remain nothing capable of feeling a loss. Nothing would be left to label the memory of his discontent "divine," and those creatures who find in nature no lack would resume their undisputed possession of the earth.

[18] Anthropoid in form some of them might continue to be, and possessed as well of all of the human brain that makes possible a cunning adaptation to the conditions of physical life. To them nature might yield up subtler secrets than any yet penetrated; their machines might be more wonderful and their bodies more healthy than any yet known—even though there had passed away, not merely all myth and poetry, but the need for them as well. Cured of his transcendental cravings, content with things as they are, accepting the universe as experience had shown it to be, man would be freed of his soul and, like the other animals, either content or at least desirous of nothing which he might not hope ultimately to obtain.

[19] Nor can it be denied that certain adumbrations of this type have before now come into being. Among those of keener intellect there are scientists to whom the test tube and its contents are all-sufficient, and among those of coarser grain, captains of finance and builders of mills, there are those to whom the acquirement of wealth and power seems to constitute a life in which no lack can be perceived. Doubtless they are not new types; doubtless they have always existed; but may they not be

the strain from which Nature will select the coming race? Is not their creed the creed of Nature, and are they not bound to triumph over those whose illusions are no longer potent because they are no longer really believed? Certain philosophers, clinging desperately to the ideal of a humanized world, have proposed a retreat into the imagination. Bertrand Russell in his popular essay, *A Free Man's Worship,* Unamuno and Santayana *passim* throughout their works, have argued that the way of salvation lay in a sort of ironic belief, in a determination to act as though one still believed the things which once were really held true. But is not this a desperate expedient, a last refuge likely to appeal only to the leaders of a lost cause? Does it not represent the last, least substantial, phase of fading faith, something which borrows what little substance it seems to have from a reality of the past? If it seems half real to the sons of those who lived in the spiritual world of which it is a shadow, will it not seem, a little further removed, only a faint futility? Surely it has but little to oppose to those who come armed with the certitudes of science and united with, not fleeing from, the nature amid which they live.

[20] And if the dilemma here described is itself a delusion it is at least as vividly present and as terribly potent as those other delusions which have shaped or deformed the human spirit. There is no significant contemporary writer upon philosophy, ethics, or aesthetics whose speculations do not lead him to it in one form or another, and even the less reflective are aware of it in their own way. Both our practical morality and our emotional lives are adjusted to a world which no longer exists. In so far as we adhere to a code of conduct, we do so largely because certain habits still persist, not because we can give any logical reason for preferring them, and in so far as we indulge ourselves in the primitive emotional satisfactions—romantic love, patriotism, zeal for justice, and so forth—our satisfaction is the result merely of the temporary suspension of our disbelief in the mythology upon which they are founded. Traditionalists in religion are fond of asserting that our moral codes are flimsy because they are rootless; but, true as this is, it is perhaps not so important as the fact that our emotional lives are rootless too.

[21] If the gloomy vision of a dehumanized world which has just been evoked is not to become a reality, some complete readjustment must be made, and at least two generations have found themselves unequal to the task. The generation of Thomas Henry Huxley, so busy with destruction as never adequately to realize how much it was destroying, fought with such zeal against frightened conservatives that it never took time to do more than assert with some vehemence that all would be well, and the generation that followed either danced amid the ruins or sought by various compromises to save the remains of a few tottering structures. But neither patches nor evasions will serve. It is not a changed world but a

new one in which man must henceforth live if he lives at all, for all his premises have been destroyed and he must proceed to new conclusions. The values which he thought established have been swept away along with the rules by which he thought they might be attained.

[22] To this fact many are not yet awake, but our novels, our poems, and our pictures are enough to reveal that a generation aware of its predicament is at hand. It has awakened to the fact that both the ends which its fathers proposed to themselves and the emotions from which they drew their strength seem irrelevant and remote. With a smile, sad or mocking, according to individual temperament, it regards those works of the past in which were summed up the values of life. The romantic ideal of a world well lost for love and the classic ideal of austere dignity seem equally ridiculous, equally meaningless when referred, not to the temper of the past, but to the temper of the present. The passions which swept through the once major poets no longer awaken any profound response, and only in the bleak, tortuous complexities of a T. S. Eliot does it find its moods given adequate expression. Here disgust speaks with a robust voice and denunciation is confident, but ecstasy, flickering and uncertain, leaps fitfully up only to sink back among the cinders. And if the poet, with his gift of keen perceptions and his power of organization, can achieve only the most momentary and unstable adjustments, what hope can there be for those whose spirit is a less powerful instrument?

[23] And yet it is with such as he, baffled, but content with nothing which plays only upon the surface, that the hope for a still humanized future must rest. No one can tell how many of the old values must go or how new the new will be. Thus, while under the influence of the old mythology the sexual instinct was transformed into romantic love and tribal solidarity into the religion of patriotism, there is nothing in the modern consciousness capable of effecting these transmutations. Neither the one nor the other is capable of being, as it once was, the *raison d'être* of a life or the motif of a poem which is not, strictly speaking, derivative and anachronistic. Each is fading, each becoming as much a shadow as devotion to the cult of purification through self-torture. Either the instincts upon which they are founded will achieve new transformations or they will remain merely instincts, regarded as having no particular emotional significance in a spiritual world which, if it exists at all, will be as different from the spiritual world of, let us say, Robert Browning as that world is different from the world of Cato the Censor.

[24] As for this present unhappy time, haunted by ghosts from a dead world and not yet at home in its own, its predicament is not, to return to the comparison with which we began, unlike the predicament of the adolescent who has not yet learned to orient himself without reference to the mythology amid which his childhood was passed. He still seeks in

the world of his experience for the values which he had found there, and he is aware only of a vast disharmony. But boys—most of them, at least— grow up, and the world of adult consciousness has always held a relation to myth intimate enough to make readjustment possible. The finest spirits have bridged the gulf, have carried over with them something of a child's faith, and only the coarsest have grown into something which was not more than finished animality. Today the gulf is broader, the adjustment more difficult, than ever it was before, and even the possibility of an actual human maturity is problematic. There impends for the human spirit either extinction or a readjustment more stupendous than any made before.

--◦◄{ COMMENT AND QUESTIONS }►◦--

1. As the title of his chapter suggests, Krutch uses both a narrative method and a cause–effect development in discussing the genesis of the modern temper. He also makes extensive use of contrast and comparison, notably in the sustained comparison of the child and the human race. What is the purpose, in the first three paragraphs, of developing so fully the experience of the child before and after birth?

2. According to Krutch, how does the world of poetry, mythology, and religion differ from the world revealed by science? What were the values of the myths and illusions which he says man has been forced to abandon?

3. Among Krutch's many skills as a writer is his way of building his paragraphs to strong endings. Re-read the final sentences of paragraphs 1–10 (the first two sections of the chapter). What identical or similar ideas are restated, and so given additional emphasis, in these emphatic end sentences?

4. In the first two sections (paragraphs 1–10), is Krutch making any assumptions about the experience of the child or of man which you are unable to accept? Explain.

5. Krutch suggests (in paragraph 17 and elsewhere) that man with his developed sensibilities and values, adjusted to a world which no longer exists, has become a "fantastic thing" for whom survival may not be possible. What kind of "dehumanized world" does the author fear?

6. What escapes from the modern dilemma does Krutch reject as unsatisfactory for intelligent men?

7. What is the general tone of the selection? Does Krutch see any hope for a happy or satisfying future for man?

8. Select one or two paragraphs in which the writing seems to you effective, and carefully analyze the author's sentence structures and use of language.

9. Writing in 1929, Krutch concludes his chapter: "There impends for the human spirit either extinction or a readjustment more stupendous than any made before." On the basis of more recent writing (i.e., since 1929) which you have read—in this book or elsewhere—would you say that the human spirit is becoming extinct, or that it is making a readjustment to a new kind of world, or neither?

[38] *Joseph Wood Krutch*: Some Unsentimental Confessions of a Nature Writer

F O R A N O T E O N Joseph Wood Krutch, see page 374. The following essay appeared in the *New York Herald Tribune Book Review*, June 15, 1952.

[1] A few years ago I first laid myself open to the charge of being a "nature writer." Perhaps in time I shall know better what it is that I am trying to do and why I do it. At the moment I still do not know precisely what a "nature writer" is.

[2] A great many people, I am afraid, do not even care to know. When they hear the phrase they think of "the birds and the bees"—a useful device in the sex education of children but hardly, they think, an occupation for a grown man. A biologist is all right and so is a sportsman. But a "nature writer" can hardly expect more than a shrug from the realistic and the robust.

[3] The more literary quote Wordsworth: "Nature never did betray the heart that loved her" or, "The meanest flower that blows for me oft holds a thought too deep for tears." But Darwin, they say, exploded such ideas nearly a century ago. Even Tennyson knew better: "Nature red in tooth and claw." We can't learn anything from all that. These are desperate times. The only hope for today lies in the study of politics, sociology, and economics. If a nature writer is some one who advocates a return to nature then he must be a sentimentalist and a very old-fashioned one at that.

[4] This is a serious charge. When I hear it I am tempted to reply only that if I discovered a certain pleasure in writing about nature and if a few like to read me, it at least does nobody any harm. My books will not contribute to juvenile delinquency, be banned in Boston, or investigated by any loyalty board. But though that satisfies some of my friends it does not entirely satisfy me. I have spent most of my life with literary criticism

and history. Why should I have discovered that my week-ends and my summers in the country were becoming more and more important; that I spent more and more time looking at and thinking about plants and animals and birds; that I began to feel the necessity of writing about what I had seen and thought? Why, finally, when I saw fifteen free months ahead of me, should I have been sure that I wanted to go back to the Southwestern desert to see what an entirely different, only half known natural environment might have to say to me?

[5] It was more than a mere casual interest in natural history as a hobby. Certainly it was also more than the mere fact that the out-of-doors is healthful and relaxing. I was not merely being soothed and refreshed by an escape from the pressures of urban life. I was seeking for something, and got at least the conviction that there was something I was actually learning. I seemed to be getting a glimpse of some wisdom of which I had less than an inkling before.

[6] Perhaps I can put the answer abstractly and a little bit pompously something like this. Man is after all a part of nature. Life is a mystery and an adventure which he shares with all living things. The only clew to himself is in them. The universe is divided into two parts: that which is living and that which remains dead. We ought to be fully aware of which side we are on and of what it means to be on that side.

[7] Yet as civilization becomes more complicated we have less and less to do with the things which are on our side. We live in cities surrounded by dead things. We deal far more with machines than we do with animals. The principal context of our lives has come to be dead matter, not living matter. And under these circumstances we tend more and more to lose sight of what we are and of what we are like. Even the graphic and plastic arts are forsaking nature so that the wheel and the lever are more familiar than the flower or the leaf. An attitude which became fully explicit at the Renaissance seems to be in the process of disappearing.

[8] Perhaps that is the real reason why we have tended more and more to think about man and society as though they were machines; why we have mechanistic theories about consciousness and about human behavior in general. Perhaps that fact is one of the things which make us unhappy and anxious because in our depths we know that we are not machines, that we are more like the animals with which we have so little to do than like the mechanical contrivances we have surrounded ourselves by. Perhaps it is even one of the reasons why totalitarianism spreads, since the theory of the totalitarian state is that men can and should be manipulated as though they were machines, not permitted to grow as organisms grow. The question used to be whether or not men had souls. The question now seems to be whether or not they are alive at all; but that is seldom asked any more. In a city we may doubt it. In the presence of nature we cannot.

[9] I do not mean that we should all go live on Walden Pond. I am not

any kind of crank or any kind of Utopian reformer. I do not believe that the solution to the world's ills is a return to some previous age of mankind. But I do doubt that any solution is possible unless we think of ourselves in the context of living nature.

[¹⁰] Perhaps that suggests an answer to the question what a "nature writer" is. He is not a sentimentalist who says that "nature never did betray the heart that loved her." Neither is he simply a scientist classifying animals or reporting on the behavior of birds just because certain facts can be ascertained. He is a writer whose subject is the natural context of human life, a man who tries to communicate his observations and his thoughts in the presence of nature as part of his attempt to make himself more aware of that context. "Nature writing" is nothing really new. It has always existed in literature. But it has tended in the course of the last century to become specialized partly because so much writing that is not specifically "nature writing" does not present the natural context at all; because so many novels and so many treatises describe man as an economic unit, a political unit, or as a member of some social class but not as a living creature surrounded by other living things.

[¹¹] There are few men who have never looked at a kitten and thought it was cute or looked at the stars and felt themselves small. Whoever has done either has been aware of the context of nature and that is good as far as it goes. But it does not go very far and there is little in modern life, not too much in modern literature or modern art, to make him go further. What the "nature writer" is really asking him to do is to explore what such thoughts and such feelings mean. Nearly every one admits that literature and art have something to say that science and sociology cannot. But nature in her turn has something to say beyond the reach of literature and art. To that something the nature writer asks us to open our minds and our hearts precisely as another kind of writer asks us to open them to art or music or literature.

[¹²] That is, at least, what I am asking myself to do when I write about a year in Connecticut or a year in the desert, about the courtship of lizards, or the desert toad who seems to spend four-fifths of his life holed up in the sand not dreading but waiting for a rainy day. He is interesting primarily because he is playing his part in an inconceivable adventure in which we are all somehow involved.

[¹³] One of the things which I remember best from my year in the West is a day spent alone on a mountain top looking down at a desert. Half seriously I said to myself that this was my great chance. Moses and Zarathustra did just that. Most of the prophets have retired either to a mountain or to a desert. If ever, I thought, you are to get The Answer it ought to be now.

[¹⁴] I did not get it. These days, I suppose, no one ever does. This is not an age when men appear to hear the voice of God. But I do not think that

I ever before understood myself so well and with the understanding came a conviction. We cannot understand other people or the world unless we do understand ourselves first. It is presumption and folly to advise, and direct, and legislate unless we at least know our own selves. But we do not understand ourselves unless we have been alone with ourselves and with that nature of which we are more a part than we usually seem to remember.

[15] Alone on a mountain top no one ever believed that Man is nothing but the product of economic forces or that production per man hour is a reliable index of human welfare. And surely no man on a mountain top ever believed that Good and Evil are nothing except the prejudices of a given society. Such dismal, such deadly, opinions are possible only to those who do not know human beings because they do not know themselves and do not know themselves because they have never been alone with themselves. This will never be a world in which a good life is possible for most people as long as dismal and deadly opinions predominate. And the nature writer, like the poet and the priest, is their enemy.

[16] I do not mean to suggest that the nature writer always is or always should be on the mountain tops, either literally or figuratively. No one who actually looks at nature rather than at some fancy projected upon or read into her can ever fail to realize that she represents some ultimate things-as-they-are not some ideal of things-as-he-thinks-they-ought-to-be. There is in her what we call cruelty and also, even more conspicuously, what we call grotesqueness and what we call comedy. If she warns the so-called realist how limited his conception of reality is she is no less likely to bring the sentimentalist back, literally, to earth.

[17] How much of the cruelty, of the grotesqueness, or of the sublimity any given man will see depends no doubt to some considerable extent upon his own temperament and I suppose it is some indication of mine when I confess that what I see most often and relish the most is, first, the intricate marvel and, second, the comedy. To be reminded that one is very much like other members of the animal kingdom is often funny though it is never, like being compared to a machine, merely humiliating. I do not too much mind being somewhat like a cat, a dog, or even an insect but I resent having it said that even an electronic calculator is like me.

[18] Not very long ago I was pointing out to a friend the courtship of two spiders in a web just outside my door. Most people know that the male is often much smaller than his mate and nearly everybody knows by now that the female of many species sometimes eats her husband. Both of these things were true of the common kind beside my door and the insignificant male was quite obviously torn between ardor and caution. He danced forward and then darted back. He approached now from one side and now from the other. He would and he wouldn't.

[19] My friend, no nature student and not much given to observing

such creatures, was gratifyingly interested. Presently he could contain himself no longer.

[20] "You know," he said thoughtfully, "there is only one difference between that spider and a human male. The spider knows it's dangerous."

[21] That, I maintain, both is and ought to be as much grist for a nature writer's mill as a sunset or a bird song.

⊷ C O M M E N T   A N D   Q U E S T I O N S ⊶

1. What is the persona revealed in the first five paragraphs of this essay? What assumptions does Krutch seem to make about his audience?

2. In the preceding selection, "The Genesis of a Mood," Krutch has discussed the "ruthless indifference" of nature to human values, and the "intolerable disharmony" between man and the world of nature which science reveals. Do the views of nature expressed in "Some Unsentimental Confessions of a Nature Writer" represent a complete abandonment of his earlier views, or are the two attitudes towards nature reconcilable? Explain.

3. What does Krutch mean (paragraph 8) by "mechanistic theories about consciousness and about human behavior in general"? To one alone on a mountain top, Krutch says later, these and other theories are "dismal and deadly opinions." What perspective is provided by a mountain top that is not provided by a city street?

4. Summarize briefly the values Krutch sees in man's awareness of nature. In this context, what is the function of the "nature writer"?

5. Krutch says (paragraph 11) that "there is little in modern life, not too much in modern literature or modern art," to make man explore the possible meaning of nature. Do you agree or disagree, and why?

6. "Nature in her turn has something to say beyond the reach of literature and art." Do you agree or disagree with this statement, and why?

7. What is the function in the essay of the closing paragraphs about the spiders?

8. Early in his essay Krutch quotes Wordsworth and Tennyson on nature. Is he rejecting either or both of their views? Explain your answer.

[39] *Joseph Wood Krutch*: Life, Liberty, and the Pursuit of Welfare

FOR A NOTE ON Joseph Wood Krutch, see page 374. The following essay was published in the *Saturday Evening Post*, July 15, 1961.

[¹] "Welfare" is one of the key words of our time. What too many men now seem to desire is not virtue or knowledge or justice, but welfare. To the majority the word sums up the principal object of government and, indeed, of all social institutions.

[²] Had you asked a Greek philosopher what the purpose of government should be, he would have said something about the maintenance of justice. And had you pressed him to say in what justice consists, he would have replied—not very satisfactorily—"In assuring to every man that which is rightfully his."

[³] A medieval theologian would have added something about the City of God and the extent to which a community of mortals might approximate it. On the other hand that brutal seventeenth-century realist, Thomas Hobbes, would have gone to the other extreme. To him the principal aim of government is simply the maintenance of order, the taming of that state of nature which is anarchy or war. And the state of anarchy, he would have added, is so terrible that any government is better than no government.

[⁴] Finally, had you posed the same question to an eighteenth-century philosopher, he would have said something to the effect that the chief purpose of government is not simply the maintenance of order, but the assurance to each man of his inalienable rights. And if you had asked him what these inalienable rights are, he would have answered in some form not too different from that of the Declaration—"Life, liberty and the pursuit of happiness."

[⁵] In any event, it is obvious that none of these formulas is entirely satisfactory to most people today. They do not explicitly reject life, liberty and the pursuit of happiness, but they obviously consider them something less than enough. The invention of the term "welfare state" to describe something more than the democratic state is an expression of this dissatisfaction. It is intended to define a new ideal, which its proponents would call an extension of the ideal of a merely democratic state.

[⁶] If it be objected that the philosophers, theologians and social critics

cited above did not actually speak for the masses and that the great majority of the people would always have preferred "welfare" to the less
easily understood goods proposed to them, the answer is that even if this
be granted, it is not crucial to the argument which follows. The fact
remains that the power of the masses is now for the first time decisive and
that the sociologists and political scientists most influential today tend
both to accept this fact and to concur in regarding "welfare" as the chief
legitimate aim of government.

[7] In a broad, general way we all know what welfare so used implies,
what specific laws and institutions are called welfare measures, and what
are the premises upon which they are advocated. No one would object
very much if I said that the welfare state assumes, not only that men
should be protected against those who would deprive them of their right
to life, liberty and the pursuit of happiness, but that it should go beyond
mere protection to something more positive. All men not only must be
guaranteed their liberties but also, to a very considerable extent, "looked
after." Many of the arguments both for and against the policy of looking
after people are too familiar to need mentioning. But certain fundamental
questions are seldom asked. What is the ultimate definition of welfare—
in what does it consist, and who decides what it is? Or, to put the question
in a simpler form: Does the promotion of welfare mean giving people
what they want or seem to want or think they want, or does it consist in
giving them what they ought to have?

[8] The answer implied in various specific welfare proposals is sometimes the one and sometimes the other. But few have ever dared to put
the question boldly and to give a positive answer one way or another. If
welfare means that people get what they want, then which wants of
which people come first? If welfare means giving them what they ought
to have, then who decides what they ought to have, and on the basis of
what criteria is the decision made?

[9] This last is a very tough question indeed for an age which has
rejected absolutes and enthusiastically embraced both cultural and moral
relativism. One of the few bold answers I have ever encountered was
given by David Thompson, a lecturer in history at Cambridge University.
"The welfare state," said he, "exists to promote whatever the community
regards as beneficial and good. If the community regards automobiles,
TV sets and football pools as of greater value than better schools, more
generous care for old people, and a creative use of leisure, then the democratic state will provide more automobiles, TV sets and football pools."

[10] In the course of the article Mr. Thompson gives the impression
that he has preferences of his own and that they are not what he believes
to be those of most people. But he does not appear to have his tongue in
his cheek when he yields to the only definition of democracy and the only
definition of welfare which his relativistic philosophy will permit. Like

most of our contemporaries, he is unwilling to consider the possibility that what the community regards as valuable is not the only possible standard by which values may be judged. Nor, as a matter of fact, can anyone escape such a conviction unless he is willing to assume what most today refuse to assume, namely, that some basis for calling one thing intrinsically and absolutely better or righter or higher than another can be found somewhere: In nature, in reason or in the law of God—all of which are independent of either custom or majority opinion.

[11] Refuse, as most sociologists, psychologists and anthropologists do refuse, to make such an assumption, and you are driven to the conclusion which Mr. Thompson accepts: That nothing is better or more desirable than anything else except insofar as more people want it. Thus he comes to defend democracy not because of any conviction that its decisions are wiser by some independent standards than those arrived at by other forms of government, but simply because any decision which has majority sanction is wise and right by the only possible definition of those terms.

[12] If, as most people seem to assume, the normal is merely the average, if the good life is whatever the majority thinks or has been persuaded to think it is, if what men should do is whatever they do do, then it must follow that the desirable is whatever is most widely desired, and that democracy means that what the majority admires is necessarily to be called excellent. Mr. Thompson himself may prefer what he calls "the creative use of leisure" to TV sets and football pools, but he is too broad-minded—as we now call it—to suppose that such a preference is anything more than just another one of those tastes about which there is no disputing.

[13] *Laissez faire* is generally supposed to describe the social theory diametrically opposed to that of the welfare state, but here one sort of *laissez faire* is exchanged for another. Though the economy is to be planned, society is to be allowed to drift intellectually and culturally with whatever economic, technological or other currents may vary in this direction or that.

[14] Under democracy of the older sort the most fundamental right of the citizen was assumed to be the pursuit of happiness. The welfare state substitutes welfare—usually defined in material terms—for happiness. But by way of compensation it assures the citizen that his right is not merely to pursue happiness but to attain welfare; and under this arrangement we lose something as well as, perhaps, gain something. Though we may pursue whatever kind of happiness seems to us most worth pursuing, the welfare which is going to be assured us must be mass-produced, whether it is defined, under a dictatorship, as what the dictator thinks we ought to have, or, as in our society, by what the majority wants or has been persuaded to want.

[15] If I object that to define welfare as whatever most people seem

to want tends to mean more things and fewer ideas and, in general, tends toward the vulgarest possible conception of what constitutes the good life, I will be told that the answer is education—that, given enough schools, and schools that are good enough, the community will want what is truly most desirable; and that, if properly educated, it will provide for itself and ultimately reach a truly acceptable definition of welfare.

[16] But despite all the schooling which Americans get, many of them do not seem to be very effectively learning any ideals or cultivating any interests other than those which seem to prevail among the uneducated. High-school graduates and college graduates also very frequently prefer television and shinier automobiles to any of the more intellectual and less material forms of welfare.

[17] This fact brings us again up against the unanswered question and it suggests that education is failing to help people to achieve an acceptable definition of welfare for the same reason that the ideal of welfare itself is failing—because, in other words, we are unable to give any definition of education except the same kind of definition we give of welfare.

[18] If students do not want classical literature, philosophy or science, if they do want sports, courses in movie appreciation and in the accepted social conventions, then, just as the other things constitute welfare, so these things must constitute education. Once the school, like the church, tended to embody a protest, or at least a countervailing influence, against what the other forces in society tended to make of that society and of man himself. The church held that man undisciplined by religion was wicked. The school held that unless he was educated, he would be ignorant and crass. But both the church and the school seem now to have fallen in love with the world as it is. They talk more and more about adjustment—and by that to mean "adjustment to things as they are."

[19] The church halfheartedly, the school with real enthusiasm, gives up the attempt to direct society and is content to follow it, like the political leader who watches where the mob is going, puts himself at the head of it and says, "Follow me." Educators so-called have said, "Don't teach literary English; teach acceptable English." If, as a New York commission recently has proposed, children are not interested in the classics, don't waste time trying to arouse their interests; give them something they are interested in—teach them how to drive automobiles, how lipstick is best applied or, and this is part of one actual course in a Midwestern institution of learning, how to order groceries over the telephone.

[20] These are the things many of the students will be doing; this is what their lives will be made up of. And if the business of education is to prepare for life, then these are the things that they ought to be taught. But the statement so commonly made, that education should be a

preparation for life, is meaningless unless the kind of life it is supposed to prepare for is specified. If education is properly defined as hardly more than what anthropologists call "acculturation," then it is worth taking account of the fact that most children get much more of their education in this sense from advertisements, moving pictures, television, popular songs and so on, than they do from school. Preparation for life as the schools are tending to define it is much better accomplished by those institutions outside the school system than by those within it.

[21] It would, of course, be inaccurate as well as unfair to leave the impression that there is no protest against the ideals and practices of the schools as typified by the examples just given. During the past few years such protests have grown from a whisper to an outcry. Various organizations, notably the Council for Basic Education, have been formed to combat the prevailing tendencies. The latter especially has conducted a vigorous campaign of propaganda, buttressed by news bulletins, which report both outrageous examples of denatured education and reforms in the directions of which it approves.

[22] Such protests have had their effect. In California, for instance, the recent report of a state-appointed commission puts itself squarely on record as finding the prevailing aims and methods of the school system to be in many instances radically undesirable.

[23] Even more important perhaps is the fact that many parents have expressed their dissatisfaction and called for reform. The National Education Association, a very powerful and well entrenched group, has bitterly resented most such criticisms, but if the tide has not actually turned, it looks as though it might be on the point of turning.

[24] Nevertheless, it is not enough merely to ridicule current extravagances, to call for a return to the three R's and to insist that education does not consist in miscellaneous instruction in such varied specific subjects as safety rules for automobilists, the use of consumer credit and the current conventions governing "dating." Neither is it enough to say only that schools should be concerned primarily with the intellect and that those who talk about "educating the whole child" seem to forget that his head is part of him. Any rational theory must be based upon some conviction that the man of whom the child is the father ought to be in mind, in taste and in convictions something more than what he will be if he is allowed to follow only his simplest inclinations and whatever happens to be the current conventions of his group. In other words, what is necessary is a standard of values. Education is simply not changing people as much as it should.

[25] Many critics of our society have said that we lack standards. This has been said so often by preachers and by the makers of commencement addresses that we have almost stopped asking what, if anything,

it means to say that our society "lacks standards." But that we do lack standards for welfare and standards for education is obvious. Welfare turns into vulgar materialism because we have no standard by which to measure it. Education fails because it also refuses to face the responsibility of saying in what education consists. Both tend to become merely what people seem to want.

[26] To any such complaint most sociologists, psychologists and educators will shrug and say, "Perhaps. But where can you find standards other than those which are set by society itself? Who is arrogant enough to set them up? Where can the authority for such standards be found?"

[27] Most periods of human history have believed that they could be found somewhere outside mere custom. They have usually been sought in one or all of three places: (1) In the revealed will of God; (2) in the operation of right reason, supposedly capable of defining good and evil; (3) in something permanent in human nature itself.

[28] If I say this to the modern relativist, he replies that none of these things will any longer do. (1) God no longer exists. (2) Though man is capable of thinking instrumentally—that is to say, capable of scheming to get what he wants—there is no such thing as pure reason capable of reaching an absolute; and whenever men have thought they were doing so, they were, in fact only rationalizing their desires or the customs of their particular country. (3) What we call "human nature" is merely the result of the conditioning of the individual, either by the society in which he lives or by the peculiar experiences which have happened to be his. Since neither God nor pure reason exists, and since human nature is infinitely variable, it is evident that morals are merely mores, or custom; that right reason is merely a rationalization of the prejudices of the individual or his society; and that human nature is merely what social circumstances have made it.

[29] If all these characteristic modern convictions—or lack of convictions—are sound, then we must agree that whatever most people want is welfare, and that whatever pupils think they would least dislike doing in school is education. It is then useless to ask whether society is going in the right direction or whether men today are leading a good life. Nothing is absolutely better than anything else; things are what they are and will be what they will be, and we cannot control or direct. We must follow where events may lead us.

[30] Before accepting this counsel of despair once and for all, it would be worth while to ask again if it really is certain that all three of the conceivable bases upon which some standard might be founded really are merely illusory. Each of them might be taken up in turn. One might ask again does God exist; one might ask again is right reason a mere figment of the imagination? Does human nature exist?

[31] I here raise only what is perhaps the least difficult of all these

questions—the last one. Granted that man may be conditioned in various ways, is it nevertheless true that there are limits to the extent to which he can be conditioned? Is it true that human nature tends to return to some norm, that it is not limitlessly conditionable? And is it possible that to some extent one thing is better or higher or more valuable than another because human nature tends persistently to think that it is? Or, to put the question in its most general form, is there a good life which might be loosely defined as "that which is in accord with the most fundamental and persistent wants, desires and needs of human nature"?

[32] If ours is the richest and most powerful civilization that has ever existed, but if it is also the most anxious and ill at ease, is that in part because human nature needs something more than the wealth and power it has acquired? Is it possibly because human nature needs to believe just what modern thought has forbidden it to believe—that is, that morals are more than mores and that value judgments are more than merely rationalized prejudices? Once you insist that human nature as such does not exist, all the relativisms of our time—cultural, moral and social—inevitably follow. So, almost in desperation, let us ask again, "How good is the evidence that there is no such thing as human nature, that it is nothing but what experience or culture has made it?"

[33] We must begin by remembering that the theory that human nature is nothing in itself is not actually new. In that enormously influential seventeenth-century book, *Leviathan* by Thomas Hobbes, the theory is already implicit. Hobbes attempts to account for all the phenomena of human life by assuming that there is nothing innate in man except the ability to receive stimuli, the ability to react to them and the desire to experience pleasure. There is, accordingly, nothing in the mind which has not been first in the senses. There are no such things as innate ideas or desires other than the simple desire to experience pleasure or to exercise power, which latter is said to be the same thing. Hence man becomes whatever experience makes him and, to use the phrase which became popular later, he is born with a blank slate upon which anything may be written.

[34] We have enormously complicated this theory. We have drawn from it many deductions. But we have added little if anything essentially new. The whole of modern relativism seems to follow logically from Hobbes. If the human mind begins as a blank slate upon which anything may be written, then morals are only mores, our ideas of what is good or evil, just or unjust, beautiful or ugly, seemly or unseemly, are simply learned from the society in which we grow up. Nothing is eternally or inherently better than anything else—cultures vary from time to time and from place to place, but there is no external standard by which one may be judged as better than another. Incidentally, this complete abandon-

ment of the right to judge we now commonly call "getting rid of our prejudices."

[35] Contemporary anthropologists are fond of pointing out that what was considered right and desirable in one society was not so considered in another. Already by the end of the nineteenth century the historian Lecky could assert in his *History of European Morals* that there is no act which has not at one time or place been commanded as a duty and at another time or place forbidden as a sin—which is to say again that morals are only mores. Or, as a contemporary college textbook on psychology, written by a professor at the University of Southern California, puts it in a very short chapter on morals, "We call a man moral when he acts in accord with the laws and customs of his society"—by which definition, no doubt, a Nazi who took part in the persecution of the Jews would be a moral man, and who did not would be an immoral one.

[36] In a world which has so definitely rejected transcendental sanctions for either codes of morals or standards of value, the question whether human nature itself might supply them becomes enormously important. Is the usual negative answer really justifiable? Shall we one day swing again in a different direction and discover evidence now neglected that human nature is something in itself and does provide certain absolutes, valid at least within the human realm?

[37] Have the anthropologists, for instance, been so preoccupied with the collection of materials to demonstrate the enormous differences between cultures that they have overlooked some things which are common to all? Have the experimental psychologists been so busy conditioning both men and animals that they have paid little attention to the resistance to conditioning which both can put up?

[38] One little breeze in psychological doctrine might seem to point in this direction. Some skeptical psychologists have begun to wonder whether instinct on the one hand and the conditioned reflex on the other really can account for all of the behavior of living organisms. Certain sufficiently obvious facts have recently been re-emphasized.

[39] Consider three of them which seem ludicrously simple. (1) Birds know by instinct how to fly and do not have to be taught, though mother birds sometimes seem to be teaching them. This is an example of instinct. (2) Seals do not instinctively know how to swim, but they learn very easily how to swim when they are taught by their parents. (3) You would have a very hard time indeed teaching most songbirds to swim. In other words, there are not just two classes of animal behavior—that which is inborn and that which is learned. There is also a third and possibly an enormously important one—namely, that behavior which is not inborn, though the ability to learn it easily is.

[40] Considering such facts, some have begun to wonder whether the same might be true not only of skills but throughout the whole psychic

realm of beliefs, tastes, motives, desires and needs. The thesis of the moral relativist is—to take an extreme case—that since no one is born with an innate idea that dishonesty and treachery are evil, then the conviction that they are evil can be nothing but the result of social education, and the opposite could just as easily have been taught, since value judgments are merely the rationalized prejudices of a given culture. May it not be true on the contrary that certain ideas are much more easily learned than others, and that what the eighteenth century called natural law, natural taste and the rest, is real—consisting in those beliefs and tastes which are most readily learned and most productive of health and happiness?

[41] Perhaps you can condition an individual or a society to think and behave unnaturally just as you might possibly teach a robin to swim, but men who have been conditioned to think or behave unnaturally are unhappy—as unhappy and as inefficient as swimming robins. Perhaps Hobbes was right to the extent that no ideas are innate; but if the capacity to entertain readily some ideas and not others is innate, then it comes down to much the same thing. As Alexander Pope wrote nearly two and a half centuries ago, "Nature affords at least a glimmering light; the lines, though touched but faintly, are drawn right"—which is to say that the faint lines on the not quite blank slate constitute the reality behind the idea of a normal human being.

[42] What Pope thought of as a metaphor may be an accurate biological statement. On the not quite blank slate the lines are touched too faintly to constitute an automatic instinct—they may even be destroyed by resolute conditioning and education—but they are rather like a latent image on a photographic plate, imperceptible until developed, though development will reveal only what already exists. If this is true, then there is such a thing as human nature. What we are born with is not a blank slate, but a film bearing already a latent image.

[43] No doubt, as Pope himself said elsewhere, as experimental psychologists prove in the laboratory and as dictators as well as educators have too often demonstrated, the lines may be overlaid, and the unnatural may cease to seem a creature of hideous mien. But the conditioners have to work hard. Men, I suspect, believe much more readily in the reality of good and evil than they accept cultural relativism. Perhaps that means that belief in the reality of good and evil is according to nature and the modern tendency to dismiss them as mere prejudices of culture is fundamentally unnatural.

[44] Such an assumption is at least one which no valid science forbids, and if we make even such a minimum assumption, we can be saved from the nihilism of the present-day social, cultural and moral relativism. We have again some point of reference now lacking in every inquiry

which sets out to determine what kind of society or education or culture would be best for us. One thing is no longer as good as another provided only it can be shown or made to exist. We would no longer need to talk only about what can be done to men or what we might possibly be able to make them into, for we would be able to talk again about what men are in themselves.

[45] We would have the beginning of a basis for a definition of welfare and a definition of education such as we now totally lack. We could say, for example, that welfare is not merely what people at a given moment believe they want, but that which experience has proved to be conducive to health and happiness.

[46] We could say that education is not whatever a pupil thinks he wants in school, but that it is that which experience has shown will lead to a true understanding of his own nature, his own needs and his own wants. We could say the ideal of education is not conformity, not acculturation, but the full development of human nature's potentialities.

[47] We could say that the normal is not the same thing as the average, but rather that the normal is normative—that is to say, that by which a thing is to be judged. And we could add that the normal human being is not the average human being, but the thing to which human nature aspires.

[48] To attempt to determine what is part of permanent human nature is to undertake no easy task. To distinguish between what is truly natural and what is merely conditioned is extremely difficult. But to conclude that the question is actually a meaningful one is already to have concluded something vastly important. We talk much today about the extent to which we can control nature and our destiny, of how we have taken the future of the human race into our hands. But control implies some idea of the direction in which you want to go. We have the power, perhaps, but what good is the power unless we know what we want to do with it? "Give me a fulcrum for my lever, and I will move the world," said Archimedes. But a fulcrum for a lever is exactly what we lack. It implies a point of support which is necessary if you are going to move the world. We are trying to lever society without having any fulcrum on which to rest the lever and, in the absence of any other, we might possibly find it in some understanding of fundamental human nature.

[49] However much there may be still to learn about human nature, certain of its characteristics seem to me obvious enough to suggest some of the ways in which our society has been going wrong.

[50] The first of these permanent characteristics seems to me to be that man is inveterately a maker of value judgments. His idea of what constitutes right and wrong conduct, of what is just or unjust, has been—perhaps will continue to be—extremely diverse. But he has nearly always believed that good and evil, justice and injustice, are realities which it

is of the first importance to define and to cherish, while moral and cultural relativism—the idea that morals are nothing but mores and that one society is not absolutely better than another is so profoundly unnatural a conviction that it has seldom been entertained for long and is destructive of human welfare when it is.

[51] Closely related to the value judgment is the idea of justice. Men have varied enormously, irreconcilably, over the question of what constitutes justice. But they have nearly always believed that there is some such thing and that they should adhere to it. Part of that feeling is, I believe, the conviction that acts should have consequences, and that the way you are treated should be in some degree affected by the way in which you behave. A spoiled child, one who never pays any penalty for his follies or misdeeds, one who is given what some of the modern educators call "uncritical love," is usually an unhappy child because something fundamental in his human nature tells him that acts should have consequences and makes him profoundly uneasy in a world where they do not.

[52] Similarly I believe that a society is unhappy if it holds—as so many sociologists now profess to hold—that no man should be held responsible for his imprudences or his crimes. He may be glad to escape those consequences, but he is finding himself in a world without justice, in a world where the way in which you act has no effect upon the way in which you are treated. And I believe that, like the spoiled child, he is profoundly uneasy in that unnatural situation.

[53] I believe that it is also in accord with fundamental human nature to want some goods other than the material, that a society which defines the good life as merely a high standard of living and then defines the high standard of living in terms of material things alone is one which, in that respect, is denying expression to a fundamental characteristic of man. Few societies, whether primitive or not, have ever accepted the belief that welfare thus narrowly defined is the one and only supreme good. Men have sought all sorts of other things—they have sought God, they have sought beauty, they have sought truth or they have sought glory, militarily or otherwise. They have sought adventure; they have even—so anthropologists tell us—sometimes believed that a large collection of dried human heads was the thing in all the world most worth having. But seldom if ever, so it seems to me, have they confessedly sought only what is now called "welfare."

[54] This is a mere beginning. You may dispute, if you like, even the few general statements I have made about permanent human nature. But if you admit that some things are and some things are not in accord

with human nature, then you have grasped an instrument capable of doing something which few men today seem able to do, namely, attempt a rational criticism of things as they are.

⸻⧉ C O M M E N T   A N D   Q U E S T I O N S ⧉⸻

1. What is the purpose, in the first six paragraphs of the essay, of Krutch's discussion of various concepts of the purpose of government? In these opening paragraphs, does Krutch express or imply his own attitudes toward welfare as the chief aim of government?

2. One of Krutch's key terms is *cultural and moral relativism*. In the context of the essay, how is the term defined and clarified? What is the relativist view of what constitutes welfare?

3. Briefly summarize Krutch's reasons (paragraphs 10–15) for believing that welfare, properly defined, should consist of giving people what they ought to have instead of what they want or think they want.

4. Explain the statement (paragraph 17) that "education is failing to help people to achieve an acceptable definition of welfare . . . because . . . we are unable to give any definition of education except the same kind of definition we give of welfare." How does Krutch support this statement? How does he qualify it?

5. In paragraphs 25–30, Krutch discusses our lack of standards and the prevalent opinion that no standards can exist outside of mere custom and conditioning. If you have read "The Genesis of a Mood," what was Krutch's attitude in that selection toward a similar "counsel of despair"? In "Life, Liberty, and the Pursuit of Welfare" (written thirty-two years later) what is his attitude? Where is he looking for standards or values?

6. Krutch introduces, at the end of paragraph 33, the figure of the human mind as a "blank slate" on which anything can be written. Trace the recurrence and development of this figure later in the essay.

7. What is the point of the discussion, beginning in paragraph 39, of birds and seals? What conclusions does Krutch draw from the "simple" facts about animal behavior?

8. Point out examples, in paragraphs 40–44, of the author's qualifications of his statements.

9. What are the characteristics which seem to Krutch a part of, or in accord with, fundamental human nature? In qualifying his assertions about these characteristics, does the author qualify them out of existence; that is, do the assertions seem meaningful and valid to you after they are so fully qualified? What is the relationship of each of the human characteristics to the concept of welfare?

10. Early in the essay (paragraphs 7 and 8), Krutch raises two basic questions: (a) "Does the promotion of welfare mean giving people what they

want or seem to want or think they want, or does it consist in giving them what they ought to have?" and (b) "If welfare means giving them what they ought to have, then who decides what they ought to have, and on the basis of what criteria is the decision made?" In the course of the essay, Krutch gives his answer to the first question. Does he also answer the second? Would you say that the general pattern of the essay is problem-to-solution? Explain.

11. What are your answers to Krutch's two questions quoted above, and how would you support your answers?

12. Krutch in this essay is dealing with a number of abstract ideas (*welfare, relativism, education, values, the good life, human nature,* for example). Study his use of concrete language—concrete words, facts, examples, quotations, allusions, and comparisons—to clarify and develop the abstractions. What instances of concrete language seem to you most effective in making or supporting a point?

[40] *Brand Blanshard*: The Case for Determinism

BRAND BLANSHARD (1892–   ) has taught at Swarthmore College and Columbia University and is a professor of philosophy at Yale University. The following selection, an argument against what is commonly called free will, was a paper delivered at the New York University Institute of Philosophy in 1957. Students who are untrained in philosophy are likely to find parts of the essay difficult; but the argument is closely reasoned, and the main ideas are clear and significant.

[1] I am a determinist. None of the arguments offered on the other side seem of much weight except one form of the moral argument, and that itself is far from decisive. Perhaps the most useful thing I can do in this paper is explain why the commoner arguments for indeterminism do not, in my mind, carry conviction. In the course of this explanation the brand of determinism to which I am inclined should become gradually apparent.

[2] But first a definition or two. Determinism is easier to define than indeterminism, and at first glance there seems to be no difficulty in saying what one means by it. It is the view that all events are caused. But unless one also says what one means by "event" and "caused," there is likely to

be trouble later. Do I include among events not only changes but the lack of change, not only the fall of water over the cataract's edge, but the persistence of ice in the frozen river? The answer is "Yes." By an event I mean any change or persistence of state or position. And what is meant by saying that an event is caused? The natural answer is that the event is so connected with some preceding event that unless the latter had occurred the former would not have occurred. Indeterminism means the denial of this. And the denial of this is the statement that there is at least one event to which no preceding event is necessary. But that gets us into trouble at once, for it is doubtful if any indeterminist would want to make such an assertion. What he wants to say is that his decision to tell the truth is undetermined, not that there is no preceding event necessary to it. He would not contend, for example, that he could tell the truth if he had never been born. No, the causal statement to which the indeterminist takes exception is a different one. He is not saying that there is any event to which some namable antecedents are not necessary; he is saying that there are some events whose antecedents do not make them necessary. He is not denying that all consequents have necessary antecedents; he is denying that all antecedents have necessary consequents. He is saying that the state of things just before he decided to tell the truth might have been exactly what it was and yet he might have decided to tell a lie.

[³] By determinism, then, I mean the view that every event *A* is so connected with a later event *B* that, given *A*, *B* must occur. By indeterminism I mean the view that there is some event *B* that is not so connected with any previous event *A* that, given *A*, it must occur. Now, what is meant here by "must"? We cannot in the end evade that question, but I hope you will not take it as an evasion if at this point I am content to let you fill in the blank in any way you wish. Make it a logical "must," if you care to, or a physical or metaphysical "must," or even the watered-down "must" that means "*A* is always in fact followed by *B*." We can discuss the issue usefully though we leave ourselves some latitude on this point.

[⁴] With these definitions in mind, let us ask what are the most important grounds for indeterminism. This is not the same as asking what commonly moves people to be indeterminists; the answer to that seems to me all too easy. Everyone vaguely knows that to be undetermined is to be free, and everyone wants to be free. My question is rather, When reflective people accept the indeterminist view nowadays, what considerations seem most cogent to them? It seems to me that there are three: first, the stubborn feeling of freedom, which seems to resist all dialectical solvents; second, the conviction that natural science itself has now gone over to the indeterminist side; and, third, that determinism would make nonsense of moral responsibility. The third of these seems to me the most important, but I must try to explain why none of them seem to me conclusive.

[5] One of the clearest heads that ever devoted itself to this old issue was Henry Sidgwick. Sidgwick noted that, if at any given moment we stop to think about it, we always feel as if more than one course were open to us, that we could speak or be silent, lift our hand or not lift it. If the determinist is right, this must be an illusion, of course, for whatever we might have done, there must have been a cause, given which we had to do what we did. Now, a mere intuitive assurance about ourselves may be a very weak ground for belief; Freud has shown us that we may be profoundly deceived about how we really feel or why we act as we do. But the curious point is that, though a man who hates his father without knowing it can usually be shown that he does and can often be cured of his feeling, no amount of dialectic seems to shake our feeling of being free to perform either of two proposed acts. By this feeling of being free I do not mean merely the freedom to do what we choose. No one on either side questions that we have that sort of freedom, but it is obviously not the sort of freedom that the indeterminist wants, since it is consistent with determinism of the most rigid sort. The real issue, so far as the will is concerned, is not whether we can do what we choose to do, but whether we can choose our own choice, whether the choice itself issues in accordance with law from some antecedent. And the feeling of freedom that is relevant as evidence is the feeling of an open future as regards the choice itself. After the noise of argument has died down, a sort of intuition stubbornly remains that we can not only lift our hand if we choose, but that the choice itself is open to us. Is this not an impressive fact?

[6] No, I do not think it is. The first reason is that when we are making a choice our faces are always turned toward the future, toward the consequences that one act or the other will bring us, never toward the past with its possible sources of constraint. Hence these sources are not noticed. Hence we remain unaware that we are under constraint at all. Hence we feel free from such constraint. The case is almost as simple as that. When you consider buying a new typewriter your thought is fixed on the pleasure and advantage you would gain from it, or the drain it would make on your budget. You are not delving into the causes that led to your taking pleasure in the prospect of owning a typewriter or to your having a complex about expenditure. You are too much preoccupied with the ends to which the choice would be a means to give any attention to the causes of which your choice may be an effect. But that is no reason for thinking that if you did preoccupy yourself with these causes you would not find them at work. You may remember that Sir Francis Galton was so much impressed with this possibility that for some time he kept account in a notebook of the occasions on which he made important choices with a full measure of this feeling of freedom; then shortly after each choice he turned his eye backward in search of constraints that might have been acting on him stealthily. He found it so easy to bring

such constraining factors to light that he surrendered to the determinist view.

[7] But this, you may say, is not enough. Our preoccupation with the future may show why we are not aware of the constraints acting on us, and hence why we do not feel bound by them; it does not explain why our sense of freedom persists after the constraints are disclosed to us. By disclosing the causes of some fear, for example, psychoanalytic therapy can remove the fear, and when these causes are brought to light, the fear commonly does go. How is it, then, that when the causes of our volition are brought to light volition continues to feel as free as before? Does this not show that it is really independent of those causes?

[8] No again. The two cases are not parallel. The man with the panic fear of dogs is investing all dogs with the qualities—remembered, though in disguised form—of the monster that frightened him as a child. When this monster and his relation to it are brought to light, so that they can be dissociated from the Fidos and Towsers around him, the fear goes, because its appropriate object has gone. It is quite different with our feeling of freedom. We feel free, it was suggested, because we are not aware of the forces acting on us. Now, in spite of the determinist's conviction that when a choice is made there are always causal influences at work, he does not pretend to reveal the influences at work in our present choice. The chooser's face is always turned forward; his present choice is always unique; and no matter how much he knows about the will and the laws, his present choice always emerges out of deep shadow. The determinist who buys a typewriter is as little interested at the moment in the strings that may be pulling at him from his physiological or subconscious cellars as his indeterminist colleague, and hence feels just as free. Thus, whereas the new knowledge gained through psychoanalysis does remove the grounds of fear, the knowledge gained by the determinist is not at all of the sort that would remove the grounds for the feeling of freedom. To make the persistence of this feeling in the determinist an argument against his case is therefore a confusion.

[9] The second reason, I suggested, why so many thoughtful persons remain indeterminists is that they are convinced that science has gone indeterminist. Well, has it? If you follow Heisenberg, Eddington, and Bron, it has. If you follow Russell, Planck, and Einstein, it has not. When such experts disagree it is no doubt folly for the layman to rush in. But since I am discussing the main reasons why people stick to indeterminism, and have admitted that the new physics is one of them, I cannot afford to be quite prudent. Let me say, then, with much hesitation that, as far as I can follow the argument, it provides no good evidence for indeterminism even in the physical world, and that, if it did, it would provide no good evidence for indeterminism in the realm of will.

[10] First as to physical indeterminism. Physicists now tell us that de-

scriptive statements about the behavior of bodies are really statistical statements. It was known long ago that the pressure that makes a football hard is not the simple quality one feels in pushing something: it is the beating on the inner surface of the football of millions of molecule bullets. We now know that each of these bullets is a swarm of atoms, themselves normally swarms of still minuter somethings, of which the proton and the electron are typical. The physicist admits that the behavior of an enormous mass of these particles, such as a billiard ball, is so stable that we may safely consider it as governed by causal law. But that is no reason, he adds, for assigning a like stability to the ultimate particles themselves. Indeed, there is good reason, namely the principle of indeterminacy, for saying that they sometimes act by mere chance. That principle tells us that whereas, when we are talking about a billiard ball, we can say that it has a certain momentum and direction at point B as a result of having a certain momentum and direction at point A, we can never say that sort of thing about an electron. Why? Because the conditions of observation are such that, when they allow us to fix the position exactly, they make it impossible to fix the momentum exactly. Suppose that we can determine the position of a moving particle with more accuracy the shorter the wave length of light we use. But suppose that the shorter the wave length, the more it interferes with the momentum of the particle, making it leap unpredictably about. And suppose there is no way of determining the position without in this way leaving the momentum vague, or of determining the momentum without leaving the position vague. It will then be impossible to state any precise law that governs the particle's movement. We can never say that such-and-such a momentum at point A was necessarily followed by such-and-such a momentum at point B, because these statements can have no precise meaning, and can be given none, for either antecedent or consequent. Hence to speak any longer of nature as governed ultimately by causal laws—*i.e.*, statements of precise connection between antecedent and consequent—is simply out of the question.

[11] This argument, as Sir David Ross has pointed out, may be interpreted in different ways. It may be taken to say that, though the particle does have a certain position and momentum, we can never tell, definitely and for both at the same time, what they are. Many interpreters thus understand the theory. But so taken, there is of course nothing in it to throw the slightest doubt on the reign of causality. It is merely a statement that in a certain region our knowledge of causal law has limits. Secondly, the theory might be taken to mean that electrons are not the sort of things that have position and momentum at all in the ordinary sense, but are fields, perhaps, or widespreading waves. This, too, has no suggestion of indeterminism. It would not mean that general statements about the nature and behavior of electrons could not be made, but only

that such statements would not contain references to position and momentum. Thirdly, the theory might mean that, though these particles do have a position and a momentum, the position or momentum is not definitely this rather than that. Even laymen must rise at this point and protest, with all respect, that this is meaningless. Vagueness in our thought of a position makes sense; vagueness of actual position makes none. Or, finally, the argument may mean that, though the particle does have a definite position and momentum, these cannot even in theory be correlated with anything that went before. But how could we possibly know this? The only ground for accepting it is that we do not know of any such correlates. And that is no reason for denying that any exist. Indeed, to deny this is to abandon the established assumption and practice of science. Science has advanced in the past precisely because, when things happened whose causes were unknown, it was assumed that they had causes nevertheless. To assume that a frustration of present knowledge, even one that looks permanent, is a sign of chance in nature is both practically uncourageous and theoretically a *non sequitur.*

[12] But let us suppose that the Eddingtonians are right and that what has been called "free will among the electrons" is the fact. Would that imply indeterminism in the realm that most nearly concerns us, the realm of choice? I cannot see that it would. The argument supposed to show that it would is as follows: Psychical processes depend on physical processes. But physical processes are themselves at bottom unpredictable. Hence the psychical processes dependent on them must share this unpredictability. Stated in the abstract, the argument sounds impressive. But what does it actually come to? We are told that, even if there is inconstancy in the behavior of single particles, there is no observable inconstancy in the behavior of masses of them; the particles of a billiard ball are never able to get together and go on a spree simultaneously. Eddington admitted that they might, just as he admitted that an army of monkeys with a million typewriters might produce all the books in the British Museum, but he admitted also that the chances of a billiard ball's behaving in this way were so astronomically remote that he would not believe it if he saw it.

[13] The question of importance for us, then, is whether, if acts of choice are dependent on physical processes at all, they depend on the behavior of particles singly or on that of masses of particles. To this there can be but one answer. They depend on mass behavior. An act of choice is an extremely complex process. It involves the idea of one or more ends, the association of that idea with more or less numerous other ideas, the presence of desires and repulsions, and the operation of habits and impulses; indeed, in those choices for which freedom is most demanded, the whole personality seems to be at work. The cortical basis for so complex a

process must be extremely broad. But if it is, the great mass of cells involved must, by the physicist's admission, act with a high stability, and the correlated psychical processes must show a similar stability. But that is what we mean by action in accordance with causal law. So, even if the physicists are right about the unstable behavior of single particles, there is no reason whatever for translating this theory into a doctrine of indeterminism for human choice.

[14] We come now to the third of the reasons commonly advanced in support of indeterminism. This is that determinism makes a mess of morality. The charge has taken many forms. We are told that determinism makes praise and blame meaningless, punishment brutal, remorse pointless, amendment hopeless, duty a deceit. All these allegations have been effectively answered except the one about duty, where I admit I am not quite satisfied. But none of them are in the form in which determinism most troubles the plain man. What most affronts him, I think, is the suggestion that he is only a machine, a big foolish clock that seems to itself to be acting freely, but whose movements are controlled completely by wheels and weights inside, a Punch-and-Judy show whose appearance of doing everything is mechanically regulated by wires from below. He has no objections to determinism as applied by physicists to atoms, by himself to machines, or by his doctor to his body. He has an emphatic objection to determinism as applied by anyone to his reflection and his will, for this seems to make him a gigantic mechanical toy, or worse, a sort of Frankenstein monster.

[15] In this objection I think we must agree with the plain man. If anyone were to show me that determinism involved either materialism or mechanism, I would renounce it at once, for that would be equivalent, in my opinion, to reducing it to absurdity. The "physicalism" once proposed by Neurath and Carnap as a basis for the scientific study of behavior I could not accept for a moment, because it is so dogmatically antiempirical. To use empirical methods means, for me, not to approach nature with a preconceived notion as to what facts must be like, but to be ready to consider all kinds of alleged facts on their merits. Among these the introspectively observable fact of reflective choice, and the inference to its existence in others, are particularly plain, however different from anything that occurs in the realm of the material or the publicly observable or the mechanically controlled.

[16] Now, what can be meant by saying that such choice, though not determined mechanically, is still determined? Are you suggesting, it will be asked, that in the realm of reflection and choice there operates a different kind of causality from any we know in the realm of bodies? My answer is: Yes, just that. To put it more particularly, I am suggesting (a) that even within the psychical realm there are different causal levels,

(*b*) that a causality of higher level may supervene on one of lower level, and (*c*) that when causality of the highest level is at work, we have precisely what the indeterminists, without knowing it, want.

[¹⁷] *a*. First, then, as to causal levels. I am assuming that even the indeterminist would admit that most mental events are causally governed. No one would want to deny that his stepping on a tack had something to do with his feeling pain, or that his touching a flame had something to do with his getting burned, or that his later thought of the flame had something to do with his experience of its hotness. A law of association is a causal law of mental events. In one respect it is like a law of physical events: in neither case have we any light as to *why* the consequent follows the antecedent. Hume was right about the billiard balls. He was right about the flame and the heat; we do not see why something bright and yellow should also be hot. He was right about association; we do not understand how one idea calls up another; we only know that it does. Causality in all such cases means to us little if anything more than a routine of regular sequence.

[¹⁸] Is all mental causation like that? Surely not. Consider a musician composing a piece or a logician making a deduction. Let us make our musician a philosopher also, who after adding a bar pauses to ask himself, "Why did I add just that?" Can we believe he would answer, "Because whenever in the past I have had the preceding bars in mind, they have always been followed by this bar"? What makes this suggestion so inept is partly that he may never have thought of the preceding bars before, partly that, if he had, the repetition of an old sequence would be precisely what he would avoid. No, his answer, I think, would be something like this: "I wrote what I did because it seemed the right thing to do. I developed my theme in the manner demanded to carry it through in an aesthetically satisfactory way." In other words, the constraint that was really at work in him was not that of association; it was something that worked distinctly against association; it was the constraint of an aesthetic ideal. And, if so, there is a causality of a different level. It is idle to say that the musician is wholly in the dark about it. He can see not only *that* B succeeded A; as he looks back, he can see in large measure *why* it did.

[¹⁹] It is the same with logical inference, only more clearly so. The thinker starts, let us say, with the idea of a regular solid whose faces are squares, and proceeds to develop in thought the further characteristics that such a solid must possess. He constructs it in imagination and then sees that it must have six faces, eight vertices, and twelve edges. Is this association merely? It may be. It is, for example, if he merely does in imagination what a child does when it counts the edges of a lump of sugar. This is not inference and does not feel like it. When a person, starting with the thought of a solid with square faces, deduces that it must have eight vertices, and then asks why he should have thought of that, the natural answer is, Because the first property entails the second. Of course this is not the only condition, but it seems to me contrary to introspectively plain fact to say that it had nothing to do with the movement of thought. It is easy to put this in such a way as to invite attack. If we say that the condition of our thinking of B is the observed necessity between A and B, we are assuming that B is already thought of as a means of explaining how it comes to be thought of. But that is not what I am saying. I am saying that in thinking at its best thought comes under the constraint of necessities in its object, so that the objective fact that A necessitates B partially determines our passing in thought from A to B. Even when the explanation is put in this form, the objection has been raised that necessity is a timeless link between concepts, while causality is a temporal bond between events, and that the two must be kept sharply apart. To which the answer is: Distinct, yes; but always apart, no. A timeless relation may serve perfectly well as the condition of a temporal passage. I hold that in the course of our thinking we can easily verify this fact, and, because I do, I am not put off by pronouncements about what we should and should not be able to see.

[20] *b.* My second point about these causal levels is that our mental processes seldom move on one level alone. The higher is always supervening on the lower and taking over partial control. Though brokenly and imperfectly rational, rational creatures we still are. It must be admitted that most of our so-called thinking moves by association, and is hardly thinking at all. But even in the dullest of us "bright shoots of everlastingness," strands of necessity, aesthetic or logical, from time to time appear. "The quarto and folio editions of mankind" can follow the argument with fewer lapses than most of us; in the texts of the greatest of all dramas, we are told, there was seldom a blot of erasure; but Ben Jonson added, and no doubt rightly, that there ought to have been a thousand. The effort of both thought and art is to escape the arbitrary, the merely personal, everything that, casual and capricious, is irrelevant, and to keep to lines appointed by the whole that one is constructing. I do not suggest that logical and aesthetic necessity are the same. I do say that they are both to be distinguished from association or habit as representing a different level of control. That control is never complete; all creation in thought or art is successful in degree only. It is successful in the degree to which it ceases to be an expression of merely personal impulses and becomes the instrument of a necessity lying in its own subject matter.

[21] *c.* This brings us to our last point. Since moral choice, like thought and art, moves on different causal levels, it achieves freedom, just as they do, only when it is determined by its own appropriate necessity. Most of our so-called choices are so clearly brought about by association, impulse, and feeling that the judicious indeterminist will raise no issue about them. When we decide to get a drink of water, to take another nibble of

chocolate, to go to bed at the usual hour, the forces at work are too plain to be denied. It is not acts like these on which the indeterminist takes his stand. It is rather on those where, with habit, impulse, and association prompting us powerfully to do X, we see that we ought to do Y and therefore do it. To suppose that in such cases we are still the puppets of habit and impulse seems to the indeterminist palpably false.

[22] So it does to us. Surely about this the indeterminist is right. Action impelled by the sense of duty, as Kant perceived, is action on a different level from anything mechanical or associative. But Kant was mistaken in supposing that when we were determined by reason we were not determined at all. This supposition seems to me wholly unwarranted. The determination is still there, but, since it is a determination by the moral necessities of the case, it is just what the moral man wants and thus is the equivalent of freedom. For the moral man, like the logician and the artist, is really seeking self-surrender. Through him as through the others an impersonal ideal is working, and to the extent that this ideal takes possession of him and molds him according to its pattern, he feels free and is free.

[23] The logician is most fully himself when the wind gets into his sails and carries him effortlessly along the line of his calculations. Many an artist and musician have left it on record that their best work was done when the whole they were creating took the brush or pen away from them and completed the work itself. It determined them, but they were free, because to be determined by this whole was at once the secret of their craft and the end of their desire. This is the condition of the moral man also. He has caught a vision, dimmer perhaps than that of the logician or the artist, but equally objective and compelling. It is a vision of the good. This good necessitates certain things, not as means to ends merely, for that is not usually a necessary link, but as integral parts of itself. It requires that he should put love above hate, that he should regard his neighbor's good as of like value with his own, that he should repair injuries, and express gratitude, and respect promises, and revere truth. Of course it does not guide him infallibly. On the values of a particular case he may easily be mistaken. But that no more shows that there are no values present to be estimated, and no ideal demanding a special mode of action, than the fact that we make a mistake in adding figures shows that there are no figures to be added, or a right way of adding them. In both instances what we want is control by the objective requirements of the case. The saint, like the thinker and the artist, has often said this in so many words. I feel most free, said St. Paul, precisely when I am most a slave.

[24] We have now dealt, as best we can in a restricted space, with the three commonest objections to determinism. They all seem to admit of answers. To the objection that we always feel free, we answer that it is

natural to feel so, even if we are determined, since our faces are set toward results and not toward causes, and the causes of present action always elude us. To the objection that science has gone indeterminist, we answer that that is only one interpretation of recent discoveries, and not the most plausible one, and that, even if it were true, it would not carry with it indeterminism for human choice. To the objection that determinism would reduce us to the level of mechanical puppets, we answer that though we are puppets in part we live, as Aristotle said, on various levels. And so far as causality in reflection, art, and moral choice involves control by immanent ideal, mechanism has passed over into that rational determinism that is the best kind of freedom.

COMMENT AND QUESTIONS

1. The first three paragraphs of this selection are characterized by a direct statement of the author's position and purpose and by careful definition of terms. Study Blanshard's methods, in paragraphs 2 and 3, of defining and making distinctions, and then state in your own words the meaning of *determinism* and *indeterminism*. For a full understanding of the essay, you will also need to understand the meaning and use of the following terms (numbers in parentheses refer to the paragraph in which the term first appears): *causal* (2) and *causal laws* (10) and *causality* (11); *antecedents* and *consequents* (2); *metaphysical* (3); *dialectical solvents* (4); *intuitive assurance* (5); *constraint* (6); *volition* (7); *antiempirical* and *empirical* (15); *mechanism* (15); *causal levels* (16); *aesthetic* (18); *immanent ideal* (24).

2. According to Blanshard, there are three main arguments against determinism: (a) the stubborn feeling that we are free when we make choices; (b) the belief that physical science has become indeterminist; (c) the idea that determinism damages or destroys morality. Explain as clearly as you can Blanshard's reply to each of these three arguments.

3. In discussing the charge that determinism "makes a mess of morality," the author assumes that his audience of philosophers is familiar with various allegations and the answers to them. Can you develop by examples the charges against determinism summarized in sentence 4 of paragraph 14? Can you explain why Blanshard might have a different attitude toward duty than he does toward praise, blame, punishment, etc.?

4. Elaborate the statement that even though choice is not determined mechanically, it is still determined.

5. Explain as clearly as you can how each of the following examples illustrates Blanshard's contention that one can believe in determinism and yet have the freedom that men want: the musician, the logician, the moral man.

6. The philosopher Philip Wheelwright says:

> If metaphysical determinism is true, then every choice I make has been absolutely necessitated by previous happenings in my body and environment, and those by yet prior happenings, and so on endlessly. I could not have chosen otherwise than as I actually did choose, and at the present moment I cannot choose otherwise than as I actually am choosing. The future is as settled as the past.[1]

Would Blanshard agree with this statement about the determinist view? Explain.

7. John Stuart Mill, in his *Autobiography*, wrote the following passage about a crisis in his mental history:

> . . . during the later returns of my dejection, the doctrine of what is called Philosophical Necessity weighed on my existence like an incubus. I felt as if I was scientifically proved to be the helpless slave of antecedent circumstances; as if my character and that of all others had been formed for us by agencies beyond our control, and was wholly out of our own power. I often said to myself, what a relief it would be if I could disbelieve the doctrine of the formation of character by circumstances. . . . I pondered painfully on the subject, till gradually I saw light through it. I perceived that the word Necessity, as a name for the doctrine of Cause and Effect applied to human action, carried with it a misleading association; and that this association was the operative force in the depressing and paralysing influence which I had experienced: I saw that though our character is formed by circumstances, our own desires can do much to shape those circumstances; and that what is really inspiriting and ennobling in the doctrine of freewill, is the conviction that we have real power over the formation of our own character; that our will, by influencing some of our circumstances, can modify our future habits or capabilities of willing. All this was entirely consistent with the doctrine of circumstances, or rather, was that doctrine itself, properly understood.

Is Mill's reconciliation of "Necessity" and free will in accord with Blanshard's ideas? Explain.

8. If you accept Blanshard's idea of determinism, do you think that a man can reasonably be held responsible for his actions—for example, for dishonesty, theft, murder? If you do think that men can be held responsible for their actions, does it follow that you believe in free will or indeterminism?

9. Granted the complexity of his subject, how has Blanshard made his essay readable for a layman?

[1] *The Way of Philosophy* (The Odyssey Press, Inc., 1960), p. 248.

[41] *Irwin Edman*: A Reasonable Life in a Mad World

IRWIN EDMAN (1896–1954) was a professor of philosophy at Columbia University; author of *Four Ways of Philosophy, Philosopher's Holiday, Candle in the Dark, Arts and the Man;* and a contributor to *The New Yorker* as well as to scholarly journals. He is one of the most readable and one of the most rewarding of modern writers-on-philosophy. The following essay was published in *The Atlantic Monthly* in 1949.

[1] That the world is mad has been the judgment of self-denominated sane philosophers from the Greeks to the present day. It is not a discovery of our own age that both the public and private lives of human beings are dominated by folly and stupidity. Philosophers pressing the point have brought such charges not against human nature only—that is, the world of human relations—but against that larger universe in which the world of human relations is set. As far back as the Book of Job and probably much further back, for there must have been at least gruntingly articulate Jobs in prehistory, it is not only men who have been declared mad: by any standards of rationality the universe itself has been called irrational, pointless, meaningless, with incidental, unintended overtones of cruelty and injustice.

[2] With the provincialism of each generation, ours imagines that the causes of cynicism and despair are new in our time. There have, of course, been modern improvements and refinements of stupidity and folly. No previous generation has been by way of organizing itself with insane efficiency for blowing the whole race to smithereens. It does not take a particularly logical mind at the present moment to discover that the world is quite mad, though a great many critics apparently think that the cruel absurdity of technical efficiency combined with moral bankruptcy is a discovery that it took great wit on their part to turn up.

[3] Reputations are being made by reiterating, to the extent of four or five hundred pages, that collective modern man is a technical genius merged with a moral imbecile.

[4] The first encouragement I can bring is the reminder that the kind of madness which we all realize to be the present state of the world is not something new. It is, just like everything else in the modern world,

bigger and more streamlined, if not better. It is a pity some of the great satirists are dead; Swift and Voltaire would have given their eyeteeth for the present situation. And Aristophanes would scarcely have believed it. But the essential charges they would bring against the present time and the essential absurdities they would show up are not different in essence now from what they were.

[5] Neither nature nor man appears reasonable by reasonable human standards. So acutely does this seem to many people to be true that in almost exuberant desperation they decide to march crazily in the insane procession. Existentialists make a cult of anxiety and despair and find a kind of wry comfort in saying, Since the world is absurd, let absurdity and irony be our standards. There are others who say—and the currency of an ersatz theological literature shows how epidemic they are—that since the world and mankind at present seem so palpably absurd it simply can't be true, and history, as Toynbee[1] now assures us, moves delightfully and progressively to fulfillment in the Church of God—a kind of quiet, English Church incorporating the best features of Islam, Buddhism, Confucianism, and a little, even, of the Hebrew prophets and the secular sciences.

[6] The excitements and confused urgencies of the present time may seem to make hysteria or mystical narcosis or hedonistic excitement tantamount to a philosophy. But the still, small voice of rationality persists. And the question still remains the same as that propounded by the Greeks long ago. How, in a world certainly not at first acquaintance rational-appearing, is it possible to lead a rational life?

[7] It seems mad now to say that anyone could believe, as the Fabians[2] did (including such unsentimental people as George Bernard Shaw and Sidney and Beatrice Webb and Graham Wallas and later H. G. Wells), that the world could be transformed into a livable, beautiful, reasonable place by the co-operation of reasonable men. It is not simply that the violent external events of the past generation have revealed to us how precarious were security and comfort, and for how few it obtained at all.

[8] But the psychological sciences have revealed to us the deep sources of violence, confusion, hysteria, and madness in ourselves. What perhaps a generation ago seemed a melodramatic aphorism when Santayana uttered it seems now to be a hitting of the nail on the head: "The normal man holds a lunatic in leash." The definition needs to be amended. In the light of the past twenty-five years, the normal man no longer *does* hold a lunatic in leash. The fact that even talk about a third world war has become standard has practically made lunacy respectable. It is now become

[1] Arnold J. Toynbee, contemporary English historian and author of *A Study of History*.

[2] English socialists who aimed to reform society gradually, avoiding revolutionary methods.

a stamp of madness to talk as if one seriously believed that a peaceful and just world were possible.

[9] And yet the sentiment of rationality persists and the hope persists also that it is not impossible, at least in imagination, to dream and in organized effort to work for what seems "an ordered, coherent world society." The most ardent workers for such a world, however, realize that there is plenty of madness left, out of which a third world war may come.

– II –

[10] The persistence of power politics, the greed for privilege, the insane clutching of wealth, the pathological tribalisms of nations, of class, and of race; it is this world in which we are actually living, and the human problem for anyone in it is to discover what is a reasonable life in such a world.

[11] Is it to forget as far as possible and to live only in the moment and to make that moment as brief and bright as possible? Is it to surrender any hope for pleasure or happiness now and give one's dedicated and ruthless devotion to work for a more reasonable world? Is it to seek Nirvana or to seek some salvation in another world? There seems to be some sense in each answer, but which answer one chooses will depend ultimately on how one answers a basic question: Is the world always and necessarily mad? Is it completely mad now, and is it possible even now to understand the madness and, through understanding, to endure or change it?

[12] Let us try as simply as possible to deal with some of these questions. First, is the world always and necessarily mad? By "the world," of course, one means both the processes of nature and the activities of human beings. For "world" in the first sense one had perhaps better use the word "universe." A thoroughly rational universe would be one which was achieving a purpose set down in advance, a purpose which in human terms made sense and which by human standards made moral sense. A rational universe might be one such as the Deists conceived in the eighteenth century, in which nature was simply reason incarnate or reason embodied in the vast machinery of things.

[13] In one respect at least the advance of knowledge of the physical world has not made the world seem more irrational. It has made it seem orderly and regular. But in another respect an understanding of the causes and consequences of nature by conventional standards made nature seem wholly irrational. "I am what I am," said Jehovah in the Old Testament, as if that announcement were sufficient explanation of his wrathful ways. "It is what it is and it does what it does" may be said to be the conclusions of empirical physical science. It is maddening to rational creatures to discover they were born into a world which is not particularly interested in human purposes, which perhaps permits and sustains these

purposes but is innocent of any solicitude concerning them. The rain notoriously falls on the just and the unjust, and the just feel highly put upon. Death is no respecter of persons; plagues fell the virtuous. The most generous and devoted enterprises are washed away by floods along with the conspiracies of the sinister and hateful.

[14] Theologians have spent a good deal of time trying to gloss away the irrationalities of the universe, explaining that God moves in a mysterious or at least salutary way, his morally therapeutic wonders to perform. Job was not greatly impressed by his comforters, and neither are we. But if exasperated humans have criticized the world in general, they have been especially critical of the madness of their fellow men. Voltaire found his greatest weapon of satire in treating cruelty, barbarism, and superstition not as evil but as absurd.

[15] The most serious and damaging charge we can bring against civilization is that by the very standards of civilization it is a ridiculous failure. It takes a high degree of sophistication and technical resources to make such an international shambles as we seem fated to do. It takes something like genius in folly to have millions starving in the midst of plenty, to have technological magic whose fruits are poverty, squalor, anarchy, and death; it takes a refinement of absurdity to use the most generous aphorism of the highest religions to justify or rationalize intolerance, violence, and our established international disorder.

[16] Now about the first irrationality: that of the universe itself. Perhaps the only reasonable attitude is that of resignation and endurance of it. Perhaps it is only the persistence of our childhood wishes and expectations that has led to an assumption that the universe must conform to human purposes and that it is shockingly unreasonable of it not so to conform. We can, within the limits of a world not made for us, make it conform to ideals and values which flower out of nature itself. Part of the life of reason is a contemplation of the unchanging and unchangeable elements in the world of nature; part of it is a sedulous attempt to discover the ways of changing the world in the interest of human values.

[17] With respect to the world of human activities there has been an accelerated desperation at the present time. In the old days when humor could still flourish in Central Europe it used to be said that the difference between the temper of Berlin and Vienna could be stated as follows: In Berlin when things went wrong it was remarked: "The situation is serious but not hopeless"; in Vienna with smiling deprecation the Viennese used to say: "The situation is hopeless but not serious." The Berlin version seems of late more greatly to have impressed the world.

[18] Though Existentialism may be said to describe the world as being both hopeless and trivial, if one so conceives the realm of human affairs the Epicurean prescription for a reasonable life is perhaps the best that one can find. However clouded and uncertain the future, there is at least

possible for the lucky and the prudent a brief, bright interval in which they may find luster and to which their refined sensibilities may give luster. In a world without meaning they may find exquisite nuances of meaning in the arts, in friendship, in love.

[19] The trouble with the Epicurean solution and abdication is that it is always haunted by a scruple of conscience and the shadow of despair. There is something already tarnished in a brightness that declares itself both ultimately meaningless and transient. Sorrow and inhibition and regret dog the footsteps of the Epicurean in a world where folly is no longer a joke but a terrifying threat to all mankind.

[20] There are those, therefore, in our own age who jump to the other extreme. One insists that one *must* give up any hope for present happiness and give one's dedicated and ruthless devotion to work for a better world. I have friends, especially in social or government work or in the social sciences, who regard humor, irony, urbanity, or relaxation with something of the same moral impatience with which a missionary might watch the natives of the Fiji Islands dance or lounge in the sun. There is so little time; it is later than you think; there is no time for comedy. Urbanity is a form of evasion, and laughter is a form of bourgeois or decadent callousness. Let us gird our loins and work together rapidly for the common good or we shall all in common be destroyed. The psychiatric departments of hospitals number among their patients a good many people who in their earnest haste to save the world from destruction ended up by destroying their equilibrium and almost themselves. The tension of moral earnestness, the refusal to permit the enjoyment of even such goods as are possible in a chaotic world, is one of the diseases of our civilization, not a sign of its health. If Epicureanism leads to dismay, unrelieved moral dedication leads to fanaticism. Neither the playboy nor the zealot is a true or adequate incarnation of the life of reason.

[21] Those who recognize the disillusion of a pleasure philosophy or the destructiveness of a moral fanaticism have begun in our age, as they have in other ages, to turn to otherworldly philosophies. They have tried to seek an inward light unquenchable by external circumstances. They have tried in spirit to follow the Indian saint into the wilderness or the monk into his cell or the mystic into his remote meditation. They have sought Nirvana, or a Oneness with the One, or an Aloneness with the Alone. The follies of society are not cured by the incantations of pure mysticism, and the search for oblivion is really a pathological attempt simply to become oblivious to the actual and remediable conflicts and disorders in society.

[22] There are still others than the pleasure-lovers, the Nirvana-seekers, the devotees of such mystics, who have sought to make a prescription for a reasonable life. Among those others now epidemic are followers of historians and zoologists who with the theological wave of a wand discover

that a palpably absurd world is somehow moving toward a cozy fulfillment where, as I heard Mr. Toynbee say, "God is Love." It would seem
a strange moment to detect the course of history as the operations of
universal love when the world is being filled with universal hate.

[23] No, I do not think any of these ersatz solutions will do. The pressure of events simply confirms again what the life of reason does consist
in: a brave contemplation of what things are discoverably like and a
resolute attempt to improve the lot of man in the conditions into which
he finds himself born. The life of reason must always have a stoic element
because there is no sign that either the follies of humanity or the uncaring
order of nature will ever be magically transformed.

[24] The life of reason must also contain an element of hope, for it is
quite clear, as the history of every improvement in man's estate has shown
us, that human intelligence accompanied by human goodwill may profoundly improve the life of mankind. The life of reason must include the
pleasure principle also, for what else gives life meaning if not joy and
delight of life, and what a folly it would be not to cherish and embrace,
not to nourish then, even in a sick society, that which yields the fruit of a
quickened, multiplied awareness, the substance of vision and of joy. The
universe may be pointless, but there are many good points in it. Our
urgencies may be intense, but the world does not end with us or even
with our own civilization; nor, if we do not quench intelligence and generosity in ourselves, is it a foregone conclusion that our civilization must
end. And the best insurance, perhaps, of maintaining both is to reaffirm
the quality of life itself, of its possibility of beauty and its intimations of
order and of justice.

⌐❦ C O M M E N T   A N D   Q U E S T I O N S ❧⌐

1. Edman begins with an assumption—that the world is mad. Would you
   expect his readers to agree? Do you agree? In the course of the essay, what
   aspects of the world and of human relations are mentioned in support of
   the assumption of madness?

2. Edman, in this essay, is frequently ironical and satirical, and he makes
   use of some highly charged language. Point out examples of irony, satire,
   and charged words, and comment on their effectiveness in achieving what
   you take to be the author's purpose.

3. In the last sentence of paragraph 7, in paragraph 8, and in the first half of
   the single sentence of paragraph 10, Edman makes some general statements about the world of human affairs. Because this essay was written
   in 1949, the specific events and instances Edman had in mind are not

exactly those of the present time. To what extent are his generalizations true today? What concrete examples can you give to support those which do seem true?

4. What seems to be Edman's answer to the question "Is the world always and necessarily mad?"

5. What are the various prescriptions for a reasonable life which the author rejects as "ersatz solutions"? Why does he reject each one?

6. If you have read Sartre's essay on existentialism, Epicurus' "Letter to a Friend," and the discussion of mysticism in Aldous Huxley's essay on the Perennial Philosophy, you are in a better position to judge what Edman is saying. Do you agree with his attitudes toward existentialism, Epicureanism, and mysticism?

7. For a study of Edman's style, read carefully paragraphs 18–21. What is distinctive in his sentence structures and in his choice and use of words?

8. State in your own words the concept of the reasonable life presented in the last two paragraphs of the essay. Does the author's conclusion follow logically from the ideas and details presented earlier in the essay? Explain.

9. To what extent do you agree or disagree with Edman's idea of the reasonable life, and why?

LANGUAGE

❦

[42] *Bergen Evans*: Grammar for Today

BERGEN EVANS (1904–   ), a professor of English at Northwestern University, is well known as the host and commentator on television and radio programs including "The Last Word" and "Of Many Things." Among his numerous publications are *Natural History of Nonsense, A Dictionary of Contemporary American Usage* (with Cornelia Evans), and *Comfortable Words.* The following article appeared in *The Atlantic Monthly* in March, 1960.

[1] In 1747 Samuel Johnson issued a plan for a new dictionary of the English language. It was supported by the most distinguished printers of the day and was dedicated to the model of all correctness, Philip Dormer Stanhope, Fourth Earl of Chesterfield. Such a book, it was felt, was urgently needed to "fix" the language, to arrest its "corruption" and "decay," a degenerative process which, then as now, was attributed to the influence of "the vulgar" and which, then as now, it was a mark of superiority and elegance to decry. And Mr. Johnson seemed the man to write it. He had an enormous knowledge of Latin, deep piety, and dogmatic convictions. He was also honest and intelligent, but the effect of these lesser qualifications was not to show until later.

[2] Oblig'd by hunger and request of friends, Mr. Johnson was willing to assume the role of linguistic dictator. He was prepared to "fix" the pronunciation of the language, "preserve the purity" of its idiom, brand "impure" words with a "note of infamy," and secure the whole "from being overrun by . . . low terms."

[³] There were, however, a few reservations. Mr. Johnson felt it necessary to warn the oversanguine that "Language is the work of man, a being from whom permanence and stability cannot be derived." English "was not formed from heaven . . . but was produced by necessity and enlarged by accident." It had, indeed, been merely "thrown together by negligence" and was in such a state of confusion that its very syntax could no longer "be taught by general rules, but [only] by special precedents."

[⁴] In 1755 the *Dictionary* appeared. The noble patron had been given a great deal more immortality than he had bargained for by the vigor of the kick Johnson had applied to his backside as he booted him overboard. And the *Plan* had been replaced by the *Preface*, a sadder but very much wiser document.

[⁵] Eight years of "sluggishly treading the track of the alphabet" had taught Johnson that the hopes of "fixing" the language and preserving its "purity" were but "the dreams of a poet doomed at last to wake a lexicographer." In "the boundless chaos of living speech," so copious and energetic in its disorder, he had found no guides except "experience and analogy." Irregularities were "inherent in the tongue" and could not be "dismissed or reformed" but must be permitted "to remain untouched." "Uniformity must be sacrificed to custom . . . in compliance with a numberless majority" and "general agreement." One of the pet projects of the age had been the establishment of an academy to regulate and improve style. "I hope," Johnson wrote in the *Preface,* that if "it should be established . . . the spirit of English liberty will hinder or destroy [it.]"

[⁶] At the outset of the work he had flattered himself, he confessed, that he would reform abuses and put a stop to alterations. But he had soon discovered that "sounds are too volatile and subtle for legal restraints" and that "to enchain syllables and to lash the wind are equally undertakings of pride unwilling to measure its desires by its strength." For "the causes of change in language are as much superior to human resistance as the revolutions of the sky or the intumescence of the tide."

[⁷] There had been an even more profound discovery: that grammarians and lexicographers "do not form, but register the language; do not teach men how they should think, but relate how they have hitherto expressed their thoughts." And with this statement Johnson ushered in the rational study of linguistics. He had entered on his task a medieval pedant. He emerged from it a modern scientist.

[⁸] Of course his discoveries were not strikingly original. Horace had observed that use was the sole arbiter and norm of speech and Montaigne had said that he who would fight custom with grammar was a fool. Doubtless thousands of other people had at one time or another perceived and said the same thing. But Johnson introduced a new principle. Finding that he could not lay down rules, he gave actual examples to show meaning and form. He offered as authority illustrative quotations, and in so doing established that language is what usage makes it and that custom, in the long run, is the ultimate and only court of appeal in linguistic matters.

[⁹] This principle, axiomatic today in grammar and lexicography, seems to exasperate a great many laymen who, apparently, find two hundred and five years too short a period in which to grasp a basic idea. They insist that there are absolute standards of correctness in speech and that these standards may be set forth in a few simple rules. To a man, they believe, of course, that they speak and write "correctly" and they are loud in their insistence that others imitate them.

[¹⁰] It is useless to argue with such people because they are not, really, interested in language at all. They are interested solely in demonstrating their own superiority. Point out to them—as has been done hundreds of times—that forms which they regard as "corrupt," "incorrect," and "vulgar" have been used by Shakespeare, Milton, and the Bible and are used daily by 180 million Americans and accepted by the best linguists and lexicographers, and they will coolly say, "Well, if they differ from me, they're wrong."

[¹¹] But if usage is not the final determinant of speech, what is? Do the inhabitants of Italy, for example, speak corrupt Latin or good Italian? Is Spanish superior to French? Would the Breton fisherman speak better if he spoke Parisian French? Can one be more fluent in Outer Mongolian than in Inner Mongolian? One has only to ask such questions in relation to languages other than one's own, languages within which our particular snobberies and struggles for prestige have no stake, to see the absurdity of them.

[¹²] The language that we do speak, if we are to accept the idea of "corruption" and "decay" in language, is a horribly decayed Anglo-Saxon, grotesquely corrupted by Norman French. Furthermore, since Standard English is a development of the London dialect of the fourteenth century, our speech, by true aristocratic standards, is woefully middle-class, commercial, and vulgar. And American speech is lower middle-class, reeking of counter and till. Where else on earth, for instance, would one find crime condemned because it didn't *pay!*

[¹³] In more innocent days a great deal of time was spent in wondering what was the "original" language of mankind, the one spoken in Eden, the language of which all modern tongues were merely degenerate remnants. Hector Boethius tells us that James I of Scotland was so interested in this problem that he had two children reared with a deaf and dumb nurse on an island in order to see what language they would "naturally" speak. James thought it would be Hebrew, and in time, to his great satisfaction, it was reported that the chidren were speaking Hebrew!

[¹⁴] Despite this experiment, however, few people today regard English as a corruption of Hebrew. But many seem to think it is a corruption of Latin and labor mightily to make it conform to this illusion. It is they and their confused followers who tell us that we can't say "I am mistaken" because translated into Latin this would mean "I am misunderstood," and we can't say "I have enjoyed myself" unless we are egotistical or worse.

[¹⁵] It is largely to this group—most of whom couldn't read a line of Latin at sight if their lives depended on it—that we owe our widespread bewilderment concerning *who* and *whom*. In Latin the accusative or dative form would always be used, regardless of the word's position in the sentence, when the pronoun was the object of a verb or a preposition. But in English, for at least four hundred years, this simply hasn't been so. When the pronoun occurs at the beginning of a question, people who speak natural, fluent, literary English use the nominative, regardless. They say "Who did you give it to?" not "Whom did you give it to?" But the semiliterate, intimidated and bewildered, are mouthing such ghastly utterances as a recent headline in a Chicago newspaper: WHOM'S HE KIDDING?

[¹⁶] Another group seems to think that in its pure state English was a Laputan tongue, with logic as its guiding principle. Early members of this sect insisted that *unloose* could only mean "to tie up," and present members have compelled the gasoline industry to label its trucks *Flammable* under the disastrous insistence, apparently, that the old *Inflammable* could only mean "not burnable."

[¹⁷] It is to them, in league with the Latinists, that we owe the bogy of the double negative. In all Teutonic languages a doubling of the negative merely emphasizes the negation. But we have been told for a century now that two negatives make a positive, though if they do and it's merely a matter of logic, then three negatives should make a negative again. So that if "It doesn't make no difference" is wrong merely because it includes two negatives, then "It doesn't never make no difference" ought to be right again. Both of these groups, in their theories at least, ignore our idiom. Yet idiom—those expressions which defy all logic but are the very essence of a tongue—plays a large part in English. We go to school and college, but we go to *the* university. We buy two dozen eggs but a couple *of* dozen. *Good and* can mean *very* ("I am good and mad!") and "a hot cup of coffee" means that the coffee, not the cup, is to be hot. It makes a world of difference to a condemned man whether his reprieve is *upheld* or *held up*.

[¹⁸] There are thousands of such expressions in English. They are the "irregularities" which Johnson found "inherent in the tongue" and which his wisdom perceived could not and should not be removed. Indeed, it is in the recognition and use of these idioms that skillful use of English lies.

[19] Many words in the form that is now mandatory were originally just mistakes, and many of these mistakes were forced into the language by eager ignoramuses determined to make it conform to some notion of their own. The *s* was put in island, for instance, in sheer pedantic ignorance. The second *r* doesn't belong in *trousers,* nor the *g* in *arraign,* nor the *t* in deviltry, nor the *n* in *passenger* and *messenger.* Nor, so far as English is concerned, does that first *c* in *arctic* which so many people twist their mouths so strenuously to pronounce.

[20] And grammar is as "corrupted" as spelling or pronunciation. "You are" is as gross a solecism as "me am." It's recent, too; you won't find it in the Authorized Version of the Bible. *Lesser, nearer,* and *more* are grammatically on a par with *gooder. Crowed is* the equivalent of *knowed* or *growed,* and *caught* and *dug* (for *catched* and *digged*) are as "corrupt" as *squoze* for *squeezed* or *snoze* for *sneezed.*

[21] Fortunately for our peace of mind most people are quite content to let English conform to English, and they are supported in their sanity by modern grammarians and linguists.

[22] Scholars agree with Puttenham (1589) that a language is simply speech "fashioned to the common understanding and accepted by consent." They believe that the only "rules" that can be stated for a language are codified observations. They hold, that is, that language is the basis of grammar, not the other way round. They do not believe that any language can become "corrupted" by the linguistic habits of those who speak it. They do not believe that anyone who is a native speaker of a standard language will get into any linguistic trouble unless he is misled by snobbishness or timidity or vanity.

[23] He may, of course, if his native language is English, speak a form of English that marks him as coming from a rural or an unread group. But if he doesn't mind being so marked, there's no reason why he should change. Johnson retained a Staffordshire burr in his speech all his life. And surely no one will deny that Robert Burns's rustic dialect was just as good as a form of speech as, and in his mouth infinitely better as a means of expression than, the "correct" English spoken by ten million of his southern contemporaries.

[24] The trouble is that people are no longer willing to be rustic or provincial. They all want to speak like educated people, though they don't want to go to the trouble of becoming truly educated. They want to believe that a special form of socially acceptable and financially valuable speech can be mastered by following a few simple rules. And there is no

lack of little books that offer to supply the rules and promise "correctness" if the rules are adhered to. But, of course, these offers are specious because you don't speak like an educated person unless you are an educated person, and the little books, if taken seriously, will not only leave the lack of education showing but will expose the pitiful yearning and the basic vulgarity as well, in such sentences as "Whom are you talking about?"

[25] As a matter of fact, the educated man uses at least three languages. With his family and his close friends, on the ordinary, unimportant occasions of daily life, he speaks, much of the time, a monosyllabic sort of shorthand. On more important occasions and when dealing with strangers in his official or business relations, he has a more formal speech, more complete, less allusive, politely qualified, wisely reserved. In addition he has some acquaintance with the literary speech of his language. He understands this when he reads it, and often enjoys it, but he hesitates to use it. In times of emotional stress hot fragments of it may come out of him like lava, and in times of feigned emotion, as when giving a commencement address, cold, greasy gobbets of it will ooze forth.

[26] The linguist differs from the amateur grammarian in recognizing all of these variations and gradations in the language. And he differs from the snob in doubting that the speech of any one small group among the language's more than 300 million daily users constitutes a model for all the rest to imitate.

[27] The methods of the modern linguist can be illustrated by the question of the grammatical number of *none*. Is it singular or plural? Should one say "None of them is ready" or "None of them are ready"?

[28] The prescriptive grammarians are emphatic that it should be singular. The Latinists point out that *nemo*, the Latin equivalent, is singular. The logicians triumphantly point out that *none* can't be more than one and hence can't be plural.

[29] The linguist knows that he hears "None of them are ready" every day, from people of all social positions, geographical areas, and degrees of education. He also hears "None is." Furthermore, literature informs him that both forms were used in the past. From Malory (1450) to Milton (1650) he finds that *none* was treated as a singular three times for every once that it was treated as a plural. That is, up to three hundred years ago men usually said *None is*. From Milton to 1917, *none* was used as a plural seven times for every four times it was used as a singular. That is, in the past three hundred years men often said *None is*, but they said *None are* almost twice as often. Since 1917, however, there has been a noticeable increase in the use of the plural, so much so that today *None are* is the preferred form.

[30] The descriptive grammarian, therefore, says the while *None is* may still be used, it is becoming increasingly peculiar. This, of course, will not be as useful to one who wants to be cultured in a hurry as a

short, emphatic permission or prohibition. But it has the advantage of describing English as it is spoken and written here and now and not as it ought to be spoken in some Cloud-Cuckoo-Land.

[31] The descriptive grammarian believes that a child should be taught English, but he would like to see the child taught the English actually used by his educated contemporaries, not some pedantic, theoretical English designed chiefly to mark the imagined superiority of the designer.

[32] He believes that a child should be taught the parts of speech, for example. But the child should be told the truth—that these are functions of use, not some quality immutably inherent in this or that word. Anyone, for instance, who tells a child—or anyone else—that *like* is used in English only as a preposition has grossly misinformed him. And anyone who complains that its use as a conjunction is a corruption introduced by Winston cigarettes ought, in all fairness, to explain how Shakespeare, Keats, and the translators of the Authorized Version of the Bible came to be in the employ of the R. J. Reynolds Tobacco Company.

[33] Whether formal grammar can be taught to advantage before the senior year of high school is doubtful; most studies—and many have been made—indicate that it can't. But when it is taught, it should be the grammar of today's English, not the obsolete grammar of yesterday's prescriptive grammarians. By that grammar, for instance, *please* in the sentence "Please reply" is the verb and *reply* its object. But by modern meaning *reply* is the verb, in the imperative, and *please* is merely a qualifying word meaning "no discourtesy intended," a mollifying or de-imperatival adverb, or whatever you will, but not the verb.

[34] This is a long way from saying "Anything goes," which is the charge that, with all the idiot repetition of a needle stuck in a groove, the uninformed ceaselessly chant against modern grammarians. But to assert that usage is the sole determinant in grammar, pronunciation, and meaning is *not* to say that anything goes. Custom is illogical and unreasonable, but it is also tyrannical. The least deviation from its dictates is usually punished with severity. And because this is so, children should be taught what the current and local customs in English are. They should not be taught that we speak a bastard Latin or a vocalized logic. And they should certainly be disabused of the stultifying illusion that after God had given Moses the Commandments He called him back and pressed on him a copy of Woolley's *Handbook of English Grammar*.

[35] The grammarian does not see it as his function to "raise the standards" set by Franklin, Lincoln, Melville, Mark Twain, and hundreds of millions of other Americans. He is content to record what they said and say.

[36] Insofar as he serves as a teacher, it is his business to point out the limits of the permissible, to indicate the confines within which the writer may exercise his choice, to report that which custom and practice

have made acceptable. It is certainly not the business of the grammarian to impose his personal taste as the only norm of good English, to set forth his prejudices as the ideal standard which everyone should copy. That would be fatal. No one person's standards are broad enough for that.

--•≼ C O M M E N T   A N D   Q U E S T I O N S ≽•--

1. In the three opening paragraphs, how does Evans communicate his attitudes toward the kind of dictionary Samuel Johnson proposed to write and toward the people who wish to "fix" language?

2. What purposes are served by the introductory section of the essay (paragraphs 1–7)? What pattern of organization does Evans use in these first seven paragraphs?

3. What is the purpose of paragraphs 8–12? In these paragraphs, how does the author support his central thesis? How successfully, in your opinion, does he support it?

4. What is the purpose of the anecdote in paragraph 13? What is the main idea of the division which it introduces (paragraphs 13–21)?

5. At the end of paragraph 15, Evans is criticizing the newspaper headline for the use of *whom*. On what other ground might one also object to this headline?

6. Look up in your dictionary the words listed in paragraph 19. Do you find support for the point Evans is making in this paragraph?

7. Evans uses some strong language in dealing with those who do not share his views. Point out examples of his verbal assaults. Do they seem to you effective? Explain.

8. What is the difference between prescriptive and descriptive grammar? Comment on Evans' use of the problem of *none* as a persuasive illustration of the methods of the descriptive grammarian.

9. In paragraph 34, Evans says emphatically that the modern grammarian is *not* saying that "anything goes." Does this statement come as a surprise to the reader? Has it been prepared for by anything in the preceding material? Explain.

10. To what extent, and on what particular points, do you agree or disagree with Evans' ideas about language and usage?

[43]   *Mario Pei*: The Dictionary as a Battlefront: English Teachers' Dilemma

MARIO PEI (1901–) is a noted author and linguist, professor of Romance philology at Columbia University. His many books include *The World's Chief Languages, The Story of Language, Voices of Man,* and *The American Heritage.* The following article, part of the controversy about *Webster's Third New International Dictionary,* appeared in the *Saturday Review,* July 21, 1962.

[¹] For some years, there have been more and more insistent rumblings from all sorts of quarters concerning the quality of the English imparted in our schools and colleges. Graduates of our educational institutions, the critics have charged, do not know how to spell, punctuate, or capitalize; to divide a thought concept into phrases, sentences, and paragraphs; or to express themselves, either in speech or writing, in the sort of English that is meaningful and acceptable. As a single sample of the many complaints that have been voiced, I may cite a friend who is a high official in WNBC-TV: "Recently we interviewed over a hundred college graduates to fill a post calling for a knowledge of good English. Not one of them made the grade. None of them knew the rules of good writing, and none of them could express himself or herself in clear, simple, forthright English sentences."

[²] The blame for this state of affairs has consistently been put upon two branches of the educational world: the teachers of English and the progressive educationists. Books such as "Why Johnny Can't Read" are indictments of modern educational practice. A cultured lay writer, J. Donald Adams of the New York *Times Book Review,* said in his column of December 20, 1959:

If more parents who were themselves the recipients of a decent education could be made aware of the asinine statements about the teaching of the English language which are being spewed forth by today's educational theorists, there would be an armed uprising among the Parent-Teacher Associations all over the United States. It would be an uprising armed by common sense and hot indignation, and it would demand and get the scalps of those so-called educators whose indefensible doctrines are rapidly producing a generation of American illiterates . . . The root responsibility for the decline in standards of English rests, I think, with the teachers of English in our primary and secondary schools, and even more so, with the teachers of education who produced them. . . . There is an organization called the National Council of Teachers of English, whose attitudes and activities constitute one of the chief threats to the cultivation of good English in our schools.

[3] What critics of present-day methods of teaching English have in the past failed to realize is that the responsibility for the situation lies deeper than the departments of English and the teachers colleges. The practices of both are merely a reflection of the philosophy and theories of a school of linguistics that is in turn linked with a school of cultural anthropology of the equalitarian persuasion whose views color far more than the teaching of languages in general or English in particular.

[4] As far back as 1948, in a New York *Herald Tribune* book review, Bernard De Voto came out with a blast at the cultural anthropologists for assuming that methods that seem to work with the Ubangi and the Trobriand Islanders will produce dependable results when applied to the English or Americans. But his was a voice crying in the wilderness. Few people were sufficiently specialized, or interested, to perceive the link between theories presented in scholarly books on anthropology or linguistics and practices that affect the daily lives of all of us.

[5] It was only with the appearance of the new third edition of "Webster's Unabridged International Dictionary" late in 1961 that the issues at stake, at least for what concerns languages, became clear to the cultured, educated layman of America. For this there was a deep, underlying reason that reaches down to the grass roots of our mores.

[6] The English language, as is well known, has no set standard and no accepted authority, in the sense that countries such as France, Italy, and Spain have language academies that undertake to tell the speakers what is and what is not good standard practice. Since the days of Dr. Johnson, who refused to embalm the language and thereby destroy liberty, English speakers have submitted to the Doctrine of Usage rather than to the Voice of Authority. But usage has its own canons. In Britain, something called the King's (or Queen's) English has been enshrined over and above local dialects that range from London's Cockney to super-cultivated Oxford, and from the harsh speech of the North Country to the mellifluous accents of Kent. In America there is no President's American, but there is the Dictionary. From the time of Noah Webster, Americans have been wont to dip into a dictionary, the more unabridged the better, to settle questions of usage and proper practice.

[7] It may be stressed at this point that at no time did the compilers of the various editions of the Merriam-Webster, the most comprehensive dictionary of America, set themselves up as authorities or arrogate the right to tell the people what was right and what was wrong in the matter of language. All they did was to record prevailing usage among the more educated classes. They listed and described plenty of variant regional

pronunciations and words. They recorded, too, speech-forms of the lower classes, carefully labeling them "colloquial," "substandard," "vulgar," or "slang." This was not meant to prescribe or proscribe the use of certain forms, but merely to inform the reader as to the distribution of their occurrence. The attitude of the earlier lexicographers seemed to be: "Go ahead and use this form if you want to; but if you do, don't complain if someone says you are using a slang term."

[8] The new 1961 edition of the Merriam-Webster has many features to commend it. Not only does it list the multitude of new terms, technological and otherwise, that have entered the language in recent years; it also has the merit of listing, with full definitions and examples, word combinations that have acquired special connotations not inherent in their component parts. The older Webster's defines both "guilt" and "association"; but the new Webster's also gives you "guilt by association." This means that the new edition is a handier tool than the older.

[9] But the new edition makes one startling innovation which has recommended itself to the attention of all reviewers and of the general public as well. It blurs to the point of obliteration the older distinction between standard, substandard, colloquial, vulgar, and slang. "Ain't," it says, is now used by many cultivated speakers; "who" in the accusative function and "me" after a copulative verb are of far more frequent occurrence than "whom" and "I," and, by implication, should be preferred. This viewpoint goes right down the line. It led the editor of the New York *Times* to compose a passage that starts:

A passel of double-domes at the G. & C. Merriam Company joint in Springfield, Mass., have been confabbing and yakking for twenty-seven years—which is not intended to infer that they have not been doing plenty work—and now they have finalized Webster's Third New International Dictionary, Unabridged, a new edition of that swell and esteemed word book.

Those who regard the foregoing paragraph as acceptable English prose will find that the new Webster's is just the dictionary for them.

[10] There is more: the older Webster's, insofar as it gave citations, used only established authors, recognized masters of the language. The new Webster's cites profusely from people who are in the public eye, but who can hardly be said to qualify as shining examples of fine speaking or writing. This leads another critic to complain that Churchill, Maritain, Oppenheimer, and Schweitzer are ranged as language sources side by side with Billy Rose, Ethel Merman, James Cagney, and Ted Williams; Shakespeare and Milton with Polly Adler and Mickey Mantle.

[11] Dr. Gove's defense, fully presented in the pages of the same New York *Times* that had thundered editorially against his product, is both able and forthright: a dictionary's function, he said in substance, is to record the language, not to judge or prescribe it. Language, like prac-

tically everything else, is in a state of constant flux. It is not responsible to expect it to remain static, to retain unchanged forms that were current at one period but are no longer current today. We have changed our point of view in many fields; why not in language? His defense is, in a sense, a counterattack against the forces of purism, conservatism, and reaction. Why disguise the true function of a dictionary by turning it into a tool of prescriptivism, a fortress of a language traditionalism that no one today really wants? Language, after all, is what people speak, not what someone, be it even Webster, thinks they ought to speak.

[12] This both clarifies and restricts the issue. But an issue still remains. Should a dictionary be merely a record of what goes on in language (all language, both high and low), or should it also be not so much a prescriptive tool as a guide for the layman, to not merely what *is* usage, but what is the *best* usage?

[13] A speaking community that has been accustomed for the better part of two centuries to rely upon the dictionary to settle questions of usage balks at finding all usage now set on an identical plane. The contention of the objectors is that there are different, clearly identifiable levels of usage, which it is the duty of the dictionary to define. Without necessarily using the terms "correct" and "incorrect," they still would like to see a distinction made between what is better and what is worse.

[14] In opposition to their stand, the new philosophy, linguistic and otherwise, seems to be summed up in this formula: "What is is good, simply because it is." Good and bad, right and wrong, correct and incorrect no longer exist. Any reference to any of these descriptive adjectives is a value judgment, and unworthy of the scientific attitude, which prescribes that we merely observe and catalogue the facts, carefully refraining from expressing either judgment or preference.

[15] This relativistic philosophy, fully divorced from both ethics and esthetics, is said to be modern, sophisticated, and scientific. Perhaps it is. Some claim that its fruits are to be seen in present-day moral standards, national, international, and personal, as well as in modern so-called art, music, literature, and permissive education.

[16] But we are concerned here only with its reflections on the language. The appearance of the new Webster's International has had several major effects. It has brought the question of permissiveness in language squarely to the attention of millions of educated laymen, who use the dictionary and refer to it for guidance. Without forcing a renunciation of Anglo-American reliance on usage rather than on the Voice of Authority, it has brought into focus the paramount question: "Whose usage? That of the cultivated speakers, or that of the semiliterates?" Finally, it has for the first time brought forth, into the view of the general public, those who are primarily responsible for the shift in attitude and point of view in matters of language—not the ordinary classroom teachers of English, not

the educationists of the teachers colleges, but the followers of the American, anthropological, descriptive, structuralistic school of linguistics, a school which for decades has been preaching that one form of language is as good as another; that there is no such thing as correct or incorrect so far as native speakers of the language are concerned; that at the age of five anyone who is not deaf or idiotic has gained a full mastery of his language; that we must not try to correct or improve language, but must leave it alone; that the only language activity worthy of the name is speech on the colloquial, slangy, even illiterate plane; that writing is a secondary, unimportant activity which cannot be dignified with the name of language; that systems of writing serve only to disguise the true nature of language; and that it would be well if we completely refrained from teaching spelling for a number of years.

[17] If these pronouncements come as a novelty to some of my readers, it is the readers themselves who are at fault. The proponents of these language theories certainly have made no mystery about them; they have been openly, even vociferously advancing them for years, and this can easily be documented from their voluminous writings.

[18] The real novelty of the situation lies in the fact that, through the publication of the new Webster's—compiled in accordance with these principles—the principles themselves and their original formulators, rather than their effects upon the younger generations, now come to the attention of the general public. Lay reviewers generally display their complete awareness.

[19] Dwight MacDonald, reviewing the new Webster extensively in the March 10, 1962 *New Yorker,* after claiming that the "scientific" revolution in linguistics has meshed gears with a trend toward permissiveness, in the name of democracy, that is debasing our language by rendering it less precise and thus less effective as communication, goes on to say:

Dr. Gove and the other makers of 3 are sympathetic to the school of language study that has become dominant since 1934. It is sometimes called Structural Linguistics Science. . . . Dr. Gove and his editors are part of the dominant movement in the professional study of language—one that has in the last few years established strong beachheads in the National Council of Teachers of English and the College English Association. . . . As a scientific discipline, Structural Linguistics can have no truck with values or standards. Its job is to deal only with The Facts.

[20] Max S. Marshall, Professor of Microbiology at the University of California, writing in *Science,* March 2, 1962, says in part:

Opposed to [believers in a standard of quality in English] with several ringleaders at the head, is a group which goes back some thirty years, but has been actively proselytizing only in relatively recent years. These are the advocates of "observing precisely what happens when native speakers speak." These are the self-styled structural linguists, presenting language in a way so foreign that it might be imposed before users of the language discover its existence. . . . Gove declares himself flatly on the side of the structural linguists, calmly assuming, as do their ringleaders, that they are about to take over.

[21] The principles of the American school of linguistics described above may come as a shock to some, but there is no need to be shocked. They are based upon definitely observable historical facts. Language invariably changes. Within our own personal experience we have noticed certain forms and expressions once considered slangy turning into regularly accepted parts of the standard language.

[22] All that the American school of linguistics advocates is that we accept the process of change in language and submit gracefully to its inevitability. If we persist in hanging on to language forms and concepts that are antiquated and superseded, then we are merely subscribing to what they call "the superstitions of the past." We should be forward-looking, and progressive-minded. We renounce imperialism and colonialism in international relations, and admit nations like Ghana and the Congo to full equality with the established countries of Europe; by the same token, we should view the languages of the Arapahoes and the Zulus as being of equal importance with Latin and French. We believe in democracy and majority rule in political elections. Then, if a majority of the speakers of American English use "aint," "knowed," "I'll learn you," "I laid on the bed," "who did you see," "between you and I," "like a cigarette should," these forms are by definition standard usage, and the corresponding minority forms, though sanctioned by traditional grammars, are, if not incorrect, at least obsolescent.

[23] It may be argued, as does our Professor of Microbiology in *Science*, that "weighing the speech of casual speakers with no pretense of expertness on the same IBM card as usages of topnotch writers of past and present is an example of what the modern linguist calls 'science.' Tabulation is not science. Public opinion polls do not settle questions of science, or even of right and wrong. . . . If the guttersnipes of language do more talking than professors of English they get proportionally more votes."

[24] But the structuralistic linguists can easily reply that language is a matter of habit and convention, not of dogma or esthetics, and that if the basic purpose of semantic communication is achieved, it matters little what linguistic form is used. In engineering, calculations as to stresses and structures must be precise and correct, under penalty of seeing the bridge collapse. In medicine, correct dosage is essential, under penalty of seeing your patient die. But in language, the use of a substandard for a standard form seldom leads to irreparable consequences; at the most, as picturesquely stated by a leader of the school, you may not be invited to tea again.

[25] On the other hand, members of the American school of linguistics are not always consistent in the application of their democratic and equalitarian principles. In reply to his critics, Dr. Gove remarked that while comments in lay newspapers and magazines had generally been unfavorable, the learned journals had not yet reviewed the new edition. The implication seemed to be that favorable reviews from a few members of his own clique, read and approved by a small circle of professional structuralistic linguists, would more than offset the generally unfavorable reaction of newspapers like the New York *Times* and magazines like the *New Yorker*, which appeal to large audiences of cultivated laymen. This not only puts the process of democracy into reverse; it comes close to setting up a hierarchy of professional linguists acting as the Voice of Authority for a recalcitrant majority of educated people.

[26] There is no doubt in my mind that widespread localisms, slang, vulgarisms, colloquialisms, even obscenities and improprieties, should be duly noted in a comprehensive dictionary, whose first duty is to record what goes on in the field of language. Should such forms be labeled and described for what they are, not in a spirit of condemnation, but merely for the guidance of the reader? That, too, seems reasonable. If this procedure helps to slow up the inevitable process of language change by encouraging the speakers to use what the older dictionaries call standard forms, and discouraging them from using substandard forms, this impresses me as a distinct advantage. Too rapid and too widespread language change is a hindrance to communications. It lends itself to confusion and misunderstanding. The use of a more or less uniform standard by all members of the speaking community is desirable in the interests of efficiency rather than of esthetics. There is no question that within the next 500 years the English language, along with all other languages spoken today, will be so changed as to be practically unrecognizable. This will happen whether we like it or not. But need we deliberately hasten and amplify the process? Between sudden revolution and stolid reaction there is a middle ground of sound conservatism and orderly change.

[27] Also, without being puristic to the point of ejecting "ain't" and kindred forms from a dictionary of recorded usage, it might be worth while to recognize the existence of a standard language, neither literary nor slangy, which has acceptance and is understood practically everywhere in the country, even if everybody does not use it. Such phrases as "Them dogs is us'uns" and "I'll call you up without I can't," which an American structural linguist claims are good, meaningful language to him, merely because they are uttered by some native American speakers, definitely do not form part of that standard language. By all means let us record them for our own information and amusement, but let us not try to palm them off on the public on the general ground that the native speaker can do no wrong, and that "correct" and "incorrect" are terms that

can be legitimately applied only to the speech of foreigners attempting to use English.

[28] Language is something more than a heritage of sentimental value. It is an indispensable tool of communication and exchange of ideas. The more standardized and universal it is, the more effective it is. The more it is allowed to degenerate into local and class forms, the less effective it becomes. It may be perfectly true that in the past language has been allowed to run its own sweet, unbridled course, with the chips falling where they might. We are now in an age where we no longer believe in letting diseases and epidemics run their natural course, but take active, artificial means to control them. In fact, we endeavor to control natural, physical, and sociological phenomena of all descriptions, from floods to business cycles, from weather to diet, from the monetary system to racial relations. Is it unreasonable for us, far from leaving our language alone, as advocated by the American school of linguistics, to wish to channel it in the directions where it will prove of maximum efficiency for its avowed function, which is that of semantic transfer?

[29] For the concern of that other burning question, standards of writing, as apart from standards of speech, ought we not to recognize that until such a time as tapes, recordings, dictaphones and spoken films altogether replace our system of written communications, the latter should be viewed and treated with respect? Again, we need not let ourselves be led too far afield by purely literary or esthetic considerations. The written language, in a modern civilization, is practically on a par with speech as a communications tool. It is incongruous to see our American structuralistic linguists devote so much painstaking attention to phonetic phenomena like pitch, stress, intonation, and juncture, to the fine distinctions between "a light housekeeper" and "a lighthouse keeper," "an iceman" and "a nice man," and yet shrug their shoulders at correct spelling, punctuation, and capitalization. More misunderstandings have occurred over misplaced commas than over misplaced junctures, and a wrong spelling can be just as fatal as a wrong intonation.

[30] Perhaps the time has come, in language as in other fields, for the return of reason, and its ascendancy over dogma, whether the latter be of the puristic or of the structuralistic variety.

[31] Above all, there is need for sound, scientific consideration of *all* the facts of language, not merely that portion which happens to suit the tastes and inclinations of a small group. Language is more than a set of phonemes, morphemes, junctures, and stresses. It also happens to be our most important instrument of semantic transfer, and the common possession of all of us. If democracy means anything, we, the speakers, have the right to have our say as to how it shall be viewed and used, and not to be forced to subscribe to the prescriptive excesses of what the European professor of linguistics describes as "the God's Truth School."

---◦◄ C O M M E N T   A N D   Q U E S T I O N S ►◦---

1. The first two paragraphs deal with a decline in the quality of English taught in schools and colleges, and with the placing of blame for this decline on teachers of English and progressive educationists. Does Pei support the statements made in these paragraphs, or does he assume that his readers agree that the situation is as he describes it? What is the relevance of these two paragraphs to the main ideas of the article?

2. For what common reasons do people consult dictionaries? What use of the dictionary is Pei emphasizing?

3. What major differences does Pei find between the older editions and the new *Webster's*? What is the substance of Dr. Gove's defense of *Webster's Third*? To Pei, what central issue still remains?

4. Look up in *Webster's Third New International Dictionary* four or five expressions which you consider either colloquial English or substandard English. Do you find any restrictive labels or comments? Does your research support Pei's statement in paragraph 13 that all usage is "set on an identical plane"?

5. Summarize in your own words what the author is saying in paragraph 15. Does his brief departure from the subject of language seem an irrelevancy in the essay? Explain.

6. Paragraph 16 is a harsh indictment of the American school of structural linguistics, an indictment supported to some extent, at least, by the quotations in paragraphs 19, 20, and 23. Does it seem to you that Pei is overstating in paragraph 16? If you have read the preceding selection by Bergen Evans, do you think that Evans would agree with Pei's summary of the linguistic philosophy?

7. Comment on the last sentence of paragraph 24. Do you agree or disagree with this linguistic stand?

8. On some matters, Pei agrees with the structural linguists. Point out examples of such agreement. How does the author qualify his agreement and emphasize his own point of view?

9. Do you agree with the statement in paragraph 28 that the more standard and universal language is, the more effective it is as a means of communication? How successful is the use of analogy in paragraph 28? Explain.

10. How would you explain the subtitle of this essay—"English Teachers' Dilemma"? What is the dilemma?

11. To what extent do you agree or disagree with Pei's argument that a good dictionary should guide the reader by making a distinction between *usage* and *best usage*?

[44] *Sheridan Baker*: Scholarly Style, or the Lack Thereof

SHERIDAN BAKER, a professor of English at the University of Michigan, is the author of *The Practical Stylist, The Complete Stylist,* and *The Essayist.* The following essay is addressed to teachers and scholarly writers, but it gives sound advice to any writer.

[¹] Teachers and scholars are constantly picking at faulty writing. Indeed, instructors in English do little else. But the writing of the college professor himself, I think, could stand one more attack, though I repeat much said before. Recently, as I was getting together a volume from different scientific and scholarly fields, several things from freshman handbooks and articles on composition came home.¹ Regardless of person or field, I saw, writing always fails in the same way. Words should count, they should make sense, and the great enemy of counting sensibly is wordiness. I saw also that behind the professor's wordiness lay a failure of attitude, a mistaken stance encouraged by both our scientific and our pedantic selves.

[²] We mistake, I think, how scholarship should look and sound in public. Picture a young man in a rusty cutaway and striped pants, a celluloid collar and flowing tie, face serious, eyes glazed, gesticulating with his gloves, mumbling long words while no one at the party pays him the slightest attention. Or perhaps he is dapper, nose-in-the-air, full of jargon and wind. Picture either one and you will have some idea of the way a great many scholars attempt to address their readers. Both have the wrong attitude. Our scientific temper has made our syntax ponderous, and our dignity strings out long words like so much bunting.

[³] Now, both scholar and scientist owe first allegiance to the scientific method. Whether he works with books or social behavior or metallic salts, the researcher collects his facts, weighs them, and shapes from probability an hypothesis about the truth. But the scientific attitude has nevertheless, I think, done much to load our sentences with nouns, and to teach us the passive voice.

¹ I am especially indebted to George Orwell, "Politics and the English Language," in *Shooting an Elephant* (New York: Harcourt, Brace and Co., 1950), pp. 77–92, and to Robert C. Waddell, *Grammar and Style* (New York: Dryden Press, 1951).

[⁴] Because the scientist, social or natural, prefers *things* to *qualities,* he prefers nouns to adjectives. Indeed, whenever he can, he makes qualities into things by building nouns around them. He will write *Spanish-type* instead of *Spanish.* He will write *in size* instead of *long.* He will always say *of a peculiar order* when he means *peculiar,* and *of an indefinite nature* when he means *indefinite,* and *of great importance* when he means *important.* He will encumber prepositions with nouns, apparently because this makes the preposition more substantial, less like a disembodied process. He will say *in order to* rather than *to,* and *by means of* rather than *by.* Where *and* or *with* would serve, he writes *in relation to.* When he wants to add a phrase, he will select the relative pronoun—usually *which*—rather than the adjective or participle: "a subject *which was* popular a decade ago" rather than "a subject popular a decade ago."

[⁵] The trouble with this is its density—more words, less light, and almost no movement. The *ofs* and the *whiches* have thrown our prose into a hundred-years' sleep. Here is a piece typically respectable and drowsy:

Many biological journals, especially those *which* regularly publish new scientific names, now state in each issue the exact date *of* publication *of* the preceding issue. In dealing with journals *which* do not follow this practice, or with volumes *which* are issued individually, the biologist often needs *to* resort *to* indexes . . . *in order to* determine the actual date *of* publication *of* a particular name.

By eliminating *ofs* and the nouns they bring, by changing *which*-phrases into participles, and nouns into verbs, we can cut this passage almost to half without touching the sense:

Many biological journals, especially those regularly *publishing* new scientific names, now give the date of each preceding issue. With journals not *following* this practice, and with some books, the biologist must turn to indexes . . . *to date* a particular name.

[⁶] Our heavy preference for nouns, moreover, leads to a habit worse than any indulgence in *whiches* and *ofs:* we modify nouns by nouns instead of by adjectives. The social sciences here sin more than most. Working with intangibles, the social scientist seems urged to stiffen his nouns with nouns, and the reader can separate main thought from modifier only after initiation. "Child sex education" stands for "the sexual education of children," I think, unless it stands for "educating someone about the sex of children." Is sex educational, or is education sexual? The noun-habit often carries us completely away from what words mean, and keeps us there by elevated sound alone. And even if by habit we learn to read these constructions, they remain lumpy and unattractive: *body consciousness, human body function, significance level, sign situation,*

population theory, art ability, teacher grades, nature–nurture evidence.
If we can't drop one of the nouns or find its related adjective, the only
cure is homeopathic—a cautious shot of *ofs*.

– II –

[⁷] Our scientific taste prefers not only the solid noun but the impersonal passive voice—an opiate which cancels responsibility, hides identity,
and numbs the reader. And our adherence to officialdom and groups
strengthens the preference.

[⁸] We have almost forgotten that the simple English sentence, the
basis of good writing, moves. It moves from *subject* through *verb* to
object: "Smith laid the cornerstone on April 1." But because we must
sound important, because the institution must be bigger than Smith, we
write "the cornerstone was laid on April 1," and the human being vanishes
from the earth. The doer and the writer both—all traces of individuality
—disappear behind elongated verbs. Men don't do things, things merely
are done; stones move into place, whole campuses emerge from the
ground, regulations crystallize overhead. Committees always write this
way—and the ecological effect on scholarly writing is deadly. "It was
moved that a conference would be held," the secretary writes, to avoid
pinning the rap on anybody.

[⁹] Unfortunately, we like this. We use the passive voice at every
opportunity, even with nothing to hide and no one to protect. The passive
voice seems dignified and authoritative, and, for all this, it makes our
writing dreary with extra *ises, beens* and *bys*. It overruns every scholarly
field:

Public concern *has also been given* a tremendous impetus *by* the findings of
the Hoover Commission in the federal government, and "little Hoover" commissions to survey the organizational structure and functions of many state
governments *have been established*. [In the federal government, the findings
of the Hoover Commission have also greatly stimulated public concern, and
many states have established "little Hoover" commissions to survey their governments.]

The algal mats *are made up of* the interwoven filaments of several genera. [The
interwoven filaments of several genera make up these algal mats.]

Many of the remedies *would probably be shown to be* "faith cures." [Many of
the remedies are probably "faith cures."]

In this way less developed countries *can be enabled* to participate in the higher
production system of the Western World. [These programs can help backward
countries to Western productivity.]

Anxiety and emotional conflict *are lessened* when latency sets in. The total
personality *is oriented* in a repressive, inhibitory fashion so as to maintain the
barriers, and what Freud has called "psychic dams," against psychological

impulses. [When latency sets in, anxiety and emotional conflict subside. The personality inhibits itself, maintaining its barriers—Freud's "psychic dams"—against psychosexual impulses.]

The passive voice, simply in its wordiness, is unclear; but, eliminating the real subject of the verb, as it does, it is intrinsically unclear also. An essay, getting started, will state, "it was demonstrated," and one can only guess as to whether the writer or his rivals had done the demonstrating.

[10] The passive voice is the natural voice of science. Not only officialdom but scientific objectivity tempts us to it. It sounds dispassionate and impersonal; it stops time and holds life still so we can catalogue it. (Flowers never grow in this dry land; they "are found.") Perhaps scientific German has had something to do with it. At any rate, since the scientist describes what *is*, since our dignity demands *is laid* instead of *laid*, *is* becomes almost our only verb. All of us, following first the natural and then the social scientist, define, partition, arrange categories, and cement our writing into blocks with an equals-sign our only predication.

[11] *Is* so besets us—we are so willing to sit back on our *ises*—that we not only replace active with passive voice, but active verbs with sedentary ones. We can almost see the roadblocks—separated by a narrow *was*, inverted to look passive—in this opening sentence:

Typical of the rationalism of the eighteenth century was a view of prose fiction which developed during the middle decades.

After a little blasting, we might get on into the essay, leaving something like this behind:

A new view of prose fiction, typically rational, developed in the middle decades of the eighteenth century.

To make matters worse, we spread our *isms* by handing out *exists* and *existences* at every opportunity. We write "this association is not known to exist," not "this association is unknown." And we like to carry phrases around in a stretcher that looks like this: "There is——which." *It* may substitute for *there. That* or *who* may substitute for *which*. But they are all equally wordy: "Moreover, *there is* one class of worker *which* never seeks regular employment." If we drop the italicized words, nothing diminishes but clumsiness.

– III –

[12] If we straighten out our syntax, however, we are still left with the ornate vocabulary we think proper to scholarship. Vocabulary is a matter of tone. Tone is a matter of attitude. All our *ofs*, our *whiches*, our passives, our clumps of substantives—all rise from the same source as our vocabulary: the pompous and circumstantial attitude so common to our

scholarly, scientific pages. Official anonymity is in our ears. We wish to be modest and objective. We want to impress other zoologists, psychologists, economists, and literary men by writing like them. And the result is an inky, back-bay fog. We should work like scholars and scientists, but we should write like writers. We should take our subjects seriously but ourselves with grains of salt, with the knowledge that we are all sinners, all wordy, and all—whether courtly or pontifical—too fond of big Latin words.

[13] Two scientific fishermen have compared numbers of bass in the pond to numbers in the basket, and have watched imported bass survive in mixed company. Their article begins:

Of the many things which influence angling success, the size of population of the species sought must be a prime factor. In order to gain information on the relationship between population and yield to fishermen in a fishery based mainly on large mouth bass, *Micropterus salmoides* (Lacépède), we have experimented. . . .

The trouble with this is not *Micropterus salmoides*. Technical Latin words are precise and useful. The trouble lies in *influence, success, population, factor, information, relationship, population,* and the ambiguous *yield to*—all slushing along together through the weedy connectives. Does your subject seem mundane or trivial? Then give it a Latin diploma and it will graduate into elegant dullness. Actually, this article soon begins to read quite well. After a Latin period or two the writers get down to ponds and fish; they leave the academic procession and get out their waders. If we traded our Latin words for Anglo-Saxon ones wherever we could make a bargain, and long words for short ones; if we wrote *find* for *determine, see* for *inquire, watch* for *observe, book* for *volume;* if we banished all words containing *tion,* and then let not more than three sneak back into any one paragraph, our writing would be clearer. Subjects needing Latin technicalities should insist the more stoutly on short English words for the writing in between.

[14] But the social sciences—especially sociology and psychology—unblessed with Latin genera, are in a bad way. They must make their own terms as they go, and few men have Freud's command of words. Some words, like *schizophrenia* and *psychosomatic,* describe what they represent; *ego* and *id* are clear enough. But, for the most part, poor writers have endowed psychology with a technical vocabulary that would put even Solomon on the couch. We hear of *reaction fixation,* of *reaction to action. Factors, aspects,* and *situations* are *functions* of every sentence, and a word like *motivation* takes on private meanings which force the writer to new definitions. *Affect* changes into a noun and affects the sanity of everyone trying to write effectively.

[15] Language is public property that must not be rough-hewn to

private ends. A real knowledge of Latin might save us from this—a real understanding of what a word means at the root. But we are not Latinists; we are merely Latinate. Always looking for an exact scientific language, we never write with an alert and delighted sense that words have more than one meaning, that our sentences can strike harmonies and still be precise. Beware of the writer who must define his terms, I say. He may be unable to use language, as it runs, to express his meaning, and—whatever his motivation—the result is pomposity. He is Humpty Dumpty, the original egghead, making words say what he wants them to mean instead of meaning what he wants to say. He is either evading the toil of finding the right word, or defining the obvious:

Let us agree to use the word *signal* as an abbreviation for the phrase "the simplest kind of sign." (This agrees fairly well with the customary meaning of the word "signal.")

[16] A definer of words is usually a bad writer. The man, above, who had to get his signals straight, a semanticist, by the way, grinds out about three parts sawdust to every one of meat. In the following excerpt, the italics are his; the brackets, mine. Read the sentence first as it was written; then read it again, omitting the bracketed words:

The moral of such examples is that *all intelligent criticism* [*of any instance*] *of language* [*in use*] *must begin with understanding* [*of*] *the motives* [*and purposes*] *of the speaker* [*in that situation*].

Here, each of the bracketed phrases is already implied in the others. Attempting to be precise, our writer has only clouded his meaning. We have reached our last infirmity of scientific mind. Naturally the speaker would be "in that situation"; naturally a sampling of language would be "an instance" of language "in use." And even if *motives* are not *purposes*, the difference is too small to dawdle over. His next sentence deserves some kind of immortality. He means "muddy language causes trouble":

Unfortunately, the type of case that causes trouble in practice is that in which the kind of use made of language is not transparently clear. . . .

— IV —

[17] Clearly, it is hard to be transparent. Writing is hard. Even divinity has found it necessary to write in the middle of the night with great commotion. Writing is probably more than half of the researcher's job, as anyone will testify who has found himself hunting up one more fact, and running one more test, postponing the awful hour when he must face the mystery of the word, to gather his thoughts and to communicate. It is a matter of finding first the right attitude, and then the right words —and no more. If we have little to say, we will be pompous, we will write in the passive voice, we will throw phrases in the air like dust.

[¹⁸] But if you have something to say and still sound tumid, we can work out our salvation. Here are some suggestions:

1. Economize. Think of explaining what you have to say clearly, simply and pleasantly to a small mixed group of intelligent people.

2. Never use a long word when you can find a short one, or a Latin word when you can find a good Old English one.

3. Suspect yourself of wordiness whenever you see an *of,* a *which* or a *that.* Inspect all areas surrounding any form of *to be.* Never use *exist.*

4. Resolve not to use the passive voice. Simply fly in the face of convention and begin your sentences with "I" or "we" or "the writer."

5. Take pains to avoid modifying a noun with a noun.

6. Make sure that each word really makes sense. No one who had inspected the meaning of his words could have written: "Every seat in the auditorium was filled to capacity."

7. Beware of the metaphor. It is the spirit of good prose. It gives the reader a picture, a glimpse of what the subject really looks like to the writer. But it is dangerous, can easily get tangled and insistent, the more so when it almost works; don't have a violent explosion pave the way for a new growth. *mixed metaphor*

[¹⁹] The important thing is, I think, to pick up each sentence in turn, asking ourselves if we can possibly make it shorter. This done, clarity will come of itself, and with it the peculiar pleasure of having wrestled— the struggle itself will be agony—with the written word, and written well. We may even live in a style in which we never dreamed we could become accustomed.

COMMENT AND QUESTIONS

1. How would you describe the style and tone of Baker's title? Is the title appropriate?

2. What is the purpose, in paragraph 3, of the distinction between the scientific method and the scientific attitude?

3. The first three paragraphs are introductory. What is the central idea of each main division of the essay? How do the opening sentences of sections II, III, and IV make transitions?

4. In the quoted and revised passage in paragraph 5, the italics show how Baker eliminates prepositions and encumbering nouns and how he changes *which*-phrases into participles. He speaks also of changing nouns into verbs. Can you find examples of this change?

5. At the end of paragraph 6, what does *homeopathic* mean? Is the word well chosen?

6. Teachers of composition would generally agree with Baker that the passive voice is often wordy, indirect, and unclear. Do you think that one might justifiably use the passive voice in writing about any of the topics mentioned in paragraph 8? Explain.

7. Can you revise the passage quoted in paragraph 13, eliminating most or all of the expressions Baker objects to?

8. What appears to be the reason for the shift in pronouns (*we, you, we, our*) in the last sentence of paragraph 17 and the first sentence of paragraph 18?

9. Which of the suggestions offered in paragraph 18 seem most important, not only for the scholarly writer, but for any writer? Why?

10. What is wrong with the metaphor at the end of item 7 in paragraph 18? Baker himself makes considerable use of metaphor. Review his essay and point out examples of metaphors, other figures of speech, and plays on words that seem to you effective.

[45]   *H. W. Fowler*: from Modern English Usage

H. W. FOWLER (1858–1933) was a British writer whose *Dictionary of Modern English Usage,* first published in 1926, has been a widely read, widely admired reference work. Much of the book is not a dictionary in the usual sense of the word but is rather a series of short essays on conventions of language and grammar. The usage Fowler described, and often condemned, has changed since 1926; and a second edition of *Modern English Usage,* revised and edited by Sir Ernest Gowers, was published in 1965. Sir Ernest Gowers, author of *The Complete Plain Words* and *H. W. Fowler: The Man and His Teaching,* has said in his preface to the new edition that he was chary of making substantial changes in Fowler's writing except for purposes of bringing it up to date; he did not wish to sacrifice the "Fowleresque flavour" which has long delighted the readers of *Modern English Usage.* The following excerpts are from the revised edition.

abstractitis.   The effect of this disease, now endemic on both sides of the Atlantic, is to make the patient write such sentences as *Participation by the men in the control of the industry is non-existent* instead of *The men have no part in the control of the industry; Early expectation of a vacancy is indicated by the firm* instead of *The firm say they expect to have a vacancy soon; The availability of this material is diminishing* instead of

This material is getting scarcer; A cessation of dredging has taken place instead of *Dredging has stopped; Was this the realization of an antici- pated liability?* instead of *Did you expect you would have to do this?* And so on, with an abstract word always in command as the subject of the sentence. Persons and what they do, things and what is done to them, are put in the background, and we can only peer at them through a glass darkly. It may no doubt be said that in these examples the meaning is clear enough; but the danger is that, once the disease gets a hold, it sets up a chain reaction. A writer uses abstract words because his thoughts are cloudy; the habit of using them clouds his thoughts still further; he may end by concealing his meaning not only from his readers but also from himself, and writing such sentences as *The actualization of the motivation of the forces must to a great extent be a matter of personal angularity.*

[1] **ambiguity.**   The word as here used includes not only those ambigui- ties that leave the reader genuinely puzzled which of two interpretations is right, but also those in which one of these, probably the more natural grammatically, is clearly not what the writer meant. The fault of this kind of writing is not so much obscurity as clumsiness. Like that described in the article FALSE SCENT, it misleads the reader only momentarily, if at all, but makes him think the writer a fool for not being able to say what he means. As the purpose of this dictionary is to help writers to express themselves clearly and accurately, and the causes of ambiguity are in- numerable, reference might perhaps here be made to its contents *passim*. But a few of the more frequent of these causes deserve special notice.

[2] "Of all the faults found in writing," wrote Cobbett in 1818, "the wrong placing of words is one of the most common, and perhaps it leads to the greatest number of misconceptions." Or, in the words of another old grammarian, the golden rule of writing is "that the words or members most nearly related should be placed in the sentence as near to one an- other as possible, so as to make their mutual relation clearly appear." Few books since published on grammar and usage have omitted to enliven an arid subject by stock examples of this fault, such as the well-worn one of the advertisement of a piano for sale by a lady going abroad in an oak case with carved legs. Nevertheless, carelessness of this kind is still so common that it may be worth while to give some modern examples by way of warning. *No child shall be employed on any weekday when the school is not open for a longer period than four hours. / Please state from what date the patient was sent to bed and totally incapacitated by your instructions. / To ask the Minister of Agriculture if he will require eggs to be stamped with the date when they are laid by the farmer. / The Committee considered again the recommendation that _____ soap be used throughout the hospital because Mr. G. had objected to it at the Medical*

Committee. / *No force was used beyond that necessary to put an end to the uproar by the stewards.* / *I can recommend this candidate for the post for which he applies with complete confidence.* / *We had a leisurely breakfast and recalled the old tales of the city and the love story of Hero and Leander, who swam the Hellespont, and spent a great deal of time just looking at the beautiful view.* All these ambiguities can be removed by rearrangement to "bring the words or members most nearly related as near to one another as possible."

[3] Some other common causes of ambiguity are:

[4] The use of a word with two meanings in a context in which it makes for uncertainty or absurdity. *Much conversation was going on about him.* / Certain *remedies are available for this condition.* / *The meeting had been* overlooked *by the police on duty.* / *Miss Pickhill grasped the pince-nez which hung from a sort of button on her* spare *bosom.*

[5] The use of pronouns in such a way that the reader cannot be sure of their antecedents.

[6] Uncertainty whether *shall* or *will,* or *should* or *would,* is used as a simple auxiliary or as implying volition or obligation. *It is of interest to note that, even as a tiro in politics, he should have taken his own line.*

[1] **genteelism.** By *genteelism* is here to be understood the rejecting of the ordinary natural word that first suggests itself to the mind, and the substitution of a synonym that is thought to be less soiled by the lips of the common herd, less familiar, less plebeian, less vulgar, less improper, less apt to come unhandsomely betwixt the wind and our nobility. The truly genteel do not *ask* but *enquire,* invite one to *step,* not to *come* this way, may detect an *unpleasant odour* but not a *nasty smell,* never *help,* but *assist* each other to potatoes, of which they may have *sufficient,* but never *enough,* do not *go to bed* but *retire for the night*: and have quite forgotten that they could ever have been guilty of *sitting-room, napkin,* and *dirty clothes* where nothing will now do for them but *lounge, serviette,* and *soiled linen.*

[2] The reader need hardly be warned that the inclusion of any particular word in the small selection of genteelisms offered below does not imply that that word should never be used. All or most of these, and of the hundreds that might be classed with them, have their proper uses, in which they are not genteel, but natural. *Lounge* is at home in hotels, *step* in the dancing class, *retire* for the superannuated man, and so forth; but out of such contexts, and in the conditions explained above, the taint of gentility is on them. To illustrate a little more in detail, "He went out without shutting the door" is plain English; with *closing* substituted for *shutting* it becomes genteel; nevertheless, to *close* the door is justified if more is implied than the mere not leaving it open: "Before beginning his story, he crossed the room and closed the door," i.e. so placed it as to

prevent eavesdropping; "Six people sleeping in a small room with closed windows," i.e. excluding air. Or again, "The schoolroom roof fell in, and two of the boys (or girls, or children) were badly injured"; *scholars* for boys etc. would be a genteelism, and a much more flagrant one than *closing* in the previous example; yet *scholar* is not an obsolete or archaic word; it is no longer the natural English for a schoolboy or schoolgirl, that is all. The point is that, when the word in the second column of the list that follows is the word of one's thought, one should not consent to displace it by the word in the first column unless an improvement in the meaning would result. The reader will easily increase the list for himself; he may also be disposed to amend it by omission. Genteelisms, if they attain a wide enough currency, soon rub their taint off by use.

[3] *Genteelisms*	*Normal words*
assist	help
bosom	breast
close	shut
couch	sofa
enquire	ask
dentifrice	tooth-powder
desire	want
expectorate	spit
hard of hearing	deaf
help	servant
lady dog	bitch
lingerie	underclothes
lounge	sitting room
odour	smell
paying guest	lodger
perspire	sweat
require	want
retire	go to bed
scholar	schoolboy, -girl
serviette	table napkin
soiled linen	dirty clothes
step, vb.	come, go
sufficient	enough

[1] **haziness.** By this is meant a writer's failure to make a clear line between different members of a sentence or clause, with the result that they run into one another. If he does not know the exact content of what he has set down or is about to set down, either the word or words that he is now writing will not fit without overlapping, or a gap will be left between them. This sounds so obvious that it may seem hardly worth an

article; but even the more flagrant transgressions of the principle are so numerous as to make it plain that a warning is called for. Those more flagrant transgressions are illustrated first.

[²] *It is a pity that an account of American activities in aircraft production cannot yet be described* (overlapping; *account* is contained in *described;* omit *an account of,* or change *described* to *given*). / *The need of some effort, a joint effort if possible, is an urgent necessity for all the interests concerned* (*need* and *necessity* overlap). / *It is almost incomprehensible to believe at present that such works as his Five Orchestral Pieces can ever undergo such a total change of character as to . . .* (*to believe* is part of the content of *incomprehensible*). / *The welfare of the poor and needy was a duty that devolved especially on those who had a seat in that House* (gap; it is not the welfare, but the securing of the welfare, that is a duty). / *The mischief aimed at by the Act was to prevent members of local authorities who had occasion to enter into contracts from being exposed to temptation.* (The mischief aimed at was the exposure to temptation, not its prevention). / *The rather heavy expense of founding it could have been more usefully spent in other ways* (spend money; incur expense). / *Hitherto the only way of tackling the evil was by means of prohibiting the exportation from certain places* (*way* and *means* overlap; the only way of tackling was to prohibit; it could only be tackled by means of).

[³] Certain words seem to lend themselves especially to this sort of haziness, as AGO with *since,* BUT with superfluous negative, PREFERABLE with *more,* REASON and CAUSE with BECAUSE or DUE, REMAIN with CONTINUE, SEEM with *appear* and TOO illogical.

[¹] **Siamese twins.** This seems a suitable term for the many words which, linked in pairs by *and* or *or,* are used to convey a single meaning. As with the human variety, some verbal twins can be divided and each partner live separately; on others this cannot be attempted without fatal results. Their abundance in English is perhaps partly attributable to legal language, where the multiplication of near-synonyms is a normal precaution against too narrow an interpretation, and also contributes a pompous sonority to ceremonial occasions. A Royal patent creating a peer, with a splendid prodigality of words, will *advance, create, and prefer* him to the *state, degree, style, dignity, title, and honour* of his rank, and guarantee that he shall *enjoy and use all the rights, principles, pre-eminences, immunities, and advantages* appertaining to it. The phraseology of the Prayer Book, seldom content with one word if two can be used, may also have something to do with it: in the first few minutes the congregation at Morning Prayer will hear *acknowledge and confess, sins and wickedness, dissemble nor cloke, assemble and meet together, requisite and necessary.*

[²] In ordinary writing Siamese twins are a fruitful source of clichés, and it may be worth while to examine a sample of the commoner of them. Many are merely tautological: a synonym or near-synonym is added for the sake of emphasis: *Alas and alack, betwixt and between, bits and pieces, gall and wormwood, heart and soul, jot or tittle, leaps and bounds, lo and behold, nerve and fibre, rags and tatters, shape or form, sort or kind, toil and moil.* These are separable twins, but others, superficially similar, are indivisible, either because one of the components is used in an archaic sense and would not now be understood by itself, or because the combination has acquired a meaning different from that of either component alone. Such are *chop and change, fair and square, hue and cry, kith and kin, might and main, rack and ruin, odds and ends, part and parcel, spick and span, use and wont.* Others again consist not of synonyms but of associated ideas (e.g. *bill and coo, bow and scrape, flotsam and jetsam, frills and furbelows, hot and strong, hum and ha, thick and fast, ways and means*) or of opposites or alternatives (e.g. *cut and thrust, fast and loose, hither and thither, by hook or by crook, thick and thin, to and fro*). Some are from the law—*act and deed, aid and abet, each and every, let or hindrance, null and void*—and some quotations or literary allusions —*fear and trembling, hip and thigh, prunes and prisms, rhyme nor reason, sackcloth and ashes, sere and yellow, whips and scorpions.* A few can be classed as HENDIADYS (*grace and favour = gracious favour, rough and ready = roughly ready*).

[³] Whenever a Siamese twin suggests itself to a writer he should be on his guard; it may be just the phrase he wants, but it is more likely to be one of those clichés that are always lying in wait to fill a vacuum in the brain.

COMMENT AND QUESTIONS

1. Examine the sentences Fowler uses as examples of "abstractitis." What particular weaknesses, besides those he points out, do you find in the sentences?
2. Can you translate into clear English the final example of "abstractitis"; or do you think that the author's purpose was to write a completely meaningless sentence?
3. Revise the sentences in paragraph 2 of **ambiguity**.
4. What are the possible meanings of the sentences in paragraphs 4 and 6 of **ambiguity**? Which sentences cause the reader uncertainty?
5. Which of Fowler's "genteelisms" would you question or remove from his list? Explain.

6. The last paragraph of **haziness** lists undesirable combinations of words. Can you give examples of each?
7. According to Fowler, what are the two kinds of Siamese twins? What is the meaning of *hendiadys*, at the end of paragraph 2 of **Siamese twins**?
8. What seem to be the principal purposes of the article on Siamese twins?
9. The purpose of *Modern English Usage* is stated in the first paragraph of **ambiguity**: to help writers to express themselves clearly and accurately. In the excerpts printed here, what evidence do you find of the author's concern with clarity and accuracy in thought as well as in expression?
10. How would you describe the "Fowleresque flavour" which Sir Ernest Gowers wished to keep in the revised edition of *Modern English Usage*?

[46]   *E. B. White*: Calculating Machine

E. B. WHITE (1899–   ), one of the best of contemporary American essayists, has written regularly for *Harper's Magazine* and for *The New Yorker*. In July, 1963, John F. Kennedy named him in the first group to receive the new Presidential Medal of Freedom, an award to those "who contribute significantly to the quality of American life." E. B. White's books include *One Man's Meat, The Wild Flag, Here Is New York, The Second Tree from the Corner,* and *The Points of My Compass.* The following short essay is from *The Second Tree from the Corner,* published in 1951.

[1] A publisher in Chicago has sent us a pocket calculating machine by which we may test our writing to see whether it is intelligible. The calculator was developed by General Motors, who, not satisfied with giving the world a Cadillac, now dream of bringing perfect understanding to men. The machine (it is simply a celluloid card with a dial) is called the Reading Ease Calculator and shows four grades of "reading ease"—Very Easy, Easy, Hard, and Very Hard. You count your words and syllables, set the dial, and an indicator lets you know whether anybody is going to understand what you have written. An instruction book came with it, and after mastering the simple rules we lost no time in running a test on the instruction book itself, to see how *that* writer was doing. The poor fellow! His leading essay, the one on the front cover, tested Very Hard.

[2] Our next step was to study the first phrase on the face of the calculator: "How to test Reading-Ease of written matter." There is, of course, no such thing as reading ease of written matter. There is the ease

with which matter can be read, but that is a condition of the reader, not of the matter. Thus the inventors and distributors of this calculator get off to a poor start, with a Very Hard instruction book and a slovenly phrase. Already they have one foot caught in the brier patch of English usage.

[3] Not only did the author of the instruction book score badly on the front cover, but inside the book he used the word "personalize" in an essay on how to improve one's writing. A man who likes the word "personalize" is entitled to his choice, but we wonder whether he should be in the business of giving advice to writers. "Whenever possible," he wrote, "personalize your writing by directing it to the reader." As for us, we would as lief Simonize our grandmother as personalize our writing.

[4] In the same envelope with the calculator, we received another training aid for writers—a booklet called "How to Write Better," by Rudolf Flesch. This, too, we studied, and it quickly demonstrated the broncolike ability of the English language to throw whoever leaps cocksurely into the saddle. The language not only can toss a rider but knows a thousand tricks for tossing him, each more gay than the last. Dr. Flesch stayed in the saddle only a moment or two. Under the heading "Think Before You Write," he wrote, "The main thing to consider is your *purpose* in writing. Why are you sitting down to write?" And Echo answered: Because, sir, it is more comfortable than standing up.

[5] Communication by the written word is a subtler (and more beautiful) thing than Dr. Flesch and General Motors imagine. They contend that the "average reader" is capable of reading only what tests Easy, and that the writer should write at or below this level. This is a presumptuous and degrading idea. There is no average reader, and to reach down toward this mythical character is to deny that each of us is on the way up, is ascending. ("Ascending," by the way, is a word Dr. Flesch advises writers to stay away from. Too unusual.)

[6] It is our belief that no writer can improve his work until he discards the dulcet notion that the reader is feeble-minded, for writing is an act of faith, not a trick of grammar. Ascent is at the heart of the matter. A country whose writers are following a calculating machine downstairs is not ascending—if you will pardon the expression—and a writer who questions the capacity of the person at the other end of the line is not a writer at all, merely a schemer. The movies long ago decided that a wider communication could be achieved by a deliberate descent to a lower level, and they walked proudly down until they reached the cellar. Now they are groping for the light switch, hoping to find the way out.

[7] We have studied Dr. Flesch's instructions diligently, but we return for guidance in these matters to an earlier American, who wrote with more patience, more confidence. "I fear chiefly," he wrote, "lest my ex-

pression may not be *extra-vagant* enough, may not wander far enough beyond the narrow limits of my daily experience, so as to be adequate to the truth of which I have been convinced . . ⌈Why level downward to our dullest perception always, and praise that as common sense? The commonest sense is the sense of men asleep, which they express by snoring." ~Thoreau

[8] Run that through your calculator! It may come out Hard, it may come out Easy. ⌈But⌉ it will come out whole, and it will last forever.

⊸⊷{ C O M M E N T A N D Q U E S T I O N S }⊶⊷

1. An informal tone and style are combined with careful use of language in this selection. Because "Calculating Machine" was originally written for *The New Yorker,* White uses the editorial *we* (*us, our*) as a matter of convention; he also, however, uses the informal *you* (in paragraph 1, for example). What other informal expressions do you find in the essay?

2. Numerous touches of humor and of irony occur in "Calculating Machine," and White also uses figurative language, often for purposes of humor or irony. Point out examples that seem to you effective.

3. Do you agree with White's criticisms, in paragraphs 2–4, of the English used on the calculator and in the accompanying books? Explain.

4. Can you accept White's statement in paragraph 5 that there is no average reader? Explain.

5. Examine the writing in paragraph 6. What stylistic traits do you notice?

6. The quotation in paragraph 7 is from Thoreau. What does White appear to mean by saying that the earlier American "wrote with more patience, more confidence"?

7. What techniques has White used to make his ending emphatic?

8. This essay illustrates a method frequently used by E. B. White, and also by other informal essayists: the method of starting with a small, particular experience or event, and proceeding to its larger implications. Briefly summarize the serious things that, for all of his humor and lightness of tone, E. B. White is saying about language and about contemporary society.

[47] *George Orwell*: The Principles of Newspeak

THE FOLLOWING essay was written as an appendix to *Nineteen Eighty-Four,* a novel depicting life in a future totalitarian state made up of countries in Europe and America. For a note on George Orwell see page 51.

[1] Newspeak was the official language of Oceania and had been devised to meet the ideological needs of Ingsoc, or English Socialism. In the year 1984 there was not as yet anyone who used Newspeak as his sole means of communication, either in speech or writing. The leading articles in the *Times* were written in it, but this was a tour de force which could only be carried out by a specialist. It was expected that Newspeak would have finally superseded Oldspeak (or Standard English, as we should call it) by about the year 2050. Meanwhile it gained ground steadily, all Party members tending to use Newspeak words and grammatical constructions more and more in their everyday speech. The version in use in 1984, and embodied in the Ninth and Tenth Editions of the Newspeak dictionary, was a provisional one, and contained many superfluous words and archaic formations which were due to be suppressed later. It is with the final, perfected version, as embodied in the Eleventh Edition of the dictionary, that we are concerned here.

[2] The purpose of Newspeak was not only to provide a medium of expression for the world-view and mental habits proper to the devotees of Ingsoc, but to make all other modes of thought impossible. It was intended that when Newspeak had been adopted once and for all and Oldspeak forgotten, a heretical thought—that is, a thought diverging from the principles of Ingsoc—should be literally unthinkable, at least so far as thought is dependent on words. Its vocabulary was so constructed as to give exact and often very subtle expression to every meaning that a Party member could properly wish to express, while excluding all other meanings and also the possibility of arriving at them by indirect methods. This was done partly by the invention of new words, but chiefly by eliminating undesirable words and by stripping such words as remained of unorthodox meanings, and so far as possible of all secondary meanings whatever. To give a single example, the word *free* still existed in Newspeak, but it could only be used in such statements as "This dog is free from lice" or "This field is free from weeds." It could not be used

in its old sense of "politically free" or "intellectually free," since political and intellectual freedom no longer existed even as concepts, and were therefore of necessity nameless. Quite apart from the suppression of definitely heretical words, reduction of vocabulary was regarded as an end in itself, and no word that could be dispensed with was allowed to survive. Newspeak was designed not to extend but to *diminish* the range of thought, and this purpose was indirectly assisted by cutting the choice of words down to a minimum.

[3] Newspeak was founded on the English language as we now know it, though many Newspeak sentences, even when not containing newly created words, would be barely intelligible to an English-speaker of our own day. Newspeak words were divided into three distinct classes, known as the A vocabulary, the B vocabulary (also called compound words), and the C vocabulary. It will be simpler to discuss each class separately, but the grammatical peculiarities of the language can be dealt with in the section devoted to the A vocabulary, since the same rules held good for all three categories.

[4] *The A vocabulary.* The A vocabulary consisted of the words needed for the business of everyday life—for such things as eating, drinking, working, putting on one's clothes, going up and down stairs, riding in vehicles, gardening, cooking, and the like. It was composed almost entirely of words that we already possess—words like *hit, run, dog, tree, sugar, house, field*—but in comparison with the present-day English vocabulary, their number was extremely small, while their meanings were far more rigidly defined. All ambiguities and shades of meaning had been purged out of them. So far as it could be achieved, a Newspeak word of this class was simply a staccato sound expressing *one* clearly understood concept. It would have been quite impossible to use the A vocabulary for literary purposes or for political or philosophical discussion. It was intended only to express simple, purposive thoughts, usually involving concrete objects or physical actions.

[5] The grammar of Newspeak had two outstanding peculiarities. The first of these was an almost complete interchangeabililty between different parts of speech. Any word in the language (in principle this applied even to very abstract words such as *if* or *when*) could be used either as verb, noun, adjective, or adverb. Between the verb and the noun form, when they were of the same root, there was never any variation, this rule of itself involving the destruction of many archaic forms. The word *thought,* for example, did not exist in Newspeak. Its place was taken by *think,* which did duty for both noun and verb. No etymological principle was involved here; in some cases it was the original noun that was chosen for retention, in other cases the verb. Even when a noun and verb of kindred meaning were not etymologically connected,

one or other of them was frequently suppressed. There was, for example, no such word as *cut,* its meaning being sufficiently covered by the noun-verb *knife.* Adjectives were formed by adding the suffix *-ful* to the noun-verb, and adverbs by adding *-wise.* Thus, for example, *speedful* meant "rapid" and *speedwise* meant "quickly." Certain of our present-day adjectives, such as *good, strong, big, black, soft,* were retained, but their total number was very small. There was little need for them, since almost any adjectival meaning could be arrived at by adding *-ful* to a noun-verb. None of the now-existing adverbs was retained, except for a very few already ending in *-wise;* the *-wise* termination was invariable. The word *well,* for example, was replaced by *goodwise.*

[6] In addition, any word—this again applied in principle to every word in the language—could be negatived by adding the affix *un-,* or could be strengthened by the affix *plus-,* or, for still greater emphasis, *doubleplus-.* Thus, for example, *uncold* meant "warm," while *pluscold* and *doublepluscold* meant, respectively, "very cold" and "superlatively cold." It was also possible, as in present-day English, to modify the meaning of almost any word by prepositional affixes such as *ante-, post-, up-, down-,* etc. By such methods it was found possible to bring about an enormous diminution of vocabulary. Given, for instance, the word *good,* there was no need for such a word as *bad,* since the required meaning was equally well—indeed, better—expressed by *ungood.* All that was necessary, in any case where two words formed a natural pair of opposites, was to decide which of them to suppress. *Dark,* for example, could be replaced by *unlight,* or *light* by *undark,* according to preference.

[7] The second distinguishing mark of Newspeak grammar was its regularity. Subject to a few exceptions which are mentioned below, all inflections followed the same rules. Thus, in all verbs the preterite and the past participle were the same and ended in *-ed.* The preterite of *steal* was *stealed,* the preterite of think was *thinked,* and so on throughout the language, all such forms as *swam, gave, brought, spoke, taken,* etc., being abolished. All plurals were made by adding *-s* or *-es* as the case might be. The plurals of *man, ox, life* were *mans, oxes, lifes.* Comparison of adjectives was invariably made by adding *-er, -est* (*good, gooder, goodest*), irregular forms and the *more, most* formation being suppressed.

[8] The only classes of words that were still allowed to inflect irregularly were the pronouns, the relatives, the demonstrative adjectives, and the auxiliary verbs. All of these followed their ancient usage, except that *whom* had been scrapped as unnecessary, and the *shall, should* tenses had been dropped, all their uses being covered by *will* and *would.* There were also certain irregularities in word-formation arising out of the need for rapid and easy speech. A word which was difficult to utter, or was liable to be incorrectly heard, was held to be ipso facto a bad word; occasionally therefore, for the sake of euphony, extra letters were

inserted into a word or an archaic formation was retained. But this need made itself felt chiefly in connection with the B vocabulary. *Why* so great an importance was attached to ease of pronunciation will be made clear later in this essay.

[9] *The B vocabulary.* The B vocabulary consisted of words which had been deliberately constructed for political purposes: words, that is to say, which not only had in every case a political implication, but were intended to impose a desirable mental attitude upon the person using them. Without a full understanding of the principles of Ingsoc it was difficult to use these words correctly. In some cases they could be translated into Oldspeak, or even into words taken from the A vocabulary, but this usually demanded a long paraphrase and always involved the loss of certain overtones. The B words were a sort of verbal shorthand, often packing whole ranges of ideas into a few syllables, and at the same time more accurate and forcible than ordinary language.

[10] The B words were in all cases compound words.[1] They consisted of two or more words, or portions of words, welded together in an easily pronounceable form. The resulting amalgam was always a noun-verb, and inflected according to the ordinary rules. To take a single example: the word *goodthink,* meaning, very roughly, "orthodoxy," or, if one chose to regard it as a verb, "to think in an orthodox manner." This inflected as follows: noun-verb, *goodthink;* past tense and past participle, *goodthinked;* present participle, *goodthinking;* adjective, *goodthinkful;* adverb, *goodthinkwise;* verbal noun, *goodthinker.*

[11] The B words were not constructed on any etymological plan. The words of which they were made up could be any parts of speech, and could be placed in any order and mutilated in any way which made them easy to pronounce while indicating their derivation. In the word *crimethink* (thought-crime), for instance, the *think* came second, whereas in *thinkpol* (Thought Police) it came first, and in the latter word *police* had lost its second syllable. Because of the greater difficulty in securing euphony, irregular formations were commoner in the B vocabulary than in the A vocabulary. For example, the adjectival forms of *Minitrue,* *Minipax,* and *Miniluv* were, respectively, *Minitruthful, Minipeaceful,* and *Minilovely,* simply because *-trueful, -paxful,* and *-loveful* were slightly awkward to pronounce. In principle, however, all B words could inflect, and all inflected in exactly the same way.

[12] Some of the B words had highly subtilized meanings, barely intelligible to anyone who had not mastered the language as a whole. Consider, for example, such a typical sentence from a *Times* leading article

---

[1] Compound words, such as *speakwrite,* were of course to be found in the A vocabulary, but these were merely convenient abbreviations and had no special ideological color.

as *Oldthinkers unbellyfeel Ingsoc.* The shortest rendering that one could make of this in Oldspeak would be: "Those whose ideas were formed before the Revolution cannot have a full emotional understanding of the principles of English Socialism." But this is not an adequate translation. To begin with, in order to grasp the full meaning of the Newspeak sentence quoted above, one would have to have a clear idea of what is meant by *Ingsoc.* And, in additon, only a person thoroughly grounded in Ingsoc could apprecate the full force of the word *bellyfeel,* which implied a blind, enthusiastic acceptance difficult to imagine today; or of the word *oldthink,* which was inextricably mixed up with the idea of wickedness and decadence. But the special function of certain Newspeak words, of which *oldthink* was one, was not so much to express meanings as to destroy them. These words, necessarily few in number, had had their meanings extended until they contained within themselves whole batteries of words which, as they were sufficiently covered by a single comprehensive term, could now be scrapped and forgotten. The greatest difficulty facing the compilers of the Newspeak dictionary was not to invent new words, but, having invented them, to make sure what they meant: to make sure, that is to say, what ranges of words they canceled by their existence.

[13] As we have already seen in the case of the word *free,* words which had once borne a heretical meaning were sometimes retained for the sake of convenience, but only with the undesirable meanings purged out of them. Countless other words such as *honor, justice, morality, internationalism, democracy, science,* and *religion* had simply ceased to exist. A few blanket words covered them, and, in covering them, abolished them. All words grouping themselves round the concepts of liberty and equality, for instance, were contained in the single word *crimethink,* while all words grouping themselves round the concepts of objectivity and rationalism were contained in the single word *oldthink.* Greater precision would have been dangerous. What was required in a Party member was an outlook similar to that of the ancient Hebrew who knew, without knowing much else, that all nations other than his own worshipped "false gods." He did not need to know that these gods were called Baal, Osiris, Moloch, Ashtaroth, and the like; probably the less he knew about them the better for his orthodoxy. He knew Jehovah and the commandments of Jehovah; he knew, therefore, that all gods with other names or other attributes were false gods. In somewhat the same way, the Party member knew what constituted right conduct, and in exceedingly vague, generalized terms he knew what kinds of departure from it were possible. His sexual life, for example was entirely regulated by the two Newspeak words *sexcrime* (sexual immorality) and *goodsex* (chastity). *Sexcrime* covered all sexual misdeeds whatever. It covered fornication, adultery, homosexuality, and other perversions, and, in addition, normal intercourse

practiced for its own sake. There was no need to enumerate them separately, since they were all equally culpable, and, in principle, all punish-
able by death. In the C vocabulary, which consisted of scientific and
technical words, it might be necessary to give specialized names to certain
sexual aberrations, but the ordinary citizen had no need of them. He knew
what was meant by *goodsex*—that is to say, normal intercourse between
man and wife, for the sole purpose of begetting children, and without
physical pleasure on the part of the woman; all else was *sexcrime*. In
Newspeak it was seldom possible to follow a heretical thought further
than the perception that is *was* heretical; beyond that point the necessary
words were nonexistent.

[14] No word in the B vocabulary was ideologically neutral. A great
many were euphemisms. Such words, for instance, as *joycamp* (forced-
labor camp) or *Minipax* (Ministry of Peace, i.e., Ministry of War) meant
almost the exact opposite of what they appeared to mean. Some words,
on the other hand, displayed a frank and contemptuous understanding of
the real nature of Oceanic society. An example was *prolefeed,* meaning
the rubbishy entertainment and spurious news which the Party handed
out to the masses. Other words, again, were ambivalent, having the connotation "good" when applied to the Party and "bad" when applied to its
enemies. But in addition there were great numbers of words which at first
sight appeared to be mere abbreviations and which derived their ideological color not from their meaning but from their structure.

[15] So far as it could be contrived, everything that had or might have
political significance of any kind was fitted into the B vocabulary. The
name of every organization, or body of people, or doctrine, or country,
or institution, or public building, was invariably cut down into the familiar
shape; that is, a single easily pronounced word with the smallest number
of syllables that would preserve the original derivation. In the Ministry of
Truth, for example, the Records Department, in which Winston Smith
worked, was called *Recdep,* the Fiction Department was called *Ficdep,*
the Teleprograms Department was called *Teledep,* and so on. This was
not done solely with the object of saving time. Even in the early decades
of the twentieth century, telescoped words and phrases had been one of
the characteristic features of political language; and it had been noticed
that the tendency to use abbreviations of this kind was most marked in
totalitarian countries and totalitarian organizations. Examples were such
words as *Nazi, Gestapo, Comintern, Inprecor, Agitprop.* In the beginning the practice had been adopted as it were instinctively, but in Newspeak it was used with a conscious purpose. It was perceived that in thus
abbreviating a name one narrowed and subtly altered its meaning, by
cutting out most of the associations that would otherwise cling to it. The
words *Communist International,* for instance, call up a composite picture
of universal human brotherhood, red flags, barricades, Karl Marx, and the

Paris Commune. The word *Comintern,* on the other hand, suggests merely a tightly knit organization and a well-defined body of doctrine. It refers to something almost as easily recognized, and as limited in purpose, as a chair or a table. *Comintern* is a word that can be uttered almost without taking thought, whereas *Communist Internatonal* is a phrase over which one is obliged to linger at least momentarily. In the same way, the associations called up by a word like *Minitrue* are fewer and more controllable than those called up by *Ministry of Truth.* This accounted not only for the habit of abbreviating whenever possible, but also for the almost exaggerated care that was taken to make every word easily pronounceable.

[16] In Newspeak, euphony outweighed every consideration other than exactitude of meaning. Regularity of grammar was always sacrificed to it when it seemed necessary. And rightly so, since what was required, above all for political purposes, were short clipped words of unmistakable meaning which could be uttered rapidly and which roused the minimum of echoes in the speaker's mind. The words of the B vocabulary even gained in force from the fact that nearly all of them were very much alike. Almost invariably these words—*goodthink, Minipax, prolefeed, sexcrime, joycamp, Ingsoc, bellyfeel, thinkpol,* and countless others —were words of two or three syllables, with the stress distributed equally between the first syllable and the last. The use of them encouraged a gabbling style of speech, at once staccato and monotonous. And this was exactly what was aimed at. The intention was to make speech, and especially speech on any subject not ideologically neutral, as nearly as possible independent of consciousness. For the purposes of everyday life it was no doubt necessary, or sometimes necessary, to reflect before speaking, but a Party member called upon to make a political or ethical judgment should be able to spray forth the correct opinions as automatically as a machine gun spraying forth bullets. His training fitted him to do this, the language gave him an almost foolproof instrument, and the texture of the words, with their harsh sound and a certain willful ugliness which was in accord with the spirit of Ingsoc, assisted the process still further.

[17] So did the fact of having very few words to choose from. Relative to our own, the Newspeak vocabulary was tiny, and new ways of reducing it were constantly being devised. Newspeak, indeed, differed from almost all other languages in that its vocabulary grew smaller instead of larger every year. Each reduction was a gain, since the smaller the area of choice, the smaller the temptation to take thought. Ultimately it was hoped to make articulate speech issue from the larynx without involving the higher brain centers at all. This aim was frankly admitted in the Newspeak word *duckspeak,* meaning "to quack like a duck." Like various other words in the B vocabulary, *duckspeak* was ambivalent in meaning.

Provided that the opinions which were quacked out were orthodox ones, it implied nothing but praise, and when the *Times* referred to one of the orators of the Party as a *doubleplusgood duckspeaker* it was paying a warm and valued compliment.

[18] *The C vocabulary.* The C vocabulary was supplementary to the others and consisted entirely of scientific and technical terms. These resembled the scientific terms in use today, and were constructed from the same roots, but the usual care was taken to define them rigidly and strip them of undesirable meanings. They followed the same grammatical rules as the words in the other two vocabularies. Very few of the C words had any currency either in everyday speech or in political speech. Any scientific worker or technician could find all the words he needed in the list devoted to his own specialty, but he seldom had more than a smattering of the words occurring in the other lists. Only a very few words were common to all lists, and there was no vocabulary expressing the function of Science as a habit of mind, or a method of thought, irrespective of its particular branches. There was, indeed, no word for "Science," any meaning that it could possibly bear being already sufficiently covered by the word *Ingsoc.*

[19] From the foregoing account it will be seen that in Newspeak the expression of unorthodox opinions, above a very low level, was well-nigh impossible. It was of course possible to utter heresies of a very crude kind, a species of blasphemy. It would have been possible, for example, to say *Big Brother is ungood.* But this statement, which to an orthodox ear merely conveyed a self-evident absurdity, could not have been sustained by reasoned argument, because the necessary words were not available. Ideas inimical to Ingsoc could only be entertained in a vague wordless form, and could only be named in very broad terms which lumped together and condemned whole groups of heresies without defining them in doing so. One could, in fact, only use Newspeak for unorthodox purposes by illegitimately translating some of the words back into Oldspeak. For example *All mans are equal* was a possible Newspeak sentence, but only in the same sense in which *All men are redhaired* is a possible Oldspeak sentence. It did not contain a grammatical error, but it expressed a palpable untruth, i.e., that all men are of equal size, weight, or strength. The concept of political equality no longer existed, and this secondary meaning had accordingly been purged out of the word *equal.* In 1984, when Oldspeak was still the normal means of communication, the danger theoretically existed that in using Newspeak words one might remember their original meanings. In practice it was not difficult for any person well grounded in *doublethink* to avoid doing this, but within a couple of generations even the possibility of such a lapse would have

vanished. A person growing up with Newspeak as his sole language would no more know that *equal* had once had the secondary meaning of "politically equal," or that *free* had once meant "intellectually free," than, for instance, a person who had never heard of chess would be aware of the secondary meanings attaching to *queen* and *rook*. There would be many crimes and errors which it would be beyond his power to commit, simply because they were nameless and therefore unimaginable. And it was to be foreseen that with the passage of time the distinguishing characteristics of Newspeak would become more and more pronounced—its words growing fewer and fewer, their meanings more and more rigid, and the chance of putting them to improper uses always diminishing.

[20] When Oldspeak had been once and for all superseded, the last link with the past would have been severed. History had already been rewritten, but fragments of the literature of the past survived here and there, imperfectly censored, and so long as one retained one's knowledge of Oldspeak it was possible to read them. In the future such fragments, even if they chanced to survive, would be unintelligible and untranslatable. It was impossible to translate any passage of Oldspeak into Newspeak unless it either referred to some technical process or some very simple everyday action, or was already orthodox (*goodthinkful* would be the Newspeak expression) in tendency. In practice this meant that no book written before approximately 1960 could be translated as a whole. Prerevolutionary literature could only be subjected to ideological translation—that is, alteration in sense as well as language. Take for example the well-known passage from the Declaration of Independence:

[21] *We hold these truths to be self-evident, that all men are created equal, that they are endowed by their Creator with certain inalienable rights, that among these are life, liberty, and the pursuit of happiness. That to secure these rights, Governments are instituted among men, deriving their powers from the consent of the governed. That whenever any form of Government becomes destructive of these ends, it is the right of the People to alter or abolish it, and to institute new Government . . .*

[22] It would have been quite impossible to render this into Newspeak while keeping to the sense of the original. The nearest one could come to doing so would be to swallow the whole passage up in the single word *crimethink*. A full translation could only be an ideological translation, whereby Jefferson's words would be changed into a panegyric on absolute government.

[23] A good deal of the literature of the past was, indeed, already being transformed in this way. Considerations of prestige made it desirable to preserve the memory of certain historical figures, while at the same time bringing their achievements into line with the philosophy of

Ingsoc. Various writers, such as Shakespeare, Milton, Swift, Bryon, Dickens and some others were therefore in process of translation; when the task had been completed, their original writing, with all else that survived of the past, would be destroyed. These translations were a slow and difficult business, and it was not expected that they would be finished before the first or second decade of the twenty-first century. There were also large quantities of merely utilitarian literature—indispensable technical manuals and the like—that had to be treated in the same way. It was chiefly in order to allow time for the preliminary work of translation that the final adoption of Newspeak had been fixed for so late a date as 2050.

COMMENT AND QUESTIONS

1. The following questions will check your understanding of the factual content and structure of Orwell's essay: (a) What are the purposes of Newspeak? (b) What are the chief characteristics of each of the three classes of words? (c) Why does the author choose to discuss the grammar of Newspeak in connection with the A vocabulary instead of discussing it in a section preceding his analysis of the three vocabularies? (d) Why is the B vocabulary discussed more fully than the other two; the C vocabulary less fully? (e) Why is easy pronunciation important in Newspeak? (f) What is meant by the ideological translation of older literature? Why is it necessary?

2. The basis of irony is contrast—contrast, for example, between what is said and what is meant, or between what is expected and what actually occurs, or between what is and what seems to be or should be. What kind or kinds of irony do you find in "The Principles of Newspeak"?

3. Consider the language of the following passages:

> Its vocabulary was so constructed as to give *exact and often very subtle expression* to every meaning that a Party member could properly wish to express. . . .

> The B words were a sort of verbal shorthand, often packing whole ranges of ideas into a few syllables, and at the same time *more accurate and forcible than ordinary language.*

> Each reduction [in vocabulary] was *a gain,* since the smaller the area of choice, the smaller the temptation to take thought.

> What sort of attitude toward the subject would normally be communicated by the italicized expressions? In the context of the essay, what do these expressions mean? What does the author gain by stating his meaning thus indirectly instead of directly?

4. Point out other examples in Orwell's essay of the kind of ironical expression illustrated in the passages above.

5. Look up in your dictionary the word *euphony*. Do the definitions clarify Orwell's use of the word at the beginning of paragraph 16?

6. Can you determine from context the meaning of *doublethink* in paragraph 19?

7. Does there appear to be a plan in the illustrations the author uses; that is, does he seem to be emphasizing any point or points with his examples comparing Newspeak to Oldspeak?

8. What tendencies toward the kind of language perfected in Newspeak do you see in present-day English? Do any of the simplifications or other changes seem to you sensible or desirable? Do you think that they would to George Orwell?

9. List as many characteristics as you can of the hypothetical society of 1984 as it appears in this selection. What is the relationship of each of these characteristics to the language of Newspeak? Do the attitudes and the practices of 1984 seem wholly remote from those of our society, or are at least some of them extensions of present practices? (If you have read the essay by John Lukacs, "It's Halfway to 1984," consider his comments on the last part of this question.)

10. Summarize what you take to be Orwell's ideas about the relationship between language and thought. To what extent do you agree with his ideas, and why?

[48] *Richard M. Weaver*: Ultimate Terms in Contemporary Rhetoric

RICHARD M. WEAVER (1910–1963) was a professor of English at the University of Chicago and author of *Ideas Have Consequences* and *Visions of Order: the Cultural Crisis of Our Time*. The following selection is the last chapter of *The Ethics of Rhetoric*, published in 1957. Footnotes are the author's.

[1] We have shown that rhetorical force must be conceived as a power transmitted through the links of a chain that extends upward toward some ultimate source. The higher links of that chain must always be of unique interest to the student of rhetoric, pointing, as they do, to some prime mover of human impulse. Here I propose to turn away from general considerations and to make an empirical study of the terms on these higher levels of force which are seen to be operating in our age.

[²] We shall define term simply here as a name capable of entering into a proposition. In our treatment of rhetorical sources, we have regarded the full predication consisting of a proposition as the true validator. But a single term is an incipient proposition, awaiting only the necessary coupling with another term; and it cannot be denied that single names set up expectancies of propositional embodiment. This causes everyone to realize the critical nature of the process of naming. Given the name "patriot," for example, we might expect to see coupled with it "Brutus," or "Washington," or "Parnell"; given the term "hot," we might expect to see "sun," "stove," and so on. In sum, single terms have their potencies, this being part of the phenomenon of names, and we shall here present a few of the most noteworthy in our time, with some remarks upon their etiology.

[³] Naturally this survey will include the "bad" terms as well as the "good" terms, since we are interested to record historically those expressions to which the populace, in its actual usage and response, appears to attribute the greatest sanction. A prescriptive rhetoric may specify those terms which, in all seasons, ought to carry the greatest potency, but since the affections of one age are frequently a source of wonder to another, the most we can do under the caption "contemporary rhetoric" is to give a descriptive account and withhold the moral until the end. For despite the variations of fashion, an age which is not simply distraught manages to achieve some system of relationship among the attractive and among the repulsive terms, so that we can work out an order of weight and precedence in the prevailing rhetoric once we have discerned the "rhetorical absolutes"—the terms to which the very highest respect is paid.

[⁴] It is best to begin boldly by asking ourselves, what is the "god term" of the present age? By "god term" we mean that expression about which all other expressions are ranked as subordinate and serving dominations and powers. Its force imparts to the others their lesser degree of force, and fixes the scale by which degrees of comparison are understood. In the absence of a strong and evenly diffused religion, there may be several terms competing for this primacy, so that the question is not always capable of definite answer. Yet if one has to select the one term which in our day carries the greatest blessing, and—to apply a useful test—whose antonym carries the greatest rebuke, one will not go far wrong in naming "progress." This seems to be the ultimate generator of force flowing down through many links of ancillary terms. If one can "make it stick," it will validate almost anything. It would be difficult to think of any type of person or of any institution which could not be recommended to the public through the enhancing power of this word. A politician is urged upon the voters as a "progressive leader"; a community is proud to style itself "progressive"; technologies and methodologies claim to be "progressive"; a peculiar kind of emphasis in modern education calls itself "progressive," and so on without limit. There is no word whose power to move is more implicitly trusted than "progressive." But unlike some other words we shall examine in the course of this chapter, its rise to supreme position is not obscure, and it possesses some intelligible referents.

[5] Before going into the story of its elevation, we must prepare ground by noting that it is the nature of the conscious life of man to revolve around some concept of value. So true is this that when the concept is withdrawn, or when it is forced into competition with another concept, the human being suffers an almost intolerable sense of being lost. He has to know where he is in the ideological cosmos in order to coordinate his activities. Probably the greatest cruelty which can be inflicted upon the psychic man is this deprivation of a sense of tendency. Accordingly every age, including those of rudest cultivation, sets up some kind of sign post. In highly cultivated ages, with individuals of exceptional intellectual strength, this may take the form of a metaphysic. But with the ordinary man, even in such advanced ages, it is likely to be some idea abstracted from religion or historical speculation, and made to inhere in a few sensible and immediate examples.

[6] Since the sixteenth century we have tended to accept as inevitable an historical development that takes the form of a changing relationship between ourselves and nature, in which we pass increasingly into the role of master of nature. When I say that this seems inevitable to us, I mean that it seems something so close to what our more religious forebears considered the working of providence that we regard as impiety any disposition to challenge or even suspect it. By a transposition of terms, "progress" becomes the salvation man is placed on earth to work out; and just as there can be no achievement more important than salvation, so there can be no activity more justified in enlisting our sympathy and support than "progress." As our historical sketch would imply, the term began to be used in the sixteenth century in the sense of continuous development or improvement; it reached an apogee in the nineteenth century, amid noisy demonstrations of man's mastery of nature, and now in the twentieth century it keeps its place as one of the least assailable of the "uncontested terms," despite critical doubts in certain philosophic quarters. It is probably the only term which gives to the average American or West European of today a concept of something bigger than himself, which he is socially impelled to accept and even to sacrifice for. This capacity to demand sacrifice is probably the surest indicator of the "god term," for when a term is so sacrosanct that the material goods of this life must be mysteriously rendered up for it, then we feel justified in saying that it is in some sense ultimate. Today no one is startled to hear of a man's sacrificing health or wealth for the "progress" of the community, whereas such sacrifices for other ends may be regarded as self-indulgent or even trea-

sonable. And this is just because "progress" is the coordinator of all socially respectable effort.

[⁷] Perhaps these observations will help the speaker who would speak against the stream of "progress," or who, on the other hand, would parry some blow aimed at him through the potency of the word, to realize what a momentum he is opposing.

[⁸] Another word of great rhetorical force which owes its origin to the same historical transformation is "fact." Today's speaker says "It is a fact" with all the gravity and air of finality with which his less secular-minded ancestor would have said "It is the truth."[1] "These are facts"; "Facts tend to show"; and "He knows the facts" will be recognized as common locutions drawing upon the rhetorical resource of this word. The word "fact" went into the ascendent when our system of verification changed during the Renaissance. Prior to that time, the type of conclusion that men felt obligated to accept came either through divine revelation, or through dialectic, which obeys logical law. But these were displaced by the system of verification through correspondence with physical reality. Since then things have been true only when measurably true, when susceptible to some kind of quantification. Quite simply, "fact" came to be the touchstone after the truth of speculative inquiry had been replaced by the truth of empirical investigation. Today when the average citizen says "It is a fact" or says that he "knows the facts in the case," he means that he has the kind of knowledge to which all other knowledges must defer. Possibly it should be pointed out that his "facts" are frequently not facts at all in the etymological sense; often they will be deductions several steps removed from simply factual data. Yet the "facts" of his case carry with them this aura of scientific irrefragability, and he will likely regard any questioning of them as sophistry. In his vocabulary a fact is a fact, and all evidence so denominated has the prestige of science.

[⁹] These last remarks will remind us at once of the strongly rhetorical character of the word "science" itself. If there is good reason for placing "progress" rather than "science" at the top of our series, it is only that the former has more scope, "science" being the methodological tool of "progress." It seems clear, moreover, that "science" owes its present status to an hypostatization. The hypostatized term is one which treats as a substance or a concrete reality that which has only conceptual existence; and every reader will be able to supply numberless illustrations of how "science" is used without any specific referent. Any utterance beginning "Science says" provides one: "Science says there is no difference in brain capacity between the races"; "Science now knows the cause of encephalitis"; "Science says that smoking does not harm the throat." Science is

---

[1] It is surely worth observing that nowhere in the King James Version of the Bible does the word "fact" occur.

not, as here it would seem to be, a single concrete entity speaking with one authoritative voice. Behind these large abstractions (and this is not an argument against abstractions as such) there are many scientists holding many different theories and employing many different methods of investigation. The whole force of the word nevertheless depends upon a bland assumption that all scientists meet periodically in synod and there decide and publish what science believes. Yet anyone with the slightest scientific training knows that this is very far from a possibility. Let us consider therefore the changed quality of the utterance when it is amended to read "a majority of scientists say"; or "Many scientists believe"; or "Some scientific experiments have indicated." The change will not do. There has to be a creature called "science"; and its creation has as a matter of practice been easy, because modern man has been conditioned to believe that the powers and processes which have transformed his material world represent a very sure form of knowledge, and that there must be a way of identifying that knowledge. Obviously the rhetorical aggrandizement of "science" here parallels that of "fact," the one representing generally and the other specifically the whole subject matter of trustworthy perception.

[¹⁰] Furthermore, the term "science" like "progress" seems to satisfy a primal need. Man feels lost without a touchstone of knowledge just as he feels lost without the direction-finder provided by progress. It is curious to note that actually the word is only another name for knowledge (L. *scientia*), so that if we should go by strict etymology, we should insist that the expression "science knows" (*i.e.*, "knowledge knows") is pure tautology. But our rhetoric seems to get around this by implying that science is *the* knowledge. Other knowledges may contain elements of quackery, and may reflect the selfish aims of the knower; but "science," once we have given the word its incorporation, is the undiluted essence of knowledge. The word as it comes to us then is a little pathetic in its appeal, inasmuch as it reflects the deeply human feeling that somewhere somehow there must be people who know things "as they are." Once God or his ministry was the depository of such knowledge, but now, with the general decay of religious faith, it is the scientists who must speak *ex cathedra*, whether they wish to or not.

[¹¹] The term "modern" shares in the rhetorical forces of the others thus far discussed, and stands not far below the top. Its place in the general ordering is intelligible through the same history. Where progress is real, there is a natural presumption that the latest will be the best. Hence it is generally thought that to describe anything as "modern" is to credit it with all the improvements which have been made up to now. Then by a transference the term is applied to realms where valuation is, or ought to be, of a different source. In consequence, we have "modern living" urged upon us as an ideal; "the modern mind" is mentioned as something superior to previous minds; sometimes the modifier stands alone as an epithet of approval: "to become modern" or "to sound modern" are expressions that carry valuation. It is of course idle not to expect an age to feel that some of its ways and habits of mind are the best; but the extensive transformations of the past hundred years seem to have given "modern" a much more decisive meaning. It is as if a difference of degree had changed into a difference of kind. But the very fact that a word is not used very analytically may increase its rhetorical potency, as we shall see later in connection with a special group of terms.

[12] Another word definitely high up in the hierarchy we have outlined is "efficient." It seems to have acquired its force through a kind of no-nonsense connotation. If a thing is efficient, it is a good adaptation of means to ends, with small loss through friction. Thus as a word expressing a good understanding and management of cause and effect, it may have a fairly definite referent; but when it is lifted above this and made to serve as a term of general endorsement, we have to be on our guard against the stratagems of evil rhetoric. When we find, to cite a familiar example, the phrase "efficiency apartments" used to give an attractive aspect to inadequate dwellings, we may suspect the motive behind such juxtaposition. In many similar cases, "efficient," which is a term above reproach in engineering and physics, is made to hold our attention where ethical and aesthetic considerations are entitled to priority. Certain notorious forms of government and certain brutal forms of warfare are undeniably efficient; but here the featuring of efficiency unfairly narrows the question.

[13] Another term which might seem to have a different provenance but which participates in the impulse we have been studying is "American." One must first recognize the element of national egotism which makes this a word of approval with us, but there are reasons for saying that the force of "American" is much more broadly based than this. "This is the American way" or "It is the American thing to do" are expressions whose intent will not seem at all curious to the average American. Now the peculiar effect that is intended here comes from the circumstance that "American" and "progressive" have an area of synonymity. The Western World has long stood as a symbol for the future; and accordingly there has been a very wide tendency in this country, and also I believe among many people in Europe, to identify that which is American with that which is destined to be. And this is much the same as identifying it with the achievements of "progress." The typical American is quite fatuous in this regard: to him America is the goal toward which all creation moves; and he judges a country's civilization by its resemblance to the American model. The matter of changing nationalities brings out this point very well. For a citizen of a European country to become a citizen of the United States is considered natural and right, and I have known those so

transferring their nationality to be congratulated upon their good sense and their anticipated good fortune. On the contrary, when an American takes out British citizenship (French or German would be worse), this transference is felt to be a little scandalous. It is regarded as somehow perverse, or as going against the stream of things. Even some of our intellectuals grow uneasy over the action of Henry James and T. S. Eliot, and the masses cannot comprehend it at all. Their adoption of British citizenship is not mere defection from a country; it is treason to history. If Americans wish to become Europeans, what has happened to the hope of the world? is, I imagine, the question at the back of their minds. The tremendous spread of American fashions in behavior and entertainment must add something to the impetus, but I believe the original source to be this prior idea that America, typifying "progress," is what the remainder of the world is trying to be like.

[14] It follows naturally that in the popular consciousness of this country, "un-American" is the ultimate in negation. An anecdote will serve to illustrate this. Several years ago a leading cigarette manufacturer in this country had reason to believe that very damaging reports were being circulated about his product. The reports were such that had they not been stopped, the sale of this brand of cigarettes might have been reduced. The company thereupon inaugurated an extensive advertising campaign, the object of which was to halt these rumors in the most effective way possible. The concocters of the advertising copy evidently concluded after due deliberation that the strongest term of condemnation which could be conceived was "un-American," for this was the term employed in the campaign. Soon the newspapers were filled with advertising rebuking this "un-American" type of depreciation which had injured their sales. From examples such as this we may infer that "American" stands not only for what is forward in history, but also for what is ethically superior, or at least for a standard of fairness not matched by other nations.

[15] And as long as the popular mind carries this impression, it will be futile to protest against such titles as "The Committee on un-American Activities." While "American" and "un-American" continue to stand for these polar distinctions, the average citizen is not going to find much wrong with a group set up to investigate what is "un-American" and therefore reprehensible. At the same time, however, it would strike him as most droll if the British were to set up a "Committee on un-British Activities" or the French a "Committee on un-French Activities." The American, like other nationals, is not apt to be much better than he has been taught, and he has been taught systematically that his country is a special creation. That is why some of his ultimate terms seem to the general view provincial, and why he may be moved to polarities which represent only local poles.

[¹⁶] If we look within the area covered by "American," however, we find significant changes in the position of terms which are reflections of cultural and ideological changes. Among the once powerful but now waning terms are those expressive of the pioneer ideal of ruggedness and self-sufficiency. In the space of fifty years or less we have seen the phrase "two-fisted American" pass from the category of highly effective images to that of comic anachronisms. Generally, whoever talks the older language of strenuosity is regarded as a reactionary, it being assumed by social democrats that a socially organized world is one in which cooperation removes the necessity for struggle. Even the rhetorical trump cards of the 1920's, which Sinclair Lewis treated with such satire, are comparatively impotent today, as the new social consciousness causes terms of centrally planned living to move toward the head of the series.

[¹⁷] Other terms not necessarily connected with the American story have passed a zenith of influence and are in decline; of these perhaps the once effective "history" is the most interesting example. It is still to be met in such expressions as "History proves" and "History teaches"; yet one feels that it has lost the force it possessed in the previous century. Then it was easy for Byron—"the orator in poetry"—to write, "History with all her volumes vast has but one page"; or for the commemorative speaker to deduce profound lessons from history. But people today seem not to find history so eloquent. A likely explanation is that history, taken as whole, is conceptual rather than factual, and therefore a skepticism has developed as to what it teaches. Moreover, since the teachings of history are principally moral, ethical, or religious, they must encounter today that threshold resentment of anything which savors of the prescriptive. Since "history" is inseparable from judgment of historical fact, there has to be a considerable community of mind before history can be allowed to have a voice. Did the overthrow of Napoleon represent "progress" in history or the reverse? I should say that the most common rhetorical uses of "history" at the present are by intellectuals, whose personal philosophy can provide it with some kind of definition, and by journalists, who seem to use it unreflectively. For the contemporary masses it is substantially true that "history is bunk."

[¹⁸] An instructive example of how a coveted term can be monopolized may be seen in "allies." Three times within the memory of those still young, "allies" (often capitalized) has been used to distinguish those fighting on our side from the enemy. During the First World War it was a supreme term; during the Second World War it was again used with effect; and at the time of the present writing it is being used to designate that nondescript combination fighting in the name of the United Nations in Korea. The curious fact about the use of this term is that in each case the enemy also has been constituted of "allies." In the First World War Germany, Austria-Hungary, and Turkey were "allies"; in the Second,

Germany and Italy; and in the present conflict the North Koreans and the Chinese and perhaps the Russians are "allies." But in the rhetorical situation it is not possible to refer to them as "allies," since we reserve that term for the alliance representing our side. The reason for such restriction is that when men or nations are "allied," it is implied that they are united on some sound principle or for some good cause. Lying at the source of this feeling is the principle discussed by Plato, that friendship can exist only among the good, since good is an integrating force and evil a disintegrating one. We do not, for example, refer to a band of thieves as "the allies" because that term would impute laudable motives. By confining the term to our side we make an evaluation in our favor. We thus style ourselves the group joined for purposes of good. If we should allow it to be felt for a moment that the opposed combination is also made up of allies, we should concede that they are united by a principle, which in war is never done. So as the usage goes, we are always allies in war and the enemy is just the enemy, regardless of how many nations he has been able to confederate. Here is clearly another instance of how tendencies may exist in even the most innocent-seeming language.

[19] Now let us turn to the terms of repulsion. Some terms of repulsion are also ultimate in the sense of standing at the end of the series, and no survey of the vocabulary can ignore these prime repellants. The counterpart of the "god term" is the "devil term," and it has already been suggested that with us "un-American" comes nearest to filling that role. Sometimes, however, currents of politics and popular feeling cause something more specific to be placed in that position. There seems indeed to be some obscure psychic law which compels every nation to have in its national imagination an enemy. Perhaps this is but a version of the tribal need for a scapegoat, or for something which will personify "the adversary." If a nation did not have an enemy, an enemy would have to be invented to take care of those expressions of scorn and hatred to which people must give vent. When another political state is not available to receive the discharge of such emotions, then a class will be chosen, or a race, or a type, or a political faction, and this will be held up to a practically standardized form of repudiation. Perhaps the truth is that we need the enemy in order to define ourselves, but I will not here venture further into psychological complexities. In this type of study it will be enough to recall that during the first half century of our nation's existence, "Tory" was such a devil term. In the period following our Civil War, "rebel" took its place in the Northern section and "Yankee" in the Southern, although in the previous epoch both of these had been terms of esteem. Most readers will remember that during the First World War "pro-German" was a term of destructive force. During the Second World War "Nazi" and "Fascist" carried about equal power to condemn, and then, following the breach with Russia, "Communist" displaced them

both. Now "Communist" is beyond any rival the devil term, and as such it is employed even by the American president when he feels the need of a strong rhetorical point.

[20] A singular truth about these terms is that, unlike several which were examined in our favorable list, they defy any real analysis. That is to say, one cannot explain how they generate their peculiar force of repudiation. One only recognizes them as publicly-agreed-upon devil terms. It is the same with all. "Tory" persists in use, though it has long lost any connection with redcoats and British domination. Analysis of "rebel" and "Yankee" only turns up embarrassing contradictions of position. Similarly we have all seen "Nazi" and "Fascist" used without rational perception; and we see this now, in even greater degree, with "Communist." However one might like to reject such usage as mere ignorance, to do so would only evade a very important problem. Most likely these are instances of the "charismatic term," which will be discussed in detail presently.

[21] No student of contemporary usage can be unmindful of the curious reprobative force which has been acquired by the term "prejudice." Etymologically it signifies nothing more than a prejudgment, or a judgment before all the facts are in; and since all of us have to proceed to a great extent on judgments of that kind, the word should not be any more exciting than "hypothesis." But in its rhetorical applications "prejudice" presumes far beyond that. It is used, as a matter of fact, to characterize unfavorably any value judgment whatever. If "blue" is said to be a better color than "red," that is prejudice. If people of outstanding cultural achievement are praised through contrast with another people, that is prejudice. If one mode of life is presented as superior to another, that is prejudice. And behind all is the implication, if not the declaration, that it is un-American to be prejudiced.

[22] I suspect that what the users of this term are attempting, whether consciously or not, is to sneak "prejudiced" forward as an uncontested term, and in this way to disarm the opposition by making all positional judgments reprehensible. It must be observed in passing that no people are so prejudiced in the sense of being committed to valuations as those who are engaged in castigating others for prejudice. What they expect is that they can nullify the prejudices of those who oppose them, and then get their own installed in the guise of the *sensus communis*. Mark Twain's statement, "I know that I am prejudiced in this matter, but I would be ashamed of myself if I weren't" is a therapeutic insight into the process; but it will take more than a witticism to make headway against the repulsive force gathered behind "prejudice."

[23] If the rhetorical use of the term has any rational content, this probably comes through a chain of deductions from the nature of democracy; and we know that in controversies centered about the meaning of

democracy, the air is usually filled with cries of "prejudice." If democracy is taken crudely to mean equality, as it very frequently is, it is then a contradiction of democracy to assign inferiority and superiority on whatever grounds. But since the whole process of evaluation is a process of such assignment, the various inequalities which are left when it has done its work are contradictions of this root notion and hence are "prejudice"—the assumption of course being that when all the facts are in, these inequalities will be found illusory. The man who dislikes a certain class or race or style has merely not taken pains to learn that it is just as good as any other. If all inequality is deception, then superiorities must be accounted the products of immature judgment. This affords plausible ground, as we have suggested, for the coupling of "prejudice" and "ignorance."

[24] Before leaving the subject of the ordered series of good and bad terms, one feels obliged to say something about the way in which hierarchies can be inverted. Under the impulse of strong frustration there is a natural tendency to institute a pretense that the best is the worst and the worst is the best—an inversion sometimes encountered in literature and in social deportment. The best illustration for purpose of study here comes from a department of speech which I shall call "GI rhetoric." The average American youth, put into uniform, translated to a new and usually barren environment, and imbued from many sources with a mission of killing, has undergone a pretty severe dislocation. All of this runs counter to the benevolent platitudes on which he was brought up, and there is little ground for wonder if he adopts the inverted pose. This is made doubly likely by the facts that he is at a passionate age and that he is thrust into an atmosphere of superinduced excitement. It would be unnatural for him not to acquire a rhetoric of strong impulse and of contumacious tendency.

[25] What he does is to make an almost complete inversion. In this special world of his he recoils from those terms used by politicians and other civilians and by the "top brass" when they are enunciating public sentiments. Dropping the conventional terms of attraction, this uprooted and specially focussed young man puts in their place terms of repulsion. To be more specific, where the others use terms reflecting love, hope, and charity, he uses almost exclusively terms connected with excretory and reproductive functions. Such terms comprise what Kenneth Burke has ingeniously called "the imagery of killing." By an apparently universal psychological law, faeces and the act of defecation are linked with the idea of killing, of destruction, of total repudiation—perhaps the word "elimination" would comprise the whole body of notions. The reproductive act is associated especially with the idea of aggressive exploitation. Consequently when the GI feels that he must give his speech a proper show of spirit, he places the symbols for these things in places which

would normally be filled by prestige terms from the "regular" list. For specimens of such language presented in literature, the reader is referred to the fiction of Ernest Hemingway and Norman Mailer.

[26] Anyone who has been compelled to listen to such rhetoric will recall the monotony of the vocabulary and the vehemence of the delivery. From these two characteristics we may infer a great need and a narrow means of satisfaction, together with the tension which must result from maintaining so arduous an inversion. Whereas previously the aim had been to love (in the broad sense) it is now to kill; whereas it had been freedom and individuality, it is now restriction and brutalization. In taking revenge for a change which so contradicts his upbringing he is quite capable, as the evidence has already proved, of defiantly placing the lower level above the higher. Sometimes a clever GI will invent combinations and will effect metaphorical departures, but the ordinary ones are limited to a reiteration of the stock terms—to a reiteration, with emphasis of intonation, upon "the imagery of killing."[2] Taken as a whole, this rhetoric is a clear if limited example of how the machine may be put in reverse—of how, consequently, a sort of devil worship may get into language.

[27] A similar inversion of hierarchy is to be seen in the world of competitive sports, although to a lesser extent. The great majority of us in the Western world have been brought up under the influence, direct or indirect, of Christianity, which is a religion of extreme altruism. Its terms of value all derive from a law of self-effacement and of consideration for others, and these terms tend to appear whenever we try to rationalize or vindicate our conduct. But in the world of competitive sports, the direction is opposite: there one is applauded for egotistic display and for success at the expense of others—should one mention in particular American professional baseball? Thus the terms with which an athlete is commended will generally point away from the direction of Christian passivity, although when an athlete's character is described for the benefit of the general public, some way is usually found to place him in the other ethos, as by calling attention to his natural kindness, his interest in children, or his readiness to share his money .

[28] Certainly many of the contradictions of our conduct may be explained through the presence of these small inverted hierarchies. When, to cite one familiar example, the acquisitive, hard-driving local capitalist

[2] Compare Sherwood Anderson's analysis of the same phenomenon in *A Story Teller's Story* (New York, 1928), p. 198: "There was in the factories where I worked and where the efficient Ford type of man was just beginning his dull reign this strange and futile outpouring of men's lives in vileness through their lips. Ennui was at work. The talk of the men about me was not Rabelaisian. In old Rabelais there was the salt of infinite wit and I have no doubt that the Rabelaisian flashes that came from our own Lincoln, Washington, and others had point and a flare to them.
But in the factories and in army camps!"

is made the chief lay official of a Christian church, one knows that in a definite area there has been a transvaluation of values.

[29] Earlier in the chapter we referred to terms of considerable potency whose referents it is virtually impossible to discover or to construct through imagination. I shall approach this group by calling them "charismatic terms." It is the nature of the charismatic term to have a power which is not derived, but which is in some mysterious way given. By this I mean to say that we cannot explain their compulsiveness through referents of objectively known character and tendency. We normally "understand" a rhetorical term's appeal through its connection with something we apprehend, even when we object morally to the source of the impulse. Now "progress" is an understandable term in this sense, since it rests upon certain observable if not always commendable aspects of our world. Likewise the referential support of "fact" needs no demonstrating. These derive their force from a reading of palpable circumstance. But in charismatic terms we are confronted with a different creation: these terms seem to have broken loose somehow and to operate independently of referential connections (although in some instances an earlier history of referential connection may be made out). Their meaning seems inexplicable unless we accept the hypothesis that their content proceeds out of a popular will that they *shall* mean something. In effect, they are rhetorical by common consent, or by "charisma." As is the case with charismatic authority, where the populace gives the leader a power which can by no means be explained through his personal attributes, and permits him to use it effectively and even arrogantly, the charismatic term is given its load of impulsion without reference, and it functions by convention. The number of such terms is small in any one period, but they are perhaps the most efficacious terms of all.

[30] Such rhetorical sensibility as I have leads me to believe that one of the principal charismatic terms of our age is "freedom." The greatest sacrifices that contemporary man is called upon to make are demanded in the name of "freedom"; yet the referent which the average man attaches to this word is most obscure. Burke's dictum that "freedom inheres in something sensible" has not prevented its breaking loose from all anchorages. And the evident truth that the average man, given a choice between exemption from responsibility and responsibility, will choose the latter, makes no impression against its power. The fact, moreover, that the most extensive use of the term is made by modern politicians and statesmen in an effort to get men to assume more responsibility (in the form of military service, increased taxes, abridgement of rights, etc.) seems to carry no weight either.[3] The fact that what the American pioneer considered freedom has become wholly impossible to the modern

---

[3] One is inevitably reminded of the slogan of Oceania in Orwell's *Nineteen Eighty-four:* "Freedom is Slavery."

apartment-dwelling metropolitan seems not to have damaged its potency. Unless we accept some philosophical interpretation, such as the proposition that freedom consists only in the discharge of responsibility, there seems no possibility of a correlation between the use of the word and circumstantial reality. Yet "freedom" remains an ultimate term, for which people are asked to yield up their first-born.

[31] There is plenty of evidence that "democracy" is becoming the same kind of term. The variety of things it is used to symbolize is too weird and too contradictory for one to find even a core meaning in present-day usages. More important than this for us is the fact, noted by George Orwell, that people resist any attempt to define democracy, as if to connect it with a clear and fixed referent were to vitiate it. It may well be that such resistance to definition of democracy arises from a subconscious fear that a term defined in the usual manner has its charisma taken away. The situation then is that "democracy" means "be democratic," and that means exhibit a certain attitude which you can learn by imitating your fellows.

[32] If rationality is measured by correlations and by analyzable content, then these terms are irrational; and there is one further modern development in the creation of such terms which is strongly suggestive of irrational impulse. This is the increasing tendency to employ in the place of the term itself an abbreviated or telescoped form—which form is nearly always used with even more reckless assumption of authority. I seldom read the abbreviation "U S" in the newspapers without wincing at the complete arrogance of its rhetorical tone. Daily we see "U S Cracks Down on Communists"; "U S Gives OK to Atomic Weapons"; "U S Shocked by Death of Official." Who or what is this "U S"? It is clear that "U S" does not suggest a union of forty-eight states having republican forms of government and held together by a constitution of expressly delimited authority. It suggests rather an abstract force out of a new world of forces, whose will is law and whom the individual citizen has no way to placate. Consider the individual citizen confronted by "U S" or "FBI." As long as terms stand for identifiable organs of government, the citizen feels that he knows the world he moves around in, but when the forces of government are referred to by these bloodless abstractions, he cannot avoid feeling that they are one thing and he another. Let us note while dealing with this subject the enormous proliferation of such forms during the past twenty years or so. If "U S" is the most powerful and prepossessing of the group, it drags behind it in train the previously mentioned "FBI," and "NPA," "ERP," "FDIC," "WPA," "HOLC," and "OSS," to take a few at random. It is a fact of ominous significance that this use of foreshortened forms is preferred by totalitarians, both the professed and the disguised. Americans were hearing the terms "OGPU," "AMTORG" and "NEP" before their own government turned to large-

scale state planning. Since then we have spawned them ourselves, and, it is to be feared, out of similar impulse. George Orwell, one of the truest humanists of our age, has described the phenomenon thus: "Even in the early decades of the twentieth century, telescoped words and phrases had been one of the characteristic features of political language; and it had been noticed that the tendency to use abbreviations of this kind was most marked in totalitarian countries and totalitarian organizations. Examples were such words as Nazi, Gestapo, Comintern, Inprecor, Agitprop."[4]

[33] I venture to suggest that what this whole trend indicates is an attempt by the government, as distinguished from the people, to confer charismatic authority. In the earlier specimens of charismatic terms we were examining, we beheld something like the creation of a spontaneous general will. But these later ones of truncated form are handed down from above, and their potency is by fiat of whatever group is administering in the name of democracy. Actually the process is no more anomalous than the issuing of pamphlets to soldiers telling them whom they shall hate and whom they shall like (or try to like), but the whole business of switching impulse on and off from a central headquarters has very much the meaning of *Gleichschaltung* as that word has been interpreted for me by a native German. Yet it is a disturbing fact that such process should increase in times of peace, because the persistent use of such abbreviations can only mean a serious divorce between rhetorical impulse and rational thought. When the ultimate terms become a series of bare abstractions, the understanding of power is supplanted by a worship of power, and in our condition this can mean only state worship.

[34] It is easy to see, however, that a group determined upon control will have as one of its first objectives the appropriation of sources of charismatic authority. Probably the surest way to detect the fabricated charismatic term is to identify those terms ordinarily of limited power which are being moved up to the front line. That is to say, we may suspect the act of fabrication when terms of secondary or even tertiary rhetorical rank are pushed forward by unnatural pressure into ultimate positions. This process can nearly always be observed in times of crisis. During the last war, for example, "defense" and "war effort" were certainly regarded as culminative terms. We may say this because almost no one thinks of these terms as the natural sanctions of his mode of life. He may think thus of "progress" or "happiness" or even "freedom"; but "defense" and "war effort" are ultimate sanctions only when measured against an emergency situation. When the United States was preparing for entry into that conflict, every departure from our normal way of life could be justified as a "defense" measure. Plants making bombs to be dropped on other continents were called "defense" plants. Correspond-

---

[4] "Principles of Newspeak," *Nineteen Eighty-four* (New York, 1949), p. 310.

ingly, once the conflict had been entered, everything that was done in military or civilian areas was judged by its contribution to the "war effort." This last became for a period of years the supreme term: not God or Heaven or happiness, but successful effort in the war. It was a term to end all other terms or a rhetoric to silence all other rhetoric. No one was able to make his claim heard against "the war effort."

[³⁵] It is most important to realize, therefore, that under the stress of feeling or preoccupation, quite secondary terms can be moved up to the position of ultimate terms, where they will remain until reflection is allowed to resume sway. There are many signs to show that the term "aggressor" is now undergoing such manipulation. Despite the fact that almost no term is more difficult to correlate with objective phenomena, it is being rapidly promoted to ultimate "bad" term. The likelihood is that "aggressor" will soon become a depository for all the resentments and fears which naturally arise in a people. As such, it will function as did "infidel" in the mediaeval period and as "reactionary" has functioned in the recent past. Manifestly it is of great advantage to a nation bent upon organizing its power to be able to stigmatize some neighbor as "aggressor," so that the term's capacity for irrational assumption is a great temptation for those who are not moral in their use of rhetoric. This passage from natural or popular to state-engendered charisma produces one of the most dangerous lesions of modern society.

[³⁶] An ethics of rhetoric requires that ultimate terms be ultimate in some rational sense. The only way to achieve that objective is through an ordering of our own minds and our own passions. Every one of psychological sophistication knows that there is a pleasure in willed perversity, and the setting up of perverse shibboleths is a fairly common source of that pleasure. War cries, school slogans, coterie passwords, and all similar expressions are examples of such creation. There may be areas of play in which these are nothing more than a diversion; but there are other areas in which such expressions lure us down the roads of hatred and tragedy. That is the tendency of all words of false or "engineered" charisma. They often sound like the very gospel of one's society, but in fact they betray us; they get us to do what the adversary of the human being wants us to do. It is worth considering whether the real civil disobedience must not begin with our language.

[³⁷] Lastly, the student of rhetoric must realize that in the contemporary world he is confronted not only by evil practitioners, but also, and probably to an unprecedented degree, by men who are conditioned by the evil created by others. The machinery of propagation and inculcation is today so immense that no one avoids entirely the assimilation and use of some terms which have a downward tendency. It is especially easy to pick up a tone without realizing its trend. Perhaps the best that any of us can do is to hold a dialectic with himself to see what the wider circumferences of his terms of persuasion are. This process will not only improve the consistency of one's thinking but it will also, if the foregoing analysis is sound, prevent his becoming a creature of evil public forces and a victim of his own thoughtless rhetoric.

--◀{ COMMENT AND QUESTIONS }▶--

1. The opening paragraphs of Weaver's chapter are transitional and also technical; they nevertheless provide a preliminary survey of the chapter. State in your own words what Weaver says, in his first three paragraphs, that he proposes to do.

2. What is the meaning of the word *ultimate* in the title?

3. What is the meaning of the word *referent*, first used at the end of paragraph 4? In what sense does *progress*, unlike some of the other words to be examined, possess "some intelligible referents"? How does Weaver account for the power of this "god term" *progress*?

4. How does the author relate the force of the words *fact* and *science* to the rhetorical force of *progress*?

5. Explain what is meant, in paragraph 9, by an *hypostatized term*. What other examples can you give of hypostatized terms?

6. What are Weaver's attitudes toward the use of the words *modern* and *efficient*? To what does he attribute the potency of the word *American*? Do you agree or disagree with his ideas about these three words? Explain.

7. What are the main points Weaver is making about the word *prejudice*? Does he appear to be defending prejudice—for example, racial or religious prejudice? Explain.

8. Review the author's lists of "god terms" and "devil terms," and think about the force of these terms at the present time. Would you remove any of the terms or make changes in Weaver's ranking of them? Would you add any terms?

9. Look up in your dictionary the word *charismatic*. What is the original meaning of *charisma*? What are the qualities of charismatic terms as Weaver describes them? Do you agree that *freedom* and *democracy* belong in this category of words?

10. What does the author find disturbing about the increasing tendency to use abbreviated or telescoped forms? What point is he making with his examples in paragraphs 34 and 35?

11. Weaver has said early that he will give a descriptive account and withhold the moral until the end. What is the "moral"? Where does it begin?

12. Examine the last sentences of the final paragraph. What is the meaning of *terms which have a downward tendency*? Why is *dialectic* a better word than *dialogue*? In what ways is Weaver's last sentence an effective ending?

[49]   *Theodore C. Sorensen*: Kennedy's Speech-Writing

THEODORE C. SORENSEN (1928–   ) was a special assistant
to President Kennedy from 1953, when Kennedy was a Senator from
Massachusetts, until the President's death in 1963. The following excerpt
is from the chapter "The Senator" in Sorensen's book *Kennedy*,
published in 1965.

[¹] He would never blindly accept or blandly deliver a text he had not
seen and edited. We always discussed the topic, the approach and the
conclusions in advance. He always had quotations or historical allusions
to include. Sometimes he would review an outline. And he always,
upon receiving my draft, altered, deleted or added phrases, paragraphs
or pages. Some drafts he rejected entirely.

[²] As the years went on, and I came to know what he thought on each
subject as well as how he wished to say it, our style and standard
became increasingly one. When the volume of both his speaking and
my duties increased in the years before 1960, we tried repeatedly but
unsuccessfully to find other wordsmiths who could write for him in the
style to which he was accustomed. The style of those whom we tried
may have been very good. It may have been superior. But it was not his.

[³] The very fact that I was involved in his other activites and decisions, and constantly present to hear his public and private utterances,
made it increasingly easy for me to fulfill the speech-writing role—and
increasingly difficult to shed or even share it. "I know you wish you could
get out of writing so many speeches," he said to me one weary night
in an Indianapolis hotel room in 1959. "I wish I could get out of giving
so many, but that's the situation we're both in for the present."

[⁴] In that situation we turned out hundreds of speeches, some good,
some bad, some mediocre. The poorer speeches, in my view, occurred
for the most part in the early days when we were learning and in later
days when we were rushed. Invariably the more time he had to edit
and rewrite, the better the speech would be.

[⁵] The Kennedy style of speech-writing—our style, I am not reluctant
to say, for he never pretended that he had time to prepare first drafts
for all his speeches—evolved gradually over the years. Prepared texts

were carefully designed for an orderly presentation of their substance but with no deliberate affectation of any certain style. We were not conscious of following the elaborate techniques later ascribed to these speeches by literary analysts. Neither of us had any special training in composition, linguistics or semantics. Our chief criterion was always audience comprehension and comfort, and this meant: (1) short speeches, short clauses and short words, wherever possible; (2) a series of points or propositions in numbered or logical sequence, wherever appropriate; and (3) the construction of sentences, phrases and paragraphs in such a manner as to simplify, clarify and emphasize.

[6] The test of a text was not how it appeared to the eye but how it sounded to the ear. His best paragraphs, when read aloud, often had a cadence not unlike blank verse—indeed at times key words would rhyme. He was fond of alliterative sentences, not solely for reasons of rhetoric but to reinforce the audience's recollection of his reasoning. Sentences began, however incorrect some may have regarded it, with "And" or "But" whenever that simplified and shortened the text. His frequent use of dashes as a means of separating clauses was of doubtful grammatical standing—but it simplified the delivery and even the publication of a speech in a manner no comma, parenthesis or semicolon could match.

[7] Words were regarded as tools of precision, to be chosen and applied with a craftsman's care to whatever the situation required. He liked to be exact. But if the situation required a certain vagueness, he would deliberately choose a word of varying interpretations rather than bury his imprecision in ponderous prose.

[8] For he disliked verbosity and pomposity in his own remarks as much as he disliked them in others. He wanted both his message and his language to be plain and unpretentious, but never patronizing. He wanted his major policy statements to be positive, specific and definite, avoiding the use of "suggest," "perhaps" and "possible alternatives for consideration." At the same time, his emphasis on a course of reason—rejecting the extremes of either side—helped produce the parallel construction and use of contrasts with which he later became identified. He had a weakness for one unnecessary phrase: "The harsh facts of the matter are . . ."—but, with few other exceptions, his sentences were lean and crisp.

[9] No speech was more than twenty to thirty minutes in duration. They were all too short and too crowded with facts to permit any excess of generalities and sentimentalities. His texts wasted no words and his delivery wasted no time. Frequently he moved from one solid fact or argument to another, without the usual repetition and elaboration, far too quickly for his audiences to digest or even applaud his conclusions. Nor would he always pause for applause when it came.

[¹⁰] He spoke at first with no gestures, though he gradually developed a short jab to emphasize his points. Often his tone was monotonous. Often his emphasis was on the wrong word. But often when his audiences were large and enthusiastic—particularly indoors, if the hall was not too vast—an almost electric charge would transmit vitality back and forth between speaker and listeners.

[¹¹] He used little or no slang, dialect, legalistic terms, contractions, clichés, elaborate metaphors or ornate figures of speech. He refused to be folksy or to include any phrase or image he considered corny, tasteless or trite. He rarely used words he considered hackneyed: "humble," "dynamic," "glorious." He used none of the customary word fillers (e.g., "And I say to you that is a legitimate question and here is my answer"). And he did not hesitate to depart from strict rules of English usage when he thought adherence to them (e.g., "Our agenda *are* long") would grate on the listener's ear.

[¹²] The intellectual level of his speeches showed erudition but not arrogance. Though he knew a little French ("very little," he commented in 1957 after a somewhat halting telephone conversation with the King of Morocco on the North African situation), he was most reluctant to include any foreign words in his addresses.

[¹³] He was not reluctant, however, particularly in those pre-1960 days, to pack his speeches with statistics and quotations—frequently too many for audiences unaccustomed to his rapid-fire delivery. While I learned to keep a *Bartlett's* and similar works handy, the Senator was the chief source of his own best quotations. Some were in the black notebooks he had kept since college—some were in favorite reference books on his desk, such as Agar's *The Price of Union*—most were in his head.

[¹⁴] He would not always be certain of the exact wording or even the author of a quotation he wanted, but he could suggest enough for his staff or the Library of Congress to find it. Preparing his brief, effective statement against the isolationist Bricker Amendment to the Constitution, for example, he told me, "Someone—was it Falkland?—gave the classic definition of conservatism which went something like 'When it is not necessary to change, it is necessary not to change.' Let's include the exact quotation and author."

[¹⁵] He also liked on occasion—especially with college audiences which he enjoyed—to include humorous illustrations and quotations in the body of his speeches. An excerpt from a particularly abusive debate between earlier Senators and statesmen always delighted him, possibly because it contrasted so vividly with his own style of understatement.

[¹⁶] Humor in the *body* of a prepared speech, however, was rare compared to its use at the *beginning* of almost every speech he made off the Senate floor. While here, too, he preferred historical or political anecdotes, both the quality and the sources of this introductory material varied widely. He believed topical, tasteful, pertinent, pointed humor at the beginning of his remarks to be a major means of establishing audience rapport; and he would work with me as diligently for the right opening witticism, or take as much pride the next day in some spontaneous barb he had flung, as he would on the more substantive paragraphs in his text.

--◄{ C O M M E N T   A N D   Q U E S T I O N S }►--

1. Sorensen is mainly concerned in this selection with Kennedy's pre-1960 speeches, though much of what he says applies to later speeches as well. What are Sorensen's attitudes toward each of the following: (a) his own role in the speech-writing; (b) the efforts of other speech-writers; (c) the whole body of speeches that he and Kennedy produced together? Do you see in Sorensen's expression of attitudes any similarity to the kind of tone Kennedy wanted in his speeches?

2. Sorensen's attitude toward Kennedy is, of course, generally admiring. Do you find any stated or implied adverse criticism in this selection?

3. This excerpt is more of a series of comments than a tightly organized discussion of Kennedy's speeches. What are the connections between paragraphs 8 and 9, 9 and 10, 11 and 12, 12 and 13?

4. What does Sorensen mean, in paragraph 6, by saying that sentences began with *And* or *But* "whenever that simplified and shortened the text"? In what sense is the use of a dash between clauses a way of simplifying?

5. List the traits of style and the kinds of usage which, according to Sorensen, Kennedy chose to avoid.

6. What are Sorensen's comments on the following characteristics of Kennedy's speeches: (a) attention to sounds and rhythms; (b) precision in choice of words; (c) use of parallelism and contrast?

7. Examine Sorensen's writing and point out examples of the traits of what he calls "our style." Does it seem to you that this style is completely natural and unselfconscious in this excerpt or that Sorensen is working consciously to illustrate the style he is discussing? Explain.

8. The text of President Kennedy's Inaugural Address is included in another selection from Sorensen, page 482. Read the address and analyze its style in terms of Sorensen's comments here on Kennedy's speeches.

[50] *F. L. Lucas*: On the Fascination of Style

F. L. LUCAS (1894–   ) is a British critic, scholar, poet, and fellow and lecturer of King's College, Cambridge. Among his many books are *Authors Dead and Living, Literature and Psychology, Greek Drama for Everyman, Style, Tennyson, The Search for Good Sense,* and *The Drama of Ibsen and Strindberg.* The following essay was published in *Holiday* in March, 1960.

[¹] When it was suggested to Walt Whitman that one of his works should be bound in vellum, he was outraged—"Pshaw!" he snorted, "—hangings, curtains, finger bowls, chinaware, Matthew Arnold!" And he might have been equally irritated by talk of style; for he boasted of "my barbaric yawp"—he would *not* be literary; his readers should touch not a book but a man. Yet Whitman took the pains to rewrite *Leaves of Grass* four times, and his style is unmistakable. Samuel Butler maintained that writers who bothered about their style became unreadable but he bothered about his own. "Style" has got a bad name by growing associated with precious and superior persons who, like Oscar Wilde, spend a morning putting in a comma, and the afternoon (so he said) taking it out again. But such abuse of "style" is misuse of English. For the word means merely "a way of expressing oneself, in language, manner, or appearance"; or, secondly, "a *good* way of so expressing oneself"—as when one says, "Her behavior never lacked style."

[²] Now there is no crime in expressing oneself (though to try to *im*-press oneself on others easily grows revolting or ridiculous). Indeed one cannot help expressing oneself, unless one passes one's life in a cup-board. Even the most rigid Communist, or Organization-man, is com-pelled by Nature to have a unique voice, unique fingerprints, unique handwriting. Even the signatures of the letters on your breakfast table may reveal more than their writers guess. There are blustering signatures that swish across the page like cornstalks bowed before a tempest. There are cryptic signatures, like a scrabble of lightning across a cloud, sug-gesting that behind is a lofty divinity whom all must know, or an aloof divinity whom none is worthy to know (though, as this might be highly inconvenient, a docile typist sometimes interprets the mystery in a bracket underneath). There are impetuous squiggles implying that the author is a sort of strenuous Sputnik streaking round the globe every eighty minutes. There are florid signatures, all curlicues and danglements and flamboyance, like the youthful Disraeli (through these seem rather out of fashion). There are humble, humdrum signatures. And there are also, sometimes, signatures that are courteously clear, yet mindful of a certain simple grace and artistic economy—in short, of style.

[3] Since, then, not one of us can put pen to paper, or even open his mouth, without giving something of himself away to shrewd observers, it seems mere common sense to give the matter a little thought. Yet it does not seem very common. Ladies may take infinite pains about having style in their clothes, but many of us remain curiously indifferent about having it in our words. How many women would dream of polishing not only their nails but also their tongues? They may play freely on that perilous little organ, but they cannot often be bothered to tune it. And how many men think of improving their talk as well as their golf handicap?

[4] No doubt strong silent men, speaking only in gruff monosyllables, may despise "mere words." No doubt the world does suffer from an endemic plague of verbal dysentery. But that, precisely, is bad style. And consider the amazing power of mere words. Adolf Hitler was a bad artist, bad statesman, bad general, and bad man. But largely because he could tune his rant, with psychological nicety, to the exact wave length of his audiences and make millions quarrelsome-drunk all at the same time by his command of windy nonsense, skilled statesmen, soldiers, scientists were blown away like chaff, and he came near to rule the world. If Sir Winston Churchill had been a mere speechifier, we might well have lost the war; yet his speeches did quite a lot to win it.

[5] No man was less of a literary aesthete than Benjamin Franklin; yet this tallow-chandler's son, who changed world history, regarded as "a principal means of my advancement" that pungent style which he acquired partly by working in youth over old *Spectators;* but mainly by being Benjamin Franklin. The squinting demagogue, John Wilkes, as ugly as his many sins, had yet a tongue so winning that he asked only half an hour's start (to counteract his face) against any rival for a woman's favor. "Vote for you!" growled a surly elector in his constituency. "I'd sooner vote for the devil!" "But in case your friend should not stand . . . ?" Cleopatra, that ensnarer of world conquerors, owed less to the shape of her nose than to the charm of her tongue. Shakespeare himself has often poor plots and thin ideas; even his mastery of character has been questioned; what does remain unchallenged in his verbal magic. Men are often taken, like rabbits, by the ears. And though the tongue has no bones, it can sometimes break millions of them.

[6] "But," the reader may grumble, "I am neither Hitler, Cleopatra, nor Shakespeare. What is all this to me?" Yet we all talk—often too much; we all have to write letters—often too many. We live not by bread alone but also by words. And not always with remarkable efficiency. Strikes, lawsuits, divorces, all sorts of public nuisance and private misery, often

come just from the gaggling incompetence with which we express our-selves. Americans and British get at cross-purposes because they use the same words with different meanings. Men have been hanged on a comma in a statute. And in the valley of Balaclava a mere verbal ambiguity, about *which* guns were to be captured, sent the whole Light Brigade to futile annihilation.

[⁷] Words can be more powerful, and more treacherous, than we some-times suspect; communication more difficult than we may think. We are all serving life sentences of solitary confinement within our own bodies; like prisoners, we have, as it were, to tap in awkward code to our fellow men in their neighboring cells. Further, when A and B converse, there take part in their dialogue not two characters, as they suppose, but six. For there is A's real self—call it A_1; there is also A's picture of himself —A_2; there is also B's picture of A—A_3. And there are three correspond-ing personalities of B. With six characters involved even in a simple tête-à-tête, no wonder we fall into muddles and misunderstandings.

[⁸] Perhaps, then, there are five main reasons for trying to gain some mastery of language:

We have no other way of understanding, informing, misinforming, or persuading one another.

Even alone, we think mainly in words; if our language is muddy, so will our thinking be.

By our handling of words we are often revealed and judged. "Has he written anything?" said Napoleon of a candidate for an appoint-ment. "Let me see his *style*."

Without a feeling for language one remains half-blind and deaf to literature.

Our mother tongue is bettered or worsened by the way each generation uses it. Languages evolve like species. They can degenerate; just as oysters and barnacles have lost their heads. Compare ancient Greek with modern. A heavy responsibility, though often forgotten.

[⁹] Why and how did I become interested in style? The main answer, I suppose, is that I was born that way. Then I was, till ten, an only child running loose in a house packed with books, and in a world (thank goodness) still undistracted by radio and television. So at three I groaned to my mother, "Oh, I *wish* I could read," and at four I read. Now travel among books is the best travel of all, and the easiest, and the cheapest. (Not that I belittle ordinary travel—which I regard as one of the three main pleasures in life.) One learns to write by reading good books, as one learns to talk by hearing good talkers. And if I have learned anything of writing, it is largely from writers like Montaigne, Dorothy Osborne, Horace Walpole, Johnson, Goldsmith, Montesquieu, Voltaire, Flaubert and Anatole France. Again, I was reared on Greek and Latin, and one can learn much from translating Homer or the Greek Anthology, Horace or Tacitus, if one is thrilled by the originals and tries, however vainly, to recapture some of that thrill in English.

[10] But at Rugby I could *not* write English essays. I believe it stupid to torment boys to write on topics that they know and care nothing about. I used to rush to the school library and cram the subject, like a python swallowing rabbits; then, still replete as a postprandial python, I would tie myself in clumsy knots to embrace those accursed themes. Bacon was wise in saying that reading makes a full man; talking, a ready one; writing, an exact one. But writing from an empty head is futile anguish.

[11] At Cambridge, my head having grown a little fuller, I suddenly found I *could* write—not with enjoyment (it is always tearing oneself in pieces)—but fairly fluently. Then came the War of 1914–18; and though soldiers have other things than pens to handle, they learn painfully to be clear and brief. Then the late Sir Desmond MacCarthy invited me to review for the *New Statesman;* it was a useful apprenticeship, and he was delightful to work for. But I think it was well after a few years to stop; reviewers remain essential, but there are too many books one *cannot* praise, and only the pugnacious enjoy amassing enemies. By then I was an ink-addict—not because writing is much pleasure, but because not to write is pain; just as some smokers do not so much enjoy tobacco as suffer without it. The positive happiness of writing comes, I think, from work when done—decently, one hopes, and not without use—and from the letters of readers which help to reassure, or delude, one that so it is.

[12] But one of my most vivid lessons came, I think, from service in a war department during the Second War. Then, if the matter one sent out was too wordy, the communication channels might choke; yet if it was not absolutely clear, the results might be serious. So I emerged, after six years of it, with more passion than ever for clarity and brevity, more loathing than ever for the obscure and the verbose.

[13] For forty years at Cambridge I have tried to teach young men to write well, and have come to think it impossible. To write really well is a gift inborn; those who have it teach themselves; one can only try to help and hasten the process. After all, the uneducated sometimes express themselves far better than their "betters." In language, as in life, it is possible to be perfectly correct—and yet perfectly tedious, or odious. The illiterate last letter of the doomed Vanzetti was more moving than most professional orators; 18th Century ladies, who should have been spanked for their spelling, could yet write far better letters than most professors of English; and the talk of Synge's Irish peasants seems to me vastly more vivid than the later styles of Henry James. Yet Synge averred that his characters owed far less of their eloquence to what he invented for them than to what he had overheard in the cottages of Wicklow and Kerry:

CHRISTY. It's little you'll think if my love's a poacher's, or an earl's itself, when you'll feel my two hands stretched around you, and I squeezing kisses on your puckered lips, till I'd feel a kind of pity for the Lord God in all ages sitting lonesome in His golden chair.

PEGEEN. That'll be right fun, Christy Mahon, and any girl would walk her heart out before she'd meet a young man was your like for eloquence, or talk at all.

[14] Well she might! It's not like that they talk in universities—more's the pity.

[15] But though one cannot teach people to write well, one can some-times teach them to write rather better. One can give a certain number of hints, which often seem boringly obvious—only experience shows they are not.

[16] One can say: Beware of pronouns—they are devils. Look at even Addison, describing the type of pedant who chatters of style without having any:

Upon enquiry I found my learned friend had dined that day with Mr. Swan, the famous punster; and desiring *him* to give me some account of Mr. Swan's conversation, *he* told me that *he* generally talked in the Paronomasia, that *he* sometimes gave it to the Plocé, but that in *his* humble opinion *he* shone most in the Antanaclasis.

What a sluttish muddle of *he* and *him* and *his!* It all needs rewording. Far better repeat a noun, or a name, than puzzle the reader, even for a moment, with ambiguous pronouns. Thou shalt not puzzle thy reader.

[17] Or one can say: Avoid jingles. The B.B.C. news bulletins seem compiled by earless persons, capable of crying round the globe: "The enemy is re*port*ed to have seized this im*port*ant *port,* and reinforcements are hurrying up in sup*port.*" Any fool, once told, can hear such things to be insupportable.

[18] Or one can say: Be sparing with relative clauses. Don't string them together like sausages, or jam them inside one another like Chinese boxes or the receptacles of Buddha's tooth. Or one can say: Don't flaunt jargon, like Addison's Mr. Swan, or the type of modern critic who gurgles more technical terms in a page than Johnson used in all his *Lives* or Sainte-Beuve in thirty volumes. But dozens of such snippety precepts, though they may sometimes save people from writing badly, will help them little toward writing well. Are there no general rules of a more positive kind, and of more positive use?

[19] Perhaps. There *are* certain basic principles which seem to me observed by many authors I admire, which I think have served me and which may serve others. I am not talking of geniuses, who are a law to themselves (and do not always write a very good style, either); nor of poetry, which has different laws from prose; nor of poetic prose, like

Sir Thomas Browne's or De Quincey's, which is often more akin to poetry; but of the plain prose of ordinary books and documents, letters and talk.

[20] The writer should respect truth and himself; therefore honesty. He should respect his readers; therefore courtesy. These are two of the cornerstones of style. Confucius saw it, twenty-five centuries ago: "The Master said, The gentleman is courteous, but not pliable: common men are pliable, but not courteous."

[21] First, honesty. In literature, as in life, one of the fundamentals is to find, and be, one's true self. One's true self may indeed be unpleasant (though one can try to better it); but a false self, sooner or later, becomes disgusting—just as a nice plain woman, painted to the eyebrows, can become horrid. In writing, in the long run, pretense does not work. As the police put it, anything you say may be used as evidence against you. If handwriting reveals character, writing reveals it still more. You cannot fool *all* your judges *all* the time.

[22] Most style is not honest enough. Easy to say, but hard to practice. A writer may take to long words, as young men to beards—to impress. But long words, like beards, are often the badge of charlatans. Or a writer may cultivate the obscure, to seem profound. But even carefully muddied puddles are soon fathomed. Or he may cultivate eccentricity, to seem original. But really original people do not have to think about being original—they can no more help it than they can help breathing. They do not need to dye their hair green. The fame of Meredith, Wilde or Bernard Shaw might now shine brighter, had they struggled less to be brilliant; whereas Johnson remains great, not merely because his gifts were formidable but also because, with all his prejudice and passion, he fought no less passionately to "clear his mind of cant."

[23] Secondly, courtesy—respect for the reader. From this follow several other basic principles of style. Clarity is one. For it is boorish to make your reader rack his brains to understand. One should aim at being impossible to misunderstand—though men's capacity for misunderstanding approaches infinity. Hence Molière and Po Chu-i tried their work on their cooks; and Swift his on his men-servants—"which, if they did not comprehend, he would alter and amend, until they understood it perfectly." Our bureaucrats and pundits, unfortunately, are less considerate.

[24] Brevity is another basic principle. For it is boorish, also, to waste your reader's time. People who would not dream of stealing a penny of one's money turn not a hair at stealing hours of one's life. But that does not make them less exasperating. Therefore there is no excuse for the sort of writer who takes as long as a marching army corps to pass a given point. Besides, brevity is often more effective; the half can say more than the whole, and to imply things may strike far deeper than to state them

at length. And because one is particularly apt to waste words on preambles before coming to the substance, there was sense in the Scots professor who always asked his pupils—"Did ye remember to tear up that fir-r-st page?"

[25] Here are some instances that would only lose by lengthening.

It is useless to go to bed to save the light, if the result is twins. (Chinese proverb.)

My barn is burnt down—

Nothing hides the moon. (Complete Japanese poem.)

Je me regrette. (Dying words of the gay Vicomtesse d'Houdetot.)

I have seen their backs before. (Wellington, when French marshals turned their backs on him at a reception.)

Continue until the tanks stop, then get out and walk. (Patton to the Twelfth Corps, halted for fuel supplies at St. Dizier, 8/30/44.)

[26] Or there is the most laconic diplomatic note on record: when Philip of Macedon wrote to the Spartans that, if he came within their borders, he would leave not one stone of their city, they wrote back the one word—"If."

[27] Clarity comes before even brevity. But it is a fallacy that wordiness is necessarily clearer. Metternich when he thought something he had written was obscure would simply go through it crossing out everything irrelevant. What remained, he found, often became clear. Wellington, asked to recommend three names for the post of Commander-in-Chief, India, took a piece of paper and wrote three times—"Napier." Pages could not have been clearer—or as forcible. On the other hand the lectures, and the sentences, of Coleridge became at times bewildering because his mind was often "wiggle-waggle"; just as he could not even walk straight on a path.

[28] But clarity and brevity, though a good beginning, are only a beginning. By themselves, they may remain bare and bleak. When Calvin Coolidge, asked by his wife what the preacher had preached on, replied "Sin," and, asked what the preacher had said, replied, "He was against it," he was brief enough. But one hardly envies Mrs. Coolidge.

[29] An attractive style requires, of course, all kinds of further gifts—such as variety, good humor, good sense, vitality, imagination. Variety means avoiding monotony of rhythm, of language, of mood. One needs to vary one's sentence length (this present article has too many short sentences; but so vast a subject grows here as cramped as a djin in a bottle); to amplify one's vocabulary; to diversify one's tone. There are books that petrify one throughout, with the rigidly pompous solemnity of an owl perched on a leafless tree. But ceaseless facetiousness can be as

bad; or perpetual irony. Even the smile of Voltaire can seem at times a fixed grin, a disagreeable wrinkle. Constant peevishness is far worse, as often in Swift; even on the stage too much irritable dialogue may irritate an audience, without its knowing why.

[30] Still more are vitality, energy, imagination gifts that must be inborn before they can be cultivated. But under the head of imagination two common devices may be mentioned that have been the making of many a style—metaphor and simile. Why such magic power should reside in simply saying, or implying, that A is like B remains a little mysterious. But even our unconscious seems to love symbols; again, language often tends to lose itself in clouds of vaporous abstraction, and simile or metaphor can bring it back to concrete solidity; and, again, such imagery can gild the gray flats of prose with sudden sun-glints of poetry.

[31] If a foreigner may for a moment be impertinent, I admire the native gift of Americans for imagery as much as I wince at their fondness for slang. (Slang seems to me a kind of linguistic fungus; as poisonous, and as shortlived, as toadstools.) When Matthew Arnold lectured in the United States, he was likened by one newspaper to "an elderly macaw pecking at a trellis of grapes"; he observed, very justly, "How lively journalistic fancy is among the Americans!" General Grant, again, unable to hear him, remarked: "Well, wife, we've paid to see the British lion, but as we can't hear him roar, we'd better go home." By simile and metaphor, these two quotations bring before us the slightly pompous, fastidious, inaudible Arnold as no direct description could have done.

[32] Or consider how language comes alive in the Chinese saying that lending to the feckless is "like pelting a stray dog with dumplings," or in the Arab proverb: "They came to shoe the pasha's horse, and the beetle stretched forth his leg"; in the Greek phrase for a perilous cape—"stepmother of ships"; or the Hebrew adage that "as the climbing up a sandy way is to the feet of the aged, so is a wife full of words to a quiet man"; in Shakespeare's phrase for a little England lost in the world's vastness— "in a great Poole, a Swan's nest"; or Fuller's libel on tall men—"Ofttimes such who are built four stories high are observed to have little in their cockloft"; in Chateaubriand's "I go yawning my life"; or in Jules Renard's portrait of a cat, "well buttoned in her fur." Or, to take a modern instance, there is Churchill on dealing with Russia:

Trying to maintain good relations with a Communist is like wooing a crocodile. You do not know whether to tickle it under the chin or beat it over the head. When it opens its mouth, you cannot tell whether it is trying to smile or preparing to eat you up.

What a miracle human speech can be, and how dull is most that one hears! Would one hold one's hearers, it is far less help, I suspect, to read manuals on style than to cultivate one's own imagination and imagery.

[33] I will end with two remarks by two wise old women of the civilized 18th Century.

[34] The first is from the blind Mme. du Deffand (the friend of Horace Walpole) to that Mlle. de Lespinasse with whom, alas, she was to quarrel so unwisely: "You must make up your mind, my queen, to live with me in the greatest truth and sincerity. You will be charming so long as you let yourself be natural, and remain without pretension and without artifice." The second is from Mme. de Charrière, the Zélide whom Boswell had once loved at Utrecht in vain, to a Swiss girl friend: "Lucinde, my clever Lucinde, while you wait for the Romeos to arrive, you have nothing better to do than become perfect. Have ideas that are clear, and expressions that are simple." (*"Ayez des idées nettes et des expressions simples."*) More than half the bad writing in the world, I believe, comes from neglecting those two very simple pieces of advice.

[35] In many ways, no doubt, our world grows more and more complex; sputniks cannot be simple; yet how many of our complexities remain futile, how many of our artificialities false. Simplicity too can be subtle—as the straight lines of a Greek temple, like the Parthenon at Athens, are delicately curved, in order to look straighter still.

COMMENT AND QUESTIONS

1. What are the purposes of Lucas' first seven paragraphs? The author later recommends brevity and speaks of not wasting words on preambles before coming to the substance. Do you think that the first seven paragraphs might have been briefer? Explain.

2. What point is Lucas making, in paragraph 7, with his analysis of the six characters involved in a dialogue? Does the analysis seem to you accurate?

3. Which of the five main reasons for gaining some mastery of language has the author discussed in the paragraphs preceding paragraph 8? Which of the five reasons seem most important to you, and why?

4. What, in your judgment, were Lucas' reasons for including the biographical information in paragraphs 9–14?

5. Paragraph 18 begins with the precept "Be sparing with relative clauses." Examine the relative clauses in paragraph 19. Could any of them be eliminated without loss?

6. What is the meaning of *pliable* in paragraph 20, and how is the word related to the topic idea of the paragraph?

7. In the discussion of honesty and courtesy, what particular kinds of dishonesty and discourtesy is the author criticizing? Why does he devote more space to courtesy than to honesty?

8. What relationships does Lucas see between brevity and clarity?

9. According to the author, what are the values of metaphor and simile? Examine Lucas' figurative language, especially in paragraphs 2, 5, 7, 18, 21, 22, 29, 30, and 35. Which figures seem to you effective, and why?

10. In what ways are the quotations in paragraph 34 well chosen to conclude the essay?

11. One of the noticeable qualities of Lucas' writing is his use, not only of figurative language, but also of quotation and of concrete example and detail. Comment on this use of quotation and illustrative detail. Is there more of it than the author needs or the reader wants? Is Lucas sacrificing brevity to clarity? Or, do you find his use of supporting detail skillful and interesting? Explain.

12. What seem to you the most significant things that Lucas communicates, directly and indirectly, to the young writer interested in improving his style?

LITERATURE
AND THE ARTS

❦

[51] *I. A. Richards*: Science and Poetry

I. A. RICHARDS (1893–   ) was born and educated in England, was a professor of English at Harvard from 1944 to 1963, and is one of the influential educators and literary critics of the twentieth century. Among his well-known books are *The Meaning of Meaning* (written with C. K. Ogden), *The Principles of Literary Criticism, Practical Criticism, Coleridge on Imagination, How to Read a Page, Basic English and Its Uses*, and *Science and Poetry*, from which the following essay is a selection.

> *The future of poetry is immense, because in poetry, where it is worthy of its high destinies, our race, as time goes on, will find an ever surer and surer stay. There is not a creed which is not shaken, not an accredited dogma which is not shown to be questionable, not a received tradition which does not threaten to dissolve. Our religion has materialised itself in the fact, in the supposed fact; it has attached its emotion to the fact, and now the fact is failing it. But for poetry the idea is everything.*
>
> MATTHEW ARNOLD

CHAPTER I: THE GENERAL SITUATION

[1] Man's prospects are not at present so rosy that he can neglect any means of improving them. He has recently made a number of changes in

his customs and ways of life, partly with intention, partly by accident. These changes are involving such widespread further changes that the fairly near future is likely to see an almost complete reorganization of our lives, in their intimate aspects as much as in their public. Man himself is changing, together with his circumstances; he has changed in the past, it is true, but never perhaps so swiftly. His circumstances are not known ever to have changed so much or so suddenly before, with psychological as well as with economic, social and political dangers. This suddenness threatens us. Some parts of human nature resist change more than others. We risk disaster if some of our customs change while others which should change with them stay as they are.

[²] Habits that have endured for many thousands of years are not easy to throw off—least of all when they are habits of thought, and when they do not come into open conflict with changing circumstances, or do not clearly involve us in loss or inconvenience. Yet the loss may be great without our knowing anything about it. Before 1590 no one knew how inconvenient were our natural habits of thought about the ways in which a stone may fall; yet the modern world began when Galileo discovered what really happens. Before 1800 only persons thought to be crazy knew that ordinary traditional ideas as to cleanliness are dangerously inadequate. The infant's average 'expectation of life' has increased by about 30 years since Lister upset them. Nobody before Sir Ronald Ross knew what were the consequences of thinking about malaria in terms of influences and miasmas instead of in terms of mosquitoes. The Roman Empire might perhaps have still been flourishing if some one had found this out before A.D. 100.

[³] With such examples all about us we can no longer, in any department of life, so easily accept what was good enough for our fathers as good enough for ourselves or for our children. We are forced to wonder whether our ideas, even upon subjects apparently of little practical importance, such as poetry, may not be dangerously inadequate. It becomes indeed somewhat alarming to recognize, as we must, that our habits of thought remain, as regards most of our affairs, much as they were 5,000 years ago. The Sciences are, of course, simply the exceptions to this rule. Outside the Sciences—and the greater part of our thinking still goes on outside the Sciences—we think very much as our ancestors thought a hundred or two hundred generations ago. Certainly this is so as regards official views about poetry. Is it not possible that these are wrong, as wrong as most ideas of an equally hoary antiquity? Is it not possible that to the men of the future our life to-day will seem a continual, ceaseless disaster due only to our own stupidity, to the nervelessness with which we accept and transmit ideas which do not apply and never have applied to anything?

[⁴] *The average educated man is growing more conscious,* an extraordinarily significant change. It is probably due to the fact that his life is becoming more complex, more intricate, his desires and needs more varied and more apt to conflict. And as he becomes more conscious he can no longer be content to drift in unreflecting obedience to custom. He is forced to reflect. And if reflection often takes the form of inconclusive worrying, that is no more than might be expected in view of the unparalleled difficulty of the task. To live reasonably is much more difficult today than it was in Dr. Johnson's time, and even then, as Boswell shows, it was difficult enough.

[5] To live reasonably is not to live by reason alone—the mistake is easy, and, if carried far, disastrous—but to live in a way of which reason, a clear full sense of the whole situation, would approve. And the most important part of the whole situation, as always, is ourselves, our own psychological make-up. The more we learn about the physical world, about our bodies, for example, the more points we find at which our ordinary behaviour is out of accord with the facts, inapplicable, wasteful, disadvantageous, dangerous or absurd. Witness our habit of boiling our vegetables. We have still to learn how to feed ourselves satisfactorily. Similarly, the little that is yet known about the mind already shows that our ways of thinking and feeling about very many of the things with which we concern ourselves are out of accord with the facts. This is pre-eminently true of our ways of thinking and feeling about poetry. We think and talk in terms of states of affairs which have never existed. We attribute to ourselves and to things, powers which neither we nor they possess. And equally we overlook or misuse powers which are all-important to us.

[6] Day by day, in recent years, man is getting more out of place in Nature. Where he is going to he does not yet know, he has not yet decided. As a consequence he finds life more and more bewildering, more and more difficult to live coherently. Thus he turns to consider himself, his own nature. For the first step towards a reasonable way of life is a better understanding of human nature.

[7] It has long been recognized that if only something could be done in psychology remotely comparable to what has been achieved in physics, practical consequences might be expected even more remarkable than any that the engineer can contrive. The first positive steps in the science of the mind have been slow in coming, but already they are beginning to change man's whole outlook.

CHAPTER II: THE POETIC EXPERIENCE

[8] Extraordinary claims have often been made for poetry—Matthew Arnold's words quoted at the head of this essay are an example—claims which very many people are inclined to view with astonishment or with the smile which tolerance gives to the enthusiast. Indeed a more repre-

sentative modern view would be that the future of poetry is *nil*. Peacock's conclusion in his *The Four Ages of Poetry* finds a more general acceptance. "A poet in our times is a semi-barbarian in a civilized community. He lives in the days that are past. . . . In whatever degree poetry is cultivated, it must necessarily be to the neglect of some branch of useful study: and it is a lamentable thing to see minds, capable of better things, running to seed in the specious indolence of these empty aimless mockeries of intellectual exertion. Poetry was the mental rattle that awakened the attention of intellect in the infancy of civil society: but for the maturity of mind to make a serious business of the playthings of its childhood, is as absurd as for a grown man to rub his gums with coral, and cry to be charmed asleep by the jingle of silver bells." And with more regret many others—Keats was among them—have thought that the inevitable effect of the advance of science would be to destroy the possibility of poetry.

[9] What is the truth in this matter? How is our estimate of poetry going to be affected by science? And how will poetry itself be influenced? The extreme importance which has in the past been assigned to poetry is a fact which must be accounted for whether we conclude that it was rightly assigned or not, and whether we consider that poetry will continue to be held in such esteem or not. It indicates that the case for poetry, whether right or wrong, is one which turns on momentous issues. We shall not have dealt adequately with it unless we have raised questions of great significance.

[10] Very much toil has gone to the endeavour to explain the high place of poetry in human affairs, with, on the whole, few satisfactory or convincing results. This is not surprising. For in order to show how poetry is important it is first necessary to discover to some extent what it is. Until recently this preliminary task could only be very incompletely carried out; the psychology of instinct and emotion was too little advanced; and, moreover, the wild speculations natural in pre-scientific enquiry definitely stood in the way. Neither the professional psychologist, whose interest in poetry is frequently not intense, nor the man of letters, who as a rule has no adequate ideas of the mind as a whole, has been equipped for the investigation. Both a passionate knowledge of poetry and a capacity for dispassionate psychological analysis are required if it is to be satisfactorily prosecuted.

[11] It will be best to begin by asking 'What *kind of a thing*, in the widest sense, is poetry?' When we have answered this we shall be ready to ask 'How can we use and misuse it?' and 'What reasons are there for thinking it valuable?'

[12] Let us take an experience, ten minutes of a person's life, and describe it in broad outline. It is now possible to indicate its general structure, to point out what is important in it, what trivial and accessory, which

features depend upon which, how it has arisen, and how it is probably going to influence his future experience. There are, of course, wide gaps in this description, none the less it *is* at last possible to understand in general how the mind works in an experience, and what sort of stream of events the experience is.

[13] A poem, let us say Wordsworth's *Westminster Bridge* sonnet, is such an experience, it is the experience the right kind of reader has when he peruses the verses. And the first step to an understanding of the place and future of poetry in human affairs is to see what the general structure of such an experience is. Let us begin by reading it very slowly, preferably aloud, giving every syllable time to make its full effect upon us. And let us read it experimentally, repeating it, varying our tone of voice until we are satisfied that we have caught its rhythm as well as we are able, and—whether our reading is such as to please other people or not— we ourselves at least are certain how it should 'go.'

> Earth has not anything to show more fair:
> Dull would he be of soul who could pass by
> A sight so touching in its majesty:
> This City now doth like a garment wear
> The beauty of the morning: silent, bare,
> Ships, towers, domes, theatres and temples lie
> Open to the fields, and to the sky;
> All bright and glittering in the smokeless air.
> Never did sun more beautifully steep
> In his first splendour valley, rock or hill;
> Ne'er saw I, never felt, a calm so deep!
> The river glideth at its own sweet will:
> Dear God! the very houses seem asleep
> And all that mighty heart is lying still!

[14] We may best make our analysis of the experience that arises through reading these lines from the surface inwards, to speak metaphorically. The surface is the impression of the printed words on the retina. This sets up an agitation which we must follow as it goes deeper and deeper.

[15] The first things to occur (if they do not, the rest of the experience will be gravely inadequate) are the sound of the words 'in the mind's ear' and the feel of the words imaginarily spoken. These together give the *full body*, as it were, to the words, and it is with the full bodies of words that the poet works, not with their printed signs. But many people lose nearly everything in poetry through these indispensable parts escaping them.

[16] Next arise various pictures 'in the mind's eye'; not of words but of things for which the words stand; perhaps of ships, perhaps of hills; and together with them, it may be, other images of various sorts. Images

of what it feels like to stand leaning on the parapet of Westminster Bridge. Perhaps that odd thing an image of 'silence.' But, unlike the image-bodies of the words themselves, those other images of things are not vitally important. Those who have them may very well think them indispensable, and *for them* they may be necessary; but other people may not require them at all. This is a point at which differences between individual minds are very marked.

[17] Thence onwards the agitation which is the experience divides into a major and a minor branch, though the two streams have innumerable interconnections and influence one another intimately. Indeed it is only as an expositor's artifice that we may speak of them as two streams.

[18] The minor branch we may call the intellectual stream; the other, which we may call the active, or emotional, stream, is made up of the play of our interests.

[19] The intellectual stream is fairly easy to follow; it follows itself, so to speak; but it is the less important of the two. In poetry it matters only *as a means;* it directs and excites the active stream. It is made up of thoughts, which are not static little entities that bob up into consciousness and down again out of it, but fluent happenings, events, which reflect or point to the things the thoughts are of. Exactly how they do this is a matter which is still much disputed.

[20] This pointing to or reflecting things is all that thoughts do. They appear to do much more; which is our chief illusion. The realm of thought is never a sovereign state. Our thoughts are the servants of our interests, and even when they seem to rebel it is usually our interests that are in disorder. Our thoughts are pointers and it is the other, the active, stream which deals with the things which thoughts reflect or point to.

[21] Some people who read verse (they do not often read much of it) are so constituted that very little more happens than this intellectual stream of thoughts. It is perhaps superfluous to point out that they miss the real poem. To exaggerate this part of the experience, and give it too much importance on its own account, is a notable current tendency, and for many people explains why they do not read poetry.

[22] The active branch is what really matters; for from it all the energy of the whole agitation comes. The thinking which goes on is somewhat like the play of an ingenious and invaluable 'governor' run by, but controlling, the main machine. Every experience is essentially some interest or group of interests swinging back to rest.

[23] To understand what an interest is we should picture the mind as a system of very delicately poised balances, a system which so long as we are in health is constantly growing. Every situation we come into disturbs some of these balances to some degree. The ways in which they swing back to a new equipoise are the impulses with which we respond to the situation. And the chief balances in the system are our chief interests.

[24] Suppose that we carry a magnetic compass about in the neighbourhood of powerful magnets. The needle waggles as we move and comes to rest pointing in a new direction whenever we stand still in a new position. Suppose that instead of a single compass we carry an arrangement of many magnetic needles, large and small, swung so that they influence one another, some able only to swing horizontally, others vertically, others hung freely. As we move, the perturbations in this system will be very complicated. But for every position in which we place it there will be a final position of rest for all the needles into which they will in the end settle down, a general poise for the whole system. But even a slight displacement may set the whole assemblage of needles busily readjusting themselves.

[25] One further complication. Suppose that while all the needles influence one another, some of them respond only to some of the outer magnets among which the system is moving. The reader can easily draw a diagram if his imagination needs a visual support.

[26] The mind is not unlike such a system if we imagine it to be incredibly complex. The needles are our interests, varying in their importance, that is in the degree to which any movement they make involves movement in the other needles. Each new disequilibrium, which a shift of position, a fresh situation, entails, corresponds to a need; and the wagglings which ensue as the system rearranges itself are our responses, the impulses through which we seek to meet the need. Often the new poise is not found until long after the original disturbance. Thus states of strain can arise which last for years.

[27] The child comes into the world as a comparatively simple arrangement. Few things affect him comparatively speaking, and his responses also are few and simple, but he very quickly becomes more complicated. His recurrent needs for food and for various attentions are constantly setting all his needles swinging. Little by little separate needs become departmentalized as it were, sub-systems are formed; hunger causes one set of responses, the sight of his toys another, loud noises yet another, and so on. But the sub-systems never become quite independent. So he grows up, becoming susceptible to ever more numerous and more delicate influences.

[28] He grows more discriminating in some respects, he is thrown out of equilibrium by slighter differences in his situation. In other respects he becomes more stable. From time to time, through growth, fresh interests develop; sex is the outstanding example. His needs increase, he becomes capable of being upset by quite new causes, he becomes responsive to quite new aspects of the situation.

[29] This development takes a very indirect course. It would be still more erratic if society did not mould and remould him at every stage, reorganising him completely two or three times over before he grows up.

He reaches maturity in the form of a vast assemblage of major and minor interests, partly a chaos, partly a system, with some tracts of his personality fully developed and free to respond, others tangled and jammed in all kinds of accidental ways. It is this incredibly complex assemblage of interests to which the printed poem has to appeal. Sometimes the poem is itself the influence which disturbs us, sometimes it is merely the means by which an already existing disturbance can right itself. More usually perhaps it is both at once.

[³⁰] We must picture then the stream of the poetic experience as the swinging back into equilibrium of these disturbed interests. We are reading the poem in the first place only because we are in some way interested in doing so, only because some interest is attempting to regain its poise thereby. And whatever happens as we read happens only for a similar reason. We understand the words (the intellectual branch of the stream goes on its way successfully) only because an interest is reacting through that means, and all the rest of the experience is equally but more evidently our adaptation working itself out.

[³¹] The rest of the experience is made up of emotions and attitudes. Emotions are what the reaction, with its reverberations in bodily changes, feels like. Attitudes are the impulses towards one kind of behaviour or another which are set ready by the response. They are, as it were, its outward going part. Sometimes, as here in *Westminster Bridge,* they are very easily overlooked. But consider a simpler case—a fit of laughter which it is absolutely essential to conceal, in Church or during a solemn interview, for example. You contrive not to laugh; but there is no doubt about the activity of the impulses in their restricted form. The much more subtle and elaborate impulses which a poem excites are not different in principle. They do not show themselves as a rule, they do not come out into the open, largely because they are so complex. When they have adjusted themselves to one another and become organized into a coherent whole, the needs concerned may be satisfied. *In a fully developed man a state of readiness for action will take the place of action when the full appropriate situation for action is not present.* The essential peculiarity of poetry as of all the arts is that the full appropriate situation is *not* present. It is an *actor* we are seeing upon the stage, not Hamlet. So readiness for action takes the place of actual behaviour.

[³²] This is the main plan then of the experience. Signs on the retina, taken up by sets of needs (remember how many other impressions all day long remain entirely *unnoticed* because no interest responds to them); thence an elaborate agitation of impulses, one branch of which is *thoughts* of what the words mean, the other an emotional response leading to the development of *attitudes,* preparations, that is, for action which may or may not take place; the two branches being in intimate connection.

[³³] We must look now a little more closely at these connections. It may seem odd that we do not more definitely make the thoughts the rulers and causes of the rest of the response. To do just this has been in fact the grand error of traditional psychology. Man prefers to stress the features which distinguish him from monkey, and chief among these are his intellectual capacities. Important though they are, he has given them a rank to which they are not entitled. Intellect is an adjunct to the interests, a means by which they adjust themselves more successfully. Man is not in any sense primarily an intelligence; he is a system of interests. Intelligence helps man but does not run him.

[³⁴] Partly through this natural mistake, and partly because intellectual operations are so much easier to study, the whole traditional analysis of the working of the mind has been turned upside down. It is largely as a remedy from the difficulties which this mistake involves that poetry may have so much importance in the future. But let us look again more closely at the poetic experience.

[³⁵] In the first place, why is it essential in reading poetry to give the words their full imagined sound and body? What is meant by saying that the poet works with this sound and body? The answer is that even before the words have been intellectually understood and the thoughts they occasion formed and followed, the movement and sound of the words is playing deeply and intimately upon the interests. How this happens is a matter which has yet to be successfully investigated, but that it happens no sensitive reader of poetry doubts. A good deal of poetry and even some great poetry exists (*e.g.*, some of Shakespeare's Songs and, in a different way, much of the best of Swinburne) in which the sense of the words can be *almost* entirely missed or neglected without loss. Never perhaps entirely without effort, however; though sometimes with advantage. But the plain fact that the relative importance of grasping the sense of the words may vary (compare Browning's *Before* with his *After*) is enough for our purpose here.

[³⁶] In nearly all poetry the sound and feel of the words, what is often called the *form* of the poem in opposition to its *content*, get to work first, and the sense in which the words are taken is subtly influenced by this fact. Most words are ambiguous as regards their plain sense, especially in poetry. We can take them as we please in a variety of senses. The sense we are pleased to choose is the one which most suits the impulses already stirred through the form of the verse. The same thing can be noticed in conversation. Not the strict logical sense of what is said, but the tone of voice and the occasion are the primary factors by which we interpret. Science, it is worth noting, endeavours with increasing success to bar out these factors. We believe a scientist because he can substantiate his remarks, not because he is eloquent or forcible in his enunciation. In fact, we distrust him when he seems to be influencing us by his manner.

[³⁷] In its use of words poetry is just the reverse of science. Very definite thoughts do occur, but not because the words are so chosen as logically to bar out all possibilities but one. No. But because the manner, the tone of voice, the cadence and the rhythm play upon our interests and make *them* pick out from among an indefinite number of possibilities the precise particular thought which they need. This is why poetical descriptions often seem so much more accurate than prose descriptions. Language logically and scientifically used cannot describe a landscape or a face. To do so it would need a prodigious apparatus of names for shades and nuances, for precise particular qualities. These names do not exist, so other means have to be used. The poet, even when, like Ruskin or De Quincey, he writes in prose, makes the reader pick out the precise particular sense required from an indefinite number of possible senses which a word, phrase or sentence may carry. The means by which he does this are many and varied. Some of them have been mentioned above, but the way in which he uses them is the poet's own secret, something which cannot be taught. He knows how to do it, but he does not himself know how it is done.

[³⁸] Misunderstanding and under-estimation of poetry is mainly due to over-estimation of the thought in it. We can see still more clearly that thought is not the prime factor if we consider for a moment not the experience of the reader but that of the poet. Why does the poet use these words and no others? Not because they stand for a series of thoughts which in themselves are what he is concerned to communicate. It is never what a poem *says* which matters, but what it *is*. The poet is not writing as a scientist. He uses these words because the interests which the situation calls into play combine to bring them, just in this form, into his consciousness *as a means of ordering, controlling and consolidating* the whole experience. The experience itself, the tide of impulses sweeping through the mind, is the source and the sanction of the words. They represent this experience itself, not any set of perceptions or reflections, though often to a reader who approaches the poem wrongly they will seem to be only a series of remarks about other things. But to a suitable reader the words—if they actually spring from experience and are not due to verbal habits, to the desire to be effective, to factitious excogitation, to imitation, to irrelevant contrivances, or to any other of the failings which prevent most people from writing poetry—the words will reproduce in his mind a similar play of interests putting him for the while into a similar situation and leading to the same response.

[³⁹] Why this should happen is still somewhat of a mystery. An extraordinarily intricate concourse of impulses brings the words together. Then in another mind the affair in part reverses itself, the words bring into being a similar concourse of impulses. The words which seem to be the effect of the experience in the first instance, seem to become the cause of a similar experience in the second. A very odd thing to happen, not exactly paralleled outside communication. But this description is not quite accurate. The words, as we have seen, are not simply the effect in one case, nor the cause in the other. In both cases they are the part of the experience which binds it together, which gives it a definite structure and keeps it from being a mere welter of disconnected impulses. They are *the key,* to borrow a useful metaphor from McDougall, for this particular combination of impulses. So regarded, it is less strange that what the poet wrote should reproduce his experience in the mind of the reader.

CHAPTER III: WHAT IS VALUABLE?

[⁴⁰] Enough perhaps as to the kind of thing a poem is, as to the general structure of these experiences. Let us now turn to the further questions 'Of what use is it?' 'Why and how is it valuable?'

[⁴¹] The first point to be made is that poetic experiences are valuable (when they are) in the same ways as any other experiences. They are to be judged by the same standards. What are these?

[⁴²] Extraordinarily diverse views have been held upon this point. Very naturally, since such very different ideas have been entertained as to what kind of thing an experience is. For our opinions as to the differences between good and bad experiences depend inevitably upon what we take an experience to be. As fashions have changed in psychology men's ethical theories have followed suit. When a created, simple and eternal soul was the pivotal point, Good was conformity with the will of the creator, Evil was rebellion. When the associationist psychologists substituted a swarm of sensations and images for the soul, Good became pleasure and Evil became pain, and so on. A long chapter of the history of opinions has still to be written tracing these changes. Now that the mind is seen to be a hierarchy of interests, what will for this account be the difference between Good and Evil?

[⁴³] It is the difference between free and wasteful organization, between fullness and narrowness of life. For if the mind is a system of interests, and if an experience is their play, the worth of any experience is a matter of the degree to which the mind, through this experience, attains a complete equilibrium.

[⁴⁴] This is a first approximation. It needs qualifying and expanding if it is to become a satisfactory theory. Let us see how some of these amendments would run.

[⁴⁵] Consider an hour of any person's life. It holds out innumerable possibilities. Which of these are realized depends upon two main groups of factors:—the external situation in which he is living, his surroundings, including the other people with whom he is in contact; and, secondly, his psychological make-up. The first of these, the external situation, is sometimes given too much importance. We have only to notice what very different experiences different people undergo when in closely similar situations to recognize this fact. A situation which is dulness itself for one may be full of excitement for another. What an individual responds to is not the whole situation but a selection from it, and as a rule few people make the same selection. What is selected is decided by the organization of the individual's interests.

[46] Now let us simplify the case by supposing that nothing which happens during this hour is going to have any further consequences either in our hypothetical person's life or in anyone else's. He is going to cease to exist when the clock strikes—but for our purposes he must be imagined not to know this—and no one is to be a whit better or worse whatever he thinks, feels or does during the hour. What shall we say it would be best for him, if he could, to do?

[47] We need not bother to imagine the detail of the external situation or the character of the man. We can answer our question in general terms without doing so. The man has a certain definite instinctive make-up— the result of his past history, including his heredity. There will be many things which he cannot do which another man could, and many things which he cannot do in this situation, whatever it is, which he could do in other situations. But given this particular man in this particular situation, our question is, which of the possibilities open to him would be better than which others? How would we as friendly observers like to see him living?

[48] Setting pain aside, we may perhaps agree that torpor would be the worst choice. Complete inertness, lifelessness, would be the sorriest spectacle—anticipating too nearly and unnecessarily what is to happen when the hour strikes. We can then perhaps agree, though here more resistance from preconceived ideas may be encountered, that the best choice would be the opposite of torpor, that is to say, the fullest, keenest, most active and completest kind of life.

[49] Such a life is one which brings into play as many as possible of the *positive* interests. We can leave out the negative interests. It would be a pity for our friend to be frightened or disgusted even for a minute of his precious hour.

[50] But this is not all. It is not enough that many interests should be stirred. There is a more important point to be noted.

> The Gods approve
> The depth and not the tumult of the soul.

The interests must come into play and remain in play with as little conflict among themselves as possible. In other words, the experience must be organized so as to give all the impulses of which it is composed the greatest possible degree of freedom.

[51] It is in this respect that people differ most from one another. It

is this which separates the good life from the bad. Far more life is wasted through muddled mental organization than through lack of opportunity. Conflicts between different impulses are the greatest evils which afflict mankind.

[⁵²] The best life then which we can wish for our friend will be one in which as much as possible of himself is engaged (as many of his impulses as possible). And this with as little conflict, as little mutual interference between different sub-systems of his activities as there can be. The more he lives and the less he thwarts himself, the better. That briefly is our answer as psychologists, as outside observers abstractly describing the state of affairs. And if it is asked, what does such life feel like, how is it to live through? the answer is that it feels like and is the experience of poetry.

[⁵³] There are two ways in which conflict can be avoided or overcome. By conquest and by conciliation. One or other of the contesting impulses can be suppressed, or they can come to a mutual arrangement, they can adjust themselves to one another. We owe to psycho-analysis—at present still a rather undisciplined branch of psychology—a great deal of striking evidence as to the extreme difficulty of suppressing any vigorous impulse. When it seems to be suppressed it is often found to be really as active as ever, but in some other form, generally a troublesome one. Persistent mental imbalances are the source of nearly all our troubles. For this reason, as well as for the simpler reason that suppression is wasteful of life, conciliation is always to be preferred to conquest. People who are always winning victories over themselves might equally well be described as always enslaving themselves. Their lives become unnecessarily narrow. The minds of many saints have been like wells; they should have been like lakes or like the sea.

[⁵⁴] Unfortunately, most of us, left to ourselves, have no option but to go in for extensive attempts at self-conquest. It is our only means of escape from chaos. Our impulses must have some order, some organisation, or we do not live ten minutes without disaster. In the past, Tradition, a kind of Treaty of Versailles assigning frontiers and spheres of influence to the different interests, and based chiefly upon conquest, ordered our lives in a moderately satisfactory manner. But Tradition is weakening. Moral authorities are not as well backed by beliefs as they were; their sanctions are declining in force. We are in need of something to take the place of the old order. Not in need of a new balance of power, a new arrangement of conquests, but of a League of Nations for the moral ordering of the impulses; a new order based on conciliation, not on attempted suppression.

[⁵⁵] Only the rarest individuals hitherto have achieved this new order, and never yet perhaps completely. But many have achieved it for a brief while, for a particular phase of experience, and many have recorded it for these phases.

[56] Of these records poetry consists.

[57] But before going on to this new point let us return for a moment to our hypothetical friend who is enjoying his last hour, and suppose this limitation removed. Instead of such an hour let us consider any hour, one which has consequences for his future and for other people. Let us consider any piece of any life. How far is our argument affected? Will our standards of good and evil be altered?

[58] Clearly the case now is, in certain respects, different; it is much more complicated. We have to take these consequences into account. We have to regard his experience not in itself alone, but as a piece of his life and as a probable factor in other people's situations. If we are to approve of the experience, it must not only be full of life and free from conflict, but it must be likely to lead to other experiences, both his own and those of other people, also full of life and free from conflict. And often, in actual fact, it has to be less full of life and more restricted than it might be in order to ensure these results. A momentary individual good has often to be sacrificed for the sake of a later or a general good. Conflicts are often necessary in order that they should not occur later. The mutual adjustment of conflicting impulses may take time, and an acute struggle may be the only way in which they learn to co-operate peacefully in the future.

[59] But all these complications and qualifications do not disturb the conclusion we arrived at through considering the simpler case. A good experience is still one full of life, in the sense which we have explained, or derivatively one conducive to experiences full of life. An evil experience is one which is self-thwarting or conducive to stultifying conflicts. So far then, all is sound and shipshape in the argument, and we can go on to consider the poet.

COMMENT AND QUESTIONS

1. Since *Science and Poetry* was written more than forty years ago, the author could not have had in mind, in writing the first chapter, many particulars we may think of now when we consider "the general situation" of man. What statements in Chapter I are still applicable to the present situation? Are any statements inapplicable or untrue today?
2. What is the relation of Chapter I to the following chapters on the experience and value of poetry?

3. In what senses does Richards use the term *science,* and how is science relevant to poetry?

4. In Chapter II, what is the structure, or the stream of events, of the experience of "the right kind of reader" when he reads a poem? Why does it seem important to Richards to analyze this experience?

5. One of the author's central ideas is that the intellectual stream of thought is less important in reading poetry than what he calls the active or emotional stream. How does he support and develop this thesis? Is it convincing to you and applicable to your own reading of poetry?

6. Comment on the analogy of the system of magnetic needles and the human mind (paragraphs 23–26). What is the function of the analogy in Richards' essay? Is the analogy effective?

7. What is the purpose, in paragraphs 27–29, of tracing the development of the child into the adult?

8. Why does Richards return, in paragraph 35, to an early stage of the poetic experience—giving words their full imagined sound as one reads?

9. Chapter III is specifically devoted to the value of poetry. By the end of Chapter II, however, what values of the poetic experience have already been established or suggested?

10. In Chapter III, what are Richards' standards for judging the worth, or the good or evil, of any experience, including the poetic experience? Are his standards acceptable to you?

11. The thesis in Chapter III about the value of the poetic experience is developed (and qualified) largely by the long concrete example (paragraphs 45 ff.) of an hour in a person's life. Why does the author at first make this the last hour of the person's life, and later (paragraphs 57 ff.) make it any hour? In this section, are there any assumptions or steps in the author's reasoning which you have difficulty in accepting? Explain.

12. Summarize briefly Richards' answer to the question of what is valuable in the poetic experience.

[52] *Joseph Conrad*: Preface to
The Nigger of the Narcissus

JOSEPH CONRAD (1857–1924) was a famous English novelist and short story writer, Polish by birth and originally named Teodor Jozef Konrad Korzeniowski. After spending twenty years at sea, first as a sailor and later as an officer in the British merchant marine, Conrad retired to live in his adopted country and devote himself to writing. The following preface to a novel published in 1897 presents his concept of art and the aims of the serious writer of fiction. Among Conrad's other works are *Almayer's Folly, Lord Jim, Nostromo, Victory, Youth, Typhoon,* and *Heart of Darkness.*

[1] A work that aspires, however humbly, to the condition of art should carry its justification in every line. And art itself may be defined as a single-minded attempt to render the highest kind of justice to the visible universe, by bringing to light the truth, manifold and one, underlying its every aspect. It is an attempt to find in its forms, in its colors, in its light, in its shadows, in the aspects of matter and in the facts of life what of each is fundamental, what is enduring and essential—their one illuminating and convincing quality—the very truth of their existence. The artist, then, like the thinker or the scientist, seeks the truth and makes his appeal. Impressed by the aspect of the world the thinker plunges into ideas, the scientist into facts—whence, presently, emerging they make their appeal to those qualities of our being that fit us best for the hazardous enterprise of living. They speak authoritatively to our commonsense, to our intelligence, to our desire of peace or to our desire of unrest; not seldom to our prejudices, sometimes to our fears, often to our egoism— but always to our credulity. And their words are heard with reverence, for their concern is with weighty matters: with the cultivation of our minds and the proper care of our bodies, with the attainment of our ambitions, with the perfection of the means and the glorification of our precious aims.

[2] It is otherwise with the artist.

[3] Confronted by the same enigmatical spectacle the artist descends within himself, and in that lonely region of stress and strife, if he be deserving and fortunate, he finds the terms of his appeal. His appeal is made to our less obvious capacities: to that part of our nature which, because of the warlike conditions of existence, is necessarily kept out of sight within the more resisting and hard qualities—like the vulnerable body within a steel armour. His appeal is less loud, more profound, less distinct, more stirring—and sooner forgotten. Yet its effect endures forever. The changing wisdom of successive generations discards ideas, questions facts, demolishes theories. But the artist appeals to that part of our being which is not dependent on wisdom: to that in us which is a gift and not an acquisition—and, therefore, more permanently enduring. He speaks to our capacity for delight and wonder, to the sense of mystery surrounding our lives; to our sense of pity, and beauty, and pain; to the latent feeling of fellowship with all creation—and to the subtle but invincible conviction of solidarity that knits together the loneliness of innumerable hearts, to the solidarity in dreams, in joy, in sorrow, in

aspirations, in illusions, in hope, in fear, which binds men to each other, which binds together all humanity—the dead to the living and the living to the unborn.

[4] It is only some such train of thought, or rather of feeling, that can in a measure explain the aim of the attempt, made in the tale which follows, to present an unrestful episode in the obscure lives of a few individuals out of all the disregarded multitude of the bewildered, the simple, and the voiceless. For, if any part of truth dwells in the belief confessed above, it becomes evident that there is not a place of splendour or a dark corner of the earth that does not deserve if only a passing glance of wonder and pity. The motive then, may be held to justify the matter of the work; but this preface, which is simply an avowal of endeavour, cannot end here—for the avowal is not yet complete.

[5] Fiction—if it at all aspires to be art—appeals to temperament. And in truth it must be, like painting, like music, like all art, the appeal of one temperament to all the other innumerable temperaments whose subtle and resistless power endows passing events with their true meaning, and creates the moral, the emotional atmosphere of the place and time. Such an appeal to be effective must be an impression conveyed through the senses; and, in fact, it cannot be made in any other way, because temperament, whether individual or collective, is not amenable to persuasion. All art, therefore, appeals primarily to the senses, and the artistic aim when expressing itself in written words must make its appeal through the senses, if its high desire is to reach the secret spring of responsive emotions. It must strenuously aspire to the plasticity of sculpture, the color of painting, and to the magic suggestiveness of music— which is the art of arts. And it is only through complete, unswerving devotion to the perfect blending of form and substance; it is only through an unremitting never-discouraged care for the shape and ring of sentences that an approach can be made to plasticity, to color, and that the light of magic suggestiveness may be brought to play for an evanescent instant over the commonplace surface of words: of the old, old words, worn thin, defaced by ages of careless usage.

[6] The sincere endeavour to accomplish that creative task, to go as far on that road as his strength will carry him, to go undeterred by faltering, weariness or reproach, is the only valid justification for the worker in prose. And if his conscience is clear, his answer to those who in the fulness of wisdom which looks for immediate profit, demand specifically to be edified, consoled, amused; who demand to be promptly improved, or encouraged, or frightened, or shocked, or charmed, must run thus:—My task which I am trying to achieve is, by the power of the written word to make you hear, to make you feel—it is, before all, to make you *see*. That —and no more, and it is everything. If I succeed, you shall find there according to your deserts: encouragement, consolation, fear, charm—all

you demand—and, perhaps, also that glimpse of truth for which you have forgotten to ask.

[7] To snatch in a moment of courage, from the remorseless rush of time, a passing phase of life, is only the beginning of the task. The task approached in tenderness and faith is to hold up unquestioningly, without choice and without fear, the rescued fragment before all eyes in the light of a sincere mood. It is to show its vibration, its color, its form; and through its movement, its form, and its color, reveal the substance of its truth—disclose its inspiring secret: the stress and passion within the core of each convincing moment. In a single-minded attempt of that kind, if one be deserving and fortunate, one may perchance attain to such clearness of sincerity that at last the presented vision of regret, or pity, of terror or mirth, shall awaken in the hearts of the beholders that feeling of unavoidable solidarity; of the solidarity in mysterious origin, in toil, in joy, in hope, in uncertain fate, which binds men to each other and all mankind to the visible world.

[8] It is evident that he who, rightly or wrongly, holds by the convictions expressed above cannot be faithful to any one of the temporary formulas of his craft. The enduring part of them—the truth which each only imperfectly veils—should abide with him as the most precious of his possessions, but they all: Realism, Romanticism, Naturalism, even the unofficial sentimentalism (which like the poor, is exceedingly difficult to get rid of), all these gods must, after a short period of fellowship, abandon him—even on the very threshold of the temple—to the stammerings of his conscience and to the outspoken consciousness of the difficulties of his work. In that uneasy solitude the supreme cry of Art for Art itself, loses the exciting ring of its apparent immorality. It sounds far off. It has ceased to be a cry, and is heard only as a whisper, often incomprehensible, but at times and faintly encouraging.

[9] Sometimes, stretched at ease in the shade of a roadside tree, we watch the motions of a labourer in a distant field, and after a time, begin to wonder languidly as to what the fellow may be at. We watch the movements of his body, the waving of his arms, we see him bend down, stand up, hesitate, begin again. It may add to the charm of an idle hour to be told the purpose of his exertions. If we know he is trying to lift a stone, to dig a ditch, to uproot a stump, we look with a more real interest at his efforts; we are disposed to condone the jar of his agitation upon the restfulness of the landscape; and even, if in a brotherly frame of mind, we may bring ourselves to forgive his failure. We understood his object, and, after all, the fellow has tried, and perhaps he had not the strength—and perhaps he had not the knowledge. We forgive, go on our way—and forget.

[10] And so it is with the workman of art. Art is long and life is short, and success is very far off. And thus, doubtful of strength to travel so far,

we talk a little about the aim—the aim of art, which, like life itself, is inspiring, difficult—obscured by mists. It is not in the clear logic of a triumphant conclusion; it is not in the unveiling of one of those heartless secrets which are called the Laws of Nature. It is not less great, but only more difficult.

[11] To arrest, for the space of a breath, the hands busy about the work of the earth, and compel men entranced by the sight of distant goals to glance for a moment at the surrounding vision of form and color, of sunshine and shadows; to make them pause for a look, for a sigh, for a smile—such is the aim, difficult and evanescent, and reserved only for a very few to achieve. But sometimes, by the deserving and the fortunate, even that task is accomplished. And when it is accomplished—behold!—all the truth of life is there: a moment of vision, a sigh, a smile—and the return to an eternal rest.

like Thoreau
"Be awake"

⊷ COMMENT AND QUESTIONS ⊷

1. Examine the definition of art in the second and third sentences of paragraph 1. In that definition and the expansion of it in paragraphs 1–3, what basic assumptions is Conrad making about life and human experience?

2. Although English was not his native language, Conrad is known as a master of English style. Comment on the sentence structures and the use of words in paragraph 1. Point out other passages in the essay in which the writing seems to you notably good, and explain why it is good.

3. Can you reconcile the statements in paragraph 3 that the appeal of the artist is "sooner forgotten" than the appeal of the thinker or the scientist, and yet that the effect of the artist's appeal "endures forever"? What is the difference in meaning between *gift* and *acquisition* in paragraph 3, and what point is Conrad making with his contrast?

4. Where and for what purposes does Conrad return to the contrast, developed in the first three paragraphs, between the thinker or the scientist and the artist?

5. Paragraph 4 briefly refers to the content of *The Nigger of the Narcissus*. How has Conrad justified writing a novel about "an unrestful episode" in a few "obscure lives"? Is his justification convincing to you? Explain.

6. What two points about the writing of fiction is Conrad emphasizing in paragraph 5? Does either principle, or do both, seem applicable to other kinds of writing? Explain.

7. A statement in paragraph 6 is often quoted: "My task which I am trying to achieve. . . ." Think of one or more novels or short stories that have impressed you. Have they made you hear, feel, and, before all, *see*? Would

you make any additions to Conrad's statement about the creative writer's task?

8. In this essay, is Conrad following his precept of making the reader hear, feel, and see? Explain.

9. What are the implications of *the very threshold of the temple* in paragraph 8?

10. In paragraph 9, what is the purpose of the experience described and commented on?

11. In paragraphs 3, 7, and 11, Conrad uses the combination of *deserving* and *fortunate* in talking about the artistic writer. What does *deserving* appear to mean or to imply?

12. Summarize in your own words what Conrad means by *art*. To what extent do you agree or disagree with his concept? Explain.

[53] *William Faulkner*: Remarks on Receiving the Nobel Prize

WILLIAM FAULKNER (1897–1962) is regarded by many critics as the most brilliant American short story writer and novelist of the twentieth century. Among his novels are *The Sound and the Fury; As I Lay Dying; Light in August; Absalom, Absalom; Intruder in the Dust; A Fable; The Hamlet; The Town; The Mansion;* and *The Reivers.* Faulkner gave the following short address in Stockholm, Sweden, in December, 1950, when he accepted the award of the 1949 Nobel Prize for Literature.

[1] I feel that this award was not made to me as a man but to my work —a life's work in the agony and sweat of the human spirit, not for glory and least of all for profit, but to create out of the materials of the human spirit something which did not exist before. So this award is only mine in trust. It will not be difficult to find a dedication for the money part of it commensurate with the purpose and significance of its origin. But I would like to do the same with the acclaim too, by using this moment as a pinnacle from which I might be listened to by the young men and women already dedicated to the same anguish and travail, among whom is already that one who will some day stand here where I am standing.

[2] Our tragedy today is a general and universal physical fear so long sustained by now that we can even bear it. There are no longer problems

of the spirit. There is only the question: when will I be blown up? Because of this, the young man or woman writing today has forgotten the problems of the human heart in conflict with itself which alone can make good writing because only that is worth writing about, worth the agony and the sweat.

[3] He must learn them again. He must teach himself that the basest of all things is to be afraid; and, teaching himself that, forget it forever, leaving no room in his workshop for anything but the old verities and truths of the heart, the old universal truths lacking which any story is ephemeral and doomed—love and honor and pity and pride and compassion and sacrifice. Until he does so he labors under a curse. He writes not of love but of lust, of defeats in which nobody loses anything of value, of victories without hope, and worst of all, without pity or compassion. His griefs grieve on no universal bones, leaving no scars. He writes not of the heart but of the glands.

[4] Until he relearns these things he will write as though he stood alone and watched the end of man. I decline to accept the end of man. It is easy enough to say that man is immortal simply because he will endure; that when the last ding-dong of doom has clanged and faded from the last worthless rock hanging tideless in the last red and dying evening, that even then there will still be one more sound: that of his puny inexhaustible voice, still talking. I refuse to accept this. I believe that man will not merely endure: he will prevail. He is immortal, not because he alone among creatures has an inexhaustible voice, but because he has a soul, a spirit capable of compassion and sacrifice and endurance. The poet's, the writer's, duty is to write about these things. It is his privilege to help man endure by lifting his heart, by reminding him of the courage and honor and hope and pride and compassion and pity and sacrifice which have been the glory of his past. The poet's voice need not merely be the record of man, it can be one of the props, the pillars to help him endure and prevail.

·⊰ COMMENT AND QUESTIONS ⊱·

1. In what phrases in the first two paragraphs does Faulkner stress the suffering a writer must endure? Why should the suffering be necessary?
2. Do the first three sentences of paragraph 2 seem to you to be true today? Explain.
3. What does Faulkner appear to mean, in paragraph 2, by "the problems of the human heart in conflict with itself"?

4. What is the meaning of *workshop* in paragraph 3? What is the literal meaning of the next-to-last sentence of this paragraph?

5. Can you think of writers of whom Faulkner's last three sentences in paragraph 3 are true? Who are they, and how does his comment fit them?

6. In the first sentence of paragraph 4, what does Faulkner mean by *as though he stood alone*? By *the end of man* in that sentence and the following sentence does Faulkner mean the literal end or destruction of the human race, or is his meaning different? Explain.

7. Comment on the structure and diction of the sentence in paragraph 4 beginning "It is easy enough . . . ."

8. What is the difference between *endure* and *prevail* as Faulkner is using the words? What does he believe to be the duty and the privilege of the writer?

9. Faulkner is addressing his remarks to young men and women interested in writing. What does he say of concern to the nonwriter about human life and values?

10. Faulkner's speech has been highly praised for its content and style and severely criticized as a piece of pompous and empty rhetoric. What is your judgment of it, and why?

[54] *Ihab Hassan*: The Anti-Hero

IHAB HASSAN (1925–   ) is a professor of English at Wesleyan University. The following essay is from *Radical Innocence: Studies in the Contemporary American Novel*, published in 1961; footnotes are the author's.

[1] "In its essence literature is concerned with the self," Lionel Trilling writes in *Freud and the Crisis of Our Culture*, "and the particular concern of the literature of the last two centuries has been with the self in its standing quarrel with culture."[1] The image of the self in its standing, and recently embittered, quarrel with culture—indeed in its quarrel with itself, as Mr. Trilling neglects to say—comes to focus in the figure of the anti-hero.

[2] In fiction, the unnerving rubric "anti-hero" refers to a ragged as-

From Ihab Hassan, *Radical Innocence: Studies in the Contemporary American Novel*. Reprinted by permission of Princeton University Press. Copyright © 1961 by Princeton University Press.

[1] Lionel Trilling, *Freud and the Crisis of Our Culture* (Boston, 1955), pp. 58 ff.

sembly of victims: the fool, the clown, the hipster, the criminal, the poor sod, the freak, the outsider, the scapegoat, the scrubby opportunist, the rebel without a cause, the "hero" in the ashcan and "hero" on the leash. If the anti-hero seems nowadays to hold us in his spell, it is because the deep and disquieting insights revealed to us by modern literature often require that we project ourselves into the predicament of victims.

[3] The gradual process of atrophy of the hero may have begun with Don Quixote, or perhaps even Job, Orestes, and Christ. It enters the critical phase, however, only late in the eighteenth century. Goethe's Werther introduces the "tragic" Romantic hero who, in his inordinate conception of himself, severs the traditional bond between the hero and his society, and points the way to such extreme stances of alienation as were to find expression in the Byronic and Sadist hero, in the gothic and demonic protagonist, in werewolf, ghoul, and vampire. But as the new bourgeois order, which the Romantic hero rejected, became a powerful social reality, the strategy of oppositon changed. The characters of Stendhal, Balzac, and Flaubert often seem, as Raymond Giraud has recognized, "heroes of ironies" whose "ideals, desires, and feelings are in disharmony" with their "adult conception of reality."[2] Similarly, the subtitle for *Vanity Fair: A Novel Without a Hero*, suggests that Victorian fiction was quietly disposing of the heroic protagonist. The ambivalences of a bourgeois hero in an overwhelmingly middle-class society raise for him problems of estrangement and communion, sincerity and simulation, ambition and acquiescence, which we recognize as the patent themes of the great novels of the last century. The wretched fate of the lower-class hero, caught between malignant Heredity and crushing Environment in the *roman experimental* of Zola, and in the less experimental but more benign novels of the brothers Goncourt, reflects the familiar bias of Naturalism and marks a further stage in the disintegration of heroism. Victim to immitigable "cosmic laws," with little or no control over his fate in the world, man turns inward again. The next development is predictable. "The way was open from the realist to the intimist novel," Mario Praz concludes in *The Hero in Eclipse in Victorian Fiction*. "Disillusioned observation of life as it really was, led to the eclipse of the hero and the disclosure of man's swarming interior world, made up of disparate and contradictory things."[3]

[4] With the retrenchment of the individual, the drama of good and evil which the hero and villain once objectified in society becomes blurred. The traditional forms of moral conflict are so internalized that no victory or defeat, where self is divided against itself, can claim to be

[2] Raymond Giraud, *The Unheroic Hero* (New Brunswick, 1957), p. 189. See also Harry Levin, "From Priam to Birotteau," *Yale French Studies*, vi (1950), p. 76.

[3] Mario Praz, *The Hero in Eclipse in Victorian Fiction* (New York, 1956), p. 383.

atrophy - wasting away

costly

more than pyrrhic. Cunningly introspective, the modern novel redefines the identity of its central character and redirects his energies toward the virtues of love or self-discovery, virtues that are a good deal more personal than social. To become someone, to know who or what one is, to reach finally another human being with love, and to do so in terms that society may censure, this is the passionate, bitter concern of the modern anti-hero. But the modern identity proved an elusive thing to capture. "You mustn't look in my novel for the old stable *ego* of the character," D. H. Lawrence wrote to Edward Garnett. "There is another *ego*, according to whose action the individual is unrecognizable, and passes through, as it were, allotropic states. . . ."[4] A new shifty ego, a new concept of man. The sad history of the anti-hero is nothing more than the history of man's changing awareness of himself. It is the record of his recoil.

[5] The encounter between the new ego and the destructive element of experience, we have insisted, lies at the dramatic center of the modern novel in Europe and America. The encounter is further illumined by some striking European images which define the modern idea of the self and clarify its responses. We shall view some concrete instances of the anti-hero—whom in hope and charity we may simply call "hero." These instances are taken from writers of very different age and background, yet they add to a remarkably persistent theme.

[6] To consider Dostoyevsky's *Notes from Underground,* 1864, modern is perhaps to stretch the idea of modernity to its permissible limit. The document so shrill and anxious, so full of spite and spleen, reveals, in any case, what the modern soul likes most to gnaw upon: itself. The dagger is turned inward, the most refined tortures are reserved for the self. Whom else are we really interested in? Listening for forty years from the crack under his floor, Dostoyevsky's hero looks at existence with a cringe and a snarl. He knows the intense pleasure of degradation and of despair and knows, while gnashing his teeth, that "there is no one even for you to feel vindictive against, that you have not, and perhaps never will have, an object for your spite. . . ."[5] Precisely the condition which Albert Camus calls, in *The Rebel,* metaphysical rebellion, and which our hero understands as a revolt against "the whole legal system of Nature."[6] But no one is to blame; "consequently there is only the same outlet left again —that is, to beat the wall as hard as you can."[7] This frenzy is not only meant to be a protest against the whole order of Nature, the terrible fact that "every sort of consciousness . . . is a disease," or merely a protest

[4] Aldous Huxley, ed., *The Letters of D. H. Lawrence* (London, 1956), p. 198.
[5] *The Short Novels of Dostoyevsky,* Introduction by Thomas Mann (New York, 1945), p. 137.
[6] *Ibid.,* p. 137.
[7] *Ibid.,* p. 140.

Meliorism

gradual progression for the better [handwritten marginalia, top right]

against the historical enemies of Dostoyevsky—rationalism, meliorism, and science, the coxcomb fact that two plus two equals four.[8] The frenzy, in the form of caprice, is also directed against our individuality. That Dostoyevsky's "insect" can establish his identity only by forcing himself to collide ignominiously with an arrogant officer who does not even recognize his existence is of no importance. The important thing is that it is *he* who *forces* the recognition. This is freedom.

[7] The grotesque image of this strange creature haunts modern literature and remains at the center of our dread. Its cracked reflections in some way or other penetrate the works of most European novelists. And its perverse truths, almost insupportable, infiltrate recent American fiction which does not stem only, as Hemingway claimed, from a book by Mark Twain called *Huckleberry Finn* but also from another, it may be argued with equal pertinence, by Dostoyevsky called *Notes from Underground.* The image, taken up, modified, and recreated by later novelists deserves further attention.

[8] Conrad, we know, shared with Dostoyevsky more than the dubious heritage of a Slavic temper. His metaphysical romances of the seven seas subject the idea of heroism to an ironic rhetoric which is peculiarly modern, and his abiding interest in the theme of the double—his *Secret Sharer* and Dostoyevsky's *The Double* come to mind—probes the distempers of the modern self in a way that seems now familiar. While no character of his strictly reminds us of the hero of the *Notes*, the state of immersion, the desperation felt in the heart of darkness or in the underground habitations of consciousness, the surrender to the "destructive element," compel our terrified assent in the novels of both authors. Kurtz, in *Heart of Darkness,* had perhaps immersed himself too deeply, there where victim and victimizer become one, till he could distinguish only the horror. But Kurtz creeping on all fours in the night-time jungle and Lord Jim erect and dazzling in spotless white are still two sides of the same image, two sides separated really by the enormous distance between action and heroic intention. Conrad does not repudiate human striving. In a celebrated passage from *Lord Jim* he simply points to the way of fulfillment. "A man that is born falls into a dream like a man who falls into the sea," Conrad writes. "If he tries to climb out into the air as inexperienced people endeavor to do, he drowns. . . . The way is to the destructive element submit yourself. . . ."[9] The unintelligent brutality of existence leaves man no other choice.

[9] It is, of course, the unintelligent brutality of existence that dominates the Dublin of Joyce's *Ulysses;* the city becomes a focus, in Eliot's famous words, to "the immense panorama of futility and anarchy which

---

[8] *Ibid.*, p. 132.

[9] Joseph Conrad, *Lord Jim* (New York, 1931), p. 214.

Jansenist - man is predestined [handwritten marginalia, bottom]

is contemporary history."[10] The proportions of the hero are further shrunken, his self pushed further underground in the world of memory and fantasy. The element to which Bloom submits himself, in humor and humility, is the ignominious element. Insult and pathos, loneliness and failure, are his familiars. Leopold Bloom, wandering Jew, mock Odysseus, and lowly Christ, finally appears to us, above all, as "Everyman or Noman."[11] He stands between Stephen Dedalus and Molly Bloom, between intelligence and nature, as a pathetic monument to the generosity of suffering. For intelligence, in the person of Stephen—he is Lucifer and Hamlet and Dedalus—can only cry: *Non serviam!* And Nature, in the person of Molly—Ceres, Hera, eternal Mother Earth—must endlessly murmur: Yes I will Yes. Man, meanwhile, goes clowning his sentimental way into eternity, unable to reconcile himself completely to one or the other.

[10] The two heroes of Joyce and of Dostoyevsky show that humility lies on the other side of spite. But the clown in man has many disguises. He is Bloom, "one lonely last sardine of summer."[12] He is also, as we shall see, an insect, a sentient tubercle, at best a shaggy wolf. The self in recoil cannot afford to be choosy.

[11] Dostoyevsky's metaphor of man as an insect inevitably calls to mind Kafka's story, "Metamorphosis," in which the narrator is transformed into a huge, hideous, and pathetic vermin. This, too, is self-degradation, a form of the self in recoil. This, too, is protest. The theme is everywhere in Kafka, in *The Castle,* in *The Trial,* in "The Penal Colony" or "The Judgment." Man is always judged, and found invariably guilty. He is the victim of an unappeasable power, a horrible and recurrent outrage, and even in his most serene moments he can only exclaim, like the Hunter Gracchus: "I am here, more than that I do not know, further than that I cannot go. My ship has no rudder, and it is driven by the wind that blows in the undermost regions of death."[13] The vision of man is as grotesque as that of Dostoyevsky; but it goes farther, denying man freedom, the sheer horror of choice, and denying him grace. Indeed, of man Kafka can only say, "He found the Archimedean point, but he used it against himself; it seems that he was permitted to find it only under this condition."[14] The lever which gives man mastery over his universe, moving worlds at the touch of a finger tip, is still the inbred dagger of the soul. In Kafka as in Dostoyevsky, the sense of compounded

[10] T. S. Eliot, "Ulysses, Order and Myth," in John W. Aldridge, ed., *Critiques and Essays on Modern Fiction* (New York, 1952), p. 426.

[11] James Joyce, *Ulysses* (New York, 1946), p. 712.

[12] *Ibid.,* p. 284.

[13] *Selected Stories of Franz Kafka,* Introduction by Philip Rahv (New York, 1952), p. 187.

[14] Franz Kafka, *Dearest Father* (New York, 1954), p 378.

guilt and absurdity defines the point at which victimization and rebellion meet.[15]

[12] This view of the human predicament will no doubt seem to many both exigent and extreme. It borders, people argue, on disease. Exactly. In the panoramic view of Thomas Mann, whose sane vision did not prevent him from cultivating a lifelong interest in Kafka and Dostoyevsky, disease and even death become an ultimate response to life. The idea informs at least two of his masterpieces, *The Magic Mountain* and *Death in Venice,* and it hovers about his latest work, *The Confessions of Felix Krull.* Hans Castorp reflects, as if prompted by the hero of Dostoyevsky's *Notes,* "Disease was a perverse, a dissolute form of life. And life? Life itself? Was it perhaps only an infection, a sickening of matter? . . . The first step toward evil, toward desire and death, was taken precisely then, when there took place that first increase in the density of the spiritual, that pathologically luxuriant morbid growth. . . ."[16] But the radical disease of consciousness, which the hero of Dostoyevsky resented to the end of his spite, and to which the Kafka hero finally submits in a lucid nightmare, is transmuted by Thomas Mann into a condition of spiritual refulgence. It is thus that Mann is able to claim, with Nietzsche and Dostoyevsky in mind, that "certain attainments of the soul and the intellect are impossible *without disease, without insanity, without spiritual crime, and* the *great invalids* are *crucified victims,* sacrificed to humanity and its advancement, to the broadening of its feeling and knowledge—in short, to its more *sublime health* [italics mine]."[17] Man, we see, pitches himself at the terrible limit of experience, as Lucifer did.

[13] Mann's statement reminds us that grace, if it is to be found at all, lies deep in the soft core of violence. The saint and the criminal stand back to back on either side of the demonic. Both are protestants, both victims. But pure violence, like the demonic, has no reality in the public realm, the domain of action. Pure violence, as we shall repeatedly observe in modern fiction, seems almost the ultimate form of introspection. That the saint and the criminal, the suppliant and psychopath—they are conjoined in the recent literature of hipsterism and in such enduring figures as Greene's Pinkie and Faulkner's Christmas—partake of violence compulsively is no surprise. For untrammelled violence is not an act, it is merely a state; it is the experience of world negation. As Miss Arendt saw, the saint and the criminal are both lonely figures: ". . . . the one being for, the other against, all men; they, therefore, remain outside the pale of human intercourse and are, politically, marginal figures who

[15] Parallels between the two novelists are well elaborated by Renato Poggioli, "Kafka and Dostoyevsky," in Angel Flores ed., *The Kafka Problem* (New York, 1946), pp. 97–107.

[16] Thomas Mann, *The Magic Mountain* (New York, 1927), pp. 285 ff.

[17] "Introduction," *The Short Novels of Dostoyevsky,* p. xv.

usually enter the historical scene in times of corruption, disintegration, and political bankruptcy. Because of its inherent tendency to disclose the agent together with the act, action needs for its full appearance the shining brightness we once called glory, and which is possible only in the public realm."[18]

[14] It is perhaps unnecessary to recover for our age the Corneillian idea of glory, but when the focus of moral energy moves so far from the center of human effort in the world, losing itself in the domain of holy silence or demonic violence, then it is time to give vent to our anxiety. The dissociation of action from intelligence, we remember, is manifest in Dostoyevsky's *Notes* whose hero openly contemns the active life. The consequences of this attitude are not limited to the cult of inactivity, living in a hole, like the man from underground, or in a jar like the hero of Beckett's *The Unnamable*, living, if you will, in the "packing-box shanty on the city dump" thoughtfully reserved by the editors of *Life* for our most promising novelists. The consequences also involve the alienation of the moral and artistic imagination from things of this world, often leading to a criminal state of autonomy.

[15] The rebel-victim, we see, is also the outsider in search of truth.[19] Harry Haller, in Hermann Hesse's *Steppenwolf*, is still an isolate genius of suffering "whose fate it is to live the whole riddle of human destiny heightened to the pitch of a personal torture, a personal hell."[20] He is still grappling with the radical multiplicities of the human ego, oscillating not merely between the wolf and the man, not merely between two poles, such as the body and the spirit, the saint and the sinner, but between "thousands and thousands."[21] In the "Treatise on the Steppenwolf," however, the outsider is finally made to reckon with the fact that man may be nothing more than a temporary agreement between warring opposites, nothing more, in fact, than "a bourgeois compromise"—such as Bloom!

[16] The idea of man as a transient compromise in the universe entails the acceptance of permanent outrage. Harry Haller could find some redemption of that condition in love or art, or even in humor which reconciles all opposites, and in whose "imaginary realm the intricate and many-faceted ideal of all Steppenwolves finds its realization."[22] Other writers—Mauriac, Bernanos, Graham Greene—sought for their characters a solution more commensurate with their religious faith; for, as

[18] Hannah Arendt, *The Human Condition* (Chicago, 1958), p. 180.

[19] See Colin Wilson, *The Outsider* (Boston, 1956), for an extended documentary more valuable for its recognition of the general problem and for its range of significant reference than for its particular insights into the crucial documents it uses.

[20] Hermann Hesse, *Steppenwolf* (New York, 1929), p. 28.

[21] *Ibid.*, p. 77.

[22] *Ibid.*, p. 73.

Colin Wilson has loudly noted, the problems of modern man, rebel, victim, or outsider, lend themselves to an intense religious apprehension which need not be specifically Christian.[23] Yet even the Christian novelists, so Jansenist they seem in their insistence on human depravity, manage to convey only the terrible intricacies of damnation. Thus, for instance, is the pursuit of damnation conceived in *Brighton Rock* as an appalling manifestation of the mercy of God. The modern Christian martyr, it seems, can aspire only to perdition.

[17] To the religious and the humanist solutions of man's plight in the universe must be added the Existentialist. The basic question here is still one of freedom, the search for identity under the aspects of violence or alienation. Freedom, we recall, is known to the hero of the *Notes* only as caprice; he understands that men, himself included, must seek freedom and must be repelled and horrified by it. The same ambivalence haunts the quest of Kafka's characters. Beginning with Gide, however, the ambivalence is seemingly resolved in favor of positive action. Man asserts his liberty in a gratuitous act of murder, as in Lafcadio's case, in acts of social repudiation, or ruthless heroism, as in the case of Michel and Theseus. Freedom consists of revolt, against morality, against the social order, against history. But the blood-curdling price is one that only heroes and supermen can afford. In this direction, the Existentialist novelists go farther than Gide was willing to go, and their view is correspondingly more special. Victory, in their novels, depends on the certainty of defeat, *is* the process of defeat. But unlike the heroes of classical tragedy, their protagonists act in full foreknowledge of their fatality, act *only* in *despite* of that fatality. And there is never any reconciliation.

[18] It is thus that Sartre understands man—a creature *condemned* to be free. Antoine Roquentin, in *The Nausea,* suffers from metaphysical disgust. His consciousness is like a decayed trap door through which the sordid impressions of his world endlessly sift. Nothing happens in his life, nothing begins or ends; Phenomena merely change, and Things, grotesque, obdurate, and unnamable, simply exist. Roquentin thinks: "I have only my body: a man entirely alone, with his lonely body, cannot indulge in memories; they pass through him. I shouldn't complain: all I wanted was to be free."[24] Thinking is his game, the famous Cartesian proof of existence his plaything. In Kafka's work, as Erich Heller perceived, a cursed Intelligence asserts its omnipresence; the Cartesian formula becomes: "I think, and therefore I am not."[25] Such negation of being is inadmissible to Sartre; the proper formula should read: "My thought is *me.* . . . At this very moment—it's frightful—if I exist, it is because I am

[23] *The Outsider,* p. 261. Also Colin Wilson, *Religion and the Rebel* (Boston, 1957).
[24] Jean-Paul Sartre, *Nausea* (Norfolk, Conn., n.d.,), p. 91.
[25] Erich Heller, *The Disinherited Mind* (New York, 1957), p. 202.

horrified at existing."[26] The change is less of an improvement than it may seem. For as Roquentin comes to believe, existence is nothing if not superfluous. Everything is *de trop,* everything is rooted in the Absurd, the irreducible condition of all reality. Man, we see, is not only a clown or a transient compromise, he is a contingency of existence. The way to true being, seldom realized, lies through Nausea.

[19] Sartre's doctrine that existence precedes essence, carried to its atheistic conclusion, defines no limit to the idea of freedom and gives no value to the concept of being. Camus, a far more accomplished artist if not a more systematic thinker, starts with his "absurdist" philosophy of man and reaches, in *The Rebel* and *The Fall,* a more complex awareness of freedom. In his early novel, *The Stranger,* Meursault surrenders to the absurd, the destructive element, and loses his life, it seems, without ever finding it. In the following novel, *The Plague,* a small light of hope, even of redemption, flickers through the night of human victimization. Doctor Rieux says: "All I maintain is that on this earth there are pestilences and there are victims, and it's up to us, as far as possible, not to join forces with the pestilences. . . . I decided to take, in every predicament, the victim's side, so as to reduce the damage done. Among them, I can at least try to understand how one attains to the third category: in other words, to peace."[27] To join the victims is an act of rebellion against and alienation from the prevalent norm. But such an act is never purely nugatory. "Rebellion," Camus wrote, "though apparently negative, since it creates nothing, is profoundly positive in that it reveals the part of man which must always be defended."[28] Rebellion is therefore an aspiration to order, a means of lifting pain and evil from personal to collective experience. For the rebel-victim, the Cartesian argument par excellence is: "I rebel—therefore *we* exist [italics mine]."[29]

[20] The problem of the anti-hero is essentially one of identity. His search is for existential fulfillment, that is, for freedom and self-definition. What he hopes to find is a position he can take within himself. Society may modulate his awareness of his situation, but only existence determines his stand. The recoil of the modern self is its way of taking a stand. The retreat weakens its involvement in the living world. It leads it in the ways of violence and alienation, augments its sense of guilt and absurdity, and affords it no objective standard for evaluating the worth of human action. But living in the world exclusively, living in what Ortega y Gasset has called the Other, is also brutish and deadening. Complete immersion in the otherness of things is a ghastlier form of alienation; it is alienation from the self. "Without a strategic retreat into the self,"

[26] *Nausea,* pp. 135 ff.
[27] Albert Camus, *The Plague* (Paris, 1948), p. 229.
[28] *The Rebel,* p. 19.
[29] *Ibid.,* p. 22.

Ortega rightly notes, "without vigilant thought, human life is impossible."[30]
It is precisely in fear of the Other—total loss of selfhood—that the
modern conscience has fallen back on its internal resources. The schizophrenic goes too far in that direction, the rebel-victim remains in the field
of our vision.

[21] Camus' statement, "I rebel—therefore we exist," brings to surface
a dialectic that has been implicit in all the works we have viewed. In
its naked form, the dialectic can be seen as an interplay between the
essential Yes and the radical No, two piercing utterances beyond which
the human voice cannot rise. Such utterances may sometimes blend. It
is only silence they equally abhor. In the modern novel, man seems to
overcome the contradictions of his experience, its destructive or demonic
element, by assuming the role of the anti-hero, the rebel-victim. The rebel
denies without saying No to life, the victim succumbs without saying
Yes to oppression. Both acts are, in a sense, identical: they affirm the
human against the nonhuman. The figure of modern man, when he
chooses to assert his full manhood, always bears the brave indissoluble
aspects of Prometheus and Sisyphus—the eternal rebel and the eternal
victim. The paradox is resolved when man cries, in the ringing words of
Jaspers, "Although I am an anvil, as a hammer I can consummate what
I must suffer."[31] Sparks from the same anvil were struck when Christ said
to his disciples, "For whosoever will save his life shall lose it; and whosoever will lose his life for my sake shall find it."[32]

[22] The condition of modern life may not be more desperate, as
relativists sapiently remind us, than those which prevailed in any earlier
age. Men, as usual, like to exaggerate their predicament to convince
themselves, if nothing else, that they are still alive. All this is beside the
point. It is certainly not the wretchedness of modern existence that we
have sought to illustrate in this chapter, but rather man's peculiar
awareness of his own situation. This awareness is both critical and adverse.
The spirit of recoil in modern literature continues to affirm itself despite
all our bounties.

--⊷{ C O M M E N T   A N D   Q U E S T I O N S }⊷--

Some of Hassan's examples of the anti-hero may be unfamiliar to you. If
this is so, do you find that the unfamiliar references make the essay unclear? Explain.

[30] Ortega y Gasset, *The Dehumanization of Art* (New York, 1956), p. 185.
[31] Karl Jaspers, *Man in the Modern Age* (New York, 1957), p. 205.
[32] Matthew 16:25.

2. Consult your dictionary, if necessary, to determine the meaning in context of the following words: *rubric* (paragraph 2), *atrophy* (paragraph 3), *pyrrhic* and *allotropic* (paragraph 4), *meliorism* (paragraph 6), *exigent* (paragraph 12), *Jansenist* (paragraph 16), *Cartesian* and *contingency* (paragraph 18), *nugatory* (paragraph 19).

3. In what ways are the two opening paragraphs an effective beginning?

4. Paragraph 3 traces the disintegration of heroism, particularly from the late eighteenth century through the nineteenth century. What do the various kinds of heroes discussed in that paragraph have in common?

5. At the end of paragraph 4, what does the author mean by saying that the history of the anti-hero is the record of man's "recoil"?

6. Paragraph 5 is an introduction to concrete instances of the anti-hero. What is Hassan's purpose in starting with a full discussion of Dostoyevsky's hero?

7. How do you interpret Conrad's advice (paragraph 8) about submitting oneself to the "destructive element"? To what extent do you agree or disagree with it? Explain.

8. What relationship does Hassan see between the saint and the criminal?

9. What is the meaning of Camus' statement, quoted in paragraphs 19 and 21: "I rebel—therefore we exist"?

10. Examine paragraph 20, a summary of the problem of the anti-hero. To what extent do you agree or disagree with the statement that "living in the world exclusively . . . . is a ghastlier form of alienation"? Explain.

11. What is the meaning of Jaspers' statement, quoted near the end of paragraph 21? How is it related to the preceding material in the paragraph?

12. The author says in his closing paragraph that he has sought to illustrate man's peculiar, critical, and adverse awareness of his situation. To what extent do you share the view of life reflected in the literature Hassan has discussed? Or, what characters or authors discussed in the essay most nearly represent your own view?

[55]   *Herbert J. Muller*: Modern Tragedy

HERBERT J. MULLER (1905–   ), a professor of English at Indiana University, is the author of many books including *Science and Criticism, The Uses of the Past, The Loom of History, Freedom in the Ancient World,* and *Freedom in the Western World.* The following selection is from *The Spirit of Tragedy,* published in 1956.

THE PECULIAR ISSUES

[1] Among the incidental oddities of our queer times is a question often discussed: is it possible for modern man to write tragedy? The common answer has been No; and literary men have then found still another reason for despairing of modern culture. Their worry may seem a little ludicrous in an atomic age. Most societies in the past managed to get along without writing tragedy, and never asked such a question. Yet it is a significant question, which finally involves the basic issues of our civilization. It must be considered, at any rate, in a chapter entitled "Modern Tragedy."

[2] The gloomiest statement of the case is Joseph Wood Krutch's well-known essay "The Tragic Fallacy." Krutch argued that modern knowledge has killed the tragic faith, and all possibility of recovering it. Man can no longer believe that his fate makes the least difference to a universe he conceives as soulless. Worse, he can no longer believe in his own nobility; he knows that he is a creature of reflexes and complexes, determined by heredity and environment. The glory both of God and of Man has departed this world. Although Krutch later modified his rather melodramatic statement of our plight, his thesis is substantially borne out by the many poets and critics who stress only the vulgarity and barbarity of modern civilization, and can see no tragic dignity in the calamities that are signaling its collapse; if it now appears that we may end with a bang, we remain hollow men who can only whimper. Even John Dewey, the incorrigible optimist, provided a text for literary despair. The best we can do, he once remarked, is to venerate what we do not really believe, and to criticize what we really live by.

[3] This side of despair, the possibilities of high tragedy are most obviously limited by the characteristic realism of modern literature. As writers faithfully portray the life of their time, the scene dwindles into a parlor, the protagonist into a petty bourgeois. Some may focus on the ordinary, commonplace individual, the Bovary or Babbitt; others on the abnormal individual, the neurotic who we have come to realize is not so abnormal after all, but a brother in the unconscious. In either case the hero is naturally unheroic. If he stirs pity, he stirs little fear—except as we feel our own littleness and helplessness. He may then illustrate a deeper irony; with increased freedom, political and intellectual, modern man has come to realize that he is not so free, but a slave to custom, to economic necessity, to class consciousness, to unconscious desire, to irrational passion— to impersonal forces that cannot inspire the awe that the will of the gods once did. Hence the hero may suffer further in becoming primarily a guinea pig, an exhibit for sociological or psychological analysis. (In the fables of Kafka he is not even granted a name.) As the terms of our problems keep shifting, his tragedy becomes outdated. And it is naturally

told in prose, the language of everyday life. It is deprived of the intensity and extensity, magnitude and lift, which poetry can give.

[⁴] A still more common complaint, especially in America, is the commercial theater. How could a tradition of high tragedy ever take root on Broadway? The show business is precisely that: a business whose commodity is a good show. Granted that Shakespeare too was in the business, his Globe was essentially different from the theaters of Broadway. It was a national theater serving the general public, not a slick industry catering to the few. Hence the Little Theaters that have sprung up all over the land, in town and on campus, have also failed to create a living theater. Mostly they produce old Broadway hits; now and then they produce arty little plays, for arty little audiences. At best, serious drama attracts a small but heterogeneous audience that is not representative of the community, and may be self-consciously aloof from the community. Critics point out that it lacks a common faith, a common moral attitude, a common tradition in art or anything else. It has no deep sense of myth or ritual.

[⁵] For such reasons Francis Fergusson sees no hope of restoring the comprehensive "idea of a theater" realized by Sophocles and Shakespeare. In his sensitive, sympathetic studies of the greater modern dramatists he demonstrates how all fall short of this idea, presenting diverse but always limited, partial, fragmentary perspectives. "And when the idea of a theater is inadequate or lacking," he concludes, "we are reduced to speculating about the plight of the whole culture."

[⁶] As we speculate, we are immediately oppressed by the uniformity of a mass culture, and in particular its standardized, synthetic entertainment: manufactured by cynical professionals, disseminated by mass media, having none of the spontaneity and genuineness of folk art, but only endless variations on a few monotonous themes, such as boy makes good, boy wins girl. Lacking a folk tradition, the masses have no use for a tragic hero. They demand a successful hero, at their most exalted a Führer; their scapegoats are villains—the Reds, the Jews, the eggheads. In another aspect, we are oppressed by the multiplicity and heterogeneity of our civilization, the immense complexity and confusion. Underlying the uniformity is a profound disorder, disharmony, disunity. In the arts the great traditions have given way to a welter of changing fashions that at best represent a self-conscious experimentation, at worst a feverish strain for originality. And the most promising innovations are not likely to be promising for tragedy, which is naturally concerned with the permanent, elemental, and universal in experience.

[⁷] Now I believe that modern writers nevertheless can write, and have written, drama worthy of being dignified by this name. It is my thesis that the realism which is the obvious source of the limitations of modern tragedy is also the chief source of its strength; or in other words, that this tragedy is at its best when it is most distinctively modern. For it is bound to be different from ancient tragedy, and in some respects is bound to suffer from the inevitable comparison with it. The responsible modern writer cannot escape the radical and continuous change that the political, industrial, and scientific revolutions have brought about. He cannot blink the new knowledge about the nature and history of man and the universe, cannot evade the terms of life in a mass society. He cannot write like Sophocles or Shakespeare. Nor is there any hope of realizing Fergusson's ideal theater. The magnificent theater of Athens was possible only because of the littleness of Athens, the intimacy of its civic life; and Shakespeare's England was still relatively cozy. Broadway can never be the focus of the national life.

[8] Yet it is possible to take such news calmly. The inevitable comparisons should also remind us how few writers have written great tragedy, and how brief were the periods of its greatness. History does not indicate that the state of drama, or the idea of a theater, is a good index to the state of culture as a whole. It does indicate the need of qualifying somewhat the laments over the plight of the modern dramatist, with his restricted audience. For Athens was a rare exception in cultural history. In almost all other societies serious drama, like poetry, was addressed to the few; the rise of an elite is the norm in the history of literature. The *Divine Comedy*—Fergusson's *ne plus ultra*—was itself written for a very small audience.

[9] We should also suspect possible sentimental exaggeration in the ideal picture of the Greek or Elizabethan theater, with a homogeneous audience united in a semi-religious experience. Although we cannot know just what the Athenian or Elizabethan man on the street thought and felt—we scarcely hear his voice—these were both ages of ferment, of lusty individualism, of underlying doubt and disillusionment, of conflict and change. An audience that gave prizes to both Sophocles and Euripides, or that applauded both *Tamburlaine* and *Hamlet*, evidently comprised considerable diversity of interest and belief; the common faith to which the dramatists appealed was more patriotic than ethical or religious. And some such faith underlies the heterogeneity of the modern audience. This audience is, after all, a group with some common interests, not an anarchic crowd. Its group spirit, as Henri Gouhier points out, is based on a common acceptance of the drama, not a common interpretation of it. Those who cherish a free society—and most of us still share this faith— should not be dismayed by diversity of belief. Those who conceive the ideal audience as a community of fellow believers, stirred by a uniform emotion, at a ritualistic performance, on a ceremonial occasion, might contemplate the crowds whom Hitler harangued. Or they might attend a revivalist meeting.

[10] The plight of our whole culture, real as it is, is likewise oversimplified. As everyone says, we live in a revolutionary world; and it is

therefore full of contradictions, still more complex than it appears. There is no mistaking, for example, the notorious pessimism that Krutch saw as the essence of the modern temper. Yet the decline of faith in the supernatural may tend to make man more self-important than he was as a fallen creature of original sin; those who display least faith in him are typically the traditionalists. Modern man has been given to as notorious a complacence about his progress. Religionists declare that the root evil of our time is man's sinful faith that he can get along without God's help. Particularly in America, optimism has smothered the tragic spirit more than has Krutch's kind of pessimism. Modern writers in general have been less given to despair of the human condition than to indignation over remediable social evils.

[11] And so with science, the ultimate source of both the pessimism and the optimism. In its triumphant advance, it introduced grave complications into the drama of civilization long before it created the problem of how to live with hydrogen bombs. Unquestionably it has undermined the traditional faith that man is the main object of the whole creation, and has therefore led to gloomy views of the meaninglessness of his life, on an insignificant planet in which life itself may be "a disease that afflicts matter in its old age," and is in any case doomed to ultimate extinction. In dealing with man himself, scientists have encouraged further indignities by their fear of the horrid word "value," and their tendency to reduce complex organic phenomena to quantitative material terms, in an effort to improve their dubious scientific status.[1] As a result, men have confused the physical basis of behavior with its essence, and so landed in the kind of "realism" reflected in Krutch's essay. Love, we hear, is "nothing but" sublimated sex, or a biological urge to reproduce the species. And in this century the role of science has become still more paradoxical. A power that men of the Enlightenment believed would banish all mystery, it has now made the universe more mysterious than ever before in the history of thought—not only queerer than we suppose, as one scientist wrote, but "queerer than we *can* suppose."

[12] Yet the new concepts represent a marvelous adventure in thought. While the critics of science picture it as another form of vulgar materialism, it remains a great imaginative enterprise that in its further reaches, as in the speculations of an Einstein, is a more spiritual activity than what commonly passes for spirituality today. It can inspire a much deeper sense of wonder and awe than we get from most modern literature. As the old story goes, the scientist said: "Astronomically speaking, man is negligible";

---

[1] The early behaviorists, for example, demonstrated the purity of their science by basing it on the mechanistic concepts that physicists had already found inadequate for the physical world. Because states of consciousness cannot be measured or objectively observed, they leaped to an elementary fallacy, denying that they existed. (Muller)

the poet replied: "Astronomically speaking, man is the astronomer." But in fact the men of science have often had to tell this to the poets. The greater scientists and philosophers of science have almost uniformly re-asserted the dignity of man, on the basis of the new knowledge. Perhaps the darkest view of man's nature, that of Freud, is still a genuinely tragic view; for if man has to struggle constantly against the dark powers of the unconscious, by the same token he is not at their mercy and may maintain his dignity.

[13] By such considerations I do not mean to minimize the very difficult problems that the responsible modern artist has to contend with, often in the face of the massive indifference of his countrymen. I am merely suggesting that the problems are also challenges, which need to be seen in perspective and from more than one point of view. Neither supported nor restricted by a common convention, writers have responded to the challenge in such diverse ways that one cannot generalize so freely about modern literature as one may about Greek, Elizabethan, or classical French, and should not approach it with set presuppositions and expectations. As for modern tragedy, critics still argue that it is not "really" tragic by some canon derived from the practice—or more often the theory—of the ancients. The fair question is whether, in the new terms imposed by modern knowledge and conditions of life, it still affirms equivalent values and affords an equivalent pleasure.

[14] In a previous work, *Modern Fiction,* I applied this test to a number of major novelists. The tragic spirit has turned to the novel for expression, since it is a form better suited than drama to a complex age, permitting both more amplitude and more inwardness. Only two or three dramatists compare in stature with the two or three dozen greater novelists over the last hundred years. But for the sake of consistency, or convenience, I shall here focus on modern drama. For the playwright the basic problems are complicated by the further need of a theater and an audience; he is not so free to write as he pleases. At the same time, he has a possible advantage in the very limitations of his form. He cannot indulge in the streams of consciousness or the involved analyses that may illumine character but blur the drama, obscure the elemental issues; he is forced to strip and come directly to grips with his theme. I propose, at any rate, to examine a number of diverse playwrights, not necessarily the best of our time, but representative of the major tendencies in modern tragedy, for better or worse. . . .

BOURGEOIS TRAGEDY: IBSEN

[15] The Ibsen who thrilled and shocked all Europe, and had so profound an influence on modern drama, is the Ibsen of *Ghosts,* the first great bourgeois tragedy. This is not strictly a representative work. He was greater than any one of his plays, and himself declared that his poetry was

to be found only in his plays as a whole, no one of which was complete by itself. Neither was *Ghosts* a sudden or complete innovation. We have seen the rise of bourgeois tragedy in the eighteenth century, and may find its beginnings in Elizabethan drama; in Ibsen's own lifetime Hebbel prepared the ground by his dramatic theory, as well as his play *Maria Magdalena*. In general, the time was ripe for Ibsen. Yet he was the genius who rose to the occasion—as genius does not invariably do. The originality of *Ghosts* is sufficiently proved by the sensation it caused. At its first performance in Berlin a Danish critic announced: "This day marks the beginning of a new literary era." Brandes wrote as truly that the play made Ibsen "the most modern of the moderns." And it was a conscious innovation, the product of a long, slow growth. Ibsen was over fifty years old when he wrote it.

[16] He had begun by writing romantic drama based on Teutonic saga, the "heroic" past of Norway. His revulsion against the sentimental romanticism that Wagner never outgrew at first found expression in poetic dramas, *Brand* and *Peer Gynt,* but finally carried all the way to realistic prose drama about contemporary life. He rejected verse as "most injurious to dramatic art," and especially unsuitable for his new purposes because of his conviction that modern life did not permit grandeur. With *Pillars of Society* and *A Doll's House* he restricted his action to topical social problems, his scene to the bourgeois parlor.

[17] These self-imposed limitations raise the immediate issues. *Ghosts* appears to be about an ordinary young man, Oswald, who falls victim to softening of the brain, due to syphilis inherited from a father who was a pillar of local society but secretly dissolute. As the play opens, the father has just died. Oswald's mother, Mrs. Alving, is resolved that after her long ordeal of keeping up false appearances, they shall now lead a life of freedom, joy, and truth. The plot thickens as she discovers that the son who she has proudly announced is hers alone, and who shall owe nothing to his father, is taking to the ways of the father. The denouement comes when she learns that he is doomed by syphilis, and wants of her only the promise of a killing dose of morphine when the next attack leaves him helpless. The play concludes with the onset of the fatal attack. Oswald tonelessly asks for "the sun, the sun." After shrieking "I cannot bear it!" Mrs. Alving stares at him in "speechless horror." The apparent thesis is the falsity of conventional bourgeois marriage—an idea that today seems less than revolutionary. This once shocking play is also dated by Ibsen's dramaturgy, which here leans heavily on coincidences, pat ironies, theatrical curtains—the tricks of the "well-made" play.

[18] Krutch made *Ghosts* a prime exhibit of the "mean misery" that passes for modern tragedy. He contrasted the wretched Oswald with the tragic heroes of yore, describing his failure as "trivial and meaningless"; the upshot is simply despair, "intolerable because it is no longer signifi-

cant or important." Fergusson also uses *Ghosts* as an exhibit of modern realism, and though he makes a much more acute study of it, he arrives at almost as melancholy a conclusion. Recognizing that the play belongs to Mrs. Alving rather than Oswald, he makes out a tragic rhythm comparable to the rhythm in *Œdipus Rex*: like Œdipus, she is "engaged in a quest for her true human condition," and as the action develops, attains to an ever clearer, fuller realization of the meaning of her past. But the all-important difference is that her tragic quest is not completed—it is "brutally truncated." Her shriek at the end drives home the thesis but in this deeper sense concludes nothing: "it is merely sensational." Neither is the action of the drama "placed in the wider context of meanings" that poetry demands. Ibsen illumines most brilliantly "the limitations of the bourgeois parlor as the scene of human life." And all critics add that the social-problem play is bound to become dated, lose point and force. Thus Nora thrilled or scandalized our parents as she slammed the door at the end of *A Doll's House,* leaving her selfish, petty husband after asserting her woman's right to a life of her own; but now we may ponder a little wearily why it took her so long to see through so transparent a husband and arrive at so elementary a decision.

[19] Yet such losses are not wholly unprecedented—else scholars would be out of a job. We wonder often enough at the behavior of Greek and Elizabethan heroes, whose dramas likewise reflect topical interests and require historical understanding; the footnotes that explain the point do not restore the whole impact. Ibsen is actually no more dated than Dante. Before deploring sociological fiction and drama, in any case, we should ask the obvious question: *why* have modern writers turned to this genre? For with Ibsen, again, it was a deliberate choice. He was not by nature or nurture given to the realism that many lesser writers have since taken for granted.

[20] To begin with, let us recognize the legitimacy and the value of timely drama. Posterity need not be the main concern of a responsible artist. He can still be respected if he speaks powerfully only to his own age, for the great majority of serious writers can hope for no more than this, and without the mass of honorable second-rate work we could not hope to have the "timeless" masterpieces. We should also acknowledge our lasting indebtedness to some dated work. "It seemed to me," wrote the Ibsen of *Ghosts,* "that the time had come for moving some boundary-posts." If the work that impressed Brandes as his "noblest deed" now seems commonplace in its thesis, the influence of Ibsen helped to make it commonplace. His sociological drama represented another landmark in the advance of consciousness. It was a stimulus to imagination, not a mere cramp. It gave writers more freedom and scope.

[21] Above all, this is a wholly natural type of tragedy—given a serious concern with man's fate. Through the rise of science, writers have become

more aware of the hereditary and environmental forces that actually determine the fate of most men. The indifference of Shakespeare and the Greeks to such forces was not wholly a matter of lofty artistic principle: it signified as well a limited understanding. In our vast, complex civilization, moreover, the individual may be more at the mercy of his social environment, or more conscious of his impotence. In short Ibsen was telling a significant tragic truth about modern life. He himself did not regard the doom of Oswald as "trivial and meaningless." Only a literary critic with a thesis could do so.

[22] Shakespeare and the Greeks also believed that they were "holding up the mirror to nature," telling the tragic truth about man's life. Modern realism is different in its closer literalness and its common concern with the ordinary man, the familiar and average in experience. But Fergusson confuses its issues by defining its "essence" in terms of its most superficial aspects, as a "strictly photographic imitation of the human scene," or in the words of T. S. Eliot, reality as "perceived by the most commonplace mind." Hence he declares that realism imposes upon the writer the "necessity" of pretending that he has no poetic purpose, but is aiming only at truth. The poetry he finds in Ibsen is always "hidden" or "evident only to the histrionic sensibility." It is a "triumph" whenever Ibsen transcends the literal, reveals an intention "more philosophical than history." Actually, all the greater realists have had such an intention, none has confined himself to the literal. If the realistic method has manifest dangers, anyone who knows Balzac, Flaubert, Hardy, Turgenev, Tolstoy, and Dostoyevsky will not equate realism with meagerness and superficiality. As for Ibsen, our immediate concern is not the wonder that he managed to smuggle some poetry and philosophy into his drama, but the scope and depth of the vision that he naturally, unmistakably did embody. Our final concern is the tragic values of a drama that deliberately eschews splendor and grandeur.

[23] Although *Ghosts* is no affair with the gods, many still find it a powerful drama, and not primarily because of its demonstration that hereditary syphilis is a damnable thing. One obvious source of its power is the tragic sense of inevitable doom, a fated action that may be associated with Greek fatalism, or with the Hebraic idea that the sins of the father are visited upon the children. In either case it may be called a "timeless" theme. Another means to wider connections is the symbolism indicated in the title (as in the typical titles of Ibsen's bourgeois dramas— *Pillars of Society, A Doll's House, The Wild Duck*). Underlying the surface thesis is the more significant idea that Mrs. Alving realizes in the course of her tragic quest:

I am half inclined to think we are all ghosts, Mr. Manders. It is not only what we have inherited from our fathers and mothers that exists again in us, but all sorts of dead ideas and all kinds of old dead beliefs and things of that kind.

They are not actually alive in us; but they are dormant all the same, and we can never be rid of them. Whenever I take up a newspaper and read it, I fancy I see ghosts creeping between the lines. There must be ghosts all over the world. They must be as countless as the grains of sand, it seems to me. And we are so miserably afraid of the light, all of us.

Such ghosts keep returning in Ibsen's drama, whose people are mostly fearful of the light or unable to endure it; and this theme has lost none of its point or force. It has always been true, though ancient writers were disposed to revere the ghosts. It is especially pertinent in a revolutionary world, when traditional beliefs are so often at variance with changed conditions and new knowledge. And Ibsen habitually set it in a still wider context. His bourgeois parlors, haunted by ghosts, are invaded by thoughts of the elemental wildness of mountain, fen, and fiord. Mrs. Alving's parlor looks out on snow-capped mountain peaks, which are lit by the rising sun as the tragedy comes to a close—the sun that Oswald begs for, the glow in which she has aspired to live with him.

[24] Yet this vision of mountain peaks produces no exhilaration: it only intensifies the "speechless horror" of Mrs. Alving. And here again is the ultimate issue of realistic tragedy. Fergusson finds this ending literal, brutal, merely sensational. Others agree that it is merely depressing, effecting no catharsis. There is no reconciliation, no equilibrium of good and evil. The issue becomes more difficult if one feels, as I do, that Ibsen was not being sensational, but had good reasons for ending his bleak play as he did. Since the tragic spirit has always been fundamentally realistic, the modern realist says in effect: Let us tell the whole tragic truth. Let us admit that there is no apparent moral order governing the universe. Let us recognize that the "true human condition" may often be helpless and hopeless, strictly irreconcilable. Tragedy cannot serve the deepest needs of modern man unless it drops such pretenses as that a Fortinbras will restore the health of Denmark—an idea as naïve as the popular faith in the U. S. Marines. Let us not have "complete actions" at the expense of the tragic truth.

[25] On this issue one must begin by speaking only for himself. Whether or not one derives the pleasure of tragedy from *Ghosts* is not primarily a matter of sure, fine esthetic taste, but again a matter of temperament, or philosophical predisposition. Neither can one dispose of the issue by an appeal to "truth." An utterly sordid or horrible story can be quite true— the newspapers are full of them. Ibsen's *Hedda Gabler* is another powerful drama, a realistic study of a neurotic, predatory woman who destroys her lover and herself; but it seems to me too abnormal and purely horrible to be a great tragic drama. Yet *Ghosts,* and Ibsen's drama as a whole, can provide an experience comparable in kind to the experience of Greek

and Shakespearean tragedy, if less rich and deep. And having granted a temperamental factor, one may point to some objective qualities of Ibsen's drama that validate this experience, and with it the judgment that he belongs among the greater writers of tragedy.

[26] For one thing, Ibsen himself clearly did not intend *Ghosts* as a message of despair. He was saying that men need not be so miserably afraid of the light. By the same token he was not the cynic or nihilist that horrified conservatives made of him. As a helpless victim of the ghosts, Oswald is a pitiable figure, far from heroic but by no means contemptible. His much more admirable mother arouses both pity and terror. Her tragic quest leads her to a belated perception of Ibsen's positive values. It bears out his explicit statement of the tragic faith that at least partly offsets the horror:

It has been said of me on different occasions that I am a pessimist. And I am in so far as I do not believe in the everlastingness of human ideals. But I am an optimist in so far as I firmly believe in the capacity for the procreation and development of ideals.

[27] Most of all Ibsen was devoted to the ideal of freedom. His bourgeois dramas illustrate his lifelong effort to emancipate the individual from bourgeois conventionality. Like Mrs. Alving, almost all his heroes are engaged in the tragic quest to realize themselves, discover in freedom their true human condition. In the light of human history, with its overwhelming preponderance of closed societies, this is not strictly a perennial, universal theme; but it is an appropriate theme for high tragedy, and surely has lost none of its pertinence for us today. And Ibsen treated it in a spirit not only liberal but tragic. He went deeper than the Marxists and other political reformers, once commenting that they wanted only liberties, not liberty. (Leftists had joined the bourgeoisie in denouncing *Ghosts*.) He was much more complex and ironic, aware of the evils that inevitably attend the quest for freedom.

[28] One witness to both the depth and the loftiness of Ibsen is Thomas Mann, who coupled him with Wagner as "northern wizards" or "weavers of spells," among the giants of the century. (It is well to remember that this century which is conventionally divided into Romantic and Victorian, both epithets of disparagement today, was in fact a century of giants— artists like Balzac, Zola, Dostoyevsky, and Tolstoy, working on a grand scale.) The most striking witness is Nicolas Berdyaev, who testified to the enormous influence Ibsen had on him during the spiritual crisis following his emancipation from Marxism. He found in the reputedly cramped realist a prophet comparable to Dostoyevsky and Nietzsche, and was fired by his scorn of the bourgeois spirit, his concern for the heroic personality, the heights, the mountaintops. As a theologian, Berdyaev was obliged to

add that Ibsen had lost sight of the living God, was ignorant of the final meaning of sin, and could not find the way to the heights—or in other words, was a tragic rather than a Christian poet; yet he linked him with Kierkegaard, in his contempt for the spirit of compromise. For Berdyaev, Ibsen's main theme was the eternal conflict between dream and reality, creativity and life, the heroic personality and the conventional collective.

⸺⊰ C O M M E N T   A N D   Q U E S T I O N S ⊱⸻

1. Joseph Wood Krutch, the author says in paragraph 2, "argued that modern knowledge has killed the tragic faith." What appears to be the meaning of *tragic faith?*

2. Muller alludes in paragraph 3 to Aristotle's definition of tragedy: "an imitation of an action that is serious, complete, and of a certain magnitude . . . through pity and fear effecting the purgation of these emotions." If you have read Ihab Hassan's essay "The Anti-Hero," do you think that an anti-hero can stir pity and fear? Explain.

3. Paragraphs 2–6 discuss the reasons for the common belief that modern man cannot write tragedy. Which, if any, of these reasons seem convincing to you? Explain.

4. Paragraph 7 states the author's thesis. In that paragraph and the following paragraphs (8–14), to what extent does Muller accept the premises of the critics who are pessimistic about modern drama? In what principal ways does he disagree with these critics?

5. Why does Muller present so fully, in paragraph 18, the adverse criticism of *Ghosts?*

6. In paragraphs 19 and 20, the author defends the timely, topical drama. To what extent do you agree or disagree with his idea that posterity need not be the main concern of the serious writer? Explain.

7. What significant tragic truths and themes does Muller find in *Ghosts?*

8. Most writers about tragedy agree that great tragedy is an affirmation of values; although the drama ends in disaster, it does not end in horror or despair, and it leaves the spectator or reader with a sense of elevation. Muller says that the end of *Ghosts* "produces no exhilaration." How does he justify Ibsen's ending?

9. In what ways does the discussion of *Ghosts* support Muller's thesis that "the realism which is the obvious source of the limitations of modern tragedy is also the chief source of its strength"?

10. If you have read *Ghosts,* to what extent do you agree or disagree with Muller's judgment of the play, and why?

11. If you have not read *Ghosts,* what is your reaction to the discussion and evaluation of the play?

12. In the whole of his chapter "Modern Tragedy," Muller discusses the work
of Wagner, Ibsen, Strindberg, Hauptmann, Chekhov, T. S. Eliot, Sartre,
O'Neill, and (briefly) Maxwell Anderson, Arthur Miller, and Tennessee
Williams. Comment on a play that you know, written by any of these
dramatists. Does the play seem to you "real" tragedy? Explain.

[56] *Martin Esslin*: The Significance of the Absurd

MARTIN ESSLIN (1918–) is a London theatrical producer and director
of drama for the B. B. C. A student of the theater in both Europe and
America, Esslin has taught in the department of dramatic arts and speech
at the University of California and is the author of *Brecht: The Man and His
Work* and *The Theatre of the Absurd* (1961), from which the following
selection is taken.

[1] When Nietzsche's Zarathustra descended from his mountains to
preach to mankind, he met a saintly hermit in the forest. This old man
invited him to stay in the wilderness rather than go into the cities of men.
When Zarathustra asked the hermit how he passed his time in his solitude, he replied:

I make up songs and sing them; and when I make up songs I laugh, I weep,
and I growl; thus do I praise God.

Zarathustra declined the old man's offer and continued on his journey:

But when he was alone, he spoke thus to his heart: "Can it be possible! This
old saint in the forest has not yet heard that God is dead!"

[2] *Zarathustra* was first published in 1883. The number of people for
whom God is dead has greatly increased since Nietzsche's day, and mankind has learned the bitter lesson of the falseness and evil nature of some
of the cheap and vulgar substitutes that have been set up to take His
place. And so, after two terrible wars, there are still many who are trying
to come to terms with the implications of Zarathustra's message, searching
for a way in which they can, with dignity, confront a universe deprived
of what was once its center and its living purpose, a world deprived of a

generally accepted integrating principle, which has become disjointed, purposeless—absurd.

[3] The Theatre of the Absurd is one of the expressions of this search. It bravely faces up to the fact that for those to whom the world has lost its central explanation and meaning, it is no longer possible to accept art forms still based on the continuation of standards and concepts that have lost their validity; that is, the possibility of knowing the laws of conduct and ultimate values, as deducible from a firm foundation of revealed certainty about the purpose of man in the universe.

[4] In expressing the tragic sense of loss at the disappearance of ultimate certainties the Theatre of the Absurd, by a strange paradox, is also a symptom of what probably comes nearest to being a genuine religious quest in our age: an effort, however timid and tentative, to sing, to laugh, to weep—and to growl—if not in praise of God (whose name, in Adamov's phrase, has for so long been degraded by usage that it has lost its meaning), at least in search of a dimension of the Ineffable; an effort to make man aware of the ultimate realities of his condition, to instill in him again the lost sense of cosmic wonder and primeval anguish, to shock him out of an existence that has become trite, mechanical, complacent, and deprived of the dignity that comes of awareness. For God is dead, above all, to the masses who live from day to day and have lost all contact with the basic facts—and mysteries—of the human condition with which, in former times, they were kept in touch through the living ritual of their religion, which made them parts of a real community and not just atoms in an atomized society.

[5] The Theatre of the Absurd forms part of the unceasing endeavor of the true artists of our time to breach this dead wall of complacency and automatism and to re-establish an awareness of man's situation when confronted with the ultimate reality of his condition. As such, the Theatre of the Absurd fulfills a dual purpose and presents its audience with a twofold absurdity.

[6] On the one hand, it castigates, satirically, the absurdity of lives lived unaware and unconscious of ultimate reality. This is the feeling of the deadness and mechanical senselessness of half-unconscious lives, the feeling of "human beings secreting inhumanity," which Camus describes in *The Myth of Sisyphus*:

> In certain hours of lucidity, the mechanical aspect of their gestures, their senseless pantomime, makes stupid everything around them. A man speaking on the telephone behind a glass partition—one cannot hear him but observes his trivial gesturing. One asks oneself, why is he alive? This malaise in front of man's own inhumanity, this incalculable letdown when faced with the image of what we are, this "nausea," as a contemporary writer calls it, also is the Absurd.

[7] This is the experience that Ionesco expresses in plays like *The Bald Soprano* or *The Chairs*, Adamov in *La Parodie*, or N. F. Simpson in *A Resounding Tinkle*. It represents the satirical, parodistic aspect of the Theatre of the Absurd, its social criticism, its pillorying of an inauthentic, petty society. This may be the most easily accessible, and therefore most widely recognized, message of the Theatre of the Absurd, but it is far from being its most essential or most significant feature.

[8] Behind the satirical exposure of the absurdity of inauthentic ways of life, the Theatre of the Absurd is facing up to a deeper layer of absurdity—the absurdity of the human condition itself in a world where the decline of religious belief has deprived man of certainties. When it is no longer possible to accept simple and complete systems of values and revelations of divine purpose, life must be faced in its ultimate, stark reality. That is why, in the analysis of the dramatists of the Absurd in this book, we have always seen man stripped of the accidental circumstances of social position or historical context, confronted with the basic choices, the basic situations of his existence: man faced with time and therefore waiting, in Beckett's plays or Gelber's, waiting between birth and death; man running away from death, climbing higher and higher, in Vian's play, or passively sinking down toward death, in Buzzati's; man rebelling against death, confronting and accepting it, in Ionesco's *Tueur Sans Gages;* man inextricably entangled in a mirage of illusions, mirrors reflecting mirrors, and forever hiding ultimate reality, in the plays of Genet; man trying to establish his position, or to break out into freedom, only to find himself newly imprisoned, in the parables of Manuel de Pedrolo; man trying to stake out a modest place for himself in the cold and darkness that envelop him, in Pinter's plays; man vainly striving to grasp the moral law forever beyond his comprehension, in Arrabal's; man caught in the inescapable dilemma that strenuous effort leads to the same result as passive indolence—complete futility and ultimate death—in the earlier work of Adamov; man forever lonely, immured in the prison of his subjectivity, unable to reach his fellow man, in the vast majority of these plays.

[9] Concerned as it is with the ultimate realities of the human condition, the relatively few fundamental problems of life and death, isolation and communication, the Theatre of the Absurd, however grotesque, frivolous, and irreverent it may appear, represents a return to the original, religious function of the theatre—the confrontation of man with the spheres of myth and religious reality. Like ancient Greek tragedy and the medieval mystery plays and baroque allegories, the Theatre of the Absurd is intent on making its audience aware of man's precarious and mysterious position in the universe. . . .

[10] In the "literary" theatre, language remains the predominant com-

ponent. In the anti-literary theatre of the circus or the music hall, language is reduced to a very subordinate role. The Theatre of the Absurd has regained the freedom of using language as merely one—sometimes dominant, sometimes submerged—component of its multidimensional poetic imagery. By putting the language of a scene in contrast to the action, by reducing it to meaningless patter, or by abandoning discursive logic for the poetic logic of association or assonance, the Theatre of the Absurd has opened up a new dimension of the stage.

[11] In its devaluation of language, the Theatre of the Absurd is in tune with the trend of our time. As George Steiner has pointed out in two radio talks entitled *The Retreat from the Word*, the devaluation of language is characteristic not only of the development of contemporary poetry or philosophical thought but, even more, of modern mathematics and the natural sciences. "It is no paradox to assert," Steiner says, "that much of reality now begins *outside* language. . . . Large areas of meaningful experience now belong to non-verbal languages such as mathematics, formulae, and logical symbolism. Others belong to 'anti-languages' such as the practice of nonobjective art or atonal music. The world of the word has shrunk." Moreover, the abandonment of language as the best instrument of notation in the spheres of mathematics and symbolic logic goes hand in hand with a marked reduction in the popular belief in its practical usefulness. Language appears more and more as being in contradiction to reality. The trends of thought that have the greatest influence on contemporary popular thinking all show this tendency.

[12] Take the case of Marxism. Here a distinction is made between *apparent* social relations and the social *reality* behind them. Objectively, an employer is seen as an exploiter, and therefore an enemy, of the working class. If an employer therefore says to a worker; "I have sympathy with your point of view," he may himself believe what he is saying, but objectively his words are meaningless. However much he asserts his sympathy for the worker, he remains his enemy. Language here belongs to the realm of the purely subjective, and is thus devoid of objective reality.

[13] The same applies to modern depth psychology and psychoanalysis. Every child today knows that there is a vast gap between what is consciously thought and asserted and the psychological reality behind the words spoken. A son who tells his father that he loves and respects him is objectively bound to be, in fact, filled with the deepest Oedipal hatred of his father. He may not know it, but he means the opposite of what he says. And the subconscious has a higher content of reality than the conscious utterance.

[14] The relativization, devaluation, and criticism of language are also the prevailing trends in contemporary philosophy, as exemplified by Wittgenstein's conviction, in the last phase of his thinking, that the phi-

losopher must endeavor to disentangle thought from the conventions and rules of grammar, which have been mistaken for the rules of logic. "A *picture* held us captive. And we could not get outside it, for it lay in our language, and language seemed to repeat it to us inexorably. . . . Where does our investigation get its importance from, since it seems only to destroy everything interesting; that is, all that is great and important? (As it were, all the buildings, leaving behind only bits of stone and rubble.) What we are destroying is nothing but houses of cards, and we are clearing up the ground of language on which they stand." By a strict criticism of language, Wittgenstein's followers have declared large categories of statements to be devoid of objective meaning. Wittgenstein's "word games" have much in common with the Theatre of the Absurd.

[15] But even more significant than these tendencies in Marxist, psychological, and philosophical thinking is the trend of the times in the workaday world of the man in the street. Exposed to the incessant, and inexorably loquacious, onslaught of the mass media, the press, and advertising, the man in the street becomes more and more skeptical toward the language he is exposed to. The citizens of totalitarian countries know full well that most of what they are told is double-talk, devoid of real meaning. They become adept at reading between the lines; that is, at guessing at the reality the language conceals rather than reveals. In the West, euphemisms and circumlocutions fill the press or resound from the pulpits. And advertising, by its constant use of superlatives, has succeeded in devaluing language to a point where it is a generally accepted axiom that most of the words one sees displayed on billboards or in the colored pages of magazine advertising are as meaningless as the jingles of television commercials. A yawning gulf has opened between language and reality.

[16] Apart from the general devaluation of language in the flood of mass communications, the growing specialization of life has made the exchange of ideas on an increasing number of subjects impossible between members of different spheres of life which have each developed its own specialized jargon. As Ionesco says, in summarizing and enlarging on, the views of Antonin Artaud:

As our knowledge becomes separated from life, our culture no longer contains ourselves (or only an insignificant part of ourselves), for it forms a "social" context into which we are not integrated. So the problem becomes that of bringing our life back into contact with our culture, making it a living culture once again. To achieve this, we shall first have to kill "the respect for what is written down in black and white" . . . to break up our language so that it can be put together again in order to re-establish contact with "the absolute," or, as I should prefer to say, "with multiple reality"; it is imperative to "push human beings again toward seeing themselves as they really are."

[17] That is why communication between human beings is so often shown in a state of breakdown in the Theatre of the Absurd. It is merely

a satirical magnification of the existing state of affairs. Language has run riot in an age of mass communication. It must be reduced to its proper function—the expression of authentic content, rather than its conceal- ment. But this will be possible only if man's reverence toward the spoken or written word as a means of communication is restored, and the ossified clichés that dominate thought (as they do in the limericks of Edward Lear or the world of Humpty Dumpty) are replaced by a living language that serves it. And this, in turn, can be achieved only if the limitations of logic and discursive language are recognized and respected, and the uses of poetic language acknowledged.

[18] The means by which the dramatists of the Absurd express their critique—largely instinctive and unintended—of our disintegrating soci- ety are based on suddenly confronting their audiences with a grotesquely heightened and distorted picture of a world that has gone mad. This is a shock therapy that achieves what Brecht's doctrine of the "alienation effect" postulated in theory but failed to achieve in practice—the inhibi- tion of the audience's identification with the characters on the stage (which is the age-old and highly effective method of the traditional theatre) and its replacement by a detached, critical attitude. . . .

[19] The madness of the times lies precisely in the existence, side by side, of a large number of unreconciled beliefs and attitudes—conven- tional morality, for example, on the one hand, and the values of adver- tising on the other; the conflicting claims of science and religion; or the loudly proclaimed striving of all sections for the general interest when in fact each is pursuing very narrow and selfish particular ends. On each page of his newspaper, the man in the street is confronted with a different and contradictory pattern of values. No wonder that the art of such an era shows a marked resemblance to the symptoms of schizophrenia. But it is not, as Jung has pointed out in an essay on Joyce's *Ulysses,* the artist who is schizophrenic: "The medical description of schizophrenia offers only an analogy, in that the schizophrenic has apparently the same tend- ency to treat reality as if it were strange to him, or, the other way around, to estrange himself from reality. In the modern artist, this tendency is not produced by any disease in the individual but is a manifestation of our time."

[20] The challenge to make sense out of what appears as a senseless and fragmented action, the recognition that the fact that the modern world has lost its unifying principle is the source of its bewildering and soul-destroying quality, is therefore more than a mere intellectual exer- cise; it has a therapeutic effect. In Greek tragedy, the spectators were made aware of man's forlorn but heroic stand against the inexorable forces of fate and the will of the gods—and this had a cathartic effect upon them and made them better able to face their time. In the Theatre

of the Absurd, the spectator is confronted with the madness of the human condition, is enabled to see his situation in all its grimness and despair, and this, in stripping him of illusions or vaguely felt fears and anxieties, enables him to face it consciously, rather than feel it vaguely below the surface of euphemisms and optimistic illusions. And this, in turn, results in the liberating effect of anxieties overcome by being formulated. This is the nature of all the gallows humor and *humour noir* of world literature, of which the Theatre of the Absurd is the latest example. It is the unease caused by the presence of illusions that are obviously out of tune with reality that is dissolved and discharged through liberating laughter at the recognition of the fundamental absurdity of the universe. The greater the anxieties and the temptation to indulge in illusions, the more beneficial is this therapeutic effect—hence the success of *Waiting for Godot* at San Quentin. It was a relief for the convicts to be made to recognize in the tragicomic situation of the tramps the hopelessness of their own waiting for a miracle. They were enabled to laugh at the tramps—and at themselves.

[21] As the reality with which the Theatre of the Absurd is concerned is a psychological reality expressed in images that are the outward projection of states of mind, fears, dreams, nightmares, and conflicts within the personality of the author, the dramatic tension produced by this kind of play differs fundamentally from the suspense created in a theatre concerned mainly with the revelation of objective characters through the unfolding of a narrative plot. The pattern of exposition, conflict, and final solution mirrors a view of the world in which solutions are possible, a view based on a recognizable and generally accepted pattern of an objective reality that can be apprehended so that the purpose of man's existence and the rules of conduct it entails can be deduced from it.

[22] This is true even of the lightest type of drawing-room comedy, in which the action proceeds on a deliberately restricted view of the world—that the sole purpose of the characters involved is for each boy to get his girl. And even in the darkest pessimistic tragedies of the naturalistic or Expressionist theatres, the final curtain enables the audience to go home with a formulated message or philosophy in their minds: the solution may have been a sad one, but it was a rationally formulated conclusion nevertheless. This, as I pointed out in the introduction, applies even to the theatre of Sartre and Camus, which is based on a philosophy of the absurdity of human existence. Even plays like *Huis Clos* (*No Exit*), *Le Diable et le Bon Dieu* (*Lucifer and the Lord*), and *Caligula* allow the audience to take home an intellectually formulated philosophical lesson.

[23] The Theatre of the Absurd, however, which proceeds not by intellectual concepts but by poetic images, neither poses an intellectual problem in its exposition nor provides any clear-cut solution that would

be reducible to a lesson or an apothegm. Many of the plays of the Theatre of the Absurd have a circular structure, ending exactly as they began; others progress merely by a growing intensification of the initial situation. And as the Theatre of the Absurd rejects the idea that it is possible to motivate all human behavior, or that human character is based on an immutable essence, it is impossible for it to base its effect on the suspense that in other dramatic conventions springs from awaiting the solution of a dramatic equation based on the working out of a problem involving clearly defined quantities introduced in the opening scenes. In most dramatic conventions, the audience is constantly asking itself the question "What is going to happen next?"

[24] In the Theatre of the Absurd, the audience is confronted with actions that lack apparent motivation, characters that are in constant flux, and often happenings that are clearly outside the realm of rational experience. Here, too, the audience can ask, "What is going to happen next?" But then *anything* may happen next, so that the answer to this question cannot be worked out according to the rules of ordinary probability based on motives and characterizations that will remain constant throughout the play. The relevant question here is not so much what is going to happen next but what *is* happening? "What does the action of the play represent?" . . .

[25] Ultimately, a phenomenon like the Theatre of the Absurd does not reflect despair or a return to dark irrational forces but expresses modern man's endeavor to come to terms with the world in which he lives. It attempts to make him face up to the human condition as it really is, to free him from illusions that are bound to cause constant maladjustment and disappointment. There are enormous pressures in our world that seek to induce mankind to bear the loss of faith and moral certainties by being drugged into oblivion—by mass entertainments, shallow material satisfactions, pseudo-explanations of reality, and cheap ideologies. At the end of that road lies Huxley's Brave New World of senseless euphoric automata. Today, when death and old age are increasingly concealed behind euphemisms and comforting baby talk, and life is threatened with being smothered in the mass consumption of hypnotic mechanized vulgarity, the need to confront man with the reality of his situation is greater than ever. For the dignity of man lies in his ability to face reality in all its senselessness; to accept it freely, without fear, without illusions—and to laugh at it.

[26] That is the cause to which, in their various individual, modest, and quixotic ways, the dramatists of the Absurd are dedicated.

--◄ COMMENT AND QUESTIONS ►--

1. The author refers, in paragraph 2, to "the falseness and evil nature of some of the cheap and vulgar substitutes" set up to take God's place in the world. What does he appear to mean by such "substitutes"?

2. Esslin several times uses the word *dignity*, although many of the characters of the Absurd dramatists lack the qualities we conventionally associate with this word. In what sense is the Theater of the Absurd concerned with human dignity?

3. What are the author's reasons for believing that the Theater of the Absurd represents a kind of religious quest? To what extent do you agree or disagree with his reasoning? Explain.

4. Paragraph 5, a transitional paragraph, introduces the two purposes or messages of the Theater of the Absurd. What are the two? How are they related? Why does Esslin consider the second message more important than the first?

5. "In its devaluation of language," Esslin says at the beginning of paragraph 11, "the Theatre of the Absurd is in tune with the trend of our time." What parts of the author's discussion of the divorce between language and reality (paragraphs 11–17) are most meaningful to you? Explain.

6. In a section that we have omitted, Esslin discusses parallels between Zen Buddhism and the Theater of the Absurd. If you have read William Barrett's "Zen for the West," what parallels can you see between Zen and the Theater of the Absurd?

7. If you have read I. A. Richards' "Science and Poetry," do you see any similarities between the experience of the good reader of poetry, as Richards describes it, and the experience of the audience at the Theater of the Absurd? Explain.

8. Paragraphs 21–24 contrast the Theater of the Absurd and conventional drama. Herbert J. Muller, in his discussion of modern tragedy and of Ibsen's *Ghosts,* is talking about conventional drama. If you have read the selection from Muller, do you think that he could agree with any or all of the premises of the Theater of the Absurd? Explain.

9. Summarize in your own words the values Esslin sees in the Theater of the Absurd.

[57] *Walter Allen*: And Now
the Mid-Atlantic Man

W A L T E R   A L L E N (1911–   ), a British critic and biographer who has
been a visiting professor at Vassar, is the author of a number of books including
Arnold Bennett, The English Novel, Six Great Novelists, Tradition and Dream,
and *The Modern Novel in Britain and the United States.* The following article
appeared in *The New York Times Book Review,* December 27, 1964.

[1] Mid-Atlantic man is a species very much on the increase. The best
English undergraduates, whatever their fields, now take it for granted
that they will do some of their post-graduate work in the United States.
For more and more young Englishmen the home town and New York
are adjacent parishes, and not only New York but a host of other cities
throughout the United States. When these young men begin to write
novels, America will be their natural scene almost as much as England.

[2] Already, the English experience of America has become a subject
for English novelists. We had three novels on the theme last year, Andrew
Sinclair's "The Hallelujah Bums," Pamela Hansford Johnson's "Night
and Silence Who Is Here?" and Kingsley Amis's "One Fat Englishman."
Despite the difference in the nature of their talents, all three of these
authors are Mid-Atlantic. At the center of all three novels is an Englishman in America.

[3] Miss Hansford Johnson's novel is perhaps the most "English" of the
three; Andrew Sinclair's, as one might expect from a historian whose field
is American history, the most "American"; his title is not the only thing
about the book reminiscent of Jack Kerouac. But in all three novels the
presentation of the American characters is essential to the authors' ends,
and here, it seems to me, the authors are notably successful. These novels
are light-hearted comedies; but they achieve what they set out to do,
and they are pointers to the future.

[4] It has never been a simple thing for English novelists to create
American characters convincing to Americans, or for American novelists
to create English characters convincing to Englishmen. Mrs. Winifred
Hurtle, in Anthony Trollope's "The Way We Live Now," may not be
among the most famous characters in English fiction but she is an extremely interesting one, especially in this connection. Mrs. Hurtle, an

American lady from the Far West, reputed to have "shot a man through the head in Oregon" and also to have fought a duel with her husband, is in love with Trollope's hero Paul Montagu, who, in a period of infatuation, has proposed marriage to her when in the United States, though he is in love with an English girl. Mrs. Hurtle crosses the Atlantic and pursues him to London in order to pin him down to his promise.

[5] She is indeed Trollope's version of the emancipated American girl Henry James dramatizes so differently in "The Portrait of a Lady" and "The Wings of the Dove." As a result of teaching Trollope's novel at Vassar to a group (the word seems inescapable) of very bright students, I have recently changed my opinion of her. In the past, I have taken her as an expression of a Victorian Englishman's horrified reaction to the 19th-century American woman's claim to freedom and sexual equality.

[6] She seemed to me a figure of melodrama, and I still find the pistol-packin' momma part a little much to swallow. What led me to revise my interpretation of Mrs. Hurtle, in part at least, was that my students at Vassar had no difficulty in accepting her as a credible representation of American 19th-century womanhood. For them, she was much more believable than her English foil in the novel, Hetta Carbury, who had seemed to me adequate, albeit unexciting. By contrast with her, my students seemed to think, Mrs. Hurtle behaved as a woman—at any rate an American woman—should.

[7] I am now inclined to chalk Mrs. Hurtle up as another of Trollope's triumphs, one, moreover, of a sort remarkably few novelists have achieved. The only novelist who has been successful equally with his American and his English characters is James. Dickens's Americans in "Martin Chuzzlewit" are merely what he meant them to be—savage caricatures relieved by no attempt at understanding, important only because they reinforced vulgar preconceptions of Americans in the British mind.

[8] And things have not been much better when we come to the fiction of our own times. I have yet to meet the American who considers Graham Greene's "quiet American," Alden Pyle, an acceptable representation of an American. There is, of course, a difficulty here. Through Pyle, Greene is making a criticism of what seems to him typical American attitudes and behavior toward other peoples. Whether it is a just criticism or not is beside the point; it is one widely held throughout the world, and Americans would be wrong to equate it with simple anti-Americanism. In fact, Pyle seems to me pretty well docketed; his attitudes and behavior are "placed," related to a specific historical and geographical context. He is, it is true, rather an old-fashioned as well as a quiet American; but since, as it seems to me, the New England spirit is still potent in the American mind, I don't think this a mistake on Greene's part.

[9] Yet, though the separate elements that go to make up Alden Pyle are accurate enough, the character as a whole seems subtly wrong.

I feel that Greene has looked at the traditonal European stereotype of the American rather than at one specific American. There is a difficulty here, too. The image that other peoples have of the nationals of a country is not necessarily false because it is unpalatable to the nation in question. Throughout Europe, and I suspect in the United States as well, the Englishman is traditionally seen as a "creature cold, reticent, buttoned-up, superior." As a generalization, this is probably as accurate as most, but the important point is that it is a generalization. If true, its truth is statistical. It is not an individual truth, and it is with individual truth that novelists are concerned.

[10] We are all much more the victims of preconceived notions, stock responses, stereotyped images, than we like to realize; and I suggest that it is here that the novelist's problem in rendering convincingly a character belonging to another people largely lies. To take an American's idea of an Englishman—one that may well, one guesses, have been based on a living model—the English big-game Lunter Wilson, in Hemingway's "The Short Happy Life of Francis Macomber." The story is one of Hemingway's most highly esteemed, and I have never heard an American criticize the truth of the portraiture of Wilson. Unlike Pyle, he is created with liking and respect; he is indeed the vehicle of Hemingway's values in the story. Yet for me he is the one false note in it, because to me as an Englishman he stands on the edge of parody; unwitting parody, but still parody.

[11] The failure lies in the dialogue Hemingway puts into Wilson's mouth. To my ear, it has too many echoes of conventional notions, almost of the comic-strip story of the "pukka sahib," the empire-builder. It is not differentiated enough: the cliché phrases produce a cliché character. It is on this rock of language that most English attempts to render Americans, and vice versa, founder. It is a difficulty implicit in the very closeness of the two branches of the language. The differences are small, subtle, and the more real and exacting because of their subtlety. It is, beyond differences of idiom and usage, a matter of speech rhythms. Few Englishmen can appreciate the poetry of William Carlos Williams, because they do not know how to read it aloud. Similarly, Americans have told me how difficult they sometimes find it to read English juvenile books aloud to their children; they are defeated in effect, by the tone of voice.

[12] This especial, characteristic tone of voice is, in the last analysis, the expression of something much deeper, what Lionel Trilling has called "a culture's hum and buzz of implication." Trilling defines this as "the whole evanescent context in which . . . explicit statements are made. It is that part of a culture which is made up of half-uttered or unuttered or unutterable expressions of value. They are hinted at by small actions, sometimes by the arts of dress or decoration, sometimes by tone, gesture, emphasis, or rhythm, sometimes by the words that are used with a special frequency or special meaning. They are the things that for good

or bad draw the people of a culture together and that separate them from the people of another culture."

[13] They are the things, in short, that the novelist writing about his own community knows unconsciously and that cannot adequately be learned of another community by any amount of reading or of traveling in the tourist sense. They can be learned only by living in the community, the culture.

[14] One comes back to James, the great exemplar. It was in 1876 he arrived in London. His great London novel, "The Princess Casamassima," did not appear until 10 years later, but, as he tells us, "It proceeded, quite directly, during the first year of a long residence in London, from the habit and interest of walking the streets. . . . It is a fact that, as I look back, the attentive exploration of London, the assault directly made by the great city upon an imagination quick to react, fully explains a large part of it."

[15] "The Princess Casamassima" is a remarkable novel, remarkable among other things for the way James caught "a culture's hum and buzz of implication," especially the hum and buzz of implications of the dark political underside of that culture, the back-street revolutionary movement one would have thought impossibly remote from James's experience.

[16] It is important to see how he did it. Hyacinth Robinson, he tells us, "sprang up for me out of the London pavement." But how untypical of Cockneydom Hyacinth is, the illegitimate offspring of a French woman who had murdered his father, an English nobleman. I suspect that by making Hyacinth so untypical by moving him right away from any conventional or Dickensian stereotype of the Cockney, James was better able to come to terms with and render the London from whose pavements Hyacinth sprang.

[17] We cannot expect another James; but James was one of the first representatives of Mid-Atlantic Man, the man, whether American or British, who is almost equally at home on either side of the Atlantic and who knows and appreciates both American and British culture without in any sense sacrificing his national identity.

[18] As I said, the species seems to be increasing. I like to think that there is already in New York a young Englishman walking the streets as James walked London's 90 years ago, experiencing on his quickly reacting imagination the direct assault of the great city.

--≈{ C O M M E N T   A N D   Q U E S T I O N S }≈--

1. What, precisely, does the author mean by the Mid-Atlantic Man? How does he support his thesis that the species is growing?
2. What purposes are served by the discussion of Trollope's character Mrs. Hurtle in paragraphs 4–7?
3. Examine the content and the tone of paragraphs 8 and 9. What different judgments is Allen making? How does he qualify his judgments?
4. The statement at the end of paragraph 9, "it is with individual truth that novelists are concerned," expresses a key idea that grows out of the preceding material and will be further developed. How is this idea related to the author's central thesis?
5. Allen's first nine paragraphs are concerned chiefly with English portrayals of American characters. Paragraphs 10 and 11 comment on an American portrayal of an Englishman. How would you describe the tone of Allen's criticism of Hemingway's story? How does this criticism make a transition into a larger idea?
6. Does Allen assume that his readers are familiar with Trollope's, Graham Greene's, and Henry James' novels and with Hemingway's story? Explain.
7. If you have read Greene's *The Quiet American* and Hemingway's "The Short Happy Life of Francis Macomber," what are your reactions to Allen's comments on those works?
8. By proportion and by position, the author emphasizes his discussion of Henry James. What appear to be his reasons for doing so?
9. In what ways is paragraph 18 a good conclusion?
10. Describe the persona revealed in this article.

[58]   *Mary McCarthy*: Settling the Colonel's Hash

MARY MCCARTHY (1912–   ) is an American novelist, short story writer, and critic. Among her books are *Cast a Cold Eye, The Company She Keeps, The Groves of Academe, Memories of a Catholic Girlhood, The Stones of Florence,* and *The Group.* The following essay, written in 1954, is from a collection of essays, *On the Contrary,* published in 1961.

[1] Seven years ago, when I taught in a progressive college, I had a pretty girl student in one of my classes who wanted to be a short-story writer. She was not studying writing with me, but she knew that I some-

times wrote short stories, and one day, breathless and glowing, she came up to me in the hall, to tell me that she had just written a story that her writing teacher, a Mr. Converse, was terribly excited about. "He thinks it's wonderful," she said, "and he's going to help me fix it up for publication."

[²] I asked what the story was about; the girl was a rather simple being who loved clothes and dates. Her answer had a deprecating tone. It was just about a girl (herself) and some sailors she had met on the train. But then her face, which had looked perturbed for a moment, gladdened.

[³] "Mr. Converse is going over it with me and we're going to put in the symbols."

[⁴] Another girl in the same college, when asked by us in her sophomore orals why she read novels (one of the pseudo-profound questions that ought never to be put) answered in a defensive flurry: "Well, *of course* I don't read them to find out what happens to the hero."

[⁵] At the time, I thought these notions were peculiar to progressive education: it was old-fashioned or regressive to read a novel to find out what happens to the hero or to have a mere experience empty of symbolic pointers. But I now discover that this attitude is quite general, and that readers and students all over the country are in a state of apprehension, lest they read a book or story literally and miss the presence of a symbol. And like everything in America, this search for meanings has become a socially competitive enterprise; the best reader is the one who detects the most symbols in a given stretch of prose. And the benighted reader who fails to find any symbols humbly assents when they are pointed out to him; he accepts his mortification.

[⁶] I had no idea how far this process had gone until last spring, when I began to get responses to a story I had published in *Harper's*. I say "story" because that was what it was called by *Harper's*. I myself would not know quite what to call it; it was a piece of reporting or a fragment of autobiography—an account of my meeting with an anti-Semitic army colonel. It began in the club car of a train going to St. Louis; I was wearing an apple-green shirtwaist and a dark-green skirt and pink earrings; we got into an argument about the Jews. The colonel was a rather dapper, flashy kind of Irish-American with a worldly blue eye; he took me, he said, for a sculptress, which made me feel, to my horror, that I looked Bohemian and therefore rather suspect. He was full of the usual profound clichés that anti-Semites air, like original epigrams, about the Jews: that he could tell a Jew, that they were different from other people, that you couldn't trust them in business, that some of his best friends were Jews, that he distinguished between a Jew and and a kike, and finally that, of course, he didn't agree with Hitler: Hitler went too far; the Jews were human beings.

[⁷] All the time we talked, and I defended the Jews, he was trying to get my angle, as he called it; he thought it was abnormal for anybody who wasn't Jewish not to feel as he did. As a matter of fact, I have a Jewish grandmother, but I decided to keep this news to myself: I did not want the colonel to think that I had any interested reason for speaking on behalf of the Jews, that is, that I was prejudiced. In the end, though, I got my comeuppance. Just as we were parting, the colonel asked me my married name, which is Broadwater, and the whole mystery was cleared up for him, instantly; he supposed I was married to a Jew and that the name was spelled B-r-o-d-w-a-t-e-r. I did not try to enlighten him; I let him think what he wanted; in a certain sense, he was right; he had unearthed my Jewish grandmother or her equivalent. There were a few details that I must mention to make the next part clear: in my car, there were two nuns, whom I talked to as a distraction from the colonel and the moral problems he raised. He and I finally had lunch together in the St. Louis railroad station, where we continued the discussion. It was a very hot day. I had a sandwich; he had roast-beef hash. We both had an old-fashioned.

[⁸] The whole point of this "story" was that it really happened; it is written in the first person; I speak of myself in my own name, McCarthy; at the end, I mention my husband's name, Broadwater. When I was thinking about writing the story, I decided not to treat it fictionally; the chief interest, I felt, lay in the fact that it happened, in real life, last summer, to the writer herself, who was a good deal at fault in the incident. I wanted to embarrass myself and, if possible, the reader too.

[⁹] Yet, strangely enough, many of my readers preferred to think of this account as fiction. I still meet people who ask me, confidentially, "That story of yours about the colonel—was it really true?" It seemed to them perfectly natural that I would write a fabrication, in which I figured under my own name, and sign it, though in my eyes this would be like perjuring yourself in court or forging checks. Shortly after the "story" was published, I got a kindly letter from a man in Mexico, in which he criticized the menu from an artistic point of view: he thought salads would be better for hot weather and it would be more in character for the narrator-heroine to have a Martini. I did not answer the letter, though I was moved to, because I had the sense that he would not understand the distinction between what *ought* to have happened and what *did* happen.

[¹⁰] Then in April I got another letter, from an English teacher in a small college in the Middle West, that reduced me to despair. I am going to cite it at length.

[¹¹] "My students in freshman English chose to analyze your story, 'Artists in Uniform,' from the March issue of *Harper's*. For a week I heard oral discussions on it and then the students wrote critical analyses. In so far as it is possible, I stayed out of their discussions, encouraging them to read the story closely with your intentions as a guide to their understanding. Although some of them insisted that the story has no other level than the realistic one, most of them decided it has symbolic overtones.

[12] "The question is: how closely do you want the symbols labeled? They wrestled with the nuns, the author's two shades of green with pink accents, with the 'materialistic godlessness' of the colonel. . . . A surprising number wanted exact symbols; for example, they searched for the significance of the colonel's eating hash and the author eating a sandwich. . . . From my standpoint, the story was an entirely satisfactory springboard for understanding the various shades of prejudice, for seeing how much of the artist goes into his painting. If it is any satisfaction to you, our campus was alive with discussions about 'Artists in Uniform.' We liked the story and we thought it amazing that an author could succeed in making readers dislike the author—for a purpose, of course!"

[13] I probably should have answered this letter, but I did not. The gulf seemed to me too wide. I could not applaud the backward students who insisted that the story has no other level than the realistic one without giving offense to their teacher, who was evidently a well-meaning person. But I shall try now to address a reply, not to this teacher and her unfortunate class, but to a whole school of misunderstanding. There were no symbols in this story; there was no deeper level. The nuns were in the story because they were on the train; the contrasting greens were the dress I happened to be wearing; the colonel had hash because he had hash; materialistic godlessness meant just what it means when a priest thunders it from the pulpit—the phrase, for the first time, had meaning for me as I watched and listened to the colonel.

[14] But to clarify the misunderstanding, one must go a little further and try to see what a literary symbol is. Now in one sense, the colonel's hash and my sandwich can be regarded as symbols; that is, they typify the colonel's food tastes and mine. (The man in Mexico had different food tastes which he wished to interpose into our reality.) The hash and the sandwich might even be said to show something very obvious about our characters and bringing-up, or about our sexes; I was a woman, he was a man. And though on another day I might have ordered hash myself, that day I did not, because the colonel and I, in our disagreement, were polarizing each other.

[15] The hash and the sandwich, then, could be regarded as symbols of our disagreement, almost conscious symbols. And underneath our discussion of the Jews, there was a thin sexual current running, as there

always is in such random encounters or pickups (for they have a strong suggestion of the illicit). The fact that I ordered something conventionally feminine and he ordered something conventionally masculine represented, no doubt, our awareness of a sexual possibility; even though I was not attracted to the colonel, nor he to me, the circumstances of our meeting made us define ourselves as a woman and a man.

[16] The sandwich and the hash were our provisional, *ad hoc* symbols of ourselves. But in this sense all human actions are symbolic because they represent the person who does them. If the colonel had ordered a fruit salad with whipped cream, this too would have represented him in some way; given his other traits, it would have pointed to a complexity in his character that the hash did not suggest.

[17] In the same way, the contrasting greens of my dress were a symbol of my taste in clothes and hence representative of me—all too representative, I suddenly saw, in the club car, when I got an "artistic" image of myself flashed back at me from the men's eyes. I had no wish to stylize myself as an artist, that is, to parade about as a symbol of flamboyant unconventionality, but apparently I had done so unwittingly when I picked those colors off a rack, under the impression that they suited me or "expressed my personality" as salesladies say.

[18] My dress, then, was a symbol of the perplexity I found myself in with the colonel; I did not want to be categorized as a member of a peculiar minority—an artist or a Jew; but brute fate and the colonel kept resolutely cramming me into both those uncomfortable pigeonholes. I wished to be regarded as ordinary or rather as universal, to be anybody and therefore everybody (that is, in one sense, I wanted to be on the colonel's side, majestically above minorities); but every time the colonel looked at my dress and me in it with my pink earrings I shrank to minority status, and felt the dress in the heat shriveling me, like the shirt of Nessus, the centaur, that consumed Hercules.

[19] But this is not what the students meant when they wanted the symbols "labeled." They were searching for a more recondite significance than that afforded by the trite symbolism of ordinary life, in which a dress is a social badge. They supposed that I was engaging in literary or artificial symbolism, which would lead the reader out of the confines of reality into the vast fairy tale of myth, in which the color green would have an emblematic meaning (or did the two greens signify for them what the teacher calls "shades" of prejudice), and the colonel's hash, I imagine, would be some sort of Eucharistic mincemeat.

[20] Apparently, the presence of the nuns assured them there were overtones of theology; it did not occur to them (a) that the nuns were there because pairs of nuns are a standardized feature of summer Pullman travel, like crying babies, and perspiring businessmen in the club car, and (b) that if I thought the nuns worth mentioning, it was also be-

cause of something very simple and directly relevant: the nuns and the colonel and I all had something in common—we had all at one time been Catholics—and I was seeking common ground with the colonel, from which to turn and attack his position.

[21] In any account of reality, even a televised one, which comes closest to being a literal transcript or replay, some details are left out as irrelevant (though nothing is really irrelevant). The details that are not eliminated have to stand as symbols of the whole, like stenographic signs, and of course there is an art of selection, even in a newspaper account: the writer, if he has any ability, is looking for the revealing detail that will sum up the picture for the reader in a flash of recognition.

[22] But the art of abridgment and condensation, which is familiar to anybody who tries to relate an anecdote, or give a direction—the art of natural symbolism, which is at the basis of speech and all representation—has at bottom a centripetal intention. It hovers over an object, an event, or series of events and tries to declare what it is. Analogy (that is, comparison to other objects) is inevitably one of its methods. "The weather was soupy," i.e., like soup. "He wedged his way in," i.e., he had to enter, thin edge first, as a wedge enters, and so on. All this is obvious. But these metaphorical aids to communication are a far cry from literary symbolism, as taught in the schools and practiced by certain fashionable writers. Literary symbolism is centrifugal and flees from the object, the event, into the incorporeal distance, where concepts are taken for substance and floating ideas and archetypes assume a hieratic authority.

[23] In this dream-forest, symbols become arbitrary; all counters are interchangeable; anything can stand for anything else. The colonel's hash can be a Eucharist or a cannibal feast or the banquet of Atreus, or all three, so long as the actual dish set before the actual man is disparaged. What is depressing about this insistent symbolization is the fact that while it claims to lead to the infinite, it quickly reaches very finite limits —there are only so many myths on record, and once you have got through Bulfinch, the Scandinavian, and the Indian, there is not much left. And if all stories reduce themselves to myth and symbol, qualitative differences vanish, and there is only a single, monotonous story.

[24] American fiction of the symbolist school demonstrates this mournful truth, without precisely intending to. A few years ago, when the mode was at its height, chic novels and stories fell into three classes: those which had a Greek myth for their framework, which the reader was supposed to detect, like finding the faces in the clouds in old newspaper puzzle contests; those which had symbolic modern figures, dwarfs, hermaphrodites, and cripples, illustrating maiming and loneliness; and those which contained symbolic animals, cougars, wild cats, and monkeys. One young novelist, a product of the Princeton school of symbolism, had

all three elements going at once, like the ringmaster of a three-ring circus, with the freaks, the animals, and the statues.

[25] The quest for symbolic referents had as its object, of course, the deepening of the writer's subject and the reader's awareness. But the result was paradoxical. At the very moment when American writing was penetrated by the symbolic urge, it ceased to be able to create symbols of its own. Babbitt, I suppose, was the last important symbol to be created by an American writer; he gave his name to a type that henceforth would be recognizable to everybody. He passed into the language. The same thing could be said, perhaps, though to a lesser degree, of Caldwell's Tobacco Road, Eliot's Prufrock, and possibly of Faulkner's Snopeses. The discovery of new symbols is not the only function of a writer, but the writer who cares about this must be fascinated by reality itself, as a butterfly collector is fascinated by the glimpse of a new specimen. Such a specimen was Mme. Bovary or M. Homais or M. de Charlus or Jupien; these specimens were precious to their discoverers, not because they repeated an age-old pattern but because their markings were new. Once the specimen has been described, the public instantly spots other examples of the kind, and the world seems suddenly full of Babbitts and Charlus, where none had been noted before.

[26] A different matter was Joyce's Mr. Bloom. Mr. Bloom can be called a symbol of eternal recurrence—the wandering Jew, Ulysses the voyager—but he is a symbol thickly incarnate, fleshed out in a Dublin advertising canvasser. He is not *like* Ulysses or vaguely suggestive of Ulysses; he is Ulysses, circa 1905. Joyce evidently believed in a cyclical theory of history, in which everything repeated itself; he also subscribed in youth to the doctrine that declares that the Host, a piece of bread, is also God's body and blood. How it can be both things at the same time, transubstantially, is a mystery, and Mr. Bloom is just such a mystery: Ulysses in the visible appearance of a Dublin advertising canvasser.

[27] Mr. Bloom is not a symbol of Ulysses, but Ulysses-Bloom together, one and indivisible, symbolize or rather demonstrate eternal recurrence. I hope I make myself clear. The point is transubstantiation: Bloom and Ulysses are transfused into each other and neither reality is diminished. Both realities are locked together, like the protons and neutrons of an atom. *Finnegans Wake* is a still more ambitious attempt to create a fusion, this time a myriad fusion, and to exemplify the mystery of how a thing can be itself and at the same time be something else. The world is many and it is also one.

[28] But the clarity and tension of Joyce's thought brought him closer in a way to the strictness of allegory than to the diffuse practices of latter-day symbolists. In Joyce, the equivalences and analogies are very sharp and distinct, as in a pun, and the real world is almost querulously audible, like the voices of the washerwomen of the Liffey that come into

Earwicker's dream. But this is not true of Joyce's imitators or of the imitators of his imitators, for whom reality is only a shadowy pretext for the introduction of a whole *corps de ballet* of dancing symbols in mythic draperies and animal skins.

[29] Let me make a distinction. There are some great writers, like Joyce or Melville, who have consciously introduced symbolic elements into their work; and there are great writers who have written fables or allegories. In both cases, the writer makes it quite clear to the reader how he is to be read; only an idiot would take *Pilgrim's Progress* for a realistic story, and even a young boy, reading *Moby Dick*, realizes that there is something more than whale-fishing here, though he may not be able to name what it is. But the great body of fiction contains only what I have called natural symbolism, in which selected events represent or typify a problem, a kind of society or psychology, a philosophical theory, in the same way that they do in real life. What happens to the hero becomes of the highest importance. This symbolism needs no abstruse interpretation, and abstruse interpretation will only lead the reader away from the reality that the writer is trying to press on his attention.

[30] I shall give an example or two of what I mean by natural symbolism and I shall begin with a rather florid one: Henry James' *The Golden Bowl*. This is the story of a rich American girl who collects European objects. One of these objects is a husband, Prince Amerigo, who proves to be unfaithful. Early in the story, there is a visit to an antique shop in which the Prince picks out a gold bowl for his fiancée and finds, to his annoyance, that it is cracked. It is not hard to see that the cracked bowl is a symbol, both of the Prince himself, who is a valuable antique but a little flawed, morally, and also of the marriage, which represents an act of acquisition or purchase on the part of the heroine and her father. If the reader should fail to notice the analogy, James calls his attention to it in the title.

[31] I myself would not regard this symbol as necessary to this particular history; it seems to me, rather, an ornament of the kind that was fashionable in the architecture and interior decoration of the period, like stylized sheaves of corn or palms on the façade of a house. Nevertheless, it is handsome and has an obvious appropriateness to the theme. It introduces the reader into the Gilded Age attitudes of the novel. I think there is also a scriptural echo in the title that conveys the idea of punishment. But having seen and felt the weight of meaning that James put into this symbol, one must not be tempted to press further and look at the bowl as a female sex symbol, a chalice, a Holy Grail, and so on; a book is not a pious excuse for reciting a litany of associations.

[32] My second example is from Tolstoy's *Anna Karenina*. Toward the beginning of the novel, Anna meets the man who will be her lover, Vronsky, on the Moscow-St. Petersburg express; as they meet, there has

been an accident; a workman has been killed by the train. This is the beginning of Anna's doom, which is completed when she throws herself under a train and is killed; and the last we see of Vronsky is in a train, with a toothache; he is off to the wars. The train is necessary to the plot of the novel, and I believe it is also symbolic, both of the iron forces of material progress that Tolstoy hated so and that played a part in Anna's moral destruction, and also of those iron laws of necessity and consequence that govern human action when it remains on the sensual level.

[33] One can read the whole novel, however, without being conscious that the train is a symbol; we do not have to "interpret" to feel the import of doom and loneliness in the train's whistle—the same import we ourselves can feel when we hear a train whistle blow in the country, even today. Tolstoy was a deeper artist than James, and we cannot be sure that the train was a conscious device with him. The appropriateness to Anna's history may have been only a *felt* appropriateness; everything in Tolstoy has such a supreme naturalness that one shrinks from attributing contrivance to him, as if it were a sort of fraud. Yet he worked very hard on his novels—I forget how many times Countess Tolstoy copied out *War and Peace* by hand.

[34] The impression one gets from his diaries is that he wrote by ear; he speaks repeatedly, even as an old man, of having to start a story over again because he has the wrong tone, and I suspect that he did not think of the train as a symbol but that it sounded "right" to him, because it was, in that day, an almost fearsome emblem of ruthless and impersonal force, not only to a writer of genius but to the poorest peasant in the fields. And in Tolstoy's case I think it would be impossible, even for the most fanciful critic, to extricate the train from the novel and try to make it say something that the novel itself does not say directly. Every detail in Tolstoy has an almost cruel and viselike meaningfulness and truth to itself that make it tautological to talk of symbolism; he was a moralist and to him the tiniest action, even the curiosities of physical appearance, Vronsky's bald spot, the small white hands of Prince Andrei, told a moral tale.

[35] It is now considered very old-fashioned and tasteless to speak of an author's "philosophy of life" as something that can be harvested from his work. Actually, most of the great authors did have a "philosophy of life" which they were eager to communicate to the public; this was one of their motives for writing. And to disentangle a moral philosophy from a work that evidently contains one is far less damaging to the author's purpose and the integrity of his art than to violate his imagery by symbol-hunting, as though reading a novel were a sort of paper-chase.

[36] The images of a novel or a story belong, as it were, to a family, very closely knit and inseparable from each other; the parent "idea" of

a story or a novel generates events and images all bearing a strong family resemblance. And to understand a story or a novel, you must look for the parent "idea," which is usually in plain view, if you read quite carefully and literally what the author says.

[37] I will go back, for a moment, to my own story, to show how this can be done. Clearly, it is about the Jewish question, for that is what the people are talking about. It also seems to be about artists, since the title is "Artists in Uniform." Then there must be some relation between artists and Jews. What it it? They are both minorities that other people claim to be able to recognize by their appearance. But artists and Jews do not care for this categorization; they want to be universal, that is, like every-body else. They do not want to wear their destiny as a badge, as the soldier wears his uniform. But this aim is really hopeless, for life has formed them as Jews or artists, in a way that immediately betrays them to the majority they are trying to melt into. In my conversation with the colonel, I was endeavoring to play a double game. I was trying to force him into a minority by treating anti-Semitism as an aberration, which, in fact, I believe it is. On his side, the colonel resisted this attempt and tried to show that anti-Semitism was normal, and he was normal, while I was the queer one. He declined to be categorized as anti-Semite; he regarded himself as an independent thinker, who by a happy chance thought the same as everybody else.

[38] I imagined I had a card up my sleeve; I had guessed that the colonel was Irish (i.e., that he belonged to a minority) and presumed that he was a Catholic. I did not see how he could possibly guess that I, with my Irish name and Irish appearance, had a Jewish grandmother in the background. Therefore when I found I had not convinced him by reasoning, I played my last card; I told him that the Church, his Church, forbade anti-Semitism. I went even further; I implied that God forbade it, though I had no right to do this, since I did not believe in God, but was only using Him as a whip to crack over the colonel, to make him feel humble and inferior, a raw Irish Catholic lad under discipline. But the colonel, it turned out, did not believe in God, either, and I lost. And since, in a sense, I had been cheating all along in this game we were play-ing, I had to concede the colonel a sort of moral victory in the end; I let him think that my husband was Jewish and that that "explained" every-thing satisfactorily.

[39] Now there are a number of morals or meanings in this little tale, starting with the simple one: don't talk to strangers on a train. The chief moral or meaning (what I learned, in other words, from the experience) was this: you cannot be a universal unless you accept the fact that you are a singular, that is, a Jew or an artist or what-have-you. What the colonel

and I were discussing, and at the same time illustrating and enacting, was the definition of a human being. I was trying to be something better than a human being; I was trying to be the voice of pure reason; and pride went before a fall. The colonel, without trying, was being something worse than a human being, and somehow we found ourselves on the same plane—facing each other, like mutually repellent twins. Or, put in another way: it is dangerous to be drawn into discussions of the Jews with anti-Semites: you delude yourself that you are spreading light, but you are really sinking into muck; if you endeavor to be dispassionate, you are really claiming for yourself a privileged position, a little mountain top, from which you look down, impartially, on both the Jews and the colonel.

[40] Anti-Semitism is a horrible disease from which nobody is immune, and it has a kind of evil fascination that makes an enlightened person draw near the source of infection, supposedly in a scientific spirit, but really to sniff the vapors and dally with the possibility. The enlightened person who lunches with the colonel in order, as she tells herself, to improve him, is cheating herself, having her cake and eating it. This attempted cheat, on my part, was related to the question of the artist and the green dress; I wanted to be an artist but not to pay the price of looking like one, just as I was willing to have Jewish blood but not willing to show it, where it would cost me something—the loss of superiority in an argument.

[41] These meanings are all there, quite patent, to anyone who consents to look *into* the story. They were *in* the experience itself, waiting to be found and considered. I did not perceive them all at the time the experience was happening; otherwise, it would not have taken place, in all probability—I should have given the colonel a wide berth. But when I went back over the experience, in order to write it, I came upon these meanings, protruding at me, as it were, from the details of the occasion. I put in the green dress and my mortification over it because they were part of the truth, just as it had occurred, but I did not see how they were related to the general question of anti-Semitism and my grandmother until they *showed* me their relation in the course of writing.

[42] Every short story, at least for me, is a little act of discovery. A cluster of details presents itself to my scrutiny, like a mystery that I will understand in the course of writing or sometimes not fully until afterward, when, if I have been honest and listened to these details carefully, I will find that they are connected and that there is a coherent pattern. This pattern is *in* experience itself; you do not impose it from the outside and if you try to you will find that the story is taking the wrong tack, dribbling away from you into artificiality or inconsequence. A story that you do not learn something from while you are writing it, that does not

illuminate something for you, is dead, finished before you started it. The "idea" of a story is implicit in it, on the one hand; on the other hand, it is always ahead of the writer, like a form dimly discerned in the distance; he is working *toward* the "idea."

[43] It can sometimes happen that you begin a story thinking that you know the "idea" of it and find, when you are finished, that you have said something quite different and utterly unexpected to you. Most writers have been haunted all their lives by the "idea" of a story or a novel that they think they want to write and see very clearly: Tolstoy always wanted to write a novel about the Decembrists and instead, almost against his will, wrote *War and Peace;* Henry James thought he wanted to write a novel about Napoleon. Probably these ideas for novels were too set in their creators' minds to inspire creative discovery.

[44] In any work that is truly creative, I believe, the writer cannot be omniscient in advance about the effects that he proposes to produce. The suspense in a novel is not only in the reader, but in the novelist himself, who is intensely curious too about what will happen to the hero. Jane Austen may know in a general way that Emma will marry Mr. Knightley in the end (the reader knows this too, as a matter of fact); the suspense for the author lies in the how, in the twists and turns of circumstance, waiting but as yet unknown, that will bring the consummation about. Hence, I would say to the student of writing that outlines, patterns, arrangements of symbols may have a certain usefulness at the outset for some kind of minds, but in the end they will have to be scrapped. If the story does not contradict the outline, overrun the pattern, break the symbols, like an insurrection against authority, it is surely a still birth. The natural symbolism of reality has more messages to communicate than the dry Morse code of the disengaged mind.

[45] The tree of life, said Hegel, is greener than the tree of thought; I have quoted this before but I cannot forbear from citing it again in this context. This is not an incitement to mindlessness or an endorsement of realism in the short story (there are several kinds of reality, including interior reality); it means only that the writer must be, first of all, a listener and observer, who can pay attention to reality, like an obedient pupil, and who is willing, always, to be surprised by the messages reality is sending through to him. And if he gets the messages correctly he will not have to go back and put in the symbols; he will find that the symbols are there, staring at him significantly from the commonplace.

--⊷ C O M M E N T   A N D   Q U E S T I O N S ⊱⊶--

1. Comment on the four opening paragraphs. What do they contribute to the whole essay?
2. What devices for emphasis does the author use in paragraph 8? Can you tell, from the summary in paragraphs 6 and 7, why the writer "was a good deal at fault in the incident"? Explain.
3. Do the two letters (paragraphs 9–12) have anything in common, or is Mary McCarthy citing the first and quoting from the second to make two different points?
4. The author says in paragraph 13 that there were no symbols in her story; in paragraphs 14–20 she qualifies the statement and then, in effect, re-affirms it. What different meanings of *symbol* is she establishing?
5. Explain the meaning of the following terms: *recondite* and *Eucharistic mincemeat* (paragraph 19); *centripetal, centrifugal, archetypes,* and *hieratic* (paragraph 22); *banquet of Atreus* (paragraph 23).
6. What are the author's principal objections to the "literary symbolism" taught in schools and practiced by certain writers? How would you de-scribe her language and tone in communicating her attitudes?
7. Examine the use of figurative language, especially in paragraph 24, the last half of paragraph 25, and paragraphs 27 and 28. Which figures seem to you most effective, and why?
8. What point is the author making with the examples of the golden bowl in James' novel and the train in *Anna Karenina*?
9. "Settling the Colonel's Hash," first given as a talk at the Breadloaf School of English in Middlebury, Vermont, is addressed both to readers and to writers or students of writing. Summarize Mary McCarthy's advice to readers in paragraphs 35–45; summarize her advice to students of writing. How does she connect the two kinds of advice?
10. In what ways are the last two paragraphs an effective ending?
11. Comment on the title of the essay. What does the title mean to you?

[59] *Deems Taylor*: The Monster

DEEMS TAYLOR (1885–1966) was a well-known American critic and music commentator and the composer of two operas and many symphonic poems and songs. "The Monster" is taken from one of his books of criticism, *Of Men and Music*, published in 1937.

[1] He was an undersized little man, with a head too big for his body —a sickly little man. His nerves were bad. He had skin trouble. It was agony for him to wear anything next to his skin coarser than silk. And he had delusions of grandeur.

[2] He was a monster of conceit. Never for one minute did he look at the world or at people, except in relation to himself. He was not only the most important person in the world, to himself; in his own eyes he was the only person who existed. He believed himself to be one of the greatest dramatists in the world, one of the greatest thinkers, and one of the greatest composers. To hear him talk, he was Shakespeare, and Beethoven, and Plato, rolled into one. And you would have had no difficulty in hearing him talk. He was one of the most exhausting conversationalists that ever lived. An evening with him was an evening spent in listening to a monologue. Sometimes he was brilliant; sometimes he was maddeningly tiresome. But whether he was being brilliant or dull, he had one sole topic of conversation: himself. What *he* thought and what *he* did.

[3] He had a mania for being in the right. The slightest hint of disagreement, from anyone, on the most trivial point, was enough to set him off on a harangue that might last for hours, in which he proved himself right in so many ways, and with such exhausting volubility, that in the end his hearer, stunned and deafened, would agree with him, for the sake of peace.

[4] It never occurred to him that he and his doings were not of the most intense and fascinating interest to anyone with whom he came in contact. He had theories about almost any subject under the sun, including vegetarianism, the drama, politics, and music; and in support of these theories he wrote pamphlets, letters, books . . . thousands upon thousands of words, hundreds and hundreds of pages. He not only wrote these things, and published them—usually at somebody else's expense—but he would sit and read them aloud, for hours, to his friends and his family.

[5] He wrote operas; and no sooner did he have the synopsis of a story, but he would invite—or rather summon—a crowd of his friends to his house and read it aloud to them. Not for criticism. For applause. When the complete poem was written, the friends had to come again, and hear *that* read aloud. Then he would publish the poem, sometime years before the music that went with it was written. He played the piano like a composer, in the worst sense of what that implies, and he would sit down at the piano before parties that included some of the finest pianists of his time, and play for them, by the hour, his own music, needless to say. He had a composer's voice. And he would invite eminent vocalists to his house, and sing them his operas, taking all the parts.

[6] He had the emotional stability of a six-year-old child. When he felt out of sorts, he would rave and stamp, or sink into suicidal gloom and talk darkly of going to the East to end his days as a Buddhist monk. Ten

minutes later, when something pleased him, he would rush out of doors and run around the garden or jump up and down on the sofa, or stand on his head. He could be grief-stricken over the death of a pet dog, and he could be callous and heartless to a degree that would have made a Roman emperor shudder.

[7] He was almost innocent of any sense of responsibility. Not only did he seem incapable of supporting himself, but it never occurred to him that he was under any obligation to do so. He was convinced that the world owed him a living. In support of this belief, he borrowed money from everybody who was good for a loan—men, women, friends, or strangers. He wrote begging letters by the score, sometimes groveling without shame, at others loftily offering his intended benefactor the privilege of contributing to his support, and being mortally offended if the recipient declined the honor. I have found no record of his ever paying or repaying money to anyone who did not have a legal claim upon it.

[8] What money he could lay his hands on he spent like an Indian rajah. The mere prospect of a performance of one of his operas was enough to set him running up bills amounting to ten times the amount of his prospective royalties. On an income that would reduce a more scrupulous man to doing his own laundry, he would keep two servants. Without enough money in his pocket to pay his rent, he would have the walls and ceiling of his study lined with pink silk. No one will ever know— certainly he never knew—how much money he owed. We do know that his greatest benefactor gave him $6,000 to pay the most pressing of his debts in one city, and a year later had to give him $16,000 to enable him to live in another city without being thrown into jail for debt.

[9] He was equally unscrupulous in other ways. An endless procession of women marches through his life. His first wife spent twenty years enduring and forgiving his infidelities. His second wife had been the wife of his most devoted friend and admirer, from whom he stole her. And even while he was trying to persuade her to leave her first husband he was writing to a friend to inquire whether he could suggest some wealthy woman—*any* wealthy woman—whom he could marry for her money.

[10] He was completely selfish in his other personal relationships. His liking for his friends was measured solely by the completeness of their devotion to him, or by their usefulness to him, whether financial or artistic. The minute they failed him—even by so much as refusing a dinner invitation—or began to lessen in usefulness, he cast them off without a second thought. At the end of his life he had exactly one friend left whom he had known even in middle age.

[11] He had a genius for making enemies. He would insult a man who disagreed with him about the weather. He would pull endless wires in order to meet some man who admired his work, and was able and anxious to be of use to him—and would proceed to make a mortal enemy of him

with some idiotic and wholly uncalled-for exhibition of arrogance and bad manners. A character in one of his operas was a caricature of one of the most powerful music critics of his day. Not content with burlesquing him, he invited the critic to his house and read him the libretto aloud in front of his friends.

[12] The name of this monster was Richard Wagner. Everything that I have said about him you can find on record—in newspapers, in police reports, in the testimony of people who knew him, in his own letters, between the lines of his autobiography. And the curious thing about this record is that it doesn't matter in the least.

[13] Because this undersized, sickly, disagreeable, fascinating little man was right all the time. The joke was on us. He *was* one of the world's great dramatists; he *was* a great thinker; he *was* one of the most stupendous musical geniuses that, up to now, the world has ever seen. The world did owe him a living. People couldn't know those things at the time, I suppose; and yet to us, who know his music, it does seem as though they should have known. What if he did talk about himself all the time? If he had talked about himself for twenty-four hours every day for the span of his life he would not have uttered half the number of words that other men have spoken and written about him since his death.

[14] When you consider what he wrote—thirteen operas and music dramas, eleven of them still holding the stage, eight of them unquestionably worth ranking among the world's great musico-dramatic masterpieces—when you listen to what he wrote, the debts and heartaches that people had to endure from him don't seem much of a price. Eduard Hanslick, the critic whom he caricatured in *Die Meistersinger* and who hated him ever after, now lives only because he was caricatured in *Die Meistersinger*. The women whose hearts he broke are long since dead; and the man who could never love anyone but himself has made them deathless atonement, I think, with *Tristan und Isolde*. Think of the luxury with which for a time, at least, fate rewarded Napoleon, the man who ruined France and looted Europe; and then perhaps you will agree that a few thousand dollars' worth of debts were not too heavy a price to pay for the *Ring* trilogy.

[15] What if he was faithless to his friends and to his wives? He had one mistress to whom he was faithful to the day of his death: Music. Not for a single moment did he ever compromise with what he believed, with what he dreamed. There is not a line of his music that could have been conceived by a little mind. Even when he is dull, or downright bad, he is dull in the grand manner. There is a greatness about his worst mistakes. Listening to his music, one does not forgive him for what he may or may not have been. It is not a matter of forgiveness. It is a matter of being dumb with wonder that his poor brain and body didn't burst under the torment of the demon of creative energy that lived inside him, strug-

gling, clawing, scratching to be released; tearing, shrieking at him to write the music that was in him. The miracle is that what he did in the little space of seventy years could have been done at all, even by a great genius. Is it any wonder that he had no time to be a man?

--◆{ C O M M E N T   A N D   Q U E S T I O N S }◆--

1. This essay is built on a pattern of contrast, with the first eleven paragraphs devoted to Wagner's unpleasant qualities and the last three, introduced by the turn in paragraph 12, to his genius. For an analysis of the essay, list in order the topic ideas in the first eleven paragraphs.

2. What is the reason for the sequence of ideas in these eleven paragraphs? Could the order be changed without loss?

3. How many of the unpleasant qualities discussed in the first section are referred to and justified in the last three paragraphs?

4. What does Taylor gain by withholding the "monster's" identity until paragraph 12?

5. The judgment of Wagner in the first eleven paragraphs is developed with a wealth of detail. In the absence of footnotes or sources introduced into the text, why do you think the reader is inclined to accept the detail and the characterization as authentic? How is the contrasting judgment in the last three paragraphs supported?

6. We have said in the "Introduction to Rhetorical Analysis" that proportion is a means of emphasis; that a writer ordinarily gives fullest development to the ideas he considers most important. In view of this general principle, can you account for the fact that Taylor devotes more than twice as much space to Wagner's unadmirable traits as to his genius?

7. Taylor's sentences are varied in structure and length, but he uses many short sentences with a simple, conventional subject–verb–complement pattern and some short incomplete sentences which he might have attached to the preceding sentence. What is the effect of these numerous short sentences? Examine some of Taylor's longer and more complex sentences. Does he use them merely to avoid monotony, or are there in some cases other reasons for the change in sentence style?

8. The author slants his writing, first against and then in favor of Wagner, by selection of material, but also by use of charged words. Point out some examples of his attitudinal language. Does it seem to you appropriate and effective in this essay? Explain.

9. State in the form of a syllogism Taylor's argument in the last three paragraphs. Do you agree with his major premise?

[60]   *Kenneth Clark*: The Blot and the Diagram

SIR KENNETH CLARK (1903–   ) is a distinguished English critic and
art historian whose books include *Leonardo da Vinci, Florentine Painting:
Fifteenth Century, Landscape into Art, Moments of Vision, The Nude,* and
Looking at Pictures. In the following essay, a discussion of modern art, the
author frequently uses the word *art* to refer, not to all the arts, but specifically
to painting.

[¹] I have been told to "look down from a high place over the whole
extensive landscape of modern art." We all know how tempting high
places can be, and how dangerous. I usually avoid them myself. But if I
must do as I am told, I shall try to find out why modern art has taken its
peculiar form, and to guess how long that form will continue.

[²] I shall begin with Leonardo da Vinci, because although all processes are gradual, he does represent one clearly marked turning point in
the history of art. Before that time, the painters' intentions were quite
simple: they were first of all to tell a story, secondly to make the invisible
visible, and thirdly to turn a plain surface into a decorated surface. Those
are all very ancient aims, going back to the earliest civilisations, or beyond; and for three hundred years painters had been instructed how to
carry them out by means of a workshop tradition. Of course, there had
been breaks in that tradition—in the fourth century, maybe, and towards
the end of the seventh century; but broadly speaking, the artist learnt
what he could about the technique of art from his master in his workshop,
and then set up shop on his own and tried to do better.

[³] As is well known, Leonardo had a different view of art. He thought
that it involved both science and the pursuit of some peculiar attribute
called beauty or grace. He was, by inclination, a scientist: he wanted to
find out how things worked, and he believed that this knowledge could
be stated mathematically. He said "Let no one who is not a mathematician
read my works," and he tried to relate this belief in measurement to his
belief in beauty. This involved him in two rather different lines of thought,
one concerned with magic—the magic of numbers—the other with science. Ever since Pythagoras had discovered that the musical scale could
be stated mathematically, by means of the length of the strings, etc., and

Originally published for the Reed and Barton Design Lecture. Subsequently published in the January 1963 issue of *Encounter.* Reprinted by permission of the author.

so had thrown a bridge between intellectual analysis and sensory perception, thinkers on art had felt that it should be possible to do the same for painting. I must say that their effort had not been very rewarding; the modulus, or golden section, and the logarithmic spiral of shells are practically the only undisputed results. But Leonardo lived at a time when it was still possible to hope great things from perspective, which should not only define space, but order it harmoniously; and he also inherited a belief that ideal mathematical combinations could be derived from the proportions of the human body. This line of thought may be called the *mystique* of measurement. The other line may be called the *use* of measurement. Leonardo wished to state mathematically various facts related to the act of seeing. How do we see light passing over a sphere? What happens when objects make themselves perceptible on our retina? Both these lines of thought involved him in drawing diagrams and taking measurements, and for this reason were closely related in his mind. No painter except perhaps Piero della Francesca has tried more strenuously to find a mathematical statement of art, nor has had a greater equipment for doing so.

[4] But Leonardo was also a man of powerful and disturbing imagination. In his notebooks, side by side with his attempts to achieve *order* by mathematics, are drawings and descriptions of the most violent scenes of *dis*order which the human mind can conceive—battles, deluges, eruptions. And he included in his treatise on painting advice on how to develop this side of the artistic faculty also. The passages in which he does so have often been quoted, but they are so incredibly foreign to the whole Renaissance idea of art, although related to a remark in Pliny, that each time I read them, they give me a fresh surprise. I will, therefore, quote them again.

I shall not refrain from including among these precepts a new and speculative idea, which although it may seem trivial and almost laughable, is none the less of great value in quickening the spirit of invention. It is this: that you should look at certain walls stained with damp or at stones of uneven colour. If you have to invent some setting you will be able to see in these the likeness of divine landscapes, adorned with mountains, ruins, rocks, woods, great plains, hills and valleys in great variety; and then again you will see there battles and strange figures in violent action, expressions of faces and clothes and an infinity of things which you will be able to reduce to their complete and proper forms. In such walls the same thing happens as in the sound of bells, in whose strokes you may find every named word which you can imagine.

[5] Later he repeats this suggestion in slightly different form, advising the painter to study not only marks on walls, but also "the embers of the fire, or clouds or mud, or other similar objects from which you will find most admirable ideas . . . because from a confusion of shapes the spirit is quickened to new inventions."

[⁶] I hardly need to insist on how relevant these passages are to modern painting. Almost every morning I receive cards inviting me to current exhibitions, and on the cards are photographs of the works exhibited. Some of them consist of blots, some of scrawls, some look like clouds, some like embers of the fire, some are like mud—some of them are mud; a great many look like stains on walls, and one of them, I remember, consisted of actual stains on walls, photographed and framed. Leonardo's famous passage has been illustrated in every particular. And yet I doubt if he would have been satisfied with the results, because he believed that we must somehow unite the two opposite poles of our faculties. Art itself was the connection between the diagram and the blot.

[⁷] Now in order to prevent the impression that I am taking advantage of a metaphor, as writers on art are often bound to do, I should explain how I am going to use these words. By "diagram" I mean a rational statement in a visible form, involving measurements, and usually done with an ulterior motive. The theorem of Pythagoras is proved by a diagram. Leonardo's drawings of light striking a sphere are diagrams; but the works of Mondrian, although made up of straight lines, are not diagrams, because they are not done in order to prove or measure some experience, but to please the eye. That they look like diagrams is due to influences which I will examine later. But diagrams can exist with no motive other than their own perfection, just as mathematical propositions can.

[⁸] By "blots" I mean marks or areas which are not intended to convey information, but which, for some reason, seem pleasant and memorable to the maker, and can be accepted in the same sense by the spectator. I said that these blots were not intended to convey information, but of course they do, and that of two kinds. First, they tell us through association, about things we had forgotten; that was the function of Leonardo's stains on walls, which as he said, quickened the spirit of invention, and it can be the function of man-made blots as well; and secondly a man-made blot will tell us about the artist. Unless it is made entirely accidentally, as by spilling an inkpot, it will be a commitment. It is quite difficult to make a non-commital blot. Although the two are connected, I think we can distinguish between analogy blots and gesture blots.

[⁹] Now let me try to apply this to modern art. Modern art is not a subject on which one can hope for a large measure of agreement, but I hope I may be allowed two assumptions. The first is that the kind of painting and architecture which we call, with varying inflections of the voice, "modern," is a true and vital expression of our own day; and the second assumption is that it differs radically from any art which has preceded it. Both these assumptions have been questioned. It has been said that modern art is "a racket" engineered by art dealers, who have exploited the incompetence of artists and the gullibility of patrons, that the whole thing is a kind of vast and very expensive practical joke. Well, fifty years is a long time to keep up a hoax of this kind, and during these years modern art has spread all over the free world and created a complete international style. I don't think that any honest-minded historian, whether he liked it or not, could pretend that modern art was the result of an accident or a conspiracy. The only doubt he could have would be whether it is, so to say, a long-term or a short-term movement. In the history of art there are stylistic changes which appear to develop from purely internal causes, and seem almost accidental in relation to the other circumstances of life and society. Such, for example, was the state of art in Italy (outside Venice) from about 1530 to 1600. When all is said about the religious disturbances of the time, the real cause of the Mannerist style was the domination of Michelangelo, who had both created an irresistible style and exhausted its possibilities. It needed the almost equally powerful pictorial imagination of Caravaggio to produce a counter-infection, which could spread from Rome to Spain and the Netherlands and prepare the way for Rembrandt. I can see nothing in the history of man's spirit to account for this episode. It seems to me to be due to an internal and specifically artistic chain of events which are easily related to one another, and comprehensible within the general framework of European art. On the other hand, there are events in the history of art which go far beyond the interaction of styles and which evidently reflect a change in the whole condition of the human spirit. Such an event took place towards the end of the fifth century, when the Hellenistic-Roman style gradually became what we call Byzantine; and again in the early thirteenth century, when the Gothic cathedrals shot up out of the ground. In each case the historian could produce a series of examples to prove that the change was inevitable, and was part of a complete spiritual revolution.

[10] Whether we think that modern art represents a transformation of style or a change of spirit depends to some extent on my second assumption, that it differs radically from anything which has preceded it. This too has been questioned; it has been said that Léger is only a logical development of Poussin, or Mondrian of Vermeer. And it is true that the element of design in each has something in common. If we pare a Poussin down to its bare bones, there are combinations of curves and cubes which are the foundations of much classical painting, and Léger had the good sense to make use of them. Similarly, in Vermeer there is a use of rectangles, large areas contrasted with very narrow ones, and a feeling for shallow recessions, which became the preferred theme of Mondrian. But such analogies are trifling compared with the differences. Poussin was a very intelligent man who thought deeply about his art, and if anyone had suggested to him that his pictures were praise-worthy solely on account of their construction, he would have been incredulous and affronted.

[11] So let us agree that the kind of painting and architecture which we find most representative of our times—say, the painting of Jackson Pollock and the architecture of the Lever building—is deeply different from the painting and architecture of the past; and is *not* a mere whim of fashion, but the result of a great change in our ways of thinking and feeling.

[12] How did this great change take place and what does it mean? To begin with, I think it is related to the development upon which all industrial civilisation depends, the differentiation of function. Leonardo was exceptional, almost unique in his integration of functions—the scientific and the imaginative. Yet he fore-shadowed more than any other artist their disintegration, by noting and treating in isolation the diagrammatic faculty and the blot-making faculty. The average artist took the unity of these faculties for granted. They were united in Leonardo, and in lesser artists, by *interest or pleasure in the thing seen*. The external object was like a magnetic pole which drew the two faculties together. At some point the external object became a negative rather than a positive charge. Instead of drawing together the two faculties, it completely dissociated them; architecture went off in one direction with the diagram, painting went in the other direction with the blot.

[13] This disintegration was related to a radical change in the philosophy of art. We all know that such changes, however harmless they sound when first enunciated, can have drastic consequences in the world of action. Rulers who wish to maintain the *status quo* are well advised to chop off the heads of all philosophers. What Hilaire Belloc called the "remote and ineffectual don" is more dangerous than the busy columnist with his eye on the day's news. The revolution in our ideas about the nature of painting seems to have been hatched by a don who was considered remote and ineffectual even by Oxford standards—Walter Pater. It was he (inspired, I believe, by Schopenhauer) who first propounded the idea of the aesthetic sensation, intuitively perceived.

In its primary aspect [Pater said] a great picture has no more difficult message for us than an accidental play of sunlight and shadow for a few moments on the wall or floor; in itself, in truth, a space of such fallen light, caught, as in the colours of an Eastern carpet, but refined upon and dealt with more subtly and exquisitely than by nature itself.

[14] It is true that his comparison with an Eastern carpet admits the possibility of "pleasant sensations" being arranged or organised; and Pater confirms this need for organisation a few lines later, when he sets down his famous dictum that "all art constantly aspires towards the condition of music." He does not believe in blots uncontrolled by the conscious mind. But he is very far from the information-giving diagram.

[15] This belief that art has its origin in our intuitive rather than our rational faculties, picturesquely asserted by Pater, was worked out historically and philosophically, in the somewhat wearisome volumes of Benedetto Croce, and owing to his authoritative tone, he is usually considered the originator of a new theory of aesthetics. It was, in fact, the reversion to a very old idea. Long before the Romantics had stressed the importance of intuition and self-expression, men had admitted the Dionysiac nature of art. But philosophers had always assumed that the frenzy of inspiration must be controlled by law and by the intellectual power of putting things into harmonious order. And this general philosophic concept of art as a combination of intuition and intellect had been supported by technical necessities. It was necessary to master certain laws and to use the intellect in order to build the Gothic cathedrals, or set up the stained glass windows of Chartres or cast the bronze doors of the Florence Baptistry. When this bracing element of craftsmanship ceased to dominate the artist's outlook, as happened soon after the time of Leonardo, new scientific disciplines had to be invented to maintain the intellectual element in art. Such were perspective and anatomy. From a purely artistic point of view, they were unnecessary. The Chinese produced some of the finest landscapes ever painted, without any systematic knowledge of perspective. Greek figure sculpture reached its highest point before the study of anatomy had been systematised. But from the Renaissance onwards, painters felt that these two sciences made their art intellectually respectable. They were two ways of connecting the diagram and the blot.

[16] In the nineteenth century, belief in art as a scientific activity declined, for a quantity of reasons. Science and technology withdrew into specialisation. Voltaire's efforts to investigate the nature of heat seem to us ludicrous; Goethe's studies of botany and physics a waste of a great poet's time. In spite of their belief in inspiration, the great Romantics were aware of the impoverishment of the imagination which would take place when science had drifted out of reach, and both Shelley and Coleridge spent much time in chemical experiments. Even Turner, whose letters reveal a singular lack of analytic faculty, annotated Goethe's theories of colour, and painted two pictures to demonstrate them. No good. The laws which govern the movement of the human spirit are inexorable. The enveloping assumption, within which the artist has to function, was that science was no longer approachable by any but the specialist. And gradually there grew up the idea that all intellectual activities were hostile to art.

[17] I have mentioned the philosophic development of this view by Croce. Let me give one example of its quiet acceptance by the official mind. The British Council sends all over the world, even to Florence and Rome, exhibitions of children's art—the point of these children's pictures

being that they have no instruction of any kind, and do not attempt the troublesome task of painting what they see. Well, why not, after all? The results are quite agreeable—sometimes strangely beautiful; and the therapeutic effect on the children is said to be excellent. It is like one of those small harmless heresies which we are shocked to find were the object of persecution by the Mediaeval Church. When, however, we hear admired modern painters saying that they draw their inspiration from the drawings of children and lunatics, as well as from stains on walls, we recognise that we have accomplices in a revolution.

[18] The lawless and intuitive character of modern art is a familiar theme and certain historians have said that it is symptomatic of a decline in Western civilisation. This is journalism—one of those statements that sound well to-day and nonsense to-morrow. It is obvious that the development of physical science in the last hundred years has been one of the most colossal efforts the human intellect has ever made. But I think it is also true that human beings can produce, in a given epoch, only a certain amount of creative energy, and that this is directed to different ends and different times—music in the eighteenth century is the obvious example; and I believe that the dazzling achievements of science during the last seventy years have deflected far more of those skills and endowments which go to the making of a work of art than is usually realised. To begin with, there is the sheer energy. In every moulding of a Renaissance palace we are conscious of an immense intellectual energy, and it is the absence of this energy in the nineteenth-century copies of Renaissance buildings which makes them seem so dead. To find a form with the same vitality as a window moulding of the Palazzo Farnese I must wait till I get back into an aeroplane, and look at the relation of the engine to the wing. That form is alive, not (as used to be said) because it is functional—many functional shapes are entirely uninteresting—but because it is animated by the breath of modern science.

[19] The deflections from art to science are the more serious because these are not, as used to be supposed, two contrary activities, but in fact draw on many of the same capacities of the human mind. In the last resort each depends on the imagination. Artist and scientist alike are both trying to give concrete form to dimly apprehended ideas. Dr. Bronowski has put it very well: "All science is the search for unity in hidden likenesses, and the starting point is an image, because then the unity is before our mind's eye." Even if we no longer have to pretend that a group of stars looks like a plough or a bear, our scientists still depend on humanly comprehensible images, and it is striking that the valid symbols of our time, invented to embody some scientific truth, have taken root in the popular imagination. Do those red and blue balls connected by rods really resemble a type of atomic structure? I am too ignorant to say. I accept the symbol just as an

early Christian accepted the Fish or the Lamb, and I find it echoed or even (it would seem) anticipated in the work of modern artists like Kandinsky and Miró.

[20] Finally, there is the question of popular interest and approval. We have grown accustomed to the idea that great artists can work in solitude and incomprehension; but that was not the way things happened in the Renaissance or the seventeenth century, still less in ancient Greece. The pictures carried through the streets by cheering crowds, the *Te Deum* sung on completion of a public building—all this indicates a state of opinion in which men could undertake great works of art with a confidence quite impossible to-day. The research scientist, on the other hand, not only has millions of pounds worth of plant and equipment for the asking, he has principalities and powers waiting for his conclusions. He goes to work, as Titian once did, confident that he will succeed because the strong tide of popular admiration is flowing with him.

[21] But although science has absorbed so many of the functions of art and deflected (I believe) so many potential artists, it obviously cannot be a *substitute* for art. Its mental processes may be similar, but its ends are different. There have been three views about the purpose of art. First that it aims simply at imitation; secondly that it should influence human conduct; and thirdly that it should produce a kind of exalted happiness. The first view, which was developed in ancient Greece, must be reckoned one of the outstanding failures of Greek thought. It is simply contrary to experience, because if the visual arts aimed solely at imitating things they would be of very little importance; where the Greeks above all people knew that they were important, and treated them as such. Yet such was the prestige of Greek thought that this theory of art was revived in the Renaissance, in an uncomfortable sort of way, and had a remarkable recrudescence in the nineteenth century. The second view, that art should influence conduct and opinions, is more respectable, and held the field throughout the Middle Ages; indeed the more we learn about the art of the past and motives of those who commissioned it, the more important this particular aim appears to be; it still dominated art theory in the time of Diderot. The third view, that art should produce a kind of exalted happiness, was invented by the Romantics at the beginning of the nineteenth century (well, perhaps *invented* by Plotinus, but given currency by the Romantics), and gradually gained ground until by the end of the century it was believed in by almost all educated people. It has held the field in Western Europe till the present day. Leaving aside the question which of these theories is correct, let me ask which of them is most likely to be a helpful background to art (for that is all that a theory of æsthetics can be) in an age when science has such an overwhelming domination

over the human mind. The first aim must be reckoned *by itself* to be pointless, since science has now discovered so many ways of imitating appearances, which are incomparably more accurate and convincing than even the most realistic picture. Painting might defend itself against the daguerreotype, but not against Cinerama.

[22] The popular application of science has also, it seems to me, invalidated the second aim of art, because it is quite obvious that no picture can influence human conduct as effectively as a television advertisement. It is quite true that in totalitarian countries artists are still instructed to influence conduct. But that is either due to technical deficiencies, as in China, where in default of T.V., broadsheets and posters are an important way of communicating with an illiterate population; or, in Russia, to a philosophic time-lag. The fact is that very few countries have had the courage to take Plato's advice and exclude works of art altogether. They have, therefore, had to invent some excuse for keeping them on, and the Russians are still using the pretext that paintings and sculpture can influence people in favour of socialist and national policies, although it must have dawned on them that these results can be obtained far more effectively by the cinema and television.

[23] So it seems to me that of these three possible purposes of art— imitation, persuasion, or exalted pleasure—only the third still holds good in an age of science; and it must be justified very largely by the fact that it is a feeling which is absent from scientific achievements—although mathematicians have told us that it is similar to the feeling aroused by their finest calculations. We might say that in the modern world the art of painting is defensible only in so far as it is complementary to science.

[24] We are propelled in the same direction by another achievement of modern science, the study of psychology. That peeling away of the psyche, which was formerly confined to spiritual instructors, or the great novelists, has become a commonplace of conversation. When a good, solid, external word like Duty is turned into a vague, uneasy, internal word like Guilt, one cannot expect artists to take much interest in good, solid, external objects. The artist has always been involved in the painful process of turning himself inside out, but in the past his inner convictions have been of such a kind that they can, so to say, re-form themselves round an object. But, as we have seen, even in Leonardo's time, there were certain obscure needs and patterns of the spirit, which could discover themselves only through less precise analogies— the analogies provided by stains on walls or the embers of a fire. Now, I think that in this inward-looking age, when we have become so much more aware of the vagaries of the spirit, and so respectful of the working of the unconscious, the artist is more likely to find his point of departure in analogies of this kind. They are more exciting because they, so to say, take us by surprise, like for-

gotten smells; and they seem to be more profound because the memories they awaken have been deeply buried in our minds. Whether Jung is right in believing that this free, undirected, illogical form of mental activity will allow us to pick up, like a magic radio station, some deep memories of our race which can be of universal interest, I do not know. The satisfaction we derive from certain combinations of shape and colour does seem to be inexplicable even by the remotest analogies, and may perhaps involve inherited memories. It is not yet time for the art-historian to venture in to that mysterious jungle. I must, however, observe that our respect for the unconscious mind not only gives us an interest in analogy blots, but in what I called "gesture blots" as well. We recognise how free and forceful such a communication can be, and this aspect of art has become more important in the last ten years. An apologist of modern art has said: "What we want to know is not what the world looks like, but what we mean to each other." So the gesture blot becomes a sort of ideogram, like primitive Chinese writing. Students of Zen assure us it is a means of communication more direct and complete than anything which our analytic system can achieve. Almost 2,000 years before Leonardo looked for images in blots, Lao-tzu had written:

> The Tao is something blurred and indistinct.
> How indistinct! How blurred!
> Yet within are images,
> How blurred! How indistinct!
> Yet within are things.

[25] I said that when the split took place between our faculties of measurement and intuition, *architecture* went off with the diagram. Of course architecture had always been involved with measurement and calculation, but we tend to forget how greatly it was also involved with the imitation of external objects. "The question to be determined," said Ruskin, "is whether architecture is a frame for the sculpture, or the sculpture an ornament of the architecture." And he came down on the first alternative. He thought that a building became architecture only in so far as it was a frame for figurative sculpture. I wonder if there is a single person alive who would agree with him. And yet Ruskin had the most sensitive eye and the keenest analytic faculty that has ever been applied to architecture. Many people disagreed with him in his own day; they thought that sculpture should be subordinate to the total design of the building. But that anything claiming to be architecture could dispense with ornament altogether never entered anyone's head till a relatively short time ago.

[26] A purely diagrammatic architecture is only about thirty years older than a purely blottesque painting; yet it has changed the face of the world and produced in every big city a growing uniformity. Perhaps because it is a little older, perhaps because it seems to have a material justification,

we have come to accept it without question. People who are still puzzled or affronted by action painting are proud of the great steel and glass boxes which have arisen so miraculously in the last ten years. And yet these two are manifestations of the same state of mind. The same difficulties of function, the same deflection from the external object, and the same triumph of science. Abstract painting and glass box architecture are related in two different ways. There is the direct relationship of style—the kind of relationship which painting and architecture had with one another in the great consistent ages of art like the 13th and 17th centuries. For modern architecture is not simply functional; at its best it has a style which is almost as definite and as arbitrary as Gothic. And this leads me back to my earlier point: that diagrams can be drawn in order to achieve some imagined perfection, similar to that of certain mathematical propositions. Thirty years after Pater's famous dictum, painters in Russia, Holland, and France began to put into practice the theory that "all art constantly aspires to the condition of music"; and curiously enough this Pythagorean mystique of measurement produced a style—the style which reached its purest expression in the Dutch painter, Mondrian. And through the influence of the *Bauhaus,* this became the leading style of modern architecture.

[27] The other relationship between contemporary architecture and painting appears to be indirect and even accidental. I am thinking of the visual impact when the whole upper part of a tall glass building mirrors the clouds or the dying embers of a sunset, and so becomes a frame for a marvellous, moving Tachiste picture. I do not think that future historians of art will find this accidental at all, but will see it as the culmination of a long process beginning in the Romantic period, in which, from Wordsworth and De Quincey onwards, poets and philosophers recognised the movement of clouds as the symbol of a newly discovered mental faculty.

[28] Such, then, would be my diagnosis of the present condition of art. I must now, by special request, say what I think will happen to art in the future. I think that the state of affairs which I have called the blot and the diagram will last for a long time. Architecture will continue to be made up of glass boxes and steel grids, without ornament of any kind. Painting will continue to be subjective and arcane, an art of accident rather than rule, of stains on walls rather than of calculation, of inscape rather than of external reality.

[29] This conclusion is rejected by those who believe in a social theory of art. They maintain that a living art must depend on the popular will, and that neither the blot nor the diagram is popular; and, since those who hold a social theory of art are usually Marxists, they point to Soviet Russia as a country where all my conditions obtain—differentiation of function,

the domination of science and so forth—and yet what we call modern art has gained no hold. This argument does not impress me. There is, of course, nothing at all in the idea that Communist doctrines inevitably produce social realism. Painting in Yugoslavia, in Poland and Hungary is in the same modern idiom as painting in the United States, and shows remarkable vitality. Whereas the official social realism of the U.S.S.R., except for a few illustrators, lacks life or conviction, and shows no evidence of representing the popular will. In fact Russian architecture has already dropped the grandiose official style, and I am told that this is now taking place in painting also. In spite of disapproval amounting to persecution, experimental painters exist and find buyers.

[30] I doubt if the Marxists are even correct in saying that the blot and the diagram are not popular. The power, size, and splendour of, say, the Seagram building in New York makes it as much the object of pride and wonder as great architecture was in the past. And one of the remarkable things about Tachisme is the speed with which it has spread throughout the world, not only in sophisticated centres, but in small local art societies. It has become as much an international style as Gothic in the 14th and Baroque in the 17th centuries. I recently visited the exhibition of a provincial academy in the north of England, a very respectable body then celebrating its hundred and fiftieth anniversary. A few years ago it had been full of Welsh mountain landscapes, and scenes of streets and harbours, carefully delineated. Now practically every picture was in the Tachiste style, and I found that many of them were painted by the same artists, often quite elderly people, who had previously painted the mountains and streets. As works of art, they seemed to me neither better nor worse. But I could not help thinking that they must have been less trouble to do, and I reflected that the painters must have had a happy time releasing the Dionysiac elements in their natures. However, we must not be too cynical about this. I do not believe that the spread of action painting is due solely to the fact that it is easy to do. Cubism, especially synthetic Cubism, also looks easy to do, and never had this immense diffusion. It remained the style of a small élite of professional painters and specialised art lovers; whereas Tachisme has spread to fabrics, to the decoration of public buildings, to the backgrounds of television programmes, to advertising of all kinds. Indeed the closest analogy to action painting is the most popular art of all—the art of jazz. The trumpeter who rises from his seat as one possessed, and squirts out his melody like a scarlet scrawl against a background of plangent dashes and dots, is not as a rule performing for a small body of intellectuals.

[31] Nevertheless, I do not think that the style of the blot and the diagram will last forever. For one thing, I believe that the imitation of

external reality is a fundamental human instinct which is bound to re-assert itself. In his admirable book on sculpture called *Aratra Pentelici,* Ruskin describes an experience which many of us could confirm. "Having been always desirous," he says,

that the education of women should begin in learning how to cook, I got leave, one day, for a little girl of eleven years old to exchange, much to her satisfaction, her schoolroom for the kitchen. But as ill fortune would have it, there was some pastry toward, and she was left unadvisedly in command of some delicately rolled paste; whereof she made no pies, but an unlimited quantity of cats and mice. . . .

Now [he continues] you may read the works of the gravest critics of art from end to end; but you will find, at last, they can give you no other true account of the spirit of sculpture than that it is an irresistible human instinct for the making of cats and mice, and other imitable living creatures, in such permanent form that one may play with the images at leisure.

I cannot help feeling that he was right. I am fond of works of art, and I collect them. But I do not want to hang them on the wall simply in order to get an electric shock every time that I pass them. I want to hold them, and turn them round and re-hang them—in short, to play with the images at leisure. And, putting aside what may be no more than a personal prejudice, I rather doubt if an art which depends solely on the first impact on our emotions is permanently valid. When the shock is exhausted, we have nothing to occupy our minds. And this is particularly troublesome with an art which depends so much on the unconscious, because, as we know from the analysis of dreams, the furniture of our unconscious minds is even more limited, repetitive, and commonplace than that of our conscious minds. The blots and stains of modern painting depend ultimately on the memories of things seen, memories sunk deep in the unconscious, overlaid, transformed, assimilated to a physical condition, but memories none the less. *Ex nihilo nihil fit.* It is not possible for a painter to lose all contact with the visible world.

[32] At this point the apes have provided valuable evidence. There is no doubt that they are Tachiste painters of considerable accomplishment. I do not myself care for the work of Congo the chimp, but Sophie, the Rotterdam gorilla, is a charming artist, whose delicate traceries remind me of early Paul Klee. As you know, apes take their painting seriously. The patterns they produce are not the result of mere accident, but of intense, if short-lived, concentration, and a lively sense of balance and space-filling. If you compare the painting of a young ape with that of a human child of relatively the same age, you will find that in the first, expressive, pattern-making stage, the ape is superior. Then, automatically and inexorably the child begins to draw *things*—man, house, truck, etc.

This the ape never does. Of course his Tachiste paintings are far more attractive than the child's crude conceptual outlines. But they cannot develop. They are monotonous and ultimately rather depressing.

[33] The difference between the child and the ape does not show itself in æsthetic perception, or in physical perception of any kind, but in the child's power to form a concept. Later, as we know, he will spend his time trying to adapt his concept to the evidence of physical sensation; in that struggle lies the whole of style. But the concept—the need to draw a line round his thought—comes first. Now it is a truism that the power to form concepts is what distinguishes man from the animals; although the prophets of modern society, Freud, Jung, D. H. Lawrence, have rightly insisted on the importance of animal perceptions in balanced human personality, the concept-forming faculty has not declined in modern man. On the contrary, it is the basis of that vast scientific achievement which, as I said earlier, seems almost to have put art out of business.

[34] Now if the desire to represent external reality depended solely on an interest in visual sensation, I would agree that it might disappear from art and never return. But if, as the evidence of children and monkeys indicates, it depends primarily on the formation of concepts, which are then modified by visual sensation, I think it is bound to return. For I consider the human faculty of forming concepts at least as "inalienable" as "life, liberty, and the pursuit of happiness. . . ."

[35] I am not, of course, suggesting that the imitation of external reality will ever again become what it was in European art from the mid-17th to the late 19th centuries. Such a subordination of the concept to the visual sensation was altogether exceptional in the history of art. Much of the territory won by modern painting will, I believe, be held. For example, freedom of association, the immediate passage from one association to another—which is so much a part of Picasso's painting and Henry Moore's sculpture, is something which has existed in music since Wagner and in poetry since Rimbaud and Mallarmé. (I mean existed consciously; of course it underlies all great poetry and music.) It need not be sacrificed in a return to external reality. Nor need the direct communication of intuition, through touch and an instinctive sense of materials. This I consider pure gain. In the words of my original metaphor, both the association blot and the gesture blot can remain. But they must be given more nourishment: they must be related to a fuller knowledge of the forms and structures which impress us most powerfully, and so become part of our concept of natural order. At the end of the passage in which Leonardo tells the painter that he can look for battles, landscapes, and animals in the stains on walls, he adds this caution, "But first be sure that you know all the members of all things you wish to depict, both the members of the animals and the members of landscapes, that is to say of rocks, plants, and

so forth." It is because one feels in Henry Moore's sculpture this knowledge of the members of animals and plants, that his work, even at its most abstract, makes an impression on us different from that of his imitators. His figures are not merely pleasing examples of design, but seem to be a part of nature, "rolled round in Earth's diurnal course with rocks and stones and trees."

[36] Those lines of Wordsworth lead me to the last reason why I feel that the intuitive blot and scribble may not dominate painting forever. Our belief in the whole purpose of art may change. I said earlier that we now believe it should aim at producing a kind of exalted happiness: this really means that art becomes an end in itself. Now it is an incontrovertible fact of history that the greatest art has always been *about* something, a means of communicating some truth which is assumed to be more important than the art itself. The truths which art has been able to communicate have been of a kind which could not be put in any other way. They have been ultimate truths, stated symbolically. Science has achieved its triumph precisely by disregarding such truths, by not asking unanswerable questions, but sticking to the question "how." I confess it looks to me as if we shall have to wait a long time before there is some new belief which requires expression through art rather than through statistics or equations. And until this happens, the visual arts will fall short of the greatest epochs, the ages of the Parthenon, the Sistine Ceiling, and Chartres Cathedral.

[37] I am afraid there is nothing we can do about it. No amount of good-will and no expenditure of money can effect that sort of change. We cannot even dimly foresee when it will happen or what form it will take. We can only be thankful for what we have got—a vigorous, popular, decorative art, complementary to our architecture and our science, somewhat monotonous, somewhat prone to charlatanism, but genuinely expressive of our time.

COMMENT AND QUESTIONS

1. What are the author's reasons for starting his discussion of modern art with Leonardo da Vinci?
2. Paragraphs 7 and 8 define the terms of the central metaphor. What synonyms or suggested meanings can you think of for *blot* and for *diagram* as the words are used in the whole essay?
3. At the end of paragraph 8, the author makes a distinction—to which he

will return later—between analogy blots and gesture blots. Explain the distinction.

4. Paragraph 9 states two assumptions. Much of the essay, however, is an effort to support these assumptions. What principal methods of development does the author use?

5. What is meant by "the differentiation of function," in the second sentence of paragraph 12? How is the phrase related to the central idea of the essay?

6. Summarize the points Clark is making about (a) the deflections from art to science, (b) the purpose of art in an age of science, (c) the effect on painting of the study of psychology.

7. The author has said that modern painting and architecture represent less a change in style than a change of spirit: "a great change in our ways of thinking and feeling." How convincingly, in your opinion, does he support this thesis? Explain.

8. Summarize the author's reasons for believing that the style of the blot and the diagram will not last forever. In his first prediction—that the style will last for a long time—Clark discusses both architecture and painting. In the second prediction, does he appear to be discussing both? How does he qualify the thesis that the style of modern art will not last forever?

9. What parallels to the style of the blot and the diagram do you know in modern literature or in modern music? What do you think may happen to these arts in the future? Explain.

10. Although the tone of "The Blot and the Diagram" is notably fair and dispassionate, the author makes, both directly and by implication, a number of value judgments—about great art, about modern art, and about modern life. What are these judgments? To what extent do you agree or disagree with them, and why?

11. Skillful use of quotation is a characteristic of this essay. What use does the author make of the quotations from Leonardo (paragraphs 4 and 5), Pater (paragraphs 13 and 14), Bronowski (paragraph 19), Lao-tzu (paragraph 24), and Ruskin (paragraph 31)?

[61] *DeWitt Parker*: The Intrinsic Value of Art

THE FOLLOWING selection discusses various forms of art—painting, sculpture, music, and literature—and the values they have in common. DeWitt Parker (1885–1949), who was a professor of philosophy at the University of Michigan, is the author of *Human Values, Analysis of Art*, and *The Principles of Aesthetics* (1946), from which this selection is taken.

[¹] Our definition of art can be complete only if it enables us to understand the value of art. The reader might very well ask, however, what possible value expression could have when it becomes an end in itself. "I can understand its value," he might say, "when it has useful effects or conveys information, but what value can it possess of its own?" At this point, moreover, we are concerned with the value immediately realized in the experience of art, not with further values that may result from it. Art, no less than practical or scientific expression, may have beneficial effects on other experiences, which must be taken into account in measuring its total worth, but these we shall leave for investigation in our last chapters, after we have reached our fullest comprehension of art; we are interested now, in order to test and complete our definition, in the resident value only. That aesthetic expression does have this value follows directly from the spontaneous delight which artist and art lover take in it. The only problem, therefore, is its source, which, we shall find, is fed from many springs, some of them underground, and all intermingled.

[²] One source of value consists of the pleasures afforded by the orderly media of expression—colors, lines and shapes, word sounds or tones, with their rhythms and relationships. As we have noted, there is no aesthetic expression without some values of this kind. These satisfactions we may call musical, because, taken by themselves, they have the vague, elusive quality of pure music. Outside of music, they are commonly fused with other satisfactions, for in literature and the plastic arts the sensuous media are symbols, verbal or representational, with definite meanings that may be agreeable; yet for purposes of analysis we can distinguish them. Thus we take pleasure in the yellow of Van Gogh's *Sunflowers,* partly because it is just that yellow, but partly because it is the color of a represented sunflower. Why we do enjoy the sensuous envelope of expression is a question we shall try to answer later; for the moment we are interested merely in setting it down as a universal spring of value in art.

[³] With this exception, the most obvious source of value in art is the imagination of objects and events which normally cause pleasure. Out of the meanings attached to his sensuous medium the artist may weave for us waking dreams of the things we like to see. We all enjoy perceiving the human form, so the sculptor offers a semblance of one; we like to see the ocean or flowers; here now is a shining vision by Winslow Homer or Van Gogh. The poet also is a magician, who may make of the meanings of words a happy dream:

> Gold wings across the sea!
> Moonlight from tree to tree,
> Sweet hair laid on my knee . . .

[⁴] In general, instincts and interests receive a partial satisfaction through imagining the objects, of which the perception or use might provide a full satisfaction. Both art and dream illustrate this principle.

[⁵] Similarly, through ideas of action or emotion suggested by the work of art, we are enabled imaginatively to perform actions, or to feel emotions, we should like to perform or feel. So, putting ourselves as it were into the represented body of the wrestler or dancer, we vicariously enjoy taking the proud poses or exerting the vigorous energies there suggested. Or, watching the play, we may find pleasure in fancying ourselves courting as eloquently as Romeo or being as charmingly responsive as Juliet. All aesthetic expression may thus become self-expression. We can understand how this is true if we remember that out of our own minds come the ideas and feelings which make up the content of the work of art; that all the artist does is to provide a set of stimuli or sensuous symbols which he hopes we will interpret as he intends. Self-expression is most readily the effect of the more subjective types of art, such as lyric poetry and music, because the emotions expressed are simple and universal; hence easily become anybody's experiences. Yet even the more objective types of art like the novel and drama, painting and sculpture, may become forms of self-expression, for we build up the worlds they contain in our imagination and emotion. We may then live in them, as it were, providing for ourselves imaginative modes of assuagement of our desires for action and passion.

[⁶] In the appreciation of the more objective types of art, however, the personality satisfied may not be the ordinary work-a-day one, but rather the self expanded by the imagination, under the suggestions of the artist. The acts represented in the landscape or genre picture, in the novel or play, may never have been performed by me; the opinions uttered may not be mine. And yet, as I look at the picture, it may be to me as if I were a shepherd moving with my sheep among the mountains or a peasant brawling with my companions. Or, watching the play, I may become as Anthony addressing the Romans or Hamlet soliloquizing on life and death. This is possible because each of us has capacities for action and emotion unrealized; the actual self is only one of many that might have been; hundreds of possible lives slumber in our souls. I remember George Herbert Palmer telling me when I was a student how many different professions he would have liked to pursue—that of ladies' tailor was one of them!—and I am sure he did not tell me all. No matter which life we may have chosen for our own, or have had forced upon us by our fate, we retain a secret longing for the others that have gone unfulfilled. Some of these—those that we deliberately rejected or that a turn of fate might have made ours—we may imagine vaguely; but many of them we have not the power to dream; yet they too beckon us from behind, and the artist provides us with their dream. Through art we may secure an imaginative realization of tendencies to think and act and feel, which, because incompatible with each other or with the conditions of our existence, cannot find free play in real life.

[7] Nevertheless, it must not be thought that the satisfactions of art are derived solely from the provision of substitute objects for the fulfillment of our own conscious or unconscious desires, through the simple process of identification with the world of persons and activities that we build up in the imagination under the artist's direction. Not all of art is "wish-fulfillment" in the ordinary sense. If the persons represented are too unlike ourselves we cannot without reservations place ourselves sympathetically within them; they therefore remain objects for us, not modes of ourselves. It would be hard for a man of simple, straightforward nature to identify himself with Hamlet or a normal woman to put herself in the place of Ophelia or [Lady] Macbeth. Even if we did identify ourselves with them imaginatively, their misfortunes were so great they would not provide us with a vicarious fulfillment of ordinary wishes: who could desire such a fate as theirs? Yet we do find satisfaction in works of art of this kind. For, strange as it may seem at first thought, objects and persons that are foreign, or even opposed to us, may provide us with an assuagement of needs not of a personal, but of a general type, like pity or curiosity, or of a negative character, such as fear, horror, wrath, hate, indignation and scorn. And if real life does not offer opportunities in sufficient abundance and perfection for our appeasement—and how can life, since our needs are immoderate, almost infinite—we will seek them in art. . . .

[8] But just to express desire, quite apart from the provision of an imaginary object or activity through which it can be fulfilled, may be of value if it assists us to satisfy that desire which is deepest of all, for inner harmony or freedom.

> Oh, to be in England
> Now that April's there . . .

sang the poet and won for himself and for all who feel themselves into his verses, some appeasement, even though there is no hint of the assuagement of longing through a homecoming. No matter how poignant be a desire, the weight, the sting of it is lightened through expression, for it is drawn from the dark depths of the self to the clear and orderly surface of the work of art, where the mind can view and master it. Otherwise fluid and chaotic, or, when orderly, too busy with its ends to know itself, experience achieves the fixed outlines of a thing by being attached to a permanent form, and there can be retained and surveyed. Everyone has verified the clarifying effect of expression upon ideas, how they thus acquire definiteness and cohesion, so that even the mind that thinks them can hold them in review. Now, a similar effect upon feeling is no less certain. The unexpressed values of experience are vague strivings, embedded in disordered sensations and images; these expression sorts and organizes by attaching them to permanent ordered symbols. Even what is most intimate and fugitive becomes a stable object to which we may return again and again. When put into patterned words, the subtlest and deepest passions of a poet, which before were felt in a dim and tangled fashion, are brought out into the light. In music the most elusive moods, by being embodied in ordered sound, remain no longer subterranean. Through the novel or drama, the writer is able not only to enact his visions of life in the imagination, but by embodying them in external words and acts, to possess them for reflection. In painting, all that is seen or wondered at in nature is perceived with more delicacy and discrimination, and felt with greater freedom; or the vague fancies which a heated imagination paints upon the background of the mind come out better controlled when sketched with care upon a canvas.

[9] The most violent and unruly passions may be the material of art, but once they are put into artistic form, they are mastered: "There is an art of passion but no passionate art"—Schiller. Through expression, the repression—the obstruction of feeling—is broken down; the mere effort to find a fitting artistic form diverts the attention and provides other occupation for the mind; an opportunity is given to reflect upon and digest the experience, through all these means bringing peace. It is impossible to cite too often the famous passage from Goethe's *Poetry and Truth:*

And thus began that bent of mind from which I could not deviate my whole life through; namely that of turning into an image, into a poem, everything that delighted me or troubled me, or otherwise occupied my attention, and of coming to some certain understanding with myself thereupon . . . All the works therefore that have been published by me are only fragments of one great confession.[1]

[10] This effect of artistic expression belongs, as we have noted, to forms of expression outside of art. Every confidential outpouring of emotion, as between two friends, every confession in and outside of the confessional provides an example of the truth that to formulate feeling is to begin to be free with regard to it; not that we thereby get rid of it, but that we are able to find some place in our world where we can be on good terms with it. The greatest difficulty in bearing any disappointment or sorrow comes not from the frustration itself—for after all we have other things to live for—but from its effect upon the presuppositions of our entire being. The mind has an unconscious set of axioms or postulates which are assumed in the process of living; now anything that seems to contradict these, as a great calamity does, by destroying the logic of life,

---

[1] English translation, edited by Park Godwin, Vol. I, p. 66.

makes it seem meaningless and corrupts that faith in life which is the spring of action. In order for the health of the mind to be restored, the contradictory fact must somehow be reconciled with the mind's presuppositions, and the rationality of existence re-affirmed. But it is indispensable that we should clearly envisage and reflect upon the fact, viewing it in its larger relations where it will lose its overwhelming significance. Now precisely this transformation of experience may be achieved through expression. A fine illustration of this is Keats' sonnet ending

> . . . then on the shore
> Of the wide world I stand alone and think,
> Till love and fame to nothingness do sink.

[11] A great many works of art besides Goethe's, and some of them the greatest, like the *Divine Comedy,* so far as they spring intimately from the life of the artist, have had the salutary value of a confession for their creators. It is not always possible to trace the personal feelings and motives lying behind the artist's fictions, for the suffering soul covers its pain with subtle disguises; yet even when we do not know them we can divine them. We are certain that Watteau's gay picture visions were the projection and confession of his own disappointed dreams. In this respect, one great advantage of art over ordinary expression is its universality. Art is the confessional of the race. The artist provides a medium through which all men may confess themselves and heal their souls. Who does not feel a revival of some old or present despair of his own when he reads

> Un grand sommeil noir   Je ne vois plus rien,
> Tombe sur ma vie;   Je perds la mémoire
> Dormez toute espoir,   Du mal et du bien . . .
> Dormez toute envie!   O, la triste histoire!

yet who does not at the same time experience its assuagement? And this effect upon the reader is not confined to lyrical art; for, when in novel and drama we put ourselves in the place of the dramatis personae, we can pour our emotional experience into them and through them find relief for ourselves. Just so, Aristotle recognized the cathartic, or healing virtue of the drama as well as of music—"through pity and fear, effecting the proper purgation of these emotions."[2]

[12] The values that may result from expression which I have been describing pertain to generalizations of experience no less than to experiences of concrete objects and events. Many poems and some works of plastic art possess what I like to call "depth meanings"—meanings of universal scope underneath relatively concrete meanings or ideas. Thus in the following line of one of Frost's little poems

> Nothing gold can stay

[2] *Poetics,* VI, 2. *Politics,* VIII, 7.

the word "gold" has its usual surface meaning, but underneath that is its depth meaning, precious; so in addition to saying that nothing golden can endure, the poet is saying that nothing valuable can abide—a more universal statement. This is the same as one of the depth meanings in Shakespeare's

> Golden lads and girls all must
> As chimney sweepers come to dust . . .

although, of course, there is another meaning here—that of the equality in death of rich and poor. That there may be a multiplicity of meanings in a single work of art was recognized in the Renaissance, and even seems to have been regarded as essential to its purpose.[3] Sometimes the satisfaction in the expression of a generalization stems from the fact that the thought is one that we like to entertain, as in the so familiar

> God's in his heaven—
> All's right with the world!

but in other cases, as when the thought is not agreeable, it accompanies that adjustment to truth which arises as we look it squarely in the face, no longer struggling against it—"coming to some certain understanding with ourselves thereupon."

> You linger your little hour and are gone,
> And still the woods sweep leafily on,
> Not even missing the coral root flower
> You took as a trophy of the hour.

[13] All the other values of expression are enhanced through the fact that the medium is orderly and delightful. To imagine such objects as those suggested in the following lines

> Charmed magic casements, opening on the foam
> Of perilous seas, in faery lands forlorn

is pleasurable in itself, but more agreeable, and therefore more spontaneous, because of the melody of sound in which they are enveloped. And when the facts imagined are not pleasant, their expression in a delightful medium helps to induce us to make them our own and accept them notwithstanding. The medium becomes a charming net to hold us, and because of its allurements, we give ourselves the more freely to its spirit within. The following is not an agreeable thought

---

[3] Cf. Dante, *Convito*, Trattato Secundo; Leone Ebreo, *Dialoghi d'Amore*, pp. 99 and 100, Bari, Laterza, 1929.

Tomorrow and tomorrow and tomorrow
Creeps in this petty pace from day to day,
To the last syllable of recorded time;
And all our yesterdays have lighted fools
The way to dusty death.

yet the expression of this thought becomes a value in part because of the rhythmic charm of language. There is no incongruity between the fair form of a work of art and its content, however repugnant; for if we esteem the sympathetic vision of life—an imagination of it which provides some assuagement of our wishes, and in particular of our desire to be reconciled with it—we shall be glad of any means to this end.

[14] The contrast between the perfection of the work of art and the drab or difficult realities of nature and personal striving, serve also to make of beauty a consoler and healer. In place of a confused medley of sense impressions, art offers orderly colors and sounds and shapes; instead of an experience distracted and at loose ends, it offers one where each element serves the pervading purpose and where none are irrelevant or distracting; instead of a life of duty hard to fulfill and ambitions painfully and only partially achieved, it provides an imagined life, which while imitating, and so appeasing, the interests of real life, remains free from its hazards and burdens. I would not base the value of art on the contrast between it and life; yet if life were not so bound and disordered, art would not seem so free and perfect; and very often those who suffer and struggle most love it best. The organic unity of the work of art, in which each element suggests another within its world, keeping you there and shutting you out momentarily from the real world to which you must presently return, and the sensuous charm of the medium, fascinating your eyes and ears, bring forgetfulness and a temporary release.

[15] The satisfactions which art provides are the greater because they are communicable; to possess them alone would be a good, but all values become enhanced when we add the joy of fellow feeling. Merely private and unutterable inspirations are not art. Beauty does for values what science does for intelligence; even as the one universalizes thought so the other universalizes feeling. In expressing himself the artist creates a form into which all similar experiences can be poured and out of which they can be shared. When we listen to the hymns of the church or read the poems of Horace the significance of our experience is magnified because we know that the feelings of millions have been there; we are in unison with a vast company living and dead. No thing of beauty is a private possession. All artists feed on one another, and into each of their products has gone the mind-work of the ages.

[16] But there are two types of universality—one by exclusion, the other by inclusion. Christian communists like Tolstoi demand that art ex-

press universal feelings only, such as the moral and religious; they would exclude all values that have not become those of the race. The aristocratic, the pathological, even the patriotic, are condemned as substance for art. But this is to diminish the importance of art; for it is art's privilege to make feelings common by providing a medium through which they can be communicated rather than merely to express those that are already common. Art is the more valuable because it encompasses the things which tend to separate and distinguish men than it would be if it were limited to those that unite them. There is nothing so bizarre that art may not express it, provided that thereby it may be communicated.

[17] The life of the imagination is, moreover, the only one that we can have in common. Actually to lead another's life would involve possessing his body, occupying his position, doing his work and so destroying him. But through the sympathetic imagination we can penetrate his life and leave him in possession. To do this thoroughly is possible, however, with the real life of a very few people, with intimates and friends. With the mass, we can share only ideal things like religion and patriotism, but these also are matters largely of imagination. Now art widens the scope of this common life by creating a new, imaginary world to which we can all belong, where action and enjoyment do not involve competition or depend on mastery and possession.

[18] Finally, the values that art provides are relatively permanent. Art not only extends life and enables us to share it, but also preserves it. Existence has a leak in it, as Plato said; experience flows in and then flows on forever. Against this flux, our belief in progress comforts us; maturity is better than youth, we think, and each generation happier and more spiritual than the last. Yet the consolations of progress are partial. For even if it were true that we always go on to something better in the future, the past had its unique value, and that is lost ineluctably. The present repeats much of the form of the past—the essential aspects of human nature and institutions remain the same; but the distinctive bloom of each phase of personal life, and of each period of the world's history is transient. We cannot again become children or possess the strenuous freedom of the Renaissance, or the unclouded integrity attributed to the Greeks.

[19] In the life of the individual, however, the flux is not absolute; for through memory we preserve something of the unique value of our past. Its vividness, its fullness, the sharp bite of its reality go; but a subtle essence remains. And the worth that we attach to our personality depends largely upon it; for the instinct of self-preservation penetrates the inner world; we strive not only to maintain our physical existence in the present but our psychic past as well. In preserving the values of the past through memory we find a satisfaction akin to that of protecting our lives from danger. Through memory we feel childhood's joys and youth's

sweet love and manhood's triumphs still our own, secure against the perils of oblivion.

[20] Now art does for the group what memory does for the individual. Only through expression can the past be preserved for all men and all time. When the individual perishes his memories go with him; unless he puts them into a form where they can be taken up into the consciousness of other men, they are lost forever. And just as the individual seeks a vicarious self-preservation by identifying himself with his children and his group, and finds compensation for his death in their continuance, so he rejoices when he knows that men who come after will appreciate the values of his life. We of the present feel ourselves enriched, in turn, as by a longer memory, in adding to the active values of our lives the imagined values of our forebears. Their desire to know themselves immortal is met by our desire to unite our lives with our whole past. Art alone makes this possible. History may tell us what men did, but only the poet or other artists can make us relive the values of their experience. For through expression they make their own memories, or their interpretation of other men's memories, ours. Art is the memory of a people, the conserver of its values.

COMMENT AND QUESTIONS

1. Paragraph 1 limits the subject: the author is concerned in this discussion "with the value immediately realized in the experience of art, not with further values that may result from it." Does it seem to you that he is, at any time in the selection, talking about "further values that may result"? Explain.

2. Briefly summarize the principal values that Parker finds in art. Which of these values are most meaningful to you? Would you add other values to his enumeration?

3. To which of the values does Parker give emphasis by proportion and position? What do you think are the reasons for his emphasis? Explain.

4. The author uses a number of examples, many of them familiar to a general audience, some perhaps not familiar. Does the reader need to know the sources of the illustrations in order to understand the principles illustrated?

5. In paragraphs 5 and 6, what is the meaning of "self-expression"? What two forms of self-expression is Parker discussing here?

6. Initially, the author is concerned with the pleasures of seeing things in art that we like to see and imagining actions and emotions that we should like to experience. How does he later qualify the idea of the *pleasures* in art?

7. Parker suggests, especially in paragraphs 10 and 13, that art can help to reaffirm the rationality of existence and help us to fulfill our desire to be

reconciled with life. What writers whom you have read would agree or disagree with the two assumptions that existence is rational and that we wish to be reconciled with life? To what extent do you agree or disagree? Explain.

8. In paragraphs 2, 8, 13, and particularly in paragraph 14, the author emphasizes the idea that art is orderly and that its order is a source of value. Sir Kenneth Clark, in "The Blot and the Diagram," describes the disorder, the free association, and the irrationality in the blots and stains of modern painting. Martin Esslin, in "The Significance of the Absurd," describes the grotesqueness, the illogic, and the disorder in Absurd drama. Do you think that Parker could find any of the values he assigns to art in the blot-style of modern painting or in Absurd plays? Explain.

9. "History may tell us what men did, but only the poet or other artists can make us relive the values of their experience." Does this statement seem valid to you? Explain.

SCIENCE AND
THE MODERN WORLD

&

[62] *J. Bronowski*: The Creative Mind

J. BRONOWSKI (1908–   ) is an English mathematician and writer,
author of *The Face of Violence*, *The Commonsense of Science*, *William Blake
and the Age of Revolution*, *The Poet's Defence*, and *The Identity of Man*.
The following selection is the first of three essays in *Science and Human
Values*, published in 1956 and revised in 1965. In paragraphs 8 and 9 of
"The Creative Mind" Bronowski summarizes the aims and content of *Science
and Human Values*.

– 1 –

[1] On a fine November day in 1945, late in the afternoon, I was landed
on an airstrip in southern Japan. From there a jeep was to take me over
the mountains to join a ship which lay in Nagasaki Harbor. I knew
nothing of the country or the distance before us. We drove off; dusk
fell; the road rose and fell away, the pine woods came down to the road,
straggled on and opened again. I did not know that we had left the open
country until unexpectedly I heard the ship's loudspeakers broadcasting
dance music. Then suddenly I was aware that we were already at the
center of damage in Nagasaki. The shadows behind me were the skele-
tons of the Mitsubishi factory buildings, pushed backwards and sideways
as if by a giant hand. What I had thought to be broken rocks was a
concrete power house with its roof punched in. I could now make out

the outline of two crumpled gasometers; there was a cold furnace festooned with service pipes; otherwise nothing but cockeyed telegraph poles and loops of wire in a bare waste of ashes. I had blundered into this desolate landscape as instantly as one might wake among the craters of the moon. The moment of recognition when I realized that I was already in Nagasaki is present to me as I write, as vividly as when I lived it. I see the warm night and the meaningless shapes; I can even remember the tune that was coming from the ship. It was a dance tune which had been popular in 1945, and it was called 'Is You Is Or Is You Ain't Ma Baby?'

[2] These essays, which I have called *Science and Human Values*, were born at that moment. For the moment I have recalled was a universal moment; what I met was, almost as abruptly, the experience of mankind. On an evening like that evening, some time in 1945, each of us in his own way learned that his imagination had been dwarfed. We looked up and saw the power of which we had been proud loom over us like the ruins of Nagasaki.

[3] The power of science for good and for evil has troubled other minds than ours. We are not here fumbling with a new dilemma; our subject and our fears are as old as the toolmaking civilizations. Men have been killed with weapons before now: what happened at Nagasaki was only more massive (for 40,000 were killed there by a flash which lasted seconds) and more ironical (for the bomb exploded over the main Christian community in Japan). Nothing happened in 1945 except that we changed the scale of our indifference to man; and conscience, in revenge, for an instant became immediate to us. Before this immediacy fades in a sequence of televised atomic tests, let us acknowledge our subject for what it is: civilization face to face with its own implications. The implications are both the industrial slum which Nagasaki was before it was bombed, and the ashy desolation which the bomb made of the slum. And civilization asks of both ruins, 'Is You Is Or Is You Ain't Ma Baby?'

– 2 –

[4] The man whom I imagine to be asking this question, wrily with a sense of shame, is not a scientist; he is civilized man. It is of course more usual for each member of civilization to take flight from its consequences by protesting that others have failed him. Those whose education and perhaps tastes have confined them to the humanities protest that the scientists alone are to blame, for plainly no mandarin ever made a bomb or an industry. The scientists say, with equal contempt, that the Greek scholars and the earnest cataloguers of cave paintings do well to wash their hands of blame; but what in fact are they doing to help direct the society whose ills grow more often from inaction than from error?

[5] This absurd division reached its *reductio ad absurdum*, I think,

when one of my teachers, G. H. Hardy, justified his great life work on the ground that it could do no one the least harm—or the least good. But Hardy was a mathematician; will humanists really let him opt out of the conspiracy of scientists? Or are scientists in their turn to forgive Hardy because, protest as he might, most of them learned their indispensable mathematics from his books?

[6] There is no comfort in such bickering. When Shelley pictured science as a modern Prometheus who would wake the world to a wonderful dream of Godwin, he was alas too simple. But it is as pointless to read what has happened since as a nightmare. Dream or nightmare, we have to live our experience as it is, and we have to live it awake. We live in a world which is penetrated through and through by science, and which is both whole and real. We cannot turn it into a game simply by taking sides.

[7] And this make-believe game might cost us what we value most: the human content of our lives. The scholar who disdains science may speak in fun, but his fun is not quite a laughing matter. To think of science as a set of special tricks, to see the scientist as the manipulator of outlandish skills—this is the root of the poison mandrake which flourishes rank in the comic strips. There is no more threatening and no more degrading doctrine than the fancy that somehow we may shelve the responsibility for making the decisions of our society by passing it to a few scientists armored with a special magic. This is another dream, the dream of H. G. Wells, in which the tall elegant engineers rule, with perfect benevolence, a humanity which has no business except to be happy. To H. G. Wells, this was a dream of heaven—a modern version of the idle, harp-resounding heaven of other childhood pieties. But in fact it is the picture of a slave society, and should make us shiver whenever we hear a man of sensibility dismiss science as someone else's concern. The world today is made, it is powered by science; and for any man to abdicate an interest in science is to walk with open eyes towards slavery.

[8] My aim in this book is to show that the parts of civilization make a whole: to display the links which give society its coherence and, more, which give it life. In particular, I want to show the place of science in the canons of conduct which it has still to perfect.

[9] This subject falls into three parts. The first is a study of the nature of the scientific activity, and with it of all those imaginative acts of understanding which exercise 'The Creative Mind.' After this it is logical to ask what is the nature of the truth, as we seek it in science and in social life; and to trace the influence which this search for empirical truth has had on conduct. This influence has prompted me to call the second part 'The Habit of Truth.' Last I shall study the conditions for the success of science, and find in them the values of man which science would have had to invent afresh if man had not otherwise known them: the values which make up 'The Sense of Human Dignity.'

[10] This, then, is a high-ranging subject which is not to be held in the narrow limits of a laboratory. It disputes the prejudice of the humanist who takes his science sourly and, equally, the petty view which many scientists take of their own activity and that of others. When men misunderstand their own work, they cannot understand the work of others; so that it is natural that these scientists have been indifferent to the arts. They have been content, with the humanists, to think science mechanical and neutral; they could therefore justify themselves only by the claim that it is practical. By this lame criterion they have of course found poetry and music and painting at least unreal and often meaningless. I challenge all these judgments.

– 3 –

[11] There is a likeness between the creative acts of the mind in art and in science. Yet, when a man uses the word science in such a sentence, it may be suspected that he does not mean what the headlines mean by science. Am I about to sidle away to those riddles in the Theory of Numbers which Hardy loved, or to the heady speculations of astrophysicists, in order to make claims for abstract science which have no bearing on its daily practice?

[12] I have no such design. My purpose is to talk about science as it is, practical and theoretical. I define science as the organization of our knowledge in such a way that it commands more of the hidden potential in nature. What I have in mind therefore is both deep and matter of fact; it reaches from the kinetic theory of gases to the telephone and the suspension bridge and medicated toothpaste. It admits no sharp boundary between knowledge and use. There are of course people who like to draw a line between pure and applied science; and oddly, they are often the same people who find art unreal. To them, the word useful is a final arbiter, either for or against a work; and they use this word as if it can mean only what makes a man feel heavier after meals.

[13] There is no sanction for confining the practice of science in this or another way. True, science is full of useful inventions. And its theories have often been made by men whose imagination was directed by the uses to which their age looked. Newton turned naturally to astronomy because it was the subject of his day, and it was so because finding one's way at sea had long been a practical preoccupation of the society into which he was born. It should be added, mischievously, that astronomy also had some standing because it was used very practically to cast horoscopes. (Kepler used it for this purpose; in the Thirty Years' War he cast the horoscope of Wallenstein which wonderfully told his character, and he predicted a universal disaster for 1634 which proved to be the murder of Wallenstein.)

[¹⁴] In a setting which is more familiar, Faraday worked all his life to link electricity with magnetism because this was the glittering problem of his day; and it was so because his society, like ours, was on the lookout for new sources of power. Consider a more modest example today: the new mathematical methods of automatic control, a subject sometimes called cybernetics, have been developed now because this is a time when communication and control have in effect become forms of power. These inventions have been directed by social needs, and they are useful inventions; yet it was not their usefulness which dominated and set light to the minds of those who made them. Neither Newton nor Faraday, nor yet Norbert Wiener, spent their time in a scramble for patents.

[¹⁵] What a scientist does is compounded of two interests: the interest of his time and his own interest. In this his behavior is no different from any other man's. The need of the age gives its shape to scientific progress as a whole. But it is not the need of the age which gives the individual scientist his sense of pleasure and of adventure, and that excitement which keeps him working late into the night when all the useful typists have gone home at five o'clock. He is personally involved in his work, as the poet is in his, and as the artist is in the painting. Paints and painting too must have been made for useful ends; and language was developed, from whatever beginnings, for practical communication. Yet you cannot have a man handle paints or language or the symbolic concepts of physics, you cannot even have him stain a microscope slide, without instantly waking in him a pleasure in the very language, a sense of exploring his own activity. This sense lies at the heart of creation.

– 4 –

[¹⁶] The sense of personal exploration is as urgent, and as delightful, to the practical scientist as to the theoretical. Those who think otherwise are confusing what is practical with what is humdrum. Good humdrum work without originality is done every day by everyone, theoretical scientists as well as practical, and writers and painters too, as well as truck drivers and bank clerks. Of course the unoriginal work keeps the world going; but it is not therefore the monopoly of practical men. And neither need the practical man be unoriginal. If he is to break out of what has been done before, he must bring to his own tools the same sense of pride and discovery which the poet brings to words. He cannot afford to be less radical in conceiving and less creative in designing a new turbine than a new world system.

[¹⁷] And this is why in turn practical discoveries are not made only by practical men. As the world's interest has shifted, since the Industrial Revolution, to the tapping of new springs of power, the theoretical scientist has shifted his interests too. His speculations about energy have been as abstract as once they were about astronomy; and they have been profound now as they were then, because the man loved to think. The Carnot cycle and the dynamo grew equally from this love, and so did nuclear physics and the German V weapons and Kelvin's interest in low temperatures. Man does not invent by following either use or tradition; he does not invent even a new form of communication by calling a conference of communication engineers. Who invented the television set? In any deep sense, it was Clerk Maxwell who foresaw the existence of radio waves, and Heinrich Hertz who proved it, and J. J. Thomson who discovered the electron. This is not said in order to rob any practical man of the invention, but from a sad sense of justice; for neither Maxwell nor Hertz nor J. J. Thomson would take pride in television just now.

[18] Man masters nature not by force but by understanding. This is why science has succeeded where magic failed: because it has looked for no spell to cast over nature. The alchemist and the magician in the Middle Ages thought, and the addict of comic strips is still encouraged to think, that nature must be mastered by a device which outrages her laws. But in four hundred years since the Scientific Revolution we have learned that we gain our ends only *with* the laws of nature; we control her only by understanding her laws. We cannot even bully nature by any insistence that our work shall be designed to give power over her. We must be content that power is the byproduct of understanding. So the Greeks said that Orpheus played the lyre with such sympathy that wild beasts were tamed by the hand on the strings. They did not suggest that he got this gift by setting out to be a lion tamer.

– 5 –

[19] What is the insight with which the scientist tries to see into nature? Can it indeed be called either imaginative or creative? To the literary man the question may seem merely silly. He has been taught that science is a large collection of facts; and if this is true, then the only seeing which scientists need do is, he supposes, seeing the facts. He pictures them, the colorless professionals of science, going off to work in the morning into the universe in a neutral, unexposed state. They then expose themselves like a photographic plate. And then in the darkroom or laboratory they develop the image, so that suddenly and startlingly it appears, printed in capital letters, as a new formula for atomic energy.

[20] Men who have read Balzac and Zola are not deceived by the claims of these writers that they do no more than record the facts. The readers of Christopher Isherwood do not take him literally when he writes 'I am a camera.' Yet the same readers solemnly carry with them from their schooldays this foolish picture of the scientist fixing by some mechanical process the facts of nature. I have had of all people

a historian tell me that science is a collection of facts, and his voice had not even the ironic rasp of one filing cabinet reproving another.

[21] It seems impossible that this historian had ever studied the beginnings of a scientific discovery. The Scientific Revolution can be held to begin in the year 1543 when there was brought to Copernicus, perhaps on his deathbed, the first printed copy of the book he had finished about a dozen years earlier. The thesis of this book is that the earth moves around the sun. When did Copernicus go out and record this fact with his camera? What appearance in nature prompted his outrageous guess? And in what odd sense is this guess to be called a neutral record of fact?

[22] Less than a hundred years after Copernicus, Kepler published (between 1609 and 1619) the three laws which described the paths of the planets. The work of Newton and with it most of our mechanics spring from these laws. They have a solid, matter of fact sound. For example, Kepler says that if one squares the year of a planet, one gets a number which is proportional to the cube of its average distance from the sun. Does anyone think that such a law is found by taking enough readings and then squaring and cubing everything in sight? If he does, then, as a scientist, he is doomed to a wasted life; he has as little prospect of making a scientific discovery as an electronic brain has.

[23] It was not this way that Copernicus and Kepler thought, or that scientists think today. Copernicus found that the orbits of the planets would look simpler if they were looked at from the sun and not from the earth. But he did not in the first place find this by routine calculation. His first step was a leap of imagination—to lift himself from the earth, and put himself wildly, speculatively into the sun. 'The earth conceives from the sun,' he wrote; and 'the sun rules the family of stars.' We catch in his mind an image, the gesture of the virile man standing in the sun, with arms outstretched, overlooking the planets. Perhaps Copernicus took the picture from the drawings of the youth with outstretched arms which the Renaissance teachers put into their books on the proportions of the body. Perhaps he had seen Leonardo's drawings of his loved pupil Salai. I do not know. To me, the gesture of Copernicus, the shining youth looking outward from the sun, is still vivid in a drawing which William Blake in 1780 based on all these: the drawing which is usually called *Glad Day*.

[24] Kepler's mind, we know, was filled with just such fanciful analogies; and we know what they were. Kepler wanted to relate the speeds of the planets to the musical intervals. He tried to fit the five regular solids into their orbits. None of these likenesses worked, and they have been forgotten; yet they have been and they remain the stepping stones of every creative mind. Kepler felt for his laws by way of metaphors, he searched mystically for likenesses with what he knew in every strange corner of nature. And when among these guesses he hit upon his laws,

he did not think of their numbers as the balancing of a cosmic bank account, but as a revelation of the unity in all nature. To us, the analogies by which Kepler listened for the movement of the planets in the music of the spheres are farfetched. Yet are they more so than the wild leap by which Rutherford and Bohr in our own century found a model for the atom in, of all places, the planetary system?

– 6 –

[25] No scientific theory is a collection of facts. It will not even do to call a theory true or false in the simple sense in which every fact is either so or not so. The Epicureans held that matter is made of atoms two thousand years ago and we are now tempted to say that their theory was true. But if we do so we confuse their notion of matter with our own. John Dalton in 1808 first saw the structure of matter as we do today, and what he took from the ancients was not their theory but something richer, their image: the atom. Much of what was in Dalton's mind was as vague as the Greek notion, and quite as mistaken. But he suddenly gave life to the new facts of chemistry and the ancient theory together, by fusing them to give what neither had: a coherent picture of how matter is linked and built up from different kinds of atoms. The act of fusion is the creative act.

[26] All science is the search for unity in hidden likenesses. The search may be on a grand scale, as in the modern theories which try to link the fields of gravitation and electromagnetism. But we do not need to be browbeaten by the scale of science. There are discoveries to be made by snatching a small likeness from the air too, if it is bold enough. In 1935 the Japanese physicist Hideki Yukawa wrote a paper which can still give heart to a young scientist. He took as his starting point the known fact that waves of light can sometimes behave as if they were separate pellets. From this he reasoned that the forces which held the nucleus of an atom together might sometimes also be observed as if they were solid pellets. A schoolboy can see how thin Yukawa's analogy is, and his teacher would be severe with it. Yet Yukawa without a blush calculated the mass of the pellet he expected to see, and waited. He was right; his meson was found, and a range of other mesons, neither the existence nor the nature of which had been suspected before. The likeness had borne fruit.

[27] The scientist looks for order in the appearances of nature by exploring such likenesses. For order does not display itself of itself; if it can be said to be there at all, it is not there for the mere looking. There is no way of pointing a finger or a camera at it; order must be discovered and, in a deep sense, it must be created. What we see, as we see it, is mere disorder.

[28] This point has been put trenchantly in a fable by Karl Popper.

Suppose that someone wished to give his whole life to science. Suppose that he therefore sat down, pencil in hand, and for the next twenty, thirty, forty years recorded in notebook after notebook everything that he could observe. He may be supposed to leave out nothing: today's humidity, the racing results, the level of cosmic radiation and the stock-market prices and the look of Mars, all would be there. He would have compiled the most careful record of nature that has ever been made; and, dying in the calm certainty of a life well spent, he would of course leave his notebooks to the Royal Society. Would the Royal Society thank him for the treasure of a lifetime of observation? It would not. The Royal Society would treat his notebooks exactly as the English bishops have treated Joanna Southcott's box. It would refuse to open them at all, because it would know without looking that the notebooks contain only a jumble of disorderly and meaningless items.

- 7 -

[29] Science finds order and meaning in our experience, and sets about this in quite a different way. It sets about it as Newton did in the story which he himself told in his old age, and of which the schoolbooks give only a caricature. In the year 1665, when Newton was twenty-two, the plague broke out in southern England, and the University of Cambridge was closed. Newton therefore spent the next eighteen months at home, removed from traditional learning, at a time when he was impatient for knowledge and, in his own phrase, 'I was in the prime of my age for invention.' In this eager, boyish mood, sitting one day in the garden of his widowed mother, he saw an apple fall. So far the books have the story right; we think we even know the kind of apple; tradition has it that it was a Flower of Kent. But now they miss the crux of the story. For what struck the young Newton at the sight was not the thought that the apple must be drawn to the earth by gravity; that conception was older than Newton. What struck him was the conjecture that the same force of gravity, which reaches to the top of the tree, might go on reaching out beyond the earth and its air, endlessly into space. Gravity might reach the moon: this was Newton's new thought; and it might be gravity which holds the moon in her orbit. There and then he calculated what force from the earth (falling off as the square of the distance) would hold the moon, and compared it with the known force of gravity at tree height. The forces agreed; Newton says laconically, 'I found them answer pretty nearly.' Yet they agreed only nearly: the likeness and the approximation go together, for no likeness is exact. In Newton's sentence modern science is full grown.

[30] It grows from a comparison. It has seized a likeness between two unlike appearances; for the apple in the summer garden and the grave moon overhead are surely as unlike in their movements as two things

can be. Newton traced in them two expressions of a single concept, gravitation: and the concept (and the unity) are in that sense his free creation. The progress of science is the discovery at each step of a new order which gives unity to what had long seemed unlike. Faraday did this when he closed the link between electricity and magnetism. Clerk Maxwell did it when he linked both with light. Einstein linked time with space, mass with energy, and the path of light past the sun with the flight of a bullet; and spent his dying years in trying to add to these likenesses another, which would find a single imaginative order between the equations of Clerk Maxwell and his own geometry of gravitation.

– 8 –

[31] When Coleridge tried to define beauty, he returned always to one deep thought: beauty, he said, is 'unity in variety.' Science is nothing else than the search to discover unity in the wild variety of nature—or more exactly, in the variety of our experience. Poetry, painting, the arts are the same search, in Coleridge's phrase, for unity in variety. Each in its own way looks for likenesses under the variety of human experience. What is a poetic image but the seizing and the exploration of a hidden likeness, in holding together two parts of a comparison which are to give depth each to the other? When Romeo finds Juliet in the tomb, and thinks her dead, he uses in his heartbreaking speech the words,

> Death that hath suckt the honey of thy breath.

The critic can only haltingly take to pieces the single shock which this image carries. The young Shakespeare admired Marlowe, and Marlowe's Faustus had said of the ghostly kiss of Helen of Troy that it sucked forth his soul. But that is a pale image; what Shakespeare has done is to fire it with the single word honey. Death is a bee at the lips of Juliet, and the bee is an insect that stings; the sting of death was a commonplace phrase when Shakespeare wrote. The sting is there, under the image; Shakespeare has packed it into the word honey; but the very word rides powerfully over its own undertones. Death is a bee that stings other people, but it comes to Juliet as if she were a flower; this is the moving thought under the instant image. The creative mind speaks in such thoughts.

[32] The poetic image here is also, and accidentally, heightened by the tenderness which town dwellers now feel for country ways. But it need not be; there are likenesses to conjure with, and images as powerful, within the man-made world. The poems of Alexander Pope belong to this world. They are not countrified, and therefore readers today find them unemotional and often artificial. Let me then quote Pope: here he is in a formal satire face to face, towards the end of his life, with his own gifts. In eight lines he looks poignantly forward towards death and back to the laborious years which made him famous.

> Years foll'wing Years, steal something ev'ry day,
> At last they steal us from our selves away;
> In one our Frolicks, one Amusements end,
> In one a Mistress drops, in one a Friend:
> This subtle Thief of Life, this paltry Time,
> What will it leave me, if it snatch my Rhime?
> If ev'ry Wheel of that unweary'd Mill
> That turn'd ten thousand Verses, now stands still.

The human mind had been compared to what the eighteenth century called a mill, that is to a machine, before; Pope's own idol Bolingbroke had compared it to a clockwork. In these lines the likeness goes deeper, for Pope is thinking of the ten thousand Verses which he had translated from Homer: what he says is sad and just at the same time, because this really had been a mechanical and at times a grinding task. Yet the clockwork is present in the image too; when the wheels stand still, time for Pope will stand still for ever; we feel that we already hear, over the horizon, Faust's defiant reply to Mephistopheles, which Goethe had not yet written—'let the clock strike and stop, let the hand fall, and time be at an end.'

> Werd ich zum Augenblicke sagen:
> Verweile doch! du bist so schön!
> Dann magst du mich in Fesseln schlagen,
> Dann will ich gern zugrunde gehn!
> Dann mag die Totenglocke schallen,
> Dann bist du deines Dienstes frei,
> Die Uhr mag stehn, der Zeiger fallen,
> Es sei die Zeit für mich vorbei![1]

[33] I have quoted Pope and Goethe because their metaphor here is not poetic; it is rather a hand reaching straight into experience and arranging it with new meaning. Metaphors of this kind need not always be written in words. The most powerful of them all is simply the presence of King Lear and his Fool in the hovel of a man who is shamming madness, while lightning rages outside. Or let me quote another clash of two conceptions of life, from a modern poet. In his later poems W. B. Yeats was troubled by the feeling that in shutting himself up to write, he was missing the active pleasures of life; and yet it seemed to him certain that

---

[1] Should I say to the moment:
  Do tarry! you are so beautiful!
  Then you may throw me in chains,
  Then I will gladly go to my perdition!
  Then Death's knell may resound,
  Then you shall be free of your service,
  The clock may stop, the hour-hand drop,
  Time may cease for me!

the man who lives for these pleasures will leave no lasting work behind him. He said this at times very simply, too:

> The intellect of man is forced to choose
> Perfection of the life, or of the work.

This problem, whether a man fulfills himself in work or in play, is of course more common than Yeats allowed; and it may be more commonplace. But it is given breadth and force by the images in which Yeats pondered it.

> Get all the gold and silver that you can,
> Satisfy ambition, or animate
> The trivial days and ram them with the sun,
> And yet upon these maxims meditate:
> All women dote upon an idle man
> Although their children need a rich estate;
> No man has ever lived that had enough
> Of children's gratitude or woman's love.

The love of women, the gratitude of children: the images fix two philosophies as nothing else can. They are tools of creative thought, as coherent and as exact as the conceptual images with which science works: as time and space, or as the proton and the neutron.

– 9 –

[34] The discoveries of science, the works of art are explorations—more, are explosions, of a hidden likeness. The discoverer or the artist presents in them two aspects of nature and fuses them into one. This is the act of creation, in which an original thought is born, and it is the same act in original science and original art. But it is not therefore the monopoly of the man who wrote the poem or who made the discovery. On the contrary, I believe this view of the creative act to be right because it alone gives a meaning to the act of appreciation. The poem or the discovery exists in two moments of vision: the moment of appreciation as much as that of creation; for the appreciator must see the movement, wake to the echo which was started in the creation of the work. In the moment of appreciation we live again the moment when the creator saw and held the hidden likeness. When a simile takes us aback and persuades us together, when we find a juxtaposition in a picture both odd and intriguing, when a theory is at once fresh and convincing, we do not merely nod over someone else's work. We re-enact the creative act, and we ourselves make the discovery again. At bottom, there is no unifying likeness there until we too have seized it, we too have made it for ourselves.

[35] How slipshod by comparison is the notion that either art or sci-

ence sets out to copy nature. If the task of the painter were to copy for men what they see, the critic could make only a single judgment: either that the copy is right or that it is wrong. And if science were a copy of fact, then every theory would be either right or wrong, and would be so for ever. There would be nothing left for us to say but this is so, or is not so. No one who has read a page by a good critic or a speculative scientist can ever again think that this barren choice of yes or no is all that the mind offers.

[36] Reality is not an exhibit for man's inspection, labelled 'Do not touch.' There are no appearances to be photographed, no experiences to be copied, in which we do not take part. Science, like art, is not a copy of nature but a re-creation of her. We re-make nature by the act of discovery, in the poem or in the theorem. And the great poem and the deep theorem are new to every reader, and yet are his own experiences, because he himself re-creates them. They are the mark of unity in variety; and in the instant when the mind seizes this for itself, in art or in science, the heart misses a beat.

----◄{ C O M M E N T   A N D   Q U E S T I O N S }►----

1. What is the purpose of the first section of Bronowski's essay? What images and figures of speech in the first three paragraphs seem to you effective in achieving the author's purpose? What does the name of the dance tune contribute?

2. The author is criticizing or rejecting a number of common attitudes toward science. What, specifically, is he criticizing, and what are the basic reasons for the criticism?

3. In paragraph 15 the author distinguishes between the two interests of the scientist. What is the main point of this distinction?

4. What idea is Bronowski emphasizing, at the end of paragraph 18, with his allusion to Orpheus, and why is he emphasizing it?

5. Sections 5 and 6 of the essay develop the thesis that scientific theory is not a collection of facts. What examples and reasons in these sections seem to you most effective in supporting the thesis? Explain.

6. In the discussion of Copernicus and Kepler (paragraphs 23 and 24) Bronowski touches on the idea of likenesses that reveal unity; at the end of paragraph 25 and the beginning of paragraph 26 he explicitly defines scientific activity: the search for unity in hidden likenesses. Where does he later return to this definition and for what purposes?

7. Section 8 is a discussion of art, chiefly of literature. How has this discussion been prepared for earlier in the essay?

8. In his concluding section, the author gives emphasis to an extension of his

ideas about creativity. State briefly the central idea of the last three paragraphs. Why do you think it is emphasized by the end-position?

9. If you have read I. A. Richards' "Science and Poetry" and DeWitt Parker's "The Intrinsic Value of Art," compare the ideas of one or both of these writers with the ideas of Bronowski on the creative act and its value.

10. What seem to you the most important things the author says to the scholar or humanist who disdains science? What are the most important things he says to the scientist who finds poetry, music, and painting unreal or meaningless? Which of Bronowski's ideas are most convincing and which are least convincing to you? Explain.

11. Near the end of his long essay *Science and Human Values,* Bronowski says that science needs to teach us not its techniques but its spirit: "the irresistible need to explore." Does this statement seem consistent with what the author is saying in "The Creative Mind"? Explain.

[63] *J. Robert Oppenheimer*: Prospects in the Arts and Sciences

J. ROBERT OPPENHEIMER (1904–1967) was a distinguished American physicist who taught at the University of California at Berkeley, the California Institute of Technology, and Princeton University, and who was early known for his work at Los Alamos, New Mexico, as head of the project to develop the atomic bomb. He was director of the Institute for Advanced Study at Princeton, and in 1963 he received the Enrico Fermi Award for his work in theoretical physics. The following essay is from *The Open Mind,* published in 1960.

[1] The words "prospects in the arts and sciences" mean two quite different things to me. One is prophecy: What will the scientists discover and the painters paint, what new forms will alter music, what parts of experience will newly yield to objective description? The other meaning is that of a view: What do we see when we look at the world today and compare it with the past? I am not a prophet; and I cannot very well speak to the first subject, though in many ways I should like to. I shall try to speak to the second, because there are some features of this view which seem to me so remarkable, so new and so arresting, that it may be worth turning our eyes to them; it may even help us to create and shape the future better, though we cannot foretell it.

[²] In the arts and in the sciences, it would be good to be a prophet. It would be a delight to know the future. I had thought for a while of my own field of physics and of those nearest to it in the natural sciences. It would not be too hard to outline the questions which natural scientists today are asking themselves and trying to answer. What, we ask in physics, is matter, what is it made of, how does it behave when it is more and more violently atomized, when we try to pound out of the stuff around us the ingredients which only violence creates and makes manifest? What, the chemist asks, are those special features of nucleic acids and proteins which make life possible and give it its characteristic endurance and mutability? What subtle chemistry, what arrangements, what reactions and controls make the cells of living organisms differentiate so that they may perform functions as oddly diverse as transmitting information throughout our nervous systems or covering our heads with hair? What happens in the brain to make a record of the past, to hide it from consciousness, to make it accessible to recall? What are the physical features which make consciousness possible?

[³] All history teaches us that these questions that we think the pressing ones will be transmuted before they are answered, that they will be replaced by others, and that the very process of discovery will shatter the concepts that we today use to describe our puzzlement.

[⁴] It is true that there are some who profess to see in matters of culture, in matters precisely of the arts and sciences, a certain macrohistorical pattern, a grand system of laws which determines the course of civilization and gives a kind of inevitable quality to the unfolding of the future. They would, for instance, see the radical, formal experimentation which characterized the music of the last half-century as an inevitable consequence of the immense flowering and enrichment of natural science; they would see a necessary order in the fact that innovation in music precedes that in painting and that in turn in poetry, and point to this sequence in older cultures. They would attribute the formal experimentation of the arts to the dissolution, in an industrial and technical society, of authority—of secular, political authority, and of the catholic authority of the church. They are thus armed to predict the future. But this, I fear, is not my dish.

[⁵] If a prospect is not a prophecy, it is a view. What does the world of the arts and sciences look like? There are two ways of looking at it: One is the view of the traveler, going by horse or foot, from village to village to town, staying in each to talk with those who live there and to gather something of the quality of its life. This is the intimate view, partial, somewhat accidental, limited by the limited life and strength and curiosity of the traveler, but intimate and human, in a human compass. The other is the vast view, showing the earth with its fields and towns and valleys as they appear to a camera carried in a high-altitude rocket. In one sense this prospect will be more complete; one will see all branches of knowledge, one will see all the arts, one will see them as part of the vastness and complication of the whole of human life on earth. But one will miss a great deal; the beauty and warmth of human life will largely be gone from that prospect.

[6] It is in this vast high-altitude survey that one sees the general surprising quantitative features that distinguish our time. This is where the listings of science and endowments and laboratories and books published show up; this is where we learn that more people are engaged in scientific research today than ever before, that the Soviet world and the free world are running neck and neck in the training of scientists, that more books are published per capita in England than in the United States, that the social sciences are pursued actively in America, Scandinavia, and England, that there are more people who hear the great music of the past, and more music composed and more paintings painted. This is where we learn that the arts and sciences are flourishing. This great map, showing the world from afar and almost as to a stranger, would show more: It would show the immense diversity of culture and life, diversity in place and tradition for the first time clearly manifest on a world-wide scale, diversity in technique and language, separating science from science and art from art, and all of one from all of the other. This great map, world-wide, culture-wide, remote, has some odd features. There are innumerable villages. Between the villages there appear to be almost no paths discernible from this high altitude. Here and there passing near a village, sometimes through its heart, there will be a superhighway, along which windy traffic moves at enormous speed. The superhighways seem to have little connection with the villages, starting anywhere, ending anywhere, and sometimes appearing almost by design to disrupt the quiet of the village. This view gives us no sense of order or of unity. To find these we must visit the villages, the quiet, busy places, the laboratories and studies and studios. We must see the paths that are barely discernible; we must understand the superhighways and their dangers.

[7] In the natural sciences these are and have been and are likely to continue to be heroic days. Discovery follows discovery, each both raising and answering questions, each ending a long search, and each providing the new instruments for a new search. There are radical ways of thinking unfamiliar to common sense and connected with it by decades or centuries of increasingly specialized and unfamiliar experience. There are lessons of how limited, for all its variety, the common experience of man has been with regard to natural phenomena, and hints and analogies as to how limited may be his experience with man. Every new finding is a part of the instrument kit of the sciences for further investigation and for penetrating into new fields. Discoveries of knowledge fructify technology and the practical arts, and these in turn pay back refined techniques, new possibilties of observation and experiment.

[8] In any science there is harmony between practitioners. A man may work as an individual, learning of what his colleagues do through reading or conversation; he may be working as a member of a group on problems whose technical equipment is too massive for individual effort. But whether he is a part of a team or solitary in his own study, he, as a professional, is a member of a community. His colleagues in his own branch of science will be grateful to him for the inventive or creative thoughts he has, will welcome his criticism. His world and work will be objectively communicable; and he will be quite sure that if there is error in it, that error will not long be undetected. In his own line of work he lives in a community where common understanding combines with common purpose and interest to bind men together both in freedom and in co-operation.

[9] This experience will make him acutely aware of how limited, how inadequate, how precious is this condition of his life; for in his relations with a wider society, there will be neither the sense of community nor of objective understanding. He will sometimes find, in returning to practical undertakings, some sense of community with men who are not expert in his science, with other scientists whose work is remote from his, and with men of action and men of art. The frontiers of science are separated now by long years of study, by specialized vocabularies, arts, techniques, and knowledge from the common heritage even of a most civilized society; and anyone working at the frontier of such science is in that sense a very long way from home, a long way too from the practical arts that were its matrix and origin, as indeed they were of what we today call art.

[10] The specialization of science is an inevitable accompaniment of progress; yet it is full of dangers, and it is cruelly wasteful, since so much that is beautiful and enlightening is cut off from most of the world. Thus it is proper to the role of the scientist that he not merely find new truth and communicate it to his fellows, but that he teach, that he try to bring the most honest and intelligible account of new knowledge to all who will try to learn. This is one reason—it is the decisive organic reason—why scientists belong in universities. It is one reason why the patronage of science by and through universities is its most proper form; for it is here, in teaching, in the association of scholars and in the friendships of teachers and taught, of men who by profession must themselves be both teachers and taught, that the narrowness of scientific life can best be moderated, and that the analogies, insights, and harmonies of scientific discovery can find their way into the wider life of man.

[11] In the situation of the artist today there are both analogies to and differences from that of the scientist; but it is the differences which are the most striking and which raise the problems that touch most on the evil of our day. For the artist it is not enough that he communicate with others who are expert in his own art. Their fellowship, their understand-

ing, and their appreciation may encourage him; but that is not the end of his work, nor its nature. The artist depends on a common sensibility and culture, on a common meaning of symbols, on a community of experience and common ways of describing and interpreting it. He need not write for everyone or paint or play for everyone. But his audience must be man; it must be man, and not a specialized set of experts among his fellows. Today that is very difficult. Often the artist has an aching sense of great loneliness, for the community to which he addresses himself is largely not there; the traditions and the culture, the symbols and the history, the myths and the common experience, which it is his function to illuminate, to harmonize, and to portray, have been dissolved in a changing world.

[12] There is, it is true, an artificial audience maintained to moderate between the artist and the world for which he works: the audience of the professional critics, popularizers, and advertisers of art. But though, as does the popularizer and promoter of science, the critic fulfills a necessary present function and introduces some order and some communication between the artist and the world, he cannot add to the intimacy and the directness and the depth with which the artist addresses his fellow men.

[13] To the artist's loneliness there is a complementary great and terrible barrenness in the lives of men. They are deprived of the illumination, the light and tenderness and insight of an intelligible interpretation, in contemporary terms, of the sorrows and wonders and gaieties and follies of man's life. This may be in part offset, and is, by the great growth of technical means for making the art of the past available. But these provide a record of past intimacies between art and life; even when they are applied to the writing and painting and composing of the day, they do not bridge the gulf between a society, too vast and too disordered, and the artist trying to give meaning and beauty to its parts.

[14] In an important sense this world of ours is a new world, in which the unity of knowledge, the nature of human communities, the order of society, the order of ideas, the very notions of society and culture have changed and will not return to what they have been in the past. What is new is new not because it has never been there before, but because it has changed in quality. One thing that is new is the prevalence of newness, the changing scale and scope of change itself, so that the world alters as we walk in it, so that the years of man's life measure not some small growth or rearrangement or moderation of what he learned in childhood, but a great upheaval. What is new is that in one generation our knowledge of the natural world engulfs, upsets, and complements all knowledge of the natural world before. The techniques, among which and by which we live, multiply and ramify, so that the whole world is bound together by communication, blocked here and there by the immense synapses of political tyranny. The global quality of the world is new: our knowledge of and sympathy with remote and diverse peoples, our involvement with

them in practical terms, and our commitment to them in terms of brother-hood. What is new in the world is the massive character of the dissolution and corruption of authority, in belief, in ritual, and in temporal order. Yet this is the world that we have come to live in. The very difficulties which it presents derive from growth in understanding, in skill, in power. To assail the changes that have unmoored us from the past is futile, and in a deep sense, I think, it is wicked. We need to recognize the change and learn what resources we have.

[15] Again I will turn to the schools and, as their end and as their center, the universities. For the problem of the scientist is in this respect not different from that of the artist or of the historian. He needs to be a part of the community, and the community can only with loss and peril be without him. Thus it is with a sense of interest and hope that we see a growing recognition that the creative artist is a proper charge on the university, and the university a proper home for him; that a composer or a poet or a playwright or painter needs the toleration, understanding, the rather local and parochial patronage that a university can give; and that this will protect him from the tyranny of man's communication and profes-sional promotion. For here there is an honest chance that what the artist has of insight and of beauty will take root in the community, and that some intimacy and some human bonds can mark his relations with his patrons. For a university rightly and inherently is a place where the in-dividual man can form new syntheses, where the accidents of friendship and association can open a man's eyes to a part of science or art which he had not known before, where parts of human life, remote and perhaps superficially incompatible, can find in men their harmony and their synthesis.

[16] These, then, in rough and far too general words, are some of the things we see as we walk through the villages of the arts and of the sci-ences and notice how thin are the paths that lead from one to another, and how little in terms of human understanding and pleasure the work of the villages comes to be shared outside.

[17] The superhighways do not help. They are the mass media—from the loud-speakers in the deserts of Asia Minor and the cities of Com-munist China to the organized professional theater of Broadway. They are the purveyors of art and science and culture for the millions upon mil-lions—the promoters who represent the arts and sciences to humanity and who represent humanity to the arts and sciences; they are the means by which we are reminded of the famine in remote places or of war or trouble or change; they are the means by which the great earth and its peoples have become one to one another, the means by which the news of discovery or honor and the stories and songs of today travel and re-sound throughout the world. But they are also the means by which the true human community, the man knowing man, the neighbor understand-

ing neighbor, the schoolboy learning a poem, the woman dancing, the individual curiosity, the individual sense of beauty are being blown dry and issueless, the means by which the passivity of the disengaged spectator presents to the man of art and science the bleak face of unhumanity.

[18] For the truth is that this is indeed, inevitably and increasingly, an open and, inevitably and increasingly, an eclectic world. We know too much for one man to know much, we live too variously to live as one. Our histories and traditions—the very means of interpreting life—are both bonds and barriers among us. Our knowledge separates as well as it unites; our orders disintegrate as well as bind; our art brings us together and sets us apart. The artist's loneliness, the scholar despairing because no one will any longer trouble to learn what he can teach, the narrowness of the scientist—these are unnatural insignia in this great time of change.

[19] For what is asked of us is not easy. The openness of this world derives its character from the irreversibility of learning; what is once learned is part of human life. We cannot close our minds to discovery; we cannot stop our ears so that the voices of far-off and strange people can no longer reach them. The great cultures of the East cannot be walled off from ours by impassable seas and defects of understanding based on ignorance and unfamiliarity. Neither our integrity as men of learning nor our humanity allows that. In this open world, what is there, any man may try to learn.

[20] This is no new problem. There has always been more to know than one man could know; there have always been modes of feeling that could not move the same heart; there have always been deeply held beliefs that could not be composed into a synthetic union. Yet never before today have the diversity, the complexity, the richness so clearly defied hierarchical order and simplification; never before have we had to understand the complementary, mutually not compatible ways of life and recognize choice between them as the only course of freedom. Never before today has the integrity of the intimate, the detailed, the true art, the integrity of craftsmanship and the preservation of the familiar, of the humorous and the beautiful stood in more massive contrast to the vastness of life, the greatness of the globe, the otherness of people, the otherness of ways, and the all-encompassing dark.

[21] This is a world in which each of us, knowing his limitations, knowing the evils of superficiality and the terrors of fatigue, will have to cling to what is close to him, to what he knows, to what he can do, to his friends and his tradition and his love, lest he be dissolved in a universal confusion and know nothing and love nothing. It is at the same time a world in which none of us can find hieratic prescription or general sanction for any ignorance, any insensitivity, any indifference. When a friend tells us of a new discovery we may not understand, we may not be able to listen without jeopardizing the work that is ours and closer to us; but we cannot find

in a book or canon—and we should not seek—grounds for hallowing our ignorance. If a man tells us that he sees differently than we, or that he finds beautiful what we find ugly, we may have to leave the room, from fatigue or trouble; but that is our weakness and our default. If we must live with a perpetual sense that the world and the men in it are greater than we and too much for us, let it be the measure of our virtue that we know this and seek no comfort. Above all, let us not proclaim that the limits of our powers correspond to some special wisdom in our choice of life, of learning, or of beauty.

[22] This balance, this perpetual, precarious, impossible balance between the infinitely open and the intimate, this time—our twentieth century—has been long in coming; but it has come. It is, I think, for us and our children, our only way.

[23] This is for all men. For the artist and for the scientist there is a special problem and a special hope, for in their extraordinarily different ways, in their lives that have increasingly divergent character, there is still a sensed bond, a sensed analogy. Both the man of science and the man of art live always at the edge of mystery, surrounded by it; both always, as the measure of their creation, have had to do with the harmonization of what is new with what is familiar, with the balance between novelty and synthesis, with the struggle to make partial order in total chaos. They can, in their work and in their lives, help themselves, help one another, and help all men. They can make the paths that connect the villages of arts and sciences with each other and with the world at large the multiple, varied, precious bonds of a true and world-wide community.

[24] This cannot be an easy life. We shall have a rugged time of it to keep our minds open and to keep them deep, to keep our sense of beauty and our ability to make it, and our occasional ability to see it in places remote and strange and unfamiliar; we shall have a rugged time of it, all of us, in keeping these gardens in our villages, in keeping open the manifold, intricate, casual paths, to keep these flourishing in a great, open, windy world; but this, as I see it, is the condition of man; and in this condition we can help, because we can love, one another.

⟪ COMMENT AND QUESTIONS ⟫

1. Oppenheimer, in his analysis of prospects in the arts and sciences, makes repeated use of contrast and comparison. Paragraph 1 briefly contrasts two meanings of *prospect* and states that the author will speak in terms of the second meaning—*view* rather than *prophecy*. Why does he, then, in paragraphs 2–4, discuss questions for the future and the theory of those

armed to predict the future? What is the relevance of these paragraphs to the whole essay?

2. Paragraph 5, contrasting two possible views of the world of arts and sciences, introduces the recurrent figure of travel and of the village. In paragraphs 5, 6, and later, what is the literal meaning of *villages*, of *paths*, and of *superhighways*?

3. Examine the language and the attitudes in paragraphs 5 and 6. What is gained and what is lost in each of the two views of the arts and sciences?

4. What is the function of the last two sentences of paragraph 6? Do they seem to you to effect a transition into the following paragraphs? Explain.

5. In what ways, according to the author, are the situations of the scientist and the artist comparable? In what ways do their situations differ? What does society at large lose by the "prospect" Oppenheimer is describing?

6. Summarize the author's ideas about the values of the universities as patrons of the arts and sciences. Is there a relationship between the universities and the figurative "paths" and "superhighways"? Explain.

7. This essay reflects a mind capable not only of highly intelligent analysis but also of fairness and reasonableness in seeing more than one side of a problem or question. The fairness accounts in part for the fact that many of Oppenheimer's paragraphs contain contrasting elements or are built on patterns of contrast. Re-read paragraphs 14, 17, 18, and 20, for example. What different kinds of contrast do you find in the four paragraphs?

8. What other traits of style are noticeable in paragraphs 14, 17, 18, and 20? Comment on the endings of these paragraphs.

9. Paragraph 21 suggests what we should and should not do in the world in which we live. To what extent do you agree with Oppenheimer's suggestions? Explain.

10. Examine paragraph 24. Is it an effective ending? If so, what makes it effective?

11. The tone of "Prospects in the Arts and Sciences"—particularly the author's attitude toward his subject—is complex. Do any of the following words seem to you to describe this attitude accurately: *pessimistic, despairing, hopeful, stoical, realistic, resigned*? Can you think of a description that seems to you more accurate than any one of these words?

[64] *Sigmund Freud*: Dreams of the Death of Persons of Whom the Dreamer Is Fond

IN THE FOLLOWING selection, a pioneer in the study of the unconscious mind presents and argues in favor of a theory which he knows will encounter opposition. Sigmund Freud (1856–1939) was an Austrian physician and the founder of psychoanalysis. Although his theories have been modified, even discarded, by some other psychiatrists, he has had a profound influence on twentieth-century thought. This selection from *The Interpretation of Dreams* (1899) deals with Freud's theory of the embodiment in dreams of repressed wishes, and with what Freud later called the "Oedipus complex." The footnotes are from subsequent editions of *The Interpretation of Dreams;* notes by the translator, James Strachey, are in brackets.

[1] Another group of dreams which may be described as typical are those containing the death of some loved relative—for instance, of a parent, of a brother or sister, or of a child. Two classes of such dreams must at once be distinguished: those in which the dreamer is unaffected by grief, so that on awakening he is astonished at his lack of feeling, and those in which the dreamer feels deeply pained by the death and may even weep bitterly in his sleep.

[2] We need not consider the dreams of the first of these classes, for they have no claim to be regarded as 'typical.' If we analyse them, we find that they have some meaning other than their apparent one, and that they are intended to conceal some other wish. Such was the dream of the aunt who saw her sister's only son lying in his coffin. It did not mean that she wished her little nephew dead; as we have seen, it merely concealed a wish to see a particular person of whom she was fond and whom she had not met for a long time—a person whom she had once before met after a similarly long interval beside the coffin of another nephew. This wish, which was the true content of the dream, gave no occasion for grief, and no grief, therefore, was felt in the dream. It will be noticed that the affect felt in the dream belongs to its latent and not to its manifest content, and that the dream's *affective* content has remained untouched by the distortion which has overtaken its *ideational* content.

[3] Very different are the dreams of the other class—those in which the dreamer imagines the death of a loved relative and is at the same time painfully affected. The meaning of such dreams, as their content indicates, is a wish that the person in question may die. And since I must expect that the feelings of all of my readers and any others who have experienced similar dreams will rebel against my assertion, I must try to base my evidence for it on the broadest possible foundation.

[4] I have already discussed a dream which taught us that the wishes which are represented in dreams as fulfilled are not always present-day wishes. They may also be wishes of the past which have been abandoned, overlaid and repressed, and to which we have to attribute some sort of continued existence only because of their re-emergence in a dream. They are not dead in our sense of the word but only like the shades in the Odyssey, which awoke to some sort of life as soon as they had tasted

blood. In the dream of the dead child in the 'case' what was involved was a wish which had been an immediate one fifteen years earlier and was frankly admitted as having existed at that time. I may add—and this may not be without its bearing upon the theory of dreams—that even behind this wish there lay a memory from the dreamer's earliest childhood. When she was a small child—the exact date could not be fixed with certainty—she had heard that her mother had fallen into a deep depression during the pregnancy of which she had been the fruit and had passionately wished that the child she was bearing might die. When the dreamer herself was grown-up and pregnant, she merely followed her mother's example.

[5] If anyone dreams, with every sign of pain, that his father or mother or brother or sister has died, I should never use the dream as evidence that he wishes for that person's death *at the present time*. The theory of dreams does not require as much as that; it is satisfied with the inference that this death has been wished for at some time or other during the dreamer's childhood. I fear, however, that this reservation will not appease the objectors; they will deny the possibility of their *ever* having had such a thought with just as much energy as they insist that they harbour no such wishes now. I must therefore reconstruct a portion of the vanished mental life of children on the basis of the evidence of the present.[1]

[6] Let us first consider the relation of children to their brothers and sisters. I do not know why we presuppose that that relation must be a loving one; for instances of hostility between adult brothers and sisters force themselves upon everyone's experience and we can often establish the fact that the disunity originated in childhood or has always existed. But it is further true that a great many adults, who are on affectionate terms with their brothers and sisters and are ready to stand by them to-day, passed their childhood on almost unbroken terms of enmity with them. The elder child ill-treats the younger, maligns him and robs him of his toys; while the younger is consumed with impotent rage against the elder, envies and fears him, or meets his oppressor with the first stirrings of a love of liberty and a sense of justice. Their parents complain that the children do not get on with one another, but cannot discover why. It is easy to see that the character of even a good child is not what we should wish to find it in an adult. Children are completely egoistic; they feel their needs intensely and strive ruthlessly to satisfy them—especially as against the rivals, other children, and first and foremost as against their

---

[1] [*Footnote added* 1909:] Cf. my 'Analysis of a Phobia in a Five-Year-Old Boy' (1909*b*) and my paper 'On the Sexual Theories of Children' (1908*c*).

brothers and sisters. But we do not on that account call a child 'bad,' we call him 'naughty'; he is no more answerable for his evil deeds in our judgment than in the eyes of the law. And it is right that this should be so; for we may expect that, before the end of the period which we count as childhood, altruistic impulses and morality will awaken in the little egoist and (to use Meynert's terms [e.g. 1892, 169 ff.]) a secondary ego will overlay and inhibit the primary one. It is true, no doubt, that morality does not set in simultaneously all along the line and that the length of non-moral childhood varies in different individuals. If this morality fails to develop, we like to talk of 'degeneracy,' though what in fact faces us is an inhibition in development. After the primary character has already been overlaid by later development, it can still be laid bare again, at all events in part, in cases of hysterical illness. There is a really striking resemblance between what is known as the hysterical character and that of a naughty child. Obsessional neurosis, on the contrary, corresponds to a super-morality imposed as a reinforcing weight upon fresh stirrings of the primary character.

[7] Many people, therefore, who love their brothers and sisters and would feel bereaved if they were to die, harbour evil wishes against them in their unconscious, dating from earlier times; and these are capable of being realized in dreams.

[8] It is of quite particular interest, however, to observe the behaviour of small children up to the age of two or three or a little older towards their younger brothers and sisters. Here, for instance, was a child who had so far been the only one; and now he was told that the stork had brought a new baby. He looked the new arrival up and down and then declared decisively: 'The stork can take him away again!'[2] I am quite seriously of the opinion that a child can form a just estimate of the set-back he has to expect at the hands of the little stranger. A lady of my acquaintance, who is on very good terms to-day with a sister four years her junior, tells me that she greeted the news of her first arrival with this qualification: 'But all the same I shan't give her my red cap!' Even if a child only comes to realize the situation later on, his hostility will date from that moment. I know of a case in which a little girl of less than three tried to strangle an infant in its cradle because she felt that its continued

---

[2] [Footnote added 1909:] The three-and-a-half-year-old Hans (whose phobia was the subject of the analysis mentioned in the preceding footnote) exclaimed shortly after the birth of a sister, while he was suffering from a feverish sore throat: 'I don't want a baby sister!' [Freud, 1909b, Section I.] During his neurosis eighteen months later he frankly confessed to a wish that his mother might drop the baby into the bath so that she would die. [Ibid., Section II (April 11).] At the same time, Hans was a good-natured and affectionate child, who soon grew fond of this same sister and particularly enjoyed taking her under his wing.

presence boded her no good. Children at that time of life are capable of jealousy of any degree of intensity and obviousness. Again, if it should happen that the baby sister does in fact disappear after a short while, the elder child will find the whole affection of the household once more concentrated upon himself. If after that the stork should bring yet another baby, it seems only logical that the little favourite should nourish a wish that his new competitor may meet with the same fate as the earlier one, so that he himself may be as happy as he was originally and during the interval.[3] Normally, of course, this attitude of a child towards a younger brother or sister is a simple function of the difference between their ages. Where the gap in time is sufficiently long, an elder girl will already begin to feel the stirring of her maternal instincts towards the helpless newborn baby.

[9] Hostile feelings towards brothers and sisters must be far more frequent in childhood than the unseeing eye of the adult observer can perceive.[4]

[10] In the case of my own children, who followed each other in rapid succession, I neglected the opportunity of carrying out observations of this kind; but I am now making up for this neglect by observing a small nephew, whose autocratic rule was upset, after lasting for fifteen months, by the appearance of a female rival. I am told, it is true, that the young man behaves in the most chivalrous manner to his little sister, that he kisses her hand and strokes her; but I have been able to convince myself that even before the end of his second year he made use of his powers of speech for the purpose of criticizing someone whom he could not fail to regard as superfluous. Whenever the conversation touched upon her he used to intervene in it and exclaim petulantly: 'Too 'ickle! too 'ickle!' During the last few months the baby's growth has made enough progress to place her beyond this particular ground for contempt, and the little boy has found a different basis for his assertion that she does not deserve so much attention: at every suitable opportunity he draws attention to the

[3] [*Footnote added* 1914:] Deaths that are experienced in this way in childhood may quickly be forgotten in the family; but psycho-analytic research shows that they have a very important influence on subsequent neuroses.

[4] [*Footnote added* 1914:] Since this was written, a large number of observations have been made and recorded in the literature of psycho-analysis upon the originally hostile attitude of children towards their brothers and sisters and one of their parents. The [Swiss] author and poet Spitteler has given us a particularly genuine and naïve account of this childish attitude, derived from his own childhood [1914, 40]: 'Moreover there was a second Adolf there: a little creature who they alleged was my brother, though I could not see what use he was and still less why they made as much fuss of him as of me myself. I was sufficient so far as I was concerned; why should I want a brother? And he was not merely useless, he was positively in the way. When I pestered my grandmother, he wanted to pester her too. When I was taken out in the perambulator, he sat opposite to me and took up half the space, so that we were bound to kick each other with our feet.'

fact that she has no teeth.[5] We all of us recollect how the eldest girl of another of my sisters, who was then a child of six, spent half-an-hour in insisting upon each of her aunts in succession agreeing with her: 'Lucie can't understand that yet, can she?' she kept asking. Lucie was her rival— two and a half years her junior.

[11] In none of my women patients, to take an example, have I failed to come upon this dream of the death of a brother or sister, which tallies with an increase in hostility. I have only found a single exception; and it was easy to interpret this as a confirmation of the rule. On one occasion during an analytic session I was explaining this subject to a lady, since in view of her symptom its discussion seemed to me relevant. To my astonishment she replied that she had never had such a dream. Another dream, however, occurred to her, which ostensibly had no connection with the topic—a dream which she had first dreamt when she was four years old and at that time the youngest of the family, and which she had dreamt repeatedly since: *A whole crowd of children—all her brothers, sisters and cousins of both sexes—were romping in a field. Suddenly they all grew wings, flew away and disappeared.* She had no idea what this dream meant; but it is not hard to recognize that in its original form it had been a dream of the death of all her brothers and sisters, and had been only slightly influenced by the censorship. I may venture to suggest the following analysis. On the occasion of the death of one of this crowd of children (in this instance the children of two brothers had been brought up together as a single family) the dreamer, not yet four years old at the time, must have asked some wise grown-up person what became of children when they were dead. The reply must have been: 'They grow wings and turn into little angels.' In the dream which followed upon this piece of information all the dreamer's brothers and sisters had wings like angels and—which is the main point—flew away. Our little baby-killer was left alone, strange to say: the only survivor of the whole crowd! We can hardly be wrong in supposing that the fact of the children romping in a *field* before flying away points to butterflies. It is as though the child was led by the same chain of thought as the peoples of antiquity to picture the soul as having a butterfly's wings.

[12] At this point someone will perhaps interrupt: 'Granted that children have hostile impulses towards their brothers and sisters, how can a child's mind reach such a pitch of depravity as to wish for the *death* of his rivals or of playmates stronger than himself, as though the death penalty were the only punishment for every crime?' Anyone who talks like this has failed to bear in mind that a child's idea of being 'dead' has nothing much in common with ours apart from the word. Children know

---

[5] [*Footnote added* 1909:] Little Hans, when he was three and a half, gave vent to a crushing criticism of his sister in the same words. It was because of her lack of teeth, he supposed, that she was unable to talk. [Freud, 1909*b*, Section I.]

nothing of the horrors of corruption, of freezing in the ice-cold grave, of the terrors of eternal nothingness—ideas which grown-up people find it so hard to tolerate, as is proved by all the myths of a future life. The fear of death has no meaning to a child; hence it is that he will play with the dreadful word and use it as a threat against a playmate: 'If you do that again, you'll die, like Franz!' Meanwhile the poor mother gives a shudder and remembers, perhaps, that the greater half of the human race fail to survive their childhood years. It was actually possible for a child, who was over eight years old at the time, coming home from a visit to the Natural History Museum, to say to his mother: 'I'm so fond of you, Mummy: when you die I'll have you stuffed and I'll keep you in this room, so that I can see you *all* the time.' So little resemblance is there between a child's idea of being dead and our own![6]

[13] To children, who, moreover, are spared the sight of the scenes of suffering which precede death, being 'dead' means approximately the same as being 'gone'—not troubling the survivors any longer. A child makes no distinction as to how this absence is brought about: whether it is due to a journey, to a dismissal, to an estrangement, or to death.[7] If, during a child's prehistoric epoch, his nurse has been dismissed, and if soon afterwards his mother has died, the two events are superimposed on each other in a single series in his memory as revealed in analysis. When people are absent, children do not miss them with any great intensity; many mothers have learnt this to their sorrow when, after being away from home for some weeks on a summer holiday, they are met on their return by the news that the children have not once asked after their mummy. If their mother does actually make the journey to that 'undiscover'd country, from whose bourn no traveller returns,' children seem at first to have forgotten her, and it is only later on that they begin to call their dead mother to mind.

---

[6] [*Footnote added* 1909:] I was astonished to hear a highly intelligent boy of ten remark after the sudden death of his father: 'I know father's dead, but what I can't understand is why he doesn't come home to supper.'—[*Added* 1919:] Further material on this subject will be found in the first [seven] volumes of the periodical *Imago* [1912–21], under the standing rubric of '*Vom wahren Wesen der Kinderseele*' ['The True Nature of the Child Mind'], edited by Frau Dr. H. von Hug-Hellmuth.

[7] [*Footnote added* 1919:] An observation made by a parent who had a knowledge of psycho-analysis caught the actual moment at which his highly intelligent four-year-old daughter perceived the distinction between being 'gone' and being 'dead.' The little girl had been troublesome at meal-time and noticed that one of the maids at the pension where they were staying was looking at her askance. 'I wish Josefine was dead,' was the child's comment to her father. 'Why dead?' enquired her father soothingly; 'wouldn't it do if she went away?' 'No,' replied the child; 'then she'd come back again.' The unbounded self-love (the narcissism) of children regards any interference as an act of *lèse majesté;* and their feelings demand (like the Draconian code) that any such crime shall receive the one form of punishment which admits of no degrees.

[¹⁴] Thus if a child has reasons for wishing the absence of another, there is nothing to restrain him from giving his wish the form of the other child being dead. And the psychical reaction to dreams containing death-wishes proves that, in spite of the different content of these wishes in the cases of children, they are nevertheless in some way or other the same as wishes expressed in the same terms by adults.[8]

[¹⁵] If, then, a child's death-wishes against his brothers and sisters are explained by the childish egoism which makes him regard them as his rivals, how are we to explain his death-wishes against his parents, who surround him with love and fulfil his needs and whose preservation that same egoism should lead him to desire?

[¹⁶] A solution of this difficulty is afforded by the observation that dreams of the death of parents apply with preponderant frequency to the parent who is of the same sex as the dreamer: that men, that is, dream mostly of their father's death and women of their mother's. I cannot pretend that this is universally so, but the preponderance in the direction I have indicated is so evident that it requires to be explained by a factor of general importance.[9] It is as though—to put it bluntly—a sexual preference were making itself felt at an early age: as though boys regarded their fathers and girls their mothers as their rivals in love, whose elimination could not fail to be to their advantage.

[¹⁷] Before this idea is rejected as a monstrous one, it is as well in this case, too, to consider the real relations obtaining—this time between parents and children. We must distinguish between what the cultural standards of filial piety demand of this relation and what everyday observation shows it in fact to be. More than one occasion for hostility lies concealed in the relation between parents and children—a relation which affords the most ample opportunities for wishes to arise which cannot pass the censorship.

[¹⁸] Let us consider first the relation between father and son. The sanctity which we attribute to the rules laid down in the Decalogue has, I think, blunted our powers of perceiving the real facts. We seem scarcely to venture to observe that the majority of mankind disobey the Fifth Commandment. Alike in the lowest and in the highest strata of human society filial piety is wont to give way to other interests. The obscure information which is brought to us by mythology and legend from the pri-

---

[8] [The adult attitude to death is discussed by Freud more particularly in the second essay of his *Totem and Taboo* (1912–13), Section 3 (c), in his paper on "The Three Caskets" (1913f) and in the second part of his "Thoughts on War and Death" (1915b).]

[9] [*Footnote added* 1925:] The situation is often obscured by the emergence of a self-punitive impulse, which threatens the dreamer, by way of a moral reaction, with the loss of the parent whom he loves.

maeval ages of human society gives an unpleasing picture of the father's despotic power and of the ruthlessness with which he made use of it. Kronos devoured his children, just as the wild boar devours the sow's litter; while Zeus emasculated his father[10] and made himself ruler in his place. The more unrestricted was the rule of the father in the ancient family, the more must the son, as his destined successor, have found himself in the position of an enemy, and the more impatient must he have been to become ruler himself through his father's death. Even in our middle-class families fathers are as a rule inclined to refuse their sons independence and the means necessary to secure it and thus to foster the growth of the germ of hostility which is inherent in their relation. A physician will often be in a position to notice how a son's grief at the loss of his father cannot suppress his satisfaction at having at length won his freedom. In our society to-day fathers are apt to cling desperately to what is left of a now sadly antiquated *potestas patris familias*; and an author who, like Ibsen, brings the immemorial struggle between fathers and sons into prominence in his writings may be certain of producing his effect.

[19] Occasions for conflict between a daughter and her mother arise when the daughter begins to grow up and long for sexual liberty, but finds herself under her mother's tutelage; while the mother, on the other hand, is warned by her daughter's growth that the time has come when she herself must abandon her claims to sexual satisfaction.

[20] All of this is patent to the eyes of everyone. But it does not help us in our endeavour to explain dreams of a parent's death in people whose piety towards their parents has long been unimpeachably established. Previous discussions, moreover, will have prepared us to learn that the death-wish against parents dates back to earliest childhood.

[21] This supposition is confirmed with a certainty beyond all doubt in the case of psychoneurotics when they are subjected to analysis. We learn from them that a child's sexual wishes—if in their embryonic stage they deserve to be so described—awaken very early, and that a girl's first affection is for her father[11] and a boy's first childish desires are for his mother. Accordingly, the father becomes a disturbing rival to the boy and the mother to the girl; and I have already shown in the case of brothers and sisters how easily such feelings can lead to a death-wish. The parents too give evidence as a rule of sexual partiality: a natural predilection

---

[10] [*Footnote added* 1909:] Or so he is reported to have done according to some myths. According to others, emasculation was only carried out by Kronos on his father Uranus. [This passage is discussed in Chapter X (3) of *The Psychopathology of Everyday Life* (Freud, 1901*b*).] For the mythological significance of this theme, cf. Rank, 1909, [*added* 1914:] and Rank, 1912*c*, Chapter IX, Section 2.—[These sentences in the text are, of course, an early hint at the line of thought developed later by Freud in his *Totem and Taboo* (1912–13).]

[11] [Freud's views on this point were later modified. Cf. Freud, 1925*j* and 1931*b*.]

usually sees to it that a man tends to spoil his little daughters, while his wife takes her sons' part; though both of them, where their judgment is not disturbed by the magic of sex, keep a strict eye upon their children's education. The child is very well aware of this partiality and turns against that one of his parents who is opposed to showing it. Being loved by an adult does not merely bring a child the satisfaction of a special need; it also means that he will get what he wants in every other respect as well. Thus he will be following his own sexual instinct and at the same time giving fresh strength to the inclination shown by his parents if his choice between them falls in with theirs.

[22] The signs of these infantile preferences are for the most part over-looked; yet some of them are to be observed even after the first years of childhood. An eight-year-old girl of my acquaintance, if her mother is called away from the table, makes use of the occasion to proclaim herself her successor: 'I'm going to be Mummy now. Do you want some more greens, Karl? Well, help yourself, then!' and so on. A particularly gifted and lively girl of four, in whom this piece of child psychology is especially transparent, declared quite openly: 'Mummy can go away now. Then Daddy must marry me and I'll be his wife.' Such a wish occurring in a child is not in the least inconsistent with her being tenderly attached to her mother. If a little boy is allowed to sleep beside his mother when his father is away from home, but has to go back to the nursery and to some-one of whom he is far less fond as soon as his father returns, he may easily begin to form a wish that his father should *always* be away, so that he himself could keep his place beside his dear, lovely Mummy. One obvious way of attaining this wish would be if his father were dead; for the child has learnt one thing by experience—namely that 'dead' people, such as Granddaddy, are always away and never come back.

[23] Though observations of this kind on small children fit in perfectly with the interpretation I have proposed, they do not carry such complete conviction as is forced upon the physician by psycho-analyses of adult neurotics. In the latter case dreams of the sort we are considering are introduced into the analysis in such a context that it is impossible to avoid interpreting them as *wishful* dreams.

[24] One day one of my women patients was in a distressed and tearful mood. 'I don't want ever to see my relations again,' she said 'they must think me horrible.' She then went on, with almost no transition, to say that she remembered a dream, though of course she had no idea what it meant. When she was four years old she had a dream that *a lynx or fox*[12] *was walking on the roof; then something had fallen down or she had fallen down; and then her mother was carried out of the house dead*—and

---

[12] [The German names for these animals are very much alike: *'Luchs'* and *'Fuchs.'*]

she wept bitterly. I told her that this dream must mean that when she was a child she had wished she could see her mother dead, and that it must be on account of the dream that she felt her relations must think her horrible. I had scarcely said this when she produced some material which threw light on the dream. 'Lynx-eye' was a term of abuse that had been thrown at her by a street-urchin when she was a very small child. When she was three years old, a tile off the roof had fallen on her mother's head and made it bleed violently.

[25] I once had an opportunity of making a detailed study of a young woman who passed through a variety of psychical conditions. Her illness began with a state of confusional excitement during which she displayed a quite special aversion to her mother, hitting and abusing her whenever she came near her bed, while at the same period she was docile and affectionate towards a sister who was many years her senior. This was followed by a state in which she was lucid but somewhat apathetic and suffered from badly disturbed sleep. It was during this phase that I began treating her and analysing her dreams. An immense number of these dreams were concerned, with a greater or less degree of disguise, with the death of her mother: at one time she would be attending an old woman's funeral, at another she and her sister would be sitting at table dressed in mourning. There could be no question as to the meaning of these dreams. As her condition improved still further, hysterical phobias developed. The most tormenting of these was a fear that something might have happened to her mother. She was obliged to hurry home, wherever she might be, to convince herself that her mother was still alive. This case, taken in conjunction with what I had learnt from other sources, was highly instructive: it exhibited, translated as it were into different languages, the various ways in which the psychical apparatus reacted to one and the same exciting idea. In the confusional state, in which, as I believe, the second psychical agency was overwhelmed by the normally suppressed first one, her unconscious hostility to her mother found a powerful *motor* expression. When the calmer condition set in, when the rebellion was suppressed and the domination of the censorship re-established, the only region left open in which her hostility could realize the wish for her mother's death was that of dreaming. When a normal state was still more firmly established, it led to the production of her exaggerated worry about her mother as a hysterical counter-reaction and defensive phenomenon. In view of this it is no longer hard to understand why hysterical girls are so often attached to their mothers with such exaggerated affection.

[26] On another occasion I had an opportunity of obtaining a deep insight into the unconscious mind of a young man whose life was made almost impossible by an obsessional neurosis. He was unable to go out into the street because he was tortured by the fear that he would kill everyone he met. He spent his days in preparing his alibi in case he might

be charged with one of the murders committed in the town. It is unnecessary to add that he was a man of equally high morals and education. The
analysis (which, incidentally, led to his recovery) showed that the basis
of this distressing obsession was an impulse to murder his somewhat over-
severe father. This impulse, to his astonishment, had been consciously
expressed when he was seven years old, but it had, of course originated
much earlier in his childhood. After his father's painful illness and death,
the patient's obsessional self-reproaches appeared—he was in his thirty-
first year at the time—taking the shape of a phobia transferred on to
strangers. A person, he felt, who was capable of wanting to push his own
father over a precipice from the top of a mountain was not to be trusted
to respect the lives of those less closely related to him; he was quite right
to shut himself up in his room.

[27] In my experience, which is already extensive, the chief part in the
mental lives of all children who later become psychoneurotics is played by
their parents. Being in love with the one parent and hating the other are
among the essential constituents of the stock of psychical impulses which
is formed at that time and which is of such importance in determining
the symptoms of the later neurosis. It is not my belief, however, that
psychoneurotics differ sharply in this respect from other human beings
who remain normal—that they are able, that is, to create something absolutely new and peculiar to themselves. It is far more probable—and this
is confirmed by occasional observations on normal children—that they are
only distinguished by exhibiting on a magnified scale feelings of love and
hatred to their parents which occur less obviously and less intensely in
the minds of most children.

[28] This discovery is confirmed by a legend that has come down to us
from classical antiquity: a legend whose profound and universal power
to move can only be understood if the hypothesis I have put forward in
regard to the psychology of children has an equally universal validity.
What I have in mind is the legend of King Oedipus and Sophocles' drama
which bears his name.

[29] Oedipus, son of Laïus, King of Thebes, and of Jocasta, was exposed
as an infant because an oracle had warned Laïus that the still unborn
child would be his father's murderer. The child was rescued, and grew
up as a prince in an alien court, until, in doubts as to his origin, he too
questioned the oracle and was warned to avoid his home since he was
destined to murder his father and take his mother in marriage. On the
road leading away from what he believed was his home, he met King
Laïus and slew him in a sudden quarrel. He came next to Thebes and
solved the riddle set him by the Sphinx who barred his way. Out of gratitude the Thebans made him their king and gave him Jocasta's hand in
marriage. He reigned long in peace and honour, and she who, unknown

to him, was his mother bore him two sons and two daughters. Then at last a plague broke out and the Thebans made enquiry once more of the oracle. It is at this point that Sophocles' tragedy opens. The messengers bring back the reply that the plague will cease when the murderer of Laïus has been driven from the land.

> But he, where is he? Where shall now be read
> The fading record of this ancient guilt?[13]

The action of the play consists in nothing other than the process of revealing, with cunning delays and ever-mounting excitement—a process that can be likened to the work of a psycho-analysis—that Oedipus himself is the murderer of Laïus, but further that he is the son of the murdered man and of Jocasta. Appalled at the abomination which he has unwittingly perpetrated, Oedipus blinds himself and forsakes his home. The oracle has been fulfilled.

[30] *Oedipus Rex* is what is known as a tragedy of destiny. Its tragic effect is said to lie in the contrast between the supreme will of the gods and the vain attempts of mankind to escape the evil that threatens them. The lesson which, it is said, the deeply moved spectator should learn from the tragedy is submission to the divine will and realization of his own impotence. Modern dramatists have accordingly tried to achieve a similar tragic effect by weaving the same contrast into a plot invented by themselves. But the spectators have looked on unmoved while a curse or an oracle was fulfilled in spite of all the efforts of some innocent man: later tragedies of destiny have failed in their effect.

[31] If *Oedipus Rex* moves a modern audience no less than it did the contemporary Greek one, the explanation can only be that its effect does not lie in the contrast between destiny and human will, but is to be looked for in the particular nature of the material on which that contrast is exemplified. There must be something which makes a voice within us ready to recognize the compelling force of destiny in the *Oedipus*, while we can dismiss as merely arbitrary such dispositions as are laid down in [Grillparzer's] *Die Ahnfrau* or other modern tragedies of destiny. And a factor of this kind is in fact involved in the story of King Oedipus. His destiny moves us only because it might have been ours—because the oracle laid the same curse upon us before our birth as upon him. It is the fate of all of us, perhaps, to direct our first sexual impulse towards our mother and our first hatred and our first murderous wish against our father. Our dreams convince us that that is so. King Oedipus, who slew his father Laïus and married his mother Jocasta, merely shows us the fulfilment of our own childhood wishes. But, more fortunate than he, we have meanwhile succeeded, in so far as we have not become psycho-

---

[13] [Lewis Campbell's translation (1883), line 108 f.]

neurotics, in detaching our sexual impulses from our mothers and in forgetting our jealousy of our fathers. Here is one in whom these primaeval wishes of our childhood have been fulfilled, and we shrink back from him with the whole force of the repression by which those wishes have since that time been held down within us. While the poet, as he unravels the past, brings to light the guilt of Oedipus, he is at the same time compelling us to recognize our own inner minds, in which those same impulses, though suppressed, are still to be found. The contrast with which the closing Chorus leaves us confronted—

> . . . Fix on Oedipus your eyes,
> Who resolved the dark enigma, noblest champion and most wise.
> Like a star his envied fortune mounted beaming far and wide:
> Now he sinks in seas of anguish, whelmed beneath a raging tide . . .[14]

—strikes as a warning at ourselves and our pride, at us who since our childhood have grown so wise and so mighty in our own eyes. Like Oedipus, we live in ignorance of these wishes, repugnant to morality, which have been forced upon us by Nature, and after their revelation we may all of us well seek to close our eyes to the scenes of our childhood.[15]

[32] There is an unmistakable indication in the text of Sophocles' tragedy itself that the legend of Oedipus sprang from some primaeval dream-material which had as its content the distressing disturbance of a child's relation to his parents owing to the first stirrings of sexuality. At a point when Oedipus, though he is not yet enlightened, has begun to feel troubled by his recollection of the oracle, Jocasta consoles him by referring to a dream which many people dream, though, as she thinks, it has no meaning:

---

[14] [Lewis Campbell's translation, line 1524 ff.]

[15] [*Footnote added* 1914:] None of the findings of psycho-analytic research has provoked such embittered denials, such fierce opposition—or such amusing contortions—on the part of critics as this indication of the childhood impulses towards incest which persist in the unconscious. An attempt has even been made recently to make out, in the face of all experience, that the incest should only be taken as 'symbolic.'— Ferenczi (1912) has proposed an ingenious 'over-interpretation' of the Oedipus myth, based on a passage in one of Schopenhauer's letters.—[*Added* 1919:] Later studies have shown that the 'Oedipus complex' which was touched upon for the first time in the above paragraphs in the *Interpretation of Dreams*, throws a light of undreamt-of importance on the history of the human race and the evolution of religion and morality. (See my *Totem and Taboo*, 1912–13 [Essay IV].)—[Actually the gist of this discussion of the Oedipus complex and of the *Oedipus Rex*, as well as of what follows on the subject of *Hamlet*, had already been put forward by Freud in a letter to Fliess as early as October 15th, 1897. (See Freud, 1950a, Letter 71.) A still earlier hint at the discovery of the Oedipus complex was included in a letter of May 31st, 1897. (Ibid., Draft N.)—The actual term 'Oedipus complex' seems to have been first used by Freud in his published writings in the first of his 'Contributions to the Psychology of Love' (1910h).]

> Many a man ere now in dreams hath lain
> With her who bare him. He hath least annoy
> Who with such omens troubleth not his mind.[16]

To-day, just as then, many men dream of having sexual relations with their mothers, and speak of the fact with indignation and astonishment. It is clearly the key to the tragedy and the complement to the dream of the dreamer's father being dead. The story of Oedipus is the reaction of the imagination to these two typical dreams. And just as these dreams, when dreamt by adults, are accompanied by feelings of repulsion, so too the legend must include horror and self-punishment. Its further modification originates once again in a misconceived secondary revision of the material, which has sought to exploit it for theological purposes. The attempt to harmonize divine omnipotence with human responsibility must naturally fail in connection with this subject-matter just as with any other.

COMMENT AND QUESTIONS

The discussion of Freud's methods and theories in "What Is a Self?" by Philip Wheelwright, page 333, may provide interesting background for thought about this selection.

1. Freud limits his discussion to dreams of the death of relatives in which the dreamer feels grief. Why does he exclude those in which the dreamer feels no grief? What is meant by the distinction, at the end of paragraph 2, between the *affective* and the *ideational* content of dreams?

2. In paragraph 3 Freud announces his thesis and anticipates opposition to it. What is his initial qualification of the thesis? What objection does he still anticipate?

3. With what kind of evidence does Freud support the theory that children feel hostility toward their brothers and sisters? How does he meet the objection that, even if they feel hostility, they would not wish for the death of the brothers and sisters?

4. With what kind of evidence and reasoning does Freud support the theory that children entertain death-wishes toward their parents?

5. According to Freud, why may exaggerated affection for or worry about a parent be a symptom of hostility?

6. What relationship does Freud see between the reactions of psychoneurotics and of people who remain normal?

7. How do the legend of Oedipus and the power of Sophocles' play seem to Freud to confirm his hypothesis?

[16] [Lewis Campbell's translation, line 982 ff.]

8. What parts of Freud's theory and reasoning strike you as being common sense, borne out by your own experience or observation? Do you resist, or do you find unconvincing, any parts of the theory or the reasoning? Explain.
9. This selection is, of course, a translation. Nevertheless, what comment can you make about the clarity, the interest, and the general quality of Freud's writing?

[65] *Julian Huxley*: The Uniqueness of Man

SIR JULIAN HUXLEY (1887–) is a distinguished English biologist, the grandson of Thomas Henry Huxley and brother of Aldous Huxley. He is the author of more than forty books including *Essays of a Biologist, The Stream of Life, Man in the Modern World, Evolution in Action,* and *New Bottles for New Wine;* the following essay is from *Man Stands Alone,* published in 1939.

[1] Man's opinion of his own position in relation to the rest of the animals has swung pendulum-wise between too great or too little a conceit of himself, fixing now too large a gap between himself and the animals, now too small. The gap, of course, can be diminished or increased at either the animal or the human end. One can, like Descartes, make animals too mechanical, or, like most unsophisticated people, humanize them too much. Or one can work at the human end of the gap, and then either dehumanize one's own species into an animal species like any other, or superhumanize it into beings a little lower than the angels.

[2] Primitive and savage man, the world over, not only accepts his obvious kinship with the animals but also projects into them many of his own attributes. So far as we can judge, he has very little pride in his own humanity. With the advent of settled civilization, economic stratification, and the development of an elaborate religion as the ideological mortar of a now class-ridden society, the pendulum began slowly to swing in the other direction. Animal divinities and various physiological functions such as fertility gradually lost their sacred importance. Gods became anthropomorphic and human psychological qualities pre-eminent. Man saw himself as a being set apart, and the rest of the animal kingdom created to serve his needs and pleasure, with no share in salvation, no position in eternity. In Western civilization this swing of the pendulum

reached its limit in developed Christian theology and in the philosophy of Descartes: both alike inserted a qualitative and unbridgeable barrier between all men and any animals.

[3] With Darwin, the reverse swing was started. Man was once again regarded as an animal, but now in the light of science rather than of unsophisticated sensibility. At the outset, the consequences of the changed outlook were not fully explored. The unconscious prejudices and attitudes of an earlier age survived, disguising many of the moral and philosophical implications of the new outlook. But gradually the pendulum reached the furthest point of its swing. What seemed the logical consequences of the Darwinian postulates were faced: man is an animal like any other; accordingly, his views as to the special meaning of human life and human ideals need merit no more consideration in the light of eternity (or of evolution) than those of a bacillus or a tapeworm. Survival is the only criterion of evolutionary success: therefore, all existing organisms are of equal value. The idea of progress is a mere anthropomorphism. Man happens to be the dominant type at the moment, but he might be replaced by the ant or the rat. And so on.

[4] The gap between man and animal was here reduced not by exaggerating the human qualities of animals, but by minimizing the human qualities of men. Of late years, however, a new tendency has become apparent. It may be that this is due mainly to the mere increase of knowledge and the extension of scientific analysis. It may be that it has been determined by social and psychological causes. Disillusionment with *laisser faire* in the human economic sphere may well have spread to the planetary system of *laisser faire* that we call natural selection. With the crash of old religious, ethical, and political systems, man's desperate need for some scheme of values and ideals may have prompted a more critical re-examination of his biological position. Whether this be so is a point that I must leave to the social historians. The fact remains that the pendulum is again on the swing, the man-animal gap again broadening. After Darwin, man could no longer avoid considering himself as an animal; but he is beginning to see himself as a very peculiar and in many ways a unique animal. The analysis of man's biological uniqueness is as yet incomplete. This essay is an attempt to review its present position.

[5] The first and most obviously unique characteristic of man is his capacity for conceptual thought; if you prefer objective terms, you will say, his employment of true speech, but that is only another way of saying the same thing. True speech involves the use of verbal signs for objects, not merely for feelings. Plenty of animals can express the fact that they are hungry; but none except man can ask for an egg or a banana. And to have words for objects at once implies conceptual thought, since an object is always one of a class. No doubt, children and savages are as unaware of using conceptual thought as Monsieur Jourdain was unaware

of speaking in prose; but they cannot avoid it. Words are tools which automatically carve concepts out of experience. The faculty of recognizing objects as members of a class provides the potential basis for the concept: the use of words at once actualizes the potentiality.

[6] This basic human property has had many consequences. The most important was the development of a cumulative tradition. The beginnings of tradition, by which experience is transmitted from one generation to the next, are to be seen in many higher animals. But in no case is the tradition cumulative. Offspring learn from parents, but they learn the same kind and quantity of lessons as they, in turn, impart: the transmission of experience never bridges more than one generation. In man, however, tradition is an independent and potentially permanent activity, capable of indefinite improvement in quality and increase in quantity. It constitutes a new accessory process of heredity in evolution, running side by side with the biological process, a heredity of experience to supplement the universal heredity of living substance.

[7] The existence of a cumulative tradition has as its chief consequence —or if you prefer, its chief objective manifestation—the progressive improvement of human tools and machinery. Many animals employ tools; but they are always crude tools employed in a crude way. Elaborate tools and skilled technique can develop only with the aid of speech and tradition.

[8] In the perspective of evolution, tradition and tools are the characters which have given man his dominant position among organisms. This biological dominance is, at present, another of man's unique properties. In each geological epoch of which we have knowledge, there have been types which must be styled biologically dominant: they multiply, they extinguish or reduce competing types, they extend their range, they radiate into new modes of life. Usually at any one time there is one such type—the placental mammals, for instance, in the Cenozoic period—but sometimes there is more than one. The Mesozoic is usually called the Age of Reptiles, but in reality the reptiles were then competing for dominance with the insects: in earlier periods we should be hard put to it to decide whether trilobites, nautiloids, or early fish were *the* dominant type. Today, however, there is general agreement that man is the sole type meriting the title. Since the early Pleistocene, widespread extinction has diminished the previously dominant group of placental mammals, and man has not merely multiplied, but has evolved, extended his range, and increased the variety of his modes of life.

[9] Biology thus reinstates man in a position analogous to that conferred on him as Lord of Creation by theology. There are, however, differences, and differences of some importance for our general outlook. In the biological view, the other animals have not been created to serve man's needs, but man has evolved in such a way that he has been able to

eliminate some competing types, to enslave others by domestication, and to modify physical and biological conditions over the larger part of the earth's land area. The theological view was not true in detail or in many of its implications; but it had a solid biological basis.

[10] Speech, tradition, and tools have led to many other unique properties of man. These are, for the most part, obvious and well known, and I propose to leave them aside until I have dealt with some less familiar human characteristics. For the human species, considered as a species, is unique in certain purely biological attributes; and these have not received the attention they deserve, either from the zoological or the sociological standpoint.

[11] In the first place, man is by far the most variable wild species known. Domesticated species like dog, horse, or fowl may rival or exceed him in this particular, but their variability has obvious reasons, and is irrelevant to our inquiry.

[12] In correlation with his wide variability, man has a far wider range than any other animal species, with the possible exception of some of his parasites. Man is also unique as a dominant type. All other dominant types have evolved into many hundreds or thousands of separate species, grouped in numerous genera, families, and larger classificatory groups. The human type has maintained its dominance without splitting: man's variety has been achieved within the limits of a single species.

[13] Finally, man is unique among higher animals in the method of his evolution. Whereas, in general, animal evolution is divergent, human evolution is reticulate. By this is meant that in animals, evolution occurs by the isolation of groups which then become progressively more different in their genetic characteristics, so that the course of evolution can be represented as a divergent radiation of separate lines, some of which become extinct, others continue unbranched, and still others divergently branch again. Whereas in man, after incipient divergence, the branches have come together again, and have generated new diversity from their Mendelian recombinations, this process being repeated until the course of human descent is like a network.

[14] All these biological peculiarities are interconnected. They depend on man's migratory propensities, which themselves arise from his fundamental peculiarities, of speech, social life, and relative independence of environment. They depend again on his capacity, when choosing mates, for neglecting large differences of color and appearance which would almost certainly be more than enough to deter more instinctive and less plastic animals. Thus divergence, though it appears to have gone quite a long way in early human evolution, generating the very distinct white, black, and yellow subspecies and perhaps others, was never permitted to attain its normal culmination. Mutually infertile groups were never pro-

duced: man remained a single species. Furthermore, crossing between distinct types, which is a rare and extraordinary phenomenon in other animals, in him became normal and of major importance. According to Mendelian laws, such crosses generate much excess variability by producing new recombinations. Man is thus more variable than other species for two reasons. First, because migration has recaptured for the single interbreeding group divergences of a magnitude that in animals would escape into the isolation of separate species; and secondly, because the resultant crossing has generated recombinations which both quantitatively and qualitatively are on a far bigger scale than is supplied by the internal variability of even the numerically most abundant animal species.

[15] We may contrast this with the state of affairs among ants, the dominant insect group. The ant type is more varied than the human type; but it has achieved this variability by intense divergent evolution. Several thousand species of ants are known, and the number is being added to each year with the increase of biological exploration. Ways of life among ants are divided among different subtypes, each rigidly confined to its own methods. Thus even if ants were capable of accumulating experience, there could exist no single world-wide ant tradition. The fact that the human type comprises but one biological species is a consequence of his capacity for tradition, and also permits his exploitation of that unique capacity to the utmost.

[16] Let us remind ourselves that superposed upon this purely biological or genetic variability is the even greater amount of variability due to differences of upbringing, profession, and personal tastes. The final result is a degree of variation that would be staggering if it were not so familiar. It would be fair to say that, in respect to mind and outlook, individual human beings are separated by differences as profound as those which distinguish the major groups of the animal kingdom. The difference between a somewhat subnormal member of a savage tribe and a Beethoven or a Newton is assuredly comparable in extent with that between a sponge and a higher mammal. Leaving aside such vertical differences, the lateral difference between the mind of, say, a distinguished general or engineer of extrovert type and of an introvert genius in mathematics or religious mysticism is no less than that between an insect and a vertebrate. This enormous range of individual variation in human minds often leads to misunderstanding and even mutual incomprehensibility; but it also provides the necessary basis for fruitful division of labor in human society.

[17] Another biological peculiarity of man is the uniqueness of his evolutionary history. Writers have indulged their speculative fancy by imagining other organisms endowed with speech and conceptual thought —talking rats, rational ants, philosophic dogs and the like. But closer

analysis shows that these fantasies are impossible. A brain capable of conceptual thought could not have been developed elsewhere than in a human body.

[18] The course followed by evolution appears to have been broadly as follows. From a generalized early type, various lines radiate out, exploiting the environment in various ways. Some of these comparatively soon reach a limit to their evolution, at least as regards major alteration. Therefore they are limited to minor changes such as the formation of new genera and species. Others, on the other hand, are so constructed that they can continue their career, generating new types which are successful in the struggle for existence because of their greater control over the environment and their greater independence of it. Such changes are legitimately called "progressive." The new type repeats the process. It radiates out into a number of lines, each specializing in a particular direction. The great majority of these come up against dead ends and can advance no further: specialization is one-sided progress, and after a longer or shorter time, reaches a biomechanical limit. The horse stock cannot reduce its digits below one; the elephants are near the limits of size for terrestrial animals; feathered flight cannot become more efficient than in existing birds, and so on.

[19] Sometimes all the branches of a given stock have come up against their limit, and then either have become extinct or have persisted without major change. This happened, for instance, to the echinoderms, which with their sea urchins, starfish, brittle stars, sea lilies, sea cucumbers, and other types now extinct had pushed the life that was in them into a series of blind alleys: they have not advanced for perhaps a hundred million years, nor have they given rise to other major types.

[20] In other cases, all but one or two of the lines suffer this fate, while the rest repeat the process. All reptilian lines were blind alleys save two —one which was transformed into the birds, and another which became the mammals. Of the bird stock, all lines came to a dead end; of the mammals, all but one—the one which became man.

[21] Evolution is thus seen as an enormous number of blind alleys, with a very occasional path of progress. It is like a maze in which almost all turnings are wrong turnings. The goal of the evolutionary maze, however, is not a central chamber, but a road which will lead indefinitely onwards.

[22] If now we look back upon the past history of life, we shall see that the avenues of progress have been steadily reduced in number, until by the Pleistocene period, or even earlier, only one was left. Let us remember that we can and must judge early progress in the light of its latest steps. The most recent step has been the acquisition of conceptual thought, which has enabled man to dethrone the non-human mammals from their previous position of dominance. It is biologically obvious that conceptual

thought could never have arisen save in an animal, so that all plants, both green and otherwise, are at once eliminated. As regards animals, I need not go through the early steps in their progressive evolution. Since some degree of bulk helps to confer independence of the forces of nature, it is obvious that the combination of many cells to form a large individual was one necessary step, thus eliminating all single-celled forms from such progress. Similarly, progress is barred to specialized animals with no blood-system, like planarian worms; to internal parasites like tapeworms; to animals with radial symmetry and consequently no head, like echinoderms.

[23] Of the three highest animal groups—the molluscs, the arthropods, and the vertebrates—the molluscs advanced least far. One condition for the later steps in biological progress was land life. The demands made upon the organism by exposure to air and gravity called forth biological mechanisms, such as limbs, sense organs, protective skin, and sheltered development, which were necessary foundations for later advance. And the molluscs have never been able to produce efficient terrestrial forms: their culmination is in marine types like squid and octopus.

[24] The arthropods, on the other hand, have scored their greatest successes on land, with the spiders and especially the insects. Yet the fossil record reveals a lack of all advance, even in the most successful types such as ants, for a long time back—certainly during the last thirty million years, probably during the whole of the Tertiary epoch. Even during the shorter of these periods, the mammals were still evolving rapidly, and man's rise is contained in a fraction of this time.

[25] What was it that cut the insects off from progress? The answer appears to lie in their breathing mechanism. The land arthropods have adopted the method of air tubes or tracheae, branching to microscopic size and conveying gases directly to and from the tissues, instead of using the dual mechanism of lungs and bloodstream. The laws of gaseous diffusion are such that respiration by tracheae is extremely efficient for very small animals, but becomes rapidly less efficient with increase of size, until it ceases to be of use at a bulk below that of a house mouse. It is for this reason that no insect has ever become, by vertebrate standards, even moderately large.

[26] It is for the same reason that no insect has ever become even moderately intelligent. The fixed pathways of instinct, however elaborate, require far fewer nerve cells than the multiple switchboards that underlie intelligence. It appears to be impossible to build a brain mechanism for flexible behavior with less than a quite large minimum of neurones; and no insect has reached a size to provide this minimum.

[27] Thus only the land vertebrates are left. The reptiles shared biological dominance with the insects in the Mesozoic. But while the insects had reached the end of their blind alley, the reptiles showed themselves

capable of further advance. Temperature regulation is a necessary basis for final progress, since without it the rate of bodily function could never be stabilized, and without such stabilization, higher mental processes could never become accurate and dependable.

[28] Two reptilian lines achieved this next step, in the guise of the birds and the mammals. The birds soon, however, came to a dead end, chiefly because their forelimbs were entirely taken up in the specialization for flight. The subhuman mammals made another fundamental advance, in the shape of internal development, permitting the young animal to arrive at a much more advanced stage before it was called upon to face the world. They also (like the birds) developed true family life.

[29] Most mammalian lines, however, cut themselves off from indefinite progress by one-sided evolution, turning their limbs and jaws into specialized and therefore limited instruments. And, for the most part, they relied mainly on the crude sense of smell, which cannot present as differentiated a pattern of detailed knowledge as can sight. Finally, the majority continued to produce their young several at a time, in litters. As J. B. S. Haldane has pointed out, this gives rise to an acute struggle for existence in the prenatal period, a considerable percentage of embryos being aborted or resorbed. Such intrauterine selection will put a premium upon rapidity of growth and differentiation, since the devil takes the hindmost; and this rapidity of development will tend automatically to be carried on into postnatal growth.

[30] As everyone knows, man is characterized by a rate of development which is abnormally slow as compared with that of any other mammal. The period from birth to the first onset of sexual maturity comprises nearly a quarter of the normal span of his life, instead of an eighth, a tenth or twelfth, as in some other animals. This again is in one sense a unique characteristic of man, although from the evolutionary point of view it represents merely the exaggeration of a tendency which is operative in other Primates. In any case, it is a necessary condition for the evolution and proper utilization of rational thought. If men and women were, like mice, confronted with the problems of adult life and parenthood after a few weeks, or even, like whales, after a couple of years, they could never acquire the skills of body and mind that they now absorb from and contribute to the social heritage of the species.

[31] This slowing (or "foetalization," as Bolk has called it, since it prolongs the foetal characteristics of earlier ancestral forms into postnatal development and even into adult life) has had other important byproducts for man. Here I will mention but one—his nakedness. The distribution of hair on man is extremely similar to that on a late foetus of a chimpanzee, and there can be little doubt that it represents an extension of this temporary anthropoid phase into permanence. Hairlessness of body is not a unique biological characteristic of man; but it is unique

among terrestrial mammals, save for a few desert creatures, and some others which have compensated for loss of hair by developing a pachydermatous skin. In any case, it has important biological consequences, since it must have encouraged the comparatively defenseless human creatures in their efforts to protect themselves against animal enemies and the elements, and so has been a spur to the improvement of intelligence.

[32] Now, foetalization could never have occurred in a mammal producing many young at a time, since intrauterine competition would have encouraged the opposing tendency. Thus we may conclude that conceptual thought could develop only in a mammalian stock which normally brings forth but one young at a birth. Such a stock is provided in the Primates—lemurs, monkeys, and apes.

[33] The Primates also have another characteristic which was necessary for the ancestor of a rational animal—they are arboreal. It may seem curious that living in trees is a prerequisite of conceptual thought. But Elliot Smith's analysis has abundantly shown that only in an arboreal mammal could the forelimb become a true hand, and sight become dominant over smell. Hands obtain an elaborate tactile pattern of what they handle, eyes an elaborate visual pattern of what they see. The combination of the two kinds of pattern, with the aid of binocular vision, in the higher centres of the brain allowed the Primate to acquire a wholly new richness of knowledge about objects, a wholly new possibility of manipulating them. Tree life laid the foundation both for the fuller definition of objects by conceptual thought and for the fuller control of them by tools and machines.

[34] Higher Primates have yet another prerequisite of human intelligence—they are all gregarious. Speech, it is obvious, could never have been evolved in a solitary type. And speech is as much the physical basis of conceptual thought as is protoplasm the physical basis of life.

[35] For the passage, however, of the critical point between subhuman and human, between the biological subordination and the biological primacy of intelligence, between a limited and a potentially unlimited tradition—for this it was necessary for the arboreal animal to descend to the ground again. Only in a terrestrial creature could fully erect posture be acquired; and this was essential for the final conversion of the arms from locomotor limbs into manipulative hands. Furthermore, just as land life, ages previously, had demanded and developed a greater variety of response than had been required in the water, so now it did the same in relation to what had been required in the trees. An arboreal animal could never have evolved the skill of the hunting savage, nor ever have proceeded to the domestication of other animals or to agriculture.

[36] We are now in a position to define the uniqueness of human evolution. The essential character of man as a dominant organism is conceptual thought. And conceptual thought could have arisen only in a multicellular

animal, an animal with bilateral symmetry, head and blood system, a
vertebrate as against a mollusc or an arthropod, a land vertebrate among
vertebrates, a mammal among land vertebrates. Finally, it could have
arisen only in a mammalian line which was gregarious, which produced
one young at a birth instead of several, and which had recently become
terrestrial after a long period of arboreal life.

[37] There is only one group of animals which fulfils these conditions
—a terrestrial offshoot of the higher Primates. Thus not merely has conceptual thought been evolved only in man: it could not have been evolved
except in man. There is but one path of unlimited progress through the
evolutionary maze. The course of human evolution is as unique as its
result. It is unique not in the trivial sense of being a different course from
that of any other organism, but in the profounder sense of being the only
path that could have achieved the essential characters of man. Conceptual
thought on this planet is inevitably associated with a particular type of
Primate body and Primate brain.

[38] A further property of man in which he is unique among higher
animals concerns his sexual life. Man is prepared to mate at any time:
animals are not. To start with, most animals have a definite breeding
season; only during this period are their reproductive organs fully developed and functional. In addition to this, higher animals have one or
more sexual cycles within their breeding seasons, and only at one phase
of the cycle are they prepared to mate. In general, either a sexual season
or a sexual cycle, or both, operates to restrict mating.

[39] In man, however, neither of these factors is at work. There appear
to be indications of a breeding season in some primitive peoples like the
Eskimo, but even there they are but relics. Similarly, while there still
exist physiological differences in sexual desire at different phases of the
female sexual cycle, these are purely quantitative, and may readily be
overridden by psychological factors. Man, to put it briefly, is continuously
sexed: animals are discontinuously sexed. If we try to imagine what a
human society would be like in which the sexes were interested in each
other only during the summer, as in songbirds, or, as in female dogs,
experienced sexual desire only once every few months, or even as in ants,
only once in a lifetime, we can realize what this peculiarity has meant.
In this, as in his slow growth and prolonged period of dependence, man
is not abruptly marked off from all other animals, but represents the
culmination of a process that can be clearly traced among other Primates.
What the biological meaning of this evolutionary trend may be is difficult
to understand. One suggestion is that it may be associated with the rise
of mind to dominance. The bodily functions, in lower mammals rigidly
determined by physiological mechanisms, come gradually under the more
plastic control of the brain. But this, for what it is worth, is a mere
speculation.

[40] Another of the purely biological characters in which man is unique is his reproductive variability. In a given species of animals, the maximum litter size may, on occasions, reach perhaps double the minimum, according to circumstances of food and temperature, or even perhaps threefold. But during a period of years, these variations will be largely equalized within a range of perhaps fifty per cent either way from the average, and the percentage of wholly infertile adults is very low. In man, on the other hand, the range of positive fertility is enormous—from one to over a dozen, and in exceptional cases to over twenty; and the number of wholly infertile adults is considerable. This fact, in addition to providing a great diversity of patterns of family life, has important bearings on evolution. It means that in the human species differential fertility is more important as a basis for selection than is differential mortality; and it provides the possibility of much more rapid selective change than that found in wild animal species. Such rapidity of evolution would, of course, be effectively realized only if the stocks with large families possessed a markedly different hereditary constitution from those with few children; but the high differential fertility of unskilled workers as against the professional classes in England, or of the French Canadians against the rest of the inhabitants of Canada, demonstrates how rapidly populations may change by this means.

[41] Still another point in which man is biologically unique is the length and relative importance of his period of what we may call "post-maturity." If we consider the female sex, in which the transition from reproductive maturity to non-reproductive post-maturity is more sharply defined than in the male, we find, in the first place, that in animals a comparatively small percentage of the population survives beyond the period of reproduction; in the second place, that such individuals rarely survive long, and so far as known never for a period equal to or greater than the period during which reproduction was possible; and thirdly, that such individuals are rarely of importance in the life of the species. The same is true of the male sex, provided we do not take the incapacity to produce fertile gametes as the criterion of post-maturity, but rather the appearance of signs of age, such as the beginnings of loss of vigor and weight, decreased sexual activity, or graying hair.

[42] It is true that in some social mammals, notably among ruminants and Primates, an old male or old female is frequently found as leader of the herd. Such cases, however, provide the only examples of the special biological utility of post-mature individuals among animals; they are confined to a very small proportion of the population, and it is uncertain to what extent such individuals are post-mature in the sense we have defined. In any event, it is improbable that the period of post-maturity is anywhere near so long as that of maturity. In civilized man, on the other hand, the average expectation of life now includes over ten years

of post-maturity, and about a quarter of the population enjoys a period of post-maturity almost as long as that of maturity. What is more, in all human societies above the lowest, a large proportion of the leaders of the community has always been post-mature.

[43] This is truly a remarkable phenomenon. Through the new social mechanisms made possible by speech and tradition, man has been able to utilize for the benefit of the species a period of life which in almost all other creatures is a mere superfluity. We know that the dominance of the old can be overemphasized; but it is equally obvious that society cannot do without the post-mature. To act on the slogan "Too old at forty"—or even at forty-five—would be to rob man of one of his unique characteristics, whereby he utilizes tradition to the best advantage.

[44] We have now dealt in a broad way with the unique properties of man both from the comparative and the evolutionary point of view. Now we can return to the present and the particular and discuss these properties and their consequences a little more in detail. First, let us remind ourselves that the gap between human and animal thought is much greater than is usually supposed. The tendency to project familiar human qualities into animals is very strong, and colors the ideas of nearly all people who have not special familiarity both with animal behavior and scientific method.

[45] Let us recall a few cases illustrating the unhuman characteristics of animal behavior. Everyone is familiar with the rigidity of instinct in insects. Worker ants emerge from their pupal case equipped not with the instincts to care for ant grubs in general, but solely with those suitable to ant grubs of their own species. They will attempt to care for the grubs of other species, but appear incapable of learning new methods if their instincts kill their foster children. Or again, a worker wasp, without food for a hungry grub, has been known to bite off its charge's tail and present it to its head. But even in the fine flowers of vertebrate evolution, the birds and mammals, behavior, though it may be more plastic than in the insects, is as essentially irrational. Birds, for instance, seem incapable of analyzing unfamiliar situations. For them some element in the situation may act as its dominant symbol, the only stimulus to which they can react. At other times, it is the organization of the situation as a whole which is the stimulus: if the whole is interfered with, analysis fails to dissect out the essential element. A hen meadowpipit feeds her young when it gapes and squeaks in the nest. But if it has been ejected by a young cuckoo, gaping and squeaking has no effect, and the rightful offspring is neglected and allowed to die, while the usurper in the nest is fed. The pipit normally cares for its own young, but not because it recognizes them as such.

[46] Mammals are no better. A cow deprived of its calf will be quieted by the provision of a crudely stuffed calfskin. Even the Primates are no

exception. Female baboons whose offspring have died will continue carrying the corpses until they have not merely putrefied but mummified. This appears to be due not to any profundity of grief, but to a contact stimulus: the mother will react similarly to any moderately small and furry object.

[47] Birds and especially mammals are, of course, capable of a certain degree of analysis, but this is effected, in the main, by means of trial and error through concrete experience. A brain capable of conceptual thought appears to be the necessary basis for speedy and habitual analysis. Without it, the practice of splitting up situations into their components and assigning real degrees of significance to the various elements remains rudimentary and rare, whereas with man, even when habit and trial and error are prevalent, conceptual thought is of major biological importance. The behavior of animals is essentially arbitrary, in that it is fixed within narrow limits. In man it has become relatively free—free at the incoming and the outgoing ends alike. His capacity for acquiring knowledge has been largely released from arbitrary symbolism, his capacity for action, from arbitrary canalizations of instinct. He can thus rearrange the patterns of experience and action in a far greater variety, and can escape from the particular into the general.

[48] Thus man is more intelligent than the animals because his brain mechanism is more plastic. This fact also gives him, of course, the opportunity of being more nonsensical and perverse: but its primary effects have been analytical knowledge and more varied control. The essential fact, from my present standpoint, is that the change has been profound and in an evolutionary sense rapid. Although it has been brought about by the gradual quantitative enlargement of the association areas of the brain, the result has been almost as abrupt as the change (also brought about quantitatively) from solid ice to liquid water. We should remember that the machinery of the change has been an increase in plasticity and potential variety: it is by a natural selection of ideas and actions that the result has been greater rationality instead of greater irrationality.

[49] This increase of flexibility has also had other psychological consequences which rational philosophers are apt to forget: and in some of these, too, man is unique. It has led, for instance, to the fact that man is the only organism normally and inevitably subject to psychological conflict. You can give a dog a neurosis as Pavlov did, by a complicated laboratory experiment: you can find cases of brief emotional conflict in the lives of wild birds and animals. But, for the most part, psychological conflict is shirked by the simple expedient of arranging that now one and now another instinct should dominate the animal's behavior. I remember in Spitsbergen finding the nest of a Red-throated Diver on the shore of an inland pool. The sitting bird was remarkably bold. After leaving the nest for water, she stayed very close. She did not, however, remain in a state of conflict between fear of intruders and desire to return to her

brooding. She would gradually approach as if to land, but eventually fear became dominant, and when a few feet from the shore she suddenly dived, and emerged a good way farther out—only to repeat the process. Here the external circumstances were such as to encourage conflict, but even so what are the most serious features of human conflict were minimized by the outlet of alternate action.

[50] Those who take up bird-watching as a hobby tend at first to be surprised at the way in which a bird will turn, apparently without transition or hesitation, from one activity to another—from fighting to peaceable feeding, from courtship to uninterested preening, from panic flight to unconcern. However, all experienced naturalists or those habitually concerned with animals recognize such behavior as characteristic of the subhuman level. It represents another aspect of the type of behavior I have just been describing for the Red-throated Diver. In this case, the internal state of the bird changes, presumably owing to some form of physiological fatigue or to a diminution of intensity of a stimulus with time or distance; the type of behavior which had been dominant ceases to have command over the machinery of action, and is replaced by another which just before had been subordinate and latent.

[51] As a matter of fact, the prevention of conflict between opposed modes of action is a very general phenomenon, of obvious biological utility, and it is only the peculiarities of the human mind which have forced its partial abandonment on man. It begins on the purely mechanical level with the nervous machinery controlling our muscles. The main muscles of a limb, for instance, are arranged in two antagonistic sets, the flexors bending and the extensors straightening it. It would obviously be futile to throw both sets into action at the same time, and economical when one set is in action to reduce to the minimum any resistance offered by the other. This has actually been provided for. The nervous connections in the spinal cord are so arranged that when a given muscle receives an impulse to contract, its antagonist receives an impulse causing it to lose some of its tone and thus, by relaxing below its normal level, to offer the least possible resistance to the action of the active muscle.

[52] Sherrington discovered that the same type of mechanism was operative in regard to the groups of muscles involved in whole reflexes. A dog, for instance, cannot very well walk and scratch itself at the same time. To avoid the waste involved in conflict between the walking and the scratching reflex, the spinal cord is constructed in such a way that throwing one reflex into action automatically inhibits the other. In both these cases, the machinery for preventing conflicts of activity resides in the spinal cord. Although the matter has not yet been analyzed physiologically, it would appear that the normal lack of conflict between instincts which we have just been discussing is due to some similar type of nervous mechanism in the brain.

[53] When we reach the human level, there are new complications; for, as we have seen, one of the peculiarities of man is the abandonment of any rigidity of instinct, and the provision of association-mechanisms by which any activity of the mind, whether in the spheres of knowing, feeling, or willing, can be brought into relation with any other. It is through this that man has acquired the possibility of a unified mental life. But, by the same token, the door is opened to the forces of disruption, which may destroy any such unity and even prevent him from enjoying the efficiency of behavior attained by animals. For, as Sherrington has emphasized, the nervous system is like a funnel, with a much larger space for intake than for outflow. The intake cone of the funnel is represented by the receptor nerves, conveying impulses inward to the central nervous system from the sense organs: the outflow tube is, then, through the effector nerves, conveying impulses outwards to the muscles, and there are many more of the former than of the latter. If we like to look at the matter from a rather different standpoint, we may say that, since action can be effected only by muscles (strictly speaking, also by the glands, which are disregarded here for simplicity's sake), and since there are a limited number of muscles in the body, the only way for useful activity to be carried out is for the nervous system to impose a particular pattern of action on them, and for all other competing or opposing patterns to be cut out. Each pattern when it has seized control of the machinery of action, *should* be in supreme command, like the captain of a ship. Animals are, in many ways, like ships which are commanded by a number of captains in turn, each specializing in one kind of action, and popping up and down between the authority of the bridge and the obscurity of their private cabins according to the business on hand. Man is on the way to achieving permanent unity of command, but the captain has a disconcerting way of dissolving into a wrangling committee.

[54] Even on the new basis, however, mechanisms exist for minimizing conflict. They are what are known by psychologists as suppression and repression. From our point of view, repression is the more interesting. It implies the forcible imprisonment of one of two conflicting impulses in the dungeons of the unconscious mind. The metaphor is, however, imperfect. For the prisoner in the mental dungeon can continue to influence the tyrant above in the daylight of consciousness. In addition to a general neurosis, compulsive thoughts and acts may be thrust upon the personality. Repression may thus be harmful; but it can also be regarded as a biological necessity for dealing with inevitable conflict in the early years of life, before rational judgment and control are possible. Better to have the capacity for more or less unimpeded action, even at the expense of possible neurosis, than an organism constantly inactivated like the ass between the two bundles of hay, balanced in irresolution.

[55] In repression, not only is the defeated impulse banished to the

unconscious, but the very process of banishment is itself unconscious. The inhibitory mechanisms concerned in it must have been evolved to counteract the more obvious possibilities of conflict, especially in early life, which arose as by-products of the human type of mind.

[56] In suppression, the banishment is conscious, so that neurosis is not likely to appear. Finally in rational judgment, neither of the conflicting impulses is relegated to the unconscious, but they are balanced in the light of reason and experience, and control of action is consciously exercised.

[57] I need not puruse the subject further. Here I am only concerned to show that the great biological advantages conferred on man by the unification of mind have inevitably brought with them certain counterbalancing defects. The freedom of association between all aspects and processes of the mind has provided the basis for conceptual thought and tradition; but it has also provided potential antagonists, which in lower organisms were carefully kept apart, with the opportunity of meeting face to face, and has thus made some degree of conflict unavoidable.

[58] In rather similar fashion, man's upright posture has brought with it certain consequential disadvantages in regard to the functioning of his internal organs and his proneness to rupture. Thus man's unique characteristics are by no means all beneficial.

[59] In close correlation with our subjection to conflict is our proneness to laughter. So characteristic of our species is laughter that man has been defined as the laughing animal. It is true that, like so much else of man's uniqueness, it has its roots among the animals, where it reveals itself as an expression of a certain kind of general pleasure—and thus in truth perhaps more of a smile than a laugh. And in a few animals—ravens, for example—there are traces of a malicious sense of humor. Laughter in man, however, is much more than this. There are many theories of laughter, most of them containing a partial truth. But biologically the important feature of human laughter seems to lie in its providing a release for conflict, a resolution of troublesome situations.

[60] This and other functions of laughter can be exaggerated so that it becomes as the crackling of thorns under the pot, and prevents men from taking anything seriously; but in due proportion its value is very great as a lubricant against troublesome friction and a lightener of the inevitable gravity and horror of life, which would otherwise become portentous and overshadowing. True laughter, like true speech, is a unique possession of man.

[61] Those of man's unique characteristics which may better be called psychological and social than narrowly biological spring from one or other of three characteristics. The first is his capacity for abstract and general thought: the second is the relative unification of his mental processes, as against the much more rigid compartmentalization of animal

mind and behavior: the third is the existence of social units, such as tribe, nation, party, and church, with a continuity of their own, based on organized tradition and culture.

[62] There are various by-products of the change from pre-human to the human type of mind which are, of course, also unique biologically. Let us enumerate a few: pure mathematics; musical gifts; artistic appreciation and creation; religion; romantic love.

[63] Mathematical ability appears, almost inevitably, as something mysterious. Yet the attainment of speech, abstraction, and logical thought, bring it into potential being. It may remain in a very rudimentary state of development; but even the simplest arithmetical calculations are a manifestation of its existence. Like any other human activity, it requires proper tools and machinery. Arabic numerals, algebraic conventions, logarithms, the differential calculus, are such tools: each one unlocks new possibilities of mathematical achievement. But just as there is no essential difference between man's conscious use of a chipped flint as an implement and his design of the most elaborate machine, so there is none between such simple operations as numeration or addition and the comprehensive flights of higher mathematics. Again, some people are by nature more gifted than others in this field; yet no normal human being is unable to perform some mathematical operations. Thus the capacity for mathematics is, as I have said, a by-product of the human type of mind.

[64] We have seen, however, that the human type of mind is distinguished by two somewhat opposed attributes. One is the capacity for abstraction, the other for synthesis. Mathematics is one of the extreme by-products of our capacity for abstraction. Arithmetic abstracts objects of all qualities save their enumerability; the symbol π abstracts in a single Greek letter a complicated relation between the parts of all circles. Art, on the other hand, is an extreme by-product of our capacity for synthesis. In one unique production, the painter can bring together form, color, arrangement, associations of memory, emotion, and idea. Dim adumbrations of art are to be found in a few creatures such as bowerbirds; but nothing is found to which the word can rightly be applied until man's mind gave the possibility of freely mingling observations, emotions, memories, and ideas, and subjecting the mixture to deliberate control.

[65] But it is not enough here to enumerate a few special activities. In point of fact, the great majority of man's activities and characteristics are by-products of his primary distinctive characteristics, and therefore, like them, biologically unique.

[66] On the one hand, conversation, organized games, education, sport, paid work, gardening, the theatre; on the other, conscience, duty, sin, humiliation, vice, penitence—these are all such unique by-products. The trouble, indeed, is to find any human activities which are not unique.

Even the fundamental biological attributes such as eating, sleeping, and mating have been tricked out by man with all kinds of unique frills and peculiarities.

[67] There may be other by-products of man's basic uniqueness which have not yet been exploited. For let us remember that such by-products may remain almost wholly latent until demand stimulates invention and invention facilitates development. It is asserted that there exist human tribes who cannot count above two; certainly some savages stop at ten. Here the mathematical faculty is restricted to numeration, and stops short at a very rudimentary stage of this rudimentary process. Similarly, there are human societies in which art has never been developed beyond the stage of personal decoration. It is probable that during the first half of the Pleistocene period, none of the human race had developed either their mathematical or their artistic potentialities beyond such a rudimentary stage.

[68] It is perfectly possible that to-day man's so-called super-normal or extra-sensory faculties are in the same case as were his mathematical faculties during the first or second glaciations of the Ice Age—barely more than a potentiality, with no technique for eliciting and developing them, no tradition behind them to give them continuity and intellectual respectability. Even such simple performances as multiplying two three-figure numbers would have appeared entirely magical to early Stone Age men.

[69] Experiments such as those of Rhine and Salter on extra-sensory guessing, experiences like those of Gilbert Murray on thought transference, and the numerous sporadic records of telepathy and clairvoyance suggest that some people at least possess possibilities of knowing which are not confined within the ordinary channels of sense perception. Salter's work is particularly interesting in this connection. As a result of an enormous number of trials with apparatus ingeniously designed to exclude all alternative explanation, he finds that those best endowed with this extra-sensory gift can guess right about once in four times when once in five would be expected on chance alone. The results are definite, and significant in the statistical sense, yet the faculty is rudimentary: it does not permit its possessor to guess right all the time or even most of the time—merely to achieve a small rise in the percentage of right guessing. If, however, we could discover in what this faculty really consists, on what mechanism it depends, and by what conditions and agencies it can be influenced, it should be capable of development like any other human faculty. Man may thus be unique in more ways than he now suspects.

[70] So far we have been considering the fact of human uniqueness. It remains to consider man's attitude to these unique qualities of his. Professor Everett, of the University of California, in an interesting paper

bearing the same title as this essay, but dealing with the topic from the standpoint of the philosopher and the humanist rather than that of the biologist, has stressed man's fear of his own uniqueness. Man has often not been able to tolerate the feeling that he inhabits an alien world, whose laws do not make sense in the light of his intelligence, and in which the writ of his human values does not run. Faced with the prospect of such intellectual and moral loneliness, he has projected personality into the cosmic scheme. Here he has found a will, there a purpose; here a creative intelligence, and there a divine compassion. At one time, he has deified animals, or personified natural forces. At others, he has created a super-human pantheon, a single tyrannical world ruler, a subtle and satisfying Trinity in Unity. Philosophers have postulated an Absolute of the same nature as mind.

[71] It is only exceptionally that men have dared to uphold their uniqueness and to be proud of their human superiority to the impersonality and irrationality of the rest of the universe. It is time now, in the light of our knowledge, to be brave and face the fact and the consequences of our uniqueness. That is Dr. Everett's view as it was also that of T. H. Huxley in his famous Romanes lecture. I agree with them; but I would suggest that the antinomy between man and the universe is not quite so sharp as they have made out. Man represents the culmination of that process of organic evolution which has been proceeding on this planet for over a thousand million years. That process, however wasteful and cruel it may be, and into however many blind alleys it may have been diverted, is also in one aspect progressive. Man has now become the sole representative of life in that progressive aspect and its sole trustee for any progress in the future.

[72] Meanwhile it is true that the appearance of the human type of mind, the latest step in evolutionary progress, has introduced both new methods and new standards. By means of his conscious reason and its chief offspring, science, man has the power of substituting less dilatory, less wasteful, and less cruel methods of effective progressive change than those of natural selection, which alone are available to lower organisms. And by means of his conscious purpose and his set of values, he has the power of substituting new and higher standards for change than those of mere survival and adaptation to immediate circumstances, which alone are inherent in pre-human evolution. To put the matter in another way, progress has hitherto been a rare and fitful by-product of evolution. Man has the possibility of making it the main feature of his own future evolution, and of guiding its course in relation to a deliberate aim.

[73] But he must not be afraid of his uniqueness. There may be other beings in this vast universe endowed with reason, purpose, and aspiration: but we know nothing of them. So far as our knowledge goes, human mind and personality are unique and constitute the highest product yet

achieved by the cosmos. Let us not put off our responsibilities onto the shoulders of mythical gods or philosophical absolutes, but shoulder them in the hopefulness of tempered pride. In the perspective of biology, our business in the world is seen to be the imposition of the best and most enduring of our human standards upon ourselves and our planet. The enjoyment of beauty and interest, the achievement of goodness and efficiency, the enhancement of life and its variety—these are the harvest which our human uniqueness should be called upon to yield.

COMMENT AND QUESTIONS

1. What is the purpose of the first four paragraphs of the essay? Writing in 1939, Julian Huxley said that the man–animal gap was broadening and that man was beginning to see himself as "a very peculiar and in many ways a unique animal." Do you think that this statement of man's view of himself is valid today? Explain.

2. What is the meaning of *conceptual thought* as Huxley uses the term in paragraph 5 and later?

3. Paragraphs 5–9 are a unit in the essay. Trace the cause–effect development in these paragraphs. What main points is the author making here about the uniqueness of man?

4. Paragraph 10 introduces a long discussion of the "purely biological attributes" in which man is unique. Briefly summarize these biological attributes. Huxley develops very fully the uniqueness of man's evolutionary history. What is the central thesis of this section (paragraphs 17–36) of the essay?

5. Examine sentence by sentence and phrase by phrase the material in paragraph 36, a summary paragraph. Explain clearly how Huxley has supported each of the points mentioned in this summary.

6. What is the purpose of the numerous examples of animal behavior in paragraphs 45–46 and 49–50?

7. Comment on the figures of speech in paragraphs 53–54: the funnel, the ship, the dungeon, the ass between two bundles of hay. Which seem to you most effective? Why does Huxley say that the dungeon figure is imperfect? If it is imperfect, why does he use it?

8. Some of the characteristics of man—his psychological conflicts and his laughter, for example—are, as the author says, psychological and social rather than narrowly biological. How are they related to man's biological uniqueness?

9. Do Huxley's conjectures, in paragraphs 67–69, about the possibility of developing other by-products of man's uniqueness seem to stem logically from the content of the essay? Explain.

10. We have mentioned a cause–effect development in an early section of the

essay. The author uses numerous methods of organizing and developing his material. What are his major methods of ordering and developing his ideas? What are specific examples of each?

11. How, according to Huxley, may man's uniqueness affect his future evolution? To what extent do you agree with the ideas and attitudes expressed in the last four paragraphs? Explain.

[66]   *Warren Weaver*: Confessions of a Scientist-Humanist

WARREN WEAVER (1894–   ) is an internationally known mathematician, author, and administrator. As vice-president of the Rockefeller Foundation and as trustee and consultant for the Alfred P. Sloan Foundation, he has been instrumental in administering millions of dollars in grants for the advance of the biological and medical sciences. He has been awarded the Public Welfare Medal of the National Academy of Sciences and the Medal of Merit of the United States Government. The following essay, from the *Saturday Review* of May 28, 1966, is one of a series of essays written by different authors and published in the *Saturday Review* under the general heading *What I Have Learned.*

[1] Observations, we have finally and painfully learned in science, depend upon the observer, and after each observation the observer is, perhaps by very little but nevertheless essentially, a different person. So I have to start by mentioning a few facts about my life.

[2] My earliest curiosity was about how things are made and why they work. This led me by semantic error—my family and friends knowing the word "engineering" but being wholly vague about the word "science"—to my graduating from college with the degree of civil engineer. But it was during my sophomore year that the blazing beauty and power of differential and integral calculus were revealed by a great teacher, and I promptly knew that I wanted to move into mathematics and, eventually, into mathematical physics. So I went on to take a doctor's degree, and spent more than a dozen years teaching undergraduate mathematics to engineers, and the classical fields of mathematical physics to graduate students of physics.

[3] Then came a reorienting. My friend and previous co-worker Max Mason had gone from the presidency of the University of Chicago to the

Rockefeller Foundation, and he caused me to be invited to join that philanthropy as Director for the Natural Sciences. The phrase "natural sciences" there meant, in principle, "everything scientific except medicine"; however, it promptly began to mean, in operational terms, something different.

[4] For, forced by the offer to think what a large philanthropic foundation ought to be doing, I rather suddenly realized that if such an agency were to have significant influence upon the development of science it ought not simply climb on a surfboard riding down a great wave that had been building for a century, and which was sweeping forward with majestic power—it ought to scan the horizon and try to help build a wave of the future.

[5] Research in the physical sciences was, in 1932 when I faced this decision, moving forward with great vigor. The discouraged and complacent prediction of 1900 that there was nothing left to do but slightly to improve the accuracy of physical measurements had been blasted by Einstein, Planck, Bohr, and the genius of the "boy physicists" of the Twenties. Relativity and quantum theory were leading to the beginnings of modern high-energy particle physics, and startling and beautiful new results were fairly bursting forth. The *Physical Review* changed from a thin monthly to a massively thick bi-monthly; and over the world dozens of new journals appeared.

[6] All this was wonderful, was amazing, and was lovely. But this wave needed no special encouragement. Interconnections with technology and with defense were assuring massive support from industry and government. The problem with that wave was not to build it up—the real problem, when one considered nuclear energy, was to determine whether this wave of unleashed physical power was becoming a tidal wave that might engulf us.

[7] There was discernible, however, another wave—one ready to swell. For centuries other able scientists had been concerned not with physical but rather with living nature. Its incredible variety and complication was such that for long, early periods little was possible beyond collection, description, and classification. Then observation became more penetrating, and scientists began to study the parts of living things, their actions and interactions, and the overall behavior of living organisms.

[8] But variety and complication, and the lack of tools with which to deal with such variety and complication, limited progress. By 1932, however, when the problem of deciding on a new program in science faced the Rockefeller Foundation, one could see that the situation had essentially changed.

[9] For the various physical sciences, notably chemistry and physics but also that non-physical and essentially mental science, mathematics,

had by then produced a whole array of new instruments, of new techniques of analysis, and of new general theories that promised to have the dexterity, precision, generality, and power to deal with the complex problems of living matter. It therefore seemed clear to me that the Rockefeller Foundation ought to concentrate upon developing modern experimental biology, or, more broadly and accurately, ought to concentrate upon financing the friendly invasion of the biological sciences by the physical sciences.

[10] It seemed equally clear to me that I was no person to head such a program, since my training and experience had all been in the physical sciences. I was wholly fascinated by the physical sciences, and was very happy in the job I already had. But the officials of the Rockefeller Foundation persuaded me; and coming to this fork in the road, I chose the unexpected and strange turning.

[11] As a result of this decision I spent twenty-eight years in the Rockefeller Foundation with a wholly new range of problems. I had to reorient myself scientifically by self-study of the various biological disciplines. As my responsibilities were enlarged to include the foundation's activities in agriculture and medicine, my contacts with scientists and with problems spread from its previous base in the United States and Europe to South America, India, and the Far East. The emphasis continued to be, broadly speaking, upon biological problems; and much of this work was rooted in the physical sciences.

[12] Thus through the lucky fortune of my work I have had an opportunity to have unusually wide exposure to the different kinds of science and to different parts of the world. At the same time I have also been intensely interested in a lot of other things—in reading, in music, in gardening, in the general experiences of travel. For more than forty-five years I have been an ardent collector of Lewis Carroll, with special interest in the translations of *Alice in Wonderland* into nearly fifty languages. I have been confused, and on the whole bored, by my attempts to read political history, but have been fascinated to read intellectual history. I have a pleasant but rather dazed curiosity about formal philosophy, a subject which I disliked for many years, until I became sensible enough to realize that it profoundly differs from science in that its interest and value do not depend upon its making progress in the solution of the problems with which it is concerned. I have a deep and sustained interest in religion.

[13] Out of all this good fortune of broad interests and exposure, what have I learned? I have a few assorted convictions, and a main conclusion.

[14] Of the widely assorted convictions I will merely list as samples: that childhood is usually an unhappy period (mine certainly was); that we do not take seriously enough the concerns, ideas, or abilities of chil-

dren; that the central purpose of education should be to teach how to learn; that life's most important goals—such as happiness, to which I give a very high rating—must be attacked indirectly; that the luckiest persons are those who enjoy their work; that fun and gaiety are seriously important—solemnity, as Tristram Shandy reports a French wit to have said, being "a mysterious carriage of the body to cover defects of the mind"; that spelling is illogical, ridiculous, and unimportant; and that there is nothing worse than badly cooked vegetables, and nothing better than good cheese and Burgundy.

[15] Turning from such trivia, the major thesis I will state is this: That as man's control of his environment has proceeded, giving him time to think and to make discoveries leading to further control, he has progressively uncovered more and more complication; but at the same time he has succeeded in discovering more and more unifying principles which accept the ever increasing variety, but recognize an underlying unity. He has, in short, discovered the many and the one.

[16] Science has been a great leader in this process of revelation. But the process is by no means limited to science.

[17] This view received a major scientific impetus when Copernicus, some four and a half centuries ago, removed the ancient but unsupportable simplicity of a fixed and central earth resting at the center of a revolving painted dome. The special position of our earth was at one stroke destroyed, and we became one of the countless billions of stars. Man should at that moment have realized that his own supposed special position in creation was also subject to challenge.

[18] Not long thereafter Galileo Galilei initiated the great series of theories that, while recognizing the wild variety with which objects can move, placed all these motions within the conceptual simplicity of the laws of dynamics. Starting with the pendulum and the falling feather and stone, he proved that the earth does indeed move; and his contemporary, Kepler, discovered the three laws that characterize the motions of all the planets. It has taken to the present to round out this ever improving story, with a major contribution from Clark Maxwell—who captured in four short and universal equations the laws that are obeyed by electrical quantities—and with a still more recent improvement provided by quantum dynamics. All of this has brought about the present-day result that for all objects whatsoever, from the elementary particles which make up atoms to the stars which make up the galaxies, however complex and various their motions may be, all these are cases included within unifying laws of austere generality.

[19] We will see in a moment that all matter is included within an even more widely embracing unity; but let us turn for a moment to the world of living things.

[20] The singularity of man was shaken by Copernicus in a manner that we have fully recognized only recently when we became aware that there may well be billions of other cold stars in the universe with earthlike properties and perhaps with sentient inhabitants. But the great blow to man's illusion of singularity came, of course, with Darwin. With many details still and stimulatively lacking, the evidence is overwhelming that all living creatures are kin. It is relatively easy to grasp superficial aspects of this tremendous fact—indeed, as one sees recent moving pictures of the great apes it cannot be judged difficult to acknowledge our kinship to them. But as one looks at the almost incredible and indeed bizarre variety and complexity of the animal world—especially the inhabitants of the sea—it requires a real effort to appreciate the interconnections and the underlying unity.

[21] The diversity, however, is a surface phenomenon: When one looks underneath and within, the universal unity again becomes apparent. We remember the name of Gregor Mendel, curious about the variety in the blossom colors of the peas in his monastery garden at Brünn. His revolutionary ideas about genetic mechanisms have cut through all of the surface diversity of the inheritance of characteristics. In its present-day formulation in molecular genetics, we recognize the universality of basic structure of the genetic apparatus, the lovely spiral molecules that store genetic information and code the messages that, passed along by a second "messenger" molecule, guide the synthesis of proteins. The DNA differs in fine detail between you and me—which is, in fact, a reason why you are you and I am I. But the main architecture of the DNA is the same in a virus, a mollusk, a rose, or a man; and the code used for the genetic messages is universal for all living things.

[22] So, inside, all living things have now become brothers. Indeed they are more profoundly similar than the comparisons of their gene mechanisms might suggest. For one of the striking universalities of the whole biological kingdom is that not only the reproductive mechanism but also the metabolic mechanisms are essentially the same in the cells of a lizard, an eagle, and a man—indeed, in the single cell which constitutes all there is of an amoeba. Thus the so-called Krebs or citric acid cycle, within which are transformed the carbohydrates, fats, and proteins to furnish the chief source of metabolic energy, occurs within the single cells of practically all creatures.

[23] Because of this striking and lovely fact that the inner patterns of life are closely similar in all forms, the biologist does not need always to experiment upon man to learn about man. He may choose convenient cases—neurospora for gene biochemistry, the giant axon of the squid for nerve conduction, the gentle albino rat for nutrition studies, the cat for a detailed study of visual patterns, flatworms or pigeons or porpoises for investigating learning.

[24] With the motions of all dead matter put into universal formulae, and the revelation that all living things have deep common traits, two further steps remained. One of these, at the moment, is not completed; but no informed and responsible scientist doubts that any gap will much longer remain between the world of dead matter and the world of living matter.

[25] That gap, previously so great, began suddenly to shrink in 1828 when the organic chemist F. Wöhler synthesized, from totally inorganic starting materials, a substance (urea) which is produced in living bodies and which, it was formerly held, could be produced only in a living body. By now chemists have synthesized thousands of these "organic" compounds. Indeed such syntheses are so common that they go unnoticed unless the case is one of great complexity and difficulty, and the basis has been removed for a biologically based distinction between "organic" and "inorganic" chemistry.

[26] A much more important narrowing of the gap, however, results from the fact that we are on the very verge of producing, in glass dishes in the laboratory and starting from wholly dead matter, an object which we will have to recognize as being alive. This object will presumably be a virus. These entities are known to share characteristic properties of both the inanimate and animate world. On the one hand they reproduce their kind; but on the other hand, as purified crystalline material they can be stored in a bottle indefinitely. The possibility of a laboratory-produced "living thing" is so tremendous, so awesome a fact, that some believe it better not to think about it.

[27] There is further evidence of this closing of the gap between deadness and life. The last quarter-century has seen the birth and lusty development of a new hybrid science—molecular biology. It seeks to explain all biological phenomena in terms of the properties of molecules—that is to say, in terms of the laws of physics. I do not add "and of chemistry," for at this fundamental level the distinction between physics and chemistry is another instance of a variety which has become unimportant.

[28] The triumphs of molecular biology have, to date, been primarily in genetics; but it is clear that a molecular biology of neurophysiology is about to evolve that will bring an explanation on the molecular level of memory, of learning, and indeed of the entire mind–brain–body relationship.

[29] Although the living world holds the record for variety, with about 1,000,000 species and subspecies of plants and perhaps 2,500,000 of animals, nevertheless the world of inanimate objects is also complex. At present the physicist recognizes 104 basic kinds of elements, of which eighty-one are stable (hydrogen, helium, oxygen, carbon, iron, etc.), and twenty-three are radioactive (radium, thorium, etc.). The total count of

nuclear species, including all the stable and unstable isotopes that are variants of the elements, is 1,511 at present, with about twenty additional ones being discovered each year.

[30] Are there relations between these inanimate units out of which everything is built? Can one be transformed into or evolve into another? The answer depends upon whom you ask and when. The Greeks, the alchemists of the thirteenth century, Dr. William Prout in 1815–16, and modern physicists all say yes. A century ago any sober scientist would have said no, and would probably have scoffed at the questioner.

[31] Indeed we now have a detailed and experimentally confirmed theory that explains how hydrogen, at the incredibly high temperatures within stars, "burns" to yield helium—and energy and more hydrogen as well, so that the process goes on and on. Three helium nuclei, in turn, can fuse to form carbon, with oxygen and helium nuclei as byproducts. And so on and so on, the theory explaining, in good general agreement with the facts as far as we know them, the relative abundance in our universe of practically all the various physical elements. Thus, granting that details are still to be worked out, the physicists' theory of inorganic evolution is much more analytical and quantitative than the biologists' theory of organic evolution. The latter, for example, could not attempt to predict the equilibrium ratios between the total numbers of amoebae, ants, robins, chimps, and men.

[32] Here again, then, is a story of the uncovering of tremendous variety and complexity—but the further discovery of the unifying relations that underlie and embrace all the complexity. The story, however, does not stop here, for there is one more major chapter.

[33] That is the chapter which truly connects the dead world with the living world. The outlines of that chapter have as yet only been sketched. We have mentioned the initial clues of the synthesis of urea and the dual nature of viruses. But we have indeed seen the border between the living and the non-living blur and become indistinct. Modern science is, in fact, now engaged in connecting the discovery of the prior act of the inorganic evolution of the elements with the second—and in our present view, culminating—act of the evolution of the living world. That is to say, science is now joining inorganic and organic evolution into a single grand pattern.

[34] This joining is by no means complete at the moment, and even the partial results are still being debated. But there is direct evidence that in a primitive atmosphere of hydrogen, methane, ammonia, and water vapor an electric discharge can bring about the formation of several amino acids. These are substances which are the building blocks of protein, and proteins, as the word indicates, are the basic stuff of life. This story is only beginning to unfold, and much detail remains unexplored; but as always, the detail, confused at first, will fall into a pattern of overall simplicity.

[35] Important as is this pageant of the discovery that the surface

diversity of all nature is in fact superficial, being underlaid by an all-embracing unity, this is not all, for the materials and mechanics of life are not life. So, it seems to me, we should take still greater satisfaction in the evidence of the growing unification of the humane aspects of life. This even shows up in that most fractionated of all fields, world politics: For though we are still in the early stages of maturation which, tragically, may not occur soon enough, the mere fact of a world organization, the mere fact that favored nations are concerned about the ill-favored—this, we must remember in moments of discouragement, represents tremendous progress.

[36] There is a sense of growing inner unity in the world of religion, with present-day ecumenical movements that would have been unbelievable even a half-century ago. The planet-wide worlds of art, of music, of literature, are unified as has never before been the case. Transport and communication bind us all together as never before. At times we resent the efficiency of communication, longing for the good old days when we did not know of the famines, plagues, riots, and insurrections that were torturing our fellow creatures. But as has been true in science, the complication must come to the surface and be recognized and faced before underlying unity can prevail.

[37] The world of science has long been an internationalized world, and now that the true nature of science is more generally realized, science can join forces with the arts and humanities and with philosophy and religion. For we now know that science is motivated by curiosity, inspired by imagination, and based on faith. We know that it seeks increasing order, and does not pretend to deal with immutable truth. Magnificent as science is, and superbly useful as are its applications, we know that its apparent objectivity is only superficial, its pronouncements always open to revision. We know that, as is all art, it is culture-bound.

[38] What then have I learned from a life spent chiefly in science, but also partly in the library and in the garden? It is that life is stimulatingly, deliciously complicated—but is all of one piece. We are built to appreciate variety, but to seek and recognize unity.

[39] The variety of life cannot be disregarded. Variety is inevitable and desirable, but variety must be either resisted or accommodated and appreciated. To resist variety leads to sinful disaster. To recognize and tolerate variety and to penetrate it so as to discover the underlying unity is the common-good way of science, the arts, and religion.

[40] When this way is pursued, what final lesson is then learned? It is that the ultimate unifying virtues are order, beauty, faith, and love. The emphasis in science is upon the first of these four words, slowly tapering off on the remaining three. The emphasis of religion, on the other hand, increases from first to last in this list, culminating on the final word. The

arts and the humanities primarily emphasize the central two. But the underlying unity being what it is, all are concerned with all.

[41] "All things," wrote Heraclitus, "come out of the one; and the one out of all things."

---◄{ COMMENT AND QUESTIONS }►◦---

1. What is the meaning of *humanist* in the title of the essay? Why, in your opinion, does Weaver call his essay *confessions*?
2. Paragraphs 2–11 supply facts about the author's life. What other kinds of information do these paragraphs give? What do paragraphs 12–14 contribute to the essay? To what extent do you agree with the "assorted convictions" in paragraph 14?
3. The author states his thesis in paragraph 15. What are the major unities underlying diversities discussed in the essay?
4. Weaver speaks, in paragraph 20, of "man's illusion of singularity." If you have read Julian Huxley's essay on the uniqueness of man, do you think that Huxley and Weaver are in disagreement about man's uniqueness? Explain.
5. What is the function of paragraph 24?
6. Some people believe, the author says at the end of paragraph 26, that it is better not to think about the possibility of producing a "living thing" in a laboratory. What are your reactions to this possibility and the reasons for your reactions?
7. Although Weaver is writing for an educated audience of nonspecialists, his allusions (to Gregor Mendel, for example) and his occasional technical terms (like *DNA* and *molecular biology*) may not be clear to all readers. If this is true, does it seem to you to interfere with the general clarity of the essay? Explain.
8. The author often uses language to express feeling; an example is *the blazing beauty and power of . . . calculus* in paragraph 2. Point out other examples in the essay. What is the effect of this use of attitudinal or emotional language?
9. Examine the concluding paragraphs of the essay, especially paragraphs 37–40. To what extent do you agree with Weaver's comments on the relationships of science, the arts and humanities, philosophy, and religion? Why?
10. The quotation from Heraclitus in the last paragraph might have been put elsewhere—for example, in paragraph 15 where Weaver states his thesis about the many and the one. What does the author gain by using the quotation at the end and by setting it in a separate short paragraph?

[67]   *Elting E. Morison*: It's Two-Thirds of a Century—We've Made It, So Far

THE FOLLOWING article, published in *The New York Times Magazine*, April 24, 1966, is not concerned solely with science; the author believes, however, that the rapid advance of scientific knowledge and the rapid application of scientific findings to human affairs are important causes of conditions and problems in the modern world. Elting E. Morison (1909–   ), author of *Admiral Sims and the Modern American Navy* and *Turmoil and Tradition,* is Sloan Fellows Professor of Industrial History at the Massachusetts Institute of Technology and chairman of the Social Studies Curriculum program of Educational Services, Inc.

[¹] The main line of argument for this article was worked out on a 707 bound east from Los Angeles. Conditions for reflection upon the shape of things to come were almost perfect. Swirling gently around me was a current of cool air projected from a small spigot in the ceiling of the plane. Overhead also, from a small box, "a first-run movie" called, I believe, "From Moment to Moment," was steadily unwinding. In my earphones, in stereophonic sound, was the music of Verdi's "Requiem." I had been told I could watch Jean Seberg and listen to Verdi at the same time without mechanical complication and so I did. On the tray in front of me, ice-cold in a small cylindrical green bottle, was the first of two complimentary martinis. We were passing over the eastern slope of the Rocky Mountains on the way to Chicago.

[²] I had a great-grandfather who had taken somewhat the same route, the other way, from Illinois to California. He had driven out at the head of a wagon train in a buckboard drawn by two bay horses and had made about as much progress in one day, if it was a good day, as I was making between sips of the martini if I sipped fast. I reflected on this and on the fact that my ancestor looking upward, perhaps, from time to time on his westward journey would not have been able to tell very precisely what interesting uses we would be making of the empty skies.

[³] This is all by way of saying that it is hard to tell about the future. Indeed, the idea, as it was put to me, that a man who has spent time studying what has happened in the past two-thirds of a century should, as a result, be able to describe what will happen in the next one-third was probably never a very sensible idea. There is a difference between telling "where all past years are"—which John Donne thought was hard enough —and locating the years to come, let alone reporting on what they will look like.

[4] And today, when the rate and variety of change seem to approach infinity, the task of relating what went before to what will come after seems immeasurable. Any shrewd man would be willing to settle for the kind of prescience Carlyle had when he observed that there was thunder upon the horizon as well as dawn and let it go at that.

[5] Henry Adams went a good deal further. He made in fact something of an intellectual career out of his attempt to bring the future within a foreseeable scheme and he produced, on the whole, some impressive results. Early in this century he said that the United States and Russia were the countries to watch—and that they should watch each other. He also told his brother Brooks in 1912 that a belt of dissolving society was stretched around the world from Peking to Sicily. In the next year, he believed, it would reach into the heart of civilization in Central Europe. At 75, he added, he was rotting to pieces in every sense, but "the damned world rots faster than I."

[6] In his minor calculation he was almost precisely right. Give or take a few months, the dissolving disease got to Sarajevo when he said it would. As for his larger divination, cast in the form of generalized calamity that increasingly attracted him as he got older, the evidence appears to offer considerable confirmation. Much of the world that Adams knew well has now, by rot or other means, disintegrated and most of the society he knew even better has dissolved. The far-flung battle lines that maintained the 19th-century order seem near the end of their long withdrawal and the peculiar fire of the time has almost sunk on all the dunes and headlands and even on the home grounds.

[7] To be more specific is hardly necessary. Everybody knows that things are not at all what they were at the beginning of this century; even the heart of society has shifted to some other not yet fully defined location. The intent here is not to describe the workings of the process— which Adams called a disease—but to discover if it has run its course.

[8] The answer is, "Probably not." For one thing, the figures of speech —disease, dissolution, rot—suggesting as they do decomposition ending in inert residues, are quite misleading. Some parts of the previous world did no doubt just fall apart or go to pieces. But more of it was torn, wrenched, blasted or blown asunder. From Verdun to Manchuria, from the Finland Station to the Sudetenland, from Omaha Beach to Hiroshima, to Dienbienphu and Vietnam, there has been a hectic destruction of ancient powers and principalities. Looked at this way, it could be said

that the damned world was not so much rotting away as going to hell in a hack and hew.

[⁹] The energy in the system, in other words, has been tremendous. It still is. We are a long way from inert residues, but also some distance from tranquillity. The available energy has not yet been brought within any very orderly or stable scheme. In the first instance, it was turned against patterns and structures that had become antiquated, irrelevant, insufficient or just in the way. And no doubt for much of the two-thirds of a century just passed, the available energy was worked out in acts of violence designed by desperate men.

[¹⁰] But much of it, too, was put in the service of certain propositions, some old—all men are created equal; some new—any five-year plan— that seemed to offer fuller promise for more lives. Working through the disorder, whether in Central Europe, Africa, India or Asia, there have been constructive intents and a purpose to reach useful accommodations politically and socially to conditions without precedent.

[¹¹] To say that such intents are not yet fully realized, that from time to time and from place to place they have been and still are in open conflict with each other, is not the same as saying that the world is dissolving. It may well be the difference between galloping consumption and labor pains.

[¹²] Thus far, nothing new or very interesting has been said about either the past or the future. It amounts to little more than saying "our little systems have their day, they have their day and cease to be." It may speed things up somewhat to ask "What next?"—or more specifically: "May we soon be entering a time of much greater stability and harmony?"

[¹³] The answer must appear to be, "No, not in this century." In the way of creating new political arrangements to take the place of the old dispensations there seems to be unfinished business in India, Africa and throughout much of the Far East. It will no doubt take considerable time and much painful experiment to get things set right in these areas. And the uncertainties in these areas will be a continuing source of further perturbation in the larger system of international relations where Russia, China, the nations of Europe, and the United States will be seeking useful accommodations to each other.

[¹⁴] If all these foreseeable activities were to be played out within the old conventional schemes of time and energy, it would be possible perhaps to make some qualified prediction about when and how the dust would settle down, as in the previous century a man might with a show of confidence forecast some sort of schedule for the colonization of Africa or the disposition of the Shantung Peninsula. But not even a bold or rash man today would dare predict when and how the dust will settle in this disturbed world.

[15] For what is going on is not simply, as so often in the past, a reorganization of familiar elements, an attempt to give modified forms to fairly constant entities. In Africa, for instance, the cement has fallen out of the seams of empire, leaving small pieces; but the effort in Africa is not directed simply to putting the pieces together again in a fairly familiar context; it is directed to putting the pieces together to fit a set of novel and complicated conditions.

[16] What is true in Africa is true of all other places; even the most ancient structures are put under the rising pressure of novelty and complication. If one searches for the cause of this pressure within the whole system, it can easily be discovered. It appears to derive from two things—the excitements produced by the steady advance of the ideas of science and the power introduced by the utilization of the scientific ideas in engineering. Indeed, the transcendent fact in the history of this century so far may well be the rapid development of a system that can produce a steadily enlarging flow of scientific findings and the increasingly rapid application of these findings to the affairs of men.

[17] By means of this system, man in the part of this century already passed has acquired an amazing domination over his natural or physical surrounding. Starting centuries ago on this effort to extend his control over his surrounding by steadily extending his skill as a tool-user, man is now close to the payoff of his long labors, the part where he can manipulate his environment to suit his own desires. Most of his progress, which has spread out over eons, is concentrated in the past two-thirds of a century.

[18] The extent and nature of this competence is, in fact, awesome; we can blow the world up, as we all know. But taken by itself, it is not a matter for unqualified pride. Thomas Huxley, who was in on the beginning of the great modern forward march, came to Baltimore near the end of the last century to say that he was not very much impressed by the existing plant—the dynamos, the open-hearth furnaces, the locomotives and all that. "The great issue," he went on, "about which hangs a true sublimity and the terror of overhanging fate is, what are you going to do with all these things?"

[19] In the short run—say 33⅓ years, to pick a figure at random—it is pretty clear what we will do and not do with some of these things. For instance, will we by the year 2,000 blow ourselves, or a considerable part of ourselves, up? The answer is almost certainly not. Indeed, it seems far more probable that the knowledge of the great destructive power we have at our disposal will tend to steady and stabilize the decision-makers.

[20] Will we have placed men upon the moon? The answer is almost certainly yes. But it is not clear that such first explorations will produce

a constant flow of traffic between ourselves and that cold and blasted heath. Will we have so refined "the spare-parts deal" in modern medicine that the brains of one man will have been transplanted into the head of another? Quite probably. Will we have developed a vehicle to take us to London in two hours on a fairly predictable commuting schedule? Quite probably.

[21] Will we have so mastered the content and purpose of the nucleic acids that we will know far more fully than we do now how to manage the selection and development of human characteristics? Quite probably. And what of the computer? It will no doubt continue to extend its competence into many regions of man's thought and increasingly invade the sectors of routine management in technical and human systems.

[22] The putting of such questions and the supplying of such answers is really not a very profitable or even very interesting exercise. What it amounts to is saying that in the next few years we will without much doubt extend our technical competence. There is a slightly different kind of question which offers room for a little more stimulating speculation and for larger difference of opinion.

[23] Will there, for instance, be enough food, enough clothes, enough houses, even enough ground for the multiplying population in the year 2000? With due regard for the difficulty of deciding what "enough" may be, and recognizing that problems of distribution are perhaps greater than problems of production, it may be said that we seem to have it in our hands to supply the support required, if we put our minds to it. And, if we use our minds a little more, we will begin at the proper end and try to work with more understanding and system at the task of controlling the number of births.

[24] And, however many people there are, will they be put out of business by the machines? This seems very doubtful indeed. Historically at least, the more work the machinery does, the more work that machines can't do there seems to be. And what of leisure? More, one hopes than now, and better used and more opportunity for education continued episodically through life to keep up with the times—which will prove to be more upwardly mobile than the Joneses ever were.

[25] And what of the North, South, East and West; the town and the country; the old and the young, the rich and the poor; the King's English and the vernacular; the upper, the middle and the lower; the black, the white and the yellow—still all there no doubt, but with a leveling off of distinctions, a flattening out of differences.

[26] This, of course, is not at all what Huxley meant when he asked what we were going to do with all these things. He wanted to know, to what end will they be used? This is a hard question and the question that

must precede it is little easier. It is the question of how or whether we can learn to handle or manage the system of ideas, forces, materials and things that we are busily constructing, whatever the end in view might be.

[27] The system at this moment is so powerful and so filled with interior change that any human organization resting upon it is subject to continuous change itself. That is why the social and political disequilibriums around the world from Cuba to Vietnam to the Congo will undoubtedly continue to perturb the equilibrium of the whole for some time to come. The task of creating a social and political structure firm enough to contain and flexible enough to be responsive to the scientific and technical changes will be difficult—and one not soon finished, because the exciting forces of science and engineering will be steadily changing as well.

[28] But one may hazard a guess that in the parts of the world where "new" societies are emerging—and in the other parts of the world where older societies are attempting to modify familiar structures to meet the new conditions—real progress will be made in the next three decades towards useful accommodations both social and political. A further guess is that, to reach these accommodations, it will be necessary to reduce a little the circumference of the circle of freedom in which each man now stands.

[29] The extent to which a man has a sense of himself in our society depends to a considerable degree on the size of that circle and what goes on in it—specifically on the extent to which a man feels free and able to make independent choices among an array of alternative opportunities. During the next 33⅓ years, and probably thereafter, this space will in all probability serve as the theater for the most interesting and significant encounters that will occur in the period. An old associate of mine, a physiologist, says occasionally that man may be looked upon in time simply as "a node in a communication network." There are a growing number of other technical systems in which man can similarly be looked upon as a small point.

[30] And if others so consider him, it is but a step to his so considering himself. So one problem will be to discover how intricate systems can be managed not only in the interests of the general whole (across-the-board decisions) but can be so ordered that they may preserve a lively concern for the particular—the single individual.

[31] A lot in this process will depend upon the people who put the intricate system together, how sensitive they will remain to the claims of single men. But a lot, too, indeed much more, will depend on the single men. If they can figure out their legitimate claims and press them upon the public consciousness with persistence, it will do much to increase the sensitivity of those who may otherwise come to believe that—in putting together a great society—general rules, inclusive systems and across-the-board decisions are enough.

[³²] And here, in the next third of a century, the load on single men will grow. For the size of the circle each man stands in as a single self is not only diminishing, but the space enclosed is filling up. The things which Emerson said were in the saddle and sufficient even in his time "to ride mankind" have now multiplied exponentially—even small and apparently insignificant things. Take what piles up in and around a seat in a 707— intercom, stereo, air conditioner, TV, and so forth. Almost all things are possible, even Miss Seberg and Giuseppe Verdi and Captain Jones' report on the weather at O'Hare all at the same time. How to sort things out and keep them in their proper places becomes a problem—too great a problem obviously in the case in point to be solved.

[³³] These are, relatively, small and weak things compared with the machines and procedures creating the general surround a man stands in today. These are powerful enough to set their own conditions and to determine their own environment if left untended. They may well do so unless the men in the environment can sort out and arrange things to suit themselves. In the old days when much that was desirable could not be done, one settled as a piece of ripe old wisdom for the possible. Today when so much is possible, the problem for the wise is to pick out from all the things that can be done what may be altogether fitting and proper—desirable to do.

[³⁴] Such selection may be done in part by higher authority. We will go to the moon and cause Appalachia to flourish as the green bay tree, but we will resist the military application of nuclear energy. And it may be done in part by the influence of the general public in the body politic. But in the end, the decisions of higher authority and the opinion of the body politic will be determined by the mood of innumerable men standing in their own small circles.

[³⁵] Their judgments will determine what kind of machines to build and what machines we can build that don't need to be built; what rules and regulations and moral codes shall govern the use of birth-control pills, nucleic acids and the procedures of the spare-parts deal; what kinds of technical systems and networks will preserve the largest play for human beings. It's a matter of selecting, as they say today, the proper targets of opportunity and designing the appropriate instrumentation to achieve the end in view.

[³⁶] To fortify the single man as he seeks to make his judgments within his small circle he must have all kinds of support—some knowledge of the potential in each new idea and machine and network; as full a knowledge as possible of his own potential, historically conceived and currently understood; a set of definitions stating, among all the things that are possible, the things especially to be hoped for; and a set of criteria which, given his own potential and the potential in the machinery, will enable him to choose the best means to fulfill his hopes.

[³⁷] Some part of this fortification will come no doubt from the decisions and aspirations set forth by those in authority and some part will certainly be found in the body of fact, attitude and timeless perception that makes up the Western culture. But more must in the future come from an educational process transformed to meet the new dispensation. In times without precedent, formal education, responsive to changing conditions, must assume much of the load borne in more static conditions by the familiar and sustaining cultures.

[³⁸] And today when, as Whitehead said, the society that does not value the trained mind will perish, the imaginative development of new content and new forms in education has a very high priority. And finally, if the single man is to do his necessary work within his small circle, he must recover the feeling that he counts.

[³⁹] In the creation of this feeling the support of the relevant parts of the old culture—the aspirations that may be defined for him by those in authority, the knowledge supplied by the new education—will all help. But in addition, he must have a sense that he has some hand in shaping the mechanical surround he will increasingly inhabit—that the character and quality of his life is not determined simply by the technically possible and economically feasible.

[⁴⁰] How to give individual men the evidence they need to make sensible judgments about the kind of world they want to live in and how to give them the power to make their judgments stick, that is the unfinished business of the next third of the century.

COMMENT AND QUESTIONS

1. The first six paragraphs might be considered introductory; paragraph 7 states the author's purpose, or part of his purpose, in writing the article. What do the first paragraphs contribute?
2. What use does Morison make of the indirect and direct quotations from Henry Adams in paragraph 5? Of the quotation from Thomas Huxley in paragraph 18?
3. A question-to-answer pattern is recurrent in this essay. Summarize the author's reasons for saying "Probably not" in answer to the indirect question at the end of paragraph 7 and his reasons for saying "No, not in this century" in answer to the question at the end of paragraph 12.
4. Paragraphs 19–21 ask and answer a number of questions, and paragraph 22 makes a transition to a "slightly different kind of question." How do the questions in paragraphs 23–25 differ from those in paragraphs 19–21? To what extent do you agree with the author's comments in paragraphs 23–25?

5. At the end of paragraph 28, Morison introduces the figure of the circle of freedom. Explain what he means by his guess that it will be necessary to reduce a little the circumference of that circle. What examples can you give of ways in which the circle of freedom for the individual has already been reduced in this century?

6. The plane on which Morison was traveling offered him a number of free choices. What were they? How, then, is the further discussion of the plane, in paragraph 32, relevant to the circle of freedom?

7. In paragraph 33 and again in paragraph 39, the author uses *surround* as a noun. Neither *The Standard College Dictionary* nor *Webster's New World Dictionary* lists the word as a noun; *Webster's Seventh New Collegiate Dictionary* does list it as a noun and defines it: "something (as a border or edging) that surrounds." If you had been editing Morison's article, would you have suggested changing the word *surround* to the more generally used word *surroundings*? Explain.

8. The author emphasizes a number of times the role of individual men in shaping the world they live in. Do you agree with what he says about the possible influence of individuals? Explain.

9. Does this article seem to you to offer a solution to the problem stated by Thomas Huxley and restated by Morison in paragraph 26? Explain.

10. Comment on the title "It's Two-Thirds of a Century—We've Made It, So Far." Does the title prepare the reader for the content of the article or emphasize what is most important in the article? Can you think of other possible titles?

[68]   *Emmanuel G. Mesthene*: Learning to Live with Science

EMMANUEL G. MESTHENE is Executive Director of the Harvard University Program on Technology and Society. The following article appeared in the *Saturday Review*, July 17, 1965.

[1] It was Gilbert Murray who first used the celebrated phrase "the failure of nerve." Writing about ancient Greek religions, Murray characterized as a failure of nerve the change of temper that occurred in Hellenistic civilization around the turn of the era. The Greeks of the fifth and fourth centuries B.C. believed in the ultimate intelligibility of the universe. There was nothing in the nature of existence or of man that was inherently unknowable. They accordingly believed also in the power

of the human intelligence to know all there was to know about the world, and to guide man's career in it.

[²] The wars, increased commerce, and infiltration of Oriental cultures that marked the subsequent period brought with them vicissitude and uncertainty that shook this classic faith in the intelligibility of the world and in the capacity of men to know and to do. There was henceforth to be a realm of knowledge available only to God, not achievable by human reason. Men, in other words, more and more turned to God to do for them what they no longer felt confident to do for themselves. That was the failure of nerve.

[³] I think things are changing. I doubt that there are many men today who would question that life will be produced in the laboratory, that psychologists and their personality drugs will soon reveal what really makes men tick, that scientific prediction is a far more promising guide to the future than divination, and that the heavens cannot long remain mysterious in the face of our ability to hit the moon today and the stars tomorrow. In a recent article, Daniel Bell characterized this new-found faith as follows: "Today we feel that there are no inherent secrets in the universe . . . and this is one of the significant changes in the modern moral temper." I would say, indeed, that this is a major implication of our new world of science and technology. We are witnessing a widespread recovery of nerve.

WE FEAR THE MACHINES

[⁴] Paradoxically, this taking on of new courage is tending at the same time to produce an opposite reaction, vague but disturbingly widespread. At the same time that we admire the new machines we build—the ones that play chess, and translate Russian, and catch and correct their own mistakes, and tend each other—we also begin to fear them. We fear them in two ways—one that we talk about, and one that we joke about.

[⁵] We talk quite openly about our fear that machines may take away jobs, deprive people of work. But we dare only to joke about our fear that machines will replace people, not only as workers, but as people. Already they do arithmetic better than any of us. How much longer can it be before they make people obsolete? This fear is part of our technological world, but I see it only as derivative. I think it has its roots in a deeper, moral implication.

[⁶] Some who have seen farthest and most clearly in recent decades have warned of a growing imbalance between man's capabilities in the physical and in the social realms. John Dewey, for example, said: "We have displayed enough intelligence in the physical field to create the new and powerful instrument of science and technology. We have not as yet had enough intelligence to use this instrument deliberately and systematically to control its social operations and consequences." Dewey said this more than thirty years ago, before television, before atomic power, before electronic computers, before space satellites. He had been saying it, moreover, for at least thirty years before that. He saw early the problems that would arise when man learned to do anything he wanted before he learned what he wanted.

WHAT SHOULD WE DO?

[7] I think the time Dewey warned about is here. My more thoughtful scientific friends tell me that we now have, or know how to acquire, the technical capability to do very nearly anything we want. Can we transplant human hearts, control personality, order the weather that suits us, travel to Mars or to Venus? Of course we can, if not now or in five or 10 years, then certainly in 25, or in 50 or a 100. If each of us examined the extent of his own restored faith in the essential intelligibility of the world, we might find that we have recovered our nerve to the point that we are becoming almost nervy. (I think, incidentally, that this recovery of nerve largely explains the current crisis of the churches. After 20 centuries of doing man's work, they are now having to learn how to do God's. The Ecumenical Council is evidence that the long but false war between religion and science is ended, and that we are once more facing Augustine's problem, to distinguish what is God's and what is man's.)

[8] If the answer to the question "What can we do?" is "Anything," then the emphasis shifts far more heavily than before onto the question "What should we do?" The commitment to universal intelligibility entails moral responsibility. Abandonment of the belief in intelligibility 2,000 years ago was justly described as a failure of nerve because it was the prelude to moral surrender. Men gave up the effort to be wise because they found it too hard. Renewed belief in intelligibility 2,000 years later means that men must take up again the hard work of becoming wise, And it is much harder work now, because we have so much more power than the Greeks. On the other hand, the benefits of wisdom are potentially greater, too, because we have the means at hand to *make* the good life, right here and now, rather than just to go on contemplating it in Plato's heaven.

[9] The question "What should we do?" is thus no idle one but challenges each one of us. That, I think, is the principal moral implication of our new world. It is what all the shouting is about in the mounting concern about the relations of science and public policy, and about the impact of technology on society. Our almost total mastery of the physical world entails a challenge to the public intelligence of a degree heretofore unknown in history.

[10] But how do we come to grips with the challenge? How do we pull together and learn to use the knowledge we already have, and in using it learn the other things we need to know? What do the implications of

our great contemporary scientific and technical spurt forward add up to? I do not have the answers, but I should like to propose some hypotheses.

WHAT HAPPENS TO THE WORKER?

[11] My first hypothesis is that the time will come when machines will put most people permanently out of work. What will happen to people when there is no longer work for them to do? Consider the foreman in a steel plant. He brings thirty years' experience to one of the half-dozen really crucial jobs in the mill. At the critical point in the process, it is his trained eye that tells him the molten metal is ready to pour, and it is his well-developed sense of timing and steady hand that tip the cauldron synchronously with the processes that precede and follow. For this he is well paid, and can provide for his family perhaps better than the average. For this, too, he is looked up to by his fellows. They seek him out as a friend. He has prestige at his work, status in the town, and the respect of his children. He belongs. He contributes. He is needed.

[12] Then you move in a machine that takes his job away, and does it better. What happens to this man? What happens to his many juniors at the mill whose aspiration was to an achievement like his? One of the pervasive characteristics of our civilization has been the identification of life's meaning with life's work. The evidence is strong in the problem of the aged: how do they fight the conviction that their life is done, that the world could do very well, perhaps better, without them? Are we heading toward a time when society will be burdened with a problem of the aged beginning in most cases at age 20, because there will no longer be work to enter upon, let alone retire from, at the age of 65?

[13] Among the suggestions for banishing this specter are two that do not impress me much. The first is essentially a cry of anguish. Stop automation! Stop making more and more complicated machines! What business have we going to the moon, or tampering with life and heredity? Life is difficult enough without going out of our way to make it more so.

[14] All the odds are against the success of that kind of solution. The technologies of the atom bomb, the automobile, the industrial revolution, gunpowder, all provoked social dislocations accompanied by similar demands that they be stopped. But there is clearly no stopping. Aristotle said a long time ago that "man by nature desires to know." He will probe and learn all that his curiosity leads him to and his brain makes possible, until he is dead. The cry of "stop" is the fear reaction I talked about earlier. It comes from those who have not yet recovered their nerve.

[15] A second suggestion, specifically aimed at the prospect of loss of work, is that we find better ways to employ leisure. There is a whole literature growing up on this theme, and I think it should be encouraged. Other things being equal, and given my own biases, it is better to read a good book than to watch television, or to play a Beethoven quartet than

listen to the Beatles. But leisure activity, no matter how uplifting and educational, is not a substitute for work. The very concept loses meaning in the absence of the correlative concept of "work." No, I do not think that is the happiest solution.

[16] But then that may not be the problem either. My second hypothesis is that my first hypothesis is wrong. Machines might not in fact put a significant number of people out of work permanently. It might just be that machines will simply take over the kinds of work that people have done up to now, and that people will then be freed, not to become problems to themselves and to society, but to do entirely new kinds of work that have hardly been thought about seriously because there has not yet been a serious possibility that they could be done.

[17] It is often said, for example, that as work in agriculture and industry is progressively mechanized, job opportunities in the service sector of the economy will increase and absorb released manpower. I assume that production processes will not be mechanized except as machines prove more efficient than human labor. There should then follow a significant increment in wealth, which, adequately distributed, could buy more of the services already available, from babysitting to education and government and from better waiters to art and religion. The structure of the work force might thus be altered significantly.

[18] Even more exciting is the possibility that the nature of service itself might be altered. I suggest a trivial, perhaps ridiculous example. Doubled police forces and quadrupled sanitation forces could give us, for the first time, really safe and really clean cities. Put 20,000 people into the streets every day to catch the cigarette butts before they even hit the ground, and you might have a clean city.

[19] Inherently, there is nothing ridiculous about a clean city. If the suggestion makes one smile, it is rather because such use of people, by today's standards, is ridiculously uneconomical. People are more efficiently employed to produce the goods we consume. But if machines will be doing most of that, then maybe people can be employed to produce the services, such as street-cleaning or teaching, that we would like to have more of if we could.

[20] Consider another example. One of the genuinely new and exciting ideas of the Kennedy Administration, I think, was the Peace Corps, the idea that young Americans in large numbers could, by example, help less favored peoples to help themselves. Imagine a Peace Corps 50,000,000 strong in Africa, released by machines to pour the kind of sweat that machines will never pour. This is the kind of service that can anticipate, peacefully and constructively, the ugly danger that the have-nots of the world will resort to uncontrollable violence as the gap between their expectations and reality widens. It is also the kind of service that might

provide to individuals a satisfaction and a goal to life undreamed of by today's assembly-line worker in Detroit, however fully employed. From such a perspective, the new machines and the new technologies may spell, not the end of the world, but the beginning of a new one. We might begin to see, for the first time, what God meant when he said that the meek shall inherit the earth.

[21] There has been a long tradition that divides work into creative and intellectual for the few, and routine and mechanical for the many. There has grown up around that distinction (although we are told that that was not yet true in the time of the Greeks) a moral judgment: that the first kind of work was for superior people, and the second for inferior people. There then occurred, I think, one of those curious inversions of history whereby an effect is later seen as cause. The reason the majority of people did routine and mechanical work, we were told was that that was the only kind of work they were fit to do, because they were inferior.

[22] It seems to me much more plausible, however, that the reason the majority of people have done routine and mechanical work is that there has been a very great deal of routine and mechanical work to do. I am not denying that some people are more gifted than other people. But it seems to me that we have not yet been motivated to inquire sufficiently into how many people of what kinds can do what, because there has up to now been so much routine and mechanical work to do that most people have necessarily been impressed into doing it.

[23] I suggest also that it is this same imperative of a great deal of routine and mechanical work to do that has led to the ivory-tower syndrome on the part of creative, intellectual workers. I doubt that artists and scientists have typically detached themselves from the world because they liked it that way. The cry for application of knowledge, at least since Francis Bacon, and the essential need of the artist to communicate preclude that view. I suspect, rather, that there may be another reversal of cause and effect here: that the ivory tower may be symptomatic of a world by necessity too preoccupied with the routine and mechanical to generate a real demand for the product of the artist and the scholar. It is no accident that art and philosophy were the exclusive province of the freemen, not the slaves, in Greece, or that science, even in our own age, has for most of its history been indulged in by the gifted amateur who was rich in fact or by philanthropy.

NEW DEMAND FOR SCHOLARS AND ARTISTS

[24] And now machines will do the routine and mechanical work of the world. Very large numbers of human resources will be released and available for services to mankind beyond those required for subsistence. The need to discover the nature of this new kind of work, to plan it and

to do it, just might overcome the traditional gap between the creative and the routine. The many will be challenged, as they have not been before, to rise to their maximum potentialities. The few—the scholars and the artists—may find that there is a new demand for them in the world, to muster, to shape, and to guide this new force. The two historical judgments that I have criticized as inverted, in other words, might become true from now on in: work could finally become the measure of man, and efficacy the measure of ideas.

[25] What will be the nature of this new work? What goals will it serve? How will it be done? What talents will be needed for it? I do not know the answers to these questions, either. Each, I think, provides an opportunity for imaginative inquiry still to be done. I have undertaken only to state a hypothesis, or, more accurately, to indicate a hunch that precedes hypothesis. My hunch is that man may have finally expiated his original sin, and might now aspire to bliss. I think also that my hunch may hang together historically. Original sin was invented after, and to account for, the failure of nerve. With the recovery of nerve, we do not need the concept any more, and the advance of technology frees us from the drudgery it has imposed.

[26] But freedom from drudgery, as I have suggested, entails a commitment to wisdom. Consider, as one example, the staggering implications for education. Education (in foot-high letters on public billboards) has become a panacean word. But education for what? For whom? What kind of education? And when? There is very little small print on the billboards to answer those questions.

[27] The response of education to the new world of science and technology up to now has taken the form of five principal proposals or goals: 1) more education for more people, 2) educational booster shots in some form of continuing adult education, 3) increased production of scientists and engineers, 4) expanded vocational training, and 5) mid-career refresher training or retraining for a different specialty.

[28] It is hard to quarrel with more education, or with continuing education. With respect to the other three goals, however, one can raise the question "For how long?" To be sure, we need more scientists and engineers than we have now, but we already hear warnings that the demand will level off, and it is perhaps not too early to start thinking about a massive effort in the social sciences and the humanities.

[29] Similarly with vocational education. Training in a trade is desirable and useful. But in which trade? Certainly not in those doomed to extinction in the next 10 to 20 years. The informal experience of the young people who have recently been crusading in Mississippi and Alabama might prove a much more relevant vocational education for the future that lies ahead of us.

[³⁰] Today's best educational judgments, in other words, might turn into tomorrow's worst mistakes, because they depend on forecasting successfully the shape of what is coming. Of course, the judgments must still be made today, despite the risk, despite the increased uncertainties of a world that changes shape rapidly and radically. This is a measure of the difficulty of the modern educator's task. Yet in this very change may lie a relative certainty, with a particular further implication for the job of education. I add a word about that.

WHAT IS REALITY?

[³¹] There were two ancient Greek philosophers, long before even Socrates haunted the streets of Athens, who had diametrically opposed views about reality. There was Parmenides, who argued that all change is illusory, transitory, imperfect, unreal. And later there was Heraclitus, who saw reality as a flowing river, apparently the same but never the same, to whom all was constant flux and change, and who dismissed the permanent as unreal, as evidence of human imperfection, as a distortion of reality.

[³²] I go back to those ancient thinkers, because each gave his name to a major and persistent theme in Western intellectual history. Parmenides, the apostle of the eternal, has had his emulators in Christian theology, in romantic idealism, and in 20th-century mathematics and logic. The followers of Heraclitus, who saw the world as flux, include the medieval nominalists, the 19th-century evolutionary philosophers, and today's existentialists.

[³³] Are we Parmenidians or Heracliteans? In our social attitudes, we certainly lean to Parmenides. In our concept of work, the real is the career that holds together, makes sense, and lasts a lifetime. If a man changes jobs too often, we consider him a drifter, or, if we like him, we say he has not yet found his proper work. We see the change as unnatural, unreal, unwanted, and feel much more comfortable with the permanent, the stable.

[³⁴] Similarly with our social institutions. Democracy, capitalism, socialism, the organized faiths—these are the real, the cherished, and any change is transitional, accidental, to be avoided, or dealt with as quickly as possible, to return to the stable, the familiar, the true.

[³⁵] The evidence is becoming compelling that we are going to have to change these attitudes and comfortable habits. Careers are increasingly becoming shorter-lived than people. The complexities of national existence lead to an increasing and inevitable mixing-up of the public and the private. States' rights, that honored mark of 18th-century federalism, has become a slogan of those who would have us return to the 18th-century. The profit motive is being introduced into the Soviet economy, and the world's religions are beginning to talk to each other. All our familiar institutions, in other words, are changing so rapidly and so constantly that the change is becoming more familiar now than the institutions that are changing. The change is the new reality. We are entering an era that might aptly be called Social Heracliteanism.

[36] The challenge to education is indeed staggering. Teachers who have been brought up to cherish the stable must take the children of parents who have been brought up to cherish the stable, and try to teach them that the stable, the unchanging, is unreal, constraining, a false goal, and that they will survive in an age of change to the degree that they become familiar with change, feel comfortable with it, understand it, master and control it.

[37] When that task is done, the recovery of nerve will be complete, because our new technical mastery will have been supplemented by the wisdom necessary to harness it to human ends. John Dewey's dream will have been realized. We will be the masters of our techniques instead of their slaves, and we might just become the first civilization since 500 B.C. to be able to look the Greeks in the face with pride, instead of just with wonder. I do not like to think of the alternative, which is that the people of a century from now will say of us: "Look at the trouble and woe they had with their technology, and look what ours has done for us."

---◄{ C O M M E N T   A N D   Q U E S T I O N S }►---

1. Explain clearly what Mesthene means by "recovery of nerve." What are the effects of this recovery, and what problems does it involve?
2. What is the meaning of the distinction in the second sentence of paragraph 5 between people as workers and people as people?
3. The author says, in paragraph 16, that his second hypothesis is that his first hypothesis is wrong; and he develops more fully and more emphatically the second hypothesis. What seem to be his reasons for including the first hypothesis and for giving it as much development as he does?
4. Comment on the examples of services in paragraphs 18–20. Are they well selected and well arranged for Mesthene's purposes? Explain.
5. State in your own words the reversals of cause and effect the author discusses in paragraphs 21–23. Does his reasoning seem to you to be clear and sound? Explain.
6. To what extent do you agree with Mesthene's ideas, in paragraphs 33–35, that we tend to be Parmenidians in our attitudes and that we need to change those attitudes?
7. Summarize the possible gains Mesthene sees for the individual and for

society if his second hypothesis proves true. What are the principal problems to be solved before the gains can be realized?

8. Examine paragraph 37. In what ways is it an effective ending?
9. If you have read the article by Elting E. Morison, compare and contrast Morison's and Mesthene's views of the future.

[69] *Norman Cousins*: The Computer and the Poet

NORMAN COUSINS (1912–   ) is the editor of the *Saturday Review* and author of many works, including *Modern Man Is Obsolete, Who Speaks for Man?, The Last Defense in a Nuclear Age,* and *In Place of Folly.* "The Computer and the Poet" is an editorial from the *Saturday Review* of July 23, 1966.

[1] The essential problem of man in a computerized age remains the same as it has always been. That problem is not solely how to be more productive, more comfortable, more content, but how to be more sensitive, more sensible, more proportionate, more alive. The computer makes possible a phenomenal leap in human proficiency; it demolishes the fences around the practical and even the theoretical intelligence. But the question persists and indeed grows whether the computer will make it easier or harder for human beings to know who they really are, to identify their real problems, to respond more fully to beauty, to place adequate value on life, and to make their world safer than it now is.

[2] Electronic brains can reduce the profusion of dead ends involved in vital research. But they can't eliminate the foolishness and decay that come from the unexamined life. Nor do they connect a man to the things he has to be connected to—the reality of pain in others; the possibilities of creative growth in himself; the memory of the race; and the rights of the next generation.

[3] The reason these matters are important in a computerized age is that there may be a tendency to mistake data for wisdom, just as there has always been a tendency to confuse logic with values, and intelligence with insight. Unobstructed access to facts can produce unlimited good only if it is matched by the desire and ability to find out what they mean and where they would lead.

[⁴] Facts are terrible things if left sprawling and unattended. They are too easily regarded as evaluated certainties rather than as the rawest of raw materials crying to be processed into the texture of logic. It requires a very unusual mind, Whitehead said, to undertake the analysis of a fact. The computer can provide a correct number, but it may be an irrelevant number until judgment is pronounced.

[⁵] To the extent, then, that man fails to make the distinction between the intermediate operations of electronic intelligence and the ultimate responsibilities of human decision and conscience, the computer could prove a digression. It could obscure man's awareness of the need to come to terms with himself. It may foster the illusion that he is asking fundamental questions when actually he is asking only functional ones. It may be regarded as a substitute for intelligence instead of an extension of it. It may promote undue confidence in concrete answers. "If we begin with certainties," Bacon said, "we shall end in doubts; but if we begin with doubts, and we are patient with them, we shall end in certainties."

[⁶] The computer knows how to vanquish error, but before we lose ourselves in celebration of the victory, we might reflect on the great advances in the human situation that have come about because men were challenged by error and would not stop thinking and probing until they found better approaches for dealing with it. "Give me a good fruitful error, full of seeds, bursting with its own corrections," Ferris Greenslet wrote. "You can keep your sterile truth for yourself."

[⁷] The biggest single need in computer technology is not for improved circuitry, or enlarged capacity, or prolonged memory, or miniaturized containers, but for better questions and better use of the answers. Without taking anything away from the technicians, we think it might be fruitful to effect some sort of junction between the computer technologist and the poet. A genuine purpose may be served by turning loose the wonders of the creative imagination on the kinds of problems being put to electronic tubes and transistors. The company of poets may enable the men who tend the machines to see a larger panorama of possibilities than technology alone may inspire.

[⁸] A poet, said Aristotle, has the advantage of expressing the universal; the specialist expresses only the particular. The poet, moreover, can remind us that man's greatest energy comes not from his dynamos but from his dreams. The notion of where a man ought to be instead of where he is; the liberation from cramped prospects; the intimations of immortality through art—all these proceed naturally out of dreams. But the quality of a man's dreams can only be a reflection of his subconscious. What he puts into his subconscious, therefore, is quite literally the most important nourishment in the world.

[⁹] Nothing really happens to a man except as it is registered in the subconscious. This is where event and feeling become memory and where the proof of life is stored. The poet—and we use the term to include all those who have respect for and speak to the human spirit—can help to supply the subconscious with material to enhance its sensitivity, thus safeguarding it. The poet, too, can help to keep man from making himself over in the image of his electronic marvels. For the danger is not so much that man will be controlled by the computer as that he may imitate it.

[¹⁰] The poet reminds men of their uniqueness. It is not necessary to possess the ultimate definition of this uniqueness. Even to speculate on it is a gain.

COMMENT AND QUESTIONS

1. Parallel structures and sentences built on patterns of contrast are marked traits of style in this well-written essay. Point out examples that seem to you effective.

2. The first two paragraphs are concerned with human problems and needs that the author says are important. What are his reasons for believing that the computer may make it harder rather than easier for men to solve their problems and fulfill their needs? To what extent do you agree, first with Cousins' statement of values, and second with his ideas about computer technology as a possible hindrance to realizing the values?

3. In paragraph 5 Cousins speaks of man's illusion "that he is asking fundamental questions when actually he is asking only functional ones"; and in paragraph 7 the author says that we need "better questions and better use of the answers." What examples can you give to illustrate the difference between functional and fundamental questions? Does it seem to you possible for a computer to answer fundamental questions? Explain.

4. Do you think that Cousins is suggesting that the poet compose the questions given to the computer, or is his meaning different? Explain.

5. What is the meaning of the statement at the end of paragraph 9 concerning the danger of man imitating the computer? If man were to imitate the computer, what might be his attitudes toward himself and toward other men?

6. Cousins says in his last paragraph that it is not necessary to have "the ultimate definition" of man's uniqueness. What are some of the qualities of this uniqueness that he apparently sees and values?

7. What other writers whom you have read in this section, "Science and the Modern World," would agree wholly or in part with Cousins' ideas?

[70] *Walter Sullivan*: What If We Succeed?

W A L T E R S U L L I V A N (1918–   ) is Science Editor of the *New York Times* and author of *White Land of Adventure, Quest for a Continent,* and *Assault on the Unknown.* The following selection is the last chapter of *We Are Not Alone: The Search for Intelligent Life on Other Worlds,* published in 1964. In preceding chapters, Sullivan has explored the history of man's attempts to communicate with other worlds and the reasons for the belief of many scientists that intelligent life exists on other planets.

[1] On the night of October 30, 1938, there were manifestions of panic in widely scattered parts of the United States. They began shortly after Orson Welles, the actor and producer, sat in front of a microphone in the New York studios of the Columbia Broadcasting System to introduce an adaptation of *The War of the Worlds,* written in 1898 by H. G. Wells. Orson Welles told his nationwide audience how, in recent years, people on earth had gone about their daily lives in complacence: "Yet across an immense ethereal gulf, minds that are to our minds as ours are to the beasts in the jungle, intellects vast, cool and unsympathetic regarded this earth with envious eyes and slowly and surely drew their plans against us. . . ."

[2] The dramatization that followed, consisting of simulated news bulletins, interviews and sometimes fearful sound effects, was so realistic that thousands believed Martians had, in fact, landed in New Jersey— hideous creatures that slew all opposing them with a sinister "heat-ray." People rushed into the streets only partially clothed or struck out aimlessly across open country. Cars raced wildly through crowded cities.

[3] Is this a hint of what might happen if we did, in fact, make contact with a superior civilization? Possibly so, according to a report submitted to the Federal government in 1960. For so dramatic an effect, the encounter would presumably have to be physical, but even radio contact would lead to profound upheavals, the report said. The document was a by-product of the historic action taken by Congress on the heels of the first Sputniks in establishing an agency for the exploration of space. The National Aeronautics and Space Act of July 29, 1958, called for "long-range studies" of the benefits and problems to be expected from space activities. Pursuant to this act, NASA set up a Committee on Long-Range Studies and awarded a study contract to the Brookings Institution. More

than 200 specialists were interviewed by a team led by Donald N. Michael, a social psychologist who later became Director of the Peace Research Institute in Washington. Pertinent portions of the resulting report were reviewed by such figures as Lloyd V. Berkner, head of the Space Science Board, Caryl P. Haskins, President of the Carnegie Institution of Washington, James R. Killian, Chairman of the Corporation of M.I.T., Oscar Schachter, Director of the General Legal Division of the United Nations, and Margaret Mead, the anthropologist.

[4] The document was submitted to NASA only a few months after Project Ozma's attempt to intercept signals from two nearby stars, and much in the minds of those who drafted it was the question of what would happen if we discovered another, far more advanced civilization. The report did not rule out the possibility of direct contact, such as the one so vividly dramatized by Orson Welles, and it suggested that artifacts left by explorers from another world "might possibly be discovered through our space activities on the Moon, Mars, or Venus." Nevertheless, it said, if intelligent life is discovered beyond the earth during the next twenty years, it most probably will be in a distant solar system and manifest itself by radio. Such circumstances, it added, would not necessarily rule out revolutionary effects:

Anthropological files [the report said] contain many examples of societies, sure of their place in the universe, which have disintegrated when they have had to associate with previously unfamiliar societies espousing different ideas and different life ways; others that survived such an experience usually did so by paying the price of changes in values and attitudes and behavior.

Since intelligent life might be discovered at any time via the radio telescope research presently under way, and since the consequences of such a discovery are presently unpredictable because of our limited knowledge of behavior under even an approximation of such dramatic circumstances, two research areas can be recommended:

1. Continuing studies to determine emotional and intellectual understanding and attitudes—and successive alterations of them if any—regarding the possibility and consequences of discovering intelligent extraterrestrial life.

2. Historical and empirical studies of the behavior of peoples and their leaders when confronted with dramatic and unfamiliar events or social pressures. . . .

[5] Such studies, the report continued, should consider public reactions to past hoaxes, "flying saucer" episodes and incidents like the Martian invasion broadcast. They should explore how to release the news of an encounter to the public—or withhold it, if this is deemed advisable. The influence on international relations might be revolutionary, the report concluded, for the discovery of alien beings "might lead to a greater unity of men on earth, based on the 'oneness' of man or on the age-old assumption that any stranger is threatening."

[6] Much would depend, of course, on the nature of the contact and the content of any message received. Man is so completely accustomed to regarding himself as supreme that to discover he is no more an intellectual match for beings elsewhere than our dogs are for us would be a shattering revelation. Carl Gustav Jung, the disciple of Freud who later went his own psychological way, has said of a direct confrontation with such creatures: The "reins would be torn from our hands and we would, as a tearful old medicine man once said to me, find ourselves 'without dreams,' that is, we would find our intellectual and spiritual aspirations so outmoded as to leave us completely paralyzed."

[7] There has been some debate recently in scientific circles as to whether our new acquaintances would, in fact, be "nice people" or the monstrous villains depicted by Orson Welles. Much of the population has been conditioned by science-fiction tales of evil genius at work among the stars, of death rays and battles between galaxies. This may, in part, have accounted for the reaction to the Welles broadcast. Some of those concerned with the search for life in other worlds have sought to counter this attitude.

[8] Thus Philip Morrison, in one of his lectures, questioned whether any civilization with a superior technology would wish to do harm to one that has just entered the community of intelligence. If he were looking through a microscope, he said, and saw a group of bacteria spell out, like a college band, "Please do not put iodine on this plate. We want to talk to you," his first inclination, he said, would certainly not be to rush the bacteria into a sterilizer. He doubted that advanced societies "crush out any competitive form of intelligence, especially when there is clearly no danger."

[9] Ronald Bracewell, in his lecture at the University of Sydney, asked whether beings in another world could covet our gold or other rare substances. Do they want us as cattle or as slaves? He replied by pointing out the literally astronomical cost of transport between solar systems. Any civilization able to cover interstellar distances would hardly need us for food or raw material, which they could far more easily synthesize at home. "The most interesting item to be transferred from star to star," he said, "is information, and this can be done by radio."

[10] Edward Purcell, who forcefully argued the impracticality of travel between solar systems, said the relations between such widely separated civilizations must be "utterly benign." Maybe journeys over such distances could be made "by magic," he added, "but you can't get there by physics."

[11] Arthur C. Clarke, one of the most knowledgeable of all science-fiction writers, has pointed out the difficulty of administering a galactic empire, be it benign or tyrannical, because the distances would make

communications so very slow. Radio messages to our nearest neighbors would take a decade or more.

[12] Nevertheless there has been at least one dissent in the scientific community and its author, as might be expected, is among those who refuse to dismiss the possibility of travel between solar systems, particularly if one does not insist that the trip be completed within a human lifetime. The dissenter was Freeman Dyson, the brilliant young physicist at the Institute for Advanced Study in Princeton. In a letter to *Scientific American* in the spring of 1964 he questioned whether one was justified in assuming that the distant creatures with whom we may converse are moral by our standards.

[13] "Intelligence may indeed be a benign influence," he said, "creating isolated groups of philosopher-kings far apart in the heavens and enabling them to share at leisure their accumulated wisdom." On the other hand, he added, "intelligence may be a cancer of purposeless technological exploitation, sweeping across a galaxy as irresistibly as it has swept across our own planet." Assuming interstellar travel at moderate speeds, he said, "the technological cancer could spread over a whole galaxy in a few million years, a time very short compared with the life of a planet."

[14] What our detectors will pick up is a technological civilization, he argued, but it will not necessarily be intelligent, in the pure sense of the word. In fact, he continued, it may even be that the society we are inherently likely to detect is more probably "a technology run wild, insane or cancerously spreading than a technology firmly under control and supporting the rational needs of a superior intelligence." It is possible that a "truly intelligent" society might no longer feel the need of, or be interested in, technology. "Our business as scientists is to search the universe and find out what is there. What is there may conform to our moral sense or it may not. . . . It is just as unscientific to impute to remote intelligences wisdom and serenity as it is to impute to them irrational and murderous impulses. We must be prepared for either possibility and conduct our searches accordingly."

[15] This point of view is reflected in the questions of those who ask: Should we reply, if we hear someone calling? Since message travel times are long, a hasty reply would be uncalled for, but it seems to this writer hard to believe that we would hear from a race of villains or a civilization run amok. As noted in the chapter entitled "Is There Intelligent Life on Earth?" an achievement of lasting peace and stability seems to be an important element in qualifying for membership in the interstellar community. While Dyson is understandably dismayed at what technology and population growth are doing to the face of our planet, a society that could not bring such trends under control would probably suffer the disintegration envisioned by Fred Hoyle.

[16] In fact, the achievement of great stability and serenity would seem a prerequisite for a society willing to make the expensive and enormously prolonged effort required to contact another world.

[17] What, indeed, do we know about the roots of evil—of greed, aggressiveness and treachery? On earth they are clearly manifestations of a complex society that has not reached stability. Animals, as a rule, are aggressive only when necessary. The well-fed lion lies near the waterhole while his traditional victims, sensing his satiety, quench their thirst in peace. Man's inherent aggressiveness has made wars possible—though it does not necessarily initiate wars—but it would appear that if man is to survive, this aspect of his personality will have to be controlled—an achievement that in the past few years has seemed increasingly possible.

[18] Because we have information on only one form of intelligent, technological life we tend to think of such life elsewhere as resembling ourselves more closely than is probably justified. The creatures in which we are interested, besides having minds, must be able to move about and to build things. That is, they must have something comparable to hands and feet. They must have senses, such as sight, touch and hearing, although the senses that evolve on any given planet will be determined by the environment. For example, it may be that, for various reasons, vision in the infrared part of the spectrum will be more useful than sight in the wavelengths visible to human eyes. Creatures fulfilling such requirements might bear little resemblance to man. As Philip Morrison has put it, they may be "blue spheres with twelve tentacles." They may be as big as a mountain or as small as a mouse, although the amount of food available would set a limit on largeness and the fixed sizes of molecules must limit the extent to which the size of a complex brain can be compressed. Life spans in some worlds might be extremely great. The cells of our bodies (with a few exceptions, such as brain cells) are constantly replenishing themselves. It would appear that, barring accident or disease, this should continue indefinitely, but because of some subtle influence the replacement process is imperfect. This, the essence of aging, is now under intensive study. It is not inconceivable that it can be controlled. Progress in the transplantation of human organs and the manufacture of other body components (such as heart valves) is such that even the most sober medical men believe we may ultimately be able to extend lifetimes considerably. Lives measured in many centuries instead of barely one would make the slowness of interstellar signaling far more acceptable. Yet even life spans comparable to our own of today should not divert our interest in message exchanges. "Imagine," says Edward Purcell of Harvard, "that a reply to one of your messages was scheduled to be received forty years from now. What a legacy for your grandchildren."

[19] Otto Struve and others have said that the current awakening of mankind to the possible existence of intelligent life in other worlds is as

much a challenge to established ways of thought as was the Copernican revolution that displaced the earth from the center of the universe. The latter set in motion a religious and philosophical upheaval that only in recent decades has run its course. It will be recalled that Giordano Bruno, the Copernican protagonist, was burned at the stake and Martin Luther argued that, since Joshua, in the Bible, commanded the sun—not the earth—to stand still, the system of Copernicus must be false.

[20] By the mid-nineteenth century great changes had taken place. Father Angelo Secchi, the great Jesuit astronomer, was helping to lay the foundations of modern astrophysics—and worrying about the religious implications of the vast universe opening before him. Could it be, he asked, that God populated only one tiny speck in this cosmos with spiritual beings: ". . . It would seem absurd to find nothing but uninhabited deserts in these limitless regions," he wrote. "No! These worlds are bound to be populated by creatures capable of recognizing, honoring and loving their Creator."

[21] Both Protestant and Catholic theologians pursued this subject during the early decades of the twentieth century, many of them viewing it in terms of man's spiritual history as set forth in their dogma. It was proposed by Catholic authorities that beings in other worlds could be in a variety of "states."

[22] For example, they might be in a state of grace, such as that enjoyed by Adam and Eve before they succumbed to the serpent's temptation. They might be in the fallen state of mankind after the expulsion from Eden. They might have undergone these stages and been redeemed by some action of God. They might be in a "state of integral nature," midway between man and angel and immune to death; or they might have proved so evil that redemption was denied them. C. S. Lewis, the Anglican lay theologian, has proposed that the vast distances between solar systems may be a form of divine quarantine: "They prevent the spiritual infection of a fallen species from spreading"; they block it from playing the role of the serpent in the Garden of Eden. Father Daniel C. Raible of Brunnendale Seminary of the Society of the Precious Blood in Canton, Ohio, said in the Catholic weekly *America* that intelligent beings elsewhere "could be as different from us, physically, as an elephant is from a gnat." To be "human" in the theological sense they need only be "composites of spirit and matter." As God could create billions of galaxies, he reasoned, "so He could create billions of human races each unique in itself." To redeem such races, he said, God could take on any bodily form. "There is nothing at all repugnant in the idea of the same Divine Person taking on the nature of many human races. Conceivably, we may learn in heaven that there has been not one incarnation of God's son but many."

[23] The idea of God incarnate in some strange, if not grotesque, creature is to some Catholics unacceptable. Such a point of view was expressed

by Joseph A. Breig, a Catholic journalist, in a dialogue published in a 1960 issue of *America*. There can have been only one incarnation, one mother of God, one race "into which God has poured His image and likeness," he said.

[24] In reply Father L. C. McHugh, an associate editor of the magazine, wrote: "Does it not seem strange to say that His power, immensity, beauty and eternity are displayed with lavish generosity through unimaginable reaches of space and time, but that the knowledge and love which alone give meaning to all this splendor are confined to this tiny globe where self-conscious life began to flourish a few millennia ago?"

[25] Like the Catholics, the Protestants have been concerned with whether or not God could have taken on bodily form elsewhere. Paul Tillich, one of the foremost Protestant theologians, argues that there is no real reason why such incarnations could not have taken place: "Incarnation is unique for the special group in which it happens, but it is not unique in the sense that other singular incarnations for other unique worlds are excluded. . . . Man cannot claim to occupy the only possible place for Incarnation. . . . The manifestation of saving power in one place implies that saving power is operating in all places."

[26] Astronomy tells us that new worlds are constantly evolving and old ones are becoming uninhabitable. The lifetime of our own world is thus limited, he said, but this "leaves open other ways of divine self-manifestation before and after our historical continuum." Elsewhere he wrote, with characteristic boldness: "Our ignorance and our prejudice should not inhibit our thoughts from transcending our earth and our history and even our Christianity."

[27] The hint of Tillich that, though worlds come and go, spiritual life somewhere in the universe goes on forever has been carried further by John Macquarrie of the University of Glasgow, in lectures that he gave in 1957 at Union Theological Seminary in New York. He took his cue from the "steady state" theory proposed by Fred Hoyle, Hermann Bondi and Thomas Gold in which, although the universe is constantly expanding, there is continuous creation of new matter to fill the resulting voids. "It might well be the case," he said, "that the universe has produced and will continue to produce countless millions of . . . histories analogous to human history." The creation would be cyclical, in that it produces "the same kind of thing over and again in endless variations.

[28] "To attempt to draw ultimate conclusions about God and the universe from a few episodes of the history which has been enacted on this planet," he continued, "would seem to be a most hazardous if not impossible proceeding."

[29] Long before Project Ozma the British mathematician and physicist Edward A. Milne proposed that only one incarnation—that of Jesus—was necessary, because, when news of it reached other worlds via radio, they

too would be saved. This was challenged by E. L. Mascall, University Lecturer in the Philosophy of Religion at Oxford, who said redemption was, in effect, not exportable. Like a number of other theologians who have taken part in this dialogue, he cited the argument of Saint Thomas Aquinas in the thirteenth century that the Incarnation could have taken one of several forms: instead of God the Son appearing on earth, he said, it might have been God the Father or God the Holy Ghost. He reasoned that none of these alternatives was ruled out on theological grounds. If so, today's scholars argue, why could there not also be incarnations elsewhere?

[30] At the conclusion of this analysis, Mascall was almost apologetic for discussing such hypothetical problems: "Theological principles tend to become torpid for lack of exercise," he said, "and there is much to be said for giving them now and then a scamper in a field where the paths are few and the boundaries undefined; they do their day-to-day work all the better for an occasional outing in the country."

[31] Actually, such "outings" have been taken by churchmen as sober as William Ralph Inge, Dean of St. Paul's Cathedral in London and known as "the gloomy dean" for his criticism of modern life. Like Father Secchi, he considered it intolerably presumptuous to believe that spiritual life exists only on this one planet. In a series of lectures given at Lincoln's Inn Chapel in 1931–33 he discussed Plato's concept of a "Universal Soul," and its parallels with Christian views on the Holy Spirit. This, he said,

raises the question whether there is soul-life in all parts of the universe. I do not think we need follow Fechner in believing that every heavenly body has a soul of its own. [Gustav Theodor Fechner, the German experimental psychologist, preached a highly animistic philosophy.] But I would rather be a star-worshipper that believe with Hegel (if he was not merely speaking impatiently, which is likely enough) that the starry heavens have no more significance than a rash on the sky, or a swarm of flies. There may be, and no doubt are, an immense number of souls in the universe, and some of them may be nearer to the divine mind than we are.

[32] It is, perhaps, a sign of the times and of the convergence of Catholicism and Protestantism that theologians of both faiths have been moved by the discussion of the Incarnation in a poem, "Christ in the Universe," by the English turn-of-the-century poetess Alice Meynell:

> . . . No planet knows that this
> Our wayside planet, carrying land and wave,
> Love and life multiplied, and pain and bliss,
> Bears, as chief treasure, one forsaken grave. . . .
>
> But, in the eternities,
> Doubtless we shall compare together, hear
> A million alien Gospels, in what guise
> He trod the Pleiades, the Lyre, the Bear.

> O, be prepared, my soul!
> To read the inconceivable, to scan
> The million forms of God those stars unroll
> When, in our turn, we show them a Man.

[33] There are some faiths that have long preached the existence of many worlds, and so for them the shock of discovery would be lessened. Notable among these are the Buddhists and Mormons. The doctrine of the latter, the Church of Jesus Christ of Latter-Day Saints, is set forth in a series of revelations including one entitled the "Visions of Moses, as revealed to Joseph Smith the Prophet, in June, 1830." This tells how Moses "beheld many lands; and each land was called earth, and there were inhabitants on the face thereof." God told Moses:

And worlds without number have I created. . . . But only an account of this earth, and the inhabitants thereof, give I unto you. For behold, there are many worlds that have passed away by the word of my power. And there are many that now stand, and innumerable are they unto man; but all things are numbered unto me, for they are mine and I know them. . . . And as one earth shall pass away, and the heavens thereof even so shall another come; and there is no end to my works, neither to my words.

[34] This is strikingly similar to the "steady state" concept advanced by such men as Tillich and Macquarrie.

[35] The holy books of Buddhism, in their own glittering way, speak of many worlds. Such a book is the *Saddharma-Pundarika* or *Lotus of the True Law*. The Lord appears before an assembly of Bodhisattvas, or wise men, gathered from countless worlds and numbering eight times the grains of sand in the river Ganges. He tells them of many worlds, of golden people, jeweled trees, perfumed winds, wafting showers of petals. To illustrate the great number of worlds, he says:

Let there be the atoms of earth of fifty hundred thousand myriads of kotis of worlds; let there exist some man who takes one of those atoms of dust and then goes in an eastern direction fifty hundred thousand myriads of kotis of worlds further on, there to deposit that atom of dust; let in this manner the man carry away from all those worlds the whole mass of earth, and in the same manner, and by the same act as supposed, deposit all those atoms in an eastern direction. Now, would you think, young men of good family, that any one should be able to imagine, weigh, count, or determine [the number of] those worlds?

[36] While the Hindus believe in the transmigration of souls into other bodies or spiritual states, their various cosmologies do not envisage other inhabited worlds. As for the Confucians, their attention has been centered on earthly matters, in particular the behavior of man, even though some early Chinese scholars spoke of other earths with their own heavens shining upon them.

[37] About a dozen centuries ago Jewish thinkers conceived of the cosmos in somewhat of a steady-state manner. This is reflected in one of the commentaries on the Bible, prepared long ago by scholarly Rabbis and entitled the *Midrash Rabba*. It states that, "The Holy One, blessed be he, builds worlds and destroys them." However, according to contemporary Jewish theologians there has not been much speculation on the religious implications of extraterrestrial life.

[38] While the Brookings report to NASA dwells on the stresses and strains that would follow our making contact with another planet, it is staggering to consider the potential gains. Life in another world would presumably be at a far more advanced stage of evolution—technological, biological and medical—than ours. Knowledge of such a civilization, its discoveries, its techniques might enable us to leap-frog thousands or even millions of years ahead along the path before us. The agonies of premature death, congenital deformity, insanity, as well as such diseases of our society as prejudice, hatred and war, might be eliminated long before otherwise possible. No matter how much another world differed from our own in superficial ways, we might learn from its history enough to understand better our own: what, for example, brought about the great revolutions in the development of life on earth, the extinction of the giant reptiles, the emergence of the mammals and finally of man.

[39] Alastair Cameron, the astrophysicist, in the introduction to his anthology on interstellar communication, describes the possibility of life in other worlds as "currently the greatest question in scientific philosophy." Already, he says, we are admitting "that there may be millions of societies more advanced than ourselves in our galaxy alone. If we can now take the next step and communicate with some of these societies, then we can expect to obtain an enormous enrichment of all phases of our sciences and arts. Perhaps we shall also receive valuable lessons in the techniques of stable world government."

[40] One question that has been raised by J. Robert Oppenheimer, the nuclear physicist, is whether or not the science of another civilization would be comprehensible to us. He cites the "uncertainty principle" first recognized a generation ago, which says that we have a choice as to which traits of an atomic system we wish to study and measure, but in any single case we cannot measure them all. For example, in an experiment, we can determine the location of a particle but, if we do so, we cannot find out its speed. Similarly our science has concentrated on asking certain questions at the expense of others, although this is so woven into the fabric of our knowledge that we are generally unaware of it. In another world the basic questions may have been asked differently.

[41] Thus, while the period of Isaac Newton taught us that scientific truth in the most distant corner of the universe is identical to that in any laboratory on earth, yet in this century it has been shown that there are

various ways in which we can seek this truth, and science in one world may be seeking it by means different from those in another. This would make it more difficult to understand the work of our distant neighbors, but it seems unlikely that such understanding would be impossible.

[42] Most exciting of all the prospects are the spiritual and philosophical enrichment to be gained from such exchanges. Our world is undergoing revolutionary changes. Our ancestors enjoyed a serenity denied to most of us. As we devastate our planet with industrialization, with highways, housing and haste, the restoration of the soul that comes from contemplating nature unmarred by human activity becomes more and more inaccessible. Furthermore, through our material achievements, we are threatened by what the French call "embourgeoisement"—domination of the world by bourgeois mediocrity, conformity and comfort-seeking.

[43] The world desperately needs a global adventure to rekindle the flame that burned so intently during the Renaissance, when new worlds were being discovered on our own planet and in the realms of science. Within a generation or less we will vicariously tread the moon and Mars, but the possibility of ultimately "seeing" worlds in other solar systems, however remote, is an awesome prospect. "The soul of man was made to walk the skies," the English poet Edward Young wrote in the eighteenth century:

> how great,
> How glorious, then, appears the mind of man,
> When in it all the stars and planets roll!
> And what it seems, it is. Great objects make
> Great minds, enlarging as their views enlarge;
> Those still more godlike, as these more divine.

[44] The realization that life is probably universal, however thinly scattered through the universe, has meaning for all who contemplate the cosmos and the mortality of man. George Wald, Professor of Biochemistry at Harvard and a long-time participant in the search for an understanding of life's origins, has said:

Life has a status in the physical universe. It is part of the order of nature. It has a high place in that order, since it probably represents the most complex state of organization that matter has achieved in our universe. We on this planet have an especially proud place as men; for in us as men matter has begun to contemplate itself. . . .

[45] Harlow Shapley, the astronomer, has likewise found spiritual wealth in the new discoveries. They have contributed, he said, "to the unfolding of a magnificent universe":

To be a participant is in itself a glory. With our confreres on distant planets; with our fellow animals and plants of land, air, and sea; with the rocks and waters of all planetary crusts, and the photons and atoms that make up the stars —with all these we are associated in an existence and an evolution that inspires respect and deep reverence. We cannot escape humility. And as groping philosophers and scientists we are thankful for the mysteries that still lie beyond our grasp.

[46] The universality of life also has meaning with regard to the mortality, not only of individuals on earth, but of our planet itself. Bertrand Russell has pointed out that "all the labours of the ages, all the devotion, all the inspirations, all the noonday brightness of human genius, are destined to extinction in the vast death of the solar system." Yet it seems that life, in a sense, may be eternal. Perhaps true wisdom is a torch—one that we have not yet received, but that can be handed to us by a civilization late in its life and passed on by our own world as its time of extinction draws near. Thus, as our children and grandchildren offer some continuity to our personal lives, so our communion with cosmic manifestations of life would join us with a far more magnificent form of continuity.

[47] The Spanish-American philosopher George Santayana, in his preface to a volume of Spinoza's works, discussed a form of immortality enjoyed by those who commune with the eternal: "He who, while he lives, lives in the eternal, does not live longer for that reason. Duration has merely dropped from his view; he is not aware of or anxious about it; and death, without losing its reality, has lost its sting. The sublimation of his interest rescues him, so far as it goes, from the mortality which he accepts and surveys."

[48] The universe that lies about us, visible only in the privacy, the intimacy of night, is incomprehensibly vast. Yet the conclusion that life exists across this vastness seems inescapable. We cannot yet be sure whether or not it lies within reach, but in any case we are a part of it all; we are not alone!

COMMENT AND QUESTIONS

1. This selection has a question-to-answer and cause–effect pattern: If we succeed in discovering intelligent extraterrestrial life, the author is asking, what will be the effects? What is the purpose of beginning the discussion with the account of Orson Welles' 1938 broadcast?
2. The author is informative and fair in presenting conflicting points of view and also skillful in emphasizing his own views. Examine the opinions presented in paragraphs 8–17 on the question of whether beings in another world would be "nice people" or villains. What is the logical and psychological order of presentation?

3. What is the function of paragraph 18—the speculations about what other forms of life might be like—in the development of the essay?
4. What are the principal religious and philosophical problems which arise from the possible existence of intelligent life in other worlds (paragraphs 19–32)? Does Sullivan appear, by selection and emphasis, to be slanting in favor of one theory or attitude?
5. Why are Catholic and Protestant theologians more concerned than members of other faiths about the religious implications of extraterrestrial life?
6. The last section of Sullivan's book (paragraphs 38–48) is devoted to the potential gains of our making contact with other planets. What kinds of gains does he foresee?
7. What is the purpose of including the question raised by Oppenheimer (paragraphs 40–41), and what is the reason for placing it here instead of in paragraph 38 or near the end of the selection?
8. What criticisms of society in our world does Sullivan make in the course of the selection? How are they related to his central idea of the possibilities inherent in communication with other worlds?

MEN AND EVENTS

##

[71]   The Imprisonment and Death of Socrates

ON THE DAY before the trial of Socrates (see the *Apology*, page 105), a sacred ship was sent on an annual mission to the shrine of Apollo at Delos; until the return of the ship, Athens observed a season of ritual purity during which no executions were allowed. Some weeks elapsed, therefore, between the trial and the death of Socrates. Although he was imprisoned, he had daily visits from his friends, and his friends had time to plan his escape. In the dialogue *Crito,* Socrates explains to his old friend Crito his reasons for refusing to escape. The action of the *Phaedo* takes place on the last day of Socrates' life. The narrator, Phaedo, describes to a friend not present that day Socrates' discussion of the soul's divinity and the importance of tending and improving the soul during life; the last section of the dialogue, which we are printing here, describes the death of Socrates. (For notes on Plato, see pages 105, 107, and 190.)

Plato: Crito

Socrates. Why have you come at this hour, Crito? it must be quite early?

Crito. Yes, certainly.

Soc. What is the exact time?

Cr. The dawn is breaking.

Both selections were translated by Benjamin Jowett. (We have arbitrarily inserted paragraph numbers here and there in the first dialogue to facilitate references to particular passages.)

Soc. I wonder that the keeper of the prison would let you in.

Cr. He knows me, because I often come, Socrates; moreover, I have done him a kindness.

Soc. And are you only just arrived?

Cr. No, I came some time ago.

Soc. Then why did you sit and say nothing, instead of at once awakening me?

Cr. I should not have liked myself, Socrates, to be in such great trouble and unrest as you are—indeed I should not: I have been watching with amazement your peaceful slumbers; and for that reason I did not awake you, because I wished to minimize the pain. I have always thought you to be of a happy disposition; but never did I see anything like the easy, tranquil manner in which you bear this calamity.

Soc. Why, Crito, when a man has reached my age he ought not to be repining at the approach of death.

Cr. And yet other old men find themselves in similar misfortunes, and age does not prevent them from repining.

Soc. That is true. But you have not told me why you come at this early hour.

Cr. I come to bring you a message which is sad and painful; not, as I believe, to yourself, but to all of us who are your friends, and saddest of all to me.

Soc. What? Has the ship come from Delos, on the arrival of which I am to die?

Cr. No, the ship has not actually arrived, but she will probably be here to-day, as persons who have come from Sunium tell me that they left her there; and therefore tomorrow, Socrates, will be the last day of your life.

Soc. Very well, Crito; if such is the will of God, I am willing; but my belief is that there will be a delay of a day.

Cr. Why do you think so?

Soc. I will tell you. I am to die on the day after the arrival of the ship.

Cr. Yes; that is what the authorities say.

Soc. But I do not think that the ship will be here until to-morrow; this I infer from a vision which I had last night, or rather only just now, when you fortunately allowed me to sleep.

Cr. And what was the nature of the vision?

Soc. There appeared to me the likeness of a woman, fair and comely, clothed in bright raiment, who called to me and said: O Socrates,

"The third day hence to fertile Phthia shalt thou go."[1]

Cr. What a singular dream, Socrates!

Soc. There can be no doubt about the meaning, Crito, I think.

[1] Homer, Il. ix. 363.

[¹] *Cr.* Yes; the meaning is only too clear. But, oh! my beloved Socrates, let me entreat you once more to take my advice and escape. For if you die I shall not only lose a friend who can never be replaced, but there is another evil: people who do not know you and me will believe that I might have saved you if I had been willing to give money, but that I did not care. Now, can there be a worse disgrace than this—that I should be thought to value money more than the life of a friend? For the many will not be persuaded that I wanted you to escape, and that you refused.

Soc. But why, my dear Crito, should we care about the opinion of the many? Good men, and they are the only persons who are worth considering, will think of these things truly as they occurred.

Cr. But you see, Socrates, that the opinion of the many must be regarded, for what is now happening shows that they can do the greatest evil to any one who has lost their good opinion.

Soc. I only wish it were so, Crito; and that the many could do the greatest evil; for then they would also be able to do the greatest good— and what a fine thing this would be! But in reality they can do neither; for they cannot make a man either wise or foolish; and whatever they do is the result of chance.

[²] *Cr.* Well, I will not dispute with you; but please to tell me, Socrates, whether you are not acting out of regard to me and your other friends: are you not afraid that if you escape from prison we may get into trouble with the informers for having stolen you away, and lose either the whole or a great part of our property; or that even a worse evil may happen to us? Now, if you fear on our account, be at ease; for in order to save you, we ought surely to run this, or even a greater risk; be persuaded, then, and do as I say.

Soc. Yes, Crito, that is one fear which you mention, but by no means the only one.

[³] *Cr.* Fear not—there are persons who are willing to get you out of prison at no great cost; and as for the informers, they are far from being exorbitant in their demands—a little money will satisfy them. My means, which are certainly ample, are at your service, and if you have a scruple about spending all mine, here are strangers who will give you the use of theirs; and one of them, Simmias the Theban, has brought a large sum of money for this very purpose; and Cebes and many others are prepared to spend their money in helping you to escape. I say, therefore, do not hesitate on our account, and do not say, as you did in the court, that you will have a difficulty in knowing what to do with yourself anywhere else. For men will love you in other places to which you may go, and not in Athens only; there are friends of mine in Thessaly, if you like to go to them, who will value and protect you, and no Thessalian will give you any trouble. Nor can I think that you are at all justified, Socrates, in betraying your own life when you might be saved; in acting thus you are playing into the hands of your enemies, who are hurrying on your destruction. And further I should say that you are deserting your own children; for you might bring them up and educate them; instead of which you go away and leave them, and they will have to take their chance; and if they do not meet with the usual fate of orphans, there will be small thanks to you. No man should bring children into the world who is unwilling to persevere to the end in their nurture and education. But you appear to be choosing the easier part, not the better and manlier, which would have been more becoming in one who professes to care for virtue in all his actions, like yourself. And, indeed, I am ashamed not only of you, but of us who are your friends, when I reflect that the whole business will be attributed entirely to our want of courage. The trial need never have come on, or might have been managed differently; and this last act, or crowning folly, will seem to have occurred through our negligence and cowardice, who might have saved you, if we had been good for anything; and you might have saved yourself, for there was no difficulty at all. See now, Socrates, how sad and discreditable are the consequences, both to us and you. Make up your mind, then, or rather have your mind already made up, for the time of deliberation is over, and there is only one thing to be done, which must be done this very night, and if we delay at all will be no longer practicable or possible; I beseech you therefore, Socrates, be persuaded by me, and do as I say.

[⁴] *Soc.* Dear Crito, your zeal is invaluable, if a right one; but if wrong, the greater the zeal the greater the danger; and therefore we ought to consider whether I shall or shall not do as you say. For I am and always have been one of those natures who must be guided by reason, whatever the reason may be which upon reflection appears to me to be the best; and now that this chance has befallen me, I cannot repudiate my own words: the principles which I have hitherto honoured and revered I still honour, and unless we can at once find other and better principles, I am certain not to agree with you; no, not even if the power of the multitude could inflict many more imprisonments, confiscations, deaths, frightening us like children with hobgoblin terrors. What will be the fairest way of considering the question? Shall I return to our old argument about the opinions of men?—we were saying that some of them are to be regarded, and others, not. Now, were we right in maintaining this before I was condemned? And has the argument which was once good now proved to be talk for the sake of talking—mere childish nonsense? That is what I want to consider with your help, Crito:—whether, under my present circumstances, the argument appears to be in any way different or not; and is to be allowed by me or disallowed. That argument, which, as I believe, is maintained by many persons of authority, was to the effect, as I was saying, that the opinions of some men are to be regarded, and of other men not to be regarded. Now you, Crito, are not going to die to-morrow—at least, there is no human probability of this—and therefore you are disinterested and not liable to be deceived by the circumstances in which you are placed. Tell me, then, whether I am right in saying that some opinions, and the opinions of some men only, are to be valued, and that other opinions, and the opinions of other men, are not to be valued. I ask you whether I was right in maintaining this?

Cr. Certainly.

Soc. The good are to be regarded, and not the bad?

Cr. Yes.

Soc. And the opinions of the wise are good, and the opinions of the unwise are evil?

Cr. Certainly.

Soc. And what was said about another matter? Is the pupil who devotes himself to the practice of gymnastic supposed to attend to the praise and blame and opinion of every man, or of one man only—his physician or trainer, whoever he may be?

Cr. Of one man only.

Soc. And he ought to fear the censure and welcome the praise of that one only, and not of the many?

Cr. Clearly so.

Soc. And he ought to act and train, and eat and drink in the way which seems good to his single master who has understanding, rather than according to the opinion of all other men put together?

Cr. True.

Soc. And if he disobeys and disregards the opinion and approval of the one, and regards the opinion of the many who have no understanding, will he not suffer evil?

Cr. Certainly he will.

Soc. And what will the evil be, whither tending and what affecting, in the disobedient person?

Cr. Clearly, affecting the body; that is what is destroyed by the evil.

Soc. Very good; and is not this true, Crito, of other things which we need not separately enumerate? In questions of just and unjust, fair and foul, good and evil, which are the subjects of our present consultation, ought we to follow the opinion of the many and to fear them; or the opinion of the one man who has understanding? ought we not to fear and reverence him more than all the rest of the world: and if we desert him shall we not destroy and injure that principle in us which may be assumed to be improved by justice and deteriorated by injustice;—there is such a principle?

Cr. Certainly there is, Socrates.

Soc. Take a parallel instance:—if, acting under the advice of those who have no understanding, we destroy that which is improved by health and is deteriorated by disease, would life be worth having? And that which has been destroyed is—the body?

Cr. Yes.

Soc. Could we live, having an evil and corrupted body?

Cr. Certainly not.

Soc. And will life be worth having, if that higher part of man be destroyed, which is improved by justice and depraved by injustice? Do we suppose that principle, whatever it may be in man, which has to do with justice and injustice, to be inferior to the body?

Cr. Certainly not.

Soc. More honourable than the body?

Cr. Far more.

Soc. Then, my friend, we must not regard what the many say of us: but what he, the one man who has understanding of just and unjust, will say, and what the truth will say. And therefore you begin in error when you advise that we should regard the opinion of the many about just and unjust, good and evil, honourable and dishonourable.—"Well," some one will say, "But the many can kill us."

Cr. Yes, Socrates; that will clearly be the answer.

[⁵] *Soc.* And it is true: but still I find with surprise that the old argument is unshaken as ever. And I should like to know whether I may say the same of another proposition—that not life, but a good life, is to be chiefly valued?

Cr. Yes, that also remains unshaken.

Soc. And a good life is equivalent to a just and honourable one—that holds also?

Cr. Yes, it does.

[⁶] *Soc.* From these premises I proceed to argue the question whether I ought or ought not to try to escape without the consent of the Athenians: and if I am clearly right in escaping, then I will make the attempt; but if not, I will abstain. The other considerations which you mention, of money and loss of character and the duty of educating one's children, are, I fear, only the doctrines of the multitude, who would be as ready to restore people to life, if they were able, as they are to put them to death —and with as little reason. But now, since the argument has thus far prevailed, the only question which remains to be considered is, whether we shall do rightly either in escaping or in suffering others to aid in our escape and paying them in money and thanks, or whether in reality we shall not do rightly; and if the latter, then death or any other calamity which may ensue on my remaining here must not be allowed to enter into the calculation.

Cr. I think that you are right, Socrates; how then shall we proceed?

Soc. Let us consider the matter together, and do you either refute me if you can, and I will be convinced; or else cease, my dear friend, from repeating to me that I ought to escape against the wishes of the Athenians: for I highly value your attempts to persuade me to do so, but I may not be persuaded against my own better judgment. And now please to consider my first position, and try how you can best answer me.

Cr. I will.

[7] *Soc.* Are we to say that we are never intentionally to do wrong, or that in one way we ought and in another way we ought not to do wrong, or is doing wrong always evil and dishonourable, as I was just now saying, and as has been already acknowledged by us? Are all our former admissions which were made within a few days to be thrown away? And have we, at our age, been earnestly discoursing with one another all our life long only to discover that we are no better than children? Or, in spite of the opinion of the many, and in spite of consequences whether better or worse, shall we insist on the truth of what was then said, that injustice is always an evil and dishonour to him who acts unjustly? Shall we say so or not?

Cr. Yes.

Soc. Then we must do no wrong?

Cr. Certainly not.

Soc. Nor when injured injure in return, as the many imagine; for we must injure no one at all?

Cr. Clearly not.

Soc. Again, Crito, may we do evil?

Cr. Surely not, Socrates.

Soc. And what of doing evil in return for evil, which is the morality of the many—is that just or not?

Cr. Not just.

Soc. For doing evil to another is the same as injuring him?

Cr. Very true.

[8] *Soc.* Then we ought not to retaliate or render evil for evil to any one, whatever evil we may have suffered from him. But I would have you consider, Crito, whether you really mean what you are saying. For this opinion has never been held, and never will be held, by any considerable number of persons; and those who are agreed and those who are not agreed upon this point have no common ground, and can only despise one another when they see how widely they differ. Tell me, then, whether you agree with and assent to my first principle, that neither injury nor retaliation nor warding off evil by evil is ever right. And shall that be the premise of our argument? Or do you decline and dissent from this? For so I have ever thought, and continue to think; but, if you are of another opinion, let me hear what you have to say. If, however, you remain of the same mind as formerly, I will proceed to the next step.

Cr. You may proceed, for I have not changed my mind.

[⁹] *Soc.* Then I will go on to the next point, which may be put in the form of a question:—Ought a man to do what he admits to be right, or ought he to betray the right?

Cr. He ought to do what he thinks right.

[¹⁰] *Soc.* But if this is true, what is the application? In leaving the prison against the will of the Athenians, do I wrong any? or rather do I not wrong those whom I ought least to wrong? Do I not desert the principles which were acknowledged by us to be just—what do you say?

Cr. I cannot tell, Socrates; for I do not know.

[¹¹] *Soc.* Then consider the matter in this way:—Imagine that I am about to play truant (you may call the proceeding by any name which you like), and the laws and the government come and interrogate me: "Tell us, Socrates," they say; "what are you about? are you not going by an act of yours to overturn us—the laws, and the whole state, as far as in you lies? Do you imagine that a state can subsist and not be overthrown, in which the decisions of law have no power, but are set aside and trampled upon by individuals?" What will be our answer, Crito, to these and the like words? Any one, and especially a rhetorician, will have a good deal to say on behalf of the law which requires a sentence to be carried out. He will argue that this law should not be set aside; and shall we reply, "Yes; but the state has injured us and given an unjust sentence." Suppose I say that?

Cr. Very good, Socrates.

[¹²] *Soc.* "And was that our agreement with you?" the laws would answer; "or were you to abide by the sentence of the state?" And if I were to express my astonishment at their words, the laws would probably add: "Answer, Socrates, instead of opening your eyes—you are in the habit of asking and answering questions. Tell us,—What complaint have you to make against us which justifies you in attempting to destroy us and the state? In the first place did we not bring you into existence? Your father married your mother by our aid and begat you. Say whether you have any objection to urge against those of us who regulate marriage?" None, I should reply. "Or against those of us who after birth regulate the nurture and education of children, in which you also were trained? Were not the laws, which have the charge of education, right in commanding your father to train you in music and gymnastic?" Right, I should reply. "Well, then, since you were brought into the world and nurtured and educated by us, can you deny in the first place that you are our child and slave, as your fathers were before you? And if this is true, you are not on equal terms with us; nor can you think that you have a right to do to us what we are doing to you. Would you have any right to strike or revile or do any other evil to your father or your master, if you had one, because you have been struck or reviled by him, or received some other evil at his hands?—you would not say this? And because we think right to destroy you, do you think that you have any right to destroy us in return, and your country as far as in you lies? Will you, O professor of true virtue, pretend that you are justified in this? Has a philosopher like you failed to discover that our country is more to be valued and higher and holier far than mother or father or any ancestor, and more to be regarded in the eyes of the gods and of men of understanding? also to be soothed, and gently and reverently entreated when angry, even more than a father, and either to be persuaded, or if not persuaded, to be obeyed? And when we are punished by her, whether with imprisonment or stripes, the punishment is to be endured in silence; and if she lead us to wounds or death in battle, thither we follow as is right; neither may any one yield or retreat or leave his rank, but whether in battle or in a court of law, or in any other place, he must do what his city and his country order him; or he must change their view of what is just: and if he may do no violence to his father or mother, much less may he do violence to his country." What answer shall we make to this, Crito? Do the laws speak truly, or do they not?

Cr. I think that they do.

[13] *Soc.* Then the laws will say: "Consider, Socrates, if we are speaking truly that in your present attempt you are going to do us an injury. For, having brought you into the world, and nurtured and educated you, and given you and every other citizen a share in every good which we had to give, we further proclaim to any Athenian by the liberty which we allow him, that if he does not like us when he has become of age and has seen the ways of the city, and made our acquaintance, he may go where he pleases and take his goods with him. None of us laws will forbid him or interfere with him. Any one who does not like us and the city, and who wants to emigrate to a colony or to any other city, may go where he likes, retaining his property. But he who has experience of the manner in which we order justice and administer the State, and still remains, has entered into an implied contract that he will do as we command him. And he who disobeys us is, as we maintain, thrice wrong; first, because in disobeying us he is disobeying his parents; secondly, because we are the authors of his education; thirdly, because he has made an agreement with us that he will duly obey our commands; and he neither obeys them nor convinces us that our commands are unjust; and we do not rudely impose them, but give him the alternative of obeying or convincing us;—that is what we offer, and he does neither.

[14] "These are the sort of accusations to which, as we were saying, you, Socrates, will be exposed if you accomplish your intentions; you, above all other Athenians." Suppose now I ask, why I rather than anybody else? they will justly retort upon me that I above all other men have acknowledged the agreement. "There is clear proof," they will say, "Socrates, that we and the city were not displeasing to you. Of all Ath-

enians you have been the most constant resident in the city, which, as you never leave, you may be supposed to love. For you never went out of the city either to see the games, except once when you went to the Isthmus, or to any other place unless when you were on military service; nor did you travel as other men do. Nor had you any curiosity to know other States or their laws: your affections did not go beyond us and our State; we were your special favourites, and you acquiesced in our government of you; and here in this city you begat your children, which is a proof of your satisfaction. Moreover, you might in the course of the trial, if you had liked, have fixed the penalty at banishment; the State which refuses to let you go now would have let you go then. But you pretended that you preferred death to exile, and that you were not unwilling to die. And now you have forgotten these fine sentiments, and pay no respect to us, the laws, of whom you are the destroyer; and are doing what only a miserable slave would do, running away and turning your back upon the compacts and agreements which you made as a citizen. And, first of all, answer this very question: Are we right in saying that you agreed to be governed according to us in deed, and not in word only? Is that true or not?" How shall we answer, Crito? Must we not assent?

Cr. We cannot help it, Socrates.

[15] *Soc.* Then will they not say: "You, Socrates, are breaking the covenants and agreements which you made with us at your leisure, not in any haste or under any compulsion or deception, but after you have had seventy years to think of them, during which time you were at liberty to leave the city, if we were not to your mind, or if our covenants appeared to you to be unfair. You had your choice, and might have gone either to Lacedaemon or Crete, both which States are often praised by you for their good government, or to some other Hellenic or foreign State. Whereas you, above all other Athenians, seemed to be so fond of the State, or, in other words, of us, her laws (and who would care about a State which has no laws?), that you never stirred out of her; the halt, the blind, the maimed were not more stationary in her than you were. And now you run away and forsake your agreements. Not so, Socrates, if you will take our advice; do not make yourself ridiculous by escaping out of the city.

[16] "For just consider, if you transgress and err in this sort of way, what good will you do either to yourself or to your friends? That your friends will be driven into exile and deprived of citizenship, or will lose their property, is tolerably certain; and you yourself, if you fly to one of the neighbouring cities, as, for example, Thebes or Megara, both of which are well governed, will come to them as an enemy, Socrates, and their government will be against you, and all patriotic citizens will cast an evil eye upon you as a subverter of the laws, and you will confirm in the minds of the judges the justice of their own condemnation of you. For he

who is a corrupter of the laws is more than likely to be a corrupter of the young and foolish portion of mankind. Will you then flee from well-ordered cities and virtuous men? and is existence worth having on these terms? Or will you go to them without shame, and talk to them, Socrates? And what will you say to them? What you say here about virtue and justice and institutions and laws being the best things among men? Would that be decent of you? Surely not. But if you go away from well-governed States to Crito's friends in Thessaly, where there is great disorder and licence, they will be charmed to hear the tale of your escape from prison, set off with ludicrous particulars of the manner in which you were wrapped in goatskin or some other disguise, and metamorphosed as the manner is of runaways; but will there be no one to remind you that in your old age you were not ashamed to violate the most sacred laws from a miserable desire of a little more life? Perhaps not, if you keep them in a good temper; but if they are out of temper you will hear many degrading things; you will live, but how?—as the flatterer of all men, and the servant of all men; and doing what?—eating and drinking in Thessaly, having gone abroad in order that you may get a dinner. And where will be your fine sentiments about justice and virtue? Say that you wish to live for the sake of your children—you want to bring them up and educate them—will you take them into Thessaly and deprive them of Athenian citizenship? Is this the benefit which you will confer upon them? Or are you under the impression that they will be better cared for and educated here if you are still alive, although absent from them; for your friends will take care of them? Do you fancy that if you are an inhabitant of Thessaly they will take care of them, and if you are an inhabitant of the other world that they will not take care of them? Nay; but if they who call themselves friends are good for anything, they will—to be sure they will.

[17] "Listen, then, Socrates, to us who have brought you up. Think not of life and children first, and of justice afterwards, but of justice first, that you may be justified before the princes of the world below. For neither will you nor any that belong to you be happier or holier or juster in this life, or happier in another, if you do as Crito bids. Now you depart in innocence, a sufferer and not a doer of evil; a victim, not of the laws but of men. But if you go forth, returning evil for evil; and injury for injury, breaking the covenants and agreements which you have made with us, and wronging those whom you ought least of all to wrong, that is to say yourself, your friends, your country, and us, we shall be angry with you while you live, and our brethren, the laws in the world below, will receive you as an enemy; for they will know that you have done your best to destroy us. Listen, then, to us and not to Crito."

This, dear Crito, is the voice which I seem to hear murmuring in my ears, like the sound of the flute in the ears of the mystic; that voice,

I say, is humming in my ears, and prevents me from hearing any other. And I know that anything more which you may say will be vain. Yet speak, if you have anything to say.

Cr. I have nothing to say, Socrates.

Soc. Leave me then, Crito, to fulfil the will of God, and to follow whither he leads.

Plato: from the Phaedo

(At the beginning of this selection, Socrates is speaking to the friends assembled in the prison.)

[1] . . . Wherefore, I say, let a man be of good cheer about his soul, who having cast away the pleasures and ornaments of the body as alien to him and working harm rather than good, has sought after the pleasures of knowledge; and has arrayed the soul, not in some foreign attire, but in her own proper jewels, temperance, and justice, and courage, and nobility, and truth—in these adorned she is ready to go on her journey to the world below, when her hour comes. You, Simmias and Cebes, and all other men, will depart at some time or other. Me already, as a tragic poet would say, the voice of fate calls. Soon I must drink the poison; and I think that I had better repair to the bath first, in order that the women may not have the trouble of washing my body after I am dead.

[2] When he had done speaking, Crito said: And have you any commands for us, Socrates—anything to say about your children, or any other matter in which we can serve you?

[3] Nothing particular, Crito, he replied: only, as I have always told you, take care of yourselves; that is a service which you may be ever rendering to me and mine and to all of us, whether you promise to do so or not. But if you have no thought for yourselves, and care not to walk according to the rule which I have prescribed for you, not now for the first time, however much you may profess or promise at the moment, it will be of no avail.

[4] We will do our best, said Crito: And in what way shall we bury you?

[5] In any way that you like; but you must get hold of me, and take care that I do not run away from you. Then he turned to us, and added with a smile:—I cannot make Crito believe that I am the same Socrates who has been talking and conducting the argument; he fancies that I am the other Socrates whom he will soon see, a dead body—and he asks, How shall he bury me? And though I have spoken many words in the endeavour to show that when I have drunk the poison I shall leave

you and go to the joys of the blessed,—these words of mine, with which I was comforting you and myself, have had, as I perceive, no effect upon Crito. And therefore I want you to be surety for me to him now, as at the trial he was surety to the judges for me: but let the promise be of another sort; for he was surety for me to the judges that I would remain, and you must be my surety to him that I shall not remain, but go away and depart; and then he will suffer less at my death, and not be grieved when he sees my body being burned or buried. I would not have him sorrow at my hard lot, or say at the burial, Thus we lay out Socrates, or, Thus we follow him to the grave or bury him; for false words are not only evil in themselves, but they inflict the soul with evil. Be of good cheer then, my dear Crito, and say that you are burying my body only, and do with that whatever is usual, and what you think best.

[6] When he had spoken these words, he arose and went into a chamber to bathe; Crito followed him and told us to wait. So we remained behind, talking and thinking of the subject of discourse, and also of the greatness of our sorrow; he was like a father of whom we were being bereaved, and we were about to pass the rest of our lives as orphans. When he had taken the bath his children were brought to him (he had two young sons and an elder one); and the women of his family also came, and he talked to them and gave them a few directions in the presence of Crito; then he dismissed them and returned to us.

[7] Now the hour of sunset was near, for a good deal of time had passed while he was within. When he came out, he sat down with us again after his bath, but not much was said. Soon the jailer, who was the servant of the Eleven, entered and stood by him, saying:—To you, Socrates, whom I know to be the noblest and gentlest and best of all who ever came to this place, I will not impute the angry feeling of other men, who rage and swear at me, when, in obedience to the authorities, I bid them drink the poison—indeed, I am sure that you will not be angry with me; for others, as you are aware, and not I, are to blame. And so fare you well, and try to bear lightly what must needs be—you know my errand. Then bursting into tears he turned away and went out.

[8] Socrates looked at him and said: I return your good wishes, and will do as you bid. Then turning to us, he said, How charming the man is: since I have been in prison he has always been coming to see me, and at times he would talk to me, and was as good to me as could be, and now see how generously he sorrows on my account. We must do as he says, Crito; and therefore let the cup be brought, if the poison is prepared: if not, let the attendant prepare some.

[9] Yet, said Crito, the sun is still upon the hill-tops, and I know that many a one has taken the draught late, and after the announcement has been made to him, he has eaten and drunk, and enjoyed the society of his beloved: do not hurry—there is time enough.

[¹⁰] Socrates said: Yes, Crito, and they of whom you speak are right in so acting, for they think that they will be gainers by the delay; but I am right in not following their example, for I do not think that I should gain anything by drinking the poison a little later; I should only be ridiculous in my own eyes for sparing and saving a life which is already forfeit. Please then to do as I say, and not to refuse me.

[¹¹] Crito made a sign to the servant, who was standing by; and he went out, and having been absent for some time, returned with the jailer carrying the cup of poison. Socrates said: You, my good friend, who are experienced in these matters, shall give me directions how I am to proceed. The man answered: You have only to walk about until your legs are heavy, and then to lie down, and the poison will act. At the same time he handed the cup to Socrates, who in the easiest and gentlest manner, without the least fear or change of colour or feature, looking at the man with all his eyes, Echecrates, as his manner was, took the cup and said: What do you say about making a libation out of this cup to any god? May I, or not? The man answered: We only prepare, Socrates, just so much as we deem enough. I understand, he said: but I may and must ask the gods to prosper my journey from this to the other world—even so—and so be it according to my prayer. Then raising the cup to his lips, quite readily and cheerfully he drank off the poison. And hitherto most of us had been able to control our sorrow; but now when we saw him drinking, and saw too that he had finished the draught, we could no longer forbear, and in spite of myself my own tears were flowing fast; so that I covered my face and wept, not for him, but at the thought of my own calamity in having to part from such a friend. Nor was I the first; for Crito, when he found himself unable to restrain his tears, had got up, and I followed; and at that moment, Apollodorus, who had been weeping all the time, broke out in a loud and passionate cry which made cowards of us all. Socrates alone retained his calmness: What is this strange outcry? he said. I sent away the women mainly in order that they might not misbehave in this way, for I have been told that a man should die in peace. Be quiet then, and have patience. When we heard his words we were ashamed, and refrained our tears; and he walked about until, as he said, his legs began to fail, and then he lay on his back, according to directions, and the man who gave him the poison now and then looked at his feet and legs; and after a while he pressed his foot hard, and asked him if he could feel; and he said, No; and then his leg, and so upwards and upwards, and showed us that he was cold and stiff. And he felt them himself, and said: When the poison reaches the heart, that will be the end. He was beginning to grow cold about the groin, when he uncovered his face, for he had covered himself up, and said—they were his last words—he said: Crito, I owe a cock to Asclepius; will you remember to pay the debt? The debt shall be paid, said Crito; is there anything else? There was no answer to this question; but in a minute or two a movement was heard, and the attendants uncovered him; his eyes were set, and Crito closed his eyes and mouth.

[12] Such was the end, Echecrates, of our friend; concerning whom I may truly say, that of all men of his time whom I have known, he was the wisest and justest and best.

--⊰{ C O M M E N T   A N D   Q U E S T I O N S }⊱--

The first nine of the following questions are on the *Crito*.

1. Plato depicts Crito as a devoted friend of Socrates but by no means a brilliant thinker. Crito's reasons for believing that Socrates should escape pour out, in a disorganized way, in the paragraphs to which we have assigned the numbers 1–3 of the *Crito*. Arrange the reasons in an orderly pattern, and summarize Crito's argument.

2. In paragraphs 4 and 5 and the short paragraphs following, Socrates begins to build his counterargument on two principles or propositions with which Crito has agreed in the past. What are the two propositions? When Crito admits that the first is still true, what parts of his own argument has he demolished? When he agrees that the second principle still holds, how has he further undermined his cause?

3. Socrates leads Crito, in paragraphs 7–9, to assent to two other principles. What are they? Do you accept the principles as true? Explain.

4. In paragraph 10, after Crito has answered the last question, the argument seems to Socrates to be settled. It might be expressed in a syllogism: To injure others is wrong; to escape would be to injure others; therefore, to escape is wrong. What part or parts of this syllogism does Crito fail to understand?

5. The core of the *Crito* lies in Socrates' concept of the relationship of the individual and the State. Summarize his reasons, beginning in paragraph 11, for believing that even though he has been given an unjust sentence, he has no right to disregard the judgment of the court and to escape from prison.

6. What is gained by personifying the laws and having them speak to Socrates?

7. If you have read the *Apology*, can you reconcile Socrates' individualism—his refusal to change his way of life and to conform to the will of the majority—with his submission to authority in the *Crito*? Perhaps see the discussion of this point in paragraphs 13–16 of "Salvation on the Campus" by J. Glenn Gray, and explain your reasons for agreeing or disagreeing with the answer suggested there.

8. Socrates' dialogue with the laws is concerned primarily with his duty to the State. How does the dialogue also counter some of Crito's initial arguments?

9. How would you describe Socrates' attitude toward Crito in the *Crito*?

10. In paragraph 3 of the selection from the *Phaedo*, what seems to be the meaning of Socrates' statement "take care of yourselves"?

11. What do paragraphs 4 and 5 in the *Phaedo* contribute?

12. Is Socrates' attitude about delaying the drinking of the poison (paragraph 10) consistent with attitudes expressed in the *Crito*? Explain.

13. Asclepius was a god of healing. It has been suggested that Socrates' last words meant that he owed a thank-offering to the god for delivering him from the sickness or fever of life. Another suggestion, made by W. H. D. Rouse, a classical scholar and translator, is that since Plato was ill and unable to be present on the day of Socrates' death, Plato may have thought of the offering as one for his recovery. Does either of these interpretations seem more reasonable than the other? Why?

14. What seem to you the most important characteristics of Socrates revealed in the *Crito* and this part of the *Phaedo*?

[72]   *Carl Sandburg*: Lincoln Speaks at Gettysburg

THE FOLLOWING account of an event in history is part of a long biography of Lincoln. One of the distinctive features of the selection is the skillful weaving of a mass of fact, evidence, and conflicting opinion into a highly readable historical narrative. Carl Sandburg, probably best known as a poet of the Midwest, was the author of *Chicago Poems; Cornhuskers; Smoke and Steel; The American Songbag; The People, Yes;* and *Remembrance Rock,* a novel. His biography of Lincoln, *The Prairie Years* (two volumes) and *The War Years* (four volumes), won the 1940 Pulitzer Prize.

[1] A printed invitation came to Lincoln's hands notifying him that on Thursday, November 19, 1863, exercises would be held for the dedication of a National Soldiers' Cemetery at Gettysburg. The same circular invitation had been mailed to Senators, Congressmen, the governors of Northern States, members of the Cabinet, by the commission of Pennsylvanians who had organized a corporation through which Maine, New Hampshire, Vermont, Massachusetts, Rhode Island, Maryland, Connecticut, New York, New Jersey, Pennsylvania, Delaware, West Virginia, Ohio, Indiana, Illinois, Michigan, Wisconsin, and Minnesota were to share the cost of a

decent burying-ground for the dust and bones of the Union and Confederate dead.

[2] In the helpless onrush of the war, it was known, too many of the fallen had lain as neglected cadavers rotting in the open fields or thrust into so shallow a resting-place that a common farm plow caught in their bones. Now by order of Governor Curtin of Pennsylvania seventeen acres had been purchased on Cemetery Hill, where the Union center stood its colors on the second and third of July, and plots of soil had been allotted each State for its graves.

[3] The sacred and delicate duties of orator of the day had fallen on Edward Everett. An eminent cultural figure, perhaps foremost of all distinguished American classical orators, he was born in 1794, had been United States Senator, Governor of Massachusetts, member of Congress, Secretary of State under Fillmore, Minister to Great Britain, Phi Beta Kappa poet at Harvard, professor of Greek at Harvard, president of Harvard. His reputation as a public speaker began in the Brattle Street Unitarian Church of Boston. Two volumes of his orations published in 1850 held eighty-one addresses, two more volumes issued in 1859 collected one hundred and five speeches. His lecture on Washington, delivered a hundred and twenty-two times in three years, had in 1859 brought a fund of $58,000, which he gave to the purchase and maintenance of Mount Vernon as a permanent shrine. Other Everett lectures had realized more than $90,000 for charity causes. . . . No ordinary trafficker in politics, Everett had in 1860 run for Vice-President on the Bell-Everett ticket of the Constitutional Union party, receiving the electoral votes of Virginia, Kentucky, and Tennessee.

[4] The Union of States was a holy concept to Everett, and the slavery issue secondary, though when president of Harvard from 1846 to 1849 he refused to draw the color line, saying in the case of a Negro applicant, Beverly Williams, that admission to Harvard College depended on examinations. "If this boy passes the examinations, he will be admitted; and if the white students choose to withdraw, all the income of the College will be devoted to his education." Not often was he so provocative.

[5] On the basis of what Everett had heard about Lincoln he wrote in his journal shortly before the inauguration in '61 that the incoming President was "evidently a person of very inferior cast of character, wholly unequal to the crisis." Then on meeting the new President he recorded that he found him of better stuff than he had expected. As a strict worshiper of the Constitution and the Union he was drawn toward Lincoln's moderate slavery policy, writing to critics after the Administration had lost in the '62 fall elections, "It is my purpose to support the President to the best of my ability." Speaking publicly as a man of no party, and as the leading founder of the Mount Vernon memorial to George Washington, he trusted he would offend no candid opponent by saying that the

main objection against Mr. Lincoln, "that personally he lacks fixedness of purpose," might on precisely the same grounds be brought against George Washington and his Administration. The President's "intellectual capacity" had been proved in his debates with Douglas. "He is one of the most laborious and indefatigable men in the country," said Everett, "and that he has been able to sustain himself under as great a load of care as was ever laid upon the head or the heart of a living man is in no small degree owing to the fact that the vindictive and angry passions form no part of his nature and that a kindly and playful spirit mingles its sweetness with the austere cup of public duty." . . .

[6] Serene, suave, handsomely venerable in his sixty-ninth year, a prominent specimen of Northern upper-class distinction, Everett was a natural choice of the Pennsylvania commissioners, who sought an orator for a solemn national occasion. When in September they notified him that the date of the occasion would be October 23, he replied that he would need more time for preparation, and the dedication was postponed till November 19.

[7] Lincoln meanwhile, in reply to the printed circular invitation, sent word to the commissioners that he would be present at the ceremonies. This made it necessary for the commissioners to consider whether the President should be asked to deliver an address when present. Clark E. Carr of Galesburg, Illinois, representing his State on the Board of Commissioners, noted that the decision of the Board to invite Lincoln to speak was an afterthought. "The question was raised as to his ability to speak upon such a grave and solemn occasion. . . . Besides, it was said that, with his important duties and responsibilities, he could not possibly have the leisure to prepare an address. . . . In answer . . . it was urged that he himself, better than any one else, could determine as to these questions, and that, if he were invited to speak, he was sure to do what, under the circumstances, would be right and proper."

[8] And so on November 2 David Wills of Gettysburg, as the special agent of Governor Curtin and also acting for the several States, by letter informed Lincoln that the several States having soldiers in the Army of the Potomac who were killed, or had since died at hospitals in the vicinity, had procured grounds for a cemetery and proper burial of their dead. "These grounds will be consecrated and set apart to this sacred purpose by appropriate ceremonies on Thursday, the 19th instant. I am authorized by the Governors of the various States to invite you to be present and participate in these ceremonies, which will doubtless be very imposing and solemnly impressive. It is the desire that after the oration, you, as Chief Executive of the nation, formally set apart these grounds to their sacred use by a few appropriate remarks."

[9] Mr. Wills proceeded farther as to the solemnity of the occasion, and when Lincoln had finished reading the letter he understood definitely that

the event called for no humor and that a long speech was not expected from him. "The invitation," wrote Clark E. Carr, "was not settled upon and sent to Mr. Lincoln until the second of November, more than six weeks after Mr. Everett had been invited to speak, and but little more than two weeks before the exercises were held."

[10] On the second Sunday before the Gettysburg ceremonies were to take place Lincoln went to the studio of the photographer Gardner for a long-delayed sitting. Noah Brooks walked with him, and he carefully explained to Brooks that he could not go to the photographer on any other day without interfering with the public business and the photographer's business, to say nothing of his liability to be hindered en route by curiosity-seekers "and other seekers." On the White House stairs Lincoln had paused, turned, walked back to his office, and rejoined Brooks with a long envelope in his hand, an advance copy of Edward Everett's address to be delivered at the Gettysburg dedication. It was thoughtful of Everett to take care they should not cover the same ground in their speeches, he remarked to Brooks, who exclaimed over the length of the Everett address, covering nearly two sides of a one-page supplement of a Boston newspaper. Lincoln quoted a line he said he had read somewhere from Daniel Webster: "Solid men of Boston, make no long orations." There was no danger that he should get upon the lines of Mr. Everett's oration, he told Brooks, for what he had ready to say was very short, or as Brooks recalled his emphasis, "Short, short, short." He had hoped to read the Everett address between sittings, but the photographer worked fast, Lincoln got interested in talk, and did not open the advance sheets while at Gardner's. In the photograph which Lincoln later gave to Brooks an envelope lay next to Lincoln's right arm resting on a table. In one other photograph made by Gardner that Sunday the envelope was still on the table. The chief difference between the two pictures was that in one Lincoln had his knees crossed and in the other the ankles.

[11] Lamon noted that Lincoln wrote part of his intended Gettysburg address at Washington, covered a sheet of foolscap paper with a memorandum of it, and before taking it out of his hat and reading it to Lamon he said that it was not at all satisfactory to him, that he was afraid he would not do himself credit nor come up to public expectation. He had been too busy to give it the time he would like to. . . .

[12] Two men, in the weeks just before the Gettysburg ceremonies, had worked on Lincoln, doing their best to make him see himself as a world spokesman of democracy, popular government, the mass of people as opposed to aristocrats, classes, and special interests. John Murray Forbes, having read Lincoln's lively stump-speech letter to the Springfield, Illinois, mass meeting, wrote to Sumner on September 3, "I delight in the President's plain letter to plain people!" Forbes followed this five days later with a letter which Sumner carried to the White House and handed to

Lincoln. It began with convincingly phrased praise of the Springfield letter, and proceeded into the unusual question: "Will you permit a suggestion from one who has nothing to ask for himself: one who would accept no office, and who seeks only to do his duty in the most private way possible?" With such an opening it could hardly be doubted that Lincoln read on into the next paragraphs—and read them more than once.

[13] An aristocracy ruled the South and controlled it for war, believed Forbes, pointing to "the aristocratic class who own twenty negroes and upwards" as numbering "about 28,000 persons, which is about the 178th part of 5,000,000" whites. So Forbes urged, "Let the people North and South see this line clearly defined between the people and the aristocrats, and the war will be over!" . . .

[14] Thus while Lincoln shaped his speech to be made at Gettysburg he did not lack specific advice that when the chance came he should stand up and be a world spokesman for those who called themselves democrats and liberals as opposed to what they termed "the aristocratic classes."

[15] Some newspapers now had it that the President was going to make a stump speech over the graves of the Gettysburg dead as a political play. Talk ran in Washington that by attending Governor Curtin's "show" the President would strengthen himself with the Curtin faction without alienating the opposing Cameron clique.

[16] Various definite motives besides vague intuitions may have guided Lincoln in his decision to attend and speak even though half his Cabinet had sent formal declinations in response to the printed circular invitations they had all received. Though the Gettysburg dedication was to be under interstate auspices, it had tremendous national significance for Lincoln because on the platform would be the State governors whose cooperation with him was of vast importance. Also a slander and a libel had been widely mouthed and printed that on his visit to the battlefield of Antietam nearly a year before he had laughed obscenely at his own funny stories and called on Lamon to sing a cheap comic song. Perhaps he might go to Gettysburg and let it be seen how he demeaned himself on a somber landscape of sacrifice.

[17] His personal touch with Gettysburg, by telegraph, mail, courier, and by a throng of associations, made it a place of great realities to him. Just after the battle there, a woman had come to his office, the doorman saying she had been "crying and taking on" for several days trying to see the President. Her husband and her three sons were in the army. On part of her husband's pay she had lived for a time, till money from him stopped coming. She was hard put to scrape a living and needed one of her boys to help.

[18] The President listened to her, standing at a fireplace, hands behind him, head bowed, motionless. The woman finished her plea for one of her

three sons in the army. He spoke. Slowly and almost as if talking to himself alone the words came and only those words:

[19] "I have two, and you have none."

[20] He crossed the room, wrote an order for the military discharge of one of her sons. On a special sheet of paper he wrote full and detailed instructions where to go and what to say in order to get her boy back.

[21] In a few days the doorman told the President that the same woman was again on hand crying and taking on. "Let her in," was the word. She had found doors opening to her and officials ready to help on seeing the President's written words she carried. She had located her boy, camp, regiment, company. She had found him, yes, wounded at Gettysburg, dying in a hospital, and had followed him to the grave. And, she begged, would the President now give her the next one of her boys?

[22] As before he stood at the fireplace, hands behind him, head bent low, motionless. Slowly and almost as if talking to himself alone the words came and as before only those words:

[23] "I have two, and you have none."

[24] He crossed the room to his desk and began writing. As though nothing else was to do she followed, stood by his chair as he wrote, put her hand on the President's head, smoothed his thick and disorderly hair with motherly fingers. He signed an order giving her the next of her boys, stood up, put the priceless paper in her hand as he choked out the one word, "There!" and with long quick steps was gone from the room with her sobs and cries of thanks in his ears.

[25] Thus the Kentuckian, James Speed, gathered the incident and told it. By many strange ways Gettysburg was to Lincoln a fact in crimson mist. . . .

[26] Benjamin B. French, officer in charge of buildings in Washington, introduced the Honorable Edward Everett, orator of the day, who rose, bowed low to Lincoln, saying, "Mr. President." Lincoln responded, "Mr. Everett."

[27] The orator of the day then stood in silence before a crowd that stretched to limits that would test his voice. Beyond and around were the wheat fields, the meadows, the peach orchards, long slopes of land, and five and seven miles farther the contemplative blue ridge of a low mountain range. His eyes could sweep them as he faced the audience. He had taken note of it in his prepared and rehearsed address. "Overlooking these broad fields now reposing from the labors of the waning year, the mighty Alleghenies dimly towering before us, the graves of our brethren beneath our feet, it is with hesitation that I raise my poor voice to break the eloquent silence of God and Nature. But the duty to which you have called me must be performed;—grant me, I pray you, your indulgence and your sympathy." Everett proceeded, "It was appointed by law in

Athens," and gave an extended sketch of the manner in which the Greeks cared for their dead who fell in battle. He spoke of the citizens assembled to consecrate the day. "As my eye ranges over the fields whose sods were so lately moistened by the blood of gallant and loyal men, I feel, as never before, how truly it was said of old that it is sweet and becoming to die for one's country."

[28] Northern cities would have been trampled in conquest but for "those who sleep beneath our feet," said the orator. He gave an outline of how the war began, traversed decisive features of the three days' battles at Gettysburg, discussed the doctrine of State sovereignty and denounced it, drew parallels from European history, and came to his peroration quoting Pericles on dead patriots: "The whole earth is the sepulchre of illustrious men." The men of nineteen sister States had stood side by side on the perilous ridges. "Seminary Ridge, the Peach-Orchard, Cemetery, Culp, and Wolf Hill, Round Top, Little Round Top, humble names, henceforward dear and famous,—no lapse of time, no distance of space, shall cause you to be forgotten." He had spoken for an hour and fifty-seven minutes, some said a trifle over two hours, repeating almost word for word an address that occupied nearly two newspaper pages, as he had written it and as it had gone in advance sheets to many newspapers.

[29] Everett came to his closing sentence without a faltering voice: "Down to the latest period of recorded time, in the glorious annals of our common country there will be no brighter page than that which relates THE BATTLE OF GETTYSBURG." It was the effort of his life and embodied the perfections of the school of oratory in which he had spent his career. His erect form and sturdy shoulders, his white hair and flung-back head at dramatic points, his voice, his poise, and chiefly some quality of inside goodheartedness, held most of his audience to him, though the people in the front rows had taken their seats three hours before his oration closed.

[30] The Baltimore Glee Club sang an ode written for the occasion by Benjamin B. French, who had introduced Everett to the audience. The poets Longfellow, Bryant, Whittier, Lowell, George Boker, had been requested but none found time to respond with a piece to be set to music. The two closing verses of the ode by French immediately preceded the introduction of the President to the audience:

> Great God in Heaven!
> Shall all this sacred blood be shed?
> Shall we thus mourn our glorious dead?
> Oh, shall the end be wrath and woe,
> The knell of Freedom's overthrow,
>   A country riven?
>
> It will not be!
> We trust, O God! thy gracious power
> To aid us in our darkest hour.

This be our prayer—"O Father! save
A people's freedom from its grave.
All praise to Thee!"

[31] Having read Everett's address, Lincoln knew when the moment drew near for him to speak. He took out his own manuscript from a coat pocket, put on his steel-bowed glasses, stirred in his chair, looked over the manuscript, and put it back in his pocket. The Baltimore Glee Club finished. The specially chosen Ward Hill Lamon rose and spoke the words "The President of the United States," who rose, and holding in one hand the two sheets of paper at which he occasionally glanced, delivered the address in his high-pitched and clear-carrying voice. The *Cincinnati Commercial* reporter wrote, "The President rises slowly, draws from his pocket a paper, and, when commotion subsides, in a sharp, unmusical treble voice, reads the brief and pithy remarks." Hay wrote in his diary, "The President, in a firm, free way, with more grace than is his wont, said his half dozen words of consecration." Charles Hale of the *Boston Advertiser,* also officially representing Governor Andrew of Massachusetts, had notebook and pencil in hand, took down the slow-spoken words of the President, as follows:

Fourscore and seven years ago, our fathers brought forth upon this continent a new nation, conceived in liberty and dedicated to the proposition that all men are created equal.

Now we are engaged in a great civil war, testing whether that nation—or any nation, so conceived and so dedicated—can long endure.

We are met on a great battle-field of that war. We are met to dedicate a portion of it as the final resting place of those who have given their lives that that nation might live.

It is altogether fitting and proper that we should do this.

But, in a larger sense, we cannot dedicate, we cannot consecrate, we cannot hallow, this ground. The brave men, living and dead, who struggled here, have consecrated it, far above our power to add or to detract.

The world will very little note nor long remember what we say here; but it can never forget what they did here.

It is for us, the living, rather, to be dedicated, here, to the unfinished work that they have thus far so nobly carried on. It is rather for us to be here dedicated to the great task remaining before us; that from these honored dead we take increased devotion to that cause for which they here gave the last full measure of devotion; that we here highly resolve that these dead shall not have died in vain; that the nation shall, under God, have a new birth of freedom, and that government of the people, by the people, for the people, shall not perish from the earth.

[32] In a speech to serenaders just after the battle of Gettysburg four and a half months before, Lincoln had referred to the founding of the republic as taking place "eighty-odd years since." Then he had hunted up

the exact date, which was eighty-seven years since, and phrased it "Four-score and seven years ago" instead of "Eighty-seven years since." Also in the final copy Lincoln wrote "We have come" instead of the second "We are met" that Hale reported.

[33] In the written copy of his speech from which he read Lincoln used the phrase "our poor power." In other copies of the speech which he wrote out later he again used the phrase "our poor power." So it was evident that he meant to use the word "poor" when speaking to his audience, but he omitted it. Also in the copy held in his hands while facing the audience he had not written the words "under God," though he did include those words in later copies which he wrote. Therefore the words "under God" were decided upon after he wrote the text the night before at the Wills residence.

[34] The *New York Tribune* and many other newspapers indicated "[Applause.]" at five places in the address and "[Long continued applause.]" at the end. The applause, however, according to most of the responsible witnesses, was formal and perfunctory, a tribute to the occasion, to the high office, to the array of important men of the nation on the platform, by persons who had sat as an audience for three hours. Ten sentences had been spoken in five minutes, and some were surprised that it should end before the orator had really begun to get his outdoor voice.

[35] A photographer had made ready to record a great historic moment, had bustled about with his dry plates, his black box on a tripod, and before he had his head under the hood for an exposure, the President had said "by the people, for the people" and the nick of time was past for a photograph.

[36] The *New York Times* reporter gave his summary of the program by writing: "The opening prayer by Reverend Mr. Stockton was touching and beautiful, and produced quite as much effect upon the audience as the classic sentences of the orator of the day. President Lincoln's address was delivered in a clear loud tone of voice, which could be distinctly heard at the extreme limits of the large assemblage. It was delivered (or rather read from a sheet of paper which the speaker held in his hand) in a very deliberate manner, with strong emphasis, and with a most business-like air."

[37] The *Philadelphia Press* man, John Russell Young, privately felt that Everett's speech was the performance of a great actor whose art was too evident, that it was "beautiful but cold as ice." The *New York Times* man noted: "Even while Mr. Everett was delivering his splendid oration, there were as many people wandering about the fields, made memorable by the fierce struggles of July, as stood around the stand listening to his eloquent periods. They seem to have considered, with President Lincoln, that it was not what was *said* here, but what was *done* here, that deserved their attention. . . . In wandering about these battlefields, one is aston-

ished and indignant to find at almost every step of his progress the carcasses of dead horses which breed pestilence in the atmosphere. I am told that more than a score of deaths have resulted from this neglect in the village of Gettysburg the past summer; in the house in which I was compelled to seek lodging, there are now two boys sick with typhoid fever attributed to this cause. Within a stone's throw of the whitewashed hut occupied as the headquarters of General Meade, I counted yesterday no less than ten carcasses of dead horses, lying on the ground where they were struck by the shells of the enemy."

[38] The audience had expected, as the printed program stipulated, "Dedicatory Remarks, by the President of the United States." No eloquence was promised. Where eloquence is in flow the orator must have time to get tuned up, to expatiate and expand while building toward his climaxes, it was supposed. The *New York Tribune* man and other like observers merely reported the words of the address with the one preceding sentence: "The dedicatory remarks were then delivered by the President." These reporters felt no urge to inform their readers about how Lincoln stood, what he did with his hands, how he moved, vocalized, or whether he emphasized or subdued any parts of the address. Strictly, no address as such was on the program from him. He was down for just a few perfunctory "dedicatory remarks."

[39] According to Lamon, Lincoln himself felt that about all he had given the audience was ordinary garden-variety dedicatory remarks, for Lamon wrote that Lincoln told him just after delivering the speech that he had regret over not having prepared it with greater care. "Lamon, that speech won't *scour*. It is a flat failure and the people are disappointed." On the farms where Lincoln grew up as a boy when wet soil stuck to the mold board of a plow they said it didn't "scour."

[40] The near-by *Patriot and Union* of Harrisburg took its fling: "The President succeeded on this occasion because he acted without sense and without constraint in a panorama that was gotten up more for the benefit of his party than for the glory of the nation and the honor of the dead. . . . We pass over the silly remarks of the President; for the credit of the nation we are willing that the veil of oblivion shall be dropped over them and that they shall no more be repeated or thought of."

[41] The *Chicago Times* held that "Mr. Lincoln did most foully traduce the motives of the men who were slain at Gettysburg" in his reference to "a new birth of freedom," the *Times* saying, "They gave their lives to maintain the old government, and the only Constitution and Union." He had perverted history, misstated the cause for which they died, and with "ignorant rudeness" insulted the memory of the dead, the *Times* alleged: "Readers will not have failed to observe the exceeding bad taste which characterized the remarks of the President and Secretary of State at the dedication of the soldiers' cemetery at Gettysburg. The cheek of every

American must tingle with shame as he reads the silly, flat, and dish-watery utterances of the man who has to be pointed out to intelligent foreigners as the President of the United States. And neither he nor Seward could refrain, even on that solemn occasion, from spouting their odious abolition doctrines. The readers of THE TIMES ought to know, too, that the valorous President did not dare to make this little journey to Gettysburg without being escorted by a bodyguard of soldiers. For the first time in the history of the country, the President of the United States, in traveling through a part of his dominions, on a peaceful, even a religious mission, had to be escorted by a bodyguard of soldiers . . . it was fear for his own personal safety which led the President to go escorted as any other military despot might go." In the pronouncement of a funeral sermon Mr. Lincoln had intruded an "offensive exhibition of boorishness and vulgarity," had alluded to tribal differences that an Indian orator eulogizing dead warriors would have omitted, "which he knew would excite unnecessarily the bitter prejudices of his hearers." Therefore the *Chicago Times* would inquire, "Is Mr. Lincoln less refined than a savage?"

[42] A Confederate outburst of war propaganda related to Lincoln and the Gettysburg exercises was set forth in a *Richmond Examiner* editorial, and probably written by its editor, Edward A. Pollard, taking a day off from his merciless and occasionally wild-eyed criticism of President Jefferson Davis of the Confederacy. And the *Chicago Times*, which seldom let a day pass without curses on Lincoln for his alleged suppression of free speech and a free press, reprinted in full the long editorial from the *Examiner*. "The dramatic exhibition at Gettysburg is in thorough keeping with Yankee character, suited to the usual dignity of their chosen chief," ran part of the editorial scorn. "Stage play, studied attitudes, and effective points were carefully elaborated and presented to the world as the honest outpourings of a nation's heart. In spite of shoddy contracts, of universal corruption, and cruel thirst for southern blood, these people have ideas . . . have read of them in books . . . and determined accordingly to have a grand imitation of them. . . . Mr. Everett was equal to the occasion. He 'took down his Thucydides,' and fancied himself a Pericles commemorating the illustrious dead. The music, the eloquence, the bottled tears and hermetically sealed grief, prepared for the occasion, were all properly brought out in honor of the heroes, whom they crimp in Ireland, inveigle in Germany, or hunt down in the streets of New York.

[43] "So far the play was strictly classic. To suit the general public, however, a little admixture of the more irregular romantic drama was allowed. A vein of comedy was permitted to mingle with the deep pathos of the piece. This singular novelty, and deviation from classic propriety, was heightened by assigning this part to the chief personage. Kings are usually made to speak in the magniloquent language supposed to be

suited to their elevated position. On the present occasion Lincoln acted the clown."

[44] This was in the customary tone of the *Chicago Times* and relished by its supporting readers. Its rival, the *Chicago Tribune,* however, had a reporter who telegraphed (unless some editor who read the address added his own independent opinion) a sentence: "The dedicatory remarks of President Lincoln will live among the annals of man."

[45] The *Cincinnati Gazette* reporter added after the text of the address, "That this was the right thing in the right place, and a perfect thing in every respect, was the universal encomium."

[46] The American correspondent of the *London Times* wrote that "the ceremony was rendered ludicrous by some of the sallies of that poor President Lincoln. . . . Anything more dull and commonplace it would not be easy to produce."

[47] Count Gurowski, the only man ever mentioned by Lincoln to Lamon as his possible assassin, wrote in a diary, "Lincoln spoke, with one eye to a future platform and to re-election."

[48] The *Philadelphia Evening Bulletin* said thousands who would not read the elaborate oration of Mr. Everett would read the President's few words "and not many will do it without a moistening of the eye and a swelling of the heart." The *Detroit Advertiser and Tribune* said Mr. Everett had nobly told the story of the battle, "but he who wants to take in the very spirit of the day, catch the unstudied pathos that animates a sincere but simple-minded man, will turn from the stately periods of the professed orator to the brief speech of the President." The *Providence Journal* reminded readers of the saying that the hardest thing in the world is to make a good five-minute speech: "We know not where to look for a more admirable speech than the brief one which the President made at the close of Mr. Everett's oration. . . . Could the most elaborate and splendid oration be more beautiful, more touching, more inspiring, than those thrilling words of the President? They had in our humble judgment the charm and power of the very highest eloquence."

[49] Later men were to find that Robert Toombs of Georgia had in 1850 opened a speech: "Sixty years ago our fathers joined together to form a more perfect Union and to establish justice. . . . We have now met to put that government on trial. . . . In my judgment the verdict is such as to give hope to the friends of liberty throughout the world."

[50] Lincoln had spoken of an idea, a proposition, a concept, worth dying for, which brought from a Richmond newspaper a countering question and answer, "For what are we fighting? An abstraction."

[51] The *Springfield Republican* had veered from its first opinion that Lincoln was honest but "a Simple Susan." Its comment ran: "Surpassingly fine as Mr. Everett's oration was in the Gettysburg consecration, the rhe-

torical honors of the occasion were won by President Lincoln. His little speech is a perfect gem; deep in feeling, compact in thought and expression, and tasteful and elegant in every word and comma. Then it has the merit of unexpectedness in its verbal perfection and beauty. We had grown so accustomed to homely and imperfect phrase in his productions that we had come to think it was the law of his utterance. But this shows he can talk handsomely as well as act sensibly. Turn back and read it over, it will repay study as a model speech. Strong feelings and a large brain were its parents—a little painstaking its *accoucheur*."

[52] That scribbler of curious touch who signed himself "The Lounger" in *Harper's Weekly* inquired why the ceremony at Gettysburg was one of the most striking events of the war. "There are grave-yards enough in the land—what is Virginia but a cemetery?—and the brave who have died for us in this fierce war consecrate the soil from the ocean to the Mississippi. But there is peculiar significance in the field of Gettysburg, for there 'thus far' was thundered to the rebellion. . . . The President and the Cabinet were there, with famous soldiers and civilians. The oration by Mr. Everett was smooth and cold. . . . The few words of the President were from the heart to the heart. They can not be read, even, without kindling emotion. 'The world will little note nor long remember what we say here, but it can never forget what they did here.' It was as simple and felicitous and earnest a word as was ever spoken. . . . Among the Governors present was Horatio Seymour. He came to honor the dead of Gettysburg. But when they were dying he stood in New York sneeringly asking where was the victory promised for the Fourth of July? These men were winning that victory, and dying for us all; and now he mourns, *ex officio*, over their graves."

[53] Everett's opinion of the speech he heard Lincoln deliver was written in a note to Lincoln the next day and was more than mere courtesy: "I should be glad if I could flatter myself that I came as near to the central idea of the occasion in two hours as you did in two minutes." Lincoln's immediate reply was: "In our respective parts yesterday, you could not have been excused to make a short address, nor I a long one. I am pleased to know that, in your judgment, the little I did say was not entirely a failure."

[54] At Everett's request Lincoln wrote with pen and ink a copy of his Gettysburg Address, which manuscript was auctioned at a Sanitary Fair in New York for the benefit of soldiers. At the request of George Bancroft, the historian, he wrote another copy for a Soldiers' and Sailors' Fair at Baltimore. He wrote still another to be lithographed as a facsimile in a publication, *Autographed Leaves of Our Country's Authors*. For Mr. Wills, his host at Gettysburg, he wrote another. The first draft, written in Washington, and the second one, held while delivering it, went into John Hay's hands to be eventually presented to the Library of Congress.

[⁵⁵] After the ceremonies at Gettysburg Lincoln lunched with Governor Curtin, Mr. Everett, and others at the Wills home, held a reception that had not been planned, handshaking nearly an hour, looking gloomy and listless but brightening sometimes as a small boy or girl came in line, and stopping one tall man for remarks as to just how high up he reached. At five o'clock he attended a patriotic meeting in the Presbyterian church, walking arm-in-arm with old John Burns, and listening to an address by Lieutenant Governor-elect Anderson of Ohio. At six-thirty he was on the departing Washington train. In the dining-car his secretary John Hay ate with Simon Cameron and Wayne MacVeagh. Hay had thought Cameron and MacVeagh hated each other, but he noted: "I was more than usually struck by the intimate, jovial relations that existed between men that hate and detest each other as cordially as do these Pennsylvania politicians."

[⁵⁶] The ride to Washington took until midnight. Lincoln was weary, talked little, stretched out on one of the side seats in the drawing-room and had a wet towel laid across his eyes and forehead.

[⁵⁷] He had stood that day, the world's foremost spokesman of popular government, saying that democracy was yet worth fighting for. He had spoken as one in mist who might head on deeper yet into mist. He incarnated the assurances and pretenses of popular government, implied that it could and might perish from the earth. What he meant by "a new birth of freedom" for the nation could have a thousand interpretations. The taller riddles of democracy stood up out of the address. It had the dream touch of vast and furious events epitomized for any foreteller to read what was to come. He did not assume that the drafted soldiers, substitutes, and bounty-paid privates had died willingly under Lee's shot and shell, in deliberate consecration of themselves to the Union cause. His cadences sang the ancient song that where there is freedom men have fought and sacrificed for it, and that freedom is worth men's dying for. For the first time since he became President he had on a dramatic occasion declaimed, howsoever it might be read, Jefferson's proposition which had been a slogan of the Revolutionary War—"All men are created equal" —leaving no other inference than that he regarded the Negro slave as a man. His outwardly smooth sentences were inside of them gnarled and tough with the enigmas of the American experiment.

[⁵⁸] Back at Gettysburg the blue haze of the Cumberland Mountains had dimmed till it was a blur in a nocturne. The moon was up and fell with a bland golden benevolence on the new-made graves of soldiers, on the sepulchers of old settlers, on the horse carcasses of which the onrush of war had not yet permitted removal. The *New York Herald* man walked amid them and ended the story he sent his paper: "The air, the trees, the graves are silent. Even the relic hunters are gone now. And the soldiers here never wake to the sound of reveille."

[⁵⁹] In many a country cottage over the land, a tall old clock in a quiet

corner told time in a tick-tock deliberation. Whether the orchard branches
hung with pink-spray blossoms or icicles of sleet, whether the outside
news was seedtime or harvest, rain or drought, births or deaths, the swing
of the pendulum was right and left and right and left in a tick-tock
deliberation.

[60] The face and dial of the clock had known the eyes of a boy who
listened to its tick-tock and learned to read its minute and hour hands.
And the boy had seen years measured off by the swinging pendulum, and
grown to man size, had gone away. And the people in the cottage knew
that the clock would stand there and the boy never again come into the
room and look at the clock with the query, "What is the time?"

[61] In a row of graves of the Unidentified the boy would sleep long in
the dedicated final resting-place at Gettysburg. Why he had gone away
and why he would never come back had roots in some mystery of flags
and drums, of national fate in which individuals sink as in a deep sea, of
men swallowed and vanished in a man-made storm of smoke and steel.

[62] The mystery deepened and moved with ancient music and inviola-
ble consolation because a solemn Man of Authority had stood at the
graves of the Unidentified and spoken the words "We cannot consecrate—
we cannot hallow—this ground. The brave men, living and dead, who
struggled here, have consecrated it far above our poor power to add or
detract. . . . From these honored dead we take increased devotion to that
cause for which they gave the last full measure of devotion."

[63] To the backward and forward pendulum swing of a tall old clock
in a quiet corner they might read those cadenced words while outside the
windows the first flurry of snow blew across the orchard and down over
the meadow, the beginnings of winter in a gun-metal gloaming to be
later arched with a star-flung sky.

⸺⸙ COMMENT AND QUESTIONS ⸙⸺

1. Most of this selection is objective reporting of verifiable facts, with the
   verification or documentation of the facts incorporated into the writing.
   There are few obvious devices for interest, no diluting or popularizing of
   the material to make it more appealing. But most readers find the packed,
   informative account very absorbing. What is the basis of its interest?
2. What sources has Sandburg apparently used in writing his biography of
   Lincoln?
3. Is the delineation of Edward Everett generally favorable or unfavorable?
   Explain.
4. In writing his historical narrative, Sandburg had the problem of pace and
   proportion. What is the purpose of the full development in paragraphs 7–9

of the invitation to Lincoln to speak at Gettysburg? What is the purpose of including in the account Lincoln's visit to the photographer (paragraph 10)?

5. What do the visits of the woman to Lincoln's office (paragraphs 17–24) contribute to the narrative? By what means does Sandburg make these visits vivid and dramatic?

6. How does Sandburg give the reader a sense of the setting in which the ceremonies at Gettysburg took place?

7. Comment on Sandburg's handling of Everett's oration, paragraphs 26–29. Do the proportion and length of development seem appropriate? Explain.

8. Study the conflicting reports and judgments of the ceremonies at Gettysburg (paragraphs 34–52) and the language of the reporters. What forces were apparently operating to influence their judgments? Do you think that some of those who disregarded or condemned Lincoln's speech were sincere? Explain.

9. How do the last seven paragraphs (57–63) differ from the rest of the account in attitude toward the subject and in style? What do they contribute to the selection? Can you summarize, in factual language, Sandburg's evaluation of the Gettysburg Address?

10. What does Sandburg mean by saying, in paragraph 57, that Lincoln's smooth sentences were "gnarled and tough with the enigmas of the American experiment"?

[73] *Winston Churchill*: Dunkirk

THE EVACUATION of Dunkirk, regarded by military experts as a miracle of World War II, has become a symbol of victory in defeat. Badly defeated in May, 1940, by the Germans in Belgium, the British and French armies fell back to Dunkirk, the only port on the French coast still in Allied hands. A fleet of rescue boats—destroyers, ferries, tugboats, fishing smacks— every boat available—set out from the British coast across the channel and, shuttling back and forth under heavy German attack, rescued 335,000 men from the beaches of Dunkirk. On June 4, 1940, Winston Churchill, Prime Minister of Great Britain, gave the following account of the evacuation to the House of Commons. His address is an informative report, an evaluation, and above all a piece of persuasion designed to inspire courage and strength for the hard days ahead.

[1] From the moment that the French defenses at Sedan and on the Meuse were broken at the end of the second week of May, only a rapid

retreat to Amiens and the south could have saved the British and French
Armies who had entered Belgium at the appeal of the Belgian King;
but this strategic fact was not immediately realized. The French High
Command hoped they would be able to close the gap, and the Armies
of the north were under their orders. Moreover, a retirement of this kind
would have involved almost certainly the destruction of the fine Belgian
Army of over 20 divisions and the abandonment of the whole of Belgium.
Therefore, when the force and scope of the German penetration were
realized and when a new French Generalissimo, General Weygand, assumed command in place of General Gamelin, an effort was made by the
French and British Armies in Belgium to keep on holding the right hand
of the Belgians and to give their own right hand to a newly created
French Army which was to have advanced across the Somme in great
strength to grasp it.

[2] However, the German eruption swept like a sharp scythe around
the right and rear of the Armies of the north. Eight or nine armored
divisions, each of about four hundred armored vehicles of different kinds,
but carefully assorted to be complementary and divisible into small
self-contained units, cut off all communications between us and the main
French Armies. It severed our own communications for food and ammunition, which ran first to Amiens and afterwards through Abbeville,
and it shore its way up the coast to Boulogne and Calais, and almost
to Dunkirk. Behind this armored and mechanized onslaught came a
number of German divisions in lorries, and behind them again there
plodded comparatively slowly the dull brute mass of the ordinary German
Army and German people, always so ready to be led to the trampling
down in other lands of liberties and comforts which they have never
known in their own.

[3] I have said this armored scythe-stroke almost reached Dunkirk
—almost but not quite. Boulogne and Calais were the scenes of desperate
fighting. The Guards defended Boulogne for a while and were then
withdrawn by orders from this country. The Rifle Brigade, the 60th Rifles,
and the Queen Victoria's Rifles, with a battalion of British tanks and a
thousand Frenchmen, in all about four thousand strong, defended Calais
to the last. The British Brigadier was given an hour to surrender. He
spurned the offer, and four days of intense street fighting passed before
silence reigned over Calais, which marked the end of a memorable
resistance. Only thirty unwounded survivors were brought off by the
Navy, and we do not know the fate of their comrades. Their sacrifice,
however, was not in vain. At least two armored divisions, which otherwise would have been turned against the British Expeditionary Force,
had to be sent to overcome them. They have added another page to the
glories of the light divisions, and the time gained enabled the Graveline
water lines to be flooded and to be held by the French troops.

[⁴] Thus it was that the port of Dunkirk was kept open. When it was found impossible for the Armies of the north to reopen their communications to Amiens with the main French Armies, only one choice remained. It seemed, indeed, forlorn. The Belgian, British and French Armies were almost surrounded. Their sole line of retreat was to a single port and to its neighboring beaches. They were pressed on every side by heavy attacks and far outnumbered in the air.

[⁵] When, a week ago today, I asked the House to fix this afternoon as the occasion for a statement, I feared it would be my hard lot to announce the greatest military disaster in our long history. I thought—and some good judges agreed with me—that perhaps 20,000 or 30,000 men might be reembarked. But it certainly seemed that the whole of the French First Army and the whole of the British Expeditionary Force north of the Amiens-Abbeville gap would be broken up in the open field or else would have to capitulate for lack of food and ammunition. These were the hard and heavy tidings for which I called upon the House and the nation to prepare themselves a week ago. The whole root and core and brain of the British Army, on which and around which we were later to build, and are to build, the great British Armies in the later years of the war, seemed about to perish upon the field or to be led into an ignominious and starving captivity.

[⁶] That was the prospect of a week ago. But another blow which might well have proved final was yet to fall upon us. The King of the Belgians had called upon us to come to his aid. Had not this Ruler and his Government severed themselves from the Allies, who rescued their country from extinction in the late war, and had they not sought refuge in what has proved to be a fatal neutrality, the French and British Armies might well at the outset have saved not only Belgium but perhaps even Poland. Yet at the last moment, when Belgium was already invaded, King Leopold called upon us to come to his aid, and even at the last moment we came. He and his brave, efficient Army, nearly half a million strong, guarded our left flank and thus kept open our only line of retreat to the sea. Suddenly, without prior consultation, with the least possible notice, without the advice of his Ministers and upon his own personal act, he sent a plenipotentiary to the German Command, surrendered his Army, and exposed our whole flank and means of retreat.

[⁷] I asked the House a week ago to suspend its judgment because the facts were not clear, but I do not feel that any reason now exists why we should not form our own opinions upon this pitiful episode. The surrender of the Belgian Army compelled the British at the shortest notice to cover a flank to the sea more than 30 miles in length. Otherwise all would have been cut off, and all would have shared the fate to which King Leopold had condemned the finest Army his country had ever formed. So in doing this and in exposing this flank, as anyone who followed the operations on the map will see, contact was lost between the British and two out of the three corps forming the First French Army, who were still farther from the coast than we were, and it seemed impossible that any large number of Allied troops could reach the coast.

[8] The enemy attacked on all sides with great strength and fierceness, and their main power, the power of their far more numerous Air Force, was thrown into battle or else concentrated upon Dunkirk and the beaches. Pressing in upon the narrow exit, both from the east and from the west, the enemy began to fire with cannon upon the beaches by which alone the shipping could approach or depart. They sowed magnetic mines in the channels and seas; they sent repeated waves of hostile aircraft, sometimes more than a hundred strong in one formation, to cast their bombs upon the single pier that remained, and upon the sand dunes upon which the troops had their eyes for shelter. Their U-boats, one of which was sunk, and their motor launches took their toll of the vast traffic which now began. For four or five days an intense struggle reigned. All their armored divisions—or what was left of them—together with great masses of infantry and artillery, hurled themselves in vain upon the ever-narrowing, ever-contracting appendix within which the British and French Armies fought.

[9] Meanwhile, the Royal Navy, with the willing help of countless merchant seamen, strained every nerve to embark the British and Allied troops; 220 light warships and 650 other vessels were engaged. They had to operate upon the difficult coast, often in adverse weather, under an almost ceaseless hail of bombs and an increasing concentration of artillery fire. Nor were the seas, as I have said, themselves free from mines and torpedoes. It was in conditions such as these that our men carried on, with little or no rest, for days and nights on end, making trip after trip across the dangerous waters, bringing with them always men whom they had rescued. The numbers they have brought back are the measure of their devotion and their courage. The hospital ships, which brought off many thousands of British and French wounded, being so plainly marked were a special target for Nazi bombs, but the men and women on board never faltered in their duty.

[10] Meanwhile, the Royal Air Force, which had already been intervening in the battle, so far as its range would allow, from home bases, now used part of its main metropolitan fighter strength, and struck at the German bombers and at the fighters which in large numbers protected them. This struggle was protracted and fierce. Suddenly the scene has cleared, the crash and thunder has for the moment—but only for the moment—died away. A miracle of deliverance, achieved by valor, by perseverance, by perfect discipline, by faultless service, by resource, by skill, by unconquerable fidelity, is manifest to us all. The enemy was hurled back by the retreating British and French troops. He was so

roughly handled that he did not hurry their departure seriously. The Royal Air Force engaged the main strength of the German Air Force, and inflicted upon them losses of at least four to one; and the Navy, using nearly a thousand ships of all kinds, carried over 335,000 men, French and British, out of the jaws of death and shame, to their native land and to the tasks which lie immediately ahead. We must be very careful not to assign to this deliverance the attributes of a victory. Wars are not won by evacuations. But there was a victory inside this deliverance, which should be noted. It was gained by the Air Force. Many of our soldiers coming back have not seen the Air Force at work; they saw only the bombers which escaped its protective attack. They underrate its achievements. I have heard much talk of this; that is why I go out of my way to say this. I will tell you about it.

[11] This was a great trial of strength between the British and German Air Forces. Can you conceive a greater objective for the Germans in the air than to make evacuation from these beaches impossible, and to sink all these ships which were displayed, almost to the extent of thousands? Could there have been an objective of greater military importance and significance for the whole purpose of the war than this? They tried hard, and they were beaten back; they were frustrated in their task. We got the Army away; and they have paid four-fold for any losses which they have inflicted. Very large formations of German aeroplanes—and we know that they are a very brave race—have turned on several occasions from the attack of one-quarter of their number of the Royal Air Force, and have dispersed in different directions. Twelve aeroplanes have been hunted by two. One aeroplane was driven into the water and cast away by the mere charge of a British aeroplane, which had no more ammunition. All of our types—the Hurricane, the Spitfire, and the new Defiant —and all our pilots have been vindicated as superior to what they have at present to face.

[12] When we consider how much greater would be our advantage in defending the air above this Island against an overseas attack, I must say that I find in these facts a sure basis upon which practical and re-assuring thoughts may rest. I will pay my tribute to these young airmen. The great French Army was very largely, for the time being, cast back and disturbed by the onrush of a few thousands of armored vehicles. May it not also be that the cause of civilization itself will be defended by the skill and devotion of a few thousand airmen? There never has been, I suppose, in all the world, in all the history of war, such an opportunity for youth. The Knights of the Round Table, the Crusaders, all fall back into the past—not only distant but prosaic; these young men, going forth every morn to guard their native land and all that we stand for, holding in their hands these instruments of colossal and shattering power, of whom it may be said that

"Every morn brought forth a noble chance
And every chance brought forth a noble knight,"

deserve our gratitude, as do all of the brave men who, in so many ways and on so many occasions, are ready, and continue ready, to give life and all for their native land.

[13] I return to the Army. In the long series of very fierce battles, now on this front, now on that, fighting on three fronts at once, battles fought by two or three divisions against an equal or somewhat larger number of the enemy, and fought fiercely on some of the old grounds that so many of us knew so well—in these battles our losses in men have exceeded 30,000 killed, wounded, and missing. I take occasion to express the sympathy of the House to all who have suffered bereavement or who are still anxious. The President of the Board of Trade is not here today. His son has been killed, and many in the House have felt the pangs of affliction in the sharpest form. But I will say this about the missing: We have had a large number of wounded come home safely to this country, but I would say about the missing that there may be very many reported missing who will come back home, some day, in one way or another. In the confusion of this fight it is inevitable that many have been left in positions where honor required no further resistance from them.

[14] Against this loss of over 30,000 men, we can set a far heavier loss certainly inflicted upon the enemy. But our losses in material are enormous. We have perhaps lost one-third of the men we lost in the opening days of the battle of 21st March, 1918, but we have lost nearly as many guns—nearly one thousand—and all our transport, all the armored vehicles that were with the Army in the north. This loss will impose a further delay on the expansion of our military strength. That expansion had not been proceeding as fast as we had hoped. The best of all we had to give had gone to the British Expeditionary Force, and although they had not the numbers of tanks and some articles of equipment which were desirable, they were a very well and finely equipped Army. They had the first-fruits of all that our industry had to give, and that is gone. And now here is this further delay. How long it will be, how long it will last, depends upon the exertions which we make in this Island. An effort the like of which has never been seen in our records is now being made. Work is proceeding everywhere, night and day, Sundays and week days. Capital and Labor have cast aside their interests, rights, and customs and put them into the common stock. Already the flow of munitions has leaped forward. There is no reason why we should not in a few months overtake the sudden and serious loss that has come upon us, without retarding the development of our general program.

[15] Nevertheless, our thankfulness at the escape of our Army and so many men, whose loved ones have passed through an agonizing week,

must not blind us to the fact that what has happened in France and Belgium is a colossal military disaster. The French Army has been weakened, the Belgian Army has been lost, a large part of those fortified lines upon which so much faith had been reposed is gone, many valuable mining districts and factories have passed into the enemy's possession, the whole of the Channel ports are in his hands, with all the tragic consequences that follow from that, and we must expect another blow to be struck almost immediately at us or at France. We are told that Herr Hitler has a plan for invading the British Isles. This has often been thought of before. When Napoleon lay at Boulogne for a year with his flat-bottomed boats and his Grand Army, he was told by someone, "There are bitter weeds in England." There are certainly a great many more of them since the British Expeditionary Force returned.

[16] The whole question of home defense against invasion is, of course, powerfully affected by the fact that we have for the time being in this Island incomparably more powerful military forces than we have ever had at any moment in this war or the last. But this will not continue. We shall not be content with a defensive war. We have our duty to our Ally. We have to reconstitute and build up the British Expeditionary Force, once again, under its gallant Commander-in-Chief, Lord Gort. All this is in train; but in the interval we must put our defenses in this Island into such a high state of organization that the fewest possible numbers will be required to give effective security and that the largest possible potential offensive effort may be realized. On this we are now engaged. It will be very convenient, if it be the desire of the House, to enter upon this subject in a secret Session. Not that the Government would necessarily be able to reveal in very great detail military secrets, but we like to have our discussions free, without the restraint imposed by the fact that they will be read the next day by the enemy; and the Government would benefit by views freely expressed in all parts of the House by Members with their knowledge of so many different parts of the country. I understand that some request is to be made upon this subject, which will be readily acceded to by His Majesty's Government.

[17] We have found it necessary to take measures of increasing stringency, not only against enemy aliens and suspicious characters of other nationalities, but also against British subjects who may become a danger or a nuisance should the war be transported to the United Kingdom. I know there are a great many people affected by the orders which we have made who are the passionate enemies of Nazi Germany. I am very sorry for them, but we cannot, at the present time and under the present stress, draw all the distinctions which we should like to do. If parachute landings were attempted and fierce fighting attendant upon them followed, these unfortunate people would be far better out of the way, for their own sakes as well as for ours. There is, however, another class, for

which I feel not the slightest sympathy. Parliament has given us the powers to put down Fifth Column activities with a strong hand, and we shall use those powers, subject to the supervision and correction of the House, without the slightest hesitation until we are satisfied, and more than satisfied, that this malignancy in our midst has been effectively stamped out.

[18] Turning once again, and this time more generally, to the question of invasion, I would observe that there has never been a period in all these long centuries of which we boast when an absolute guarantee against invasion, still less against serious raids, could have been given to our people. In the days of Napoleon the same wind which would have carried his transports across the Channel might have driven away the blockading fleet. There was always the chance, and it is that chance which has excited and befooled the imaginations of many Continental tyrants. Many are the tales that are told. We are assured that novel methods will be adopted, and when we see the originality of malice, the ingenuity of aggression, which our enemy displays, we may certainly prepare ourselves for every kind of novel stratagem and every kind of brutal and treacherous maneuver. I think that no idea is so outlandish that it should not be considered and viewed with a searching, but at the same time, I hope, with a steady eye. We must never forget the solid assurances of sea power and those which belong to air power if it can be locally exercised.

[19] I have, myself, full confidence that if all do their duty, if nothing is neglected, and if the best arrangements are made, as they are being made, we shall prove ourselves once again able to defend our Island home, to ride out the storm of war, and to outlive the menace of tyranny, if necessary for years, if necessary alone. At any rate, that is what we are going to try to do. That is the resolve of His Majesty's Government— every man of them. That is the will of Parliament and the nation. The British Empire and the French Republic, linked together in their cause and in their need, will defend to the death their native soil, aiding each other like good comrades to the utmost of their strength. Even though large tracts of Europe and many old and famous States have fallen or may fall into the grip of the Gestapo and all the odious apparatus of Nazi rule, we shall not flag or fail. We shall go on to the end, we shall fight in France, we shall fight on the seas and oceans, we shall fight with growing confidence and growing strength in the air, we shall defend our Island, whatever the cost may be, we shall fight on the beaches, we shall fight on the landing grounds, we shall fight in the fields and in the streets, we shall fight in the hills; we shall never surrender, and even if, which I do not for a moment believe, this Island or a large part of it were sub-jugated and starving, then our Empire beyond the seas, armed and guarded by the British Fleet, would carry on the struggle, until, in God's

good time, the New World, with all its power and might, steps forth to the rescue and the liberation of the old.

--◦⸲{ COMMENT AND QUESTIONS }⸱◦--

1. The opening paragraphs of "Dunkirk" are chiefly informative, but with elements of evaluation and persuasion. Where, in the first three paragraphs, does Churchill subtly or clearly place blame and award praise? Would a French statesman have given exactly the same account? How does Churchill treat the King of the Belgians (in paragraphs 6 and 7), and why? Paragraph 5 is not essential to the report of events; what purpose does this paragraph serve?

2. Paragraphs 8–10 are interesting examples of dramatic narration. What techniques does Churchill use to make the reported action intense and vivid?

3. What seem to be Churchill's reasons for paying particular tribute to the Air Force?

4. Summarize Churchill's evaluation of the events he is reporting to the House of Commons.

5. What are Churchill's attitudes toward the possible invasion of England?

6. What passages in the speech do you think would have been most effective in arousing zeal and determination for carrying on the war effort? Explain.

7. Churchill's prose, though more formal and rhetorical than most modern expression, is excellent and worth study for its style. We have commented in the "Introduction to Rhetorical Analysis" on the opening sentence of the last paragraph of "Dunkirk." Examine the whole of the last paragraph, noticing the diction and the length, structure, and rhythm of sentences. Look with particular care at the famous long last sentence, and notice the techniques of parallelism, repetition, variety within the parallel structures, subordination, and emphasis. To what different groups is this last paragraph addressed? To what emotions does it appeal?

8. The story is told that Churchill was forced by the wild cheering in the House of Commons to pause in the delivery of his conclusion, and that, under cover of the uproar, he added, "And beat the **** over the head with bottles. That's all we've got." If this story is true, what does it reveal about Churchill?

[74]   *Adlai E. Stevenson*: Speech of Acceptance

ADLAI E. STEVENSON (1900–1965), Governor of Illinois, Democratic nominee for the Presidency of the United States in 1952 and 1956, and in the last years of his life United States Ambassador to the United Nations, had an influence on political life perhaps not yet fully appraised. Unsuccessful in his two presidential campaigns against General Eisenhower, Stevenson nevertheless brought to American politics an idealism, an eloquence, an intelligence and candor, and a humanity and humor which aroused interest in the political scene and rekindled hope for millions of Americans. George W. Ball, in *The Atlantic Monthly* of May, 1966, said that Stevenson, by sending up "flaming arrows to light the sky," raised political discussion to a new level of literacy; John Fischer, editor of *Harper's Magazine,* said in the November, 1965, issue of that magazine that Stevenson made politics intellectually respectable once again; Elmo Roper wrote in the *Saturday Review* of July 9, 1966, that at a crucial time in our history Stevenson, an "embodiment of humane and civilized intelligence," gave us a new vision and a new "respect for the intellectual life"; in an editorial published soon after his death, *Life* magazine concluded that Stevenson's qualities of integrity, doubt, humility, wit, and belief in the obligations of power helped defeat him in his presidential campaigns, and yet he carried these elements of America's moral strength beyond his own country, and although he never held the highest office at home "he died the first gentleman of the world." We are printing here an early speech, the acceptance of the Democratic nomination for the Presidency, delivered in Chicago, July 26, 1952; this speech, though necessarily limited by some of the established conventions for acceptance speeches, set the tone for the 1952 campaign, and it demonstrates a number of the qualities of Adlai Stevenson's mind and style.

[1] I accept your nomination—and your program.

[2] I should have preferred to hear those words uttered by a stronger, a wiser, a better man than myself. But, after listening to the President's speech, I feel better about myself!

[3] None of you, my friends, can wholly appreciate what is in my heart. I can only hope that you may understand my words. They will be few.

[4] I have not sought the honor you have done me. I *could* not seek it because I aspired to another office, which was the full measure of my ambition. One does not treat the highest office within the gift of the people of Illinois as an alternative or as a consolation prize.

[⁵] I *would* not seek your nomination for the Presidency because the burdens of that office stagger the imagination. Its potential for good or evil now and in the years of our lives smothers exultation and converts vanity to prayer.

[⁶] I have asked the Merciful Father—the Father of us all—to let this cup pass from me. But from such dread responsibility one does not shrink in fear, in self-interest, or in false humility.

[⁷] So, "If this cup may not pass from me, except I drink it, Thy will be done."

[⁸] That my heart has been troubled, that I have not sought this nomination, that I could not seek it in good conscience, that I would not seek it in honest self-appraisal, is not to say that I value it the less. Rather it is that I revere the office of the Presidency of the United States.

[⁹] And now, my friends, that you have made your decision, I will fight to win that office with all my heart and soul. And, with your help, I have no doubt that we will win.

[¹⁰] You have summoned me to the highest mission within the gift of any people. I could not be more proud. Better men than I were at hand for this mighty task, and I owe to you and to them every resource of mind and of strength that I possess to make your deed today a good one for our country and for our party. I am confident too, that your selection of a candidate for Vice-President will strengthen me and our party immeasurably in the hard, the implacable work that lies ahead for all of us.

[¹¹] I know you join me in gratitude and respect for the great Democrats and the leaders of our generation whose names you have considered here in this Convention, whose vigor, whose character, whose devotion to the Republic we love so well have won the respect of countless Americans and have enriched our party. I shall need them, we shall need them, because I have not changed in any respect since yesterday. Your nomination, awesome as I find it, has not enlarged my capacities. So I am profoundly grateful and emboldened by their comradeship and their fealty, and I have been deeply moved by their expressions of good will and support. And I cannot, my friends, resist the urge to take the one opportunity that has been afforded me to pay my humble respects to a very great and good American, whom I am proud to call my kinsman, Alben Barkley¹ of Kentucky.

[¹²] Let me say, too, that I have been heartened by the conduct of this Convention. You have argued and disagreed, because as Democrats you care and you care deeply. But you have disagreed and argued without calling each other liars and thieves, without despoiling our best traditions in any naked struggles for power.

[¹³] And you have written a platform that neither equivocates, con-

¹ Vice-President of the United States.

tradicts nor evades. You have restated our party's record, its principles and its purposes, in language that none can mistake, and with a firm confidence in justice, freedom and peace on earth that will raise the hearts and the hopes of mankind for that distant day when no one rattles a saber and no one drags a chain.

[¹⁴] For all these things I am grateful to you. But I feel no exultation, no sense of triumph. Our troubles are all ahead of us. Some will call us appeasers; others will say we are the war party. Some will say we are reactionary. Others will say that we stand for socialism. There will be the inevitable cries of "throw the rascals out"; "it's time for a change"; and so on and so on.

[¹⁵] We'll hear all those things and many more besides. But we will hear nothing that we have not heard before. I am not too much concerned with partisan denunciation, with epithets and abuse, because the working-man, the farmer, the thoughtful businessmen, all know that they are better off than ever before and they all know that the greatest danger to free enterprise in this country died with the great depression under the hammer blows of the Democratic Party.

[¹⁶] Nor am I afraid that the precious two-party system is in danger. Certainly the Republican Party looked brutally alive a couple of weeks ago, and I mean both Republican parties!² Nor am I afraid that the Democratic Party is old and fat and indolent. After 150 years it has been old for a long time; and it will never be indolent as long as it looks forward and not back, as long as it commands the allegiance of the young and the hopeful who dream the dreams and see the visions of a better America and a better world.

[¹⁷] You will hear many sincere and thoughtful people express concern about the continuation of one party in power for twenty years. I don't belittle this attitude. But change for the sake of change has no absolute merit in itself. If our greatest hazard is preservation of the values of Western civilization, in our self-interest alone, if you please, is it the part of wisdom to change for the sake of change to a party with a split personality; to a leader, whom we all respect, but who has been called upon to minister to a hopeless case of political schizophrenia?

[¹⁸] If the fear is corruption in official position, do you believe with Charles Evans Hughes that guilt is personal and knows no party? Do you doubt the power of any political leader, if he has the will to do so, to set his own house in order without his neighbors having to burn it down?

[¹⁹] What does concern me, in common with thinking partisans of both parties, is not just winning the election, but how it is won, how well we can take advantage of this great quadrennial opportunity to debate issues

---

² A reference to the split in 1952 between the conservative and liberal wings of the Republican Party.

sensibly and soberly. I hope and pray that we Democrats, win or lose, can campaign not as a crusade to exterminate the opposing party, as our opponents seem to prefer, but as a great opportunity to educate and elevate a people whose destiny is leadership, not alone of a rich and prosperous, contented country as in the past, but of a world in ferment.

[20] And, my friends, more important than winning the election is governing the nation. That is the test of a political party—the acid, final test. When the tumult and the shouting die, when the bands are gone and the lights are dimmed, there is the stark reality of responsibility in an hour of history haunted with those gaunt, grim specters of strife, dissension and materialism at home, and ruthless, inscrutable and hostile power abroad.

[21] The ordeal of the twentieth century—the bloodiest, most turbulent era of the Christian age—is far from over. Sacrifice, patience, understanding and implacable purpose may be our lot for years to come. Let's face it. Let's talk sense to the American people. Let's tell them the truth, that there are no gains without pains, that we are now on the eve of great decisions, not easy decisions, like resistance when you're attacked, but a long, patient, costly struggle which alone can assure triumph over the great enemies of man—war, poverty and tyranny—and the assaults upon human dignity which are the most grievous consequences of each.

[22] Let's tell them that the victory to be won in the twentieth century, this portal to the Golden Age, mocks the pretensions of individual acumen and ingenuity. For it is a citadel guarded by thick walls of ignorance and of mistrust which do not fall before the trumpets' blast or the politicians' imprecations or even a general's baton. They are, my friends, walls that must be directly stormed by the hosts of courage, of morality and of vision, standing shoulder to shoulder, unafraid of ugly truth, contemptuous of lies, half truths, circuses and demagoguery.

[23] The people are wise—wiser than the Republicans think. And the Democratic Party is the people's party, not the labor party, not the farmers' party, not the employers' party—it is the party of no one because it is the party of everyone.

[24] That, I think, is our ancient mission. Where we have deserted it we have failed. With your help there will be no desertion now. Better we lose the election than mislead the people; and better we lose than misgovern the people. Help me to do the job in this autumn of conflict and of campaign; help me to do the job in these years of darkness, of doubt and of crisis which stretch beyond the horizon of tonight's happy vision, and we will justify our glorious past and the loyalty of silent millions who look to us for compassion, for understanding and for honest purpose. Thus we will serve our great tradition greatly.

[25] I ask of you all you have; I will give to you all I have, even as he who came here tonight and honored me, as he has honored you—the

Democratic Party—by a lifetime of service and bravery that will find him an imperishable page in the history of the Republic and of the Democratic Party—President Harry S. Truman.

[26] And finally, my friends, in the staggering task you have assigned me, I shall always try "to do justly and to love mercy and to walk humbly with my God."

---⊸ COMMENT AND QUESTIONS ⊱⋅-

1. Early in 1952, Stevenson had announced his candidacy for a second term as Governor of Illinois, and he had said repeatedly that he was not a candidate for the Presidency; he was drafted by the Democratic National Convention against his often expressed wishes. The first nine paragraphs of the acceptance speech therefore explain his situation and the reasons for his reluctance, and also affirm his resolve to fight now for the office he had not sought. The introductory paragraphs reveal, too, a characteristic modesty. Where else in the speech do you find evidence of this modesty?

2. The content of paragraphs 10–13 is in many ways conventional: a nominee conventionally expresses his feeling about the honor accorded him, pays tribute to other members of his party, attempts to establish unity for the coming campaign, and praises the party's platform. Examine the language in paragraph 13. What qualities of style do you notice? What is the literal meaning of "when no one rattles a saber and no one drags a chain"?

3. This is a serious speech. Are there traces in it of the wit and humor for which Stevenson was famous?

4. Paragraph 14 makes a transition and introduces a block of material. What is the unifying idea in paragraphs 15–18? Notice the endings of these four paragraphs. In what ways are the endings effective?

5. Paragraph 19 is an initial statement of Stevenson's purpose in the 1952 campaign, a purpose embodied in speeches that electrified many who had come to expect meaningless emotional oratory in political campaigns. Comment on the structure of the last sentence of paragraph 19 and on the effectiveness of the sentence as a statement of hope and purpose.

6. Examine the last sentence of paragraph 20, and comment on its structure and its style.

7. What are the implications, in paragraph 22, of "a general's *baton*"? In the whole speech, what are Stevenson's attitudes toward Eisenhower?

8. Paragraphs 21 and 24 supplied campaign slogans, and they are perhaps the best examples in this speech of Stevenson's mastery of language. Carefully analyze the writing in these two paragraphs.

9. In what ways is the final quotation a good ending?

10. Describe the persona revealed in Stevenson's speech.

[75]   The Kennedy Inauguration: Two Accounts

Theodore C. Sorensen: Inauguration

Arthur M. Schlesinger, Jr.: Prologue: January 1961

THE FIRST OF THESE two accounts is from *Kennedy*, the second from *A Thousand Days: John F. Kennedy in the White House*, both books published in 1965. For a note on Theodore C. Sorensen, see page 482; for a note on Arthur M. Schlesinger, Jr., see page 78.

Theodore C. Sorensen: Inauguration

[¹] Early in January, with work on his program well under way and his principal nominees named, the President-elect's thoughts turned more and more to his inauguration. He took a lively interest in plans for the Inaugural Concert and five simultaneous Inaugural Balls (all of which he would attend), in plans for the four-hour-long Inaugural Parade (all of which he would watch in twenty-degree temperature), the million-dollar Democratic fund-raising Inaugural Gala (which he greatly enjoyed, despite a two-hour delay due to blizzards) and in all the other festivities. He asked Robert Frost to deliver a poem at the inauguration ceremony. He wanted Marian Anderson to sing "The Star-Spangled Banner." He sought a family Bible on which he could take the oath of office without arousing the POAU. He indicated that top hats instead of Homburgs would be in order for the official party. And, finally and most importantly, he began to work on his Inaugural Address.

[²] He had first mentioned it to me in November. He wanted suggestions from everyone. He wanted it short. He wanted it focused on foreign policy. He did not want it to sound partisan, pessimistic or critical of his predecessor. He wanted neither the customary cold war rhetoric about the Communist menace nor any weasel words that Khrushchev might misinterpret. And he wanted it to set a tone for the era about to begin.

[³] He asked me to read all the past Inaugural Addresses (which I discovered to be a largely undistinguished lot, with some of the best eloquence emanating from some of our worst Presidents). He asked me to study the secret of Lincoln's Gettysburg Address (my conclusion, which his Inaugural applied, was that Lincoln never used a two- or three-syllable word where a one-syllable word would do, and never used two or three words where one word would do).

[4] Actual drafting did not get under way until the week before it was due. As had been true of his acceptance speech at Los Angeles, pages, paragraphs and complete drafts had poured in, solicited from Kraft, Galbraith, Stevenson, Bowles and others, unsolicited from newsmen, friends and total strangers. From Billy Graham he obtained a list of possible Biblical quotations, and I secured a similar list from the director of Washington's Jewish Community Council, Isaac Franck.

[5] The final text included several phrases, sentences and themes suggested by these sources, as did his address to the Massachusetts legislature. He was, in fact, concerned that the Massachusetts speech had pre-empted some of his best material and had set a mark that would be hard to top. Credit should also go to other Kennedy advisers who reviewed the early drafts and offered suggestions or encouragement.

[6] But however numerous the assistant artisans, the principal architect of the Inaugural Address was John Fitzgerald Kennedy. Many of its most memorable passages can be traced to earlier Kennedy speeches and writings. For example:

Inaugural Address	*Other Addresses*
For man holds in his mortal hands the power to abolish all forms of human poverty and all forms of human life.	. . . man . . . has taken into his mortal hands the power to exterminate the entire species some seven times over. *—Acceptance speech at Los Angeles*
. . . the torch has been passed to a new generation of Americans. . . .	It is time, in short, for a new generation of Americans. *—Acceptance speech and several campaign speeches*
And so, my fellow Americans, ask not what your country can do for you; ask what you can do for your country.	We do not campaign stressing what our country is going to do for us as a people. We stress what we can do for the country, all of us. *—Televised campaign address from Washington, September 20, 1960*

[7] No Kennedy speech ever underwent so many drafts. Each paragraph was reworded, reworked and reduced. The following table illustrates the attention paid to detailed changes:

First Draft	Next-to-Last Draft	Final Text
We celebrate today not a victory of party but the sacrament of democracy.	We celebrate today not a victory of party but a convention of freedom.	We observe today not a victory of party but a celebration of freedom.
Each of us, whether we hold office or not, shares the responsibility for guiding this most difficult of all societies along the path of self-discipline and self-government.	In your hands, my fellow citizens, more than in mine, will be determined the success or failure of our course.	In your hands, my fellow citizens, more than mine, will rest the final success or failure of our course.
Nor can two great and powerful nations forever continue on this reckless course, both overburdened by the staggering cost of modern weapons . . .	. . . neither can two great and powerful nations long endure their present reckless course, both overburdened by the staggering cost of modern weapons . . .	. . . neither can two great and powerful groups of nations take comfort from our present course—both sides overburdened by the cost of modern weapons . . .
And if the fruits of cooperation prove sweeter than the dregs of suspicion, let both sides join ultimately in creating a true world order—neither a Pax Americana, nor a Pax Russiana, nor even a balance of power—but a community of power.	And if a beachhead of cooperation can be made in the jungles of suspicion, let both sides join some day in creating, not a new balance of power but a new world of law . . .	And if a beachhead of cooperation can push back the jungle of suspicion, let both sides join in creating a new endeavor, not a new balance of power, but a new world of law . . .

[8] Initially, while he worked on his thoughts at Palm Beach, I worked at my home in a Washington suburb with telephoned instructions from the President-elect and the material collected from other sources. Then I flew down, was driven to his father's oceanside home, and gave him my notes for the actual drafting and assembling. We worked through the morning seated on the patio overlooking the Atlantic.

[9] He was dissatisfied with each attempt to outline domestic goals. It sounded partisan, he said, divisive, too much like the campaign. Finally he said, "Let's drop out the domestic stuff altogether. It's too long anyway." He wanted it to be the shortest in the twentieth century, he said. "It's more effective that way and I don't want people to think I'm a

windbag." He couldn't beat FDR's abbreviated wartime remarks in 1944, I said—and he settled for the shortest (less than nineteen hundred words) since 1905.

[¹⁰] "I'm sick of reading how we're planning another 'hundred days' of miracles," he said, "and I'd like to know who on the staff is talking that up. Let's put in that this won't all be finished in a hundred days or a thousand."

[¹¹] That afternoon, as he was busy with other meetings at the house, I put his notes, changes and additions into a clean draft, working beside the Palm Beach Towers Hotel swimming pool.

[¹²] The next morning, on the patio in sport clothes, he reworked it further. "Let's eliminate all the 'I's,'" he said. "Just say what 'we' will do. You'll have to leave it in about the oath and the responsibility, but let's cut it everywhere else." The ending, he said, "sounds an awful lot like the ending of the Massachusetts legislature speech, but I guess it's OK." He worked and reworked the "ask not" sentence, with the three campaign speeches containing a similar phrase (Anchorage, Detroit, Washington) spread out on a low glass coffee table beside him.

[¹³] Later that day—January 17—as we flew back to Washington from Palm Beach, working in his cabin on the *Caroline*, the final phrasing was emerging. A biblical quotation that was later used in his American University speech was deleted. The opening paragraphs were redictated by the President-elect to Evelyn Lincoln en route, and he smilingly placed in the plane's desk drawer his handwritten notes from which he had dictated, saying, "An early draft of Roosevelt's Inaugural was discovered the other day—and brought $200,000 at an auction."

[¹⁴] Arriving back in Washington, the work went on at his house and in our Senate offices. Kenneth Galbraith suggested "cooperative ventures" with our allies in place of "joint ventures," which sounded like a mining partnership. Dean Rusk suggested that the other peoples of the world be challenged to ask "what together we can do for freedom" instead of "what you can do for freedom." Walter Lippmann suggested that references to the Communist bloc be changed from "enemy" to "adversary." The President-elect inserted a phrase he had used in a campaign speech on Latin America—"a new alliance for progress." At the last moment, concerned that his emphasis on foreign affairs would be interpreted as an evasion on civil rights, he added to his commitment on human rights the words "at home and around the world."

[¹⁵] On January 19, one day before inauguration, it was finished. The Arrangements Committee was asked to check on the height of the reading lectern. A large-type reading copy was encased in a loose-leaf notebook. A copy sat beside the Kennedy chair at home, and by his seat on a quick trip to New York, so that any spare moment could be used to familiarize himself with it. (He never memorized a speech.) It was beside him when he took time out, amidst the last day's hectic schedule of conferences and arrangements, to meet seven of my little nieces and nephews as well as their parents.

[16] Inauguration morning dawned cold but clear. Three thousand servicemen stationed in the Washington area had done an amazing job of working through the night with seven hundred plows and trucks to remove the eight inches of snow which, on the previous day, had nearly strangled the city. (On hearing the order go out for snow shovelers, one new Kennedy economic adviser, already burdened with a dozen assignments, had wearily remarked to his chairman, "Don't be surprised if they call us.") Visitors from every state, jubilant Kennedy workers we had hardly seen since the primaries, foreign diplomats and dignitaries, outgoing and incoming officials, a specially invited group of 155 writers, artists and scholars, and thousands of ordinary citizens of every age and background, all crowded the capital city and Capitol Hill. On the temporary wooden grandstands raised on the east front of the newly painted Capitol, under a glittering sun but in bitter cold, the Cabinet and White House officers of the New Frontier assembled. We bore some resemblance to "frontiersmen," wearing sweaters beneath our formal togs and woolen gloves along with top hats. As we greeted each other gaily, the chill in the air merely added a certain warmth to the spirit of youth and vigor.

[17] Few will forget the memorable moments of that solemn ceremony at twelve noon:

[18] Robert Frost, with the glare of the sun and the snow making it impossible for his aging eyes to read a new dedication (". . . a Golden Age of poetry and power, of which this noonday's the beginning hour . . ."), resolutely reciting his older poem from memory . . .

[19] Richard Cardinal Cushing, delivering a proud (and prolonged) prayer for his famous parishioner while firemen and Secret Servicemen contended with smoldering short-circuited wires in the lectern . . .

[20] John Fitzgerald Kennedy, thirty-fifth President of the United States, in that marvelously clear voice, repeating after Chief Justice Earl Warren the oath of office he had told the Houston ministers he could take without condition or reservation, "so help me God."

[21] Few will forget the striking contrast presented by the outgoing and incoming Presidents. One was the likeable, dedicated product of the rural Midwest and the Military Academy. The other was the urbane product of the urban East. Both had spent their entire adult careers in the service of their country, yet they were vastly different, not only in age, religion and political philosophy, but in their views of politics as a profession and the Presidency as power. Every eye watched them take their places, the oldest man ever to serve in the office of the Presidency and the youngest man ever elected to it. Dwight Eisenhower, aged seventy— still looking remarkably ruddy, his successor observed—sat next to John

Kennedy, aged forty-three, bareheaded as always in the twenty-two-degree air, carrying the top hat he had decreed all should wear. Their contrast lent added meaning to the phrase: "Let the word go forth from this time and place, to friend and foe alike, that the torch has been passed to a new generation of Americans."

[22] Grouped behind Kennedy as he removed his overcoat to speak were the young men of his new administration—men with strikingly successful backgrounds in business, law, politics, government and academic affairs—men who were, with few exceptions, unschooled in the old pre-World War I dogmas and pre-depression doctrines—men who had witnessed the folly of unpreparedness and appeasement, the tragedy of war, the dawn of the nuclear age, and the harmful rejection of intellectuals by McCarthyism and the new materialism. These were men who had been concerned about the lack of ideas and idealism in the sterile clash between repressive Communism and narrowly negative anti-Communism, but who were also determined, as their leader put it that day, to "pay any price, bear any burden, meet any hardship, support any friend [or] oppose any foe in order to assure the survival and the success of liberty."

[23] I know of no way to summarize, condense or excerpt the Kennedy Inaugural Address. It was itself a compact summary of the new President's hopes and resolves—his pledges to our friends and allies, old and new—his request to the Communists for a new quest for peace—and his summons to his fellow citizens to bear with him the burdens of freedom. Each of these imperatives was contained in phrases too brief to be summarized and too important to be omitted. They were addressed to the American people of our time but have meaning for all people for all time. For they embody the best of our heritage from the past and the best of our hopes for the future. This one speech, of all John Kennedy's speeches, must be set forth here in full:

1. We observe today not a victory of party but a celebration of freedom, symbolizing an end as well as a beginning, signifying renewal as well as change. For I have sworn before you and Almighty God the same solemn oath our forebears prescribed nearly a century and three-quarters ago.

2. The world is very different now. For man holds in his mortal hands the power to abolish all forms of human poverty and all forms of human life. And yet the same revolutionary belief for which our forebears fought is still at issue around the globe, the belief that the rights of man come not from the generosity of the state but from the hand of God.

3. We dare not forget today that we are the heirs of that first revolution. Let the word go forth from this time and place, to friend and foe alike, that the torch has been passed to a new generation of Americans, born in this century, tempered by war, disciplined by a hard and bitter

peace, proud of our ancient heritage, and unwilling to witness or permit the slow undoing of those human rights to which this nation has always been committed, and to which we are committed today at home and around the world.

4. Let every nation know, whether it wishes us well or ill, that we shall pay any price, bear any burden, meet any hardship, support any friend, oppose any foe to assure the survival and the success of liberty.

5. This much we pledge—and more.

6. To those old allies whose cultural and spiritual origins we share, we pledge the loyalty of faithful friends. United, there is little we cannot do in a host of cooperative ventures. Divided, there is little we can do, for we dare not meet a powerful challenge at odds and split asunder.

7. To those new states whom we welcome to the ranks of the free, we pledge our word that one form of colonial control shall not have passed away merely to be replaced by a far more iron tyranny. We shall not always expect to find them supporting our view. But we shall always hope to find them strongly supporting their own freedom, and to remember that, in the past, those who foolishly sought power by riding the back of the tiger ended up inside.

8. To those peoples in the huts and villages of half the globe struggling to break the bonds of mass misery, we pledge our best efforts to help them help themselves, for whatever period is required, not because the Communists may be doing it, not because we seek their votes, but because it is right. If a free society cannot help the many who are poor, it cannot save the few who are rich.

9. To our sister republics south of our border, we offer a special pledge: to convert our good words into good deeds, in a new alliance for progress, to assist free men and free governments in casting off the chains of poverty. But this peaceful revolution of hope cannot become the prey of hostile powers. Let all our neighbors know that we shall join with them to oppose aggression or subversion anywhere in the Americas. And let every other power know that this hemisphere intends to remain the master of its own house.

10. To that world assembly of sovereign states, the United Nations, our last best hope in an age where the instruments of war have far outpaced the instruments of peace, we renew our pledge of support: to prevent it from becoming merely a forum for invective, to strengthen its shield of the new and the weak, and to enlarge the area in which its writ may run.

11. Finally, to those nations who would make themselves our adversary, we offer not a pledge but a request: that both sides begin anew the quest for peace, before the dark powers of destruction unleashed by science engulf all humanity in planned or accidental self-destruction.

12. We dare not tempt them with weakness. For only when our arms are sufficient beyond doubt can we be certain beyond doubt that they will never be employed.

13. But neither can two great and powerful groups of nations take comfort from our present course—both sides overburdened by the cost of modern weapons, both rightly alarmed by the steady spread of the deadly atom, yet both racing to alter that uncertain balance of terror that stays the hand of mankind's final war.

14. So let us begin anew, remembering on both sides that civility is not a sign of weakness, and sincerity is always subject to proof. Let us never negotiate out of fear, but let us never fear to negotiate.

15. Let both sides explore what problems unite us instead of belaboring those problems which divide us.

16. Let both sides, for the first time, formulate serious and precise proposals for the inspection and control of arms, and bring the absolute power to destroy other nations under the absolute control of all nations.

17. Let both sides seek to invoke the wonders of science instead of its terrors. Together let us explore the stars, conquer the deserts, eradicate disease, tap the ocean depths and encourage the arts and commerce.

18. Let both sides unite to heed in all corners of the earth the command of Isaiah to "undo the heavy burdens . . . [and] let the oppressed go free."

19. And if a beachhead of cooperation may push back the jungle of suspicion, let both sides join in creating a new endeavor, not a new balance of power, but a new world of law, where the strong are just and the weak secure and the peace preserved.

20. All this will not be finished in the first one hundred days. Nor will it be finished in the first one thousand days, nor in the life of this Administration, nor even perhaps in our lifetime on this planet. But let us begin.

21. In your hands, my fellow citizens, more than mine, will rest the final success or failure of our course. Since this country was founded, each generation of Americans has been summoned to give testimony to its national loyalty. The graves of young Americans who answered the call to service surround the globe.

22. Now the trumpet summons us again—not as a call to bear arms, though arms we need; not as a call to battle, though embattled we are; but a call to bear the burden of a long twilight struggle, year in and year out, "rejoicing in hope, patient in tribulation," a struggle against the common enemies of man: tyranny, poverty, disease and war itself.

23. Can we forge against these enemies a grand and global alliance, North and South, East and West, that can assure a more fruitful life for all mankind? Will you join in that historic effort?

24. In the long history of the world, only a few generations have been granted the role of defending freedom in its hour of maximum danger. I do not shrink from this responsibility; I welcome it. I do not believe that any of us would exchange places with any other people or any other generation. The energy, the faith, the devotion which we bring to this endeavor will light our country and all who serve it, and the glow from that fire can truly light the world.

25. And so, my fellow Americans, ask not what your country can do for you; ask what you can do for your country.

26. My fellow citizens of the world, ask not what America will do for you, but what together we can do for the freedom of man.

27. Finally, whether you are citizens of America or citizens of the world, ask of us here the same high standards of strength and sacrifice which we ask of you. With a good conscience our only sure reward, with history the final judge of our deeds, let us go forth to lead the land we love, asking His blessing and His help, but knowing that here on earth God's work must truly be our own.

[24] It seemed to me, as I watched the faces of the crowd, that they had forgotten the cold, forgotten party lines and forgotten all the old divisions of race, religion and nation. It was time to begin.

Arthur M. Schlesinger, Jr.: Prologue: January 1961

[1] It all began in the cold.

[2] It had been cold all week in Washington. Then early Thursday afternoon the snow came. The winds blew in icy, stinging gusts and whipped the snow down the frigid streets. Washingtonians do not know how to drive in the snow: they slide and skid and spin their wheels and panic. By six o'clock traffic had stopped all over town. People abandoned their cars in snowdrifts and marched grimly into the gale, heads down, newspapers wrapped around necks and stuffed under coats. And still the snow fell and the winds blew.

[3] At eight o'clock the young President-elect and his wife went to the Inaugural Concert at Constitution Hall. An hour later they left at the intermission to go on to the Inaugural Gala at the Armory. The limousine made its careful way through the blinding snow down the Mall. Bonfires had been lit along the path in a vain effort to keep the avenue clear. Great floodlights around the Washington Monument glittered through the white storm. It was a scene of eerie beauty. As stranded motorists cheered the presidential car, the President-elect told his friend William Walton, "Turn on the lights so they can see Jackie." With the light on inside the car, he settled back to read Jefferson's First Inaugural, which

had been printed in the concert program. When he finished, he shook his head and said wryly, "Better than mine."

[4] By midnight the city was choked with snow. Workmen labored to clear Pennsylvania Avenue for next day's parade. Soldiers used flame throwers to melt the frozen drifts around the inaugural stand in the Capitol Plaza. At quarter to four in the morning, the President-elect returned to his house in Georgetown from a supper given him downtown by his father after the Gala. His wife, recuperating from the birth of their second child, had gone home hours earlier; but he found her awake, too excited to sleep, and they talked for a moment about the day that had passed and the day yet to come.

[5] Toward dawn the snow began to stop. It covered houses and clung to trees and filled the windswept streets: the white city faintly shimmered in the pale sunrise. The President-elect arose at eight, read over the text of his inaugural address, pencil in hand, and then left to attend mass at a neighboring church. The crowd began to gather in the Capitol Plaza long before noon. At eleven the President-elect and his wife drank coffee with the retiring President and Vice-President and their wives in the Red Room of the White House. They talked formally and inconsequentially. In morning coats and top hats they entered limousines to drive along the snowy streets to the Capitol. The wife of the retiring President said, "Look at Ike in his top hat. He looks just like Paddy the Irishman."

[6] The skies were now blue and cloudless, and the Plaza glistened in the sun, but the wind had not fallen and the temperature was barely twenty degrees above zero. The waiting crowd huddled and shivered. They enveloped themselves in sweaters and mufflers, blankets and sleeping bags. They stamped their feet to keep out the chill. They watched restlessly as the dignitaries slowly took their places on the platform. When the Vice President-elect entered, a man in a ten-gallon hat shouted, "All the way with L.B.J."; the Vice President-elect acknowledged the shout with a slight inclination of his head. Noon passed, and the crowd shuffled with impatience when the ceremony failed to begin. The President-elect, starting to come from the Capitol onto the platform, was instructed to wait. Then, at twenty minutes after twelve, he appeared, and the spectators warmed themselves with applause.

[7] Now they listened with stoicism as the Cardinal boomed out an interminable invocation. They looked with envy as blue smoke thinly curled up from a short circuit in the electric wires underneath the lectern: where there was fire, there must be heat. The Chief of the Secret Service watched the smoke with apprehension, fearful that the whole inaugural stand might go up in flames. Three times he started to give the order to clear the stand, and three times he paused; then the

smoke stopped. The Chief mused that his Service would be in for a lively era protecting the athletic and fearless new President.*

[8] On the platform, the breath of the old poet congealed in the freezing air; and now, when he stepped forth to speak, the glare from the sun and snow blinded him. He read three lines from a manuscript:

> *Summoning artists to participate*
> *In the august occasions of the state*
> *Seems something artists ought to celebrate.*

Then he stopped and said, "I'm not having a good light here at all. I can't see in this light." The Vice President-elect held out his hat to shield the old man's eyes; Robert Frost still could not see, could not conclude the poem:

> *It makes the prophet in us all presage*
> *The glory of a next Augustan age*
> *Of a power leading from its strength and pride,*
> *Of young ambition eager to be tried,*
> *Firm in our free beliefs without dismay,*
> *In any game the nations want to play.*
> *A golden age of poetry and power*
> *Of which this noonday's the beginning hour.*

Instead he said, "This was to have been a preface to a poem which I do not have to read," and from memory he recited "The Gift Outright"— "The land was ours before we were the land's"—changing the last line:

> *Such as we were we gave ourselves outright*
> *(The deed of gift was many deeds of war)*
> *To the land vaguely realizing westward,*
> *But still unstoried, artless, unenhanced,*
> *Such as she was, such as she will become.*

[9] At nine minutes before one the Chief Justice came forward to administer the oath. The President-elect, without hat or coat, the old Douay Bible of the Fitzgerald family open before him, gave his responses in firm tones. At last he began his inaugural address, his voice ringing out in the frosty air. "Let the word go forth from this time and place, to friend and foe alike, that the torch has been passed to a new generation of Americans—born in this century, tempered by war, disciplined by a hard and bitter peace, proud of our ancient heritage." And so he continued, striking notes of strength, conciliation and hope. "Let us begin anew," he said, "—remembering on both sides that civility is not a sign of weakness, and sincerity is always subject to proof. Let us never negotiate out of fear. But let us never fear to negotiate." The prospect would not be

* U. E. Baughman, *Secret Service Chief* (New York, 1962), 3, 12.

easy. "All this will not be finished in the first hundred days. Nor will it be finished in the first thousand days, nor in the life of this Administration, nor even perhaps in our lifetime on this planet. But let us begin." The burden of the "long twilight struggle" lay on this people and this generation. "And so, my fellow Americans: ask not what your country can do for you—ask what you can do for your country."* (That morning, reading over his text, he had scratched out "will" and replaced it by "can.") He concluded: "My fellow citizens of the world: ask not what America will do for you, but what together we can do for the freedom of man."

[10] The applause was strong and sustained. The President left the platform. His young wife joined him in the Capitol, whispered, "Oh, Jack, what a day," and softly touched his face. Then the inaugural parade marched through the freezing afternoon, and the thirty-fifth Presidentiad, as Walt Whitman would say, began.

----◄{ COMMENT AND QUESTIONS }►----

Sorensen's comments on Kennedy's speech-writing, page 482, may be of interest as you think about the Inaugural Address.

1. These two accounts of the same event are good examples of the way different observers may select and emphasize different things. What aspects of the inauguration do both authors include in their accounts? What major differences do you see in selection, development, and tone? (Sorensen not

---

* This thought had lain in Kennedy's mind for a long time. As far back as 1945 he had noted down in a looseleaf notebook a quotation from Rousseau: "As soon as any man says of the affairs of the state, What does it matter to me? the state may be given up as lost." In his address accepting the Democratic nomination in 1960, he said of the New Frontier, "It sums up not what I intend to *offer* the American people, but what I intend to *ask* of them." On September 5 at Cadillac Square in Detroit, Kennedy departed from his prepared text to say: "The new frontier is not what I promise I am going to do for you. The new frontier is what I ask you to do for our country." He continued to polish the thought in the back of his mind until he was ready to put it in final form in the inaugural address.

Though this line was clearly Kennedy's own, like all such lines it had its historic analogues. Gilbert Seldes cites the remarks of the mayor of Haverhill at the funeral of John Greenleaf Whittier as quoted by Van Wyck Brooks in *New England: Indian Summer:* "Here may we be reminded that man is most honored, not by that which a city may do for him, but by that which he has done for the city." And James Rowe, Jr., Oliver Wendell Holmes's last law clerk, points out the following lines from a Memorial Day address delivered by Justice Holmes in 1884: "It is now the moment when by common consent we pause to become conscious of our national life and to rejoice in it, to recall what our country has done for each of us, and to ask ourselves what we can do for our country in return."

only helped with the drafting of the Inaugural Address but also had been Kennedy's assistant speech-writer since 1953. "Prologue: January 1961" is the beginning of Schlesinger's book, and the book ends with comment on the bitter cold and the snow in Washington a month after President Kennedy's assassination; Schlesinger's concluding, one-sentence paragraph is: "It all ended, as it began, in the cold." Do these facts help to explain some of the different emphases of the two writers?)

2. Examine the changes in phrasing that Sorensen illustrates in paragraph 7 of his account. In what ways is the final text of the Inaugural Address superior to the earlier drafts?

3. Which of the two accounts of the inauguration seems better to you, and why?

4. This question and the following questions are on the Inaugural Address. A marked characteristic of style is the use of parallelism and patterns of contrast or antithesis, often involving the repetition of words, as in *ask not what your country can do for you; ask what you can do for your country.* Point out other examples of parallelism or antithesis or both.

5. In paragraphs 5–11, the word *pledge* is used seven times. Why is *pledge* a better word than *promise?* Paragraphs 6–11 have similar beginnings, and paragraphs 15–18 have the same beginnings: *Let both sides . . . .* What is the purpose of these repetitions? What other repetitions can you find? Do they seem to you effective?

6. Repeated patterns of sound as well as of words and sentence patterns are also characteristic of the Address. Point out examples of alliteration. Can you find examples of other repeated sounds or internal rhyme in any sentences?

7. For all of the repetitions, the Address is varied in sentence structure and sentence length. The longest sentence (80 words) is at the end of paragraph 3; the shortest (4 words) is at the end of paragraph 20. Can you see a reason for the length of these two sentences?

8. What are the connotations of *torch* (paragraph 3), *iron tyranny* (paragraph 7), and *balance of terror* (paragraph 13)?

9. President Kennedy makes considerable use of figurative language. What figures seem to you most effective, and why?

CURRENT PROBLEMS
AND ATTITUDES

ᝣ

[76] *Lewis Mumford*: The American Way of Death

LEWIS MUMFORD (1895–) is an American critic and author of a number of well-known studies of American life. Among his books are *Sticks and Stones, The Brown Decades, Technics and Civilization, The Culture of Cities,* and *The City in History*. The following article, from *The New York Review of Books,* April 28, 1966, is a review of two books—*Unsafe at Any Speed: The Designed-in Dangers of the American Automobile* by Ralph Nader, and *Safety Last: An Indictment of the Auto Industry* by Jeffrey O'Connell and Arthur Myers. The article is also Mumford's own indictment of the motor car industry and of some values of American society.

[¹] As so often happens, when the minds of many people have been silently brooding over the same subject, there has recently been an outbreak of books, articles, and legislative investigations, all devoted to assessing the mechanical defects, the bodily hazards, and the mounting social disadvantages of the motor car. The tone of this discussion has been critical, not to say sacrilegious. Some of the critics have dared to say that the Sacred Cow of the American Way of Life is overfed and bloated; that the daily milk she supplies is poisonous; that the pasturage this species requires wastes acres of land that could be used for more significant human purposes; and that the vast herds of sacred cows, allowed to roam everywhere, like their Hindu counterparts, are trampling down the vegetation, depleting wild life, and turning both urban and rural areas into a single smudgy wasteland, whose fancy sociological name is Megalopolis.

[2] The priesthood of the Sacred Cow, very sensitive to the mildest heresy, now shows definite signs of alarm, alternating plaintive moos with savage bellows; for in their religion, the cult of the Sacred Cow is closely affiliated with an older object of worship, the Golden Calf. With justified trepidation, the priestly establishment feels religion itself (capitalized) is being challenged—that religion for whose evidences of power and glory the American people, with eyes devoutly closed, are prepared to sacrifice some 45,000 lives every year, and to maim, often irreparably, more than a million and a half more. Only war can claim so many premature deaths; for the death rate from motor cars is greater than the combined death rate from falls, burnings, drownings, railroads, firearms, and poisonous gases, plus some two thousand other deaths from unidentifiable causes. And though only roughly half as many Americans were killed outright by autos in the last four-year period as were killed in our armed forces during a similar term in the Second World War, nearly three times as many were injured.

[3] The current uprising against the miscarriage of the horseless carriage has long been brewing; John Keats's *The Insolent Chariots* broke the painful silence as far back as 1958. Only childish petulance on the part of the car manufacturers and their allies makes them attribute this spreading dissatisfaction with their product to the outspoken criticisms of a few mischievous critics, since the latter, till now a sorry few, have had none of the auto industry's facilities for commanding public attention and suppressing debate. The roots of the current revolt spread over a wide area, and they go much deeper than even the most impassioned advocates of safer motor car design yet realize.

[4] If the temple of the Sacred Cow is crumbling, it is because the whole mode of existence for which it is the prime mover has become antagonistic to the genuine human needs it was once supposed to serve and enhance. The fact is that the great American dream of a nation on wheels, which began with the covered wagon, has come to a dreary terminus. The very success of the auto industry in fulfilling the mechanical conditions for that dream has turned it, ironically, into a nightmare. An essential part of the American's delight over the auto was a happy leftover from pioneer days: the ingratiating idea of private freedom, in the sense of being able to go anywhere one willed, at any time one willed, at any speed one willed, up hill and down dale exploring the great open spaces, and at least getting away from the familiar habitat, the daily round, the mechanical grind. In what has belatedly been called "auto-

mobility," now that we are losing it, the personal "auto" was even more essential than the mechanical "mobility."

[5] Until about 1930, this dream bore more than a faint resemblance to actuality. Even such a fastidious soul as Henry James hailed the aristocratic joys of travel by motor car, which opened up the landscape and refreshed the spirit; so much so, that such usual interruptions as a leaky tire or a boggy road, if not too frequent, only added an extra spice to the adventure. Unfortunately, one of the conditions for enjoying this freedom was the existence of other possible modes of transportation, to handle mass demands, such as the wonderful transportation network, of railroads, electric trolleys, and steamboats that once spanned the country and not merely took up much of the travel load but met different human needs at different speeds. By now people have fallen into the habit of characterizing the pre-motor-car era as the "horse-and-buggy" age, as if fast transportation were unknown till the auto came. Actually, electric trolleys, in New England and the Middle West, travelled over their own rights of ways at speeds of fifty miles an hour: I cherish a picture post-card, c. 1910, showing such a trolleycar, sensibly streamlined, that served Indianapolis. As with the mass movement into suburbia, which coincided with the mass production of motor cars, the desired freedom depended upon creating a more complex pattern of both movement and settlement, maintaining and improving a balanced transportation system, and maintaining and improving old cities. Had those two essential factors been understood and respected, the motor car could have made an invaluable contribution in creating a regional distribution of population. As in the Netherlands today, this would give the countryside the social advantages of the city, and multiply the number of cities with easy access to the countryside, without the compulsive and wasteful routines that have now been developed to cope with the uncontrolled explosion of motor cars.

[6] The huge success of the auto industry, not merely in multiplying the number of cars, but in utilizing its quasi-monopolistic resources and public monies to elbow out competing forms of locomotion and transportation, has turned the dream of automobility into the anxiety nightmare it has become today. From that nightmare Americans are now belatedly struggling to awake: the nightmare of the air becoming toxic with poisonous exhausts, including the highly lethal carbon monoxide; of the water supply, polluted with deadly lead from gasoline exhausts already half way to the danger point even in the Arctic wastes; the nightmare of diurnal mass commutation by car, along freeways where speed is compulsory, where the constant tensions demonstrably produce higher blood pressure, where a single car, stopping in time to avert an accident, may trigger a succession of more serious accidents in the tail-

gateing cars behind, even when traveling at the usual drugged crawl of rush hours.

[7] The motor car, it goes without saying, has brought many pleasant and desirable benefits; and certain by-products, like the beautiful Taconic Parkway in New York, remain permanent contributions to amenity and esthetic delight. But the whole picture has become increasingly dismal, and the most attractive feature of the American dream, freedom of movement and settlement, is turning into a system of choiceless compulsion. Just as old Henry Ford graciously said the consumer could have a car of any color he wanted as long as it was black, so motor travel is reaching a point where the driver can go anywhere he wants to, at a high speed, so long as he demands no change in either the environment or the destination. G. K. Chesterton's epigram "Nothing fails like success" may yet prove the epitaph of the motor industry. Though danger and death have played a part in the awakening, frustration and boredom have perhaps played a greater part—if only because courting danger has unfortunately proved one of the chronic modes of faking real life and finding momentary relief from its emptiness and its grim routines.

[8] The signs of this revolt are multiplying. Just a few years ago the motorcar owners of the San Francisco Bay region voted $750 million to rebuild the fast public transportation system which the worshippers of the Sacred Cow had cleverly scrapped only twenty years before. But even more significantly, at the moment I write, news comes from San Francisco that "an overflow crowd of spectators cheered wildly at the City Hall here . . . as the Board of Supervisors voted down two proposed freeways on which the Federal Government was willing to put up two hundred and eighty million dollars." Even worse, these delirious iconoclasts are demanding that the Embarcadero Freeway, whose construction, half-way through, was brought to an end by public demand, should be torn down. Is it not indeed time that Detroit began to pay a little attention to the feedback? If the current disillusion with the motor car keeps on growing, auto industry investments may not remain so profitable, unless Detroit's current representative in the Defense Department manages to involve the country in even more extensive military aggressions than Vietnam.

[9] But to go back to the American dream. In the 1920s when a score of small corporations still gave the color of "free enterprise" to the auto industry, the automobile was a crude but relatively honest machine: clumsy in its transmission system and gear shift, capricious in its starting devices, unreliable in its braking capability, decidedly old-fashioned in its reliance upon the gas engine, but still, for all its adolescent gawkiness, a functional machine, designed for transportation and recreation. Around 1930, just when the "new capitalism" suddenly slumped down to earth, the motor car industry picked itself up by exchanging economy for style.

General Motors led the way here, and even Ford was compelled to follow. In the new hierarchy of values, recreation, reliability, safety, efficiency, economy all took a lower place. Style and speed were what counted. At this point, the automotive engineer took his orders from beauty specialists, whose job was to give the car a new look every year, in order to make last year's model unfashionable, that is, prematurely obsolete. The pioneer's dream wagon entered Madison Avenue's fairyland.

[10] Within the next two decades, the motor car became a status symbol, a religious icon, an erotic fetish: in short, "something out of this world," increasingly voluptuous and tumescent, as if on the verge of an orgasm. What words other than Madison Avenue's can adequately describe these exciting confections, glittering with chrome, pillowed in comfort, sleepy-soft to ride in, equipped with mirrors, cigarette lighters, radios, telephones, floor carpeting; liquor bars and tape-recorders are still optional. But in achieving these delights the designers so far turned their backs on the sordid realities of life as to increase the dangers through accidents by displaying jutting knobs, projecting, often knife-edged, instrument panels, murderous wings, confusing shift levers, soft suspension coils, undersized wheels, flimsy hardtops, utterly inadequate front and rear fenders, such broad, barge-like hoods as to give the driver minimum visibility in passing or parking, not to mention sun-reflecting chrome on windshield wipers and window frames to blind either the driver or an approaching car.

[11] In the process of styling the motor car for flashy sales appeal, the designers not only increased the dangers but gratuitously cancelled out good features that earlier cars had had. By lowering its center of gravity, they made the car impossible to enter except by acrobatic maneuvers—this in an age that boasts more elderly people and more arthritic limbs than ever before. Likewise they reduced the six-person capacity that had been happily achieved by eliminating the running board, to a four-person size. To speak plainly, the present motor car has been the result of a secret collaboration between the beautician and the mortician; and according to sales and accident statistics both have reason to be satisfied.

[12] With all the vast resources available for fundamental engineering research, the American motor car industry has not succeeded in producing a single original over-all design since 1930, except the Army Jeep, an honest job unfortunately built with no attention to passenger comfort. In neither shapes nor sizes has it pioneered any car as sensible as the small Volkswagen or the VW autobus. While many able engineers doubtless remain in the automotive industry, they might stop the fashion parade if they came up with a car as rugged as a Rover; and if they sought to

make even bolder departures, they would be rated as unemployable. But fortunately there are still honest men in the industry, even at the upper levels, such as a vice-president of Ford who publicly admitted as late as 1964 that "the automatic transmission"—adopted on a mass production basis in 1939—"was the last major improvement." This change-over from working machines to beauty salon dummies bears the hallmark of the affluent society and its expanding economy: compulsive spending and conspicuous waste. Unfortunately, the waste extends to human lives.

[13] The motor car industry's studious indifference to safety, as a possible deterrent to marketability, has at last produced a public reaction; and a still greater one will possibly follow. The damning evidence against motordom, particularly against General Motors, which dominates the field, has now been marshalled together by two lawyers, Ralph Nader, who was an adviser to the Senate sub-committee investigating automobile hazards, and Jeffrey O'Connell, a professor of law at the University of Illinois, and erstwhile associate Director of the Automobile Claims Study at the Harvard Law School. Much of this evidence comes from public spirited physicians, faced with the dire human consequences of engineering negligence; and it is to the activity of a handful of zealous legislators, like New York State Senator Edward J. Speno and United States Senators Ribicoff and Gaylord Nelson, that we are indebted for the public airing of the auto industry's shocking behavior.

[14] Now to assault the integrity of the great motor car producers is almost as audacious an enterprise as challenging the military judgment of the Pentagon; and incidentally, if we value our lives, quite as essential. The three great corporations—General Motors, Ford, and Chrysler— have a virtual monopoly of the American market as pace-setters and tastemakers, so that Studebaker, American Motors, and Willis-Overland had to follow their bad examples or go under. These three corporations do not stand alone, but reach out into a whole series of ancillary industries, beginning with steel, rubber, and oil, which depend upon them for their existence: Likewise these giant enterprises spread their devastating glamor through go-go Highway Departments heavy with Federal Subsidies, and through all the current media of publicity and advertisement; while by judicious grants for "research" the auto industry does not a little to seduce the judgment and sully the objectivity of the research institutes and universities that accept their dubiously philanthropic support.

[15] In the face of this massive vested interest, it says something for the tough original fabric of American life, and not least for the Fathers of the Constitution, that any open discussion of this seemingly all-powerful megamachine can still take place. Yet, despite many early warning signals, the motor industry was so deeply entrenched, so assured of

popular approval by its mounting profits that the present criticism of its aims and its methods has caught it off guard. If motordom knew how to silence this discussion, it would do so. General Motors has already demonstrated, with a stupidity that amounts to genius, that it is prepared to go to any lengths to prevent a rational public assessment of the changes that must be made in the American motor car to ensure its safety on the road. If General Motors' position were not so vulnerable and damnable they would not have hired detectives in the hope of digging up something unsavory about the character of the young lawyer who wrote *Unsafe at Any Speed.* By this action, they not merely made a public confession of guilt, but added an extra count to the indictment: attempted character assassination with intent to kill.

[16] The reaction of the motor industry to criticism of its product shows that those in control exhibit the same weaknesses that General Matthew Ridgway, that gallant and intelligent officer, has pointed out in relation to the Vietnam-Chinese policy of the Pentagon: Their judgments are devoid of human understanding. And no wonder; for they issue from the same type of mind, the computer mind, programmed strictly for money and power. But since the subject of the motor car's deficiencies has been opened up there is no telling where the assault will stop: Even computers may come in for a ribbing.

[17] Now it is both the strength and the weakness of the two sober books under review that they are mainly concerned with a narrow segment of the motor car problem: the defects and dangers of bad mechanical design. Their positive value lies in their bringing together various suggestions, from engineers and physicians, for reducing the accident rate from mechanical defects, and for lessening the injuries that come from normal human error and from incalculable, uncontrollable incidents, such as a bee suddenly stinging the driver. These are indeed life-and-death matters; and the authors' common approach to the subject is probably the shortest and quickest way to open up the much larger problems that must sooner or later be faced.

[18] On the whole matter of safety, the evidence that both books summarize is both appalling and incontrovertible. Every device for increasing the safety of the motor car has been resisted by the manufacturers, even when, like the safety door catch, it has been finally accepted; while the most dangerous part of the car in a serious accident, the chief cause of fatalities, is the steering assemblage, which still has serious defects besides the tight squeeze that most cars inflict upon the driver. What is worse than the mere failure to take urgent safety measures, is the fact that even when the automotive engineers have provided them at an early stage of the design, they have been removed, either to reduce

costs, give emphasis to some meretricious selling point, or just to eliminate any concern for danger from the prospective buyer's mind.

[19] What both books reveal is that the great motor car corporations,
with all the insolence born of their supreme financial position in the
economy, have not merely been careless about essential safety features in
design: They have been criminally negligent, to the point of being
homicidal. If these facts were not solidly established, no publisher in
his senses would dare to publish these books; for every chapter would
give ground for libel.

[20] Since the authors cover nearly the same ground, use substantially
the same evidence, and exhibit similar well-justified indignation over the
auto industry's refusal to mend its ways, so long as those ways are
profitable, I hardly know how to advise the reader as to making a choice
of them; though I should warn him that the data in either book are
warranted, for a week or two, to make even the loveliest motor ride taste
a little gritty, as with sand in the spinach. With regard to the main points
about safety and air pollution, these books are in general agreement;
though since Myers is a journalist, he does not make Nader's rhetorical
error of using the Corvair case as the opening argument, since such an
extreme example of bad engineering and obstinate contempt for evidence
serves best as a clincher to a more widely based indictment. If all motor
cars were as bad as Chevrolet's early Corvairs (1960–1963) no one with
any instinct for self-preservation would dare to put his foot into any
machine. Apart from this, *Unsafe at Any Speed* is as well-balanced as
Safety Last; but the first has an Index without a list of cited sources, while
the other has lists of references with every chapter but no index.

[21] Both books are driven by the evidence to point to the ultimate
source of the motor car's structural defects, namely, that the cars are
built with a single thought uppermost in the mind of the manufacturers:
What will make them sell? And by what pinching and paring on essentials can more money be spent on styling and on advertising the nonessentials, those glossy features that will catch the eye, flatter the ego,
coddle a neurosis—and open the purse.

[22] What these books demonstrate is that most American motor cars,
even of the latest vintage, are still unfit vehicles for coping with the
normal mischances of the road. When one considers the wide range of
competence in licensed drivers, at different ages with different road
experience, and the wide daily fluctuations in their general health, their
eyesight, their inner tensions and pressures, it is obvious that the one
factor that can and should be standardized and normalized rigorously,
and raised to the highest degree of mechanical efficiency and structural
safety, is the vehicle itself. That is the responsibility of the motor car

companies, not of the motorist. And if the fulfillment of that responsibility means that the profits of General Motors must be cut down from a billion and a half dollars a year to as little as a third of that amount, this is still no reason why this responsibility should not be imposed—by legislation if necessary—as a mandatory condition for earning any profits whatever.

[23] In stressing the need for introducing every possible mechanical dodge to make the car and its occupants less vulnerable to accidents, both books carry their stern indictments to various sensible conclusions; and I would not, by what follows, lessen the sting of their indictment, qualify their arguments, or minimize the value of their recommendations: quite the contrary. Most of the structural changes they suggest are desirable; and some, like seatbelts, are so cheap and simple that one wonders why so much effort had to go into making them standard equipment.

[24] As if to show their open contempt for the whole safety argument, the manufacturers have lately souped up their cars and their advertising slogans in order to appeal to the least safe group of motor car drivers, the newly licensed adolescents and the perpetual adolescents; and they have underlined their incitement to calculated recklessness by giving the cars appropriate names, Thunderbirds, Wildcats, Tempests, Furies, to emphasize hell-bent power and aggressiveness, while their allies in the oil industry, for good measure, offer to place a tiger in the tank. Speed is the pep pill that the motor car manufacturers are now cannily offering to adolescents like any dope peddler; and since power and speed are both regarded as absolute goods by the worshippers of the Sacred Cow, both as good in themselves and as the surest way to expand the industry and maximize the profits, why should anyone suppose that any other human considerations will modify their homicidal incitements? Speed, marijuana, heroin, and lysergic acid, are all attempts to use a scientific technology to overcome the existential nausea that the lopsided development of this very technology is the main cause of. Have Messrs. Nader, O'Connell, and Myers sufficiently reckoned with the vast irrational opposition that their sound and rational arguments will encounter? Will safety alone appeal to a public that, in the face of indisputable cancer statistics, now consumes more cigarettes than ever before?

[25] But suppose the rational argument for safer cars nevertheless wins out. I don't think that the writers of these books fully realize where their proposals will ultimately lead them unless they place these essential changes within a much wider framework. Both the desire for safety and for the enjoyment of the motor car demand a broader restatement of the whole problem. What is the place of the motor car in a rational scheme of transportation? By what system of control at source can we handle the motor car explosion, which is as badly in need of birth control as the population explosion? And what measures are needed to restore to both

transportation and travel—including air travel—some of the humanly desirable qualities that an exclusive concern with speed has already robbed them of?

[26] As to the enjoyment of the motor car, some of the safety devices that have been suggested, crash helmets, shoulder straps as well as a seat belt, padded leg protection, may have unfortunate results in opposite directions; either by reducing the pleasurable sense of freedom, or by prompting those who submit to these constraints to seek a compensatory release in aiming at higher speeds with greater impunity—despite the fact that this in turn will raise the accident rate. Nothing could be worse in the long run for the auto industry than to eliminate the very things that made the automobile, at the beginning, so attractive: the sense of freedom and variety that motor travel once gave. In the interests of speed, the highway designers have steadily been taking away the visual pleasure and environmental stimulus of a long journey, and every other "improvement" conspires to the same end. The same compulsory high speed, the same wide monotonous road, producing the same hypnotic drowsiness, the same air-conditioned climate in the car, the same Howard Johnsons, the same clutter of parking lots, the same motels. No matter how fast he travels or how far he goes, the motorist never actually leaves home: Indeed no effort is spared to eliminate variety in the landscape, and to make famous beauty spots by mountain or sea into as close a counterpart of the familiar shopping center as the original landscape will permit. In short, automobility has turned out to be the most static form of mobility that the mind of man has yet devised.

[27] If speed and safety were the only considerations, there is no reason why the auto industry, once it awakened from its self-induced narcosis, should not "go with" this movement and make greater profits than ever. For it is easy to foresee the theoretic ideal limit toward which both the automotive engineer and the highway engineer have begun to move: to make the surface of this planet no better for any form of organic life than the surface of the moon. To minimize road accidents, the highway engineers have already advocated cutting down all trees and telegraph poles within a hundred feet of each side of the road. But that is only a beginning. To provide maximum safety at high speed, the car will either have to be taken out of the motorist's hands and placed under automatic control, as M.I.T. researchers have, on purely mechanical assumptions, worked out; or else turned into an armored vehicle, windowless, completely padded on the inside, with front and rear vision provided on a screen, and a television set installed to amuse the non-drivers, just as if they were in a jet-plane. Along those lines, the motor car in a not-too-distant future would become a space capsule, a mobile prison, and the earth itself a featureless asteroid. Meanwhile, a further consolidation of the megamachine, with autos, jet planes, and rockets forming a single

industry; the profits of that ultimate combine should exceed the wildest expectations of even General Motors.

[28] But who wants speed at that price or safety at that price? one is tempted to ask. Buckminster Fuller and Jacques Ellul will doubtless answer, Everyone: or at all events, that is what is coming, whether anyone wants it or not. This answer is naive, but not disarming. For these backward assumptions which are really the leftovers of the Victorian avant garde are precisely what must now be questioned. Beyond the area of safety and freedom of movement lies the need for a conception of what constitutes a valid human life, and how much of life will be left if we go on ever more rapidly in the present direction. What has to be challenged is an economy that is based not on organic needs, historic experience, human aptitudes, ecological complexity and variety, but upon a system of empty abstractions: money, power, speed, quantity, progress, vanguardism, expansion. The overvaluation of these abstractions, taken as goods in themselves, has produced the unbalanced, purposeless, sick-making, and ultimately suicidal existence we now confront.

[28] In short, the crimes and the misdemeanors of the motor car manufacturers are significant, not because they are exceptional but because they are typical. These indictments of the auto industry pin down the same evils as were exposed by Rachel Carson's survey of the chemical industry's proliferation of pesticides and herbicides, and by Senator Kefauver's exposure of the pharmaceutical industry. The insolence of the Detroit chariotmakers and the masochistic submissiveness of the American consumer are symptoms of a larger disorder: a society that is no longer rooted in the complex realities of an organic and personal world; a society made in the image of machines, by machines, for machines; a society in which any form of delinquency or criminality may be practiced, from meretriciously designed motor cars or insufficiently tested wonder drugs to the wholesale distribution of narcotics and printed pornography, provided that the profits sufficiently justify their exploitation. If those remain the premises of the Great Society we shall never be out of danger —and never really alive.

--⊰{ C O M M E N T   A N D   Q U E S T I O N S }⊱--

1. How would you describe the tone of this essay?
2. In paragraphs 1 and 2, what does Mumford mean by the Sacred Cow and the Golden Calf, and what is the effect of his sustained figure of speech?

3. The first sentence of paragraph 4 is a statement of the author's thesis. To what "genuine human needs" is the mode of existence developed in the essay antagonistic?

4. Examine Mumford's use of charged language in, for example, paragraphs 10, 15, 19, and 24. Where else do you find examples of highly emotive words? Comment on the purpose and the effectiveness of the author's charged language.

5. Mumford uses a generally formal vocabulary and some very informal expressions; examples of the latter are *go-go, digging up, souped up, hell-bent, "go with."* The words listed below are part of the author's formal vocabulary. If they are unfamiliar to you, examine them in their context (paragraph references are in parentheses after each word) and see if the context establishes their meaning; if the meaning is still unclear, look up the word in your dictionary. Can you justify Mumford's mixture of levels of language?

quasi-monopolistic (6)	fetish (10)	meretricious (18)
diurnal (6)	gratuitously (11)	mandatory (22)
amenity (7)	ancillary (14)	narcosis (27)
iconoclasts (8)	sully (14)	ecological (28)

6. Various methods of development are used in this essay. What use is made of contrast and comparison? Of cause–effect development?

7. Although Mumford praises the two books which are the springboard for his essay, he says that they are concerned with a narrow segment of the motor car problem. Why, in his opinion, are safer cars not the whole answer to the problem? What larger problems must be faced?

8. The authors of the two books Mumford comments on apparently describe and give convincing evidence of the structural defects of modern cars, and then make recommendations for remedying the situation. Does Mumford follow a similar procedure of describing, giving evidence, and suggesting remedies for a situation? Explain.

9. In this essay, the author is probably less concerned with cars than with values. What values does he attack as false or unworthy? What values does he approve?

10. The title of this review is the title of a widely read book, a criticism of the funeral industry in the United States, written by Jessica Mitford and published in 1963. Why do you think Mumford chose to use this well-known title? Does *death* in the title of the review have implications beyond the death rate on the highways? If so, what direct or indirect references to other kinds of death can you find in the selection?

[77]   *Roger Revelle*: The Problem of People

ROGER REVELLE (1909–   ), who has been Director of the Scripps
Oceanographic Institute in California, is the Richard Saltonstall Professor of
Population Policy and Director of the Center for Population Studies in the
School of Public Health at Harvard. The following article, published in
the Autumn 1965 issue of *Harvard Today*, is a detailed description and
analysis of a frequently discussed problem; it also describes an approach to
solving the problem.

[1] Present rates of human population growth confront us with a problem that is unique in the long history of our species.

[2] Hundreds of thousands of years were required to produce, by
1850 A.D., a living population of one billion people. The second billion
took 75 years more, from 1850 to 1925, but only another 35 years until
1960 were needed for the third billion. The fourth billion will be here by
1980, and the fifth 10 years later, by 1990. Unless drastic changes in birth
or death rates occur, the population increase between now and the year
2,000 will be larger than the entire present population of the earth.

[3] Bringing down rates of population growth to a manageably low
level will require far more knowledge and experience than we now possess. Economic, sociological, medical, and educational research on a large
scale and a wide front are urgently required. The problem may well be
the most difficult mankind has ever faced, for its solution lies in controlling
one of the basic drives of all living things—to reproduce.

[4] When we try to bring down death rates, every human instinct is on
our side. Nearly everyone wants to live longer. Everyone thinks other
people should live longer. When we try to bring down birth rates, most
human instincts work against us. It is not merely a question of the sex
instinct; it is a question of the meaning of life—the joy of having children,
the feeling that one is a complete human being only if he has children.

[5] The number of human beings on the earth may ultimately be
limited by one or more of many factors—the total energy available for
food and material production, the biological and psychosomatic results
of crowding, or, more hopefully, the conscious and deliberate decisions
of individual men and women.

[6] At least a temporary check on population growth could come from
the increased area of cities. During the next century, most people will

live in cities. The farm population of the world will not increase very much, because we are approaching the limit of the number of farmers who can be effectively employed. At present rates of increase city populations would multiply perhaps 40 times within the next 100 years. Even in the next 50 years, the Indian city of Calcutta could grow to 60 million. Calcutta today is a house of misery. What would it be like with 60 million people? Our own cities in the United States might reach sizes that we can hardly imagine.

[7] As a city becomes bigger, the density of population within it tends to diminish; consequently the total area covered by cities in the middle of the 21st century could be 100 times larger than today, and equal to perhaps one-fifth of the entire land surface of the earth. The problems of supplying the wants and removing the waste of such sprawling monster cities would require wholly new levels of technology.

[8] Although population growth clearly cannot continue indefinitely, it is equally clear that given the right social and economic conditions, and a sufficiently high technology, the resources of the earth could support a much larger number of human beings than are now alive. The real and present question is not population size in the future but the rate of increase today. How shall we provide decent conditions of life for the living generation, conditions in which men and women can live, and children can grow up, free of the desperate want experienced by the majority of human beings in this century? This is the urgent thrust of the population problem.

[9] Present rates of population growth in India, Pakistan, and Egypt are probably between two and one-half per cent and three per cent per year. In Brazil and some other South American countries, annual rates are more than three per cent. The populations of Costa Rica and the Philippines are growing by perhaps four per cent per year. A three per cent growth rate means a doubling of population in 23 years; with a four per cent rate the doubling time is 17 years. These figures are typical of many of the underdeveloped countries. They underlie the fact that the world population, which increased by one per cent a year in 1940, is now increasing by two per cent. Although total national incomes are rising, the increased production must be divided among ever larger numbers of people, and standards of living remain nearly static. Men have to run faster and faster just to stay where they are.

[10] In the two American continents today, about as many people live north of the Rio Grande as south of it. But by the year 2,000, there will be twice as many people in Latin America as in the United States and Canada. In the world as a whole, unless a drastic change occurs, people who live in desperate misery and poverty will constitute the overwhelming fraction of the human population.

[11] Compared with 1935, food production in many countries has barely

kept up with population growth, and in some cases has fallen behind. Average food production per capita for Latin America is less now than it was before World War II. Were it not for food imports from the United States and other Western countries, the diets of the people of India and Pakistan would be even more deficient today than in 1935. The average person in the sub continent is getting less food than he needs, by perhaps 20 per cent. His diet is particularly deficient in high quality protein. Without sufficient protein of the right kind, the health of adults is worsened and their life span shortened, but, what may be even more disastrous, the mental development of children probably is retarded.

[12] Egypt is a large country in terms of area but nearly all of it is a lifeless desert. Only the delta and the flat flood plain of the Nile are suitable for agriculture. This arable region covers about six million acres, approximately equal to the area of Massachusetts. Today there are 30 million Egyptians, most of whom are trying to make a living on these fertile acres. This is the highest density for a rural population anywhere in the world, about 3,000 people per square mile.

[13] The population is increasing at such a rate that there will be 60 million Egyptians by the year 1988—just 23 years from now. One dreads the possibility that the population will become stabilized at some figure short of this by malnutrition and disease, that situation of "misery and vice" foreseen by Thomas Robert Malthus, the prophetic 18th century demographer. The Aswan High Dam will provide about a 40 per cent increase in agricultural production, which means that unless they can halt their population increase Egyptians will be able to feed themselves at present levels only for another 10 to 12 years.

[14] In India, with a growth rate of around two and one-half per cent per year, the number of children below 15 years of age is 45 per cent of the entire population. Nearly one person in two is a child or younger adolescent, whereas with a slowly growing population under modern conditions of life expectancy, this proportion is less than 25 per cent. The high proportion of children and adolescents to adults means that the nation cannot save for capital investment without great difficulty, because most of what the adults produce is needed for immediate consumption. Yet the ability to invest savings in order to increase the means of production is an essential requirement for economic development.

[15] We in the United States need to examine more closely the social and economic costs of rising numbers of people in our own country. Our population is increasing at about one and one-half per cent a year, considerably less than the rate in the less developed parts of the world. Yet even this rate of growth brings many problems. Increases in per capita costs of pollution abatement, municipal water supplies, outdoor recreation, and urban transportation are all consequences of our increasing numbers. Perhaps more serious is the decline in the quality of life: the

crowding and dangers in our parks; the fact that our water does not taste as good as it used to; that many of our fellow citizens waste one or two hours each day driving to and from work under what can only be described as miserable conditions. One has to ask whether juvenile delinquency, student alienation in the universities, and unemployment among untrained youth, are not also partly related to our rapid population growth and, if so, how should this affect our national thought and action?

[16] During the past two decades our rate of population growth was considerably higher than it is today. As a result the number of high school students will increase from 10 million in 1960 to 15 million in 1970. Within these 10 years we must build new high schools equal in capacity to half of all those now in use in the United States. This is a hard thing for the taxpayers to face, and in general they do not seem really willing to face it. In many communities the quality of our high school facilities is going down.

[17] The number of college and university students is growing from about four million in 1960 to about 12 million in 1980. Everybody who has children of college age realizes how hard this is on young people. It is equally hard on the colleges. Both the necessary construction of facilities and the required increase in the numbers of able teachers seem to be almost insoluble problems.

[18] In the first edition of his famous "Essay on Population," published in 1798, Malthus reached the pessimistic conclusion that an equilibrium between human births and deaths could be established only at a relatively high death rate. That is, war, famine, and disease, or "misery and vice," as he put it, would kill people off as fast as others were born. Man's fate was to reproduce himself right up to the limit of disease and starvation, and he had no control over what would happen to him.

[19] Some modern "Neo-Malthusians," who share Malthus' early views, claim that the population of any organism will continue to increase until it reaches the edge of subsistence or of control by enemy organisms. They believe this is as true of men as it is of mice or elephants—the only difference being that with different organisms different amounts of time might be required.

[20] History and experience show that this doctrine is bad sociology; recent biological research shows it is bad biology. Experiments with laboratory rats demonstrate that when too many of these animals are forced to live together in too small a space, their behavior patterns become radically abnormal and they effectively cease to reproduce themselves. Wild animals, particularly predators, seem to limit their own numbers in various ways. Some species do this by exercising territoriality: each dominant male controls an area of a certain size, on which he will not allow other males of the same species to encroach, even though he may be indifferent to the presence of males of a different species.

[21] Malthus himself changed his mind before he published the second edition of his "Essay" in 1803. In gathering data for the second edition, he observed that the population of Switzerland had remained nearly static for several generations, even though death rates had substantially declined. He concluded that birth rates must have decreased in proportion to the decline in death rates, and that this was due to the postponement of marriage by Swiss couples until they could inherit or buy enough farm land to support a family. He then added a third process, "moral restraint," to the dismal duo, "misery and vice," which he had previously believed were the only causes of population limitation. His new edition concluded with these (for Malthus) optimistic words:

". . . it is hoped that the general result of the inquiry is such as not to make us give up the improvement of human society in despair. The partial good which seems to be attainable is worthy of all our exertions; is sufficient to direct our efforts, and animate our prospects. And although we cannot expect that the virtue and happiness of mankind will keep pace with the brilliant career of physical discovery; yet, if we are not wanting ourselves, we may confidently indulge the hope that, to no unimportant extent, they will be influenced by its progress and will partake in its success."

[22] In both ancient and medieval times, there were occasions when human beings exercised control over their own populations, through the aggregate of the individual decisions of many couples.

[23] During the last two or three centuries before the fall of the Roman Empire (476 A.D.) the population of Italy steadily declined. Despite governmental attempts, by means of penalties and rewards, to increase the population, the people just did not reproduce themselves in sufficient numbers.

[24] In Tuscany, between 1200 and 1400 A.D., the population decreased by nearly 75 per cent. The tax rolls and other sources of vital statistics are very good for this period in Tuscany, and they show that throughout most of these two centuries the average number of children per household was two or less. We do not know what kept the people from reproducing, but a factor that may have strongly influenced them was a decline in the prices of farm products compared to interest rates on farm mortgages. This brought increasing poverty and misery to the countryside.

[25] Throughout the 19th Century, there was in Europe and North America a steady fall in death rates from disease, due perhaps primarily to the introduction of such public health practices as smallpox vaccination and improved sanitation. The excess of births over deaths was eventually succeeded by a decline in birth rates. As both birth rates and death rates diminished they grew closer together, so that rates of population growth, especially in certain European nations, gradually but markedly decreased

during the 100 years before World War II. Demographers have called this series of events the "Demographic Transition."

[26] Several developed nations in our own time, notably Japan, Hungary, Sweden, and Italy, have essentially stabilized their populations. For example, in Japan the birth rate is not much more than 15 per thousand per year, while the death rate is about seven per thousand, so that the population is growing at around 0.8 per cent a year. But a moment's thought will show that an annual death rate of seven per thousand cannot continue for very long. Otherwise people would live to be 150 years old. The death rate must rise to around 15 per thousand if the human life span is to remain at about 70 years.

[27] Today we know something that Malthus did not: Nearly all societies attempt some population control, though the methods used may be relatively ineffective. Among the most effective of the traditional methods is abortion.

[28] In some countries, such as Japan, Hungary, and the Soviet Union, that have legalized abortion and have introduced new, comparatively safe techniques, the number of abortions each year is believed to be about the same as the number of live births. We know less about the ratio of abortions to live births in countries where abortions are illegal. In Chile and Colombia, and perhaps in other South American nations, a high percentage of all hospital admissions in the obstetric wards is of women suffering from infections or injuries as a result of illegal abortions.

[29] In the last few years, two very effective contraceptive methods have been introduced—the steroid pills and the intra-uterine loops or coils, commonly called IUD's. IUD's can be manufactured very cheaply, since they are simply small pieces of polyethylene plastic, and they can be inserted fairly inexpensively. These devices are already being widely used in Taiwan and South Korea. The Indian Medical Council has accepted them as a safe and effective contraceptive method, and plans are now under way for nationwide programs of introducing the devices in both India and Pakistan. Although IUD's can be retained by only about four out of five women who attempt to use them—the other 20 per cent involuntarily expel them or the devices have to be removed for medical reasons—it should nevertheless be possible with their use to bring about a significant reduction in birth rates throughout the subcontinent during the next 15 years.

[30] One must not be too optimistic, however, concerning the resulting decline in the rate of population growth, because the death rate can be expected to fall during this time from the present 17 to 25 per thousand to perhaps 10 or below, which would mean that for some time to come the rate of population growth would still be more than two per cent, or a doubling within one generation.

[31] In ancient Rome, medieval Tuscany, and 18th Century Switzerland, death rates were high, and only a slight pressure for population control was needed to tip the balance between birth and deaths. In 19th Century Europe and North America, the early stages of the demographic transition took place in an environment of increasing prosperity and rapidly spreading literacy. The 20th Century countries that have stabilized their populations are comparatively well developed both educationally and economically.

[32] But none of these conditions exist today in the countries where rapid rates of population growth are a tragically serious problem. Most of their people are illiterate and nearly all are desperately poor. Their death rates are actually or potentially lower than were death rates in any country prior to the last few decades. Consequently, population control methods must be much more effective than in the past, if population growth is to be sufficiently diminished. On the positive side, there is evidence that significant numbers of village women and their husbands strongly desire not to have more children, and are eager to use effective birth control methods that are within their physical and educational capabilities.

[33] Although there are great differences between the problems of death control and birth control, a direct relationship exists between birth rates and death rates, particularly rates of infant and child mortality. In many countries, grown-up children who will support their aged parents are the chief form of social security. If a man and his wife do not have at least one adult male child, they have little to look forward to when they can no longer work to support themselves. Under conditions of high child mortality, the average married couple needs to produce many children to be sufficiently certain that at least one boy will survive to become a man. Only in this way can they ensure their own future security. Whenever infant and child mortality can be brought down to a low level, the probability in an individual family that a male child will survive becomes very much greater, and the pressure for large numbers of children will correspondingly lessen. This is one of the principal reasons the profession of public health needs to be deeply involved in programs of family planning and population control.

[34] In some less-developed countries, rates of population growth might be reduced by the introduction of a social security system, whereby the government helped men to be their brothers' keepers. Here we come up against a moral problem—public versus private morality. In the Western world we believe we have a responsibility toward society as a whole, toward all men and all women in our society. In many less-developed countries, the individual's responsibility toward other human beings is just as intense, but it does not extend beyond the family or the blood relations.

[35] These are problems that universities may be able to do something about. One reason for thinking so is that universities have in the past helped to solve other problems that look somewhat like these: problems in medicine and public health, sanitation, human behavior, and social structure.

[36] Accordingly, Harvard has established during the past year a new university-wide Center for Population Studies, under the leadership of the School of Public Health.

[37] The need to reduce rates of population growth is so urgent in many countries that immediate action on a large scale should be undertaken. Yet we in the University must try at the same time to deepen our understanding and improve our practice. We need to work in real societies with all their environmental and cultural differences, not only to discover underlying generalities, but also to learn how to adapt our actions to fit the range of human conditions. Much of the needed understanding will come from experience gained in birth control and family planning programs; members of the University should participate in these programs if they are to learn as much as possible from them. Because of its long experience and broad involvement in field projects throughout the world, the School of Public Health is uniquely fitted to work out appropriate means of participation.

[38] Within the University, the principal strategic problem is to find ways whereby scholars and scientists in different fields can join in a common attack on population problems. One way is through joint appointment of faculty members in existing Departments and in the Center for Population Studies, and some promising starts have been made in this direction.

[39] Two young specialists in Social Ethics, Ralph B. Potter and Arthur J. Dyck, have been appointed Assistant Professors in the Divinity School and in the Center. They will teach and do research on moral values in family life, and on religious and social attitudes toward family planning and fertility control. Among the questions they will ask is: Why does the number of children desired by married couples vary widely at different times in the same society?

[40] An alliance with the Medical School has been formed through the appointment of Dr. Hilton A. Salhanick as a Member of the Center for Population Studies, as well as Professor of Obstetrics and Gynecology. Dr. Salhanick will conduct basic research in the Laboratory for Human Reproduction which is being established in the Medical School, and he will also develop a program of clinical research and teaching in problems of human fertility control.

[41] The object of a birth control method is simply to prevent the union of the male and female reproductive cells. Yet in one of the most certain methods developed to date, the use of the steroid pills, fertility control is

accomplished by suppressing the entire normal menstrual cycle and substituting an artificial one. In effect, we are using a cannon where a .22 rifle should do. One of the ultimate practical goals of the research by Dr. Salhanick and his colleagues will be to obtain the knowledge needed to devise more direct and less drastic methods of fertility control. He is studying the menstrual cycle of normal women, the combined hormonal and neural communication systems that control this cycle, and the mechanisms of action of the hormones that prevent ovulation or conception. Our knowledge of all these phenomena is very incomplete.

[42] In the Faculty of Arts and Sciences, Professor Harvey Leibenstein of Berkeley has received a joint appointment as Visiting Professor in the Department of Economics and in the Center for Population Studies to continue his theoretical studies of the effects of population increase on economic growth at different levels of economic development. Professor Harold Thomas of the Division of Engineering and Applied Physics has focussed his research in the Center. He is studying the relationships between resource utilization and human population changes, and the application of new statistical methods, using large computers, to population problems. He has recently used these methods to analyze the complex range of relationships in different countries among birth rates, numbers of children in individual families, and rates of infant and child mortality.

[43] In the School of Public Health, teaching of physicians and public health specialists is being carried out by the Department of Demography and Human Ecology, which was formed prior to the establishment of the Center. Faculty members and research fellows in the Department are involved in a variety of research projects, both in the University and in the field, including work on problems of illegal abortion in Chile and studies of physiological factors affecting fertility in villages of the Indian Punjab. In cooperation with the Ford Foundation, the Center is undertaking a study of resources development in Egypt and its potential effect on population problems. It is hoped that this study can be expanded to include a cooperative research program on sociological factors involved in family planning. Professor Laila Shukry El Hamamsy, Director of the Social Science Research Center of the American University of Cairo, is at present a Visiting Member of the Center for Population Studies in order to work out plans for this program.

[44] Greece is one of the relatively poor European countries in which the population is nearly stable. The Center is beginning a field investigation, in cooperation with the University of Athens, of the reasons for low human fertility in Greece.

[45] Our immediate concerns are family planning, population control, and the balancing of resources development against population growth, but the members of the Center will also inevitably be interested in some

long range questions. Among these are: How many human beings would it be good to have on the earth?

[46] We have little information and less understanding about the psychosomatic results of crowding among human beings, but at present it appears that a population density as high as that in Harlem today is simply not good for people. Possibly we could devise some way to make it good, but the prospect does not look very promising.

[47] In essence, we are dealing with qualitative and not quantitative questions, with the quality of human life, and only incidentally with the quantity of people. In the long run, the Harvard Center for Population Studies will focus on the drama of living human beings, rather than on their entrances and their exits on the stage of life. We will be concerned with the physical health of human populations, with improvement of nutrition, reduction of vitality-sapping disease, and amelioration of genetic burdens. We will be concerned with relating the education of human populations to the changing needs of individuals and their societies. We will want to find better ways to fit environments to human beings—not only the earthly environment of air, water, and land, but also the social environment created by interactions among men.

[48] It is sometimes said that man is a wild animal. Though he has domesticated many other animals, he has never been able to domesticate himself. The underlying question for the Center for Population Studies is, "Can man domesticate himself?" Throughout most of his existence, man was simply one among many species on the earth. But during the last few millennia he has preempted the planet, its space and its resources. Of far greater importance, we are perhaps the first form of matter in the 20 billion years of the lifetime of our galaxy that has had the ability to understand not only the world but itself. It does not seem too large a step from self-understanding to self-control.

--◄[**COMMENT AND QUESTIONS**]►--

1. Not until paragraph 8 does the author come to what he calls the "real and present question"—the rate of increase in population today rather than the size of population in the future. What purposes are served by the first seven paragraphs?
2. What, according to Revelle, are or soon will be the serious effects of increasing population in the developing countries? What different effects does he see in this country?

3. To what extent do you agree with the author's comments, in paragraph 15, on life in the United States? Explain.
4. What is the purpose of the discussion of Malthus' theories, in paragraphs 18–22?
5. What different relationships does Revelle see between declining death rates and the problem of population?
6. The work of the Center for Population Studies represents an effort of the kind John Dewey recommended years ago—the application of knowledge and technology to human needs and social problems. What seem to be Revelle's reasons for giving as much information as he does, in paragraphs 39–44, about the people and the programs connected with the Center?
7. In paragraphs 45–47 the author discusses the larger concerns of the Center. In what ways do these larger concerns stem logically from the earlier content of the article?
8. "The Problem of People" emphasizes the gravity and urgency of the problem. Does the article on the whole seem to you to be optimistic or pessimistic? Explain.
9. Do you know of any attitudes toward the problem of population other than those expressed in this article? Explain.

[78]   *James Baldwin*: Notes of a Native Son

JAMES BALDWIN (1924–   ) is an American novelist and essayist, author of *Go Tell It on the Mountain, Giovanni's Room, Another Country, Notes of a Native Son,* and *The Fire Next Time.* The following essay is from the book of the same name, a collection of essays published in 1955.

[1] On the 29th of July, in 1943, my father died. On the same day, a few hours later, his last child was born. Over a month before this, while all our energies were concentrated in waiting for these events, there had been, in Detroit, one of the bloodiest race riots of the century. A few hours after my father's funeral, while he lay in state in the undertakers's chapel, a race riot broke out in Harlem. On the morning of the 3rd of August, we drove my father to the graveyard through a wilderness of smashed plate glass.

[2] The day of my father's funeral had also been my nineteenth birthday. As we drove him to the graveyard, the spoils of injustice, anarchy, discontent, and hatred were all round us. It seemed to me that God himself had devised, to mark my father's end, the most sustained and

brutally dissonant of codas. And it seemed to me, too, that the violence which rose all about us as my father left the world had been devised as a corrective for the pride of his eldest son. I had declined to believe in that apocalypse which had been central to my father's vision; very well, life seemed to be saying, here is something that will certainly pass for an apocalypse until the real thing comes along. I had inclined to be contemptuous of my father for the conditions of his life, for the conditions of our lives. When his life had ended I began to wonder about that life and also, in a new way, to be apprehensive about my own.

[3] I had not known my father very well. We had got on badly, partly because we shared, in our different fashions, the vice of stubborn pride. When he was dead I realized that I had hardly ever spoken to him. When he had been dead a long time I began to wish I had. It seems to be typical of life in America, where opportunities, real and fancied, are thicker than anywhere else on the globe, that the second generation has no time to talk to the first. No one, including my father, seems to have known exactly how old he was, but his mother had been born during slavery. He was of the first generation of free men. He, along with thousands of other Negroes, came North after 1919 and I was part of that generation which had never seen the landscape of what Negroes sometimes call the Old Country.

[4] He had been born in New Orleans and had been a quite young man there during the time that Louis Armstrong, a boy, was running errands for the dives and honky-tonks of what was always presented to me as one of the most wicked of cities—to this day, whenever I think of New Orleans, I also helplessly think of Sodom and Gomorrah. My father never mentioned Louis Armstrong, except to forbid us to play his records; but there was a picture of him on our wall for a long time. One of my father's strongwilled female relatives had placed it there and forbade my father to take it down. He never did, but he eventually maneuvered her out of the house and when, some years later, she was in trouble and near death, he refused to do anything to help her.

[5] He was, I think, very handsome. I gather this from photographs and from my own memories of him, dressed in his Sunday best and on his way to preach a sermon somewhere, when I was little. Handsome, proud, and ingrown, "like a᾽ toe-nail," somebody said. But he looked to me, as I grew older, like pictures I had seen of African tribal chieftains: he really should have been naked, with war-paint on and barbaric mementos, standing among spears. He could be chilling in the pulpit and indescribably cruel in his personal life and he was certainly the most bitter man I have ever met; yet it must be said that there was something else in him, buried in him, which lent him his tremendous power and, even, a rather crushing charm. It had something to do with his blackness, I think—he was very black—with his blackness and his beauty,

and with the fact that he knew that he was black but did not know that he was beautiful. He claimed to be proud of his blackness but it had also been the cause of much humiliation and it had fixed bleak boundaries to his life. He was not a young man when we were growing up and he had already suffered many kinds of ruin; in his outrageously demanding and protective way he loved his children, who were black like him and menaced, like him; and all these things sometimes showed in his face when he tried, never to my knowledge with any success, to establish contact with any of us. When he took one of his children on his knee to play, the child always became fretful and began to cry; when he tried to help one of us with our homework the absolutely unabating tension which emanated from him caused our minds and our tongues to become paralyzed, so that he, scarcely knowing why, flew into a rage and the child, not knowing why, was punished. If it ever entered his head to bring a surprise home for his children, it was, almost unfailingly, the wrong surprise and even the big watermelons he often brought home on his back in the summertime led to the most appalling scenes. I do not remember, in all those years, that one of his children was ever glad to see him come home. From what I was able to gather of his early life, it seemed that this inability to establish contact with other people had always marked him and had been one of the things which had driven him out of New Orleans. There was something in him, therefore, groping and tentative, which was never expressed and was buried with him. One saw it most clearly when he was facing new people and hoping to impress them. But he never did, not for long. We went from church to smaller and more improbable church, he found himself in less and less demand as a minister, and by the time he died none of his friends had come to see him for a long time. He had lived and died in an intolerable bitterness of spirit and it frightened me, as we drove him to the graveyard through those unquiet, ruined streets, to see how powerful and over-flowing this bitterness could be and to realize that this bitterness now was mine.

[6] When he died I had been away from home for a little over a year. In that year I had had time to become aware of the meaning of all my father's bitter warnings, had discovered the secret of his proudly pursed lips and rigid carriage: I had discovered the weight of white people in the world. I saw that this had been for my ancestors and now would be for me an awful thing to live with and that the bitterness which had helped to kill my father could also kill me.

[7] He had been ill a long time—in the mind, as we now realized, reliving instances of his fantastic intransigence in the new light of his affliction and endeavoring to feel a sorrow for him which never, quite, came true. We had not known that he was being eaten up by paranoia, and the discovery that his cruelty, to our bodies and our minds, had been

one of the symptoms of his illness was not, then, enough to enable us to forgive him. The younger children felt, quite simply, relief that he would not be coming home anymore. My mother's observation that it was he, after all, who had kept them alive all these years meant nothing because the problems of keeping children alive are not real for children. The older children felt, with my father gone, that they could invite their friends to the house without fear that their friends would be insulted or, as had sometimes happened with me, being told that their friends were in league with the devil and intended to rob our family of everything we owned. (I didn't fail to wonder, and it made me hate him, what on earth we owned that anybody else would want.)

[8] His illness was beyond all hope of healing before anyone realized that he was ill. He had always been so strange and had lived, like a prophet, in such unimaginably close communion with the Lord that his long silences which were punctuated by moans and hallelujahs and snatches of old songs while he sat at the living-room window never seemed odd to us. It was not until he refused to eat because, he said, his family was trying to poison him that my mother was forced to accept as a fact what had, until then, been only a unwilling suspicion. When he was committed, it was discovered that he had tuberculosis and, as it turned out, the disease of his mind allowed the disease of his body to destroy him. For the doctors could not force him to eat, either, and, though he was fed intravenously, it was clear from the beginning that there was no hope for him.

[9] In my mind's eye I could see him, sitting at the window, locked up in his terrors; hating and fearing every living soul including his children who had betrayed him, too, by reaching towards the world which had despised him. There were nine of us. I began to wonder what it could have felt like for such a man to have had nine children whom he could barely feed. He used to make little jokes about our poverty, which never, of course, seemed very funny to us; they could not have seemed very funny to him, either, or else our all too feeble response to them would never have caused such rages. He spent great energy and achieved, to our chagrin, no small amount of success in keeping us away from the people who surrounded us, people who had all-night rent parties to which we listened when we should have been sleeping, people who cursed and drank and flashed razor blades on Lenox Avenue. He could not understand why, if they had so much energy to spare, they could not use it to make their lives better. He treated almost everybody on our block with a most uncharitable asperity and neither they, nor, of course, their children were slow to reciprocate.

[10] The only white people who came to our house were welfare workers and bill collectors. It was almost always my mother who dealt with them, for my father's temper, which was at the mercy of his pride,

was never to be trusted. It was clear that he felt their very presence in his home to be a violation: this was conveyed by his carriage, almost ludicrously stiff, and by his voice, harsh and vindictively polite. When I was around nine or ten I wrote a play which was directed by a young, white schoolteacher, a woman, who then took an interest in me, and gave me books to read and, in order to corroborate my theatrical bent, decided to take me to see what she somewhat tactlessly referred to as "real" plays. Theater-going was forbidden in our house, but, with the really cruel intuitiveness of a child, I suspected that the color of this woman's skin would carry the day for me. When, at school, she suggested taking me to the theater, I did not, as I might have done if she had been a Negro, find a way of discouraging her, but agreed that she should pick me up at my house one evening. I then, very cleverly, left all the rest to my mother, who suggested to my father, as I knew she would, that it would not be very nice to let such a kind woman make the trip for nothing. Also, since it was a schoolteacher, I imagine that my mother countered the idea of sin with the idea of "education," which word, even with my father, carried a kind of bitter weight.

[11] Before the teacher came my father took me aside to ask *why* she was coming, what *interest* she could possibly have in our house, in a boy like me. I said I didn't know but I, too, suggested that it had something to do with education. And I understood that my father was waiting for me to say something—I didn't quite know what; perhaps that I wanted his protection against this teacher and her "education." I said none of these things and the teacher came and we went out. It was clear, during the brief interview in our living room, that my father was agreeing very much against his will and that he would have refused permission if he had dared. The fact that he did not dare caused me to despise him: I had no way of knowing that he was facing in that living room a wholly unprecedented and frightening situation.

[12] Later, when my father had been laid off from his job, this woman became very important to us. She was really a very sweet and generous woman and went to a great deal of trouble to be of help to us, particularly during one awful winter. My mother called her by the highest name she knew: she said she was a "christian." My father could scarcely disagree but during the four or five years of our relatively close association he never trusted her and was always trying to surprise in her open, Midwestern face the genuine, cunningly hidden, and hideous motivation. In later years, particularly when it began to be clear that this "education" of mine was going to lead me to perdition, he became more explicit and warned me that my white friends in high school were not really my friends and that I would see, when I was older, how white people would do anything to keep a Negro down. Some of them could be nice, he admitted, but none of them were to be trusted and most of them were not even nice.

The best thing was to have as little to do with them as possible. I did not feel this way and I was certain, in my innocence, that I never would.

[13] But the year which preceded my father's death had made a great change in my life. I had been living in New Jersey, working in defense plants, working and living among southerners, white and black. I knew about the south, of course, and about how southerners treated Negroes and how they expected them to behave, but it had never entered my mind that anyone would look at me and expect *me* to behave that way. I learned in New Jersey that to be a Negro meant, precisely, that one was never looked at but was simply at the mercy of the reflexes the color of one's skin caused in other people. I acted in New Jersey as I had always acted, that is as though I thought a great deal of myself—I had to *act* that way—with results that were, simply, unbelievable. I had scarcely arrived before I had earned the enmity, which was extraordinarily ingenious, of all my superiors and nearly all my co-workers. In the beginning, to make matters worse, I simply did not know what was happening. I did not know what I had done, and I shortly began to wonder what *anyone* could possibly do, to bring about such unanimous, active, and unbearably vocal hostility. I knew about jim-crow but I had never experienced it. I went to the same self-service restaurant three times and stood with all the Princeton boys before the counter, waiting for a hamburger and coffee; it was always an extraordinarily long time before anything was set before me; but it was not until the fourth visit that I learned that, in fact, nothing had ever been set before me: I had simply picked something up. Negroes were not served there, I was told, and they had been waiting for me to realize that I was always the only Negro present. Once I was told this, I determined to go there all the time. But now they were ready for me and, though some dreadful scenes were subsequently enacted in that restaurant, I never ate there again.

[14] It was the same story all over New Jersey, in bars, bowling alleys, diners, places to live. I was always being forced to leave, silently, or with mutual imprecations. I very shortly became notorious and children giggled behind me when I passed and their elders whispered or shouted —they really believed that I was mad. And it did begin to work on my mind, of course; I began to be afraid to go anywhere and to compensate for this I went places to which I really should not have gone and where, God knows, I had no desire to be. My reputation in town naturally enhanced my reputation at work and my working day became one long series of acrobatics designed to keep me out of trouble. I cannot say that these acrobatics succeeded. It began to seem that the machinery of the organization I worked for was turning over, day and night, with but one aim: to eject me. I was fired once, and contrived, with the aid of a friend from New York, to get back on the payroll; was fired again, and bounced back again. It took a while to fire me for the third time, but the third

time took. There were no loopholes anywhere. There was not even any way of getting back inside the gates.

[15] That year in New Jersey lives in my mind as though it were the year during which, having an unsuspected predilection for it, I first contracted some dread, chronic disease, the unfailing symptom of which is a kind of blind fever, a pounding in the skull and fire in the bowels. Once this disease is contracted, one can never be really carefree again, for the fever, without an instant's warning, can recur at any moment. It can wreck more important things than race relations. There is not a Negro alive who does not have this rage in his blood—one has the choice, merely, of living with it consciously or surrendering to it. As for me, this fever has recurred in me, and does, and will until the day I die.

[16] My last night in New Jersey, a white friend from New York took me to the nearest big town, Trenton, to go to the movies and have a few drinks. As it turned out, he also saved me from, at the very least, a violent whipping. Almost every detail of that night stands out very clearly in my memory. I even remember the name of the movie we saw because its title impressed me as being so patly ironical. It was a movie about the German occupation of France, starring Maureen O'Hara and Charles Laughton and called *This Land Is Mine*. I remember the name of the diner we walked into when the movie ended: it was the "American Diner." When we walked in the counterman asked what we wanted and I remember answering with the casual sharpness which had become my habit: "We want a hamburger and a cup of coffee, what do you think we want?" I do not know why, after a year of such rebuffs, I so completely failed to anticipate his answer, which was, of course, "We don't serve Negroes here." This reply failed to discompose me, at least for the moment. I made some sardonic comment about the name of the diner and we walked out into the streets.

[17] This was the time of what was called the "brown-out," when the lights in all American cities were very dim. When we re-entered the streets something happened to me which had the force of an optical illusion, or a nightmare. The streets were very crowded and I was facing north. People were moving in every direction but it seemed to me, in that instant, that all of the people I could see, and many more than that, were moving toward me, against me, and that everyone was white. I remember how their faces gleamed. And I felt, like a physical sensation, a *click* at the nape of my neck as though some interior string connecting my head to my body had been cut. I began to walk. I heard my friend call after me, but I ignored him. Heaven only knows what was going on in his mind, but he had the good sense not to touch me—I don't know what would have happened if he had—and to keep me in sight. I don't know what was going on in my mind, either; I certainly had no conscious plan. I wanted to do something to crush these white faces, which were crushing

me. I walked for perhaps a block or two until I came to an enormous, glittering, and fashionable restaurant in which I knew not even the intercession of the Virgin would cause me to be served. I pushed through the doors and took the first vacant seat I saw, at a table for two, and waited.

[18] I do not know how long I waited and I rather wonder, until today, what I could possibly have looked like. Whatever I looked like, I frightened the waitress who shortly appeared, and the moment she appeared all of my fury flowed towards her. I hated her for her white face, and for her great, astounded, frightened eyes. I felt that if she found a black man so frightening I would make her fright worth-while.

[19] She did not ask me what I wanted, but repeated, as though she had learned it somewhere, "We don't serve Negroes here." She did not say it with the blunt, derisive hostility to which I had grown so accustomed, but, rather, with a note of apology in her voice, and fear. This made me colder and more murderous than ever. I felt I had to do something with my hands. I wanted her to come close enough for me to get her neck between my hands.

[20] So I pretended not to have understood her, hoping to draw her closer. And she did step a very short step closer, with her pencil poised incongruously over her pad, and repeated the formula: ". . . don't serve Negroes here."

[21] Somehow, with the repetition of that phrase, which was already ringing in my head like a thousand bells of a nightmare, I realized that she would never come any closer and that I would have to strike from a distance. There was nothing on the table but an ordinary watermug half full of water, and I picked this up and hurled it with all my strength at her. She ducked and it missed her and shattered against the mirror behind the bar. And, with that sound, my frozen blood abruptly thawed, I returned from wherever I had been, I *saw,* for the first time, the restaurant, the people with their mouths open, already, as it seemed to me, rising as one man, and I realized what I had done, and where I was, and I was frightened. I rose and began running for the door. A round, potbellied man grabbed me by the nape of the neck just as I reached the doors and began to beat me about the face. I kicked him and got loose and ran into the streets. My friend whispered, *"Run!"* and I ran.

[22] My friend stayed outside the restaurant long enough to misdirect my pursuers and the police, who arrived, he told me, at once. I do not know what I said to him when he came to my room that night. I could not have said much. I felt, in the oldest, most awful way, that I had somehow betrayed him. I lived it over and over and over again, the way one relives an automobile accident after it has happened and one finds oneself alone and safe. I could not get over two facts, both equally difficult for the imagination to grasp, and one was that I could have been

murdered. But the other was that I had been ready to commit murder. I saw nothing very clearly but I did see this: that my life, my *real* life, was in danger, and not from anything other people might do but from the hatred I carried in my own heart.

– II –

[²³] I had returned home around the second week in June—in great haste because it seemed that my father's death and my mother's confinement were both but a matter of hours. In the case of my mother, it soon became clear that she had simply made a miscalculation. This had always been her tendency and I don't believe that a single one of us arrived in the world, or has since arrived anywhere else, on time. But none of us dawdled so intolerably about the business of being born as did my baby sister. We sometimes amused ourselves, during those endless, stifling weeks, by picturing the baby sitting within in the safe, warm dark, bitterly regretting the necessity of becoming a part of our chaos and stubbornly putting it off as long as possible. I understood her perfectly and congratulated her on showing such good sense so soon. Death, however, sat as purposefully at my father's bedside as life stirred within my mother's womb and it was harder to understand why he so lingered in that long shadow. It seemed that he had bent, and for a long time, too, all of his energies towards dying. Now death was ready for him but my father held back.

[²⁴] All of Harlem, indeed, seemed to be infected by waiting. I had never before known it to be so violently still. Racial tensions throughout this country were exacerbated during the early years of the war, partly because the labor market brought together hundreds of thousands of ill-prepared people and partly because Negro soldiers, regardless of where they were born, received their military training in the south. What happened in defense plants and army camps had repercussions, naturally, in every Negro ghetto. The situation in Harlem had grown bad enough for clergymen, policemen, educators, politicians, and social workers to assert in one breath that there was no "crime wave" and to offer, in the very next breath, suggestions as to how to combat it. These suggestions always seemed to involve playgrounds, despite the fact that racial skirmishes were occurring in the playgrounds, too. Playground or not, crime wave or not, the Harlem police force had been augmented in March, and the unrest grew—perhaps, in fact, partly as a result of the ghetto's instinctive hatred of policemen. Perhaps the most revealing news item, out of the steady parade of reports of muggings, stabbings, shootings, assaults, gang wars, and accusations of police brutality, is the item concerning six Negro girls who set upon a white girl in the subway because, as they all too accurately put it, she was stepping on their toes. Indeed she was, all over the nation.

[25] I had never before been so aware of policemen, on foot, on horse-back, on corners, everywhere, always two by two. Nor had I ever been so aware of small knots of people. They were on stoops and on corners and in doorways, and what was striking about them, I think, was that they did not seem to be talking. Never, when I passed these groups, did the usual sound of a curse or a laugh ring out and neither did there seem to be any hum of gossip. There was certainly, on the other hand, occurring between them communication extraordinarily intense. Another thing that was striking was the unexpected diversity of the people who made up these groups. Usually, for example, one would see a group of sharpies standing on the street corner, jiving the passing chicks; or a group of older men, usually, for some reason, in the vicinity of a barber shop, discussing baseball scores, or the numbers, or making rather chilling ob-servations about women they had known. Women, in a general way, tended to be seen less often together—unless they were church women, or very young girls, or prostitutes met together for an unprofessional instant. But that summer I saw the strangest combinations: large, respect-able, churchly matrons standing on the stoops or the corners with their hair tied up, together with a girl in sleazy satin whose face bore the marks of gin and the razor, or heavy-set, abrupt, no-nonsense older men, in company with the most disreputable and fanatical "race" men, or these same "race" men with the sharpies, or these sharpies with the churchly women. Seventh Day Adventists and Methodists and Spiritualists seemed to be hobnobbing with Holyrollers and they were all, alike, entangled with the most flagrant disbelievers; something heavy in their stance seemed to indicate that they had all, incredibly, seen a common vision, and on each face there seemed to be the same strange, bitter shadow.

[26] The churchly women and the matter-of-fact, no-nonsense men had children in the Army. The sleazy girls they talked to had lovers there, the sharpies and the "race" men had friends and brothers there. It would have demanded an unquestioning patriotism, happily as uncommon in this country as it is undersirable, for these people not to have been disturbed by the bitter letters they received, by the newspaper stories they read, not to have been enraged by the posters, then to be found all over New York, which described the Japanese as "yellow-bellied Japs." It was only the "race" men, to be sure, who spoke ceaselessly of being revenged—how this vengeance was to be exacted was not clear—for the indignities and dangers suffered by Negro boys in uniform; but every-body felt a directionless, hopeless bitterness, as well as that panic which can scarcely be suppressed when one knows that a human being one loves is beyond one's reach, and in danger. This helplessness and this gnawing uneasiness does something, at length, to even the toughest mind. Perhaps the best way to sum all this up is to say that the people I knew felt, mainly, a peculiar kind of relief when they knew that their boys

were being shipped out of the south, to do battle overseas. It was, perhaps, like feeling that the most dangerous part of a dangerous journey had been passed and that now, even if death should come, it would come with honor and without the complicity of their countrymen. Such a death would be, in short, a fact with which one could hope to live.

[27] It was on the 28th of July, which I believe was a Wednesday, that I visited my father for the first time during his illness and for the last time in his life. The moment I saw him I knew why I had put off this visit so long. I had told my mother that I did not want to see him because I hated him. But this was not true. It was only that I *had* hated him and I wanted to hold on to this hatred. I did not want to look on him as a ruin: it was not a ruin I had hated. I imagine that one of the reasons people cling to their hates so stubbornly is because they sense, once hate is gone, that they will be forced to deal with pain.

[28] We traveled out to him, his older sister and myself, to what seemed to be the very end of a very Long Island. It was hot and dusty and we wrangled, my aunt and I, all the way out, over the fact that I had recently begun to smoke and, as she said, to give myself airs. But I knew that she wrangled with me because she could not bear to face the fact of her brother's dying. Neither could I endure the reality of her despair, her unstated bafflement as to what had happened to her brother's life, and her own. So we wrangled and I smoked and from time to time she fell into a heavy reverie. Covertly, I watched her face, which was the face of an old woman; it had fallen in, the eyes were sunken and lightless; soon she would be dying, too.

[29] In my childhood—it had not been so long ago—I had thought her beautiful. She had been quick-witted and quick-moving and very generous with all the children and each of her visits had been an event. At one time one of my brothers and myself had thought of running away to live with her. Now she could no longer produce out of her handbag some unexpected and yet familiar delight. She made me feel pity and revulsion and fear. It was awful to realize that she no longer caused me to feel affection. The closer we came to the hospital the more querulous she became and at the same time, naturally, grew more dependent on me. Between pity and guilt and fear I began to feel that there was another me trapped in my skull like a jack-in-the-box who might escape my control at any moment and fill the air with screaming.

[30] She began to cry the moment we entered the room and she saw him lying there, all shriveled and still, like a little black monkey. The great, gleaming apparatus which fed him and would have compelled him to be still even if he had been able to move brought to mind, not beneficence, but torture; the tubes entering his arm made me think of pictures I had seen when a child, of Gulliver, tied down by the pygmies on that island. My aunt wept and wept, there was a whistling sound in my

father's throat; nothing was said; he could not speak. I wanted to take his hand, to say something. But I do not know what I could have said, even if he could have heard me. He was not really in that room with us, he had at last really embarked on his journey; and though my aunt told me that he said he was going to meet Jesus, I did not hear anything except that whistling in his throat. The doctor came back and we left, into that unbearable train again, and home. In the morning came the telegram saying that he was dead. Then the house was suddenly full of relatives, friends, hysteria, and confusion and I quickly left my mother and the children to the care of those impressive women, who, in Negro communities at least, automatically appear at times of bereavement armed with lotions, proverbs, and patience, and an ability to cook. I went downtown. By the time I returned, later the same day, my mother had been carried to the hospital and the baby had been born.

– III –

[31] For my father's funeral I had nothing black to wear and this posed a nagging problem all day long. It was one of those problems, simple, or impossible of solution, to which the mind insanely clings in order to avoid the mind's real trouble. I spent most of that day at the downtown apartment of a girl I knew, celebrating my birthday with whiskey and wondering what to wear that night. When planning a birthday celebration one naturally does not expect that it will be up against competition from a funeral and this girl had anticipated taking me out that night, for a big dinner and a night club afterwards. Sometime during the course of that long day we decided that we would go out anyway, when my father's funeral service was over. I imagine I decided it, since, as the funeral hour approached, it became clearer and clearer to me that I would not know what to do with myself when it was over. The girl, stifling her very lively concern as to the possible effects of the whiskey on one of my father's chief mourners, concentrated on being conciliatory and practically helpful. She found a black shirt for me somewhere and ironed it and, dressed in the darkest pants and jacket I owned, and slightly drunk, I made my way to my father's funeral.

[32] The chapel was full, but not packed, and very quiet. There were, mainly, my father's relatives, and his children, and here and there I saw faces I had not seen since childhood, the faces of my father's one-time friends. They were very dark and solemn now, seeming somehow to suggest that they had known all along that something like this would happen. Chief among the mourners was my aunt, who had quarreled with my father all his life; by which I do not mean to suggest that her mourning was insincere or that she had not loved him. I suppose that she was one of the few people in the world who had, and their incessant quarreling proved precisely the strength of the tie that bound them. The only other

person in the world, as far as I knew, whose relationship to my father rivaled my aunt's in depth was my mother, who was not there.

[33] It seemed to me, of course, that it was a very long funeral. But it was, if anything, a rather shorter funeral than most, nor, since there were no overwhelming, uncontrollable expressions of grief, could it be called— if I dare to use the word—successful. The minister who preached my father's funeral sermon was one of the few my father had still been seeing as he neared his end. He presented to us in his sermon a man whom none of us had ever seen—a man thoughtful, patient, and forbearing, a Christian inspiration to all who knew him, and a model for his children. And no doubt the children, in their disturbed and guilty state, were almost ready to believe this; he had been remote enough to be anything and, anyway, the shock of the incontrovertible, that it was really our father lying up there in that casket, prepared the mind for anything. His sister moaned and this grief-stricken moaning was taken as corroboration. The other faces held a dark, non-committal thoughtfulness. This was not the man they had known, but they had scarcely expected to be confronted with *him;* this was, in a sense deeper than questions of fact, the man they had not known, and the man they had not known may have been the real one. The real man, whoever he had been, had suffered and now he was dead: this was all that was sure and all that mattered now. Every man in the chapel hoped that when his hour came he, too, would be eulogized, which is to say forgiven, and that all of his lapses, greeds, errors, and strayings from the truth would be invested with coherence and looked upon with charity. This was perhaps the last thing human beings could give each other and it was what they demanded, after all, of the Lord. Only the Lord saw the midnight tears, only He was present when one of His children, moaning and wringing hands, paced up and down the room. When one slapped one's child in anger the recoil in the heart reverberated through heaven and became part of the pain of the universe. And when the children were hungry and sullen and distrustful and one watched them, daily, growing wilder, and further away, and running headlong into danger, it was the Lord who knew what the charged heart endured as the strap was laid to the backside; the Lord alone who knew what one *would* have said if one had had, like the Lord, the gift of the living word. It was the Lord who knew of the impossibility every parent in that room faced: how to prepare the child for the day when the child would be despised and how to *create* in the child—by what means?—a stronger antidote to this poison than one had found for oneself. The avenues, side streets, bars, billiard halls, hospitals, police stations, and even the playgrounds of Harlem—not to mention the houses of correction, the jails, and the morgue—testified to the potency of the poison while remaining silent as to the efficacy of whatever antidote, irresistibly raising the question of whether or not such an antidote existed;

raising, which was worse, the question of whether or not an antidote was desirable; perhaps poison should be fought with poison. With these several schisms in the mind and with more terrors in the heart than could be named, it was better not to judge the man who had gone down under an impossible burden. It was better to remember: *Thou knowest this man's fall; but thou knowest not his wrassling.*

[34] While the preacher talked and I watched the children—years of changing their diapers, scrubbing them, slapping them, taking them to school, and scolding them had had the perhaps inevitable result of making me love them, though I am not sure I knew this then—my mind was busily breaking out with a rash of disconnected impressions. Snatches of popular songs, indecent jokes, bits of books I had read, movie sequences, faces, voices, political issues—I thought I was going mad; all these impressions suspended, as it were, in the solution of the faint nausea produced in me by the heat and liquor. For a moment I had the impression that my alcoholic breath, inefficiently disguised with chewing gum, filled the entire chapel. Then someone began singing one of my father's favorite songs and, abruptly, I was with him, sitting on his knee, in the hot, enormous, crowded church which was the first church we attended. It was the Abyssinia Baptist Church on 138th Street. We had not gone there long. With this image, a host of others came. I had forgotten, in the rage of my growing up, how proud my father had been of me when I was little. Apparently, I had had a voice and my father had liked to show me off before the members of the church. I had forgotten what he had looked like when he was pleased but now I remembered that he had always been grinning with pleasure when my solos ended. I even remembered certain expressions on his face when he teased my mother—had he loved her? I would never know. And when had it all begun to change? For now it seemed that he had not always been cruel. I remembered being taken for a haircut and scraping my knee on the footrest of the barber's chair and I remembered my father's face as he soothed my crying and applied the stinging iodine. Then I remembered our fights, fights which had been of the worst possible kind because my technique had been silence.

[35] I remembered the one time in all our life together when we had really spoken to each other.

[36] It was on a Sunday and it must have been shortly before I left home. We were walking, just the two of us, in our usual silence, to or from church. I was in high school and had been doing a lot of writing and I was, at about this time, the editor of the high school magazine. But I had also been a Young Minister and had been preaching from the pulpit. Lately, I had been taking fewer engagements and preached as rarely as possible. It was said in the church, quite truthfully, that I was "cooling off."

[37] My father asked me abruptly, "You'd rather write than preach, wouldn't you?"

[38] I was astonished at his question—because it was a real question. I answered, "Yes."

[39] That was all we said. It was awful to remember that that was all we had *ever* said.

[40] The casket now was opened and the mourners were being led up the aisle to look for the last time on the deceased. The assumption was that the family was too overcome with grief to be allowed to make this journey alone and I watched while my aunt was led to the casket and, muffled in black, and shaking, led back to her seat. I disapproved of forcing the children to look on their dead father, considering that the shock of his death, or, more truthfully, the shock of death as a reality, was already a little more than a child could bear, but my judgment in this matter had been overruled and there they were, bewildered and frightened and very small, being led, one by one, to the casket. But there is also something very gallant about children at such moments. It has something to do with their silence and gravity and with the fact that one cannot help them. Their legs, somehow, seem *exposed*, so that it is at once incredible and terribly clear that their legs are all they have to hold them up.

[41] I had not wanted to go to the casket myself and I certainly had not wished to be led there, but there was no way of avoiding either of these forms. One of the deacons led me up and I looked on my father's face. I cannot say that it looked like him at all. His blackness had been equivocated by powder and there was no suggestion in that casket of what his power had or could have been. He was simply an old man dead, and it was hard to believe that he had ever given anyone either joy or pain. Yet, his life filled that room. Further up the avenue his wife was holding his newborn child. Life and death so close together, and love and hatred, and right and wrong, said something to me which I did not want to hear concerning man, concerning the life of man.

[42] After the funeral, while I was downtown desperately celebrating my birthday, a Negro soldier, in the lobby of the Hotel Braddock, got into a fight with a white policeman over a Negro girl. Negro girls, white policemen, in or out of uniform, and Negro males—in or out of uniform —were part of the furniture of the lobby of the Hotel Braddock and this was certainly not the first time such an incident had occurred. It was destined, however, to receive an unprecedented publicity, for the fight between the policeman and the soldier ended with the shooting of the soldier. Rumor, flowing immediately to the streets outside, stated that the soldier had been shot in the back, an instantaneous and revealing invention, and that the soldier had died protecting a Negro woman. The facts were somewhat different—for example, the soldier had not been shot in the back, and was not dead, and the girl seems to have been as

dubious a symbol of womanhood as her white counterpart in Georgia usually is, but no one was interested in the facts. They preferred the invention because this invention expressed and corroborated their hates and fears so perfectly. It is just as well to remember that people are always doing this. Perhaps many of those legends, including Christianity, to which the world clings began their conquest of the world with just some such concerted surrender to distortion. The effect, in Harlem, of this particular legend was like the effect of a lit match in a tin of gasoline. The mob gathered before the doors of the Hotel Braddock simply began to swell and to spread in every direction, and Harlem exploded.

[43] The mob did not cross the ghetto lines. It would have been easy, for example, to have gone over Morningside Park on the west side or to have crossed the Grand Central railroad tracks at 125th Street on the east side, to wreak havoc in white neighborhoods. The mob seems to have been mainly interested in something more potent and real than the white face, that is, in white power, and the principal damage done during the riot of the summer of 1943 was to white business establishments in Harlem. It might have been a far bloodier story, of course, if, at the hour the riot began, these establishments had still been open. From the Hotel Braddock the mob fanned out, east and west along 125th Street, and for the entire length of Lenox, Seventh, and Eighth avenues. Along each of these avenues, and along each major side street—116th, 125th, 138th, and so on—bars, stores, pawnshops, restaurants, even little luncheonettes had been smashed open and entered and looted—looted, it might be added, with more haste than efficiency. The shelves really looked as though a bomb had struck them. Cans of beans and soup and dog food, along with toilet paper, corn flakes, sardines, and milk tumbled every which way, and abandoned cash registers and cases of beer leaned crazily out of the splintered windows and were strewn along the avenues. Sheets, blankets, and clothing of every description formed a kind of path, as though people had dropped them while running. I truly had not realized that Harlem *had* so many stores until I saw them all smashed open; the first time the word *wealth* ever entered my mind in relation to Harlem was when I saw it scattered in the streets. But one's first, incongruous impression of plenty was countered immediately by an impression of waste. None of this was doing anybody any good. It would have been better to have left the plate glass as it had been and the goods lying in the stores.

[44] It would have been better, but it would also have been intolerable, for Harlem had needed something to smash. To smash something is the ghetto's chronic need. Most of the time it is the members of the ghetto who smash each other, and themselves. But as long as the ghetto walls are standing there will always come a moment when these outlets do not work. That summer, for example, it was not enough to get into a fight on Lenox Avenue, or curse out one's cronies in the barber shops. If ever,

indeed, the violence which fills Harlem's churches, pool halls, and bars erupts outward in a more direct fashion, Harlem and its citizens are likely to vanish in an apocalyptic flood. That this is not likely to happen is due to a great many reasons, most hidden and powerful among them the Negro's real relation to the white American. This relation prohibits, simply, anything as uncomplicated and satisfactory as pure hatred. In order really to hate white people, one has to blot so much out of the mind—and the heart—that this hatred itself becomes an exhausting and self-destructive pose. But this does not mean, on the other hand, that love comes easily: the white world is too powerful, too complacent, too ready with gratuitous humiliation, and, above all, too ignorant and too innocent for that. One is absolutely forced to make perpetual qualifications and one's own reactions are always canceling each other out. It is this, really, which has driven so many people mad, both white and black. One is always in the position of having to decide between amputation and gangrene. Amputation is swift but time may prove that the amputation was not necessary—or one may delay the amputation too long. Gangrene is slow, but it is impossible to be sure that one is reading one's symptoms right. The idea of going through life as a cripple is more than one can bear, and equally unbearable is the risk of swelling up slowly, in agony, with poison. And the trouble, finally, is that the risks are real even if the choices do not exist.

[45] "But as for me and my house," my father had said, "we will serve the Lord." I wondered, as we drove him to his resting place, what this line had meant for him. I had heard him preach it many times. I had preached it once myself, proudly giving it an interpretation different from my father's. Now the whole thing came back to me, as though my father and I were on our way to Sunday school and I were memorizing the golden text: *And if it seem evil unto you to serve the Lord, choose you this day whom you will serve; whether the gods which your fathers served that were on the other side of the flood, or the gods of the Amorites, in whose land ye dwell: but as for me and my house, we will serve the Lord.* I suspected in these familiar lines a meaning which had never been there for me before. All of my father's texts and songs, which I had decided were meaningless, were arranged before me at his death like empty bottles, waiting to hold the meaning which life would give them for me. This was his legacy: nothing is ever escaped. That bleakly memorable morning I hated the unbelievable streets and the Negroes and whites who had, equally, made them that way. But I knew that it was folly, as my father would have said, this bitterness was folly. It was necessary to hold on to the things that mattered. The dead man mattered, the new life mattered; blackness and whiteness did not matter; to believe that they did was to acquiesce in one's own destruction. Hatred,

which could destroy so much, never failed to destroy the man who hated and this was an immutable law.

[46] It began to seem that one would have to hold in the mind forever two ideas which seemed to be in opposition. The first idea was acceptance, the acceptance, totally without rancor, of life as it is, and men as they are: in the light of this idea, it goes without saying that injustice is a commonplace. But this did not mean that one could be complacent, for the second idea was of equal power: that one must never, in one's own life, accept these injustices as commonplace but must fight them with all one's strength. This fight begins, however, in the heart and it now had been laid to my charge to keep my own heart free of hatred and despair. This intimation made my heart heavy and, now that my father was irrecoverable, I wished that he had been beside me so that I could have searched his face for the answers which only the future would give me now.

COMMENT AND QUESTIONS

1. The title of Baldwin's essay echoes Richard Wright's novel *Native Son,* an attack on race prejudice in the United States. What are the connotations of *Notes?* Does the word seem well chosen to describe the form and structure of the essay?

2. The first paragraph associates the death of the author's father, the birth of his sister, and race riots. It therefore introduces some of the merging themes woven through the essay—oppositions of death–birth, blackness–whiteness, hate–love, parent–child, innocence–experience, and reality–unreality. Is paragraph 1 coherent?

3. How does paragraph 2 further develop some of the themes? What is the meaning of *codas* in that paragraph? Of *apocalypse?* Does the paragraph indicate what kind of apocalypse Baldwin experienced?

4. Paragraph 5 is interesting for its style as well as for its graphic picture of the author's father. Point out sentence structures, combinations of words, and repetitions of words and sounds that seem to you effective.

5. What is the function of paragraph 6?

6. How are recurrent themes stressed and developed in paragraphs 7–12? What is the purpose of developing fully the experience with the white schoolteacher?

7. During the year in New Jersey (paragraphs 13–22), experience replaces innocence; and, for the author, hate and the opposition of blackness–whiteness become one. What other theme recurs in these paragraphs? Why do you think Baldwin develops as fully as he does the episode in the

restaurant, paragraphs 18–21? In the last sentence of section I, what is the meaning of "my *real* life"?

8. "Notes of a Native Son" is an example of narration which departs from chronological order. Analyze the time-structure of the essay. In what ways is this structure more effective for Baldwin's purposes than a setting down of events in the time-order in which they occurred?

9. Section II begins with the death–birth opposition. What other oppositions are woven into this part of the essay and in some respects changed?

10. Examine the imagery and the sentence structures in paragraph 30. What makes the paragraph a good section ending?

11. The opening paragraph of section III brings together death and birth in a different way, and the second sentence of the paragraph refers to "the mind's real trouble." What is this "real trouble"?

12. Paragraphs 33–41 further develop some of the basic themes. What changes in feeling and tone do these paragraphs establish?

13. How are the themes of reality–unreality and of hate–love associated, in paragraphs 42–44, with the riot in Harlem? What does Baldwin mean by saying, in paragraph 44, that the white world is "too ignorant and too innocent"?

14. By the end of the essay, some of the themes have coalesced; the oppositions have been modified and have shifted into new oppositions. For the author, what realizations have emerged from the experience of his father's death?

15. Baldwin is, of course, writing about a Negro son, his Negro father, and the experience of being a Negro. In what ways do his experiences transcend the particular and his themes become universal themes?

[79] *Norman Podhoretz*: My Negro Problem— and Ours

NORMAN PODHORETZ (1930–   ), an American writer and critic, is the editor of *Commentary*. A collection of his articles, called *Doings and Undoings: The Fifties and After in American Writing*, was published in 1964; the following essay first appeared in the February, 1963, issue of *Commentary*. Footnotes are the author's.

If we—and . . . I mean the relatively conscious whites and the relatively conscious blacks, who must, like lovers, insist on, or create, the consciousness of the others—do not falter in our duty

*now, we may be able, handful that we are, to end the racial
nightmare, and achieve our country, and change the history of
the world.*—JAMES BALDWIN

[¹] Two ideas puzzled me deeply as a child growing up in Brooklyn
during the 1930's in what today would be called an integrated neighborhood. One of them was that all Jews were rich; the other was that all
Negroes were persecuted. These ideas had appeared in print; therefore
they must be true. My own experience and the evidence of my senses told
me they were not true, but that only confirmed what a day-dreaming boy
in the provinces—for the lower-class neighborhoods of New York belong
as surely to the provinces as any rural town in North Dakota—discovers
very early: *his* experience is unreal and the evidence of his senses is not
to be trusted. Yet even a boy with a head full of fantasies incongruously
synthesized out of Hollywood movies and English novels cannot altogether deny the reality of his own experience—especially when there is
so much deprivation in that experience. Nor can he altogether gainsay the
evidence of his own senses—especially such evidence of the senses as
comes from being repeatedly beaten up, robbed, and in general hated,
terrorized, and humiliated.

[²] And so for a long time I was puzzled to think that Jews were supposed to be rich when the only Jews I knew were poor, and that Negroes
were supposed to be persecuted when it was the Negroes who were doing
the only persecuting I knew about—and doing it, moreover, to *me*. During the early years of the war, when my older sister joined a left-wing
youth organization, I remember my astonishment at hearing her passionately denounce my father for thinking that Jews were worse off than
Negroes. To me, at the age of twelve, it seemed very clear that Negroes
were better off than Jews—indeed, than *all* whites. A city boy's world
is contained within three or four square blocks, and in my world it was
the whites, the Italians and Jews, who feared the Negroes, not the other
way around. The Negroes were tougher than we were, more ruthless,
and on the whole they were better athletes. What could it mean, then, to
say that they were badly off and that we were more fortunate? Yet my
sister's opinions, like print, were sacred, and when she told me about
exploitation and economic forces I believed her. I believed her, but I
was still afraid of Negroes. And I still hated them with all my heart.

[³] It had not always been so—that much I can recall from early
childhood. When did it start, this fear and this hatred? There was a
kindergarten in the local public school, and given the character of the
neighborhood, at least half of the children in my class must have been
Negroes. Yet I have no memory of being aware of color differences at
that age, and I know from observing my own children that they attribute
no significance to such differences even when they begin noticing them.

I think there was a day—first grade? second grade?—when my best friend Carl hit me on the way home from school and announced that he wouldn't play with me any more because I had killed Jesus. When I ran home to my mother crying for an explanation, she told me not to pay any attention to such foolishness, and then in Yiddish she cursed the *goyim* and the *schwartzes*, the *schwartzes* and the *goyim*. Carl, it turned out, was a *schwartze,* and so was added a third to the categories into which people were mysteriously divided.

[4] Sometimes I wonder whether this is a true memory at all. It is blazingly vivid, but perhaps it never happened: can anyone really remember back to the age of six? There is no uncertainty in my mind, however, about the years that followed. Carl and I hardly ever spoke, though we met in school every day up through the eighth or ninth grade. There would be embarrassed moments of catching his eye or of his catching mine—for whatever it was that had attracted us to one another as very small children remained alive in spite of the fantastic barrier of hostility that had grown up between us, suddenly and out of nowhere. Nevertheless, friendship would have been impossible, and even if it had been possible, it would have been unthinkable. About that, there was nothing anyone could do by the time we were eight years old.

[5]*Item:* The orphanage across the street is torn down, a city housing project begins to rise in its place, and on the marvelous vacant lot next to the old orphanage they are building a playground. Much excitement and anticipation as Opening Day draws near. Mayor LaGuardia himself comes to dedicate this great gesture of public benevolence. He speaks of neighborliness and borrowing cups of sugar, and of the playground he says that children of all races, colors, and creeds will learn to live together in harmony. A week later, some of us are swatting flies on the playground's inadequate little ball field. A gang of Negro kids, pretty much our own age, enter from the other side and order us out of the park. We refuse, proudly and indignantly, with superb masculine fervor. There is a fight, they win, and we retreat, half whimpering, half with bravado. My first nauseating experience of cowardice. And my first appalled realization that there are people in the world who do not seem to be afraid of anything, who act as though they have nothing to lose. Thereafter the playground becomes a battleground, sometimes quiet, sometimes the scene of athletic competition between Them and Us. But rocks are thrown as often as baseballs. Gradually we abandon the place and use the streets instead. The streets are safer, though we do not admit this to ourselves. We are not, after all, sissies—that most dreaded epithet of an American boyhood.

[6] *Item:* I am standing alone in front of the building in which I live. It is late afternoon and getting dark. That day in school the teacher had asked a surly Negro boy named Quentin a question he was unable to

answer. As usual I had waved my arm eagerly ("Be a good boy, get good marks, be smart, go to college, become a doctor") and, the right answer bursting from my lips, I was held up lovingly by the teacher as an example to the class. I had seen Quentin's face—a very dark, very cruel, very Oriental-looking face—harden, and there had been enough threat in his eyes to make me run all the way home for fear that he might catch me outside.

[7] Now, standing idly in front of my own house, I see him approaching from the project accompanied by his little brother who is carrying a baseball bat and wearing a grin of malicious anticipation. As in a nightmare, I am trapped. The surroundings are secure and familiar, but terror is suddenly present and there is no one around to help. I am locked to the spot. I will not cry out or run away like a sissy, and I stand there, my heart wild, my throat clogged. He walks up, hurls the familiar epithet ("Hey, mo'f——r"), and to my surprise only pushes me. It is a violent push, but not a punch. A push is not as serious as a punch. Maybe I can still back out without entirely losing my dignity. Maybe I can still say, "Hey, c'mon Quentin, whaddya wanna do *that* for. I dint do nothin' to *you*," and walk away, not too rapidly. Instead, before I can stop myself, I push him back—a token gesture—and I say, "Cut that out, I don't wanna fight, I ain't got nothin' to fight about." As I turn to walk back into the building, the corner of my eye catches the motion of the bat his little brother has handed him. I try to duck, but the bat crashes colored lights into my head.

[8] The next thing I know, my mother and sister are standing over me, both of them hysterical. My sister—she who was later to join the "progressive" youth organization—is shouting for the police and screaming imprecations at those dirty little black bastards. They take me upstairs, the doctor comes, the police come. I tell them that the boy who did it was a stranger, that he had been trying to get money from me. They do not believe me, but I am too scared to give them Quentin's name. When I return to school a few days later, Quentin avoids my eyes. He knows that I have not squealed, and he is ashamed. I try to feel proud, but in my heart I know that it was fear of what his friends might do to me that had kept me silent, and not the code of the street.

[9] *Item:* There is an athletic meet in which the whole of our junior high school is participating. I am in one of the seventh-grade rapid-advance classes, and "segregation" has now set in with a vengeance. In the last three or four years of the elementary school from which we have just graduated, each grade had been divided into three classes, according to "intelligence." (In the earlier grades the divisions had either been arbitrary or else unrecognized by us as having anything to do with brains.) These divisions by IQ, or however it was arranged, had resulted in a preponderance of Jews in the "1" classes and a corresponding pre-

ponderance of Negroes in the "3's," with the Italians split unevenly along
the spectrum. At least a few Negroes had always made the "1's," just as
there had always been a few Jewish kids among the "3's" and more
among the "2's" (where Italians dominated). But the junior high's rapid-
advance class of which I am now a member is overwhelmingly Jewish
and entirely white—except for a shy lonely Negro girl with light skin
and reddish hair.

[¹⁰] The athletic meet takes place in a city-owned stadium far from
the school. It is an important event to which a whole day is given over.
The winners are to get those precious little medallions stamped with the
New York City emblem that can be screwed into a belt and that prove
the wearer to be a distinguished personage. I am a fast runner, and so
I am assigned the position of anchor man on my class's team in the relay
race. There are three other seventh-grade teams in the race, two of them
all Negro, as ours is all white. One of the all-Negro teams is very tall—
their anchor man waiting silently next to me on the line looks years older
than I am, and I do not recognize him. He is the first to get the baton and
crosses the finishing line in a walk. Our team comes in second, but a few
minutes later we are declared the winners, for it has been discovered that
the anchor man on the first-place team is not a member of the class. We
are awarded the medallions, and the following day our home-room
teacher makes a speech about how proud she is of us for being superior
athletes as well as superior students. We want to believe that we deserve
the praise, but we know that we could not have won even if the other
class had not cheated.

[¹¹] That afternoon, walking home, I am waylaid and surrounded by
five Negroes, among whom is the anchor man of the disqualified team.
"Gimme my medal, mo'f——r," he grunts. I do not have it with me and
I tell him so. "Anyway, it ain't yours," I say foolishly. He calls me a liar
on both counts and pushes me up against the wall on which we sometimes play handball. "Gimme my mo'f——n' medal," he says again. I
repeat that I have left it home. "Le's search the li'l mo'f——r," one of
them suggests, "he prolly got it *hid* in his mo'f——n' *pants*." My panic
is now unmanageable. (How many times had I been surrounded like this
and asked in soft tones, "Len' me a nickel, boy." How many times had I
been called a liar for pleading poverty and pushed around, or searched,
or beaten up, unless there happened to be someone in the marauding
gang like Carl who liked me across that enormous divide of hatred and
who would therefore say, "Aaah, c'mon, le's git someone else, *this* boy
ain't got no money on 'im.") I scream at them through tears of rage and
self-contempt, "Keep your f——n' filthy lousy black hands offa me! I
swear I'll get the cops." This is all they need to hear, and the five of them
set upon me. They bang me around, mostly in the stomach and on the
arms and shoulders, and when several adults loitering near the candy

store down the block notice what is going on and begin to shout, they run off and away.

[¹²] I do not tell my parents about the incident. My team-mates, who have also been waylaid, each by a gang led by his opposite number from the disqualified team, have had their medallions taken from them, and they never squeal either. For days, I walk home in terror, expecting to be caught again, but nothing happens. The medallion is put away into a drawer, never to be worn by anyone.

[¹³] Obviously experiences like these have always been a common feature of childhood life in working-class and immigrant neighborhoods, and Negroes do not necessarily figure in them. Wherever, and in whatever combination, they have lived together in the cities, kids of different groups have been at war, beating up and being beaten up: micks against kikes against wops against spicks against polacks. And even relatively homogeneous areas have not been spared the warring of the young: one block against another, one gang (called in my day, in a pathetic effort at gentility, an "S.A.C.," or social-athletic club) against another. But the Negro-white conflict had—and no doubt still has—a special intensity and was conducted with a ferocity unmatched by intramural white battling.

[¹⁴] In my own neighborhood, a good deal of animosity existed between the Italian kids (most of whose parents were immigrants from Sicily) and the Jewish kids (who came largely from East European immigrant families). Yet everyone had friends, sometimes close friends, in the other "camp," and we often visited one another's strange-smelling houses, if not for meals, then for glasses of milk, and occasionally for some special event like a wedding or a wake. If it happened that we divided into warring factions and did battle, it would invariably be half-hearted and soon patched up. Our parents, to be sure, had nothing to do with one another and were mutually suspicious and hostile. But we, the kids, who all spoke Yiddish or Italian at home, were Americans, or New Yorkers, or Brooklyn boys: we shared a culture, the culture of the street, and at least for a while this culture proved to be more powerful than the opposing cultures of the home.

[¹⁵] Why, *why* should it have been so different as between the Negroes and us? How was it borne in upon us so early, white and black alike, that we were enemies beyond any possibility of reconciliation? Why did we hate one another so?

[¹⁶] I suppose if I tried, I could answer those questions more or less adequately from the perspective of what I have since learned. I could draw upon James Baldwin—what better witness is there?—to describe the sense of entrapment that poisons the soul of the Negro with hatred for the white man whom he knows to be his jailer. On the other side, if I wanted to understand how the white man comes to hate the Negro,

I could call upon the psychologists who have spoken of the guilt that white Americans feel toward Negroes and that turns into hatred for lack of acknowledging itself as guilt. These are plausible answers and certainly there is truth in them. Yet when I think back upon my own experience of the Negro and his of me, I find myself troubled and puzzled, much as I was as a child when I heard that all Jews were rich and all Negroes persecuted. How could the Negroes in my neighborhood have regarded the whites across the street and around the corner as jailers? On the whole, the whites were not so poor as the Negroes, but they were quite poor enough, and the years were years of Depression. As for white hatred of the Negro, how could guilt have had anything to do with it? What share had these Italian and Jewish immigrants in the enslavement of the Negro? What share had they—downtrodden people themselves breaking their own necks to eke out a living—in the exploitation of the Negro?

[17] No, I cannot believe that we hated each other back there in Brooklyn because they thought of us as jailers and we felt guilty toward them. But does it matter, given the fact that we all went through an unrepresentative confrontation? I think it matters profoundly, for if we managed the job of hating each other so well without benefit of the aids to hatred that are supposedly at the root of this madness everywhere else, it must mean that the madness is not yet properly understood. I am far from pretending that I understand it, but I would insist that no view of the problem will begin to approach the truth unless it can account for a case like the one I have been trying to describe. Are the elements of any such view available to us?

[18] At least two, I would say, are. One of them is a point we frequently come upon in the work of James Baldwin, and the other is a related point always stressed by psychologists who have studied the mechanisms of prejudice. Baldwin tells us that of the reasons Negroes hate the white man is that the white man refuses to *look* at him: the Negro knows that in white eyes all Negroes are alike; they are faceless and therefore not altogether human. The psychologists, in their turn, tell us that the white man hates the Negro because he tends to project those wild impulses that he fears in himself onto an alien group which he then punishes with his contempt. What Baldwin does *not* tell us, however, is that the principle of facelessness is a two-way street and can operate in both directions with no difficulty at all. Thus, in my neighborhood in Brooklyn, *I* was as faceless to the Negroes as they were to me, and if they hated me because I never looked at them, I must also have hated them for never looking at *me*. To the Negroes, my white skin was enough to define me as the enemy, and in a war it is only the uniform that counts and not the person.

[19] So with the mechanism of projection that the psychologists talk

about: it too works in both directions at once. There is no question that the psychologists are right about what the Negro represents symbolically to the white man. For me as a child the life lived on the other side of the playground and down the block on Ralph Avenue seemed the very embodiment of the values of the street—free, independent, reckless, brave, masculine, erotic. I put the word "erotic" last, though it is usually stressed above all others, because in fact it came last, in consciousness as in importance. What mainly counted for me about Negro kids of my own age was that they were "bad boys." There were plenty of bad boys among the whites—this was, after all, a neighborhood with a long tradition of crime as a career open to aspiring talents—but the Negroes were *really* bad, bad in a way that beckoned to one, and made one feel inadequate. *We* all went home every day for a lunch of spinach-and-potatoes; *they* roamed around during lunch hour, munching on candy bars. In winter *we* had to wear itchy woolen hats and mittens and cumbersome galoshes; *they* were bare-headed and loose as they pleased. *We* rarely played hookey, or got into serious trouble in school, for all our street-corner bravado; *they* were defiant, forever staying out (to do what delicious things?), forever making disturbances in class and in the halls, forever being sent to the principal and returning uncowed. But most important of all, they were *tough*; beautifully, enviably tough, not giving a damn for anyone or anything. To hell with the teacher, the truant officer, the cop; to hell with the whole of the adult world that held *us* in its grip and that we never had the courage to rebel against except sporadically and in petty ways.

[20] This is what I saw and envied and feared in the Negro: this is what finally made him faceless to me, though some of it, of course, was actually there. (The psychologists also tell us that the alien group which becomes the object of a projection will tend to respond by trying to live up to what is expected of them.) But what, on his side, did the Negro see in me that made me faceless to *him?* Did he envy me my lunches of spinach-and-potatoes and my itchy woolen caps and my prudent behavior in the face of authority, as I envied him his noon-time candy bars and his bare head in winter and his magnificent rebelliousness? Did those lunches and caps spell for him the prospect of power and riches in the future? Did they mean that there were possibilities open to me that were denied to him? Very likely they did. But if so, one also supposes that he feared the impulses within himself toward submission to authority no less powerfully than I feared the impulses in myself toward defiance. If I represented the jailer to him, it was not because I was oppressing him or keeping him down: it was because I symbolized for him the dangerous and probably pointless temptation toward greater repression, just as he symbolized for me the equally perilous tug toward greater freedom. I

personally was to be rewarded for this repression with a new and better life in the future, but how many of my friends paid an even higher price and were given only gall in return.

[21] We have it on the authority of James Baldwin that all Negroes hate whites. I am trying to suggest that on their side all whites—all American whites, that is—are sick in their feelings about Negroes. There are Negroes, no doubt, who would say that Baldwin is wrong, but I suspect them of being less honest than he is, just as I suspect whites of self-deception who tell me they have no special feeling toward Negroes. Special feelings about color are a contagion to which white Americans seem susceptible even when there is nothing in their background to account for the susceptibility. Thus everywhere we look today in the North, we find the curious phenomenon of white middle-class liberals with no previous personal experience of Negroes—people to whom Negroes have always been faceless in virtue rather than faceless in vice— discovering that their abstract commitment to the cause of Negro rights will not stand the test of a direct confrontation. We find such people fleeing in droves to the suburbs as the Negro population in the inner city grows; and when they stay in the city we find them sending their children to private school rather than to the "integrated" public school in the neighborhood. We find them resisting the demand that gerrymandered school districts be re-zoned for the purpose of overcoming de facto segregation; we find them judiciously considering whether the Negroes (for their own good, of course) are not perhaps pushing too hard; we find them clucking their tongues over Negro militancy; we find them speculating on the question of whether there may not, after all, be something in the theory that the races are biologically different; we find them saying that it will take a very long time for Negroes to achieve full equality, no matter what anyone does; we find them deploring the rise of black nationalism and expressing the solemn hope that the leaders of the Negro community will discover ways of containing the impatience and incipient violence with the Negro ghettos.[1]

[22] But that is by no means the whole story; there is also the phenomenon of what Kenneth Rexroth once called "crow-jimism." There are the broken-down white boys like Vivaldo Moore in Baldwin's *Another Country* who go to Harlem in search of sex or simply to brush up against something that looks like primitive vitality, and who are so often punished by the Negro they meet for crimes that they would have been the last ever to commit and of which they themselves have been as sorry victims as any of the Negroes who take it out on them. There are the writers and intellectuals and artists who romanticize Negroes and pander

---

[1] For an account of developments like these, see "The White Liberal's Retreat" by Murray Friedman in the January 1963 *Atlantic Monthly*.

to them, assuming a guilt that is not properly theirs. And there are all the white liberals who permit Negroes to blackmail them into adopting a double standard of moral judgment, and who lend themselves—again assuming the responsibility for crimes they never committed—to cunning and contemptuous exploitation by Negroes they employ or try to befriend.

[23] And what about me? What kind of feelings do I have about Negroes today? What happened to me, from Brooklyn, who grew up fearing and envying and hating Negroes? Now that Brooklyn is behind me, do I fear them and envy them and hate them still? The answer is yes, but not in the same proportions and certainly not in the same way. I now live on the upper west side of Manhattan, where there are many Negroes and many Puerto Ricans, and there are nights when I experience the old apprehensiveness again, and there are streets that I avoid when I am walking in the dark, as there were streets that I avoided when I was a child. I find that I am not afraid of Puerto Ricans, but I cannot restrain my nervousness whenever I pass a group of Negroes standing in front of a bar or sauntering down the street. I know now, as I did not know when I was a child, that power is on my side, that the police are working for me and not for them. And knowing this I feel ashamed and guilty, like the good liberal I have grown up to be. Yet the twinges of fear and the resentment they bring and the self-contempt they arouse are not to be gainsaid.

[24] But envy? Why envy? And hatred? Why hatred? Here again the intensities have lessened and everything has been complicated and qualified by the guilts and the resulting over-compensations that are the heritage of the enlightened middle-class world of which I am now a member. Yet just as in childhood I envied Negroes for what seemed to me their superior masculinity, so I envy them today for what seems to me their superior physical grace and beauty. I have come to value physical grace very highly, and I am now capable of aching with all my being when I watch a Negro couple on the dance floor, or a Negro playing baseball or basketball. They are on the kind of terms with their own bodies that I should like to be on with mine, and for that precious quality they seem blessed to me.

[25] The hatred I still feel for Negroes is the hardest of all the old feelings to face or admit, and it is the most hidden and the most overlarded by the conscious attitudes into which I have succeeded in willing myself. It no longer has, as for me it once did, any cause or justification (except, perhaps, that I am constantly being denied my right to an honest expression of the things I earned the right as a child to feel). How, then, do I know that this hatred has never entirely disappeared? I know it from the insane rage that can stir in me at the thought of Negro anti-Semitism; I know it from the disgusting prurience that can stir in me at the sight of a mixed couple; and I know it from the violence that can stir in me

whenever I encounter that special brand of paranoid touchiness to which many Negroes are prone.

[26] This, then, is where I am; it is not exactly where I think all other white liberals are, but it cannot be so very far away either. And it is because I am convinced that we white Americans are—for whatever reason, it no longer matters—so twisted and sick in our feelings about Negroes that I despair of the present push toward integration. If the pace of progress were not a factor here, there would perhaps be no cause for despair: time and the law and even the international political situation are on the side of the Negroes, and ultimately, therefore, victory—of a sort, anyway—must come. But from everything we have learned from observers who ought to know, pace has become as important to the Negroes as substance. They want equality and they want it *now,* and the white world is yielding to their demand only as much and as fast as it is absolutely being compelled to do. The Negroes know this in the most concrete terms imaginable, and it is thus becoming increasingly difficult to buy them off with rhetoric and promises and pious assurances of support. And so within the Negro community we find more and more people declaring—as Harold R. Isaacs recently put it in these pages[2]—that they want *out:* people who say that integration will never come, or that it will take a hundred or a thousand years to come, or that it will come at too high a price in suffering and struggle for the pallid and sodden life of the American middle class that at the very best it may bring.

[27] The most numerous, influential, and dangerous movement that has grown out of Negro despair with the goal of integration is, of course, the Black Muslims. This movement, whatever else we may say about it, must be credited with one enduring achievement: it inspired James Baldwin to write an essay[3] which deserves to be placed among the classics of our language. Everything Baldwin has ever been trying to tell us is distilled here into a statement of overwhelming persuasiveness and prophetic magnificence. Baldwin's message is and always has been simple. It is this: "Color is not a human or personal reality; it is a political reality." And Baldwin's demand is correspondingly simple: color must be forgotten, lest we all be smited with a vengeance "that does not really depend on, and cannot really be executed by, any person or organization, and that cannot be prevented by any police force or army: historical vengeance, a cosmic vengeance based on the law that we recognize when we say, 'Whatever goes up must come down.'" The Black Muslims Baldwin portrays as a sign and a warning to the intransigent white world. They come to proclaim how deep is the Negro's disaffection with the

[2] "Integration and the Negro Mood," December 1962.

[3] Originally published last November in the *New Yorker* under the title "Letter From a Region in My Mind," it has just been reprinted (along with a new introduction) by Dial Press under the title *The Fire Next Time.*

white world and all its works, and Baldwin implies that no American Negro can fail to respond somewhere in his being to their message: that the white man is the devil, that Allah has doomed him to destruction, and that the black man is about to inherit the earth. Baldwin of course knows that this nightmare inversion of the racism from which the black man has suffered can neither win nor even point to the neighborhood in which victory might be located. For in his view the neighborhood of victory lies in exactly the opposite direction: the transcendence of color through love.

[28] Yet the tragic fact is that love is not the answer to hate—not in the world of politics, at any rate. Color is indeed a political rather than a human or a personal reality and if politics (which is to say power) has made it into a human and a personal reality, then only politics (which is to say power) can unmake it once again. But the way of politics is slow and bitter, and as impatience on the one side is matched by a setting of the jaw on the other, we move closer and closer to an explosion and blood may yet run in the streets.

[29] Will this madness in which we are all caught never find a resting-place? Is there never to be an end to it? In thinking about the Jews I have often wondered whether their survival as a distinct group was worth one hair on the head of a single infant. Did the Jews have to survive so that six million innocent people should one day be burned in the ovens of Auschwitz? It is a terrible question and no one, not God himself, could ever answer it to my satisfaction. And when I think about the Negroes in America and about the image of integration as a state in which the Negroes would take their rightful place as another of the protected minorities in a pluralistic society, I wonder whether they really believe in their hearts that such a state can actually be attained, and if so *why* they should wish to survive as a distinct group. I think I know why the Jews once wished to survive (though I am less certain as to why we still do): they not only believed that God had given them no choice, but they were tied to a memory of past glory and a dream of imminent redemption. What does the American Negro have that might correspond to this? His past is a stigma, his color is a stigma, and his vision of the future is the hope of erasing the stigma by making color irrelevant, by making it disappear as a fact of consciousness.

[30] I share this hope, but I cannot see how it will ever be realized unless color does *in fact* disappear: and that means not integration, it means assimilation, it means—let the brutal word come out—miscegenation. The Black Muslims, like their racist counterparts in the white world, accuse the "so-called Negro leaders" of secretly pursuing miscegenation as a goal. The racists are wrong, but I wish they were right, for I believe that the wholesale merging of the two races is the most desirable alternative for everyone concerned. I am not claiming that this alternative can

be pursued programmatically or that it is immediately feasible as a solution; obviously there are even greater barriers to its achievement than to the achievement of integration. What I am saying, however, is that in my opinion the Negro problem can be solved in this country in no other way.

[³¹] I have told the story of my own twisted feelings about Negroes here, and of how they conflict with the moral convictions I have since developed, in order to assert that such feelings must be acknowledged as honestly as possible so that they can be controlled and ultimately disregarded in favor of the convictions. It is *wrong* for a man to suffer because of the color of his skin. Beside that clichéd proposition of liberal thought, what argument can stand and be respected? If the arguments are the arguments of feeling, they must be made to yield; and one's own soul is not the worst place to begin working a huge social transformation. Not so long ago, it used to be asked of white liberals, "Would you like your sister to marry one?" When I was a boy and my sister was still unmarried, I would certainly have said no to that question. But now I am a man, my sister is already married, and I have daughters. If I were to be asked today whether I would like a daughter of mine "to marry one," I would have to answer: "No, I wouldn't *like* it at all. I would rail and rave and rant and tear my hair. And then I hope I would have the courage to curse myself for raving and ranting, and to give her my blessing. How dare I withhold it at the behest of the child I once was and against the man I now have a duty to be?"

COMMENT AND QUESTIONS

1. The author begins with the conflict between commonly accepted ideas and the evidence of his senses and his experience. Where and for what purpose does he discuss a similar conflict later in the essay?
2. The childhood experiences with Negroes are presented in great detail. Why does Podhoretz develop them so fully? What is gained by narrating the "items" in the present tense?
3. What is meant by "the culture of the street," near the end of paragraph 14?
4. The author asks a number of questions in his essay. Point out examples of the use of questions to introduce new aspects of the whole problem.
5. Podhoretz moves from his personal experience to generalizations about people, Negro and white. Does this shift from the particular to the general seem to you justifiable and logical? Explain.
6. Explain how Podhoretz thinks the "mechanism of projection" worked for

him and probably for the Negro boys. How is this projection related to "the principle of facelessness"?

7. How does the author support his ideas that all Negroes hate whites and that all American whites are sick and twisted in their feelings about Negroes? Are the ideas convincing to you? Explain.

8. In paragraph 26 and later, Podhoretz expresses a despair about the push toward integration. Do you agree with his views? Explain.

9. What is the meaning of James Baldwin's statement, with which Podhoretz agrees, that color is not a human or personal reality but is a political reality? How is the statement related to the author's concluding paragraphs?

10. Paragraph 30 suggests what Podhoretz believes is the only solution to the Negro problem. What does paragraph 31 contribute to the essay? Comment on the effectiveness of the last sentence.

11. When "My Negro Problem—and Ours" was published in *Commentary*, it provoked sharply different reactions from readers. What is your reaction to the essay, and why?

[80]   *The Economist*: Not Just America

THE FOLLOWING article was printed August 21, 1965, in *The Economist* of London and was reprinted in the November, 1965, issue of *Harper's Magazine* under the title "The Worldwide Plague of City Riots: A British View." (Articles in *The Economist* are by tradition unsigned.)

[1] It is not just an American tragedy. The riots in Los Angeles have sent the editorial writers reaching for that good old standby from Dreiser. The Communists have seen it less as a tragedy than as a morality play, but have been just as ready to claim that the outbreak was peculiarly American; the Peking *People's Daily* even salutes it as a rebellion against President Johnson's imperialist foreign policy. All this is nonsense. What happened in Los Angeles is pretty certainly going to happen in many other countries, both capitalist and communist, as the conditions that caused it spread to them. This was an American phenomenon only in the sense that the United States is half a generation ahead of the rest of the world in the development of an industrial urban society with the special problems that brings. It has the first taste of both the pleasures and the terrors of this new sort of life.

[²] For the Los Angeles riots were the product of two causes, neither of which is peculiar to America. The first has nothing to do with race. For all the anti-white slogans shouted by some of the rioters, the essential news from Los Angeles is that many of them were moved by something quite unconnected with the color of their skin. "This was no race riot; they were just stealing," one Negro store owner is quoted as saying. That is too simple; they were also, after all, sniping and fire-raising and generally rampaging. But as in Harlem and Rochester last year—quiet so far this year—the majority of the rioters were young people caught up in an explosion of violence against authority—any authority, but usually the police, the authoritarians they have run foul of in their everyday lives. This was an insurrection, but not against the economic order (which is the Marxist fallacy) and not even chiefly against white men's domination (which is going to be the Afro-Asian fallacy). It was an insurrection of anarchy, an outburst against any kind of system by the people left at the bottom.

[³] Outbreaks like this are part of the price we are going to pay for a society in which more and more people live in cities and do deadly dull work and waste their leisure. One of the problems of urban-industrial life is that it creates communities of the left-behind. These are the people who do the dullest jobs of all, and are the worst paid, and live in the ugliest parts of crumbling old towns. They have a high rate of illegitimacy and broken marriages. Their religious and cultural roots have been cut. Materially, they are better off than their peasant grandfathers were, but cramming a man with distressful bread has never made him contented —quite the reverse. These people know they are a community of the un-talented, because a modern state needs to skim off the people with talent and by and large does skim them off. The rest sit and simmer. They know they are the natural bottom layer; they have been deprived of the social and religious consolations of the old rural life; there is no legal outlet for young male violence; and every now and then they go bang.

[⁴] Many of the Los Angeles rioters are brothers under the skin to the baffled young men from London and its suburbs who spend their holidays stomping along the beach front at Brighton and Margate, or breaking up bars in Calais and Ostend. Their fathers got into fights at football games or satisfied a dim ancestral prejudice by chasing second-generation Irishmen in Glasgow or Jews in Dalston. They were trying to prove that they belonged to something. The elder sons ripped up railway carriages: it was their way of not belonging.

[⁵] Now the youth of the bottom layer takes it out on the town—and even the seedy parts of their towns have more than ever before to take it out on. The Swedish police were having trouble a decade ago with young toughs raising hell in the center of Stockholm; in the bad things as well as the good, Sweden is America's closest follower on the march to the sort of society most of us will be living in by the year 2000. The Czech police had a first taste of the problem a year ago when young hooligans disrupted Wenceslas Square in Prague. Not even the Russians are immune. The passionate violence of the riots in Novocherkassk a couple of years ago, which probably killed more people than the Los Angeles riots, can no more be wholly explained by their ostensible cause—a rise in food prices—than the Los Angeles outburst can be wholly explained in racial terms.

[6] What has happened since 1945 is that the youngest members of this community of the left-behind now have better means of transport and a wider range of weapons, at any rate in Western Europe and North America. This makes the violence more noticeable; motorbikes and flick-knives on a British south-coast esplanade, or car-drivers lobbing fire bombs into Los Angeles stores, make for bigger headlines, especially in the silly season, than a fists-and-boots brawl outside a back-street pub. But at the same time the frustration that lies behind it all has grown sharper, as the hierarchy of modern industrial society takes clearer shape. For those at the bottom, life presents a still more dismal picture when it is not God who calls men to their stations in life, but the unappealable selection processes of economic life.

[7] Russian sociologists have told Western colleagues that they are deeply worried about this. So they should be. Communism and capitalism are rival mechanisms for supplying material plenty. What neither of them has thought out, and what both are going to run headlong into by the end of the century, is the problem of the needs left unsatisfied by relative abundance: how to make routine work bearable, how to help people use their leisure, how to stop them dying of boredom—or killing from it.

[8] But there is the second factor. If part of what made Los Angeles go bang had nothing to do with race, the other part certainly had. Outbursts like this can and will happen when the frustrated bottom-layer people are racially indistinguishable from those who live around them. When they are picked out by the color of their skin as well, the worst happens. They believe—some of them rightly—that they could have risen out of the ghetto of the left-behind but for their color; they band together with a double grievance. Los Angeles is a model of the most explosive sort of situation that the growingly urbanized, growingly race-mixed world of the 1970s and 1980s will have to cope with.

[9] In one way, it may be a help for a pressured community to be able to identify itself by its color. The white proletariat of America and Europe is leaderless; the best of each generation are plucked away from it to take a comfortable place higher up—in the communist world, where they are absorbed into the ranks of the *apparatchiks*, just as much as in the West. The potential leaders of a colored community, by contrast, stay attached

to their community by their color, and may be a force for moderation. But even this hope is a limited one. The potential leaders may not be able to take command of their communities. And if they can take command, they may not stay moderate, or they may be pushed aside if they do. What could Martin Luther King, effective in the disciplined South, do for the troubles of rootless Los Angeles?

[10] The mistake no one should make is to think that this is only someone else's problem. People still talk as if the racial conflict in America were in a category of its own; or as if the only significant race confrontation were the one between black and white men. The whites are certainly going to be in the middle of a rolling race row for years to come, if only because for the last couple of centuries they have been in a position to be beastly to everybody else, and everybody else is now in a mood to get his own back.

[11] But the world's record even this year should explode the idea that this is all there is to it. The week of the Los Angeles riots was also the week when Malaysia broke apart because brown men could not control their dark suspicions of yellow men, and when black and brown men resumed their efforts to slug it out in southern Sudan. All the evidence is that there is potential trouble wherever people of different colors rub shoulders uneasily together. The history of the black-brown dividing line in independent Africa in the last five years—with splits opening up in Sudan, in Mauretania, in Chad, and between Somalia and Kenya—makes a man's heart sink into his boots.

[12] Race is the most visible, and thus the most potent of the things that make one lot of men feel different from another lot; and as long as they feel different, they find it difficult to muck in together in any common venture, whether it is sharing a boardinghouse or running a country. This is lamentable, but it is not much help lamenting it; it is one of the rock-bottom facts of political life. The communist Europeans have been learning the lesson since communities of colored students began to live among them.

[13] Even relatively minor distinctions within what is generally accepted as a single race produce the same effect. Nobody who has listened to the comfortable burghers of Germany or Switzerland talking about their Italian, Greek, and Spanish workers—or the workers talking about them—can help wondering how long it will be before these countries suffer their own minor-key variations on the Los Angeles theme.

[14] Heaven knows how it will work out; certainly no politician, communist or democratic, shows the faintest sign of knowing. It is the most preposterous counsel of despair to argue that each race should henceforth retire to its own corner of the earth, and stay there. The industrialized

world needs workers from the developing world to keep up the momentum of economic expansion. It is in the interest of the developing world that this momentum should be kept up, and that communities of white men should live in colored countries to start them on the same way.

[¹⁵] The only hope—and it is a thin straw to clutch at—is that as people of different colors mix with each other they will gradually lose the sense of difference that inhibits collaboration between them. There are some people—the ones around the Mediterranean, for instance—who have never felt the sense of difference very keenly, though even that is not true of Palestine or Kabylia. There are others, like the West Indians, who have slowly come to find it a little less important than others find it. There is the East Indian community in Holland, where the Dutch have made a better effort than anyone at integration. It is something. Meanwhile, as the races go on jostling each other, and as the race problem exacerbates the other problems of our industrial society, anyone who points a finger of scorn at the Americans over Los Angeles is calling the same beastly experience down on his own head.

--◄{ C O M M E N T   A N D   Q U E S T I O N S }►--

1. Starting with an effect, the riots in Los Angeles, the author examines the causes. How does he support his repeated statement (and the statement in the title) that what happened in Los Angeles was not a peculiarly American phenomenon?
2. What were the probable reasons for discussing the two causes of the riots in the order followed?
3. Examine the language in paragraphs 3–6. Does the author seem wholly unsympathetic with the young rioters? Explain.
4. Does the article suggest, directly or indirectly, any solution for the problems that are the first cause of the city riots? Can you suggest any solution?
5. Examine the last sentence of paragraph 10. How would you describe its tone? What are the connotations of *rolling*?
6. "Race is the most visible and thus the most potent of the things that make one lot of men feel different from another lot." To what extent do you agree or disagree with this statement, and why?
7. The beginning of paragraph 15 expresses some hope ("a thin straw to clutch at") for a gradual lessening of race conflict. Does the author seem more hopeful about solving this problem than he does about solving the problems of an industrial society?
8. Explain the meaning of the last half of the final sentence in the article.

[81]   *John Fischer*: Substitutes for Violence

J O H N   F I S H E R (1910–   ) is an American writer and publisher, editor in chief of *Harper's Magazine* from 1953 to 1967. The following essay was published in that magazine in January, 1966. Footnotes are the author's.

Scoundrels and in some cases even ruffians terrified the citizens. Young mothers had to take their babies to Central Park in armored cars. Old women went to the theater in tanks, and no pretty woman would venture forth after dark unless convoyed by a regiment of troops . . . the police wore bullet-proof underwear and were armed with mortars and fifteen-inch howitzers . . . — J A M E S   R E S T O N
The New York Times, Oct. 29, 1965

[¹] Like most fables, Mr. Reston's moral tale exaggerates a little. But not much; for all of us are uneasily aware that violence is becoming a central fact of American life. Year after year the official graph for crimes of violence—murder, rape, assault, robbery, and riot—inches a little higher.* Many of these crimes seem to be entirely senseless: a California sniper blazes away at random at passing motorists . . . Bronx youngsters pillage the Botanical Garden and wreck their own schoolrooms . . . a subway rider suddenly pulls a knife and starts slashing at his fellow passengers . . . a gang of roaming teen-agers comes across an old man drowsing on a park bench; they club and burn him to death without even bothering to rifle his pockets.

[²] It is hardly surprising, then, that violence is becoming a dominant concern in our politics, literature, and conversation. Every campaigning candidate promises to chase the hoodlums off the city streets. Murder and mayhem—usually aimless, inexplicable, "existential"—are a growing preoccupation of American novelists: witness the recent work of Norman Mailer, Nelson Algren, and a hundred less-publicized writers. And not only the novelists; one of the most memorable nonfiction books of the past year was Truman Capote's *In Cold Blood,* a factual account of the pecu-

---

* According to the annual reports of the Federal Bureau of Investigation. But its figures are based on voluntary reports by more than eight thousand local law-enforcement agencies, using different definitions of crime and widely varying statistical methods; therefore the FBI does not vouch for their accuracy. In fact, nobody knows precisely how much crime is committed in the United States, or its rate of increase, if any.

liarly brutal murder of the Clutter family by two young sadists. Significantly, the scene was not a city street but a Kansas farm.

[³] Nor is the carnage limited to the United States. As *The Economist* of London pointed out in a recent article (reprinted in the November issue of *Harper's*), rioting and hooliganism are on the rise in nearly every country, including England, Sweden, and Russia. Bloodshed in the big cities naturally gets most of the headlines, but it seems to be almost as widespread in predominantly rural areas—the Sudan, for example, India, the Congo, and Colombia, where *la violencia* has taken hundreds of thousands of lives during the last two decades.

[⁴] Explanations for all this are easy to come by, from nearly every clergyman, sociologist, and politician. Unfortunately they are seldom consistent. Some blame the miseries of slum life, others the breakdown of the family, or religion, or our national moral fiber. Racial and religious frictions apparently account for much free-floating hostility—in Watts and Calcutta, Capetown and Hué, even in Moscow and Peking, where African students report a lot of rough treatment from their hosts. Marxists, naturally, explain it all in terms of bourgeois decadence (although that would hardly account for the outbreaks in Prague and Novocherkassk, where the wicked bourgeoisie were liquidated long ago). While the Black Muslims decry police brutality, J. Edgar Hoover is prescribing more policemen, armed with wider powers. The Freudians suggest that sexual frustration may be the root of the trouble, while Billy Graham is just as sure that it is sexual laxity. Nearly everybody points an indignant finger at the dope peddlers, and William Buckley gets cheers whenever he proclaims that nothing will save us short of a universal moral regeneration.

[⁵] Perhaps there is some truth in all these explanations. But I am beginning to wonder whether, far beneath them all, there may not lie another, more primordial reason. Just possibly the global surge of antisocial violence may result from the fact that nearly all societies—especially those we describe as "advanced"—suddenly have been forced to change a key commandment in their traditional codes of behavior; and many people, particularly the young males, have not yet been able to adjust themselves to this reversal.

[⁶] That commandment was simple: "Be a fighter." Ever since human beings began to emerge as a separate species, something over a million years ago, it has been our first law of survival. For the earliest men, life was an incessant battle: against the hostile Pleistocene environment, against other mammals for food, against their own kind for a sheltering cave, a water hole, a hunting range, a mate. The fiercest, wiliest, and strongest lived to raise children. The meek, weak, slow, and stupid made an early breakfast—for a local tiger or, perhaps oftener, for a neighboring family, since archaeological evidence suggests that cannibalism was common among primeval man. The result was that "our ancestors have bred pugnacity into our bone and marrow. . . ."*

[7] As civilization began to dawn, fighting became more organized—a community enterprise rather than a family one. In addition to their daily skirmishes with wolves, cattle thieves, and passing strangers, the able-bodied men of the village (or polis, kingdom, or pueblo) normally banded together at least once a year for a joint killing venture. The convenient time for settled farming people was early fall, after the harvest was in; then they had both enough leisure and enough surplus food to mount an expedition. So it was about September when the Assyrian swept down like a wolf on the fold, when Gideon smote the Philistines, when Vikings ravaged the Kentish coast, when the Greeks shoved off for Troy, when the Dorians swept into the Argive plain, irresistibly armed with that first mass weapon, the iron sword. (Because iron ore was much more plentiful than copper, it could be used—once the secret of smelting it was learned —to equip every man in the ranks. The victims of the Dorians, still lingering in the Bronze Age, normally armed only their officers with metal blades; the rest carried flint-tipped spears and arrows.) Tribes in the preagricultural stage sometimes found other seasons more suitable for rapine. The War Moon of the Great Plains Indians, for example, came in May—since the spring grass was then just high enough to graze the horses of a raiding party, and the full moon made it easy to travel fast at night. Regardless of timing, however, warfare was for centuries the main social enterprise, absorbing virtually all of the community's surplus time, energy, and resources. "History," as William James put it, "is a bath of blood . . . war for war's sake, all the citizens being warriors . . . To hunt a neighboring tribe, kill the males, loot the village, and possess the females was the most profitable, as well as the most exciting, way of living."

[8] As soon as warfare became socialized, the premium on belligerence was redoubled. Always highly favored by the processes of natural selection, it was now celebrated as a prime civic virtue as well. The Great Fighter was enshrined as the universal hero. His name might be Hercules or Rustum, Beowulf or David, Kiyomori or Hiawatha, but his characteristics remained the same: physical strength, reckless courage, skill with weapons, and a bottomless appetite for bloodshed. From earliest boyhood the males of the community were taught to emulate him. Their training for combat began as soon as they could lift a spear, and by eighteen they normally would be full-fledged warriors—whether in Athens or Cuzco— equally ready to defend their city's walls or to pillage a weaker neighbor.

---

* As William James put it in his classic essay, "The Moral Equivalent of War," published in 1910. His other comments on this grisly topic will be noted in a moment.

Success in battle was the basic status symbol. The best fighters were feted in victory celebrations, heaped with honors and plunder, endowed with the lushest women, both homegrown and captive. The weak and timid, on the other hand, were scorned by elders and girls alike, and in many societies cowardice was punished by death.

[9] For nearly all of human history, then, the aggressive impulse—so deeply embedded in our genes—had no trouble in finding an outlet. This outlet was not only socially acceptable; it was encouraged and rewarded by every resource at society's disposal.

[10] This remained true until roughly a hundred years ago. (When my grandfathers were boys, the martial virtues were still applauded about as much as ever, and both of them marched off to the Civil War with the joyous spirit of an Alcibiades bound for Syracuse.)

[11] Then, with stunning abruptness, the rules changed. Within about a century—a mere eye-blink in terms of evolutionary development—the traditional outlet for violence closed up. Fighting, so long encouraged by society, suddenly became intolerable.

[12] One reason, of course, was the industrialization of war. It not only made warfare ruinously expensive; it took all the fun out of it. Long before the invention of the atom bomb, farsighted men such as William James had come to see that war was no longer "the most profitable, as well as the most exciting, way of living"; and by 1918 the lesson was plain to nearly everyone. In retrospect, our Civil War seems to have been the last in which physical strength, raw courage, and individual prowess could be (sometimes, at least) decisive; perhaps that is why it is written about so much, and so nostalgically.

[13] For there is a certain animal satisfaction (as every football player knows) in bopping another man over the head. By all accounts, our ancestors thoroughly enjoyed hammering at each other with sword and mace; it exercised the large muscles, burned up the adrenalin in the system, relieved pent-up frustrations, and demonstrated virility in the most elemental fashion. But nobody can get that kind of satisfaction out of pulling the lanyard on a cannon, pointed at an unseen enemy miles away; you might as well be pulling a light switch in a factory. Indeed, in a modern army not one man in ten ever gets near combat; the great majority of the troops are cranking mimeograph machines, driving trucks, and tending the PX far to the rear. As a consequence, warfare—aside from its other disadvantages—no longer satisfies the primitive instinct for violence as it did for uncountable thousands of years.

[14] At about the same time—that is, roughly a century ago—the other socially approved outlets for pugnacity also began to close up. For example, so long as our society was mostly rural and small-town, a good deal

of purely personal, casual brawling was easily tolerated. When Lincoln was a young man, the main public amusement seemed to be watching (and often joining in) the donnybrooks which boiled up regularly in the village street; and during his New Salem days, Abe more than held his own. Our literature of the last century, from *Huckleberry Finn* to the story of the OK Wagon Yard, is studded with this kind of spontaneous combat. And our chronicles memorialize the violent men (whether fur trappers, river boatmen, forty-niners, lumberjacks, or cowboys) in the same admiring tone as the sagas of Achilles and Roland. As recently as my own boyhood, fist-fighting was considered a normal after-school activity, like marbles and run-sheep-run; nobody thought of us as juvenile delinquents, in need of a corps of Youth Workers to hound us into docility. A tight-packed urban society, however, simply can't put up with this kind of random combat. It disturbs the peace, endangers bystanders, and obstructs traffic.

[15] As we turned into a nation of city dwellers, we lost another traditional testing ground for masculine prowess: the struggle against nature. Since the beginning of history, when men weren't fighting each other they spent most of their time fighting the elements. To survive, they had to hack down forests, kill off predatory animals, battle with every ounce of strength and cunning against blizzards, droughts, deserts, and gales. When Richard Henry Dana came home after two years before the mast, he knew he was a man. So too with the striplings who rafted logs down rivers in a spate, drove a wagon over the Natchez Trace, pulled a fishing dory on the Grand Banks, or broke sod on the Nebraska prairies. Not long after he started shaving, my father went off alone to homestead a farm in what eventually became the state of Oklahoma. If he had been bothered by an "identity crisis"—something he couldn't even conceive—it would have evaporated long before he got his final papers.

[16] Today of course the strenuous life, which Theodore Roosevelt thought essential for a healthy man, has all but vanished. Probably not 5 per cent of our youngsters grow up to outdoor work, in farming, forests, or fisheries; and even for them, although the work may be hard, it is rarely either exciting or dangerous. (The modern cowboy does most of his work in a pickup truck, while Captain Ahab's successor goes to sea in a floating oil factory.) This final conquest of nature has had some results both comic and a little sad. Among the Masai tribesmen, for instance, when a boy comes of age it has always been customary for him to prove his manhood by killing a lion with a spear; but according to recent reports from Africa, there are no longer enough lions to go around.

[17] In our tamer culture, we have shown remarkable ingenuity in inventing lion-substitutes. The most fashionable surrogates for violence are the strenuous and risky sports—skiing, skin diving, surfing, mountain

climbing, drag racing, sailing small boats in rough weather—which have burgeoned so remarkably in recent years. When a middle-aged Cleveland copy editor crosses the Atlantic alone in a twelve-foot sloop, nobody accuses him of suicidal impulses; on the contrary, millions of sedentary males understand all too well his yearning for at least one adventure in life, however self-imposed and unnecessary. (Women, of course, generally do not understand; most of the wives I've overheard discussing the Manry voyage wondered, not how he made it, but why Mrs. Manry ever let him try.)

[18] But these devices serve only the middle class. For the poor, they ordinarily are too expensive. When Robert Benchley remarked that there was enough suffering in life without people tying boards on their feet and sliding down mountains, he missed the point; the real trouble with skiing is that slum kids can't afford it. Consequently, they try to get their kicks vicariously, by watching murder, football, boxing, and phony wrestling matches on television. When that palls, their next resort usually is reckless driving. That is why access to a car (his own, his family's, or a stolen one) is as precious to the adolescent male—rich or poor—in our culture as possession of a shield was in fifth-century Athens. It is a similar badge of manhood, the equipment necessary to demonstrate that he is a fearless and dashing fellow. (It also is the reason why insurance premiums are so high on autos driven by males under twenty-five years old.)

[19] Such games are socially useful, because they absorb in a relatively harmless way some of our pent-up aggressions. But they all have one great drawback: they are merely games. They are contrived; they are artificial adjuncts to life, rather than the core of life itself. When our ancestors harpooned a whale, pillaged a city, or held the pass at Thermopylae, they knew they were playing for keeps. When our sons break their legs on a ski slope or play "chicken" on the highway, they know that the challenge is a made-up one, and therefore never wholly satisfying. They still yearn for a genuine challenge, a chance to prove their hardihood in a way that really means something.

[20] Lacking anything better, some of them—a growing number, apparently—turn to crimes of violence. Gang fights, vandalism, robbery are, in an important sense, more "real" than any game. And for large groups of disadvantaged people, any form of antisocial violence is a way of striking back, in blind fury, at the community which has condemned them to disappointment and frustration. This is equally true, I suspect, of the Negro rioters in Watts and the poor whites of the South, who take so readily to the murders, church burnings, and assorted barbarities of the Klan.

[21] This sort of thing may well continue, on a rising scale, until we can discover what James called a "moral equivalent for war." He thought he

had found it. He wanted to draft "the whole youthful population" into a peacetime army to serve in "the immemorial human warfare against nature." What he had in mind was a sort of gigantic Civilian Conservation Corps, in which every youngster would spend a few years at hard and dangerous labor—consigned to "coal and iron mines, to freight trains, to fishing fleets in December . . . to road-building and tunnel-making." When he wrote, a half-century ago, this idea sounded plausible, because the need for such work seemed limitless.

[22] Today, however, his prescription is harder to apply. In many parts of the globe, the war against nature has ended, with nature's unconditional surrender. Automation, moreover, has eliminated most dangerous and physically demanding jobs; our mines and freight trains are over-manned, our roads are now built with earth-moving machines rather than pick and shovel.

[23] Nevertheless, so far as I can see James's idea is still our best starting point. And already an encouraging number of people are groping for ways to make it work, in the different and more difficult circumstances of our time.

[24] A few have found personal, unofficial answers. The young people who join the civil-rights movement in the South, for example, are encountering hardship, violence, and occasionally death in a cause that is obviously genuine; they aren't playing games. But The Movement can accommodate only a limited number of volunteers, and presumably it will go out of business eventually, when the white Southerners reconcile themselves to rejoining the United States. In the North, civil-rights work has often turned out to be less satisfying, emotionally, because The Enemy is harder to identify and the goals are less clear. As a result its young partisans sometimes have drifted into a kind of generalized protest, carrying placards for almost anything from SNCC to Free Speech to World Peace: that is, they have ended up with another form of game playing.

[25] President Kennedy, who understood thoroughly the youthful need for struggle and self-sacrifice, had the Jamesian principle in mind when he started the Peace Corps. It remains the most successful official experiment in this direction, and it led to the Job Corps and several related experiments in the domestic Antipoverty Program. How they will work out is still an open question, as William Haddad pointed out last month in *Harper's*. At least they are a public recognition that the country has to do *something*. If we don't—if we continue to let millions of young men sit around, while the adrenalin bubbles and every muscle screams for action, with no outlet in sight but a desk job at best and an unemployment check at worst—then we are asking for bad trouble. Either we can find ways to give them action, in some useful fashion, or we can look forward

to a rising surge of antisocial violence. In the latter case we may, a decade from now, remember the Fort Lauderdale beach riots as a mere boyish prank.

[²⁶] What I am suggesting, of course, is that all of us—especially our businessmen, sociologists, and political leaders—ought to invest a good deal more effort, ingenuity, and money in the search for acceptable substitutes for violence. How many industries have really tried to create interesting and physically demanding jobs for young people? Have the paper companies, for instance, figured out how many foresters they might use, if they were to develop their timber reserves for camping, hunting, and fishing, as well as for wood pulp? And are they sure such a venture would not be profitable?

[²⁷] To take care of the population explosion, we are going to have to duplicate all of our present college buildings within the next twenty years. Has any university looked into the possibility of using prospective students to do some of the building? Maybe every able-bodied boy should be required to labor on the campus for six months as a bricklayer or carpenter before he is admitted to classes?

[²⁸] Cleaning up our polluted rivers is a task worthy of Paul Bunyan, and one we can't postpone much longer. What governor has thought of mobilizing a state Youth Corps to do part of the job? Has Ladybird Johnson calculated how many husky youngsters might be deployed, axes in hand, to chop down billboards along our highways and replace them with trees?

[²⁹] The possibilities aren't as easy to spot as they were in William James's day, but even in our overcrowded and overdeveloped society some of them still exist. No single one of them will provide the kind of simple, large-scale panacea that James had in mind—yet if we can discover a few hundred such projects, they might add up to a pretty fair Moral Equivalent. In any case, the search is worth a more serious try than anyone has made yet.

[³⁰] Why, my wife asks me, is all that necessary? Wouldn't it be simpler for you men to stop acting like savages? Since you realize that belligerence is no longer a socially useful trait, why don't you try to cultivate your gentler and more humane instincts? Are you saying that You Can't Change Human Nature?

[³¹] No, that isn't quite what I'm saying. I recognize that human nature changes all the time. Cannibalism, for example, is now fairly rare, and polygamy (at least in its more open form) has been abandoned by a number of cultures. Someday (I hope and believe) the craving for violence will leach out of the human system. But the reversal of an evolutionary process takes a long time. For a good many generations, then, the Old Adam is likely to linger in our genes; and during that transitional period, probably the best we can hope for is to keep him reasonably quiet with some variant of William James's prescription.

--⊰{ C O M M E N T   A N D   Q U E S T I O N S }⊱--

1. The basic pattern of this essay might be called problem-to-solution: the problem of violence to ways of providing substitutes for violence. Where in the essay does Fischer also use patterns of narration, of contrast, and of cause and effect?

2. The author announces a thesis in paragraph 5 and clarifies it in paragraph 6. What are the purposes of the first four paragraphs? How would you describe the tone of paragraph 5?

3. How does Fischer make the survey of human history, in paragraphs 6–10, interesting?

4. Briefly summarize the author's main points about why advanced societies have been forced to change a traditional "key commandment."

5. Examine the last sentence of paragraph 14. What makes it an effective sentence?

6. What is the function in the essay of the report about the lions in paragraph 16? Of the comment on women's attitudes at the end of paragraph 17?

7. Some of our present substitutes for violence, the author says, are socially useful outlets for aggressiveness. What deficiencies does he see in them? To what extent do you agree or disagree with his analysis in paragraphs 17–20?

8. What is your reaction to Fischer's general proposal of a large-scale program to provide substitutes for violence? Comment on his particular suggestions in paragraphs 26–28. How many young men whom you know would probably like to participate in such a program? What might be the major difficulties in making it work?

9. If you have read John Dewey's essay "Does Human Nature Change?" what similarities do you see between Dewey's and Fischer's ideas?

[82]   *Leon H. Keyserling*: Something for Everybody

THE FOLLOWING article, from *The New York Times Book Review* of February 27, 1966, is a review of a book edited by Robert Theobald and called *The Guaranteed Income: Next Step in Economic Evolution?* Since the reviewer does not wholly agree with the general thesis of the book, the article presents two attitudes toward a current question. Leon H. Keyserling (1908–   ), an attorney and economist, has been Chairman of the Council of Economic Advisers and President of the Conference on Economic Progress. His publications include *The Federal Budget and the General Welfare, Food and Freedom, Progress on Poverty,* and *Agriculture and the Public Interest.*

[¹] The central proposition of the Preface and 10 essays in this book is that society, presumably starting in the United States, should guarantee to everyone a socially acceptable level of income. This guaranteed income would not be made available solely to those unable to work for reasons such as age or disability, or debarred from work by involuntary unemployment. It would extend to *all*, regardless of whether they are or should be "gainfully employed" in the production of goods and services as this term has come to be understood. It would include all who, for reasons of their own, prefer leisure to gainful employment.

[²] I assume that this guaranteed income should be far above the currently defined poverty-income ceiling of $3,000-plus for a family. For while only about 34 million Americans lived in poverty in 1964, another 49 million lived in deprivation, with incomes below the requirements for a "modest but adequate" budget. The concept of what is "modest but adequate" changes with advances in the industrial arts; today, it implies in the U.S. a family income of about $6,000.

[³] Interest in these essays is heightened by the Feb. 4 release of the long-awaited Report of the National Commission on Technology, Automation, and Economic Progress. This Report advocates guaranteed incomes for all, but evidently in the same context as this reviewer, rather than in the different context underlying these essays.

[⁴] The essays are valuable on several counts, aside from being very readable throughout. The espousal of a guaranteed annual income for all, while not entirely novel, has so little acceptance to date that it should be rated as enterprising and courageous. We do need these virtues today. The position is unassailable that the U.S. economy is already powerful enough to assure a "modest but adequate" standard of living for all our people. In my view, we therefore have a moral obligation to furnish this assurance, and the authors are most commendable in bringing moral considerations to the forefront at a time when they are being seriously neglected in most approaches to economic problems.

[5] Still another merit is that the book brings together a wide range of disciplines; economic and related social policies are too important to be left, even in their technical or professional aspects, to economists alone. The authors' challenge to the conventional economics is telling, notably Meno Lovenstein's. The contributors include four economists (Robert Theobald, Clarence E. Ayers, Lovenstein and Ben B. Seligman); an anthropologist (Conrad M. Arensberg); a psychologist (Robert H. Davis); a psychiatrist (Erich Fromm); an administrator and scholar in the field of culture and technology (Marshall McLuhan); a social-welfare expert (Edward Schwartz); and a conservationist (William Vogt).

[6] My dissent from the general theme of the volume is partial but vital. When I join in the view that all of our people should be guaranteed a "modest but adequate" income and standard of living, I envisage this as stemming primarily from a full-employment policy coupled with adequate compensation, and secondarily from guaranteed incomes for those not qualified for gainful employment because of age or other disability. But the authors go far beyond this. With probably two exceptions (Mr. Ayers and Mr. Seligman) they appear to relegate far to the rear the goal of sustained full employment and the ever-increasing national output which would result from full utilization of a growing labor force plus an advancing technology. Most of them are mainly interested in incomes, not jobs.

[7] The economic basis of the case is stated simply and with candor by the book's editor, Mr. Theobald, in the Preface, consistently with his voluminous other writings on the same subject. He is a British socio-economist, formerly with the Organization for European Economic Co-operation and now living in New York. As he would have it, the onrush of technology, automation and cybernation is so overwhelming that massive unemployment is utterly unavoidable and full employment a pious dream. This presents to him no difficulties from the viewpoint of available output: advances in industrial techniques are such that, even with only a moderate fraction of the population of working age gainfully employed in the production of conventional goods and services, we will enjoy "an overwhelming abundance" of them. Under these assumptions, it is mani-

festly more desirable that everybody should live nicely on a guaranteed income rather than that poverty should be the lot of those who cannot be gainfully employed.

[8] In evaluating this case, I am not particularly impressed with the standard argument that income without employment as customarily defined would for motivational and psychological reasons be corrosive of the human spirit. Fromm, McLuhan and Arensberg offer reasons at least worthy of careful consideration to the effect that freedom from the obligation to work, equating with the freedom of every individual to do what he thinks he likes best, might have real value in terms of individual development. Vogt adds the point that the guaranteed income for all would not accentuate the problem of overpopulation. And at least for those who cannot be gainfully employed, Schwartz castigates the "means test" along lines which should help to propel much-needed revision of the prevalent approaches to many current welfare programs which tend to encourage pauperization.

[9] Before going all the way with the authors, we must examine Mr. Theobald's proposition (which most of the others in the group seem to share) that sustained full employment and the ever-increasing production of goods and services which would result as technology advances are neither feasible nor highly desirable. The first difficulty with this proposition is that those among the authors (primarily Mr. Davis and Mr. Seligman) who pick up the task of giving us the facts do not in my view come through convincingly. They offer relevant data with respect to computers and other innovations, and valid evidence of long-term acceleration in the rate of increase in output per man-hour worked. But even if they are talking only about the U.S. and its domestic needs, they offer no comprehensive quantitative appraisal as to how long it would take us, even if fully employed, to turn out so much goods and services that we would no longer be concerned about the increased output which would result from sustained full employment.

[10] Let us look at some facts that seem to be most pertinent, first with respect to *when* we might be able to produce more than we would need or want. The average disposable per-capita income in the U.S. in 1965 was about $2,400, or about $7,500–8,000 on an average consumer-unit basis. I do not suppose that most of the professors and others who write books would regard a family income of about three times this as more than could be used wisely and well (and without corruption of soul) for the needs and niceties of life, including a trip to Europe now and then. Most of them would aspire toward achieving this income and living standard, if they have not already done so, before they would plunk for "retirement" on a guaranteed income of even $6,000 or thereabouts. In all probability, nonintellectuals would make the same choice with even

more alacrity, although I have never noted that the intellectual community is congenitally opposed to more income and "material" things.

[11] During the years 1955–1965, U.S. per-capita disposable income in real terms increased less than 23 per cent. On this basis, allowing for compounding, it would take more than five decades for average U.S. incomes and living standards to reach levels which the professors and other writers certainly would not regard as "too high" even now. To attain these levels requires just that much more national production of goods and services on a per-capita basis.

[12] Besides, increased output must serve many purposes other than personal incomes and outlays. It must help to build plant and equipment; finance research; conserve and replenish our neglected natural resources; purify our polluted air and waters; modernize our obsolescent transportation systems; rebuild our decaying cities; rehouse the at least one-sixth of the total population who still live in urban and rural slums; generate the additional hospitals and personnel needed to bring adequate medical care to the two-fifths of our people who do not now obtain it at costs within their means. It must also help to overcome enormous deficiencies in educational plant and teachers, and enable to go to college the half of our young people who have the ability and ambition but lack the means; and support (as far as we can see ahead) immense outlays for defense and space exploration and international policies fraught with great uncertainties. This is not the whole list.

[13] All of these things are paid for, in the final analysis, not with money but with production. One of the writers in the volume, Mr. Ayers, does intimate that the guaranteed income for all would provide the purchasing power to stimulate full production and full employment. But this reverses the core theme of the volume: that the guaranteed income for all is essential because massive unemployment is in the cards, and because output per employed worker will soon be so fabulous that high employment will no longer be needed.

[14] And even if we in the U.S. should reach, 50 years hence, a situation where our production at full employment led to genuine saturation of needs and desires at home, what about the rest of the world? This brings us back to 1966, not forward to 2016. While the rich nations get richer, the poor get poorer. The widening gap threatens us no less than them. The prospect is that, by 1970, there will be a billion people in the world who are literally starving. What should we now and henceforth be doing to help them avoid this, not only with know-how, but also with exports of food and hardware and capital, in immensely increased amounts? Are Africa, Asia and South America shuddering at the prospect of an "overwhelming abundance" of goods and services? Is it the advance of technology which explains their massive unemployment?

[15] Before we even talk about dulling the greatest nonsecret weapon in the world, our soaring productive powers, we should reexamine and reconstruct our worldwide economic policies. The Administration has just done much of this in qualitative terms. But we do not yet realize that the quality of what we do to help those who need help most is quantitative at its very foundation.

[16] In the full perspective of human needs, we have room and to spare for all we can produce at full employment, as far ahead as we can see. It would thus be one of the greatest tragedies in human history, if, when the prophets' dreams of abundance (not surfeit) are for the first time feasible in terms of our productive powers and potentials, we should bury these instead of using them to the hilt.

[17] Nor is there any merit in the argument that we have not the organizing skills, economic tools and experience to assure sustained full employment (and the full production that goes with it) in the U.S. Even with some very deficient policies, and despite the advances of the new technology, we have reduced unemployment from 6.7 per cent in 1961 to 4 per cent now. If 4 per cent, why not 3, or even 2?

[18] I project ahead at a more rapid rate than most other economists the likely advances in productivity, or output per man-hour worked, resulting from technological change. Even so, I estimate that we need, for the decade ahead, an average annual economic growth rate of only about 5 to 6 per cent to absorb all increases in productivity plus a rapidly growing labor force. This is far below the 9 per cent average annual rate of economic growth which we maintained for four years during World War II, despite the dislocation of wartime.

[19] The utilization of our burgeoning productive powers is not an insoluble problem. It is a relatively easy problem, if we apply to it, in the cause of winning the war against poverty at home and disaster overseas, with the added frosting of large material progress for the rest of us, a modicum of the energy and determination we applied during World War II.

[20] The question may legitimately be posed: If the authors are correct in the limited objective of a guaranteed annual income for those who really cannot be employed, what harm is done by going as much further as they do? My concern is that, by attempting to advance a thesis which seems indefensible when pushed so far, they are undermining their effectiveness in winning acceptance of their more limited and splendid theme: that the American economy is powerful enough, and should be socially-minded enough, to guarantee an American standard of living to all those who really cannot participate in the functioning economy, and also to those who are employed but at substandard wages.

[21] We are now paying to our senior citizens, more than three-quarters

of whom live in abject poverty and who constitute about 27 per cent of all the U.S. poor, Social Security benefits averaging half of what they ought to be within five years. We are grossly neglecting the 25 per cent of all the U.S. poor who live in fatherless families, with at least half headed by mothers who cannot or should not work. For these, we should establish decent systems of family allowances, similar to those in some European countries. We should commence, for the first time, to make large Federal contributions in the general welfare category. Also with Federal contributions, we should greatly improve our unemployment insurance and workmen's compensation systems.

[22] About 60 per cent of the poor are poor because their breadwinners are unemployed, or employed only part-time, or paid substandard wages when employed, or because of some combination of these situations. The remedy here is an adequate, national, full-employment-and-income policy. This type of "guarantee" was really the mandate of the Employment Act of 1946. But we have moved toward its full implementation only with mincing steps. Grafted upon this rather than pursued independently, guaranteed incomes to those who cannot or should not be employed is eminently desirable. This would also enlarge aggregate demand, and thereby stimulate employment to counteract the displacements due to technological advance.

[23] What I urge, in essence, is that we build upon what we have, more courageously and comprehensively than we are now doing. We really have in place the institutions, the machinery and even the stated purposes to build a Great Society, strong and just. We need only to use them.

[24] This seems to me more promising—economically, financially, politically, and psychologically—than to blur the dividing line between evolution and revolution. It may seem appealing to write an entirely new prescription on a white sheet of paper, but entirely "new approaches" are not meritorious per se.

[25] Even the current "war on poverty" suffers from too much bright new experimentalism. Poverty is not a new problem nor even a recent discovery. There is a wealth of revealed experience, both at home and abroad, bearing upon what works toward reducing poverty. The poor should not be made the victims of a farrago of "new approaches."

[26] Too much of the recent and current writing on economic and related social problems seems to manifest the sentiment that nobody will listen unless there are iconoclastic shockers in the story. We have plenty of real economic problems, some requiring drastic solutions, without ranging off into the wild blue yonder. My good friend John K. Galbraith, in his most famous book, "The Affluent Society," made a tremendous contribution in his plea for more attention to the "public

sector." Unfortunately, he elected to spice up his text with forays to the effect that economic growth and full employment are no longer essential in an affluent society. I fear that the heritage of this mistake is reflected in the volume under review.

[27] Speculative but remote thinking and writing about the highly improbable would be more welcome were we not now confronted by so many unmet problems and so many aberrations in national policies that call for quick, precision readjustment. The 1967 Federal Budget makes it clear that we are willing, if need be, to cut back on nonessentials in order to finance an expanding war in Vietnam (I imply no dissent from that). But we are not yet willing, through tax increases, to cut back on scores of billions of dollars of wasteful private consumption (and the private investment designed to feed it), in order to finance adequately the most urgent of our domestic public priorities—the very bricks and mortar of a Great Society.

[28] The servicing of these priorities requires intense efforts to expand production, combined with unalloyed determination to allocate the product in accord with what we need most, not what we need least. We have gone too far already on the assumption that stimulating any kind of demand through incontinent tax reductions can turn the trick.

[29] The tasks ahead will require changes in the structure of the labor force and employment, but no surrender of the goal of full employment. It will require many alterations in the structure of demand, but even firmer commitment than we now have to a high enough level of total demand to expand total output even more rapidly than we are now doing.

[30] The development of the economic means suitable to these tasks, and the enlargement of the popular understanding and support which is so essential, call for the best that the intellectual community can offer. If we make long-range budgets of our needs and resources, and use fiscal and other policies sufficiently to redirect our energies in accord with our needs, we can create a Great Society at home, and do our full share toward spreading its seeds among the 3 billion people of the earth.

COMMENT AND QUESTIONS

1. Paragraph 1 explains the central proposition of the book the author is reviewing; paragraph 2 clarifies the meaning of "modest but adequate" income; and paragraphs 3–5 are generally commendatory of the interest and value of the book. Does anything in the first paragraph prepare for Keyserling's "partial but vital" dissent from the central thesis of the book?

2. With what ideas in the volume he is reviewing does the author apparently agree? What is his dissent and his own thesis?

3. In paragraph 7 and again in paragraph 9, the author summarizes the assumptions underlying *The Guaranteed Income:* (a) that technology and automation make massive unemployment inevitable, and (b) that advances in industrial techniques will, even with a small fraction of the population working, produce an overwhelming and even undesirable abundance of goods and services. What are Keyserling's main arguments against these assumptions? Which of his arguments seem most convincing to you, and why?

4. What is the function in the article of paragraph 12?

5. Later in his review, Keyserling is critical of the extremism in the book he is discussing and critical of "new approaches." What seem to be the reasons for his criticism and his concern?

6. As the author says, a standard argument against the kind of guaranteed income recommended in Theobald's book is that unearned income would be psychologically damaging and damaging to character. Does this seem to you a valid argument? Explain.

7. Robert Theobald, in a letter to *The New York Times Book Review* after Keyserling's review appeared, wrote that in his opinion everyone should have a right either to an income or to a job and that unless the income was absolutely guaranteed to everyone, rules for determining eligibility for a guaranteed income would be necessary; the administrators of the eligibility rules would then have an enormous and potentially dangerous power. Does this point seem to you to strengthen the case for the guaranteed income for all? Explain.

8. The following advertisement appeared in national magazines at about the time *The Guaranteed Income* was published. Comment on the language and the point of view.

WHEN WE ALL TAKE IN EACH OTHER'S WASHING UTOPIA WILL HAVE ARRIVED

Let's tax the whole country so New Yorkers won't have to pay as much as the true cost of their train rides. Let's all pay more for our breakfast coffee so the rich planters of South America will stay rich and won't have to pay the taxes you pay. Let's continue to forgive France the 4 billion dollars we lent them almost 50 years ago (plus the billions we have given them since) so they can drain away our gold. Let's all continue to pay more for gasoline taxes to build superhighways for states who refuse to build their own. Let's all keep on paying more for food than it costs to raise it, so some farmers can be paid billions they don't earn. Let's continue to pay billions to "veterans" who never saw a battle. Let's keep on paying more for our homes so building trades unionists can continue to get as much as $30 for a 6 hour day.

Who's kidding whom?

If we all did our own work, paid our own bills instead of insisting others pay them, we'd get more done, and save the billions of dollars every year in handling charges—charges that have so boosted our debt that *interest alone* is more than 11 billion dollars a year.

Sharing the wealth (i.e., socialism) is nothing but sharing the poverty, and don't let any politician steal your vote by telling you differently.

[83] *John Lear*: Men, Moonships, and Morality

JOHN LEAR (1909–   ) is an American writer and editor who, since 1956, has been science editor of the *Saturday Review*. The following article was published in the January 7, 1967, issue of that magazine.

[¹] Three hundred and fifty-eight years ago Johannes Kepler—the great German mathematician who figured out how the earth and its sister planets orbit the sun—wrote the first scientific treatise on the problems man must solve in traveling to the moon. He considered the perils of the solar wind. He correctly described the influence of gravity in both the earthly and lunar phases of the voyage. He anticipated the use of inertial power. And he predicted that when earth was finally seen from the moon the geographical features of the planet would be recognizable.

[²] At the time Kepler wrote that manuscript, in the year 1609, the very idea of going to the moon so unsettled his superstitious contemporaries that his mother (who had been named allegorically in his script) was imprisoned as a witch and put on trial for her life.

[³] By the end of the month of September in the year 1967, the inertial power that Kepler foresaw will have been in use for ten years. Moonships designed to carry a crew of three men are already built and christened with the name *Apollo*. Considerably smaller and lighter craft have been rocketed to the moon's surface, and others have been placed in orbit around the moon. One of the latter, called *Orbiter I*, has photographed both hemispheres of the moon: the one earth never sees as well as the one that is continually in earthlings' sight. While pursuing its course around the moon, *Orbiter* I has also photographed the earth. The first of those pictures confirms Kepler's prediction of 358 years ago. Although not clearly distinguishable by the untrained eye, features discerned in the crescent image of the planet by photo-analysts of the National Aeronautics and Space Administration at Langley, Virginia, include the eastern coast of the United States, southern Europe, and Antarctica.

[⁴] The appearance of the earth from the moon, then, at 4:35 P.M.

Greenwich Mean Time on August 23, 1966 (the date of the photograph), was not vastly different from what Kepler had expected from looking at the moon in 1609. But three and a half centuries of technological change had to intervene before confirmation of his vision became possible. During that interim, the art of transportation has undergone several successive revolutions. People today are able to move over long distances at speeds that would have been thought incredible in Kepler's day. Their political inventions have not kept pace with their growing mobility, but in the main kings have given way to popularly elected agents of the people, empires have crumbled into independent states, and nations have banded together in free associations of free individuals.

[5] What has been the fate of moral wisdom meanwhile?

[6] Dr. Robert S. Morison, director of Cornell University's Division of Biological Sciences, commented on this most fundamental of all human questions at the public celebration of California Institute of Technology's seventy-fifth birthday two months ago.

[7] "Compared to our views on the nature of matter, the origin of the seasons, the control of the weather, and even on the creation and nature of man himself," he said, "our views on private property, murder, rape, and adultery have changed very little since the time of Moses."

[8] Casting a long look backward into history, he continued: "In earlier times, the repositories of knowledge, wisdom, and morals were inextricably intertwined. The high priests of the early riverine societies were the astronomers, the biologists, the philosophers, the lawyers, and the religious leaders all wrapped into one. To a large extent, scientific and theological knowledge coincided.

[9] "The rapid growth of scientific knowledge in our time has resulted in a greater and greater gulf between natural and theological knowledge and a considerable decline in interest in the latter. Ethics and morality occupy an uneasy position somewhere in between."

[10] Noting that the explosion in technological information in recent decades has left many parents unable to pass on to their children the practical knowledge the children need to confront the future confidently, Dr. Morison went on:

[11] "The astonishing thing is that the decline in respect for fathers, mothers, and priests as repositories of expert scientific knowledge has not been accompanied by more of a decline in respect for their moral influence."

[12] Only the first five pages of Dr. Morison's message at Caltech were concerned with the past and present state of morality, however. The remaining eleven pages spelled out a warning of impending change,

"the social consequences of which are not easy to see." At the end of his remarks an inescapable question loomed:

Can the family survive as the fundamental reproductive cell of the great and sprawling body of civilization?

[13] Without going so far as to enunciate a flat negative answer, the Cornell biologist suggested three reasons for expecting at least a diminution in the family's social role:

[14] 1) While it is "a fine mechanism for transmitting conventional wisdom in a relatively static society," the family "is relatively poor at assimilating and transmitting new knowledge essential to survival" in a rapidly altering environment.

[15] 2) Birth control—now deemed necessary to give all earth's peoples enough food to eat, water to drink, and air to breathe—and growth of knowledge about genetically transmitted disease are together separating "the phenomena associated with sexual attraction and those involving reproduction *per se*."

[16] Since "much of the conventional moral apparatus of almost all societies has been based on the assumption of an extremely close tie between the two," and since the family has been the traditional repository of the tie, it is prudent to try to evaluate what changes may come in the institution of the family "if sexual behavior and reproduction become completely separated from one another." Should such a final break occur, society "would have to struggle on the one hand with defining the nature of interpersonal relationships which have no long-term social point other than the satisfaction of the individuals concerned. On the other hand, it must seek new ways to ensure reasonable care for infants and children in an emotional atmosphere which lacks biological reinforcement through basic sexual and parental drives."

[17] 3) Our increasing knowledge of the biology and psychology of infancy and early childhood fortifies an old belief in the importance of shaping the first five or six years of a child's life.

[18] "These are the years which the child ordinarily spends in the bosom of his family, and the evidence is accumulating that it is this fact that is primarily responsible for the relative fixity of the socio-economic class structure of a country like the United States." And "just as a wider appreciation of the science of genetics has made a pleasant eighteenth century fantasy of the stirring phrase 'all men are created equal' . . . it is quite clear that it is idle to talk of a society of equal opportunity as long as that society abandons its newcomers solely to their families for their most impressionable years."

[19] Many will fear the effects on children of the accelerated erosion of parental responsibility for bringing up the children. The apprehensions spring from a conviction that freedom of the individual will be circum-

scribed and that the ultimate consequences will be a colorless, conformist society.

[20] Dr. Morison conceded the fears, but did not share them. Instead, he expressed his faith in "the almost infinite adaptability of the human nervous system." He emphasized: "It is hard to see how enriching the environment and increasing the contacts of young children can do other than increase their capacity for intelligent choices later in life and thus free them from both external and internal constraints that normally limit personal freedom."

[21] Parents rather than children will be most likely to suffer deprivation from the decline of family influence, he predicted. Fathers and mothers will lose a sense of importance in relation to the future. And "if all this is even approximately right, it would seem essential to set about devising substitutes or sublimations. Somehow people must be made to expand their sense of loyalty and responsibility to include a larger share of the human race."

[22] Now directors of divisions of modern universities do not make pronouncements of this magnitude without due deliberation. Before drafting his Caltech birthday address, Dr. Morison not only consulted many fellow members of the Cornell faculty individually but gathered about him at night a gifted group with out-of-the-ordinary communicative ability. Among this party was a man who knows at least as much as and perhaps more than any other American scientist does about the changing role of the family in societies competitive with our own. This person was Urie Bronfenbrenner, Cornell professor of psychology and of child development and family relationships, a frequent professional visitor to the Soviet Union, chairman of the research advisory committee to UNESCO's cross-cultural study of prejudice, and member of the social science advisory board of the U.S. Disarmament and Arms Control Agency.

[23] Professor Bronfenbrenner during the half year prior to Dr. Morison's appearance at Caltech had been reporting on his Soviet experiences and observations at scientific symposia scattered from Moscow to Winnipeg to Miami to Boston. On each occasion he had told how the Communist society had been taking over traditional functions of the Russian family for the last decade. Following an order issued by Nikita Khrushchev in 1956, children were put into collective schools at the age of three months and brought up through nurseries, kindergartens, and boarding schools under conditions designed to create "the new Soviet man." Seven million boys and girls, almost 10 per cent of the present Soviet population of preschool and school age, are now being reared in these institutions; by 1970, one-third of all Soviet children will be involved; by the 1980's, all.

[24] The principles and methods employed in the collective schools were developed by a Communist social psychologist, A. S. Makarenko, who died in 1939 after setting up fantastically successful camps for rehabilitation of wild gangs of juvenile delinquents who pillaged the Russian countryside in the 1920s. Makarenko's posthumous glory in the U.S.S.R. is so radiant that Professor Bronfenbrenner says the American equivalent can be arrived at only by imagining Dr. Benjamin Spock and John Dewey combined into one man.

[25] Makarenko's books have been best sellers throughout Russia for a quarter century. Thousands of copies have also been sold in eastern Europe, Cuba, and China. Mao's notorious Red Guards are an extreme example of the pitch to which youth can be disciplined by the Makarenko system. Virtually every language has its editions of Makarenko's works— English included. The United States is the only major nation on earth that has not published a translation.

[26] This last-mentioned omission will be corrected next month, when Doubleday, through an arrangement with the Am-Rus Literary Agency, will release an Americanized version of Makarenko's handbook for Russian parents under a new title: *The Collective Family*. An Anchor paperback original, translated by Robert Daglish, the volume will sell for $1.45 per copy.

[27] Professor Bronfenbrenner's introduction to *The Collective Family* will not be reassuring to American readers. For he reminds the forgetful that it was just ten years ago come October that Soviet technologists startled people everywhere by putting the first man-made moon into orbit around planet earth. *Sputnik I* stayed up until January 4, 1958, and *Sputnik II* was orbiting for two months with the dog Laika as passenger before American rocketeers lofted *Explorer I,* the first capitalist moon, on January 31, 1958.

[28] Ever since that traumatic humbling of American pride, curricula in American schools have been repeatedly shock-proofed against future anguish with the new math, the new physics, the new chemistry, and the new biology.

[29] So Professor Bronfenbrenner's message inevitably must come as a profoundly rude shock: During our ten-year preoccupation with the teaching of technical skill—accompanied, as it has been, with long-haired campus rebellions of sometimes riotous proportions—the Russians have been concentrating on the inculcation of character!

[30] The Soviet process begins at the age of three months, in collective playpens shared by six to eight infants. "Upbringers" (one for every four charges among the younger children) stimulate sensory, motor, mental, and social responses with special exercises. Devotion to the ideal of com-

mon ownership of property is fostered from the beginning through use of phrases like "mine is ours; ours is mine." By the time the children are eighteen months old, they control their excretory functions and wash, dress, and feed themselves. As soon as they can talk, they are encouraged to judge and criticize each other's behavior from the group's perspective. It is the "upbringer's" job to see that individual and collective self-reliance develop together. In kindergarten, there is group play at keeping store, going to the doctor, and similar real-life simulations; there is actual responsibility for gardening and care of animals; and some kindergartens teach foreign languages. In the collective boarding schools, each student must choose a vocation (automotive mechanics, dressmaking, radio repair, computer programming are among subjects available) in which to receive daily training not only in school shops but in affiliated factories, institutes, and farms.

[31] "In the collective, by the collective, for the collective" was the motto Makarenko wrote to guide what Khrushchev later described as "engineering of the soul."

[32] What has Soviet collective schooling accomplished to date?

[33] Professor Bronfenbrenner has reported to his scientific colleagues on comparative studies of Soviet children and age-mates in the United States and Western Europe. The preschoolers, he said, "cry far less frequently, are more obedient, and appear to be better able to take care of themselves." Yet, although they are "clearly normal, and perhaps even advanced, physically and mentally," the Soviet children display "emotional blandness." Older children in the collective boarding schools "are well-mannered, attentive, and industrious. In informal conversations, they reveal strong motivation to learn, a readiness to serve their society, and what is perhaps best described as an idealistic and even sentimental attitude toward life."

[34] What implications has the Soviet schooling experiment for our own democratic society?

[35] Although research on the subject is still too limited to allow firm judgment, "a recently completed experiment . . . has yielded sobering results." More than 150 sixth-graders (six classrooms) in each country [U.S. and U.S.S.R.] were placed in situations revelatory of their readiness to engage in morally disapproved behavior such as cheating on an exam, denying responsibility for property damage, etc. The American children were "far more ready to take part in such actions."

[36] Now Soviet collective schooling was established deliberately for an ideological purpose. Soviet parents accepted it willingly because it freed living space in crowded homes, cut food costs (which run up to 70 per cent of the Russian family budget), raised family income by allowing mothers to work, and offered deprived children opportunities otherwise denied them.

[³⁷] The American family meanwhile has been losing its traditional influence over the children by default. Mothers work to augment strained domestic budgets, children are left on their own, and offspring of poorer families—particularly those of the Negro community—drop out of school and become delinquents.

[³⁸] "The question therefore arises whether we cannot profit by taking to heart Makarenko's injunctions regarding the constructive influence of imposing communal responsibility within both family and peer-groups," the introduction to *The Collective Family* says. "This does not mean subscribing to his insistence on the primacy of the collective over the individual. It does mean giving the children, from early ages on, genuine responsibilities from which they learn the meaning of self-respect and respect for others. Such responsibilities can and must extend beyond the home to the neighborhood, the school, the community, and—in due course—the larger society. They should involve not only parents and friends but the full range of human beings who make up the society, including those who most need and deserve the service of others—old people, young children, the handicapped, and the underprivileged. . . . We, too, must teach morality . . . consistent with the welfare of all and the dignity of each."

COMMENT AND QUESTIONS

1. What seem to be the purposes of the first four paragraphs of Lear's article?
2. Examine paragraph 9. Do you agree that "ethics and morality occupy an uneasy position" somewhere between scientific and theological knowledge? Explain.
3. Paragraph 12 seems to shift from the idea of morality, and the question about the survival of the family as a dominant force may not at first seem relevant to the author's central theme. When does the discussion of the family become clearly relevant?
4. Comment on Dr. Morison's reasons, in paragraphs 14–18, for expecting some diminution in the family's role. Do the reasons seem to you logical? Explain.
5. What is the meaning of the statement at the end of paragraph 18 that "it is idle to talk of a society of equal opportunity as long as that society abandons its newcomers solely to their families for their most impressionable years"? To what extent do you agree with the statement, and why?
6. Paragraphs 27–29 bring into new relationship the men, moonships, and morality of Lear's alliterative title. Why do you think the author included, in paragraph 29, the reference to campus rebellions?
7. According to this article, what seem to be the significant advantages of

the Russian system of collective schooling? Are any disadvantages suggested? Do you see disadvantages? Explain.

8. Examine the quotation in the last paragraph from Professor Bronfenbrenner's introduction to *The Collective Family*. Do his proposals seem reasonable and feasible to you? How, specifically, might they be put into effect?

9. If you have read "Substitutes for Violence" by John Fischer, do you think that some modified version of Russian collective schooling might provide the substitutes for violence that Fischer is recommending? Explain.

PART THREE

Autobiography and

Personal Essays

[84] *Lincoln Steffens*: I Get a Colt to Break In

THE FOLLOWING autobiographical narrative presents a series of episodes in a single phase (probably a year) of a boy's life. Lincoln Steffens (1866–1936) was a prominent American journalist and editor, best known in the early twentieth century for his exposés of corruption in business and government. "I Get a Colt to Break In" is one of the early chapters of his well-written and interesting *Autobiography*, published in 1931.

[¹] Colonel Carter gave me a colt. I had my pony, and my father meanwhile had bought a pair of black carriage horses and a cow, all of which I had to attend to when we had no "man." And servants were hard to get and to keep in those days; the women married, and the men soon quit service to seize opportunities always opening. My hands were pretty full, and so was the stable. But Colonel Carter seemed to think that he had promised me a horse. He had not; I would have known it if he had. No matter. He thought he had, and maybe he did promise himself to give me one. That was enough. The kind of man that led immigrant trains across the continent and delivered them safe, sound, and together where he promised would keep his word. One day he drove over from Stockton, leading a two-year-old which he brought to our front door and turned over to me as mine. Such a horse!

[²] She was a cream-colored mare with a black forelock, mane, and tail and a black stripe along the middle of her back. Tall, slender, high-spirited, I thought then—I think now—that she was the most beautiful of horses. Colonel Carter had bred and reared her with me and my uses in mind. She was a careful cross of a mustang mare and thoroughbred stallion, with the stamina of the wild horse and the speed and grace of the racer. And she had a sense of fun. As Colonel Carter got down out of his buggy and went up to her, she snorted, reared, flung her head high in the air, and, coming down beside him, tucked her nose affectionately under his arm.

[³] "I have handled her a lot," he said. "She is as kind as a kitten, but she is as sensitive as a lady. You can spoil her by one mistake. If you ever lose your temper, if you ever abuse her, she will be ruined forever. And she is unbroken. I might have had her broken to ride for you, but I didn't want to. I want you to do it. I have taught her to lead, as you can see; had to, to get her over here. But here she is, an unbroken colt; yours. You take and you break her. You're only a boy, but if you break this colt right, you'll be a man—a young man, but a man. And I'll tell you how."

[4] Now, out West, as everyone knows, they break in a horse by riding out to him in his wild state, lassoing, throwing, and saddling him; then they let him up, frightened and shocked, with a yelling broncho-buster astride of him. The wild beast bucks, the cowboy drives his spurs into him, and off they go, jumping, kicking, rearing, falling, till by the weight of the man, the lash, and the rowels, the horse is broken—in body and spirit. This was not the way I was to break my colt.

[5] "You must break her to ride without her ever knowing it," Colonel Carter said. "You feed and you clean her—you; not the stable man. You lead her out to water and to walk. You put her on a long rope and let her play, calling her to you and gently pulling on the rope. Then you turn her loose in the grass lot there and, when she has romped till tired, call her. If she won't come, leave her. When she wants water or food, she will run to your call, and you will pet and feed and care for her." He went on for half an hour, advising me in great detail how to proceed. I wanted to begin right away. He laughed. He let me lead her around to the stable, water her, and put her in the stable and feed her.

There I saw my pony. My father, sisters, and Colonel Carter saw me stop and look at my pony.

"What'll you do with him?" one of my sisters asked. I was bewildered for a moment. What should I do with the little red horse? I decided at once.

"You can have him," I said to my sisters.

"No," said Colonel Carter, "not yet. You can give your sisters the pony by and by, but you'll need him till you have taught the colt to carry you and a saddle—months; and you must not hurry. You must learn patience, and you will if you give the colt time to learn it, too. Patience and control. You can't control a young horse unless you can control yourself. Can you shoot?" he asked suddenly.

I couldn't. I had a gun and I had used it some, but it was a rifle, and I could not bring down with it such game as there was around Sacramento —birds and hares. Colonel Carter looked at my father, and I caught the look. So did my father. I soon had a shotgun. But at the time Colonel Carter turned to me and said:

"Can't shoot straight, eh? Do you know what that means? That means that you can't control a gun, and that means you can't control yourself, your eye, your hands, your nerves. You are wriggling now. I tell you that a good shot is always a good man. He may be a 'bad man' too, but he is quiet, strong, steady in speech, gait, and mind. No matter, though. If you break in this colt right, if you teach her her paces, she will teach you to shoot and be quiet."

[⁶] He went off downtown with my father, and I started away with my colt. I fed, I led, I cleaned her, gently, as if she were made of glass; she was playful and willing, a delight. When Colonel Carter came home with my father for supper, he questioned me.

"You should not have worked her today," he said. "She has come all the way from Stockton and must be tired. Yes, yes, she would not show her fatigue; too fine for that, and too young to be wise. You have got to think for her, consider her as you would your sisters."

Sisters! I thought; I had never considered my sisters. I did not say that, but Colonel Carter laughed and nodded to my sisters. It was just as if he had read my thought. But he went on to draw on my imagination a centaur; the colt as a horse's body—me, a boy, as the head and brains of one united creature. I liked that. I would be that. I and the colt: a centaur.

[⁷] After Colonel Carter was gone home I went to work on my new horse. The old one, the pony, I used only for business: to go to fires, to see my friends, run errands, and go hunting with my new shotgun. But the game that had all my attention was the breaking in of the colt, the beautiful cream-colored mare, who soon knew me—and my pockets. I carried sugar to reward her when she did right, and she discovered where I carried it; so did the pony, and when I was busy they would push their noses into my pockets, both of which were torn down a good deal of the time. But the colt learned. I taught her to run around a circle, turn and go the other way at a signal. My sisters helped me. I held the long rope and the whip (for signaling), while one of the girls led the colt; it was hard work for them, but they took it in turns. One would lead the colt round and round till I snapped the whip; then she would turn, turning the colt, till the colt did it all by herself. And she was very quick. She shook hands with each of her four feet. She let us run under her, back and forth. She was slow only to carry me. Following Colonel Carter's instructions, I began by laying my arm or a surcingle over her back. If she trembled, I drew it slowly off. When she could abide it, I tried buckling it, tighter and tighter. I laid over her, too, a blanket, folded at first, then open, and, at last, I slipped up on her myself, sat there a second, and as she trembled, slid off. My sisters held her for me, and when I could get up and sit there a moment or two, I tied her at a block, and we, my sisters and I, made a procession of mounting and dismounting. She soon got used to this, and would let us slide off over her rump, but it was a long, long time before she would carry me.

That we practiced by leading her along a high curb where I could get on as she walked, ride a few steps, and then, as she felt me and crouched, slip off. She never did learn to carry a girl on her back; my sisters had to lead her while I rode. This was not purposeful. I don't know just how it happened, but I do remember the first time I rode on my colt all the way round the lot and how, when I put one of the girls up, she refused to repeat. She shuddered, shook and frightened them off.

[8] While we were breaking in the colt a circus came to town. The ring was across the street from our house. Wonderful! I lived in that circus for a week. I saw the show but once, but I marked the horse-trainers, and in the mornings when they were not too busy I told them about my colt, showed her to them, and asked them how to train her to do circus tricks. With their hints I taught the colt to stand up on her hind legs, kneel, lie down, and balance on a small box. This last was easier than it looked. I put her first on a low big box and taught her to turn on it; then got a little smaller box upon which she repeated what she did on the big one. By and by we had her so that she would step up on a high box so small that her four feet were almost touching, and there also she would turn.

[9] The circus man gave me one hint that was worth all the other tricks put together. "You catch her doing something of herself that looks good," he said, "and then you keep her at it." It was thus that I taught her to bow to people. The first day I rode her out on to the streets was a proud one for me and for the colt, too, apparently. She did not walk, she danced; perhaps she was excited, nervous; anyhow I liked the way she threw up her head, champed at the bit, and went, dancing, prancing down the street. Everybody stopped to watch us, and so, when she began to sober down, I picked her up again with heel and rein, saying, "Here's people, Lady," and she would show off to my delight. By constant repetition I had her so trained that she would single-foot, head down, along a country road till we came to a house or a group of people. Then I'd say, "People, Lady," and up would go her head, and her feet would dance.

[10] But the trick that set the town talking was her bowing to anyone I spoke to. "Lennie Steffens' horse bows to you," people said, and she did. I never told how it was done; by accident. Dogs used to run out at us and the colt enjoyed it; she kicked at them sometimes with both hind hoofs. I joined her in the game, and being able to look behind more conveniently than she could, I watched the dogs until they were in range, then gave the colt a signal to kick. "Kick, gal," I'd say, and tap her ribs with my heel. We used to get dogs together that way; the colt would kick them over and over and leave them yelping in the road. Well, one day when I met a girl I knew I lifted my hat, probably muttered a "Good day," and I must have touched the colt with my heel. Anyway, she dropped her head and kicked—not much; there was no dog near, so she had responded to my unexpected signal by what looked like a bow. I caught the idea and kept her at it. Whenever I wanted to bow to a girl or anyone else, instead of saying "Good day," I muttered "Kick, gal," spurred her lightly, and—the whole centaur bowed and was covered with glory and conceit.

[11] Yes, conceit. I was full of it, and the colt was quite as bad. One day

my chum Hjalmar came into town on his Black Bess, blanketed. She had had a great fistula cut out of her shoulder and had to be kept warm. I expected to see her weak and dull, but no, the good old mare was champing and dancing, like my colt.

"What is it makes her so?" I asked, and Hjalmar said he didn't know, but he thought she was proud of the blanket. A great idea. I had a gaudy horse blanket. I put it on the colt, and I could hardly hold her. We rode down the main street together, both horses, and both boys, so full of vanity that everybody stopped to smile. We thought they admired, and maybe they did. But some boys on the street gave us another angle. They, too, stopped and looked, and as we passed, one of them said, "Think you're hell, don't you?"

Spoilsport!

[12] We did, as a matter of fact; we thought we were hell. The recognition of it dashed us for a moment; not for long, and the horses paid no heed. We pranced, the black and the yellow, all the way down J Street, up K Street, and agreed that we'd do it again, often. Only, I said, we wouldn't use blankets. If the horses were proud of a blanket, they'd be proud of anything unusually conspicuous. We tried a flower next time. I fixed a big rose on my colt's bridle just under her ear and it was great—she pranced downtown with her head turned, literally, to show off her flower. We had to change the decorations from time to time, put on a ribbon, or a bell, or a feather, but, really, it was not necessary for my horse. Old Black Bess needed an incentive to act up, but all I had to do to my horse was to pick up the reins, touch her with my heel, and say, "People"; she would dance from one side of the street to the other, asking to be admired. As she was. As we were.

[13] I would ride down to my father's store, jump off my prancing colt in the middle of the street, and run up into the shop. The colt, free, would stop short, turn, and follow me right up on the sidewalk, unless I bade her wait. If anyone approached her while I was gone, she would snort, rear, and strike. No stranger could get near her. She became a frightened, frightening animal, and yet when I came into sight, she would run up to me, put her head down, and as I straddled her neck, she would throw up her head and pitch me into my seat, facing backwards, of course. I whirled around right, and off we'd go, the vainest boy and the proudest horse in the State.

"Hey, give me a ride, will you?" some boy would ask.

[14] "Sure," I'd say, and jump down and watch the boy try to catch and mount my colt. He couldn't. Once a cowboy wanted to try her, and he caught her; he dodged her forefeet, grabbed the reins, and in one spring was on her back. I never did that again. My colt reared, then bucked, and, as the cowboy kept his seat, she shuddered, sank to the

ground, and rolled over. He slipped aside and would have risen with her, but I was alarmed and begged him not to. She got up at my touch and followed me so close that she stepped on my heel and hurt me. The cowboy saw the point.

"If I were you, kid," he said, "I'd never let anybody mount that colt. She's too good."

[15] That, I think, was the only mistake I made in the rearing of Colonel Carter's gift-horse. My father differed from me. He discovered another error or sin, and thrashed me for it. My practice was to work hard on a trick, privately, and when it was perfect, let him see it. I would have the horse out in our vacant lot doing it as he came home to supper. One evening, as he approached the house, I was standing, whip in hand, while the colt, quite free, was stepping carefully over the bodies of a lot of girls, all my sisters and all their girl friends. (Grace Gallatin, later Mrs. Thompson-Seton, was among them.) My father did not express the admiration I expected; he was frightened and furious. "Stop that," he called, and he came running around into the lot, took the whip, and lashed me with it. I tried to explain; the girls tried to help me explain.

[16] I had seen in the circus a horse that stepped thus over a row of prostrate clowns. It looked dangerous for the clowns, but the trainer had told me how to do it. You begin with logs, laid out a certain distance apart; the horse walks over them under your lead, and whenever he touches one you rebuke him. By and by he will learn to step with such care that he never trips. Then you substitute clowns. I had no clowns, but I did get logs, and with the girls helping, we taught the colt to step over the obstacles even at a trot. Walking, she touched nothing. All ready thus with the logs, I had my sisters lie down in the grass, and again and again the colt stepped over them. None was ever touched. My father would not listen to any of this; he just walloped me, and when he was tired or satisfied and I was in tears, I blubbered a short excuse: "They were only girls." And he whipped me some more.

[17] My father was not given to whipping; he did it very seldom, but he did it hard when he did it at all. My mother was just the opposite. She did not whip me, but she often smacked me, and she had a most annoying habit of thumping me on the head with her thimbled finger. This I resented more than my father's thoroughgoing thrashings, and I can tell why now. I would be playing Napoleon and as I was reviewing my Old Guard, she would crack my skull with that thimble. No doubt I was in the way; it took a lot of furniture and sisters to represent properly a victorious army; and you might think as my mother did that a thimble is a small weapon. But imagine Napoleon at the height of his power, the ruler of the world on parade, getting a sharp rap on his crown from a woman's thimble. No. My father's way was more appropriate. It was hard. "I'll attend to you in the morning," he would say, and I lay awake wonder-

ing which of my crimes he had discovered. I know what it is to be sentenced to be shot at sunrise. And it hurt, in the morning, when he was not angry but very fresh and strong. But you see, he walloped me in my own person; he never humiliated Napoleon or my knighthood, as my mother did. And I learned something from his discipline, something useful.

[18] I learned what tyranny is and the pain of being misunderstood and wronged, or, if you please, understood and set right; they are pretty much the same. He and most parents and teachers do not break in their boys as carefully as I broke in my colt. They haven't the time that I had, and they have not some other incentives I had. I saw this that day when I rubbed my sore legs. He had to explain to my indignant mother what had happened. When he had told it his way, I gave my version: how long and cautiously I had been teaching my horse to walk over logs and girls. And having shown how sure I was of myself and the colt, while my mother was boring into his silence with one of her reproachful looks, I said something that hit my father hard.

"I taught the colt that trick, I have taught her all that you see she knows, without whipping her. I have never struck her; not once. Colonel Carter said I mustn't, and I haven't."

And my mother, backing me up, gave him a rap: "There," she said, "I told you so." He walked off, looking like a thimble-rapped Napoleon.

COMMENT AND QUESTIONS

1. What is the purpose of presenting so fully, in paragraphs 3 to 7, Colonel Carter's comment and advice? Notice that at the end of paragraph 5 Steffens summarizes some of the advice. What were his probable reasons for changing from direct presentation to brief summary?

2. The author does not say explicitly that he practiced the patience and control Colonel Carter advised. How does the reader know that he did? How does Steffens make clear, before the closing paragraphs, that he never whipped the colt?

3. What is the function of the episode with the cowboy in paragraph 14?

4. After he presents the talk of Colonel Carter, the author uses little direct discourse. What are the effects of his occasional direct quotations and of using dialogue rather than summary or indirect discourse in the last two paragraphs? Comment on the word *rap* in the last paragraph.

5. Lincoln Steffens writes very well, in a generally informal style but with carefully structured sentences and precise choice of words. Examine paragraphs 4, 6 (and the short paragraphs following), 9, and 17. In what particular ways is the writing good?

6. What central idea emerges from the story of Steffens and his colt? Do you agree with the idea? Explain.
7. What seem to you the qualities that make this autobiographical essay interesting?

[85] *Mark Twain*: from The Autobiography of Mark Twain

MARK TWAIN is the pseudonym of Samuel Langhorne Clemens (1835–1910), American author, journalist, and humorist, whose works include *The Innocents Abroad, The Adventures of Tom Sawyer, The Adventures of Huckleberry Finn, Life on the Mississippi,* and *A Connecticut Yankee in King Arthur's Court.* The following selection is chapter 9 of *The Autobiography* as arranged and edited by Charles Neider in 1959.

[1] In 1849, when I was fourteen years old, we were still living in Hannibal, on the banks of the Mississippi, in the new "frame" house built by my father five years before. That is, some of us lived in the new part, the rest in the old part back of it and attached to it. In the autumn my sister gave a party and invited all the marriageable young people of the village. I was too young for this society and was too bashful to mingle with young ladies, anyway, therefore I was not invited—at least not for the whole evening. Ten minutes of it was to be my whole share. I was to do the part of a bear in a small fairy play. I was to be disguised all over in a close-fitting brown hairy stuff proper for a bear. About half past ten I was told to go to my room and put on this disguise and be ready in half an hour. I started but changed my mind, for I wanted to practice a little and that room was very small. I crossed over to the large unoccupied house on the corner of Main Street, unaware that a dozen of the young people were also going there to dress for their parts. I took the little black boy, Sandy, with me and we selected a roomy and empty chamber on the second floor. We entered it talking and this gave a couple of half-dressed young ladies an opportunity to take refuge behind a screen undiscovered. Their gowns and things were hanging on hooks behind the door but I did not see them; it was Sandy that shut the door but all his heart was in the theatricals and he was as unlikely to notice them as I was myself.

[2] That was a rickety screen with many holes in it but as I did not know there were girls behind it I was not disturbed by that detail. If I had known, I could not have undressed in the flood of cruel moonlight that was pouring in at the curtainless windows; I should have died of shame. Untroubled by apprehensions, I stripped to the skin and began my practice. I was full of ambition, I was determined to make a hit, I was burning to establish a reputation as a bear and get further engagements; so I threw myself into my work with an abandon that promised great things. I capered back and forth from one end of the room to the other on all fours, Sandy applauding with enthusiasm; I walked upright and growled and snapped and snarled, I stood on my head, I flung hand-springs, I danced a lubberly dance with my paws bent and my imaginary snout sniffing from side to side, I did everything a bear could do and many things which no bear could ever do and no bear with any dignity would want to do, anyway; and of course I never suspected that I was making a spectacle of myself to anyone but Sandy. At last, standing on my head, I paused in that attitude to take a minute's rest. There was a moment's silence, then Sandy spoke up with excited interest and said:

"Mars Sam, has you ever seed a dried herring?"

"No. What is that?"

"It's a fish."

"Well, what of it? Anything peculiar about it?"

"Yes, suh, you bet you dey is. *Dey* eats 'em innards and all!"

[3] There was a smothered burst of feminine snickers from behind the screen! All the strength went out of me and I toppled forward like an undermined tower and brought the screen down with my weight, burying the young ladies under it. In their fright they discharged a couple of piercing screams—and possibly others—but I did not wait to count. I snatched my clothes and fled to the dark hall below, Sandy following. I was dressed in half a minute and out the back way. I swore Sandy to eternal silence, then we went away and hid until the party was over. The ambition was all out of me. I could not have faced that giddy company after my adventure, for there would be two performers there who knew my secret and would be privately laughing at me all the time. I was searched for but not found, and the bear had to be played by a young gentleman in his civilized clothes. The house was still and everybody asleep when I finally ventured home. I was very heavy-hearted and full of a bitter sense of disgrace. Pinned to my pillow I found a slip of paper which bore a line which did not lighten my heart but only made my face burn. It was written in a laboriously disguised hand and these were its mocking terms:

You probably couldn't have played bear but you played bare very well—oh, very *very* well!

[⁴] We think boys are rude, unsensitive anmials but it is not so in all cases. Each boy has one or two sensitive spots and if you can find out where they are located you have only to touch them and you can scorch him as with fire. I suffered miserably over that episode. I expected that the facts would be all over the village in the morning but it was not so. The secret remained confined to the two girls and Sandy and me. That was some appeasement of my pain but it was far from sufficient—the main trouble remained: I was under four mocking eyes and it might as well have been a thousand, for I suspected all girls' eyes of being the ones I so dreaded. During several weeks I could not look any young lady in the face; I dropped my eyes in confusion when any one of them smiled upon me and gave me greeting; I said to myself, "That is one of them," and got quickly away. Of course I was meeting the right girls everywhere but if they ever let slip any betraying sign I was not bright enough to catch it. When I left Hannibal four years later the secret was still a secret; I had never guessed those girls out and was no longer hoping or expecting to do it.

[⁵] One of the dearest and prettiest girls in the village at the time of my mishap was one whom I will call Mary Wilson, because that was not her name. She was twenty years old; she was dainty and sweet, peach-blooming and exquisite, gracious and lovely in character. I stood in awe of her, for she seemed to me to be made out of angel clay and rightfully unapproachable by just any unholy ordinary kind of boy like me. I probably never suspected *her*. But—

[⁶] The scene changes to Calcutta—forty-seven years later. It was in 1896. I arrived there on a lecturing trip. As I entered the hotel a vision passed out of it, clothed in the glory of the Indian sunshine—the Mary Wilson of my long-vanished boyhood! It was a startling thing. Before I could recover from the pleasant shock and speak to her she was gone. I thought maybe I had seen an apparition but it was not so, she was flesh. She was the granddaughter of the other Mary. The other Mary, now a widow, was upstairs and presently sent for me. She was old and gray-haired but she looked young and was very handsome. We sat down and talked. We steeped our thirsty souls in the reviving wine of the past, the pathetic past, the beautiful past, the dear and lamented past; we uttered the names that had been silent upon our lips for fifty years and it was as if they were made of music; with reverent hands we unburied our dead, the mates of our youth, and caressed them with our speech; we searched the dusty chambers of our memories and dragged forth incident after incident, episode after episode, folly after folly, and laughed such good laughs over them, with the tears running down; and finally Mary said, suddenly, and without any leading up:

"Tell me! What is the special peculiarity of dried herrings?"

[7] It seemed a strange question at such a hallowed time as this. And so inconsequential, too. I was a little shocked. And yet I was aware of a stir of some kind away back in the deeps of my memory somewhere. It set me to musing—thinking—searching. Dried herrings? Dried herrings? The peculiarity of dri . . . I glanced up. Her face was grave, but there was a dim and shadowy twinkle in her eye which—All of a sudden I knew and far away down in the hoary past I heard a remembered voice murmur, "Dey eats 'em innards and all!"

"At—last! I've found one of you, anyway! Who was the other girl?"

[8] But she drew the line there. She wouldn't tell me.

[9] But a boy's life is not all comedy; much of the tragic enters into it. The drunken tramp who was burned up in the village jail lay upon my conscience a hundred nights afterward and filled them with hideous dreams—dreams in which I saw his appealing face as I had seen it in the pathetic reality, pressed against the window bars, with the red hell glowing behind him—a face which seemed to say to me, "If you had not given me the matches this would not have happened; you are responsible for my death." I was *not* responsible for it, for I had meant him no harm but only good, when I let him have the matches; but no matter, mine was a trained Presbyterian conscience and knew but the one duty—to hunt and harry its slave upon all pretexts and on all occasions, particularly when there was no sense nor reason in it. The tramp—who was to blame—suffered ten minutes; I, who was not to blame, suffered three months.

[10] The shooting down of poor old Smarr in the main street at noonday supplied me with some more dreams; and in them I always saw again the grotesque closing picture—the great family Bible spread open on the profane old man's breast by some thoughtful idiot and rising and sinking to the labored breathings and adding the torture of its leaden weight to the dying struggles. We are curiously made. In all the throng of gaping and sympathetic onlookers there was not one with common sense enough to perceive that an anvil would have been in better taste there than the Bible, less open to sarcastic criticism and swifter in its atrocious work. In my nightmares I gasped and struggled for breath under the crush of that vast book for many a night.

[11] All within the space of a couple of years we had two or three other tragedies and I had the ill luck to be too near by on each occasion. There was the slave man who was struck down with a chunk of slag for some small offense; I saw him die. And the young Californian emigrant who was stabbed with a bowie knife by a drunken comrade; I saw the red life gush from his breast. And the case of the rowdy young brothers and their harmless old uncle; one of them held the old man down with his knees on his breast while the other one tried repeatedly to kill him with an Allen revolver which wouldn't go off. I happened along just then, of course.

[¹²] Then there was the case of the young Californian emigrant who got drunk and proposed to raid the "Welshman's house" all alone one dark and threatening night. This house stood halfway up Holliday's Hill and its sole occupants were a poor but quite respectable widow and her blameless daughter. The invading ruffian woke the whole village with his ribald yells and coarse challenges and obscenities. I went up there with a comrade—John Briggs, I think—to look and listen. The figure of the man was dimly visible; the women were on their porch, not visible in the deep shadow of its roof, but we heard the elder woman's voice. She had loaded an old musket with slugs and she warned the man that if he stayed where he was while she counted ten it would cost him his life. She began to count, slowly; he began to laugh. He stopped laughing at "six"; then through the deep stillness, in a steady voice, followed the rest of the tale: "Seven . . . eight . . . nine"—a long pause, we holding our breaths— "ten!" A red spout of flame gushed out into the night and the man dropped with his breast riddled to rags. Then the rain and the thunder burst loose and the waiting town swarmed up the hill in the glare of the lightning like an invasion of ants. Those people saw the rest; I had had my share and was satisfied. I went home to dream and was not disappointed.

[¹³] My teaching and training enabled me to see deeper into these tragedies than an ignorant person could have done. I knew what they were for. I tried to disguise it from myself but down in the secret deeps of my troubled heart I knew—and I *knew* I knew. They were inventions of Providence to beguile me to a better life. It sounds curiously innocent and conceited now, but to me there was nothing strange about it; it was quite in accordance with the thoughtful and judicious ways of Providence as I understood them. It would not have surprised me nor even overflattered me if Providence had killed off that whole community in trying to save an asset like me. Educated as I had been, it would have seemed just the thing and well worth the expense. *Why* Providence should take such an anxious interest in such a property, that idea never entered my head, and there was no one in that simple hamlet who would have dreamed of putting it there. For one thing, no one was equipped with it.

[¹⁴] It is quite true, I took all the tragedies to myself and tallied them off in turn as they happened, saying to myself in each case, with a sigh, "Another one gone—and on my account; this ought to bring me to repentance; the patience of God will not always endure." And yet privately I believed it would. That is, I believed it in the daytime; but not in the night. With the going down of the sun my faith failed and the clammy fears gathered about my heart. It was then that I repented. Those were awful nights, nights of despair, nights charged with the bitterness of death. After each tragedy I recognized the warning and repented; repented and begged; begged like a coward, begged like a dog; and not in the interest of those poor people who had been extinguished for my sake but only in my *own* interest. It seems selfish when I look back on it now.

[15] My repentances were very real, very earnest; and after each trag- edy they happened every night for a long time. But as a rule they could not stand the daylight. They faded out and shredded away and disap- peared in the glad splendor of the sun. They were the creatures of fear and darkness and they could not live out of their own place. The day gave me cheer and peace and at night I repented again. In all my boyhood life I am not sure that I ever tried to lead a better life in the daytime—or wanted to. In my age I should never think of wishing to do such a thing. But in my age, as in my youth, night brings me many a deep remorse. I realize that from the cradle up I have been like the rest of the race— never quite sane in the night. When "Injun Joe" died . . . But never mind. Somewhere I have already described what a raging hell of repentance I passed through then. I believe that for months I was as pure as the driven snow. After dark.

---◄ C O M M E N T   A N D   Q U E S T I O N S ►---

1. This chapter has two main parts—the comedy of the rehearsal and the village tragedies. Is there a relationship between the comic and the tragic other than the fact that the episodes all took place in Hannibal within a few years? Explain.

2. Mark Twain said of his autobiography that he intended to use a tech- nique of bringing the past and the present face to face and so establishing interesting contrasts. Where in this chapter does he use that technique? Does it add to the interest of the material?

3. Examine the "bear" rehearsal in paragraph 2. Why do you think it is developed as fully as it is? What are the characteristics of Twain's style in this paragraph?

4. How does the author make real and believable the tragedies and acts of violence in paragraphs 9–12?

5. Twain says, at the beginning of paragraph 13, that his religious training enabled him to see deeper into the tragedies than an ignorant person could have done. Is the statement ironical? How did he interpret the tragedies?

6. The last paragraphs contrast the author's boyhood resolve to lead a better life with his failure to do so, and also contrast night—the time of remorse, repentance, and despair—with day—the time of faith, cheer, and peace. Does the night–day contrast seem to you symbolic or simply realistic? Explain.

7. Near the end of paragraph 15 Twain says that he has been "like the rest of the race—never quite sane in the night." Does this seem to you a valid generalization about mankind or true only of the author? Explain.

8. Mark Twain wrote his autobiography many years after the events recorded here. At the time of writing, what was his attitude, apparently, toward his "trained Presbyterian conscience"?

[86] *Clarence Day*: Father Opens My Mail

THE FOLLOWING autobiographical essay narrates a sequence of events covering a period of years but focused on one aspect of a father–son relationship. Clarence Day (1874–1935) is best known for his humorous autobiographical works, *God and My Father, Life with Father, Life with Mother,* and *Father and I.* "Father Opens My Mail" is a chapter of *Life with Father,* which was published in 1935 and dramatized in 1939.

[1] There was a time in my boyhood when I felt that Father had handicapped me severely in life by naming me after him, "Clarence." All literature, so far as I could see, thronged with objectionable persons named Clarence. Percy was bad enough, but there had been some good fighters named Percy. The only Clarence in history was a duke who did something dirty at Tewkesbury, and who died a ridiculous death afterwards in a barrel of malmsey.

[2] As for the Clarences in the fiction I read, they were horrible. In one story, for instance, there were two brothers, Clarence and Frank. Clarence was a "vain, disagreeable little fellow" who was proud of his curly hair and fine clothes, while Frank was a "rollicking boy who was ready to play games with anybody." Clarence didn't like to play games, of course. He just minced around looking on.

[3] One day when the mother of these boys had gone out, this story went on, Clarence "tempted" Frank to disobey her and fly their kite on the roof. Frank didn't want to, but Clarence kept taunting him and daring him until Frank was stung into doing it. After the two boys went up to the roof, Frank got good and dirty, running up and down and stumbling over scuttles, while Clarence sat there, giving him orders, and kept his natty clothes tidy. To my horror, he even spread out his handkerchief on the trapdoor to sit on. And to crown it all, this sneak told on Frank as soon as their mother came in.

[4] This wasn't an exceptionally mean Clarence, either. He was just run-of-the-mill. Some were worse.

[5] So far as I could ever learn, however, Father had never heard of

these stories, and had never dreamed of there being anything objectionable in his name. Quite the contrary. And yet as a boy he had lived a good rough-and-tumble boy's life. He had played and fought on the city streets, and kept a dog in Grandpa's stable, and stolen rides to Greenpoint Ferry on the high, lurching bus. In the summer he had gone to West Springfield and had run down Shad Lane through the trees to the house where Grandpa was born, and had gone barefoot and driven the cows home just as though he had been named Tom or Bill.

[6] He had the same character as a boy, I suppose, that he had as a man, and he was too independent to care if people thought his name fancy. He paid no attention to the prejudices of others, except to disapprove of them. He had plenty of prejudices himself, of course, but they were his own. He was humorous and confident and level-headed, and I imagine that if any boy had tried to make fun of him for being named Clarence, Father would simply have laughed and told him he didn't know what he was talking about.

[7] I asked Mother how this name had ever happened to spring up in our family. She explained that my great-great-grandfather was Benjamin Day, and my great-grandfather was Henry, and consequently my grandfather had been named Benjamin Henry. He in turn had named his eldest son Henry and his second son Benjamin. The result was that when Father was born there was no family name left. The privilege of choosing a name for Father had thereupon been given to Grandma, and unluckily for the Day family she had been reading a novel, the hero of which was named Clarence.

[8] I knew that Grandma, though very like Grandpa in some respects, had a dreamy side which he hadn't, a side that she usually kept to herself, in her serene, quiet way. Her romantic choice of this name probably made Grandpa smile, but he was a detached sort of man who didn't take small matters seriously, and who drew a good deal of private amusement from the happenings of everyday life. Besides, he was partly to blame in this case, because that novel was one he had published himself in his magazine.

[9] I asked Mother, when she had finished, why I had been named Clarence too.

[10] It hadn't been her choice, Mother said. She had suggested all sorts of names to Father, but there seemed to be something wrong with each one. When she had at last spoken of naming me after him, however, he had said at once that that was the best suggestion yet—he said it sounded just right.

[11] Father and I would have had plenty of friction in any case. This identity of names made things worse. Every time that I had been more of a fool than he liked, Father would try to impress on me my responsibilities as his eldest son, and above all as the son to whom he had given

his name, as he put it. A great deal was expected, it seemed to me, of a boy who was named after his father. I used to envy my brothers, who didn't have anything expected of them on this score at all.

[¹²] I envied them still more after I was old enough to begin getting letters. I then discovered that when Father "gave" me his name he had also, not unnaturally, I had to admit, retained it himself, and when anything came for Clarence S. Day he opened it, though it was something for me.

[¹³] He also opened everything that came addressed to Clarence S. Day, Jr. He didn't do this intentionally, but unless the "Jr." was clearly written, it looked like "Esq.," and anyhow Father was too accustomed to open all Clarence Day letters to remember about looking carefully every time for a "Jr." So far as mail and express went, I had no name at all of my own.

[¹⁴] For the most part nobody wrote to me when I was a small boy except firms whose advertisements I had read in the *Youth's Companion* and to whom I had written requesting them to send me their circulars. These circulars described remarkable bargains in magicians' card outfits, stamps and coins, pocket knives, trick spiders, and imitation fried eggs, and they seemed interesting and valuable to me when I got them. The trouble was that Father usually got them and at once tore them up. I then had to write for such circulars again, and if Father got the second one too, he would sometimes explode with annoyance. He became particularly indignant one year, I remember, when he was repeatedly urged to take advantage of a special bargain sale of false whiskers. He said he couldn't understand why these offerings kept pouring in. I knew why, in this case, but at other times I was often surprised myself at the number he got, not realizing that as a result of my postcard requests my or our name had been automatically put on several large general mailing lists.

[¹⁵] During this period I got more of my mail out of Father's wastebasket than I did from the postman.

[¹⁶] At the age of twelve or thirteen, I stopped writing for these childish things and turned to a new field. Father and I, whichever of us got at the mail first, began then to receive not merely circulars but personal letters beginning:

Dear Friend Day:
    In reply to your valued request for one of our Mammoth Agents' Outfits, kindly forward postoffice order for $1.49 to cover cost of postage and packing, and we will put you in a position to earn a large income in your spare time with absolutely no labor on your part, by taking subscriptions for *The Secret Handbook of Mesmerism,* and our *Tales of Blood* series.

And one spring, I remember, as the result of what I had intended to be a secret application on my part, Father was assigned "the exclusive rights for Staten Island and Hoboken of selling the Gem Home Popper for Pop Corn. Housewives buy it at sight."

[17] After Father had stormily endured these afflictions for a while, he and I began to get letters from girls. Fortunately for our feelings, these were rare, but they were ordeals for both of us. Father had forgotten, if he ever knew, how silly young girls sound, and I got my first lesson in how unsystematic they were. No matter how private and playful they meant their letters to be, they forgot to put "Jr." on the envelope every once in so often. When Father opened these letters, he read them all the way through, sometimes twice, muttering to himself over and over: "This is very peculiar. I don't understand this at all. Here's a letter to me from some person I never heard of. I can't see what it's all about." By the time it had occurred to him that possibly the letter might be for me, I was red and embarrassed and even angrier at the girl than at Father. And on days when he had read some of the phrases aloud to the family, it nearly killed me to claim it.

[18] Lots of fellows whom I knew had been named after their fathers without having such troubles. But although Father couldn't have been kinder-hearted or had any better intentions, when he saw his name on a package or envelope it never dawned on him that it might not be for him. He was too active in his habits to wait until I had a chance to get at it. And as he was also single-minded and prompt to attend to unfinished business, he opened everything automatically and then did his best to dispose of it.

[19] This went on even after I grew up until I had a home of my own. Father was always perfectly decent about it, but he never changed. When he saw I felt sulky, he was genuinely sorry and said so, but he couldn't see why all this should annoy me, and he was surprised and amused that it did. I used to get angry once in a while when something came for me which I particularly hadn't wished him to see and which I would find lying, opened, on the hall table marked "For Jr.?" when I came in; but nobody could stay angry with Father—he was too utterly guiltless of having meant to offend.

[20] He often got angry himself, but it was mostly at things, not at persons, and he didn't mind a bit (as a rule) when persons got angry at him. He even declared, when I got back from college, feeling dignified, and told him I wished he'd be more careful, that he suffered from these mistakes more than I did. It wasn't *his* fault, he pointed out, if my stupid correspondents couldn't remember my name, and it wasn't any pleasure to him to be upset at his breakfast by finding that a damned lunatic company in Battle Creek had sent him a box of dry bread crumbs, with a letter asserting that this rubbish would be good for his stomach. "I admit I threw it into the fireplace, Clarence, but what else could I do? If you valued this preposterous concoction, my dear boy, I'm sorry. I'll

buy another box for you today, if you'll tell me where I can get it. Don't feel badly! I'll buy you a barrel. Only I hope you won't eat it."

[21] In the days when Mrs. Pankhurst and her friends were chaining themselves to lamp posts in London, in their campaign for the vote, a letter came from Frances Hand trustfully asking "Dear Clarence" to do something to help Woman Suffrage—speak at a meeting, I think. Father got red in the face. "Speak at one of their meetings!" he roared at Mother. "I'd like nothing better! You can tell Mrs. Hand that it would give me great pleasure to inform all those crackpots in petticoats exactly what I think of their antics."

[22] "Now, Clare," Mother said, "you mustn't talk that way. I like that nice Mrs. Hand, and anyhow this letter must be for Clarence."

[23] One time I asked Father for his opinion of a low-priced stock I'd been watching. His opinion was that it was not worth a damn. I thought this over, but still wished to buy it, so I placed a scale order with another firm instead of with Father's office, and said nothing about it. At the end of the month this other firm sent me a statement setting forth each of my little transactions in full, and of course they forgot to put the "Jr." at the end of my name. When Father opened the envelope, he thought at first in his excitement that this firm had actually opened an account for him without being asked. I found him telling Mother that he'd like to wring their damned necks.

"That must be for me, Father," I said, when I took in what had happened.

We looked at each other.

"You bought this stuff?" he said incredulously. "After all I said about it?"

"Yes, Father."

He handed over the statement and walked out of the room.

Both he and I felt offended and angry. We stayed so for several days, too, but then we made up.

[24] Once in a while when I got a letter that I had no time to answer I used to address an envelope to the sender and then put anything in it that happened to be lying around on my desk—a circular about books, a piece of newspaper, an old laundry bill—anything at all, just to be amiable, and yet at the same time to save myself the trouble of writing. I happened to tell several people about this private habit of mine at a dinner one night— a dinner at which Alice Duer Miller and one or two other writers were present. A little later she wrote me a criticism of Henry James and ended by saying that I needn't send her any of my old laundry bills because she wouldn't stand it. And she forgot to put on the "Jr."

[25] "In the name of God," Father said bleakly, "this is the worst yet. Here's a woman who says I'd better not read *The Golden Bowl*, which I

have no intention whatever of doing, and she also warns me for some unknown reason not to send her my laundry bills."

[26] The good part of all these experiences, as I realize now, was that in the end they drew Father and me closer together. My brothers had only chance battles with him. I had a war. Neither he nor I relished its clashes, but they made us surprisingly intimate.

--◦◄{ COMMENT AND QUESTIONS }►◦--

1. "Father Opens My Mail" has at first a very informal organization, both because it is one chapter of a book about the author and his father and because informality is part of the tone. What do the first four paragraphs, about the author's attitude toward the name "Clarence," contribute to the essay?
2. Examine paragraphs 11–12. What is the double transition between them?
3. What are the main stages or periods in the struggle between Clarence Day and his father?
4. The narrative pace of this essay is worth study. Because the account covers a long period of time, the author necessarily summarizes much of the material, but he is very skillful in breaking and illustrating his summary with the presentation of little scenes or parts of scenes. Paragraphs 14–15 and paragraph 16 are essentially summaries of the events of several years. How does Day make the summaries interesting?
5. In the presented scenes—in paragraph 17 and later—the author uses direct quotation to bring the scene to life and to characterize Father. Day also uses some indirect discourse: an example, in paragraph 14, is "He said he couldn't understand why these offerings kept pouring in." Point out examples of indirect discourse which still keeps the flavor of Father's language.
6. What is the effect of the expanded development of the episodes or scenes near the end of the essay (paragraphs 21–25)? What were the author's probable reasons for ending the series with the letter from Alice Duer Miller and Father's response to it? Comment on the word *bleakly* in the first sentence of paragraph 25.
7. Does the final paragraph seem to you an effective ending? Explain.

[87] *Colette*: My Mother and the Animals

THE FOLLOWING autobiographical selection is concentrated in time. The author recalls a brief experience (her return to her country home after a visit in Paris) in which immediate impressions called up associated memories. Colette (1873–1954) was a French novelist whose work has long been acclaimed in her native country, and who has been widely read in this country too; she was the first woman to be elected to the Académie Goncourt, a French literary society consisting of ten members. Among her short novels which have been translated into English are *The Vagabond, The Cat, Gigi, Julie de Carneilhan, Chéri,* and *The Last of Chéri.* "My Mother and the Animals" is a chapter of *La Maison de Claudine,* first published in 1922, and published in this country in 1953 under the title *My Mother's House.*

[¹] A succession of harsh sounds, made by the train, cabs, and omnibuses, is all that my memory retains of a brief visit to Paris when I was six years old. Of a week in Paris five years later I remember nothing but arid heat, panting thirst, feverish fatigue and fleas in a hotel bedroom in the Rue St. Roch.

[²] I remember also that I kept on gazing upwards, vaguely oppressed by the height of the houses, and that a photographer won my heart by calling me, as he doubtless called every child, a "wonder."

[³] Five years in the country followed without so much as a thought of Paris.

[⁴] But when I was sixteen, on returning to Puisaye after a fortnight of theatres, museums and shops, I brought home with me, among memories of finery and greediness, mixed with hopes, regrets, and feelings of scorn, as innocent and awkward as myself, the surprise and the melancholy aversion aroused in me by what I called houses without animals.

[⁵] Mere cubes without gardens, flowerless abodes where no cat mews behind the dining-room door, where one never treads near the fireside on some part of a dog sprawling like a rug; rooms devoid of familiar spirits, wherein the hand seeking a friendly caress encounters only inanimate wood, or marble, or velvet; I felt all these with famished senses, with a vehement need to touch once again fleeces and leaves, warm feathers and the exciting dewiness of flowers.

[⁶] As if I were discovering them all together again, I extended my composite greeting to my mother, the garden and the circle of animals.

854

[⁷] My return coincided with the watering of the garden, and I still cherish happy memories of the sixth hour of the evening, the green watering-can soaking the blue sateen frock, the strong smell of leaf-mould, and the afterglow that cast a pink reflection on the pages of a forgotten book, the white petals of the tobacco flowers and the white fur of the cat in her basket.

[⁸] Nonoche the tortoiseshell had had kittens two days earlier, and Bijou her daughter the following evening, and as for Musette, the Havanese bitch, perennial breeder of bastards. . . .

"Minet-Chéri, go and see Musette's puppy!"

[⁹] So I went off to the kitchen where Musette was engaged in feeding an ash-colored monster, still half blind and nearly as big as herself. Fathered by some local gun-dog, he tugged like a calf at the delicate teats, strawberry-pink against the silver-pale fur, and trampled rhythmically with extended claws a silky belly that would have suffered severely if . . . if my mother had not cut out and sewed for him, from an old pair of white gloves, suede mittens reaching to his elbows. I never saw a ten days' pup look so much like a gendarme.

[¹⁰] How many treasures had bloomed in my absence! I ran to the great basket overflowing with indistinguishable cats. That orange ear certainly belonged to Nonoche, but that plume of a black angora tail could only belong to her daughter Bijou, intolerant as a pretty woman. One long slim dry paw, like that of a black rabbit, threatened the heavens; and a tiny kitten spotted like a civet-cat, slumbering replete and prostrate on its back in the middle of this disorder, looked as though it has been assassinated.

[¹¹] I set to work happily to disentangle the mass of nurses and well-licked nurslings from which arose a pleasant smell of new-mown hay, fresh milk and well-tended fur, and I discovered that Bijou, four times a mother in three years, from whose teats hung a chaplet of newborn off-spring, was herself engaged in noisily sucking, with an over-large tongue and a purring not unlike the roar of a log fire, the milk of the aged Nonoche, who lay inert with comfort, one paw across her eyes. Bending nearer, I listened to the double purring, treble and bass, that is the mysterious prerogative of the feline race; a rumbling as of a distant factory, a whirring as of a captive moth, a frail mill whose profound slumber stops its grinding. I was not surprised at the chain of mutually suckling cats. To those who live in the country and use their eyes everything becomes alike miraculous and simple. We had long considered it natural that a bitch should nourish a kitten, that a cat should select as her lair the top of the cage wherein trustful green canaries sang happily, their beaks from time to time plucking from the sleeper an occasional silky hair for nesting purposes.

[¹²] A whole year of my childhood was devoted to the task of capturing, in the kitchen or the cow-house, the rare flies of winter for the benefit of two swallows, October nestlings thrown down to us by a gale. Was it not essential to preserve them and to find provender for their insatiable beaks that disdained any but living prey?

[13] It was thanks to them that I learned how infinitely a tame swallow can surpass, in insolent sociability, even the most pampered of dogs. Our two swallows spent their time perching on a shoulder or a head, nestling in the work-basket, running about under the table like chickens, pecking at the nonplussed dog or chirping in the very face of the disconcerted cat. They came to school in my pocket and returned home by air. As soon as the shining sickle of their wings grew and sharpened, they would vanish at any time into the vault of the spring sky, but a single shrill call of "Ti-i-inies" would bring them cleaving the wind like two arrows, to alight in my hair, to which they would cling with all the strength of their little curved black steel claws.

[14] All was faery and yet simple among the fauna of my early home. You could never believe that a cat could eat strawberries? And yet, because I have seen him so many times, I know that Babou, that black Satan, interminable and as sinuous as an eel, would carefully select in Madame Pomié's kitchen garden the ripest of the Royal Sovereigns or the Early Scarlets. He it was, too, who would be discovered poetically absorbed in smelling newly-opened violets.

[15] Have you ever heard tell of Pelisson's spider that so passionately loved music? I for one am ready to believe it and also to add, as my slender contribution to the sum of human knowledge, the story of the spider that my mother kept—as my father expressed it—on her ceiling, in that year that ushered in my sixteenth spring. A handsome garden spider she was, her belly like a clove of garlic emblazoned with an ornate cross. In the daytime she slept, or hunted in the web that she had spun across the bedroom ceiling. But during the night, towards three o'clock in the morning, at the moment when her chronic insomnia caused my mother to relight the lamp and open her bedside book, the great spider would also wake, and after a careful survey would lower herself from the ceiling by a thread, directly above the little oil lamp upon which a bowl of chocolate simmered through the night. Slowly she would descend, swinging limply to and fro like a big bead, and grasping the edge of the cup with all her eight legs, she would bend over head foremost and drink to satiety. Then she would draw herself ceilingwards again, heavy with creamy chocolate, her ascent punctuated by the pauses and meditations imposed by an overloaded stomach, and would resume her post in the centre of her silken rigging.

[16] Still wearing my travelling coat, I sat dreaming, weary, enchanted and re-enslaved in the midst of my kingdom.

"Where is your spider, mother?"

My mother's gray eyes, magnified by her glasses, clouded:

"Have you come back from Paris only to ask for news of the spider, you ungrateful child?"

I hung my head, awkward in my affection, ashamed of that which was best in me:

"I couldn't help remembering sometimes, at night, at the spider's hour, when I couldn't sleep. . . ."

"Minet-Chéri, you couldn't sleep? Was your bed uncomfortable? The spider's in her web, I suppose. But do come and see if my caterpillar is hibernating. I really think she's going to become a chrysalis, and I've given her a little box of dry sand. She's an Emperor moth caterpillar and I think a bird must have pecked her stomach but she's quite well again now."

[17] The caterpillar was perhaps asleep, moulded to the form of a supporting twig of box thorn. The ravages around her testified to her vitality. There were nothing but shreds of leaves, gnawed stems and barren shoots. Plump, as thick as my thumb and over four inches long, she swelled the fat rolls of her cabbage-green body, adorned at intervals with hairy warts of turquoise blue. I detached her gently from her twig and she writhed in anger, exposing her paler stomach and all her spiky little paws that clung leechlike to the branch to which I returned her.

"But, mother, she has devoured everything!"

The grey eyes behind the spectacles wavered perplexedly from the denuded twigs to the caterpillar and thence to my face:

"But what can I do about it? And after all, the box thorn she's eating, you know, is the one that strangles honeysuckle."

"Yes, but won't the caterpillar eat the honeysuckle too?"

"I don't know. But in any case, what can I do about it? I can hardly kill the creature."

[18] The scene is before me as I write, the garden with its sun-warmed walls, the last of the black cherries hanging on the tree, the sky webbed with long pink clouds. I can feel again beneath my fingers the vigorous resentment of the caterpillar, the wet, leathery hydrangea leaves, and my mother's little work-worn hand.

[19] I can evoke the wind at will and make it rustle the stiff papery blades of the bamboos and sing, through the comb-like leaves of the yew, as a worthy accompaniment to the voice that on that day and on all the other days, even to the final silence, spoke words that had always the same meaning.

[20] "That child must have proper care. Can't we save that woman? Have those people got enough to eat? I can hardly kill the creature."

---◄{ C O M M E N T   A N D   Q U E S T I O N S }►---

1. The basis of good description is close observation and vivid concrete detail which enable the reader to share the writer's experience; the skillful writer chooses details that produce a unified effect or dominant impression. In the first five paragraphs of "My Mother and the Animals," what is the dominant impression of Paris? What seem to be the author's reasons for starting with Paris instead of with her return home?

2. Another principle of good description is that it appeals to the reader's senses; the writer vitalizes a scene, brings it to life and reality, by including sights, colors, sounds, and other physical impressions that are part of experiencing the scene. Examine paragraphs 7–11. How many sense appeals or sensory impressions do you find in them?

3. Paragraphs 11 and 13, among others, contain figures of speech. Which figures seem to you most effective, and why?

4. What is the dominant impression of Colette's home to which the many details contribute? What details and images in the selection are most vivid and interesting to you?

5. What is the dominant impression of the author's mother, and how is it established?

6. Comment on paragraphs 18–20. In what ways are they a good ending?

[88]   *Alfred Kazin*: from A Walker in the City

ALFRED KAZIN (1915–   ), is a writer, critic, and teacher; his works include *On Native Grounds, A Walker in the City, The Inmost Leaf, Contemporaries,* and *Starting Out in the Thirties. A Walker in the City,* published in 1951, is the first volume of a long autobiography; the city is New York.

[¹] In Brownsville tenements the kitchen is always the largest room and the center of the household. As a child I felt that we lived in a kitchen to which four other rooms were annexed. My mother, a "home" dressmaker, had her workshop in the kitchen. She told me once that she had begun dressmaking in Poland at thirteen; as far back as I can remember, she was always making dresses for the local women. She had an innate sense of design, a quick eye for all the subtleties in the latest fashions, even when she despised them, and great boldness. For three or four dollars she would study the fashion magazines with a customer, go with the customer to the remnants store on Belmont Avenue to pick out the material, argue the owner down—all remnants stores, for some reason, were supposed to be shady, as if the owners dealt in stolen goods —and then for days would patiently fit and baste and sew and fit again. Our apartment was always full of women in their housedresses sitting around the kitchen table waiting for a fitting. My little bedroom next to the kitchen was the fitting room. The sewing machine, an old nut-brown Singer with golden scrolls painted along the black arm and engraved along the two tiers of little drawers massed with needles and thread on each side of the treadle, stood next to the window and the great coal-black stove which up to my last year in college was our main source of heat. By December the two outer bedrooms were closed off, and used to chill bottles of milk and cream, cold borscht and jellied calves' feet.

[²] The kitchen held our lives together. My mother worked in it all day long, we ate in it almost all meals except the Passover *seder*, I did my homework and first writing at the kitchen table, and in winter I often had a bed made up for me on three kitchen chairs near the stove. On the wall just over the table hung a long horizontal mirror that sloped to a ship's prow at each end and was lined in cherry wood. It took up the whole wall, and drew every object in the kitchen to itself. The walls were a fiercely stippled whitewash, so often rewhitened by my father in slack seasons that the paint looked as if it had been squeezed and cracked into the walls. A large electric bulb hung down the center of the kitchen at the end of a chain that had been hooked into the ceiling; the old gas ring and key still jutted out of the wall like antlers. In the corner next to the toilet was the sink at which we washed, and the square tub in which my mother did our clothes. Above it, tacked to the shelf on which were pleasantly ranged square, blue-bordered white sugar and spice jars, hung calendars from the Public National Bank on Pitkin Avenue and the Minsker Progressive Branch of the Workman's Circle; receipts for the payment of insurance premiums, and household bills on a spindle; two little boxes engraved with Hebrew letters. One of these was for the poor, the other to buy back the Land of Israel. Each spring a bearded little man would suddenly appear in our kitchen, salute us with a hurried Hebrew blessing, empty the boxes (sometimes with a sidelong look of disdain if they were not full), hurriedly bless us again for remembering our less fortunate Jewish brothers and sisters, and so take his departure until the next spring, after vainly trying to persuade my mother to take still another box. We did occasionally remember to drop coins in the boxes, but this was usually only on the dreaded morning of "midterms" and final examinations, because my mother thought it would bring me luck. She was extremely superstitious, but embarrassed about it, and always laughed at herself whenever, on the morning of an examination, she counseled me to leave the house on my right foot. "I know it's silly," her smile seem to say, "but what harm can it do? It may calm God down."

[3] The kitchen gave a special character to our lives; my mother's character. All my memories of that kitchen are dominated by the nearness of my mother sitting all day long at her sewing machine, by the clacking of the treadle against the linoleum floor, by the patient twist of her right shoulder as she automatically pushed at the wheel with one hand or lifted the foot to free the needle where it had got stuck in a thick piece of material. The kitchen was her life. Year by year, as I began to take in her fantastic capacity for labor and her anxious zeal, I realized it was ourselves she kept stitched together. I can never remember a time when she was not working. She worked because the law of her life was work, work and anxiety; she worked because she would have found life meaningless without work. She read almost no English; she could read the Yiddish paper, but never felt she had time to. We were always talking of a time when I would teach her how to read, but somehow there was never time. When I awoke in the morning she was already at her machine, or in the great morning crowd of housewives at the grocery getting fresh rolls for breakfast. When I returned from school she was at her machine, or conferring over *McCall's* with some neighborhood woman who had come in pointing hopefully to an illustration—"Mrs. Kazin! Mrs. Kazin! Make me a dress like it shows here in the picture!" When my father came home from work she had somehow mysteriously interrupted herself to make supper for us, and the dishes cleared and washed, was back at her machine. When I went to bed at night, often she was still there, pounding away at the treadle, hunched over the wheel, her hands steering a piece of gauze under the needle with a finesse that always contrasted sharply with her swollen hands and broken nails. Her left hand had been pierced through when as a girl she had worked in the infamous Triangle Shirtwaist Factory on the East Side. A needle had gone straight through the palm, severing a large vein. They had sewn it up for her so clumsily that a tuft of flesh always lay folded over the palm.

[4] The kitchen was the great machine that set our lives running; it whirred down a little only on Saturdays and holy days. From my mother's kitchen I gained my first picture of life as a white, overheated, starkly lit workshop redolent with Jewish cooking, crowded with women in housedresses, strewn with fashion magazines, patterns, dress material, spools of thread—and at whose center, so lashed to her machine that bolts of energy seemed to dance out of her hands and feet as she worked, my mother stamped the treadle hard against the floor, hard, hard, and silently, grimly at war, beat out the first rhythm of the world for me.

[5] Every sound from the street roared and trembled at our windows

—a mother feeding her child on the doorstep, the screech of the trolley car on Rockaway Avenue, the eternal smash of a handball against the wall of our house, the clatter of *"der Italyéner"*'s cart packed with watermelons, the sing-song of the old-clothes men walking Chester Street, the cries *"Árbes! Árbes! Kinder! Kinder! Heyse gute árbes!"* All day long people streamed into our apartment as a matter of course—"customers," upstairs neighbors, downstairs neighbors, women who would stop in for a half-hour's talk, salesmen, relatives, insurance agents. Usually they came in without ringing the bell—everyone knew my mother was always at home. I would hear the front door opening, the wind whistling through our front hall, and then some familiar face would appear in our kitchen with the same bland, matter-of-fact inquiring look: no need to stand on ceremony: my mother and her kitchen were available to everyone all day long.

[6] At night the kitchen contracted around the blaze of light on the cloth, the patterns, the ironing board where the iron had burned a black border around the tear in the muslin cover; the finished dresses looked so frilly as they jostled on their wire hangers after all the work my mother had put into them. And then I would get that strangely ominous smell of tension from the dress fabrics and the burn in the cover of the ironing board—as if each piece of cloth and paper crushed with light under the naked bulb might suddenly go up in flames. Whenever I pass some small tailoring shop still lit up at night and see the owner hunched over his steam press; whenever in some poorer neighborhood of the city I see through a window some small crowded kitchen naked under the harsh light glittering in the ceiling, I still smell that fiery breath, that warning of imminent fire. I was always holding my breath. What I must have felt most about ourselves, I see now, was that we ourselves were like kindling—that all the hard-pressed pieces of ourselves and all the hard-used objects in that kitchen were like so many slivers of wood that might go up in flames if we came too near the white-blazing filament in that naked bulb. Our tension itself was fire, we ourselves were forever burning—to live, to get down the foreboding in our souls, to make good.

[7] Twice a year, on the anniversaries of her parents' deaths, my mother placed on top of the ice-box an ordinary kitchen glass packed with wax, the *yortsayt*, and lit the candle in it. Sitting at the kitchen table over my homework, I would look across the threshold to that mourning-glass, and sense that for my mother the distance from our kitchen to *der heym*, from life to death, was only a flame's length away. Poor as we were, it was not poverty that drove my mother so hard; it was loneliness —some endless bitter brooding over all those left behind, dead or dying or soon to die; a loneliness locked up in her kitchen that dwelt every day on the hazardousness of life and the nearness of death, but still kept struggling in the lock, trying to get us through by endless labor.

[⁸] With us, life started up again only on the last shore. There seemed to be no middle ground between despair and the fury of our ambition. Whenever my mother spoke of her hopes for us, it was with such unbelievingness that the likes of us would ever come to anything, such abashed hope and readiness for pain, that I finally came to see in the flame burning on top of the ice-box death itself burning away the bones of poor Jews, burning out in us everything but courage, the blind resolution to live. In the light of that mourning-candle, there were ranged around me how many dead and dying—how many eras of pain, of exile, of dispersion, of cringing before the powers of this world!

[⁹] It was always at dusk that my mother's loneliness came home most to me. Painfully alert to every shift in the light at her window, she would suddenly confess her fatigue by removing her pince-nez, and then wearily pushing aside the great mound of fabrics on her machine, would stare at the street as if to warm herself in the last of the sun. "How sad it is!" I once heard her say. "It grips me! It grips me!" Twilight was the bottommost part of the day, the chillest and loneliest time for her. Always so near to her moods, I knew she was fighting some deep inner dread, struggling against the returning tide of darkness along the streets that invariably assailed her heart with the same foreboding—Where? Where now? Where is the day taking us now?

[¹⁰] Yet one good look at the street would revive her. I see her now, perched against the windowsill, with her face against the glass, her eyes almost asleep in enjoyment, just as she starts up with the guilty cry— "What foolishness is this in me!"—and goes to the stove to prepare supper for us: a moment, only a moment, watching the evening crowd of women gathering at the grocery for fresh bread and milk. But between my mother's pent-up face at the window and the winter sun dying in the fabrics—"Alfred, see how beautiful!"—she has drawn for me one single line of sentience.

⌁ COMMENT AND QUESTIONS ⌁

1. Note that the first four paragraphs begin with statements about the kitchen. Are these opening sentences topic sentences for the four paragraphs? Explain.
2. What does the detailed description of the kitchen, in paragraph 2, contribute?
3. As the selection goes on, we learn more and more about the author's mother. What characteristics are introduced or further developed in paragraph 3?

4. What kind of transition, if any, is there between paragraphs 3 and 4?
5. Examine and comment on the style of the last long sentence in paragraph 4.
6. In paragraph 6 the images of burning and light take on a larger meaning. Does this expanded meaning tell us anything more about the mother, or only more about the author? Explain.
7. How are paragraphs 7 and 8 related to paragraph 6?
8. What qualities of Kazin's mother are re-emphasized in the last two paragraphs? What new qualities do we see?
9. If you have read other essays in this section, you know that they illustrate different techniques, among them the author's method of handling time: some discuss or present a sequence of events that took place over a period of time, and others are focused on a single experience; some have a chronological order, and others do not. Comment on Kazin's handling of time in this selection. What is the effect of the technique he uses?

[89] *Irwin Edman*: Former Teachers

IN THE FOLLOWING essay, a philosopher and teacher looks back on his own student days and comments on the personalities, methods, and ideas of those who taught him. "Former Teachers" is Chapter Twelve of *Philosopher's Holiday* (1938), and is preceded by a chapter entitled "Former Students." For a further note on Irwin Edman, see page 415.

[1] By an easy transition I am led from reflection about former students to meditation on former teachers. For I have had teachers as well as pupils, and in considering what effect one has had, or failed to have, on one's one-time students, I cannot help looking back on teachers who, though they might be embarrassed to acknowledge it, or insistent on denying it, had an influence over me. I shall leave out my early love for Miss Foley in 4A, or Miss Carpendale in 7B, whom I feared horribly, partly because she taught me the impossible subject of arithmetic, and partly because of her immense height and blazing red hair and unrelenting expression and deep mannish voice. I felt rather sorry for the trim little teacher of shopwork (another impossible subject) when I heard Miss Carpendale had married him. I was sure even then that that was the way it had happened.

[2] I shall begin rather with high school, for I don't remember that in grade school anybody aroused my mind and imagination. That event

came in my first term at Townsend Harris Hall, the preparatory school, called at the time the academic department, of the College of the City of New York. The man involved was named Michael J. Kelleher, an enthusiastic, curly-haired Irishman, who, at the top of his voice but with a winning cadence, dragooned us into liking *The Ancient Mariner* and *Ivanhoe*. He also dragooned some of us into liking our own writing. He was the first one, save, perhaps, Miss Foley, to make me think I could write. Miss Foley's observation had been based on one sentence. I had written a self-portrait of a camel. The last sentence was: "I do not need water for days at a time; I have it with me." She said that was very good and very well informed. Mr. Michael Kelleher wrote in a large bold hand on a theme of mine: "This has the sweet breath of the country about it." It was an essay on Central Park.

[3] But I recall Mr. Michael Kelleher chiefly because he gave us the contagious impression of so liking poetry that he simply had to tell us about it. Since we were the fourth class he had each morning, it occurred to me even then that it was very remarkable that he should be able to care so deeply and vividly about Rebecca and Rowena still. But he did. It was, I found out, the first year he had taught. I have often thought since it might be well to have a big turn-over in the teaching profession. But that is not really necessary. For, years later, finding myself in the neighbourhood of my old school, I decided to hunt out my old teacher. It was not quite the end of the hour and I heard the powerful cadenced voice of Mr. Kelleher still making clear to fourteen-year-olds the wonder and mystery of *The Ancient Mariner*. I could hear him and even see his figure outlined through the transparent glass of the door:

> "Alone, alone, all, all alone,
> Alone on a wide, wide sea,
> And never a saint took pity on
> My soul in agony. . . ."

The remembered shiver went up my spine. Mr. Kelleher was a born teacher of poetry. He did not explain it; he communicated it by contagion.

[4] There were three other high school teachers I remember. One was the beautifully dressed, slim Mr. Knickerbocker who taught us French. His technique belied his debonair appearance. There was no languid elegance about his methods. He spent the first fifteen minutes of each hour rapidly going around the class making certain that we knew the new words in each lesson. It was a martinet method, but it worked. One did not twice come to class unprepared, to have Mr. Knickerbocker's clear blue eyes briefly stare one into humiliation if one guessed, or could not even guess, the meaning of a word. There was not much about appreciation of French literature, and I presume such methods now would be

regarded as unimaginative drill. But one knew a great many words with precision before the term was over.

[5] My third debt to my high school teachers is to Bird W. Stair, now a professor in the College of the City of New York. He had just come to New York from Indiana; he used the English class as an introduction to ideas, and I suspect my feeling that literature was the vehicle, sensuous and imaginative, of ideas came from him. After three terms with him I had learned once and for all that books, even old ones, were distillations of life, and began to think less of literature with a capital L. As I look back on it now, I am quite sure that Mr. Stair found Burke's Speech on Conciliation and *Macbeth* the springboards for various ideas that had a rather tenuous connexion with them. "English" became at his hands an introduction to philosophy, manners, contemporary political ideas, journalism, and love. These ideas were not always directly germane to the text; but they were ideas, and though their accent and their origin were Middle-Western—Middle-Western *révolté*—they were an introduction to the great world and to the realm of mind.

[6] The fourth teacher I recall in high school is one who, if he still lives, may possibly remember me. If he does, he recalls me as the worst student of mathematics he ever had. Rumor circulated in the school that Mr. Powell, an urbane, sad man who looked like a banker, was a very wealthy man who taught simply to occupy his time. I never believed it; no one would, I thought, teach solid geometry for amusement. If I were rich, I kept on thinking during the class, I should buy a yacht; I should go around the world. I should, if I must teach, teach English. Mr. Powell noticed my mind wandering; he also noticed when I came up to the blackboard for a demonstration that mathematics was not my *forte*. He called me to him once at the end of the hour. "You do not seem stupid," he said, "but mathematics seems a lot of hocus pocus to you." For the most part, it still does; and I regret it very much. For I am told on good authority that in the logistic symbols of the newer mathematics lies hid the secret of the universe. I recall also that Plato said a gift for mathematics was essential to a philosopher. But it is too late to do anything about it now; it was too late then. And when it came to trigonometry, I, too, was "alone on a wide, wide sea," and Mr. Powell I always remember as the only teacher of mathematics ever to take pity on my soul in agony.

[7] When one speaks of one's old teachers, it is generally to one's college teachers that one refers. For it is then, if one is lucky, that one comes in contact with men who communicate and articulate the things and ideas which become the seeds of one's later intellectual and imaginative life. Every college has five or six men who in essence are its educational system. I was very lucky. For during my undergraduate days at Columbia,

there was a galaxy of teachers available to the student who in their respective ways and as a group would be hard to duplicate at any college
in any period. As a freshman straight from high school, I heard Charles A.
Beard lecture on American Government; as a sophomore—and in 1914—
I heard Carlton Hayes lecture on European History; as a junior I heard
John Erskine talk on Shakespeare, and was in a small class where he
taught us, really taught us, writing; and in my senior year I had the unique
and irrecoverable experience of traversing the history of philosophy with
Frederick J. E. Woodbridge. It was not until my graduate study that I
came to know John Dewey.

[8] Charles A. Beard illustrates something very remarkable about the
art of teaching. Today everybody, even the literary youngsters, are interested in government. For even literature seems less in the Ivory Tower
than it did in 1913. But the study of government, then officially known
at Columbia as "Politics," did not, to most of us addicted to poetry and
music, seem to be our meat, and there was nothing in the dark blue tome,
Beard's *American Government and Politics,* that seemed arresting. There
were endless details about the mechanisms and structure of State and
Federal government. It was not the Beard of the *Economic Interpretation
of the Constitution.*

[9] But his lectures were another matter. The lanky figure leaning
against the wall, drawling wittily with half-closed eyes, made the questions of government seem the most vital that anyone could broach, and
touched matters that lay far deeper than the mere forms of constitutional
government.

[10] Every good teacher has his own special art; with some, it is a
genius for a clarity that sometimes is more lucid than the complexities of
the subject justify. Sometimes it is a talent for apophthegm or leading
suggestion, a word that evokes a vista or an idea that opens a world.
I cannot now quite remember what Professor Beard's special technique
was. He was clear, he was suggestive, he was witty. But none of these
things could quite account for the hold he had on the smug and the rebels
alike, on both the pre-lawyers and pre-poets. I suspect it was a certain
combination of poetry, philosophy, and honesty in the man himself, a
sense he communicated that politics mattered far beyond the realm commonly called political, and an insight he conveyed into the life that forms
of government furthered or betrayed. One morning he came into class as
usual, stood against the wall, and, half-closing his eyes, said:

[11] "Gentlemen, today we are to discuss the budget system in State
government. I am sure that must seem to you a dull subject. But if you
will tell me, gentlemen, how much *per capita* a nation spends on its Army,
on its Navy, on education, on public works, I shall be able to tell you,
I think, as much about that nation as if you gave me the works of its
poets and philosophers."

[¹²] We listened with revised and revived attention to an exposition, full of figures and detail, of the State budget system. Charles A. Beard showed us what politics had to do with the life beyond it and which it made possible. And he taught us, too, the difference between the forms of government and the living substance of its operations. Under his easy, drawling manner, we sensed a passionate concern for an understanding of the realities of government, the economic forces and the interested persons involved in it, and the ideal of government: the liberation of the energies of men. Nobody who has ever listened to Beard can disdain the study of politics in favour of the study of "higher things." He has been too well taught, as tragic world events have since shown, how government may nourish or destroy "higher things."

[¹³] Up to the autumn of 1914 Europe seemed to most American college students a solar system away. In the autumn of 1914, when the war had been going on two months, Europe came for the first time in the imagination of many Americans to be vivid and near. European history ceased to be the anthropology and the archaeology of distant peoples who spoke remote languages. It became as alive as yesterday's events: it was what explained today's news. It was, therefore, no wonder that at the beginning of the college year Carlton Hayes's course in "Europe since 1815" had become the most popular course in Columbia College. But it was not only the war that accounted for that. Carlton Hayes had for some time been one of the most popular professors in the college. His lectures were the most famous dramatic spectacle on the campus. Nor was it as a performance alone that they were famous. Everyone had heard that Hayes could actually make clear French political parties; I have never met anybody since who could or can.

[¹⁴] The complicated history of Germany in the second half of the nineteenth century took shape as well as drama under his presentation of it. And in the midst of being taught and taught clearly, one had the incidental and additional pleasure of hearing a man to whom the great catastrophe of war had its roots in a past he knew, in the traditions of nations among whom he had lived familiarly, and in the desperate mythologies of nationalism, to which he had given special study and concern. One was treated, besides, to unforgettable vignettes of Disraeli dropping his morning walking stick as the cannons boomed noon at Gibraltar; of the Manchester school of economists, the "spiritual advisers" to the robber barons of early nineteenth-century England; of the black walnut furniture of the Victorian period; of the times and the manners of Louis Napoleon; of the studies that produced the *Communist Manifesto*. One was shaken out of the smugness of the middle-class world in which most students were brought up and out of the provincial Americanism in which most of us had lived.

[¹⁵] It did not matter, it served only as spice, that some of the barbs delivered in a dry voice by this baldish, sharp-featured man in his thirties were directed at us, at our very smugness, at our laziness, or at our fathers: when he was explaining the attitude of the manufacturers of the early Industrial Revolution, he reminded us that we all knew manu-facturers; "some of your fathers," he drawled, "are manufacturers." It did matter a little to some of us that he mocked poetry and philosophy (this *in re* Shelley and Godwin) . . . "philosophy is what is taught in Philosophy Hall . . ." But it did not matter much. For during a whole year, we sat through a whole century of European history, and Bismarck, Garibaldi, Social Legislation in England, Benevolent Tories like Shaftesbury and reformers like Cobden and Bright, "nationalism"—what devastating force Carlton Hayes put and can still put into the word—democracy, the Third Republic, became familiar parts of our imagination. In the midst of cries of "pro-German" and "pro-Ally," "preparedness" and "pacifism," during the three years before America went into the war, we knew somewhat better than many of our older compatriots what had brought the tornado about. Carlton Hayes had brought European history, as Charles Beard had brought American government, from the abstraction of a textbook to an experience lived and a problem to be faced. And it always surprised some of us that, in the midst of the lectures—first-rate theatrical perform-ances, words shot out for emphasis, silences sustained for a moment, gestures and movements deployed like those of a good actor—when we looked down at our notes, they were as ordered and clear as if we had listened to a scholastic metronome . . . I confess with shame that I achieved only a B.

[16] You were allowed, if you had a fairly good academic record, to take in the senior year a graduate course that was at the time one of the famous academic enterprises of the period. It was James Harvey Robin-son's course in the History of the Intellectual Classes in Western Europe. Everyone who had gone to high school knew the two volumes of Robin-son and Beard's *Development of Modern Europe.* But the Robinson we came to know as a legend and a rumour by the time we were sophomores was the Robinson who had invented the "new history"—the history of causes and consequences, the history that treated politics as the surface of more fundamental matters, economic and social and cultural, and that regarded the date of the invention of the steam engine as more important than the dates of a king, and the industrial use of steam as more signifi-cant than monarchies and dynasties. We had also heard of Robinson, along with Dewey and Beard, as among the intellectual-liberal forces that were making our university famous in some quarters, notorious in others. And, finally, we had heard of the remarkable brilliance of the lectures in History 72.

[17] The latter was a graduate course to which undergraduates, a hand-

ful of us, were admitted on sufferance. The majority of the class of over two hundred were graduate students of history, many of them women high school teachers from all over the country, particularly the West and South. Professor Robinson was a short man, with thin, greying hair and a deprecating, half-tired, half-amused, drawling voice. He seemed to be having a half-weary good time examining the origins of human stupidity, and those vestigial remains of our culture that blocked the free and hopeful functioning of human intelligence. It took us a few weeks in the course to get to the beginnings of *intellectual* history. For Robinson, with saturnine delight, liked to show us the mind of the child, the slave, and the animal still functioning in us. Once he brought in a leading editorial from the New York *Times* to illustrate the theme, and another time quoted from a batch of Sunday sermons reported in that journal the next day. The course was not a course in intellectual heroes, but a course in the changing fashions of adult follies taken seriously in various ages. It only gradually became clear what intellectual heroes were presiding over the whole story as he gave it. They were Freud and Marx and Dewey and the anthropologists, and H. G. Wells, the prophet, then, of intelligence reshaping the world. There were only two or three gods of the past left unbesmirched, or whose clay feet were not recognized. They were Lucretius, who saw the diabolism of religion; Francis Bacon, who saw the human possibilities of science; Voltaire, who exhibited the foolishness of superstition. Plato was a man who believed in Truth, Goodness, the Beauty because he saw the actual world as a chaos which, Robinson loved to remind us, he compared to "a man with a running nose. . . ." Aristotle's science was childish (Robinson did not know how soon again it was to be fashionable and how more fundamental than fashion it is): St. Augustine was a most amusingly and scandalously human saint. It was not until the enlightenment of the eighteenth century that anybody, so most of us gathered from the course, was very enlightened.

[18] Many of the graduate students were shocked, especially by the treatment of religion. The undergraduates from Columbia College had heard much of this before and had no faith (as did some of the graduate students) to have taken away. One of the young women complained to Professor Robinson: "You are taking away my faith." He looked at her oddly. "But if I took away a headache," he said simply, "you would not complain."

[19] We undergraduates enjoyed the sallies, the freshness, the irreverence, and enjoyed, too, the fundamental feeling that lay at the basis of it all—that man, if he took his own intelligence into his hands—could make the world less a shambles and an idiocy than it had so often been. It was in the great days of the liberal faith when trust in intelligence was in the ascendant. If Robinson made the world appear a satire to intelligent observation, he made it seem a lyric hope to generosity and

understanding. Dixon Ryan Fox, now President of Union College, was the young instructor who took the third quiz hour with the undergraduates. He felt it his special obligation to let us see the other side. And after a week, when he knew Robinson had been "exposing" modern Protestantism, he called in the chaplain as a counterweight. He need not have bothered; we had our own grains of salt. One of the reasons we had grains of salt was that some of us had been studying with a man who will go down, I am quite certain, as one of the great philosophical teachers of our generation. His slender published writings will live, but they will live for a small circle of students. But Frederick J. E. Woodbridge had educated a whole generation of students in philosophy; and a whole circle of them scattered over the country, including Morris Cohen and Sidney Hook and J. H. Randall, Jr., and Herbert Schneider (to mention only a few), are living testimonies to his influence and his power. In my college days, the great thing was to have taken his course in the History of Philosophy. Some of us were taking it at the same time that we took Robinson's History of the Intellectual Classes in Western Europe. It was rather a different story we were told. It was not a story, but a succession of experiences of philosophers whose importance lay "not in their truth but in their power." It was a shock that turned into a liberation for those of us who had come to philosophy looking for *the* Truth with a dogmatic capital letter. There were other shocks, too. Much that was said in the textbooks we never heard in class, or we heard the contrary. Professor Woodbridge, who looked like a bishop and would have made a very eloquent one, talked like a poet whose theme happened to be the human mind. He talked most like a poet on the days when he was most interested; one remembers what days those were: the early Greeks, Plato, Aristotle, Marcus Aurelius, Lucretius, Spinoza with his sovereign detachment, and Locke with his sovereign common sense. He was not an unprejudiced observer and we rather liked the frankness and the brevity with which he dismissed the Germans and Rousseau. But what one was most moved by was the things by which he himself was most moved: the Plato who was the son of Apollo, the poet and the dramatist of ideas; Marcus Aurelius, the disillusioned statesman whistling to keep up his comical courage; Lucretius looking out with dramatic sympathy and equable understanding on the eternal nature of things. We were impressed by a mind whose maturity had not dulled its enthusiasms, and an understanding uncorrupted by the technical controversies of the academy, by the routine of the classroom, by the burden of administration of an elder statesman, for Woodbridge was graduate Dean of the University. He taught a whole generation of students of philosophy to keep their eye on the object, to see a thinker in his own terms, to cease to raise foolish and irrelevant questions, and above all, to raise the central and relevant ones about a man's teaching. On Aristotle's metaphysics, he began by reminding us that Aristotle was asking the simple and the ultimate question: "What does it mean to be? . . ." We found ourselves astonished to be reminded that the Middle Ages were in their own time not the Middle Ages at all. We were made aware of Locke's simple English attempt to be sensible, tolerant, and direct, and learned to understand what Spinoza meant and why he saw it as a liberation to see all things under the form of eternity. For in that wonderful class, as Will Durant (sitting next to me in alphabetical order) remarked, we were listening not to a professor of philosophy but to philosophy itself. It was impossible to feel you were listening to a doctrine; Professor Woodbridge has never founded a school. You were hearing philosophy itself and came to understand it as an attempt to speak in the categories of mind of the categories of things.

[20] I did not—I think not many of us did—understand it all. But we began to understand what understanding meant, in words that had eloquence without rhetoric. We heard great things nobly uttered. We learnt no doctrine but we grasped the significance of intellectual procedure; and to a whole generation of philosophers, though Professor Woodbridge has long since ceased to be their teacher, he remains their teacher still. He made us understand as none else had done, to use one of his own phrases, "the enterprise of learning."

[21] A figure more widely known outside purely academic circles was and is John Dewey. In 1915 his name was already, if not a household, certainly a schoolroom word. His *How We Think* was used in all the normal schools of the country, and even fashionable ladies dipped into his far from easy books. I had read almost all of Dewey I could get hold of by the time I was a senior, but it was not until my first year as a graduate student that I heard, or, I believe, saw him. His familiar figure and speech, seeming at first that of a Vermont farmer, the casual gait, the keen but often absent eyes, seem so familiar now that I can scarcely believe I did not know them before.

[22] I admit the first lecture was quite a shock, a shock of dullness and confusion, if that can be said. It was at any rate a disappointment. I had not found Dewey's prose easy, but I had learned that its difficulty lay for the most part in its intellectual honesty, which led him to qualify an idea in one sentence half a page long. In part also it lay in the fact that this profoundly original philosopher was struggling to find a vocabulary to say what had never been said in philosophy before, to find a diction that would express with exactness the reality of change and novelty, philosophical words having been used for centuries to express the absolute and the fixed. Once one had got used to the long sentences, with their strings of qualifying clauses, to the sobriety, to the lack of image and of colour, one sensed the liberating force of this philosophy. Here was was not an answer but a quest for light in the living movement of

human experience; in the very precariousness of experience there lay open to the perplexed human creature the possibilities that peril itself provocatively suggested. I had found here, as have so many of my generation, a philosophy that, instead of laying down a diagram of an ideal universe that had nothing to do with the one of actual human doings and sufferings, opened a vision of conscious control of life, of a democracy operating through creative intelligence in the liberation of human capacities and natural goods. In *How We Think* I had learned that thinking itself was simply a discipline of the animal habit of trial and error, and of the possible human habit of imagination and foresight. In *Democracy and Education* I had gathered that it was not in the forms of democratic government that true democracy lay, but in the substance of intelligent co-operation, largely dependent on education. Dewey was not easy, but once one had mastered his syntax, a vision of a liberal and liberated commonwealth was one's reward, and a philosophy that was not only a vision but a challenge.

[23] I was naturally prepared, therefore, to expect something of intellectual excitement from the lectures in "Psychological Ethics." Intellectual excitement was the last term to describe what I experienced that September afternoon. The course came, in the first place, directly after lunch. It was well attended; there were even some fashionably dressed society ladies, for Dewey had become a vogue. But this famous philosopher who had written so much on "Interest in Education" as the essence of the educational process could not, save by a radical distortion of the term, be said at first hearing to sound interesting. He had none of the usual tricks or gifts of the effective lecturer. He sat at his desk, fumbling with a few crumpled yellow sheets and looking abstractedly out the window. He spoke very slowly in a Vermont drawl. He looked both very kindly and very abstracted. He hardly seemed aware of the presence of a class. He took little pains to underline a phrase, or emphasize a point, or, so at first it seemed to me, to make any. Occasionally he would apparently realize that people in the back of the room might not hear his quiet voice: he would then accent the next word, as likely as not a preposition or a conjunction. He seemed to be saying whatever came into his head next, and at one o'clock on an autumn afternoon to at least one undergraduate what came next did not always have or seem to have a very clear connexion with what had just gone before. The end of the hour finally came and he simply stopped; it seemed to me he might have stopped anywhere. But I soon found that it was my mind that had wandered, not John Dewey's. I began very soon to do what I had seldom done in college courses—to take notes. It was then a remarkable discovery to make on looking over my notes to find that what had seemed so casual, so rambling, so unexciting, was of an extraordinary coherence, texture, and brilliance. I had been listening to a man actually *thinking*

in the presence of a class. As one became accustomed to Dewey's technique, it was this last aspect of his teaching that was most impressive— and educative. To attend a lecture of John Dewey was to participate in the actual business of thought. Those pauses were delays in creative thinking, when the next step was really being considered, and for the glib dramatics of the teacher-actor was substituted the enterprise, careful and candid, of the genuine thinker. Those hours came to seem the most arresting educational experiences, almost, I have ever had. One had to be scrupulously attentive and one learned to be so. Not every day or in every teacher does one overhear the palpable processes of thought. One came to enjoy and appreciate the homely metaphor, "the fork in the road," the child and his first attempts to speak, the New England town meeting, instead of the classical images one had been accustomed to from more obviously eloquent lips. Moreover, if one listened attentively one discovered apophthegm and epigram delivered as casually and sleepily as if they were clichés. I remember one instance. It had been rather a long lecture designed to show that the crucial tests of the morals of a group came in what that group regarded as violations of its conventions. The bell rang. Professor Dewey began to crumple up his notes. "And so," he said, " I think sometimes one can tell more about the morals of our society from the inmates of its jails than from the inmates of its universities." The student next to me who had been semi-dozing stirred in half-alarmed surprise.

[24] I learned later in a seminar to see Dewey's greatest gift as a teacher, that of initiating inquiry rather than that of disseminating a doctrine. The subject matter of the seminar was innocent enough and removed from the immediacies of current controversy. It was a year's course, meeting every Tuesday afternoon, on "The Logic of John Stuart Mill." The seminar remains in my memory, it must be added, not simply for John Dewey or John Stuart Mill. It consisted, looking back on it and indeed as it appeared then, of a very remarkable group. It included two now well-known professors of philosophy, Brand Blanshard of Swarthmore College and Sterling Lamprecht of Amherst, Paul Blanshard, later to become Commissioner of Accounts under Mayor LaGuardia, and Albert C. Barnes, the inventor and manufacturer of Argyrol and collector of French paintings, even then a grey-haired man who used to come up from Philadelphia every week with his secretary expressly to study philosophy with his friend John Dewey.

[25] I do not suppose Professor Dewey said more than five percent of the words actually uttered in that seminar. For the latter consisted largely of papers presented by various members of the group. But one remembered what he said. The subject matter was obviously close to him, for had not Mill been one of the great nineteenth century leaders of the empirical school of thought; had he not been, in his way, a prag-

matist and, like Dewey himself, a liberal? But one noticed particularly
Dewey's gift for pointing to the exact difficulty or the exact limitations
of a man or a paper; his capacity for sympathetically seeing what a
student was driving at, even when he did not quite succeed in saying it,
and Dewey's candid expression of his own position or his own prejudices.

[26] One instance of Dewey's frankness comes to my mind. There was
among the group a young lady who had come from England where she
had studied philosophy with Bertrand Russell at Cambridge. She listened
patiently for weeks to Dewey's varied insistence that the truth of an idea
was tested by its use. One day she burst out toward the close of the
seminar in the sharp, clipped speech of the educated Englishwoman:
"But, professor, I have been taught to believe that true means true; that
false means false, that good means good and bad means bad; I don't
understand all this talk about more or less true, more or less good. Could
you explain more exactly?"

[27] Professor Dewey looked at her mildly for a moment and said:
"Let me tell you a parable. Once upon a time in Philadelphia there was a
paranoiac. He thought he was dead. Nobody could convince him he was
alive. Finally, one of the doctors thought of an ingenious idea. He pricked
the patient's finger. 'Now,' he said, 'are you dead?' 'Sure,' said the
paranoiac, 'that proves that dead men bleed. . . .' Now I'll say true or
false if you want me to, but I'll mean better or worse."

[28] There are all kinds of talents that go to make up a great teacher.
Among those not commonly noted in the textbooks are simplicity and
candour. These qualities in Dewey even an undergraduate could recognize and understand.

[29] I cannot say that John Erskine seemed to me a great man in the
sense that Woodbridge and Dewey did and do, nor did *The Private Life
of Helen of Troy*, for all its bright entertainment, lead me to think I had
been obtuse on this point as an undergraduate. But I am convinced he
was a very remarkable teacher and it has always seemed to me a pity
that he gave up the profession of distinguished teaching for that of the
popular novelist. Erskine's quality as a teacher was that of communication by contagion; you felt the quality of the authors he talked about
and books seemed to have something to do with life rather than libraries.

[30] Literature was an exercise in imagination, not in archaeology, and
there must be thousands of students besides myself who learned to read
authors in their own terms, to enjoy them for their own sakes, from John
Erskine's famous course in Elizabethan Literature. It is true that one
enjoyed Professor Erskine for other reasons. He had wit—often malicious
—in his own right, and, when he was in the vein, poetry and philosophy,
too. He obviously loved poetry and it seemed to him both to matter and
a matter of course that we should love it, too. One felt about him some-

thing of the prima donna lecturer; it was evidenced by the pointed silence that would occur while some unfortunate late-comer found his way to his seat. It was clear, too, from the way in which, not infrequently, Shakespeare or Marlowe or Castiglione would be the springboards for little bravura lectures by our teacher on the importance of love or of being a cultivated gentleman, the latter one of his favourite themes. But if he was sometimes the prima donna, he always respected the materials he taught, and for many years no one at Columbia was a more devoted servant to the art and to the love of literature than he. And not the least of his services to that art were, first, the noble and musical way in which he read poetry itself; and secondly, the pains he took to encourage signs of that art among undergraduates. Other teachers might make literature seem a set of documents to be investigated; no one quite knew why. Erskine made it an art to be lived and loved.

[31] It is occasionally said that a good student needs no teachers and that all that he does need is a library and leisure. Neither the poor nor the good student needs bad teachers or bored ones; he is better off without them. But he is very fortunate indeed if he can look back on his college days and enumerate half a dozen men who, by their passion for ideas, their clarity about them, their love for the communication of them, their exemplification in their own being of intellectual discipline and candour, have given a meaning to facts that, even with leisure and libraries, he would not have been as likely to find by himself.

[32] I feel my college generation at Columbia was very fortunate. Half a dozen good teachers in a college are enough to make it distinguished. We had more than half a dozen very exceptional ones. But then I think current undergraduates at Columbia, if they are discerning, will, looking back, be able to say the same.

--◄{ COMMENT AND QUESTIONS }►--

The writing in "Former Teachers" is a product of wide knowledge, sharp observation, deep and lively interest in people and ideas, and careful attention to style. Such writing is not easy to imitate, but one can, by examining it closely, learn much that is applicable to his own writing.

1. The first section of the essay (paragraphs 1–6) may appear to end anti-climactically with the teacher who was unable to teach Edman mathematics; paragraph 6, however, makes an important contribution to tone. Where else in the essay do you find evidence of the author's modesty about his achievements and of his lack of complacency about what he does not

understand? What besides the tone makes paragraph 6 a good section ending?

2. Paragraph 7 lists, in the order in which Edman took their courses, five of his teachers: Charles A. Beard, Carlton Hayes, John Erskine, Frederick J. E. Woodbridge, and John Dewey. This essay is clearly and skillfully organized, but the author departs from strict chronology and discusses his teachers in this order: Beard, Hayes, James Harvey Robinson, Woodbridge, Dewey, and Erskine. What seem to be the reasons for Edman's organization? Why do you think he ends with John Erskine who, he says, did not seem to him a great man in the sense that Woodbridge and Dewey did?

3. Re-read paragraphs 9–12 to see Edman's techniques of vitalizing people by describing them and showing them in action as well as by telling the reader about their teaching. Where else in the essay does the author use these and other techniques with particular success?

4. Edman shows a special admiration for Frederick J. E. Woodbridge. Examine the sequence of three sentences (near the middle of paragraph 19) beginning *But what one was most moved by,* and examine the whole of paragraph 20. Does the author meaningfully communicate the reasons for his admiration? How do the style and sentence structure in these passages contribute to the meaning?

5. The treatment of John Dewey in paragraphs 21–23 produces a kind of suspense. What is the nature of this suspense, and how is it achieved?

6. Edman includes in his essay a considerable amount of detail about the content of his courses—names, works, and schools of thought not all of which may be familiar to all readers. What is the effect of this detail?

7. Do you think that Edman enjoyed his courses more than most college students do? If so, was it simply because he had such good teachers?

8. What appear to be the important qualities of Edman's best teachers? Of these qualities which one or ones do you value most in a teacher, and why?

9. In paragraph 31 Edman makes a carefully qualified judgment about students and teachers. To what extent do you agree with that judgment, and why?

[90]   *E. B. White*: Walden, 1939

THIS PERSONAL ESSAY, written after a visit to the woods and pond where Thoreau had lived nearly a hundred years before, is a tribute by one writer to another, and a commentary on modern society. For a note on E. B. White, see page 452.

Miss Nims, take a letter to Henry David Thoreau.

[1] Dear Henry: I thought of you the other afternoon as I was approaching Concord doing fifty on Route 62. That is a high speed at which to hold a philosopher in one's mind, but in this century we are a nimble bunch.

[2] On one of the lawns in the outskirts of the village a woman was cutting the grass with a motorized lawn mower. What made me think of you was that the machine had rather got away from her, although she was game enough, and in the brief glimpse I had of the scene it appeared to me that the lawn was mowing the lady. She kept a tight grip on the handles, which throbbed violently with every explosion of the one-cylinder motor, and as she sheered around bushes and lurched along at a reluctant trot behind her impetuous servant, she looked like a puppy who had grabbed something that was too much for him. Concord hasn't changed much, Henry; the farm implements and the animals still have the upper hand.

[3] I may as well admit that I was journeying to Concord with the deliberate intention of visiting your woods; for although I have never knelt at the grave of a philosopher nor placed wreaths on moldy poets, and have often gone a mile out of my way to avoid some place of historical interest, I have always wanted to see Walden Pond. The account which you left of your sojourn there is, you will be amused to learn, a document of increasing pertinence; each year it seems to gain a little headway, as the world loses ground. We may all be transcendental yet, whether we like it or not. As our common complexities increase, any tale of individual simplicity (and yours is the best written and the cockiest) acquires a new fascination; as our goods accumulate, but not our well-being, your report of an existence without material adornment takes on a certain awkward credibility.

[4] My purpose in going to Walden Pond, like yours, was not to live cheaply or to live dearly there, but to transact some private business with the fewest obstacles. Approaching Concord, doing forty, forty-five, doing fifty, the steering wheel held snug in my palms, the highway held grimly in my vision, the crown of the road now serving me (on the righthand curves), now defeating me (on the lefthand curves), I began to rouse myself from the stupefaction which a day's motor journey induces. It was a delicious evening, Henry, when the whole body is one sense, and imbibes delight through every pore, if I may coin a phrase. Fields were richly brown where the harrow, drawn by the stripped Ford, had lately sunk its teeth; pastures were green; and overhead the sky had that same everlasting great look which you will find on Page 144 of the Oxford pocket edition. I could feel the road entering me, through tire, wheel,

spring, and cushion; shall I not have intelligence with earth too? Am I not partly leaves and vegetable mold myself?—a man of infinite horse-power, yet partly leaves.

[5] Stay with me on 62 and it will take you into Concord. As I say, it was a delicious evening. The snake had come forth to die a bloody S on the highway, the wheel upon its head, its bowels flat now and exposed. The turtle had come up too to cross the road and die in the attempt, its hard shell smashed under the rubber blow, its intestinal yearning (for the other side of the road) forever squashed. There was a sign by the wayside which announced that the road had a "cotton surface." You wouldn't know what that is, but neither, for that matter, did I. There is a cryptic ingredient in many of our modern improvements—we are awed and pleased without knowing quite what we are enjoying. It is something to be traveling on a road with a cotton surface.

[6] The civilization round Concord to-day is an odd distillation of city, village, farm, and manor. The houses, yards, fields look not quite suburban, not quite rural. Under the bronze beech and the blue spruce of the departed baron grazes the milch goat of the heirs. Under the porte-cochère stands the reconditioned station wagon; under the grape arbor sit the puppies for sale. (But why do men degenerate ever? What makes families run out?)

[7] It was June and everywhere June was publishing her immemorial stanza; in the lilacs, in the syringa, in the freshly edged paths and the sweetness of moist beloved gardens, and the little wire wickets that preserve the tulips' front. Farmers were already moving the fruits of their toil into their yards, arranging the rhubarb, the asparagus, the strictly fresh eggs on the painted stands under the little shed roofs with the patent shingles. And though it was almost a hundred years since you had taken your ax and started cutting out your home on Walden Pond, I was interested to observe that the philosophical spirit was still alive in Massachusetts; in the center of a vacant lot some boys were assembling the framework of a rude shelter, their whole mind and skill concentrated in the rather inauspicious helter-skeleton of studs and rafters. They too were escaping from town, to live naturally, in a rich blend of savagery and philosophy.

[8] That evening, after supper at the inn, I strolled out into the twilight to dream my shapeless transcendental dreams and see that the car was locked up for the night (first open the right front door, then reach over, straining, and pull up the handles of the left rear and the left front till you hear the click, then the handle of the right rear, then shut the right front but open it again, remembering that the key is still in the ignition switch, remove the key, shut the right front again with a bang, push the tiny keyhole cover to one side, insert key, turn, and withdraw). It is what we all do, Henry. It is called locking the car. It is said to confuse thieves

and keep them from making off with the laprobe. Four doors to lock behind one robe. The driver himself never uses a laprobe, the free movement of his legs being vital to the operation of the vehicle; so that when he locks the car it is a pure and unselfish act. I have in my life gained very little essential heat from laprobes, yet I have ever been at pains to lock them up.

[9] The evening was full of sounds, some of which would have stirred your memory. The robins still love the elms of New England villages at sundown. There is enough of the thrush in them to make song inevitable at the end of day, and enough of the tramp to make them hang round the dwellings of men. A robin, like many another American, dearly loves a white house with green blinds. Concord is still full of them.

[10] Your fellow-townsmen were stirring abroad—not many afoot, most of them in their cars; and the sound which they made in Concord at evening was a rustling and a whispering. The sound lacks steadfastness and is wholly unlike that of a train. A train, as you know who lived so near the Fitchburg line, whistles once or twice sadly and is gone, trailing a memory in smoke, soothing to ear and mind. Automobiles, skirting a village green, are like flies that have gained the inner ear—they buzz, cease, pause, start, shift, stop, halt, brake, and the whole effect is a nervous polytone curiously disturbing.

[11] As I wandered along, the toc toc of ping pong balls drifted from an attic window. In front of the Reuben Brown house a Buick was drawn up. At the wheel, motionless, his hat upon his head, a man sat, listening to Amos and Andy on the radio (it is a drama of many scenes and without an end). The deep voice of Andrew Brown, emerging from the car, although it originated more than two hundred miles away, was unstrained by distance. When you used to sit on the shore of your pond on Sunday morning, listening to the church bells of Acton and Concord, you were aware of the excellent filter of the intervening atmosphere. Science has attended to that, and sound now maintains its intensity without regard for distance. Properly sponsored, it goes on forever.

[12] A fire engine, out for a trial spin, roared past Emerson's house, hot with readiness for public duty. Over the barn roofs the martins dipped and chittered. A swarthy daughter of an asparagus grower, in culottes, shirt, and bandanna, pedaled past on her bicycle. It was indeed a delicious evening, and I returned to the inn (I believe it was your house once) to rock with the old ladies on the concrete veranda.

[13] Next morning early I started afoot for Walden, out Main Street and down Thoreau, past the depot and the Minuteman Chevrolet Company. The morning was fresh, and in a bean field along the way I flushed an agriculturist, quietly studying his beans. Thoreau Street soon joined Number 126, an artery of the State. We number our highways nowadays, our speed being so great we can remember little of their quality or

character and are lucky to remember their number. (Men have an in-distinct notion that if they keep up this activity long enough all will at length ride somewhere, in next to no time.) Your pond is on 126.

[14] I knew I must be nearing your woodland retreat when the Golden Pheasant lunchroom came into view—Sealtest ice cream, toasted sand-wiches, hot frankfurters, waffles, tonics, and lunches. Were I the pro-prietor, I should add rice, Indian meal, and molasses—just for old time's sake. The Pheasant, incidentally, is for sale: a chance for some nature lover who wishes to set himself up beside a pond in the Concord atmos-phere and live deliberately, fronting only the essential facts of life on Number 126. Beyond the Pheasant was a place called Walden Breezes, an oasis whose porch pillars were made of old green shutters sawed into lengths. On the porch was a distorting mirror, to give the traveler a comical image of himself, who had miraculously learned to gaze in an ordinary glass without smiling. Behind the Breezes, in a sun-parched clearing, dwelt your philosophical descendants in their trailers, each trailer the size of your hut, but all grouped together for the sake of congeniality. Trailer people leave the city, as you did, to discover solitude and in any weather, at any hour of the day or night, to improve the nick of time; but they soon collect in villages and get bogged deeper in the mud than ever. The camp behind Walden Breezes was just rousing itself to the morning. The ground was packed hard under the heel, and the sun came through the clearing to bake the soil and enlarge the wry smell of cramped housekeeping. Cushman's bakery truck had stopped to deliver an early basket of rolls. A camp dog, seeing me in the road, barked petu-lantly. A man emerged from one of the trailers and set forth with a bucket to draw water from some forest tap.

[15] Leaving the highway I turned off into the woods toward the pond, which was apparent through the foliage. The floor of the forest was strewn with dried old oak leaves and *Transcripts*. From beneath the flat-tened popcorn wrapper (*granum explosum*) peeped the frail violet. I followed a footpath and descended to the water's edge. The pond lay clear and blue in the morning light, as you have seen it so many times. In the shallows a man's waterlogged shirt undulated gently. A few flies came out to greet me and convoy me to your cove, past the No Bathing signs on which the fellows and the girls had scrawled their names. I felt strangely excited suddenly to be snooping around your premises, tiptoe-ing along watchfully, as though not to tread by mistake upon the inter-vening century. Before I got to the cove I heard something which seemed to me quite wonderful: I heard your frog, a full clear *troonk*, guiding me, still hoarse and solemn, bridging the years as the robins had bridged them in the sweetness of the village evening. But he soon quit, and I came on a couple of young boys throwing stones at him.

[16] Your front yard is marked by a bronze tablet set in a stone. Four

small granite posts, a few feet away, show where the house was. On top of the tablet was a pair of faded blue bathing trunks with a white stripe. Back of it is a pile of stones, a sort of cairn, left by your visitors as a tribute I suppose. It is a rather ugly little heap of stones, Henry. In fact the hillside itself seems faded, browbeaten; a few tall skinny pines, bare of lower limbs, a smattering of young maples in suitable green, some birches and oaks, and a number of trees felled by the last big wind. It was from the bole of one of these fallen pines, torn up by the roots, that I extracted the stone which I added to the cairn—a sentimental act in which I was interrupted by a small terrier from a nearby picnic group, who confronted me and wanted to know about the stone.

[17] I sat down for a while on one of the posts of your house to listen to the bluebottles and the dragonflies. The invaded glade sprawled shabby and mean at my feet, but the flies were tuned to the old vibration. There were the remains of a fire in your ruins, but I doubt that it was yours; also two beer bottles trodden into the soil and become part of earth. A young oak had taken root in your house, and two or three ferns, unrolling like the ticklers at a banquet. The only other furnishings were a DuBarry pattern sheet, a page torn from a picture magazine, and some crusts in wax paper.

[18] Before I quit I walked clear round the pond and found the place where you used to sit on the northeast side to get the sun in the fall, and the beach where you got sand for scrubbing your floor. On the eastern side of the pond, where the highway borders it, the State has built dressing rooms for swimmers, a float with diving towers, drinking fountains of porcelain, and rowboats for hire. The pond is in fact a State Preserve, and carries a twenty-dollar fine for picking wild flowers, a decree signed in all solemnity by your fellow-citizens Walter C. Wardwell, Erson B. Barlow, and Nathaniel I. Bowditch. There was a smell of creosote where they had been building a wide wooden stairway to the road and the parking area. Swimmers and boaters were arriving; bodies plunged vigorously into the water and emerged wet and beautiful in the bright air. As I left, a boatload of town boys were splashing about in mid-pond, kidding and fooling, the young fellows singing at the top of their lungs in a wild chorus:

> Amer-ica, Amer-i-ca, God shed his grace on thee,
> And crown thy good with brotherhood
> From sea to shi-ning sea!

[19] I walked back to town along the railroad, following your custom. The rails were expanding noisily in the hot sun, and on the slope of the roadbed the wild grape and the blackberry sent up their creepers to the track.

[20] The expense of my brief sojourn in Concord was:

Canvas shoes $1.95
Baseball bat ....   .25 } gifts to take back to a boy
Left-handed fielder's glove 1.25
Hotel and meals 4.25
In all $7.70

As you see, this amount was almost what you spent for food for eight months. I cannot defend the shoes or the expenditure for shelter and food: they reveal a meanness and grossness in my nature which you would find contemptible. The baseball equipment, however, is the kind of impediment with which you were never on even terms. You must remember that the house where you practiced the sort of economy which I respect was haunted only by mice and squirrels. You never had to cope with a shortstop.

⟁ COMMENT AND QUESTIONS ⟁

This essay will have more meaning if you have read the selection from Thoreau's *Walden* on page 259. To one familiar with the whole of *Walden*, E. B. White's essay is rich in allusions to and echoes of Thoreau's work. For example, the end of paragraph 4 echoes a passage in which Thoreau, writing about the beneficence of Nature and his sense of oneness with Nature, asks, "Shall I not have intelligence with the earth? Am I not partly leaves and vegetable mould myself?" And E. B. White's record of his expenses in paragraph 20 recalls Thoreau's meticulous records in *Walden*—in all, a cost of $28.12½ for building his house; a profit of $8.71½ from his beans, etc.

1. What does White gain, first by writing his essay as a letter, and second by suggesting that he is dictating the letter?

2. Why do you think the author has included each of the following: the woman and the lawn mower (paragraph 2); the death of the snake and the turtle (paragraph 5); the "cotton surface" of the road (paragraph 5); the business of locking the car (paragraph 8); the numbering of highways (paragraph 13); the trailer camp (paragraph 14)?

3. Comment on the style of sentence 2 in paragraph 4. What is the effect of the last sentence of that paragraph?

4. Examine the structure of the first sentence of paragraph 8. How does the structure help to communicate meaning? Comment on the structure and diction of the last sentence of paragraph 10.

5. This essay has a wealth of concrete detail, and White is very skillful in arranging the details. Notice that in paragraph 15, for example, he brings together contrasting items: oak leaves and *Transcripts* (copies of a Boston

newspaper), the popcorn wrapper and the violet. Point out other examples of juxtaposing incongruous details. What is the effect of this technique?

6. As the author leaves, the boys splashing in the pond are singing part of "America the Beautiful." Do you think that White included this detail simply because he was recording everything he saw and heard or that he had a special reason for including it?

7. Does White state explicitly his judgment of present-day civilization and progress? What particular passages or what parts of the essay seem to you best to convey his judgment?

8. How would you describe the tone of the essay? For example, is the author sad, cynical, bitter, good-humored, resigned, or nostalgic for a way of life no longer possible? Or is the tone complex?

9. When White speaks in the last paragraph of "the sort of economy which I respect," what might he mean besides economy with money?

[91] *Robert Louis Stevenson*: The Lantern-Bearers

THE FOLLOWING reflective essay is built on a personal experience which becomes the symbol of a larger idea. Robert Louis Stevenson (1850–1894), Scottish novelist, essayist, and poet, was one of the distinguished stylists of the late nineteenth century. He is probably best known today for his stories of fantasy and romantic adventure, among them *Treasure Island, Kidnapped, The Master of Ballantrae,* and *The Strange Case of Dr. Jekyll and Mr. Hyde.* "The Lantern-Bearers" was published in 1888.

– I –

[1] These boys congregated every autumn about a certain easterly fisher-village, where they tasted in a high degree the glory of existence. The place was created seemingly on purpose for the diversion of young gentlemen. A street or two of houses, mostly red and many of them tiled; a number of fine trees clustered about the manse and the kirkyard, and turning the chief street into a shady alley; many little gardens more than usually bright with flowers; nets a-drying, and fisher-wives scolding in the backward parts; a smell of fish, a genial smell of seaweed; whiffs of blowing sand at the streetcorners; shops with golf-balls and bottled lollipops; another shop with penny pickwicks (that remarkable cigar) and the *London Journal,* dear to me for its startling pictures, and a few novels, dear for their suggestive names: such, as well as memory serves

me, were the ingredients of the town. These, you are to conceive posted on a spit between two sandy bays, and sparsely flanked with villas— enough for the boys to lodge in with their subsidiary parents, not enough (not yet enough) to cocknify the scene: a haven in the rocks in front: in front of that, a file of gray islets: to the left, endless links and sand-wreaths, a wilderness of hiding-holes, alive with popping rabbits and soaring gulls: to the right, a range of seaward crags, one rugged brow beyond another; the ruins of a mighty and ancient fortress on the brink of one; coves between—now charmed into sunshine quiet, now whistling with wind and clamorous and bursting surges; the dens and sheltered hollows redolent of thyme and southernwood, the air at the cliff's edge brisk and clean and pungent of the sea—in front of all, the Bass Rock, tilted seaward like a doubtful bather, and surf ringing it with white, the solan-geese hanging round its summit like a great and glittering smoke. This choice piece of seaboard was sacred, besides, to the wrecker; and the Bass, in the eye of fancy, still flew the colors of King James; and in the ear of fancy the arches of Tantallon still rang with horseshoe iron, and echoed to the commands of Bell-the-Cat.

[2] There was nothing to mar your days, if you were a boy summering in that part, but the embarrassment of pleasure. You might golf if you wanted; but I seem to have been better employed. You might secrete yourself in the Lady's Walk, a certain sunless dingle of elders, all mossed over by the damp as green as grass, and dotted here and there by the stream-side with roofless walls, the cold homes of anchorites. To fit themselves for life, and with a special eye to acquire the art of smoking, it was even common for the boys to harbor there; and you might have seen a single penny pickwick, honestly shared in lengths with a blunt knife, bestrew the glen with the apprentices. Again, you might join our fishing-parties, where we sat perched as thick as solan-geese, a covey of little anglers, boy and girl, angling over each other's heads, to the much entanglement of lines and loss of podleys and consequent shrill recrimination—shrill as the geese themselves. Indeed, had that been all, you might have done this often; but though fishing be a fine pastime, the podley is scarce to be regarded as a dainty for the table; and it was a point of honor that a boy should eat all that he had taken. Or again, you might climb the Law, where the whale's jawbone stood landmark in the buzzing wind, and behold the face of many counties, and the smokes and spires of many towns, and the sails of distant ships. You might bathe, now in the flaws of fine weather, that we pathetically call our summer, now in a gale of wind, with the sand scourging your bare hide, your clothes thrashing abroad from underneath their guardian stone, the froth of the great breakers casting you headlong ere it had drowned your knees. Or you might explore the tidal rocks, above all in the ebb of springs, when the very roots of the hills were for the nonce

discovered; following my leader from one group to another, groping in slippery tangle for the wreck of ships, wading in pools after the abominable creatures of the sea, and ever with an eye cast backward on the march of the tide and the menaced line of your retreat. And then you might go Crusoeing, a word that covers all extempore eating in the open air; digging perhaps a house under the margin of the links, kindling a fire of the sea-ware, and cooking apples there—if they were truly apples, for I sometimes suppose the merchant must have played us off with some inferior and quite local fruit, capable of resolving, in the neighborhood of fire, into mere sand and smoke and iodine; or perhaps pushing to Tantallon, you might lunch on sandwiches and visions in the grassy court, while the wind hummed in the crumbling turrets; or clambering along the coast, eat geans[1] (the worst, I must suppose, in Christendom) from an adventurous gean-tree that had taken root under a cliff, where it was shaken with an ague of east wind, and silvered after gales with salt, and grew so foreign among its bleak surroundings that to eat of its produce was an adventure in itself.

[3] There are mingled some dismal memories with so many that were joyous. Of the fisher-wife, for instance, who had cut her throat at Canty Bay; and of how I ran with the other children to the top of the Quadrant, and beheld a posse of silent people escorting a cart, and on the cart, bound in a chair, her throat bandaged, and the bandage all bloody—horror!—the fisher-wife herself, who continued thenceforth to hag-ride my thoughts, and even to-day (as I recall the scene) darkens daylight. She was lodged in the little old jail in the chief street; but whether or no she died there, with a wise terror of the worst, I never inquired. She had been tippling; it was but a dingy tragedy; and it seems strange and hard that, after all these years, the poor crazy sinner should be still pilloried on her cart in the scrap-book of my memory. Nor shall I readily forget a certain house in the Quadrant where a visitor died, and a dark old woman continued to dwell alone with the dead body; nor how this old woman conceived a hatred to myself and one of my cousins, and in the dread hour of the dusk, as we were clambering on the garden-walls, opened a window in that house of mortality and cursed us in a shrill voice and with a marrowy choice of language. It was a pair of very colorless urchins that fled down the lane from this remarkable experience! But I recall with a more doubtful sentiment, compounded out of fear and exultation, the coil of equinoctial tempests; trumpeting squalls, scouring flaws of rain; the boats with their reefed lugsails scudding for the harbor mouth, where danger lay, for it was hard to make when the wind had any east in it; the wives clustered with blowing shawls at the pierhead, where (if fate was against them) they might see boat and husband

---

[1] Wild cherries.

and sons—their whole wealth and their whole family—engulfed under their eyes; and (what I saw but once) a troop of neighbors forcing such an unfortunate homeward, and she squalling and battling in their midst, a figure scarcely human, a tragic Maenad.

[4] These are things that I recall with interest; but what my memory dwells upon the most, I have been all this while withholding. It was a sport peculiar to the place, and indeed to a week or so of our two months' holiday there. Maybe it still flourishes in its native spot; for boys and their pastimes are swayed by periodic forces inscrutable to man; so that tops and marbles reappear in their due season, regular like the sun and moon; and the harmless art of knucklebones has seen the fall of the Roman empire and the rise of the United States. It may still flourish in its native spot, but nowhere else, I am persuaded; for I tried myself to introduce it on Tweedside, and was defeated lamentably; its charm being quite local, like a country wine that cannot be exported.

[5] The idle manner of it was this:—

[6] Toward the end of September, when school-time was drawing near and the nights were already black, we would begin to sally from our respective villas, each equipped with a tin bull's-eye lantern. The thing was so well known that it had worn a rut in the commerce of Great Britain; and the grocers, about the due time, began to garnish their windows with our particular brand of luminary. We wore them buckled to the waist upon a cricket belt, and over them, such was the rigor of the game, a buttoned topcoat. They smelled noisomely of blistered tin; they never burned aright, though they would always burn our fingers; their use was naught; the pleasure of them merely fanciful; and yet a boy with a bull's-eye under his top-coat asked for nothing more. The fishermen used lanterns about their boats, and it was from them, I suppose, that we had got the hint; but theirs were not bull's-eyes, nor did we ever play at being fishermen. The police carried them at their belts, and we had plainly copied them in that; yet we did not pretend to be policemen. Burglars, indeed, we may have had some haunting thoughts of; and we had certainly an eye to past ages when lanterns were more common, and to certain storybooks in which we had found them to figure very largely. But take it for all in all, the pleasure of the thing was substantive; and to be a boy with a bull's-eye under his top-coat was good enough for us.

[7] When two of these asses met, there would be an anxious "Have you got your lantern?" and a gratified "Yes!" That was the shibboleth, and very needful too; for, as it was the rule to keep our glory contained, none could recognize a lantern-bearer, unless (like the polecat) by the smell. Four or five would sometimes climb into the belly of a ten-man lugger, with nothing but the thwarts above them—for the cabin was usually locked, or choose out some hollow of the links where the wind might

whistle overhead. There the coats would be unbuttoned and the bull's-eye discovered, and in the checkering glimmer, under the huge windy hall of the night, and cheered by a rich steam of toasting tinware, these fortunate young gentlemen would crouch together in the cold sand of the links or on the scaly bilges of the fishing-boat, and delight themselves with inappropriate talk. Woe is me that I may not give some specimens —some of their foresights of life, or deep inquiries into the rudiments of man and nature, these were so fiery and so innocent, they were so richly silly, so romantically young. But the talk, at any rate, was but a condiment; and these gatherings themselves only accidents in the career of the lantern-bearer. The essence of this bliss was to walk by yourself in the black night; the slide shut, the top-coat buttoned; not a ray escaping, whether to conduct your footsteps or to make your glory public: a mere pillar of darkness in the dark; and all the while, deep down in the privacy of your fool's heart, to know you had a bull's-eye at your belt, and to exult and sing over the knowledge.

– II –

[8] It is said that a poet has died young in the breast of the most stolid. It may be contended, rather, that this (somewhat minor) bard in almost every case survives, and is the spice of life to his possessor. Justice is not done to the versatility and the unplumbed childishness of man's imagination. His life from without may seem but a rude mound of mud; there will be some golden chamber at the heart of it, in which he dwells delighted; and for as dark as his pathway seems to the observer, he will have some kind of bull's-eye at his belt.

[9] It would be hard to pick out a career more cheerless than that of Dancer, the miser, as he figures in the "Old Bailey Reports," a prey to the most sordid persecutions, the butt of his neighborhood; betrayed by his hired man, his house beleaguered by the impish schoolboy, and he himself grinding and fuming and impotently fleeing to the law against these pin-pricks. You marvel at first that any one should willingly prolong a life so destitute of charm and dignity; and then you call to memory that had he chosen, had he ceased to be a miser, he could have been freed at once from these trials, and might have built himself a castle and gone escorted by a squadron. For the love of more recondite joys, which we cannot estimate, which, it may be, we should envy, the man had willingly foregone both comfort and consideration. "His mind to him a kingdom was"; and sure enough, digging into that mind, which seems at first a dust-heap, we unearth some priceless jewels. For Dancer must have had the love of power and the disdain of using it, a noble character in itself; disdain of many pleasures, a chief part of what is commonly called wisdom; disdain of the inevitable end, that finest trait of mankind; scorn of men's opinions, another element of virtue; and at the back of

all, a conscience just like yours and mine, whining like a cur, swindling like a thimble-rigger, but still pointing (there or thereabout) to some conventional standard. Here was a cabinet portrait to which Hawthorne perhaps had done justice; and yet not Hawthorne either, for he was mildly minded, and it lay not in him to create for us that throb of the miser's pulse, his fretful energy of gusto, his vast arms of ambition clutching in he knows not what: insatiable, insane, a god with a muck-rake. Thus, at least, looking in the bosom of the miser, consideration detects the poet in the full tide of life, with more, indeed, of the poetic fire than usually goes to epics; and tracing that mean man about his cold hearth, and to and fro in his discomfortable house, spies within him a blazing bonfire of delight. And so with others, who do not live by bread alone, but by some cherished and perhaps fantastic pleasure; who are meat salesmen to the external eye, and possibly to themselves are Shakespeares, Napoleons, or Beethovens; who have not one virtue to rub against another in the field of active life, and yet perhaps, in the life of contemplation, sit with the saints. We see them on the street, and we can count their buttons; but Heaven knows in what they pride themselves! Heaven knows where they have set their treasure!

[10] There is one fable that touches very near the quick of life: the fable of the monk who passed into the woods, heard a bird break into song, hearkened for a trill or two, and found himself on his return a stranger at his convent gates; for he had been absent fifty years, and of all his comrades there survived but one to recognize him. It is not only in the woods that this enchanter carols, though perhaps he is native there. He sings in the most doleful places. The miser hears him and chuckles, and the days are moments. With no more apparatus than an ill-smelling lantern I have evoked him on the naked links. All life that is not merely mechanical is spun out of two strands: seeking for that bird and hearing him. And it is just this that makes life so hard to value, and the delight of each so incommunicable. And just a knowledge of this, and a remembrance of those fortunate hours in which the bird has sung to us, that fills us with such wonder when we turn the pages of the realist. There, to be sure, we find a picture of life in so far as it consists of mud and of old iron, cheap desires and cheap fears, that which we are ashamed to remember and that which we are careless whether we forget; but of the note of that time-devouring nightingale we hear no news.

[11] The case of these writers of romance is most obscure. They have been boys and youths; they have lingered outside the window of the beloved, who was then most probably writing to some one else; they have sat before a sheet of paper, and felt themselves mere continents of congested poetry, not one line of which would flow; they have walked alone in the woods, they have walked in cities under the countless lamps; they have been to sea, they have hated, they have feared, they have longed

to knife a man and maybe done it; the wild taste of life has stung their palate. Or, if you deny them all the rest, one pleasure at least they have tasted to the full—their books are there to prove it—the keen pleasure of successful literary composition. And yet they fill the globe with volumes, whose cleverness inspires me with despairing admiration, and whose consistent falsity to all I care to call existence, with despairing wrath. If I had no better hope than to continue to revolve among the dreary and petty businesses, and to be moved by the paltry hopes and fears with which they surround and animate their heroes, I declare I would die now. But there has never an hour of mine gone quite so dully yet; if it were spent waiting at a railway junction, I would have some scattering thoughts, I could count some grains of memory, compared to which the whole of one of these romances seems but dross.

[12] These writers would retort (if I take them properly) that this was very true; that it was the same with themselves and other persons of (what they call) the artistic temperament; that in this we were exceptional, and should apparently be ashamed of ourselves; but that our works must deal exclusively with (what they call) the average man, who was a prodigious dull fellow, and quite dead to all but the paltriest considerations. I accept the issue. We can only know others by ourselves. The artistic temperament (a plague on the expression!) does not make us different from our fellow-men, or it would make us incapable of writing novels; and the average man (a murrain on the word!) is just like you and me, or he would not be average. It was Whitman who stamped a kind of Birmingham sacredness upon the latter phrase; but Whitman knew very well, and showed very nobly, that the average man was full of joys and full of a poetry of his own. And this harping on life's dulness and man's meanness is a loud profession of incompetence; it is one of two things: the cry of the blind eye, *I cannot see*, or the complaint of the dumb tongue, *I cannot utter*. To draw a life without delights is to prove that I have not realized it. To picture a man without some sort of poetry —well, it goes near to prove my case, for it shows an author may have little enough. To see Dancer only as a dirty, old, small-minded, impotently fuming man, in a dirty house, besieged by Harrow boys, and probably beset by small attorneys, is to show myself as keen an observer as . . . the Harrow boys. But these young gentlemen (with a more becoming modesty) were content to pluck Dancer by the coat-tails; they did not suppose they had surprised his secret or could put him living in a book; and it is there my error would have lain. Or say that in the same romance—I continue to call these books romances, in the hope of giving pain—say that in the same romance which now begins really to take shape, I should leave to speak of Dancer, and follow instead the Harrow boys; and say that I came on some such business as that of my lantern-bearers on the links; and described the boys as very cold, spat upon by

flurries of rain, and drearily surrounded, all of which they were; and their talk as silly and indecent, which it certainly was. I might upon these lines, and had I Zola's genius, turn out, in a page or so, a gem of literary art, render the lantern-light with the touches of a master, and lay on the indecency with the ungrudging hand of love; and when all was done, what a triumph would my picture be of shallowness and dulness! how it would have missed the point! how it would have belied the boys! To the ear of the stenographer, the talk is merely silly and indecent; but ask the boys themselves, and they are discussing (as it is highly proper they should) the possibilities of existence. To the eye of the observer they are wet and cold and drearily surrounded; but ask themselves, and they are in the heaven of a recondite pleasure, the ground of which is an ill-smelling lantern.

– III –

[¹³] For, to repeat, the ground of a man's joy is often hard to hit. It may hinge at times upon a mere accessory, like the lantern, it may reside, like Dancer's, in the mysterious inwards of psychology. It may consist with perpetual failure, and find exercise in the continued chase. It has so little bond with externals (such as the observer scribbles in his note-book) that it may even touch them not; and the man's true life, for which he consents to live, lie altogether in the field of fancy. The clergyman, in his spare hours, may be winning battles, the farmer sailing ships, the banker reaping triumph in the arts; all leading another life, plying another trade from that they choose; like the poet's housebuilder, who, after all is cased in stone,

> "By his fireside, as impotent fancy prompts,
> Rebuilds it to his liking."

In such a case the poetry runs underground. The observer (poor soul, with his documents!) is all abroad. For to look at the man is but to court deception. We shall see the trunk from which he draws his nourishment; but he himself is above and abroad in the green dome of foliage, hummed through by winds and nested in by nightingales. And the true realism were that of the poets, to climb up after him like a squirrel, and catch some glimpse of the heaven for which he lives. And the true realism, always and everywhere, is that of the poets: to find out where joy resides, and give it a voice far beyond singing.

[¹⁴] For to miss the joy is to miss all. In the joy of the actors lies the sense of any action. That is the explanation, that the excuse. To one who has not the secret of the lanterns, the scene upon the links is meaningless. And hence the haunting and truly spectral unreality of realistic books. Hence, when we read the English realists, the incredulous wonder with which we observe the hero's constancy under the submerging tide of dulness, and how he bears up with his jibbing sweetheart, and endures the chatter of idiot girls, and stands by his whole unfeatured wilderness of an existence, instead of seeking relief in drink or foreign travel. Hence in the French, in that meat-market of middle-aged sensuality, the disgusted surprise with which we see the hero drift sidelong, and practically quite untempted, into every description of misconduct and dishonor. In each, we miss the personal poetry, the enchanted atmosphere, that rainbow work of fancy that clothes what is naked and seems to ennoble what is base; in each, life falls dead like dough, instead of soaring away like a balloon into the colors of the sunset; each is true, each inconceivable; for no man lives in the external truth, among salts and acids, but in the warm, phantasmagoric chamber of his brain, with the painted windows and the storied walls.

[15] Of this falsity we have had a recent example from a man who knows far better—Tolstoi's *Powers of Darkness*. Here is a piece full of force and truth, yet quite untrue. For before Mikita was led into so dire a situation he was tempted, and temptations are beautiful at least in part; and a work which dwells on the ugliness of crime and gives no hint of any loveliness in the temptation, sins against the modesty of life, and even when a Tolstoi writes it, sinks to melodrama. The peasants are not understood; they saw their life in fairer colors; even the deaf girl was clothed in poetry for Mikita, or he had never fallen. And so, once again, even an Old Bailey melodrama, without some brightness of poetry and lustre of existence, falls into the inconceivable and ranks with fairy tales.

– IV –

[16] In nobler books we are moved with something like the emotions of life; and this emotion is very variously provoked. We are so moved when Levine labors in the field, when Andre sinks beyond emotion, when Richard Feverel and Lucy Desborough meet beside the river, when Antony, "not cowardly, puts off his helmet," when Kent has infinite pity on the dying Lear, when, in Dostoieffsky's *Despised and Rejected*, the uncomplaining hero drains his cup of suffering and virtue. These are notes that please the great heart of man. Not only love, and the fields, and the bright face of danger, but sacrifice and death and unmerited suffering humbly supported, touch in us the vein of the poetic. We love to think of them, we long to try them, we are humbly hopeful that we may prove heroes also.

[17] We have heard, perhaps, too much of lesser matters. Here is the door, here is the open air. *Itur in antiquam silvam.*[2]

---

[2] One goes into the ancient forest.

---•◦{ C O M M E N T   A N D   Q U E S T I O N S }◦•---

This reflective essay—rich (perhaps too rich) in concrete detail, in language, and in its picture of human life—requires careful reading. First you need to follow its general development. In paragraphs 1–3 Stevenson describes his boyhood experiences as he remembers them; the reasons for the fullness and variety of details become evident later. In paragraphs 4–7 he introduces the bull's-eye lantern, then tells what it is and how the boys feel about it. In section II, paragraphs 8 and 9, he further clarifies the meaning or symbolism of the lantern and shows that the miser, Dancer, has his lantern too. In paragraph 10 he introduces another symbol, the bird's song, which you will need to interpret. In the same paragraph he begins his attack on writers of realistic fiction by saying that they portray only the mud and fears of life. In paragraphs 11 and 12 he continues to argue against what he considers the false picture of life that realists present. At the end of section II he returns to his lantern figure to show what realists fail to include in their writings. In section III he continues to discuss the mysterious inner life of man and the deceptive appearance of man's outer life. In section IV he deals with the way life is presented in what he calls "nobler books," and the spirit and the view of life that they contain.

Much of this essay may appear to be mere description, or mere argument, sometimes intemperately stated, against a type of literature which Stevenson, himself an avowed romanticist, did not like. A critical reader may question the amount of descriptive detail, and may disagree with Stevenson's opinions of the realistic novelists; but he will also see that Stevenson is dealing with things more significant than bull's-eye lanterns and literary differences.

1. State in a sentence what you take to be the central idea of the essay.
2. Where and how does Stevenson begin to relate the lantern to this central idea? Does the lantern figure seem to you a good one for his purposes?
3. Can you see any reason why Stevenson wrote three long paragraphs before he introduced the boys and the lanterns? Why do you think he included in these paragraphs details that show not only the pleasantness but also the unpleasantness and even the sordidness of life?
4. What techniques of description are used in paragraph 1?
5. Comment on Stevenson's interpretation of Dancer's character (paragraph 9). Where in this paragraph does the author refer directly or indirectly to the lantern symbol?
6. How does Stevenson interpret the fable of the monk and the bird song, and how is the fable related to the main idea of the essay? Do you think that the essay would have been equally clear and effective if Stevenson had omitted the fable and had been content to use only the lantern figure? Explain.
7. For what explicit purpose does the author return near the end of section II to the boys and the lanterns?

8. From paragraph 10 to the end of the essay, Stevenson is stating his own view of life and is attacking the view of "realistic" novelists. Do you find places where his reasoning seems questionable? In what passages do you find the most heavily charged language?

9. If you have read the work of such contemporaries of Stevenson as Zola, Flaubert, and Hardy, what is your opinion of his indictment of their novels?

10. Examine and comment on Stevenson's choice of words, the movement and rhythm of his sentences, his use of details and of figures of speech, especially in paragraphs 3, 6, 10, and 14. Do you see why Stevenson is considered one of the distinguished prose writers of the nineteenth century?

11. When you think of the essay as a whole, what is your judgment of it, and why?

A Glossary of Rhetorical Terms

Abstract Words. Words which generally name qualities, concepts, and conditions. See pages 11–12.

Alliteration. The repetition of consonant sounds, usually at the beginnings of words: "The *furrow followed free.*"

Analogy. A sustained comparison of two dissimilar ideas or situations.

Antithesis. A stylistic arrangement of opposed elements to heighten the contrast between them: "I wish to preach not the doctrine of ignoble ease, but the doctrine of the strenuous life."

Appositives and Appositive Structures. An appositive is a noun, pronoun, noun phrase, noun clause, or noun plus modifiers standing beside another noun and denoting the same person or thing: "The spring flowers, *daffodils and scillas*, brighten the yard." An apposed adjective is an adjective, or an expression used as an adjective, that occupies the same position as an appositive: "The dog, *playful and gay*, jumped over the fence."

Assumptions. What a communicator conjectures or takes for granted about his subject or about the interests, attitudes, and beliefs of his audience. See pages 5–6.

Attitudinal Language. Language which expresses the feelings or attitudes of a communicator toward himself, his audience, and his subject. See **Charged Language** and **Tone.**

Balance. See Parallelism. When parallel expressions are similar in length and rhythm as well as in grammatical construction, they are said to be *balanced:* "The world is *a comedy to those who think, a tragedy to those who feel.*"

Charged Words and **Charged Language.** Words which carry strong emotional or attitudinal meaning are called charged words; and language intended to produce emotional charges—attractions or repulsions—in the hearer or reader is called charged language. See page 6.

Climactic Arrangement. The arrangement of sentence elements (or of elements in a paragraph or a whole composition) to build to a climax or strong ending. See page 13.

Complement. A noun or adjective structure that completes the thought and establishes the meaning of a verb: "Bert is *chairman;* he looks *tired.*"

Concrete Words. Words which generally refer to things that exist in the physical world, on the nature and meaning of which people can agree. See pages 11–12.

Connotation. The implied or associated meanings of a word. "Home," for example, carries suggestions of comfort and security; "house" does not.

Context. The surrounding words or circumstances which establish the meaning of a particular expression.

Denotation. The factual meaning of a word used to identify something by naming it. See **Connotation.**

Direct Discourse. Quotation of a person's exact words.

Dominant Impression. In narrative or descriptive writing, the unified effect to which details contribute.

Economy. A trait of good style, achieved by avoiding unnecessary and verbose expressions, cutting weak clauses to phrases or single words, and using exact words.

WORDY: She rendered a vocal selection.

REVISED: She sang.

WORDY: The wind which blew through the cracks made a whistling sound.

REVISED: The wind whistled through the cracks.

WORDY: He lifted the stick that he uses to conduct the orchestra.

REVISED: He lifted his baton.

Emphasis. Stress on important words and ideas by means of position, proportion, repetition, and other techniques. See pages 10, 12–14.

Figurative Language. Language in which words are used nonliterally. See pages 11–12.

Formal and Informal Style. Formal English, more often written than spoken, is likely to have the following characteristics: long sentences, parallel and balanced constructions, a wide and exact vocabulary, the absence of contractions (*can't, don't*), and an impersonal tone. In informal English, the sentences are likely to be shorter and to have the rhythms and uncomplicated constructions of speech, and the tone is more often personal than impersonal. For examples of formal and informal style, see pages 7–8.

Heavy Words. Formal or pretentious words used unnecessarily in an informal context. They have too much bulk or weight for the situation.

Indirect Discourse. Statement of what a person said without quotation of his exact words: "He said that he did not approve."

Inversion or **Inverted Order.** A departure from the normal subject–verb–object order of English sentences: "The solstice he does not observe, the equinox he knows as little." *Inversion* is sometimes used to refer to the moving of any sentence element from its most normal or common position: "Desperately he struggled, but to no avail."

Irony. A manner of expression in which the real meaning is different from, sometimes the opposite of, the apparent or literal meaning.

Loose Sentence. A sentence which continues after the main idea has been expressed: *"They returned to camp* after a long and exhausting walk through the woods." See **Periodic Sentence.**

Motif. A repeated detail (sound, visual image, sensation, or condition) used to give texture and unity to a piece of writing.

Normal Order. The conventional pattern of English sentences in which the subject precedes the verb and the object or complement follows the verb.

Pace. The movement of a piece of writing. Pace depends, in narrative writing, on the balance between summary and presentation of material. In non-narrative writing it may depend on the fullness of development and detail. See pages 13–14.

Paradox. A statement that seems contradictory or unbelievable but that may in fact be true: "My life closed twice before its close."

Parallelism. The principle of usage which requires that coordinate elements in a compound construction be given the same grammatical form: "The world will little note nor long remember what we say here; but it can never forget what they did here." For further examples, see pages 8–10.

Periodic Sentence. A sentence, more characteristic of formal than of informal style, in which the meaning is suspended until the end: "About his disappointments, his anxieties, and the reasons for his action, *we have little knowledge.*"

Persona. The "voice," role, or personality which a speaker or writer adopts in a particular communication. See pages 6–7.

Premise. An assertion or previous statement that is the basis of an argument. See **Syllogism.**

Repetition. In skillful writing, a means of emphasizing important words and ideas, of binding together the sentences in a passage, and of creating emotional effects. See pages 10–11.

Slanting. The process of selecting facts, words, and emphasis to achieve the communicator's intention.

Slanting by selection of facts:

FAVORABLE: Tom is an honor student.
UNFAVORABLE: Tom hasn't shaved for two weeks.

Slanting by selection of charged words:

FAVORABLE: Jean is a slender blonde.
UNFAVORABLE: Jean is a skinny girl with brassy hair.

Slanting by emphasis:

MORE FAVORABLE: Although Tom hasn't shaved for two weeks, he is an honor student.
LESS FAVORABLE: Tom may be an honor student, but he hasn't shaved for two weeks.

Style. A quality of excellence or distinction. See pages 7–14.

Subordination. Expressing in dependent clauses, or phrases, or single words, ideas which are not significant enough to be expressed in a main clause or an independent sentence.

LACKING SUBORDINATION: The quarterback was tired. He was also battered. He was determined to win.

SUBORDINATION: The quarterback, though tired and battered, was determined to win.

Syllogism. In formal logic, the pattern in which a deductive argument is expressed: All men are mortal (major premise). John is a man (minor premise). Therefore John is mortal (conclusion). See page 15.

Symbol. A particular object, person, experience, or situation which stands for, or is associated with, some larger relationship or idea.

Tone. The manner of verbal expression; the expression of a communicator's attitudes toward himself, his audience, and his material. See pages 5–7.

Topic Sentence. A sentence which expresses the central idea of a paragraph.

Transitions. Words, phrases, sentences, or even paragraphs, which show the reader the connections between the writer's ideas. See page 5.

Triad.   A sequence of three parallel constructions: ". . . to defend our island home, to ride out the storm of war, and to outlive the menace of tyranny. . . ."

Variety.   Variation in the length and construction of sentences to avoid monotony and to suit style to sense. See pages 8–10.

Vitalizing.   Bringing people and scenes to life. Vitalizing a person usually involves showing him in some typical pose or activity. Vitalizing a scene means carrying the reader into it by providing him with some of the sights, sounds, and other sense impressions that are part of experiencing that scene.

Index to Authors and Titles

[FOR AN INDEX TO RHETORICAL TERMS, SEE THE GLOSSARY, PAGES 895–99.]